WHITE COLLAR CRIME

by

Ellen S. Podgor

Gary R. Trombley Family White-Collar Research Professor
Professor of Law
Stetson University College of Law

Peter J. Henning

Professor of Law
Wayne State University Law School

Jerold H. Israel

Alene and Allan F. Smith Professor of Law Emeritus,
University of Michigan Law School
Ed Rood Eminent Scholar Emeritus,
University of Florida, Levin College of Law

Nancy J. King

Lee S. and Charles A. Speir Professor of Law
Vanderbilt University Law School

HORNBOOK SERIES®

WEST®

Mat #40930089

Hornbook Series is a trademark registered in the U.S. Patent and Trademark Office.

© 2013 by LEG, Inc. d/b/a West Academic Publishing

    610 Opperman Drive
    St. Paul, MN 55123
    1-800-313-9378

West, West Academic Publishing, and West Academic are trademarks of West Publishing Corporation, used under license.

Printed in the United States of America

ISBN: 978–0–314–26271–4

Dedicated –

To the Gary R. Trombley Family

To Karen, who is everything to me, and Alexandra, Molly, and Grace

To Paul Borman, who introduced me to the special character of white collar enforcement and defense over 30 years ago and continues to provide invaluable insights

To the late, great Don Hall, inspiration to generations of Vanderbilt lawyers

Preface

This hornbook is intended to provide to students and lawyers a general overview of the growing area of white collar criminal law. Because of the general focus of this book, it is not recommended as a source for deciding a specific legal issue. Cases were selected for this book to be illustrative, rather than comprehensive of each area being discussed. It is important to note that white collar crime is a continuing study, with ever-changing rules and precedents. Many of the issues within white collar crime, as noted throughout this book, continue to evolve.

The book is divided into four parts: Part I - A General Overview; Part II - Specific Crimes; Part III - Procedure; and Part IV – Sanctions. In Part II, specific crimes were selected to provide a sampling of the wide array of offenses encompassed within this enormous body of law. In Part III, coverage similarly is not comprehensive, but selective. For example, we do not have a chapter concerning discovery, an important topic in all criminal matters. The selection of substantive and procedural topics was made to highlight the key areas that arise in white collar matters. It should also be noted that this book focuses on white collar crime in the federal criminal context, with some exceptions, and does not delve into developments at the state and local level.

The authors recommend that for additional materials on criminal procedure one can consult the LaFave, Israel, King, & Kerr Criminal Procedure Hornbook or Treatise. The full treatise is available on Westlaw at database CRIMPROC. It should also be noted that some of the material from this book originated from Podgor & Israel, Nutshell on White Collar Crime (4th ed).

There are many to thank for assisting with this project and the authors particularly thank Elizabeth Andary, Rachel M. Batten, Paul D. Borman, Darby Dickerson, Shannon Edgar, Alison Hightower, Olive A. Hyman, Adam Labonte, Paul J. Mayer, Katherine Morris, Rachel A. Morris (Kestenbaum), Brian Morrison, Darcie Mulay, Christopher M. Pietruszkiewicz, Stetson University College of Law, Wayne State University Law School, University of Michigan Law School, The University of Florida Levin College of Law, and Vanderbilt University Law School.

ELLEN S. PODGOR
PETER J. HENNING
JEROLD H. ISRAEL
NANCY J. KING

May 2013

Summary of Contents

Table of Contents

___

WHITE COLLAR CRIME

Chapter 1

SCOPE OF WHITE COLLAR CRIME

§ 1.1   INTRODUCTION

A. Sociological Origins

"White collar crime" is a term coined by Edwin Sutherland in a speech he gave in 1939 to the American Sociological Society.[1] In this speech he focused on "crime in relation to business." He claimed that it was "misleading and incorrect" to think of crime as being "closely correlated with poverty or with the psychopathic and sociopathic conditions associated with poverty." Thus, he centered his talk on a "neglected" area of crime, that being "the criminal behavior of business and professional men."

In his book published the following year, Sutherland defined "white-collar crime" as, "a crime committed by a person of respectability and high social status in the course of his occupation."[2] Although Sutherland's focus was on social status and occupation, he noted that the concept was "not intended to be definitive, but merely to call attention to crimes which are not ordinarily included within the scope of criminology." Some, however, questioned whether Sutherland's definition had artificial distinctions based on class and occupation.[3] For example, focusing on the offender, as opposed to the offense, may result in gender disparities as there are fewer women than men who serve in positions of power within major companies.

Many years later, there still is no definitive definition of what is encompassed within the term white collar crime.[4] Author Susan Shapiro notes that "literature yields fundamental inconsistencies and incompatibilities." She states that, "[i]t is unclear whether the term characterizes acts or actors, types of offenses or types of offenders; or whether it refers to the social location of deviant behavior, the social role or social status of the actor, the *modus operandi* of the behavior, or the social relationship of victim and offender."[5]

---

[1] Reprinted in Edwin H. Sutherland, White–Collar Criminality, 5 Am. Soc. Rev. 1 (1940).

[2] Edwin H. Sutherland, White Collar Crime: The Uncut Version 7 (1983).

[3] See Stanton Wheeler, White–Collar Crime: History of an Idea, 4 Encyclopedia of Crime and Justice 1652, 1653 (1983).

[4] See James William Coleman, The Theory of White–Collar Crime: From Sutherland to the 1990s, White–Collar Crime Reconsidered 53 (Kip Schlegel & David Weisburd, eds.) (1992); see also David T. Johnson & Richard A. Leo, The Yale White–Collar Crime Project: A Review and Critique, Law and Social Inquiry 63 (1993) (review of varying definitions of white collar crime).

[5] Susan Shapiro, Thinking About White–Collar Crime: Matters of Conceptualization and Research 1 (1980).

B. Modern Legal Definitions

Herbert Edelhertz, former chief of the Fraud Section of the Department of Justice's Criminal Division, was a leader in moving the definition from its sociological roots to a legal term. He defined white collar crime as "an illegal act or series of illegal acts committed by nonphysical means and by concealment or guile, to obtain money or property, to avoid the payment or loss of money or property, or to obtain business or personal advantage."[6] His definition moved the focus to the *offense*, as opposed to Sutherland's emphasis on the *offender*. The factors used by Edelhertz as indicative of it being categorized as white collar were:

(a) Intent to commit a wrongful act or to achieve a purpose inconsistent with law or public policy.

(b) Disguise of purpose or intent.

(c) Reliance by perpetrator on ignorance or carelessness of victim.

(d) Acquiescence by victim in what he believes to be the true nature and content of the transaction.

(e) Concealment of crime by—

(1) Preventing the victim from realizing that he has been victimized, or

(2) Relying on the fact that only a small percentage of victims will react to what has happened, and making provisions for restitution to or other handling of the disgruntled victim, or

(3) Creation of a deceptive paper, organizational, or transactional facade to disguise the true nature of what has occurred.

But acceptance of the Edelhertz approach was not universal. Some sociologists argued that this legal definition omitted the ingredient of "abuse of power." There was also the argument that certain violent crimes should be considered white collar, such as health related crimes that cause physical injury. An example of this would be "the failure to label poisonous substances at the workplace."[7]

In looking at white collar crime, the American Bar Association also focused on "economic offenses." But they noted in a footnote that the term "non-violent" went to the means by which the crime was committed even though "the harm to society can frequently be described as violent."[8]

The term white collar crime is also prevalent in a variety of law enforcement contexts. In some instances it is considered strictly from the legal perspective, while some definitions incorporate a reference to the sociological approach. For example, the

---

[6] Herbert Edelhertz, The Nature, Impact and Prosecution of White–Collar Crime 3, 12 (1970).

[7] Gilbert Geis, White–Collar Crime—What Is It?, White–Collar Crime Reconsidered 31, 39 (Kip Schlegel & David Weisburd, eds.) (1992).

[8] Id.

Department of Justice, Attorney General's Report of 1983 defined white collar crime as:

> White collar crimes are illegal acts that use deceit and concealment—rather than the application or threat of physical force or violence—to obtain money, property, or service; to avoid the payment or loss of money; or to secure a business or personal advantage. White-collar criminals occupy positions of responsibility and trust in government, industry, the professions, and civic organizations.

This definition has many of the same attributes as the definition used by the Bureau of Justice Statistics, which provides:

> *White-collar crime: Definition.* Nonviolent crime for financial gain committed by means of deception by persons whose occupational status is entrepreneurial, professional or semi-professional and utilizing their special occupational skills and opportunities; also, nonviolent crime for financial gain utilizing deception and committed by anyone having special technical and professional knowledge of business and government, irrespective of the person's occupation.[9]

The FBI also uses an offense-based approach, with a definition that includes "illegal acts which are characterized by deceit, concealment, or violation of trust and which are not dependent upon the application or threat of physical force or violence." The FBI, however, does not include reference to "occupation or the socioeconomic position of the 'white-collar' offender."[10]

Thus, the term white collar crime, although commonly used, has many different definitions.[11] In some instances white collar crime is referenced through use of phrases such as "crime in the suites,"[12] "Wall Street crimes," "business crimes," "economic crimes," or "financial crimes."

§ 1.2   STATISTICAL REPORTING OF WHITE COLLAR CRIME

It is difficult to assess the extent of white collar crime when there is no consistent definition of what is encompassed within the term. Without a clear definition of what is included within the term, one cannot accurately say whether white collar crime has increased or decreased.

One of the reporting entities, Trac Reports, notes the difficulty of defining white collar crime for statistical purposes. It adopts the government's definition of "a non-violent event involving deceit, concealment, subterfuge and other fraudulent activity." But then it notes that because of subcategories that have been created, some non-

---

[9] Bureau of Justice Statistics, U.S. Department of Justice, Dictionary of Criminal Justice Data Terminology 215 (2d Ed. 1981).

[10] Federal Bureau of Investigation (Cynthia Barnett, The Measurement of White Collar Crime Using Uniform Crime Reporting (UCR) Data) (2002).

[11] *See* Stuart P. Green, LYING, CHEATING, AND STEALING 18 (2006) ("[w]e would do better to think of the term 'white-collar crime' as referring to a set of offenses connected by a series of what philosophers call 'family resemblances,' rather than as susceptible to definition through a precise set of necessary and sufficient conditions.").

[12] Remarks of Attorney General Dick Thornburgh Before the Annual Luncheon Meeting of the Merchants and Manufacturer Association, June 27, 1990, available at http://www.justice.gov/ag/aghistory/thornburgh/1990/06–27–90a.pdf.

violent crimes may be reported under a specific designation as opposed to the generic term of white collar crime. For example,

> Although the government official stuffing an illegal payoff in his pocket may have been wearing a white collar, for example, he probably will be counted under another category: official corruption. And while the high-level corporate executive who orders his workers to dump illegal toxic materials in a nearby river also may be wearing a white collar, he probably will be classified as an environmental violator.[13]

Trac Reporting does note that although the definition of white collar crime presents assessment problems, the statistics of these activities can be compared "because the classification system used by U.S. Attorneys all over the country has been reasonably consistent for the last three decades."

The United States Sentencing Commission, which compiles statistics on federal criminal sentencing, noted that in the year 2009 there were 81,549 new federal criminal cases and of this number "81,372 involved an individual defendant and 177 involved a corporation or other 'organizational' defendant."[14] Drug and immigration cases represented the highest percentage of cases. 13.2% of the total cases for 2009 were considered white collar related, with fraud representing 9.5% and non-fraud white collar being 3.7%. But the accuracy of any statistical numbers related to white collar offenses always remains with the definition. For example, there is no explanation provided as to whether FDA (Food and Drug Administration) prosecutions are being reported as drug cases or as white collar non-fraud matters.

§ 1.3   WHITE COLLAR CRIMES

If white collar crime is defined as a legal term, the question becomes which of the estimated 4,000-4,500 federal crimes should be considered white collar crimes.[15] Federal crimes, both white-collar and non-white-collar, are found scattered throughout the United States Code. They are not limited in the Code to Title 18—Crimes. There are even more criminal statutes if one looks at state legal systems. Additionally, there are both federal and state regulations that may carry criminal responsibility. For example, some environmental regulations may impose criminal penalties. There is, however, no list of crimes that one can call definitively white collar crimes.

Because there are a host of different entities that may be categorizing the activity, the included offenses may vary. In many circumstances, the same criminal activity can be the subject of both a state and federal prosecution. Because white collar crime is an area of current concern, designating criminality as white collar crime may enhance

---

[13] Trac Reports, White Collar Crime, available at http://trac.syr.edu/tracreports/bulletins/white_collar_crime/side_80.html (2006).

[14] United States Sentencing Commission, Overview of Federal Criminal Cases, Fiscal Year 2009 2 (Dec. 2010), available at http://www.ussc.gov/Research/Research_Publications/2010/20101230_FY09_Overview_Federal_Criminal_Cases.pdf

[15] See Brian W. Walsh & Tiffany M. Joslyn, Without Intent: How Congress Is Eroding the Criminal Intent Requirement in Federal Law 6 (2010), available at http://www.nacdl.org/criminaldefense.aspx?id=10287 & terms=withoutintent; John S. Baker, Jr., Measuring the Explosive Growth of Federal Crime Legislation, Crime Report (Federalist Soc'y for Law & Pub. Pol'y Studies), 2004, at 3.

funding for its investigation and prosecution. In addition, agencies may investigate and pursue white collar criminality. For example, Congress passed the Emergency Economic Stabilization Act of 2008, which authorized the Office of the Special Inspector General for the Troubled Asset Relief Program (SIGTARP) and provided this agency with both civil and criminal powers to investigate fraud related to the $700 billion Troubled Asset Relief Program (TARP) funds.

From the federal perspective, there are many possible agencies that may be investigating white collar criminal activity including the Federal Bureau of Investigations (FBI), Securities Exchange Commission (SEC), Internal Revenue Service (IRS), and Food and Drug Administration (FDA). The Department of Justice through the use of grand juries (see Chapter 16) also plays a significant role in the investigation of white collar criminal activity.

Although there is no general designation of white collar crime, making it difficult to determine which crimes fit within this category, crimes considered to be white collar offenses include: Antitrust (e.g., price-fixing), Bank Thefts or Embezzlement, Counterfeiting, Environmental Crimes, Fraud (Bank, Mail, Wire, Health Care, Securities, Computer and other Fraud offenses), Food & Drug Crimes, False Statements, Bribery (including the Foreign Corrupt Practices Act), Forgery, Identity Theft, Tax Offenses, and Obstruction of Justice. But even when specifying crimes it can be difficult to determine what gets included and what should be omitted. For example, the Racketeer Influenced and Corrupt Organization Act (RICO) has many predicate acts that are street crimes, such as murder. (See Chapter 8). On the other hand, RICO can also be charged using predicate acts of mail and wire fraud, crimes that are white collar offenses. The same may be true for currency reporting crimes, which can accompany drug charges, but may also be tacked onto crimes like fraud, which are clearly considered white collar offenses. So even designating by crime may not accurately depict what is a white collar crime.

§ 1.4 WHITE COLLAR CRIMINALS

Who is considered a white collar criminal is contingent upon what is considered a white collar crime. Using a generic legal definition, one finds that the individuals come from all walks of society. Individuals prosecuted for white collar crimes include corporate executives like Jeffrey Skilling, the former CEO of Enron, and Richard Scrushy, the former CEO of HealthSouth. They include governors like former Louisiana Governor Edwin Edwards and former Illinois Governor George Ryan. Ponzi schemers like Bernie Madoff have received high sentences for white collar criminal activity. Business woman and television star Martha Stewart was convicted and sent to prison for a false statement to the Securities Exchange Commission. Now deceased hotel entrepreneur Leona Helmsley was convicted and served time for tax crimes. The list of celebrity offenders is very long and it dates back prior to the coining of the term white collar crime. For example, Charles Ponzi, the namesake for Ponzi schemes, engaged in activities in the early 1920s.

Not all white collar criminals are celebrities. One finds many cases of low-level corporate personnel who are charged with crimes such as accounting and land frauds. If using a legal definition, the waiter who fails to report his tips and gets charged with tax fraud might be considered a white collar offender. Additionally, some state prosecutors have opened up white collar units, charging individuals with crimes such as welfare fraud or false statements to the state government.

One characteristic that does repeat itself, is that white collar offenders seldom have an extended criminal history. Unlike some who are charged with drug or other street crimes, white collar offenders usually fall in the lowest level criminal history category in the federal sentencing system. (See Chapter 24).

§ 1.5　WHITE COLLAR ATTORNEYS

A.　Government

The Judiciary Act of 1789 created the Department of Justice (DOJ). With its main office in Washington, D.C., the DOJ is headed by the Attorney General, a presidential appointee. The Deputy Attorney General serves under the Attorney General, and associate attorney generals below him or her. There are divisions within the DOJ structure, including the antitrust division, tax division, and the national security division.[16] There is no separate division or department bearing the label white collar crime. Within the DOJ, the criminal division investigates and prosecutes some of the federal white collar cases, but most importantly serves as the central office for enforcing federal criminal laws. Some responsibility for criminal matters also rests in other places within DOJ, such as the Antitrust Division or the Tax Division. Most white collar crime prosecutions are handled through the ninety-three U.S. Attorneys' Offices (USAOs), located within each federal district.[17] The umbrella of the Department of Justice, located in Washington, D.C. is often called Main Justice.[18]

Federal statutes and regulations with criminal provisions provide the basis for prosecutions in the federal system. In addition to the statutory mandates and legal ethics rules, federal government attorneys are guided by internal guidelines found in the United States Attorneys' Manual (USAM). The Manual serves "as a quick and ready reference for United States Attorneys (USAs), Assistant United States Attorneys (AUSAs), and Department attorneys responsible for the prosecution of violations of federal law." This Manual offers guidance on charging practices and also provides when it is necessary to obtain permission of the Criminal Division, or a specific section, prior to proceeding on a prosecution or other activity, such as an international extradition. These guidelines are not static and are revised by the Executive Office for the United States Attorneys in consultation with the Attorney General, Deputy Attorney General and Associate Attorney General. The United States Attorneys' Manual covers both criminal and civil areas, with Title Nine, the final section of the Manual, pertaining to criminal prosecutions. These guidelines are strictly internal policy and are not enforceable at law.[19]

---

[16] Department Organization Chart—http://www.justice.gov/agencies/index-org.html

[17] The Executive Office for the United States Attorneys (EOUSA) serves as the liaison between the DOJ and the 93 U.S. Attorneys. See Executive Office for United States Attorneys, available at http://www.justice.gov/usao/eousa/

[18] Department of Justice Organization Chart, available at http://www.justice.gov/agencies/index-org.html

[19] See Ellen S. Podgor, Department of Justice Guidelines: Balancing "Discretionary Justice", 13 Cornell Jrl. L. & Pub. Pol'y 167, 170–75 (2004) (discussing the history and status of guidelines in the Department of Justice).

A Criminal Resource Manual (CRM) offers federal government prosecutors further in-depth guidance on legal issues. There are also policy statements issued by the Attorney General or Deputy Attorney General that provide guidance to AUSAs on subjects such as charging of corporations or proper protocol in responding to discovery requests. These Memos often bear the name of the Attorney General or Deputy Attorney General, so one finds memos such as the Thompson Memo (See § 2.4(A)).

In many jurisdictions, white collar crimes are prosecuted along with other crimes. But a growing number of State Attorney Generals and local prosecutors have started separate white collar crime units. For example, the 2008 Florida Report of the Statewide Prosecutor stated that they targeted mortgage fraud, health care fraud, and securities fraud.[20] Like the federal system, some local and state jurisdictions have internal guidelines to assist prosecutors with their decision-making.[21]

B. Defense

For many years, major law firms shied away from handling white collar cases. They did not want the "taint" of handling criminal matters. These cases were sent to firms that often specialized in criminal law and were perhaps sole practitioners or boutique law firms.

More recently, firms created "special matters" sections that kept white collar matters internally within the firms. Corporate investigations with possible criminal liability would be handled by these law firm sections.

Today, the handling of white collar cases carries a certain prestige. Major law firms regularly advertise their expertise in this area and commonly tout their hiring of key individuals who were previously employed by the DOJ or the SEC. The size of the white collar practice area is seen by looking at the 26th Annual American Bar Association White Collar Crime National Institute of 2012 which had an attendance that exceeded one thousand. This program included both prosecutors and defense counsel. There is also a growth in the Continuing Legal Education world, with the start of many new white collar related programs.

Defense counsel may also be involved in handling internal investigations, also a white collar growth area. Criminal defense counsel may be assisting corporations in the investigation of improper activities within the company and compliance measures to assure that individuals within the corporation comply with their legal mandates.

The handling of federal white collar cases by defense counsel is not limited to private attorneys. One finds an increasing number of federal defenders handling white collar cases. For example, many mortgage fraud cases were handled by federal defender's offices. The cost involved in handling a highly complex white collar case can result in the need to appoint indigent counsel for the accused.

---

[20] http://myfloridalegal.com/webfiles.nsf/WF/MRAY-7PULWN/$file/2008SWPAnnualReport.pdf

[21] http://manhattanda.org/sites/default/files/Considerations%20in%20Charging%20Organizations.pdf (Memorandum of Daniel R. Alonso, District Attorney of the County of New York, May 27, 2010, Considerations in Charging Organizations).

§ 1.6 WHITE COLLAR PROSECUTIONS

A street crime occurs and often the police investigate and the individual is arrested. In many instances the time between the criminal activity and the arrest is minimal. Although some cases may require time to determine the perpetrator of the crime, or to secure all the necessary evidence, the police investigation is a crucial component of the case and it usually occurs prior to charging the accused with the criminal activity.

In contrast, in a white collar case the investigation can be lengthy and the government prosecutor may be a crucial player in the investigation. The grand jury is often a key investigative tool in assembling the evidence pre-indictment. (See Chapter 16). Many white collar cases include extensive documentation, and experts such as forensic accountants and computer specialists may be necessary to explain the complexities of the activities.

Prosecutors will often charge crimes that are not the focus of the investigation. For example, prosecutors may charge the perpetrator with an obstruction of justice (see Chapter 6) or false statement (see Chapter 9) offense, as it may be easier to prove these crimes than the fraudulent accounting practices that caused the initial investigation. Prosecutors have learned that keeping a case simple may enhance the likelihood of it being a successful prosecution.

White collar cases can also have parallel proceedings (see Chapter 18) or an investigation by an administrative agency (see Chapter 17). Thus, in addition to a criminal investigation, an agency such as the SEC or IRS may also be doing their own investigation or they may have a civil action that is also pending against the accused. A key issue that can arise here is whether evidence can be shared between the two entities.

Few white collar cases actually go to trial as most are resolved by the defendant entering into a plea agreement with the government or pleading guilty to the charge and arguing mitigation with the court. For example, in 2011 in the federal system, 94.5% of the fraud cases, 94.6% of the bribery cases, and 100% of the antitrust cases were resolved by pleas of guilty.[22] These numbers are not unique to white collar crime, as a very high percentage of federal and state criminal matters are resolved by a plea agreement.

§ 1.7 FEDERAL JURISDICTION

A. Constitutional Powers

Jurisdiction is important because it serves to determine who can prosecute the criminal activity, the possible charges that can be brought, the applicable law, and the rights of the accused. Jurisdiction might be found in the federal system, a state, or perhaps within the jurisdiction of an agency action.

---

[22] U.S. Sentencing Commission, 2007 Datafiles, Table 11, available at http://www.ussc.gov/Data_and_Statistics/Annual_Reports_and_Sourcebooks/2011/Table11.pdf.

Federal criminal statutes are limited in that they need to be tied to one of the express or implied powers in the United States Constitution. In this regard, Congress has used its broad commerce powers as the hook for many federal criminal statutes. One also finds federal statutes premised on the postal and taxing powers in the Constitution.

The commerce power provides that "Congress may regulate the use of the channels of interstate commerce," "regulate and protect the instrumentalities of interstate commerce, or persons or things in interstate commerce, even though the threat may come only from intrastate activities," and "regulate those activities having a substantial relation to interstate commerce, *i.e.,* those activities that substantially affect interstate commerce."[23] Thus, one finds federal criminal statutes that call for the activities to be "in interstate commerce," "affecting interstate commerce," or part of a "class of activities" that affect interstate commerce. For example, the federal wire fraud statute (18 U.S.C. § 1343) requires the government to demonstrate that the "wires" are in interstate commerce. (See § 4.9(B)). Some statutes permit alternate methods for finding the commerce connection. For example, a prosecution under the Racketeer Influenced and Corrupt Organizations Act (RICO) (18 U.S.C. §§ 1962 et seq.) requires the prosecutor to prove an "enterprise which is engaged in, or the activities of which affect, interstate or foreign commerce." (See § 8.3). Thus prosecutors have the choice of proving either that the activities were in or that they substantially affected interstate commerce.

Although the Supreme Court gives deference to Congress in the passage of legislation and often finds a sufficient commerce authority basis for a criminal statute, there are occasional instances when the Court has limited federal jurisdiction. For example, in *United States v. Lopez,*[24] the Court held that the Gun–Free School Zones Act exceeded Congress' Commerce Clause authority in that it involved intrastate activity that was not an economic activity. Chief Justice Rehnquist, writing for the majority held "that the proper test requires an analysis of whether the regulated activity 'substantially affects' interstate commerce." Likewise, in *United States v. Morrison,*[25] the Court limited a provision of the Violence Against Women Act of 1994 as it "contain[ed] no jurisdictional element establishing that the federal cause of action is in pursuance of Congress' power to regulate interstate commerce." The Court stated, "[t]he regulation and punishment of intrastate violence that is not directed at the instrumentalities, channels, or goods involved in interstate commerce has always been the province of the States."

But *Lopez* and *Morrison* do not apply when the activities regulated by Congress are "quintessentially economic." The Supreme Court has "firmly establish[ed] Congress' power to regulate purely local activities that are part of an economic 'class of activities' that have a substantial effect on interstate commerce."[26] It is important that the Congressional act be used to regulate "activity" as "[a]llowing Congress to justify federal regulation by pointing to the effect of inaction on commerce would bring

---

[23] United States v. Lopez, 514 U.S. 549 (1995).

[24] Id.

[25] 529 U.S. 598 (2000).

[26] Gonzales v. Raich, 545 U.S. 1 (2005); Perez v. United States, 402 U.S. 146 (1971).

countless decisions an individual could *potentially* make within the scope of federal regulation."[27]

Thus, while the state may reach in its criminal code all behavior within its jurisdiction that threatens the health, safety, welfare or morals of the public, Congress can criminalize behavior only when expressly provided by the Constitution or when doing so is "necessary and proper" to the implementation of one of the powers specifically given to it by the Constitution. The offense must relate to an operational function (e.g., to operate a postal system or coin money) or to a regulatory authority (e.g., to "regulate commerce . . . among the several states").

Although federal commerce power is expansive, recent attacks on overfederalization have focused on the increased number of federal statutes, the weak *mens rea* in many of these statutes, and the disorganization of the federal criminal code. One finds growing scholarship and programs on topics such as "smart on crime" and "right on crime," initiatives to convince legislators to restrain from using federal or state law-making powers to add unnecessary criminal statutes.

B. Federal Priorities

With the vast amount of prosecutorial power in bringing federal criminal charges, and the increased number of federal statutes available to prosecutors, the Department of Justice (DOJ) creates priorities, which can change by administration and by surrounding events. For example, following 9–11 a key focus of the office was terrorism. Some areas have been prominent areas of concern for lengthy periods of time, such as drugs and immigration offenses. In the late 1990s, violent crime was considered a top DOJ priority.[28]

With respect to white collar crime, in addition to public corruption, the following are considered the 2011 white collar crime national priorities:

Based upon FBI field office threat strategies and directives established by the president, the attorney general, the Director, and the Criminal Investigative Division (CID), the following national priorities for the WCC program (WCCP) have been established: public corruption, corporate fraud/securities fraud (to include Ponzi schemes), health care fraud, FIF (to include bank failures and mortgage fraud), insurance fraud, money laundering, and mass marketing fraud.[29]

Equally apparent among federal priorities in recent years is corporate criminality, which under President George W. Bush caused the creation of a Corporate Fraud Task Force. President Barak Obama's administration focuses on financial fraud, with the renaming of the Corporate Fraud Task Force as the Financial Fraud Enforcement Task Force.[30]

---

[27] National Federation of Independent Business v. Sebelius, 132 S.Ct. 2566 (2012).

[28] See, e.g., Senator Arlen Specter (former Philadelphia D.A.) and Paul Michel (former Associate Deputy Atty. Gen.), The Need For A New Federalism In Criminal Justice, July 1982, Annals of the AAPSS.

[29] FBI Financial Crimes Report to the Public, Fiscal Years 2010–2011 (October 1, 2099—September 30, 2011), http://www.fbi.gov/stats-services/publications/financial-crimes-report–2010–2011.

[30] http://www.stopfraud.gov/

C. Federal/State Prosecution

1. Dual Sovereignty Rule

Often both the federal government and a state entity may have jurisdiction to prosecute the same criminal activity. For example, corruption activity causing theft of government property might be charged via a federal statute or by a state theft statute. For a federal prosecution, the statute needs to emanate from an enumerated constitutional power (see supra A). But the same activity often falls under both jurisdictions and both may have the power and ability to proceed. Double jeopardy does not preclude this from happening.

Under the dual sovereignty rule, both the federal and state entities may proceed with the prosecution as "an act denounced as a crime by both national and state sovereignties is an offense against the peace and dignity of both and may be punished by each."[31] In *Abbate v. United States*,[32] the Supreme Court affirmed this principle as set forth in *United States v. Lanza*, noting that "if the States are free to prosecute criminal acts violating their laws, and the resultant state prosecutions bar federal prosecutions based on the same acts, federal law enforcement must necessarily be hindered."

A state, however, may have a statute that expressly precludes dual prosecutions. For example, Georgia bars prosecutions "if the accused was formerly prosecuted in a district court of the United States for a crime which is within the concurrent jurisdiction of this state if such former prosecution resulted in either a conviction or an acquittal and the subsequent prosecution is for the same conduct."[33] There are, however, limits to this state statute such as it not applying if "each prosecution requires proof of a fact not required in the other prosecution or unless the crime was not consummated when the former trial began."

2. Petite Policy

Although in most instances the ability of federal and state prosecutors to charge overlapping crimes exists, the DOJ has guidelines that limit this from happening. Referred to as the *Petite* policy, from the Supreme Court case of *Petite v. United States*,[34] the DOJ policy on dual and successive prosecution:

> precludes the initiation or continuation of a federal prosecution, following a prior state or federal prosecution based on substantially the same act(s) or transaction(s) unless three substantive prerequisites are satisfied: first, the matter must involve a substantial federal interest; second, the prior prosecution must have left that interest demonstrably unvindicated; and third, applying the same test that is applicable to all federal prosecutions, the government must believe that the defendant's conduct constitutes a federal offense, and that the admissible evidence probably will be sufficient to obtain and sustain a conviction by an unbiased trier of fact. In addition, there is a procedural prerequisite to be

---

[31] United States v. Lanza, 260 U.S. 377 (1922).

[32] 359 U.S. 187 (1959).

[33] Ga. Code Ann. § 16–1–8.

[34] 361 U.S. 529 (1960).

satisfied, that is, the prosecution must be approved by the appropriate Assistant Attorney General.[35]

The policy recommends that

> [i]n order to insure the most efficient use of law enforcement resources, whenever a matter involves overlapping federal and state jurisdiction, federal prosecutors should, as soon as possible, consult with their state counterparts to determine the most appropriate single forum in which to proceed to satisfy the substantial federal and state interests involved, and, if possible, to resolve all criminal liability for the acts in question.

The Manual does limit this policy to charging decisions, and notes that it does not apply "where the prior prosecution involved only a minor part of the contemplated federal charges."

Further, because this is a DOJ guideline, there is little ability to enforce the *Petite* policy at law. Prosecutors who violate this department policy may face internal sanctions, but the defense may have limited remedies in court. (See § 1.5(A)). Federal prosecutors who fail to adhere to the office rules or act unethically may find the conduct the subject of an Office of Professional Responsibility (OPR) investigation.[36]

3.   *Federalism Challenges*

Some federal statutes may explicitly provide for the federal government to use state conduct as part of the federal prosecution. For example, the Racketeer Influenced and Corrupt Organizations Act (18 U.S.C. §§ 1961 et seq.) explicitly includes state offenses as predicate acts for the federal crime. (See § 8.4(A)). The federal prosecution of local corruption is sometimes seen as justified since local law enforcement may not have the resources, the inclination, or the political neutrality to properly proceed against this conduct.

When state conduct is the basis of the federal charge, the defendant may challenge the federal jurisdiction for the prosecution. In *Sabri v. United States*,[37] the defendant challenged on federalism grounds the government's use of 18 U.S.C. § 666(a)(2) a statute "proscribing bribery of state, local, and tribal officials of entities that receive at least $10,000 in federal funds." The defendant, a real estate developer who offered bribes to a member of the Board of Commissioners of the Minneapolis Community Development Agency, argued that the statute was facially unconstitutional because it did not require a nexus between the local corruption and the federal funds received by the organization or agency, and therefore violated the limitations imposed by federalism on congressional power to punish local crimes.

The Court in *Sabri* upheld the constitutionality of § 666, finding that:

Congress has authority under the Spending Clause to appropriate federal monies to promote the general welfare, Art. I, § 8, cl. 1, and it has corresponding authority

---

[35] U.S. Attorneys' Manual § 9–2.031 (hereinafter cited as USAM).

[36] http://www.justice.gov/opr/.

[37] 541 U.S. 600 (2004).

under the Necessary and Proper Clause, Art. I, § 8, cl. 18, to see to it that taxpayer dollars appropriated under that power are in fact spent for the general welfare, and not frittered away in graft or on projects undermined when funds are siphoned off or corrupt public officers are derelict about demanding value for dollars.

The Court noted that "[i]t is certainly enough that the statutes condition the offense on a threshold amount of federal dollars defining the federal interest, such as that provided here."

D. Extraterritorial Jurisdiction

1. Factors for Extraterritorial Jurisdiction

Territorial jurisdiction, the place where the crime occurs, usually serves as the place of jurisdiction for the prosecution of the criminal activity. With globalization there is an increased number of extraterritorial activities, leaving the question of who should prosecute and where that prosecution should occur. There are two factors to consider in deciding the extraterritoriality of a federal criminal statute. First is whether the statute explicitly or by implication allows for the extraterritorial prosecution. Second is whether international law allows the United States to prosecute the conduct.[38]

2. Statutory Authority for Extraterritoriality

There is explicit statutory authority when Congress either provides an extraterritorial focus for the crime or states within the statute that extraterritorial conduct is covered. For example, the Foreign Corrupt Practices Act (FCPA) is very clearly focused on bribery that occurs outside the United States. (See § 5.7, § 7.7). Some statutes may not have an extraterritorial focus, but Congress will have explicitly provided language in the statute to let the courts know that extraterritorial conduct can be prosecuted under this law. For example, a key perjury statute provides that it "is applicable whether the statement or subscription is made within or without the United States."[39] (See Chapter 10).

Many statutes, especially older ones, fail to state whether extraterritorial jurisdiction will be allowed. Courts are left to judicially interpret whether it was the congressional intent to allow for an extraterritorial application.

In *United States v. Bowman*[40] the Court looked at whether the United States had jurisdiction in a case involving a conspiracy to defraud a corporation, of which the United States was the sole stockholder. In finding extraterritorial jurisdiction proper, the Court stated that "[t]he necessary locus, when not specifically defined, depends upon the purpose of Congress as evinced by the description and nature of the crime and upon the territorial limitations upon the power and jurisdiction of a government to punish crime under the law of nations." The Court noted that crimes against individuals, such as "assaults, murder, burglary, larceny, robbery, arson,

---

[38] Ellen S. Podgor & Roger S. Clark, Understanding International Criminal Law 2d Ed. 14–25 (2008).

[39] 18 U.S.C. § 1621.

[40] 260 U.S. 94 (1922).

embezzlement and frauds of all kinds" were left for prosecution by the territorial jurisdiction where the act occurred. But they contrasted this with crimes "not logically dependent on their locality for the Government's jurisdiction," and found that these offenses would be subject to extraterritorial application.

Extraterritoriality was an issue in the Supreme Court decision in *Pasquantino v. United States*.[41] The Court looked at whether it was appropriate to apply the federal wire fraud statute to conduct in the United States that was aimed at defrauding a foreign government of taxes. Justice Thomas, writing the majority's opinion, found that the prosecution was properly brought here because the conduct occurred in the United States. It did not matter that the reason for this conduct may have been to defraud Canada of revenue. A dissent by Justice Ginsburg took issue with the majority's conclusion concerning the revenue rule, a canon of statutory construction amounting to a presumption against enforcing foreign revenue laws. She also argued for use of the "rule of lenity" (see § 1.8 (C)) and a "presumption against extraterritoriality."

At the same time the Court issued the *Pasquantino* opinion, it also decided *Small v. United States*,[42] a case examining whether a foreign conviction could be used as a predicate for a gun possession statute that used the language making it "unlawful for any person . . . who has been convicted in any court, or a crime punishable by imprisonment for a term exceeding one year . . . to . . . possess . . . any firearm." The Court found that a Japanese conviction could not be used to satisfy the "convicted in any court" language of the statute. In deciding this case, the Court started by noting that there was a presumption against extraterritoriality in criminal matters.

More recently in *Morrison v. National Australia Bank LTD,*[43] the Court looked at whether there should be an extraterritorial application given to statute § 10(b), despite the Securities Exchange Act's silence as to whether the language applied beyond the United States. The Court found, in this civil action, that section 10(b) is limited to the "purchase or sale of a security listed on an American stock exchange, and the purchase or sale of any other security in the United States." The Court reaffirmed precedent that noted the "longstanding principle of American law 'that legislation of Congress, unless a contrary intent appears, is meant to apply only within the territorial jurisdiction of the United States.'"[44]

Lower courts have allowed some white collar prosecutions for conduct occurring outside the United States. For example, in *United States v. Campbell*,[45] the indictment alleged "criminal acts committed entirely beyond the borders of the United States—in Afghanistan." The government did not premise the case upon territorial jurisdiction. Distinguishing the case from *Morrison,* the D.C. district court allowed this prosecution to proceed finding that "[b]ribery in connection with contracts backed by U.S. financing is illegal precisely because it implicates and adversely affects the interests and purse of the United States." The court found that the "Defendant's alleged violation of 18 U.S.C.

---

[41] 544 U.S. 349 (2005).

[42] 544 U.S. 385 (2005).

[43] 130 S.Ct. 2869 (2010).

[44] Id. at 2877 (citing EEOC v. Arabian American Oil Co., 499 U.S. 244 (1991) (Aramco), quoting Foley Bros., Inc. v. Filardo, 336 U.S. 281 (1949).

[45] 798 F. Supp.2d 293 (D.D.C. 2011).

§ 666(a)(1)(B) in a foreign country may be prosecuted in this country without violating the principle against extraterritorial application of U.S. law, Defendants due process rights, or customary international law."

3. *International Norms*

In some instances courts will look at basic international law principles in deciding whether an extraterritorial application is proper. Five international law principles are often referred to here.[46] The most common comes from the territorial principle, and is called objective territoriality or "effects" jurisdiction. Under this principle, if the conduct affects the United States then jurisdiction may be found in this country. For example, an antitrust case that is built on the conduct having an effect on prices in the United States has been found to be a sufficient basis for an extraterritorial application.[47]

In addition to the territorial principle and its expansion based on objective territoriality, other international norms that courts have used are the nationality principle, the passive personality principle, the protective principle, and the universality principle. The nationality principle is premised on the nationality of the perpetrator. This contrasts with the passive personality principle, which looks at the nationality of the victim. The protective principle focuses on the need to protect the United States. Finally the universality principle, an unlikely one to be used in the white collar crime context, is focused on conduct that is a human rights violation.[48]

The international principle of comity can also play a role in determining the proper country to proceed with the prosecution. Although a term of several meanings, it offers a concept of reciprocity and respect for the laws of another country. In *United States v. Nippon*,[49] the First Circuit held that "[c]omity is more an aspiration than a fixed rule, more a matter of grace than a matter of obligation."

§ 1.8   STATUTORY INTERPRETATION

A. General Principles

Basic issues of statutory interpretation arise in the white collar crime context. There are many approaches to statutory interpretation, and the white collar context is equally subject to courts conflicting in the analysis of legislative language. In some instances a single word, like "willfulness," will have different meanings in different contexts. For example, in *Bryan v. United States*,[50] the Court held the term "willfully" in a firearm statute required "the defendant acted with an evil-meaning mind, that is to say, that he acted with knowledge that his conduct was unlawful." Yet in interpreting a currency reporting statute, the Court in *Ratzlaf v. United States*,[51] held that "willfully" required proof that that defendant knew that his conduct violated the

---

[46] Harvard Research in International Law, Jurisdiction With Respect to Crime, 29 Am. J.Int'l L. 437, 445 (Supp. 1935).

[47] United States v. Nippon, 109 F.3d 1 (1st Cir. 1997).

[48] The Restatement (Third) of the Foreign Relations Law of the United States, § 402 (1987).

[49] 109 F.3d 1 (1st Cir. 1997).

[50] 524 U.S. 184 (1998).

[51] 510 U.S. 135 (1994).

particular statute rather than just that he knew it was generally unlawful. It is no wonder that the Supreme Court in *Spies v. United States*[52] noted that "willful" is a word of many meanings and that "its construction [is often] influenced by its context."

Key to statutory interpretation is discerning the legislative intent.[53] Obviously, the plain language of the statute is the first place to look to ascertain what the legislators meant when writing the statute. If the language is clear, interpretation of the statute is made easier. Many courts will also look at the legislative history to see why the statute was created and the problem it sought to alleviate. Courts and scholars conflict on what role that legislative history should play in statutory interpretation. Some may argue that congressional debates are not passed by the legislative body and therefore should not be used as definitive of the legislative meaning. Others will say that legislative history provides clues as to what Congress meant when the statute was passed.

Changes in the law may prove helpful in ascertaining the legislative intent. For example, a congressional modification to 18 U.S.C. § 1030, the Computer Fraud and Abuse Act of 1986, caused the Second Circuit to find in *United States v. Morris*,[54] that the deliberate change in some portions of the statute meant that it did not intend to change the statutory portion that was being questioned by the defendant.

The statute's title may also provide guidance to a court seeking to interpret the statute. Additionally courts may look at how the term is used in comparable statutes. Other statutory interpretation tools may apply, such as *ejusdem generis*, a rule that applies when general language in a statute follows specific terms in the statute. According to this principle, the general language is limited by the specific terms. *Expressio unius est exclusion alterius* means that "the expression of one thing is the exclusion of another."

Discerning the intent of Congress may go beyond the mere words used in the statute. For example, in *United States v. Singleton*,[55] a Tenth Circuit en banc opinion vacated a panel decision that had ruled that it was a violation of the anti-gratuity statute when a prosecutor "offered leniency to a co-defendant in exchange for truthful testimony." The court noted the absurdity of applying section 201(c)(2) to the government's prosecutorial powers, which included a "longstanding practice of leniency for testimony." "[I]f Congress had intended that section 201(c)(2) overturn this ingrained aspect of American legal culture, it would have done so in clear, unmistakable, and unarguable language." (See Chapter 10).

White collar criminal cases are no different from other criminal matters in that they can require statutory interpretation. As noted in *Dowling v. United States*,[56] a case interpreting language in the National Stolen Property Act, "when assessing the reach of a federal criminal statute, we must pay close heed to language, legislative history, and purpose in order strictly to determine the scope of the conduct the

---

[52] 317 U.S. 492, 497 (1943).

[53] Wayne R. LaFave, Criminal Law 5th Ed. § 2.2 (2010).

[54] 928 F.2d 504 (2d Cir. 1991).

[55] 165 F.3d 1297 (10th Cir. 1999).

[56] 473 U.S. 207 (1985).

enactment forbids." White collar cases may also involve administrative regulations, and administrative interpretations may influence how it will be resolved.

B. Rule of Lenity

Penal laws are strictly construed with "ambiguity concerning the ambit of criminal statutes" "resolved in favor of lenity."[57] Thus, when there are two constitutional meanings that can be given to a statute, the rule of lenity requires giving the benefit to the defendant in how the statute gets interpreted. A rationale for the using the rule of lenity is that a defendant should be provided with due process (notice) of the charges against him or her. If the statute is unclear, it is problematic to the individual's understanding that the conduct they engaged in is wrong and criminal in nature. One finds lenity arguments being made by defendants, and courts have used this principle in interpreting white collar cases. For example, the Supreme Court has looked to the rule of lenity on several occasions when interpreting the mail fraud statute. In *Cleveland v. United States*,[58] a case involving the interpretation of what constitutes "property" for purposes of mail fraud, the Court noted the importance of using the rule of lenity with a statute that could be used as a predicate act for the crimes such as RICO and money laundering. The Court held that "[i]n deciding what is 'property' under § 1341, we think 'it is appropriate, before we choose the harsher alternative, to require that Congress should have spoken in language that is clear and definite.'" (See § 4.4).

C. *Mens Rea* Element

1. *Generally*

It is common for *mens rea* to be an issue in a white collar case, as defendants may argue that they did not intend any wrongdoing. The concern in some cases may be whether the defendant knew that the conduct was criminal. The level of intent that the prosecutor needs to prove to obtain a conviction will depend upon the statute charged against the accused. Some white collar offenses require that the defendant act knowingly or recklessly. Others may allow for strict liability.

Obviously, the first place for determining the *mens rea* will be in looking at the statute itself, and perhaps legislative history that may assist with interpretation of the wording of the statute. Case law and policy considerations also play a role in interpreting the statute. (See supra A).

Having no *mens rea* term within the language of the statute does not mean that it is strict liability. As noted by Chief Justice Burger in *United States v. United States Gypsum Co.*,[59] "the existence of a *mens rea* is the rule of, rather than the exception to, the principles of Anglo–American criminal jurisprudence."[60] Thus, courts will often read a *mens rea* term into a statute that might omit the explicit intent language.

---

[57] United States v. Bass, 404 U.S. 336 (1971); Rewis v. United States, 401 U.S. 808 (1971).

[58] 531 U.S. 12 (2000).

[59] 438 U.S. 422 (1978).

[60] Citing Dennis v. United States, 341 U.S. 494 (1951).

That said, there are many white collar statutes that do not require a showing of a *mens rea* and have been found to be strict liability. Public welfare offenses often are classified as white collar crimes, and these offenses may be strict liability. For example, Section 13 of the Rivers and Harbors Act (Refuse Act) is considered strict liability. (See § 14.3).

Although the principle of "ignorance of the law generally is no defense to a criminal charge," white collar statutes that are highly complex and technical may call for the defendant to have acted knowingly. In *Cheek v. United States*,[61] the defendant was charged with tax crimes for failing to file tax returns, claiming an "increasing number of withholding allowances," and seeking a refund on withheld tax. The Supreme Court in reversing the defendant's conviction and remanding the case for retrial noted that "[w]illfulness, as construed by our prior decisions in criminal tax cases, requires the Government to prove that the law imposed a duty on the defendant, that the defendant knew of this duty, and that he voluntarily and intentionally violated that duty." (See § 11.2(B)(5)). The Court took a similar position in *Ratzlaf v. United States*[62] in holding that "currency structuring is not inevitably nefarious." (See § 12.2(F)(2)). Like tax, the Court was concerned that "highly technical statutes" present a "danger of ensnaring individuals engaged in apparently innocent conduct."[63]

2. *Willful Blindness*

White collar cases can include government claims that the accused should be held criminally liable, despite saying that he or she did not know of the criminal activities, because the defendant was willfully blind. The government may request that the court give an instruction saying that knowledge can be demonstrated when the defendant avoids learning the truth. Willful blindness, sometimes call the "ostrich instruction," is premised on the theory that the defendant avoids learning the truth by burying his or her head in the sand.[64] This can arise in a white collar case when a corporate executive may be claiming that he or she did not know about the criminal conduct of an employee, and therefore, that they should not be held criminally accountable.

The Supreme Court in *Global–Tech Appliances, Inc. v. SEB*,[65] a civil patent infringement case, examined the criminal law of willful blindness. The Court held that mere recklessness or negligence would not suffice for willful blindness. For a showing of willful blindness it is necessary to show that "First, the defendant must subjectively believe that there is a high probability that a fact exists. Second, the defendant must take deliberate actions to avoid learning of that fact." The Court noted that "a willfully blind defendant is one who takes deliberate actions to avoid confirming a high probability of wrongdoing and who can almost be said to have actually known the critical facts." A dissent by Justice Kennedy questioned willful blindness being knowledge.

---

[61] 498 U.S. 192 (1991).

[62] 510 U.S. 135 (1994).

[63] Bryan v. United States, 524 U.S. 184, 194–95 (1998).

[64] See United States v. Giovannetti, 919 F.2d 1223 (7th Cir. 1990); United States v. Black, 530 F.3d 596, 604 (7th Cir. 2008).

[65] 131 S.Ct. 2060 (2011).

3. *Good Faith Reliance on Counsel*

Just as the prosecution may be seeking an instruction that the defendant was willfully blind, the defense may want an instruction that the accused relied upon counsel. Courts have looked at a variety of factors in deciding whether to allow this defense argument. In the *Cheek* retrial this issue arose and the Seventh Circuit provided a list of considerations to be used in determining whether it was appropriate to allow an advice of counsel defense.[66] The court held that to use this defense a defendant must establish that:

> (1) before taking action, (2) he in good faith sought the advice of an attorney whom he considered competent, (3) for the purpose of securing advice of the lawfulness of his possible future conduct, (4) and made a full and accurate report to his attorney of all material facts which the defendant knew, (5) and acted strictly in accordance with the advice of his attorney who had been given a full report.

Courts have limited the good faith reliance on counsel to crimes that require willfulness.[67] This includes, however, criminal prosecutions under the Securities Act of 1933.[68] Good faith reliance on counsel is "not a complete defense, but is merely one factor a jury may consider when determining whether a defendant acted willfully."[69]

§ 1.9   CONSTITUTIONAL CONSIDERATIONS

A. Vagueness

When the meaning of a statute is unclear, courts may find the statute vague. A statute cannot be so "vague that men of common intelligence must necessarily guess at its meaning and differ as to its application."[70] When a "person of ordinary intelligence" cannot understand the meaning of a statute, it violates the due process clause of the Fifth Amendment of the United States Constitution, or the Fourteenth Amendment if the statute is a state statute. Court precedent that provides meaning to the statute can serve to avoid the statute being held vague as the court interpretation provides notice to the individuals that the conduct is prohibited. Fair warning of the statute is needed, as well as there being no arbitrary and discriminatory enforcement.[71]

White collar crime cases have included vagueness challenges. The complexity of some white collar statutes can intensify the need for clarity. Although courts commonly employ the rule of lenity in white collar cases, vagueness challenges have been less successful.

---

[66] United States v. Cheek, 3 F.3d 1057 (7th Cir. 1993).

[67] United States v. Langston, 590 F.3d 1226, 1235 (11th Cir. 2009);

[68] United States v. Wenger, 427 F.3d 840, 853 (10th Cir. 2005).

[69] Id.

[70] Connally v. General Const. Co., 269 U.S. 385 (1926).

[71] Lafave, supra note 53, § 2.3.

B. Speech and Debate Clause

The Speech and Debate Clause provides immunity to members of Congress from being questioned regarding their legislative acts. As the Court noted in *Gravel v. United States*,[72]

> the Speech and Debate Clause was designed to assure a co-equal branch of the government wide freedom of speech, debate, and deliberation without intimidation or threats from the Executive Branch. It thus protects Members against prosecutions that directly impinge upon or threaten the legislative process.

Several courts have noted that the "pervasive" use of materials before a grand jury that violates the Speech and Debate Clause of the Constitution, warrants the invalidation of the indictment.[73]

Courts have noted limitations to this constitutional provision. For example, in *United States v. Brewster*[74] the Court held that the Clause prohibits "inquiry only into those things generally said or done in the House or the Senate in the performance of official duties and into the motivation for those acts." It does not affect "inquiry into activities that are casually or incidentally related to legislative affairs but not a part of the legislative process itself."

In *United States v. Jefferson*,[75] the defendant, a then sitting U.S. Congressman, argued that the indictment against him violated the Speech and Debate Clause of the Constitution.[76] He was charged with crimes including bribery, wire fraud, violation of the Foreign Corrupt Practices Act, money laundering, obstruction of justice, and racketeering. The Fourth Circuit affirmed the decision of the district court "that neither the Indictment nor the grand jury proceedings infringed the Speech or Debate Clause." The court noted that the trial court had gone beyond what was necessary to review the grand jury materials to make certain there was no use of any Speech and Debate Clause material by the grand jury.

The *Jefferson* court contrasted its decision with the Eleventh Circuit holding in *United States v. Swindall*,[77] where the government used a congressman's committee memberships as evidence to show that he had knowledge of certain statutes and that he was therefore committing perjury before the grand jury. In *Swindall*, the court reversed three of the ten counts against the defendant because it was improper for the government to use as critical evidence Speech and Debate material and also to question the defendant in the grand jury about Speech and Debate matters. The court in *Swindall* stated, "[t]he only way to vindicate a member's privilege to be free from improper questioning is to exclude the fruits of such questioning. If the questioning occurs at trial, a conviction cannot stand. If the questioning occurs before the grand jury, the affected counts of the indictment cannot stand."

---

[72] 408 U.S. 606 (1972).

[73] See United States v. Helstoski, 635 F.2d 200, 205 (3d Cir. 1980).

[74] 408 U.S. 501 (1972).

[75] 546 F.3d 300 (4th Cir. 2008).

[76] U.S. Const. Art. I, § 6, cl.1.

[77] 971 F.2d 1531, 1549 (11th Cir. 1992).

C. Other Constitutional Requirements

Other constitutional standards applicable in criminal cases apply equally to white collar matters. For example, the statute cannot violate the First Amendment. In *United States v. Alvarez,*[78] the accused reserved the right on appeal to question the constitutionality of the Stolen Valor Act of 2005.[79] He had lied about having received the Congressional Medal of Honor, a direct violation of this criminal statute. The Court noted that there are certain content-based restrictions that are permitted,

> [a]mong these categories are advocacy intended, and likely, to incite imminent lawless action, obscenity, defamation, speech integral to criminal conduct; so-called 'fighting words'; child pornography; fraud; true threats; and speech presenting some grave and imminent threat the government has the power to prevent (citations and parentheticals omitted).

Falsity alone, however, was found insufficient as a basis for criminal conduct as there is no "general exception to the First Amendment for false statements." The Court noted that in defamation matters, the statement had to be a "knowing and reckless falsehood." The Court distinguished false statements made in violation of the false statement[80] and perjury[81] statutes, as these statements are linked to important government injuries. "Perjury undermines the function and province of the law and threatens the integrity of judgments that are the basis of the legal system." The key test to be used in finding that a false statement has not violated the First Amendment is whether there is "a direct causal link between the restriction imposed and the injury being prevented." The Court found that the Stolen Valor Act "did not satisfy exacting scrutiny" and was unconstitutional.

In white collar cases, as in other criminal matters, it is also important to consider the prohibitions against laws that are ex post facto and bills of attainder.[82] Defendants also bring challenges to laws and government conduct premised on violations of due process.

In *United States v. Williams,*[83] the defendant went beyond arguing a traditional entrapment defense. Senator Williams was convicted of charges related to bribery as part of an undercover government operation called Operation Abscam. In addition to arguing that he was entrapped, he argued that outrageous government conduct violated his due process rights. Unlike entrapment where the defendant's predisposition is a focal point of the inquiry, a claim of outrageous government conduct looks at the conduct of the government officials. The court did not find a due process violation with regard to the government conduct in Operation Abscam.

---

[78] 132 S.Ct. 2537 (2012).

[79] 18 U.S.C. § 704.

[80] 18 U.S.C. § 1001; see also Chapter 9.

[81] 18 U.S.C. § 1623; see also Chapter 10.

[82] LaFave, supra note 53, § 2.4.

[83] 705 F.2d 603 (2d Cir. 1983).

Chapter 2

CORPORATE CRIMINAL LIABILITY

§ 2.1   OVERVIEW

A. History

Despite the fact that corporations have no body, no mind, and cannot be imprisoned, they can be held criminally liable.[1] But historically, this was not the case. At common law, corporations were not subject to criminal liability.[2]

The first stage in the development of corporate criminal liability was when courts found corporate criminal liability for violations of regulatory offenses involving acts of omission. This was a logical extension of the common law in that the conduct required no act and also no *mens rea*. These regulatory offenses did not require prison time, so courts considered it acceptable to expand corporate criminal liability for a punishment of fines for the improper corporate behavior.

The second stage of corporate criminal liability came when liability was allowed for strict liability offenses that were not merely omission conduct. This development was also logical to courts in that there seemed little basis to differentiate between active and passive conduct, or as some termed it, misfeasance and nonfeasance. There was still no *mens rea* required and no imprisonment could be given for these regulatory offenses that would be subject to corporate criminal liability, so the extension of this criminal liability was considered justified.

The third stage of corporate criminal liability came when the extension of liability moved beyond strict liability crimes to those that had a *mens rea* element. Even in this new arena, corporations, obviously, were not able to be imprisoned. But the ability to proceed against them for substantive crimes that required intentional acts was now held to be acceptable under law.

B. New York Central

New York Central & Hudson River Railroad Co. v. United States[3] is the landmark decision for the acceptance of corporate criminal liability for crimes requiring a *mens rea*. The defendant company was accused of violating the Elkins Act, which prohibited a person or corporation from granting or receiving rebates for the transportation of property in interstate commerce by common carrier. The act was not premised on omission conduct and the intent of the actor was an element of the crime. The Act provided "if done or omitted to be done by any director or officer thereof, or any

---

[1] Wayne R. LaFave, Criminal Law 5th Ed. 740–41 (2010).

[2] Jerold H. Israel, Ellen S. Podgor, Paul D. Borman, & Peter J. Henning, White Collar Crime: Law and Practice 3d Ed. 52 (2009).

[3] 212 U.S. 481 (1909).

23

receiver, trustee, lessee, agent, or person acting for or employed by such corporation, would constitute a misdemeanor under said acts, or under this act, shall also be held to be a misdemeanor committed by such corporation . . . "

The corporation argued against such liability, questioning the constitutionality of subjecting a corporation to criminal prosecution. It claimed that "Congress [had] no authority to impute to a corporation the commission of criminal offenses" and that it was a due process violation to "punish the innocent stockholders, and to deprive them of their property without [an] opportunity to be heard."

Rejecting these arguments, the Court reflected on how civil tort law holds a corporation liable for the acts of its agents. The Court, in using this same standard for corporate criminal liability stated,

> [a]pplying the principle governing civil liability, we go only a step farther in holding that

> the act of the agent, while exercising the authority delegated to him to make rates for transportation, may be controlled, in the interest of public policy, by imputing his act to his employer and imposing penalties upon the corporation for which he is acting in the premises.

The Court also stated that there was "no valid objection in law, and every reason in public policy, why the corporation, which profits by the transaction, and can only act through its agents and officers," should be held criminally liable and punished with a fine.

In finding corporate criminal liability applicable to violations of the Elkins Act, the Court did not say that all criminal acts would allow for this type of criminal liability. "Some crimes," they noted, "cannot be committed by corporations." But the Court did not elaborate on which crimes would not be subject to corporate criminal liability.

C. Corporate Crimes

There is no definitive list of offenses that are subject to corporate criminal liability. In the federal law one finds an array of different charges against corporations, such as conspiracy, RICO, mail and wire fraud, environmental offenses, and obstruction of justice. Federal prosecutors continually use many different white collar crimes to prosecute corporations. In the wake of corporate scandals, several recent statutes such as the Foreign Corrupt Practices Act (FCPA) have been used to prosecute criminal liability in the corporate sphere. (See § 5.7, § 7.7).

Outside the United States, one does not find as widespread an acceptance of corporate criminal liability. Some western countries have moved slower in adopting corporate criminal liability, and some have resisted its adoption, opting in some cases for "quasi-criminal administrative liability."[4]

---

[4] Sara Sun Beale & Adam G. Safwat, White Collar Criminal Law in Comparative Perspective: The Sarbanes–Oxley Act of 2002, 8 Buff. Crim. L. Rev. 89 (2004).

The federal government is not the only body involved in punishing corporate misconduct. States also proceed against corporations. There is, however, no uniform agreement among the states on whether corporate criminal liability should apply to personal crimes such as homicide offenses. Often the resolution is dependent on whether the state statute specifies that the crime be committed against a "person" "by another person."

In *Granite Construction Co. v. Superior Court of Fresno County*[5] a California Appellate Court permitted a corporate prosecution for manslaughter as the legislative language found in the California Penal Code defined "person" to include corporations. The court noted that "[i]f corporations are liable for crimes of specific intent, then they should be equally liable for crimes of criminal negligence or recklessness." In contrast, in *State v. Pacific Powder Co.*,[6] the Oregon Supreme Court refused to extend corporate criminal liability for acts of involuntary manslaughter as the word "person" as used in the involuntary manslaughter statute did not include corporations.[7]

D. Corporations as "Persons"

In the federal code, 1 U.S.C. § 1 provides that "the words 'person' and 'whoever' as used throughout the federal code, include corporations, companies, associations, firms, partnerships, societies, and joint stock companies, as well as individuals." Many states use comparable language in their statutes.[8]

As previously noted (supra § C), one finds corporations regularly prosecuted under many different federal criminal statutes. Likewise, states also pursue criminal charges against corporations.

Corporate criminal liability may have been further cemented in the law with the Supreme Court's decision in *Citizens United v. Federal Election Commission,*[9] where the Court held that corporations have the same constitutional First Amendment rights as those of people. The Court stated, "political speech does not lose First Amendment protection 'simply because its source is a corporation.'" The Court noted that prior decisions "rejected the argument that political speech of corporations or other associations should be treated differently under the First Amendment simply because such associations are not 'natural persons.'"[10] Although this decision focused on federal campaign finance law, election law, and constitutional law, it is possible that this opinion will become a source of reference in the corporate criminal world.[11]

---

[5] 149 Cal.App.3d 465, 197 Cal.Rptr. 3 (Cal. App. 1983).

[6] 360 P.2d 530 (Or. 1961).

[7] See also State v. Richard Knutson, Inc., 537 N.W.2d 420 (Wis.Ct. App. 1995).

[8] See, e.g., 1 Del.C. § 302 (15) ("person" and "whoever" respectively include corporations, companies, associations, firms, partnerships, societies and joint-stock companies, as well as individuals).

[9] 558 U.S. 310 (2010).

[10] Id. at 900.

[11] See Christopher Slobogin, Citizens United and Corporate & Human Crime, 41 Stetson L. Rev. 127 (2011) (discussing corporate procedural issues that may arise as a result of this decision); Joan MacLeod Heminway, Thoughts on the Corporation as a Person for Purposes of Corporate Criminal Liability, 41 Stetson L.Rev. 137 (2011) (discussing connections between *Citizens United* and corporate criminal liability).

E. Challenges to Corporate Criminality

Although corporate criminal liability is widely accepted in both the federal and state systems, scholars continue to argue against this legal doctrine. Arguments include that corporate civil liability could achieve the same benefits as criminal responsibility,[12] that corporate criminal liability does not advance accepted punishment theories like deterrence,[13] and that the present use of vicarious liability in prosecuting corporations places prosecutors with enormous power and "inordinate leverage."[14] Other arguments include that vicarious liability will ultimately place the penalty on innocent stockholders and that it "results in a disparity between businesses conducted in the corporate form and those run as a proprietorship."[15] This is because "individual proprietor[s] will not be criminally liable for independent acts of his employees."[16]

Many have argued that a "good faith" defense should be allowed to corporations who are charged with criminality.[17] The argument is made that the "good faith" defense provided to corporations in civil harassment cases should be allowed when a corporation is charged with criminal conduct.[18] This defense would provide some relief to corporations who were victimized by a rogue employee.

It has also been argued that when *respondeat superior* is used to impute corporate criminal liability to a company, it looks only at the *mens rea* of the agent who commits a crime, as opposed to the non-criminal acts of other corporate parties. Thus, the corporate criminal liability is argued as having "overinclusiveness" problems.[19]

A recent federal court challenge to corporate criminal liability included the argument that there was a failure to restrict the doctrine to acts of "managerial" employees. In *United States v. Ionia Management S.A.*,[20] the Second Circuit held that there was no requirement to show that the criminal acts were by managerial employees. The court in *Ionia Management* also found that there was no requirement

---

[12] V.S. Khanna, Corporate Criminal Liability: What Purpose Does it Serve, 109 Harv. L. Rev. 1477 (1996); Eliezer Lederman, Criminal Law, Perpetrator and Corporation: Rethinking a Complex Triangle, 76 J. Crim. L. & Criminology 285 (1983).

[13] John Hasnas, The Centenary of a Mistake: One Hundred Years of Corporate Criminal Liability, 46 Am. Crim. L. Rev. 1329 (2009).

[14] Andrew Weissmann, A New Approach to Corporate Criminal Liability, 44 Am. Crim. L. Rev. 1319 (2007).

[15] John C. Coffee, Jr., Corporate Criminal Responsibility, 1 Encyclopedia of Crime and Justice 257 (1983).

[16] Id.

[17] See Ellen S. Podgor, A New Corporate World Mandates a "Good Faith" Affirmative Defense, 44 Am. Crim. L. Rev. 1537, 1538 (2007) (discussing the scholars who have advocated for a "good faith" defense in corporate criminal law).

[18] See Burlington Industries, Inc. v. Ellerth, 524 U.S. 742 (1998) (allowing an affirmative defense when an employer is being sued for sexual harassment premised upon acts of a manager); Faragher v. City of Boca Raton, 524 U.S. 775, 807 (1998) (same). These cases provide that "[t]he defense comprises two necessary elements: (a) that the employer exercised reasonable care to prevent and correct promptly any sexually harassing behavior, and (b) that the plaintiff employee unreasonably failed to take advantage of any preventive or corrective opportunities provided by the employer or to avoid harm otherwise."

[19] Jennifer Moore, Corporate Culpability Under the Federal Sentencing Guidelines, 34 Ariz. L. Rev. 743, 759–60 (1992).

[20] 555 F.3d 303 (2d Cir. 2009); see also United States v. Twentieth Century Fox Film Corp., 882 F.2d 656 (2d Cir. 1989).

for the prosecution to prove that the "corporation lacked effective policies and procedures to deter and detect criminal actions by its employees."

In state courts one may find claims that the state statute fails to expressly provide for corporate criminal liability, and therefore the courts should not allow this form of liability. For example, in *State v. Shepherd Const. Co., Inc.*,[21] defendants argued that a Georgia restraint in trade statute did not provide a sentence applicable to a corporation. The sentences were to be for a term of years, subject to suspension. Since a corporation is incapable of being imprisoned, the argument was made that the statute did not intend for corporate criminality.

The Georgia Supreme Court rejected the argument made in *Shepherd* saying that the state code defined "person" to include corporations and also provided courts with the power to suspend a prison sentence and impose a fine of up to ten thousand dollars. Thus, imposing a fine was in keeping with the legislative intent. To hold otherwise, the court noted, would result in "corporate immunity" for serious crimes. One of the dissenters, Justice Smith, said "that corporations should be accountable under a criminal bid-rigging statute," but that the legislature should be the ones to make the decision of corporate accountability.

F. Targeting Corporate Fraud

Several legislative initiatives have targeted corporate fraud. For example, the Watergate Investigation in the 1970s disclosed illegal corporate payments, which resulted in the passage of the Foreign Corrupt Practices Act to curtail international bribery by public companies. (See § 5.7, § 7.7). The Enron debacle produced both the Sarbanes–Oxley legislation and the creation of a Corporate Fraud Task Force by President George W. Bush.

The Corporate Fraud Task Force, created on July 9, 2002, had as its purpose "to restore public and investor confidence in America's corporations following a wave of major corporate scandals."[22] In the five year period from 2002–2007, this Task Force had 1,236 corporate fraud convictions, which included "214 chief executive officers and presidents; 53 chief financial officers; 23 corporate counsels or attorneys; and 129 vice presidents."[23] In addition to prosecutions against corporate officers and employees, the government also proceeded against several corporations. For example, AEP Energy Services "agreed to pay a $30 million criminal penalty." "PNC entered into a deferred prosecution agreement and PNC and ICLC agreed to pay a total of $115 million in restitution and penalties." A long list of companies have now entered into deferred or non-prosecution agreements. (See § 2.4(C)).

In November 2009, President Barak Obama, targeting financial institution fraud, changed the focus of the Corporate Fraud Task Force renaming it the Financial Fraud Enforcement Task Force. This task force is "[c]omposed of more than 25 federal

---

[21] 281 S.E.2d 151 (Ga. 1981).

[22] Department of Justice, Fact Sheet: President's Corporate Fraud Task Force Marks Five Years of Ensuring Corporate Integrity, July 17, 2007, available at http://www.justice.gov/opa/pr/2007/July/07_odag_507.html.

[23] Id.

agencies, regulators and inspectors general, as well as state and local partners." The executive order creating this task force directs it:

> (1) to investigate and prosecute financial crimes and other violations relating to the current financial crisis and economic recovery efforts; (2) to recover the proceeds for such crimes and violations; (3) to address discrimination in the lending and financial markets; (4) to enhance coordination and cooperation among federal, state and local authorities responsible for the investigation and prosecution of financial crimes and violations; and (5) to conduct outreach to the public, victims, financial institutions, non-profit organizations, state and local governments and agencies, and other interested partners to enhance detection and prevention of financial fraud schemes.

The Task Force issued its first report in 2010.[24]

In FY 2011, the Sentencing Commission reported that 160 cases had used the organizational guidelines, Chapter 8 of the Federal Sentencing Guidelines. This number was close to the average for years immediately prior to FY 2011. Of those cases, 151 entities plead guilty and 9 were convicted after a jury trial. (See § 24.7). These numbers do not reflect some corporate agreements with the government. For example, non-prosecution agreements may have no plea, no court hearing, and therefore may not be having a court's use of the Organizational Guidelines of the Federal Sentencing Guidelines.

§ 2.2   STANDARDS FOR LIABILITY

A.   Respondeat Superior

Federal courts and some states use the civil law tort principle of *respondeat superior* in applying corporate criminal liability. The corporation is held criminally liable for the criminal acts of its agent within the scope of his or her employment that are intended to benefit the corporation.[25] "No distinctions are made in these cases between officers and agents, or between persons holding positions involving varying degrees of responsibility."[26] As previously noted, there is also no good faith defense for acts by a rogue employee or acts that are directly opposed to company policy. It is, however, necessary that the agent have acted for the benefit of the company. An agent that acts for his or her own personal benefit is not acting on behalf of the corporation. (See § 2.3(A)).

Prosecutors have the burden to prove the agency relationship that allows the corporation to be found guilty of the crime. Typically courts look at whether the agent is "performing acts of the kind which he is authorized to perform," and those acts are

---

[24] First Year Report, Financial Fraud Enforcement Task Force, available at http://www.stopfraud. gov/docs/FFETF–Report–LR.pdf.

[25] United States v. George F. Fish, Inc., 154 F.2d 798 (2d Cir. 1946).

[26] Id. Although courts have used the term "employee" and "agent" interchangeable when discussing corporate criminal liability. United States v. Singh, 518 F.3d 236 (4th Cir. 2008).

"motivated—at least in part—by an intent to benefit the corporation.[27] The agency relationship can be demonstrated by either a showing of actual or apparent authority.

In the case of *United States v. Bi–Co Pavers, Inc.*,[28] the court stated that "[a]pparent authority is the authority which outsiders would normally assume the agent to have, judging from his position with the company and the circumstances surrounding his past conduct." This was a case where the company was charged with bid rigging and there was evidence that showed that an individual had bid for contracts in the company name and signed contracts on behalf of the company. An accountant also confirmed that the employee had authority to bid on the projects. This demonstrated to the court, authority to act for the company.

B. Model Penal Code

1. *Generally*

In contrast to the *respondeat superior* theory of corporate criminal liability, the Model Penal Code adds the language of a "high managerial agent."[29] The Model Penal Code was adopted by the American Law Institute in 1962. The approach of the Model Penal Code is three-fold dependent upon the crime involved. Although the federal system does not endorse the Model Penal Code standard, some states have adopted this provision.

Section 2.07 of the Model Penal Code permits a conviction for corporate criminal liability:

> 1) for violations (minor offenses not classified as crimes that are punishable by fine only) or offenses defined by statute outside the criminal code where the legislature has clearly imposed liability on the corporation "and the conduct is performed by an agent acting in behalf of the corporation within the scope of his office or employment;" (2) where there is an omission of a specific duty of affirmative performance imposed on corporations by law; or (3) where the offense was authorized, performed, or recklessly tolerated by the board of directors or by a high managerial agent acting in behalf of the corporation within the scope of employment.[30]

The Model Penal Code provides that "[w]hen absolute liability is imposed for the commission of an offense, a legislative purpose to impose liability on a corporation shall be assumed, unless the contrary plainly appears." Thus, corporations can be held strictly liable under the Model Penal Code.

The Model Penal Code includes both corporations and other unincorporated associations. For both corporations and unincorporated associations, when the legislature designates an accountable agent, or has specified the circumstances of accountability, the legislature's designation will control.

---

[27] United States v. Potter, 463 F.3d 9, 25 (1st Cir. 2006) (citing United States v. Cincotta, 689 F.2d 238, 241–242 (1st Cir. 1982).

[28] 741 F.2d 730 (5th Cir. 1984).

[29] Francis Bowes Sayre, Criminal Responsibility for the Acts of Another, 43 Harv. L. Rev. 689 (1930).

[30] Ellen S. Podgor & Jerold H. Israel, White Collar Crime in a Nutshell 4th Ed. 20 (2009).

2. High Managerial Agent

States that have endorsed a Model Penal Code view have not been free of controversies. Determinations often have to be made as to who serves as a "high managerial agent." The Model Penal Code defines this agent as one "having duties of such responsibility that his conduct may fairly be assumed to represent the policy of the corporation or association."

When the agent is the CEO, it is usually easy to say that this suffices as someone who is a high managerial agent. But it becomes more problematic as one goes further down the corporate ladder. One court focused on intent, saying that complicity by the officers or directors of the corporation was needed. Although the intent may be clear when the crime results from a direct authorization of the board of directors, a criminal act committed by an employee with no authorization or knowledge by the corporation is insufficient. In *State v. Chapman Dodge Center, Inc.*,[31] the manager handled the operations of an automobile dealership. The Louisiana Supreme Court said that there was no corporate criminal liability in this case in that the president had no real knowledge and control of the day-to-day business operations.

In contrast, the Minnesota Supreme Court in *State v. Christy Pontiac–GMC, Inc.*[32] found corporate criminal liability for conduct involving a rebate scheme in an automobile dealership where the individual directly accused of having committed the criminal acts was a salesperson and fleet manager. The court stated that the individual "was acting in furtherance of the corporation's business interests." Since the benefits went to the corporation, and not the individual, plus the fact that there was participation by a corporate officer and acknowledgement of the problem by the president, provided sufficient evidence to support a finding of corporate criminal liability.

3. Rejecting the Model Penal Code

Some states struggle with whether to use a respondeat superior approach or alternatively require the Model Penal Code's high managerial agent. In *Commonwealth v. Beneficial Finance Co.*,[33] the Massachusetts Supreme Court struggled with this issue when the corporate defendants advocated for the Model Penal Code's requirement of a high managerial agent. In contrast the Commonwealth stated, "[i]t isn't the name of the office that counts, but it's the position in which the corporation placed that person with relation to its business, with regard to the powers and duties and responsibilities and authority which it gave to him which counts."

In affirming the trial court's jury instruction premised on respondeat superior, the Supreme Court of Massachusetts noted evidentiary deficiencies in using a Model Penal Code approach. The Court also used strong public policy interests for rejecting the Model Penal Code, noting that "[i]t is very difficult to obtain the conviction of the true policy formulators in large, complex corporations. The top executive[s] do not ordinarily

---

[31] 428 So. 2d 413 (La. 1983). (In this case the dealership was owned by a corporation that was the subsidiary of another corporation which in turn was owned by the president).

[32] 354 N.W.2d 17 (Minn. 1984).

[33] 275 N.E.2d 33 (Mass. 1971).

carry out the overt criminal acts—it is the lower or middle management officials who, for example, attend price-fixing meetings." The court stated:

> In a large corporation, with many numerous and distinct departments, a high ranking corporate officer or agent may have no authority or involvement in a particular sphere of corporate activity, whereas a lower ranking corporate executive might have much broader power in dealing with a matter peculiarly within the scope of his authority. Employees who are in the lower echelon of the corporate hierarchy often exercise more responsibility in the everyday operations of the corporation than the directors or officers. Assuredly, the title or office that the person holds may be considered, but it should not be the decisive criterion upon which to predicate corporate responsibility.

C. Other Scholarly Approaches

Many have written about how best to approach corporate criminal liability and when to hold a corporation liable. For example, Professor Pamela Bucy advocates for an approach premised on looking at the "distinct and identifiable personality or 'ethos'" of the corporation. She states that "[t]he government can convict a corporation under this standard only if it proves that the corporate ethos encouraged agents of the corporation to commit the criminal act."[34] Professor Eli Lederman proposes a "self-identity" approach that recognizes that "a large organization is not only a collection of people who shape it and activate it, but also a set of attributes and positions, which influence, constrain, and at times even define the modes of thinking and behavior of the people who populate it . . . "[35]

§ 2.3   PROVING CORPORATE CRIMINAL LIABILITY

A. For the Benefit

Corporate criminality requires that the act be "for the benefit" of the corporation. Thus, when an employee does not act on behalf of the company or acts for his or her own personal benefit, it may be insufficient for finding the corporation criminally liable. It is not, however, necessary for the company to have actually benefitted. Although an actual corporate benefit is not necessary, its existence or its absence, may provide "evidential value in determining whether or not the corporate officer or agent actually intended to benefit the corporation through her illegal conduct."[36] It is possible, however, to have an agent acting to benefit both him or herself and the corporation.[37]

In *Standard Oil Company of Texas v. United States*,[38] the Fifth Circuit reversed convictions under the Connally Hot Oil Act. One of the issues on appeal was whether the corporation should be held liable when the actions did not benefit the corporation.

---

[34] Professor Pamela H. Bucy, Corporate Ethos: A Standard for Imposing Corporate Criminal Liability, 75 Minn. L. Rev. 1095, 1099 (1991).

[35] Eli Lederman, Models for Imposing Corporate Criminal Liability: From Adaptation and Imitation Toward Aggregation and the Search for Self–Identity, 4 Buff. Crim. L. Rev. 641, 678 (2000).

[36] United States v. Halpin, 145 F.R.D. 447 (N.D. Ohio 1992).

[37] United States v. Automated Medical Laboratories, Inc. 770 F.2d 399 (4th Cir. 1985).

[38] 307 F.2d 120 (5th Cir. 1962).

The court stated, "[u]nder a statute requiring that there be 'a specific wrongful intent,' . . . the corporation does not acquire that knowledge or possess the requisite 'state of mind essential for responsibility' through the activities of unfaithful servants whose conduct was undertaken to advance the interests of parties other than their corporate employer."

An employee can be acting on behalf of a company despite the fact that the company has issued directives prohibiting the conduct in question. When the offense is a regulatory offense, such as a prohibition against throwing garbage from a ship into navigable waters, the corporation can be held liable despite the fact that personnel were told not to engage in these acts.[39]

Likewise, in *United States v. Hilton Hotels Corp.*,[40] the Ninth Circuit examined a case where purchasing agents participated in a boycott by threatening a supplier with loss of the hotel's business if the supplier refused to pay a fee to an association organized to attract conventions to the city. This kickback type of conduct violated the Sherman Act, and was a per se violation. Thus, no intent was required to be proven by the government.

Despite the agent's improper conduct in this case being directly against the corporate policy and instructions of Hilton Hotels Corporation, corporate criminal liability was allowed. The court, in imputing liability to the corporation, noted that agents can be pressured to maximize profits for a corporation and that violations of the Sherman Act result in profit to the corporation and not the individual. The court also stressed the difficulty the government might have if they needed to identify the particular agents responsible for the violation. The court believed that punishment of the agents would not likely be a deterrent, while punishment of the corporation would be an effective deterrent.

The *Hilton* case was decided prior to the enactment of the U.S. Sentencing Guidelines. (See Chapter 24). Today companies are encouraged to have an effective compliance program that will diminish criminal responsibility both to avoid being charged and to lessen the punishment if they are in fact indicted. (See § 2.4 (B), § 24.7(C)).

B. Collective Knowledge

In finding that corporate criminal liability extends beyond strict liability, courts have looked at what level of intent is necessary to hold a corporation criminally liable and what acts will suffice for achieving the *mens rea* of the crime. In this regard, courts have allowed corporate criminal liability using the collective knowledge of employees.[41]

---

[39] The President Coolidge (Dollar Steamship Co. v. U.S.), 101 F.2d 638 (9th Cir.1939).

[40] 467 F.2d 1000 (9th Cir. 1972).

[41] Courts have not extended the "collective knowledge" doctrine to corporate civil actions. See United States v. Science Applications International Corporation, 626 F.3d 1257 (D.C. Cir. 2010) (collective knowledge inapplicable in a civil false claims act case); United States ex rel. Heathcote Holdings Corp., Inc. v. William K. Walthers, Inc., 779 F. Supp.2d 735 (N.D. Ill. 2011) (collective knowledge inapplicable to a qui tam action under 35 U.S.C. § 292, a false markings statute concerned with patents); Southerland Securities Corp. v. INSpire Ins. Solutions, Inc., 365 F.3d 353 (5th Cir. 2004) (finding liability under 10(b)(5) as requiring specific intent and this could not be aggregated). See also Gutter v. E.I. Dupont De Nemours, 124 F. Supp.2d 1291 (S.D. Fl. 2000) ("The knowledge necessary to form the requisite intent must be possessed by

One rationale for allowing collective knowledge to be used is that without it, a corporation could designate a corporate officer as the "vice president in charge of going to jail."[42]

In *United States v. Bank of New England*,[43] the government indicted the Bank of New England for violating the Currency Transaction Reporting Act.[44] The Act imposed criminal liability when a bank failed to file a currency transaction report (CTR) for money received by the bank within the limits of the regulation.[45] The individual who was alleged to have withdrawn from a branch of the bank more than $10,000 in cash using multiple checks was acquitted. The bank, however, was convicted of 31 counts for these CTR violations.

In affirming the decision, the First Circuit started by saying, "knowledge of individual employees acting within the scope of their employment is imputed to the Bank." The court stated that there are two possible ways to acquire knowledge— knowledge by either "one of its individual employees or the aggregate knowledge of all its employees." The First Circuit court endorsed the trial court's instruction on aggregate knowledge which said that the bank's knowledge "is the sum of the knowledge of all of the employees"—"the totality of what all of the employees know within the scope of their employment." In describing this to the jury, the trial court had instructed that, "if Employee A knows one facet of the currency reporting requirement, B knows another facet of it, and C a third facet of it, the bank knows them all." Calling this approach "collective knowledge," the First Circuit said that

> [c]orporations compartmentalize knowledge, subdividing the elements of specific duties and operations into smaller components. The aggregate of those components constitutes the corporation's knowledge of a particular operation. It is irrelevant whether employees administering one component of an operation know the specific activities of employees administering another aspect of the operation.

Arguably computerization makes it easier to use a collective knowledge approach in corporate criminal cases. Without computers to assemble all the corporate data, it would be difficult to aggregate all of the individual knowledge.[46]

Few district and appellate court decisions have explicitly referenced "collective knowledge" in the corporate criminal liability context. But this may be a function of the reality that many corporations reach a settlement with the government as opposed to proceeding to trial. (See § 2.4 (C)). It may also be because collective knowledge only becomes relevant when the government's proof is through other than direct evidence of one person, who while acting within the scope of his or her employment and on behalf of the corporation, committed criminal activity.

---

at least one agent and cannot be inferred and imputed to a corporation based on disconnected facts known by different agents.").

[42] Martin J. Weinstein & Patricia Bennett Ball, Criminal Law's Greatest Mystery Thriller: Corporate Guilt Through Collective Knowledge, 29 N. Eng. L. Rev. 65 (1994).

[43] 821 F.2d 844 (1st Cir. 1987).

[44] 31 C.F.R. § 103.33 (1986).

[45] 31 U.S.C. § 5322(b).

[46] See Jerold H. Israel, Ellen S. Podgor, Paul D. Borman, & Peter J. Henning, White Collar Crime: Law & Practice 3d Ed. 65 (2009).

A theory of "collective knowledge" is not always endorsed by states. For example, in *Commonwealth v. Life Care Centers of America*,[47] a case involving a charge of involuntary manslaughter against a corporation, the Supreme Court of Massachusetts held that "collective knowledge" could not be used for neglect of a resident of a long-care facility when there was no evidence that a single specific employee was criminally liable. Using the "collective knowledge" of multiple employees will not be sufficient for the commission of this crime.

§ 2.4   PROSECUTING CORPORATIONS

A.   Charging—DOJ Guidelines

Prosecutors have enormous discretion in making charging decisions. They decide who will be charged, when they will be charged, and what will be the charged conduct. They also have discretion in the plea bargaining role and in deciding whether to dismiss a case. The Constitution, applicable statutes, and court precedent provide constraints on this power. Limited resources can also influence their charging decisions. Prosecutors have this same charging discretion and considerations when it comes to the charging of corporations.

Department of Justice (DOJ) policy provides general guidance in making these decisions. (See   § 1.5(A)). Individual Attorney Generals or their Deputy Attorney Generals may issue Department Memorandum that can expound on the charging practices of the office. For example, in May 2010, Attorney General Eric H. Holder, Jr. issued a Memorandum to all Federal Prosecutors on the department's policy on charging and sentencing.[48] The Principles of Federal Prosecution as set forth in Title 9 of the U.S. Attorneys' Manual, Chapter 27, have been the main guidance for prosecutors for approximately thirty years.

The U.S. Attorneys' Manual also provides specific guidance on corporate prosecutions. General Considerations of Corporate Liability are found in the United States Attorneys Manual, § 9–28.200. DOJ policy, however, is not law, and defendants have no rights when trying to enforce these internal policies within courts.

In charging corporations, the U.S. Attorneys Manual instructs federal prosecutors to "weigh all of the factors normally considered in the sound exercise of prosecutorial judgment: the sufficiency of the evidence; the likelihood of success at trial; the probable deterrent, rehabilitative, and other consequences of conviction; and the adequacy of noncriminal approaches." Nine additional factors are then to be considered, although the list is illustrative as opposed to being an exhaustive list of all potential relevant considerations. The nine factors listed in § 9–28.200 are:

1.   the nature and seriousness of the offense, including the risk of harm to the public, and applicable policies and priorities, if any, governing the prosecution of corporations for particular categories of crime

---

[47] 926 N.E.2d 206 (Mass. 2010).

[48] Eric H. Holder, Jr., Attorney General, Memorandum to all Federal Prosecutors, Department Policy on Charging and Sentencing, May 19, 2010, available at http://lawprofessors.typepad.com/files/holdermemo.pdf.

2.　　the pervasiveness of wrongdoing within the corporation, including the complicity in, or the condoning of, the wrongdoing by corporate management;

3.　　the corporation's history of similar misconduct, including prior criminal, civil, and regulatory enforcement actions against it;

4.　　the corporation's timely and voluntary disclosure of wrongdoing and its willingness to cooperate in the investigation of its agents;

5.　　the existence and effectiveness of the corporation's pre-existing compliance program;

6.　　the corporation's remedial actions, including any efforts to implement an effective corporate compliance program or to improve an existing one, to replace responsible management, to discipline or terminate wrongdoers, to pay restitution, and to cooperate with the relevant government agencies;

7.　　collateral consequences, including whether there is disproportionate harm to shareholders, pension holders, employees, and others not proven personally culpable, as well as impact on the public arising from the prosecution;

8.　　the adequacy of the prosecution of individuals responsible for the corporation's malfeasance; and

9.　　the adequacy of remedies such as civil or regulatory enforcement actions

Later sections in the Manual provide detailed guidance on each of these nine factors. But the factors and the later guidance present a strong picture that prevention, disclosure, and cooperation are influential considerations for the government in their decision-making process. For example, obstructing the investigation is weighed by the prosecutor in deciding whether to proceed. The Manual notes as examples of impeding an investigation, "inappropriate directions to employees or their counsel, such as directions not to be truthful or to conceal relevant facts; making representations or submissions that contain misleading assertions or material omissions; and incomplete or delayed production of records."[49]

"The nature and seriousness of the crime, including the risk of harm to the public from the criminal misconduct, are obviously primary factors in determining whether to charge a corporation."[50] It is also noted that because *respondeat superior* is the method of achieving corporate criminal liability, the most important factor when examining the pervasiveness of the wrongdoing within the corporation "is the role and conduct of the management."[51]

Although disclosure is an important component to the DOJ decision-making process, there is now recognition that the waiver of the attorney-client privilege is not a "prerequisite under the Department's prosecution guidelines for a corporation to be

---

[49] USAM § 9–28.730 (2008).
[50] USAM § 9–28.400 (2008).
[51] USAM § 9–28.500 (2008).

viewed as cooperative."[52] Significant concerns were raised under a prior Department Memorandum, issued by Deputy Attorney General Larry Thompson, that waiver of the attorney-client privilege was a consideration in receiving favorable government treatment. (See § 22.6(A)).[53]

Also of concern under this prior memo was whether the payment by a corporation of employees' attorney fees was a factor in a corporation receiving favorable treatment. The current guidance now provides that "[i]n evaluating cooperation, . . . , prosecutors should not take into account whether a corporation is advancing or reimbursing attorneys' fees or providing counsel to employees, officers, or directors under investigation or indictment." It also notes that "prosecutors may not request that a corporation refrain from taking such action."[54]

This change in policy concurred with the Second Circuit's decision in *United States v. Stein*.[55] The court in *Stein* examined whether the government had improperly pressured accounting firm KPMG from paying the attorney fees of the employees from the company who were indicted. The court found the government's conduct violated the Sixth Amendment as it interfered with the defendant's right to counsel. The court noted that "KPMG itself represented to the court that the Thompson Memorandum and the prosecutors' conduct 'substantially influenced [its] determination(s) with respect to the advancement of legal fees.'" It was clear to both the trial and appellate courts that KPMG had ceased advancing legal fees to the indicted employees as "a direct consequence of the government's overwhelming influence." The court noted that this was a highly complex white collar case and that the "[d]efendants were indicted based on a fairly novel theory of criminal liability, they faced substantial penalties; [and] the relevant facts [were] scattered throughout 22 million documents." This meant that the defendants were facing an enormous legal cost in preparing their defense.

B. Compliance Programs

Corporations receive benefits in the charging process if they have a corporate compliance program. (See § 24.7(C)). An effective program is also helpful if a charged company faces sentencing. Both the government's charging policy and the sentencing guidelines provide some guidance to companies in creating and maintaining their corporate compliance programs. This is extremely important to companies because a factor used by government prosecutors in deciding whether to charge a corporation for its misconduct is "the existence and effectiveness of the corporation's pre-existing compliance program."[56] Compliance programs serve the purpose of educating corporate personnel so that misconduct does not occur, and if it does, that it gets detected and reported promptly. The U.S. Attorneys' Manual is clear that having a compliance program does not mean that a corporation will not be prosecuted.[57]

---

[52] USAM § 9–28.710 (2008).

[53] There is, however, a continuing factor of cooperation that includes disclosing relevant facts. See USAM § 9–28.720 (2008).

[54] USAM § 9–28.730 (2008).

[55] 541 F.3d 130 (2d Cir. 2008).

[56] USAM § 9–28.300 (2008).

[57] USAM § 9–28.800 (2008).

Both the United States Attorneys' Manual and the U.S. Sentencing Guidelines provide guidance on what will be considered an effective compliance program. The Manual states that "[t]he Department has no formulaic requirements regarding corporate compliance programs. The fundamental questions any prosecutor should ask are: Is the corporation's compliance program well designed? Is the program being applied earnestly and in good faith? Does the corporation's compliance program work?"[58] In this regard, it states that:

> Prosecutors should therefore attempt to determine whether a corporation's compliance program is merely a "paper program" or whether it was designed, implemented, reviewed, and revised, as appropriate, in an effective manner. In addition, prosecutors should determine whether the corporation has provided for a staff sufficient to audit, document, analyze, and utilize the results of the corporation's compliance efforts. Prosecutors also should determine whether the corporation's employees are adequately informed about the compliance program and are convinced of the corporation's commitment to it.[59]

A corporation's compliance program, or lack thereof, is considered by the court in sentencing when a corporation enters into a plea agreement or proceeds to trial and is convicted. Chapter Eight of the federal sentencing guidelines apply when sentencing organizations. (See § 24.7). An effective compliance and ethics program affects the culpability score given to a corporation and also what conditions of probation will apply. To be an effective compliance and ethics program "an organization shall (1) exercise due diligence to prevent and detect criminal conduct; and (2) otherwise promote an organizational culture that encourages ethical conduct and a commitment to compliance with the law."[60] The fact the program does not correct all offenses does not render it ineffective.

Due diligence under the sentencing guidelines "minimally require[s]" standards and procedures, a program with high-level corporate oversight that has specific individuals "delegated day-to-day operational responsibility for the compliance and ethics program." Those who have engaged in misconduct within the entity should not be involved in the program. The guidelines call for training programs, periodic evaluation of the program's effectiveness, and a system for whistleblowers to anonymously report misconduct. Due diligence also requires promotion of the program in the entity and reasonable steps taken upon the detection of improper conduct. Commentary to the sentencing guidelines provides detailed factors for consideration in making certain that the effective compliance and ethics program meets the requirements of the guidelines.[61] (See Chapter 24).

Civil cases have emphasized the importance of having a corporate compliance program.[62] In *In re Caremark International Inc. Derivative Litigation*,[63] the Delaware Chancery court stated, "a director's obligation includes a duty to attempt in good faith

---

[58] USAM § 9–28.800(B) (2008).

[59] Id.

[60] U.S.S.G. § 8B2.1.

[61] Id.

[62] See Jerold H. Israel, Ellen S. Podgor, Paul D. Borman, & Peter J. Henning, White Collar Crime: Law & Practice 3d Ed. 85 (2009).

[63] 698 A.2d 959, 970 (Del.Ch. 1996).

to assure that a corporate information and reporting system, which the board concludes is adequate, exists, and that failure to do so under some circumstances may, in theory at least, render a director liable for losses caused by non-compliance with applicable legal standards." This position was reaffirmed in *McCall v. Scott*,[64] when the Sixth Circuit court after referring to the *Caremark* decision, stated that, "[u]nconsidered inaction can be the basis for director liability because, even though most corporate decisions are not subject to director attention, ordinary business decisions of officers and employees deeper in the corporation can significantly injure the corporation and make it subject to criminal sanctions."

The importance of having a corporate compliance program was also emphasized by the Delaware Supreme Court in *Stone v. Ritter*,[65] when it stated:

We hold that *Caremark* articulates the necessary conditions predicate for director oversight liability: (a) the directors utterly failed to implement any reporting or information system or controls; *or* (b) having implemented such a system or controls, consciously failed to monitor or oversee its operations thus disabling themselves from being informed of risks or problems requiring their attention. In either case, imposition of liability requires a showing that the directors knew that they were not discharging their fiduciary obligations. Where directors fail to act in the face of a known duty to act, thereby demonstrating a conscious disregard for their responsibilities, they breach their duty of loyalty by failing to discharge that fiduciary obligation in good faith.

C. Deferred and Non–Prosecution Agreements

1. DOJ Agreements

The ramifications of a corporate prosecution can be huge to a corporation. Findings of misconduct can result in derivative civil actions against the company. The ramifications of a criminal prosecution can be even more devastating. Merely charging a company can have a devastating effect as was seen in the prosecution of Arthur Andersen, LLP. Proceeding criminally against a major-accounting firm for allegedly obstructing justice resulted in the company's bankruptcy when other companies and individuals could not hire Arthur Andersen LLP because of the pending criminal action. Even when the company eventually succeeded in getting the conviction overturned, the collateral consequences of the indictment and its resulting publicity destroyed the company.

Such collateral consequences are especially felt by those who do business with the government. Thus, businesses engaged in defense procurement or receiving health care benefits from the government may face exclusion and debarment if they are convicted.

Recognizing the collateral consequences of an indictment and possible conviction causes many companies who are facing criminal prosecution to enter into a deferred or non-prosecution agreement with the government. These are sometimes referred to as DPAs (deferred prosecution agreements) and NPAs (non-prosecution agreements). (See

---

[64] 239 F.3d 808 (6th Cir. 2001) Amended 250 F.3d 997 (6th Cir. 2001).
[65] 911 A.2d 362 (Del. 2006).

§ 24.7(D)). The difference between a DPA and NPA is that a DPA occurs after indictment[66] and an NPA occurs pre-indictment.[67]

NPAs, often accomplished through a letter between the Department of Justice and the company, provides terms and conditions that the company will adhere to in order for a criminal action not to be filed against them. A failure to abide by the terms could mean that the DOJ might proceed with the criminal matter. In contrast, in the case of a deferred prosecution, the government already has the criminal case prepared and agrees not to move forward with the action subject to the conditions agreed to by the parties. DPAs are often agreements entered into before a court. Both NPA and DPAs typically provide for the company to pay a fine and often provide for the appointment of a corporate monitor to assure future compliance.

There has been significant growth in companies entering into these agreements with the government.[68] In the year 2003, the DOJ entered into four agreements, while in 2007 there were 38 corporate deferred or non-prosecution agreements entered into by the government.[69] One finds agreements reached with companies like Swiss bank UBS paying $780 million and agreeing to identify customers who violated United States tax laws.[70] Even law firms have entered into these agreements, such as the Milberg firm paying $75 million as part of a non-prosecution agreement.[71] Some agreements are plea agreements, as opposed to being deferred or non-prosecution agreements. For example, Siemens AG and three subsidiaries agreed to pay $450 million in fines to the U.S. government as part of a plea agreement. The coordinated enforcement actions in this case by DOJ, the Securities Exchange Commission and the German government resulted in penalties of 1.6 billion dollars.[72]

In addition to paying fines and oftentimes agreeing to a monitorship, corporate agreements can provide for dismissal of employees who fail to cooperate,[73] or they may create a fund for civil settlements. This latter provision can alleviate some of the civil

---

[66] See Jerold H. Israel, Ellen S. Podgor, Paul D. Borman, & Peter J. Henning, 2009 Statutory, Documentary and Case Supplement to White Collar Crime: Law and Practice 3d Ed., Documentary Material 216 (2009).

[67] Id. at 235.

[68] See Brandon L. Garrett, Globalized Corporate Prosecutions, 97 Virginia L. Rev. 1775 (2011); Peter Spivack, Sujit Raman, Regulating the 'New Regulators': Current Trends in Deferred Prosecution Agreements, 45 Am. Crim. L. Rev. 159 (2008). See also Brandon Garrett & Jon Ashley, Federal Organizational Plea Agreements, available at http://lib.law.virginia.edu/Garrett/plea_agreements/home.php (containing a library of 1729 agreements as of October 10, 2011).

[69] DOJ Has Taken Steps to Better Track Its Use of Deferred and Non–Prosecution Agreements But Should Evaluate Effectiveness, GAO–10–110 Report (2009), available at http://www.gao.gov/highlights/d10110high.pdf. The Report notes that in the fiscal years 2008 and 2009 this number declined slightly with 24 and 23 agreements entered into each year respectively.

[70] DOJ Press Release, UBS Enters into Deferred Prosecution Agreement, (Feb. 18, 2009), available at http://www.justice.gov/opa/pr/2009/February/09–tax–136.html.

[71] DOJ Press Release, Milberg Law Firm Admits Role in Four–Decade–Long Secret Kickback Scheme in Class–Action Lawsuits, June 16, 2008, available at http://lawprofessors.typepad.com/whitecollarcrime_blog/files/milberg_firm_settlement.083.pdf.

[72] DOJ Press Release, Siemens AG and Three Subsidiaries Plead Guilty to Foreign Corrupt Practices Act Violations and Agree to Pay $450 Million in Combined Criminal Fines, Dec. 15, 2008, available at http://www.justice.gov/opa/pr/2008/December/08–crm–1105.html.

[73] The DOJ plea agreement with Archer Daniels required dismissal of employees who failed to cooperate. Kurt Eichenwald, Archer Daniels Agrees to Big Fine for Price Fixing, NYTimes, Oct. 15, 1996, available at http://www.nytimes.com/1996/10/15/business/archer-daniels-agrees-to-big-fine-for-price-fixing.html?pagewanted=all & src=pm.

litigation that can follow the admission of corporate misconduct. For example, in an agreement reached between the government and Drexel Burnham Lambert, the company agreed to plead guilty to six felony counts and pay a total of $650 million. That sum was divided as a criminal penalty of $300 million and a fund of $350 million for shareholders and other plaintiffs who were able to claim injury by Drexel's criminal conduct.[74]

DPAs and NPAs have been the subject of controversy. Specifically terms within these agreements have sometimes raised concerns. For example terms included in a DPA have been a provision for the establishment of a law school chair, for waiving the attorney-client privilege, and agreements that allowed the government the exclusive control of determining when an agreement had been breached.[75] There have also been concerns raised about the cost and influence of monitors who are appointed to assure future corporate compliance.[76]

One of the implications of these agreements is that it shifts the role of the corporation to be aligned with the government. Professor Harry First refers to the corporation being a "branch-office" of the government as the agreements calls for the company's cooperation in the prosecution of corporate individuals who committed criminal acts.[77] It has also been argued that these agreements do not carry a significant deterrent effect and that prosecutions need to be more robust in the corporate realm.

2.   SEC Agreements

In January 2010, the Securities Exchange Commission instituted new rules. These rules allow for cooperation and also institute "new cooperation tools" which include deferred prosecution and non-prosecution agreements with the SEC.[78] The deferred prosecution agreements are when the SEC "agrees among other things, to cooperate fully and truthfully and to comply with express prohibitions and undertakings during a period of deferred prosecution." The non-prosecution agreement, also a formal written agreement, is "entered into under limited and appropriate circumstances, in which the Commission agrees not to pursue an enforcement action against a cooperator if the individual or company agrees, among other things, to cooperate fully and truthfully and comply with express undertakings."

---

[74] Stephen J. Adler, Guilty Pleas Increase Likelihood of Settlements in Civil Lawsuits, Wall St. Jrl., Dec. 22, 1988, at A5.

[75] Candace Zierdt & Ellen S. Podgor, Corporate Deferred Prosecutions Through the Looking Glass of Contract Policing, 96 Kentucky L.J. 1 (2008) (discussing problematic terms within DPAs and NPAs).

[76] See Carrie Johnson, Mukasey Had Been Overseer Finalist, Wash Post, Jan. 30, 2008, available at http://www.washingtonpost.com/wp-dyn/content/article/2008/01/29/AR2008012903203.html?hpid=topnews (discussing former Attorney General John Ashcroft receiving a fee of $52 million as a monitor).

[77] Harry First, Branch Office of the Prosecutor: The New Role of the Corporation in Business Crime Prosecutions, 89 N.C. L.Rev. 23 (2010).

[78] SEC Press Release, SEC Announces Initiative to Encourage Individuals and Companies to Cooperate and Assist in Investigations (Jan. 13, 2010), available at http://www.sec.gov/news/press/2010/2010–6.htm.

D. Jury Questions

1. Verdict Consistency

A question can arise when both the corporation and individual are being prosecuted by the government and the verdicts in the cases are inconsistent. Since corporate criminal liability is premised on *respondeat superior* liability, the issue considered is whether an acquittal of the individual should serve as an acquittal of the corporation. On the flip side, is the question of whether an acquittal of the corporation should serve as an acquittal of the individual.

In *United States v. Hughes Aircraft Co., Inc.*,[79] the Ninth Circuit rejected corporate Hughes' argument that the acquittal of an "indispensable co-conspirator" "of the identical charges on identical evidence" should preclude the corporate conviction from remaining. The corporate argument was that the individual was the "sole employee for whose actions Hughes could be found vicariously guilty and that the evidence against each of the two defendants was necessarily identical." The court rejected this argument as existing Supreme Court precedent in different contexts allowed for inconsistent jury verdicts.[80]

In *United States v. Dotterweich*,[81] the Supreme Court looked at whether the individual should be held criminally liable when the company is acquitted. The Court rejected Dotterweich's claim as baseless saying, "[w]hether the jury's verdict was the result of carelessness or compromise or a belief that the responsible individual should suffer the penalty instead of merely increasing, as it were, the cost of running the business of the corporation, is immaterial." The Court stated that, "[j]uries may indulge in precisely such motives or vagaries." (See § 2.7(B)(1)).

2. Jury Unanimity

Questions can also arise as to whether the jury has to agree on who within the entity may have violated the law. There are two components of jury unanimity analysis: (1) statutory construction to determine what the legislature intended for the jury to be unanimous about; (2) due process.[82] In the trial of Arthur Andersen LLP,[83] the auditor of Enron who was indicted for obstruction of justice when the company "instructed employees to destroy documents pursuant to its document retention policy," the trial court instructed the jury that it was not necessary for them to agree as to who within the company had committed the wrongful conduct as long as "at least one employee of Andersen had the specific intent to impede an official investigation." Agreement on the identity of this individual was not necessary.[84] The Supreme Court

---

[79] 20 F.3d 974 (9th Cir. 1994).

[80] See Dunn v. United States, 284 U.S. 390, 393 (1932); United States v. Powell, 469 U.S. 57, 64–65 (1984).

[81] 320 U.S. 277 (1943).

[82] Jacobsen v. State, 325 S.W.3d 733 (Tex. App. 2010).

[83] United States v. Arthur Andersen, LLP, 544 U.S. 696 (2005) (reversed on other grounds) (see chapter 6).

[84] Kurt Eichenwald, Judge's Ruling on Andersen Hurts Defense, N.Y.Times, June 15, 2002, available at http://www.nytimes.com/2002/06/15/business/judge-s-ruling-on-andersen-hurts-defense.html?pagewanted=all & src=pm.

reversed the conviction against Arthur Andersen, LLP, although this issue was not a focus of the decision.

Cases in other contexts have required jury unanimity on the government proving the elements of the crime. For example, in *Richardson v. United States*,[85] the Supreme Court held that "a jury in a federal criminal case brought under [21 U.S.C.] § 848 must unanimously agree not only that the defendant committed some 'continuing series of violations' but also that the defendant committed each of the individual 'violations' necessary to make up that 'continuing series.'"

§ 2.5   DEAD CORPORATIONS

Cases have examined the issue of whether corporate criminal liability extends to corporations that no longer exist. Whether via dissolution, bankruptcy, mergers, or sales, the original corporation may no longer be present and it may be necessary to determine whether the criminal matter can proceed. Although the death of an individual terminates his or her criminal case, corporations can still be subject to liability even through the corporate entity may be defunct.

In *Melrose Distillers, Inc. v. United States*,[86] the Supreme Court examined whether a dissolved corporation is subject to criminal liability. Prior to *Melrose* jurisdictions were split on whether criminal liability extended beyond its dissolution. Some courts treated the corporation as individuals and refused to allow the criminal case to proceed, while others extended the criminal liability beyond the life of the entity.[87]

In *Melrose*, the corporations were indicted for "restraining trade, conspiring to monopolize and attempting to monopolize commerce in violation of §§ 1 and 2 of the Sherman Act." Two of the corporations were organized under Maryland law and one under Delaware law, with both being subsidiaries of another company, Schenley Industries, Inc. After indictment, the three subsidiary corporations were dissolved under their respective state law, Maryland or Delaware, and they "became divisions of a new corporation under the same ultimate ownership." Justice Douglas, writing for the Supreme Court, held that "[i]n this situation there is no more reason for allowing them to escape criminal penalties than damages in civil suits." The Court found that both Maryland and Delaware law allowed for the continued existence of the corporation for purposes of this provision of the Sherman Act.

A key to finding criminal liability of a dissolved corporation often lies with the existence of a state statute that permits extending the criminal liability beyond the life of the entity. This is because corporations are created and dissolved pursuant to state law and therefore state law may control the legal obligations of the entity. Courts

---

[85] 526 U.S. 813 (1999).

[86] 359 U.S. 271 (1959).

[87] See United States v. Line Material Co., 202 F.2d 929 (6th Cir. 1953) ("the result of dissolution cannot be distinguished from the death of a natural person"); United States v. Safeway Stores, Inc. 140 F.2d 834 (10th Cir. 1944) (same), but see United States v. P.F. Collier & Son Corp., 208 F.2d 936 (7th Cir. 1953) (no rationale to relieve a corporation of its criminal liability).

examining state statutes have read them liberally to permit criminal prosecutions after the corporation has been dissolved.[88]

Courts have used this same analysis in holding that corporations that merge cannot escape criminal liability.[89] In *United States v. Alamo Bank of Texas*,[90] the Fifth Circuit allowed a corporation to be held criminally liable despite its merger with another company. Affirming a bank's conviction for failing to file currency transaction reports, despite its merger with another bank, the court held that a "bank could not escape this liability by assuming another bank's corporate persona."

§ 2.6   NON–CORPORATE ENTITY LIABILITY

Entity liability extends beyond corporations to include entities such as partnerships. In *United States v. A & P Trucking Co.*[91] the government charged a partnership with violations of the Interstate Commerce Commission regulations and the Motor Carrier Act. The trial court dismissed the charging information finding that "a partnership entity cannot be guilty of violating" these statutes.

On direct appeal the Supreme Court reversed the district court, holding that the information had been "erroneously dismissed." Justice Harlan, writing for the Court's majority, stated, "it certainly makes no difference whether the carrier which commits the infraction is organized as a corporation, a joint stock company, a partnership, or an individual proprietorship." He noted that, "[t]he mischief is the same, and we think that Congress intended to make the consequences of infraction the same." The Court did not accept the argument that partnerships, as opposed to its individual partners, cannot act "knowingly and willfully."

A four-person concurrence and dissent objected to applying the Motor Carrier Act to partnerships. It called for Congress to speak more clearly if its desire was to impose criminal liability on partnership assets.

A & P Trucking Co.'s holding, permitting partnerships to be held criminally liable, has been extended to limited partnerships and to crimes requiring specific intent.[92] It has also been used to hold law firm partnerships criminally liable. In *People v. Lessoff & Berger*,[93] a New York State court examined whether a law firm partnership could be held criminally liable. In finding that it could, the court stated, "[n]ot only do law partners, as any partners, benefit financially from the fruits of one partner's fraudulent conduct committed in the name of the firm, but there is a strong public interest in regulating the ethics of the legal profession."

---

[88] See United States v. Arcos Corp., 234 F.Supp. 355 (D.C. Ohio 1964); United States v. Brakes, Inc., 157 F.Supp. 916 (D.C. N.Y. 1958) (holding "that violation of the federal criminal statues was one of the 'obligations or liabilities' for satisfaction and discharge of which the New York law continues the existence of defendant corporation after voluntary dissolution").

[89] See H. Lowell Brown, Successor Corporate Criminal Liability: The Emerging Federal Common Law, 49 Ark. L. Rev. 469 (1996).

[90] 880 F.2d 828 (5th Cir. 1989).

[91] 358 U.S. 121 (1958).

[92] See United States v. Heffner, 916 F.Supp. 1010 (S.D. Cal. 1996).

[93] 159 Misc.2d 1096, 608 N.Y.S.2d 54 (N.Y. Sup. 1994).

§ 2.7   PERSONAL LIABILITY OF CORPORATE AGENTS

A. Generally

In recent years, corporations typically enter into deferred prosecution or non-prosecution agreements with the government. Alternatively, they will negotiate a plea agreement with the government. A common component to these settlements is that the corporation will provide to the government evidence of wrongdoing by individuals within the company. Thus, the corporation will often be assisting the government in the prosecution of individual employees who committed illegal acts. These corporate agents may be prosecuted under many different criminal statutes. The fact that the agent was acting on behalf of the company does not negate his or her personal criminal culpability.

Many high level executives, including CEOs of major companies have been criminally prosecuted. One finds prosecutions against the former CEO of Enron—Jeffrey Skilling, the former CEO of Worldcom—Bernard Ebbers, the former CEO of Adelphia Communications Corporation—John Rigas, the former CEO of Qwest Communications—Joseph Nacchio, and the former CEO of Computer Associates—Sanjay Kumar. Mid and lower level executives have also been charged and convicted of white collar crimes, and the convictions have included a range of different crimes such as mail fraud, wire fraud, bank fraud, money laundering, securities fraud, insider trading, environmental crimes, bankruptcy crimes, and more. (See § 2.1(F))

Individual criminal liability may be a function of statutory interpretation. In *United States v. Wise*,[94] the Supreme Court, in a case of first impression, examined whether the Sherman Act applied to corporate officers acting in a representative capacity. It was argued that since the Sherman Act defined "person" "to include corporations and associations," the omission of individuals in the criminal statute should be interpreted to exclude them. In this case, the lower court dismissed the case against a corporate officer and the government appealed. In reversing the lower court's holding, the Supreme Court looked at the legislative history and also at this statute's relation to the Clayton Act. The Court noted that the Sherman Act's inclusion of corporations in its definition of "persons" did not serve to exclude prosecutions against individuals who have a responsible share in the criminal conduct. The Court held "that a corporate officer is subject to prosecution under § 1 of the Sherman Act whenever he knowingly participates in effecting the illegal contract, combination, or conspiracy—be the one who authorizes, orders, or helps perpetrate the crime—regardless of whether he is acting in a representative capacity."

Personal liability for corporate agents is also supported by the Model Penal Code in § 2.07(6) which imposes individual liability on the corporate agent for conduct performed on behalf of the corporation "to the same extent as if it were performed in his own name or behalf." When there is an affirmative duty to act, the agent "having primary responsibility for the discharge of the duty is legally accountable for a reckless omission to perform the required act to the same extent as if the duty were imposed by law directly upon himself."

---

[94] 370 U.S. 405 (1962).

When the corporate agent performs the criminal act, it is relatively easy to impose criminal liability. Federal law does not require the agent to be an officer, director, or manager of the company. And merely holding a corporate position does not impute corporate criminal liability to the individual. Courts do require that the individual have the necessary *mens rea* for the crime. This may require participation in the criminal conduct or at a minimum a showing that that there is knowledge of the wrongfulness of the conduct.[95] Claims of willful blindness will require that the government show that "(1) the defendant must subjectively believe that there is a high probability that a fact exists and (2) the defendant must take deliberate actions to avoid learning of that fact."[96] (See § 1.8(C)(1)).

Agents have argued that they should not be held criminally liable as they acted at the behest of a corporate superior. If they are aware of the "illegality of the conduct, the fact that it was authorized by a superior clearly cannot insulate him from criminal liability." But if there is no knowledge, then the agent lacks the specific intent for the commission of the crime and cannot be held guilty.[97]

B. Responsible Corporate Officer

1. *Generally*

In determining whether an individual has personal criminal liability under the responsible corporate officer doctrine, it is necessary to ascertain whether the crime is a strict liability-negligence violation, a crime with a "knowing" element, or a statute that explicitly provides for criminal liability for responsible corporate officers. The doctrine has been applied in many different contexts, such as Federal Food, Drug and Cosmetic Act cases, securities violations, and environmental cases.

2. *Strict Liability/Negligence*

If the criminal offense is strict liability, the knowledge of the corporate agent is irrelevant. The key question becomes whether he or she committed the act. A factor for consideration, however, may be whether the corporate officer was powerless to prevent or correct the problem. Two Supreme Court decisions have played an influential role in the development of this doctrine: *United States v. Dotterweich*[98] and *United States v. Park*.[99]

Joseph P. Dotterweich was the president and general manager of the Buffalo Pharmacal Company. He was accused, along with the company, of violations of the Federal Food, Drug, and Cosmetic Act involving the shipping in interstate commerce of adulterated and misbranded drugs. The evidence was that the drugs had been purchased from the manufacturer, repacked under the Buffalo Pharmacal Company

---

[95] Bourgeois v. Commonwealth, 227 S.E.2d 714 (Va.1976) (holding that absent evidence of participation in the criminal conduct or knowledge imputed from the business procedures of the corporation or the personnel, there was no basis for imputing knowledge of wrongdoing to the president)

[96] Global–Tech Appliances, Inc. v. SEB, 131 S.Ct. 2060 (2011).

[97] United States v. Gold, 743 F.2d 800 (C.A. Fl. 1984).

[98] 320 U.S. 277 (1943).

[99] 421 U.S. 658 (1975).

name, and shipped in interstate commerce. After a jury trial, Dotterweich was convicted, although the company was not.

Justice Frankfurter, writing for the majority found the crime to be strict liability, thus eliminating any requirement for the government to show knowledge on the part of Dotterweich. Being that this was a strict liability crime, Dotterweich was a "person" punishable for violations of the Federal Food, Drug, and Cosmetic Act. The key, according to the court, was whether Dotterweich had a "responsible share in the furtherance of the transaction." The Court did not, however, provide a definition of "responsible share" leaving the definition to "the good sense of prosecutors, the wise guidance of trial judges, and the ultimate judgment of juries."

This was not a unanimous decision of the Supreme Court and there was a strong dissent by four justices. The dissent believed that guilt was being "imputed to the respondent solely on the basis of his authority and responsibility as president and general manager of the corporation." Since there was no statutory authority, the dissent argued that it is "inconsistent with established canons of criminal law to rest liability on an act in which the accused did not participate and of which he had no personal knowledge."

Thirty-two years later in the case of *United States v. Park*,[100] the Court re-examined the "responsible share" doctrine. Park, the CEO of Acme Markets, Inc. was charged with violations of the Federal Food, Drug, and Cosmetic Act. Acme, "a national retail food chain with approximately 36,000 employees, 874 retail outlets, 12 general warehouses, and four special warehouses," had its headquarters in Philadelphia. A warehouse in Baltimore had problems which included the building being accessible to rodents. The company pleaded guilty, and Park went to trial. He was convicted and his sentence was a fine of $50 on each count.

The court of appeals reversed the conviction and the case proceeded to the Supreme Court. In reinstating Park's conviction, the Supreme Court expounded upon its prior holding in *Dotterweich*. It noted that merely being in the position of CEO did not mean that Park was guilty of the crimes in question. Corporate employees who have a responsible share in the acts that the statute prohibits, can be criminally liable.

Park questioned the jury instruction given in his case, specifically regarding the lack of a definition of "responsible relationship." The Court stated:

> The concept of a "responsible relationship" to, or a "responsible share" in, a violation of the Act indeed imports some measure of blameworthiness; but it is equally clear that the Government establishes a prima facie case when it introduces evidence sufficient to warrant a finding by the trier of the facts that the defendant had, by reason of his position in the corporation, responsibility and authority either to prevent in the first instance, or promptly to correct, the violation complained of, and that he failed to do so.

The Court noted that individuals who have a "responsible relationship" have a duty under the Act not only "to seek out and remedy violations" but also a duty "to

---

[100] 421 U.S. 658 (1975).

implement measures that will insure that violations will not occur." The Court did state that a defendant can present a defense that he or she was "'powerless' to prevent or correct the violation."

The Court noted that "isolated parts" of the jury instructions might be "read as intimating that a finding of guilt could be predicated solely on respondent's corporate position." But this was insufficient for the court to rule in favor of Park. Jury instructions, the Court said, should "be viewed in the context of the overall charge" and not "judged in artificial isolation."

The dissent in *Park* agreed with the Court that negligence was the correct standard. But the dissent believed that the jury instruction given did not match this standard.

Scholars have debated whether the Court in *Park* expresses a strict liability or negligence standard. One argument is that because a defense of powerlessness exists, it is not strict liability. But this position is questioned because the Court does not give a jury instruction that matches a negligence standard.[101]

3. Powerlessness

The Court in *Park* stated that the accused is not required to do what is "objectively impossible." Being "'powerless' to prevent or correct the violation" is something the defendant can raise at trial. This includes a request for an instruction that explains this legal theory to the jury. In the *Park* case, there was no request for such an instruction.

When requests for a powerless instruction are made and denied, courts do not necessarily find error. In *United States v. Y. Hata & Co., Ltd*,[102] the defendants requested an "objective impossibility" instruction. The Ninth Circuit affirmed the conviction as the facts of the case did not warrant the instruction. In *United States v. Starr*,[103] the Ninth Circuit also rejected the giving of an "objective impossibility" instruction when the defendant's argument was that the "contamination resulted from a 'natural phenomenon'" and that an employee was sabotaging his compliance efforts. The court noted that the accused had the "duty of 'foresight and vigilance,'" which "requires the defendant to foresee and prepare for such an occurrence, whether it be deemed 'natural' or 'artificial.'" Here again, the evidence did not support the giving of the instruction premised on a claim of sabotage.

4. Knowing Element in Statute

When a statute has an element requiring proof of knowledge, merely showing that an individual is a responsible corporate officer does not suffice to conclusively prove that element. This differs from the *Dotterweich* and *Park* cases, as both of these cases involved misdemeanors that did not require the prosecution to prove the defendant's

---

[101] See Norman Abrams, Criminal Liability of Corporate Officers for Strict Liability Offenses—A Comment on Dotterweich and Park, 28 U.C.L.A. L. Rev. 463 (1981); Kathleen F. Brickey, Criminal Liability of Corporate Officers for Strict Liability Offenses—Another View, 35 Vand. L. Rev. 1337 (1982).

[102] 535 F.2d 508 (9th Cir.1976).

[103] 535 F.2d 512 (9th Cir. 1976).

knowledge. Although knowledge may be inferred from the evidence, including circumstantial evidence of the corporate individual's position and responsibility within the company, simply being a responsible corporate officer does not equate with having knowledge of the criminal activity.[104]

5. *Statutory Designation*

Designating a responsible corporate officer as someone who can be found criminally liable, may also be a function of what is included within a statute. For example, both the Clean Water Act[105] and Clean Air Act[106] explicitly incorporate "responsible corporate officer" within the definition of "person" for purposes of the statute. (See chapter 14). In *United States v. Iverson*[107] the Ninth Circuit examined the attributes of what constitutes a responsible corporate officer for purposes of the Clean Water Act. The court stated that "a person is a 'responsible corporate officer' if the person has authority to exercise control over the corporation's activity that is causing the discharges." The court noted, however, that "[t]here is no requirement that the officer in fact exercise such authority or that the corporation expressly vest a duty in the officer to oversee the activity."

C. Indemnification

Corporate officers, directors, and employees may seek indemnification for actions brought against them. (See § 22.4). In some cases the corporation will be paying these costs. Often there are Directors and Officers (D & O) Liability insurance policies that may assume payments of these amounts.[108] Having a D & O policy or assuring indemnification can be important factors in executive compensation as the attorney fee cost when someone is being investigated or is charged with criminal conduct can be enormously costly, especially in a document intensive white collar case. A rationale for companies providing indemnification to employees is to protect the company's officers and directors from shareholder lawsuits. It also can be a bargaining factor when negotiating the employment of key personnel.

Government interference with these contractual relations can be seen as depriving the employees of their Sixth Amendment Right to Counsel. Even when there may be no written agreement between a company and its individual employees, a longstanding practice of paying attorney fees may be respected by courts.[109] That said, indemnification in criminal cases may have contractual limitations that may limit payment or require repayment if the employee failed to act in good faith.[110]

---

[104] See United States v. MacDonald & Watson Waste Oil Co., 933 F.2d 35 (1st Cir. 1991).

[105] 33 U.S.C. § 1319 (c)(6).

[106] 42 U.S.C. § 7413(c)(6).

[107] 162 F.3d 1015 (9th Cir. 1998).

[108] See Pamela H. Bucy, Indemnification of Corporate Executives Who Have Been Convicted of Crimes: An Assessment and Proposal, 24 Ind. L. Rev. 279 (1991).

[109] United States v. Stein, 541 F.3d 130 (2d Cir. 2008) (See supra § 2.4(A)).

[110] See Norwood P. Beveridge, Does the Corporate Director Have a Duty Always to Obey the Law?, 45 DePaul L. Rev. 729 (1996).

Chapter 3

CONSPIRACY

§ 3.1   OVERVIEW

A. Generally

Conspiracy targets group criminality as the united group poses a grave danger. The phrase often cited here is "[i]n union there is strength." Francis Sayre, an early scholar on conspiracy stated, "[g]roup association for criminal purposes often, if not normally, makes possible the attainment of ends more complex than those which one criminal could accomplish."[1]

The crime of conspiracy dates back to the early common law when statutes were passed to target individuals who would bond together to bring a false indictment. In some instances children were used as participants in the conduct as their age precluded recovering damages from them. The statutes prohibiting these activities allowed prosecutors to bring in multiple individuals in the crime.

Over the years the conspiracy doctrine was expanded through judicial interpretation, and it came to include many different types of criminal activity.[2] But from its inception one can see the breadth provided in conspiracy statutes. Despite its breadth, it has survived constitutional challenges,[3] including vagueness challenges.[4]

B. Statutes

There are many conspiracy statutes scattered throughout the United States Code. Often conspiracy language is inserted in a statute so that the specific conduct being prohibited has an expanded application to group criminality. Examples of conspiracy provisions in white collar related statutes include a conspiracy in restraint of trade (15 U.S.C. § 1), conspiracy to monopolize trade (15 U.S.C. § 2), conspiracy to retaliate against a witness, victim or an informant (18 U.S.C. § 1513(f)), RICO conspiracies (18 U.S.C. § 1962(d)), and conspiracies to commit securities fraud offenses (18 U.S.C. § 3301).

Many conspiracy cases in the federal system use 18 U.S.C. § 371, a general conspiracy statute that has two alternate approaches for charging the crime: 1) conspiracy to commit any offense against the United States, or 2) a conspiracy to defraud the United States. A conspiracy to commit any offense against the United States allows the government to take almost any criminal statute and make it into a conspiracy count assuming the other elements of the crime are present. The second

---

[1] Callanan v. United States, 364 U.S. 587 (1961).

[2] See Francis B. Sayre, Criminal Conspiracy, 35 Harv. L. Rev. 393 (1922).

[3] See United States v. Heck, 499 F.2d 778 (9th Cir. 1974).

[4] See United States v. Cueto, 151 F.3d 620, 635–36 (7th Cir. 1998).

approach of § 371 does not require that the activity be connected to a specific federal offense. Rather, defrauding the government will be sufficient to bring the charge when the other statutory elements are met.

The elements of a § 371 conspiracy are: 1) an agreement; 2) unlawful object; 3) knowledge and intent; and 4) an overt act.[5] Some courts specify that there has to be "interdependence among the alleged conspirators."[6] Interdependence is achieved when "the activities of a defendant charged with conspiracy facilitated the endeavors of other alleged co-conspirators or facilitated the venture as a whole."[7]

Conspiracies that are premised upon felonies, like a conspiracy to commit mail fraud, carry a maximum imprisonment of five years. When the crime is a misdemeanor, the penalty cannot exceed the "maximum punishment for such misdemeanor." (See Chapter 24).

There are numerous white collar prosecutions that include § 371 charges. One finds conspiracies to commit wire fraud, immigration fraud, tax fraud, money laundering[8] and many other substantive crimes. One also finds conspiracies to defraud the government, such as conspiracies premised on agreements to defraud the government in the defense procurement area.

Some white collar offenses are charged under specific conspiracy statutes other than § 371. These crimes may have unique elements or omit some of the elements required in proving a case under § 371. For example, § 371 requires proof of an overt act, but a conspiracy to commit money laundering, 18 U.S.C. § 1956(h), does not require the government to prove an overt act by the perpetrator. The Supreme Court in *Whitfield v. United States*,[9] rejecting the defense argument that the money laundering statute should require the prosecution to present evidence that the accused committed an overt act in furtherance of the crime, noted that the language in § 371 required an overt act, where no such language existed in the money laundering statute. It is not unusual in the federal system to have conspiracy statutes in the federal code omitting a requirement of an overt act. The most obvious example of this is the lack of an overt act required for drug conspiracies. (see infra § 3.6).

Another difference between § 371 and other conspiracy statutes may be in the penalty allotted for the crime. For example, the statutory maximum for imprisonment for money laundering conspiracy under § 1956(h) is twenty years, a number far higher than the five years offered by § 371.

One also finds conspiracy as a crime in many state systems. Differences may occur, however, in whether both the substantive crime and conspiracy can be prosecuted. In the federal system conspiracy is a separate offense and there is no

---

[5] Some courts word the elements as "(1) the defendant entered into an agreement; (2) the agreement involved a violation of the law; (3) one of the members of the conspiracy committed an overt act; (4) the overt act was in furtherance of the conspiracy's object; and (5) the defendant willfully entered the conspiracy." United States v. Wittig, 575 F.3d 1085 (10th Cir. 2009).

[6] United States v. Wardell, 591 F.3d 1279 (10th Cir. 2009).

[7] United States v. Horn, 946 F.2d 738, 740–41 (10th Cir. 1991).

[8] See, e.g., United States v. O'Connor, 158 F.Supp.2d 697 (E.D. Va. 2001) (conspiracy to commit immigration, tax and wire fraud).

[9] 543 U.S. 209 (2005).

double jeopardy violation in charging it along with the underlying substantive offense. In the federal system, the defendant can be tried and convicted for both crimes. This is not always true for the states, as the crimes of conspiracy and the underlying substantive offense may merge.

C. Prosecutorial Advantages

Judge Learned Hand called conspiracy "that darling of the modern prosecutor's nursery."[10] He emphasized the enormous power given to prosecutors by the breadth of this crime. There are substantive, procedural, and evidentiary advantages offered to prosecutors for using conspiracy as a charge against a defendant.

One of the key benefits to prosecutors in using a crime of conspiracy is that the crime is inchoate. The government does not have to wait until the completion of the crime to proceed against the defendants. Merely having an agreement with the appropriate *mens rea*, and an overt act, if the statute provides for one, may suffice as sufficient proof of the crime. The defendants may not have succeeded with their intended conduct, but this does not mean that the conspiracy charge fails.[11]

In charging conspiracy, prosecutors can join co-conspirators, trying them as a group. From a trial advocacy perspective this offers prosecutors an advantage in that they can enhance their case through "guilt by association" among multiple defendants. Having more culpable defendants tried with ones with only minimal evidence may present a stronger case to the jury that all the defendants participated in the criminal conduct.

The prosecutor also has enhanced venue options when a conspiracy charge is added to the indictment. Conspiracy allows the government to proceed in the district where the agreement took place or where any overt act occurred. With multiple defendants the number of locations can significantly increase. Prosecutors can choose a venue with stronger evidentiary rules for their case or a place where the jury will be more attuned to the particular form of criminal conduct alleged in the indictment.

The prosecutor also has a helpful evidentiary rule that provides an important trial advantage. Rule 801(d)(2)(E) of the Federal Rules of Evidence provides an exception to the hearsay rule. The hearsay rule normally limits the admission of certain evidence at trial. The exception here allows statements "by a co-conspirator of a party during the course and in furtherance of the conspiracy." Thus, out of court statements by co-conspirators that would normally be excluded, and not heard by the jury, may now be permitted as acceptable evidence in court.[12]

The prosecutor can also expand allowable evidence at trial under relevancy rules. With more defendants, more overt acts, and additional criminality being charged, the scope of what is relevant to the case increases.

---

[10] Harrison v. United States, 7 F.2d 259 (2d Cir. 1925).

[11] United States v. Wittig, 575 F.3d 1085 (10th Cir. 2009).

[12] In United States v. Holmes, 406 F.3d 337 (5th Cir. 2005), the issue was raised whether a co-conspirator's hearsay statement could include a statement that was "from a formalized testimonial source-recorded and sworn civil deposition testimony." The court did not reach whether this was problem under Crawford v. Washington, 541 U.S. 36 (2004), because the testimony was not offered for the truth of the matter asserted therein.

The federal conspiracy statute and many states allow for prosecutions under both the conspiracy statute and the substantive offense.[13] With no merger of the conspiracy and the substantive offense, one can find increased charges against the defendant and no double jeopardy violation.[14] It may even be possible to charge more than one conspiracy. Thus, a defendant can be convicted of both a conspiracy under § 371 and 372 as the legislature intended for these to be separate crimes and thus no double jeopardy violation occurs.[15]

Defendants facing lengthy sentences because of multiple charges may be quick to enter into a plea agreement. Prosecutors may also benefit with those who do not plead and decide to go to trial, as there may be an increased chance of a jury reaching a compromise verdict when the jury has multiple counts for consideration.

Prosecutors may also have the benefit of obtaining a conviction without needing to prove each underlying overt act. The Supreme Court stated in *Griffin v. United States*,[16] that there is no due process violation when a jury reaches a general verdict of guilt in a case with multiple objects or overt acts, and the evidence is later found insufficient for one of the objects.[17] The Supreme Court, citing a lower court, stated:

> It is one thing to negate a verdict that, while supported by evidence, may have been based on an erroneous view of the law; it is another to do so merely on the chance-remote, it seems to us-that the jury convicted on a ground that was not supported by adequate evidence when there existed alternative grounds for which the evidence was sufficient.[18]

The Court did not use the due process clause here in reaching the decision, as this was premised on an evidence inadequacy, as opposed to a legal error.

There is also a longer possible statute of limitations when conspiracy is charged. The time is computed from the last overt act allowing for an expanded time frame for consideration by a jury.[19]

D. Variance

In some cases the conspiracy alleged in the charging document differs from what is presented at trial. There can be many different types of variances. For example, there can be differences in the charging document and the evidence at trial as to who are the parties to the agreement, what are the specified overt acts, and whether there were single or multiple conspiracies involved. Variances in proof can become more complicated when the evidence that is presented meets the statutory requirements, but is different from the evidence initially brought against an accused.

---

[13] The Model Penal Code differs in this regard, as the crimes merge.

[14] United States v. Felix, 503 U.S. 378 (1992) (finding in a drug case that double jeopardy did not preclude a prosecution for the conspiracy and substantive charge).

[15] See United States v. Gerhard, 615 F.3d 7 (1st Cir. 2010).

[16] 502 U.S. 46 (1991).

[17] See also infra § 3.4(A).

[18] Citing United States v. Townsend, 924 F.2d 1385, 1414 (1991).

[19] See Fiswick v. United States, 329 U.S. 211, 216 (1946); Brown v. Elliott, 225 U.S. 392, 401 (1912).

In considering whether there was a variance in proof from the charging document that warrants a reversal, courts look at whether there is in fact a variance and then whether that variance affects the substantial rights of the accused. When the variance involves whether there was a single or multiple conspiracy, the Fifth Circuit held in *United States v. Tilton*,[20] that "[t]he principal factors that this court examines when resolving the issue of a prejudicial variance are the existence of a common goal, the nature of the scheme, and an overlapping of participants in the various dealings." (See § 3.7). When the evidence at trial demonstrates the existence of multiple conspiracies and the government charged it as a single conspiracy, the variance can be problematic to the government's case. (See § 3.7 (B)).

Courts do, however, require a showing that that the defendant was prejudiced. "[T]he danger of prejudice increases along with the number of conspiracies and individuals that make up the wrongly charged single conspiracy."[21] A case with "eight different conspiracies between 13 and 43 individuals" was held to prejudice the defendant. In contrast, cases with "two conspiracies involving four individuals" and three conspiracies involving five individuals were found not to prejudice the accused.[22]

§ 3.2   AGREEMENT

A.   Form of Agreement

The agreement formed by the co-conspirators is the essence of the crime of conspiracy. It is not necessary that this agreement be in writing, oral, or even explicit. A mere nod of the head may be sufficient to prove an agreement between the parties. An agreement has been found even when a co-conspirator testifies that there was no agreement, as long as there is circumstantial evidence of its existence.[23] Courts regularly accept evidence based on the facts and circumstances as proof that an agreement exists.[24] Although courts allow circumstantial evidence for proof of a conspiracy, the government does have the burden of showing that there was a meeting of the minds. A failure to do so can result in the reversal of a conspiracy conviction.[25]

The key is whether the co-conspirators reached an agreement to the "essential nature of the plan." It is not necessary for each of the co-conspirators to know all of the plans details or even who is included within the conspiracy.[26] Thus, there can be a conspiracy to violate the money laundering statute even though one co-conspirator believed the money was from narcotics trafficking and the other co-conspirator thought it came from gambling. Since they both agreed to launder money, the agreement element of the crime was met.[27] It is necessary, however, that the agreement be to an unlawful objective. (See § 3.4).

---

[20] 610 F.2d 302 (5th Cir. 1980).

[21] See United States v. Kemp, 500 F.3d 257, 291 (3d Cir. 2007).

[22] Id. at 292 (citing Berger v. United States, 295 U.S. 78 (1935)).

[23] See United States v. Murphy, 957 F.2d 550 (8th Cir. 1992).

[24] Iannelli v. United States, 420 U.S. 770, 777 n.10 (1975) ("The agreement need not be shown to have been explicit. It can instead be inferred from the facts and circumstances of the case").

[25] United States v. Melchor–Lopez, 627 F.2d 886 (9th Cir. 1980).

[26] Blumenthal v. United States, 332 U.S. 539 (1947); Rogers v. United States, 340 U.S. 367 (1951) (stating that the names of co-conspirators does not need to be known).

[27] See United States v. Stavroulakis, 952 F.2d 686 (2d Cir. 1992).

B. Knowledge

It is necessary that the defendant have knowledge of the agreement. In *United States v. Chandler*,[28] the Eleventh Circuit stated that "[p]roof of a true agreement is the only way to prevent individuals who are not actually members of the group from being swept into the conspiratorial net." The co-conspirators must knowingly participate in the conspiracy. Although they do not have to agree to every step or every conspiratorial act, they have to have knowledge and agree to the overall objectives of the conspiracy.

C. Withdrawal

Can an individual withdraw from the agreement and the conspiracy? In order to withdraw, the defendant has to "disavow the unlawful goal of the conspiracy, affirmatively act to defeat the purpose of the conspiracy, or take 'definite, decisive, and positive' steps to show that the [defendant's] disassociation from the conspiracy is sufficient."[29] Merely ceasing participating in activities in furtherance of the conspiracy will not be enough to demonstrate withdrawal from the conspiracy. Courts typically will require there to be notification of the conspiracy's existence to authorities and communication to the co-conspirators letting them know that he or she has abandoned the conspiracy.[30]

In *United States v. Read*,[31] the defendant-appellants were convicted of conspiracy, mail fraud, and securities fraud. The indictment alleged a "scheme to artificially inflate the year-end inventory of" a medical supply company. The Seventh Circuit noted that "[t]he ultimate result of the fraud was to overstate the profitability" of the company "thereby defrauding its board, its stockholders, and the SEC." One of the defendants argued that he "withdrew from the conspiracy more than five years before the indictment was filed. He questioned the court's instruction on withdrawal from a conspiracy. The court remanded for an erroneous instruction on the conspiracy count, but affirmed with regard to the instructions on the substantive crimes. The Seventh Circuit noted that "[w]ithdrawal marks a conspirator's disavowal or abandonment of the conspiratorial agreement."

Courts have scrutinized what acts will constitute a withdrawal for a conspiracy and who has the burden of proof in demonstrating a withdrawal. The Supreme Court in *Smith v. United States*,[32] held that "[a] defendant who withdraws outside the relevant statute-of-limitations period has a complete defense to prosecution." Although Congress can include within a statute that the government has the burden of proving the defendant's withdrawal from a conspiracy, when it is not designated it is an affirmative defense which rests with the defendant. This analysis was found to also apply when the withdrawal is coupled with a defense regarding the statute of limitations and there is no due process violation in placing this burden on the defendant.

---

[28] 388 F.3d 796 (11th Cir. 2004).

[29] United States v. Lothian, 976 F.2d 1257 (9th Cir. 1992).

[30] United States v. Nippon Paper Industries Co., LTD, 62 F. Supp.2d 173, 190 (D. Mass. 1999).

[31] 658 F.2d 1225 (7th Cir. 1981).

[32] Smith v. United States, 133 S.Ct. 714 (2013).

§ 3.3   PLURALITY

A. Generally

Conspiracy requires two or more individuals forming the agreement to further the unlawful objective. The government, however, does not need to charge all the individuals. Many cases will include unindicted co-conspirators. Sometimes these unindicted co-conspirators will be government cooperating witnesses.

B. Inconsistent Verdicts

An issue that has arisen over the years is what happens when a sole defendant is convicted and his or her co-conspirators are acquitted.[33] Historically courts rejected the use of conspiracy when all parties to the conspiracy, except the defendant, were acquitted. Inconsistent verdicts were untenable because an agreement was required and the acquittal negated the agreement. This rule did not apply when there was an unindicted co-conspirator. It also did not apply when two individuals who were alleged to be part of the conspiracy were convicted and one was acquitted. Since two remained for the agreement, the courts allowed the conspiracy to stand.

Some courts have held that "[w]hen multiple defendants are charged with conspiracy, a jury may convict just one of them."[34] This is an easier answer when the indictment alleges that the defendant conspired with "other individuals" as a jury could find that a defendant conspired "with people other than his co-defendants."[35]

Some courts have moved away from rejecting conspiracies with inconsistent verdicts.[36] In *United States v. Powell*,[37] the Supreme Court held that "there is no reason to vacate respondent's conviction merely because the verdicts cannot rationally be reconciled." *Powell* extends the Court's prior holding in *Dunn v. United States*,[38] where the court "held that a criminal defendant convicted by a jury on one count could not attack that conviction because it was inconsistent with the jury's verdict of acquittal on another count."

Both *Powell* and *Dunn*, however, do not address the contextual setting of inconsistency in conspiracy verdicts between co-conspirators. Lower courts that have examined this question have been unwilling to reverse a conspiracy conviction solely because of the co-conspirator's acquittal, finding that *Powell* should apply to this situation.[39] In *United States v. Suntar Roofing, Inc.*,[40] however, the Tenth Circuit found that consistency of verdicts was necessary when a single co-conspirator is acquitted in the same prosecution as the convicted defendant. In *Suntar Roofing, Inc.* the court

---

[33] See Eric L. Muller, The Hobgoblin of Little Minds? Our Foolish Law of Inconsistent Verdicts, 111 Harv. L. Rev. 771 (1998).

[34] United States v. Gerhard, 615 F.3d 7, 30 (1st Cir. 2010).

[35] Id.

[36] Generally, inconsistent verdicts have been permitted. See Dunn v. United States, 284 U.S. 390 (1932).

[37] 469 U.S. 57, 69 (1984).

[38] 284 U.S. 390 (1932).

[39] See United States v. Bucuvalas, 909 F.2d 593, 596 (1st Cir. 1990) (discussing cases from other jurisdictions).

[40] 897 F.2d 469 (10th Cir. 1990).

affirmed the conviction because there were unindicted co-conspirators also involved in the case. Several courts have criticized the language in *Suntar Roofing Inc.* claiming that the court's reliance on a case prior to *Powell* is misplaced.[41]

C. Corporate Conspiracies

Plurality is also an issue when both parties to the conspiracy are a corporation. In *United States v. Santa Rita Store Co.*,[42] the Supreme Court of New Mexico held that "a conspiracy might be formed by two corporations acting through agents." But in reversing the conviction, the Court noted that "there must be more than one agent or more than one person actually engaged in the formation of the conspiracy." The Court stated that "[h]ad some other officer or agent of either corporation participated in, or had knowledge of, the scheme, then a conspiracy might have been formed between the two defendant corporations."

Courts have held that a corporation can conspire with its own employees, officers, and agents.[43] It has been stated that "[t]he fiction was never intended to prohibit the imposition of criminal liability by allowing a corporation or its agents to hide behind the identity of the other."[44]

Plurality, however, can be a problem when there is a corporation and one individual who is internal to the corporation. In *United States v. Stevens*,[45] the Eleventh Circuit held "that a sole stockholder who completely controls a corporation and is the sole actor in performance of corporate activities, cannot be guilty of a criminal conspiracy with that corporation in the absence of another human actor."

D. Wharton's Rule

Wharton's Rule prohibits conspiracies "when the crime is of such a nature as to necessarily require the participation of two persons for its commission." Historically crimes of bribery, adultery, incest or bigamy, which by their very nature require two individuals, could not be charged as conspiracy. The rule initiates from a case, *Shannon v. Commonwealth*,[46] in which the court dismissed an indictment for conspiracy to commit adultery. Francis Wharton, a leading scholar and author of a treatise, wrote about the rule and in later editions developed its application. The initial approach to Wharton's Rule was to dismiss the indictment prior to trial.

In more recent years, courts have limited Wharton's Rule in several ways. If more than the minimum number of individuals necessary for the crime alleged actually participate in the activity, courts have not allowed Wharton's Rule to preclude the conspiracy charge against these individuals. Likewise, if the substantive offense of the conspiracy requires less than two individuals, it will not apply. So in *United States v.*

---

[41] See United States v. Crayton, 357 F.3d 560, 566 (6th Cir. 2004) (finding *Suntar Roofing, Inc's* reliance on Hartzel v. United States, 322 U.S. 680 (1944) fails to recognize that the case did not involve inconsistent jury verdicts); United States v. Bucuvalas, 909 F.2d 593, 596 (1st Cir. 1990).

[42] 113 P. 620, 621 (N.M. 1911).

[43] See United States v. Hartley, 678 F.2d 961, 972 (11th Cir. 1982). Later cases have abrogated Hartley's holding on other grounds.

[44] Id. at 970.

[45] 909 F.2d 431 (11th Cir. 1990).

[46] 14 Pa. 226 (1850) (cited in Iannelli v. United States, 420 U.S. 770 (1975).

Rone,[47] the Ninth Circuit in a Racketeer Influenced and Corrupt Organizations Act (RICO) case, limited the use of Wharton's Rule by holding it inapplicable as the crime itself by its definition allowed the substantive offense to be "committed by an individual acting alone." Finally, the Model Penal Code, as used by some states, does not endorse Wharton's Rule.

Courts have moved to using Wharton's Rule as a judicial presumption rather than a hard and fast disqualifier. In *Iannelli v. United States*,[48] the Supreme Court considered Wharton's Rule in the context of a gambling case, specifically a violation of 18 U.S.C. § 1955. Prior to this decision, the circuits had expressed differing views on the application of Wharton's Rule to this statute. In *Iannelli*, the Court focused on three factors:

> (1) Are the parties to the agreement the only persons who participate in the substantive offense? (2) Does the crime have consequences only on those parties or also on society at large? (3) Does the agreement connected with the substantive offense pose the same threat to society "that the law of conspiracy seeks to avert?"

The Court in *Iannelli* held that "Wharton's Rule applies only to offenses that require concerted criminal activity, a plurality of criminal agents." It acts, the Court stated, "as a judicial presumption, to be applied in the absence of legislative intent to the contrary," and it requires not only that the parties to the agreement be the only parties to participate in the commission of the offense, but also that "the immediate consequences of the crime rest on the parties themselves rather than on society at large." Wharton's Rule "is essentially an aid to the determination of legislative intent." The *Iannelli* Court held Wharton's Rule inapplicable to the gambling offense in question in that the crime differed from the traditional Wharton Rule crimes. Additionally, there were additional individuals involved in the criminal activities that took it beyond the limited context used for Wharton's Rule.

Examples of white collar cases with claims of violations under Wharton's Rule, can be seen in cases involving bribery prosecutions under 18 U.S.C. §§ 201 and 666. Several circuits have held that "Wharton's Rule does not bar prosecution for both conspiracy under § 371 and bribery under § 666."[49] In *United States v. McNair*,[50] the Eleventh Circuit stated that there is nothing in the legislative history that demonstrates that "Congress intended to foreclose prosecuting § 371 conspiracy offenses in § 666 crimes." The court also noted that "the effect of the crime of § 666 bribery is not limited to the bribe-payor and recipient, as the crime involves public corruption, which harms society as a whole." Wharton's Rule has also been found not to apply to claims of bribery under 18 U.S.C. § 201.[51]

---

[47] 598 F.2d 564 (9th Cir. 1979).

[48] 420 U.S. 770 (1975).

[49] See, e.g., United States v. Bornman, 559 F.3d 150, 156 (3d Cir. 2009); United States v. Hines, 541 F.3d 833, 838 (8th Cir. 2008); United States v. Morris, 957 F.2d 1391, 1403 (7th Cir. 1992); United States v. Aubrey, 2010 WL 5314802 * 1–2 (D. Nev. 2010).

[50] 605 F.3d 1152, 1215–16 (11th Cir. 2010).

[51] See, e.g., United States v. Evans, 344 F.3d 1131, 1133 n.3 (11th Cir. 2003); United States v. Finazzo, 704 F.2d 300 (6th Cir. 1983); United States v. Previte, 648 F.2d 73, 76–78 (1st Cir. 1981).

E. Victims

When a party is protected by statute because of his or her role as a victim of the crime, the individual should not be considered for purposes of plurality for charging conspiracy. In *Gebardi v. United States*,[52] the Supreme Court rejected a Mann Act case (18 U.S.C. § 2421) involving a defendant's transporting of a woman across state lines for an immoral purpose. Even though the woman being transported consented, the Court held that this should not be the basis of a conspiracy charge. The Court found that "an affirmative legislative policy to leave her acquiescence unpunished," meant that she could not be used for purposes of conspiracy. Since there were no other individuals involved for the man to have conspired with, the conspiracy conviction was improper.

In a white collar context, the Seventh Circuit in *United States v. Nasser*,[53] examined a conspiracy to commit a conflict of interest in violation of 18 U.S.C. § 207(a) in a case involving an attorney who was employed by the IRS. The court held that although it could see differences between this case and the *Gebardi* decision where a woman is transported for immoral purposes with her consent," the "intent of Congress in failing to prescribe a penalty in § 207(a) for the client, regardless of his degree of guilty knowledge or culpable intent," should cause the "omission as precluding punishment for the client" and therefore precluding the conspiracy.

Although courts have held that an individual is not a co-conspirator when they are statutorily the victim of a crime, this has not caused courts to omit their testimony under the co-conspirator exception to Federal Rule of Evidence 801(d)(2)(E). In *United States v. Kendall*,[54] the Seventh Circuit examined a Hobbs Act case where the appellants argued that because the intent and purpose of the Hobbs Act (18 U.S.C. § 1951) was to protect victims, conversations with those victims should not be admitted under the co-conspirator exception to the hearsay rule. The court rejected this argument saying that "'conspiracy' as an evidentiary concept, embodied in Rule 801(d)(2)(E), and 'conspiracy' as a concept of substantive criminal law are coterminous."

F. Bilateral and Unilateral Conspiracies

Plurality can be questioned when one of the parties to the conspiracy is not a bona fide co-conspirator. This can occur when one party to the conspiracy is a government agent who feigns agreement for a law enforcement purpose. 18 U.S.C. § 371 takes a bilateral approach to conspiracy and requires there to be two actual parties agreeing to the conspiracy, thus not allowing the agreement element of the conspiracy to be met with a government agent who is pretending to agree.[55] This is sometimes, referred to as the *Sears* rule from the case of *Sears v. United States*,[56] which held that "as it takes two to conspire, there can be no indictable conspiracy with a government informer who

---

[52] 287 U.S. 112, 118–23 (1932).

[53] 476 F.2d 1111 (7th Cir. 1973).

[54] 665 F.2d 126, 130 (7th Cir. 1981).

[55] See United States v. Schmidt, 947 F.2d 362, 367 (9th Cir. 1991); United States v. Escobar De Bright, 742 F.2d 1196 (9th Cir. 1984).

[56] Sears v. United States, 343 F.2d 139 (5th Cir. 1965).

secretly intends to frustrate the conspiracy."[57] The rationale here is that the dangers that promote the crime of conspiracy do not exist when the conspiracy is with a government agent.

If, however, there are additional members of the conspiracy beyond the government agent, courts have found this sufficient to meet the agreement element of the crime of conspiracy.[58] Some states, following the Model Penal Code position, allow unilateral conspiracies to meet the agreement element.

§ 3.4   UNLAWFUL OBJECT OF CONSPIRACY

A.   Generally

A conspiracy under § 371 can be either a conspiracy to commit a specific *offense* or a conspiracy to *defraud* the United States or its agencies. Under the offense provision of the statute, prosecutors will charge violations of provisions in the criminal code. For example, it is common to see charges such as conspiracy to commit mail or wire fraud. The offense provision, however, does not require that the object be a crime, as it may be acts Congress "prohibited in the interest of the public policy of the United States but is made punishable only by a civil suit for a statutory penalty."[59] Under the defraud provision of § 371 the focus is on defrauding the government.

When a conspiracy has multiple objects of the offense, the question arises as to when there is sufficient evidence to support a conspiracy conviction. (see § 3.1(D)). The Supreme Court in *Griffin v. United States*,[60] allows for a verdict to stand when the charges are in the conjunctive and there is evidence to support any of the charged acts. The Second Circuit, however, has permitted a "caveat" to this rule when there is "an overwhelming amount of evidence relevant only to the unproved part of the conspiracy [that] may have prejudiced the jury."[61]

B.   Conspiracy to Defraud

1.   *General Principles*

Conspiracy to defraud has enormous breadth, giving prosecutors significant discretion.[62] The term "defraud" is considered broader than the use of the term "defraud" in the mail and wire fraud statutes.[63] (See Chapter 4). Conspiracies to defraud do not require a showing of a "knowing violation of a federal agency's rules,

---

[57] This position has been accepted by several circuits. See United States v. Escobar De Bright, 742 F.2d 1196, 1198–1200 (9th Cir. 1984) (reversible error in not instructing that on defendant conspiring with a government agent); United States v. Moss, 591 F.2d 428, 434 n.8 (8th Cir. 1979); United States v. Chase, 372 F.2d 453, 459 (4th Cir. 1967).

[58] See United States v. Si, 343 F.3d 1116 (9th Cir. 2003).

[59] See United States v. Hutto, 256 U.S. 524 (1921); Hunsaker v. United States, 279 F.2d 111 (9th Cir. 1960); United States v. Touhey, 867 F.2d 534 (9th Cir. 1989).

[60] 502 U.S. 46, 59 (1991).

[61] United States v. Desnoyers, 637 F.3d 105 (2d Cir. 2011) (citing United States v. Papadakis, 510 F.2d 287, 297 (2d Cir. 1975).

[62] See generally Abraham S. Goldstein, Conspiracy to Defraud the United States, 68 Yale L.J. 405 (1959).

[63] See United States v. Herron, 825 F.2d 50 (5th Cir. 1987).

regulations, or procedures."[64] Nor is it necessary to show a "financial loss to an agency of the government."[65]

In *Hammerschmidt v. United States*,[66] the Supreme Court explored the reach of the defraud clause of the statute and stated:

> To conspire to defraud the United States means primarily to cheat the government out of property or money, but it also means to interfere with or obstruct one of its lawful governmental functions by deceit, craft or trickery, or at least by means that are dishonest. It is not necessary that the government shall be subjected to property or pecuniary loss by the fraud, but only that its legitimate official action and purpose shall be defeated by misrepresentation, chicane, or the overreaching of those charged with carrying out the governmental intention.[67]

The aim of the conspiracy to defraud statute is to "protect the integrity of the United States and its agencies, programs and policies."[68] The government does not need to prove that the accused committed or agreed to commit a specific substantive provision. It is only necessary for the government to show that he or she "agreed to interfere with or to obstruct one of the government's lawful functions."[69]

2. *Limitations of Conspiracy to Defraud*

Courts, recognizing the broad language in the defraud clause of the statute, sometimes have given a careful reading in cases to limit the reach of this clause. In *Dennis v. United States*,[70] the Supreme Court stressed the need to review the "indictments under the broad language of the general conspiracy statute," noting that it needed to be "scrutinized carefully as to each of the charged defendants because of the possibility, inherent in a criminal conspiracy charge, that its wide net may ensnare the innocent as well as the culpable." Courts have also used the rule of lenity, a rule that leans to the defendant when there are multiple readings of a statute. (See § 1.8(B)). Thus, in *Tanner v. United States*,[71] the Supreme Court used the rule of lenity to reject the "government's sweeping interpretation of § 371—which would have, in effect, substituted 'anyone receiving federal financial assistance and supervision' for the phrase 'the United States or any agency thereof.'"

The alleged conspiracy to defraud conduct does not have to be unlawful under a statute or rule.[72] In *United States v. Porter*,[73] however, the Fifth Circuit Court of Appeals reversed convictions involving an alleged Medicare conspiracy to defraud the United States as between eight doctors and one laboratory assistant. Six doctors pled guilty and the remaining defendants went to trial. The government could not point to

---

[64] United States v. Conover, 772 F.2d 765, 770 (11th Cir. 1985).

[65] Id. at 771.

[66] 265 U.S. 182 (1924).

[67] Id. at 188.

[68] United States v. Hopkins, 916 F.2d 207 (5th Cir. 1990).

[69] See United States v. Nersesian, 824 F.2d 1294 (2d Cir. 1987).

[70] 384 U.S. 855 (1966).

[71] 483 U.S. 107, 132 (1987).

[72] United States v. Winkle, 587 F.2d 705 (5th Cir. 1979).

[73] 591 F.2d 1048 (5th Cir. 1979).

any statute or regulation that had been violated by the doctors and laboratory assistant. In reversing the convictions of these three, the Fifth Circuit stated that "[s]ince it is conceded that the government has not been subjected to any property or pecuniary loss by the activities set forth in the indictment, the conspiracy count can stand only if the government can point to some lawful function which has been impaired, obstructed or defeated."[74]

3. *Klein Conspiracies*

Conspiracies to defraud the Internal Revenue Service (IRS) under § 371 are often termed "*Klein*" conspiracies. In *United States v. Klein*,[75] several individuals were charged with defrauding the United States "by impeding and obstructing the lawful functions of the Treasury Department and concealing the nature of their business activities and source of income."[76] The Second Circuit in *Klein* held that "[m]ere failure to disclose income would not be sufficient to show a Section 371 conspiracy to defraud the United States." In order to have sufficient evidence of a conspiracy to defraud the United States there needs to be an agreement with the intent to "obstruct the government's knowledge and collection of revenue due."[77] Although the court in *Klein* found sufficient evidence, later decisions have emphasized the need for evidence beyond a showing of a failure to disclose evidence to the IRS.[78] Likewise, "[a] conspiracy to conceal the source of illegally obtained money is not automatically a *Klein* conspiracy, even if it collaterally impedes the IRS in the collection of taxes."[79] Claims of improper use of the conspiracy in tax cases result from the fact that some tax offenses carry lower penalties then provided by the conspiracy to defraud clause of § 371.[80] (see also § 11.1(E)(1)).

In *United States v. Sturman*,[81] defendants argued that the conspiracy violations should have been charged under the offense provisions of § 371 and not the defraud clause of the conspiracy statute. Sturman was alleged to have "set up a complex system of foreign and domestic organizations, transactions among the corporations, and foreign bank accounts to prevent the IRS from performing its auditing and assessment functions." The Sixth Circuit in *Sturman* found that this activity went beyond tax statutes 26 U.S.C. § 7206(1) or 7206(4) and because "[n]o provision of the Tax Code covers the totality and scope of the conspiracy, the government was therefore entitled to use the defraud clause of § 371."[82]

C. Prosecuting Under Both Offense and Defraud Clauses

Courts have not resolved whether a defendant can be prosecuted under both the offense and defraud clauses of § 371. Some courts allow prosecutors to proceed under both provisions but then state that the government cannot have two convictions or

---

[74] Id. at 1055–56.

[75] 247 F.2d 908 (2d Cir. 1957).

[76] United States v. Sturman, 951 F.2d 1466, 1472 (6th Cir. 1991).

[77] Id. at 918.

[78] See United States v. Adkinson, 158 F.3d 1147 (11th Cir. 1998).

[79] Id. at 1159.

[80] See United States v. Shermetaro, 625 F.2d 104 (6th Cir. 1980).

[81] 951 F.2d 1466, 1472 (6th Cir. 1991).

[82] Id. at 1473.

punish the defendant two times for the same conduct.[83] Thus, prosecutors would have the choice of proceeding with both aspects of this statute, but upon a guilty finding they can only convict for one aspect and likewise only punish for one.

But in *United States v. Minarik*,[84] the Sixth Circuit noted that § 371 creates one crime with two alternate ways of proceeding, and not two separate crimes. The court stated that "prosecutors and courts are required to determine and acknowledge exactly what the alleged crime *is*. They may not allow the facts to define the crime through hindsight after the case is over." The court noted that "[o]nly by treating conspiracies to commit specific offenses (which are also arguably general frauds) exclusively under the offense clause of § 371 can multiple convictions and unnecessary convictions be avoided."

Courts have distinguished the *Minarik* decision saying the holding should be limited because "the prosecution had 'used the defraud clause in a way that created great confusion about the conduct claimed to be illegal."[85] Cases in the Sixth Circuit have noted that when a defendant is given ample notice of the charges against him or her, and the conduct fits within the defraud clause of § 371, the *Minarik* case can be distinguished.[86]

D. Impossibility

It is not necessary that the agreement to commit the unlawful act actually be able to be achieved. It is also unnecessary that there be any loss suffered.[87] The impossibility of actually being able to achieve the unlawful purpose is irrelevant as the crux of the crime is the agreement to form the unlawful act, not the actual commission of this act. In *United States v. Jimenez Recio*,[88] the Supreme Court held that conspiracy does not contain an "automatic termination" rule. So if the government successfully terminates the conspiracy's objective, it does not provide immunity from prosecution. But if the agreement is to something other than a crime or some type of unlawful act, then the elements of the conspiracy may not have been met.

§ 3.5 KNOWLEDGE AND INTENT

A. Generally

As conspiracy is a specific intent crime, it is incumbent on the prosecution to prove that the defendant specifically intended to commit the crime of conspiracy. In proving the *mens rea* of the crime of conspiracy, the prosecution must show that the defendant had knowledge of the conspiracy's existence and knowledge of the objective of the conspiracy. If the conspiracy charge is premised on a conspiracy to commit a specific offense, the Supreme Court in *Ingram v. United States* held that you need to have "at

---

[83] See United States v. Bilzerian, 926 F.2d 1285 (2d Cir. 1991).

[84] 875 F.2d 1186, 1195–96 (1989).

[85] See, e.g., United States v. Arch Trading Co., 987 F.2d 1087 (4th Cir. 1993).

[86] See, e.g, United States v. Kraig, 99 F.3d 1361 (6th Cir. 1996); United States v. Sturman, 951 F.2d 1466 (6th Cir. 1991); United States v. Mohnet, 949 F.2d 899 (6th Cir. 1991).

[87] Haas v. Henkel, 216 U.S. 462 (1910).

[88] 537 U.S. 270 (2003).

least the degree of criminal intent necessary for the substantive offense itself."[89] If the conspiracy is premised upon a conspiracy to defraud, the government has to prove that the accused intended to defraud the federal government. Merely intending to defraud a state government will not suffice.[90]

There is no requirement that this knowledge extend to all the details of the conspiracy or to knowing all the individuals involved in the conspiracy. There is also no requirement that the accused have knowledge of an attendant circumstance, such as a jurisdictional element.[91] As previously noted, it is, however, necessary that the accused have knowledge of the agreement. (See § 3.2(B)).

Willful blindness or deliberate indifference can establish knowledge. This requires deliberate acts to avoid learning the truth. Additionally, the "defendant must subjectively believe that there is a high probability that a fact exists." Mere negligence or recklessness will not suffice for willful blindness.[92] (See § 1.8 (C)(1)).

B.   Merchants and Suppliers

Merchants and suppliers present unique issues in that the question can arise as to how much knowledge is necessary when the goods in question are to be used for an illicit purpose. In *United States v. Falcone*,[93] the Second Circuit held that the seller of goods does not become a co-conspirator simply because he fails to stop selling the goods when the goods might be used for an illegal purpose. To be held criminally liable in these circumstances, he "must in some sense promote their venture himself, make it his own, have a stake in its outcome."

The *Falcone* decision does not provide merchants and suppliers immunity in all instances. As noted in the later Supreme Court decision of *Direct Sales Co. v. United States*,[94] it might be possible to show that there "was a conspiracy between the buyer and the seller alone." In this regard, courts have looked at several different factors to determine whether the merchant or seller had sufficient intent for a conspiracy charge. These can include factors such as whether there was an inflated price for the goods.[95]

§ 3.6   OVERT ACT

Prosecutions under § 371 require proof of an overt act. This differs from many other conspiracy statutes in the criminal code. For example, there is no requirement for an overt act with drug[96] or money laundering conspiracies. Conspiracies under the Racketeer Influenced and Corrupt Organizations Act also do not require an overt act.[97]

---

[89] 360 U.S. 672, 678 (1959).

[90] See United States v. Mendez, 528 F.3d 811 (11th Cir. 2008).

[91] United States v. Feola, 420 U.S. 671 (1975) (finding it is not necessary to prove knowledge that the defendants knew it was a federal officer for a crime of conspiracy to assault a federal officer).

[92] See Global–Tech Applicances, Inc. v. SEB, 131 S.Ct. 2060 (2011).

[93] 109 F.2d 579 (2d Cir. 1940).

[94] 319 U.S. 703 (1943).

[95] Ellen S. Podgor, Peter J. Henning, & Neil P. Cohen, Mastering Criminal Law 283 (2008).

[96] See United States v. Shabani, 513 U.S. 10 (1994).

[97] See Salinas v. United States, 522 U.S. 52 (1997).

Although an overt act is needed for a § 371 prosecution, it is not necessary that the overt act be a crime. There is also no requirement that the jury agree on a single overt act. In *United States v. Kozeny*,[98] Defendant–Bourke was convicted of conspiring to violate the Foreign Corrupt Practices Act (FCPA), the Travel Act, and making False Statements. The Second Circuit held that the government had to prove at least one overt act, as this was an element of the crime. But the court also stated that it was not necessary to show "which overt act among multiple such acts supports proof of a conspiracy conviction." This, the court stated, is a "brute fact and not itself an element of the crime." Thus, the jury did not have to "reach unanimous agreement on which particular overt act was committed in furtherance of the conspiracy." The court's reasoning in *Kozeny* relies on the Supreme Court's decision in *Richardson v. United States*,[99] which held in a case involving a continuing criminal enterprise under 21 U.S.C. § 848(c) that a "jury must agree that a defendant committed each of the violations comprising the 'continuing series of violations'" but that they need not always decide unanimously which of several possible sets of underlying brute facts make up a particular element."

Both the Fifth and Seventh Circuits have clearly supported the position that jury unanimity is not needed on which specific overt act was committed in furtherance of the conspiracy.[100] Less certain are decisions in the Eighth and Ninth Circuit where courts gave jury instructions requiring jury unanimity and the wording of the instructions was questioned by the defense.[101]

§ 3.7   SINGLE OR MULTIPLE CONSPIRACIES

A.   Generally

A common issue in conspiracy cases is how many conspiracies exist, and whether the acts of the parties are part of a single conspiracy or multiple conspiracies. The government may seek to have one conspiracy, as opposed to multiple conspiracies, as the joinder of overt acts can work to its advantage in presenting a wider breadth of evidence. The cost of a unified trial also is a strong incentive to have all the overt acts tried together as part of one conspiracy case. On the other hand, the defense may prefer a single conspiracy if the charges are in multiple jurisdictions, overlapping, and perhaps infringing on the defendant's double jeopardy rights.

Since there is no requirement for all members of the conspiracy to be aware of who is part of the conspiracy or all the specific acts encompassed within the conspiracy, a failure to have full information does not mean that there are multiple conspiracies. Courts have held that "separate conspiracies with different memberships may still be

---

[98] 667 F.3d 122 (2d Cir. 2011).

[99] 526 U.S. 813, 815 (1999).

[100] See United States v. Sutherland, 656 F.2d 1181, 1202 (5th Cir. 1981); United States v. Griggs, 569 F.3d 341, 343 (7th Cir. 2009).

[101] See United States v. Haskell, 468 F.3d 1064, 1074 (8th Cir. 2006); United States v. Jones, 712 F.2d 1316, 1322 (9th Cir. 1983).

joined if they are part of the same series of acts or transactions."[102] The key is whether they all agreed to the "essential nature of the plan."

Some courts use a three-part test in determining whether it should be a single or multiple conspiracy. The factors are:

> 1) whether there was a common goal among the conspirators; 2) whether, looking at the nature of the scheme, the agreement contemplated bringing to pass a continuous result that would not continue without the continuous cooperation of the conspirators; and 3) the extent to which the participants overlap in the various dealings.[103]

But courts note that if one of these factors is not present, that is not determinative of it not being a single conspiracy. There is a variance if the charging document provides for a single conspiracy and the government then presents multiple conspiracies. (See § 3.1(D)).

Although it is considered a variance when the government charges a single conspiracy and then presents evidence of multiple conspiracies, it is not an impermissible variance when there is "a master conspiracy with sub-schemes." The decision of whether it is a single conspiracy or multiple conspiracies is considered a question of fact for the jury to decide.[104]

Courts instruct prosecutors to charge a single conspiracy when there is only one agreement involved.[105] If, however, there are several different conspiracy statutes violated, it is not a double jeopardy violation to charge separate conspiracy violations for each statute.[106] In *United States v. Broce,*[107] a case in which the respondents entered pleas to two separate counts of conspiracy under the Sherman Act, the Supreme Court held

> A single agreement to commit several crimes constitutes one conspiracy. By the same reasoning, multiple agreements to commit separate crimes constitute multiple conspiracies. When respondents pleaded guilty to two charges of conspiracy on the explicit premise of two agreements which started at different times and embraced separate objectives, they conceded guilt to two separate offenses.[108]

The majority of courts also hold that it is not duplicitous to join into one conspiracy, charges under the offense and defraud prongs of § 371. "Because these

---

[102] See, e.g., United States v. Hill, 643 F.3d 807 (11th Cir. 2011) (involving a bank fraud, false credit applications, wire fraud, mail fraud, and money laundering); United States v. Weaver, 905 F.2d 1466, 1476 (11th Cir. 1990).

[103] United States v. Edwards, 2011 WL 816894 (E.D. 2011); United States v. Greenidge, 495 F.3d 85 (3d Cir. 2007); United States v. Kelly, 892 F.2d 255 (3d Cir. 1989); United States v. Padilla, 982 F.2d 110, 115 (3d Cir. 1992).

[104] See United States v. Smith, 789 F.2d 196 (3d Cir. 1986).

[105] Braverman v. United States, 317 U.S. 49 (1942).

[106] Albernaz v. United States, 450 U.S. 333 (1981).

[107] 488 U.S. 563 (1989).

[108] Id. at 570–71.

counts charge one crime, not two, it logically follows that § 371 creates a single offense."[109]

When multiple jurisdictions charge conspiracy, the defendant may claim that there is a double jeopardy violation and that the conspiracies should be a single conspiracy. In these instances a defendant has the burden of going forward with a claim that the multiple conspiracies should have been charged by the government as a single conspiracy. "After a defendant establishes a prima facie nonfrivolous case that a single conspiracy exists, the burden of persuasion shifts, and the government must show by a preponderance of the evidence that the defendant has been charged in separate conspiracies."[110] The rationale for placing the burden on the government is that prosecutors control the charging function.

In the case of John Rigas, the founder of Adelphia, and his son Timothy Rigas, the CFO of the company, the defendants were indicted in the Southern District of New York in 2002 and then in Middle District of Pennsylvania in 2005. Both cases included charges under 18 U.S.C. § 371. The defendants argued that the successive prosecutions were a single offense as opposed to multiple conspiracies and therefore violated double jeopardy. In remanding the case for the government to meet the burden of why this should not be a single offense, the Third Circuit Court of Appeals stated that it was necessary to review this case, "because both indictments concern the same underlying transactions, they relate to the same time and place, and involve the same core group of participants." The court also noted that "[b]oth indictments have a common goal, and individual overt acts in both indictments were interdependent."[111] Since the government could have brought the Pennsylvania charges in the New York indictment, the government needs to demonstrate why this should be multiple conspiracies.[112]

B. Wheel and Spoke Conspiracies

In *Kotteakos v. United States*,[113] defendants were convicted of a conspiracy to obtain loans under the National Housing Act. The indictment named thirty-two defendants who were accused of "induc[ing] various financial institutions to grant credit with the intent that the loans or advances would then be offered to the Federal Housing Administration for insurance upon applications containing false and fraudulent information." Simon Brown was the key link between all the individuals. In many cases, Brown was the sole link for individuals, as they had no relationship with the other individuals alleged to be part of this conspiracy.

The Supreme Court analogized this to the hub of a wheel with its spokes. Brown was the hub of the wheel and the individual defendants were the spokes of the wheel. Because the individual defendants had no interest in any of the other defendants (the

---

[109] "The Second, Ninth, Eleventh, and District of Columbia Circuits have reached the same conclusion and held that single counts alleging violations of both the 'offense' and 'defraud' prong of § 371 are not duplicitous." United States v. Rigas, 605 F.3d 194 (3d Cir. 2010).

[110] United States v. Rabhan, 628 F.3d 200 (5th Cir. 2010).

[111] United States v. Rigas, 605 F.3d 194, 217 (3d Cir. 2010).

[112] The court affirmed the district court's denial of the Rigases' motion premised on collateral estoppel. Id. at 219.

[113] 328 U.S. 750 (1946).

other spokes of the wheel), this was not a single conspiracy. Rather the Court held that the individual defendants were involved in multiple conspiracies with Brown.

In *United States v. Chandler*,[114] a case involving a mail fraud conspiracy, the Eleventh Circuit said that "[f]or a wheel conspiracy to exist, those people who form the wheel's spokes must have been *aware* and must do something in furtherance of some single, illegal enterprise. If not there is no rim to enclose the spokes."[115]

C. Chain Conspiracies

A chain conspiracy finds one conspiracy if the individuals are links to the overall chain. In *Blumenthal v. United States*,[116] the Supreme Court held that parties who agreed to sell liquor at prices exceeding the ceiling set by regulations of the Office of Price Administration, were all acting as steps in one general conspiracy. The Court stated that "[b]y their separate agreements, if such they were, they became parties to the larger common plan, joined together by their knowledge of its essential features and broad scope, though not of its exact limits, and by their common single goal."[117]

§ 3.8   PINKERTON RULE

The Pinkerton rule, emanating from the case of *Pinkerton v. United States*,[118] places responsibility on each member of the conspiracy in that it holds each member of the conspiracy criminally liable for the reasonably foreseeable crimes of co-conspirators committed in furtherance of the conspiracy. Thus, a defendant who did not commit the specific substantive criminal act can be prosecuted for that conduct if a co-conspirator committed the act and it is reasonably foreseeable as part of the conspiracy and in furtherance of the conspiracy.[119]

In *Pinkerton*, an incarcerated defendant was convicted for violations of the Internal Revenue Code that were committed by his brother outside of the prison housing him. There was no direct evidence demonstrating that this defendant participated in these substantive offenses for which he was convicted. The Court found that the acts were within the scope and in furtherance of the conspiracy, were committed by one or more members of the conspiracy, and at the time the offense was committed, the defendant was a member of the conspiracy. Finding the "overt act[s] of one partner in crime" attributable to all, the Court said that:

> A different case would arise if the substantive offense committed by one of the conspirators was not in fact done in furtherance of the conspiracy, did not fall within the scope of the unlawful project, or was merely a part of the ramifications

---

[114] 388 F.3d 796 (11th Cir. 2004).

[115] Id. at 808 (citing United States v. Levine, 546 F.2d 658, 663 (5th Cir. 1977).

[116] 332 U.S. 539, 558 (1947).

[117] Id.

[118] 328 U.S. 640 (1946).

[119] See United States v. Tilton, 610 F.2d 302 (5th Cir. 1980) (finding that even though defendant did not participate in mailing and did not even know about it, he could he held as a member of a mail fraud conspiracy in that the act was committed by a co-conspirator in furtherance of the conspiracy).

of the plan which could not be reasonably foreseen as a necessary or natural consequence of the unlawful agreement.[120]

In *United States v. Alvarez*,[121] the Eleventh Circuit extended *Pinkerton* to acts that were not within the originally intended conspiracy by the parties. But in so doing, the court made it clear that this was a narrow extension "limited to conspirators who played more than a 'minor' role in the conspiracy, or who had actual knowledge of at least some of the circumstances and events culminating in the reasonably foreseeable but originally unintended substantive crime."

Many states do not employ the Pinkerton Rule. It also is not accepted in the Model Penal Code.

§ 3.9   ANTITRUST CONSPIRACIES

A. Statutes

Two sections of the Sherman Act contain conspiracy provisions. 15 U.S.C. § 1 criminalizes conspiracies "in restraint of trade or commence" and 15 U.S.C. § 2 criminalizes monopolizing "any part of the trade or commerce among the several States, or with foreign nations." Section one requires plurality, while section two can be met absent plurality in that it prohibits "every person" from monopolizing any part of trade or commerce. Although there are several exemptions to antitrust liability, courts construe these exemptions narrowly.[122]

B. Plurality

1.   Generally

The issue of plurality arises when the antitrust conspiracy is inter-enterprise or intra-corporate. Inter-enterprise is often a situation of a corporation and its wholly owned subsidiary and intra-corporate typically involves a corporation with an agent of that same corporation.

2.   Inter–Enterprise Conspiracies

Initially, the Supreme Court in *United States v. Yellow Cab*[123] held that a corporation "affiliated or integrated under common ownership" would not preclude antitrust liability. The Court stated that "[t]he corporate interrelationships of the conspirators. . . are not determinative of the applicability of the Sherman Act." Sometimes called "vertically integrated enterprises," the Court was reluctant to allow these restraints of trade to be beyond the reach of the law.

---

[120] Pinkerton, 328 U.S. at 647–48.

[121] 755 F.2d 830, 851 n.27 (11th Cir. 1985).

[122] See United States v. Gosselin World Wide Moving, N.V., 411 F.3d 502 (4th Cir. 2005) (holding that a bid-rigging scheme did not fall with the antitrust exemption under the Shipping Act, tariff filing exemptions, or existing grace periods).

[123] 332 U.S. 218 (1947).

The Supreme Court in *Copperweld Corporation v. Independence Tube Corporation*,[124] modified its position in *Yellow Cab*, holding that "Copperweld and its wholly owned subsidiary" were "incapable of conspiring with each other for purposes of § 1 of the Sherman Act." The Court now found that Section 1 of the Sherman Act "does not reach conduct that is 'wholly unilateral.'" The Court noted that "[b]ecause coordination between a corporation and its division does not represent a sudden joining of two independent sources of economic power previously pursuing separate interests, it is not an activity that warrants § 1 scrutiny." The Court stated:

> it is perfectly plain that an internal "agreement" to implement a single, unitary firm's policies does not raise the antitrust dangers that § 1 was designed to police. The officers of a single firm are not separate economic actors pursuing separate economic interests, so agreements among them do not suddenly bring together economic power that was previously pursuing divergent goals. Coordination within a firm is as likely to result from an effort to compete as from an effort to stifle competition. In the marketplace, such coordination may be necessary if a business enterprise is to compete effectively. For these reasons, officers or employees of the same firm do not provide the plurality of actors imperative for a § 1 conspiracy[125]

The *Copperweld* decision did not, however, resolve whether this prohibition extended to intra-enterprise conspiracies where the parent corporation is accused of conspiring with an affiliated corporation that it does not completely own.

State antitrust laws may differ from this approach. For example, in *Louisiana Power and Light Company v. United Gas Pipe Line Company*,[126] the Supreme Court of Louisiana noted that federal antitrust law should normally be influential in the Court's holdings. But the Louisiana Supreme Court held in this case that a "flexible approach" better serves the goals of the Louisiana statute and this would allow for "antitrust scrutiny of affiliated corporations as well as of independent firms acting in concert." Thus, the Louisiana statute was found to permit antitrust actions premised on "unreasonable restraints of trade committed by a parent corporation and its partially or wholly owned subsidiary corporation."

3.   *Intra–Corporate Conspiracies*

There can also be questions as to whether antitrust law applies to intra-corporate conspiracies based upon a corporation and an individual within that same corporation. In *Nelson Radio & Supply Co. v. Motorola*,[127] the Fifth Circuit Court of Appeals held that under § 1 of the Sherman Act "[a] corporation cannot conspire with itself any more than a private individual can, and it is the general rule that the acts of the agent are the acts of the corporation." The court in *Nelson Radio and Supply Co.* refused to extend § 1 antitrust liability absent a showing that the "agents of the corporation were acting in other than their normal capacities. This position may differ if the allegation refers to § 2 of the Sherman Act as this section "covers an attempt to monopolize."

---

[124] 467 U.S. 752 (1984).

[125] Id. at 769.

[126] 493 So.2d 1149 (La. 1986).

[127] 200 F.2d 911 (5th Cir. 1952).

C. Intent

If the offense in question is not a per se violation, intent is required. Sherman Act cases that involve per se illegal conduct only require a showing that the defendant knowingly engaged in the conduct that violated the law.

In *United States v. United States Gypsum Company*,[128] the Supreme Court looked at the question of whether intent was a necessary element in a § 1 Sherman Act case. Noting that "[t]he existence of *mens rea* is the rule of, rather than the exception to, the principles of Anglo–American jurisprudence,"[129] the Court was unwilling to find this statute strict liability. The Court stated:

> The imposition of criminal liability on a corporate official, or for that matter on a corporation directly, for engaging in such conduct which only after the fact is determined to violate the statute because of anticompetitive effects, without inquiring into the intent with which it was undertaken, holds out the distinct possibility of overdeterrence; salutary and procompetitive conduct lying close to the borderline of impermissible conduct might be shunned by businessmen who chose to be excessively cautious in the face of uncertainty regarding possible exposure to criminal punishment for even a good-faith error of judgment.[130]

After determining that intent was necessary, the Court next turned to the level of intent that would be required. Using the Model Penal Code, the Court held that "action undertaken with knowledge of its probable consequences and having the requisite anticompetitive effects can be a sufficient predicate for a finding of criminal liability under the antitrust laws."

There is no *mens rea* requirement when the act is a per se Sherman Act violation. In *United States v. Socony–Vacuum Oil Co.*,[131] the Supreme Court held that price-fixing agreements are per se violations under the Sherman Act.

In *United States v. Cargo Service Stations, Inc.*,[132] the Fifth Circuit examined the difference between the Supreme Court's holding in *Gypsum* that mandates a showing of intent in antitrust cases, with a case that involves per se evidence of price fixing. The court noted that even though price fixing had been alleged in *Gypsum*, there was no direct evidence presented by the government. Instead, the government had looked at "the exchange among competitors of price information as providing circumstantial evidence of price fixing." The Fifth Circuit in *Cargo Service Station* noted that "the mere exchange of price information has been held not to be a per se violation of the Sherman Act." But when a clear price fixing exists, then it can be considered a per se violation of the Sherman Act. Finding this present in *Cargo Service Station* the Fifth Circuit said that "because fixing prices is by itself an unreasonable restraint of trade, an intent to fix prices is equivalent to an intent to unreasonably restrain trade; therefore, a finding that appellants intended to fix prices supplies the criminal intent necessary for a conviction of a criminal antitrust offense."

---

[128] 438 U.S. 422 (1978).

[129] Dennis v. United States, 341 U.S. 494 (1951).

[130] United States v. Gypsum, 438 U.S. at 441.

[131] 310 U.S. 150 (1940).

[132] 657 F.2d 676 (5th Cir. 1981).

Chapter 4

MAIL, WIRE, BANK & OTHER FRAUDS

§ 4.1   INTRODUCTION

A. History

The mail fraud statute emanates from an 1872 recodification of the Postal Act. It was section 301 of the 327—section Act and there was no congressional debate and therefore no legislative history at the time of its passage. Earlier editions of the statute targeted lottery schemes.[1] The statute when eventually enacted prohibited use of the mails by "any person having devised or intending to devise any scheme or artifice to defraud."[2]

Early cases using the mail fraud statute show that the initial focus of the statute was on the misuse of the Post Office Establishment by counterfeit schemes. Courts differed in using a narrow[3] or broad approach[4] in interpreting the statute's language. To rectify this disparity, Congress in 1889 passed a mail fraud statute that explicitly listed all the possible schemes to defraud. The long list included schemes such as "sawdust swindle[s]", "counterfeit money fraud" and "green coin[s]."[5]

A second modification to the statute occurred in 1909 following the case of *Durland v. United States*,[6] a case that took a broad approach to interpreting the statute.[7] The Supreme Court in *Durland* stated that mail fraud would include "everything designed to defraud by representations as to the past or present, or suggestions and promises as to the future."[8] The statutory modification following this decision, basically codified its holding. The legislature removed specific obsolete terms from the statute, such as "sawdust swindle[s]" and reworded the statute by adding the words "or for obtaining money or property by means of false or fraudulent pretenses,

---

[1] See generally Jed S. Rakoff, The Federal Mail Fraud Statute (pt. 1), 18 Duq. L. Rev. 771 (1980) (providing a comprehensive history of the mail fraud statute).

[2] Act of June 8, 1872, ch. 335, § 301, 17 Stat. 283, 323, Act to Revise, Consolidate, and Amend the Statutes Relating to the Post Office Department.

[3] See, e.g., United States v. Clark, 121 F. 190 (M.D. Pa. 1903) (covering only instances where the mailing is an essential part of the scheme); United States v. Owens, 17 F. 72 (E.D. Mo. 1883) (finding an improper use of the mail fraud statute).

[4] See, e.g., United States v. Horman, 118 F. 780 (S.D. Ohio 1901) (finding that blackmail could be a scheme to defraud).

[5] Act of March 2, 1889, ch. 393, § 1, 25 Stat. 873, Act to Punish Dealers and Pretended Dealers in Counterfeit Money and other Fraudulent Devices for Using the United States Mails.

[6] 161 U.S. 306 (1896).

[7] See Ellen S. Podgor, Tax–Fraud–Mail Fraud: Synonymous, Cumulative or Diverse?, 57 U. Cinn. L. Rev. 903, 905 (1989); see also Ellen S. Podgor, Mail Fraud: Opening Letters, 43 S. Carolina L. Rev. 223 (1992).

[8] Id. at 313.

representations, or promises,"[9] This language later became significant when the Court was examining the scope of mail fraud and whether there was a requirement of "money or property" to meet the statute. (See § 4.3(B)).

The mail fraud statute, now located at 18 U.S.C. § 1341 is credited with having enormous breadth. The emphasis now is on "schemes to defraud" as opposed to post office misuse, its initial focus. It was described in 1974 by Chief Justice Burger in a dissenting opinion, *United States v. Maze*,[10] as a "stopgap device to deal on a temporary basis with the new phenomenon, until particularized legislation can be developed and passed to deal directly with the evil."

The language of the statute has been expanded in more recent years. In 1987, following the Supreme Court's decision in *McNally v. United States*,[11] Congress passed a new statute, 18 U.S.C. § 1346, that allowed mail fraud to go beyond the 1909 amendment of "money or property" to now include intangible rights to honest services. (See § 4.5(A)). This amendment has proved to be extremely controversial. (See § 4.5(B) & (C)). Additionally, as part of the Violent Crime Control and Law Enforcement Act of 1994, Congress inserted the language "or deposits or causes to be deposited any matter or thing whatever to be sent or delivered by any private or commercial interstate carrier."[12] This language allowed for prosecutions beyond those sent via the U.S. Postal system, such as those using UPS or Federal Express.[13]

As part of the Sarbanes–Oxley Act of 2002, a new statute, 18 U.S.C. § 1349, was added to expand the fraud statutes to include attempts and conspiracies. It states that "[a]ny person who attempts or conspires any offense under this chapter shall be subject to the same penalties as those prescribed for the offense, the commission of which was the object of the attempt or conspiracy." Conspiracies to commit mail, wire, and other frauds are no longer limited to being brought under the general conspiracy statute, 18 U.S.C. § 371. It remains to be seen whether the elements of this conspiracy will match the elements of section 371 or require a lesser standard, such as not requiring an overt act. One court ruled that an overt act is not required for prosecutions brought under § 1349.[14]

The statute has also been amended to increase the penalty. What initially was a penalty of five years is now twenty years. If the fraud affects a financial institution, imprisonment can be increased to not more than thirty years. Substantial fines can also accompany the imprisonment. Following Hurricane Katrina, Congress also increased penalties to a thirty year maximum sentence for frauds connected with "a presidentially declared major disaster or emergency."

---

[9] Offenses Against the Postal Service, ch. 321, § 215, 35 Stat. 1123, 1130 (1909) (codified as amended at 18 U.S.C. § 338 (1940).

[10] United States v. Maze, 414 U.S. 395 (1974) (C.J. Burger, dissenting).

[11] 483 U.S. 350 (1987).

[12] Violent Crime Control and Law Enforcement Act of 1994 § 250006.

[13] See Ellen S. Podgor, Mail Fraud: Limiting the Limitless, 18 Champion 4 (Dec. 1994); Peter J. Henning, Maybe It Should Just Be Called Federal Fraud: The Changing Nature of the Mail Fraud Statute, 36 Boston Col. L. Rev. 435 (1995).

[14] See United States v. Chinasa, 789 F. Supp.2d 691 (E.D.Va. 2011).

Many, like Justice Burger in his dissent in *United States v. Maze*, continue to remark on the breadth of the mail fraud statute. Hon. Jed S. Rakoff, in an article written well before he took the bench, called mail fraud the prosecutor's "Stradivarius our Colt 45, our Louisville Slugger, our Cuisinart—and our true love."[15] Hon. Ralph K. Winter, also writing in a law review article, noted in talking about "federal fraud statutes—in particular, the mail and wire fraud statutes," that "[w]ith regard to the statutory weapons available to prosecutors, they rank by analogy with hydrogen bombs on stealth aircraft."[16] Although the language of the statute has been criticized as being broad, it has survived constitutional vagueness challenges.[17]

The mail fraud statute has served as the model for many different fraud statutes. The language used in § 1341 is replicated in later statutes such as statutes for prohibiting wire fraud (see § 4.9), bank fraud (see § 4.10), and health care fraud (see § 4.11). Each of these statutes, however, have unique elements. Prosecutors find these statutes particularly useful as the broad language of "scheme to defraud" encompasses a wide breadth of conduct. The U.S. Attorneys' Manual does state that "[p]rosecutions of fraud ordinarily should not be undertaken if the scheme employed consists of some isolated transactions between individuals, involving minor loss to the victims, in which case the parties should be left to settle their differences by civil or criminal litigation in state courts."[18]

Not all fraud statutes in the United States Code are modeled after the mail fraud statute. For example, the marriage fraud statute at 8 U.S.C. § 1325(c) does not require a scheme to defraud. Rather it provides that "[a]ny individual who knowingly enters into a marriage for the purpose of evading any provision of the immigration laws shall be imprisoned for not more than 5 years, or fined not more than $250,000, or both." The computer fraud statute, 18 U.S.C. § 1030, although having several provisions that require an intent to defraud, lists specific activities that can be prosecuted as opposed to a generic category of a scheme to defraud as found in the mail and wire fraud statutes.

B. Elements

The mail fraud statute found at 18 U.S.C. § 1341 reads as follows:

Whoever, having devised or intending to devise any scheme or artifice to defraud, or for obtaining money or property by means of false or fraudulent pretenses, representations, or promises, or to sell, dispose of, loan, exchange, alter, give away, distribute, supply, or furnish or procure for unlawful use any counterfeit or spurious coin, obligation, security, or other article, or anything represented to be or intimated or held out to be such counterfeit or spurious article, for the purpose of executing such scheme or artifice or attempting so to do, places in any post office or authorized depository for mail matter, any matter or thing whatever to be sent or delivered by the Postal Service, or deposits or causes to be deposited any

---

[15] Rakoff, supra note 1 at 771.

[16] Ralph K. Winter, Paying Lawyers, Empowering Prosecutors and Protecting Managers: the Cost of Capital in America, 42 Duke L.J. 945, 954 (1993).

[17] See, e.g., United States v. Stewart, 872 F.2d 957 (10th Cir. 1989); United States v. Feinberg, 535 F.2d 1004 (7th Cir. 1976).

[18] USAM § 9–43.100.

matter or thing whatever to be sent or delivered by any private or commercial interstate carrier, or takes or receives therefrom, any such matter or thing, or knowingly causes to be delivered by mail or such carrier according to the direction thereon, or at the place at which it is directed to be delivered by the person to whom it is addressed, any such matter or thing, shall be fined under this title or imprisoned not more than 20 years, or both. If the violation occurs in relation to, or involving any benefit authorized, transported, transmitted, transferred, disbursed, or paid in connection with, a presidentially declared major disaster or emergency (as those terms are defined in section 102 of the Robert T. Stafford Disaster Relief and Emergency Assistance Act (42 U.S.C. 5122)), or affects a financial institution, such person shall be fined not more than $1,000,000 or imprisoned not more than 30 years, or both.

The key elements of the statute are: 1) a scheme devised or intending to defraud or for obtaining money or property by fraudulent means, 2) intent, 3) materiality, and 4) use or causing to use the mails (or private interstate carrier) in furtherance of the fraudulent scheme. Each of these elements are discussed in detail below.

§ 4.2   SCHEME TO DEFRAUD

The scheme to defraud element of the statute is the heart of the present-day statutory offense. It may be easier to say what is not a scheme to defraud, than what is encompassed within the statute, as this element has few restrictions. One finds an ever increasing number of different types of schemes to defraud. For example, prosecutions have been premised on credit card fraud,[19] divorce mill fraud,[20] franchise fraud,[21] insurance fraud,[22] securities fraud,[23] medical drug fraud[24] and fraud premised upon political malfeasance.[25] One even finds schemes to defraud premised on the sale of grades for classes that foreign students did not attend.[26] Schemes premised upon election fraud require prior consultation with the Public Integrity Section of the Department of Justice.[27]

One restriction was found when the Supreme Court refused to allow mail fraud for extortion conduct. In *Fasulo v. United States*,[28] the Court stated that a "use of the mails for the purpose of obtaining money by means of threats or murder or bodily harm" was not a scheme to defraud for purposes of mail fraud.

Some courts find that there is insufficient evidence of a scheme to defraud. Examples of courts that have limited the scheme to defraud element of the mail fraud statute include a court that held that a mere "breach of contract in itself [did not]

---

[19] See United States v. Stein, 500 F.2d 678 (9th Cir. 1974).

[20] See United States v. Edwards, 458 F.2d 875 (5th Cir. 1972).

[21] See United States v. Serlin, 538 F.2d 737 (7th Cir. 1976).

[22] See United States v. Cavalier, 17 F.3d 90 (5th Cir. 1994).

[23] See Carpenter v. United States, 484 U.S. 19 (1987) (see infra § 4.3(C)).

[24] See United States v. Livdahl, 459 F. Supp.2d 1255 (S.D. Fl. 2005).

[25] See United States v. Diggs, 613 F.2d 988 (D.C. Cir. 1979).

[26] See United States v. Hayes, 231 F.3d 663 (9th Cir. 2000).

[27] USAM § 9–85.210.

[28] 272 U.S. 620, 625 (1926).

constitute a scheme to defraud."[29] In *United States v. Goodman*,[30] the Eighth Circuit held that not all promotion schemes are schemes to defraud. The court stated, "without some objective evidence demonstrating a scheme to defraud, all promotional schemes to make money, even if 'sleazy' or 'shrewd,' would be subject to prosecution on the mere whim of the prosecutor."

When looking at the "scheme to defraud" element of the statute, it is important to realize that the scheme to defraud is tied to the requirement of "money or property." In this regard, a common issue is whether the scheme satisfies the "money or property" element of the statute. (see infra § 4.4) Alternatively is whether this is a case predicated on an intangible right to honest services. (See infra § 4.3, § 4.5)

§ 4.3   INTANGIBLE RIGHTS

A. History

Starting in the 1940s[31] and being used more extensively in the 1970s[32] and 1980s[33] were prosecutions premised on a deprivation of intangible rights. These cases did not have prosecutors proving that the victim suffered a money or property loss. Mail fraud was used when the "scheme or artifice to defraud" involved a breach of a fiduciary duty. The deprivation of "honest services," or a "right to good government," were the basis for the scheme to defraud. A long list of cases premised on this theory are highlighted in the dissenting opinion of Justice Stevens, joined by Justice O'Connor, in the later case of *McNally v. United States*[34] that put an end to this charging practice.

B. McNally v. United States

In *McNally v. United States*, the Supreme Court considered a case where the government had charged the defendants with a violation of the mail fraud statute for their participation in a self-dealing patronage scheme. The government argued that the patronage insurance scheme deprived the "citizens and government of Kentucky of certain 'intangible rights,' such as the right to have the Commonwealth's affairs conducted honestly."[35] In addition to the indictment being premised on intangible rights, the instructions given to the jury also used this theory.

The jury convicted the defendants on both the mail fraud and conspiracy counts, and the court of appeals rejected the appellants' arguments on the mail fraud convictions. In reversing this decision, the Supreme Court examined the history of the mail fraud statute, specifically focusing on Congress' 1909 amendment that added the words "money or property" to the statute. The Court found that "the original impetus

---

[29] See McEvoy Travel Bureau, Inc. v. Heritage Travel, Inc., 904 F.2d 786 (1st Cir. 1990) (using the mail fraud as a predicate act in a civil RICO matter).

[30] 984 F.2d 235 (8th Cir. 1993).

[31] See, e.g., United States v. Classic, 35 F.Supp. 457 (E.D. La. 1940) (using intangible rights in an election case).

[32] See, e.g., United States v. States, 488 F.2d 761 (8th Cir. 1973) (using intangible rights in case of fraud by candidates for city office).

[33] See, e.g., United States v. Margiotta, 688 F.2d 108 (2d Cir. 1982) (applying intangible rights with a political leader).

[34] 483 U.S. 350, 362n.1 (1987) (Dissenting, J. Stevens).

[35] Id. at 352.

behind the mail fraud statute was to protect the people from schemes to deprive them of their money or property."[36] Since the defendants had not been charged with this language and the jury instruction did not instruct them to make such as finding, a reversal was in order.

The Court also referenced the rule of lenity in finding that "when there are two rational readings of a criminal statute, one harsher than the other, we are to choose the harsher only when Congress has spoken in clear and definite language." In this case the government conceded that if the convictions for mail fraud could not stand, then the conspiracy convictions could not stand.

The dissent also examined the statute, but argued that the use of the word "or" in the statute should be read in the disjunctive. They presented the long line of cases that endorsed the intangible rights theory in the lower courts.

The Court's finding in *McNally* that mail fraud could not be premised on "intangible rights" left many cases subject to reversal. Courts examined cases to determine whether the *McNally* decision should be applied retroactively.[37] Most courts found that the decision could be applied retroactively.[38] They also looked at the individual cases to determine whether the charge and instructions focused solely on intangible rights. Because some individuals had already served their sentences, but still suffered the consequences of the criminal conviction, there were writs of *coram nobis* filed to alleviate the collateral consequences of the conviction.

C. Kickback Schemes

Although *McNally* mandated "money or property," the Court did not decide the question of what constituted money or property. Later cases distinguished intangible property (see § 4.4(A)) and licenses (see § 4.4(B)). New theories developed that attempted to push the limits on what should be considered property for purposes of the mail fraud statute.[39]

Several cases wrestled with this question in the context of kickback schemes. There were cases involving kickback schemes premised on faithful services. For example, following Stevens' dissent in *McNally*, a defendant argued that kickback schemes deprived the employer "of the salary and benefits paid to the employee in reliance on his faithful services free from conflict of interest."[40]

There were also cases involving kickback schemes where the government argued that the employer suffered a loss because, had it known of the supplier's willingness to

---

[36] Id. at 356.

[37] See generally Craig M. Bradley, Foreward: Mail Fraud After McNally and Carpenter: The Essence of Fraud, 79 J. Crim. L. & Criminology 573 (1988).

[38] See Deborah Sprenger, Annotation, Effect Upon Prior Convictions of McNally v. United States Rule that Mail Fraud Statute (18 U.S.C. § 1341) Is Directed Solely at Deprivation of Property Rights, 97 A.L.R.Fed. 797 (1990).

[39] See, e.g., United States v. Shyres, 898 F.2d 647 (8th Cir. 1990) (discussing corporation's spending as property right); United States v. Little, 889 F.2d 1367 (5th Cir. 1989) (selling pipe and giving kickbacks to county officials).

[40] See United States v. Johns, 688 F.Supp. 1017 (E.D. Pa. 1988).

pay kickbacks, it might have used this information to drive a harder bargain.[41] Finally there were kickback schemes premised on a "constructive trust," arguing that the profits, which were kickbacks, derived from the abuse of a fiduciary relationship belonged to the principal, not the corrupt agent.[42]

§ 4.4   INTANGIBLE PROPERTY

A.   Carpenter v. United States

Within months of the Supreme Court issuing its decision in *McNally* finding that *intangible rights* were not covered under the mail fraud statute, the Court accepted the case of *Carpenter v. United States*,[43] which held that *intangible property* was covered within the scheme to defraud language of the statute. Where *McNally* restricted the use of 18 U.S.C. § 1341, *Carpenter* limited the *McNally* holding to allow for more prosecutions under this statute.

Carpenter was the roommate of defendant Winans, an employee and columnist at the Wall Street Journal. Winans was one of the two writers of "*Heard on the Street*," a highly recognized column of the Journal that provided information to readers about different stocks. Winans, along with his roommate and several others including two connected with a brokerage company, decided to trade on the information prior to its publication in the newspaper. This was against "official policy and practice at the Journal." They profited from these trades in an amount of about $690,000. After the start of an SEC investigation, Winans and Carpenter revealed the scheme to the SEC.

The Supreme had two issues in the *Carpenter* case: the propriety of using a misappropriation theory in securities fraud cases and whether this conduct fit the "scheme to defraud" requirement for mail and wire fraud. An evenly divided court resulted in an affirmation of the securities violations (see § 5.6(3)).

With respect to the "scheme to defraud" issue, the Supreme Court noted that The Wall Street Journal had an official policy that held that pre-publication, the contents of the "*Heard on the Street*" column were the newspaper's confidential information. Even though the information in the articles was truthful, and had not been altered in any way to secure a profit, the Court found that this was a scheme to defraud of "money or property" with the property being *intangible property*.

The Court reaffirmed its position in *McNally* that *intangible rights* were not covered by the mail fraud statute. The Court stated, however, that here "the Journal, as Winans' employer, was defrauded of much more than its contractual right to his honest and faithful service, an interest too ethereal in itself to fall within the protection of the mail fraud statute, which 'had its origin in the desire to protect individual property rights.'"

The *Carpenter* case opened the door for allowing schemes to defraud that were premised on a deprivation of intangible property. But the issue soon arose of what constituted intangible property. Scholars debated the effect of *Carpenter* with some

---

[41] See United States v. Perholtz, 842 F.2d 343 (D.C. Cir. 1988).

[42] See United States v. Miller, 997 F.2d 1010, 1019–1020 (2d Cir. 1993).

[43] 484 U.S. 19 (1987).

questioning the breadth of this decision[44] and the fact that it was criminalizing embezzlement conduct.[45]

B. Licenses

District and Circuit courts struggled with the question of whether licenses were property. The issue arose in a host of different settings, such as taxi licenses, gambling licenses, arms export licenses, and bail bond licenses. The Supreme Court selected a case involving a video poker license to provide guidance on the issue of whether licenses could be property for purposes of the mail fraud statute.

In *Cleveland v. United States*,[46] the Court looked at whether the mail fraud statute reached false statements made in an application for a state video poker license. At this time, Louisiana law allowed certain businesses to operate video poker machines but a state license was required. The defendants were accused of making a false statement in their application for a license.

The government argued that "the State receives a substantial sum of money in exchange for each license and continues to receive payments from the licensee as long as the license remains in effect." They also argued that "the State has significant control over the issuance, renewal, suspension, and revocation of licenses."

The Court noted that pursuant to *McNally*, intangible rights were not property for purposes of the mail fraud statute. In contrast, pursuant to *Carpenter*, intangible property could be sufficient evidence of a mail fraud violation. Here, however, the Court noted that the "State's core concern is regulatory." In rejecting this interest as property, The Court in *Cleveland* stated:

> We reject the Government's theories of property rights not simply because they stray from traditional concepts of property. We resist the Government's reading of § 1341 as well because it invites us to approve a sweeping expansion of federal criminal jurisdiction in the absence of a clear statement by Congress. Equating issuance of licenses or permits with deprivation of property would subject to federal mail fraud prosecution a wide range of conduct traditionally regulated by state and local authorities.[47]

The *Cleveland* Court reversed the conviction of the lower court holding that "§ 1341 requires the object of the fraud to be 'property' in the victim's hands and that a Louisiana video poker license in the State's hands is not 'property' under § 1341."

C. Foreign Property

In *Pasquantino v. United States*,[48] the Court examined the scope of property for the wire fraud statute, a statute that works the same as mail fraud with regard to the

---

[44] John C. Coffee, Jr., Hush!: The Criminal Status of Confidential Information After McNally and Carpenter and the Enduring Problem of Overcriminalization, 26 Am. Crim. L. Rev. 121 (1988).

[45] Foreward: Mail Fraud After McNally and Carpenter: The Essence of Fraud, 79 J. Crim. L. & Criminology 573 (1988).

[46] 531 U.S. 12 (2000).

[47] Id. at 24.

[48] 544 U.S. 349 (2005).

scheme to defraud element. Defendants were accused of smuggling liquor to Canada to avoid Canadian taxation. One of the issues in the case was whether a scheme to defraud a foreign government of tax revenue could serve as the scheme to defraud element of the wire fraud statute. The Court held that "[u]nlike the treaties and the antismuggling statute, the wire fraud statute punishes fraudulent use of domestic wires, whether or not such conduct constitutes smuggling, occurs aboard a vessel, or evades foreign taxes."[49]

§ 4.5   INTANGIBLE RIGHTS STATUTE—SECTION 1346

A. Passage of Statute

In the *McNally* decision the Court had stated that "[i]f Congress desires to go further, it must speak more clearly than it has."[50] Congress accepted this invitation the same year as the *McNally* case was decided. As part of the Anti–Drug Abuse Act of 1988, Congress enacted 18 U.S.C. § 1346 which provides that, "[f]or purposes of this chapter, the term 'scheme or artifice to defraud' includes a scheme or artifice to deprive another of the intangible right to honest services."

This statute was used in prosecutions of both public officials and those in the private sector. There were claims that the statute was void for vagueness, since the statute did not define "honest services." For example, in *United States v. Gray*,[51] members of the men's basketball coaching staff at Baylor University, along with others, were charged with a violation of § 1346. They were accused of "executing a fraudulent scheme to establish academic eligibility for five transfer students to play basketball at Baylor during the 1993–94 academic year." Several of the defendants argued that § 1346 was unconstitutionally vague. The Fifth Circuit rejected defendant's arguments, holding that § 1346 was not unconstitutionally vague as applied to these defendants.

In one case, *Sorich v. United States*,[52] Justice Scalia wrote a dissent to a denial of certiorari. He stated, "[i]n light of the conflicts among the Circuits; the longstanding confusion over the scope of the statute; and the serious due process and federalism interests affected by the expansion of criminal liability that this case exemplifies, I would grant the petition for certiorari and squarely confront both the meaning and the constitutionality of § 1346."

Outlined in a dissent in the en banc Second Circuit decision in *United States v. Rybicki*,[53] were the many issues concerning section 1346 within the circuits that needed resolution. The dissenting judges stated that

> [i]n sum, the circuits are fractured on the basic issues: (1) the requisite *mens rea* to commit the crime, (2) whether the defendant must cause actual tangible harm, (3) the duty that must be breached, (4) the source of that duty, and (5) which body of law informs us of the statute's meaning. This lack of coherence has created "a

---

[49] Id. at 352.

[50] Id. at 360.

[51] 96 F.3d 769 (5th Cir. 1996).

[52] 555 U.S. 1204 (2009).

[53] 354 F.3d 124, 156 (2d Cir. 2003).

truly extraordinary statute, in which the substantive force of the statute varie[s] in each judicial circuit."

Other cases looked at issues with respect to private sector frauds, specifically as to whether honest services should encompass violations in this area.[54] There were also questions regarding whether it was necessary to have a violation of state law.

B. Skilling, Black & Weyrauch

In 2010, the Supreme Court decided three cases, *Skilling v. United States*,[55] *Black v. United States*,[56] and *Weyhrauch v. United States*,[57] all pertaining to § 1346—honest services. The main decision issued was in *Skilling*.

The Skilling case concerned former CEO of Enron Corp., Jeffrey Skilling. Two issues were presented to the Supreme Court: 1) whether pretrial publicity and community prejudice prevented him from receiving a fair trial; 2) whether he was improperly convicted of conspiracy to commit honest services wire fraud under section 1346. With respect to the first argument the Court held that "Skilling did not establish that a presumption of juror prejudice arose or that actual bias infected the jury that tried him." The Court rejected this argument 6–3 with Justices Sotomayor, joined by Stevens and Breyer dissenting.

He was, however, successful with respect to his argument on section 1346. Skilling was alleged to have committed a conspiracy to deprive Enron and its shareholders of the intangible right to honest services. He was also charged with other crimes, namely, securities fraud, wire fraud, making false representations and insider trading. He was convicted of nineteen counts and acquitted of nine insider-trading counts. Skilling received a sentence of 292 months in prison, 3 years supervised release, and $45 million in restitution.

On appeal he argued that § 1346 was unconstitutional or alternatively that his conduct did not violate the statute. The Court's opinion provided a history of the mail fraud statute including the decision in *McNally* and the passage of 18 U.S.C. § 1346 following the Supreme Court's decision. Although the Supreme Court in *Skilling* failed to find the statute unconstitutional, it did decide that it was important to provide interpretation of the statute. The Court stated that "§ 1346 should be construed rather than invalidated." In so doing, the Court carved out an exception for this provision to be allowed in cases involving bribes and kickbacks. The Court stated that the "vast majority" of the honest-services cases involved offenders who, in violation of a fiduciary duty, participated in bribery or kickback schemes." The Court stated that "Congress' reversal of *McNally* and reinstatement of the honest-services doctrine . . . can and should be salvaged by confining its scope to the core pre-McNally applications."

To reach a larger range of conduct, the Court stated, "would raise the due process concerns underlying the vagueness doctrine." Thus, the majority refused to include, as requested by the government, cases involving "undisclosed self-dealing by a public

---

[54] See United States v. DeVegter, 198 F.3d 1324, 1328–29 (11th Cir. 1999).

[55] 130 S.Ct. 2896 (2010).

[56] 130 S.Ct. 2963 (2010).

[57] 130 S.Ct. 2971 (2010).

official or private employee." But the Court was clear that "[a] criminal defendant who participated in a bribery or kickback scheme, in short, cannot tenably complain about prosecution under § 1346 on vagueness grounds."

Justices Scalia and Thomas offered a concurring opinion that was joined in part by Justice Kennedy. They accused the Court of rewriting the statute in finding that § 1346 criminalized only bribery and kickbacks. They would have preferred a reversal premised on the statute providing no "'ascertainable standard' for the conduct it condemns."

The Supreme Court vacated and remanded all three cases: *Skilling*, *Black*, and *Weyhrauch*. In *Skilling*'s case the remand was needed to determine whether his conduct violated § 1346. But the Supreme Court did state that "as we read § 1346, Skilling did not commit honest-services fraud." In a footnote in the *Skilling* decision, the Court gave a warning to Congress should they decide to redraft the statute to include "undisclosed self-dealing." The Court said "it would have to employ standards of sufficient definiteness and specificity to overcome due process concerns."[58] In response to a standard offered by the government, the Court said,

> That formulation, however, leaves many questions unanswered. How direct or significant does the conflicting financial interest have to be? To what extent does the official action have to further that interest in order to amount to fraud? To whom should the disclosure be made and what information should it convey? These questions and others call for particular care in attempting to formulate an adequate criminal prohibition in this context.[59]

The Supreme Court referenced the *Skilling* decision in the opinion it issued in Conrad Black's case. It vacated Black's conviction because, like *Skilling*, it rested on an improper construction of § 1346 and like, *Skilling*, the Supreme Court ordered a remand. But there was one issue that they needed to resolve in addition to what had been presented in *Skilling*.

In *Black*,[60] the government had pursued alternative theories of money or property or honest services fraud. The government requested special interrogatories to accompany the verdict so that the jury could determine which basis the jury's decision rested upon. But they acquiesced when the defendant argued a preference for an unelaborated general verdict.

On appeal the government in *Black* argued that the defense had waived their objection to the honest services instruction because they failed to agree to special interrogatories that would have allowed findings by the jury as to which theory their decision actually rested upon. The Supreme Court, however, rejected the government's argument stating that "[a] criminal defendant, we hold, need not request special interrogatories, nor need he acquiesce in the Government's request for discrete findings by the jury, in order to preserve in full a timely raised objection to jury instructions on an alternative theory of guilt." The Court stated that "by properly objecting to the

---

[58] 130 S.Ct. at 2933 n.44.

[59] Id.

[60] 130 S.Ct. 2963 (2010).

honest-services jury instructions at trial, Defendants secured their right to challenge those instructions on appeal. They did not forfeit that right by declining to acquiesce in the Government-proposed special-verdict forms."

The third case accepted by the Court, *Weyhrauch v. United States*,[61] asked the Court to consider whether § 1346 required that the accused violate a duty imposed by state law. The Court merely vacated this judgment and remanded the case in light of the *Skilling* decision. There was no specific ruling other than the holding in *Skilling* to guide future decisions on this issue.

C. Post–Skilling

Several cases were remanded as a result of the *Skilling* decision, including the cases of *Skilling*, *Black* and *Weyrauch*. In *Skilling* the defendant had been charged with conspiracy and the objects of the conspiracy included honest services fraud and securities fraud. The jury had returned a general verdict on the conspiracy count. The Fifth Circuit on remand refused to modify the decision finding that the evidence supported a conviction for conspiracy to commit securities fraud. The honest services instruction was therefore found to be harmless error.[62]

A somewhat similar result occurred in the *Black* case, before the Seventh Circuit.[63] The court found that there was no prejudicial spillover from the honest services to the pecuniary fraud and obstruction of justice. But the court did find that one of the alleged frauds was questionable after the Supreme Court's decision in *Skilling* and that this count needed to be reversed. But the Seventh Circuit then offered advice to the government that they might not want to retry this count and instead when resentencing the defendant use it as uncharged conduct for purposes of sentencing.[64]

Weyrauch's case was dismissed by the government. He did, however, enter a plea of guilty to a state lobbying charge, receiving a suspended three month sentence, a fine of $1,000, and a year's probation.[65]

In reexamining cases in light of the *Skilling* decision, lower courts often looked first at whether there were references to honest services fraud in the indictment and the instructions. Courts also examined whether there were references by the government to honest services fraud during the trial proceedings. This was the first step in the plain error analysis. The second step was often met because the *Skilling* decision clearly limited honest services fraud to bribes and kickbacks, thus clarifying the law. The final step was to examine whether the error affected the defendant's substantial rights.

---

[61] 130 S.Ct. 2971 (2010).

[62] 638 F.3d 480 (5th Cir. 2011). The sentence was previously vacated and remanded and the court reaffirmed its prior holding. See United States v. Skilling, 554 F.3d 529 (5th Cir. 2009). Skilling was later resentenced to 168 months (14 years).

[63] 625 F.3d 386 (7th Cir. 2010).

[64] Id. at 394.

[65] See Richard Mauer, Anchorage Daily News, Mar. 16, 2011, available at http://www.adn.com/2011/03/15/1756695/weyhrauch-gets-suspended-jail.html.

For example, in *United States v. Andrews*,[66] the Third Circuit found that the defendant would have still been convicted of wire fraud as the government "presented overwhelming evidence that Andrews committed tangible wire fraud." It was found to be harmless error, despite the fact that the district court had referenced "honest services" in its final instructions.

Some cases would lose on the initial step, finding that the honest services fraud was not the basis of the court's decision. Others found that the evidence presented bribes and kickbacks, thus not contrary to the *Skilling* decision. Finally, some like the *Skilling* remand, found that any error was harmless. Some of the cases being reconsidered in light of the Supreme Court's decision in *Skilling* were reviewed under a writ of corum nobis.[67]

In *United States v. Siegelman*,[68] the former governor of Alabama's case was remanded by the Supreme Court in light of the *Skilling* decision. Also being re-examined in this case was the case against Richard Scrushy, the former CEO of HealthSouth Corporation. The defendants had been convicted of federal funds bribery, five counts of honest services fraud, and conspiracy. Siegelman also had a conviction for obstruction of justice. The federal funds bribery counts were affirmed. Likewise, honest services fraud counts that were explicitly premised on bribery met the test set forth in the *Skilling* decision, and were therefore affirmed. They alleged a "pay-to-play scheme" and that was sufficient for the Eleventh Circuit. The court did reverse, due to lack of evidence, two other counts that were premised on self-dealing.

There have been several cases that required reversal as a result of the *Skilling* decision.[69] For example, In *United States v. Riley*,[70] the Third Circuit found it necessary to reverse convictions premised on honest services fraud, although it found there was no spillover effect warranting reversal on other counts. The court stated, "[i]n the context of this case, where the fraudulent act is the non-disclosure of a conflict of interest, it would demean the judicial process to attempt to put the genie back in the bottle by essentially rewriting the charge to the jury on Count 5 and assuming the jury made distinctions the Government did not bring out in its summation."[71]

§ 4.6   INTENT

Mail fraud requires the knowing and willful participation in the scheme with the specific intent to defraud.[72] Although an actual fraud does not need to be shown, most

---

[66] 681 F.3d 509 (3d Cir. 2012).

[67] See United States v. George, 676 F.3d 249 (1st Cir. 2012).

[68] 640 F.3d 1159 (11th Cir. 2011).

[69] See, e.g., United States v. Wright, 665 F.3d 560, 571 (3d Cir. 2012) (finding improper honest services fraud counts and prejudicial spillover effect); United States v. Hornsby, 666 F.3d 296, 307 (4th Cir. 2012) (finding error on honest services fraud convictions but not spillover onto remaining counts).

[70] 621 F.3d 312, 324 (3d Cir. 2010).

[71] Id. at 324.

[72] See, e.g., United States v. Stergios, 659 F.3d 127 (1st Cir. 2011); United States v. Bryant, 655 F.3d 232 (3d Cir. 2011); United States v. Gelb, 700 F.2d 875, 879 (2d Cir. 1983) (requiring specific intent); United States v. Martin–Trigona, 684 F.2d 485, 492 (7th Cir. 1982) (holding that specific intent is needed for mail fraud).

courts state that the prosecution needs to prove that the defendant contemplated a defrauding.[73] Courts have allowed intent to be inferred from the evidence.

Some courts have stated that an intent to deceive differs from an intent to defraud, and an intent to deceive is not sufficient for mail fraud.[74] Mere puffing has been found insufficient for mail fraud. If defendants "in no way misrepresented to their customers the nature or quality of the service they were providing" the elements of mail fraud would not be met. The "harm contemplated [in a scheme to defraud] must affect the very nature of the bargain itself."[75]

The statute does not require the government to prove an intent "to inflict economic harm or to injure the property rights of another."[76] Nor is it necessary to present a scheme that is calculated to deceive a person of ordinary prudence.[77]

In *United States v. D'Amato*,[78] the Second Circuit explored the level of intent necessary for mail fraud. Armand D'Amato's conviction for seven counts of mail fraud was reversed by the Second Circuit because the evidence did not support either a "right to control theory" or a "false pretenses theory." D'Amato, an attorney, had been charged premised upon his bills to a company.

Under the "right to control" theory, it is necessary to show "that some person or entity has been deprived of potentially economic information." The Second Circuit stated that "[m]ail fraud cannot be charged against a corporate agent who in good faith believes that his or her (otherwise legal) misleading or inaccurate conduct is in the corporation's best interests." Some individuals may find it necessary to conceal certain matters for a corporation. In such cases, it needs to be determined, "(i) whether corporate management has made an otherwise lawful decision that concealment or a failure to disclose is in the corporation's best interests and (ii) whether management acted in good faith in making, and did not personally profit from, the decision." The court stated that:

> In the instant matter, of course, the defendant is not someone in corporate management but a person hired to perform services for the corporation. Such a person cannot be found to intend to harm a corporation or its shareholders through otherwise lawful misleading conduct if he or she follows the instructions of an appropriate corporate agent who appears to be unconflicted and acting in good faith.

The court also rejected the false pretenses theory used by the government. The government had claimed that the defendant did not perform the services he was hired to perform. But the court found that the defendant was paid for lobbying his brother, a senator, and there was no evidence that he did not perform this work.

---

[73] See United States v. Andreadis, 366 F.2d 423, 431 (2d Cir. 1966).

[74] See, e.g., United States v. Regent Supply Co., Inc., 421 F.2d 1174 (2d Cir. 1970).

[75] United States v. Starr, 816 F.2d 94 (2d Cir. 1987) ("misrepresentations amounting only to deceit are insufficient to maintain a mail or wire fraud prosecution").

[76] See United States v. Welch, 327 F.3d 1081 (10th Cir. 2003).

[77] See United States v. Svete, 556 F.3d 1157, 1168–69 (11th Cir. 2009) (citing other circuits that held that the scheme did not need to deceive individuals of ordinary prudence).

[78] 39 F.3d 1249 (2d Cir. 1994).

Although this court did not find criminality in the billing practices of D'Amato, other courts have allowed mail fraud to be used for false billing by attorneys. In *United States v. Myerson*,[79] the defendant was convicted and sentenced to 60 months imprisonment after being charged with "defrauding six clients and his own law firm while he was a partner at the New York law firm he founded." The fraud in this case was based on Myerson's submission of a "legal fee that overbilled his clients by millions of dollars and by his fraudulent claims that personal charges were legitimate business expenses."

§ 4.7   MATERIALITY

Materiality is an essential element of the crime of mail fraud. In *Neder v. United States*,[80] the Supreme Court examined a case involving an attorney and real estate developer who was alleged to be engaged "in a number of real estate transactions financed by fraudulently obtained bank loans." He was indicted on nine counts of mail fraud, nine counts of wire fraud, twelve counts of bank fraud, and two counts of filing a false income tax return. The trial court told the jury that the question of materiality was not for the jury to decide on the tax and bank fraud counts. Additionally, the trial court did not provide an instruction on materiality with respect to the mail and wire fraud counts. Neder's conviction for which he received a sentence of 147 months imprisonment, 5 years supervised release and $25 million in restitution, was affirmed by the Eleventh Circuit although it said that it was harmless error in failing to submit the materiality issue to the jury.

The Supreme Court in an opinion authored by Chief Justice Rehnquist found that failure to submit materiality as an issue for the jury on the tax charges was harmless error. With respect to not offering the jury instructions on mail, wire, and bank fraud, the court disagreed with the lower court. The Court noted that the "well-settled meaning of 'fraud' required a misrepresentation or concealment of *material* fact." Thus, the case was remanded to determine the harmlessness of any error in failing to instruct the jury on materiality.

Justice Stevens, in a concurring in part opinion, agreed that materiality was required for the mail, wire, and bank fraud statutes, but he disagreed with the majority's analysis of the "harmless-error issue." An even stronger concurrence and dissent came from Justices Scalia, Souter and Ginsburg who said "that depriving a criminal defendant of the right to have the jury determine his guilt of the crime charged—which necessarily means his commission of *every element* of the crime charged—can never be harmless." On remand the Eleventh Circuit found that the failure to instruct on materiality in the *Neder* case was harmless error.[81]

---

[79] 18 F.3d 153, 156 (2d Cir. 1994)

[80] 527 U.S. 1 (1999).

[81] United States v. Neder, 197 F.3d 1122 (1999).

§ 4.8   USE OF THE MAILS IN FURTHERANCE

A.   Mailing

1.   *Generally*

Mail fraud requires a mailing, or that the item was sent by private or commercial interstate carrier. The mailing must be by the defendant or caused to be mailed by him or her. The mailing also needs to be in furtherance of the scheme to defraud. The mailing can be the basis of determining the venue for the prosecution.

When initially enacted the emphasis of the statute was on the mail and the fraudulent use of the postal system. For example, one of the early mail fraud cases, *United States v. Clark*,[82] held that the mailing needed to be an essential part of the scheme and a mailing which was merely "adjunct or incident" to the scheme was insufficient.[83] Courts used a subjective test to ascertain what the perpetrator intended with respect to mailing.[84]

Today, the mailing has become a jurisdictional hook necessary for bringing the charge, but having little importance once demonstrated by the government. The Supreme Court has said that it is sufficient for the mailing to be "incident to an essential part of the scheme"[85] or "a step in [the] plot."[86] An objective test is employed that looks at the tangential relationship between the scheme and the mailing.

2.   *Mailing or Interstate Carrier*

Although the mailing is a mere jurisdictional hook for the crime, it is necessary for the government to prove that something was actually mailed. The mailing may be between innocent parties, and routine mailings may be sufficient to supply the basis for the mailing element of the crime.[87] A failure to show a mailing, however, will be held as insufficient evidence for the crime charged.

Courts have permitted circumstantial evidence of office practice and procedure to prove that a mailing occurred.[88] That said, some courts have found that "reliance upon inferences drawn from evidence of standard business practice without specific reference to the mailing in question is insufficient."[89] Also if usual office practices are not followed, then proof of a mailing by circumstantial evidence will be rendered suspect.[90] When the government fails to show that that as a routine practice the United States mailed are used, and there is no showing that the correspondence was

---

[82] 121 Fed. 190 (M.D. Pa. 1903).

[83] Id. at 191.

[84] Ellen S. Podgor, Mail Fraud: Opening Letters, 43 S. Carolina L. Rev. 223, 241 (1992).

[85] Pereira v. United States, 347 U.S. 1, 8 (1954).

[86] Badders v. United States, 240 U.S. 391, 394 (1916).

[87] See, e.g., United States v. Draiman, 784 F.2d 248 (7th Cir. 1986); Schmuck v. United States, 489 U.S. 705 (1989).

[88] See United States v. Flaxman, 495 F.2d 344, 349 (7th Cir. 1974).

[89] United States v. Burks, 867 F.2d 795, 797 (3rd Cir. 1989).

[90] See United States v. Swinson, 993 F.2d 1299 (7th Cir. 1993).

mailed, it will be held as insufficient evidence to meet the mailing element of this statute.[91]

In 1994, as part of the Violent Crime Control and Law Enforcement Act of 1994, the mail fraud statute was amended to add the language "or deposits or causes to be deposited any matter or thing whatever to be sent or delivered by any private or commercial interstate carrier."[92] One of the key purposes of this addition was to assure that mailings using Federal Express or UPS would not be excluded from prosecution because of it not being through the U.S. Postal system. What constitutes a private commercial carrier and whether this new provision uses the commerce clause, as opposed to Congress' postal powers, remains to be decided.[93]

3.   By the Defendant or Caused by the Defendant

In addition to a showing of a mailing, it is necessary that the mailing be by the defendant or caused to be mailed by him or her. The Supreme Court held in *Pereira v. United States*[94] that "[w]here one does an act with knowledge that the use of the mails will follow in the ordinary course of business or where such use can reasonably be foreseen, even though not actually intended, then he 'causes' the mails to be used."

There are few cases finding that the government failed to prove that the defendant mailed the item or caused the item to be mailed. In *United States v. Smith*,[95] the Eleventh Circuit did state, that the "government failed to show that Smith knew or should have foreseen that the mails would actually be used." And *in United States v. Walters*,[96] the Seventh Circuit held that "[t]he prosecutor must prove that the use of the mails was foreseeable, rather than calling on judicial intuition to repair a rickety case." But in *United States v. Pimental*,[97] the First Circuit said "it is simply the 'use of the mails' in the course of the scheme rather than the particular mailing at issue that must be reasonably foreseeable for the causation element of a mail fraud offense to be satisfied."

4.   Venue

The mailing can become a source for determining the venue for the charge. In this regard courts use different approaches. Some courts focus on the use of the mails in determining venue and require that the mailing have passed through the district that is prosecuting the case. In *United States v. Wood*, the Sixth Circuit stated that "venue in a mail fraud case is limited to districts where the mail is deposited, received, or moves through, even if the fraud was elsewhere."[98]

---

[91] See, e.g., United States v. Hannigan, 27 F.3d 890 (3rd Cir. 1994) United States v. Oldenburg, 762 F.Supp. 272 (N.D. Cal. 1991); United States v. Scott, 730 F.2d 143 (4th Cir. 1984).

[92] Violent Crime Control and Law Enforcement Act of 1994 § 250006.

[93] See Ellen S. Podgor, Mail Fraud: Limiting the Limitless, 18 Champion 4 (Dec. 1994); see also Peter J. Henning, Maybe It Should Just Be Called Federal Fraud: The Changing Nature of the Mail Fraud Statute, 36 Boston Col. L. Rev. 435 (1995).

[94] 347 U.S. 1 (1954).

[95] 934 F.2d 270 (11th Cir. 1991).

[96] 997 F.2d 1219 (7th Cir. 1993).

[97] 380 F.3d 575, 589–90 (1st Cir. 2004).

[98] 364 F.3d 704, 713 (6th Cir. 2004).

Another view is to find mail fraud prosecutions permissible only in the districts where the mailing actually occurs. For example, in *United States v. Brennan*,[99] the Second Circuit stated that "[r]ather than make a defendant like Brennan subject to prosecution in any district through which a mail truck carrying his mail happened to drive (or perhaps even in any district over which an airplane carrying the mail happened to fly, or in which it happened to make an interim stop), we think Congress's more particularized and careful phrasing in the mail fraud statute takes it outside the scope of § 3237(a) and is best read less expansively." The test for venue used by this court was that "the mail fraud statute is permissible only in those districts in which a proscribed act occurs, *i.e.,* in which the defendant 'places,' 'deposits,' 'causes to be deposited,' 'takes,' or 'receives' mail or 'knowingly causes' mail 'to be delivered."[100]

B. In Furtherance

1. Generally

In addition to having a mailing, or interstate transmission, by the defendant or caused by him or her, it is also necessary that this mailing be in furtherance of the scheme to defraud.

2. Limitations to "In Furtherance"

Historically there were several limitations to what would be considered in furtherance of a scheme to defraud. Mailings which conflicted with the scheme were an imperative command of duty imposed by the state, occurred prior to commencement of the scheme, or occurred after fruition of the scheme, were found not to be in furtherance of the scheme to defraud. Several of these limitations to the "in furtherance" doctrine came from three Supreme Court decisions.

In *United States v. Kann*[101] the defendant, a president of a corporation that manufactured munitions, was indicted for diverting company funds for his personal use. The mailings were checks cashed by the defendant that were presented to the drawee banks for collection. The Supreme Court found that the mailings were after the fraud and therefore they could not be the basis for a mail fraud prosecution. From the *Kann* case arose the rejection of mailings that were after the scheme to defraud as being a proper basis for a mail fraud case.

A second Supreme Court decision that placed limits on whether the mailing was in furtherance of the scheme to defraud was the case of *Parr v. United States*.[102] This case involved a scheme to defraud a school district of money and the mailings included required letters pertaining to assessment and collection of school taxes. Because the mailings were required, the Court found that they were not in furtherance of the scheme to defraud. The Court stated that "we think it cannot be said that mailings made or caused to be made under the imperative command of duty imposed by state law are criminal under the federal mail fraud statute."[103] Thus, from *Parr*, we again

---

[99] 183 F.3d 139, 147 (2d Cir. 1999).

[100] Id.

[101] 323 U.S. 88 (1944)

[102] 363 U.S. 370 (1960).

[103] Id. at 391.

see that mails that are after the fruition of the scheme to defraud are not in furtherance of the scheme. Additionally, compelled mailings by law are not considered in furtherance of a scheme to defraud.

A third Supreme Court decision, *United States v. Maze*,[104] involved mail fraud convictions where the defendant had stolen his roommate's credit card and used the card for various expenses. The government argued that the mailing of the sales slips to the issuing banks was the mailing in furtherance of the scheme to defraud. The Supreme Court rejected this argument, affirming the reversal of the circuit court. The Court found that this mailing was not in furtherance because it was after fruition of the scheme to defraud. Additionally, the Court stated that the mailing conflicted with the defendant's purpose. They said, "[i]ndeed from his point of view, he probably would have preferred to have the invoices misplaced by the various motel personnel and never mailed at all."[105] Thus, from *Maze*, we see a reaffirmation that mailings after the scheme to defraud will not be allowed and also that mailings that are counterproductive to the scheme are not in furtherance of the scheme.

Often there was a strong dissent accompanying the decisions in these three cases, *Kann, Parr,* and *Maze*. For example, in *United States v. Maze*, Chief Justice Burger argued in dissent that mail fraud needed to be a "stopgap" device for newer frauds. A second dissent in this case, by Justice White, argued that the criminality was continuing and that the bank was the actual victim so that the defendant's acts were in furtherance of the scheme to defraud.

From these three Supreme Court cases were many lower decisions that refused to allow "post-fraud accounting" as a part of a scheme to defraud. Several circuit court decisions refused to allow schemes that conflicted with defendant's purpose.[106] Others extended mailings after the scheme to defraud, to not allowing mailings that were prior to the scheme to defraud. Thus, mailings that were part of a legitimate fundraising campaign for the Infantile Paralysis Foundation, could not be the basis of a mail fraud conviction when the mailings were clearly for a lawful purpose, despite the fact that the defendant was accused of a later embezzlement of the money.[107]

The issue of "compelled documents" was raised in the *McNally* case in footnote two where the Court noted that six counts had been dismissed because they were premised on the mailing of tax returns. The Court cited to the *Parr* decision and stated that "[t]he Court of Appeals held that mailings required by law cannot be made the basis for liability under § 1341 unless the documents are themselves false."[108] It was noted that the government had not sought review of this issue.

---

[104] 414 U.S. 395 (1974).

[105] Id. at 402.

[106] See, e.g., United States v. Castile, 795 F.2d 1273 (6th Cir. 1986); United States v. Pietri Giraldi, 864 F.2d 222 (1st Cir. 1988).

[107] See United States v. Beall, 126 F.Supp. 363 (N.D. Cal. 1954); see also United States v. Tarnopol, 561 F.2d 466 (3d Cir. 1977).

[108] 483 U.S. 350, 354 n.2 (1987).

3. Schmuck—"In Furtherance Test"

In 1989, the Supreme Court revisited the limits to "in furtherance" in accepting the case of *Schmuck v. United States*.[109] Wayne Schmuck, a used car salesman, was indicted on 12 counts of mail fraud for rolling back odometers and selling the vehicles at an artificially inflated price. The mailings were the title applications submitted by the dealers to the Department of Transportation. Although Schmuck did not mail these letters, he was accused of causing the dealers to mail these letters.

Schmuck contested the mailings as not being in furtherance of the scheme to defraud. But the district court rejected this argument. The Seventh Circuit, likewise, rejected this argument, although it did initially accept the defendant's claim that it was improper for the trial court to have refused to give an instruction on the lesser misdemeanor offense of odometer tampering.[110] On rehearing en banc, the Seventh Circuit affirmed the trial court's convictions, rejecting the earlier panel decision on the issue of whether it was necessary to give the jury a lesser offense instruction of odometer tampering.

The Supreme Court examined both the lesser instruction issue and what satisfies the "in furtherance" aspect of this statute. In an opinion that distinguishes the prior decisions of *Kann*, *Parr*, and *Maze*, the Court said that "the title-registrations at issue here served a function different from the mailings" in these prior cases. The Court said that the "intrabank mailings in *Kann* and the credit card invoice mailings in *Parr* and *Maze* involved little more than post-fraud accounting among the potential victims of the various schemes, and the long-term success of the fraud did not turn on which of the potential victims bore the ultimate loss." Here the Court said the "mailing of the title-registration forms was an essential step in the successful passage of title to the retail purchasers."

The Court, in affirming Schmuck's mail fraud convictions, set forth a test as follows:

> The relevant question at all times is whether the mailing is part of the execution of the scheme as conceived by perpetrator at the time, regardless of whether the mailing later, through hindsight, may prove to have been counterproductive and return to haunt the perpetrator of the fraud.

This test appears to reject the prior limitation to "in furtherance" that was premised on counterproductively. But it did not speak to whether compelled documents can be "in furtherance" of a scheme to defraud.

Courts have continued to preclude mailings that are required by law. In *United States v. Lake*,[111] the Tenth Circuit stated that "[m]ost other circuits to address the issue have interpreted *Parr* to hold that 'mailings of documents which are required by

---

[109] 489 U.S. 705 (1989).

[110] The statute for odometer tampering has since been modified to increase the possible penalty for this charge. See 49 U.S.C. § 32709.

[111] 472 F.3d 1247 (10th Cir. 2007).

law to be mailed, and which are not themselves false and fraudulent, cannot be regarded as mailed for the purpose of executing a fraudulent scheme."[112]

4. *Lulling Doctrine*

Two cases by the Supreme Court went unmentioned in the *Schmuck* decision, so it remains uncertain as to whether they continue to offer viable precedent for showing that the defendant acted in furtherance. These cases present what has been called the "lulling doctrine."

Although *Kann, Parr,* and *Maze,* precluded after-the-fact mailings, a recognized exception was when the mailings were to "lull" the victims into the defendant's scheme. In both *United States v. Sampson*[113] and *United States v. Lane,*[114] the Supreme Court allowed mailings as "in furtherance" of the scheme to defraud if they "were designed to lull the victims into a false sense of security." *Lane* has been rejected when the mailings themselves were not false.[115] Lulling has also been rejected when the lulling device was not a "fundamental part of the basic scheme and its desired continued perpetration."[116]

§ 4.9   WIRE FRAUD

A. History

Congress added the wire fraud statute in 1952. It has the same scheme to defraud element as mail fraud and the same in furtherance requirement. It is commonly stated that it works in *pari materia* to mail fraud. But unlike the use of the postal system, wire fraud uses a transmission "by means of wire, radio, or television communication." In 1956 Congress added "foreign commerce" to the statute.[117] Like the mail fraud statute, it also had the penalty increased to thirty years when the fraud involved a financial institution. Post–Hurricane Katrina the thirty year penalty also included schemes to defraud that are connected with "a presidentially declared major disaster or emergency." (See § 4.1(A)).

18 U.S.C. § 1343 provides:

Whoever, having devised or intending to devise any scheme or artifice to defraud, or for obtaining money or property by means of false or fraudulent pretenses, representations, or promises, transmits or causes to be transmitted by means of wire, radio, or television communication in interstate or foreign commerce, any writings, signs, signals, pictures, or sounds for the purpose of executing such scheme or artifice, shall be fined under this title or imprisoned not more than 20 years, or both. If the violation occurs in relation to, or involving any benefit authorized, transported, transmitted, transferred, disbursed, or paid in connection with, a presidentially declared major disaster or emergency (as those terms are

---

[112] Id. at 1256.

[113] 371 U.S. 75 (1962).

[114] 474 U.S. 438 (1986).

[115] See Wade v. Gaither, 2011 WL 112270 (D. Utah 2011).

[116] See Henderson v. United States, 425 F.2d 134, 143 (5th Cir. 1970).

[117] Pub. L. No. 84–688, 70 Stat. 523 (1956).

defined in section 102 of the Robert T. Stafford Disaster Relief and Emergency Assistance Act (42 U.S.C. 5122)), or affects a financial institution, such person shall be fined not more than $1,000,000 or imprisoned not more than 30 years, or both.

One finds wire fraud charges premised on telephone calls, microwaves, fax transmissions, and electronic transmissions. Because of the high use of computers, wire fraud is also a common charge in a white collar case involving a transmission via the Internet.

B. Interstate and Foreign Commerce

It is incumbent upon the government to prove that there was an interstate wire. This is the jurisdictional hook that provides the basis for a federal prosecution of the fraudulent scheme. "Purely intrastate communications are not sufficient under the statute."[118]

In *United States v. Phillips*,[119] the court rejected the government argument that "in order to satisfy the elements of this offense, it was *not* necessary to present evidence that the pertinent wire communications themselves actually crossed state lines, as long as the communications (whether interstate or intrastate) traveled via an 'instrument of an integrated system of interstate commerce,' such as the interstate phone system." The court stated that the text of the statute makes "no reference" "to mere 'use' of the mechanisms of interstate commerce." The court in *Phillips* therefore found that "the transmission must be 'in interstate or foreign commerce.'" The court also noted how Congress had declined to enact amendments that would have extended "the law to cover simple use of an interstate instrumentality."

This issue becomes particularly problematic when the wire is via the WorldWideWeb. In *United States v. Schaefer*,[120] the Tenth Circuit held, like other circuits, that the wire has to actually cross state lines and that one person's use of the internet, "standing alone" was insufficient evidence that the item "traveled across state lines in interstate commerce." One case, however, that has extended this holding is *United States v. Kieffer*,[121] where the court stated that "[t]he presence of end users in different states, coupled with the very character of the internet, render this inference permissible even absent evidence that only one host server delivered web content in these two states."[122] The court in *Kieffer* affirmed that defendant's use of interstate wires, which involved him running a criminal law practice without a license or law degree, as being sufficient for wire fraud.

Courts uniformly hold that it is not necessary for the defendant to know that the wire went interstate. As long as the communication traveled "from one location within

---

[118] Defazio v. Wallis, 500 F. Supp.2d 197 (E.D. N.Y. 2007) (finding an insufficient basis for wire fraud in a civil RICO action); McCoy v. Goldberg, 748 F.Supp. 146 (S.D. N.Y. 1990) ("The federal wire fraud statute does not cover telephone communications between persons within the same state."); Boruff v. United States, 310 F.2d 918, 922 (5th Cir. 1962) (noting that § 1343 requires and interstate transmission).

[119] 376 F. Supp.2d 6 (D. Mass. 2005).

[120] 501 F.3d 1197 (10th Cir. 2007).

[121] 681 F.3d 1143 (10th Cir. 2012).

[122] Id. at 1154.

a state to another location within that same state which passes through another state [it] may satisfy the interstate requirement, even if the defendant has no reason to know of the interstate character of the communication."[123]

In *United States v. Bryant*,[124] the Eighth Circuit examined a case where the defendant sent two telegrams from Kansas City, Missouri to Bridgetown, Missouri. The telegrams, unbeknownst to the defendant, had been routed through Middletown, Virginia. The court held that this was sufficient for wire fraud as "the accused need not know or foresee that the communication was interstate."[125]

What will be considered foreign commerce was an issue in the case of *United States v. Goldberg*,[126] where the Third Circuit looked at whether wire transfers between two countries outside the United States would suffice for foreign commerce. 18 U.S.C. § 10 specifies that "'foreign commerce' includes commerce with a foreign country." The defendant argued that jurisdiction was lacking because the wire communications were between the cities of Montreal and Nassau, as opposed to being between the United States and a foreign country. But the court was able to avoid the issue because there were telephone calls made by the defendant from prison to a bank in Canada. But Judge Sloviter, in a concurring in part and dissenting in part opinion, did not agree with the majority on this issue, finding that the charging document referenced wire communications from Montreal to Nassau and therefore the government failed to present sufficient proof of wires in foreign commerce.

C. Intent

Like mail fraud, wire fraud also requires that the government prove an intent to defraud. (See § 4.6). One finds mail fraud cases regarding intent used in interpreting what constitutes an intent to defraud for purposes of mail fraud. On occasion, the use of the wires presents some unique issues.

For example, in *United States v. Czubinski*,[127] the defendant, employed as a representative in an Internal Revenue Service (IRS) office, was convicted of wire fraud, honest services fraud, and four counts of computer fraud. The evidence produced at his trial was that he "disregarded IRS rules by looking at confidential information obtained by performing computer searches that were outside of the scope of his duties." He was accused of accessing files of social acquaintances, two individuals involved in a political campaign, and others. In reversing the convictions, the First Circuit said that there was no evidence that he created dossiers with the information that he was alleged to have accessed. The court held that although confidential information can be property for purposes of wire fraud, there was no showing here "that merely accessing confidential information, without doing, or clearly intending to do, more, is tantamount to a deprivation of IRS property under the wire fraud statute." The court stated that "[m]ere browsing of the records of people about whom one might have a particular

---

[123] United States v. Siembida, 604 F. Supp.2d 589 (S.D. N.Y. 2008).

[124] 766 F.2d 370 (8th Cir. 1985).

[125] Id. at 374.

[126] 830 F.2d 459 (3d Cir. 1987).

[127] 106 F.3d 1069 (1st Cir. 1997).

interest, although reprehensible, is not enough to sustain a wire fraud conviction on a 'deprivation of intangible property' theory."

§ 4.10 BANK FRAUD

A. History

In 1984 Congress passed the Bank Fraud statute, a statute that is also modeled after mail and wire fraud.[128] The statute was passed to "protect the financial integrity of [federally guaranteed financial] institutions, and . . . assure a basis for Federal prosecution of those who victimize these banks through fraudulent schemes."[129] Some attribute its passage as a reaction to the Supreme Court's decision in *Williams v. United States*, where the Court reversed a conviction under a false statement statute finding that the statute did not cover a misapplication of bank funds and a check kiting scheme.[130] Bank fraud is often a lead charge in the white collar arena. For example, in March 2012 there were 101 bank fraud convictions and it had the highest number of convictions when compared with other white collar offenses. This ranking was not unique for the category of bank fraud, as one year and five year statistics demonstrate that it held a similar position as the lead charge for white collar crimes.[131]

The statute passed to cover schemes to defraud against banks can be found at 18 U.S.C. § 1344, which provides—

Whoever knowingly executes, or attempts to execute, a scheme or artifice—

(1) to defraud a financial institution; or

(2) to obtain any of the moneys, funds, credits, assets, securities, or other property owned

by, or under the custody or control of, a financial institution, by means of false or fraudulent pretenses, representations, or promises;

shall be fined not more than $1,000,000 or imprisoned not more than 30 years, or both.

The statute has been amended on two occasions, raising the penalty to its present maximum of thirty years and also now referencing financial institutions as opposed to "federally chartered or insured financial institution." Despite its comparable appearance to mail and wire fraud, the statute has occasionally proved controversial on unique grounds.

One controversy is whether subsection (1) and (2) present two distinct offenses, or whether like mail and wire fraud, they operate conjunctively. This interpretation can effect the scheme to defraud element of the statute, the intent requirement, and even

---

[128] United States v. Mason, 902 F.2d 1434 (9th Cir. 1990).

[129] United States v. Jacobs, 117 F.3d 82, 93 (2d Cir. 1997).

[130] 458 U.S. 279 (1982).

[131] See Trac Reports, White Collar Crime Convictions for March 2012, available at http://trac.syr.edu/tracreports/bulletins/white_collar_crime/monthlymar12/gui/.

materiality.[132] For example, if read disjunctively, "bare" check-kiting schemes have been found to be subject to prosecution only under subsection one of the statute, while "embellished" check-kiting schemes could be prosecuted under subsection two.[133]

B. Execution of a Scheme

Courts have wrestled with what constitutes an "execution" of a scheme and whether the conduct is an execution "or merely a component of the scheme." In *United States v. De La Mata*,[134] the Eleventh Circuit held that "each part of the scheme that creates a separate financial risk for the financial institution constitutes a separate execution." Several cases exploring this issue have used factors such as "the ultimate goal of the scheme, the nature of the scheme, the benefits intended, the interdependence of the acts, and the number of parties involved."[135] The determination of whether conduct is an execution of a fraudulent scheme rather than an act in furtherance of the scheme can raise issues of whether charged counts should be dismissed as multiplicitous.[136]

Courts have noted that the term "scheme to defraud" "is not capable of precise definition." In *United States v. Goldblatt*,[137] the Third Circuit noted that "fraud [ ] is measured in a particular case by determining whether the scheme demonstrated a departure from fundamental honesty, moral uprightness, or fair play and candid dealings in the general life of the community."

C. Victim of the Fraud

Bank fraud requires that the fraud be against the bank, and that the bank be a federally insured bank. The term financial institution is defined in 18 U.S.C. § 20 and it includes ten different possibilities such as "an insured depository institution," "a credit union with accounts insured by the National Credit Union Share Insurance Fund" and "a depository institution holding company."

In *United States v. Blackmon*,[138] the Second Circuit referenced the Senate and House reports at the time of the passage of this statute, both of which emphasized the limited intent of the legislation. The Senate Report stated that the "victims are financial institutions that are federally created, controlled or insured."[139] The House Report noted that the section was concerned with "fraudulent schemes where banks were the victims."[140] In *Blackmon*, the court was concerned that extending the statute beyond this legislative intent would "implicate concerns of federalism." This was

---

[132] Neder v. United States, 527 U.S. 1, where the court held that materiality was required, was a case with mail, wire, and bank fraud charges. (See supra § 4.6). In United States v. Rice, 2011 WL 3841973 (E.D. Tenn. 2011), the court in a footnote stated that *Neder* only applied to the second prong of the statute.

[133] See United States v. Burnett, 10 F.3d 74 (2d Cir. 1993).

[134] 266 F.3d 1275 (11th Cir. 2001).

[135] See United States v. Longfellow, 43 F.3d 318 (7th Cir. 1994).

[136] See United States v. Harris, 79 F.3d 223 (2d Cir. 1996).

[137] 813 F.2d 619 (3d Cir. 1987).

[138] 839 F.2d 900 (2d Cir. 1988).

[139] S.Rep. No. 225, 98th Cong., 2nd Sess. 377 (1983), reprinted in 1984 U.S.Code Cong. & Admin.News 3182, 3517.

[140] H.R.Rep. No. 901, 98th Cong., 2d Sess. 2 (1984).

equally a concern in *United States v. Orr*,[141] where the Fourth Circuit vacated bank fraud convictions in a case where the bank had not been the victim of the fraud. The case involved the alleged passing of a bad check. The court stated that "[h]ere is presented a simple bad check case for criminal prosecution in the proper state court to the extent state law allows."[142]

Orr has been distinguished when the activity is not merely a routine bad check case, but rather involves a forgery. In *United States v. Brandon*,[143] the Fourth Circuit allowed a bank fraud conviction where the individual "stole the checks and forged the signatures." The court said that "there is a clear distinction between a check that bears an authorized signature and a check that bears a forged signature or has been altered in some way."

Likewise in *United States v. Morganfield*,[144] the Fifth Circuit held that "the bank does not have to be the central target of the alleged scheme for there to be bank fraud liability." But the court did note that in these cases it was necessary for the government to present "other facts evincing an intent to victimize the financial institution." In *Morganfield*, the court found that it was not a "simple insufficient check funds scheme," but rather included many other factors such as obtaining "certificates in the names of nonexistent business entities," using "false personal identifications in opening the checking accounts so as to not be personally connected to the checking accounts," and "signing the checks in the names of nonexistent persons."[145]

There is no requirement for the government to show that the bank was actually victimized. The statute also includes conduct that is an attempt to execute a scheme that will victimize a bank.[146]

D. Intent

As with mail fraud, it is necessary for the government to prove that the accused acted with specific intent. Often circumstantial evidence is used to show the defendant's intent. For example, in a bank fraud case, the evidence may be a showing that the defendant falsified information on a loan document.[147] Where there is no evidence to show that the accused intended to victimize the financial institution so that it would have an actual or potential loss, the court will not allow the conviction to stand.[148]

Courts have split on whether the "intent to defraud the bank" element applied to both subsection (1) and (2) of the statute. At issue here is whether one should read the two prongs of the statute conjunctively or disjunctively. In *United States v. Thomas*,[149]

---

[141] 932 F.2d 330 (4th Cir. 1991).

[142] Id. at 332.

[143] 298 F.3d 307 (4th Cir. 2002).

[144] 501 F.3d 453 (5th Cir. 2007).

[145] Id. at 465.

[146] See United States v. Stavroulakis, 952 F.2d 686 (2d Cir. 1992).

[147] See United States v. Jackson, 540 F.3d 578 (7th Cir. 2008).

[148] See, e.g., United States v. Rodriguez, 140 F.3d 163 (2d Cir. 1998); United States v. Laljie, 184 F.3d 180 (2d Cir. 1999).

[149] 315 F.3d 190 (3d Cir. 2002).

the Third Circuit read the statute conjunctively holding that "the *sine qua non* of a bank fraud violation, no matter what subdivision of the statute it is pled under, is the intent to defraud the bank."[150] In reading the statute this way, courts are saying that there is "no such thing as an independent violation of subsection (2)."[151]

In contrast, in *United States v. Everett*,[152] the Sixth Circuit found that "to have the specific intent required for bank fraud the defendant need not have put the bank at risk of loss in the usual sense or intended to do so." The court stated that "it is sufficient if the defendant in the course of committing fraud on someone causes a federally insured bank to transfer funds under its possession and control."[153]

The defendant does not need to know the federally insured status of the bank. This element is a jurisdictional hook requiring proof by the government that the bank was federally insured, but it does not require knowledge of this element on the part of the accused.[154] A court has allowed the inference to be made that the bank was insured at the time of the crime, when there is testimony at trial that they are presently an insured bank.[155]

§ 4.11 HEALTH CARE FRAUD

Health Care fraud has been a top priority of recent Department of Justice administrations. There were "1,235 new health care fraud prosecutions in FY 2011, equating to a 68.9% increase over the prior year."[156] In addition to the Department of Justice, the Health and Human Services (HHS) Department of the federal government has been heavily involved in this area. There are several different federal statutes that focus on health care fraud.[157] There include medical false claims statutes, anti-kickback statutes, and other statutes that are used with health care fraud prosecutions.

One statute, enacted in 1996 as part of the Health Insurance Portability and Accountability Act of 1996, and amended in 2010, is the health care fraud statute that is modeled after mail fraud.

18 U.S.C. § 1347 provides that

(a) Whoever knowingly and willfully executes, or attempts to execute, a scheme or artifice—

(1) to defraud any health care benefit program; or

---

[150] Id. at 197.

[151] See United States v. Leahy, 445 F.3d 634 (3d Cir. 2006).

[152] 270 F.3d 986 (6th Cir. 2001).

[153] Id. at 991.

[154] See United States v. Key, 76 F.3d 350 (11th Cir. 1996).

[155] See United States v. Ayewoh, 627 F.3d 914 (1st Cir. 2010).

[156] Joel R. Levin & Charles W. (Chip) Mulany, Practical Tips for Navigating the Newly Revised Sentencing Guidelines for Health Care Fraud Prosecutions, ABA Criminal Justice Newsletter, at 12 (Spring 2012) (citing Trac Reports, Record Number of Federal Criminal Health Care Fraud prosecutions Filed in FY 2011, available at http://trac.syr.edu/tracreports/crim/270/).

[157] See, e.g., 42 U.S.C. § 1320a–7b(a) & (b); 42 U.S.C. § 1395nn.

(2) to obtain, by means of false or fraudulent pretenses, representations, or promises, any of the money or property owned by, or under the custody or control or, any health care benefit program,

in connection with the delivery of or payment for health care benefits, items, or services, shall be fined under this title or imprisoned not more than 10 years, or both. If the violation results in serious bodily injury (as defined in section 1365 of this title), such person shall be fined under this title or imprisoned not more than 20 years, or both; and if the violation results in death, such person shall be fined under this title, or imprisoned for any term of years or for life, or both.

This statute has a subdivision (b) that provides that "with respect to violations of this section, a person need not have actual knowledge of this section or specific intent to commit a violation of this section."

In most other respects this health care fraud statute operates the same as mail fraud, wire fraud, and the other fraud statutes in the fraud section of the federal code. It has survived as applied vagueness challenges in specific cases.[158] It also has been interpreted broadly to cover private health care providers. In *United States v. Baldwin*,[159] a district court ruled that Congress intended to "combat health care fraud without limitation."

Many different schemes to defraud have been alleged under section 1347. For example, this statute has been used to prosecute an individual for "submitting Medicare claims for numerous wheelchairs that were never delivered, were unnecessary, or were not properly prescribed."[160] Improper billing practices are often a basis for a violation of section 1347.[161] In many cases one finds this charge used with additional counts for false statements under 18 U.S.C. § 1035, false statements relating to health care matters.[162]

Several cases have examined whether there was a sufficient scheme to defraud for purposes of health care fraud. For example, in *United States v. Wallace*,[163] the Seventh Circuit looked at whether there was sufficient evidence of a scheme to defraud in a case where a company that transported patients, and was supposed to receive reimbursement at the "community rate" for "loaded miles," had committed a scheme to fraud for charging the Medicaid program for trips that included only the driver. The jury convicted Wallace of both mail fraud and health care fraud under § 1347 and rejected his argument that this rural area had a rate that allowed for payment from the taxi's dispatch point to the passenger's destination plus a set fee. The court noted that Wallace had "collected from Medicaid about $500,000 more than he was entitled to" under provided terms.

---

[158] See United States v. Franklin–El, 554 F.3d 903 (10th Cir. 2009) (finding it constitutional when reviewing it as an as-applied basis)

[159] 277 F. Supp.2d 67 (D.D.C. 2003).

[160] See United States v. Srapyan, 2012 WL 1355016 (9th Cir. 2012).

[161] See, e.g., United States v. Poulin, 461 Fed. Appx. 272 (4th Cir. 2012); United States v. Jones, 641 F.3d 706 (6th Cir. 2011).

[162] See United States v. Akhigbe, 642 F.3d 1078 (D.C. Cir. 2011).

[163] 531 F.3d 504 (7th Cir. 2008); see also United States v. Dearing, 504 F.3d 897 (9th Cir. 2007) (finding sufficient evidence of willfulness).

In a case where mail fraud was also charged, a court allowed the scheme to defraud for mail fraud to also serve as the scheme to defraud for the health care fraud statute.[164] Further in *United States v. Martinez*,[165] the Sixth Circuit found that a "lack of individualized patient testimony for each count in the indictment alone does not render the evidence before the court insufficient." A showing that unnecessary procedures and prescribed medicine were given was sufficient to support the scheme to defraud element of a jury's verdict.

As billing codes can be an aspect of a health care fraud case, a defendant may argue that the codes or rules are ambiguous, thus not supporting him or her having sufficient intent to commit the crime. In *United States v. Singh*,[166] the Second Circuit looked at circumstantial evidence such as the doctor's instructions to his staff to find sufficient evidence of intent. But when a different statute had been used, and the government used different theories for alleging guilt in billing practices, the Second Circuit did find it necessary to vacate the conviction for Medicare billing fraud.[167]

A lack of causation has been argued when a patient uses illegal narcotics and it is claimed that this is an intervening cause of the person dying and that therefore the enhanced penalty for a death under this statute should not be permitted. In *United States v. Hancock*,[168] the Sixth Circuit held that "a patient's use of illegal narcotics is not an intervening cause which breaks the chain of proximate causation if it is a foreseeable and natural result of the defendant physician's criminal conduct." The court held that there was sufficient evidence of the defendant defrauding a health care program in violation of section 1347 and that proximate cause was the appropriate standard for the enhanced penalty provision under this section.

§ 4.12   MAJOR FRAUD ACT

18 U.S.C. § 1031, passed as the Major Fraud Act of 1988,[169] prohibits in part (a):

Whoever knowingly executes, or attempts to execute, any scheme or artifice with the intent—

(1) to defraud the United States; or

(2) to obtain money or property by means of false or fraudulent pretenses, representations, or promises,

in any grant, contract, subcontract, subsidy, loan, guarantee, insurance, or other form of Federal assistance, including through the Troubled Asset Relief Program, an economic stimulus, recovery or rescue plan provided by the Government, or the Government's purchase of any troubled asset as defined in the Emergency Economic Stabilization Act of 2008, or in any procurement of property or services as a prime contractor with the United States or as a subcontractor or supplier on a

---

[164] See United States v. Jones, 641 F.3d 706 (6th Cir. 2011).

[165] 588 F.3d 301 (6th Cir. 2009).

[166] 390 F.3d 168 (2d Cir. 2004).

[167] Siddiqi v. United States, 98 F.3d 1427 (2d Cir. 1996).

[168] 2012 WL 1058422 (6th Cir. 2012).

[169] Pub. L. No. 100–700, § 2, 102 Stat. 4631 (1988).

contract in which there is a prime contract with the United States, if the value of such grant, contract, subcontract, subsidy, loan, guarantee, insurance, or other form of Federal assistance, or any constituent part thereof, is $1,000,000 or more shall, subject to the applicability of subsection (c) of this section, be fined not more than $1,000,000, or imprisoned not more than 10 years, or both.

The portion pertaining to the "any grant, contract, subcontract, subsidy, loan, guarantee, insurance, or other form of Federal assistance, including through the Troubled Asset Relief Program, an economic stimulus, recovery or rescue plan provided by the Government, or the Government's purchase of any troubled asset as defined in the Emergency Economic Stabilization Act of 2008" was added as part of the Emergency Economic Stabilization Act of 2008.[170]

Other provisions within this statute provide for maximums and methods for determining fines,[171] statutes of limitations,[172] and a "bounty-hunter" type of provision.[173] A final subsection offers protection to whistle-blowers.[174]

The statute has a one million dollar threshold. Courts do not always agree on how this threshold can be met. In *United States v. Brooks*,[175] defendants argued that "their two subcontracts did not satisfy the $1 million value prescribed by the statute." The government in this case agreed that "the defendants' subcontracts were for amounts less than $1 million," but they argued in response to the defendant that "the statute's jurisdictional requirement is established so long as the prime contract with the United States or any part thereof is worth $1 million."

The Fourth Circuit in *Brooks* takes a different position than found in the Second Circuit decision in *United States v. Nadi*.[176] In *Brooks,* the court states that "regardless of its privity with the United States, any contractor or supplier involved with a prime contract with the United States who commits fraud with the requisite intent is guilty so long as the prime contract, a subcontract, a supply agreement, or any constituent part of such a contract is valued at $1 million or more."[177] In contrast, in *Nadi*, the court stated that in ascertaining the jurisdictional amount for this statute "the value of the contract is determined by looking to the specific contract upon which the fraud is based."[178]

The statute has been found constitutional, surviving vagueness attacks.[179] This has included a vagueness challenge premised on an argument that the statute does not define the phrase "value of the contract" and courts have disagreed on how to interpret

---

[170] Pub. L. 111–21, § 2(d)(1).

[171] 18 U.S.C. § 1031(b), (c), (d), (e).

[172] 18 U.S.C. § 1031(f).

[173] 18 U.S.C. § 1031(g).

[174] 18 U.S.C. § 1031(h).

[175] 111 F.3d 365 (4th Cir. 1997).

[176] 996 F.2d 548 (2d Cir. 1993).

[177] 111 F.3d at 368–69.

[178] 996 F.2d at 551.

[179] See United States v. Nadi, 996 F.2d 548 (2d Cir. 1993); United States v. Frequency Electronics, 862 F.Supp. 834 (E.D. N.Y. 1994).

this phrase. In *United States v. Sain*,[180] the Third Circuit held that it did not need to decide whether the *Brooks* or *Nadi* approach was accurate because there was only one contract in the *Sain* case and that contract involved approximately 7 million dollars.

The statute has been interpreted as allowing for each knowing "execution" of the fraudulent scheme to be a separate count. Interpreting it in a fashion similar to the bank fraud statute, when there is a claim of multiplicity in counts it has been stated that each execution of a fraudulent scheme rather than each act in furtherance of such a scheme is allowed.[181] Determining the time of execution can be significant in determining the statute's seven year statute of limitations.[182]

§ 4.13   MAIL FRAUD AND OTHER CRIMES

A.   Mail and Wire Fraud Instead of Specific Legislation

One issue that can arise is whether the mail fraud statute can be used when there is more specific legislation prohibiting the conduct. For example, should a prosecutor be allowed to continue to use mail fraud even though there is a specific Medicaid fraud statute that has been enacted by Congress to combat the alleged criminal conduct.

The majority of courts find that despite specific legislation, prosecutors can continue to use the generic mail fraud statute. For example, In *United States v. Simon*,[183] a district court found that a mail fraud charge was permitted despite the fact that a specific Medicaid fraud statute now existed. Likewise, in *Edwards v. United States*,[184] the Supreme Court stated that the Securities Act of 1933 does not preclude mail fraud charges for the fraudulent sale of securities via the mail. The Court stated that "[w]e see no basis for a conclusion that Congress intended to repeal the earlier statute in so far as they cover securities. The two can exist and be useful, side by side."

Not all courts accept this position. For example, in *United States v. Gallant*,[185] the district court held that it was improper to charge mail fraud where particularized legislation existed within the Copyright Act.

B.   Mail and Wire Fraud in Addition to Specific Legislation

The question also arises as to whether mail fraud can be used as an additional charge to more specific legislation that covers the criminal conduct. For example, in *United States v. Weatherspoon*,[186] the Seventh Circuit permitted convictions for both mail fraud and false statements.

Using mail fraud with another criminal charge arises in the context of tax cases. Prior to electronic filing, most individuals filed their tax returns by mailing them through the U.S. Postal system. The question was therefore whether prosecutors could

---

[180] 141 F.3d 463 (3rd Cir. 1998).

[181] Id. at 473.

[182] See United States v. Reitmeyer, 356 F.3d 1313 (10th Cir. 2004).

[183] 510 F.Supp. 232 (E.D. Pa. 1981).

[184] 312 U.S. 473 (1941).

[185] 570 F.Supp. 303 (S.D. N.Y. 1983).

[186] 581 F.2d 595 (7th Cir. 1978).

charge both tax fraud and mail fraud for the mailing of a fraudulent tax return. Here again, the majority view was that mail could be used in conjunction with tax fraud.[187]

One case where a court failed to allow the use of both tax fraud and mail fraud is seen in *United States v. Henderson*.[188] In this 1974 Southern District of New York case, musician Skitch Henderson was charged with both tax fraud and mail fraud for deductions for charitable donations of 1,000 musical scores and arrangements to the University of Wisconsin. Judge Weinfeld, the author of this opinion, refused to allow both charges noting the harms of "pyramiding of sentences" that could be "staggering" and "utterly unrealistic."[189] But this case has received criticism in other court decisions.[190]

There can also be an issue when mail fraud is used to circumvent the fact that tax fraud is not a predicate act for a charge under the Racketeer Influenced and Corrupt Organizations Act (RICO). In contrast mail fraud serves as a predicate act for a RICO charge. Thus, by using the mail fraud statute for the filing of fraudulent tax returns, prosecutors could have acceptable predicate acts for a RICO charge even though Congress did not include tax fraud in the list of predicate acts. The Department of Justice has frowned upon prosecutors who attempt to charge mail fraud for purposes of RICO when the mailings are fraudulent tax returns. In 1990 DOJ issued a guideline instructing prosecutors that only in "exceptional circumstances" will tax fraud be approved for a mail fraud prosecution.[191] This was later updated and the Tax Guidelines of DOJ now provide that, "[t]he Tax Division will not authorize the use of mail, wire or bank fraud charges to convert routine tax prosecutions into RICO or money laundering cases, but will authorize prosecution of tax-related RICO and money laundering offenses when unusual circumstances warrant such a prosecution."[192]

---

[187] See, e.g., United States v. Miller, 545 F.2d 1204, 1216 (9th Cir. 1976).

[188] 386 F.Supp. 1048 (S.D. N.Y. 1974); see also United States v. Boyd, 606 F.2d 792 (8th Cir. 1979) (rejecting use of both tax fraud and mail fraud because the mailings were "legally compelled" documents); see also Ellen S. Podgor, Tax–Fraud–Mail Fraud: Synonymous, Cumulative or Diverse?, 57 U. Cinn. L. Rev. 903, 905 (1989).

[189] Id. at 1054.

[190] See, e.g., United States v. Ohle, 678 F. Supp.2d 215 (S.D.N.Y. 2010) (allowing wire fraud for tax conspiracy); Fountain v. United States, 357 F.3d 250 (2d Cir. 2004).

[191] USAM § 6–4.211(1) (1990).

[192] USAM § 6–4.210(A) (2007).

Chapter 5

SECURITIES FRAUD

§ 5.1   INTRODUCTION

Calamities in the financial markets have occurred throughout history, from the collapse of the Dutch tulip bulb market in the seventeenth century through the massive decline in real estate values that led many banks to the brink of failure in 2008. The modern financial world involves a range of securities that are the basis for trillions of dollars of investments, from common stocks and bonds to mutual funds to more exotic investments, like credit default swaps and index futures. Unlike other types of assets, such as precious metals or real estate, securities are intangible property that can be bought and sold in a number of venues. The government plays a key role in regulating the securities markets and pursuing prosecutions for fraud.

Oversight of the securities markets in the United States was first undertaken by the states, which still retain a small role in modern securities regulation under so-called "blue sky laws."[1] The federal government is now the primary regulator of securities, a development that began at the dawn of the New Deal era with the adoption of the first federal law governing the issuance of securities. Many in Congress believed the Great Depression was triggered by the market crash in October 1929, and hearings about abuses on Wall Street led to the enactment of a series of measures designed to provide national regulation of securities and those who assist investors.

There are five principal federal statutes that govern different aspects of the securities markets: the Securities Act of 1933 (commonly referred to as the 1933 Act), which covers the issuance of securities by corporations and large shareholders;[2] the Securities Exchange Act of 1934 (commonly referred to as the 1934 Act), which regulates the securities markets and imposes disclosure requirements on companies whose securities are publicly traded in the market;[3] the Trust Indenture Act of 1939, which governs debt securities;[4] the Investment Company Act of 1940, which regulates mutual funds;[5] and, the Investment Advisers Act of 1940, which regulates investment advisory firms, including larger hedge funds.[6]

Each of the federal securities laws has a provision prohibiting schemes or artifices to defraud. The two primary statutory provisions used in most civil and criminal securities fraud cases are § 17(a) of the 1933 Act and § 10(b) of the 1934 Act, along with

---

[1] The term "blue sky law" refers to state regulation of securities, and is derived from the desire of states to prevent "speculative schemes which have no more basis than so many feet of blue sky." Hall v. Geiger–Jones Co., 242 U.S. 539 (1917).

[2] 15 U.S.C. §§ 77a et seq.

[3] 15 U.S.C. §§ 78a et seq.

[4] 15 U.S.C. §§ 77aaa et seq.

[5] 15 U.S.C. §§ 80a–1 et seq.

[6] 15 U.S.C. §§ 80b–1 et seq.

Rule 10b–5 issued under that section. The 1934 Act also created the Securities & Exchange Commission, which is the primary civil regulator of the securities markets. A second important regulator of the financial markets is the Commodity Futures Trading Commission, created in 1974, which has oversight authority over the futures markets and many derivatives contracts through enforcement of the Commodity Exchange Act.[7]

The Supreme Court has applied the common law of fraud in defining the elements of a violation of the antifraud provisions, requiring proof that a defendant made a misstatement or omission of a material fact with *scienter* in connection with the issuance of a security (§ 17(a)) or the purchase or sale of a security (§ 10(b)). Section 10(b) and Rule 10b–5 have been the most widely used basis for pursuing securities fraud cases, ranging from insider trading to market manipulation to misleading statements by corporate executives about a company's prospects. A company could even be found liable for securities fraud based on misstatements contained in a report written by an independent investment analyst if the company was "sufficiently entangled" in its drafting.[8]

The Sarbanes–Oxley Act, adopted in 2002 in the wake of financial scandals at companies like Enron, WorldCom, and Adelphia Communications, added a broad securities fraud provision that is patterned on the mail and wire fraud statutes. The statute, 18 U.S.C. § 1348, provides that any person who "knowingly executes, or attempts to execute, a scheme or artifice . . . to defraud any person in connection with any commodity for future delivery, or any option on a commodity for future delivery, or any security" can be punished by up to 25 years imprisonment. The statute does not affect the application of § 10(b) and Rule 10b–5, which remain the mainstays of federal securities fraud prosecutions.

Under the common law, fraud was a type of larceny, and the elements of that offense are a trespassory taking and carrying away (asportation) of the personal property of another with the intent to permanently deprive (steal).[9] The type of property subject to larceny was limited to goods and chattels, so that intangible property could not be the subject of a prosecution. While most larcenies involve a thief personally removing the property, the common law also recognized that the deprivation could be by a false statement of past or present fact that induced a person to voluntarily part with the property, called "larceny by trick."[10]

Securities fraud has its roots in the common law offense of larceny by trick, but there are important differences in how this modern violation is understood. The property involved is intangible, and there is no asportation requirement. In fact, the antifraud provisions of the federal securities law apply to any "scheme or artifice to defraud," so the violation can be established by showing a design to obtain (or dispose of) securities by false or fraudulent statements or omissions, without regard to whether the conduct involved an actual deprivation of property from the victim. The false or misleading statement requirement applies not only to past or present facts, but also

---

[7] 7 U.S.C. §§ 1 et seq.

[8] See Elkind v. Liggett & Myers, Inc., 635 F.2d 156 (2d Cir. 1980).

[9] See Wayne R. LaFave, Criminal Law § 19.2 (5th ed. 2010).

[10] The classic English common law case outlining the elements of "larceny by trick" was Rex v. Pear, 168 Eng.Rep. 208 (1779).

assertions of future conduct or results, allowing the antifraud provisions to be applied much more broadly than the common law larceny offense. It is sometimes difficult to identify a particular victim of a securities fraud violation, especially in insider trading cases when the transactions in financial markets are largely anonymous, and buyers and sellers rarely have any direct dealings with one another.

§ 5.2   DEFINITION OF A SECURITY

A. Generally

The definition of what constitutes a "security" covered by federal law is quite broad. Section 2(1) of the 1933 Act provides:

> [A]ny note, stock, treasury stock, security future, bond, debenture, evidence of indebtedness, certificate of interest or participation in any profit-sharing agreement, collateral-trust certificate, preorganization certificate or subscription, transferable share, investment contract, voting-trust certificate, certificate of deposit for a security, fractional undivided interest in oil, gas, or other mineral rights, any put, call, straddle, option, or privilege on any security, certificate of deposit, or group or index of securities (including any interest therein or based on the value thereof), or any put, call, straddle, option, or privilege entered into on a national securities exchange relating to foreign currency, or, in general, any interest or instrument commonly known as a "security", or any certificate of interest or participation in, temporary or interim certificate for, receipt for, guarantee of, or warrant or right to subscribe to or purchase, any of the foregoing.[11]

This definition does not include everything that could possibly be considered a "security" because § 2(1) begins with the proviso that it applies "unless the context otherwise requires," which means that courts look to the economic reality of a transaction to determine whether there is a "security" involved.

B. Investment Contract

The most flexible item listed in the definition is an "investment contract," which courts have interpreted to cover a wide range of items not usually thought of as a security. In *SEC v. W.J. Howey Co.*,[12] the Supreme Court explained that the term "investment contract" was a "flexible rather than a static principle," and Congress intended that "[f]orm was disregarded for substance and emphasis was placed upon economic reality." In *Howey*, the Court adopted the following approach for determining whether a transaction involved an "investment contract" and so was subject to the federal securities laws: "The test is whether the scheme involves an investment of money in a common enterprise with profits to come solely from the efforts of others." The Court found that an investment in a citrus grove constituted a security. Subsequent lower court decisions have applied the *Howey* test to a broad range of transactions to find that they come within the federal securities laws, from ownership

---

[11] 15 U.S.C. § 77b(1). The definition of a "security" in § 3(a)(10) of the 1934 Act, 15 U.S.C. § 78c(a)(10), is slightly different, but courts have interpreted the two provisions identically.

[12] 328 U.S. 293 (1946).

interests in limited liability companies and partnerships to much more esoteric investment schemes like growing earthworms.[13]

C. Stock

The underlying economic reality of the transaction is crucial to determining whether the item involved rises to the level of a security so that it is covered by the federal securities laws. In *Landreth Timber Co. v. Landreth*,[14] involving the sale of a family-owned business, the Court found that the structure of the transaction involving the transfer of all the shares of a corporation came under the federal securities laws because the purchasers acquired "stock," even though that was not a significant aspect of the deal. In *United Housing Foundation, Inc. v. Forman*,[15] however, the Court held that shares in a cooperative housing complex that were bought by residents in order to live there were not securities, even though their ownership interest was denominated as "stock." The Court found that they were not investment contracts because the purchasers were motivated "by a desire to use or consume the item" rather than treating it as an investment with the prospect of economic gains.

In *SEC v. Edwards*,[16] the Court found that a transaction in which an investor bought an interest in a pay telephone, with a promised annual return of 14 percent, constituted an investment contract even though the rate of return was ostensibly guaranteed and there was no opportunity for capital appreciation, unlike an investment in equity securities. It held that there "is no reason to distinguish between promises of fixed returns and promises of variable returns for purposes of the [*Howey*] test" for an investment contract.

D. Note

In *Reves v. Ernst & Young*,[17] the Court considered whether particular debt instruments came within the definition of a security as "any note." The Court pointed out that "the phrase 'any note' should not be interpreted to mean literally 'any note,' but must be understood against the backdrop of what Congress was attempting to accomplish in enacting the Securities Acts." Unlike *Landreth Timber*, in which the Court applied the term "stock" in an almost literal fashion, for debt instruments it adopted a more nuanced approach that looked to a variety of factors to determine whether the federal securities laws covered the transaction.

Reves held that "[a] note is presumed to be a 'security'" unless one of four factors, called the "family resemblance test,"[18] were shown to take it outside the definition: (1) whether the investor's motive was to invest for a profit, or just to facilitate the purchase of a minor asset or good; (2) whether it was an instrument in which there was "common trading for speculation or investment"; (3) the public expectations whether

---

[13] See Smith v. Gross, 604 F.2d 639 (9th Cir. 1979).

[14] 471 U.S. 681 (1985).

[15] 421 U.S. 837 (1975).

[16] 540 U.S. 389 (2004).

[17] 494 U.S. 56 (1990).

[18] The Court cited to the Second Circuit's decision in Exchange Nat. Bank of Chicago v. Touche Ross & Co., 544 F.2d 1126 (2d Cir. 1976), which enumerated certain types of notes that did not constitute securities, so that if the note at issue bore a "family resemblance" to one of these then it fell outside the scope of the securities laws.

the instrument was a security; and (4) "the existence of another regulatory scheme significantly reduces the risk of the instrument, thereby rendering application of the Securities Acts unnecessary." The Court concluded that the demand notes at issue were securities, finding that the financial institution "sold the notes in an effort to raise capital for its general business operations, and purchasers bought them in order to earn a profit in the form of interest."

In *Pollack v. Laidlaw Holdings, Inc.,*[19] the Second Circuit applied the "family resemblance" test to investments in mortgage participation notes to determine whether they were securities. Although a note tied to a mortgage usually would not qualify as a security, the circuit court found that these did come under the federal securities laws by considering the motivation was for investment rather than commercial purposes, there was broad-based marketing of the notes so that "neither the fixed interest rate nor the personal guarantees (assuming they existed) justified characterizing appellants' motivations as anything but investment," and that the protections afforded by state law for mortgages provided insufficient protection because the instruments were "uncollateralized, speculative participations in mortgages" rather than the actual debt instrument covering the property. Other courts have applied *Reves* similarly in looking at the particular circumstances of the transaction to determine whether an instrument comes within the definition of a security.[20]

Finding that a transaction involves a security rather than some other form of instrument is crucial for the application of the federal securities laws to the transaction. If a court finds that there was not a "security" involved, then federal jurisdiction would have to be based on another fraud provision, such as the mail or wire fraud statutes (see Chapter 4). Transactions found not to involve a security include a noncontributory, compulsory union pension plan which was already subject to regulation under the Employee Retirement Income Security Act of 1974,[21] and certificates of deposit issued by a bank subject to federal regulation.[22]

If the instrument is a security, then "§ 10(b) and Rule 10b–5 prohibit all fraudulent schemes in connection with the purchase or sale of securities, whether the artifices employed involve a garden type variety of fraud, or present a unique form of deception. Novel or atypical methods should not provide immunity from the securities laws."[23] Therefore, Ponzi schemes and other types of investment frauds come within the broad prohibitions of the 1933 and 1934 Acts, even if no investment in a security was ever actually made.

---

[19] 27 F.3d 808 (2d Cir. 1994).

[20] See S.E.C. v. Wallenbrock, 313 F.3d 532 (9th Cir. 2002) (promissory notes purportedly secured by accounts receivable of foreign latex glove manufacturers were securities); Bass v. Janney Montgomery Scott, Inc., 210 F.3d 577 (6th Cir. 2000) (bridge loan to complete transaction was not a security, but warrants issued in connection with the loan were securities); Stoiber v. S.E.C., 161 F.3d 745 (D.C. Cir. 1998) (promissory notes given to broker's customers for funds used to invest in commodities were securities).

[21] International Broth. of Teamsters, Chauffeurs, Warehousemen & Helpers of Am. v. Daniel, 439 U.S. 551 (1979).

[22] Marine Bank v. Weaver, 455 U.S. 551 (1982).

[23] A. T. Brod & Co. v. Perlow, 375 F.2d 393 (2d Cir. 1967).

§ 5.3   CRIMINAL AND CIVIL ENFORCEMENT

A.   Criminal Enforcement

A violation of a provision of the federal securities laws can be prosecuted as a criminal offense, and is also subject to a civil enforcement action by the SEC. In addition, certain antifraud provisions can be the basis for private lawsuits by investors.

Section 32(a) of the 1934 Act makes it a crime for any person

> who willfully violates any provision of this chapter . . . or any rule or regulation thereunder the violation of which is made unlawful or the observance of which is required under the terms of this chapter, or any person who willfully and knowingly makes, or causes to be made, any statement in any application, report, or document required to be filed under this chapter or any rule or regulation thereunder or any undertaking contained in a registration statement . . . which statement was false or misleading with respect to any material fact. . . . [24]

This provision contains two intent requirements: "willfully" for violations of any section of the Act, and "willfully and knowingly" for making a false or misleading statement of material fact in a filing with the SEC. The other securities acts have similar provisions permitting criminal prosecution for any person who "willfully" violates the law or any rule or regulation issued pursuant to it, but the provisions do not incorporate a knowledge element for false or misleading statements.[25]

In *United States v. Dixon*,[26] the Second Circuit pointed out that "[t]he difference seems to have been deliberate since the second clause covers violations of the Act that involve misrepresentations; hence the inclusion of the term 'knowingly,' a concept typically associated with prosecution for acts grounded in fraudulent intent." The 1934 Act is also unique in providing a limited ignorance defense in criminal prosecutions to limit the punishment for a violation: "no person shall be subject to imprisonment under this section for the violation of any rule or regulation if he proves that he had no knowledge of such rule or regulation."[27]

The Supreme Court once noted that "[t]he word 'willfully' is sometimes said to be 'a word of many meanings' whose construction is often dependent on the context in which it appears."[28] The Court has not directly addressed the meaning of "willfully" in criminal prosecutions under the securities laws, although it did state in a case construing the term for civil liability that "[w]hen the term 'willful' or 'willfully' has

---

[24] 15 U.S.C. § 78ff(a). A violation is punishable by up to a $5 million fine and twenty years imprisonment for an individual, and up to a $25 million fine for an organization.

[25] See Investment Advisers Act of 1940, 15 U.S.C. § 80b–17; Investment Company Act of 1940, 15 U.S.C. § 80a–48; Securities Act of 1933, 15 U.S.C. § 77x; Trust Indenture Act of 1939, 15 U.S.C. § 77yyy.

[26] 536 F.2d 1388 (2d Cir. 1976).

[27] 15 U.S.C. § 78ff(a).

[28] Bryan v. United States, 524 U.S. 184 (1998).

been used in a criminal statute, we have regularly read the modifier as limiting liability to knowing violations."[29]

In *United States v. Peltz*,[30] the Second Circuit analyzed the "willfully" and "knowingly" elements for a criminal prosecution under § 32(a). The case involved a conspiracy to obtain confidential information from the SEC about companies being investigated and then trade on their shares. The circuit court stated, "A person can willfully violate an SEC rule even if he does not know of its existence. This conclusion follows from the difference between the standard for violation of the statute or a rule or regulation, to wit, 'willfully,' and that for false or misleading statements, namely, 'willfully and knowingly.'" Proof of willfulness requires that "the prosecution establishes a realization on the defendant's part that he was doing a wrongful act . . . [and] the act be wrongful under the securities laws and that the knowingly wrongful act involve a significant risk of effecting the violation that has occurred."

The same court concluded in *United States v. Dixon*[31] that a corporate officer who sought to avoid disclosure rules in a required filing acted "willfully" because "[w]e do not have here the case of a defendant manifesting an honest belief that he was complying with the law. Dixon did a 'wrongful act,' in the sense of our decision in *Peltz*. . . . " Even though the defendant believed his conduct could be permissible under other reporting rules, the Second Circuit stated:

> [S]uch acts are wrongful 'under the Securities Acts' if they lead, as here, to the very violations that would have been prevented if the defendant had acted with the aim of scrupulously obeying the rules (which would have necessarily involved correctly ascertaining them) rather than of avoiding them. Such an intention to deceive is enough to meet the modest requirements of the first clause of § 32(a) when violations occur.

In *United States v. Kaiser*,[32] the Second Circuit rejected a defendant's argument that willfulness required proof of the defendant's knowledge of the illegality of his conduct, holding that "*Peltz* and *Dixon* do not require a showing that a defendant had awareness of the general unlawfulness of his conduct, but rather, that he had an awareness of the general wrongfulness of his conduct."

The Ninth Circuit reached the same conclusion in *United States v. Tarallo*,[33] stating that "'willfully' as it is used in § [32](a) means intentionally undertaking an act that one knows to be wrongful; 'willfully' in this context does not require that the actor know specifically that the conduct was unlawful." The circuit court explained how the ignorance defense provided in § 32(a) impacts the meaning of willfully:

> If "willfully" meant "with knowledge that one's conduct violates a rule or regulation," the last clause proscribing imprisonment-but not a fine-in cases where

---

[29] Safeco Ins. Co. of America v. Burr, 551 U.S. 47 (2007). The Court explained that "where willfulness is a statutory condition of civil liability, we have generally taken it to cover not only knowing violations of a standard, but reckless ones as well."

[30] 433 F.2d 48 (2d Cir. 1970).

[31] 536 F.2d 1388 (2d Cir. 1976).

[32] 609 F.3d 556 (2d Cir. 2010).

[33] 380 F.3d 1174 (9th Cir. 2004).

a defendant did not know of the rule or regulation would be nonsensical: If willfully meant "with knowledge that one is breaking the law," there would be no need to proscribe imprisonment (but permit imposition of a fine) for someone who acted without knowing that he or she was violating a rule or regulation. Such a person could not have been convicted in the first place.

The "no knowledge" defense provided by § 32(a) does not operate as a true defense to criminal liability because it only limits the punishment that may be imposed for a violation but does not relieve a defendant of liability. In those cases in which the defendant seeks to limit punishment for a conviction by arguing ignorance, the lower courts have found that the defendant has the burden of establishing the lack of knowledge of the rule or regulation. In *United States v. O'Hagan*,[34] the Supreme Court noted that "lack of knowledge of the relevant rule is an affirmative defense to a sentence of imprisonment."

Most fraud prosecutions are brought pursuant to both the substantive provision of the federal securities act and a rule adopted pursuant to that provision, such as § 10(b) and Rule 10b–5, both of which prohibit fraudulent schemes in connection with the purchase or sale of a security. There is a question whether the ignorance defense would be available to a charge of violating the statutory provision. In *United States v. Behrens*,[35] the Eighth Circuit held that a defendant could offer the "no knowledge" defense at sentencing to a charge of violating § 10(b) and Rule 10b–5 because the statutory language was clear that it applied to any violation and was not limited to only those cases involving a violation of a rule or regulation. The circuit court based its conclusion on "the unambiguous plain language of § [10(b)], which requires the violation of a rule or regulation in order to establish a violation of the statutory provision, and § [32(a)], which draws no distinction for mere technical violations of a rule or regulation." *Behrens* rejected the district court's analysis in *United States v. Sloan*,[36] which explained how § 32(a) operates in this context:

> This clause is rather unique in that it permits a defendant prior to sentencing to rebut the presumption that he had knowledge of the rule or regulation of which he had been convicted of violating. It was included in the 1934 Act as a compromise measure to allay certain fears in Congress that, by enacting a vast new securities statute giving broad rule-making authority to the SEC, and by making violations of such rules criminal, the legislators were subjecting totally 'innocent' people— persons who might act without knowledge that their conduct was now prohibited by a rule—to possible incarceration. The compromise impliedly recognized that under such circumstances, strict adherence to the presumption of knowledge of the law would be unwarranted.

> It is equally clear, however, that Congress did intend to maintain the usual presumption of knowledge with respect to the standards prescribed in the securities acts themselves. The 'no knowledge' proviso is explicitly limited to lack of knowledge of a 'rule or regulation'. Congress did not intend that the protection of the 'no knowledge' clause would extend to persons who were charged with

---

[34] United States v. O'Hagan, 521 U.S. 642 (1997).

[35] 644 F.3d 754 (8th Cir. 2011).

[36] 399 F.Supp. 982 (S.D.N.Y. 1975).

knowing their conduct to be in violation of law, but did not happen to know that it was also in violation of a particular SEC rule or regulation.

In *United States v. Lilley*,[37] the district court concluded that "[i]t would frustrate the intent of Congress to permit a person whose conduct is expressly prohibited by statute to attempt to prove no knowledge of a parallel rule provision."

The antifraud provisions of the federal securities laws have been supplemented by 18 U.S.C. § 1348, adopted in 2002 as part of the Sarbanes–Oxley Act. That provision provides:

Whoever knowingly executes, or attempts to execute, a scheme or artifice—

(1) to defraud any person in connection with any commodity for future delivery, or any option on a commodity for future delivery, or any security of an issuer with a class of securities registered under section 12 of the Securities Exchange Act of 1934 (15 U.S.C. 78l) or that is required to file reports under section 15(d) of the Securities Exchange Act of 1934 (15 U.S.C. § 78o(d)); or

(2) to obtain, by means of false or fraudulent pretenses, representations, or promises, any money or property in connection with the purchase or sale of any commodity for future delivery, or any option on a commodity for future delivery, or any security of an issuer with a class of securities registered under section 12 of the Securities Exchange Act of 1934 (15 U.S.C. 78l) or that is required to file reports under section 15(d) of the Securities Exchange Act of 1934 (15 U.S.C. 78o(d));

shall be fined under this title, or imprisoned not more than 25 years, or both.

This general securities fraud provision does not supplant § 10(b) and Rule 10b–5, which remain the primary vehicles for most securities fraud cases. The three substantive elements of a § 1348 offense are: (1) fraudulent intent; (2) a scheme or artifice to defraud; and (3) a nexus with a security.[38] The only significant difference is that the criminal provision does not require that the fraud be "in connection with the purchase or sale of a security," which may allow for a slightly broader range of conduct to come within § 1348 as opposed to § 10(b) and Rule 10b–5. There are no significant decisions interpreting this provision, and given its substantial overlap with the antifraud provisions of the federal securities laws it is unlikely the lower courts will recognize any significant substantive differences from those provisions. The new provision requires a defendant act "knowingly" rather than "willfully" as required by § 32, but the latter term has been interpreted to require proof of knowledge so it is unlikely the different *mens rea* terminology will trigger broader application of § 1348.

B. Civil Enforcement

The SEC has broad authority to investigate violations of the federal securities laws, including violations of any rules or regulations issued pursuant to these

---

[37] 291 F.Supp. 989 (S.D. Tex. 1968).
[38] United States v. Hatfield, 724 F. Supp. 2d 321 (E.D.N.Y. 2010).

statutes.[39] This investigative authority includes the power to "administer oaths and affirmations, subpoena witnesses, compel their attendance, take evidence, and require the production of any books, papers, correspondence, memoranda, or other records which the Commission deems relevant or material to the inquiry."[40] Like other federal agencies, SEC subpoenas are not self-executing and so the Commission must resort to a federal court to seek enforcement (see § 17.4).[41]

If the SEC staff concludes after completing its investigation that there is sufficient evidence that a violation occurred, its usual practice is to notify the putative defendant of its intent to file charges, called a "Wells Notice." This invites the recipient to submit a response explaining why civil charges should not be filed. If the Commission decides to pursue an enforcement action, it can file its case in the appropriate federal district court by requesting an injunction prohibiting future violations,[42] or institute an administrative proceeding for a cease-and-desist order prohibiting the respondent from further violations of the law.[43] SEC enforcement proceedings are civil rather than criminal, so the standard of proof of a violation is by a preponderance of the evidence rather than the elevated requirement of proof beyond a reasonable doubt for criminal prosecutions. A civil or administrative proceeding has no impact on a separate criminal prosecution under double jeopardy, and the SEC often coordinates its filings with the Department of Justice (see § 18.7).

In addition to prospective remedies like an injunction or cease-and-desist order, a number of other civil penalties can be imposed on a defendant for a violation of the federal securities laws. The SEC can seek a bar against an individual from serving as an officer or director of a company whose shares are registered, and monetary penalties for violations based on a three-tiered structure depending on the severity of the violation.[44] If the violation involved insider trading, the SEC can seek up to a triple penalty in addition to disgorgement of ill-gotten gains.[45] The Dodd–Frank Act, adopted in 2010, allows the Commission to impose a monetary penalty in an administrative proceeding against any defendant, in addition to seeking such penalties in a federal district court action.[46] In *Gabelli v. SEC*,[47] the Supreme Court examined the question of whether the five-year statute of limitations clock for the SEC to bring civil enforcement actions "begins to tick when the fraud is complete or when the fraud is discovered." The Court held that "[g]iven the lack of textual, historical, or equitable reasons to graft a discovery rule onto the statute of limitations of § 2462, we decline to do so."

C. Private Rights of Action

The federal securities laws explicitly authorize private damages claims in certain limited circumstances. Under the 1933 Act, those who acquire shares in an offering of

---

[39] 15 U.S.C. § 78u(a)(1).

[40] 15 U.S.C. § 78u(b).

[41] 15 U.S.C. § 78u(c).

[42] 15 U.S.C. § 78u(d)(1).

[43] 15 U.S.C. § 78u–3(a).

[44] 15 U.S.C. § 78u(d)(2)–(3).

[45] 15 U.S.C. § 78u–1.

[46] 15 U.S.C. § 78u–2(a), as amended by Pub.L. No. 111–203, Title IX, § 985(b)(8), 124 Stat. 1934 (2010).

[47] 568 U.S. ___, 133 S.Ct. 1216, 185 L.Ed.2d 297 (2013).

stock in which there is a misstatement or omission in the registration statement or a prospectus can sue to recover the amount of their investment against an array of potential defendants, if they meet strict requirements for standing to sue.[48] The 1934 Act has a similar provision, § 18, permitting a suit for damages caused by actual reliance on a misstatement or omission "in any application, report, or document" filed with the SEC.[49]

Of much greater importance are the implied rights of action recognized by the Supreme Court for violations of certain provisions, most importantly § 10(b) and Rule 10b–5. The Court explained that "[t]hough the text of the Securities Exchange Act does not provide for a private cause of action for § 10(b) violations, the Court has found a right of action implied in the words of the statute and its implementing regulation."[50] The private cause of action for a violation of § 10(b) is so well established that the Court once noted that "[t]he existence of this implied remedy is simply beyond peradventure."[51] Unlike § 18, which is limited to misstatements or omissions in corporate filings and requires a plaintiff to prove actual reliance, § 10(b) applies to *any* fraud related to transactions in securities, regardless of the context of the alleged misstatement or omission, and a plaintiff need not establish actual reliance but can prove that element through the "fraud on the market" theory.[52] Shareholders of a corporation can also pursue a private claim for fraud in a proxy solicitation under Section 14(a) and Rule 14a–9.[53]

The rationale for allowing private suits even though the statute does not expressly authorize them is that "[p]rivate enforcement . . . provides a necessary supplement to Commission action." Yet, not all provisions of the federal securities laws have been found to permit a private claim for a violation. The broad antifraud provision in the 1933 Act, § 17(a), has been found not to provide a private cause of action, even though its scope is similar to § 10(b) of the 1934 Act.[54] The Supreme Court has also declined to recognize an implied private cause of action for damages arising from a violation of § 14(e) of the 1934 Act related to fraud in a tender offer,[55] or for a violation of the antifraud provision of the Investment Advisers Act.[56]

Private securities fraud cases far outnumber criminal and SEC actions, and many are class actions brought on behalf of purchasers or sellers of a company's shares during the period when allegedly false information was in the market and effectively incorporated into the price of the shares. Many of the leading Supreme Court decisions on the scope and elements of § 10(b) and Rule 10b–5 have come in private actions, and these decisions are applicable to criminal and administrative cases because the statutes apply to all forms of action.

---

[48] 15 U.S.C. § 77k–l.

[49] 15 U.S.C. § 78r.

[50] Stoneridge Inv. Partners, LLC v. Scientific–Atlanta, 552 U.S. 148 (2008).

[51] Herman & MacLean v. Huddleston, 459 U.S. 375 (1983).

[52] See Basic, Inc. v. Levinson, 485 U.S. 224 (1988).

[53] J.I. Case Co. v. Borak, 377 U.S. 426 (1964).

[54] Touche Ross & Co. v. Redington, 442 U.S. 560 (1979).

[55] Piper v. Chris–Craft Industries, Inc., 430 U.S. 1 (1977).

[56] Transamerica Mortgage Advisors, Inc. v. Lewis, 444 U.S. 11 (1979)

Congress has restricted the availability of private securities fraud class actions by adopting legislation that imposes significant pleading requirements on plaintiffs and limits the availability of state courts to seek redress for misconduct that involves the purchase or sale of a security.[57] The Supreme Court has also taken a more restrictive view of the scope of the implied private cause of action under § 10(b) and Rule 10b–5, most importantly by rejecting the application of aiding and abetting liability and requiring a private plaintiff to show that a defendant was a "primary violator" to establish liability for a violation.[58] Congress explicitly provided authority for the SEC to pursue enforcement actions based on aiding and abetting a violation, and federal prosecutors can rely on the general federal accomplice liability statute.[59] In *Nye & Nissen v. United States*,[60] the Supreme Court stated, "In order to aid and abet another to commit a crime it is necessary that a defendant 'in some sort associate himself with the venture, that he participate in it as in something that he wishes to bring about, that he seek by his action to make it succeed.'"

§ 5.4 ELEMENTS OF SECURITIES FRAUD

A. Generally

The federal securities laws contain broad antifraud prohibitions related to particular forms of transactions. The two most important are in § 17(a) of the 1933 Act and § 10(b) of the 1934 Act. Section 17(a) prohibits any person "in the offer or sale of any securities" from using the means or instruments of interstate commerce:

1.   to employ any device, scheme, or artifice to defraud, or

2.   to obtain money or property by means of any untrue statement of a material fact or any omission to state a material fact necessary in order to make the statements made, in light of the circumstances under which they were made, not misleading; or

3.   to engage in any transaction, practice, or course of business which operates or would operate as a fraud or deceit upon the purchaser.[61]

Section 10(b) of the 1934 Act is similarly broad, prohibiting any person:

To use or employ, in connection with the purchase or sale of any security registered on a national securities exchange or any security not so registered, or any securities-based swap agreement . . . , any manipulative or deceptive device or contrivance in contravention of such rules and regulations as the Commission may prescribe as necessary or appropriate in the public interest or for the protection of investors.[62]

---

[57] Private Securities Litigation Reform Act, Pub. L. No. 104–67, 109 Stat. 737 (1995); Securities Litigation Uniform Standards Act, Pub. L. No. 105–353, 112 Stat. 3227 (1998).

[58] Central Bank of Denver, N.A. v. First Interstate Bank of Denver, N.A., 511 U.S. 164 (1994).

[59] 15 U.S.C. § 78t(e).

[60] 336 U.S. 613 (1949) (quoting United States v. Peoni, 100 F.2d 401 (2d Cir. 1938)).

[61] 15 U.S.C. § 77q(a).

[62] 15 U.S.C. § 78j(b).

Most securities fraud cases that impact the stock markets or trading in the shares of a company include a claimed violation of Rule 10b–5, promulgated by the SEC under its authority to prescribe "any manipulative or deceptive device or contrivance." The Rule provides:

> It shall be unlawful for any person, directly or indirectly . . . [t]o employ any device, scheme, or artifice to defraud, . . . or [t]o engage in any act, practice, or course of business which operates or would operate as a fraud or deceit upon any person, in connection with the purchase or sale of any security.[63]

The SEC adopted Rule 10b–5 in 1942 to deal with a situation in which the president of a company was publicly downplaying its prospects while secretly buying up shares at a depressed price, conduct that fell outside of § 17(a) because it did not involve the company's issuance of shares in the market. The proposed rule in large part mimics the scope of § 17(a) to deal with fraudulent schemes, with terminology not used in § 10(b). SEC adopted the rule without any significant consideration of its language or scope, with one Commissioner merely stating, "Well, we are against fraud, aren't we?"[64]

In analyzing securities fraud under § 17(a) and § 10(b), courts generally rely on the common law tort of fraud or deceit for the essential elements to establish a violation. Those elements are: (1) a misstatement or omission (2) of a material fact (3) made with *scienter*, along with two additional elements required by § 10(b), that the transaction be (4) "in connection with" (5) the "purchase or sale of any security."[65] For a § 17(a) violation, it must occur "in the offer or sale" of a security, so that purchases would not be covered because the 1933 Act only regulates corporate issuance of securities and not after-market transactions. Note also that § 17(a) prohibits fraud in an "offer" of securities, so unlike § 10(b) there need not be a completed transaction for a violation.

The jurisdictional basis for a prosecution or civil enforcement action under § 10(b) is use of an "any means or instrumentality of interstate commerce or of the mails, or of any facility of any national securities exchange," and under § 17(a) is use of "any means or instruments of transportation or communication in interstate commerce or by use of the mails." The jurisdictional language of the two provisions has been interpreted identically by the courts.

B. Misstatement or Omission

The first step in proving a fraud is that the defendant made, or is responsible for, an untrue statement of fact or omitted a fact that rendered the statement misleading.[66] The distinction between a misstatement and omission is often negligible when the alleged fraud involved information that was not fully truthful but was also not a complete falsehood. For example, a company that inflates its earnings is misstating

---

[63] 17 C.F.R. § 240.10b–5.

[64] Milton V. Freeman, Conference on Codification of the Federal Securities Laws, 22 Bus. Law. 793 (1967).

[65] See Stoneridge Investment Partners, LLC v. Scientific–Atlanta, 552 U.S. 148 (2008); Dura Pharmaceuticals, Inc. v. Broudo, 544 U.S. 336 (2005). Three additional elements required for private claims, but not for criminal or SEC cases, are reliance, economic loss, and loss causation.

[66] Robin v. Arthur Young & Co., 915 F.2d 1120 (7th Cir. 1990).

them but also has omitted information about its true earnings. The distinction is often unimportant because the concept of fraud covers both types of conduct, unlike the perjury statutes that require proof of an actual false statement rather than just misleading or incomplete disclosure (see § 10.5). Nor is there a "literal truth" defense under the securities laws, which is available in perjury prosecutions to avoid liability when a statement is misleading.

In *Santa Fe Industries, Inc. v. Green*,[67] the Supreme Court held that § 10(b)'s language prohibiting any "manipulative or deceptive device or contrivance" required proof of an *actual* misstatement or omission and not just a breach of fiduciary duty, so that liability for a violation of Section 10(b) could not be established absent proof of some deception or manipulation. The Court noted that "nondisclosure is usually essential to the success of a manipulative scheme" constituting the omission for a violation.

An omission can be the basis for securities fraud only if there is an obligation to disclose information. In *Basic, Inc. v. Levinson*,[68] the Court stated that "[s]ilence, absent a duty to disclose, is not misleading under Rule 10b–5." A statement of "no comment" is the functional equivalent of silence, and some lower courts recognize a duty to correct or update a statement due to a change in circumstances to prevent the prior statement from becoming misleading. In *United States v. Skelly*,[69] the Second Circuit noted that "a seller or middleman may be liable for fraud if he lies to the purchaser or tells him misleading half-truths, but not if he simply fails to disclose information that he is under no obligation to reveal." But in *Stransky v. Cummins Engine Co.*,[70] the Seventh Circuit stated:

> No duty to update an historical statement can logically exist. By definition an historical statement is addressing only matters at the time of the statement. Thus, that circumstances subsequently change cannot render an historical statement false or misleading. Absent a duty to speak, a company cannot commit fraud by failing to disclose changed circumstances, with respect to an historical statement.

C. Materiality

The concept of materiality is a familiar one in fraud prosecutions. For cases under the mail, wire, and bank fraud statutes, the Supreme Court held in *Neder v. United States*[71] that "under the rule that Congress intends to incorporate the well-settled meaning of the common-law terms it uses, we cannot infer from the absence of an express reference to materiality that Congress intended to drop that element from the fraud statutes." Section 10(b)'s prohibition on "manipulative and deceptive devices," as implemented by Rule 10b–5, has also required proof that a scheme or artifice to defraud involved material information.

---

[67] 430 U.S. 462 (1977).

[68] 485 U.S. 224 (1988).

[69] 442 F.3d 94 (2d Cir. 2006).

[70] 51 F.3d 1329 (7th Cir. 1995).

[71] 527 U.S. 1 (1999) (see also § 4.7).

In the context of the federal securities laws, the Court first addressed materiality in *TSC Industries, Inc. v. Northway, Inc.*,[72] involving an alleged violation of § 14(a) related to soliciting proxies from shareholders, when it stated that an omission was material if there was "a substantial likelihood that the disclosure of the omitted fact would have been viewed by the reasonable investor as having significantly altered the 'total mix' of information made available" so that "a reasonable shareholder would consider it important. . . . " Note that materiality is not a matter of speculation about what an investor *might* have believed was important, only applying to information that will have some appreciable effect on the value of the securities or how an investor might act in response to it.

In *Basic, Inc. v. Levinson*,[73] the Court applied the materiality standard of *TSC v. Northway* for cases arising under § 10(b) and Rule 10b–5 for fraud. The case involved a claim that the company failed to disclose merger negotiations when it had previously denied there were any significant corporate developments. The Court refined the materiality standard by applying the probability-magnitude test adopted by the Second Circuit in one of the first insider trading cases filed, *SEC v. Texas Gulf Sulphur Co.*[74] It stated, "[M]ateriality will depend at any given time upon a balancing of both the indicated probability that the event will occur and the anticipated magnitude of the event in light of the totality of the company activity." *Basic* explained that the materiality standard is designed "to filter out essentially useless information that a reasonable investor would not consider significant, even as part of a larger 'mix' of factors to consider in making his investment decision." As the First Circuit noted in *In re Boston Scientific Corp. Securities Litigation*:[75]

> Why companies do not have to disclose immediately all information that might conceivably affect stock prices is apparent: the burden and risks to management of an unlimited and general obligation would be extreme and could easily disadvantage shareholders in numerous ways (e.g., if a new invention were prematurely disclosed to competitors or a take-over plan to the target company).

In *Matrixx Initiatives, Inc. v. Siracusano*,[76] the Court considered whether information was material regarding a pharmaceutical company's failure to disclose reports of adverse reactions to a drug that caused a loss of the sense of smell. The company claimed that the plaintiffs failed to allege a "statistically significant correlation between the use of Zicam and [loss of smell] so as to make failure to publicly disclose complaints and [the doctors' reports] a material omission." The Court found that the company was proposing a "bright-line rule that reports of adverse events associated with a pharmaceutical company's products cannot be material absent a sufficient number of such reports to establish a statistically significant risk that the product is in fact causing the events." This approach was inconsistent with *Basic* and *TSC* because it would "artificially exclude information that would otherwise be considered significant to the trading decision of a reasonable investor." In assessing whether information is material, the Court explained, "[g]iven that medical

---

[72] 426 U.S. 438 (1976).

[73] 485 U.S. 224 (1988).

[74] 401 F.2d 833 (2d Cir. 1968).

[75] 686 F.3d 21 (1st Cir. 2012).

[76] 131 S.Ct. 1309 (2011).

professionals and regulators act on the basis of evidence of causation that is not statistically significant, it stands to reason that in certain cases reasonable investors would as well."

The Court's approach in *Mattrix Initiatives* shows that it takes a very flexible view of what can constitute material information that largely leaves that assessment to the trier of fact. There is no bright-line test, and the issue is whether a *reasonable* investor would consider it important based on the information made available by the defendant. In *SEC v. Morgan Keegan & Co., Inc.*,[77] the Eleventh Circuit rejected a brokerage firm's argument that the SEC could not establish materiality based on statements made to individual customers that were not made generally to the public. The circuit court held, "This argument fails because the Supreme Court's materiality standard analyzes the 'total mix' of information available to a hypothetical reasonable investor, not just to the public at large." But in *SEC v. Goble*,[78] the same court found that false information about the financial condition of a brokerage firm was not material because it did not relate to an investment decision in securities, only the investor's choice of a broker. It stated, "We hold that a misrepresentation that would only influence an individual's choice of broker-dealers cannot form the basis for § 10(b) securities fraud liability."

In criminal prosecutions, materiality is an element of the offense, so a defendant can contest whether information was actually important to investors once it is shown that a misstatement or omission took place. The question is whether full disclosure of the information, the cornerstone of the federal securities laws, would have made any difference to a purchaser or seller of the securities allegedly defrauded. If not, then materiality has not been established and there is no violation of § 10(b) and Rule 10b–5.

Under the common law, the misstatement or omission had to involve a past or present fact, but courts have not adhered to that limitation and permit statements about future events to be the basis for securities fraud violations. A defendant can argue that a statement was not material because it only involved a matter of opinion, such as a prediction about a future event, and so was incapable of misleading investors. In *Virginia Bankshares, Inc. v. Sandberg*,[79] the Supreme Court found that statements of belief or opinion can be sufficiently factual to come within § 10(b) and Rule 10b–5 because "[s]uch statements are factual in two senses: as statements that the directors do act for the reasons given or hold the belief stated and as statements about the subject matter of the reason or belief expressed." The statements at issue were given in a disclosure document sent to minority shareholders in which the board stated in its proxy solicitation that an offer to buy their minority interest in a bank holding company provided a "high value" and a "fair price."

Not every statement about the future value of a company or its securities is necessarily material. For example, a district court stated that "vague and general statements of optimism constitute no more than puffery and are understood by reasonable investors as such" so they cannot be the basis for a securities fraud

---

[77] 678 F.3d 1233 (11th Cir. 2012).

[78] 682 F.3d 934 (11th Cir. 2012).

[79] 501 U.S. 1083 (1991).

violation.[80] Whether a statement is puffing or material is a matter for the jury, and courts rarely find a particular statement (or failure to disclose) to be immaterial as a matter of law. In *United States v. Skilling*,[81] the Fifth Circuit held that a jury could find statements made by a company's chief executive that one division had "uniquely strong franchises with sustainable high earnings power" and another was a "stable, high-growth business" were not mere puffery but could be found by a jury to be misstatements of material fact under *Virginia Bankshares* to support a securities fraud conviction.

In insider trading cases, the materiality of confidential information received in connection with trading is often judged by the impact of the information on a company's stock price once it was revealed. In *United States v. Mylett*,[82] the Second Circuit rejected the defendant's argument that information about a potential merger was not material under the probability-magnitude test, finding that "the sharp jump in NCR's stock price after a formal acquisition announcement was made suffices to support a finding that the event in this case was one of major magnitude."

It is often the case that there is information circulating in the market regarding a particular transaction or corporate development, and defendants often point to public reports as a basis to claim they did trade on material information. Whether additional nonpublic information from an inside source can be considered material depends on the reliability of the information and its specificity in creating assurances that an event will come to pass. In *United States v. Contorinis*,[83] the Second Circuit stated that the "trier of fact may find that information obtained from a particular insider, even if it mirrors rumors or press reports, is sufficiently more reliable, and, therefore, is material and nonpublic, because the insider tip alters the mix by confirming the rumor or reports." In upholding the conviction, the circuit court noted that a jury instruction should convey "that material, nonpublic information is information that either is not publicly available or is sufficiently more detailed and/or reliable than publicly available information to be deemed significant, in and of itself, by reasonable investors."

The materiality determination also involves the question of whether information is nonpublic. Once out in the market, information is assumed to be reflected within a very short period into the price of the stock, so that trading on it would not constitute securities fraud. In *Contorinis*, the Second Circuit pointed out that information is publicly available not only when it is reported in the media or contained in an SEC filing, but also "if it is known only by a few securities analysts or professional investors. This is so because their trading will set a share price incorporating such information." In *SEC v. Mayhew*,[84] the same court rejected a defendant's argument that significant media speculation about a potential acquisition of a company meant that a tip about management's consideration of an actual offer was neither confidential nor material. The Second Circuit held, "To a reasonable investor, this combination of new information, acquired privately, transformed the likelihood of a . . . merger from one

---

[80] S.E.C. v. Kearns, 691 F. Supp. 2d 601 (D.N.J. 2010).

[81] United States v. Skilling, 554 F.3d 529 (5th Cir. 2009), rev'd in part on other grounds 130 S.Ct. 2896 (2010).

[82] 97 F.3d 663 (2d Cir. 1996).

[83] 692 F.3d 136 (2d Cir. 2012).

[84] 121 F.3d 44 (2d Cir. 1997).

that was certainly possible at some future time to one that was highly probable quite soon.

D. Scienter

The third element for a securities fraud violation is proof of *scienter*, which means "a mental state embracing intent to deceive, manipulate, or defraud." In determining whether *scienter* is an element of a private securities fraud cause of action, the Supreme Court held in *Ernst & Ernst v. Hochfelder*[85] that "[w]hen a statute speaks so specifically in terms of manipulation and deception, and of implementing devices and contrivances—the commonly understood terminology of intentional wrongdoing—and when its history reflects no more expansive intent, we are quite unwilling to extend the scope of the statute to negligent conduct." In a subsequent case, *Aaron v. SEC*,[86] the Court extended *Hochfelder* to an SEC injunctive action, stating that "the rationale of *Hochfelder* ineluctably leads to the conclusion that scienter is an element of a violation of § 10(b) and Rule 10b–5, regardless of the identity of the plaintiff or the nature of the relief sought."

While the Court described *scienter* as requiring proof of an intent to manipulate or deceive, in *Hochfelder* it noted that "[i]n certain areas of the law recklessness is considered to be a form of intentional conduct for purposes of imposing liability for some act." The Court reserved decision on whether recklessness sufficed in both *Hochfelder* and *Aaron*, but most lower courts have recognized that recklessness can establish *scienter* for a civil securities fraud claim.[87] In private securities fraud cases, there is also a heightened pleading standard for *scienter*, under which a plaintiff is required to include sufficient facts giving rise to a "strong inference that the defendant acted with the required state of mind."[88]

The issue of what constitutes proof of *scienter* is largely subsumed in criminal prosecutions by the requirement of § 32 that the government prove the defendant acted willfully, or willfully and knowingly if the charge relates to a false statement in a filing with the SEC. While recklessness can establish *scienter* in a private or SEC civil injunctive action, it would not suffice to prove a defendant's criminal intent for a violation of § 10(b) and Rule 10b–5.

For a violation of § 17(a) of the Securities Act, *Aaron* applied the *scienter* requirement only to claims under subsection (a)(1), which prohibits anyone "to employ any device, scheme, or artifice to defraud." The Court explained that this provision "plainly evinces an intent on the part of Congress to proscribe only knowing or intentional misconduct" because "the terms 'device,' 'scheme,' and 'artifice' all connote knowing or intentional practices." Section 17(a)(2) prohibits conduct "to obtain money or property by means of any untrue statement of a material fact or any omission to state a material fact necessary in order to make the statements made, in light of the circumstances under which they were made, not misleading," which the Court found was "devoid of any suggestion whatsoever of a scienter requirement." Similarly,

---

[85] 425 U.S. 185 (1976).

[86] 446 U.S. 680 (1980).

[87] See Thomas Lee Hazen, The Law of Securities Regulation 6th Ed. § 12.8[3].

[88] 15 U.S.C. § 78u–4(b)(2).

§ 17(a)(3) makes it unlawful "to engage in any transaction, practice, or course of business which operates or would operate as a fraud or deceit upon the purchaser," language *Aaron* found "quite plainly focuses upon the *effect* of particular conduct on members of the investing public, rather than upon the culpability of the person responsible." Thus, a violation of these two provisions only requires proof of negligence, rather than *scienter*. As with prosecutions under the 1934 Act, § 24 of the 1933 Act requires that a defendant act willfully in order to be convicted for a criminal violation of any provision of § 17(a).

E.　"In Connection With"

Along with the common law fraud requirements, § 10(b) has a transactional element for a violation, requiring proof that the misstatement or omission of a material fact occurred "in connection with" the purchase or sale of a security. The Supreme Court has taken a rather lenient approach to this nexus requirement, essentially requiring that the underlying securities transactions bear some relationship to the fraud, but not that the wrongdoer actual participated in the transaction, or that the misstatement or omission related specifically to the purchase or sale.

In *Superintendent of Insurance v. Bankers Life & Casualty Co.,*[89] the Court rejected a claim that the defendant's conduct was not in connection with a purchase or sale of securities because it was not directly involved in the sale of treasury bonds alleged by the plaintiff to meet the requirements for a violation of § 10(b) and Rule 10b–5. The transaction involved a complex web of maneuvers by the purchasers of a subsidiary from its parent, so that in the end they diverted the subsidiary's assets to fund the transaction but made it appear that they had put up the money for the purchase. In rejecting the parent company's claim that it could not be sued for securities fraud because it was not involved with those who engaged in the financial shenanigans, the Court found that the subsidiary "suffered an injury as a result of deceptive practices *touching* its sale of securities as an investor," which was sufficient to bring the claim within the antifraud provision. It did not explain how close the transaction had to be to the alleged fraud to be "touching" it, and the language of *Bankers Life* clearly implied a very broad reading of the "in connection with" requirement.

That view was affirmed in the Court's subsequent decision on this issue in *SEC v. Zandford.*[90] The defendant was a securities broker who defrauded his client, an elderly father seeking to secure financial arrangements for his disabled daughter, by selling the securities in their account and then transferring the proceeds to his own account, an embezzlement. The SEC sued him for violating § 10(b) and Rule 10b–5 for fraud, and the lower court held that the "in connection with" element had not been met because there was no fraud in the defendant's sales of the securities in the customer's account, only his subsequent transfer of the money for personal use which did not involve any securities. The Supreme Court rejected that analysis, holding that "the SEC complaint describes a fraudulent scheme in which the securities transactions and breaches of fiduciary duty *coincide*. Those breaches were therefore 'in connection with' securities sales within the meaning of § 10(b)."

---

[89] 404 U.S. 6 (1971).

[90] 535 U.S. 813 (2002).

Zandford used "coincide" to describe the relationship between the material misstatement or omission, while *Bankers Life* referred to the "in connection with" element as requiring some "touching." Both terms connote significant flexibility for establishing this element in cases under § 10(b) and Rule 10b–5 because the violation need not specifically arise from the transfer of the securities so long as a purchase or sale of securities played at least some role in the overall fraudulent scheme. In *Zandford*, the Court found a sufficient connection between the securities sales and the fraud, stating:

> [E]ach sale was made to further respondent's fraudulent scheme; each was deceptive because it was neither authorized by, nor disclosed to, the Woods. With regard to the sales of shares in the Woods' mutual fund, respondent initiated these transactions by writing a check to himself from that account, knowing that redeeming the check would require the sale of securities.

As the Court explained in *Merrill Lynch v. Dabit*,[91] "Under our precedents, it is enough that the fraud alleged 'coincide' with a securities transaction—whether by the plaintiff or by someone else."

The determination of whether particular conduct is "in connection with" a purchase or sale is determined on a case-by-case basis.[92] As an element of the violation, the jury decides whether the evidence is sufficient to establish the conduct touched or coincided with the securities transaction. In *SEC v. Pirate Investor LLC*,[93] the Fourth Circuit identified four factors to consider to determine whether the fraud coincides or touches a purchase or sale of securities: "(1) whether a securities sale was necessary to the completion of the fraudulent scheme"; "(2) whether the parties' relationship was such that it would necessarily involve trading in securities"; "(3) whether the defendant intended to induce a securities transaction"; and, "(4) whether material misrepresentations were disseminated to the public in a medium upon which a reasonable investor would rely." The circuit court noted that these factors are "merely to guide the inquiry, and we do not presume to exclude other factors that could help distinguish between fraud in the securities industry and common law fraud that happens to involve securities." It found the defendant's conduct in disseminating a research report about a company, which would result in inflating its stock price which in turn would drive more investors to buy its reports, violated § 10(b) and Rule 10b–5 because "securities transactions helped Appellants to maximize the profitability of their scheme." Similarly, in *SEC v. Santos*,[94] the district court found that "Burns and Hollendoner allegedly made illegal payments to Santos to secure the City's investment business, invested the City money allocated to them by Santos, and made commissions on those investments. Burns and Hollendoner's alleged fraudulent payment scheme, thus, directly coincided with the security transactions made on behalf of the City."

---

[91] 547 U.S. 71 (2006).

[92] Semerenko v. Cendant Corp., 223 F.3d 165 (3d Cir. 2000).

[93] 580 F.3d 233 (4th Cir. 2009).

[94] 355 F. Supp. 2d 917 (N.D. Ill. 2003).

F. Purchase or Sale

The fraud must coincide or touch an actual purchase or sale of a security, and not just involve a misstatement or omission that discourages an investor from buying or selling. In *Blue Chip Stamps v. Manor Drug Stores*,[95] the Supreme Court rejected a fraud claim by potential investors alleging that the controlling owners of a company disseminated pessimistic information to discourage plaintiffs from buying shares as part of an antitrust settlement that required competitors be given an opportunity to invest in shares of a trading stamps corporation. The Court applied the so-called *Birnbaum* rule, a Second Circuit decision holding that "the plaintiff class in a Rule 10b–5 action was limited to actual purchasers and sellers."[96]

While the *Blue Chip* requirement limits the class of potential plaintiffs in private actions, it has only a modest impact on criminal and civil enforcement actions, requiring proof of some transaction in securities and not just a hypothetical harm to potential investors. In *SEC v. Goble*,[97] the Eleventh Circuit held that a sham transaction by a broker that listed a purchase of a mutual fund money market account so that the firm could obtain a loan did not meet the purchase or sale requirement. The circuit court concluded that "the alleged 'purchase' did not involve a change of ownership, an exchange of value, or a promise to purchase a security. And, recording a fake transaction in [the firm's]books had no effect on the broader securities market and would not impact an investor's decision to purchase a security."

G. Jurisdictional Requirements

Section 10(b) reaches transactions that involve "directly or indirectly, by the use of any means or instrumentality of interstate commerce of or the mails, or of any facility of any national securities exchange. . . . "[98] Similarly, § 17(a) proscribes "the use of any means or instruments of transportation or communication in interstate commerce or by use of the mails, directly or indirectly. . . ."[99] The link between any mailing or use of an instrumentality of interstate commerce and the underlying fraud requires only that there be some relationship between them, not that the mailing or use of an interstate instrumentality be crucial to the completion of the fraud. This is similar to the interpretation of the mailing and interstate wire elements of § 1341 and § 1343 that it be a step in completing the fraud (see §§ 4.8–9).

In *United States v. MacKay*,[100] the Tenth Circuit explained that "an accused need not carry out the mailing or use of an instrumentality of commerce. If he causes it to be carried out by setting forces in motion which foreseeably result in use of the mails, his action is sufficient." Even post-fraud mailings can be sufficient if they are designed to lull the victims or the SEC into not perceiving the violation. In *United States v. Ferguson*,[101] a district court rejected the defendants' argument that mailing a corporation's annual reports and making filings with the SEC could not constitute a

---

[95] 421 U.S. 723 (1975).

[96] Birnbaum v. Newport Steel Corp., 193 F.2d 461 (2d Cir. 1952).

[97] 682 F.3d 934 (11th Cir. 2012).

[98] 15 U.S.C. § 78j.

[99] 15 U.S.C. § 77q(a).

[100] 491 F.2d 616 (10th Cir. 1973).

[101] 478 F. Supp. 2d 220 (D. Conn. 2007).

sufficient use of the mails for securities fraud when the underlying transaction had occurred years earlier. The court explained:

> [T]he success of the allegedly fraudulent reinsurance transaction depended on AIG sending out its annual reports and mandatory SEC filings without any seeming irregularities. Without these mailings perpetuating the false loss reserves figures from 2000 and 2001, the value of the company would decline (the fear of which allegedly motivated the fraudulent transaction). Given the connection between these mailings and the underlying fraud, the mailings were sufficiently part of the fraudulent scheme to satisfy those elements of the mail fraud and securities fraud statutes.

Even intrastate conduct, such as a local telephone call, can be sufficient for federal jurisdiction so long as the instrumentality is part of the interstate system, such as highways or wire transmissions that can be used for interstate transportation and communication. In *United States v. Kunzman*,[102] the Tenth Circuit found sufficient evidence for jurisdiction under the federal securities laws based on the travel of victims into Colorado to provide the funds for the fraudulent scheme, stating that "[a]s long as the instrumentality used is itself an integral part of an interstate system, Congress may regulate intrastate activities involving the use of the instrumentality under the federal securities laws." The "in connection with" requirement for a violation of § 10(b) and Rule 10b–5 does not require proof that the mailing or use of an instrumentality of interstate commerce be related to the actual purchase or sale of the security, only that it be one part of the overall fraudulent scheme. In *S.E.C. v. Merrill Scott & Associates, Ltd.*,[103] a district court held, "The fraud or misrepresentation itself need not have been communicated over the telephone or through the mail, as long as the defendant's use of the telephone or mail furthered the fraudulent scheme."

H. Aiding and Abetting

In 1994, the Supreme Court's decision in *Central Bank of Denver, N.A. v. First Interstate Bank of Denver, N.A.*[104] found that private litigants could not allege liability for a violation of § 10(b) and Rule 10b–5 based on an aiding and abetting theory. Only those who were, in the Court's terminology, "primary violators" could be sued for damages. It was not clear whether *Central Bank* also limited the SEC's authority to pursue securities fraud actions based on an aiding and abetting theory. Congress resolved the issue in 1995 when it added § 20(e) to the 1934 Act to extend liability to "any person who knowingly provides substantial assistance to another in violation. . . . " There was a split in the circuit courts regarding whether the "knowing" requirement also included recklessness, much the same as *scienter* has been interpreted to include that type of conduct.[105]

In the Dodd–Frank Act, adopted in 2010, Congress clarified the question of the requisite intent for aiding and abetting liability to provide that "any person that knowingly or recklessly provides substantial assistance to another person . . . shall be

---

[102] 54 F.3d 1522 (10th Cir. 1995).

[103] 505 F. Supp. 2d 1193 (D. Utah 2007).

[104] 511 U.S. 164 (1994).

[105] Compare SEC v. Fehn, 97 F.3d 1276 (9th Cir. 1996) (requiring knowledge) with Graham v. S.E.C., 222 F.3d 994 (D.C. Cir. 2000) (knowledge or recklessness).

deemed to be in violation of such provision to the same extent as the person to whom such assistance is provided."[106] The same test for aiding and abetting liability in an SEC action applies to violations of the 1933 Act and those by investment advisers.[107] In criminal cases, a charge of aiding and abetting is governed by the standards under 18 U.S.C. § 2, which requires proof of an intent to provide assistance in the commission of a crime and the intent required for the target offense. Proof of recklessness would not suffice to establish criminal liability as an accomplice to securities fraud.

§ 5.5   DISCLOSURE OBLIGATIONS

Companies that issue securities to the public have a number of disclosure obligations on a continuing basis. It is not the case that a company must disclose all material information as soon as it receives (or develops) it, but many items must be disclosed at some point in time, which in some instances may be required immediately if the information will have a significant impact on a company. Any reporting of information must not be misleading or omit information a reasonable investor would consider important.

Section 13 of the 1934 Act contains many of the principle disclosure obligations imposed on companies and other investors, which are designed to further the goal of the federal securities laws to provide the public with adequate information to judge the quality of an investment. Among the disclosures required by § 13 are:

• Quarterly and annual reports by companies, including management's discussion and analysis of various issues and prospects for the firm and its financial statements;

• Disclosure by owners of more than 5% of a company's securities, or a class of its securities, of the source of the funds for the acquisition, the investors intention(s) in making the purchase, any plans for restructuring or selling the company, and any change in share ownership or the reason for the investment;

• Reports by institutional investors managing over $100 million and "large traders" that detail the types of investments held.[108]

The law requires companies to "disclose to the public on a rapid and current basis such additional information concerning material changes in the financial condition or operations of the issuer, in plain English, which . . . is necessary or useful for the protection of investors and in the public interest."[109] This continuous disclosure requirement means companies must constantly monitor the business and report to investors anything that will have a significant impact on its operations or financial position. The SEC also adopted Regulation FD to curtail a practice by companies of making selective disclosure to certain investors before unveiling information to the general public. Under the Rule, if a company discloses material nonpublic information to market professionals and sizeable holders of its securities, then it "must make public disclosure of that same information: (a) simultaneously (for intentional disclosures), or

---

[106] 15 U.S.C. § 78t(e).

[107] 15 U.S.C. § 77o(b) (1933 Act violations); 15 U.S.C. § 80b–9(f) (investment advisers).

[108] 15 U.S.C. § 78m.

[109] 15 U.S.C. § 78m(l)

(b) promptly (for non-intentional disclosures)."[110] The SEC defined "promptly" in the Rule to mean "as soon as reasonably practicable (but in no event after the later of 24 hours or the commencement of the next day's trading on the New York Stock Exchange) after a senior official of the issuer . . . learns that there has been a non-intentional disclosure. . . . " Certain types of financial firms that provide services to investors also have regular disclosure obligations, such as mutual funds and investment advisors.[111]

A fiduciary relationship imposes certain disclosure obligations on a person involved in a securities transaction. In *United States v. Skelly*,[112] the Second Circuit upheld the conviction of two brokers who engaged in a "pump-and-dump" scheme in which they artificially inflated the price of shares of a thinly-traded company in which they held a substantial interest and then sold out their shares by using high-pressure sales tactics without disclosing to their customers the profits from the transactions or the ownership position they held. The circuit court pointed out that "[b]ecause a registered representative is under no inherent duty to reveal his compensation, otherwise truthful statements made by him about the merits of a particular investment are not transformed into misleading 'half-truths' simply by the broker's failure to reveal that he is receiving added compensation for promoting a particular investment." In order to engage in a fraudulent transaction, the brokers had to breach a fiduciary duty, and "this relationship exists in situations in which a broker has discretionary authority over the customer's account, but we have recognized that particular factual circumstances may serve to create a fiduciary duty between a broker and his customer even in the absence of a discretionary account."

In *United States v. Wolfson*,[113] the same court explained that for a fraud charge against a broker for trades conducted in client accounts based on incomplete disclosure, '[I]t is well settled in this Circuit that the presence of a discretionary account automatically implies a general fiduciary duty between a broker and customer, but the absence of a discretionary account does not mean that no fiduciary duty exists."

§ 5.6 INSIDER TRADING

A. Generally

The usual description of insider trading is "purchasing or selling a security while in possession of material, non-public information."[114] It is a type of securities fraud, so the traditional elements of a material misstatement or omission made with *scienter* also apply, and they have been incorporated into this description. Judicial interpretations have added a significant gloss to the analysis, addressing potential liability for tipping another person who trades on the information and extending the prohibition to those with no direct connection to the issuer of the securities.

Individual investors not directly affiliated with a company or one of its advisers generally do not have any obligation to reveal information to the public about their

---

[110] 17 C.F.R. § 243.100(a).

[111] 15 U.S.C. § 80a–29 (mutual funds); 15 U.S.C. § 80b–7 (investment advisers).

[112] 442 F.3d 94 (2d Cir. 2006).

[113] 642 F.3d 293 (2d Cir. 2011).

[114] 15 U.S.C. § 78t–1(a).

investments except when the person receives confidential information and has an obligation not to trade for their own benefit. This is the basis for the insider trading prohibition under what is called the "abstain or disclose rule." Based on certain relationships, a person cannot trade in a stock while in possession of material nonpublic information about the company until it has been disclosed to the market, after which anyone can trade because the information would no longer be confidential.

While insider trading is a frequent basis for criminal and civil enforcement actions, with approximately 50 civil cases brought by the SEC each year, insider trading is not specifically identified as a type of securities fraud in § 10(b) and Rule 10b–5, which only address in broad terms deceptive devices and schemes. Instead, it is a judicially-developed doctrine that has been endorsed by Congress, which has provided a private right to action for contemporaneous traders to recover profits (or losses avoided) from insider trading.[115] Questions have been raised about the purpose served by the prohibition, and the SEC has resisted calls to define what constitutes insider trading, relying for the most part on judicial proceedings to shape the scope of the doctrine. It has issued rules to provide a framework for analyzing certain elements of the proscription, such as when trading is "on the basis of" inside information, but those do not provide a concrete definition of what does—and more importantly does not—constitute a violation.

B. Development of Insider Trading Law

State law remains the primary source of laws governing the internal operations of a corporation, imposing fiduciary duties on directors and officers to ensure they act in the best interests of the organization. Out of those fiduciary duties arose the first state prohibition on insider trading, which viewed misuse of corporate information as a type of fraud when an investor was misled into buying or selling the company's shares. The Supreme Court, in *Strong v. Repide*,[116] stated:

> [T]he ordinary relations between directors and shareholders in a business corporation are not of such a fiduciary nature as to make it the duty of a director to disclose to a shareholder the general knowledge which he may possess regarding the value of the shares of the company before he purchases any from a shareholder, yet there are cases where, by reason of the special facts, such duty exists.

This came to be known as the "special facts" or "special circumstances" rule that allowed for the person on the opposite side of the transaction to sue the corporate official for fraud. Not all states provided for such liability, however, finding that at least where the transaction did not involve face-to-face dealings there was no breach of duty in trading on confidential corporate information.[117] A derivative claim on behalf of the corporation against a director or officer for misuse of corporate information for personal gain can be brought as a breach of the duty of loyalty.[118]

---

[115] 15 U.S.C. § 78t–1.

[116] 213 U.S. 419 (1909).

[117] Goodwin v. Agassiz, 186 N.E. 659 (Mass. 1933).

[118] See Diamond v. Oreamuno, 248 N.E.2d 910 (N.Y. 1969), Brophy v. Cities Service Co., 70 A.2d 5 (Del. Ch. 1949).

Insider trading does not appear to have been considered by Congress as a form of fraud when it adopted § 10(b). There is a reference in the legislative history to directors and officers using confidential corporate information "to aid them in their market activities," this does not appear to be directed at insider trading so much as the manipulation of stock prices by pumping up demand while insiders dumped their shares on the market.[119] The only provision of the 1934 Act directly addressing trading by officers, directors, and 10% shareholders is § 16, which requires disclosure of purchases and sales and gives the company a claim on profits from certain transactions that occur within a six-month window.[120]

The first reported insider trading case was an SEC administrative enforcement action against a brokerage firm in *In the Matter of Cady, Roberts & Co.* in 1961.[121] A broker learned from an associate at the firm who was a director of a publicly-traded company that its board planned to reduce the dividend, which would cause the stock price to drop. The broker then directed accounts at the brokerage firm over which he held discretionary trading authority to sell the company's shares and put in short-sale orders before the information became public. The SEC concluded that the trading violated § 10(b) and Rule 10b–5, explaining:

> [I]nsiders must disclose material facts which are known to them by virtue of their position but which are not known to persons with whom they deal and which, if known, would affect their investment judgment. Failure to make disclosure in these circumstances constitutes a violation of the anti-fraud provisions. If, on the other hand, disclosure prior to effecting a purchase or sale would be improper or unrealistic under the circumstances, we believe the alternative is to forego the transaction.

This analysis become known as the "abstain or disclose" rule under which a person who possesses material nonpublic information may not trade until the information becomes publicly available to all investors, and therefore incorporated in to the stock price.

It was not clear whether *Cady, Roberts* applied beyond transactions by securities brokers until the Second Circuit's 1968 decision in *SEC v. Texas Gulf Sulphur Co.*,[122] the first broad insider trading enforcement case brought by the SEC against corporate officers and employees. The circuit court applied the "abstain or disclose" rule of *Cady, Roberts* to trading by insiders who learned about the company's massive ore strike in Canada and proceeded to purchase a number of shares and call options, betting that the share price would increase once information about the discovery became public. The Second Circuit explained the rationale for the insider trading prohibition as "based in policy on [the] justifiable expectation of the securities market place that all investors trading on impersonal exchanges have relatively equal access to material information." Applying this "parity of information" approach, the circuit court held that the insider trading prohibition reached

---

[119] Hearing on H.R. 7852 and H.R. 8720 Before the House Committee on Interstate and Foreign Commerce, 73d Cong., 2d Sess. 115 (1934).

[120] 15 U.S.C. § 78p.

[121] In the Matter of Cady, Roberts 7 Co., 40 S.E.C. 907 (1961).

[122] 401 F.2d 833 (2d Cir. 1968) (en banc).

anyone in possession of material inside information [who] must either disclose it to the investing public, or, if he is disabled from disclosing it in order to protect a corporate confidence, or he chooses not to do so, must abstain from trading in or recommending the securities concerned while such inside information remains undisclosed.

The focus of *Texas Gulf Sulphur* was on possession of the information, and the Second Circuit did not limit its analysis to corporate insiders, even though those were the only persons involved in the case. Under this approach, *any* person who comes into possession of material nonpublic information, regardless of the source, must abstain from trading on it or disclose it publicly.

C. *Chiarella*: The "Classical" Theory of Insider Trading

The Supreme Court first dealt with insider trading in *Chiarella v. United States*,[123] a criminal prosecution of an employee of a financial printer working on behalf of investment bankers. Chiarella was able to decipher the identities of the targets of takeover offers before an announcement of the transaction, after which the company's stock would increase. His employer had no direct relationship with the targets of the offers, providing its services to the offeror in printing the documents that would be filed in connection with the offer. The defendant made approximately $30,000 from the trading, and he settled a civil enforcement action with the SEC in which he returned his profits. He was then charged and convicted on 17 counts of violating § 10(b) and Rule 10b–5.

The Court began by citing the SEC's decision in *Cady, Roberts*, for the requirement that "a corporate insider must abstain from trading in the shares of his corporation unless he has first disclosed all material inside information known to him," noting that "the relationship between a corporate insider and the stockholders of his corporation gives rise to a disclosure obligation is not a novel twist of the law." In explaining why this violated § 10(b), the Court found that "one who fails to disclose material information prior to the consummation of a transaction commits fraud only when he is under a duty to do so." Thus, "a purchaser of stock who has no duty to a prospective seller because he is neither an insider nor a fiduciary has been held to have no obligation to reveal material facts."

Putting the emphasis on the disclosure duty was consistent with the Court's earlier decision in *Santa Fe Industries v. Green*, in which it held that a mere breach of fiduciary duty was insufficient to establish a violation of § 10(b) absent a misstatement or omission. The failure to disclose material nonpublic information prior to trading could only be a fraud when "such liability is premised upon a duty to disclose arising from a *relationship of trust and confidence* between parties to a transaction." In reviewing the conviction, the Court determined that the defendant's "use of that information was not a fraud under § 10(b) unless he was subject to an affirmative duty to disclose it before trading." Because he did not work for the targets of the offers, or have any connection to those companies, he did not defraud their investors by purchasing the company's shares while in possession of material nonpublic information.

---

[123] 445 U.S. 222 (1980).

By requiring a pre-existing "relationship of trust and confidence" before liability could attach for insider trading, the Court rejected the parity of information approach of the Second Circuit in *Texas Gulf Sulphur* that would impose liability just upon possession of information and subsequent trading without disclosure. It explained that

> the element required to make silence fraudulent—a duty to disclose—is absent in this case. No duty could arise from petitioner's relationship with the sellers of the target company's securities, for petitioner had no prior dealings with them. He was not their agent, he was not a fiduciary, he was not a person in whom the sellers had placed their trust and confidence. He was, in fact, a complete stranger who dealt with the sellers only through impersonal market transactions.

Thus, the Court concluded that "neither the Congress nor the Commission ever has adopted a parity-of-information rule," and it was unwilling to find one in § 10(b) absent explicit evidence of congressional intent that the provision provided such a broad prohibition on the use of material nonpublic information. It overturned the conviction, stating "[w]e hold that a duty to disclose under § 10(b) does not arise from the mere possession of nonpublic market information."

The Court rejected an alternative argument offered by the government that the defendant breached a duty owed to the companies that used the printer for whom he worked by misusing information he received in his job for personal gain. This approach, which has come to be known as the "misappropriation theory" of liability for insider trading, had not been offered to the jury as a basis for convicting the defendant, so it could not be a ground for upholding the conviction. The Court noted that "we will not speculate upon whether such a duty exists, whether it has been breached, or whether such a breach constitutes a violation of § 10(b)." Chief Justice Burger, in a dissenting opinion, would have affirmed the conviction under the theory that "a person who has misappropriated nonpublic information has an absolute duty to disclose that information or to refrain from trading."

The "relationship of trust and confidence" referred to in *Chiarella* is often described as a "fiduciary duty." The common law recognizes certain legal relationships as imposing a fiduciary obligation on a person, such as the executor of an estate, an attorney, or a corporate officer or director. The Supreme Court did not simply adopt state common law, however, instead creating a special category under the federal securities laws of relationships that can satisfy the requirement for imposing a duty sufficient to trigger the abstain-or-disclose rule when the person traded on material nonpublic information. Thus, a corporate employee who is neither a director nor officer of a company is considered to have the requisite relationship to come within *Chiarella's* requirement. For example, in *SEC v. Texas Gulf Sulphur*,[124] the defendants included company geologists, an engineer, and a lawyer.

In *Dirks v. SEC*,[125] the Supreme Court recognized that not just actual corporate insiders, like employees, have the requisite relationship of trust and confidence, expanding the category of those subject to the abstain-or-disclose rule to include the following:

---

[124] 401 F.2d 833 (2d Cir. 1968).

[125] 463 U.S. 646 (1983).

Under certain circumstances, such as where corporate information is revealed legitimately to an underwriter, accountant, lawyer, or consultant working for the corporation, these outsiders may become fiduciaries of the shareholders. The basis for recognizing this fiduciary duty is not simply that such persons acquired nonpublic corporate information, but rather that they have entered into a special confidential relationship in the conduct of the business of the enterprise and are given access to information solely for corporate purposes . . . For such a duty to be imposed, however, the corporation must expect the outsider to keep the disclosed nonpublic information confidential, and the relationship at least must imply such a duty.

Often referred to as "temporary insiders," these outside advisers and independent contractors acting on behalf of the corporation are treated as an extension of it, so the same obligation to abstain from trading prior to disclosure of material nonpublic information also applies to those who act on behalf of a company.

The lower courts have not been consistent about whether a person who receives confidential information from a company and then trades on it might become a temporary insider because of the relationship through which the confidential information was disclosed. In *SEC v. Lund*,[126] a district court found that an officer of a company approached by the chief executive of another company about a potential investment by his company in a joint venture violated § 10(b) and Rule 10b–5 when he bought shares in the other company, even though he had no other relationship to it aside from learning about the project. The district court held that the defendant "knew or should have known that the information he received was confidential and that it had been disclosed to him solely for legitimate corporate purposes." In *Moss v. Morgan Stanley Inc.*,[127] on the other hand, the Second Circuit found that information provided by a target of an offer to the investment adviser for the offering company did not create the requisite relationship despite the receipt of confidential information that was subsequently used to profit from buying shares in the target.

D. *O'Hagan*: The Misappropriation Theory

Chiarella opened a substantial loophole in the application of § 10(b) and Rule 10b–5 to insider trading because only those with a direct relationship to the company whose shares were traded could be charged with securities fraud. Those in a position like Chiarella, who were unaffiliated with the company whose securities they traded, were immune from prosecution because the transactions were in the target of an offer, thus creating an incentive to limit trading to companies to whom the person had no pre-existing relationship of trust and confidence. In *SEC v. Clark*,[128] the Ninth Circuit explained that "the classical theory does not extend to trading on material nonpublic information by 'outsiders,' *i.e.* persons who are neither insiders of the companies whose shares are being traded, nor tippees of such insiders."

To address this gap in the law, the Department of Justice and the SEC brought cases under the misappropriation theory first advanced in *Chiarella*. To make it

---

[126] 570 F.Supp. 1397 (C.D. Cal. 1983).

[127] 719 F.2d 5 (2d Cir. 1983).

[128] 915 F.2d 439 (9th Cir. 1990).

consonant with the Supreme Court's emphasis on the breach of a relationship of trust and confidence as the prerequisite for fraud, the focus was on finding a relationship in which information was transmitted with the expectation of maintaining its confidentiality, so that the person's subsequent trading would violate that duty even though there was no direct relationship with the shareholders of the corporation whose securities were bought or sold.

In *United States v. Newman*,[129] the Second Circuit affirmed the insider trading conviction of an investment banker who bought shares in companies that were the intended targets of offers by the firm's clients, despite the absence of any relationship with the targets' shareholders. The circuit court held, "[D]eceitful misappropriation of confidential information by a fiduciary, whether described as theft, conversion, or breach of trust, has consistently been held to be unlawful . . . Appellee would have had to be most ingenuous to believe that Congress intended to establish a less rigorous code of conduct under the Securities Acts." Under this analysis, it was the breach of duty owed to the holder of the information, not the company whose securities were traded, that created the basis for liability for securities fraud. In *SEC v. Materia*,[130] the Second Circuit upheld under the misappropriation theory a lower court's finding of a violation of § 10(b) and Rule 10b–5 in a civil enforcement action against a printer who deciphered the identities of targets of offers, the exact same circumstances that were rejected in *Chiarella*.

The misappropriation theory first reached the Supreme Court in *Carpenter v. United States*[131] in 1987. A reporter for the *Wall Street Journal* passed along information about companies that he was going to discuss in future columns to others, who then traded in advance of the publication of his articles. The published stories usually had an impact on the stock price of the companies discussed, and the defendants made profits of almost $700,000 on their trading. The Court noted that "[t]he official policy and practice at the Journal was that prior to publication, the contents of the column were the Journal's confidential information." The defendants were convicted for both securities and wire fraud violations. While the Court upheld the wire fraud convictions, it was evenly divided on the securities fraud counts and so did not reach the defense argument that the misappropriation theory was an impermissible extension of liability under § 10(b) and Rule 10b–5.

The Seventh and Ninth Circuits followed the lead of the Second Circuit in adopting the misappropriation theory,[132] but it was later rejected by the Fourth and Eighth Circuits, creating a split. In *United States v. Bryan*,[133] the Fourth Circuit held, "We conclude that neither the language of section 10(b), Rule 10b–5, the Supreme Court authority interpreting these provisions, nor the purpose of these securities fraud prohibitions, will support convictions resting on the particular theory of misappropriation adopted by our sister circuits." In *United States v. O'Hagan*,[134] the Eighth Circuit found that "contrary to § 10(b)'s explicit requirements, the

---

[129] 664 F.2d 12 (2d Cir. 1981).

[130] 745 F.2d 197 (2d Cir. 1984).

[131] 484 U.S. 19 (1987).

[132] See SEC v. Cherif, 933 F.2d 403 (7th Cir. 1991); SEC v. Clark, 915 F.2d 439 (9th Cir. 1990).

[133] 58 F.3d 933 (4th Cir. 1995).

[134] 92 F.3d 612 (8th Cir. 1996), rev'd 521 U.S. 642 (1997).

misappropriation theory does not require 'deception,' and, even assuming that it does, it renders nugatory the requirement that the 'deception' be 'in connection with the purchase or sale of any security.'" The Supreme Court granted certiorari in *O'Hagan* to resolve the question that remained open since *Carpenter* regarding whether the misappropriation theory constituted fraud under § 10(b) and Rule 10b–5.

O'Hagan was a partner in a law firm retained by a foreign company to advise it on a possible tender offer for the shares of a rival food producer. Although he was not involved in representing the client, O'Hagan obtained information about the potential transaction and purchased call options and stock in the target of the offer. Although his law firm withdrew from representing the offeror a short time later, O'Hagan held on to the securities he purchased, and after announcement of the offer he sold them for a profit of approximately $4.3 million. One reason why he bought the securities was that he had been misusing funds from case settlements of his clients, which later resulted in his conviction for theft in state court, and needed the money to cover up his conduct.[135] He was charged in a 57–count indictment in federal court with mail fraud, securities fraud, and money laundering.

Under *Chiarella*'s classical theory of insider trading, O'Hagan could not have been charged with a violation of § 10(b) and Rule 10b–5 because he did not have a relationship of trust and confidence with the shareholders of the target when his firm only represented the potential offeror. In upholding the securities fraud convictions as a proper application of the prohibition on any "manipulative or deceptive device," the Supreme Court noted the incongruity if liability were limited solely to *Chiarella*'s analysis because "it makes scant sense to hold a lawyer like O'Hagan a § 10(b) violator if he works for a law firm representing the target of a tender offer, but not if he works for a law firm representing the bidder."

The Court explained the application of the misappropriation theory this way, quoting with approval from the government's brief:

> The "misappropriation theory" holds that a person commits fraud "in connection with" a securities transaction, and thereby violates § 10(b) and Rule 10b–5, when he misappropriates confidential information for securities trading purposes, in breach of a duty owed to the source of the information. See Brief for United States 14. Under this theory, a fiduciary's undisclosed, self-serving use of a principal's information to purchase or sell securities, in breach of a duty of loyalty and confidentiality, defrauds the principal of the exclusive use of that information. In lieu of premising liability on a fiduciary relationship between company insider and purchaser or seller of the company's stock, the misappropriation theory premises liability on a fiduciary-turned-trader's deception of those who entrusted him with access to confidential information.

The Court stated that the classical and misappropriation theories are "complementary," noting that *Chiarella* "targets a corporate insider's breach of duty to shareholders with whom the insider transacts; the misappropriation theory outlaws trading on the basis of nonpublic information by a corporate 'outsider' in breach of a

---

[135] State v. O'Hagan, 474 N.W.2d 613 (Minn. Ct. App. 1991). O'Hagan received a 30–month prison term for the theft conviction.

duty owed not to a trading party, but to the source of the information." Thus, the randomness of who the person received information from by means of the fiduciary relationship required for liability is eliminated because *any* breach of a duty of trust and confidence can be sufficient to trigger liability for trading on confidential information.

The misappropriation theory is a type of fraud in which "[d]eception through nondisclosure is central" to it because a defendant like O'Hagan did not disclose his misuse of the confidential information for personal gain. The Court found this analysis was consistent with the requirement outlined in *Santa Fe* that there be a misstatement or omission to trigger liability under § 10(b) for a deception. This means the party controlling the confidential information, who is owed the duty of trust and confidence, is the victim of the fraud, and not the person on the other side of the transaction or— more broadly—the securities market. In *SEC v. Rocklage*,[136] the First Circuit stated that the misappropriation theory "is based on deception of the source of the information, rather than on deception of the shareholders; it is that deception which brings this trading within the statutory language."

The misuse of confidential information only violates § 10(b) and Rule 10b–5 when the trading occurs, not when the information is received. The Court stated that the "in connection with" requirement "is satisfied because the fiduciary's fraud is consummated, not when the fiduciary gains the confidential information, but when, without disclosure to his principal, he uses the information to purchase or sell securities. The securities transaction and the breach of duty thus coincide." Thus, there are two steps to the misappropriation analysis: (1) gaining the confidential information from a person owed a fiduciary duty; and (2) the violation of that duty when the trading takes place while in possession of the information. The victim of the fraud is the person deprived of the confidential information, much like the wire fraud in *Carpenter* was a theft of the newspaper's intangible property through misuse of the information for personal gain.

This analysis led the Court to recognize an interesting limitation to the misappropriation theory:

> [F]ull disclosure forecloses liability under the misappropriation theory: Because the deception essential to the misappropriation theory involves feigning fidelity to the source of information, if the fiduciary discloses to the source that he plans to trade on the nonpublic information, there is no "deceptive device" and thus no § 10(b) violation—although the fiduciary-turned-trader may remain liable under state law for breach of a duty of loyalty.

Under this approach, disclosure could "cure" any securities violation because the party owed the fiduciary duty would not have been deceived, the prerequisite for a violation of § 10(b) and Rule 10b–5. Professor Donna Nagy labeled this person the "brazen fiduciary" because the person may not be authorized to trade on confidential information but does so anyway by disclosing the intended personal use of the information, which may violate other laws or private agreements but is not securities

---

[136] 470 F.3d 1 (1st Cir. 2006).

fraud.[137] This limitation on the misappropriation theory does not apply to the classical theory of insider trading liability established by *Chiarella*, which is premised on a breach of a duty owed to the shareholders of the company whose securities are traded.

One reason for the Court's finding that disclosure could remove the case from the proscription of § 10(b) would be the availability of other remedies to the principal to prevent, or recover damages for, improper use of confidential information. Thus, disclosure could negate any deception even though the trading might cause another legal violation. In *SEC v. Rocklage*, however, the First Circuit took a narrow view of this limitation on the misappropriation theory. The circuit court found that a wife's conduct in obtaining information from her husband and then tipping her brother was deceptive within the meaning of the misappropriation theory even though she told her husband about her intention to disclose the information in advance. The circuit court explained:

> In light of her disclosure to her husband, Mrs. Rocklage's mechanism for "distributing" the information to her brother may or may not have been rendered non-deceptive by her stated intention to tip. But because of the way in which Mrs. Rocklage first acquired this information, her overall scheme was still deceptive: it had as part of it at least one deceptive device. Thus as a matter of the facts alleged in the complaint, and taking all facts and inferences in favor of the plaintiff, a § 10(b) claim is stated.

In *O'Hagan*, the Supreme Court rejected the defendant's argument that the misappropriation theory was too indefinite to permit criminal liability to be imposed. The Court referenced two important limitations on the application of § 10(b) and Rule 10b–5 to insider trading that obviated any claim of vagueness: first, "the theory is limited to those who breach a recognized duty"; and, second, a criminal prosecution requires proof the defendant acted "willfully," meaning there would be evidence of a "culpable intent" to overcome any claim that imposition of criminal liability would be unjust by reaching those with an innocent mind. The attorney-client relationship at issue in *O'Hagan* is one commonly recognized in the law as imposing the highest duty of trust and confidence, so the Court did not explain what it meant by a "recognized duty" or whether it was looking to federal or state law to define when such a duty exists for liability for insider trading.

Some relationships clearly meet the requirement to establish liability for misuse of confidential information gained through the relationship. In *Carpenter*, the employer-employee relation was sufficient for liability in the Second Circuit's decision. The Ninth Circuit similarly applied the misappropriation theory to the president of an American subsidiary of a foreign corporation who traded in advance of disclosure that the parent was going to acquire another company.[138] In *United States v. Libera*,[139] the Second Circuit found that an employee of a printing company who took an advance copy of *BusinessWeek* magazine prior to its release and passed it on to others so they could trade on the stocks discussed in it was a sufficient breach for insider trading

---

[137] Donna M. Nagy, Reframing the Misappropriation Theory of Insider Trading Liability: A Post–O'Hagan Suggestion, 59 Ohio St. L.J. 1223 (1998).

[138] SEC v. Clark, 915 F.2d 439 (9th Cir. 1990).

[139] 989 F.2d 596 (2d Cir. 1993).

liability when the printer and magazine publisher had explicit policies prohibiting removal of the magazine prior to its public release.

The Seventh Circuit in *SEC v. Cherif*[140] found the employer-employee relationship continued even after its termination when the former employee of a bank used a passcard to enter its offices and obtain information about pending undisclosed corporate transactions. The breach was not the misuse of the confidential deal information, but instead the misuse of knowledge about how to enter the former employer's premises and where to obtain the information about transactions, in violation of an obligation "to protect any confidential information entrusted to him by his employer during his employment . . . [and] to continue to protect such information after his termination."

The fiduciary duty need not be owed directly to the original source of the confidential information, and the misappropriation theory applies so long as the confidential information is used to trade in breach of *a* duty of trust and confidence owed by the defendant. In *SEC v. Talbot*,[141] the defendant was a director of Fidelity National, which owned 10% of the shares of another company, Lending Tree, considering whether to put itself up for sale. Lending Tree informed Fidelity National about its plans because of that company's large ownership stake, and the defendant learned of the transaction in his role as a corporate director, although there was no statement that the information should be kept confidential. The defendant then bought shares in Lending Tree, and the district court granted his motion to dismiss the complaint because he did not have any fiduciary relationship with Lending Tree. The Ninth Circuit reversed, holding that "[t]he district court misinterpreted the misappropriation theory as requiring that the duty of confidentiality be owed to the 'originating source' of the information. *O'Hagan* stated quite clearly that the duty must be owed only to the 'source'; we decline to read an 'originating source' requirement into *O'Hagan*."

In *United States v. Willis*,[142] a pre-*O'Hagan* district court decision, the defendant was a psychiatrist who learned information from his patient about a potential offer by her husband's company that, if successful, would result in their moving to another city. The court rejected the defendant's motion to dismiss on the ground that there was no breach of a duty to investors, holding that "the only significant relationship for purposes of the misappropriation theory is the relationship between the misappropriator and the person to whom he owes an obligation of confidentiality."

The more difficult question is determining what other relationships entail a duty of trust and confidence that can be a basis for insider trading liability based on the misappropriation theory. *United States v. Chestman*,[143] an en banc Second Circuit decision issued before *O'Hagan*, set forth the factors for assessing whether a relationship of trust and confidence existed that would be sufficient to be the basis for liability under § 10(b) and Rule 10b–5 if it were breached by use of confidential information in trading. *Chestman* involved information a husband received from his

---

[140] 933 F.2d 403 (7th Cir. 1991).

[141] 530 F.3d 1085 (9th Cir. 2008).

[142] 778 F.Supp. 205 (S.D.N.Y. 1991).

[143] 947 F.2d 551 (2d Cir. 1991).

wife—whose family controlled a company that was going to be purchased—and then bought shares for himself and tipped another defendant, a stock broker, who traded in advance of its disclosure. He was admonished not to disclose the information to others, which he agreed to do but proceeded to trade on his own behalf and tipped the broker. The circuit court described what constitutes the requisite relationship for the misappropriation theory:

> A fiduciary relationship involves discretionary authority and dependency: One person depends on another—the fiduciary—to serve his interests. In relying on a fiduciary to act for his benefit, the beneficiary of the relationship may entrust the fiduciary with custody over property of one sort or another. Because the fiduciary obtains access to this property to serve the ends of the fiduciary relationship, he becomes duty-bound not to appropriate the property for his own use.

The Second Circuit held that the marital relationship alone did not rise to the level of being a fiduciary one that could be the basis for liability for insider trading, finding that "[defendant]'s status as [wife]'s husband could not itself establish fiduciary status."

The Second Circuit also rejected the government's argument that the husband agreed not to disclose the information. It noted that "[i]n the absence of evidence of an explicit acceptance by [husband] of a duty of confidentiality, the context of the disclosure takes on special import. While acceptance may be implied, it must be implied from a pre-existing fiduciary-like relationship between the parties." Thus, simply entrusting another person with confidential information would not create the requisite duty of trust and confidence. In *United States v. Falcone*,[144] the Second Circuit stated:

> [A] fiduciary duty cannot be imposed unilaterally by entrusting a person with confidential information, and ... a fiduciary relationship, or its functional equivalent, exists only where there is explicit acceptance of a duty of confidentiality or where such acceptance may be implied from a similar relationship of trust and confidence between the parties.

In *United States v. Reed*,[145] decided before *Chestman*, a district court found the requisite duty of confidentiality in a situation in which a father and son routinely exchanged confidential business information, such that there developed the relationship of trust and confidence that went beyond just the typical parent-child relation. In *Chestman*, the Second Circuit restated the holding in *Reed* to reach the situation in which "the repeated disclosure of business secrets between family members may substitute for a factual finding of dependence and influence and thereby sustain a finding of the functional equivalent of a fiduciary relationship."

The Eleventh Circuit disagreed with *Chestman*'s narrower reading of the relationship between spouses that can form the basis for the duty of trust and

---

[144] 257 F.3d 226 (2nd Cir. 2001)

[145] 601 F.Supp. 685 (S.D.N.Y. 1985).

confidence, finding that an expectation of confidentiality was sufficient. In *SEC v. Yun*,[146] the circuit court held:

> [A] spouse who trades in breach of a reasonable and legitimate expectation of confidentiality held by the other spouse sufficiently subjects the former to insider trading liability. If the SEC can prove that the husband and wife had a history or practice of sharing business confidences, and those confidences generally were maintained by the spouse receiving the information, then in most instances the conveying spouse would have a reasonable expectation of confidentiality such that the breach of the expectation would suffice to yield insider trading liability. Of course, a breach of an agreement to maintain business confidences would also suffice.

Two district court opinions, relying on *Chestman*, concluded that the government could not establish the requisite duty under circumstances that did not involve familial relationships. In *United States v. Kim*,[147] the court dismissed insider trading charges against a defendant who learned about an impending transaction when the president of the company could not attend a meeting of the Young Presidents Organization. It found that the relationship among the members of the organization, which was a type of social club, "was not characterized by any measure of superiority, control, or dominance. It was not the functional equivalent of a fiduciary relationship. While the rules of the club may have forbid defendant's actions, the federal securities laws—at least in this instance—did not."

In *United States v. Cassese*,[148] the defendant had negotiated on behalf of his company for it to be acquired by another corporation, but then learned the transactions would not occur when the chief executive of the other corporation (Karmanos) said it would be acquiring a different company. The defendant bought shares in the target of the acquisition before the announcement of the deal. In dismissing the insider trading charge, the court found no evidence of any fiduciary-like relationship between executives who were actually competitors, and "thus not inherent fiduciaries, but rather potential arms-length business partners . . . This is very far from a relationship marked by 'de facto control' and 'dominance' or entailing 'discretionary authority and dependency.'"

In *SEC v. Kornman*,[149] on the other hand, a district court rejected a motion to dismiss a complaint alleging that a tax and estate planner who learned confidential information from two clients and traded on it did not have a duty of trust and confidence with the clients. Distinguishing *Chestman* and *Kim*, the court found that "Kornman possessed superior knowledge as to the subject matter of tax and estate-planning [which] may serve as an indicator that a duty of trust and confidence had developed between Kornman and the two executives." In *SEC v. Kirch*,[150] a district court distinguished the organization in *Kim* from one involving industry executives that called "for imparting information of a sensitive and confidential nature, the

---

[146] 327 F.3d 1263 (11th Cir. 2003).

[147] 184 F.Supp.2d 1006 (N.D. Cal. 2002).

[148] 273 F.Supp.2d 481 (S.D.N.Y. 2003).

[149] 391 F.Supp.2d 477 (N.D. Tex. 2005).

[150] 263 F. Supp. 2d 1144 (N.D. Ill. 2003).

Roundtable and its members had an express policy and understanding that such matters were indeed to be kept confidential." The court found that the defendant had a duty of trust and confidence regarding information received through the organization sufficient for insider trading liability.

After *O'Hagan*, the SEC issued Rule 10b5–2[151] to expand the framework for establishing the duty sufficient for liability under the misappropriation theory, moving beyond the more narrow view offered in *Chestman* that focused on "discretionary authority and dependency." In a release accompanying its proposed rule, the SEC stated:

> In our view, however, the *Chestman* majority's approach does not fully recognize the degree to which parties to close family and personal relationships have reasonable and legitimate expectations of confidentiality in their communications. For this reason, we believe the *Chestman* majority view does not sufficiently protect investors and the securities markets from the misappropriation and resulting misuse of inside information.[152]

Rule 10b5–2(b) provides that a "duty of trust and confidence" exists in the following non-exclusive list of circumstances:

> (1) Whenever a person agrees to maintain information in confidence;
>
> (2) Whenever the person communicating the material nonpublic information and the person to whom it is communicated have a history, pattern, or practice of sharing confidences, such that the recipient of the information knows or reasonably should know that the person communicating the material nonpublic information expects that the recipient will maintain its confidentiality; or
>
> (3) Whenever a person receives or obtains material nonpublic information from his or her spouse, parent, child, or sibling; provided, however, that the person receiving or obtaining the information may demonstrate that no duty of trust or confidence existed with respect to the information, by establishing that he or she neither knew nor reasonably should have known that the person who was the source of the information expected that the person would keep the information confidential, because of the parties' history, pattern, or practice of sharing and maintaining confidences, and because there was no agreement or understanding to maintain the confidentiality of the information.

Rule 10b5–2(b)(3) establishes a familial relationship as sufficient for insider trading liability, unless the person trading (or tipping) can establish the absence of any expectation of confidentiality by the family member communicating the information. This changes the analysis by putting the onus on the trading party to demonstrate there was no breach of the duty, rather than placing the burden on the government to show that the family relationship included an understanding that business information

---

[151] 17 C.F.R. § 240.10b5–2.

[152] Selective Disclosure and Insider Trading, 1999 WL 1217849 (SEC Release Nos. 33–7787, 34–42259, and IC–24,209) (Dec. 20, 1999).

received in that circumstance would remain confidential to establish the requisite duty. Whether this change in the burden of proof for an element of a § 10(b) and Rule 10b–5 violation would be proper in a criminal prosecution under established principles of due process, which places the burden on the government beyond a reasonable doubt, has not been decided by any courts. In *United States v. Corbin*,[153] a district court concluded "that the affirmative defense provided in Rule 10b5–2(b)(3) does not shift from the Government its heavy burden to prove each element of illicit insider trading beyond a reasonable doubt at trial and thus does not render the statute unconstitutional."

The first two circumstances outlined in Rule 10b5–2(b) go beyond *Chestman* to deal with the situation in which the recipient is asked to maintain the confidentiality of information, or there is a "history, pattern, or practice of sharing confidences" such that the recipient knew or should have known of an expectation of confidentiality when information is shared. This type of arrangement is not dependent on a pre-existing fiduciary relationship between the parties to the information, and can be created among strangers or in an arms-length business transaction. The agreement or course of conduct establishes the scope of the duty of trust and confidence, not evidence of a particular relationship between the parties, such as attorney-client, employer-employee, or others seen in insider trading cases. In *Corbin*, the district court rejected a defendant's contention that Rule 10b5–2(b) was unconstitutional because it did not involve a "manipulative or deceptive device" within the meaning of § 10(b), finding:

> [T]he SEC's exercise of its rulemaking authority to promulgate Rule 10b5–2 under § 10(b) is far from arbitrary, capricious, or contrary to § 10(b). Rather, it was buttressed by a thorough and careful consideration—one that far surpasses mere reasonableness—of the ends of § 10(b), the state of the current insider trading case law which included Supreme Court and Second Circuit decisions, and the need to protect investors and the market generally.

In *SEC v. Cuban*,[154] the Fifth Circuit found that an agreement not to trade could be sufficient to establish the duty of trust and confidence required for liability under the misappropriation theory. The defendant, a well-known investor who also owns a professional basketball team, owned a large stake in a company that was struggling financially. The company's chief executive informed the defendant that it planned to sell a block of its shares in a PIPE (private investment in public equity) transaction, which usually results in a significant drop in the stock price because of the market's perception that this is a desperate financial move. The defendant objected to the transaction, and according to the SEC's complaint he agreed to keep the information confidential. A short time later, he sold his shares, thereby avoiding a $750,000 loss once the PIPE transaction became public and the stock price dropped. The district court dismissed the complaint on the ground that an agreement to maintain the confidentiality of information without a concurrent commitment not to trade the shares was insufficient to establish the requisite duty for insider trading liability, and there was insufficient evidence to establish an agreement not to sell.

The Fifth Circuit reversed the dismissal, finding that the pleadings sufficiently alleged at least an implicit agreement not to trade as a condition for receiving the

---

[153] 729 F.Supp.2d 607 (S.D.N.Y. 2010).

[154] 620 F.3d 551 (5th Cir. 2010).

details of the PIPE transaction. The circuit court found that "[t]he allegations, taken in their entirety, provide more than a plausible basis to find that the understanding between the CEO and Cuban was that he was not to trade, that it was more than a simple confidentiality agreement." Importantly, liability under the misappropriation theory was premised on an agreement to maintain confidentiality *and* not trade on the information for personal gain, which is more than what Rule 10b5–2(b)(1)–(2) requires. *Cuban* noted that the agreement not to trade did not have to be explicit, which reflects *O'Hagan*'s focus on the trading as triggering the breach of fiduciary duty required for liability under § 10(b) and Rule 10b–5 and not just acquisition of the confidential information. The Fifth Circuit's recognition of the requirements for a confidentiality agreement to form the basis for a duty of trust and confidence is a sensible application of *O'Hagan* that premises liability for fraud on the trade.

E. *Dirks*: Tipper/Tippee Liability

In *Dirks v. SEC*,[155] decided shortly after *Chiarella*, the Supreme Court dealt with the situation in which an insider disclosed material nonpublic information to another person, who then traded on the information. The Court analyzed the requirements for establishing a violation of § 10(b) and Rule 10b–5 for the tipper, who provided the information, and the tippee who traded on it, and perhaps tipped others about the information before its disclosure so they could profit (or avoid losses).

Dirks was an analyst at a brokerage firm who received information from an officer at Equity Funding of America, a large financial firm, that the company was engaging in significant fraudulent practices and was on the verge of collapse. Dirks investigated further and determined that the information was true. He informed others at his firm about his findings, and they sold Equity Funding shares in their client accounts, avoiding significant losses when the truth about its precarious financial situation emerged, which ultimately led to the company's collapse in one of the largest bankruptcies at the time. The SEC pursued an administrative enforcement action against Dirks for aiding and abetting violations of the antifraud provision by using inside information he had received as a tip and then disclosing it to others in his firm who benefited.[156] The SEC found him in violation of § 17(a) of the 1933 Act and § 10(b) of the 1934 Act, and imposed a censure on him, recognizing that he helped expose a significant fraud that the SEC itself had failed to uncover—shades of the Bernie Madoff Ponzi scheme debacle 30 years later.

The Court began by noting that tippees do not have any relationship with the shareholders of the companies whose securities they trade, and so under *Chiarella*'s analysis the absence of the requisite duty of trust and confidence would prevent any liability for insider trading. It rejected the SEC suggestion, also made in *Chiarella*, "that anyone who knowingly receives nonpublic material information from an insider has a fiduciary duty to disclose before trading," pointing out that insider trading liability was premised on a breach of duty sufficient to constitute the deceptive conduct required for fraud. The absence of a direct link between the tippee and the company's shareholders did not insulate the transaction, however, because insiders "may not give

---

[155] 463 U.S. 646 (1983).

[156] Interestingly, when the case reached the Supreme Court, the Solicitor General opposed the SEC, one of the few times that different offices of the federal government took opposite sides before the Court.

such information to an outsider for the same improper purpose of exploiting the information for their personal gain."

The Court held that "a tippee assumes a fiduciary duty to the shareholders of a corporation not to trade on material nonpublic information only when the insider has breached his fiduciary duty to the shareholders by disclosing the information to the tippee and the tippee knows or should know that there has been a breach." The first step requires a determination of the tipper's breach of a fiduciary duty, and "the test is whether the insider personally will benefit, directly or indirectly, from his disclosure. Absent some personal gain, there has been no breach of duty to stockholders. And absent a breach by the insider, there is no derivative breach." The Court explained what the "personal gain" analysis entailed:

> This requires courts to focus on objective criteria, i.e., whether the insider receives a direct or indirect personal benefit from the disclosure, such as a pecuniary gain or a reputational benefit that will translate into future earnings . . . There are objective facts and circumstances that often justify such an inference. For example, there may be a relationship between the insider and the recipient that suggests a *quid pro quo* from the latter, or an intention to benefit the particular recipient. The elements of fiduciary duty and exploitation of nonpublic information also exist when an insider makes a gift of confidential information to a trading relative or friend. The tip and trade resemble trading by the insider himself followed by a gift of the profits to the recipient.

The simplest situation involves a financial transfer from the tippee to the tipper, such as a bribe—the clearest *quid pro quo* arrangement—or providing a portion of the profits from the transaction. A friend or family situation may be harder to assess because the Court did not explain how close the relationship had to be to meet the benefit requirement, but in most cases it can be established by objective evidence. Much more difficult is the "reputational benefit" that can be the basis for finding the breach of duty by the tipper. The Court did not explain this concept further, and proof of more ethereal benefits could suffice to establish this step in the analysis.

Once the breach of a fiduciary duty by the tipper is established, the tippee's liability then depends on whether that person knew or should have known the tipper breached a duty by disclosing the confidential information. This aspect of the analysis effectively heightens the *scienter* element for a violation of § 10(b) and Rule 10b–5 to incorporate proof of knowledge or reckless disregard of facts that would have shown the tipper breached a duty through the disclosure. The knowledge requirement on the tippee's part is not an additional intent element for a criminal prosecution, but an enhanced standard of proof of willfulness required to establish a particular instance of securities fraud.

Applying the tipper/tippee test, the Supreme Court in *Dirks* found there was no violation of § 10(b) and Rule 10b–5 by the officer of Equity Funding who provided the information to Dirks. It explained that "[t]he tippers received no monetary or personal benefit for revealing Equity Funding's secrets, nor was their purpose to make a gift of valuable information to Dirks . . . In the absence of a breach of duty to shareholders by the insiders, there was no derivative breach by Dirks." In a dissenting opinion, Justice Blackmun claimed that the additional knowledge requirement for the tippee "engrafts a special motivational requirement on the fiduciary duty doctrine," arguing that "[t]he fact that the insider himself does not benefit from the breach does not eradicate the shareholder's injury."

As with most offenses requiring proof of a defendant's knowledge, the jury can infer the requisite intent from circumstantial evidence. In *SEC v. Warde*,[157] the Second Circuit found sufficient evidence to establish defendant's knowledge that information came from a corporate director because "Downe and Warde were good friends who often discussed their business and investing interests, and . . . Warde habitually discovered who was on the board of directors of a company before investing in it." The circuit court noted that "[w]hile this evidence does not compel the conclusion that Warde knew Downe was a Kidde director, it certainly allows that inference."

While the tippee must know or have reason to know the information was disclosed in breach of the tipper's fiduciary duty, there is no requirement that the tipper know specifically that the tippee intends to trade. Establishing the breach of fiduciary duty only requires that the tipper intend there be some misuse of the information, which makes its disclosure improper. In *United States v. Libera*,[158] the Second Circuit held that "[t]o allow a tippee to escape liability solely because the government cannot prove to a jury's satisfaction that the tipper knew exactly what misuse would result from the tipper's wrongdoing would not fulfill the purpose of the misappropriation theory, which is to protect property rights in information."

There must be some basis to find a benefit flowing back to the tipper, which often focuses on the nature of the relationship between the tipper and tippee and how passing the information might be viewed objectively as enhancing the tipper's position in the tippee's eyes, absent any tangible transfer between them. The lower courts have taken a broad view of what constitutes the benefit to the tipper from disclosure of confidential information. In *Warde*, the Second Circuit explained that "the SEC need not show that the tipper expected or received a specific or tangible benefit in exchange for the tip." In *SEC v. Yun*, the Eleventh Circuit stated that "[a] reputational benefit that translates into future earnings, a quid pro quo, or a gift to a trading friend or relative all could suffice to show the tipper personally benefitted."[159]

In *SEC v. Sargent*,[160] the First Circuit found the requisite benefit could be inferred by looking at various components of the relationship between the tipper and tippee. The circuit court explained:

> Shepard testified that he and Sargent were "friendly." Shepard had referred over 75 people to Sargent for their dental work. Further, Shepard stated that he often went to Sargent for help in connection with Shepard's service to the local chamber of commerce. Shepard's sister-in-law owed Sargent money and another of Shepard's relatives was threatening to harm Sargent's business. From this evidence, a jury could infer that Shepard tipped Sargent about Purolator in an effort to effect a reconciliation with his friend and to maintain a useful networking contact.

---

[157] 151 F.3d 42 (2d Cir. 1998).

[158] 989 F.2d 596 (2d Cir. 1993).

[159] 327 F.3d 1263 (11th Cir.2003).

[160] 229 F.3d 68 (1st Cir. 2000).

In *United States v. Larrabee*,[161] the same court found sufficient evidence to the benefit required by *Dirks* when the tipper and tippee had an extensive personal, financial, and professional relationship, including their families spending weekends together and the tippee paying college tuition costs for the tipper's children.

In *SEC v. Maio*,[162] the Seventh Circuit concluded that a gift could be inferred because the tipper and tippee were friends and there was no better explanation why the tipper, a chief executive, would disclose the information to the tippee. The circuit court stated, "Absent some legitimate reason for Ferrero's disclosure, however, the inference that Ferrero's disclosure was an improper gift of confidential corporate information is unassailable. After all, he did not have to make any disclosure, so why tell Maio anything?"

In *SEC v. Maxwell*,[163] on the other hand, a district court dismissed civil insider trading charges against a tipper, a corporate executive, and his tippee, who was his barber, explaining:

> Given the parties' relative stations in life, any reputational benefit to Defendant Maxwell in the eyes of his barber is extremely unlikely to have translated into any meaningful future advantage. *Dirks* requires an intended benefit of at least some consequence. While the requisite personal benefit may be shown by the intent to provide a gift to benefit the tippee, there is absolutely no evidence that Defendant Maxwell had any reason or intent to give a gift—especially a gift of this magnitude—to Defendant Jehn.

Similarly, in *SEC v. Rorech*,[164] the district found the defendants did not violate § 10(b) and Rule 10b–5 because they "had a purely professional working relationship; they were not friends," and "the SEC has failed to establish that Mr. Rorech obtained any quantifiable or direct financial benefit as a result of Mr. Negrin's . . . trades in July and August 2006."

Dirks involved information passed on by an insider at a company about his own firm, meeting the requirements of the classical theory adopted in *Chiarella* because the shareholders were allegedly harmed by the disclosure. The misappropriation theory takes a different view of who the victim of the breach of fiduciary duty is, and so it is not clear whether the benefit requirement for tipping should also be applied under that approach to insider trading liability.

In *SEC v. Yun*,[165] the SEC argued that "it is unnecessary in misappropriation cases that it show that an outsider intended to benefit from his disclosure; since outsiders owe no duty to corporate shareholders to begin with, applying the *Dirks* test to determine if there was a breach of a duty to those same shareholders would be nonsensical." The Eleventh Circuit noted "the plausibility of the SEC's logic," but rejected that approach "because it constructs an arbitrary fence between insider trading liability based upon classical and misappropriation theories." The circuit court

---

[161] 240 F.3d 18 (1st Cir. 2001).

[162] 51 F.3d 623 (7th Cir. 1995).

[163] 341 F. Supp. 2d 941 (S.D. Ohio 2004).

[164] 720 F. Supp. 2d 367 (S.D.N.Y. 2010).

[165] 327 F.3d 1263 (11th Cir. 2003).

explained that "[o]ur goal should be like that of the Court in *O'Hagan*, which sought to explain how the two theories work together to promote the policies underlying the securities laws. We believe . . . that requiring the SEC to establish that the misappropriator intended to benefit from his tip will develop consistency in insider trading caselaw."

In light of *Yun*'s conclusion, the *Dirks* analysis applies regardless of whether the case involves the classical or misappropriation theory for a violation of § 10(b) and Rule 10b–5. That makes sense because some cases involve multiple instances of trading on the basis of material nonpublic information, some of which comes from a source in the company whose shares are traded and others from outside sources, such as the offeror seeking to take over another company, so it would be odd to have different standards applied when the alleged violations involve the same statutory provision and rule.

Once the tippee "steps into" the tipper's fiduciary duty, that person may be held liable as a tipper for telling others, which requires another application of the *Dirks* tipping analysis to the second-level tip. As the information gets passed along further down the chain from the original tipper, it may be difficult to establish the tippee's knowledge of the breach of fiduciary duty by the tipper. In *SEC v. Musella*,[166] the district court stated:

> Scienter in insider trading cases is not, and as a matter of public policy should not, be limited to those in direct contact with the primary tipper. Rather, the issue is whether a tippee, wherever he stood in a chain of tippees, either knew or should have known that he was trading on improperly obtained non-public information.

In *SEC v. Thrasher*,[167] the district court rejected a defendant's motion to dismiss the complaint because he did not know who the source of the confidential information was. The court explained that the tippee "may not have known the identity of the insider, but he was on notice that the information revealed was 'privileged'[;] arguably he should have known that it was disclosed in breach of that insider's fiduciary duty." It noted that to establish the liability of a tippee who did not deal directly with the original source of the confidential information the government "need not prove that [the tippee] knew of the details of [tipper]'s involvement; to require such knowledge would effectively insulate remote tippers from liability in many instances."

While a remote tippee can be held liable, it may be the case that the original tipper and the remote tippees have no knowledge of one another, and so were not members of the same conspiracy. Unlike insider trading, conspiracy requires proof that the defendants entered into a single agreement (see § 3.2). In *United States v. Geibel*,[168] the Second Circuit overturned the conspiracy conviction of the defendants alleged to be members of a single conspiracy because the goal of the original tippers was to avoid further disclosure of the information, so that "the scope of the conspiratorial agreement between Freeman and Cooper was narrow and did not encompass disclosure of inside information to unknown remote tippees such as Conner, Allen, and Geibel." In *United*

---

[166] 678 F.Supp. 1060 (S.D.N.Y. 1988).

[167] 152 F. Supp. 2d 291 (S.D.N.Y. 2001).

[168] 369 F.3d 682 (2d Cir. 2004).

States v. McDermott,[169] the same court overturned the conspiracy conviction of an investment banker who provided confidential information about deals involving his clients to his mistress, who bought shares and also passed it on to another boyfriend who traded in the companies. The circuit court noted, in a catchy turn of phrase, "We decline to hold as a matter of law that a cheating heart must foresee a cheating heart."

F.   On the Basis of Inside Information

Under both the classical and misappropriation theories, the defendant must trade "on the basis of" material nonpublic information. There is a split, fueled in part by Rule 10b5–1 adopted by the SEC in 2000, over whether this element requires only proof of possession of the information, or whether the government must show in addition that the defendant used the information. This "use versus possession" issue relates to proof of *scienter* and, in a criminal prosecution, willfulness for the violation. If all the government must show is that the defendant received the information, then its burden may be much lighter than if it also must establish that the information had a causal relation to the trading, such that the defendant used it in deciding to purchase or sell the securities that triggers the breach of fiduciary duty necessary for liability under § 10(b) and Rule 10b–5.

Because insider trading is not based on a specific statute, the courts have developed the inside trading prohibition in a haphazard fashion, and none of the typical interpretive tools available to courts to assess its elements or the scope of the prohibition are available. Nor is insider trading analogous to any common law crime that could provide a framework for the analysis.

Congress has adopted two statutes which refer to trading "while in possession of material, nonpublic information," providing support for the argument that the government need not prove a defendant used the information, only received it.[170] Neither provision, however, defined "possession," and the legislative reference to the elements is more a summary description of what courts had found to constitute insider trading rather than a definition of the elements of a violation of § 10(b) and Rule 10b–5 for such trading.

In *O'Hagan*, the Supreme Court described the violation under both the classical and misappropriation theories as involving "trading on the basis of nonpublic information" and that "the fiduciary's fraud is consummated . . .   when, without disclosure to his principal, he uses the information to purchase or sell securities."[171] Much like Congress, the Court was not analyzing this element of the violation, instead providing a description of how the conduct would trigger a breach of fiduciary duty required for liability for violating § 10(b) and Rule 10b–5.

The lower court decisions that have directly confronted this issue have largely required that the government must prove the defendant used the information, and not merely possessed it, although possession can be circumstantial evidence of its

---

[169] 245 F.3d 133 (2d Cir. 2001).

[170] See § 20A of the 1934 Act, 15 U.S.C. § 78t–1(a), adopted as part of the Insider Trading and Securities Fraud Enforcement Act of 1988, and § 21A of the 1934 Act, 15 U.S.C. § 78u–1(a), adopted as part of the Insider Trading Sanctions Act of 1984.

[171] 521 U.S. 642 (1997).

subsequent use in trading the securities. In *SEC v. Adler*,[172] the Eleventh Circuit succinctly described the test for determining whether a defendant used material nonpublic information:

> We believe that the use test best comports with precedent and Congressional intent, and that mere knowing possession—i.e., proof that an insider traded while in possession of material nonpublic information—is not a *per se* violation. However, when an insider trades while in possession of material nonpublic information, a strong inference arises that such information was used by the insider in trading. The insider can attempt to rebut the inference by adducing evidence that there was no causal connection between the information and the trade-i.e., that the information was not used. The factfinder would then weigh all of the evidence and make a finding of fact as to whether the inside information was used.

The circuit court explained that references in statutes to trading "while in possession" of insider information did not dictate the possession standard because "numerous statements in the legislative history of ISTA [Insider Trading Sanctions Act] disclaim any intent to modify the common law definition of an insider trading violation."

The Ninth Circuit adopted *Adler*'s analysis in *United States v. Smith*,[173] pointing out that "we are concerned that the SEC's 'knowing possession' standard would not be—indeed, could not be—strictly limited to those situations actually involving intentional fraud." The circuit court questioned what it called the "presumption" from possession described in *Adler* in a criminal case because the government's burden of proving every element beyond a reasonable doubt prohibits any mandatory presumptions. It is not clear that was what the Eleventh Circuit intended, however, because *Adler* referenced the jury's role in determining whether confidential information was used based on its possession, which is certainly permissible in a criminal case as well as a civil enforcement action. But using a term like "strong inference" to describe evidence of possession, coupled with reference to the defendant's "attempt to rebut" it, certainly conveys the impression that the burden of proof is shifted to the defendant as a matter of law, which is strictly prohibited in criminal prosecutions.

In rejecting the possession approach, *Smith* pointed out that to establish use of the information "[i]t is certainly not necessary that the government present a smoking gun in every insider trading prosecution." The Ninth Circuit explained how the government could establish use through circumstantial evidence:

> Suppose, for instance, that an individual who has never before invested comes into possession of material nonpublic information and the very next day invests a significant sum of money in substantially out-of-the-money call options. We are confident that the government would have little trouble demonstrating "use" in such a situation, or in other situations in which unique trading patterns or unusually large trading quantities suggest that an investor had used inside information.

---

[172] 137 F.3d 1325 (11th Cir. 1998).
[173] 155 F.3d 1051 (9th Cir. 1998).

The Seventh Circuit applied the "use" analysis in *SEC v. Lipson*,[174] agreeing with *Adler*'s "strong inference" in a civil enforcement matter. The circuit court explained how the inference operated, and why it was unobjectionable:

> It allows the jury to infer that if he had inside information, the trades were influenced by it. To infer Y from X just means that, if X happened, Y probably happened. If Lipson possessed nonpublic information which showed that Supercuts stock was overpriced, and having this information he sold a large quantity of that stock shortly before the information became public and the stock dropped sharply in value, common sense tells us that it is probable that his decision to sell when he did and how much he did (rather than sell later or sell less) was influenced by the information.

In *SEC v. Ginsburg*,[175] the Eleventh Circuit found that a jury's verdict against the defendants in a civil enforcement action was proper when the SEC produced sufficient circumstantial evidence of use of material nonpublic information based on its possession and the jury chose not to credit the defense evidence that the trading was based on publicly-available information. The circuit court stated,

> "Evidence of the innocent explanations for the calls between the parties in this case and of Mark's trading habits is not enough to justify overturning the jury's verdict. If it were otherwise, family members who regularly traded in a particular stock or type of stock could trade based on insider information with impunity."

Not every court has adopted the "use" requirement for insider trading liability. In *United States v. Teicher*,[176] the Second Circuit endorsed the possession approach, requiring proof of knowledge that the person received confidential information but not that it played a role in the investment decision. The circuit court stated that this rule had the benefit of "simplicity," noting rather colorfully that "[u]nlike a loaded weapon which may stand ready but unused, material information can not lay idle in the human brain." That analysis was only *dictum*, however, as the Second Circuit stated "we find that it is unnecessary to determine whether proof of securities fraud requires a causal connection, because any alleged defect in the instruction was harmless beyond doubt." Interestingly, *Teicher* was a criminal case, yet it adopted a lower standard for proving an element of the offense than *Adler* and *Lipson*, which were SEC enforcement actions.

The Second Circuit affirmed its "knowing possession" standard in *United States v. Royer*,[177] pointing out that while *Teicher* "was arguably dictum, it was the product of sustained and detailed consideration as set forth in the opinion. Nothing that has developed since persuades us of any different resolution." The circuit court also relied on SEC Rule 10b5–1,[178] adopted in 2000, that adopted the possession requirement for establishing a person traded on the basis of inside information.

Rule 10b5–1 is an application of the SEC's authority to define what constitutes a "manipulative or deceptive device" in violation of § 10(b), although whether it goes

---

[174] 278 F.3d 656 (7th Cir. 2002).

[175] 362 F.3d 1292 (11th Cir. 2004).

[176] 987 F.2d 112 (2nd Cir. 1993).

[177] 549 F.3d 886 (2d Cir. 2008).

[178] 17 C.F.R. § 240.10b5–1.

beyond the Commission's authority is an issue that has not been completely resolved by the courts. The Rule provides that a trade is "on the basis of" inside information "if the person making the purchase or sale was aware of the material nonpublic information when the person made the purchase or sale." The SEC made it clear that the definition was not intended to alter the *scienter* element for securities fraud, pointing out in a "Preliminary Note" to Rule 10b5–1 that "[s]cienter remains a necessary element for liability under Section 10(b) of the Exchange Act and Rule 10b–5 thereunder, and Rule 10b5–1 does not change this."

Rule 10b5–1 also provides an affirmative defense to a claim that trading constituted securities fraud in the following circumstances:

Before becoming aware of the information, the person had:

(1) Entered into a binding contract to purchase or sell the security,

(2) Instructed another person to purchase or sell the security for the instructing person's account, or

(3) Adopted a written plan for trading securities.

Rule 10b5–1(c)(1)(i) provides detailed requirements for what is required of a "written plan" to qualify for the affirmative defense. These have come to be known as "10b5–1 Plans," and many corporate executives have them in place as a means to protect themselves from potential insider trading liability while regularly selling shares in their employers. Because it is an affirmative defense, the burden of proof is on the executive to establish that the plan meets the Rule's requirements.

In *United States v. Nacchio*,[179] a panel of the Tenth Circuit found that a trial judge's jury instruction requiring the government to prove the defendant used material nonpublic information, rather than following Rule 10b5–1's awareness standard, "was arguably incorrect because it was too favorable to Mr. Nacchio." The panel noted that "the district court may have implicitly held that Rule 10b5–1 is not a lawful interpretation of the securities laws," but it was willing to assume it was lawful because the issue of the Rule's validity had not been raised on appeal. The full Tenth Circuit, sitting en banc, overturned the panel's decision on other grounds, affirming the conviction for insider trading, so the earlier opinion does not have precedential effect but does show a court willing to apply the SEC's more relaxed standard rather than the more demanding "use" requirement.[180]

G. Illicit Access to Information

In *SEC v. Dorozhko*,[181] the defendant was sued for violating Rule 10b–5 when he hacked into a computer network and accessed undisclosed corporate earnings information before its release to the public, on which he then traded, realizing an overnight profit of nearly $300,000. The defendant was a foreign national, and had no relationship with the company whose shares he traded—he stole information by

---

[179] 519 F.3d 1140 (10th Cir. 2008), rev'd on other grounds, 555 F.3d 1234 (10th Cir. 2009).

[180] 555 F.3d 1234 (10th Cir. 2009).

[181] 574 F.3d 42 (2d Cir. 2009).

misrepresenting himself as an authorized user of the network storing the computer files. The district court denied the SEC's motion for a preliminary injunction prohibiting future violations of § 10(b) and Rule 10b–5, finding that it was unlikely to succeed on the merits of its claim for insider trading when the defendant had not engaged in any deception by violating a fiduciary duty because he did not owe one to any party to the transaction or the source of the information.

The Second Circuit reversed, finding that the Supreme Court's decisions in *Chiarella* and *O'Hagan* did not establish a blanket "fiduciary-duty requirement as an element of every violation of Section 10(b)." It pointed out that the Court's insider trading cases all dealt with the situation in which a person kept silent about the information received as part of a duty of trust and confidence. The SEC's theory of fraud was different from the typical case because it argued "that defendant affirmatively misrepresented himself in order to gain access to material, nonpublic information, which he then used to trade." This was not a failure to disclose in breach of a fiduciary duty, but instead a deception used to obtain information that was subsequently employed for trading that was part of a scheme to defraud. According to the circuit court:

> In our view, misrepresenting one's identity in order to gain access to information that is otherwise off limits, and then stealing that information is plainly "deceptive" within the ordinary meaning of the word. It is unclear, however, that exploiting a weakness in an electronic code to gain unauthorized access is "deceptive," rather than being mere theft. Accordingly, depending on how the hacker gained access, it seems to us entirely possible that computer hacking could be, by definition, a "deceptive device or contrivance" that is prohibited by Section 10(b) and Rule 10b–5.

The case was remanded to determine whether the defendant engaged in deceit to gain access to the computer files to constitute the deception required for fraud.

Dorozhko presents an interesting theory of fraud that focuses on the affirmative steps a defendant took to establish the deception rather than the fiduciary relationship between the source of the information and the person who traded or tipped. Under this approach, a case could be made for violating § 10(b) and Rule 10b–5 if a defendant obtains information by means of some type of deception and then uses it, regardless of the existence of a duty of trust and confidence owed to the source. For example, a law firm associate could take another lawyer's password to access a computer file to learn about a pending transaction, which may be in violation of the firm's policy against reviewing information unrelated to the person's work. A case for violating § 10(b) and Rule 10b–5 could be brought under both the breach of fiduciary duty standard, because the lawyer owes a duty of trust and confidence to the firm and its clients, and for an affirmative misrepresentation by taking the password of another person to access the information, a type of deception. For those cases in which proving a breach of a fiduciary duty might be difficult, the government might rely on *Dorozhko*'s analysis as an alternative avenue to establishing liability for securities fraud if there was other conduct that could be deceptive.

H. Insider Trading in Tender Offers (Rule 14e–3)

A tender offer is a means by which a person or entity can acquire some or all of the shares of a company by making an offer directly to the shareholders to sell their shares at the bid price, rather than working with a corporation's board of directors to acquire the company or its assets. Information about this type of transaction is often quite valuable, particularly when the offer is a hostile one, because the amount offered to the shareholders is usually a premium above the market price of a company's shares before the announcement, making it quite tempting to those who learn of an impending deal.

The Williams Act, added as an amendment to the 1934 Act, created extensive federal guidelines for how a tender offer can be made, the communication of its terms, and the availability of the offer for a prescribed period along with related disclosures. Section 14(e)[182] of the Williams Act is a general antifraud provision that prohibits any "fraudulent, deceptive, or manipulative acts or practices in connection with any tender offer."[183] Importantly, that provision grants the SEC the authority to issue rules to "define, and prescribe means reasonably designed to prevent, such acts and practices as are fraudulent, deceptive, or manipulative."

Shortly after the Supreme Court's decision in *Chiarella* rejected the possession theory for insider trading and instead required proof of a breach of fiduciary duty, the SEC approved Rule 14e–3 to impose the possession theory of insider trading for transactions based on material nonpublic information about a pending or proposed tender offer for a company's shares. According to the Commission, *Chiarella* "did not suggest any limitation on the Commission's authority under Section 14(e) to adopt a rule regulating trading while in possession of material, nonpublic information relating to a tender offer."[184] Thus, for information about a particular type of transaction—a tender offer—the SEC's broader approach to liability that only requires proof that the person received the information and subsequently traded on it can be sufficient to establish a violation.

The operative provision of Rule 14e–3(a) provides:

If any person has taken a substantial step or steps to commence, or has commenced, a tender offer (the "offering person"), it shall constitute a fraudulent, deceptive or manipulative act or practice within the meaning of section 14(e) of the Act for any other person who is in possession of material information relating to such tender offer which information he knows or has reason to know is nonpublic and which he knows or has reason to know has been acquired directly or indirectly from:

(1) The offering person,

(2) The issuer of the securities sought or to be sought by such tender offer, or

(3) Any officer, director, partner or employee or any other person acting on behalf of the offering person or such issuer, to purchase or sell or cause to be purchased

---

[182] 15 U.S.C. § 78n(e).

[183] 17 C.F.R. § 240.14e–3.

[184] Exchange Act Rel. No. 17120 (Sept. 4 1980).

or sold any of such securities or any securities convertible into or exchangeable for any such securities or any option or right to obtain or to dispose of any of the foregoing securities, unless within a reasonable time prior to any purchase or sale such information and its source are publicly disclosed by press release or otherwise.

Rule 14e–3(d) also prohibits tipping about a tender offer by making it a violation "to communicate material, nonpublic information relating to a tender offer to any other person under circumstances in which it is reasonably foreseeable that such communication is likely to result in a violation of this section. . . . "[185]

Rule 14e–3 covers any person who acts on behalf of the party making the tender offer or the target of the offer, including any affiliated advisers, so that each side of the transaction is subject to the trading (and tipping) prohibition. The Rule goes even further by also applying to any person possessing the information who "knows or has reason to know is nonpublic and which he knows or has reason to know has been acquired directly or indirectly" by someone affiliated with a party to the tender offer. Importantly, Rule 14e–3 does not require proof of any breach of a fiduciary duty for liability to attach, unlike the requirement for the classical or misappropriation theories for a violation of § 10(b) and Rule 10b–5.

Questions were raised about whether Rule 14e–3 was consistent with the Supreme Court's analysis in *Chiarella* and *Dirks* that focused on the breach of a duty of trust and confidence as the prerequisite to establishing that silence constituted a "deceptive" act for liability for securities fraud. In *O'Hagan*, however, the Court upheld the validity of Rule 14e–3, thereby giving the SEC and federal prosecutors a potentially more expeditious avenue to pursue insider trading in those cases in which a tender offer was involved.

The Eighth Circuit had held in *O'Hagan* that Rule 14e–3 exceeded the SEC's authority because it did not meet the requirement of *Chiarella* for a fraud that involved a breach of fiduciary duty. The Supreme Court rejected that approach because § 14(e) gives the SEC broader power to proscribe practices that are akin to fraud but may not necessarily meet all the elements of that type of violation. In upholding the Rule, the Court held that "under § 14(e), the Commission may prohibit acts not themselves fraudulent under the common law or § 10(b), if the prohibition is 'reasonably designed to prevent . . . acts and practices [that] are fraudulent.'" It explained that "[a] prophylactic measure, because its mission is to prevent, typically encompasses more than the core activity prohibited."[186] Thus, while the rule dispenses with proof of a breach of duty, the information is likely to come from someone with such a duty, so that the

> SEC, cognizant of the proof problem that could enable sophisticated traders to escape responsibility, placed in Rule 14e–3(a) a "disclose or abstain from trading" command that does not require specific proof of a breach of fiduciary duty. That prescription, we are satisfied, applied to this case, is a "means reasonably

---

[185] 17 C.F.R. § 240–14e–3(d)(1).

[186] 521 U.S. 642 (1997).

designed to prevent" fraudulent trading on material, nonpublic information in the tender offer context.

A violation of Rule 14e–3 does not require that a tender offer actually commence because the Rule covers trading on information when a "substantial step" has been taken for a tender offer at the time of the transaction. What constitutes a "substantial step" is not defined in Rule 14e–3, although the SEC included a nonexclusive list of examples in a release accompanying the rule that describe various steps that it viewed as sufficient, such as a letter sent to the target proposing a tender offer at a specified price or disclosure of an intention to commence a tender offer.

The term "substantial step" is a familiar one in the criminal law, found most prominently in the Model Penal Code's definition of an attempt crime that requires proof a defendant undertook "a substantial step in a course of conduct planned to culminate in his commission of the crime."[187] Courts generally look for some type of purposeful action which can demonstrate a defendant's intent to commit a crime. Using that analysis for Rule 14e–3 would focus on the types of financial and legal preparations that indicate a tender offer is being prepared for the shareholders of the target corporation.

O'Hagan did not reach the issue of whether there was a substantial step taken toward a tender offer at the time of the trading because the defendant only raised that issue for the first time before the Supreme Court.[188] A few lower court decisions have considered whether the requisite "substantial step" for a tender offer has occurred to permit application of Rule 14e–3 to the trading. In *SEC v. Warde*,[189] the Second Circuit found the evidence "comfortably satisfied" the substantial step requirement when the defendant bought shares in the target of the tender offer at the time its chief executive had convened an emergency board meeting with investment bankers and counsel to deal with a potential hostile takeover, and additional trading occurred after a meeting between executives of the two corporations involved. In *SEC v. Mayhew*,[190] the same court rejected a defendant's argument that his trading two months before the commencement of a tender offer meant that the substantial step requirement had not been met. The circuit court rejected the proposition that Rule 14e–3 incorporates any specific timing requirement, explaining that "[a]ny arbitrary temporal limit would frustrate" its purpose. There was sufficient evidence even at an earlier point in time to establish this element of a violation when the offeror had "retained a consulting firm, signed confidentiality agreements, and held meetings between top officials. These steps satisfy the substantiality requirement of Rule 14e–3."

Courts assess how far along in the negotiation process the companies were in determining whether a substantial step had been taken. In *SEC v. Ginsburg*,[191] the Eleventh Circuit explained why the evidence was sufficient for a Rule 14e–3 violation,

---

[187] Model Penal Code § 5.01(2).

[188] On remand, the Eighth Circuit found that defendant's failure to raise the issue in the district court or in his original appeal meant that he had waived his argument that there was not a substantial step taken toward a tender offer. United States v. O'Hagan, 139 F.3d 641 (8th Cir. 1998).

[189] 151 F.3d 42 (2d Cir. 1998).

[190] 121 F.3d 44 (2d Cir. 1997).

[191] 362 F.3d 1292 (11th Cir. 2004).

and warned against a too-rigid approach that focuses only on whether the technical requirements for a tender offer had been met:

> In this case there was a meeting between executives, which was followed by due diligence procedures, a confidentiality agreement, and by a meeting between Ginsburg and Olds—from which Ginsburg realized that the deal had to go down fast. These activities, which did result in a tender offer, were substantial steps for purposes of Rule 14e–3. Were it otherwise, liability could be avoided by taking care to tip only before the formal steps finalizing the acquisition are completed, leaving a substantial gap between the acquisition of inside information and the regulation of its disbursement.

Similarly, the Seventh Circuit in *SEC v. Maio*[192] found that a solicitation of an offer for a company was a substantial step toward a tender offer, even though the exact form of the transaction was not decided at the meeting that took place shortly before the defendant's trading.

A violation of Rule 14e–3 requires proof of a defendant's knowledge that the information was confidential and that the source was connected to one of the parties to the tender offer, but it does not require that the person knew that the transaction was likely to be structured as a tender offer as opposed to other types of acquisitions at the time of the trade. In *SEC v. Sargent*,[193] the First Circuit found that the evidence of the defendants' knowledge that the potential acquisition would be by means of a tender offer was only speculative, but that was not fatal to the government's case because "[t]here is simply no language in the Rule indicating that a defendant must know that the nonpublic information in his possession relates to a tender offer." The Eleventh Circuit, in *Ginsburg*, agreed with *Sargent*'s analysis, stating that "Rule 14e–3, by its terms, does not require that the offender know or have reason to know that the information relates to a tender offer, so long as the information in fact does relate to a tender offer and the offender knows or has reason to know the information is nonpublic and was acquired by a person with the required status."

§ 5.7   ACCOUNTING AND BOOKS-AND-RECORDS VIOLATIONS

Once a business achieves a certain scale, lenders, suppliers, and customers will require that it adhere to accounting principles so that there are assurances it is being operated properly. Accountants are usually retained to organize the records and provide reports on a company's operations, expenditures, and profits (or losses). For publicly-traded corporations, the 1934 Act imposes certain reporting and internal control requirements that mandate the use of an independent accountant to certify that the financial report complies with Generally Accepted Accounting Principles (GAAP). Violation of these provisions can result in liability, and can also be the basis for proving a violation of the antifraud provisions based on any misstatement or omission in required reports.

---

[192] 51 F.3d 623 (7th Cir. 1995).

[193] 229 F.3d 68 (1st Cir. 2000).

The primary rules regarding internal accounting controls were adopted as part of the Foreign Corrupt Practices Act (FCPA),[194] discussed in § 7.7. Congress enacted the FCPA in 1977 in response to SEC investigations into payments by American corporations to foreign officials and politicians as part of an effort to obtain contracts and maintain business relationships.[195] The FCPA regulates two related areas: foreign bribery and the requirements for publicly-traded corporations to provide proper accounting and internal controls. When the law was enacted, there was no explicit requirement that corporations comply with accounting procedures or present their financial statements and other information about its business to investors pursuant to any particular standards.

The record-keeping provisions require every issuer to "make and keep books, records, and accounts, which, in reasonable detail, accurately and fairly reflect the transactions and dispositions of the assets of the issuer."[196] One reason for adding this requirement as part of the FCPA was to prevent off-the-books transactions or the creation of corporate "slush funds" that could be used to pay bribes, kickbacks, and other types of corrupt transfers. A violation of the record-keeping provision is not limited to unlawful payments because it requires a corporation's financial records accurately reflect the financial information related to all corporate transactions along with other information that may be necessary to give a complete picture of any significant aspects of a transaction. Thus, records are "inaccurate" if they fail to record illegal or otherwise improper transactions, or falsify or disguise the nature or purpose of revenues or expenditures.

The accurate books-and-records requirement can help prevent three types of financial impropriety: (a) the failure to record illegal transactions, such as an overseas bribe; (b) the falsification of records to conceal illegal transactions, such as kickbacks paid to suppliers or transfers of assets designed to create the impression of higher sales or profitability; and, (c) the creation of records that are quantitatively accurate, but fail to specify qualitative aspects of the transaction, such as the backdating of a sale so that it is recorded in a different reporting period. The record-keeping requirement applies to all corporate transactions and is not limited only to material events, and is designed to ensure that investors receive reliable information about a company's operations and financial situation.

The internal controls provision of the FCPA requires public companies to devise and maintain a system of internal accounting controls sufficient to provide reasonable assurances that:

> • transactions are executed according to management's general or specific authorization;

---

[194] Pub. L. No. 95–213, 91 Stat. 1494 (1977). Congress amended the FCPA twice, in 1988 as part of the Omnibus Trade and Competitiveness Act, Pub. L. No. 100–418, 102 Stat. 1107, 1415–25 (1988), and again in 1998 to conform to the OECD Convention in the International Antibribery and Fair Competition Act of 1998, Pub. L. No. 105–366, 112 Stat. 3302 (1998).

[195] 15 U.S.C. §§ 78dd–1, 78dd–2, and 78ff.

[196] 15 U.S.C. § 78m(b)(2)(A). Similar record-keeping obligations are imposed on broker-dealers, see 15 U.S.C. § 78o(d), mutual funds, see 15 U.S.C. § 80a–30, and investment advisers, see 15 U.S.C. § 80b–4.

• transactions are recorded as necessary to permit preparation of financial statements according to GAAP; and

• the recorded accountability for assets is compared with the existing assets at reasonable intervals, and appropriate action is taken with respect to any differences.[197]

The SEC adopted Rules 13b2–1 and 13b2–2 to implement the accounting records provisions. Rule 13b2–1 is a general prohibition providing that "[n]o person shall directly or indirectly, falsify or cause to be falsified, any book, record or account. . . . "[198] Rule 13b2–2 concerns the representations by a company's management to its accountants in connection with the preparation of the required reports that must be provided:

No director or officer of an issuer shall, directly or indirectly:

(1) Make or cause to be made a materially false or misleading statement to an accountant in connection with; or

(2) Omit to state, or cause another person to omit to state, any material fact necessary in order to make statements made, in light of the circumstances under which such statements were made, not misleading, to an accountant in connection with:

(i) Any audit, review or examination of the financial statements of the issuer required to be made pursuant to this subpart; or

(ii) The preparation or filing of any document or report required to be filed with the Commission pursuant to this subpart or otherwise.

The SEC routinely relies on these accounting provisions and rules in civil or administrative enforcement actions against companies and their outside auditors for transactions that were falsely reflected in the corporate records. *Scienter* is not an element of a violation of the books-and-records provisions of § 13, as the Second Circuit noted in *SEC v. McNulty* in stating that "the court's ruling that lack of scienter would not be a defense to the claims under § 13 and the regulations thereunder was consistent with precedent in this Circuit and with the Commission's interpretive regulations indicating that scienter is not an element of civil claims under those provisions."[199] The SEC must show a defendant acted unreasonably in reporting, or failing to report, information in the corporate records. In many cases, this involves establishing a violation of GAAP.

For a criminal prosecution, however, the government must prove the defendant knowingly circumvented or failed to implement a system of internal controls, or knowingly falsified any book, record or account.[200] A defendant can offer the "no knowledge" defense contained in § 32 of the 1934 Act for a charge of violating Rule

---

[197] 15 U.S.C. § 78m(b)(2)(B).

[198] 17 C.F.R. § 240.13b2–1.

[199] 137 F.3d 732 (2d Cir. 1998).

[200] 15 U.S.C. § 78m(b)(4)–(5).

13b2–1 or Rule 13b2–2, but not for a violation of § 13b, which is the basis for the Rules. The books-and-records provisions were used in a number of high-profile criminal prosecutions involving significant accounting fraud at companies like Enron, WorldCom, and Adelphia Communications.[201]

In *United States v. Lake*,[202] the Tenth Circuit reversed the conviction of two corporate executives for circumventing the company's internal controls because the trial court failed to properly instruct the jury on what was required to prove their knowledge of the circumvention. The defendants did not report their personal use of a corporate jet, which the government alleged was done in violation of § 13b(2)(B), but the trial judge refused to give the defendants' proposed instruction that the SEC's rules did not require that they report the benefits received from flying on the company plane. This undermined the defense argument that they did not knowingly violate the internal controls provision: "When a defendant's defense is so dependent on an understanding of an applicable law, the court has a duty to instruct the jury on that law, rather than requiring the jury to decide whether to believe a witness on the subject or one of the attorneys presenting closing argument."

The obligation to maintain adequate books and records falls on company management, most importantly its chief financial officer. In *McConville v. SEC*,[203] the defendant argued that she was not responsible for problems in a publicly-traded corporation's financial records, even though she was its chief financial officer. The Seventh Circuit rejected that argument: "As chief financial officer, McConville's very job at Akorn was to manage its financial department and ensure its records and accounts were accurately and fairly maintained, and there is substantial evidence that she failed to do so. The record indicates that Akorn's financial records were in an ongoing state of disarray." Similarly, in *SEC v. Softpoint, Inc.*,[204] the district court held that "[a]s president of Softpoint, Stoecklein was responsible for the accuracy of Softpoint's books and records."

To prove a criminal violation of the books-and-records provisions, the government will usually try to demonstrate that the reporting of the company's transactions did not comply with GAAP, making the proper accounting treatment the key to establishing a defendant's guilt. While a defendant's position in the company can be relevant to proving knowledge of a GAAP violation, it is not sufficient in itself that the person served as the chief financial officer to establish intent.

In *United States v. Goyal*,[205] the Ninth Circuit reversed the conviction of a company's chief financial officer because no reasonable juror could have found that accounting treatment for certain transactions violated GAAP. While the defendant had the company take an aggressive position regarding booking revenues from sales, the circuit court explained that this did not prove his knowledge of a violation of GAAP, so that "Goyal's desire to meet NAI's revenue targets, and his knowledge of and

---

[201] See United States v. Skilling, 638 F.3d 480 (5th Cir. 2011) (former Enron CEO Jeffrey Skilling); United States v. Ebbers, 458 F.3d 110 (2d Cir. 2006) (former WorldCom CEO Bernard Ebbers); United States v. Rigas, 490 F.3d 208 (2d Cir. 2007) (former Adelphia Communications CEO John Rigas).

[202] 472 F.3d 1247 (10th Cir. 2007).

[203] 465 F.3d 780 (7th Cir. 2006).

[204] 958 F.Supp. 846 (S.D.N.Y. 1997).

[205] 629 F.3d 912 (9th Cir. 2010).

participation in deals to help make that happen, is simply evidence of Goyal's doing his job diligently." The defendant's position as chief financial officer also was insufficient standing alone to prove his intent: "If simply understanding accounting rules or optimizing a company's performance were enough to establish scienter, then any action by a company's chief financial officer that a juror could conclude in hindsight was false or misleading could subject him to fraud liability without regard to intent to deceive. That cannot be." *Goyal* demonstrates how difficult it can be to establish intent for a criminal violation of the books-and-records provisions because GAAP can be subject to conflicting interpretations, so a particular accounting treatment may not be improper even though it may be considered aggressive.

The Sarbanes–Oxley Act, passed in 2002 in the wake of the accounting scandals at Enron, WorldCom, and other publicly-traded corporations, added new provisions designed to enhance proper accounting at publicly-traded corporations. Congress added 18 U.S.C. § 1520, which requires "[a]ny accountant who conducts an audit of an issuer of securities . . . shall maintain all audit or review workpapers for a period of 5 years from the end of the fiscal period in which the audit or review was concluded," and any person who "knowingly and willfully" violates the provision or rules issued pursuant to it can be prosecuted. This provision ensures that documents will be preserved, an issue that arose during the SEC's investigation of Enron and the conduct of the company's accountant, Arthur Andersen.

Another provision, 18 U.S.C. § 1350, requires the chief executive officer and chief financial officer to file a written report with the financial statements of the company filed on a quarterly and annual basis with the SEC "that information contained in the periodic report fairly presents, in all material respects, the financial condition and results of operations of the issuer." The statute provides for two tiers of punishment for filing a statement when the company's financial statements do not comport with the requirements for a proper disclosure, depending on the executive's intent level. For a "knowing" violation, the penalty is up to 10 years imprisonment, but if an executive "willfully" files the certification "knowing that the periodic report accompanying the statement does not comport with all the requirements set forth in this section," then the potential punishment is up to 20 years in prison. The provision does not define what "willfully" means, and the addition of this intent element on top of proof of knowledge to trigger a potential prison sentence twice as long indicates that Congress wanted to require proof that the defendant intended a violation of a known legal provision, not just that there was knowledge the conduct was wrongful.

§ 5.8   MARKET MANIPULATION

Transactions in securities can impact the market through the use of tactics that artificially inflate or depress the price other investors pay, effectively deceiving them through manipulation of the public markets in which most trading occurs. The Supreme Court, in *Ernst & Ernst v. Hochfelder*, described the term "manipulative" as used in the federal securities laws as "virtually a term of art when used in connection with securities markets. It connotes intentional or willful conduct designed to deceive or defraud investors by controlling or artificially affecting the price of securities."[206] In *Santa Fe Industries Inc. v. Green*, the Court noted that manipulative "refers generally

---

[206] 425 U.S. 185 (1976).

to practices, such as wash sales, matched orders, or rigged prices, that are intended to mislead investors by artificially affecting market activity."[207] The manipulation prohibition is based on a free market approach as described in *United States v. Stein* when the Second Circuit stated, "The purpose of [§ 9 of the 1934 Act] is to prevent rigging of the market and to permit operation of the natural law of supply and demand."[208]

The two principle provisions used to police manipulative practices are § 9 and § 10(b) of the 1934 Act, both of which reach market manipulation. Section 9 prohibits specified practices that are usually associated with efforts to artificially affect the market price of securities, while § 10(b) merely includes the term "manipulative" along with "deceptive" as a type of fraud without further definition. A Senate Report described manipulative market practices as creating "a 'mirage" rather than 'the reflection of a genuine demand.'"[209] The two provisions are not mutually exclusive, so violations can be charged under both. Another provision, § 15(c) of the 1934 Act, prohibits manipulative conduct by broker-dealers who buy and sell securities on behalf of customers.

Section 9 prohibits a range of activities in the market designed to improperly affect the price at which other investors buy or sell securities. Section 9(a)(1) prohibits the following:

> For the purpose of creating a false or misleading appearance of active trading in any security other than a government security, or a false or misleading appearance with respect to the market for any such security, (A) to effect any transaction in such security which involves no change in the beneficial ownership thereof, or (B) to enter an order or orders for the purchase of such security with the knowledge that an order or orders of substantially the same size, at substantially the same time, and at substantially the same price, for the sale of any such security, has been or will be entered by or for the same or different parties, or (C) to enter any order or orders for the sale of any such security with the knowledge that an order or orders of substantially the same size, at substantially the same time, and at substantially the same price, for the purchase of such security, has been or will be entered by or for the same or different parties.

Section 9(a)(2) is a general catch-all provision, making it unlawful "[t]o effect, alone or with one or more other persons, a series of transactions in any security . . . creating actual or apparent active trading in such security, or raising or depressing the price of such security, for the purpose of inducing the purchase or sale of such security by others." In addition to criminal and civil enforcement of the provision, § 9 also contains a private right of action for those who traded in the manipulated securities.

A significant limitation on pursuing actions under § 9(a) for market manipulation is the requirement to prove the defendant's act were "for the purpose" of "inducing the purchase or sale" or "creating a false or misleading appearance of active trading" in the

---

[207] 430 U.S. 462 (1977).

[208] 456 F.2d 844 (2d Cir. 1972).

[209] Senate Comm. on Banking & Currency, Stock Exchange Practices, S.Rep. No. 1455, 73d Cong., 2d Sess. 54 (1934).

security affected, a much higher threshold for establishing a violation than the *scienter* requirement for cases brought under § 10(b) and Rule 10b–5. In *SEC v. U.S. Environmental, Inc.*,[210] the Second Circuit held that a § 10(b) manipulation complaint was proper because "[i]t is well-settled that knowledge of the proscribed activity is sufficient scienter under § 10(b)." Merely buying or selling shares in the hope that the market price will change is not manipulation, however, and the law "does not condemn extensive buying or buying which raises the price of a security in itself."[211]

Separating manipulative market activity from permissible securities trading can be difficult when the requisite intent is to show the "purpose" to manipulate the price of shares, especially when the transactions involve ostensibly legal open market purchases of a large publicly-traded corporation. Even when the case is brought under § 10(b), courts require proof of actual manipulation or reckless conduct showing a significant impact on the price of the securities that misled investors. The District of Columbia Circuit described the quandary of dealing with open-market purchases as proof of manipulation this way:

> Liability for manipulation wholly independent of fictitious transactions in fact raises interesting questions. Without such transactions, the core of the offense can be obscure. It may be hard to separate a "manipulative" investor from one who is simply over-enthusiastic, a true believer in the object of investment. Both may amass huge inventories and place high bids, even though there are scant objective data supporting the implicit estimate of the stock's value. Legality would thus depend entirely on whether the investor's intent was "an investment purpose" or "solely to affect the price of [the] security."[212]

In *United States v. Mulheren*,[213] the Second Circuit held that a claim of market manipulation required the government to prove that the defendant's "sole purpose" was to artificially affect the market price, and that the transactions were not for investment purposes. None of the typical indicia of a manipulative purpose were present in the case, such as the use of fictitious accounts to hide the true identity of the purchaser, a dominant position in the market, and profits from the trading. Matched trades and wash sales can be strong circumstantial evidence of a manipulative purpose.[214] The Second Circuit described these transactions as follows: "In a wash sale transaction, beneficial ownership of the stock does not change. A matched order involves the prearranged purchase and sale, usually through different brokers, of the same amount of securities at substantially the same price and time. Both practices give the appearance of legitimate market activity."

The Third Circuit took the position in a private fraud action that open-market purchases alone were not "manipulative" because otherwise lawful conduct would

---

[210] 155 F.3d 107 (2d Cir. 1998).

[211] Crane Co. v. Westinghouse Air Brake Co., 419 F.2d 787 (2d Cir. 1969).

[212] Markowski v. S.E.C., 274 F.3d 525 (D.C. Cir. 2001).

[213] 938 F.2d 364 (2d Cir. 1991).

[214] See United States v. Scop, 846 F.2d 135 (2d Cir. 1988) (matched orders through fictitious nominee accounts); United States v. Gilbert, 668 F.2d 94 (2d Cir.1981) (matched orders and wash sales).

constitute a violation based solely on a person's intent to artificially affect the market price of a security.[215] Instead, the circuit court required proof that

> the alleged manipulator injected "inaccurate information" into the market or created a false impression of market activity ... Such a construction permits courts to differentiate between legitimate trading activities that permissibly may influence prices, such as short sales, and "ingenious devices that might be used to manipulate securities prices," *Santa Fe Indus.,* such as wash sales and matched orders.

The District of Columbia Circuit took the opposite position in *Markowski v. SEC* regarding open-market purchases, finding that "[w]hatever the practical concerns, we cannot find the Commission's interpretation to be unreasonable in light of what appears to be Congress's determination that 'manipulation' can be illegal solely because of the actor's purpose."[216] In *SEC v. Masri,* the district court summarized the manipulation analysis this way:

> [I]f an investor conducts an open-market transaction with the intent of artificially affecting the price of the security, and not for any legitimate economic reason, it can constitute market manipulation ... Allegations of other deceptive conduct or features of the transaction are only required to the extent that they render plausible allegations of manipulative intent.[217]

In *SEC v. Kwak,*[218] the district court, in an unpublished opinion, upheld a jury finding of violations of § 9(a), rejecting the argument that open-market stock purchases can never be considered "manipulative" after *Mulheren.* The court described the market manipulation as follows:

> The kind of manipulation involved here was a manipulation in which the defendants, and others, bought stock in order to prevent the stock from being delisted (which would have made the stock less attractive to investors) and/or to create an illusion that the stock price was more stable than it really was (which it was hoped would attract more investment in CTT stock). While unorthodox, such a manipulation is plainly still deceptive under section 10(b) because it tricks investors into believing that the reported prices for CTT stock reflect transactions that are solely the product of independent forces of supply and demand.

---

[215] GFL Advantage Fund, Ltd. v. Colkitt, 272 F.3d 189 (3d Cir. 2001).

[216] 274 F.3d 525 (D.C. Cir. 2001).

[217] 523 F. Supp. 2d 361 (S.D.N.Y. 2007).

[218] 2008 WL 410427 (D.Conn. 2008).

Chapter 6

OBSTRUCTION OF JUSTICE

§ 6.1 INTRODUCTION

A. Generally

Obstruction of justice is a common charge used by the government in white collar cases. It is a crime that is relatively easy to prove in comparison to some sophisticated white collar crimes, particularly conduct that may be difficult to explain to a jury. It is often easier for the government to prove the destruction of documents, lying to investigators, or lying to a grand jury, then to present fraudulent complicated financial transactions. Thus "cover-up"[1] or "short-cut"[2] offenses like false statements, perjury, or obstruction of justice are common crimes. In many instances one will see one or more of these crimes in conjunction with substantive offenses like mail, wire, or securities fraud.

One finds several high-profile individuals like Martha Stewart and I. Lewis "Scooter" Libby charged with crimes of obstruction of justice. One also finds corporations, such as Arthur Andersen LLP, prosecuted under one of the obstruction statutes.

B. Obstruction Statutes

There are a host of different obstruction statutes, most of which are located in chapter 73 of Title 18. The goal of many of these statutes is to protect government proceedings. For example, the federal code includes specific statutes pertaining to assault on a process server (18 U.S.C. § 1501), resistance to an extradition agent (18 U.S.C. § 1502); influencing a juror through a writing (18 U.S.C. § 1504), theft or alteration of a record or process (18 U.S.C. § 1506), picketing, parading, using sound equipment, or demonstrating in or near a courthouse of "a building or residence occupied or used by such judge, juror, witness or court officer (18 U.S.C. § 1507), "[r]ecording, listening to or observing proceedings of grand or petit juries while [they are] deliberating or voting" (18 U.S.C. § 1508), obstruction relating to court orders (18 U.S.C. § 1509), obstruction pertaining to state and local law enforcement (18 U.S.C. § 1511), and retaliating against a federal judge or federal law enforcement officer by false claim or slander of title (18 U.S.C. § 1521).

There are also civil obstruction statutes that allow for restraining orders to protect against harassment of a victim or witness (18 U.S.C. § 1514). Added, as part of the Sarbanes–Oxley Act is a statute to protect retaliation in fraud cases (18 U.S.C. § 1514A). This statute offers protection to whistleblowers who are employees of

---

[1] See Stuart P. Green, Uncovering the Cover–Up Crimes, 42 Am. Crim. L. Rev. 9 (2005).

[2] See Ellen S. Podgor, Arthur Andersen, LLP and Martha Stewart: Should Materiality be an Element of Obstruction of Justice?, 44 Washburn L.J. 583 (2005).

publicly traded companies, when they come forward to assist in a fraud investigation. Section 1514A provides that an individual can file a complaint with the Secretary of Labor and bring a civil action in court for relief.

Focusing on white collar crime, there is the generic obstruction statute found in 18 U.S.C. § 1503, which protects against obstructions against the due administration of justice. (See § 6.2). Initially the focus of this statute was on protection for officers, jurors, and witnesses. But in 1982, Congress passed as part of the Victim and Witness Protection Act, §§ 1512 and 1513 that focused on obstructions involving witnesses. It remains controversial whether the generic statute, § 1503, can be used when the conduct involves activities covered by the more specific statutes, §§ 1512 and 1513. (See § 6.4). Other statutes that are commonly used in white collar cases include sections 1505, 1510, 1516, 1517, 1518, 1519, and 1520. These, as well as sections 1512 and 1513 are discussed below. (See § 6.3)

A definition statute is offered in 18 U.S.C. § 1515. For the most part it covers terms used in 18 U.S.C. § 1512 and18 U.S.C. § 1513, statutes that concern tampering and retaliating against witnesses. But section 1515 also provides clarifying language for one term in 18 U.S.C. § 1505. Finally, in the final provision of 1515 it states that "[t]his chapter does not prohibit or punish the providing of lawful, bona fide, legal representation services in connection with or anticipation of an official proceeding." (18 U.S.C. § 1515(c)). This provision protects attorneys in their lawful representation of clients.

C. Sentencing as an Obstruction Enhancement

Obstruction of justice is a crime and as a crime the federal sentencing guidelines provides guideline penalties for those convicted of this crime. In addition to noting how obstruction of justice conduct gets treated generally in the sentencing guidelines (§ 2J1.2), it is also important to note that obstruction conduct can serve to increase other sentences. (See § 24.4(D)(4)). The U.S. Sentencing guidelines provide in § 3C1.1that:

> If (1) the defendant willfully obstructed or impeded, or attempted to obstruct or impede, the administration of justice with respect to the investigation, prosecution, or sentencing of the instant offense of conviction, and (2) the obstructive conduct related to (A) the defendant's offense of conviction and any relevant conduct; or (B) a closely related offense, increase the offense level by 2 levels.

§ 6.2   SECTION 1503

A. Overview

The most commonly used obstruction charge for many years has been the generic statute found in 18 U.S.C. § 1503. Although it still remains a common selection by prosecutors, one now finds many charges brought under statutes enacted later, namely, 18 U.S.C. § 1512 and 1513. (See § 6.3(C) & (D)).

Section 1503 emanates from the Act of March 2, 1831,[3] a contempt statute. There were two parts to the Act. The first part dealt with conduct within the courtroom and the second part outside the courtroom.[4] Eventually it was split into two distinct offenses with 18 U.S.C. § 401 being obstruction in the court's presence and 18 U.S.C. § 1503 being obstruction away from the court.[5]

Today, Section 1503 states:

(a) Whoever corruptly, or by threats or force, or by any threatening letter or communication, endeavors to influence, intimidate, or impede any grand or petit juror, or officer in or of any court of the United States, or officer who may be serving at any examination or other proceeding before any United States magistrate judge or other committing magistrate, in the discharge of his duty, or injures any such grand or petit juror in his person or property on account of any verdict or indictment assented to by him, or on account of his being or having been such juror, or injures any such officer, magistrate judge, or other committing magistrate in his person or property on account of the performance of his official duties, or corruptly or by threats or force, or by any threatening letter or communication, influences, obstructs, or impedes, or endeavors to influence, obstruct, or impede, the due administration of justice, shall be punished as provided in subsection (b). If the offense under this section occurs in connection with a trial of a criminal case, and the act in violation of this section involves the threat of physical force or physical force, the maximum term of imprisonment which may be imposed for the offense shall be the higher of that otherwise provided by law or the maximum term that could have been imposed for any offense charged in such case.

(b) The punishment for an offense under this section is—

(1) in the case of a killing, the punishment provided in sections 1111 and 1112;

(2) in the case of an attempted killing, or a case in which the offense was committed against a petit juror and in which a class A or B felony was charged, imprisonment for not more than 20 years, a fine under this title, or both; and

(3) in any other case, imprisonment for not more than 10 years, a fine under this title, or both.

Section 1503 involves two forms of conduct: (a) acts of obstruction to jurors or court officers, and (b) obstruction of the "due administration of justice."

This statute is concerned with "preserving the integrity of the jury trial."[6] Acts of obstruction to jurors or court officers includes threats or force that endeavor to "influence, intimidate, or impede any grand or petit juror" or court officer in the

---

[3] 4 Stat. 487 (1831).

[4] See United States v. Williams, 874 F.2d 968, 978–80 (5th Cir. 1989) (providing a detailed discussion of the history of the this statute).

[5] United States v. Essex, 407 F.2d 214 (6th Cir. 1969).

[6] See United States v. Osborn, 350 F.2d 497, 503 (6th Cir. 1965).

discharge of their duties or alternatively, acts of obstruction that injure jurors or court officers. Bribing a juror constitutes obstructive conduct violating this section. But the conduct does not have to reach this level to violate this portion of the statute. For example, contacting someone on the jury to influence them may suffice.[7]

Success with the obstruction is not necessary. In *United States v. Neiswender*,[8] the Fourth Circuit stated, "the defendant need only have had knowledge or notice that success in his fraud would have likely resulted in an obstruction of justice. Notice is provided by the reasonable foreseeability of the natural and probable consequences of one's acts."

The term "jurors" has been interpreted to include prospective jurors.[9] So one finds prosecutions premised on obstruction against a member of the jury venire.[10] Courts have interpreted "officer[s] in or of any court" to include a federal district court judge[11] and also a bankruptcy trustee.[12]

The basic elements under the omnibus clause of the statute are: (1) "corruptly or by threats or force," (2) endeavored, (3) "to influence, obstruct, or impede, the due administration of justice." It is also necessary that there be a "nexus" between the act and the judicial proceeding. Meeting the element of influencing, obstructing, or impeding the due administration of justice, often referred to as the omnibus clause of the statute, requires (a) a pending proceeding, (b) that the accused knew or had notice of, and (c) that the accused intended to influence, obstruct, or impede its administration. The evidence presented may overlap on different elements, as these elements are not always distinct, but are often intertwined. In essence the omnibus clause is thought of as a "'catch-all provision' which generally prohibits conduct that interferes with the due administration of justice."[13]

B. Corruptly or by Threats or Force

1. Level of Intent

An element of section 1503 is that the prosecution prove that the defendant engaged in the conduct either "corruptly" or "by threats or force, or by any threatening letter or communication." Courts, however, do not always agree on the level of proof required to meet the statutory requirement of acting "corruptly."

Some courts find that the term "corruptly" does not require there to be a showing of "an evil, something bad, wicked or having an evil purpose." It is an act that is done with an attempt to influence a juror or court officer. For example in *United States v.*

---

[7] See United States v. Lazzerini, 611 F.2d 940 (1st Cir. 1979).

[8] 590 F.2d 1269, 1273 (4th Cir. 1979).

[9] See United States v. Russell, 255 U.S. 138 (1921).

[10] See United States v. Jackson, 607 F.2d 1219 (8th Cir. 1979).

[11] See United States v. Margoles, 294 F.2d 371 (7th Cir. 1961).

[12] See United States v. Crispo, 306 F.3d 71 (2d Cir. 2002).

[13] United States v. Benson, 104 F.3d 1267 (11th Cir. 1997) (citing United States v. Thomas, 916 F.2d 647, 651 n.3 (11th Cir. 1990).

Ogle[14] the Tenth Circuit agreed with the trial judge's position that "an endeavor to influence a juror in the performance of his or her duty or to influence, obstruct or impede the due administration of justice is per se unlawful and is tantamount to doing the act corruptly." The court in *Ogle* noted "that the term 'corruptly' does not superimpose a special and additional element on the offense such as a desire to undermine the moral character of a juror."

In contrast, some courts require the government to specifically prove that the accused acted "corruptly." They strictly construe the obstruction statute and require the government to show that the accused acted with "an evil or wicked purpose."[15] In *United States v. Brand*,[16] the Eleventh Circuit found insufficient evidence of the defendant obstructing justice. The court stated that "[t]he offending conduct must be prompted, at least in part, by a 'corrupt motive.'" Using the rule of lenity in interpreting the statute, the court found there was not enough to support the conviction. It was stated:

> It is common practice for attorneys, investigators, insurance adjusters, and law enforcement agents, both state and federal, to attempt to obtain signed statements of witnesses in criminal and civil cases. If they are to be confronted (as they frequently are), with charges of persons claiming that a statement was false, thus resulting in an obstruction of justice charge even though the statement was never submitted to a prosecutor or to the court, a new wave of cases will be filed by federal or state authorities.[17]

Other courts recognize that the term "corruptly" can have different meanings. One court stated that as used in section 1503 it includes "any endeavor to influence a witness or to impede and obstruct justice."[18] In *United States v. Thomas*,[19] the Eleventh Circuit combined some of the varying approaches used in defining the element of "corruptly" and stated this was "the specific intent of the crime," but noted that its meaning can vary with the prosecution. The court stated that, "[g]enerally, the government must show that the defendant knowingly and intentionally undertook an action from which an obstruction of justice was a reasonably foreseeable result." The court noted that "[a]lthough the government is not required to prove that the defendant had the specific purpose of obstructing justice" "it must establish that the conduct was prompted, at least in part, by a 'corrupt motive.'"[20]

2. *Corrupt Conduct*

Courts have found a wide assortment of activities as meeting the definition of "corruptly." For example "the destruction or concealment of documents can fall within the prohibition of the statute."[21] Acts of bribery, including convincing another to bribe a

---

[14] 613 F.2d 233 (10th Cir. 1979).

[15] United States v. Ryan, 455 F.2d 728 (9th Cir. 1971).

[16] 775 F.2d 1460 (11th Cir. 1985).

[17] Id. at 1468.

[18] United States v. Cohen, 202 F.Supp. 587 (D.C. Conn. 1962).

[19] 916 F.2d 647 (11th Cir. 1990).

[20] Id. at 651.

[21] United States v. Rasheed, 663 F.2d 843, 852 (9th Cir. 1981).

potential juror violates section 1503.[22] Fraudulent conduct can also be considered obstructive. As stated in *United States v. Polakoff*,[23] "[i]t is as 'corrupt' to persuade a public officer by lies as by bribes; indeed, to influence him by fraud is not far afield from influencing him by 'threats or force' as prohibited by the statute."[24] An individual who falsely represents him or herself to be a lawyer may be committing a section 1503 violation as it impedes the due administration of justice.[25] Violating the grand jury secrecy rules such as improperly obtaining or selling confidential grand jury testimony can also be an obstruction of justice.[26]

3. *Constitutional Rights*

Obstruction of justice charges are sometimes filed for corrupt acts toward a witness who has been called to testify before a grand or petit jury. A question can arise as to where is the line between lawful conduct of advising someone to assert their constitutional rights under the Fifth Amendment and acting in violation of section 1503 by obstructing justice. In *Cole v. United States*[27] the Ninth Circuit discussed the relationship between advising someone to claim the constitutional privilege against self-incrimination and violating section 1503. Although exercising this constitutional right is lawful, where one "bribes, coerces, forces or threatens a witness to claim it, or advises with corrupt motive the witness to take it," it can be found to be an obstruction of justice. In affirming the defendant's conviction in *Cole*, the court noted that the jury had been instructed "that only *corrupt* methods were prohibited; that *corrupt* influence was the only influence proscribed;—that only any act committed *corruptly* was to be considered."

The line between proper lawyering and obstructive conduct can also arise in the context of an attorney advising a client on his or her constitutional rights against self-incrimination. In *United States v. Cintolo*,[28] the First Circuit affirmed defendant defense attorney's conviction for section 1503 violations, and stated:

> To urge another-whether guilty or not-to plead the fifth amendment because immunity has been withheld and because a reasonable fear of self-inculpation exists is one thing. It is quite another to advise a fully immunized client to claim fifth amendment rights which are no longer live, not because of any fear of self-inculpation, but for the sole purpose of shielding *other* individuals.[29]

4. *Question of Law or Fact*

The question of whether a defendant endeavored to influence a witness "corruptly" has been held by one court to be a "mixed question of law and fact, if not one of fact

---

[22] United States v. Osborn, 350 F.2d 497, 505 (6th Cir. 1965).

[23] 121 F.2d 333 (2d Cir. 1941).

[24] Id. at 335.

[25] United States v. Richardson, 676 F.3d 491 (5th Cir. 2012).

[26] See, e.g., United States v. Saget, 991 F.2d 702 (11th Cir. 1993); United States v. Jeter, 775 F.2d 670 (6th Cir. 1985); United States v. Howard, 569 F.2d 1331 (5th Cir. 1978).

[27] 329 F.2d 437 (9th Cir. 1964).

[28] 818 F.2d 980 (1st Cir. 1987).

[29] Id. at 994.

alone."[30] Most courts hold that whether the endeavor was "corrupt" is a question for the jury to determine.[31]

C. Endeavors

Obstruction of justice does not require an actual obstruction. It does, however, require that the accused "endeavored" to obstruct justice. It has been stated that "[t]he 'endeavor' component of the offense 'describes any effort or assay' to obstruct justice."[32] "[A] section 1503 offense is complete when one corruptly *endeavors* to obstruct or impede the due administration of justice; the prosecution need not prove that the due administration of justice was actually obstructed or impeded."[33]

This element has been described as being similar to a criminal solicitation statute.[34] As such the success of the conduct is irrelevant.[35] It also does not need to rise to the level of being an attempt. In *United States v. Buffalano*,[36] the Second Circuit stated that by using the term "endeavor" "Congress purged from the statute the technicalities associated with distinguishing between preparation for an attempt and the attempt itself."[37]

In *United States v. Aguilar*,[38] the Supreme Court explained the importance of the "endeavor" element of the statute stating:

> Our reading of the statute gives the term "endeavor" a useful function to fulfill: It makes conduct punishable where the defendant acts with an intent to obstruct justice, and in a manner that is likely to obstruct justice, but is foiled in some way. Were a defendant with the requisite intent to lie to a subpoenaed witness who is ultimately not called to testify, or who testifies but does not transmit the defendant's version of the story, the defendant has endeavored to obstruct, but has not actually obstructed, justice. Under our approach, a jury could find such defendant guilty.[39]

In *Ethridge v. United States*[40] the Ninth Circuit reversed a section 1503 conviction where an individual promised a person awaiting sentencing that he could ensure the defendant would receive probation for the sum of $1,000. The fact that the offer was not accepted did not deter the jury from convicting him. But in reversing this conviction, the Ninth Circuit said that an endeavor requires "the defendant's act must

---

[30] United States v. Fayer, 523 F.2d 661, 664 (2d Cir. 1975).

[31] United States v. Fasolino, 586 F.2d 939 (2d Cir. 1978).

[32] United States v. Barfield, 999 F.2d 1520 (11th Cir. 1993).

[33] United States v. Silverman, 745 F.2d 1386, 1395 (11th Cir. 1984).

[34] United States v. Fasolino, 586 F.2d 939 (2d Cir. 1978).

[35] See, e.g., United States v. Richardson, 676 F.3d 491 (5th Cir. 2012); United States v. Russell, 255 U.S. 138 (1921).

[36] 727 F.2d 50 (2d Cir. 1984).

[37] Id. at 53.

[38] 515 U.S. 593, 601–02 (1995).

[39] Id. at 602–03.

[40] 258 F.2d 234 (9th Cir. 1958) (citing Catrino v. United States, 176 F.2d 884, 886 (9th Cir. 1949).

have been directed at, or brought to bear upon, some person who had legal authority to do, or not to do, some act which would or could affect the final outcome of the trial."[41]

This case is contrasted with *United States v. Neiswender*,[42] a case coming from the criminal trial of former Maryland Governor Marvin Mandel. Defendant Neiswender contacted an individual named Arnold Weiner, who served as Mandel's chief defense attorney, saying that "he could 'guarantee' an acquittal of Mandel if 'proper financial arrangements were made.'" Attorney Weiner turned this matter over to the United States Attorney and the court, which led to the eventual conviction of *Neiswender* for obstruction of justice. The issue was then raised on appeal whether the evidence of the element of "endeavor" met the statutory requirements. The court distinguished the *Ethridge* decision saying that "[t]he case is entirely unlike this one in which the jury has found that a reasonable person in Mr. Weiner's position would have considered Neiswender's proposal a serious proposal and not a simple attempt to defraud." But the court in *Neiswender* was also unwilling to endorse the holding in *Ethridge*. The Fourth Circuit court stated, "[t]he statute speaks specifically to an endeavor, and the statute is violated whether or not success of the endeavor would require a high degree of gullibility in the target victim so long as the endeavor itself was done seriously and with the hope of success."

False statements to court officers have been questioned as to whether these meet the "endeavor" element of the statute. In *United States v. Brand*,[43] the Eleventh Circuit reversed a conviction where the false statement had not been submitted to the prosecutor and it was shown that it never existed.

This has been contrasted with *United States v. Fields*[44] where the Eleventh Circuit noted that the false statement existed, despite the fact that it was not actually used in court. The *Fields* court, in distinguishing the *Brand* case, noted that "*Brand* places most of its analysis on the fact that no false statement was ever obtained, and even if a false statement had been obtained, it was not clear that the defendant would have known the statement to be false." The *Fields* court then went on to say that "[i]n this case, the false statement did exist, and its existence in combination with the circumstances of its existence made it far more likely that the statement would have been produced in court and that justice would be obstructed in this case than in *Brand*." But the court also noted that "a false statement need not be actually used in court or delivered to a court officer to satisfy the 'endeavor' element in the obstruction of justice statute."[45]

---

[41] Id. at 236 n.2.

[42] 590 F.2d 1269 (4th Cir. 1979).

[43] 775 F.2d 1460 (11th Cir. 1985).

[44] 838 F.2d 1571 (11th Cir. 1988).

[45] Id. at 1575.

D. To Influence, Obstruct or Impede the Due Administration of Justice

1. *Pending Proceeding*

There are three parts to the "influence, obstruct, or impeded the due administration of justice" element of the statute: 1) a pending proceeding; 2) that the accused knew or had notice of, and 3) that the accused intended to influence, obstruct, or impede its administration. It is a longstanding principle that the accused needs to know or have notice of the judicial proceeding.

Courts have liberally construed the term "pending proceeding." It is not limited to an actual court trial. It includes grand jury proceedings and matters on appeal. Although a matter on appeal is covered, even when the appeal may be frivolous,[46] when the time has passed for the filing of an appeal, a court found that it was no longer a pending proceeding.[47] Some courts have used the filing of a complaint as the point of demarcation, and acts after that time fall within the language of a pending proceeding.

Obstructions to agency investigations are not covered by this statute.[48] So obstructions to the FBI, IRS or other government agencies prior to the filing of a complaint or indictment might not be sufficient for a "pending proceeding."[49] An obstruction to a wiretap order is considered to be like a search warrant and not like a grand jury, thus not within the pending judicial proceedings provision of section 1503.[50]

But a court was unwilling to set aside a plea agreement when an individual pled guilty to obstruction under section 1503 for the statements he gave to the FBI who were conducting an investigation as "part of ongoing official proceedings in the Eastern District of Wisconsin, including grand jury and other criminal proceedings."[51] So, too, obstructive conduct to a probation officer conducting a presentence interview has been found to be within the confines of a pending proceeding.[52] Also obstructive conduct when there is a petition to revoke the defendant's supervised release and issuance of a warrant for his arrest has been considered a "revival of proceedings" that will be considered pending.[53]

Courts have also looked at what constitutes a duly impaneled grand jury and when an investigation crosses the line of becoming a pending grand jury investigation for purposes of section 1503. It is not necessary for the grand jury to have actually heard evidence pursuant to an issued subpoena.[54] In *United States v. Simmons*,[55] the

---

[46] United States v. Fleming, 215 F.3d 930, 936 (9th Cir. 2000).

[47] United States v. Fulbright,105 F.3d 443 (9th Cir. 1997).

[48] See United States v. Scoratow, 137 F.Supp. 620 (W.D. Pa. 1956).

[49] See, e.g., United States v. Tham, 960 F.2d 1391 (9th Cir. 1991); United States v. Ryan, 455 F.2d 728 (9th Cir. 1971).

[50] See United States v. Davis, 183 F.3d 231 (3d Cir. 1999).

[51] Torzala v. United States, 545 F.3d 517 (7th Cir. 2008).

[52] United States v. Gonzalez–Mares, 752 F.2d 1485, 1490–91 (9th Cir. 1985).

[53] United States v. Weber, 320 F.3d 1047 (9th Cir. 2003).

[54] United States v. Walasek, 527 F.2d 676 (3d Cir. 1975).

Third Circuit was unwilling to adopt a "rigid rule that a grand jury proceeding is not 'pending' until a grand jury has actually heard testimony or has in some way taken a role in the decision to issue the subpoena." The court said that the "remedy against potential abuses is not to establish a rule, easily circumvented, by which some formal act of the grand jury will be required to establish 'pendency.'" Instead the court said the "[r]emedy is rather to continue to inquire, in each case, whether the subpoena is issued in furtherance of an actual grand jury investigation, i.e, to secure a presently contemplated presentation of evidence before the grand jury."[56]

This can be distinguished from the Ninth Circuit position in *United States v. Ryan*[57] a case where an Assistant United State Attorney issued subpoenas for IRS agents for information that they were unable to obtain through use of administrative subpoenas. There was no evidence in this case that the grand jury was investigating these matters and the defendant was not indicted until fourteen months after this grand jury had ended. The court said that "the acts complained of must bear a reasonable relationship to the subject of the grand jury inquiry."[58] Other courts limit the *Ryan* decision and are unwilling to accept a test of whether the subpoenaed documents were relevant to the grand-jury investigation." They focus on the fact that in *Ryan* the "IRS had improperly commandeered a grand jury's subpoena power for its own purposes."[59]

Courts examining the question of whether a judicial proceeding is in fact a pending judicial proceeding, have found this to be a question of law.[60]

2.   *Knowledge or Notice*

It is necessary that the defendant know that there is an ongoing criminal proceeding. In *Pettibone v. United States*[61] the Court noted that a person that does not have knowledge of a pending proceeding does not necessarily have the evil intent required for an obstruction charge.

But courts have said that it is not necessary that a defendant know that the witness will appear before the grand jury. Nor is it necessary for the defendant to know "every detail of the actual pending proceeding." It is only necessary on appellate review to determine that a jury "could conclude beyond a reasonable doubt that" the defendant believed that the witness would go before the grand jury.[62]

It is necessary that the defendant's obstructive acts involve a federal proceeding and merely having a federal proceeding does not support the inference that the accused

---

[55] 591 F.2d 206 (3d Cir. 1979).

[56] Id. at 208–09.

[57] 455 F.2d 728 (9th Cir. 1971).

[58] Id. at 734–35.

[59] United States v. Erickson, 561 F.3d 1150 (10th Cir. 2009); see also United States v. Mullins, 22 F.3d 1365 (6th Cir. 1994).

[60] United States v. Gonzalez–Mares, 752 F.2d 1485, 1490 (9th Cir. 1985).

[61] 148 U.S. 197 (1893).

[62] See United States v. Vesich, 724 F.2d 451, 457–58 (5th Cir. 1984).

focused his or her alleged threat toward that proceeding.[63] But it is not necessary for the defendant to know that the proceeding is federal.[64] In this regard, knowledge of the federal element matches cases outside the obstruction of justice area that have held that federal jurisdiction is necessary, but the defendant is not required to know the federal aspect of the attendant circumstance, such as it being a federal officer in a case charging assault on the federal officer.[65]

3. *Intent to Influence, Obstruct, or Impede*

It is necessary that the accused must act with the intent to influence the judicial or grand jury proceeding. "If the defendant lacks knowledge that his actions are likely to affect the judicial proceeding, he lacks the requisite intent to obstruct."[66] (see infra § 6.2(E)). As noted in *United States v. Aguilar* "[r]ecent decisions of Courts of Appeals have likewise tended to place metes and bounds on the very broad language of the catchall provision."[67] The Court stated that "[t]he action taken by the accused must be with an intent to influence judicial or grand jury proceedings; it is not enough that there be an intent to influence some ancillary proceeding, such as an investigation independent of the court's or grand jury's authority."[68]

A brother of a defendant who threatens jurors who finished their jury service was found not to have impeded the due administration of justice. The Sixth Circuit in *United States v. Bashaw*[69] stated that "because the jury's duties already had been completed, his statements could not have had as their 'natural and probable effect' the obstruction of justice nor was such an obstruction 'reasonably foreseeable.'" Although the case was still pending with sentencing and an appeal yet to be had, the jurors no longer had an involvement with the case. There was also no evidence that these jurors would be "affected by fear or intimidation" in other cases.[70]

This is distinguished from a situation when a prosecutor is threatened by a defendant's brother following a trial. The Eleventh Circuit noted that since "the prosecutor was still responsible for representing the government on appeal or against a motion to reduce the sentence of the defendant, the brother had attempted to obstruct justice."[71]

E. Nexus

Merely having a false statement and an obstruction of the administration of justice is not enough for a section 1503 violation. It is also necessary for the

---

[63] United States v. Baker, 494 F.2d 1262, 1265 (6th Cir. 1974).

[64] United States v. Ardito, 782 F.2d 358 (2d Cir. 1986).

[65] See United States v. Feola, 420 U.S. 671 (1975); United States v. Yermian, 468 U.S. 63 (1984) (finding that proof of defendant knowing that it was federal agency, was not required for a violation of a false statement within the jurisdiction of a federal agency). (See Chap. 9).

[66] United States v. Aguilar, 515 U.S. 593, 599 (1995).

[67] Id.

[68] Id. at 593.

[69] 982 F.2d 168 (6th Cir. 1992).

[70] Id. at 172.

[71] United States v. Bashaw, 982 F.2d 168 (6th Cir. 1992) (citing United States v. Fernandez, 837 F.2d 1031 (11th Cir. 1988).

government to prove that there is a nexus between the false statements and the obstruction of the administration of justice.[72]

A leading decision on the importance of the "nexus" requirement is the Supreme Court's decision in *United States v. Aguilar*.[73] United States District Court Judge Robert Aguilar was convicted of illegally disclosing a wiretap and obstruction of justice under section 1503. The testimony was that the defendant made a false statement to an investigating officer. There was no evidence, however, that he knew the false statement would be used by a grand jury. The Ninth Circuit, on rehearing en banc reversed both convictions. The Supreme affirmed the reversal of the section 1503 conviction, but reversed the wiretap holding of the lower court.

The Supreme Court held that there is a nexus requirement for obstruction of justice and that requirement is "that the act must have a relationship in time, causation, or logic with the judicial proceedings."[74] The Court stated that "the endeavor must have the 'natural and probable effect' of interfering with the due administration of justice."[75] As noted, this does not mean that the endeavor is required to be successful. It simply means that that "if the defendant lacks knowledge that his actions are likely to affect the judicial proceeding, he lacks the requisite intent to obstruct."[76] Merely uttering false statements to agents is not enough for an obstruction of justice conviction under § 1503.

Justice Scalia, joined by Justices Kennedy and Thomas dissented to the obstruction part of the Court's decision. This dissent states that "[t]he 'nexus' requirement that the Court today engrafts into § 1503 has no basis in the words Congress enacted."[77]

The nexus requirement also proved an issue in the Supreme Court decision in *Arthur Andersen LLP v. United States*.[78] This case was brought under section 1512(b)(2), as opposed to section 1503. The Supreme Court reversed the convictions because of improper jury instructions. Particularly, the Court noted that the jury instructions did not properly present the requisite consciousness of wrongdoing. (See § 6.3(C)). But the Court also discussed an instruction regarding the "nexus" requirement for obstruction of justice. Upholding its prior decision in *Aguilar*, the Court stated that the instruction was infirm because, "[t]hey led the jury to believe that it did not have to find *any* nexus between the 'persua[sion]' to destroy documents and any particular proceeding."[79]

In *United States v. Byrne*,[80] the First Circuit was unwilling to extend the nexus requirement for section 1512(b)(2) to section 1512(b)(3). The court stated in discussing

---

[72] United States v. Thomas, 916 F.2d 647 (11th Cir. 1990).

[73] 515 U.S. 593 (1995).

[74] Id. at 593.

[75] Id.

[76] Id. at 599.

[77] Id. at 617.

[78] 544 U.S. 696 (2005).

[79] Id. at 707–08.

[80] 435 F.3d 16 (1st Cir. 2006).

the holding from *Arthur Andersen LLP*, that "subsection (b)(3) does not refer to an 'official proceeding,'" but rather "refers to a defendant intending to hinder, delay, or prevent communication to a 'law enforcement officer or judge of the United States.'"

§ 6.3   OTHER WHITE COLLAR CRIMINAL OBSTRUCTION STATUTES

A.   Section 1505

Several other obstruction statutes are commonly used in white collar cases. For example, section 1505 is an obstruction statute that one sees in the white collar context. The crux of the statute pertains to proceedings before departments, agencies and committees of the government. The statute was used against Martha Stewart for her obstructive conduct in an SEC investigation into her sale of Imclone stock.

One also finds the statute used for obstructive conduct before legislative bodies. This statute was used against John Poindexter, albeit unsuccessfully, for his congressional testimony in the Iran–Contra affair. The District of Columbia Circuit Court reversed in *United States v. Poindexter*,[81] because the Independent Counsel had not demonstrated that Poindexter's compelled testimony provided under an immunity grant was not being used against him. This would violate the immunity statute, 18 U.S.C. § 6002, and also the Fifth Amendment of the U.S. Constitution.

Additionally, the court in *Poindexter* reversed the two obstruction counts premised on 18 U.S.C. § 1505 "on the ground that the statute as written cannot constitutionally be applied to some of the conduct, specifically lying to or misleading the Congress." Looking at the history of the statute and the specific legislative history with regard to the term "corruptly," the court stated "the legislative history gives no better notice than does the statutory test that lying to or misleading a Member of the Congress (or an agency) violates § 1505. If anything, the 1940 legislative history suggests that such behavior is excluded from the scope of that section." The court found that the statute had also not been clarified by judicial decisions, and was therefore "unconstitutionally vague as applied to Poindexter's conduct."

Congress modified § 1505 by adding a definition for the term "corruptly" in a new definitions statute located at 18 U.S.C. § 1515(b). It states that "as used in section 1505, the term 'corruptly' means acting with an improper purpose, personally or by influencing another, including making a false or misleading statement, or withholding, concealing, altering, or destroying a document or other information." The Victim and Witness Protection Act also modified § 1505 by moving obstructive witness conduct to §§ 1512 and 1513.

Many of the elements for 18 U.S.C. § 1505 are synonymous with the elements of § 1503. (See § 6.2) In *United States v. Price*,[82] the Ninth Circuit described the elements of § 1505 as:

---

[81] 951 F.2d 369 (D.C.Cir. 1991).

[82] 951 F.2d 1028 (9th Cir. 1991).

"[t]he crime of obstruction of proceedings has three essential elements. First, there must be a proceeding pending before a department or agency of the United States. Second, the defendant must be aware of the pending proceeding. Third, the defendant must have intentionally endeavored corruptly to influence, obstruct or impede the pending proceeding."[83]

It should also be noted that "[t]he obstruction need not be successful; the jury may convict one who 'endeavors' to obstruct such a proceeding."[84]

In *United States v. Quattrone*,[85] the Second Circuit examined the defendant's obstruction of justice convictions under sections 1503 for grand jury obstruction, 1505 for SEC investigation obstruction, and 1512 for "knowingly and corruptly persuading or endeavoring to persuade others to withhold or destroy documents with intent to interfere with the proceedings." The case was on a retrial as the first jury was unable to reach a verdict. The Second Circuit vacated the convictions entered from the second jury trial, finding improper jury instructions. With respect to §§ 1503 and 1505, the court stated that the jury instruction was improper as "a defendant must know that his corrupt actions 'are likely to affect the . . . proceeding.'" Merely calling for the destruction of documents that are within an agency's proceeding is not the same as corrupt actions when the defendant knows his actions are likely to affect those proceedings.

Some cases will question whether the agency is in fact a sufficient one for purposes of section 1505. For example, in *United States v. Leo*,[86] the Third Circuit was faced with the question of whether the Defense Contract Audit Agency, an agency that the defendant claimed lacked "rule-making or adjudicative authority" would be sufficient for a "proceeding" as the term is used in section 1505. Specifically, it was noted that a later statute, 18 U.S.C. § 1516 focused on obstructive conduct against a federal auditor. Since section 1516 did not exist at the time of the defendant's crime, he claimed that he could not be charged with a violation of 1505. In rejecting the defendant's argument, the court also stated that "[t]he Defense Contract Audit Agency does not operate within a vacuum inside the Department of Defense; instead, as this case makes clear, the Agency serves an important role within the Department in uncovering and reporting serious fraud."[87]

B. Section 1510

Section 1510 pertains to obstruction of criminal investigations. It focuses on bribery acts that are used "to obstruct, delay, or prevent the communication of information relating to a violation of any criminal statute of the United States by any person to a criminal investigator." (18 U.S.C. § 1510(a)). This statute also protects secrecy of investigations by making it criminal for officers of a financial institution to notify individuals of subpoenas for records of that financial institution or information

---

[83] Id. at 1031 (citations omitted).

[84] United States v. Vixie, 532 F.2d 1277, 1278 (9th Cir. 1976).

[85] 441 F.3d 153 (2d Cir. 2006).

[86] 941 F.2d 181 (3d Cir. 1991).

[87] Id. at 199.

given in response to a subpoena. (18 U.S.C. § 1510(b)). Thus, the bank official that contacts the customer to tell them that their bank records have been subpoenaed by the government can face criminal penalties. When the information is given intentionally to obstruct a judicial proceeding, the crime carries a penalty of a fine and imprisonment of up to five years. (18 U.S.C. § 1510(b)(1)). Mere direct or indirect notification to the customer or person named in the subpoena, without proof of specific intent to obstruct a judicial proceeding, carries a penalty of a fine and imprisonment of not more than one year. (18 U.S.C. § 1510(b)(2)).

Section 1510 also provides a specific offense for intentional obstruction conduct by individuals engaged in the insurance industry who "directly or indirectly notifies any other person about the existence or contents of a subpoena for records of that person engaged in such business or information that has been furnished to a Federal grand jury in response to that subpoena." (18 U.S.C. § 1510(d)). A final section of 1510 provides for obstruction conduct by individuals who fail to adhere to certain federal disclosure prohibitions or confidentiality requirements as set forth in several different acts.

C. Section 1512

18 U.S.C. § 1512 is a key obstruction statute coming from the Victim and Witness Protection Act of 1982, that were enacted to focus on witness tampering conduct. Unlike the generic provision found in section 1503 (see § 6.2), this statute goes beyond judicial proceedings to cover obstructive conduct surrounding grand jury proceedings. Section 1512 concerns tampering with a witness, victim or an informant. Some of the terms used in this statute are defined in the definition statute, 18 U.S.C. § 1515. Concerns have been raised about whether section 1512 can be used with the general obstruction statute found in 1503. (See § 6.4).

18 U.S.C. 1512's section (a)–(d) provides the different levels of conduct. Section (a)(1) of the statute pertains to individuals who intentionally kill or attempt to kill someone to

(A) prevent the attendance or testimony of any person in an official proceeding;

(B) present the production of a record, document, or other object, in an official proceeding; or

(C) prevent the communication by any person to a law enforcement officer or judge of the United States of information relating to the commission or possible commission of a Federal offense or a violation of conditions of probation, parole, or release pending judicial proceedings;

Section (a)(2) focuses on the use or attempted used of physical force or threat of physical force with an intent to "influence, delay, or prevent the testimony of any person in an official proceeding;" or "causes or induce[s] a person to"

(i) withhold testimony, or withhold a record, document, or other object, from an official proceeding;

(ii) alter, destroy, mutilate, or conceal an object with intent to impair the integrity or availability of the object for use in an official proceeding;

(iii) evade legal process summoning that person to appear as a witness, or to produce a record, document, or other object, in an official proceeding; or

(iv) be absent from an official proceeding to which that person has been summoned by legal process; or

Or "hinder, delay, or prevent the communication to a law enforcement officer or judge of the United States of information relating to the commission or possible commission of a Federal offense or a violation of conditions of probation, supervised release, parole, or release pending judicial proceedings."

Under subsection (a)(1) and (2) the penalties offered include the death penalty when a death occurred. Attempts to murder or to use physical force have a maximum imprisonment of thirty years. Threats of the use of physical force have a maximum term of imprisonment of up to twenty years.

More common in white collar cases are subsections (b), (c) and (d). Subsection (b) involves the same acts noted in subsection (a)(2) such as withholding testimony, altering, concealing or doing acts which hinder. But instead of involving physical force, threats of force, or such attempted conduct, this subsection pertains to "[w]hoever knowingly uses intimidation, threatens, or corruptly persuades another person or attempts to do so, or engages in misleading conduct toward another person, with intent" to do these acts. Although initially this subsection had a maximum penalty of ten years, it was raised and now stands at a maximum penalty of twenty years.

Thus, one who asks witnesses to lie to investigators about the source of down payments on loans, can be convicted under § 1512(b)(3) for "corruptly persuading [ ] another person, or attempt [ ] to do so ... with intent to ... hinder, delay, or prevent the communication to a law enforcement officer or judge of the United States of information relation to the commission or possible commission of a Federal offense."[88] However, asking witnesses to withhold information from investigators is not sufficient for a § 1512(b) violation.[89]

Subsection (c) concerns corrupt actions, with again a penalty of up to twenty years. It prohibits the following obstructive conduct by an individual who:

(1) alters, destroys, mutilates, or conceals a record, document, or other object, or attempts to do so, with the intent to impair the object's integrity or availability for use in an official proceeding; or

(2) otherwise obstructs, influences, or impedes any official proceeding, or attempts to do so,

---

[88] United States v. Weiss, 630 F.3d 1263 (10th Cir. 2010) (citing 18 U.S.C. § 1512(b)(3)).

[89] See United States v. Farrell, 126 F.3d 484, 489 (3d Cir. 1997).

This subsection was added as part of the Sarbanes–Oxley Act of 2002 and some attribute this addition to *United States v. Arthur Andersen, LLP*. Most noticeably, this subsection adds to the criminal activity, conduct regarding records and documents.

Finally subsection (d) involves intentional harassment that "hinders, delays, prevents, or dissuades any person from:

(1) attending or testifying in an official proceeding; (2) reporting to a law enforcement officer or judge of the United States the commission or possible commission of a Federal offense or a violation of conditions of probation supervised release, parole, or release pending judicial proceedings; (3) arresting or seeking the arrest of another person in connection with a Federal offense; or (4) causing a criminal prosecution, or a parole or probation revocation proceeding, to be sought or instituted, or assisting in such prosecution or proceeding;

This subsection includes attempt conduct. Subsection (d) initially carried a maximum penalty of imprisonment of up to one year, but this was increased in 2008 to three years.

Section 1512 allows an affirmative defense for a defendant who was attempting to "encourage, induce, or cause the other person to testify truthfully."[90] The statute does not require that at the time of the offense, that the official proceeding be pending or even that it is about to be instituted. It is necessary that that the proceeding at least be foreseen.[91] Nor is it necessary that the item in question, whether it be testimony, record, document, or other object, have to be "admissible in evidence or free of a claim of privilege."[92] Thus, even when the item in question could not have been used in a court proceeding, an individual who destroys or alters it can still be prosecuted.

The statute also explicitly removes a *mens rea* requirement for one element of the crime. It states that "no state of mind need be proved with respect to the circumstance"—

(1) that the official proceeding before a judge, court, magistrate judge, grand jury, or government agency is before a judge or court of the United States, a United States magistrate judge, a bankruptcy judge, a Federal grand jury, or a Federal Government agency; or (2) that the judge is a judge of the United States or that the law enforcement officer is an officer or employee of the Federal Government or a person authorized to act for or on behalf of the Federal Government or serving the Federal Government as an adviser or consultant.[93]

18 U.S.C. § 1512 permits the prosecution of extraterritorial conduct.[94]

The penalties, as previously noted, differ dependent upon which portion of the statute was violated. But if the offense "occurs in connection with a trial of a criminal

---

[90] 18 U.S.C. § 1512(e).
[91] Arthur Andersen, LLP. v. United States, 544 U.S. 696, 707–08 (2005).
[92] 18 U.S.C. § 1512(f).
[93] 18 U.S.C. § 1512(g).
[94] 18 U.S.C. § 1512(h).

case, the maximum term of imprisonment which may be imposed for the offense shall be the higher of that otherwise provided by law or the maximum term that could have been imposed for any offense charged in such case."[95] Likewise, conspiracies charged with an obstruction provision will incur "the same penalties as those proscribed for the offense the commission of which was the object of the conspiracy."[96]

Because there have been many cases brought under section 1512, there are a good number of appellate decisions that offer guidance in interpreting this statute. Many of these cases involve white collar activity. For example in *United States v. Shotts*,[97] a criminal defense attorney who ran a bail bond business was charged with obstruction under section 1512, as well as other crimes. Although the Eleventh Circuit reversed the mail fraud counts, it affirmed the obstruction of justice counts finding that "corrupt" as used in this statute was not vague. Although that term had been found vague in *United States v. Poindexter*,[98] a case brought under section 1505, it was clear to the court in *Shotts* that the holding in *Poindexter* was limited to that specific statute and did not apply to a prosecution under § 1512.

Many cases that are brought under § 1512 use the interpretations provided by other obstruction statutes. For example, courts often look to cases brought under § 1503 in interpreting § 1512's provisions of "corrupt,"[99] "nexus,"[100] and "proceedings."[101]

There can be differences between § 1503 and § 1512. For example, unlike section 1503, section 1512 does not require that the official proceeding be instituted at the time of the offense. Courts also differ on whether section 1512's use of the term "corruptly persuades" should have a different meaning than the term "corruptly" as used in section 1503. Some take the posture that these terms should be interpreted differently.[102] One court noted that this view finds support in the Supreme Court's opinion in *Arthur Andersen, LLP*.[103] Others, however, prefer to refer to how the term "corruptly" is interpreted for purposes of section 1503.[104]

In *Arthur Andersen LLP. v. United States*,[105] the Supreme Court reviewed an obstruction conviction under section 1512(b)(2)(A) that was premised on the alleged shredding of documents by the accounting company at the time of the Enron investigation. Arthur Andersen argued that it was destroying documents as part of its regular retention policy. This indictment was prior to the enactment of the existing document destruction statute found in § 1512(c). The Supreme Court noted that "'document retention policies' which are created in part to keep certain information

---

[95] 18 U.S.C. § 1512(j).

[96] 18 U.S.C. § 1512(k).

[97] 145 F.3d 1289 (11th Cir. 1998).

[98] 951 F.2d 369, 378 (D.C. Cir. 1991); see also § 6.3(A).

[99] See § 6.2(B).

[100] See § 6.2(E).

[101] See infra § 6.2(D).

[102] See, e.g., United States v. Farrell, 126 F.3d 484, 489–90 (3d Cir. 1997).

[103] United States v. Doss, 630 F.3d 1181, 1189–90 (9th Cir. 2011).

[104] See, e.g., United States v. Thompson, 76 F.3d 442 (2d Cir. 1996).

[105] 544 U.S. 696 (2005).

from getting into the hands of others, including the Government, are common in business." The Court in reversing this conviction discussed the term "corruptly" and noted:

> The outer limits of this element need not be explored here because the jury instructions at issue simply failed to convey the requisite consciousness of wrongdoing. Indeed, it is striking how little culpability the instructions required. For example, the jury was told that, "even if [petitioner] honestly and sincerely believed that its conduct was lawful, you may find [petitioner] guilty."[106]

The Supreme Court also repeated from *Aguilar* that there must be a "'nexus' between the obstructive act and the proceeding."[107]

In *United States v. Black*,[108] the Seventh Circuit reaffirmed the obstruction of justice conviction following the Supreme Court's ruling remanding mail fraud convictions premised on intangible rights. The remand was to determine whether the convictions were from permissible conduct, namely bribery or kickbacks."[109] (See supra chapter 4). Charged under 18 U.S.C. § 1512(c)(1) Conrad Black was found to have obstructed justice by knowing that he and his co-defendants "were being investigated by a grand jury and by the SEC," and that he removed along with others "13 boxes of documents from his office."

D. Section 1513

18 U.S.C. § 1513 is also an obstruction statute coming from the Victim and Witness Protection Act of 1982. It concerns retaliation against a witness, victim, or informant. Like section 1512, some of the terms used in this statute are defined in the definition statute, 18 U.S.C. § 1515. Also like section 1512, it allows for extraterritorial federal jurisdiction[110] and provides that conspiracies "shall be subject to the same penalties as those prescribed for the offense the commission of which was the object of the conspiracy."[111] Many of the provisions from section 1512 are replicated in this statute, except the focus now is on retaliation. Thus, in section 1513(b) it provides for a maximum penalty of twenty years when the defendant "knowingly engages in any conduct and thereby causes bodily injury to another person or damages the tangible property of another person, or threatens to do so, with intent to retaliate against any person for":

> (1) the attendance of a witness or party at an official proceeding, or any testimony given or any record, document, or other object produced by a witness in an official proceeding; or

> (2) any information relating to the commission or possible commission of a Federal offense or a violation of conditions of probation, supervised release, parole, or

---

[106] Id. at 707 (citations omitted).
[107] Id. at 708; see also § 6.2(E).
[108] 625 F.3d 386 (7th Cir. 2010).
[109] 130 S.Ct. 2963 (2010).
[110] 18 U.S.C. § 1513(d).
[111] 18 U.S.C. § 1513(f).

release pending judicial proceedings given by a person to a law enforcement officer;

One does not find this statute used in white collar cases to the extent seen with section 1512, although section 1513 was used as a basis of discussing what constitutes retaliation in a civil action of an employee against an employer and others for retaliating against him for his testimony in federal court.[112]

E. Section 1516

18 U.S.C. §§ 1516–1520 provide obstruction statutes pertaining to specific conduct. Most of the crimes prohibited are in the white collar realm.

Section 1516 pertains to obstruction of a federal audit, and prohibits anyone who obstructs a "federal auditor in the performance of official duties relating to a person, entity, or program receiving in excess of $100,000, directly or indirectly, from the United States in any 1 year period." The statute defines "federal auditor to as "any person employed on a full- or part-time or contractual basis to reform an audit or a quality assurance inspection for or on behalf of the United States. The one year time period is defined pursuant to 18 U.S.C. § 666.

In *United States v. Plasser American Corp.*,[113] the Eastern District of Pennsylvania examined the question of whether Amtrak qualified as a federal agency for purposes of section 1516. The court noted that Congress had explicitly legislated that "Amtrak 'is not a department, agency, or instrumentality of the United States Government.'"[114] Although case law supports this view, there are cases holding that Amtrak is "an agency or instrumentality of the United States for the purpose of individual rights guaranteed against the Government by the Constitution."

The court in *Plasser* turned to the definition in 18 U.S.C. § 6, enacted in 1948, finding that under this section Amtrak comes within the definition of an agency, but that under 49 U.S.C. § 24301(a)(3), enacted in 1970, it does not. The court, turning to the rule of lenity, held that "[d]efendants no doubt knew that Amtrak was the recipient of federal funds, but that knowledge by itself does not overcome the statute construction problems of § 1516 that are posed by these facts."

Auditors paid by an outside company who are reimbursed by the federal government can meet the definition of a "federal auditor" for purposes of the statute. The key is whether the auditor is performing the work on behalf of the federal government.[115]

F. Section 1517

18 U.S.C. § 1517 prohibits obstructing an examination of a financial institution. It carries a maximum penalty of five years. The statute was found not to be

---

[112] See Odum v. Rayonier, Inc., 316 Fed. Appx. 855 (11th Cir. 2008).

[113] 57 F.Supp. 2d 140 (E.D. Pa. 1999).

[114] 49 U.S.C. § 24301(a)(3).

[115] United States v. Hames, 185 Fed. Appx. 318 (5th Cir. 2006).

unconstitutionally vague when challenged by a defendant who had "directed bank employees to alter records sought by bank investigators, provide some documents while concealing others, and misrepresent to bank investigators certain bank transactions."[116]

G. Section 1518

18 U.S.C. § 1518 is a specific obstruction statute targeting obstructive conduct in criminal investigations of health care offenses. The statute is limited to "information or records relating to a violation of a Federal health care offense to a criminal investigator." This crime carries a penalty of a maximum of five years imprisonment. The statute explicitly defines "criminal investigator" to include "any individual duly authorized by a department, agency, or armed force of the United States to conduct or engage in investigations for prosecutions for violations of health care offenses." A definition of what is considered a "federal health care offense" is found in 18 U.S.C. § 24.

In *United States v. Franklin–El*,[117] the Tenth Circuit affirmed seventeen counts of health care fraud, but reversed for insufficient evidence the one count for obstruction of justice that had been brought under 18 U.S.C. § 1518. The statute required the government to prove that the defendant obstructed or attempted to obstruct justice, which meant that "the government needed to show he willfully prevented, obstructed, misled, or delayed 'the communication of information or records relating to a violation of a Federal health care offense to a criminal investigator' or attempted to do so." When there was no proof of willfulness or intent, the court found there was insufficient evidence.

H. Section 1519

18 U.S.C. § 1519, added as part of the Sarbanes–Oxley Act of 2002, relates to obstruction conduct that involves destruction, alteration, or falsification of records in federal investigations and bankruptcy.[118] It is sometimes referred to as the "anti-shredding" statute. It carries imprisonment of up to twenty years. In *United States v. Perraud*,[119] a Southern District of Florida court noted the lack of cases that break down the elements of the statute, thereafter describing them as follows:

> (1) An investigation or other matter within the jurisdiction of a department of agency or the United States must have been pending or contemplated by such department or agency of the United States; (2) the defendant must have been aware of the pending or contemplated matter or investigation; and (3) the defendant must have knowingly altered, concealed, mutilated, or destroyed something with the intent to impede, obstruct, or influence the pending or

---

[116] United States v. Church, 11 Fed. Appx. 264 (4th Cir. 2001).

[117] 555 F.3d 1115 (10th Cir. 2009).

[118] See generally Dana E. Hill, Note, Anticipatory Obstruction of Justice: Pre–Emptive Document Destruction Under the Sarbanes–Oxley Anti Shredding Statute, 18 U.S.C. § 1519, 89 Cornell L. Rev. 1519 (2004).

[119] See United States v. Perraud, 672 F. Supp. 2d 1328 (S.D. Fl. 2009).

contemplated matter or investigation, or any matter in relation to the pending or contemplated matter or investigation.[120]

Some cases brought under this statute relate generally to federal investigations, while others are focused on obstructions in bankruptcy matters.[121] Courts have been clear that acting "knowingly" is not sufficient, and that "knowingly with the intent to obstruct justice" is needed.[122] The defendant does not need to know of the pending proceeding.[123]

The statute has been found to not be unconstitutionally vague.[124] In *United States v. Kernell*,[125] the defendant was convicted for obstruction of justice under section 1519 for "deleting information from his computer that related to his effort to gain access to the email account of then-Alaska governor and Vice Presidential candidate Sarah Palin." The Sixth Circuit rejected the two constitutional challenges of the defendant, "that the structure of the statute creates an ambiguity as to the application of *mens rea* to various elements of the statute" and "that the defendant act 'in contemplation of an investigation' is vague as to the required state of mind."[126]

Courts are not always in agreement on whether § 1519 requires a nexus between the defendant's conduct and the proceeding. In *United States v. Gray*,[127] the Second Circuit examined section 1519 to determine whether a nexus between the defendants' conduct and an official proceeding was required for this obstruction statute. The defendant argued that this nexus was necessary in light of how courts had narrowly interpreted section 1503 requiring the obstruction of justice to be "closely tied to a pending judicial proceeding. (See § 6.6). The Second Circuit, however, found otherwise in looking at the statute's legislative history. The court stated:

> Section 1519 is meant to apply broadly to any acts to destroy or fabricate physical evidence so long as they are done with the intent to obstruct, impede or influence the investigation or proper administration of any matter, and such matter is within the jurisdiction of an agency of the United States, or such acts done either in relation to or in contemplation of such a matter or investigation. *This statute is specifically meant not to include any technical requirement, which some courts have read into other obstruction of justice statutes, to tie the obstructive conduct to a pending or imminent proceeding or matter.* It is also sufficient that the act is done "in contemplation" of or in relation to a matter or investigation. *It is also meant to do away with the distinctions, which some courts have read into*

---

[120] Id. at 1350.

[121] See United States v. Holstein, 618 F.3d 610 (7th Cir. 2010) (finding sufficient evidence for § 1519 for bankruptcy obstruction).

[122] See, e.g., United States v. Kernell, 667 F.3d 746 (6th Cir. 2012); United States v. Jho, 465 F. Supp.2d 618, 637 n.9 (E.D. Tex. 2006) rev'd on other grounds 534 F.3d 398 (5th Cir. 2008).

[123] United States v. Gray, 642 F.3d 371, 378 (2d Cir. 2011); see also United States v. Ionia Management S.A., 526 F. Supp.2d 319 (D. Conn. 2007), affirmed by United States v. Ionia Management S.A., 555 F.3d 303 (2d Cir. 2009).

[124] See United States v. Hunt, 526 F.3d 739 (11th Cir. 2008).

[125] 667 F.3d 746 (6th Cir. 2012).

[126] Id. at 754–56.

[127] 642 F.3d 371 (2d Cir. 2011).

obstruction statutes, between court proceedings, investigations, regulatory or administrative proceedings (whether formal or not), and less formal government inquiries, regardless of their title. Destroying or falsifying documents to obstruct any of these types of matters or investigations, which in fact are proved to be within the jurisdiction of any federal agency are covered by this statute.[128]

In contrast, another court explicitly held that § 1519 required a nexus requirement.[129]

Defendant Hunt, in *United States v. Hunt,*[130] questioned his conviction under § 1519 arguing that the statute is concerned with evidence preservation. He said that since he created the evidence it was outside the scope of the statute. In rejecting this argument and affirming Hunt's conviction under § 1519, the Eleventh Circuit stated that "[a]lteration, destruction, mutilation and concealment certainly suggest § 1519 is concerned partially with evidence destruction, but it is not *solely* concerned with destruction or tampering." Despite the fact the Hunt had created the document in question, the court stated that "[n]othing suggests the document mentioned in § 1519 must be already existing at the time the false entry was made."[131]

I.   Section 1520

Also coming from the Sarbanes–Oxley Act is 18 U.S.C. § 1520, a statute pertaining to obstructive conduct in the form of destruction of corporate audit records. The statute requires "accountant[s] who conduct an audit of an issuer of securities" to "maintain all audit or review workpapers for five years. 18 U.S.C. § 1520(a)(1). The statute also calls for the SEC to promulgate rules and regulations "regarding the retention of relevant records." 18 U.S.C. § 1520(a)(2). The statute carries a maximum of ten years imprisonment for either the violation of the provision requiring accountants to maintain audit records or a violation of an SEC regulation promulgated pursuant to the authority granted it by this statute. 18 U.S.C. § 1520(b). The statute provides that the requirements of this law do not serve to relieve a person of other retention laws provided by state or federal authority. 18 U.S.C. § 1520(c).

§ 6.4   SECTION 1503 AS IT RELATES TO OTHER OBSTRUCTION STATUTES

With many obstruction statutes, a question can arise as to which statute is the more appropriate charge. Specifically there has been the question of whether the omnibus clause found in section 1503 can still be used for obstruction conduct against witnesses, in light of Congress passing sections 1512 and 1513, statutes that relate to obstruction against witnesses. When sections 1512 and 1513 were passed as part of the Victim and Witness Protection Act, Congress removed obstructions to witnesses and parties from section 1503. Despite the removal of this language in 1503, prosecutors

---

[128] Id. (citing S.Rep. No. 107–146, at 14–15 (2002), 2002 WL 863249, at *12–13 (emphases added) (footnotes omitted)).

[129] See United States v. Moyer, 726 F. Supp.2d 498, 505–06 (M.D. Pa. 2010), but see United States v. Yielding, 657 F.3d 688, 713 n.4 (8th Cir. 2011).

[130] 526 F.3d 739 (11th Cir. 2008).

[131] Id. at 744.

continue to bring these actions under 1503's omnibus clause for obstruction impeding the due administration of justice.

Courts typically have taken the position that section 1503 may continue to be charged, despite the specific language regarding "witnesses" in sections 1512 and 1513. One finds decisions in the First, Fourth, Sixth, Ninth, and Eleventh Circuits that allow for obstruction conduct against witnesses to be prosecuted under section 1503 despite the passage of sections 1512 and 1513.[132] Some of these decisions are limited to specific forms of witness tampering. For example, in *United States v. Lester*[133] the Ninth Circuit rejected the argument that the removal from section1503 of all references to witnesses was an indication that the statute had been replaced by section 1512. The court noted that "noncoercive witness tampering-including hiding a witness-would fall outside both section 1512 and section 1513." The Ninth Circuit stated:

> [I]t would be improper to hold that Congress silently decriminalized noncoercive, but nevertheless corrupt, efforts to interfere with witnesses. Rather, we believe that Congress enacted section 1512 to prohibit specific conduct comprising various forms of coercion of witnesses, leaving the omnibus provision of section 1503 to handle more imaginative forms of criminal behavior, including forms of witness tampering, that defy enumeration.[134]

In 1988 Congress "amended section 1512 to cover non-coecive witness tampering." At the time of this amendment Senator Biden stated that the new legislation was:

> intended . . . merely to include in section 1512 the same protection of witnesses from non-coercive influence that *was (and is)* found in section 1503. It would permit prosecution of such conduct in the Second Circuit, where it is not now permitted, and would *allow* such prosecutions in other circuits to be brought under section 1512 rather than under the catch-all provision of section 1503.[135]

One jurisdiction has been vocal in prohibiting the charging of 1503 witness obstruction conduct after the passage of section 1512. In *United States v. Hernandez*,[136] the Second Circuit reversed a conviction finding that it was improper to charge 1503 for conduct involving the threatening of a witness. The court stated that "congress affirmatively intended to remove witnesses entirely from the scope of § 1503." The Second Circuit said this was "graphically demonstrated by examining those portions of § 1503 that congress expressly deleted."[137] This position was reaffirmed by the Second

---

[132] See, e.g., United States v. LeMoure, 474 F.3d 37 (1st Cir. 2007); United States v. Tackett, 113 F.3d 603 (6th Cir. 1997); United States v. Maloney, 71 F.3d 645 (7th Cir. 1995); United States v. Moody, 977 F.2d 1420 (11th Cir. 1992); United States v. Kenny, 973 F.2d 339, 343–43 (4th Cir. 1992).

[133] 749 F.2d 1288 (9th Cir. 1984).

[134] Id. at 1294.

[135] United States v. Lamoure, 474 F.3d 37 (1st Cir. 2007) (citing 134 Cong. Rec. S17,369 (1988) (statement of Sen. Biden) (emphasis added)).

[136] 730 F.2d 895 (2d Cir. 1984).

[137] Id. at 898.

Circuit in *United States v. Masterpol*, where the court held that witness tampering covered by section 1512 cannot be prosecuted under section 1503.[138]

When section 1503 is examined with section 1512(c), a provision added as part of the Sarbanes–Oxley Act of 2002, the position expressed in *Hernandez* has been distinguished. In *United States v. Jahedi*,[139] the defendant argued that it was improper to use section 1503 to punish document destruction now covered in section 1512(c). A district court in the Southern District of New York held that "Congress did not make any express change to section 1503 when it enacted section 1512(c)(1)." The court noted that "[g]iven that courts have consistently construed section 1503 to apply to document destruction, no language in the statute was suitable for deletion." Distinguishing *Hernandez*, the court stated that "[u]nlike in *Hernandez*, Jahedi has identified no legislative history that indicates with any rigor-let alone expressly states-that Congress affirmatively intended section 1512(c)(1) to be the exclusive vehicle for prosecution of obstruction of justice based on document destruction."[140]

Justice Scalia, in an opinion that was concurring in part and dissenting in part[141] in *United States v. Aguilar*[142] referenced the overlap between sections 1503 and 1512. He stated, "[t]he fact that there is now some overlap between § 1503 and § 1512 is no more intolerable than the fact that there is some overlap between the omnibus clause of § 1503 and the other provisions of § 1503 itself. It hardly leads to the conclusion that § 1503 was, to the extent of the overlap, silently repealed."

---

[138] United States v. Masterpol, 940 F.2d 760 (2d Cir. 1991).

[139] 681 F. Supp.2d 430 (S.D.N.Y. 2009).

[140] Id. at 439.

[141] Justices Kennedy and Thomas joined his opinion.

[142] 515 U.S. 593, 616 (1995).

Chapter 7

BRIBERY, EXTORTION, AND CONFLICTS OF INTEREST

§ 7.1   INTRODUCTION

The corruption of government officials is a problem as old as organized society. It was bemoaned in the Bible, which said "[y]ou shall not take a bribe, for a bribe blinds the clear-sighted and subverts the cause of the just."[1] Every nation outlaws bribery of government officials, although in some countries it is a common occurrence that even the most basic public services require some type of facilitating payment. International conventions have been adopted to address corruption in both domestic and international business transactions, and the Department of Justice has targeted multinational businesses for payments to foreign officials to facilitate transactions under the Foreign Corrupt Practices Act.

Corruption can occur at every level of government, and in the United States it has ranged as high as governors and senators all the way down to local school boards, road commissions, and building inspection agencies. Since the early 1970s, the federal government has played a central role in the investigation and prosecution of corruption. While this has raised federalism concerns, the Department of Justice has made public corruption one of its primary targets because it has the resources to devote to these cases.

Cases involving elected officials can become quite complicated because of the ways in which campaigns are financed in the United States, largely through voluntary donations, and the potential for partisan political concerns to play a role in the decision whether to investigate and prosecute an individual. The Fifth Circuit pointed out in *United States v. Tomblin*[2] that "[i]ntending to make a campaign contribution does not constitute bribery, even though many contributors hope that the official will act favorably because of their contribution." Simply designating a payment as a campaign contribution does not necessarily insulate it from being prosecuted as a bribe. Proving a corrupt intent on the part of the donor or official, however, can be very difficult when a number of contributors are giving money to candidates, who often spend significant time raising money for their campaigns. The role of politics in the process is also problematic because the term "corruption" can be so potent, yet it has no single clear definition. In American history, the election of 1824 that put John Quincy Adams in the White House was described by the losing side as the "corrupt bargain," although in reality it was mainly political "horse trading" that was certainly not illegal.

The focus in this Chapter is on the main federal corruption statutes that are used to prosecute a wide range of misconduct by government officials at all levels. While

---

[1] Exodus 23:8.
[2] 46 F.3d 1369 (5th Cir. 1995).

some explicitly target bribery and illegal gifts, others reach corruption in a more indirect way, relating the violation to extortion or interstate travel and conflicts of interest that do not rise to the level of being a bribe. The Chapter also reviews the Foreign Corrupt Practices Act involving payments to foreign officials from the private sector designed to obtain or retain business in the country. There are a number of specialized statutes targeting bribery in particular offices or industries, including bribery of a bank officer (18 U.S.C. § 215) and payments affecting port security (18 U.S.C. § 226). The federal corruption laws have significant overlap, and it is not uncommon for different statutes to be charged for the same underlying transactions, which can also include the right of honest services theory of mail and wire fraud (discussed in § 4.5).

§ 7.2   BRIBERY AND UNLAWFUL GRATUITIES (18 U.S.C. § 201)

A. History

Among the first laws adopted by Congress was a statute making it a federal crime to bribe a customs officer or federal judge.[3] A broader provision enacted in 1853, called "An Act to Prevent Frauds on the Treasury," made it a crime to offer or give a thing of value to any federal officer "with intent to influence his vote or decision" on an official action.[4] In *Dixson v. United States*,[5] the Supreme Court described the broadening of the federal prohibition on bribery:

> Although primarily concerned with individuals who were bringing fraudulent claims against the United States, Congress did not limit this early statute to fraudulent claims, but chose to draft a general provision encompassing the bribery not only of Members of Congress, but also of "any officer of the United States, *or person holding any place of [public] trust or profit, or discharging any official function* under, or in connection with, any department of the Government of the United States."

Ten years later, during the Civil War, Congress expanded the anti-corruption laws to prohibit giving a gratuity to customs officers by any person "engaged in the importation of goods, wares or merchandise" into the United States.[6] This moved the federal law beyond just bribes to incorporate giving benefits related to an official's position even if there was no *quid pro quo*.

Congress reorganized the federal bribery laws in 1962[7] in order to create "a single comprehensive section of the Criminal Code for a number of existing statutes concerned with bribery. This consolidation would make no significant changes of

---

[3] Act of July 30, 1789, ch. 5, § 35, 1 Stat. 46 (1789); Act of Apr. 30, 1790, ch. 9, § 21, 1 Stat. 117 (1790).

[4] Act of Feb. 26, 1853, ch. 81, § 6, 10 Stat. 171 (1853).

[5] 465 U.S. 482 (1984).

[6] Act of Mar. 3, 1863, ch. 76, § 6, 12 Stat. 740 (1863)

[7] Pub. L. No. 87–849, 76 Stat. 1119 (1962) (codified as amended at 18 U.S.C. § 201).

substance and, more particularly, would not restrict the broad scope of the present bribery statutes as construed by the courts."[8]

B. Scope of § 201

1. Overview

Section 201 covers two corruption offenses involving federal and District of Columbia officials—bribery and unlawful gratuities—that includes both the offer and payment of a thing of value to an official, and the solicitation and receipt of the benefit.[9] The statute defines three terms: "public official," "person who has been selected to be a public official," and "official act." The provision uses the term "any thing of value," which is not defined but has been broadly construed by courts, and covers both actual transfers and any "offer to pay."

2. Public Official

The statute defines a "public official" as

Member of Congress, Delegate, or Resident Commissioner, either before or after such official has qualified, or an officer or employee or person acting for or on behalf of the United States, or any department, agency or branch of Government thereof, including the District of Columbia, in any official function, under or by authority of any such department, agency, or branch of Government, or a juror;

The use of the phrase "in any official function" has raised a question whether the bribe or unlawful gratuity must be connected to the public official's authority when provided or offered.

In *Krichman v. United States*,[10] the Supreme Court construed an earlier version of the statute covering bribery of "any officer of the United States, or to any person acting for or on behalf of the United States in any official function. . . . " The defendant was charged with offering a bribe to a railroad porter to deliver trunks containing furs, and the railroads had been placed under federal control during World War I so the porter was technically an employee of the United States. The Court overturned the conviction because the porter was not a government official and was not acting in any official capacity when the payment was made. The Court stated, "Not every person performing any service for the government, however humble, is embraced within the terms of the statute. It includes those, not officers, who are performing duties of an official character." The Court then quoted from the dissenting opinion in the lower court arguing that if a porter was acting "in any official function" then "window cleaners, scrub women, elevator boys, doorkeepers, pages—in short, any one employed by the

---

[8] S. Rep. No. 87–2213 (1962), reprinted in 1962 U.S.C.C.A.N. 3852.

[9] In 1986, Congress amended § 201 by renumbering the subsections, so that the bribery provisions are now in subsection (b), and the prohibition on giving a gratuity is in subsection (c). Act of Nov. 10, 1986, 100 Stat. 3592 (1986). Prior to 1986, bribery was in subsections (b) and (c) and unlawful gratuities were treated in subsections (f) and (g). Prosecutions for violations occurring between 1962 and 1986 reference these subsections, and the reorganization did not make any substantive changes in the law.

[10] 256 U.S. 363 (1921).

United States to do anything—is included." *Krichman* noted that "if [the statute] is to include every governmental employee, it must be amended by act of Congress."

It is not clear whether Congress responded to the Court's invitation in 1948 in the recodification of federal criminal statutes. The revised statute now included the term "employee" after "officer," which arguably could allow a bribery charge for the conduct in *Krichman*. The legislative history, however, was silent on the reason for adding "employee" to the provision, and as the District of Columbia Circuit noted in *United States v. Neville*,[11] "This silence suggests that Congress did not intend to expand the bribery statute in 1948 to cover all government employees."

Although the expansion of the statutory definition would appear to render *Krichman* moot, the case continues to be cited as a basis for limiting the application of § 201 to conduct related to official authority. But some lower courts have viewed the term "employee" as covering anyone working in the direct employ of the United States without regard to their authority. In *United States v. Romano*,[12] a defendant challenged his bribery conviction on the ground that he only offered a bribe to an employee of a federal agency who was acting as an informant after entering a guilty plea, and so he had no official duties. The defense argued that the informant could not be influenced or induced to act on behalf of the government. The Second Circuit rejected the argument, holding that "[t]he fact that he had agreed to plead guilty to a crime does not change the fact that he remained a federal employee . . . We believe that [the informant]'s status as an employee is sufficient to make him a 'public official' under the statute."

In *United States v. Gjieli*,[13] the Sixth Circuit upheld a conviction for offering a bribe to a federal agent to secure the release of a state prisoner, even though the agent had no authority to affect the prisoner's detention. The circuit court explained that "§ 201(a) imposes no requirement that a bribed 'employee' be acting in 'any official function' before the 'public official' requirement may be satisfied. Rather, the phrase 'in any official function' was intended to modify only "person acting for or on behalf of the United States . . . " In *United States v. Kidd*,[14] the Ninth Circuit held that an Army private came within the statutory definition, despite the modest authority the person had, because "Section 201(a) defines 'public official' to include any government employee."

The more frequently litigated issue is whether a person not directly employed by the United States government who solicited or received a bribe is a "public official" by acting "for or on behalf of the United States . . . in any official function, under or by authority of any such department, agency, or branch of Government." The leading case on the issue is *Dixson v. United States*,[15] involving officers of a nonprofit corporation who solicited payments from businesses in exchange for awarding contracts funded by the federal government. The defendants argued that § 201 did not apply because they

---

[11] 82 F.3d 1101 (D.C. Cir. 1996).

[12] 879 F.2d 1056 (2d Cir. 1989).

[13] 717 F.2d 968 (6th Cir. 1983).

[14] 734 F.2d 409 (9th Cir. 1984).

[15] 465 U.S. 482 (1984).

did not have a "formal bond" with the United States, such as an agency relationship, employment agreement, or other direct contractual obligation. The Supreme Court found the sparse legislative history unhelpful, although its review of prior versions of the legislation indicated that Congress did not intend to limit the definition of a "public official" to require some level of formal or legal relationship.

The Court set forth the following test: "[T]he proper inquiry is not simply whether the person had signed a contract with the United States or agreed to serve as the Government's agent, but rather whether the person occupies a position of public trust with official federal responsibilities." It explained that simply working for an organization receiving federal funds standing alone would be insufficient to bring the person within the prohibition of § 201, so that "an individual must possess some degree of official responsibility for carrying out a federal program or policy" to be a "public official." In finding the defendants were covered by § 201(a)(1), the Court explained that they were "charged with abiding by federal guidelines" regarding the distribution of federal funds, and "[b]y accepting the responsibility for distributing these federal fiscal resources, petitioners assumed the quintessentially official role of administering a social service program established by the United States Congress."

Dixson's "position of public trust" test for whether a person is acting "for or on behalf of" the federal government is designed to be comprehensive because of the need to protect federal funds. Lower courts usually focus on a combination of the degree of federal involvement in an organization's funding, oversight of the program, and the individual's authority to implement policies and procedures reflective of the goals of the federal government.

In *United States v. Hang*,[16] the Eighth Circuit held that an "eligibility technician" working for a local public housing authority was a "public official" under § 201(a)(1) based on the level of federal low-income housing funds administered by the agency and the defendant's discretionary authority to admit applicants into the program. The circuit court focused on the actual discretionary authority of the official and not the person's formal title, noting that "Hang had primary authority for determining who would be the beneficiaries of federal funds. Obviously, this is an undertaking in which Hang could not have engaged had he not possessed some federal authority." Private sector employees can also fall under the statute if they work on behalf of the federal government to help administer one of its programs.

In *United States v. Kenney*,[17] the defendant was a manager at a corporation contracted to provide services to the Air Force who told a supplier he would approve the use of cheaper materials if he was given some of the cost savings. The Fourth Circuit found that he held a "position of trust" regarding the exercise of federal authority, stating that the defendant's position involved "federal responsibilities in that he was responsible for monitoring and providing information regarding the technical aspects of the edge-marker contract. In providing such information, . . . his opinion was highly regarded, the decision makers relied upon his technical expertise and deferred to him on many day-to-day decisions." Other private sector employees

---

[16] 75 F.3d 1275 (8th Cir. 1996).
[17] 185 F.3d 1217 (11th Cir. 1999).

found to be a "public official" under § 201 include a real estate appraiser,[18] a guard working for a private correctional management company,[19] and a grain inspector.[20]

A person can qualify as a "public official" even though the program received funding from multiple sources and the official also has state-imposed duties. In *United States v. Strissel*,[21] the Fourth Circuit rejected a defendant's argument that he could not be prosecuted under § 201 because his agency administered state-funded programs in addition to a federally-funded housing program. The bribes paid by contractors involved contracts receiving federal funds, and the circuit court upheld the conviction by noting: "True, Strissel also had some state responsibilities and state funding. However, he does not argue that he was not distributing federal monies in a program established by the federal government."

It is not clear whether the same result would be reached if the bribes were related to contracts funded by the state or privately, so that federal resources were not directly affected. The focus in *Dixson* on protecting the integrity of federal authority and funding supports the position that a prosecution under § 201 of a non-employee of the federal government must involve proof of substantial federal involvement in the program affected by the bribe. For state and local officials, federal prosecutors can also pursue charges for violating 18 U.S.C. § 666, discussed below.

Section 201 does not require that the person occupying a "position of public trust" be responsible for directing the expenditure of federal funds or award of contracts involving federal money so long as the bribe impacts the integrity of the federal funding. In *United States v. Velazquez*,[22] federal inmates housed in a county facility bribed a guard as part of a plan to escape. In response to their argument that the guard was not a "public official" because he was neither a federal employee nor responsible for administering any federal funds, the Fourth Circuit noted that the county jail received payments from the federal government, was subject to federal regulations, and the guard "supervised the federal prisoners as a federal jailer would." In *United States v. Thomas*,[23] the Fifth Circuit relied on *Velazquez* in finding that a guard employed by a corporation that contracted with the federal government to supervise federal inmates came under § 201. The circuit court explained that "[a]lthough he did not have any authority to allocate federal resources, Thomas nevertheless occupied a position of public trust with official federal responsibilities, because he acted on behalf of the United States under the authority of a federal agency which had contracted with his employer."

3.   *Selected to Be a Public Official*

Section 201(a)(2) also covers persons "who have been selected to be a public official" as coming within the criminal prohibition. The term is defined as "any person

---

[18] United States v. Madeoy, 912 F.2d 1486 (D.C. Cir. 1990).

[19] United States v. Franco, 632 F.3d 880 (5th Cir. 2011).

[20] United States v. Kirby, 587 F.2d 876 (7th Cir. 1978).

[21] 920 F.2d 1162 (4th Cir. 1990).

[22] 847 F.2d 140 (4th Cir. 1988).

[23] 240 F.3d 445 (5th Cir. 2001).

who has been nominated or appointed to be a public official, or has been officially informed that such person will be so nominated or appointed." There is minimal legislative history of the provision, with a Senate Report stating unhelpfully that the definition is "self-explanatory."[24]

The only published case to discuss the provision is *United States v. Williams*,[25] a district court decision denying a motion to dismiss an unlawful gratuity charge against two defendants for giving tickets to a presidential inauguration ball to the man who would later be nominated as secretary of agriculture. The future cabinet officer had not yet been officially nominated to the position because the President-elect had not yet taken the oath of office, and the defendants argued that "officially informed" required that the president have taken office so that he had the authority to act "officially." The district court rejected the argument:

> The gratuities statute does not require, however, that it be the President who "officially" informs a Cabinet officer of his prospective nomination. Congress held hearings on the Espy nomination as early as January 14, 1993. If someone acting in an official capacity informed Secretary Espy of his impending nomination before January 18, 1993, the statutory element of official notice is satisfied.

While the statute does not require a specific official inform the person about the pending nomination or appointment, there must be some action taken by a person with federal authority to inform the nominee before § 201 applies to any bribe or gratuity. Whether *Williams* has any precedential value is an open question because one of the defendants was acquitted at trial, and the other died during the appeal of his conviction, so the charges were dismissed and prior opinions in the case vacated as moot.[26]

4. *Official Act*

The benefit provided to the public official must be connected to an actual or proposed exercise of governmental authority to violate § 201. The statute defines an "official act" as "any decision or action on any question, matter, cause, suit, proceeding or controversy, which may at any time be pending, or which may by law be brought before any public official, in such official's official capacity, or in such official's place of trust or profit." This definition has been largely unchanged since passage of a bribery statute in 1866.[27]

In *United States v. Birdsall*,[28] the Supreme Court gave a broad reading to what constituted an "official act" under a predecessor to § 201, rejecting the argument that an exercise of authority must be specifically authorized by statute before it can be the subject of a bribery prosecution. The Court stated:

---

[24] S. Rep. No. 87–2213, reprinted in 1962 U.S.C.C.A.N. 3852 (1962).

[25] 7 F.Supp.2d 40, 51 (D.D.C. 1998), rev'd as moot, United States v. Schaffer, 240 F.3d 35 (D.C. Cir. 2001).

[26] United States v. Schaffer, 240 F.3d 35 (D.C. Cir. 2001).

[27] Act of July 13, 1866, 14 Stat. 168 (1866).

[28] 233 U.S. 223 (1911).

To constitute official action, it was not necessary that it should be prescribed by statute; it was sufficient that it was governed by a lawful requirement of the Department under whose authority the officer was acting. Nor was it necessary that the requirement should be prescribed by a written rule or regulation. It might also be found in an established usage which constituted the common law of the Department and fixed the duties of those engaged in its activities. In numerous instances, duties not completely defined by written rules are clearly established by settled practice, and action taken in the course of their performance must be regarded as within the provisions of the above-mentioned statutes against bribery.

This analysis would encompass any action taken by a federal official in connection with the person's employment. In *United States v. Sun–Diamond Growers of California*,[29] the Court seemed to impose at least a modest limit on the meaning of "official act" in explaining that not every action by a federal official comes within the statutory definition. The issue in *Sun–Diamond* concerned gratuities provided to the Secretary of Agriculture by lobbyists seeking to curry favor. The Court required the government to identify a specific official act involving a "question, matter, cause, suit, proceeding or controversy" related to the benefit, explaining that if any conduct by a federal official were an "official act," it would lead to absurd results. The Court used the example of a championship sports team visiting the White House and presenting the president with one of its jerseys that is certainly a gratuity given for hosting the team and would violate the statute if the event constituted an "official act." It held that this would not come within the statutory definition:

> [W]hen the violation is linked to a particular "official act," it is possible to eliminate the absurdities *through the definition of that term*. When, however, no particular "official act" need be identified, and the giving of gifts by reason of the recipient's mere tenure in office constitutes a violation, nothing but the Government's discretion prevents the foregoing examples from being prosecuted.

After *Sun–Diamond*, the government must identify a specific exercise of governmental authority for an unlawful gratuities charge, but that same linkage is not necessarily required for a bribery theory because of the *quid pro quo* element of the offense. Nor is it necessary that the official have the actual authority to implement a particular policy or exercise of governmental power in order for a bribe or unlawful gratuity to be made for an "official act."

Courts have taken a pragmatic view of a government employee's scope of authority to determine whether there was an "official act" connected to the payment. In *United States v. Biaggi*,[30] the Second Circuit upheld the conviction of a Congressman for accepting an unlawful gratuity for writing letters on behalf of a company to local officials seeking benefits for the company from the New York City government. The circuit court noted that the authority of a member of Congress involves more than just federal legislative acts, so § 201 covers "all of the acts normally thought to constitute a congressman's legitimate use of his office."

---

[29] 526 U.S. 398 (1999).

[30] 853 F.2d 89 (2nd Cir. 1988).

In *United States v. Valdes*,[31] a closely-divided District of Columbia Circuit, sitting en banc, relied on *Sun–Diamond* to adopt a narrower view of what constitutes an "official act," questioning whether the *Birdsall* analysis of "official act" should still be applicable to almost any use of government authority. The defendant in *Valdes* was a District of Columbia police officer convicted of accepting gifts for looking up the criminal history of individuals in police databases. The information was otherwise publicly available, and the defendant's conduct did not affect any investigations or interfere with his duties. In overturning the conviction, the circuit court stated that *Birdsall* "did not, however, stand for the proposition that every action within the range of official duties *automatically* satisfies § 201's definition; it merely made clear the coverage of activities performed as a matter of custom." The defendant clearly used his position for self-enrichment but there was not an unlawful gratuity because the gifts were not made in connection with the implementation of any government policy or exercise of power. According to *Valdes*, "§ 201 is not about officials' moonlighting, or their misuse of government resources, or the two in combination." A dissenting opinion argued that "*stare decisis* requires us to comply with the United States Supreme Court's broad interpretation of the term 'official act' as set forth in *United States v. Birdsall*."

The Eleventh Circuit, in *United States v. Moore*,[32] disagreed with the narrow reading of "official act" in *Valdes*, holding that it conflicted with *Birdsall*'s broad statement as the proper test. The prosecution involved federal correctional officers who made arrangements to engage in sexual relations with female inmates in exchange for allowing them to receive contraband. The circuit court found that when the officers changed their work assignments, permitted prisoners to contact officers, and provided keys to an office to meet with an inmate, "[a]ll of these actions fall within the broad definition of 'official act' set forth in *Birdsall*."

In *United States v. Jefferson*,[33] the Fourth Circuit rejected a Congressman's argument in favor of a limited view of "official act" that would restrict it "to those activities involving questions pending or brought before Congress, such as voting on proposed legislation or conducting committee work." The defendant was charged with soliciting bribes to assist companies in securing business from foreign governments. The circuit court noted that "the bribery statute does not encompass every action taken in one's official capacity," and that *Birdsall*'s broad definition still controlled in interpreting the scope of "official act." In upholding the conviction, the Fourth Circuit explained "that an official act need not be prescribed by statute, but rather may include acts that a congressman customarily performs, even if the act falls outside the formal legislative process." The circuit court did not disagree with *Valdes* so much as read its outcome as consistent with *Birdsall*, rejecting the defense argument that the District of Columbia Circuit viewed *Sun–Diamond*'s discussion of "official act" as a *sub silentio* overruling of *Birdsall*.

The opinions in *Moore* and *Jefferson* can be reconciled with the *Valdes* analysis of "official act." The conduct of the corrections officers in *Moore* was much more than

---

[31] 475 F.3d 1319 (D.C. Cir. 2007).
[32] 525 F.3d 1033 (11th Cir. 2008).
[33] 674 F.3d 332 (4th Cir. 2012).

simply moonlighting, involving the direct exercise of authority to manipulate the system to arrange sexual encounters with the inmates. Changing work assignments, allowing otherwise unauthorized contacts with guards, and accessing prison offices are all matters or questions determined by a government official, and indeed are part of the day-to-day operation of a correctional facility. Similarly, advocating on behalf of companies with foreign governments in *Jefferson* has become part of the "settled practice" of a member of Congress in which constituency service and advocacy on behalf of American business is commonplace. In *Valdes*, on the other hand, the officer did not interfere with the operation of the police department or alter how any cases were conducted. There was no abuse of government authority, only misuse of the resources available to an employee, much like accessing the internet while at the office to conduct a small-scale betting pool.

Lower-level employees who misuse their access to other offices can engage in an "official act" even if they do not have the authority to approve benefits or implement policy. In *United States v. Parker*,[34] the Fifth Circuit upheld the conviction of a clerk to an Administrative Law Judge who took money to alter records so that social security benefits were provided. The circuit court stated, "We therefore hold that the term 'official act' encompasses use of governmental computer systems to fraudulently create documents for the benefit of the employee or a third party for compensation, even when the employee's scope of authority does not formally encompass the act." In *United States v. Carson*,[35] the Second Circuit rejected the argument of a defendant, an aide to a senator, who stated that he was not using his official power but instead was on a "personal frolic" when he accepted money to intercede with the Department of Justice in a criminal case. The circuit court upheld his conviction under § 201(b):

> [E]ven if the objective of the use of influence here might be categorized as "personal," the determinative factor is that the primary source of any conceivable influence on the Justice Department was the official position held by appellant, enhanced as it was by the status of his employer's membership in the one most powerful congressional committee affecting that Department's operations.

5.   Anything of Value

Section 201(a) does not define "anything of value," but it is a term appearing in other statutes.[36] The direct payment (or offer) of money or tangible property clearly constitutes a thing of value. Even a loan that an official repaid can constitute a thing of value when the person was experiencing financial difficulty and could not otherwise have obtained credit.[37] In *United States v. Kemp*, a mail fraud prosecution premised on bribery of a local official, the Third Circuit held that "as a legal matter, we conclude that providing a loan to a public official (or his friends or family) that would have

---

[34] 133 F.3d 322 (5th Cir. 1998).

[35] 464 F.2d 424 (2d Cir. 1972).

[36] Criminal statutes listing the term as an element include 18 U.S.C. § 657 (embezzlement and misapplication of bank funds), § 704 (sale of military medals), § 875 (interstate extortion threat), and § 912 (impersonating a federal officer).

[37] United States v. Gorman, 807 F.2d 1299 (6th Cir. 1986).

otherwise been unavailable to that official or available at a higher interest rate may constitute a bribe."[38]

Section 201 also covers the receipt of intangible benefits or services that have a subjective value to the recipient, even if they would not constitute property in the traditional sense. In *United States v. Nilsen*,[39] the Eleventh Circuit noted that "Congress' frequent use of 'thing of value' in various criminal statutes has evolved the phrase into a term of art which the courts generally construe to envelope both tangibles and intangibles." In *United States v. Williams*,[40] the Second Circuit upheld the conviction of a Senator prosecuted for accepting shares in a corporation as part of the Abscam investigation even though the stock had no commercial value, stating that "[c]orruption of office occurs when the officeholder agrees to misuse his office in the expectation of gain, whether or not he has correctly assessed the worth of the bribe."

In assessing whether an intangible can be a thing of value, courts emphasize that value—like beauty—is in the eye of the beholder. In *United States v. Moore*,[41] the Eleventh Circuit explained that "monetary worth is not the sole measure of value" in finding that the district court did not commit plain error in instructing the jury that sexual relations can constitute "anything of value" under § 201(a). Courts do not focus solely on objective measures, such as monetary worth of the benefit conferred, in assessing value. In *United States v. Gorman*,[42] the Sixth Circuit stated, "All that is required is that there be a real, as opposed to a speculative, possibility of benefit or detriment." In *United States v. McDade*,[43] a district court found that a replica of the Master's golf tournament's famous green jacket would have a high value to a fan of the sport.

There is a difference between who must receive the thing of value under § 201(b)'s bribery provision, which encompasses the receipt "personally or for any other person or entity," and an unlawful gratuity violation under § 201(c), which can be prosecuted only if the public official "personally" receives the benefit. This distinction requires a more nuanced analysis of the transaction in an unlawful gratuity prosecution to identify the specific benefit provided to the official "for or because of" the official action, and not just that another person connected to the official received the gift. In *United States v. Sun–Diamond Growers*,[44] the government identified the benefit to the Secretary of Agriculture as the companionship of his girlfriend, who actually received the funds to pay for a ticket to accompany him to a conference abroad. In *McDade*, the district court rejected the defendant's motion to dismiss an unlawful gratuities charge that identified the receipt of a scholarship by a congressman's son as the thing of value. It held that the state law obligated the congressman to provide for his son's education, so there was personal receipt of a thing of value because "the payment of scholarship money to a child bestowed a personal benefit on the scholarship recipient's parents,

---

[38] 500 F.3d 257 (3d Cir. 2007).

[39] 967 F.2d 539 (11th Cir. 1992).

[40] 705 F.2d 603 (2d Cir. 1983).

[41] 525 F.3d 1033 (11th Cir. 2008).

[42] 807 F.2d 1299 (6th Cir. 1986).

[43] 827 F.Supp. 1153 (E.D. Pa. 1993).

[44] 941 F.Supp. 1262 (D.D.C. 1996), rev'd on other grounds, 526 U.S. 398 (1999).

since the parents were relieved, at least partially, of their duty to pay for the child's education."

Whether a future job offer constitutes a thing of value has also been considered by the lower courts. In *United States v. Biaggi*,[45] a Small Business Administration (SBA) official received an offer of a job in a law firm that would be paid for in part by a company receiving SBA loans on which the official had provided assistance. The Second Circuit questioned whether the offer of a job constituted a thing of value for § 201 when the conduct was already prohibited by 18 U.S.C. § 208, which bars a federal employee from being involved in any decision regarding a company "with whom he is negotiating or has any arrangement concerning prospective employment." Although the circuit court found the job offer constituted a thing of value in this instance, it noted that "the issue is close not only because a job promise is not unlawful under all circumstances but also because it was part of [defendant]'s duties as an SBA official to assist companies participating in the section 8(a) program." In *United States v. Gorman*,[46] the Sixth Circuit found that an offer of future employment was a thing of value because the defendant would receive a salary three times his government pay and "[c]onsidering Gorman's precarious financial situation, such future employment would clearly be a thing of value for purposes of Section 201."

6.   Offer to Pay

To constitute a bribe or unlawful gratuity, there need not be an actual transfer of the thing of value, and the crime is complete upon an offer or promise to pay or the solicitation of the payment. The statute thus reaches conduct that meets the requirements of an attempt to commit the crime or a solicitation of the offense. A conviction can be secured regardless of the other party's intention to comply with the request. The Seventh Circuit pointed out in *United States v. Muhammad*[47] that "§ 201 does not require the Government to prove that Muhammad took a substantial step towards receiving the bribe. Rather, the statute criminalizes the mere solicitation of a bribe."

In *United States v. Shulman*,[48] the Second Circuit held that a statement that money to be paid to an IRS agent "was . . . available" was sufficient to constitute an offer to pay. But in *United States v. Hernandez*,[49] the Fifth Circuit found merely saying that "some people . . . want to know if you can be bought, if you will change your testimony" was not enough because it was "mere preparation to commit the crime—a 'feel out'" that did not rise to the level of an offer. The term "offer" has a fairly well-established meaning in the law of contracts, but courts do not require that the offer meet the traditional terms for a legally enforceable agreement to come within § 201. In *United States v. Synowiec*,[50] the Seventh Circuit explained that "[i]t is not necessary for a briber to be familiar with *Williston on Contracts* in order to make an illegal offer."

---

[45] 909 F.2d 662 (2d Cir. 1990).
[46] 807 F.2d 1299 (6th Cir. 1986).
[47] 120 F.3d 688 (7th Cir. 1997).
[48] 624 F.2d 384 (2d Cir. 1980).
[49] 731 F.2d 1147 (5th Cir. 1984).
[50] 333 F.3d 786 (7th Cir. 2003).

The circuit court found that a defendant's statements coupled with rubbing his index finger and thumb together "in a universally understood gesture implying money[] passes the test" of being an offer of a bribe, and "[u]sing technical civil law hornbook definitions of 'offer' would be at odds with the goal that § 201 be an effective net for snaring those who would subvert the public good."

C. Bribery

1. Generally

Section 201(b) prohibits both the offer and payment to, and solicitation and acceptance by, a public official to corruptly engage in a transaction in anything of value with the intent:

(A) to influence any official act; or

(B) to influence such public official . . . to commit or aid in committing, or collude in, or allow, any fraud, or make opportunity for the commission of any fraud, on the United States; or

(C) to induce such public official or such person who has been selected to be a public official to do or omit to do any act in violation of the lawful duty of such official or person. . . .

The government must show the defendant acted "corruptly," which requires proof of a *quid pro quo* arrangement between the offeror and the public official to influence an official act. There is no requirement that the public official undertake the exercise of public authority in response to the bribe, as the Supreme Court explained in *United States v. Brewster*[51] when it noted "acceptance of the bribe is the violation of the statute, not performance of the illegal promise." The primary distinction between a bribe and an unlawful gratuity is the corrupt intent element of the offense. The Supreme Court stated in *United States v. Sun–Diamond Growers of California*:[52]

> [F]or bribery there must be a *quid pro quo*—a specific intent to give or receive something of value in exchange for an official act. An illegal gratuity, on the other hand, may constitute merely a reward for some future act that the public official will take (and may already have determined to take), or for a past act that he has already taken.

For an unlawful gratuity, on the other hand, the Second Circuit stated in *United States v. Alfisi*,[53] "The element of a quid pro quo or a direct exchange is absent from the offense of paying an unlawful gratuity. To commit that offense, it is enough that the payment be a reward for a past official act or made in the hope of obtaining general good will. . . . "

---

[51] 408 U.S. 501 (1972).

[52] 526 U.S. 398 (1999).

[53] 308 F.3d 144 (2d Cir. 2002).

2. *Quid Pro Quo*

The "corrupt" intent element requires proof that the defendant had a specific intent to engage in the transaction, which means the prosecution must introduce evidence from which the jury can infer the defendant's subjective state of mind, usually by circumstantial evidence. The Fourth Circuit in *United States v. Jennings*[54] stated the *quid pro quo* that establishes the defendant acted corruptly is "the intent to receive a specific benefit in return for the payment." In *Alfisi*, the Second Circuit noted "bribery involves the giving of value to procure a specific official action from a public official."

The Supreme Court stated in *Evans v. United States,*[55] a Hobbs Act prosecution, that "fulfillment of the *quid pro quo* is not an element of the offense" of bribery, while in *United States v. Brewster*[56] the Court concluded "it is taking the bribe, not performance of the illicit compact, that is a criminal act." Courts sometimes refer to the *quid pro quo* as a "meeting of the minds," but the offeror and the public official do not have to reach an otherwise enforceable agreement. Indeed, it can be tacit, so that a "wink and a nod" may suffice to establish a corrupt intent. In *United States v. Massey*,[57] the Eleventh Circuit stated that direct evidence of an agreement is unnecessary because "[t]o hold otherwise would allow [defendants] to escape liability . . . with winks and nods, even when the evidence as a whole proves that there has been a meeting of the minds to exchange official action for money."

In *United States v. Bonito*,[58] the Second Circuit explained that "the corrupt agreement, offer or payment must precede the official act to be influenced or rewarded," but there does not have to be an actual payment prior to the exercise of authority if there is proof that the parties had a sufficient understanding about the nature of the exchange. Similarly, the public official need not implement or affect a particular government action for the offense to be complete. In *Jennings*, the Fourth Circuit held "it is sufficient to show that the payor intended for each payment to induce the official to adopt a specific course of action."

Although most bribes are paid in advance of the expected exercise of government authority, only the agreement itself must have been made and any actual payment could be made after the official act. *Jennings* noted that "the timing of the payment in relation to the official act for which it is made is (in theory) irrelevant. Bribes often are paid before the fact, but it is only logical that in certain situations the bribe will not actually be conveyed until the act is done." In *United States v. Harvey*,[59] the same court rejected the defendant's argument that a bribe could not be inferred from payments made after the approval of a contract, stating "reliance on the timing of the alleged bribes is misplaced."

---

[54] 160 F.3d 1006 (4th Cir. 1998).

[55] 504 U.S. 255 (1992). Although *Evans* was a Hobbs Act prosecution, the Court's analysis of bribery applies to other provisions.

[56] 408 U.S. 501 (1972).

[57] 89 F.3d 1433 (11th Cir. 1996).

[58] 57 F.3d 167 (2d Cir. 1995).

[59] 532 F.3d 326 (4th Cir. 2008).

The public official need not agree to change the government's position in order for a bribe to occur, nor must the exercise of authority be harmful or otherwise violate the law. In *United States v. Orenuga*,[60] the District of Columbia Circuit upheld a trial court jury instruction that "[i]t is not a defense to the crime of bribery that had there been no bribe, the public official might have lawfully and properly performed the same act." In *United States v. Quinn*,[61] the Fourth Circuit held "[i]t is not necessary for conviction under § 201(b) that the official act offered in exchange for the bribe be harmful to the government or inconsistent with the official's legal obligations." Similarly, even if the official could have a lawful claim to the payment received, if there is a *quid pro quo* agreement then there has been a bribe. In *Palliser v. United States*,[62] an 1890 decision involving a different statute, the Supreme Court stated:

> A promise to a public officer that, if he will do a certain unlawful act, he shall be paid a certain compensation, is an offer to bribe him to do the unlawful act; and an offer of a contract to pay money to a postmaster for an unlawful sale by him of postage stamps on credit is not the less within the statute because the portion of that money which he would ultimately have the right to retain, by way of commission, from the United States, would be no greater than he would have upon a lawful sale for cash of an equal amount of postage stamps.

Not all misconduct by a government official related to the improper receipt of funds constitutes bribery. In *United States v. Dean*,[63] the District of Columbia Circuit overturned the conviction of an employee of the District of Columbia who asked businesses seeking to renew licenses to pay any late fees in cash, which she then kept for herself. The circuit court held, "[T]here must be an agreement between the public official and the other party that the official will perform an official act in return for a personal benefit to the official. Here there was no such agreement. . . . " It noted that the defendant could have been charged with fraud or embezzlement, so "[i]t would appear that the evidence might easily have supported such charges, but the absence of any *quid pro quo* arrangement to issue the license for the payment meant the § 201 charge failed."

While the government must prove a *quid pro quo*, it is not clear whether it must also show that the public official intended to undertake the conduct that would complete the agreement when entering into it. If that intent on the part of the official is required, then it could be a defense to a bribery charge if the official did not have the authority or power to complete the *quid pro quo* and therefore could not have intended to be influenced or induced. The Fifth Circuit rejected this argument in *United States v. Valle*,[64] however, a case in which an Immigration and Customs Enforcement (ICE) officer was charged under § 201(b)(2)(C) for demanding a $20,000 payment to remove criminal charges from an alien's record. There were no pending charges against the alien at the time and the defendant did not have the authority to remove them even if

---

[60] 430 F.3d 1158 (D.C. Cir. 2005).

[61] 359 F.3d 666 (4th Cir. 2004).

[62] 136 U.S. 257 (1890).

[63] 629 F.3d 257 (D.C. Cir. 2011).

[64] 538 F.3d 341 (5th Cir. 2008).

they had existed. Rejecting the argument that the defendant did not intend to commit the official act, the circuit court held:

> [T]hat an official may be convicted under § 201(b)(2), if he has corruptly entered into a quid pro quo, knowing that the purpose behind the payment that he has received, or agreed to receive, is to induce or influence him in an official act, even if he has no intention of actually fulfilling his end of the bargain.

A Congressman tried an interesting approach, dubbed the "playacting" defense, in a prosecution from the Abscam investigation. The FBI recorded him taking money from an undercover agent while promising to provide assistance on immigration matters, claiming at trial that he had no intention of ever doing so. The Representative admitted to being a thief for defrauding the payer but argued he never accepted a bribe because he would not have engaged in any official act. Rejecting this argument, the Second Circuit in *United States v. Myers*[65] stated that for a violation of § 201(b) "'being influenced' does not describe the Congressman's true intent, it describes the intention he conveys to the briber in exchange for the bribe." The circuit court relied on the Supreme Court's statement in *United States v. Hood,*[66] a prosecution for soliciting bribes in exchange for appointments to office, that "[w]hether the corrupt transaction would or could ever be performed is immaterial. We find no basis for allowing a breach of warranty to be a defense to corruption." The Second Circuit concluded that a fraud defense to bribery was unavailable, and "[i]f Myers was 'playacting' and giving false promises of assistance to people he believed were offering him money to influence his official actions, he violated the bribery statute."

An official could seek a payment for a legitimate purpose, such as a fee for work performed, and at the same time for an illegitimate reason, such as to secure continued support for a program. In *United States v. Biaggi,*[67] the Second Circuit stated, "A valid purpose that partially motivates a transaction does not insulate participants in an unlawful transaction from criminal liability." The circuit court noted, however, that "the evidence must suffice to permit the jury to find beyond a reasonable doubt that the unlawful purposes were of substance, not merely vague possibilities that might attend an otherwise legitimate transaction."

3.   *Official Duty*

Section 201(b)(2)(C) makes it a crime to offer or solicit a bribe to induce a public official "to do or omit to do any act in violation of the official duty of such official or person." Courts take an expansive view of what constitutes an "official duty," usually rejecting the defense argument that the official's lack of explicit authority to implement the object of the bribe prevents a conviction. In *United States v. Gjieli,*[68] the Sixth Circuit held "[t]here is simply no requirement here that the act induced fall within the federal employee's official function." Similarly, in *United States v.*

---

[65] 692 F.2d 823 (2d Cir. 1982).

[66] 343 U.S. 148 (1952).

[67] 909 F.2d 662 (2d Cir. 1990).

[68] 717 F.2d 968 (6th Cir. 1983).

Analytis,[69] a district court stated "it is now clear that to support a conviction for federal bribery, it is not necessary that the bribee have the authority to actually achieve the object of the bribe." There are nineteenth-century cases, however, which found an official's lack of authority to carry out the object of the bribe a basis for dismissing the charge.[70]

The offer or solicitation must relate to an exercise of government authority and not just that official's ethical obligation to act in conformity with applicable rules and not engage in misconduct. In *United States v. Morlang,*[71] the Fourth Circuit held that jury instructions which referenced broad ethical standards for an official's duty were improper to deciding whether there was a bribe. The circuit court stated, "in order to be relevant in a criminal prosecution for conspiracy, these standards must prescribe duties and modes of conduct as opposed to broad ethical and moral precepts."

4.   *Witness Bribery and Unlawful Gratuities*

While the primary focus of § 201 is the offer and acceptance of "anything of value" in connection with the exercise of governmental authority, the statute also prohibits the payment of a bribe or unlawful gratuity to a witness in a federal judicial, administrative, or congressional proceeding. The statute makes it a crime for a person who

> directly or indirectly, corruptly gives, offers, or promises anything of value to any person, or offers or promises such person to give anything of value to any other person or entity, with intent to influence the testimony under oath or affirmation of such first-mentioned person as a witness upon a trial, hearing, or other proceeding, before any court, any committee of either House or both Houses of Congress, or any agency, commission, or officer authorized by the laws of the United States to hear evidence or take testimony, or with intent to influence such person to absent himself therefrom. . . .

The unlawful gratuities provision makes it a crime to give anything of value "for or because of" the testimony.

The fact that a witness's testimony was claimed to be truthful does not affect whether the solicitation or acceptance of a bribe violated § 201. In *United States v. Donathan,*[72] the defendant offered to provide favorable testimony in a civil sexual harassment lawsuit in exchange for a payment. The Sixth Circuit rejected the argument that the government could not show the payment influenced the testimony because the witness would testify truthfully: "That she ultimately accepted money to tell what she now claims to be the truth does not negate her corrupt motive. The government was not required to prove that the testimony she agreed to give was false."

The witness bribery provision became a source of significant, albeit brief, controversy in 1998 when a panel of the Tenth Circuit held in *United States v.*

---

[69] 687 F.Supp. 87, 90 (S.D.N.Y. 1988).

[70] See In re Yee Gee, 83 F. 145 (D. Wash. 1897); United States v. Gibson, 47 F. 833 (N.D. Ill. 1891).

[71] 531 F.2d 183, 192 (4th Cir. 1975).

[72] 65 F.3d 537 (6th Cir. 1995).

Singleton[73] that testimony given in exchange for a promise of leniency from federal prosecutors violated § 201 as an unlawful gratuity. The circuit court, sitting en banc, vacated the decision and later issued an opinion finding no violation of the statute, holding that "in light of the longstanding practice of leniency for testimony, we must presume if Congress had intended that section 201(c)(2) overturn this ingrained aspect of American legal culture, it would have done so in clear, unmistakable, and unarguable language."[74] Although the panel decision in *Singleton* was only on the books for about a week, it led to the federal courts being "inundated with a flood of what have come to be called '*Singleton* arguments.'" . . . "[75]

All of the circuit courts have rejected defense claims that § 201 applies to the offer of leniency by federal prosecutors in exchange for testimony. Since *Singleton*, lower courts have rejected challenges under § 201 to agreements in which a witness testified in exchange for cash payments,[76] a reduced sentence,[77] a decision not to prosecute,[78] a plea bargain,[79] and leniency in immigration proceedings.[80]

Despite rejection of *Singleton*'s analysis of § 201, lower courts have also noted that the statute imposes limits on what federal prosecutors are permitted to do to secure testimony. The statute does not impinge on the government's right to seek testimony to aid its prosecutions, but § 201 would clearly apply if a prosecutor actually bribed a witness to testify. In addition, courts have expressed concern about whether the government can pay a witness only for favorable testimony. In *United States v. Condon*,[81] the Seventh Circuit noted that if prosecutors were completely outside the proscription of § 201, then "[t]hat approach, if taken seriously, would permit prosecutors to pay cash for favorable testimony, a practice that lacks the statutory and historical support of immunity and sentence reduction." Whenever the government provides a benefit to a witness, prosecutors must ensure that they fulfill the obligation imposed by *Brady v. Maryland* to timely disclose exculpatory evidence so that the defense has an opportunity to examine the witness for any possible bias.

D. Unlawful Gratuities

In addition to prohibiting the offer and receipt of a bribe, § 201 makes it a crime to provide (or accept) a gratuity to an official "for or because of" the person engaging in an official act "otherwise than as provided by law for the proper discharge of official duty." In *United States v. Sun–Diamond Growers of California*,[82] the Supreme Court stated "[t]he distinguishing feature of each crime is its intent element": bribery requires proof of a *quid pro quo* entered into "corruptly," while the unlawful gratuities offense only involves an official accepting (or soliciting) anything of value in connection with the

---

[73] 144 F.3d 1343 (10th Cir. 1998).

[74] 165 F.3d 1297 (10th Cir. 1999).

[75] United States v. Lara, 181 F.3d 183 (1st Cir. 1999).

[76] United States v. Ihnatenko, 482 F.3d 1097 (9th Cir. 2007).

[77] United States v. McGee, 189 F.3d 626 (7th Cir. 1999).

[78] United States v. Harris, 210 F.3d 165 (3d Cir. 2000).

[79] United States v. Harmon, 194 F.3d 890 (8th Cir. 1999).

[80] United States v. Feng, 277 F.3d 1151 (9th Cir. 2002).

[81] 170 F.3d 687 (7th Cir. 1999).

[82] United States v. Sun–Diamond Growers of California, 526 U.S. 398 (1999).

exercise of authority. Prosecutors must prove the defendant's knowledge of the relationship between the gift and an official act, but need not show it was given to influence an exercise of governmental authority or to induce a violation of the official's duty. Thus, the unlawful gratuity can be given after the official act occurs, when there would be no question of an impermissible influence over the decision. In *United States v. Brewster,*[83] the District of Columbia Circuit explained, "It appears entirely possible that a public official could accept a thing of value 'otherwise than as provided by law for the proper discharge of official duty,' and at the same time not do it 'corruptly.'"

The authorized maximum punishments for violating § 201 are substantially different for the two offenses. A bribery conviction is punishable by up to fifteen years in prison, and a defendant "may be disqualified from holding any office of honor, trust, or profit under the United States." An unlawful gratuity conviction can lead to a prison term of no more than two years.

As with the bribery offense under § 201(b), the unlawful gratuities crime in § 201(c) reaches both parties to the arrangement. Because it does not require a *quid pro quo,* however, prosecutors do not have to show any agreement between the offeror (or payer) and the public official. As the Fifth Circuit stated in *United States v. Evans,*[84] "§ 201[(c)] makes it criminal for a public official to accept a thing of value to which he is not lawfully entitled, regardless of the intent of the donor or donee."

It is possible for the person providing the benefit to view it as a bribe, while the public official may understand it only as a gift or reward, and both can be convicted despite the disparate intents. In *United States v. Anderson,*[85] the District of Columbia Circuit pointed out that "[t]he payment and the receipt of a bribe are not interdependent offenses, for obviously the donor's intent may differ completely from the donee's." The circuit court upheld the convictions of the defendants for different violations, finding that "the jury could reasonably conclude that Anderson gave [Senator] Brewster monies with corrupt intent to influence his vote on the proposed rate-increase legislation, and that Brewster, though insensitive to any influence, accepted the monies with knowledge that Anderson's purpose was to reward him for his stance on such legislation."

Two other important differences between the bribery and unlawful gratuity offenses are (1) the timing of providing the benefit and (2) the recipient. First, the gratuity provision can be violated by a gift given before or after the official act, so that rewarding an official for "any official act performed or to be performed" is a violation. The District of Columbia Circuit noted in *United States v. Schaffer*[86] that "[b]ribery is entirely future-oriented, while gratuities can be either forward or backward looking." Second, a benefit provided after an official act can be made to a former official, even though the person no longer has any authority. Because a bribe requires a *quid pro quo* agreement, it can only be made in anticipation of the recipient engaging in an official act or in violation of a governmental duty. In addition, § 201(c) provides that the

---

[83] 506 F.2d 62 (D.C. Cir. 1974).

[84] 572 F.2d 455 (5th Cir. 1978).

[85] United States v. Anderson, 509 F.2d 312 (D.C. Cir. 1974).

[86] 183 F.3d 833 (D.C. Cir. 1999).

gratuity must be given to the public official personally and not through a third party, unlike the bribery section that reaches the transfer of "anything of value" to the official or "for any other person or entity."

An issue that divided the circuit courts was whether a violation required proof of a benefit given for a specifically identified official act, or whether gifts designed to curry favor with an official were sufficient, even if there were no particular decision motivating the gift. The Supreme Court resolved the issue in *United States v. Sun–Diamond Growers*,[87] the principle case interpreting the scope of the unlawful gratuities provision.

The defendant was a trade association convicted for giving a number of gifts to the Secretary of Agriculture to generate goodwill with him on behalf of the agricultural cooperatives that comprised its membership. The gifts totaled less than $6,000, comprised of tennis tournament tickets, luggage, meals, a framed print, and a crystal bowl. While the indictment identified two matters that the Secretary would decide that affected the association's members, the Court noted "the indictment did not allege a specific connection between either of them—or between any other action of the Secretary—and the gratuities conferred." It found that the district court gave a flawed instruction by allowing the jury to find an unlawful gratuity just "because of his official position—perhaps, for example, to build a reservoir of goodwill that might ultimately affect one or more of a multitude of unspecified acts, now and in the future." The Court found this instruction effectively removed the "for or because of" element of the offense by allowing a conviction without linking the gift to a particular official act that had been undertaken or would be in the future.

The Court read the "for or because of" language to mean "for or because of some particular official act of whatever identity," analogizing this phrase to the question "Do you like any composer?" as typically meaning "Do you like some particular composer?" To avoid making any gift—regardless of its value or the context of the transaction—to a federal official a violation of § 201(c), the Court held that "the Government must prove a link between a thing of value conferred upon a public official and a specific 'official act' for or because of which it was given." The Court took this approach to avoid "absurdities" if the prohibition on unlawful gratuities was read as broadly as the government suggested. It said that a broader approach

> would criminalize, for example, token gifts to the President based on his official position and not linked to any identifiable act—such as the replica jerseys given by championship sports teams each year during ceremonial White House visits. Similarly, it would criminalize a high school principal's gift of a school baseball cap to the Secretary of Education, by reason of his office, on the occasion of the latter's visit to the school.

Sun–Diamond Growers effectively rewrote this gratuities prohibition to require proof that the gratuity was "for or because of *an* official act." The Court clearly found troubling the government's argument that a free lunch provided to the Secretary of Agriculture in conjunction with a speech to a farm organization would be a criminal

---

[87] 526 U.S. 398 (1999).

violation because the secretary could decide a matter affecting farmers at some later point in time. The Court was concerned that adopting a broad interpretation of § 201(c) could make any innocuous gift a crime, regardless of its motive, because the gratuity offense does not have an intent requirement to limit its application to only gifts designed to compromise the integrity of an official. It stated, "When, however, no particular 'official act' need be identified, and the giving of gifts by reason of the recipient's mere tenure in office constitutes a violation, nothing but the Government's discretion prevents the foregoing examples from being prosecuted." The Court refused to rely on the reasonable exercise of prosecutorial discretion as the primary protection for otherwise innocent conduct.

Sun–Diamond Growers did not prohibit prosecution of a before-the-fact gift to a government official, but the Supreme Court rejected the "meat axe" approach of prosecutors. The Court did not want a broad interpretation of the law to undermine the extensive administrative regulations on gifts to federal officials already in place. These regulations were adopted to ensure a high level of ethics when officials interact with private parties, especially those subject to the official's authority. For example, a federal regulation provides that a government worker "may accept unsolicited gifts having an aggregate market value of $20 or less per source per occasion, provided that the aggregate market value of individual gifts received from any one person under the authority of this paragraph shall not exceed $50 in a calendar year."[88] The Court pointed out that there were numerous similar regulations "littering this field" so a broad interpretation of § 201(c) could "expand this one piece of the regulatory puzzle so dramatically as to make many other pieces misfits."

Sun–Diamond Growers did not explain what evidence would be necessary to establish the "link" between a gift and an official act. As the District of Columbia Circuit noted in *Schaffer*, "the magnitude of the necessary link, and its proper translation into a concrete rule of decision, remains in some doubt."[89] The defendant in that case was a lobbyist for a large food processing company who gave tickets to a Presidential Inaugural Ball to the same Secretary of Agriculture involved in *Sun–Diamond Growers*.[90] The circuit court explained that in light of the Supreme Court's analysis of § 201(c), three types of gifts would constitute a crime:

> First, a gratuity can take the form of a reward for past action—i.e. for a performed official act. Second, a gratuity can be intended to entice a public official who has already staked out a position favorable to the giver to maintain that position. Finally, a gratuity can be given with the intent to induce a public official to propose, take, or shy away from some future official act. This third category would additionally encompass gifts given in the hope that, when the particular official actions move to the forefront, the public official will listen hard to, and hopefully be swayed by, the giver's proposals, suggestions, and/or concerns.

---

[88] 5 C.F.R. § 2635.204(a).

[89] 183 F.3d 833, 840 (D.C. Cir. 1999).

[90] The defendant later received a pardon while his appeal on other issues was pending, and the case was dismissed as moot. United States v. Schaffer, 240 F.3d 35 (D.C. Cir. 2001).

In each circumstance, once a gift is shown, then the issue is whether the subjective intent of the provider and the official is related to a particular identified exercise of government authority. To prove the "for or because of" element, the government must show "the acts in question were substantially, or in large part motivated by the requisite intent to influence the Secretary." As with any jury assessment of intent, circumstantial evidence could be the primary basis to meet this requirement for a conviction.

The District of Columbia Circuit concluded that the evidence was insufficient to establish the requisite link to an official act. While there were issues the Secretary of Agriculture was likely to take up in which the defendant's employer had a current interest, they were too remote to meet the *Sun–Diamond Growers* test that a particular official act be shown as the basis for the gift. The circuit court explained:

> To hold otherwise would mean that any time a regulated entity became aware of any inchoate government proposal that could affect its interests, and subsequently provided something of value to a relevant official, it could be held to violate the gratuity statute in the event that the inchoate proposal later appeared in a more concretized form.

In *United States v. Hoffman*,[91] the Eighth Circuit rejected a defendant's argument that the government must show the defendant reasonably believed the official would undertake the official act connected to the gift. In *Hoffman*, the defendant, who worked for a government contractor, gave golf clubs to a government official when he was seeking a high rating of the contractor's work in order to obtain future awards. The circuit court stated that it "has never interpreted § 201(c)(1)(A) to require a 'reasonable belief' element" for an unlawful gratuity conviction.

The Supreme Court stated in *Sun–Diamond Growers* that § 201 sets forth "two separate crimes . . . with two different sets of elements and authorized punishments." This would seem to prevent finding the unlawful gratuity crime as a lesser-included offense of bribery because they have different elements, but the Court also noted that the crucial distinction between a bribe and an unlawful gratuity is the higher intent requiring proof of a *quid pro quo* for a § 201(b) conviction. A number of circuit courts have held that, in certain instances, a jury can convict the defendant for a § 201(c) violation as a lesser offense of bribery. This can only occur when the charge is a before-the-act benefit that is provided or accepted, because bribery requires a *quid pro quo* agreement reached in advance of when an official act takes place. Therefore, for any benefit given after the governmental action, the only possible charge is for an unlawful gratuity under § 201(c).

In *United States v. Brewster*,[92] the District of Columbia Circuit stated that "as a matter of semantics, . . . we would think that if the gratuity offense is narrower than the bribery offense (and it is), then the narrower could fit within the greater, *i.e*, the gratuity offense is a lesser included offense of bribery." In *United States v. Jennings*,[93]

---

[91] 556 F.3d 871 (8th Cir. 2009).

[92] 506 F.2d 62 (D.C. Cir. 1974).

[93] 160 F.3d 1006 (4th Cir. 1998);

decided after *Sun–Diamond Growers*, the Fourth Circuit held that "[p]ayment of an illegal gratuity is a lesser included offense of bribery . . . because corrupt intent is a 'different and higher' degree of criminal intent than that necessary for an illegal gratuity." The circuit court explained "it is important that a jury be properly instructed on the difference between a bribe and a gratuity in cases when there is a question about the nature of the payment alleged." Other circuit courts have upheld convictions under § 201(c) as a lesser-included offense of § 201(b).[94]

§ 7.3   THEFT OR BRIBERY CONCERNING PROGRAMS RECEIVING FEDERAL FUNDS (18 U.S.C. § 666)

A. Generally

Section 666 is a broad statute targeting corruption in state and local governments, Indian tribal governments, and private organizations that receive federal funds. Congress adopted it out of fear that the Supreme Court would issue a restrictive interpretation of the scope of § 201 in *Dixson v. United States* on who constituted a "public official" subject to prosecution. The increasing number of programs funded, at least in part, by the federal government raised the question of whether § 201 was broad enough to reach corruption at the local level. Before the Court decided *Dixson*, a Senate report[95] on the legislation asserted that a narrow interpretation of § 201 would give "rise to a serious gap in the law, since even though title to the monies may have passed, the federal government clearly retains a strong interest in assuring the integrity of such program funds." Congress enacted § 666 to augment "the ability of the United States to vindicate significant acts of theft, fraud, and bribery involving federal monies that are disbursed to private organizations or state and local governments pursuant to a federal program."

Unlike § 201, which covers only federal and District of Columbia employees along with those who directly exercise federal authority, § 666 applies to any "agent of an organization, or of a State, local, or Indian tribal government, or any agency thereof. . . . "[96] Rather than applying to those holding a specified office, § 666 conditions federal jurisdiction on the requirement that the defendant be an agent of an "organization, government, or agency [that] receives, in any one-year period, benefits in excess of $10,000 under a Federal program involving a grant, contract, subsidy, loan, guarantee, insurance, or other form of Federal assistance."[97]

The statute also limits federal jurisdiction by requiring proof that the bribe occurred in connection with transactions of the agency or governmental unit with a value of $5,000 or more. The corrupt payment itself need not have any specific value because the statute only requires the offer and acceptance of "anything of value," and it is the subject matter of the corruption that must meet the $5,000 threshold for federal

---

[94] See United States v. Patel, 32 F.3d 340 (8th Cir. 1994); United States v. Lasanta, 978 F.2d 1300 (2d Cir. 1992); United States v. Kenny, 645 F.2d 1323 (9th Cir. 1981); United States v. Evans, 572 F.2d 455 (5th Cir. 1978).

[95] S. Rep. No. 98–225 (1983).

[96] The original statute did not include Indian tribal governments, which were added in 1986. Pub. L. No. 99–646, § 59(a), 100 Stat. 3612 (1986).

[97] 18 U.S.C. § 666(b).

jurisdiction. Section 666 reaches the offer and acceptance of a bribe and gratuity "with the intent to influence or reward" the agent, and also punishes conduct in which the defendant "embezzles, steals, obtains by fraud, or . . . converts" property valued at $5,000. Thus, the statute targets corruption by means of bribes and illegal gifts along with theft and misappropriation by governmental employees, so it can be applied to a wider range of misconduct than § 201.

B.   Federal Benefits of $10,000 in a One–Year Period

1.   Overview

The first element the government must prove is the "circumstance" of federal funding for the agency, government, or organization that is the basis for federal jurisdiction over the offense. The federal power to prosecute bribery at lower levels of government is grounded in the congressional power to oversee the expenditure of the national government's resources. Section 666(b) requires proof that the federal government provided "benefits" in excess of $10,000 in any one-year period "under a Federal program involving a grant, contract, subsidy, loan, guarantee, insurance, or other form of Federal assistance." The Supreme Court has dealt with the connection between the federal funding and the offense in three cases that raised the question whether the statute comes within the power of Congress to enact legislation reaching corrupt actions of state and local officials under principles of federalism.

2.   Federal Nexus

In *Salinas v. United States*,[98] the government convicted a deputy sheriff of accepting bribes from a federal prisoner housed in the county jail to give him preferential treatment. The federal funding provided to the jail easily exceeded the statutory $10,000 minimum, so the monetary threshold was undisputed. The Court rejected the defendant's argument that, to establish federal jurisdiction, the government must also prove that the subject matter of the bribe involved the federal funds provided to the agency or government. The Court held, "The prohibition is not confined to a business or transaction which affects federal funds. The word 'any,' which prefaces the business or transaction clause, undercuts the attempt to impose this narrowing construction."

The Court recognized that Congress adopted § 666 to expand federal anticorruption law, so limiting its application to only cases involving the direct expenditure of federal funds "would be incongruous" with the legislative intent. The Court also rejected the defendant's argument that the statute implicitly required a nexus between the alleged misconduct and federal funds because it did not plainly state the contrary. It dodged the issue of whether the government needed to prove any other type of nexus to the federal funds, stating that "[w]e need not consider whether the statute requires some other kind of connection between a bribe and the expenditure of federal funds, for in this case the bribe was related to [a program] paid for in significant part by federal funds themselves." Although the Court found the statute

---

[98] 522 U.S. 52 (1997).

unambiguous, it also pointed out that "there is no serious doubt about the constitutionality of § 666(a)(1)(B) as applied to the facts of this case."

Despite holding that the government need not show a connection between the bribe and the federal funds, *Salinas* also referred obliquely to federalism, stating that "[w]hatever might be said about § 666(a)(1)(B)'s application in other cases, the application of § 666(a)(1)(B) to Salinas did not extend federal power beyond its proper bounds." Lower courts faced constitutional challenges to § 666 prosecutions based on federalism concerns because the statute did not require proof of an effect from the corruption on federal funds. Defendants argued in favor of imposing a nexus requirement between the violation and the federal funds, and a split in the circuit courts developed after *Salinas* on what prosecutors must prove about the connection between the corruption and federal funding. Some courts adopted a narrow interpretation of the statute to require the government to establish some connection, although not a direct effect, between the corruption and the federal role in the program or organization.[99] Other circuit courts rejected any nexus requirement as an element of the offense.[100]

In *Sabri v. United States*,[101] the Supreme Court resolved the split, largely putting an end to federalism challenges to § 666 prosecutions, by rejecting a requirement that prosecutors prove a nexus between the corrupt acts and federal funding. The defendant was convicted of offering bribes to a city council member for assistance in securing approval to build a hotel and retail development. He brought a facial challenge to § 666, arguing that the statute failed to require as an element of the crime proof of any connection between the bribe and the federal funds received by the local government. The Court rejected the argument:

> Congress has authority under the Spending Clause to appropriate federal moneys to promote the general welfare, Art. I, § 8, cl. 1, and it has corresponding authority under the Necessary and Proper Clause, Art. I, § 8, cl. 18, to see to it that taxpayer dollars appropriated under that power are in fact spent for the general welfare, and not frittered away in graft or on projects undermined when funds are siphoned off or corrupt public officers are derelict about demanding value for dollars.

The Court explained that corruption can have a broad impact beyond just the misuse of federal dollars or dereliction of a duty funded by the federal government. The scope of § 666 is a permissible exercise of legislative authority because "[m]oney is fungible, bribed officials are untrustworthy stewards of federal funds, and corrupt contractors do not deliver dollar-for-dollar value. Liquidity is not a financial term for nothing; money can be drained off here because a federal grant is pouring in there."

---

[99] See United States v. Zwick, 199 F.3d 672 (3d Cir. 1999); United States v. Santopietro, 166 F.3d 88 (2d Cir. 1999).

[100] See United States v. Valentine, 63 F.3d 459 (6th Cir. 1995); United States v. Westmorland, 841 F.2d 572 (5th Cir. 1988).

[101] 541 U.S. 600 (2004).

3.   Federal Benefits

In *Fischer v. United States*,[102] the Supreme Court read the term "benefits" broadly in determining whether an organization or agency meets the $10,000 federal benefits requirement in § 666(b). A jury convicted the defendant for defrauding a hospital receiving funds under the Medicare program and paying kickbacks to an officer of an organization receiving Medicare funding. The Court stated that determining when a government payment constituted a "benefit" under § 666 depended on examining the program's "nature and purposes." It rejected the argument that because Medicare funds are only reimbursement for services rendered to the ultimate beneficiaries so there is no benefit to the hospital. Instead, the Court held the funding was provided "not simply to reimburse for treatment of qualifying patients but to assist the hospital in making available and maintaining a certain level and quality of medical care, all in the interest of both the hospital and the greater community." The Court pointed to the fact that providers dealing with patients covered by the program "derive significant advantage" from their participation in Medicare, so "[t]hese advantages constitute benefits within the meaning of the federal bribery statute. . . . " It distinguished payments made under Medicare from a government contract for services, focusing on the degree and nature of the government regulations for the program in concluding that the payments constituted benefits. It stated:

> Medicare is designed to the end that the Government receives not only reciprocal value from isolated transactions but also long-term advantages from the existence of a sound and effective health care system for the elderly and disabled. The Government enacted specific statutes and regulations to secure its own interests in promoting the well being and advantage of the health care provider, in addition to the patient who receives care. The health care provider is receiving a benefit in the conventional sense of the term, unlike the case of a contractor whom the Government does not regulate or assist for long-term objectives or for significant purposes beyond performance of an immediate transaction. Adequate payment and assistance to the health care provider is itself one of the objectives of the program. These purposes and effects suffice to make the payment a benefit within the meaning of the statute.

Although the approach to benefits was broad, the Court in *Fischer* also made it clear that just receiving federal funds was insufficient standing alone to bring a case within § 666. It stated, "Any receipt of federal funds can, at some level of generality, be characterized as a benefit. The statute does not employ this broad, almost limitless use of the term." Taking such an expansive view of a federal benefit "would turn almost every act of fraud or bribery into a federal offense, upsetting the proper federal balance." Instead, determining whether a program received federal benefits requires "an examination . . . of the program's structure, operation, and purpose. The inquiry should examine the conditions under which the organization receives the federal payment. The answer could depend, as it does here, on whether the recipient's own operations are one of the reasons for maintaining the program."

---

[102] 529 U.S. 667 (2000).

The Court did not explain what it meant by the "proper federal balance," but like *Salinas*, the reference to a constraint on federal authority may have been meant to allay apprehension that the statute authorized the Department of Justice to prosecute any corruption case almost without regard to the federal interest in the program beyond finding the $10,000 in benefits. In a dissenting opinion, Justice Thomas argued that the breadth of the Court's analysis made him "doubt that there is any federal assistance program that does not provide 'benefits' to organizations . . . "

4. *Linking Federal Funding*

An issue in § 666 prosecutions is establishing the nature of the organization and its relationship to federal funding. If the funds appear to be provided as part of a standard contractual agreement in which the government is a purchaser or seller of goods and services, then the organization would not come within § 666 on that basis alone. For example, in *United States v. Stewart*,[103] a pre-*Fischer* decision, a district court granted a motion to dismiss § 666 charges alleging theft of tools and parts from the defendant's employer, a large military contractor. The government argued that contracts with the company fell outside the typical supplier arrangement because it provided custom manufactured goods that could not be sold to others due to their classified nature. The district court rejected that argument, finding "the statute was not intended to apply to purely commercial transactions," so that "monies paid in consideration for goods provided, even if customized, are not benefits within the meaning of the statute."

After *Fischer*, the federal benefits analysis focuses on the type of program involved rather than just tracing money directly from federal coffers to an organization's bank account. In *United States v. Dubón–Otero*,[104] the First Circuit upheld the conviction of two owners of a for-profit corporation called Health Services receiving federal funds only through a local government with which it contracted to provide AIDS testing and education. The circuit court stated, "It makes no difference that Health Services received this money indirectly. It is now well established that benefits under § 666 are not limited solely to primary target recipients or beneficiaries." Looking at the nature of the relationship, the First Circuit found that the contract "contemplated a relationship between Health Services and the Federal Government" that would further the federal interest in disease control and AIDS prevention, and therefore § 666 applied to the company.

United States v. Hildenbrand[105] illustrated the expansive view of benefits that brought defendants under § 666 despite not receiving federal funds directly. The defendants purchased homes at a discount through an organization participating in the Department of Housing and Urban Development's Single Family Affordable Housing Program (SFAHP) and then improperly inflated the value of the repairs they made to the properties to increase the allowable price at which the homes could be resold. The case involved fraud, not a bribe, and defendants argued that § 666 did not apply because they neither received nor disbursed federal funds through SFAHP, and the

---

[103] 727 F.Supp. 1068 (N.D. Tex. 1989).

[104] 292 F.3d 1 (1st Cir. 2002).

[105] 527 F.3d 466 (5th Cir. 2008).

discounts represented purely commercial transactions between HUD and the organization. The Fifth Circuit rejected the argument, finding that the organization "received a quantitative monetary benefit from HUD through the discounts," and the program "furthers the public policy objectives of both expanding home ownership opportunities for low-and moderate-income purchasers and strengthening neighborhoods. . . . " While the ultimate purchasers were also beneficiaries of the discounts, as in *Fischer*, the circuit court explained that there can be multiple beneficiaries of a government program. The fact that an organization acts as a conduit to transfer a benefit from the government to the ultimate recipient does not preclude the middleman from liability for violating § 666.

But not every organization receiving benefits from a federal program automatically comes within § 666. In *United States v. Wyncoop*,[106] decided before *Fischer*, the Ninth Circuit held that embezzling from a private college that did not directly receive federal funds fell outside the statutory proscription. The government's theory was that the statute applied to the school because of its participation in the federal student loan program, which guarantees loans made by banks to the college's students, with the funds ultimately being paid to the school. The Ninth Circuit held that "the statute was not intended to cover thefts from institutions like Trend College that do not themselves receive and administer federal funds." The circuit court explained that the school was only an "indirect" beneficiary of the federal funds, an analysis that does not remain good law in light of *Fischer*'s focus on the structure, operation, and purpose of the organization rather than how the funding is actually received or disbursed. But the tenuous connection to federal funds is still applicable in light of the admonition in *Fischer* that not every instance of fraud should come within § 666. The embezzlement in *Wyncoop* was unrelated to the student loan program, nor was the integrity of the federal program affected by the diversion of money from the school's bank account, so the circuit court's decision overturning the conviction appears to be the correct result after *Fischer*.

5.   *One–Year Period*

The federal jurisdictional requirement requires receiving at least $10,000 of benefits from the federal government by the state or local government, agency, or organization within one year of the offense. This nexus is defined in § 666(d)(5) as "a continuous period that commences no earlier than twelve months before the commission of the offense or that ends no later than twelve months after the commission of the offense. Such period may include time both before and after the commission of the offense."[107] The statutory requirement is effectively a swinging door, so that the receipt of identified benefits from the federal government can occur in *any* twelve-month period the prosecutor chooses to prove so long as the offense occurred at some point during that period. The statute does not peg the one-year period to a fiscal or calendar year, nor must all of the criminal activity occur within that one-year period.

---

[106] 11 F.3d 119 (9th Cir. 1993).

[107] Crime Control Act of 1990, Pub. L. No. 101–647, Title XII, § 1208, 104 Stat. 4832 (1990).

A § 666 violation can be a continuing crime, so the offense conduct, such as solicitation of a bribe or fraud, need not take place at a specific time but can occur over weeks or months. For example, misapplication of funds often requires multiple financial transactions, and so one step in the violation must take place within the one-year period identified in the indictment to establish federal jurisdiction.

As an element of the offense, the government must prove beyond a reasonable doubt that the organization, government, or agency identified in the indictment received over $10,000 in benefits during the specified one-year period. While that may appear to be something easily established, the Fifth Circuit's decision in *United States v. Jackson*[108] illustrates that this element requires more than just introducing evidence that an unrelated unit of the agency or organization received federal funds. The circuit court reversed convictions because prosecutors failed to offer sufficient proof of the actual amounts received by the city during the one-year period when the offense occurred. The government introduced evidence of indirect benefits to the city based on amounts paid by the federal government to the state for local or regional arts projects. But prosecutors did not show the actual amounts received, the dates of disbursements to the city, or how much was traceable to federal grants. The circuit court stated that "the Government must present more than a mere scintilla of evidence" of the federal benefits by introducing evidence that "affords a substantial basis" to support the jury's finding.

C. Agent

1. *Overview*

Section 666 covers any "agent of an organization, or of a State, local, or Indian tribal government, or any agency thereof" that receives $10,000 of federal benefits in the one-year period. An agent is defined in § 666(d)(1) as "a person authorized to act on behalf of another person or a government and, in the case of an organization or government, includes a servant or employee, and a partner, director, officer, manager, and representative." Whether a person is an "agent" is frequently litigated because the Supreme Court's rejection of the federal nexus requirement in *Fischer* makes this one of the few elements that can be a legal basis for avoiding a conviction.

2. *Agency*

Prior to the Supreme Court's decision in *Salinas*, a district court in *United States v. Frega*[109] limited the scope of § 666 by requiring that the government prove the agent was responsible for administering the organization's funds, although it was not necessary to show that federal funds were involved in the violation. The district judge dismissed a conspiracy to violate § 666 charge against two state court judges and an attorney arising from bribery of the judges to make favorable rulings for the lawyer's clients. The trial court found the charge insufficient because it did "not allege that federal funds were corruptly administered, were in danger of being corruptly administered, or even could have been corruptly administered."

---

[108] 313 F.3d 231 (5th Cir. 2002).
[109] 933 F.Supp. 1536 (S.D. Cal. 1996).

The Supreme Court in *Salinas* held that the organization or agency's receipt of the $10,000 in federal funds was sufficient to establish federal jurisdiction, and did not require any further proof of a federal nexus. In *United States v. Vitillo*,[110] the Third Circuit stated, "§ 666(d)(1) does not define an 'agent' as someone who necessarily controls federal funds." The same court stated in *United States v. Andrews*[111] that "Harris, who qualified as an 'agent' under § 666, did not have to possess actual authority over the business, transaction, or series of transactions, that Andrews sought to influence."

Nevertheless, the Eleventh Circuit relied on *Frega* in *United States v. Whitfield*[112] to overturn the conviction of two state court judges and the attorney who bribed them in exchange for favorable treatment in two cases, concluding there was an insufficient nexus between the bribery and the federal funding. Prosecutors identified the agency receiving the federal funding as the Administrative Office of the Courts (AOC), but the circuit court found that the judges acted only in a nonjudicial role in hiring staff and administering funds provided by that office. The bribes involved judicial authority, which was unrelated to the federal funds. The Eleventh Circuit held that "insofar as [Judges] Whitfield and Teel may have been agents of the AOC, their role as such had nothing to do with their capacity as judicial decisionmakers." The circuit court noted that the analysis would be different if the judges had been bribed to hire someone to work their chambers, while corruption related to judicial decisionmaking had no connection with the state agency.

Whitfield takes a bifurcated view of the term "agent," finding that an individual may be acting as an agent in one capacity but not in another, even if the person only occupied a single position and acted in that capacity. This supports the argument that a bribe or gratuity can be unrelated to the person's role as an agent of the program receiving federal funding, thus opening a potential avenue to avoid liability under the statute.

3. *Employees*

There is no requirement that the defendant be in a particular position or have specified responsibilities, such as authority over budgets or management of the organization, to be an agent. Once it is shown that the person is an employee, their position in the organization does not appear to matter in applying § 666. In *United States v. Brann*,[113] the Third Circuit stated, "The definition thus includes in the term 'agent' an employee of any level from the lowest clerk to the highest administrator. It does not, however, include or require that the employee hold a position of trust." In *United States v. Keen*,[114] the Eleventh Circuit rejected the argument that the government must show the defendant had some measure of authority over the organization's funding to come within § 666:

---

[110] 490 F.3d 314 (3d Cir. 2007).

[111] 681 F.3d 509 (3d Cir. 2012).

[112] 590 F.3d 325 (5th Cir. 2009).

[113] 990 F.2d 98 (3rd Cir. 1993).

[114] 676 F.3d 981 (11th Cir. 2012).

Nowhere does the statutory text either mention or imply an additional qualifying requirement that the person be authorized to act *specifically with respect to the entity's funds* . . . we must decline to read into the definition of "agent" a requirement that the person be authorized to act with respect to the entity's funds. Instead, we conclude that to qualify as an agent of an entity, an individual need only be authorized to act on behalf of that entity.

In *United States v. Ollison*,[115] the Fifth Circuit rejected a similar argument by a secretary to a school district superintendent that she did not come within § 666 because she was a low-level employee without authority over any programs that would affect the federal funds received by the district. The circuit court found that the defendant's misuse of district funds for personal expenses had a relationship to the federal funding, rejecting a constitutional as-applied challenge arguing that application of the statute to any governmental employee was beyond congressional power.

4. Non–Employees

For cases that do not involve employees, the defendant's relationship to the organization or agency's exercise of authority is important in determining whether the label "agent" can be applied. In *United States v. Ferber*,[116] a district court dismissed § 666 charges against an outside financial adviser to a state agency accused of taking bribes in connection with the award of securities underwriting business on the agency's behalf. The district judge, applying general principles of agency law, found that the defendant was not "authorized to act" on the agency's behalf because he only provided financial planning advice, and "[t]here was no evidence presented in the government's case that tended to show that Ferber was ever given the authority to alter the legal relationship between the [agency] and third parties."

In *United States v. Vitillo*,[117] the individual defendant and corporations he controlled argued that as independent contractors they were not agents of a government-owned airport. The Third Circuit found that the use of the word "includes" in § 666(d)(1) meant that the list of relationships that make someone an agent was "not exhaustive," and "as a matter of statutory interpretation, § 666(d)(1) does not by definition exclude an independent contractor who acts on behalf of a § 666(b) entity as a manager or representative of that entity." The Seventh Circuit reached the same conclusion in *United States v. Lupton*[118] regarding a real estate broker retained by the state to assist in the sale of one of its buildings charged with soliciting a kickback from a potential purchaser. The contract between the state and the real estate agency provided that it was only an "independent contractor" and did not have any authority to act on behalf of the state in a transaction, but the circuit court stated that whether a person was an "agent" should be determined by the statute and "not by the terms of a private contract." The circuit court explained that "[p]arties cannot contract around definitions provided in criminal statutes; even if Lupton could not be considered a common law agent under Equis's contract, it is nonetheless possible for him to be an

---

[115] 555 F.3d 152 (5th Cir. 2009).
[116] 966 F.Supp. 90 (D. Mass. 1997).
[117] 490 F.3d 314 (3d Cir. 2007).
[118] 620 F.3d 790 (7th Cir. 2010).

'agent' under the terms of 18 U.S.C. § 666(d)(1)." Similarly, the Sixth Circuit in *United States v. Hudson*[119] found that "[e]mployment labels . . . may bring some employment relationships within the sphere of agency status but they do not necessarily squeeze all other employment relationships out of that sphere."

5.   *Scope of Authority*

The agency element focuses on the person's relationship to the organization, and the effect of corruption on federal funds. The Supreme Court's emphasis in *Sabri* on the rationale of § 666 as designed to preserve the integrity of the organization and its federal support shows that the agent must be acting on behalf of the organization that receives the federal funds in order to come within the statute. In *United States v. Abu–Shawish*, the Seventh Circuit explained that "the agent who is potentially criminally liable must have fraudulently obtained property that is under the care, custody or control of the same organization for which he is an agent."[120]

The government must prove that the defendant is an agent of the organization, government, or agency identified in the indictment as receiving the $10,000 of federal funding during the twelve-month period. In *United States v. Phillips*,[121] the Fifth Circuit reversed the conviction of a Louisiana parish tax assessor because he did not act as an agent of the parish but instead worked for the state tax assessor's office, a separate governmental unit. The prosecution introduced evidence that the parish received over $10,000 in funding for food stamps from the federal government, but

> because Phillips, as a matter of law, was not an employee or officer of the parish and because he was not authorized to act on behalf of the parish with respect to its funds, Phillips's actions did not and could not have threatened the integrity of federal funds or programs. Without an agency relationship to the recipient of federal funds, § 666 does not reach the misconduct of local officials. Courts can rely on state and local laws to ascertain whether the person was acting as an agent of the organization.

In *United States v. Pretty*,[122] the Tenth Circuit found that a deputy state treasurer acted on behalf of the state, and not just the Treasurer's Office, because she invested funds provided to the state that were placed in a general account for all of its agencies. In *United States v. Madrzyk*,[123] the district court cited to the City of Chicago Municipal Code as authority that an alderman was an agent of the city itself and not just the city council.

Determining which state agency actually employed the defendant was crucial in *United States v. Langston*.[124] The Eleventh Circuit reversed the defendant's conviction for diverting funds from the Alabama Fire College, where he was the executive director, because the indictment only charged that he was an agent of the State of

---

[119] 491 F.3d 590 (6th Cir. 2007).

[120] 507 F.3d 550 (7th Cir. 2007).

[121] 219 F.3d 404 (5th Cir. 2000).

[122] 98 F.3d 1213 (10th Cir. 1996).

[123] 970 F.Supp. 642 (N.D. Ill. 1997).

[124] 590 F.3d 1226 (11th Cir. 2009).

Alabama. The circuit court reviewed the statute creating the organization and found that the Fire College was independent, so that he was not a dual agent of both, unlike *Moeller*. The Eleventh Circuit found that "[b]ecause Langston's employment with the Fire College does not authorize him to act on behalf of the state under the applicable state law, evidence of his employment with the Fire College is not relevant to the charges asserting he acted as an agent of the state."

D. Offense Conduct

1. Overview

Section 666 covers two different types of criminal conduct: theft and corruption. Section 666(a)(1)(A) punishes any person who "embezzles, steals, obtains by fraud, or otherwise without authority knowingly converts to the use of any person other than the rightful owner or intentionally misapplies property" worth $5,000 that is owned by, or under the care, custody, or control of an organization. Section 666(a)(1)(B) reaches bribery and unlawful gratuities, making it a crime for any person who

> corruptly solicits or demands for the benefit of any person, or accepts or agrees to accept, anything of value from any person, intending to be influenced or rewarded in connection with any business, transaction, or series of transactions of such organization, government, or agency involving any thing of value of $5,000 or more.

2. Embezzlement, Theft, Fraud, Conversion, or Misapplication

Embezzlement, theft, and fraud are common law offenses incorporated into § 666, and the traditional elements of those crimes apply to cases in which the victim is an organization receiving the requisite federal funding. These crimes are not often charged in federal court because violations involving local governments and organizations are usually pursued by state or local prosecutors. There are no reported federal cases analyzing the scope and application of embezzlement and theft in a § 666 prosecution. There are other federal statutes covering these offenses, and courts are likely to look to them in analyzing the elements of a crime.

Fraud is a much broader offense than embezzlement and theft, and has been prosecuted under a number of federal statutes involving omissions that resulted in a loss and even the deprivation of the right of honest services under 18 U.S.C. § 1346 (discussed in § 4.5). Fraud prosecutions under § 666 usually involve fairly straightforward schemes that could also be charged under the federal mail and wire fraud statutes.

The prohibition on conversion or misapplication is another offense that can be committed in a number of different ways. The legislative history of § 666 makes no mention of these crimes, and a Senate Report on the legislation states only that the provision "create[d] new offenses to augment the ability of the United States to vindicate significant acts of theft, fraud, and bribery involving Federal monies that are disbursed to private organizations of State and local governments pursuant to a

Federal program."[125] This violation is set off from embezzlement, theft, and fraud, requiring proof that a person "otherwise without authority knowingly converts to the use of any person other than the rightful owner or intentionally misapplies." These are really two different offenses: larceny by conversion and misapplication of property. Under the common law, conversion involved lawfully obtaining possession of property and then subsequently converting it to one's own use, similar to embezzlement. Under 18 U.S.C. § 641, which punishes conversion of federal government property, the crime does not require proof that a defendant actually kept the property for personal use, so that a violation can be shown by intentional and knowing abuse or unauthorized use of the property.[126]

Misapplication does not require taking possession of the property or making any unlawful personal use of it; instead, it involves directing its use improperly. Unlike the other offenses in § 666(a)(1)(A), which all relate in some way to theft, misapplication focuses on the misuse of authority, such as directing the expenditure of funds for a purpose other than that designated by the organization. In *United States v. Thompson*,[127] the Seventh Circuit analyzed the misapplication offense in a case in which the defendant was a state official convicted for violating administrative rules related to the selection of a travel agent for state agencies. After bids were received, a travel agency from outside the state was the lowest bidder, but the defendant wanted the contract awarded to an in-state agency, referring to "politics" or how "political" the decision would be in ordering that the contract be re-bid. The owner of the in-state travel agency had been a contributor to the governor's campaign. After reviewing the new bids, a board on which the defendant served awarded the contract to the in-state travel agency based on scores each bidder received, which was done properly, and three months later the defendant received a $1,000 raise. Prosecutors argued that the raise was in reality a reward for the misapplication of state funds when the contract was given to the in-state travel agency.

The Seventh Circuit explained that a "mistake" in the bidding process that violated the state's rules would not prove a misapplication of state funds. It stated, "Approving a payment for goods or services not supplied would be a misapplication, but hiring the low bidder does not sound like 'misapplication' of funds." The circuit court explained that there were two possible readings of "misapplies" in § 666, a term that is not defined in the statute:

> We could read that word broadly, so that it means any disbursement that would not have occurred had all state laws been enforced without any political considerations. Or we could read it narrowly, so that it means a disbursement in exchange for services not rendered (as with ghost workers), or to suppliers that would not have received any contract but for bribes, or for services that were overpriced (to cover the cost of baksheesh), or for shoddy goods at the price prevailing for high-quality goods.

---

[125] S. Rep. No. 225, reprinted in 1984 U.S.C.C.A.N. 3182.

[126] See United States v. Fogel, 901 F.2d 23 (4th Cir. 1990).

[127] 484 F.3d 877 (7th Cir. 2007).

Relying on the caption for § 666 that connotes targeting corruption, and referencing the Rule of Lenity to interpret an ambiguous term, the Seventh Circuit opted for the narrower reading. The focus on harm from the violation is consistent with *Sabri*'s emphasis on the statute's role in preserving the integrity of the organization receiving federal funds. The circuit court stated:

> An error—even a deliberate one, in which the employee winks at the rules in order to help out someone he believes deserving but barely over the eligibility threshold—is a civil rather than a criminal transgression. Likewise the sin is civil (if it is any wrong at all) when a public employee manipulates the rules, as Thompson did, to save the state money or favor a home-state producer that supports elected officials.

The notion of harm advanced in *Thompson* does not require that the government lose money, only that the misapplication must involve a corrupt decision or a diversion of resources from their proper application.

In *United States v. Urlacher*,[128] the Second Circuit rejected a police official's defense that there was no violation of § 666(a)(1)(A) when funds were applied to other purposes of the police department than those for which they were supposed to be used. The circuit court stated, "Intentional misapplication, in order to avoid redundancy, must mean intentional misapplication for otherwise legitimate purposes; if it were for illegitimate purposes, it would be covered by the prohibitions against embezzlement, stealing, obtaining by fraud, or conversion."

A misapplication violation does not require a personal benefit to the agent from the misconduct. In *United States v. Frazier*,[129] the Tenth Circuit affirmed a defendant's misapplication conviction for diverting funds from a federal job training grant to purchase computers for his organization rather than providing the computer training required by the grant. In *United States v. Cornier–Ortiz*,[130] the First Circuit affirmed the defendant's conviction for misapplying funds to hire the brother of a government employee to perform work in violation of a conflict-of-interest policy. The circuit court stated, "The prohibition against intentional misapplication covers the situation presented here: payments made for what was an underlying legitimate purpose but intentionally misapplied to undermine a conflict of interest prohibition."

The misapplication must be done "intentionally," so the government is required to prove the defendant's specific intent to misapply the property of the organization and not just that the defendant was negligent about its use. If a particular use of the property was authorized, then that can be strong evidence the defendant did not have the requisite specific intent to misapply property. In *United States v. De La Cruz*,[131] the Seventh Circuit stated, "Authorization, or ratification, from those with authority can be an important evidentiary factor in favor of the defense, militating against a finding of intentional misapplication." Authorization does not bar a prosecution, however,

---

[128] 979 F.2d 935 (2d Cir. 1992).
[129] 53 F.3d 1105 (10th Cir. 1995).
[130] 361 F.3d 29 (1st Cir. 2004).
[131] 469 F.3d 1064 (7th Cir. 2006).

because in *De la Cruz* the circuit court questioned the ratification of the contracts when it appeared that "officials attempted to immunize themselves from federal prosecution by simply stamping their criminal misapplication of funds as approved."

3.   Bribery and Unlawful Gratuities

Congress enacted § 666 to extend the prohibition on bribery and unlawful gratuities of federal officials in 18 U.S.C. § 201 to state and local governments, along with organizations receiving significant federal funding. Like its federal counterpart, § 666(a)(1) reaches the official demanding or accepting the bribe or gratuity, while § 666(a)(2) punishes any person who "corruptly gives, offers, or agrees to give anything of value to any person, with intent to influence or reward an agent of an organization or of a State, local or Indian tribal government, or any agency thereof. . . . " The two statutes are not coextensive, however, and § 666(a)(1)(B) is broader than § 201 by including any corrupt solicitation of a bribe or gratuity.

Including the term "solicit" in § 666 expands the statute's coverage beyond *quid pro quo* arrangements. The Sixth Circuit explained in *United States v. Abbey*[132] that "the statute does not require the government to prove that Abbey contemplated a specific act when he received the bribe; the text says nothing of a quid pro quo requirement to sustain a conviction, express or otherwise. . . . " The Seventh Circuit, in *United States v. Gee*,[133] summarized the scope of § 666(a)(1)(B) when it stated that a "*quid pro quo* of money for a specific legislative act is *sufficient* to violate the statute, but it is not *necessary*." The Eleventh Circuit, in *United States v. McNair*, rejected imposing a requirement that the government prove a *quid pro quo* agreement, finding that the plain language of § 666 did not require that the solicitation or receipt of a bribe be "in exchange for a specific official act." The circuit court pointed out that "[t]o accept the defendants' argument would permit a person to pay a significant sum to a Court employee intending the payment to produce a future, as yet unidentified favor without violating § 666."[134] Like the Seventh Circuit, the Eleventh Circuit explained that "[t]o be sure, many § 666 bribery cases will involve an identifiable and particularized official act, but that is not required to convict." Thus, a payment to a public official to provide assistance "as opportunities arise" can be a violation even if there is no specific governmental action contemplated at the time of the arrangement.[135]

Including "solicit" in the statute means that even preliminary steps leading up to a *quid pro quo* arrangement can be enough to violate the statute, so long as the solicitation was corrupt. Like proving an attempt, establishing solicitation of a corrupt payment will be easier as the parties get closer to the transfer and evidence of a specific official action being undertaken can establish the necessary intent.

The original language of § 666 mimicked § 201 by making it a crime to solicit, demand, or accept anything of value "*for or because of* the recipient's conduct in any

---

[132] 560 F.3d 513 (6th Cir. 2009).

[133] 432 F.3d 713 (7th Cir. 2005).

[134] 605 F.3d 1152 (11th Cir. 2010).

[135] See United States v. Rosen, 716 F.3d 691 (2d Cir. 2013).

transaction or matter or a series of transactions or matters."[136] A 1986 amendment changed the language of the offense to its current form that covers any corrupt solicitation or demand by an agent "intending to be influenced or rewarded."[137] The use of the term "reward" means that § 666 applies to both bribes ("influenced") and gratuities ("rewarded"). In *United States v. Bonito*,[138] the Second Circuit held that the language of the amended provision was to the same effect as the original statute, so that "the current statute continues to cover payments made with intent to reward past official conduct, so long as the intent to reward is corrupt." It reiterated that conclusion in *United States v. Bahel*,[139] stating that "[§]666 is broad enough to encompass an illegal gratuity theory of liability." In *United States v. Boender,*[140] the Seventh Circuit stated that "by its plain text, [§ 666(a)(2)] already covers both bribes and rewards."

By deleting the "for or because of" element of the offense, the Supreme Court's decision in *United States v. Sun–Diamond Growers of California*[141] is not relevant to a gratuity prosecution under § 666. In that case, as discussed above, the Court required the government to prove "a link between a thing of value conferred upon a public official and a specific 'official act' for or because of which it was given." In *United States v. Abbey*,[142] the Sixth Circuit stated, "*Sun–Diamond* . . . is not germane to our decision," and that "[t]here is thus no good reason, either in text or policy, to inject *Sun–Diamond*'s heightened requirements into § 666. . . . " In *United States v. Redzic*, the Eighth Circuit explained:

> To prove the payment of an illegal bribe, the government must present evidence of a *quid pro quo*, but an illegal bribe may be paid with the intent to influence a general course of conduct. It was not necessary for the government to link any particular payment to any particular action undertaken [by the defendant].[143]

The Eleventh Circuit in *United States v. McNair*[144] rejected reliance on *Sun–Diamond* to limit the scope of § 666 by requiring proof of a specific official act, pointing out that the statute "sweeps more broadly than §§ 201(b) or (c). Section 666 requires only that money be given with intent to influence or reward a government agent 'in connection with any business, transaction, or series of transactions.'"

The requirement that the solicitation or payment be sought with the intent "to be influenced" does not mean that the agent must be shown to have the actual authority to undertake action on behalf of the organization. In *United States v. Gee*,[145] the Seventh Circuit rejected the argument that the payments to a state senator did not come within § 666 because the official "had no power or authority to influence" a final

---

[136] Pub. L. No. 98–473, § 1104(a), 98 Stat. 2143 (1984).

[137] Pub. L. No. 99–646, § 59(a), 100 Stat. 3612 (1986).

[138] 57 F.3d 167 (2d Cir. 1995).

[139] 662 F.3d 610 (2d Cir. 2011).

[140] 649 F.3d 650 (7th Cir. 2011).

[141] 526 U.S. 398 (1999).

[142] 560 F.3d 513 (6th Cir. 2009).

[143] 569 F.3d 841 (8th Cir. 2009).

[144] 605 F.3d 1152 (11th Cir. 2010).

[145] 432 F.3d 713 (7th Cir. 2005).

decision, stating that "[t]his confuses influence with power to act unilaterally." The circuit court explained:

> A legislator with the ability to control the senate's agenda can throw a monkey wrench into a Governor's program, and this power confers influence over executive decisions even when the legislature does not pass any particular law. The absence of new laws may show the successful application of influence. One does not need to live in Chicago to know that a job description is not a complete measure of clout. The evidence permitted a reasonable jury to find that George had plenty of clout and used it to OIC's benefit, for which he was well paid.

Section 666(a)(1)(B) requires proof of two intents: that the defendant acted "corruptly" in soliciting or demanding anything of value, and that it be done "intending to be influenced or rewarded." The original language in § 666 did not include any express intent element for a conviction, so that it could have been read to require only a general intent. In *United States v. Ford*,[146] the Second Circuit held that "intending to be influenced" means "there must be a *quid pro quo*" to show the intent of the person demanding bribe. The jury had been instructed that the defendant's awareness of the offeror's purpose in giving a thing of value was sufficient to establish an intent to be influenced, which the Second Circuit rejected as insufficient to meet the mens rea requirement. The statement about the need to show a *quid pro quo* should not be read to impose a requirement on the government to prove the existence of an agreement between the offeror and agent because § 666(a)(1)(B) also covers solicitation, which would take place before the formation of an agreement. The Second Circuit apparently meant that there must be evidence to show the person entered into, or at least sought to enter into, a *quid pro quo* agreement. The circuit court explained:

> The recipient's "awareness" that the donor gave something of value for the purpose of influencing the recipient might well constitute strong circumstantial evidence that the recipient acted with the requisite culpable state of mind in accepting the item, but a jury should be clearly instructed that it is the recipient's intent to make good on the bargain, not simply her awareness of the donor's intent that is essential to establishing guilt under Section 666.

"Corruptly" is a term used in a number of federal statutes, and courts have struggled to give it any definite meaning. In *Arthur Andersen LLP v. United States*,[147] a case involving an obstruction of justice provision, the Supreme Court stated that "'[c]orrupt' and 'corruptly' are normally associated with wrongful, immoral, depraved, or evil." Interpreting a statute that required proof of "knowingly . . . corruptly persuading" another person to obstruct justice as "limiting criminality to persuaders *conscious of their wrongdoing*" was the most sensible interpretation. In *United States v. Ogle*,[148] the Tenth Circuit described "corruptly" as "[a]n act done with an intent to give some advantage inconsistent with official duty and the rights of others. . . . It includes bribery but is more comprehensive; because an act may be corruptly done though the advantage to be derived from it be not offered by another." In *United States v.*

---

[146] 435 F.3d 204 (2d Cir. 2006).

[147] 544 U.S. 696 (2005).

[148] 613 F.2d 233 (10th Cir. 1979).

Jennings,[149] the Fourth Circuit pointed out that "corruptly" can be read to require proof of a *quid pro quo* agreement, which would limit § 666 to bribes and not gratuities.

Proof that a defendant acted "corruptly" in a § 666 prosecution usually involves showing that the person consciously deviated from the duties and responsibilities of the position or authority, or that the offer or solicitation of a thing of value was to induce such deviation. In *United States v. Rooney*,[150] the Second Circuit held that "a fundamental component of a 'corrupt' act is a breach of some official duty owed to the government or the public at large." In *United States v. Ford*,[151] the same court stated that "[a] recipient who knows of the donor's intent to arrange a *quid-pro-quo* or to seek special consideration may, in certain circumstances, be said to be acting 'corruptly'" when the person accepts the thing of value.

But it is not necessary to show that the official acted contrary to the public interest. In *United States v. Bryant*,[152] the Third Circuit upheld the conviction of a state senator for taking bribes from a state medical school in exchange for protecting its interests in the legislative appropriations process. The circuit court stated, "Bryant intended to accept a 'stream of benefits' in the form of a salary and benefits from SOM [School of Osteopathic Medicine] in exchange for his official acts over the course of his nearly three-year employment there. That his actions may also have benefited his constituents is irrelevant." In *United States v. Rosen*,[153] the Second Circuit held, "[T]he corrupt intent that is central to an illegal quid pro quo exchange persists even though the State legislator's acts also benefit constituents other than the defendant."

The Third Circuit in *United States v. Cicco*[154] considered whether a public official's demand for political support in exchange for retaining a government position constituted a bribe under § 666(a)(1)(B). The defendants, a mayor and a town councilman, denied two special police officers further work because they had not supported the party's candidates in a recent election. The circuit court held that the officials had not violated § 666 by demanding political support in exchange for a governmental position because that conduct did not come within the usual meaning of bribery. Soliciting campaign contributions as a requirement for a government position, however, can violate the statute as the solicitation of a bribe. In *United States v. Grubb*,[155] the Fourth Circuit upheld § 666 convictions because the payment to the campaign was clearly designed to obtain the government job, a form of bribery that came "squarely within the literal meaning of section 666[(a)(1)(B)]." Unlike party loyalty, which is not the typical "thing of value" used in a bribe, campaign contributions can be the basis for a bribery prosecution.

---

[149] 160 F.3d 1006 (4th Cir. 1998).

[150] 37 F.3d 847 (2d Cir. 1994).

[151] 435 F.3d 204 (2d Cir. 2006).

[152] 655 F.3d 232 (3d Cir. 2011).

[153] 716 F.3d 691 (2d Cir. 2013).

[154] 938 F.2d 441 (3d Cir. 1991).

[155] 11 F.3d 426 (4th Cir. 1993).

4.   The $5,000 Requirement

Congress imposed a minimum threshold of $5,000 to trigger liability for violating § 666 in order to limit federal prosecutions to substantial cases and not those involving petty amounts. In *United States v. Webb*,[156] a district court explained that "Congress recognized that the statute constituted a significant intrusion of federal law enforcement into traditional areas of local concern; thus, it made the new statute applicable only to crimes involving substantial sums of money."

For violations of § 666(a)(1)(A) for embezzlement, theft, fraud, and misapplication, the government must prove that the property involved had a value of $5,000 or more, and that it was "owned by, or is under the care, custody, or control of such organization, government, or agency" at the time of the offense. The use of the term "property" can be read to connote only tangible property, similar to common law larceny that was limited to theft of physical property. The Sixth Circuit in *United States v. Sanderson*,[157] however, interpreted the statute as having the same broad coverage as the federal property theft statute, 18 U.S.C. § 641. The circuit court stated, "Congress seems to have intended section 666 to *expand* the ability of prosecutors to prosecute persons who were for technical reasons out of section 641's reach." It upheld the theft conviction of a supervisor in a county sheriff's office who had deputies do work on behalf of his private construction firm even though there was no taking of tangible property, only the time of the employees.

For a bribery or unlawful gratuity violation under § 666(a)(1)(B), the corruption must be "in connection with any business, transaction, or series of transactions of such organization, government, or agency involving any thing of value of $5,000 or more." In *United States v. Marmolejo*,[158] the Fifth Circuit held "that the plain meaning of the statute compels our conclusion that the term 'anything of value' in § 666(a)(1)(B) includes transactions involving intangible items, such as the conjugal visits at issue in this case." In *United States v. Mongelli*,[159] the district court found a bribery scheme involving the award of licenses came within the statute because the "term 'thing of value,' used in § 666 but not in 18 U.S.C. §§ 1341–4[3], has long been construed in other federal criminal statutes to embrace intangibles." This is different from the Supreme Court's analysis in *Cleveland v. United States*[160] where it held that unissued licenses of were not "property" under the mail and wire fraud statutes (see § 4.4).

To meet the $5,000 requirement for theft and misapplication, the government can aggregate separate acts so long as they are part of a single scheme or plan. In *Sanderson*, the Sixth Circuit stated "under section 666, where multiple conversions are part of a single scheme, it seems appropriate to aggregate the value of property stolen in order to reach the $5,000 minimum required for prosecution." In *United States v. Webb*, the district court stated that "[b]ecause aggregation is permissible where the

---

[156] 691 F.Supp. 1164 (N.D. Ill. 1988).

[157] 966 F.2d 184 (6th Cir. 1992).

[158] 89 F.3d 1185 (5th Cir. 1996).

[159] 794 F.Supp. 529 (S.D.N.Y. 1992).

[160] 531 U.S. 12 (2000),

thefts are part of a single plan, an individual who seeks to avoid the statute by so structuring his crime will find his efforts unavailing."

The Eighth Circuit in *United States v. Hines*[161] applied the aggregation approach to a bribery charge under § 666(a)(1)(B), holding that the statute "permits the government to aggregate multiple transactions in [a] single count to reach the $5,000 minimum as long as they were part of a single plan or scheme." When aggregating to establish the monetary impact element, the government must show that the conduct occurred in the same one-year period during which the organization received the $10,000 in federal benefits. In *United States v. Valentine*,[162] the Sixth Circuit held "that a natural reading of the statute requires the $5,000 theft to occur during a one-year period."

For bribery and unlawful gratuities charges under § 666(a)(1)(B), the thing of value solicited or demanded need not be worth $5,000, although if it was, then that can establish the requisite value for this element of the offense. The statute requires only that the solicitation or demand be made "in connection with any business, transaction, or series of transactions of such organization, government, or agency involving any thing of value of $5,000 or more." The focus is on the underlying business or transactions of the organization tainted by the corruption, so that a small bribe could be prosecuted if the underlying business affected by the corruption had a value of $5,000.

A wide range of evidence can establish the $5,000 value. In *United States v. Townsend*,[163] the Eleventh Circuit described a "market approach" to determining the value of an intangible, in that case securing freedom from conditions imposed during pre-trial release of a defendant. The circuit court stated:

> [T]he value of an intangible in the black market of corruption is set at the monetary value of what a willing bribe-giver gives and what a willing bribe-taker takes in exchange for the intangible. The value of the market value approach is that it does not require courts to struggle with putting a price on an intangible. The parties do it themselves.

In *United States v. Fernandes*,[164] the Seventh Circuit upheld the conviction of a deputy prosecutor who maintained a list of the amounts paid to help defendants avoid drunk driving convictions that totalled over $5,000, even though some defendants did not make the payments while another paid more than what was listed. The circuit court stated, "The overpayment and the existence of the list, in and of themselves, could allow a jury to conclude, beyond a reasonable doubt, that the 'thing of value' in this bribery scheme exceeded $5,000." In *United States v. Mills*,[165] however, the Sixth Circuit found that the only evidence sufficient to establish the value was the amounts paid as bribes, and "[t]he indictment returned against the defendants clearly and

---

[161] 541 F.3d 833 (8th Cir. 2008).

[162] 63 F.3d 459 (6th Cir. 1995).

[163] 630 F.3d 1003 (11th Cir. 2011).

[164] 272 F.3d 938 (7th Cir. 2001).

[165] 140 F.3d 630 (6th Cir. 1998).

specifically assigns values ranging from $3,500 to $3,930 to those jobs. Because those amounts are below the $5,000 statutory floor, the district court correctly dismissed those counts premised upon alleged violations of 18 U.S.C. § 666."

In *United States v. Marmolejo*,[166] the Fifth Circuit rejected the argument that payments to allow a federal prisoner to receive separate conjugal visits from his wife and girlfriend could not meet the $5,000 value requirement. The circuit court stated, "We conclude that the conjugal visits in this case did have a value which exceeded $5,000. We arrive at this estimate in the same way that an appraiser would value an asset—by looking at how much a person in the market would be willing to pay for them." The district court in *United States v. Mongelli*[167] explained that licenses issued by the state could be valued in a variety of ways, including looking at the amount of the bribes paid, the amount of business or profits obtainable under the license, or the market value of the license if it were sold.

Proof of the value of the business or transaction is not limited to just the amount that the organization, government, or agency involved in the corruption would pay for it. In *United States v. Zwick*,[168] the Third Circuit held that "the plain language of the statute does not require that value be measured from the perspective of the organization, government, or agency." In assessing the jury's value determination, the circuit court stated:

> There is substantial evidence establishing that the present value of the transactions and business involved in each of counts one, two, and three was at least $5,000. The sewer taps that Zwick offered to obtain for Kaclik were clearly worth more than $5,000, as Kaclik was willing to pay $17,500 to ensure that he received them; the contracts that were the subject of the bribery at count three were worth $45,000; and the permits in count two were worth more than $5,000 to the Fosnights, because, as detailed above, they were willing to pay Zwick $15,000 to ensure that they received them and would have lost $10,000 if they did not receive them in a timely manner.

The Second Circuit took the same approach in *United States v. Santopietro*,[169] holding that "there is no requirement that the corrupt transactions are worth $5,000 or more to the entity receiving the federal funds," and the evidence of value showed that the "favorable treatment was clearly worth more than $5,000 to" the defendants. In *United States v. Hines*, the Eighth Circuit rejected the argument that value is limited to what the briber or recipient considered it worth, holding that "[t]he plain language of the statute does not require a restricted, technical interpretation that would prevent the consideration of the 'thing's' value to other parties with an immediate interest in the transaction."[170]

---

[166] 89 F.3d 1185 (5th Cir. 1996).

[167] 794 F.Supp. 529 (S.D. N.Y. 1992).

[168] 199 F.3d 672 (3d Cir. 1999).

[169] 166 F.3d 88 (2d Cir. 1999).

[170] 541 F.3d 833 (8th Cir. 2008).

The valuation of the business or transactions can include the potential value of property if the corrupted official took the favorable action. In *United States v. Zimmermann*, the Eighth Circuit found that although the alleged gratuities to a city councilman were only $1,200 and $1,000, a developer provided them to rezone property to build condominiums the developer hoped to sell for $200,000 each. The circuit court stated, "Since there was sufficient evidence that the benefit to Carlson from the gratuities paid to Zimmerman for the development of a new Somali mall was of greater value than $5,000, the jury could reasonably find Zimmerman guilty of those counts."[171]

While there are a variety of means to establish the $5,000 value element, the government is not required to prove that the defendant intended or knew the value of the business or transactions affected by a bribe or gratuity. This element is jurisdictional, establishing a minimum threshold for the federal interest in the prosecution, but it does not require proof of a defendant's awareness of that value. In *United States v. Abbey*,[172] the Sixth Circuit rejected the defendant's argument that the government failed to prove that a city administrator understood the gift of land he received from a developer was worth more than $5,000. The circuit court stated:

> Indeed, it is not evident how § 666's mens rea element ("corruptly") would modify a person's subjective interpretation of how much something was worth. (No one would say that someone "nefariously" believed that some property was worth over $5000.) Instead, that term does the job Congress intended it to do: officials are only guilty if they take a bribe with corrupt intent. The government and jury need not read Abbey's mind to know how much he thought the property was worth to sustain a proper conviction.

E. Exemption for Bona Fide Salary

Section 666(c) limits the scope of the crime by providing that it "does not apply to bona fide salary, wages, fees, or other compensation paid, or expenses paid or reimbursed, in the usual course of business." Congress added this subsection in the 1986 amendment of the statute, and the only legislative history is a statement in a House Report that the provision "amends 18 U.S.C. § 666 to avoid its possible application to acceptable commercial and business practices."[173]

The key issue for the exemption is whether the payment was "bona fide," which can be defined as "good faith" or a transaction "without fraud or deceit." Defendants usually raise the issue in connection with misapplication or fraud charges under § 666(a)(1)(A) involving inflated salaries or payments to "ghost" employees. For example, in *United States v. Tampas*,[174] the Eleventh Circuit rejected a claim that payments to a defendant were bona fide for using an organization's funds to pay employees for work done at his home and using an organizational credit card for

---

[171] 509 F.3d 920 (8th Cir. 2007).

[172] 560 F.3d 513 (6th Cir. 2009).

[173] H.R. Rep. No. 99–797 (1986), reprinted in 1986 U.S.C.C.A.N. 6138.

[174] 493 F.3d 1291 (11th Cir. 2007).

personal purchases. In *United States v. Baldridge*,[175] the Tenth Circuit upheld a misapplication conviction "[b]ecause this was not work for which [the employee] could have been paid by the County, the payment was not a bona fide wage paid in the usual course of business."

Determining whether a payment was legitimate compensation or involved the misuse of an organization's resources that constituted theft or misapplication often depends on looking at the work performed in comparison to the amount paid. In *United States v. Williams*,[176] the Fifth Circuit upheld the embezzlement conviction of a deputy city clerk who authorized the issuance of extra paychecks to herself and her supervisor. The circuit court rejected the argument that the payments were only an "advance" on her pay, holding "a salary is not bona fide or earned in the usual course of business under § 666(c) if the employee is not entitled to the money." It also pointed out that "[a]n employee who receives three years of additional compensation amounting to over $30,000—which represents more than twice Williams's regular annual salary—is more culpable than an employee who simply works fewer hours than her regular paycheck requires."

Even if the decision to hire a worker is based on an improper purpose, such as giving a job because of a bribe, the salary is bona fide so long as the person does the work required for the position. In *United States v. Mills*,[177] the defendant accepted money in exchange for having the payers hired as deputy sheriffs. The Sixth Circuit rejected the government's argument that the salaries were not bona fide because the appointments were tainted:

> [T]he indictment does not allege that the jobs in question were unnecessary or that the individuals who obtained those employment positions did not responsibly fulfill the duties associated with their employment. In the absence of such allegations, the government has no support for its claims that the salaries paid to the deputy sheriffs were not properly earned 'in the usual course of business.'

Section 666(c) requires that the payment be made "in the usual course of business" of the organization. A bribe can take the form of a salary given to a government official, and the exemption does not provide protection for this means of giving a thing of value in exchange for influencing the exercise of authority. In *United States v. Bryant*,[178] the government alleged that a state medical school hired an influential state legislator to ensure it continued to receive funding. The district court refused to dismiss the charge, holding that

> because the . . . salary itself constitutes the bribe—the "thing of value" accepted with the intent to be influenced for purposes of § 666(a)(1)(B), and offered with the intent to influence for purposes of § 666(a)(2)—it was not "bona fide" or paid "in the regular course of business."

---

[175] 559 F.3d 1126 (10th Cir. 2009).

[176] 507 F.3d 905 (5th Cir. 2007).

[177] 140 F.3d 630 (6th Cir. 1998).

[178] 556 F.Supp. 2d 378 (D. N.J. 2008). The defendant's subsequent conviction for violating § 666 was affirmed. 655 F.3d 232 (3d Cir. 2011).

In *United States v. Cornier–Ortiz*,[179] the First Circuit concluded that payments for work actually performed were not protected by § 666(c) when they were "made for what was an underlying legitimate purpose but intentionally misapplied to undermine a conflict of interest prohibition" of the organization. The misapplication of funds was not made in the usual course of business, even if the transaction involved payment of a salary. In *United States v. Urciuoli*,[180] the same circuit upheld a bribery conviction charged under § 1346 for payments in the form of salary to a state legislator, holding "[t]hat Celona performed some marketing services did not prevent the jury from regarding the payments as primarily intended by Urciuoli to secure Celona's legislative help" in passing favorable legislation.

§ 7.4   EXTORTION UNDER COLOR OF OFFICIAL RIGHT (HOBBS ACT 18 U.S.C. § 1951)

A. Generally

The Hobbs Act developed in the early 1970s into an important tool in federal corruption prosecutions. The statute specifically prohibits extortion and robbery, and does not refer directly to bribery. Judicial interpretation expanded its scope to permit the prosecution of public officials for taking or soliciting bribes as a form of extortion "under color of official right."

Congress adopted the Hobbs Act after the Supreme Court took a narrow view of the Anti–Racketeering Act of 1934, which targeted extortion and violence by criminal organizations.[181] In *United States v. Teamsters Local 807*,[182] the Court held that the Anti–Racketeering Act did not apply to extortion committed by unionized truckers demanding payments from out-of-town drivers. Congress responded by adopting the Hobbs Act to effectively overturn the Court's decision.

The statute prohibits robbery and extortion to obtain property that has an impact on interstate commerce:

> Whoever in any way or degree obstructs, delays, or affects commerce or the movement of any article or commodity in commerce, by robbery or extortion or attempts or conspires so to do, or commits or threatens physical violence to any person or property in furtherance of a plan or purpose to do anything in violation of this section shall be fined under this title or imprisoned not more than twenty years, or both.

Section 1951(b)(2) defines extortion as obtaining property with the consent of the victim in two ways: first, by physical coercion through the "wrongful use of actual or threatened force, violence, or fear"; and second, "under color of official right." The meaning of this second type of extortion involving the use of public office was unclear because the common law did not distinguish between bribery and extortion. The

---

[179] 361 F.3d 29 (1st Cir. 2004).
[180] 613 F.3d 11 (1st Cir. 2010).
[181] Act of June 18, 1934, 48 Stat. 979 (1934).
[182] 315 U.S. 521 (1942).

Supreme Court explained the historical development of the Hobbs Act in *Scheidler v. National Organization for Women, Inc.*:[183]

> Congress used two sources of law as models in formulating the Hobbs Act: the Penal Code of New York and the Field Code, a 19th-century model penal code. Both the New York statute and the Field Code defined extortion as "the obtaining of property from another, with his consent, induced by a wrongful use of force or fear, or under color of official right." 4 Commissioners of the Code, Proposed Penal Code of the State of New York § 613 (1865) (reprint 1998) (Field Code); N.Y. Penal Law § 850 (1909). The Field Code explained that extortion was one of four property crimes, along with robbery, larceny, and embezzlement, that included "the criminal acquisition of . . . property."

Federal prosecutors first applied the Hobbs Act to reach corruption by local officials in 1972 in *United States v. Kenny*,[184] the prosecution of a political "boss" who required that a percentage of all government contracts be paid to him for the privilege of doing business with local governments. The defendants argued on appeal that the government had to prove they used force or threats to obtain money, but the Third Circuit held that extortion could be proven either by evidence of a threat or that the defendants obtained the money because of their official authority. The circuit court upheld the conviction because "while private persons may violate the statute only by use of fear and public officials may violate the act by use of fear, persons holding public office may also violate the statute by a wrongful taking under color of official right."

The elements of a Hobbs Act extortion violation are: (1) that the defendant induced someone to part with property; (2) that the defendant knowingly and willfully did so by extortionate means; and (3) that the transaction affected interstate commerce. For corruption prosecutions, proof of extortion requires showing the defendant acted "under color of official right." That form of extortion means the defendant either occupied a position of public authority, or aided and abetted (or conspired) with someone in that position to misuse authority to wrongfully obtain the consent of the victim to part with property.

Elected officials accept money from individuals and organizations on a regular basis in the form of campaign contributions. These transactions have presented difficulties in applying the Hobbs Act because it requires drawing a line between bribery and permissible payments in the form of campaign contributions that are designed, at least in part, to influence an official.

B.   The *Quid Pro Quo* Requirement

1.   *McCormick v. United States*

The interpretation of extortion "under color of official right" as a form of bribery in *Kenny* and subsequent cases raised the issue of distinguishing between lawful campaign contributions and bribes. The Supreme Court first considered the problem in

---

[183] 537 U.S. 393 (2003).

[184] 462 F.2d 1205 (3d Cir. 1972).

McCormick v. United States.[185] The defendant, a state legislator, sponsored legislation to permit doctors with degrees from foreign medical schools to practice with a state-issued temporary permit while studying for a permanent license in the United States. During his reelection campaign, McCormick contacted a lobbyist for the doctors and said "his campaign was expensive, that he had paid considerable sums out of his own pocket, and that he had not heard anything from the foreign doctors." The lobbyist gave McCormick five cash gifts, and the state prohibited cash contributions in excess of $50 so none of the payments were listed on campaign disclosure forms.

The defendant argued that the payments were campaign contributions, and therefore they were not extorted "under color of official right." The Court described the central role voluntary donations play in American elections, and the resulting problem a broad criminal prohibition on extortion "under color of official right" would present to candidates:

> Serving constituents and supporting legislation that will benefit the district and individuals and groups therein is the everyday business of a legislator. It is also true that campaigns must be run and financed. Money is constantly being solicited on behalf of candidates, who run on platforms and who claim support on the basis of their views and what they intend to do or have done. Whatever ethical considerations and appearances may indicate, to hold that legislators commit the federal crime of extortion when they act for the benefit of constituents or support legislation furthering the interests of some of their constituents, shortly before or after campaign contributions are solicited and received from those beneficiaries, is an unrealistic assessment of what Congress could have meant by making it a crime to obtain property from another, with his consent, "under color of official right."

The Court held that a Hobbs Act violation involving the payment of funds that appear to be campaign contributions required proof that "the payments were made in return for an explicit promise or undertaking by the official to perform or not to perform an official act." The Court noted that this was a special case because the defendant was an elected official, and that "if the payments to McCormick were campaign contributions, proof of a *quid pro quo* would be essential for an extortion conviction." It pointed out that "[t]his is not to say that it is impossible for an elected official to commit extortion in the course of financing an election campaign." But the requirement of an "explicit promise or undertaking" effectively mandated a higher level of proof than would normally be required to prove bribery under the Hobbs Act when the payment appeared to be a campaign contribution.

The Court took a limited approach to the Hobbs Act in *McCormick* by noting that it was only deciding a campaign contribution case and not one involving "payments made to nonelected officials or to payments made to elected officials that are properly determined not to be campaign contributions." It pointed out that "we do not decide whether a *quid pro quo* requirement exists in other contexts, such as when an elected official receives gifts, meals, travel expenses, or other items of value." The Court held

---

[185] 500 U.S. 257 (1991).

that failing to charge the jury on the *quid pro quo* element required reversal of the conviction.

2.   *Evans v. United States*

The similarity between the Hobbs Act's extortion "under color of official right" provision and bribery was further illuminated in *Evans v. United States*,[186] decided a year after *McCormick*. An elected official took $8,000 from an undercover agent seeking assistance in rezoning a tract of land, an issue that normally would come before the defendant for a vote. Evans claimed the funds he received were campaign contributions, including a check for $1,000 that was made payable to his campaign committee. The Court first rejected the argument that the Hobbs Act requires an official to affirmatively induce the payment to qualify as extortion under color of official right. It held that the word "induced" only applied to obtaining property by "force, violence, or fear," and that even if it did apply to the "under color of official right" form of extortion, it did not require "that the transaction must be *initiated* by the recipient of the bribe." According to the Court, "[T]he wrongful acceptance of a bribe establishes all the inducement that the statute requires."

Turning to the issue of whether a *quid pro quo* must be shown, the author of the majority opinion, Justice Stevens, reiterated an argument he made in a dissenting opinion in *McCormick* that "fulfillment of the *quid pro quo* is not an element of the offense." Instead, proof of the agreement meant "the Government need only show that a public official has obtained a payment to which he was not entitled, knowing that the payment was made in return for official acts." Justice Kennedy, in a concurring opinion, viewed the majority as acknowledging that proof of a *quid pro quo* was required for any Hobbs Act charge involving extortion "under color of official right," although "[t]he official and the payer need not state the *quid pro quo* in express terms, for otherwise the law's effect could be frustrated by knowing winks and nods."

3.   *Scope of McCormick and Evans*

There were two unresolved issues after *McCormick* and *Evans*: (1) what level of proof must the prosecution meet to establish a *quid pro quo* agreement when the payment appeared to be a campaign contribution; and, (2) did the *quid pro quo* requirement apply to all Hobbs Act prosecutions for extortion "under color of official right." *McCormick* stated that the illegal exchange must involve "an explicit promise or undertaking" by the elected official to take action. If by "explicit" the Court meant "express," then that would be a significant, and perhaps insurmountable, evidentiary burden to prove a violation. As Justice Stevens's dissenting opinion in *McCormick* pointed out, "Subtle extortion is just as wrongful—and probably much more common— than the kind of express understanding that the Court's opinion seems to require." In *Evans*, the Court appeared to soften the *quid pro quo* element by finding sufficient proof that the payment was in exchange for the defendant's agreement to perform an official act, so that "fulfillment of the *quid pro quo* is not an element of the offense."

---

[186] 504 U.S. 255 (1992).

The lower courts have interpreted *Evans* to mean the prosecution must introduce proof of a *quid pro quo* agreement in all Hobbs Act bribery cases, and the level of proof necessary to establish this element depends on the type of transaction involved. In *United States v. Kincaid–Chauncey*,[187] the Ninth Circuit joined the other circuits[188] addressing the issue in holding "that a conviction for extortion under color of official right, whether in the campaign or non-campaign contribution context, requires that the government prove a quid pro quo." That requires proof of an agreement to engage in a specific action, and not merely buying access or goodwill through a campaign contribution. In *United States v. Siegelman*,[189] a § 666 case, the Eleventh Circuit explained, "The official must agree to take or forego some specific action in order for the doing of it to be criminal under § 666. In the absence of such an agreement on a specific action, even a close-in-time relationship between the donation and the act will not suffice."

Beyond the campaign contribution arena, lower courts have concluded that there need not be an explicit agreement between the parties, so circumstantial proof of the arrangement can be sufficient to establish a *quid pro quo*. In *United States v. Antico*,[190] a case involving the prosecution of an official in a city's licensing department, the Third Circuit held, "The *quid pro quo* can be implicit, that is, a conviction can occur if the Government shows that Antico accepted payments or other consideration with the implied understanding that he would perform or not perform an act in his official capacity 'under color of official right.'" In *United States v. Rosen*,[191] a § 666 and § 1346 case involving payments to state legislators to watch out for the interests of a healthcare company, the Second Circuit stated, "Outside the unique context of campaign contributions, we have not, in the context of bribery cases, required proof of an express promise regarding the specific official acts to be undertaken as part of the exchange." The circuit court noted that "our reluctance to require such proof is consistent with providing the Government significant flexibility in its efforts to prosecute political corruption."

Courts have rejected arguments to make proof of the *quid pro quo* dependent on linking the payment or benefit to a specified exercise of authority. In *United States v. Abbey*,[192] a developer provided a city official with a lot for free in the hope that his company would be favourably considered for a future property development. The Sixth Circuit explained:

> So Abbey is wrong in contending that, to sustain a Hobbs Act conviction, the benefits received must have some explicit, direct link with a promise to perform a particular, identifiable act when the illegal gift is given to the official. Instead, it is sufficient if the public official understood that he or she was expected to exercise

---

[187] 556 F.3d 923 (9th Cir. 2009).

[188] See United States v. Ganim, 510 F.3d 134 (2d Cir. 2007); United States v. Antico, 275 F.3d 245 (3d Cir. 2001); United States v. Hairston, 46 F.3d 361 (4th Cir. 1995); United States v. Collins, 78 F.3d 1021 (6th Cir. 1996); United States v. Giles, 246 F.3d 966 (7th Cir. 2001); United States v. Martinez, 14 F.3d 543 (11th Cir. 1994).

[189] 640 F.3d 1159 (11th Cir. 2011).

[190] 275 F.3d 245 (3d Cir. 2001).

[191] 716 F.3d 691 (2d Cir. 2013).

[192] 560 F.3d 513 (6th Cir. 2009).

some influence on the payor's behalf as opportunities arose. The public official need not even have any intention of actually exerting his influence on the payor's behalf.

In *United States v. Ganim*,[193] authored by then-Circuit Judge Sotomayor, the Second Circuit rejected a similar argument in a case involving a series of gifts, payments, and other benefits provided to the mayor of a city, a type of influence-peddling that in which the benefits were not conditioned on performance of a specific act but instead had become the normal operation of the municipality. Referred to as the "as opportunities arise" theory of bribery, the circuit court stated:

> [S]o long as the jury finds that an official accepted gifts in exchange for a promise to perform official acts for the giver, it need not find that the specific act to be performed was identified at the time of the promise, nor need it link each specific benefit to a single official act. To require otherwise could subvert the ends of justice in cases—such as the one before us—involving ongoing schemes. In our view, a scheme involving payments at regular intervals in exchange for specific official's acts as the opportunities to commit those acts arise does not dilute the requisite criminal intent or make the scheme any less "extortionate." Indeed, a reading of the statute that excluded such schemes would legalize some of the most pervasive and entrenched corruption, and cannot be what Congress intended.

In *United States v. Rosen*, the Second Circuit rejected the argument that this theory only applies to inherently corrupt acts and not routine conduct by government officials, The circuit court held, "Payments to State legislators may constitute bribes even if the legislator's resulting actions are otherwise 'routine'—such as voting in a certain manner or supporting grants to certain businesses."

C. Campaign Contributions

Perhaps the most difficult issue in determining whether a bribe had been paid, whether under the Hobbs Act, § 201, or § 666, is when the payment appears to be a campaign contribution. When a donor gives money to a political candidate, it is usually with some expectation that if the person is elected, he or she will support (or oppose) certain policies and legislation. The payment is often "for or because of" the candidate's potential exercise of authority, and indeed many candidates solicit contributions with the promise that they will take certain actions when elected. As the Fifth Circuit noted in *United States v. Tomblin*,[194] "Intending to make a campaign contribution does not constitute bribery, even though many contributors hope that the official will act favorably because of their contribution." Although campaign contributions have all the hallmarks of a bribe, the American political system could not survive if such payments were subject to prosecution as a bribe.

Courts have been careful to distinguish campaign contributions from bribes, requiring that juries be instructed clearly that a campaign contribution does not come within the statutory prohibition. An official being investigated for a Hobbs Act

---

[193] 510 F.3d 134 (2d Cir. 2007).
[194] 46 F.3d 1369 (5th Cir. 1995).

violation has an incentive to characterize any allegedly corrupt payment as a campaign contribution in the hope that it precludes a criminal prosecution. The key is whether the payment or solicitation was a legitimate campaign contribution or whether there was a *quid pro quo* that satisfies the corrupt intent element of the offense. In *Tomblin*, the Fifth Circuit stated that "a jury instruction must adequately distinguish between the lawful intent associated with making a campaign contribution and the unlawful intent associated with bribery."

Distinguishing lawful conduct—a voluntary donation to a candidate—from a corrupt payment is difficult when the underlying transaction is essentially the same. In *United States v. Biaggi*, the Second Circuit observed that "[t]here is a line between money contributed lawfully because of a candidate's position on issues and money contributed unlawfully as part of an arrangement to secure or reward official action, though its location is not always clear." Courts have emphasized that the *quid pro quo* agreement needs to be clear so that just the timing of the payment standing along does not establish a corrupt intent. In *United States v. Allen*,[195] a § 201 prosecution, the Seventh Circuit relied on *McCormick* and stated, "accepting a campaign contribution does not equal taking a bribe unless the payment is made in exchange for an explicit promise to perform or not perform an official act. Vague expectations of some future benefit should not be sufficient to make a payment a bribe."

McCormick erected a high evidentiary threshold for proving a Hobbs Act violation when the payments appear to be campaign contributions by requiring proof of an "explicit promise or undertaking" in exchange for the funds, but a conviction does not require proof of an express agreement. In *United States v. Siegelman*,[196] the Eleventh Circuit held "there is no requirement that this agreement be memorialized in a writing, or even, as defendants suggest, be overheard by a third party. Since the agreement is for some specific action or inaction, the agreement must be *explicit,* but there is no requirement that it be *express.*"

In *United States v. Carpenter*,[197] the Ninth Circuit rejected a former state senator's argument that an elected official cannot be convicted under the Hobbs Act "unless an official has specifically stated that he will exchange official action for a contribution." The circuit court held, "To read *McCormick* as imposing such a requirement would allow officials to escape liability under the Hobbs Act with winks and nods, even when the evidence as a whole proves that there has been a meeting of the minds to exchange official action for money." While a specific statement is not required to show a *quid pro quo* involving campaign contributions, *Carpenter* also point out that the agreement must "be *clear and unambiguous*, leaving no uncertainty about the terms of the bargain." The Ninth Circuit distinguished between campaign contributions given only in "anticipation" of official action, and those that are made in exchange for the official's "promise" of that action. To prove a Hobbs Act violation, the government must show the latter:

---

[195] 10 F.3d 405 (7th Cir. 1993).

[196] 640 F.3d 1159 (11th Cir. 2011).

[197] 961 F.2d 824 (9th Cir. 1992).

When a contributor and an official clearly understand the terms of a bargain to exchange official action for money, they have moved beyond "anticipation" and into an arrangement that the Hobbs Act forbids. This understanding need not be verbally explicit. The jury may consider both direct and circumstantial evidence, including the context in which a conversation took place, to determine if there was a meeting of the minds on a *quid pro quo*. As we read *McCormick*, the explicitness requirement is satisfied so long as the terms of the *quid pro quo* are clear and unambiguous.

In *United States v. Inzunza*,[198] the Ninth Circuit confessed to "considerable uneasiness in applying this standard [in *Carpenter*] to the acceptance of campaign contributions because, in our flawed but nearly universal system of private campaign financing, large contributions are commonly given in expectation of favorable official action." The circuit court nevertheless upheld a Hobbs Act conviction of a city council member for soliciting campaign contributions in exchange for sponsoring legislation to relax the city's laws on lap-dancing at the contributor's clubs. The Ninth Circuit explained:

> How, then, in the potentially polluted atmosphere of campaign contributions, can we tell a criminal agreement from a large campaign contribution accepted from a contributor who expects favorable results? The Supreme Court's answer lies in the level of explicitness, which permits a line to be drawn legally if not according to ethical perfection.

The circuit court explained that the explicitness requirement of *McCormick* applies to the official's agreement to act, not the connection between the promise and the payment:

> An official may be convicted without evidence equivalent to a statement such as: "Thank you for the $10,000 campaign contribution. In return for it, I promise to introduce your bill tomorrow." The connection between the explicit promise of official action and the contribution must be proved, but the proof may be circumstantial.

D. Authority for a *Quid Pro Quo*

Defendants have argued that they did not have the authority to provide a benefit to the person making the payment, and therefore could not engage in extortion "under color of official right." Although this argument has generally been unavailing, in *United States v. Rabbitt*,[199] an early Hobbs Act bribery prosecution, the Eighth Circuit recognized an outer limit to the authority that can be exercised by a defendant which limits application of the statute. Rabbitt, then the speaker of the Missouri House of Representatives, was convicted of assisting an architectural firm in seeking a contract from the state. While the defendant did not have the power to award contracts, the government argued that he had the "apparent power" to do so, which was why the firm retained him. Although his advocacy would be helpful, the Eighth Circuit found that

---

[198] 580 F.3d 894 (9th Cir. 2009).

[199] 583 F.2d 1014 (8th Cir. 1978).

"no testimony established that any state contracting officer awarded any contract to Berger–Field because of Rabbitt's influence or that Berger–Field believed Rabbitt's introduction was enough to secure the work." The circuit court explained that "[t]he official need not control the function in question if the extorted party possesses a reasonable belief in the official's powers." There was no Hobbs Act violation in this instance because the firm retained Rabbitt in the hope that being associated with him would be helpful, but did not involve the exercise of any official authority rising to the level of extortion "under color of official right."

Subsequent decisions have held that a Hobbs Act violation does not require proof that the official had actual authority over the particular result sought by the *quid pro quo* arrangement. In *United States v. Loftus*,[200] the Eighth Circuit stated, "Actual authority over the end result—rezoning—is not controlling if Loftus, through his official position, had influence and authority over a means to that end." In *United States v. Bibby*,[201] the Sixth Circuit held:

> What matters is not whether the official has "actual de jure" power to secure the desired item, but whether the person paying him held, and defendant exploited, a reasonable belief that the state system so operated that the power in fact of defendant's office included the authority to determine recipients of the [contracts] here involved.

Similarly, in *United States v. Rubio*,[202] the Fifth Circuit stated, "When a defendant holds an office, it is not necessary that the person from whom the money was taken be aware of the extortionist's official position as long as the victim believes that the individual had the power to carry out the threat or promise made to the victim."

In establishing a *quid pro quo* agreement, the issue is whether the payer had a reasonable belief about the official's authority and not the actual power of the official. In *United States v. Freeman*,[203] the Ninth Circuit explained, "[T]he Hobbs Act reaches those public employees who may lack the actual power to bring about official action, but create the reasonable impression that they do possess such power and seek to exploit that impression to induce payments." The defendant was an aide to a state legislator, and the circuit court found "[t]here was ample evidence that legislative aides exercise a degree of control over pending bills in the legislative process." The Third Circuit, in *United States v. Mazzei*,[204] rejected the argument of a state senator that there was no extortion "under color of official right" when the defendant told a property owner that it was customary to pay 10 percent of the lease for a legislative office back to his campaign committee. The circuit court held:

> [T]he jury need not have concluded that he had actual de jure power to secure grant of the lease so long as it found that [the property owner] held, and defendant exploited, a reasonable belief that the state system so operated that the power in

---

[200] 992 F.2d 793 (8th Cir. 1993).

[201] 752 F.2d 1116 (6th Cir. 1985).

[202] 321 F.3d 517 (5th Cir. 2003)

[203] 6 F.3d 586 (9th Cir. 1993).

[204] 521 F.2d 639 (3d Cir. 1975).

fact of defendant's office included the effective authority to determine recipients of the state leases here involved.

In *United States v. Carter*,[205] the Seventh Circuit focused on the payer's understanding, stating:

> [I]t is irrelevant whether providing the property lists or the Purge of Lien Notice did in fact fall under the Recorder of Deeds's duties and responsibilities, or whether Carter did in fact deliver what he promised. Instead, the question is whether sufficient evidence was presented for the jury to conclude that [the payer], when he provided Carter with the payments, reasonably believed that Carter could deliver these items based on his position as the Recorder of Deeds.

The victim's understanding is important if the defendant's claim to have the power to exercise authority in exchange for a payment was not credible. In *United States v. Tomblin*,[206] the Fifth Circuit overturned a Hobbs Act conviction of a defendant who claimed he had influence over a United States senator, but was only a private citizen and did not otherwise exercise any official authority. The circuit court explained, "[A]lthough he may have 'cloaked' himself in the Senator's authority . . . no one believed that he was a public official, especially not his purported victims."

Because the public official need not demand or request the payment, determining when there was extortion "under color of official right" often turns on the payer's motive for making the payment along with the official's understanding of its purpose. In *United States v. Braasch*,[207] the Seventh Circuit held, "[s]o long as the motivation for the payment focuses on the recipient's office, the conduct falls within the ambit of 18 U.S.C. § 1951."

The Hobbs Act has been applied to cases with less formal arrangements involving outsiders who effectively control the exercise of governmental authority. In *United States v. Margiotta*,[208] a local political party official who did not hold a government office was convicted based on his positions that "afforded him sufficient power and prestige to exert substantial control over public officials in Hempstead and Nassau County who had been elected to office" from his party. The Second Circuit explained that officials who did the defendant's bidding could not be prosecuted for extortion because they were unaware of the kickbacks sought, but the defendant caused the officials to make the appointments and so he could violate the Hobbs Act. According to the circuit court, "[H]e could be found guilty of having caused the public officials unknowingly to use their power of office in such a manner that would induce the payments." In *United States v. Collins*,[209] the Sixth Circuit upheld the conviction of the husband of the Kentucky Governor who received kickbacks from firms seeking business with the state. The circuit court explained, "Although Collins held no state office, he held himself out to officers of various engineering firms and investment

---

[205] 530 F.3d 565 (7th Cir. 2008).

[206] 46 F.3d 1369 (5th Cir. 1995).

[207] 505 F.2d 139 (7th Cir. 1974).

[208] 688 F.2d 108 (2d Cir. 1982).

[209] 78 F.3d 1021 (6th Cir. 1996).

banking firms as being capable of controlling the award of certain contracts and other state business."

E. Personal Gain

In *Scheidler v. National Organization for Women, Inc.*,[210] the Supreme Court explained that "[a]t common law, extortion was a property offense committed by a public official who took 'any money or thing of value' that was not due to him under the pretense that he was entitled to such property by virtue of his office." In that regard, extortion bears some similarities to larceny because for each crime a victim has been deprived of property improperly. In *Wilkie v. Robbins*,[211] the Court stated, "[T]he crime of extortion focused on the harm of public corruption, by the sale of public favors for private gain, not on the harm caused by overzealous efforts to obtain property on behalf of the Government." In *Wilkie*, the owner of a ranch sued federal officials under the Racketeer Influenced and Corrupt Organizations Act (RICO) for attempting to force him to grant an easement to an agency through a campaign of harassment and intimidation. Finding there was no Hobbs Act violation by the federal officials, the Court noted there were no cases finding extortion under the common law or the Hobbs Act for conduct "undertaken for the sole benefit of the Government" and not to enrich the official.

Relying on *Wilkie,* a district court in *United States v. Peterson*[212] dismissed a Hobbs Act charge against a sheriff who required inmates in the county jail to pay for their room and board. The defendant remitted the funds to the county commissioners, and therefore "[a] public official who obtains property on behalf of the government does not commit the offense of extortion, even if the government does not have a lawful or legal claim to the property." Extortion "under color of official right" involves misuse of authority for someone's personal gain, not simply depriving a victim of property through an exercise of governmental power. Although that type of conduct could be a taking in violation of the Fifth Amendment,, it would not be a Hobbs Act violation.

Wilkie does not require, however, that the official realize the benefit directly from the extortion. In *United States v. Green*,[213] the Supreme Court stated, "[E]xtortion as defined in the statute in no way depends upon having a direct benefit conferred on the person who obtains the property." In *Green*, the defendants, a union and one of its officers, were charged with coercing employers to pay wages for "superfluous and fictitious services," and the Court stated that nothing in the labor laws "indicates any protection for unions or their officials in attempts to get personal property through threats of force or violence. Those are not legitimate means for improving labor conditions." Coercing an employer to pay in response to a threat violated the Hobbs Act even if the money did not go directly to the defendants. The Court rejected the trial court's statement that "the charged acts would be criminal only if they were used to obtain property for the personal benefit of the union or its agent, in this case Green. This latter holding is also erroneous."

---

[210] 537 U.S. 393 (2003).

[211] 551 U.S. 537 (2007).

[212] 544 F.Supp. 2d 1363 (M.D. Ga. 2008).

[213] 350 U.S. 415 (1956).

F. Nonofficials

The Hobbs Act prohibits conduct that involves "obtaining of property from another" with the person's "consent," so the victim of the offense is the person who pays the money or confers the benefit. This is so even though that person may, in fact, be the one who initiated the bribe and sought to gain an unfair advantage from the corrupt official. Thus, in many cases the payer of the bribe cannot be charged with a violation because that person is the victim of the extortion. But that does not mean only public officials can be charged with violating the Hobbs Act. Under 18 U.S.C. § 2, a defendant can be charged with aiding and abetting an offense, and both the statute and 18 U.S.C. § 371 punish any conspiracy to extort.

In *United States v. Hairston*,[214] the Fourth Circuit stated, "A private person can be convicted of aiding and abetting a public official who extorts under color of official right. One who collects the extorted payments is no less guilty than the official he serves." But in *United States v. Saadey*,[215] the Sixth Circuit overturned a Hobbs Act conviction when the government only showed the defendant solicited money under the pretense that it would be paid to an assistant prosecutor to reduce criminal charges, but failed to allege he aided the prosecutor in a violation or conspired with him. The circuit court explained that "a private citizen who is not in the process of becoming a public official may be convicted of Hobbs Act extortion under the 'color of official right' theory only if that private citizen either conspires with, or aids and abets, a public official in the act of extortion."

Building on *Saadey*, the Sixth Circuit adopted a bright line test that a private citizen who pays a bribe cannot be charged under the Hobbs Act as either an accomplice to the crime or as a conspirator. In *United States v. Brock*,[216] the circuit court rejected the government's argument that the payer of a bribe could be charged with conspiring with the public official to violate the Hobbs Act. It held that expanding the Hobbs Act "through a conspiracy theory effectively transforms the Act into a prohibition on paying bribes to public officials," and "Congress knows how to prohibit the giving or offering of bribes directly," as it did in § 201. The Sixth Circuit focused on the "property from another" and consent requirements for a Hobbs Act violation, finding that these elements supported excluding the bribe-payer from prosecution because otherwise "[h]ow do (or why would) people conspire to obtain their own consent?"[217] The circuit court also held in *United States v. Gray* that the person making the payment did not automatically avoid liability for a Hobbs Act violation if that person aids in the extortion by serving as a conduit. The circuit court stated, "Gray's corporate clients, seeking government contracts, funneled the illegal payments through [him] to [the public official]. We therefore conclude that the evidence was sufficient to sustain defendants' convictions on these counts."

---

[214] 46 F.3d 361 (4th Cir. 1995).

[215] 393 F.3d 669 (6th Cir. 2005).

[216] 501 F.3d 762 (6th Cir. 2007).

[217] 521 F.3d 514 (6th Cir. 2008).

Not all courts have taken the bright-line approach that limits the liability of the payer of the bribe. In *United States v. Spitler*,[218] the Fourth Circuit held that "[w]hen an individual protected by [the Hobbs Act] exhibits conduct more active than mere acquiescence, however, he or she may depart the realm of a victim and may unquestionably be subject to conviction for aiding and abetting and conspiracy." In *United States v. Cornier–Ortiz*,[219] the First Circuit rejected an "innocent victim" defense, holding that the "evidence supported the conclusion that some sort of *quid pro quo* arrangement was in place and that Cornier did more than merely acquiesce to it." The circuit court relied on evidence of a close personal relationship between the defendant and the official, and that the defendant gained numerous benefits from the official, so that "it would only take a small inference for the jury to conclude that Cornier agreed to the . . . payment arrangement with [the official] in gratitude for this help."

In *United States v. Manzo*,[220] the Third Circuit affirmed dismissal of Hobbs Act charges against an unsuccessful mayoral candidate and his brother, who served as his campaign manager, alleging that they took bribes during the campaign in exchange for a promise to provide assistance to a real estate developer if elected. The circuit court held that "because the Manzos neither acted nor pretended to act in an official capacity, their conduct was not 'under color of official right.'" It also rejected allowing an attempt or conspiracy charge because the Hobbs Act "does not prohibit a private person who is a candidate from attempting or conspiring to use a future public office to extort money at a future date." The Third Circuit contrasted its analysis with the Seventh Circuit's approach in *United States v. Meyers*,[221] which upheld a conspiracy conviction because the solicitation of the bribes began while the defendant was a candidate for office and continued after his successful election. Because the conspiracy continued until the defendant took office, it could be prosecuted, while an unsuccessful candidate would not be able to agree to extortion by use of public authority.

G. Interstate Commerce Element

The Hobbs Act reaches offenses like robbery and extortion that are already punishable under state law. Congressional authority to enact the provision is based on the power to regulate interstate commerce under the Commerce Clause.[222] The statute defines the offense as engaging in the prohibited conduct that "in any way or degree obstructs, delays, or affects commerce or the movement of any article or commodity in commerce." In *Stirone v. United States*,[223] the Supreme Court explained that the Hobbs Act "speaks in broad language, manifesting a purpose to use all the constitutional power Congress has to punish interference with interstate commerce by extortion, robbery or physical violence." By extending to the outer limits of Congress's commerce power, the government need not prove a substantial impact on interstate commerce from the activity, only a *de minimis* effect. The Ninth Circuit explained in *United*

---

[218] 800 F.2d 1267 (4th Cir. 1986).

[219] 361 F.3d 29 (1st Cir. 2004).

[220] 636 F.3d 56 (3d Cir. 2011).

[221] 529 F.2d 1033 (7th Cir. 1976).

[222] U.S. Const. Art. I, § 8, cl. 3.

[223] 361 U.S. 212 (1960).

States v. Atcheson[224] that "[t]o establish a *de minimis* effect on interstate commerce, the Government need not show that a defendant's acts actually affected interstate commerce. Rather, the jurisdictional requirement is satisfied by proof of a probable or potential impact." The requisite impact on interstate commerce is an element of the offense that must be proven beyond a reasonable doubt.

Courts have distinguished between direct and indirect effects on interstate commerce, with either being sufficient to establish this element. For direct effects, courts have focused on whether there was actual business crossing state lines, or at least the strong likelihood that those engaged in interstate commerce were impacted by the extortion. If there is evidence of a direct effect on commerce, then a court need not consider whether there was also an indirect effect.

If extortion results in a transfer of money or property across state lines, then the commerce element can be easily established because of the transaction's clear impact on interstate commerce. It is not necessary for the government to show any physical movement of funds across a state line, however, and the potential financial impact of extortionate conduct can be a sufficient. In *United States v. Staszcuk*,[225] an early Hobbs Act corruption case, a person interested in building an animal hospital paid $5,000 to a middleman who passed $3,000 to a Chicago alderman because his support to change the zoning of the property was necessary for the facility to be built in his district. Although the city never adopted the zoning change and the hospital was not built, the Seventh Circuit, sitting en banc, found a sufficient effect on interstate commerce to uphold the conviction. The circuit court stated:

> An effective prohibition against blackmail must be broad enough to include the case in which the tribute is paid as well as the one in which a victim is harmed for refusing to submit. Since the payment would normally enable the business to continue without interruption, the inference is inescapable that Congress was as much concerned with the threatened impact of the prohibited conduct as with its actual effect.

More difficult issues can arise in cases involving proof of only an indirect effect on commerce. To establish that effect, courts have held that conduct which depleted the assets of a business can be sufficient to show an impact on interstate commerce, at least if a commercial entity was the victim. In *United States v. Collins*,[226] the Fifth Circuit stated, "The government's 'depletion-of-assets' theory falls into the indirect category. This theory relies on a minimal adverse effect upon interstate commerce caused by a depletion of the resources of the business which permits the reasonable inference that its operations are obstructed or delayed." Under this theory, extortion resulting in the transfer of funds or other valuable property that could have been used by the victim to conduct an interstate business satisfies the commerce element. The Fifth Circuit in *United States v. Elders*[227] stated that "commerce is affected when an enterprise, which either is actively engaged in interstate commerce or customarily

---

[224] 94 F.3d 1237 (9th Cir. 1996).

[225] 517 F.2d 53 (7th Cir. 1975).

[226] 40 F.3d 95 (5th Cir. 1994).

[227] 569 F.2d 1020 (7th Cir. 1978).

purchases items in interstate commerce, has its assets depleted through extortion, thereby curtailing the victim's potential as a purchaser of such goods." In *United States v. Carter*,[228] the Seventh Circuit explained the "depletion of assets" theory this way:

> [I]t is sufficient for the Government to show that a business that customarily purchases items through interstate commerce had its assets depleted through the acts of extortion, thus limiting its ability to purchase goods in interstate commerce. There is no requirement that the business directly purchase its items through interstate commerce, rather, it is enough if the business purchases such items through a wholesaler or other intermediary.

Courts usually allow the "depletion of assets" theory when a business is the victim, but it can be more difficult to establish when an individual is the one targeted for extortion. In *United States v. Mattson*,[229] an extortion "under color of official right" case, the Seventh Circuit concluded the government failed to establish the commerce element through the depletion of assets theory. According to the court:

> The victim in this case was an individual who had no connection with interstate commerce at all, but whose only connection was with a business which was engaged in interstate commerce. Thus, to find an effect on interstate commerce, we would be required not only to consider indirect effects within a single business entity, but also effects arising from the business entity's relationship with an employee not engaged in interstate commerce.

Mattson refused to find that the commerce element reached every economic transaction, explaining that such a broad reading of the Hobbs Act "would mean that the extortion of money from any individual in our society could arguably affect interstate commerce eventually." Similarly, the Fourth Circuit overturned Hobbs Act convictions in *United States v. Buffey*[230] for defendants who extorted money from a wealthy business owner by threatening to reveal "somewhat indiscreet sexual activity." The circuit court rejected application of the "depletion of assets" theory because "[i]t is much more likely that [the victim] would have resorted to his readily available personal assets to satisfy any extortion demand."

In addition to the "depletion of assets" theory, the Hobbs Act applies to anyone who "attempts or conspires" to engage in extortion. A person can be found guilty of an attempt if a substantial step is taken toward completing the crime, so a Hobbs Act violation can occur even if the defendant never actually obtained property by extortion. Without an actual transaction, the impact on interstate commerce would appear to be non-existent. However, the lower courts have not read the commerce element to preclude attempt prosecutions. In *United States v. Peete*,[231] the Sixth Circuit stated the commerce element in attempt cases "has been read broadly to allow purely intrastate activity to be regulated under the theory that there was a *realistic probability* that the

---

[228] 530 F.3d 565 (7th Cir. 2008).

[229] 671 F.2d 1020 (7th Cir. 1982).

[230] 899 F.2d 1402 (4th Cir. 1990).

[231] 919 F.2d 1168 (6th Cir. 1990)

activity would have affected interstate commerce." In *United States v. Mills*,[232] the same circuit court found the impact on interstate commerce had been established when a county sheriff offered appointments as a deputy sheriff to those willing to pay $3,500, directing them to borrow the money from a loan company. The circuit court accepted the government's argument that "the proofs showed a realistic probability that the bribe money would be borrowed from a company engaged in interstate commerce."

Some courts distinguish between an attempted and completed Hobbs Act offense. They usually permit proof of a potential effect on interstate commerce only for attempt cases, while an actual impact on interstate commerce—even if only *de minimis*—is required if the defendant engaged in the substantive offense. In *United States v. Williams*,[233] the Eighth Circuit overturned a robbery conviction involving a taxicab driver because the government only proved a potential effect, and "the statute's plain language requires an actual effect on interstate commerce, not just a probable or potential impact." The Eleventh Circuit took a similar approach in *United States v. Carcione*,[234] holding that a "substantive violation of the Hobbs Act requires an actual, *de minimis* affect on commerce."

The source of the funds does not alter the analysis of the impact on interstate commerce from extortion. Where the government supplies the money for the bribe as part of a sting operation, or uses a shell corporation to pursue an undercover investigation, the potential effect on interstate commerce is sufficient for an attempt charge, but not for a substantive violation. In *United States v. Rindone*,[235] the Seventh Circuit held that "the fortuitous use of FBI funds after completion of the extortion attempt does not in any way diminish the 'realistic probability' that, at the time of the attempt, Harper's assets would be potentially depleted." For a charge of conspiracy to violate the Hobbs Act, the same analysis applies. The Third Circuit, in *United States v. Jannotti*,[236] one of the Abscam cases, held:

> [W]e see no reason to interpret Congress' legislative power as dependent upon whether the F.B.I. agents actually contract for a hotel site, purchase machinery to dump garbage, or establish their own fencing operation for the purchase of stolen goods. To require that the government take that additional step before it can constitutionally reach a proven conspiracy which would have affected interstate commerce had the facts been as represented misdirects the focus of the conspiracy cases.

The government is not required to show any adverse impact on a business in proving the interstate commerce element. In *United States v. Bailey*,[237] the Fourth Circuit point out that "[a]lthough the word 'adverse' has been loosely used in expressing the effect on interstate commerce, such adverse effect is not an essential element of the crime that must be proved by the prosecution in a Hobbs Act case." The

---

[232] 204 F.3d 669 (6th Cir. 2000).

[233] 308 F.3d 833 (8th Cir. 2002).

[234] 272 F.3d 1297 (11th Cir. 2001).

[235] 631 F.2d 491 (7th Cir. 1980).

[236] 673 F.2d 578 (3d Cir. 1982) (en banc).

[237] 990 F.2d 119 (4th Cir. 1993).

Eleventh Circuit made a similar point in *United States v. Kaplan*,[238] noting that the Hobbs Act's "language is broad, and it is evidence that Congress intended to protect commerce from any and all forms of effects, whether they are direct or indirect, actual or potential, beneficial or adverse. For courts to require the effect on commerce to be adverse would significantly narrow the statute."

Questions have been raised in the lower courts about whether the broad reach of the Hobbs Act improperly extends federal power in violation of the Constitution's limitation on the authority of the national government under federalism principles. The question of the federal government's role in enforcing criminal laws against state and local officials was raised after Supreme Court's decisions in *United States v. Lopez*[239] and *United States v. Morrison*[240] invalidated federal statutes for exceeding congressional authority to regulate in areas already subject to the police power of the states. The broad commerce element in the Hobbs Act, which allows almost any real or imagined impact on interstate commerce to suffice for federal prosecution, raised questions about the use of the statute to prosecute robberies, a crime predominantly prosecuted at the local level. In *United States v. McFarland*,[241] a substantial block of Fifth Circuit judges dissented from a decision upholding a conviction for robbery in violation of the Hobbs Act, questioning the statute's application to small-scale crimes:

> There is no sufficient rational basis to aggregate the effects on interstate commerce of any of the four individual prototypically local crimes of violence here prosecuted with the effects on interstate commerce of all the undifferentiated mass of robberies covered by the Hobbs Act's general proscription of any and all robberies that "in any way or degree . . . affect . . . commerce."

In *United States v. Rivera–Rivera*,[242] a dissenting opinion in the First Circuit argued that "virtually every business uses some item that was made in another state—perhaps a table or a rug or paint on the walls. If speculation about future replacement of such items suffices to establish the interstate commerce nexus, the Hobbs Act would embrace virtually all local robberies." These cases did not involve bribery or even extortion by force or fear, and the dissenting judges relied on the need to limit federal authority over crimes of violence that involved only minimal commercial activity to argue for limiting the Hobbs Act.

Justice Clarence Thomas also raised federalism concerns about the application of the Hobbs Act to local officials in *Evans v. United States*.[243] He asserted that "[o]ver the past 20 years, the Hobbs Act has served as the engine for a stunning expansion of federal criminal jurisdiction into a field traditionally policed by state and local laws— acts of public corruption by state and local officials." Justice Thomas claimed that application of the Hobbs Act to local officials amounted to federal regulation of state

---

[238] 171 F.3d 1351 (11th Cir. 1999) (en banc).
[239] 514 U.S. 549 (1995).
[240] 529 U.S. 598 (2000).
[241] 311 F.3d 376 (5th Cir. 2002) (en banc).
[242] 555 F.3d 277 (1st Cir. 2009).
[243] 504 U.S. 255 (1992).

governments that "mocks" earlier decisions limiting the power of Congress over the states.

§ 7.5   TRAVEL ACT (18 U.S.C. § 1952)

A. Overview

The Travel Act was part of a broad federal law targeting criminal organizations operating across state lines. The name of the statute is a bit of a misnomer because it does not require proof the defendant actually travelled as part of the violation by including use of a facility in interstate commerce or the mail as a means to a violation. The statute incorporates state law bribery as one of the predicate acts, and it has been used to prosecute public corruption, although not nearly to the degree as other provisions, like § 666 and the Hobbs Act.

To prove a Travel Act violation, the government must establish: (1) travel in interstate commerce, or use of the mails or facilities of interstate commerce (2) with intent to "promote, manage, establish, carry on or facilitate" (3) an "unlawful act" that constitutes, *inter alia,* bribery, extortion, or arson in violation of the laws of the state in which the crime is committed, or in violation of federal law, and (4) subsequent performance of or an attempt to perform the unlawful activity. Although used less frequently in public corruption cases, the Travel Act is nearly as broad as other statutes, and the commerce element can easily be met in most cases. And while the provision was designed to deal with organized crime, there is no requirement to show a connection to that type of criminal activity, so that bribery and extortion can be the basis for charges without regard to whether the conduct involved any violence.

B. Jurisdictional Element

The statute provides three different means to establish federal jurisdiction: (1) a person "travels in interstate or foreign commerce," (2) "uses the mail," or (3) uses "any facility in interstate or foreign commerce." The Travel Act as initially adopted was an exercise of the congressional power under the Commerce Clause to reach activities affecting interstate commerce. Congress amended the statute in 1990 to resolve a split in the circuit courts by clarifying the scope of its coverage involving use of the mail as the means for engaging in the illegal activity. The original language reached the use of "any facility in interstate or foreign commerce, *including the mail.*" One circuit court required proof that the mailing actually crossed state lines, a position rejected by another circuit court.[244] The amendment provided that any defendant who "uses the mail" in relation to the illegal conduct comes within the Travel Act, thereby making it clear that any mailing, and not just one moving between two states, would be sufficient to establish this element of the offense.[245] By adding the mailing as a jurisdictional basis for a prosecution, Congress relied on the exclusive federal authority over the post office as a basis for federal jurisdiction.[246]

---

[244] Compare United States v. Barry, 888 F.2d 1092 (6th Cir. 1989) (mailing must cross state line) with United States v. Riccardelli, 794 F.2d 829 (2d Cir. 1986) (mailing need not cross state line).

[245] Pub.L. No. 101–647, Title XVI, § 1604, 104 Stat. 4831 (1990).

[246] U.S. Const. Art. 1, § 8, cl. 7

The statutory language on the commerce and mailing elements is straightforward and in most cases can be easily established. For example, in *United States v. Nader*,[247] the Ninth Circuit held "that intrastate telephone calls made with intent to further unlawful activity can violate the Travel Act because the telephone is a facility in interstate commerce." Unlike the Hobbs Act, however, the Travel Act has a narrower jurisdictional reach.

The Supreme Court in *Rewis v. United States*[248] rejected the position that any conduct involving interstate travel, however tangential to the criminal violation, was sufficient for federal jurisdiction. The prosecution involved two defendants charged with gambling in a small town in Florida located close to the Georgia border. There was no evidence the defendants had crossed the state line in connection with their numbers operation, and jurisdiction was based on travel by bettors into Florida. According to the Court, the statute prohibits interstate travel undertaken with the intent to "promote, manage, establish, carry on, or facilitate" the illegal conduct, "and the ordinary meaning of this language suggests that the traveler's purpose must involve more than the desire to patronize the illegal activity." The Court noted that Congress "would certainly recognize that an expansive Travel Act would alter sensitive federal-state relationships, could overextend limited federal police resources, and might well produce situations in which the geographic origin of customers, a matter of happenstance, would transform relatively minor state offenses into federal felonies."

Rewis also pointed out that the active encouragement of interstate travel that was "more than merely conducting the illegal operation" could support jurisdiction, at least when the travel was undertaken by agents or employees of the illegal operation. The Court did not foreclose a Travel Act prosecution based on encouragement to cross state lines when "the conduct encouraging interstate patronage so closely appropriates the conduct of a principal in a criminal agency relationship that the Travel Act is violated."

Shortly thereafter, in *Erlenbaugh v. United States*,[249] the Court considered whether the use of a facility of interstate commerce was sufficient for a Travel Act conspiracy charge. It rejected the argument that transmitting gambling information contained in a sports news publication by having it shipped from where it was published in Illinois to a bookmaker in Indiana was insufficient for federal jurisdiction. The Court noted that the information in the publication was "important" to the gambling operation. The main issue was whether a companion to the Travel Act prohibiting transportation of wagering paraphernalia that exempted "the carriage or transportation in interstate or foreign commerce of any newspaper or similar publication" should also be applied to § 1952.[250] The Court held that "[t]o introduce into § 1952 an exception based upon the nature of the material transported in interstate commerce would carve a substantial slice from the intended coverage of the statute."

Rewis involved interstate travel that was tangential to the underlying criminal conduct, while *Erlenbaugh* involved the use of a facility of interstate commerce to

---

[247] 542 F.3d 713 (9th Cir. 2008).

[248] 401 U.S. 808 (1971).

[249] 409 U.S. 239 (1972).

[250] 18 U.S.C. § 1953.

obtain information necessary for the gambling operation to continue. In neither case did the Court squarely address how closely the interstate movement had to be to the criminal conduct to establish the requisite federal interest in prosecuting crimes that are based on state law. The interstate travel in *Rewis* was too attenuated, while the interstate shipment in *Erlenbaugh* was "important" for the crime. There is much that comes between those two poles, and the Court did not shed much light on how close the relationship had to be for a proper Travel Act prosecution. The lower courts have taken different approaches on how closely the jurisdictional element must be to the illegal activity, with more recent cases not applying *Rewis* strictly.

C. Bribery and Extortion

The Travel Act was the first statute to make conduct violating a state law an element of a separate federal offense. Other provisions that rely on state law violations in federal prosecutions include the Racketeer Influenced and Corrupt Organizations Act (RICO) and the money laundering statute. The Travel Act defines "unlawful activity" in § 1952(b)(i)(2) to include "extortion, bribery, or arson in violation of the laws of the State in which committed or of the United States." Congress did not provide a further explanation of what constitutes the three offenses, so the courts have been left to determine what conduct comes within the Travel Act.

In *United States v. Nardello*,[251] defendants were charged with violating the Travel Act for extorting money from victims who had been put in compromising sexual situations and then threatened with exposure if they did not make payments. The scheme took place in Pennsylvania, and the defendants travelled from other states on three occasions. Under Pennsylvania law, "extortion" followed the common law offense that was limited to conduct by public officials, similar to extortion "under color of official right" punishable under the Hobbs Act. Although Pennsylvania had statutes prohibiting blackmail that appeared to apply to the "shakedown" scheme, the district court held that Congress intended the Travel Act "to track closely the legal understanding under state law" of the offense, and therefore dismissed the indictment. The Supreme Court rejected the claim that Congress meant to limit "extortion" to its common law meaning that would exclude private parties, finding that this analysis conflicted with the congressional intent to deal with the activities of organized crime on a national level to supplement state law enforcement efforts.

The Court also rejected the argument that the label a state applied to an offense controlled application of the Travel Act because that would tie the federal statute to the peculiarities of different state laws. It pointed out that the scheme would be a violation in Utah because its statute was titled "extortion" but not in Pennsylvania because it was called "blackmail." The Court stated, "We can discern no reason why Congress would wish to have § 1952 aid local law enforcement efforts in Utah but to deny that aid to Pennsylvania when both States have statutes covering the same offense." Rather than limit the Travel Act to the vagaries of individual states, the Court held that "the acts for which [defendants] have been indicted fall within the generic term extortion as used in the Travel Act."

---

[251] 393 U.S. 286 (1969).

Reinstating the charges, the Court said the conduct was of "a type of activity generally known as extortionate," so that "extortion" in the Travel Act should be understood by reference to what acts fall under the broad prohibition without relying on the particular limitations a state may recognize in its own statutes. What constitutes "generic" extortion required lower courts to first look at the state's law where the crime occurred and then compare it to a broader understanding of the offense.

The Court further refined the analysis of what type of misconduct comes within the crime of bribery in *Perrin v. United States*,[252] where it stated that "the generic definition of bribery, rather than a narrow common-law definition, was intended by Congress." The issue was whether the Travel Act incorporated commercial bribery, which was an offense under Louisiana law—where the crime occurred—but was not a common law crime, which limited bribery prosecutions to public officials. The Court surveyed the development of bribery laws in various states when Congress adopted the Travel Act, noting that fourteen states punished commercial bribery and another twenty-eight made it a crime to engage in corrupt payments involving particular private employees, such as telephone company workers and labor officials. This survey of state laws led the Court to find that "by the time the Travel Act was enacted in 1961, federal and state statutes had extended the term bribery well beyond its common-law meaning." In looking at the legislative history, *Perrin* held that the congressional purpose in enacting the Travel Act to enhance the fight against organized crime supported a broad reading of the term, so Congress "used 'bribery' to include payments to private individuals to influence their actions."

Although the Travel Act requires the government to show a defendant's conduct violated either federal or state law that comes within the generic offenses of bribery, extortion, or arson, it need not prove beyond a reasonable doubt that the defendant actually violated the state statute referenced as the basis for the federal violation. In *United States v. Welch*,[253] the Tenth Circuit concluded that a violation of a state's bribery law named in an indictment "is not an element of the alleged Travel Act violations in this case and need not have occurred to support the Government's § 1952 prosecution." Reference to state law "is necessary only to identify the type of illegal activity involved," so that "the underlying state law merely serves a definitional purpose in characterizing the proscribed conduct." In *United States v. Campione*,[254] the Seventh Circuit explained how the state law analysis operates:

> But § 1952 refers to state law only to identify the defendant's unlawful activity, the federal crime to be proved in § 1952 is the use of interstate facilities in furtherance of the unlawful activity, not the violation of state law; therefore, § 1952 does not require that the state crime ever be completed. . . . Since § 1952 does not incorporate state law as part of the federal offense, violation of the Act does not require proof of a violation of state law.

---

[252] 444 U.S. 37 (1979).

[253] 327 F.3d 1081 (10th Cir. 2003).

[254] 942 F.2d 429 (7th Cir. 1991).

In *United States v. Jones*,[255] the District of Columbia Circuit described the appropriate jury instruction that should be given on the state law issue:

> A proper instruction would make it clear to the jury that in order to convict, they must find that the defendant specifically intended to promote (et cetera) an activity that involves all of the elements of the relevant state offense. Such an instruction would inform the jury that the defendant must have performed or attempted to perform an act in furtherance of the business, with the intent that each element of the underlying state crime be completed, but that they need not conclude that each was in fact completed.

Bribery and extortion are continuing crimes that can take place in multiple locations, and an issue in Travel Act prosecutions can arise over which state's law should be referenced in the indictment and at trial. In *United States v. Woodward*,[256] a Massachusetts state legislator argued that Florida law governed the case because the gifts identified in the indictment were received there and not in his home state. The First Circuit upheld the conviction because "where the evidence demonstrates 'unlawful activity' in violation of the laws of the state where the effects of the fraudulent scheme are felt, in this case, the state whose citizens are defrauded of their legislator's honest services." Similarly, in *United States v. Walsh*,[257] the Second Circuit upheld a Travel Act conviction based on a violation of New Jersey's bribery law because the *quid pro quo* agreement was reached in that state, even though the bribe was actually paid in New York.

D. Intent

The Travel Act prohibits a defendant from acting with the "intent to . . . otherwise promote, manage, establish, carry on, or facilitate the promotion, management, establishment, or carrying on, of any unlawful activity." The statute requires proof of a specific intent to engage in the bribery, extortion, or arson, even if the state law provision does not require proof at that intent level.

All circuits, save one, have found that the intent element does not include the interstate travel or use of a facility in interstate commerce, for which no intent is required. In *United States v. LeFaivre*,[258] the Fourth Circuit explained the reason for not requiring proof of intent regarding the jurisdictional element:

> Congress's omission of any knowledge requirement with respect to the use of facilities in interstate commerce makes good sense. The use of facilities in interstate commerce is, as we noted above in this opinion, nothing more than the jurisdictional peg on which Congress based federal jurisdiction over the unlawful activities enumerated in the Travel Act. The use of interstate facilities adds nothing whatsoever to the "criminality" of the person who is already engaged in one of the named unlawful activities. Thus, there is no need to require any mental

---

[255] 909 F.2d 533 (D.C. Cir. 1990).

[256] 149 F.3d 46 (1st Cir. 1998).

[257] 700 F.2d 846 (2d Cir. 1983).

[258] 507 F.2d 1288 (4th Cir. 1974).

element with respect to use of interstate facilities, since any mental element that Congress did write in would still not be any part of the *mens rea* of the criminal activity itself.

The Sixth Circuit has taken the opposite approach to the intent issue, holding in *United States v. Prince* that "the Travel Act only reaches those who engage in interstate activities with intent to perform other illegal acts. Thus there is a requirement of a separate intent related to the use of interstate facilities which is different from the intent required to commit the underlying State offense."[259] Although it later described this analysis as "questionable" in *United States v. Winters*,[260] it has not overruled *Prince* so it remains good law in Travel Act prosecutions in the circuit.

E. Subsequent Act

The Travel Act requires the government to prove that upon the interstate travel or use of a facility of interstate commerce the defendant "thereafter performs or attempts to perform" bribery, extortion, or arson. The criminal conduct must come *after* the acts establishing the interstate commerce element of the offense. In *United States v. Hayes*,[261] the Fourth Circuit dismissed a Travel Act indictment because the government did not properly allege the subsequent act, holding that the indictment "does not state on its face a violation of § 1952(a), for it omits a necessary element of the offense charged." Therefore, the timing is crucial for a successful prosecution. In *United States v. Botticello*,[262] the Second Circuit overturned a conviction because the interstate travel occurred after the defendant extorted money from the victim. The circuit court held that "Botticello's return to New York did nothing to further his scheme of extortion; no overt act was performed in New York to make the scheme's success more likely. The threat made in New Jersey bore no relationship at all to Botticello's return to New York."

Courts have also determined that the entire offense need not occur after the travel or use of an interstate facility. In *United States v. Arruda*,[263] the First Circuit upheld the defendant's conviction when an employee of a company travelled from New York to Massachusetts to deliver $5,000 to a government official as a kickback. The circuit court stated, "[I]t seems obvious that [the official]'s mere acceptance of the money was a sufficient overt act following the travel; acceptance is an act taken in furtherance of the distribution of the proceeds of an unlawful bribery scheme." Nor does interstate travel or use of a facility of interstate commerce have to be important for committing the crime so long as it is related to the bribery or extortion to facilitate its commission. In *United States v. Jones*,[264] the Fifth Circuit stated:

> [T]he facilitating act in the other state need not be unlawful itself. As long as the interstate travel or use of the interstate facilities and subsequent facilitating act

---

[259] 529 F.2d 1108 (6th Cir. 1976).

[260] 33 F.3d 720 (6th Cir. 1994).

[261] 775 F.2d 1279 (4th Cir. 1985).

[262] 422 F.2d 832 (2d Cir. 1970).

[263] 715 F.2d 671 (1st Cir. 1983).

[264] 642 F.2d 909 (5th Cir.1981).

make the unlawful activity easier, the jurisdictional requisites under § 1952 are complete. . . . Thus, we do not accept the appellant's contention that the subsequent facilitating conduct must be illegal, much less illegal in the state of destination.

§ 7.6   CONFLICTS OF INTEREST

A. Overview

The federal conflict of interest laws reach conduct that could result in corruption without requiring any showing that an exercise of public authority was actually or intended to be affected. In *United States v. Mississippi Valley Generating Co.*,[265] the Supreme Court stated that the conflict of interest provisions "attempt[] to prevent honest government agents from succumbing to temptation by making it illegal for them to enter into relationships which are fraught with temptation." Prohibitions on conflicts of interest date back to 1853, with a number of statutes adopted during the Civil War. The focus of the earlier provisions was on federal officials representing private interests in prosecuting claims against the government and in seeking the award of contracts. In the late 1950s, there was a push to expand federal conflict of interest laws to reach beyond representation in claims proceedings and contract decisions. The size and reach of the federal government had expanded starting in the New Deal era, so there were greater possibilities for conflicts between the public obligations of federal employees and their private interests.

In 1962, Congress streamlined the scattered corruption and conflict of interest laws into a comprehensive set of statutes in the federal code.[266] In addition to § 201 prohibiting bribery and unlawful gratuities, the law also included provisions prohibiting conflicts of interest for all federal employees that can arise from the following: unauthorized compensation (§ 203); outside activities involving the United States (§ 205); activity after government service (§ 207); conduct affecting financial interests (§ 208); and, salary supplementation by third parties (§ 209). The two provisions that have been used most frequently are the financial conflict of interest statute and the salary supplementation prohibition.

B. Conduct Affecting Financial Interests (18 U.S.C. § 208)

Section 208 addresses the issue of conflicts of interest that arise from the personal financial interests of a federal employee. The most basic means of favoring oneself is to accept a bribe or gratuity, conduct proscribed by § 201. Potential self-aggrandizement is covered by § 208, which prohibits a federal official from participating in government activities in which the employee, his or her "spouse, minor child, general partner, organization in which he is serving as officer, director, trustee, general partner or employee, or any person or organization with whom he is negotiating or has any arrangement concerning prospective employment, has a financial interest. . . . " The statute covers a broader range of interests than direct investments and ownership

---

[265] 364 U.S. 520 (1961).

[266] Pub. L. No. 87–849, 76 Stat. 1119–26 (1962).

interests by including situations in which the person is negotiating future employment and exercises governmental authority that could favor the future employer.

In *United States v. Mississippi Valley Generating Co.*, the Supreme Court explained the goal of the predecessor to § 208: "The statute is directed at an evil which endangers the very fabric of a democratic society, for a democracy is effective only if the people have faith in those who govern, and that faith is bound to be shattered when high officials and their appointees engage in activities which arouse suspicions of malfeasance and corruption." The Court pointed out that a violation does not require proof of actual corruption, or that the government suffered a loss from conflict of interest, so that "[t]he statute is thus directed not only at dishonor, but also at conduct that tempts dishonor."

Section 208 traces its roots to an 1863 statute prohibiting federal employees with a financial interest in a corporation or other type of organization from acting on behalf of the government in the "transaction of business with such business entity."[267] Having the prohibition apply to just the "transaction of business" meant that it had a narrow application, and Congress expanded its scope significantly in § 208. The House Report[268] on the provision stated:

> Section 208 supplants 18 U.S.C. § 434 which disqualifies government officials who are pecuniarily interested in business entities from transacting business with such entity on behalf of the Government. Section 208(a) would prohibit not merely "transacting business" with a business entity in which the government employee is interested but would bar any significant participation in government action in the consequences of which to his knowledge the employee has a financial interest."

Similarly, the Senate Report[269] concluded the new statute improved current law "by abandoning the limiting concept of the 'transaction of business.' The disqualification of the subsection embraces any participation on behalf of the Government in a matter in which the employee has an outside financial interest, even though his participation does not involve the transaction of business."

Section 208 covers preparatory activity well in advance of any final decision and not just conduct involving the actual exercise of government authority. As the Seventh Circuit explained in *United States v. Irons*,[270] "[T]he legislative history could not be more persuasive in suggesting that, while the former § 434 covered the 'transaction of business' including acts performed by way of execution of a contract involving a conflict of interest, the new Section 208 was explicit in addressing prior or more remote acts of advice or investigation."

Federal employees are prohibited from "personally and substantially" participating in any "decision, approval, disapproval, recommendation, the rendering of advice, investigation, or otherwise, in a judicial or other proceeding, application,

---

[267] Act of March 2, 1863, ch. 67, § 8, 12 Stat. 696 (1863).

[268] H.R. Rep. No. 748 (1961).

[269] S. Rep. No. 2213 (1961).

[270] 640 F.2d 872 (7th Cir. 1981).

request for a ruling or other determination, contract, claim, controversy, charge, accusation, arrest, or other particular matter" in which the employee has a financial interest. The question of whether a person is a federal employee is usually apparent from the outset. In *United States v. Smith*,[271] the District of Columbia Circuit held that the statute applied to any employee and not just those with authority to make decisions, explaining that "§ 208(a) was intended, and generally has been interpreted to have a broad reach, to cover all that a commonsense reading of its language would suggest."

The statute broadly describes the scope of the federal employee's conduct that is subject to prosecution under § 208. It reaches any "decision, approval, disapproval, recommendation, the rendering of advice, investigation, or otherwise. . . . " In *United States v. Irons*, the Seventh Circuit explained that "the 'or otherwise' language of Section 208 includes acts which execute or carry to completion a contract or matter as to which the acts of rendering advice or making recommendations are specifically proscribed." In *United States v. Lund*,[272] the Fourth Circuit upheld the conviction of a federal employee who recommended his wife for pay increases and a promotion after disclosing their marriage when regulations prohibited him from any involvement with her job or salary. The circuit court rejected the argument that "contract" and "arrangement" only apply to the government's dealings with third parties, holding that § 208 was "not restricted to conflicts of interest in matters involving outside entities, and nothing in the legislative history reveals a congressional intent to limit that broad language to less than its normal span. To the contrary, the legislative history indicates that Congress was fully aware of the potential breadth of the new statute."

The Ninth Circuit, in *United States v. Selby*,[273] rejected a narrow interpretation of "contract" to mean only negotiating its terms in a case in which the defendant participated in internal agency deliberations about expanding the scope of an agreement with a company that employed her husband that would result in additional sales commissions for him. The circuit court held that "where, as here, an employee suffers from a conflict of interest, liability may lie for actions taken after the initial procurement is authorized."

The employee's conduct must also involve participating "personally and substantially" in the action. In *United States v. Ponnapula*,[274] a civil contract action, the Sixth Circuit stated that "[a] statute aimed at preserving the integrity of the decisionmaking process does not need to extend to employees who have no discretion to affect that process."

Section 208(a) expanded the scope of potential conflicts of interest to include a prohibition on involvement in a government action while a federal employee "is negotiating or has any arrangement concerning prospective employment" with the person or organization that would be affected by the act. The District of Columbia Circuit rejected a vagueness challenge to this provision in *United States v. Conlon*,

---

[271] 267 F.3d 1154 (D.C. Cir. 2001).

[272] 853 F.2d 242 (4th Cir. 1988).

[273] 557 F.3d 968 (9th Cir. 2009).

[274] 246 F.3d 576 (6th Cir. 2001).

holding that "the terms 'negotiating' and 'arrangement' are not exotic or abstruse words, requiring etymological study or judicial analysis. They are common words of universal usage."[275] In overturning dismissal of a charge, the circuit court explained that "we must conclude that Congress meant the words 'negotiating' and 'arrangement' in § 208(a) to be given a broad reading, rather than the narrow reading accorded them by the district court."

A violation does not require proof of an actual or even likely gain or benefit from the action taken. In *United States v. Gorman*,[276] the Sixth Circuit held, "A financial interest exists on the part of a party to a Section 208 action where there is a real possibility of gain or loss as a result of developments in or resolution of a matter. Gain or loss need not be probable for the prohibition against official action to apply." This is consistent with the Supreme Court's analysis of the predecessor to § 208 in *Mississippi Valley Generating Co.*[277] that "the statute does not specify as elements of the crime that there be actual corruption or that there be any actual loss suffered by the Government as a result of the defendant's conflict of interest."

The only intent specified in § 208 is that the act on behalf of the government "to his knowledge" involve the employee's financial interest or others covered by the provision. The reference to "knowledge" is separated by commas, so this intent only applies to a financial interest and not other elements of the crime. In *United States v. Hedges*,[278] the Eleventh Circuit rejected the defendant's argument that the government must show "knowledge" of each element, holding that "the statute specifically places the mental state requirement of knowledge in the last element and thus requires that the government official have knowledge of the conflicting financial interest."

C. Salary of Government Officials and Employees Payable Only by United States (18 U.S.C. § 209)

Section 209 deals with supplementation of a federal employee's salary by an outside party. The statute makes it a crime to receive "any salary, or any contribution to or supplementation of salary, as compensation for his services as an officer or employee ... from any source other than the Government of the United States. . . . " Unlike a bribe or gratuity under § 201 that must be tied to a particular exercise of government authority, either as a *quid pro quo* or "for or because of" official action, § 209(a) prohibits any payment to "an officer or employee" regardless of whether the federal official could favor the payer or the benefit affected the performance of any official duty.

The predecessor to § 209 was 18 U.S.C. § 1914, which prohibited payments to a federal employee "in connection with his services as such an official or employee." Congress enacted the statute during World War I when executives from private organizations were assisting the government's war effort as "dollar-a-year men" still being paid by their previous employer. The fear was that these organizations would

---

[275] 628 F.2d 150 (D.C. Cir. 1980).
[276] 807 F.2d 1299 (6th Cir. 1986).
[277] 364 U.S. 520 (1961).
[278] 912 F.2d 1397 (11th Cir. 1990).

exercise control over government policy. The statute reaches both the federal employee receiving a payment and the individual or organization making it.

A violation does not require proof of a corrupt intent, nor must the party paying the salary have any connection to the office or agency where the employee works. In *Crandon v. United States*,[279] the Supreme Court pointed out that "[n]either good faith, nor full disclosure, nor exemplary performance of public office will excuse the making or receipt of a prohibited payment." In that case, the Court reviewed lump sum severance payments made by a company to five former employees who left it to work for the federal government. The purpose of the payments was to mitigate the financial loss from leaving private employment for government service, where they would receive greatly reduced salaries and retirement benefits. In a civil suit to recover the payments, the government claimed the payments violated § 209 because they were for the employee's service on behalf of the federal government although none had become federal employees at the time of the payments. Rejecting that argument, the Court held that a "literal reading of the second paragraph [of § 209(a)]—particularly the use of the term 'any such officer or employee'—supports the conclusion that the payee must be a Government employee at the time the payment is made."

Crandon only addressed pre-employment payments, but the Court's focus on the timing of any alleged salary supplementation would seem to preclude a charge for violating § 209(a) for payments made after the person left the federal government. If the payments were made "for or because of" an identified official act, then that would be a violation of § 201(c) as an unlawful gratuity prohibition, but it would not be an illegal salary supplementation.

Section 209(a) prohibits payment of compensation to a federal employee "for his services as an officer or employee," so there must be a nexus between the payment and the federal employee's work. In *United States v. Muntain*,[280] the District of Columbia Circuit held that reimbursing travel expenses for a government employee and his wife were not related to his government employment. The circuit court stated, "[T]he payment to Muntain was for services having nothing to do with HUD business or with any responsibilities Muntain may have had to the Government as an employee of the United States. Indeed, at the time of the trip, Muntain was on leave from his Government position."

The statutory language does not require proof of a particular intent, and the Supreme Court stated in *Crandon* that "[n]either good faith nor full disclosure, nor exemplary performance of public office will excuse the making or receipt of a prohibited payment." The statute appears to require proof of a general intent, otherwise good faith or lack of knowledge about the purpose of the payment would be viable defenses to the charge. Although not an intent element, the purpose of the payment can be relevant to whether it was "for his services" or was unrelated to federal employment.

---

[279] 494 U.S. 152 (1990).
[280] 610 F.2d 964 (D.C. Cir. 1979).

In *United States v. Project on Government Oversight*,[281] a civil case, a nonprofit organization gave a monetary award to a federal employee for exposing the underpayment of royalties to the government. The organization claimed that the money was a reward to a whistleblower that was unrelated to his official duties, while the government asserted it constituted compensation for work on behalf of his agency. The district judge noted that "'subjective intent' is not a relevant issue in this case. That is not to say, however, that 'intent' may never be a factor in the § 209(a) analysis." The district court stated that the parties' intent in making and receiving the payment "would be helpful to establish what 'services' the award was 'as compensation for' under § 209(a)."

The First Circuit took the same approach in *United States v. Alfonzo–Reyes*,[282] a criminal case, stating that there were two issues to be decided: "(1) what the disputed payment is for, i.e., what activity prompted the compensation; and (2) the subjective intent of the parties to determine what the payment was actually for, especially where there are various activities that could have motivated the payment." The circuit court rejected the defendant's argument that he only received a gift that was not compensation for work as a federal employee, looking at the reason of the payers, which gave the money and provided free repairs for his wife's car to put themselves in a better position to obtain future benefits and get on his "good side," as sufficient to support the conviction.

§ 7.7　FOREIGN CORRUPT PRACTICES ACT

The Foreign Corrupt Practices Act (FCPA)[283] was enacted in 1977 after over 400 American companies disclosed to the SEC that they had made payments to foreign government officials, politicians, and political parties to obtain contracts. The United States was the first country to prohibit overseas bribery by domestic businesses, making it a crime to make a corrupt payment without regard to whether the foreign government undertook to prosecute the conduct.

In the 1990s, the Organisation for Economic Cooperation and Development adopted the Convention on Combating Bribery of Foreign Public Officials in International Business Transactions that required signatories to outlaw bribes and other payments to foreign officials for business purposes, including providing for the liability of corporations.[284] Since then, all of the leading industrialized nations have adopted provisions similar to the FCPA in their domestic statutes. In addition, Congress amended the FCPA in response to the Convention by expanding it to reach

[281] 531 F.Supp.2d 59 (D.D.C. 2008).

[282] 592 F.3d 280, 292 (1st Cir. 2010).

[283] Pub. L. No. 95–213, 91 Stat. 1494, codified at 15 U.S.C. §§ 78dd–1, 78dd–2, and 78ff. Congress has amended the FCPA twice, in 1988 as part of the Omnibus Trade and Competitiveness Act, Pub. L. No. 100–418, 102 Stat. 1107, 1415–25 (1988), and again in 1998 to conform to the OECD Convention in the International Antibribery and Fair Competition Act of 1998, Pub. L. No. 105–366, 112 Stat. 3302 (1998).

[284] Convention on Combating Bribery of Foreign Public Officials in International Business Transactions, Nov. 21, 1997, 37 I.L.M. 1.

"any person" who engages in conduct that comes within the jurisdiction of the United States.[285]

In addition to the prohibition on foreign bribery, the FCPA imposed requirements for publicly traded corporations to implement proper accounting standards and create and apply internal controls (see § 5.7). As a provision of the federal securities laws, the FCPA is enforced by both the SEC in civil actions and the Department of Justice in criminal prosecutions.

The antibribery provisions apply to three groups, which may be overlapping:

• "issuers": American and foreign companies listed on United States securities exchanges, and their employees;

• "domestic concerns:" United States citizens and resident aliens, and business entities organized under state or federal law or with their principal place of business in the United States, plus their officers, directors, employees, and agents;

• "any person:" a non-citizen or resident who commits an act in furtherance of a foreign bribe within the territorial jurisdiction of the United States, and American businesses and citizens when acting abroad.

The FCPA prohibits authorizing, paying or offering to pay money or anything of value, directly or indirectly, to any foreign official or foreign political party, including a party official, in order to obtain or retain business.[286] Although the phrase "anything of value" could be construed to cover even a minor give, the Department of Justice and the SEC issued a Resource Guide[287] to the statute in 2012 stating that modest gifts and promotional items would not be the subject of an enforcement proceeding. The Guide states, "[I]t is difficult to envision any scenario in which the provision of cups of coffee, taxi fare, or company promotional items of nominal value would ever evidence corrupt intent, and neither DOJ nor SEC has ever pursued an investigation on the basis of such conduct."

To prove a violation, the government must establish the defendant made the payment or provided the benefit with a corrupt intent to

(1) influence any act or decision of such party, official, or candidate in its or his official capacity;

(2) induce such party, official, or candidate to do or omit to do an act in violation of the lawful duty of such party, official, or candidate;

(3) secure any improper advantage; or

---

[285] 15 U.S.C. § 78dd–3.

[286] 15 U.S.C. § 78dd–1.

[287] Dept. of Justice and Securities & Exchange Comm'n, A Resource Guide to the U.S. Foreign Corrupt Practices Act (2012), available at http://www.justice.gov/criminal/fraud/fcpa/guide.pdf.

(4) induce such party, official, or candidate to use its or his influence with a foreign government or instrumentality thereof to affect or influence any act or decision of such government or instrumentality. . . .

Most FCPA cases involve payments to secure a contract or favorable decision from a foreign government or one of its officials, but it can also be applied to cases in which the American company seeks favorable business conditions to assist its foreign operation. In *United States v. Kay*,[288] the Fifth Circuit held that bribes paid to foreign government officials to secure lower customs duties or sales taxes violated the FCPA so long as the reduction was intended to produce an effect that would assist the company to obtain or retain business. The circuit court stated:

> [W]e cannot hold as a matter of law that Congress meant to limit the FCPA's applicability to cover only bribes that lead directly to the award or renewal of contracts. Instead, we hold that Congress intended for the FCPA to apply broadly to payments intended to assist the payor, either directly or indirectly, in obtaining or retaining business for some person, and that bribes paid to foreign tax officials to secure illegally reduced customs and tax liability constitute a type of payment that can fall within this broad coverage.

Determining whether the person receiving the bribe was a "foreign official" has been the source of some controversy because it is not always clear whether the recipient held a governmental position. The FCPA defines a "foreign official" as

> any officer or employee of a foreign government or any department, agency, or instrumentality thereof, or of a public international organization, or any person acting in an official capacity for or on behalf of any such government or department, agency, or instrumentality, or for or on behalf of any such public international organization.

In many countries, especially those with authoritarian regimes or extensive government control over business and financial services, the line between the public and private sectors can be blurred. The statute does not define what an "instrumentality" is, and courts have been left to ascertain the scope of the public sector in other countries.

In *United States v. Aguilar*,[289] a district court considered whether a state-owned electric utility was an "instrumentality" of a foreign government in a prosecution for bribing high-ranking officials of the utility to obtain contracts. The court provided a list of "non-exclusive" factors for determining whether a government-controlled corporation was an "instrumentality" with characteristics sufficiently similar to a "department" or "agency" so that payments to its officials come within the FCPA's bribery prohibition:

> • The entity provides a service to the citizens—indeed, in many cases to all the inhabitants—of the jurisdiction.

---

[288] 359 F.3d 738 (5th Cir. 2004).
[289] 783 F. Supp. 2d 1108 (C.D. Cal. 2011).

• The key officers and directors of the entity are, or are appointed by, government officials.

• The entity is financed, at least in large measure, through governmental appropriations or through revenues obtained as a result of government-mandated taxes, licenses, fees or royalties, such as entrance fees to a national park.

• The entity is vested with and exercises exclusive or controlling power to administer its designated functions.

• The entity is widely perceived and understood to be performing official (*i.e.,* governmental) functions.

The FCPA exempts payments "to expedite or to secure the performance of a routine governmental action" by a foreign official.[290] The types of payments generally recognized as permissible include those to obtain permits, licenses, or other official documents, process government-issued documents, such as visas and work orders, to secure police protection, mail pick-up and delivery and other routine services; to obtain telephone service, power, water, the loading and unloading of cargo, protection of perishable products, and scheduled inspections.[291] The statute also provides that a "routine governmental action" does not involve "any decision by a foreign official whether, or on what terms, to award new business to or to continue business with a particular party, or any action taken by a foreign official involved in the decision-making process to encourage a decision to award new business to or continue business. . . . "

The FCPA provides an affirmative defense in two circumstances: (1) if the payment or promise to pay was lawful under the written laws and regulations of the foreign official's country; or (2) it was a reasonable and bona fide expenditure, such as travel and lodging expenses, designed for "(A) the promotion, demonstration, or explanation of products or services; or (B) the execution or performance of a contract with a foreign government or agency thereof."[292]

Another important limitation on the scope of the FCPA is the foreign official receiving the payment cannot be charged with a violation. Congress expressly excluded foreign officials from being prosecuted for a violation, leaving any legal redress to their own government. In *United States v. Castle,*[293] the Fifth Circuit adopted a district court decision that the general federal conspiracy statute could not be used as a way to avoid this limitation on the FCPA to allow the prosecution of foreign officials who agreed to accept corrupt payments to award contracts. Prosecutors can use other statutes, such as the money laundering law and the Travel Act, to prosecute foreign officials for conduct related to receiving bribes that violate the FCPA for the payer.

---

[290] 15 U.S.C. § 78dd–2(h)(4)(A).

[291] 15 U.S.C. § 78dd–1(f)(3)(A).

[292] 15 U.S.C. § 78dd–1(c).

[293] 925 F.2d 831 (5th Cir. 1991).

Chapter 8

RACKETEER INFLUENCED AND CORRUPT ORGANIZATIONS (RICO)

§ 8.1   INTRODUCTION

A. History

The Racketeer Influenced and Corrupt Organizations Act, commonly referred to as RICO, was passed in 1970 as part of the Organized Crime Control Act.[1] The Organized Crime Control Act included many important criminal justice initiatives such as creating the witness protection program, providing immunity to witnesses, and adding a new crime for false declarations (see Chapter 10). The statement of findings and purpose for the Organized Crime Control Act of 1970 notes five findings, including the first that states that "organized crime in the United States is highly sophisticated, diversified, and widespread activity that annually drains billions of dollars from America's economy by unlawful conduct and the illegal use of force, fraud, and corruption." It notes that:

> It is the purpose of this Act to seek the eradication of organized crime in the United States by strengthening the legal tools in the evidence-gathering process, by establishing new penal prohibitions, and by providing enhanced sanctions and new remedies to deal with the unlawful activities of those engaged in organized crime.[2]

The Organized Crime Control Act of 1970 is perhaps best known for its creation in Title IX of the crime called RICO.

There are several RICO statutes encompassed within Title IX. These statutes can be traced to a 1967 Report of the President's Commission on Law Enforcement and Administration of Justice (Katzenbach Commission).[3] This Commission's Report included recommendations and these served as the later basis for the creation of the RICO statutes. At the heart of the RICO statutes was Congress' attempt to criminalize organized crime's infiltration of legitimate businesses. Some opponents to RICO expressed concerns that it would "provide[ ] too easy a weapon against 'innocent businessmen'[4] . . . and would be prone to abuse."[5]

---

[1] Pub. L. 91–452 (1970).

[2] Id. at Statement of Findings and Purpose.

[3] Gerard E. Lynch, RICO: The Crime of Being a Criminal, Parts I & II, 87 Colum. L. Rev. 661, 666–67 (1987).

[4] Sedima, S.P.R.L. v. Imrex Co., Inc., 473 U.S. 479, 498 (1985) (citing R. Rep. No. 91–1549, p. 187 (1970).

[5] Id. (citing 116 Cong. Rec. 35227 (1970)).

B. Statutory Overview

RICO is a highly complex set of statutes and when initially enacted it was seldom used in criminal prosecutions. In contrast, today it serves as a strong basis for federal criminal prosecutions and is also commonly used in civil actions by private parties. It offers federal prosecutors the ability to take state criminal activity and bring it into the federal system. It also offers federal criminal prosecutors strong penalties and forfeiture provisions. The statutes are found in the federal code in statutes 18 U.S.C. §§ 1961–1968.

The initial RICO statute, found in 18 U.S.C. § 1961, is a statute that provides definitions to a host of different terms. It covers the meaning of racketeering activity, which includes nine possible state offenses and over fifty federal crimes that can serve as predicate acts for RICO charges. (See § 8.4). Section 1961 also provides the definition of the term "enterprise" a key aspect of this statute. (See § 8.2). Two possible ways to proceed with charges, namely through a "pattern of racketeering activity" (see infra § 8.4) or an "unlawful debt," are defined in section 1961. Courts have helped shape the contours of many of the terms used in this and the later RICO statutes.

18 U.S.C. § 1962 provides four types of prohibited activities and they are listed as subsections (a), (b), (c), and (d) of the prohibited conduct statute. These are: (a) using income from a pattern of racketeering activity to acquire an interest in an enterprise engaged in, or the activities of which affect interstate or foreign commerce; (b) acquiring or maintaining through a pattern of racketeering activity an interest in an enterprise engaged in, or the activities of which affect interstate or foreign commerce; (c) conducting or participating in the conduct, through a pattern of racketeering activity, of such affairs of an enterprise of which affect interstate or foreign commerce; and (d) conspiring to further any of the activities listed in (a), (b), or (c). It is common for federal prosecutors to insert more than one of these subsections as the basis for charging.

Each of these prohibited activities can be premised on a pattern of racketeering activity or alternatively on an "unlawful debt." Section 1961 defines the term "unlawful debt" to mean debts relating to either gambling or usurious loans that are incurred in connection with an illegal gambling business or in connection with a business of lending money where the usurious rate is at least twice the enforceable rate.[6] Actions related to an "unlawful debt" are usually beyond the definition of what constitutes a white collar crime.

18 U.S.C. § 1963 provides the criminal penalties for RICO violations. RICO carries a maximum imprisonment of twenty years.[7] (See Chapter 24). However, if the predicate act was for an offense that carried life imprisonment, then the penalty can be increased to match this predicate offense receiving a maximum sentence of life imprisonment. RICO also provides for forfeiture. Section 1963 outlines the basis for forfeiture proceedings and describes the types of property that can be forfeited. It also describes some of the procedural aspects to obtaining relief in forfeiture. (See § 8.7).

---

[6] 18 U.S.C. § 1961(7).

[7] 18 U.S.C. § 1963(a).

Section 1963 also allows for both temporary and permanent restraining orders and also provides injunction relief.

At the time of its passage, 18 U.S.C. § 1964 was unique in that it provided for civil actions, yet the statute was located in the criminal code. These actions can be brought by federal prosecutors and also by civil litigants. The rationale behind this section is to encourage private parties to assist the government in attacking the economic power of organized crime. Private litigants can receive treble damages, costs and reasonable attorney fees.[8] One exception here is that private parties may not rely as a basis of their action upon "fraud in the purpose of sale of securities to establish a violation of section 1962," unless the action targets a person "that is criminally convicted in connection with the fraud." Under this exception, the statute of limitations runs from the "date on which the conviction becomes final."[9] Section 1964 also provides that "[a] final judgment or decree in favor of the United States in any criminal proceeding brought by the United States under this chapter shall estop the defendant from denying the essential allegations of the criminal offense in any subsequent civil proceeding brought by the United States."[10] (See § 8.8).

Section 1964 has been controversial as civil litigants are not subject to Department of Justice guidelines that restrict the bringing of RICO charges. (See § 8.1(C)). Much of the controversy in the civil arena has been over the bringing of what have been called "garden variety" fraud cases. Congress has considered proposals to cut back on the civil use of RICO.[11] The restriction of RICO not being used by civil litigants for securities fraud matters unless there is a criminal conviction, was one successful action to limit the statute's civil use, while retaining its status for criminal matters.[12]

The remaining RICO statutes offer guidance on venue and process,[13] expedition of actions,[14] evidence issues regarding having the case closed to the public,[15] and civil investigative demands.[16] The main focus here is on criminal RICO, although civil cases often provide guidance on RICO law.

C. Prosecution Approvals for RICO

Bringing a RICO action requires the prior approval of the criminal division of the Department of Justice.[17] The United States Attorney's Manual states in part:

> The decision to institute a federal criminal prosecution involves balancing society's interest in effective law enforcement against the consequences for the accused. Utilization of the RICO statute, more so than most other federal criminal

---

[8] 18 U.S.C. § 1964(c).

[9] Id.

[10] 18 U.S.C. § 1964(d).

[11] See, e.g., H.R. 2943, 99th Cong., 1st Sess. (1985).

[12] 18 U.S.C. § 1964(c).

[13] 18 U.S.C. § 1965.

[14] 18 U.S.C. § 1966.

[15] 18 U.S.C. § 1967.

[16] 18 U.S.C. § 1968.

[17] USAM § 9–110.101.

sanctions, requires particularly careful and reasoned application, because, among other things, RICO incorporates certain state crimes.[18]

Although Department of Justice guidelines are unenforceable at law, they do offer internal guidance to federal prosecutors. (See § 1.5(A)). This guidance emphasizes the selectivity used with respect to RICO prosecutions. For example, it states that "[a] RICO count which merely duplicates the elements of proof of traditional Hobbs Act, Travel Act, mail fraud, wire fraud, gambling or controlled substances cases, will not be approved unless it serves some special RICO purpose."[19] Federal prosecutors are instructed that "'imaginative' prosecutions under RICO which are far afield from the congressional purpose of the RICO statute" will not be approved by the Criminal Division of Department of Justice.

The guidelines are particularly instructive when the predicate acts of the RICO charge are premised upon one or more of the nine state offenses. These RICO charges will not be approved except when, "(A) Local law enforcement officials are unlikely to investigate and prosecute otherwise meritorious cases in which the Federal government has significant interest; (B) Significant organized crime involvement exists; or (C) The prosecution of significant political or governmental individuals may pose special problems for local prosecutors."[20]

RICO does not offer as one of its predicate acts, tax offenses. In some instances, the government has attempted to circumvent this exclusion by charging mail fraud for the mailing of false tax returns. Thus, although RICO could not be premised on the filing of a false tax return, by making the predicate mail fraud, it becomes a viable RICO case. This, however, is frowned upon by the Department of Justice. They provide that Tax Division approvals are necessary for such an action and approvals are also needed for any internal revenue matter that is charged under RICO. A Directive of the Tax Division provides that "[a]bsent unusual circumstances, however, the Tax Division will not approve mail or wire fraud charges in cases involving only one person's tax liability, or when all submissions to the IRS were truthful."[21] Absent unusual circumstances, the Tax Division also will not approve tax-related RICO and money laundering offenses.[22]

D. Elements

The elements of a RICO charge are that the accused (1) invested the proceeds of a pattern of racketeering in, or acquired or maintained an interest in through a pattern of racketeering, or participated in through a pattern of racketeering, (2) an enterprise, (3) engaged in, or the activities of which affect, commerce. The complicated nature of

---

[18] Id.

[19] Id.

[20] USAM § 9–110.330.

[21] Eileen J. O'Connor, Assistant Attorney General, Tax Division Directive No. 128 (Oct. 29, 2004) available at http://www.justice.gov/usao/eousa/foia_reading_room/usam/title6/tax00014.htm. The U.S. Attorneys' Manual 6–4.210 (B) also provides [t]he Tax Division will not authorize the use of mail, wire or bank fraud charges to convert routine tax prosecutions into RICO or money laundering cases, but will authorize prosecution of tax-related RICO and money laundering offenses when unusual circumstances warrant such a prosecution."

[22] Eileen J. O'Connor, Assistant Attorney General, Tax Division Directive No. 128 (Oct. 29, 2004) available at http://www.justice.gov/usao/eousa/foia_reading_room/usam/title6/tax00014.htm.

this statute comes to light when one matches these elements to the four specific prohibited conduct provisions in section 1962.

Courts also wrestle with the scope of various aspects of RICO. For example, under section 1962(c), courts have struggled with interpreting what it means "to conduct or participate, directly or indirectly, in the conduct of such enterprise's affairs through a pattern of racketeering activity." There are also questions about specific terms used in the statute. For example, with respect to the enterprise element, what is required for an enterprise and what is the relationship between the enterprise and the individual defendant. (See § 8.2).

E. Interpreting RICO

Although RICO was drafted as a statute targeting organized crime, it has not been limited to this context.[23] As was stated in *United States v. Mandel*,[24] "the legislative history of Title IX shows that Congress had taken pains to make a conviction dependent upon behavior, and not 'status.'"[25]

Congress noted in drafting the statute that RICO should be "liberally construed to effectuate its remedial purposes."[26] In *Sedima, S.P.R.L. v. Imrex Co., Inc.*,[27] the Supreme Court held that it is not necessary for there to be a prior conviction of the predicate act in order for it to be used in a RICO case. In *Sedima*, Justice White examined the legislative history of this statute in the context of a civil RICO action brought under section 1962(c). He stated that "RICO was an aggressive initiative to supplement old remedies and develop new methods for fighting crime." He stated further that "[w]hile few of the legislative statements about novel remedies and attacking crime on all fronts, . . . were made with direct reference to § 1964(c), it is in this spirit that all of the Act's provisions should be read."[28] Cases routinely give RICO a broad reading when interpreting terms used within the statute.

F. Constitutionality

RICO has been challenged as unconstitutional with several different legal arguments made. It has survived challenges that it violates state sovereignty, is vague, and punishes associational status.[29] It has been found that it does not operate ex post facto when the prohibited conduct under state law did not exist at the time of the RICO charge. In *United States v. Vaccaro*,[30] the Fifth Circuit stated that it would require a showing that the conduct was legal at the time of the allegations in the indictment. The court noted that "[t]he reference to state law in a RICO indictment serves a 'definitional purpose.'"[31] But Justice Scalia's concurring opinion in *H.J. Inc. v.*

---

[23] See United States v. Uni Oil, Inc., 646 F.2d 946 (5th Cir. 1981).

[24] 415 F.Supp. 997 (D.C. Md. 1976).

[25] Id. at 1018.

[26] Pub. L. No. 91–452 § 904.

[27] 473 U.S. 479 (1985).

[28] Id. at 498.

[29] See, e.g., United States v. Martino, 648 F.2d 367 (5th Cir. 1981).

[30] 115 F.3d 1211 (5th Cir. 1997).

[31] Id. at 1221.

Northwestern Bell Telephone Co.,[32] invites a vagueness challenge on how to interpret a "pattern of racketeering activity."

G. Extraterritoriality

In some cases the enterprise or the racketeering activity may be outside the United States. Courts have wrestled with whether there can be prosecutions under RICO when the conduct is extraterritorial.[33] The RICO statute does not specify an extraterritorial application. Courts in some cases allowed prosecutions when the enterprise was outside the United States.

In *Morrison v. National Australia Bank Ltd*,[34] the Supreme Court examined extraterritoriality in the context of a civil securities fraud case premised on § 10(b) of the Securities Exchange Act of 1934. The Court held that "[i]t is a longstanding principle of American law 'that legislation of Congress, unless a contrary intent appears, is meant to apply only within the territorial jurisdiction of the United States.'" The presumption is that it is concerned with domestic concerns unless Congress speaks clearly indicating an extraterritorial application.

Although the *Morrison* case did not involve RICO, this case has been looked to in deciding whether to give an extraterritorial application to RICO. Uniformly, courts have rejected an extraterritorial application of RICO, although courts may focus on different aspects of the RICO statute in examining this question.[35] The *Morrison* Court, however, did clearly reject arguments premised on the statute providing for foreign commerce, stating that "[t]he general reference to foreign commerce in the definition of 'interstate commerce' does not defeat the presumption against extraterritoriality."

§ 8.2 ENTERPRISE

A. Nature of the Enterprise

1. *Generally*

RICO requires that the accused have invested in, maintained an interest in, or participated in the affairs of an enterprise. It has been held, however, that there is no requirement that the enterprise or predicate acts have an economic motive. In *National Organization for Women, Inc. v. Scheidler*,[36] the Supreme Court examined pre-trial whether RICO required an economic motive. The case involved a civil lawsuit brought by the National Organization of Women and others affected by antiabortion groups protesting at clinics. The Court rejected the position of the Second Circuit and respondents, noting that they "overlook the fact that predicate acts, such as the alleged extortion, may not benefit the protesters financially but still may drain money from the

---

[32] 492 U.S. 229, 251–56 (1989).

[33] See supra § 8.2(A)(2).

[34] 130 S.Ct. 2869 (2010); see also § 1.7(D)(2).

[35] Patricia A. Leonard & Gerardo J. Rodriguez–Albizu, Do Extraterritorial RICO Claims Still Exist in a Post–Morrison World?, 59 The Federal Lawyer 60 (Oct/Nov 2012) (arguing that courts have "disagreed on how to determine the focus of the RICO Statute for purposes of extraterritoriality" and that two approaches have emerged: an enterprise approach and predicate acts approach).

[36] 510 U.S. 249 (1994).

economy by harming businesses such as the clinics which are petitioners in this case."[37]

In *United States v. Turkette*,[38] the Supreme Court addressed the question of whether RICO was limited to legitimate businesses. The defendant in this case "argued that RICO was intended solely to protect legitimate business enterprises," basing this assumption on the legislative history and the goals of the statute.[39] In rejecting this position, the Supreme Court stated:

> [N]either the language nor structure of RICO limits its application to legitimate "enterprises." Applying it also to criminal organizations does not render any portion of the statute superfluous nor does it create any structural incongruities within the framework of the Act. The result is neither absurd nor surprising. On the contrary, insulating the wholly criminal enterprise from prosecution under RICO is the more incongruous position.[40]

The term enterprise is described in 18 U.S.C. § 1961(4) as including "any individual, partnership, corporation, association, or other legal entity, and any union or group of individuals associated-in-fact although not a legal entity." This provides two basic groups of entities: those that are legal entities and those that are associations in fact but not legal entities.

2. *Legal Entities*

Legal entities tend to be easier for the government to prove than an association-in-fact enterprise. A legal entity often will have a corporate or partnership structure with Secretary of State or tax filings that provide proof of the existence of the entity. Business entities may have filed paperwork to provide notice of doing business under a specified name within a state, and this too can offer proof of the existence of a legal entity.

The range of different legal entities that have been used by prosecutors provides an incredible list.[41] It has been applied to both small and large entities.[42] The statute does not reference whether state and local entities can be used as the enterprise, but many cases have allowed this to happen. For example, courts allowed the Philadelphia Traffic Court,[43] the Pennsylvania Bureau of Cigarette and Beverage Taxes,[44] police departments,[45] the Office of a Governor,[46] a local prosecutor's office,[47] and state legislators[48] to be enterprises for the purposes of RICO.

---

[37] Id. at 260.

[38] 452 U.S. 576 (1981).

[39] Id. at 579–80.

[40] Id. at 587.

[41] See generally Ellen S. Podgor, State and Local Entities as RICO Enterprises: A Matter of Perception, 98 W. Vir. L. Rev. 853, 857–58 (1996).

[42] See United States v. Campanale, 518 F.2d 352 (9th Cir. 1975).

[43] See United States v. Vignola, 464 F.Supp. 1091 (D.C. Pa. 1979).

[44] See United States v. Frumento, 563 F.2d 1083 (3d Cir. 1977).

[45] See, e.g., United States v. Davis, 707 F.2d 880 (6th Cir. 1983); United States v. Kovic, 684 F.2d 512 (7th Cir. 1982); United States v. Brown, 555 F.2d 407 (5th Cir. 1977).

[46] See United States v. Thompson, 685 F.2d 993 (6th Cir. 1982).

Federalism concerns have been raised with the use of state agencies as the enterprise for a RICO charge. For the most part these arguments have been unsuccessful. Courts, on occasion, express concern with it being "disruptive of comity in federal-state relations."[49] In the case of *United States v. Mandel*,[50] the former Governor Mandel of Maryland argued this point successfully to a district court in Maryland. The Maryland District Court stated that "the remedies provided for in the civil and criminal provisions clearly imply that Congress had only private entities in minds when defining 'enterprise.'"[51] The court noted that "[s]tates have their own adequate resources to combat threats to their integrity leveled by organized crime; states have laws regulating the behavior of public officials that are adequate to protect a state from any racketeering acts engaged in by that official."[52] But this decision that refused to allow the State of Maryland as a RICO enterprise has been criticized by the Fourth Circuit in later opinions.[53]

In *United States v. Warner*,[54] former Illinois Governor George H. Ryan and his associate Lawrence E. Warner raised the issue of whether the State of Illinois could be the enterprise for purposes of RICO and whether the court erred in instructing the jury that the State of Illinois was a "legal entity."[55] The Seventh Circuit in its opinion referenced the *Mandel* decision and noted how the Seventh Circuit had previously taken an opposite position from this case and held that public bodies may be enterprises for purposes of RICO. The *Warner* court also noted how even the Fourth Circuit no longer adhered to the position taken by the district court in the *Mandel* case. The Court in *Warner* found that RICO did apply to public entities, although it expressed concern with using a state as the entity for purposes of RICO. It noted that this case was exceptional in that prosecutors may not have a choice in naming anything other than the state as the enterprise. The court also found that the district court did not err in instructing the jury that the State of Illinois was a legal entity.[56]

Prior to *Morrison v. National Australia Bank Ltd*,[57] courts allowed international bodies to be the legal entity for purposes of a RICO enterprise. In *United States v. Parness*,[58] the Second Circuit, in finding it acceptable to have an Antillean corporation as the enterprise, stated that it found "no indication that Congress intended to limit Title IX (RICO) to infiltration of domestic enterprises."[59] Noting that the statute was intended to be construed broadly, the court stated that "the salutary purposes of the

---

[47] See, e.g., United States v. Goot, 894 F.2d 231, 239 (7th Cir. 1990); United States v. Altomare, 625 F.2d 5, 7 (4th Cir. 1980).

[48] See, e.g., United States v. Blandford, 33 F.3d 685, 703 (6th Cir. 1994); United States v. Long, 651 F.2d 239 (4th Cir. 1981).

[49] United States v. Thompson, 685 F.2d 993, 1000 (6th Cir. 1982).

[50] 415 F.Supp. 997 (D. Md. 1976).

[51] Id. at 1021.

[52] Id.

[53] See, e.g., United States v. Long, 651 F.2d 239, 241 (4th Cir. 1981); United States v. Altomare, 625 F.2d 5, 7 (4th Cir. 1980).

[54] 498 F.3d 666 (7th Cir. 2007).

[55] Id. at 694

[56] Id. at 696.

[57] 130 S.Ct. 2869 (2010); see also § 1.7(D)(2).

[58] 503 F.2d 430 (2d Cir. 1974); see also Alfadda v. Fenn, 935 F.2d 475 (2d Cir. 1991).

[59] Id. at 438–440.

Act would be frustrated by" a construction that limited RICO to domestic entities. In referencing the legislative history of RICO, the Second Circuit noted that the "legislative history leaves no room for doubt that Congress intended to deal generally with the influences of organized crime on the American economy and not merely with its infiltration into domestic enterprises."[60]

The *Morrison* case, now referenced in extraterritorial RICO cases, changed this landscape. As a result of this decision, courts have not permitted RICO to be used for foreign enterprises. See § 8.1(G). In *Cedeno v. Intech Group, Inc.*,[61] a Southern District of New York court held that RICO did not apply extraterritorially as "nowhere does the statute evidence any concern with foreign enterprises, let alone a concern sufficiently clear to overcome the presumption against extraterritoriality." This decision explicitly states that *Parness* is "no longer good precedent in light of *Morrison*."[62] A similar approach has been taken in other cases.[63]

3. Association-in-Fact Enterprises

In addition to presenting the enterprise through a legal entity, it is also possible for a prosecutor to charge it as a "group of individuals associated in fact although not a legal entity."[64] Courts struggled for many years in determining what would be sufficient to be called an association-in-fact. Most agreed that an association-in-fact needed to have a common purpose and must function as a continuing unit, but there was a jurisdictional split on whether an ascertainable structure was required and the essence of that structure.

Examples of three different views can be found in the cases of *United States v. Bledsoe*,[65] *United States v. Perholtz*,[66] and *United States v. Riccobene*.[67] In *Bledsoe*, the Eighth Circuit held that "the enterprise element requires proof of some structure separate from the racketeering activity and distinct from the organization."[68] It said that, in addition to having a common or shared purpose, it needed to "function as a continuing unit."[69] In contrast, in *Perholtz*, the court chose to "follow those courts that [ ] held that the government satisfies its burden if it proves the existence of the enterprise and of the pattern, and refuse[d] to require the government to prove each by separate evidence."[70] *Riccobene* took a position between *Bedsoe* and *Perholtz* in finding that there needed to be an "ongoing organization," "continuing unit," and the "entity separate and apart from the pattern of activity in which it engages."[71]

---

[60] Id. at 439.

[61] 733 F. Supp.2d 471 (S.D.N.Y. 2010).

[62] Id. at 474 n.3. See also Norex Petroleum Ltd. v. Access Industries, Inc., 631 F.3d 29 (2d Cir. 2010) (finding that RICO does not apply extraterritorially).

[63] See Sorota v. Sosa, 842 F. Supp. 2d 1345 (2012) (holding that RICO does not apply extraterritorially).

[64] 18 U.S.C. § 1961(4).

[65] 674 F.2d 647 (8th Cir. 1982).

[66] 842 F.2d 343 (D.C. Cir. 1988).

[67] 709 F.2d 214 (3d Cir. 1983).

[68] 674 F.2d 647, 664 (8th Cir. 1982).

[69] Id. at 665.

[70] 842 F.2d 343, 363 (D.C.Cir. 1988).

[71] 709 F.2d 214, 221–25 (3d Cir. 1983).

The issue of what constituted an ascertainable structure was the focus of the Supreme Court's decision in the 2009 case of *Boyle v. United States*.[72] Boyle was convicted under § 1962(c)[73] and the question on appeal concerned the instruction the Court gave regarding the association-in-fact element of this crime and its failure to give the defendant's requested instruction "that the Government was required to prove that the enterprise 'had an ongoing organization, a core membership that functioned as a continuing unit, and an ascertainable structural hierarchy distinct from the charged predicate acts.'"[74]

The Supreme Court looked at three questions in examining "whether an association-in-fact enterprise must have 'an ascertainable structure beyond that inherent in the pattern of racketeering activity in which it engages." Those questions were:

> First, must an association-in-fact enterprise have a "structure"? Second, must the structure be "ascertainable"? Third, must the "structure" go "beyond that inherent in the pattern of racketeering activity" in which its members engage?[75]

In answering the question of "structure" the Court noted "that an association-in-fact enterprise must have at least three structural features: a purpose, relationships among those associated with the enterprise, and longevity sufficient to permit these associates to pursue the enterprise's purpose."[76] That said, it was not necessary for the judge's instruction to have this precise language. Likewise, telling the jury that "they had to ascertain the existence of an 'ascertainable structure' would have been redundant and potentially misleading."[77] The Court also referenced the *Turkette* case holding that "the evidence used to prove the pattern of racketeering activity and the evidence establishing an enterprise 'may in particular cases coalesce.'"[78]

The Court in *Boyle* stated:

> Members of the group need not have fixed roles; different members may perform different roles at different times. The group need not have a name, regular meetings, dues, established rules and regulations, disciplinary procedures, or induction or initiation ceremonies. While the group must function as a continuing unit and remain in existence long enough to pursue a course of conduct, nothing in RICO exempts an enterprise whose associates engage in spurts of activity punctuated by periods of quiescence. Nor is the statute limited to groups whose crimes are sophisticated, diverse, complex, or unique; for example, a group that does nothing but engage in extortion through old-fashioned, unsophisticated, and brutal means may fall squarely within the statute's reach.[79]

---

[72] 556 U.S. 938 (2009).

[73] In United States v. Wilson, 605 F.3d 985 (D.C. Cir. 2010), the court limited Boyle to § 1962(c), not extending it for § 1962(d).

[74] Id. at 943.

[75] Id. at 946.

[76] Id.

[77] Id.

[78] Id. at 948.

[79] Id.

The Court held that the "trial judge did not err in instructing the jury that 'the existence of an association-in-fact is oftentimes more readily proven by what it does, rather than by abstract analysis of its structure.'"[80] Justices Stevens and Breyer, dissenting, stated that "the instructions and evidence in this case did not satisfy the requirement that an alleged enterprise have an existence separate and apart from the pattern of activity in which it engages."[81]

B.   Distinctiveness of the Enterprise and the Defendant

18 U.S.C. § 1962(c) makes it "unlawful for any person employed by or associated with any enterprise . . . to conduct or participate, directly or indirectly, in the conduct of such enterprise's affairs through a pattern of racketeering activity . . . " In *Cedric Kushner Promotions, Ltd. v. King*,[82] the Supreme Court held that this provision of the RICO statute requires two separate entities: a "person" and an "enterprise."

The *Cedric Kushner* Court explored, in the context of a civil RICO matter, whether a corporation and individual met this "person-enterprise" rule when the individual is the president and sole shareholder of a closely held corporation. Specifically Cedric Kushner Promotions, Ltd, a corporation that promoted boxing matches, "sued Don King, the president and sole shareholder of Don King Productions."[83] The lower courts had dismissed the complaint finding that it did not meet § 1962(c).[84] At the time the case went to the Court, other circuits disagreed with this resolution.[85]

Justice Breyer, writing for a unanimous Supreme Court, reversed and remanded the lower court's dismissal finding that the "person" and "enterprise" were distinct here. The Court stated:

> The corporate owner/employee, a natural person, is distinct from the corporation itself, a legally different entity with different rights and responsibilities due to its different legal status. And we can find nothing in the statute that requires more "separateness" than that.

§ 8.3   INTERSTATE COMMERCE

A.   Affecting Interstate Commerce

RICO requires that the enterprise be "engaged in, or the activities of which affect, interstate or foreign commerce." This requirement is irrespective of whether the RICO case is brought under § 1962(a), (b), (c), or (d).

In 1995, the Supreme Court decided the case of *United States v. Lopez*[86] which held that the Gun–Free School Zones Act exceeded Congress' Commerce Clause authority in that it involved intrastate activity that was not involved in commerce and

---

[80] Id. at 951.

[81] Id. at 959.

[82] 533 U.S. 158 (2001).

[83] Id. at 160.

[84] 219 F.3d 115 (2d Cir. 2000).

[85] See, e.g., Brannon v. Boatmen's First Nat. Bank of Oklahoma, 153 F.3d 1144 (10th Cir. 1998).

[86] 514 U.S. 549 (1995).

was not an economic activity. The Court looked at the three categories of conduct within Congress' commerce authority which included "those activities having a substantial relation to interstate commerce." The Court noted that within this category it was necessary that the regulated activity "substantially affects" interstate commerce. (See supra § 1.7(A)). The Supreme Court further examined interstate commerce in *United States v. Morrison*,[87] finding that a provision of the Violence Against Women Act of 1994 "contain[ed] no jurisdictional element establishing that the federal cause of action is in pursuance of Congress' power to regulate interstate commerce." The Court stated, "[t]he regulation and punishment of intrastate violence that is not directed at the instrumentalities, channels, or goods involved in interstate commerce has always been the province of the States." In *Gonzales v. Raich*,[88] however, the Court recognized "Congress' power to regulate purely local activities that are part of an economic 'class of activities' that have a substantial effect on interstate commerce."

Courts in applying "affecting interstate commerce" in the context of RICO have found a sufficient nexus with interstate commerce when the connection is minimal. Some of these cases were prior to the Court opinion in *Lopez* and *Morrison*. For example, in *United States v. Joseph*,[89] the defendant, the Clerk of Courts of Lehigh County, Pennsylvania, was alleged to have violated RICO "by soliciting and accepting various amounts of cash from a bailbondsman in consideration for defendant's favorable recommendations and exercise of discretion in his official decisions." The court found the interstate commerce sufficient here as "most courts do have an effect upon interstate commerce, as do sheriff's departments and the offices of prosecuting attorneys, all of which place interstate telephone calls, purchase supplies and materials through interstate commerce and involve non-citizens of the forum state in litigation."

Other cases after *Lopez* have also allowed for a minimal connection in interstate commerce to meet the interstate requirement for RICO. For example, in *United States v. Gardiner*,[90] the Sixth Circuit stated that "[f]or purposes of a conviction under 18 U.S.C. §§ 1962(c) & (d) the government need only prove that the enterprise's racketeering activities had a *de minimis* connection with interstate commerce."[91]

The Sixth Circuit in *Waucaush v. United States*[92] distinguished these interstate commerce principles stating that a minimal connection suffices for RICO when the enterprise itself engages in economic activity. But when the economic activity is not present and all you have "left is violence qua violence" this is non-economic and using a minimal effect in commerce will be insufficient for RICO's interstate commerce element.[93]

---

[87] 529 U.S. 598 (2000).

[88] 545 U.S. 1 (2005); see also Perez v. United States, 402 U.S. 146 (1971).

[89] 510 F.Supp. 1001 (E.D. Pa. 1981).

[90] 463 F.3d 445 (6th Cir. 2006).

[91] Id. at 458; see also United States v. Riddle, 249 F.3d 529 (6th Cir. 2001).

[92] 380 F.3d 251 (6th Cir. 2004).

[93] Id. at 263.

B. Engaged in Interstate Commerce

Shortly after *Lopez* was decided, the Supreme Court looked at the interstate commerce issue from the perspective of RICO. In *United States v. Robertson*,[94] the Supreme Court examined a RICO case noting that interstate commerce under RICO could be achieved in two possible ways: 1) affecting interstate commerce; or 2) engaged in interstate commerce. The defendant in this case was involved in a gold mining operation in Alaska. The Court noted the many activities that the defendant was *"engaged in"* that were in interstate commerce and therefore meeting this element of the crime. The Court stated:

> Robertson, who resided in Arizona, made a cash payment of $125,000 for placer gold mining claims near Fairbanks. He paid approximately $100,000 (in cash) for mining equipment and supplies, some of which were purchased in Los Angeles and transported to Alaska for use in the mine. Robertson also hired and paid the expenses for seven out-of-state employees to travel to Alaska to work in the mine. The partnership dissolved during the first mining season, but Robertson continued to operate the mine through 1987 as a sole proprietorship. He again hired a number of employees from outside Alaska to work in the mine. During its operating life, the mine produced between $200,000 and $290,000 worth of gold, most of which was sold to refiners within Alaska, although Robertson personally transported approximately $30,000 worth of gold out of the State.[95]

C. Enterprise Affecting Commerce

Courts have looked at the question of whether the predicate acts or the enterprise needs to be engaged in or affecting interstate commerce. Courts examining this question have held that it is the activity of the enterprise and not each predicate act that needs to be engaged in or affecting commerce.[96] Additionally, courts note that the enterprise must affect interstate commerce, not the conduct of the defendant.[97]

§ 8.4   PATTERN OF RACKETEERING ACTIVITY

A. Predicate Acts

RICO describes a "pattern of racketeering activity" as requiring "at least two acts of racketeering activity, one of which occurred after the effective date of this chapter and the last of which occurred within ten years (excluding any period of imprisonment after the commission of a prior act of racketeering activity."[98] The acts that constitute "racketeering activity" are listed in § 1961(1). Seven different groups of offenses are listed here.

The first group found in § 1961(1)(A) provides the nine offenses under state law that can be predicate acts for RICO. These are: "any act or threat involving murder,

---

[94] 514 U.S. 669 (1995).

[95] Id. at 670–71.

[96] See, e.g., United States v. Rone, 598 F.2d 564, 573 (9th Cir. 1979); United States v. Bagnariol, 665 F.2d 877, 892 (9th Cir. 1981).

[97] See, e.g., United States v. Robinson, 763 F.2d 778, 781 (6th Cir. 1985); United States v. Groff, 643 F.2d 396, 400 (6th Cir. 1981).

[98] 18 U.S.C. § 1961(5).

kidnapping, gambling, arson, robbery, bribery, extortion, dealing in obscene matter, or dealing in a controlled substance or listed chemical (as defined in section 102 of the Controlled Substances Act), which is chargeable under State law and punishable by imprisonment for more than one year." The state offenses are merely descriptive of the conduct and are not meant to restrict the use of a state crime that may use a different label for this conduct. For example, in *United States v. Garner*,[99] the Seventh Circuit examined a case in which the defendant was convicted of RICO with a predicate of an Illinois official misconduct statute.[100] The defendants argued that violations of this statute were not predicate acts for RICO. The court noted the legislative history of RICO that "[s]tate offenses are included by generic designation."[101] In allowing this to be bribery for purposes of a state predicate for RICO the court stated that "[t]he labels placed on a state statute do not determine whether that statute proscribes bribery for purposes of the RICO statute."[102]

Subsection B lists an array of different federal crimes that are located in Title 18 of the federal code. It includes key offenses such as bribery, mail fraud, wire fraud, bank fraud, obstruction of justice, Hobbs Act, and money laundering. Subsection C–F selects crimes that fall outside of Title 18. For example, subsection C pertains to labor crimes, subsection D to crimes within title 11that are connected to fraud, subsection E to crimes under the Currency and Foreign Transactions Reporting Act, and subsection F to Immigration. More depth as to each is provided in the statute. Subsection G relates to section 2332b(g)(5)(B), activities related to terrorism. This latter provision was added as part of the United and Strengthening America by Providing Appropriate Tools Required to Intercept and Obstruct Terrorism Act of 2001 (Patriot Act).

Although it is necessary to have at least two predicate acts for charging RICO, there is no requirement the defendant have been charged or convicted of these acts. In *Bridge v. Phoenix Bond & Indem. Co*,[103] the Supreme Court limited the proof required for RICO to the specific predicate act. The Court found that a plaintiff in a civil RICO case, who used mail fraud predicates, did not have to plead or prove that it relied on the defendant's alleged misrepresentations. (See § 8.8).

In those instances when the defendant has been charged under state law with a predicate act, and also charged with RICO in the federal system, courts have allowed both proceedings as the dual sovereignty rule provides concurrent jurisdiction to both the state and federal governments. This has been permitted even when the defendant was acquitted of the crime in the state system.[104] The double jeopardy clause also has not barred a subsequent RICO prosecution based upon a federal predicate offense previously used to prosecute the defendant. Since RICO requires proof of a pattern of racketeering, courts have found that it is not the same offense as the predicate act.

---

[99] 837 F.2d 1404 (7th Cir. 1987).

[100] Ill. Rev. Stat. ch. 38, para. 33–3(d).

[101] 837 F.2d 1404, 1418 (7th Cir. 1987) (citing H.R.Rep. No. 1549, 91st Cong., 2d Sess. (1970), reprinted in 1970 U.S.Code Cong. & Admin.News 4007, 4032).

[102] 837 F.2d 1404, 1418.

[103] 553 U.S. 639 (2008).

[104] United States v. Coonan, 938 F.2d 1553 (2d Cir. 1991).

Additionally courts have stated that prosecuting both RICO and the predicate substantive offense as separate charges does not violate double jeopardy.[105]

B. Continuity Plus Relationship

1.   *H.J. Inc. v. Northwestern Bell Telephone Co.*

Merely having two predicate acts within the applicable statute of limitations does not suffice for purposes of RICO. It is also necessary that you have a pattern of this racketeering activity. Case law has provided interpretation of what constitutes a pattern of racketeering activity.

In *H.J. Inc. v. Northwestern Bell Telephone Co.*,[106] the Supreme Court examined what constitutes a pattern of racketeering activity in a civil case where the petitioners alleged violations of sections 1962(a), (b), (c), and (d). The Court looked at the legislative history and dictionary definitions of the terms used in the RICO statute and decided that the two components of a pattern were "continuity plus relationship." The Court noted that although these "two constituents of RICO's pattern requirement must be stated separately, . . . in practice their proof will often overlap."[107]

Justice Brennan, delivering the opinion of the Court, referenced Title X of the Organized Crime Control Act of 1970 to ascertain the definition of "relatedness." According to this statute, "[c]riminal conduct forms a pattern if it embraces criminal acts that have the same or similar purposes, results, participants, victims, or methods of commission, or otherwise are interrelated by distinguishing characteristics and are not isolated events."[108]

Next the Court looked at the component of "continuity," which could be achieved in one of two ways. It could be "closed" of "open-ended." If the continuity is "closed" it requires proof of "a series of related predicates extending over a substantial period of time." The Court noted that "[p]redicate acts extending over a few weeks or months and threatening no future criminal conduct do not satisfy this requirement: Congress was concerned in RICO with long-term criminal conduct." But this does not mean that RICO will always require a long period of time. Shorter periods will be allowed when the conduct is "open-ended." The Court stated that "in such cases liability depends on whether the *threat* of continuity is demonstrated."[109] But the Court also noted that "the development of these concepts must await future cases, absent a decision by Congress to revisit RICO to provide clearer guidance as to the Act's intended scope."[110]

Four justices, concurring in this decision, expressed dismay that the Court had elevated "a phrase taken from the legislative history," namely, "continuity plus relationship." The concurring Justices state that this seems "as helpful to the conduct of their affairs as 'life is a fountain.'" Although they note that a constitutional challenge was not raised in this case, they invite this challenge in future cases by saying, "[t]hat

---

[105] United States v. Pungitore, 910 F.2d 1084 (3d Cir. 1990).

[106] 492 U.S. 229 (1989).

[107] Id. at 239.

[108] Id. at 240 (citing 18 U.S.C. § 3575(e)).

[109] Id. at 241–42.

[110] Id. at 243.

the highest Court in the land has been unable to derive from this statute anything more than today's meager guidance bodes ill for the day when that challenge is presented."[111] Although the Supreme Court has not accepted certiorari on a RICO vagueness challenge, there have been a fair number of lower court decisions that have provided additional guidance on how to interpret a "pattern of racketeering activity" and "continuity plus relationship."

2. Relationship

Courts have looked at when the predicate acts should be considered related for purposes of RICO. A single criminal episode has been held not to be a pattern, even when that episode "amounts to several crimes."[112] Most jurisdictions use the language from *H.J., Inc.* to instruct the jury on what constitutes relatedness.[113] In *United States v. Cain*,[114] the Second Circuit reinforced decisions that "labeled the requirement that the predicate acts be related to one another 'horizontal relatedness' and the requirement they have a nexus to the enterprise 'vertical relatedness.'"[115] Courts have stated that "both vertical and horizontal relatedness can be established simply by connecting diverse predicate acts to an enterprise whose business is racketeering activity, such as an organized crime family."[116]

Some jurisdictions have taken a broad view on what will constitute relatedness.[117] For example, in *United States v. Eppolito*[118] the Second Circuit stated that "[t]o prove relatedness, the government may show either that the individual predicate acts were directly related to each other or that they were related to the enterprise in a way that made them "*indirectly* connected to each other."[119] In *United States v. Corrado*,[120] the Sixth Circuit in discussing "relationship or relatedness" stated that "[t]he predicate acts do not necessarily need to be directly interrelated; they must, however, be connected to the affairs and operations of the criminal enterprise."[121]

3. Continuity

Courts have also looked at continuity, discussing both the close-ended and continuing threats approaches that cases can take to meet this aspect of a pattern of racketeering activity. Specifically courts have provided guidance on when there is sufficient time for the activities to meet a "close-ended" period. Courts have found the amount of time insufficient for a close-ended pattern of racketeering when the time span was nine months,[122] ten months,[123] eleven months,[124] sixteen months,[125]

---

[111] Id. at 256.

[112] See Apparel Art International Inc. v. Jacobson, 967 F.2d 720 (1st Cir. 1992).

[113] United States v. Knight, 659 F.3d 1285, 1289–90 (10th Cir. 2011).

[114] 671 F.3d 271 (2d Cir. 2012)

[115] Id. at 284–85.

[116] United States v. Coppola, 671 F.3d 220, 243 (2d Cir. 2012); United States v. Indelicato, 865 F.2d 1370, 1383 (2d Cir. 1989).

[117] Id. at 1292.

[118] 543 F.3d 25 (2d Cir. 2008).

[119] Id. at 57 (citing United States v. Locascio, 6 F.3d 924 (2d Cir. 1993).

[120] 227 F.3d 543 (6th Cir. 2000).

[121] Id. at 554.

[122] See Jackson v. BellSouth Telecommunications, 372 F.3d 1250 (11th Cir. 2004).

[123] See Wisdom v. First Midwest Bank of Poplar Bluff, 167 F.3d 402, 407 (8th Cir. 1999).

seventeen months,[126] twenty-one months,[127] and less than two years.[128] But it has been noted that various factors beside a temporal span should be used in assessing whether there is continuity.[129]

Courts have also examined whether there was a sufficient threat for it to allow a shorter period of time under *H.J., Inc.*'s "open-ended" pattern of racketeering activity. In *United States v. Busacca*,[130] the Sixth Circuit looked at six predicate acts involving the misappropriation of funds over a period of two and one half months. Since the period of time was short, it could not be considered "closed-ended." It was therefore necessary to determine if it was open-ended and whether there was a continued threat. The court stated that "[t]he threat of continued criminal activity is a fact specific concept. It may be established by any number of possibilities, such as by showing that the related predicates themselves involve a distinct threat of long term racketeering activity, either implicit or explicit, or by showing that the predicate acts or offenses are a part of an ongoing entity's regular way of doing business."[131] The court said that one needs to look at the "totality of the circumstances surrounding the commission of the predicate acts" in order to determine if "those acts pose a threat of continuing criminal activity."[132] In this case this was met by:

> Busacca's willingness to disregard established Board procedures for the disbursement of checks, his position of control over the Union and the Funds, his secretive concealment and affirmative misrepresentations to the Board regarding the advanced monies, and his obvious attorney shopping for a legal opinion consistent with his objectives were sufficient to establish a threat of long term, continuing criminal activity. The manner in which the embezzlements occurred was capable of repetition indefinitely into the future, as long as there were either legal fees or other expenses which Busacca wanted paid.[133]

§ 8.5   NEXUS REQUIREMENT

In 18 U.S.C. § 1962(a) a person is using income from a pattern of racketeering activity to acquire an interest in an enterprise and in 18 U.S.C. § 1962(b) the accused is acquiring or maintaining through a pattern of racketeering an interest in an enterprise. Thus, in these two provisions the relationship between the racketeering and enterprise is apparent. Unlike §§ 1962(a) and (b), § 1962(c) requires that there be a nexus between the racketeering and the enterprise. Prior to the Supreme Court's ruling in 1993 in *Reves v. Ernst & Young*,[134] courts disagreed on the relationship required between the enterprise and the racketeering activity or person engaged in the

---

[124] See GICC Capital Corp. v. Technology Fin. Group, Inc., 67 F.3d 463, 467–68 (2d Cir. 1995).

[125] Spool v. World Child Intern. Adoption Agency, 520 F.3d 178 (2d Cir. 2008).

[126] See Vemco, Inc. v. Camardella, 23 F.3d 129, 134 (6th Cir. 1994).

[127] See Efron v. Embassy Suites (P.R.), Inc., 223 F.3d 12 (1st Cir. 2000).

[128] See Cofacredit, S.A. v. Windsor Plumbing Supply Co., 187 F.3d 229, 242 (2d Cir. 1999).

[129] See Vicom, Inc. v. Harbridge Merchant Servs., 20 F.3d 771, 780 (7th Cir. 1994).

[130] 936 F.2d 232 (6th Cir. 1991).

[131] Id. at 237–38.

[132] Id. at 238.

[133] Id.

[134] 507 U.S. 170 (1993).

racketeering activity. Courts varied on whether a defendant needed to participate in the "operation or management" of the company.[135]

In *Reves*, the Court decided to resolve the issue of whether § 1962(c) required that "one must participate in the operation or management of the enterprise itself to be subject to liability under this provision." The issue presented in this case was whether there was civil RICO liability for an independent accounting firm who prepared audit reports for the company. The Court looked at the meaning of the phrase "to conduct or participate, directly or indirectly, in the conduct of such enterprise's affairs." The *Reves* Court considered the terminology used in the statute and also looked at its legislative history to find that one is not liable under § 1962(c) "unless one has participated in the operation or management of the enterprise itself."[136]

In endorsing an "operation or management" test, the Court stated that "[a]n enterprise is 'operated' not just by upper management but also by lower rung participants in the enterprise who are under the direction of upper management."[137] The Court noted that "[a]n enterprise also might be 'operated' or 'managed' by others 'associated with' the enterprise who exert control over it as, for example, by bribery."[138] But generally the decision limits when "outsiders" can be held liable under § 1962(c).

The Court in *Reves* did not resolve "how far § 1962(c) extends down the ladder of operations,"[139] as the facts presented by the case made it "clear that Arthur Young was not acting under the direction of the Co-ops's officers or board."[140] This can be seen as determining the vertical connection of how far down liability extends. There is also the horizontal question of who is considered part of the operation or management and who is an outsider. Courts have looked at both of these issues.

In *United States v. Oreto*[141] the First Circuit looked at whether company employees would be considered part of the "operation or management." The court stated:

> *Reves* is a case about the liability of *outsiders* who may assist the enterprise's affairs. Special care is required in translating *Reves'* concern with "horizontal" connections-focusing on the liability of an outside adviser-into the "vertical" question of how far RICO liability may extend within the enterprise but down the organizational ladder. In our view, the reason the accountants were not liable in *Reves* is that, while they were undeniably involved in the enterprise's decisions, they neither made those decisions nor carried them out; in other words, the

---

[135] See Bennett v. Berg, 710 F.2d 1361 (8th Cir. 1983) (holding an operation or management test applied); but see Bank of America National Trust & Savings Assn. v. Touche Ross & Co., 782 F.2d 966, 970 (11th Cir. 1986) (finding that it was not necessary for a defendant to participate in the operation or management of an enterprise.).

[136] 507 U.S. 179, 183 (1993).

[137] Id. at 1173.

[138] Id.

[139] Id. at 1173 n.9.

[140] Id. Justices Souter and White dissented, arguing that the Court was misapplying its own "operation or management" test. Id. at 195–96.

[141] 37 F.3d 739 (1st Cir. 1994).

accountants were outside the chain of command through which the enterprise's affairs were conducted.[142]

The court believed that the *Oreto* case presented a different circumstance than *Reves* in that the individuals were employees of the company involved in the collection process. The court stated "[w]e think Congress intended to reach all who participate in the conduct of that enterprise, whether they are generals or foot soldiers."[143]

Likewise, in *United States v. Shifman*,[144] the First Circuit held that individuals who were "plainly integral to carrying out" the enterprises activities could be liable under RICO. The Second Circuit, when considering this issue, found sufficient evidence when a defendant "carries out the decisions of the enterprise bosses and has 'broad discretion when doing so.'"[145] But the "simple taking of directions and performance of tasks that are 'necessary and helpful' to the enterprise, without more, is insufficient to bring a defendant within the scope of § 1962(c)."[146]

In contrast, in *United States v. Cummings*,[147] the Seventh Circuit examining a vertical question, refused to hold defendants liable under RICO finding that at most, the accused "'controlled' his accomplices." Despite a concession "that their scheme likely violated state bribery and official misconduct laws" as well as Illinois Department of Employment Security, the court found insufficient evidence that they met the *Reves* test of participating in the operation or management of the enterprise. Liability is not limited to those in positions of upper management,[148] but "mere participation in the activities of the enterprise is insufficient; the defendant must participate in the operation or management of the enterprise."[149]

The *Reves* case proves a significant benefit to outside accountants and lawyers who are not a direct part of the "management or control" of a company. In *Department of Economic Development v. Arthur Andersen, Co*,[150] a British government agency sued under RICO an automobile manufacturer's outside accounting firm. The district court dismissed the suit finding that *Reves* precluded this action. The court noted that "[m]any other courts faced with post-*Reves* § 1962(c) claims against outside professionals have agreed that providing important services to a racketeering enterprise is not the same as directing the affairs of the enterprise."[151] The court noted that "[a]n outsider who merely enjoys 'substantial persuasive power to induce management to take certain actions,' . . . unlike an outsider who bribes, does not exercise control over the enterprise within the meaning of *Reves*."[152]

---

[142] Id. at 750.

[143] Id. at 751.

[144] 124 F.3d 31 (1st Cir. 1997).

[145] See United States v. Hutchinson, 573 F.3d 1011 (10th Cir. 2009).

[146] United States v. Viola, 35 F.3d 37 (2d Cir. 1994).

[147] 395 F.3d 392 (7th Cir. 2005).

[148] See United States v. Shamah, 624 F.3d 449 (7th Cir. 2010).

[149] Goren v. New Vision Intern., Inc., 156 F.3d 721 (7th Cir. 1998).

[150] 924 F.Supp. 449 (S.D. N.Y. 1996).

[151] Id. at 466.

[152] Id. at 467 (citations omitted).

§ 8.6   RICO CONSPIRACY

RICO's prohibited conduct statute has a separate provision that allows for a RICO conspiracy. 18 U.S.C. § 1962(d) prohibits a conspiracy to commit the conduct stated in sections (a), (b), or (c). Unlike the generic conspiracy statute found in 18 U.S.C. § 371, it does not require an agreement to commit a specific offense or even an agreement to defraud. (See supra § 3.1(B)). The object of the conspiracy is the alleged prohibited acts of sections (a), (b), or (c), although in some cases the conspiracy will include more than one of these provisions.

In *United States v. Elliott*,[153] the Fifth Circuit held that "the object of a RICO conspiracy is to violate a substantive RICO provision . . . , to conduct or participate in the affairs of an enterprise through a pattern of racketeering activity and not merely to commit each of the predicate crimes necessary to demonstrate a pattern of racketeering activity."[154] The court noted that the "[t]he gravamen of the conspiracy charge in this case is not that each defendant agreed to commit arson, to steal goods from interstate commerce, to obstruct justice, and to sell narcotics; rather, it is that each agreed to participate, directly and indirectly, in the affairs of the enterprise by committing two or more predicate crimes." The court stated that "it is irrelevant that each defendant participated in the enterprise's affairs through different, even unrelated crimes, so long as we may reasonably infer that each crime was intended to further the enterprise's affairs."[155] In *United States v. Adams*,[156] the Third Circuit held that "a defendant must agree only to the commission of the predicate acts, and need not agree to commit personally those acts."

Unlike the general conspiracy statute found in 18 U.S.C. § 371, RICO conspiracies do not require an overt act. In *Salinas v. United States*[157] the Supreme Court held that the RICO statute was "even more comprehensive than the general conspiracy offense in § 371."[158]

§ 8.7   FORFEITURE

A. Overview

An important aspect of the crime of RICO is that it provides prosecutors with the ability to proceed against an individual's property in forfeiture. The government may proceed with either a civil or criminal forfeiture. Criminal forfeitures are called *in personam* and civil forfeitures are called *in rem*. It is required that prosecutors consult with the Department of Justice's Asset Forfeiture and Money Laundering Section if they plan to initiate "a forfeiture action against, or seeking the seizure of, or moving to retrain an ongoing business." This is out of concern that seizing an ongoing business could result in substantial losses.[159]

---

[153] 571 F.2d 880 (5th Cir. 1978).

[154] Id. at 902–03.

[155] Id.

[156] 759 F.2d 1099, 1116 (3d Cir. 1985).

[157] 522 U.S. 52 (1997).

[158] Id. at 477.

[159] USAM § 9–111.124.

The three different forfeitable properties are outlined in 18 U.S.C. § 1963(a) as follows:

1) any interest the person has acquired or maintained in violation of section 1962;

2) any

(A) interest in,

(B) security of

(C) claim against; or

(D) property or contractual right of any kind affording a source of influence over; any enterprise which the person has established, operated, controlled, conducted, or participated in the conduct of, in violation of section 1962; and

3) any property constituting, or derived from, any proceeds which the person obtained, directly or indirectly, from racketeering activity or the unlawful debt collection in violation of 1962.

Additionally, 18 U.S.C. § 1963(b) provides that both real property, including items affixed to real property, and "tangible and intangible personal property, including rights, privileges, interests, claims, and securities" are subject to criminal forfeiture under this section. Section 1963(d) provides the procedure for obtaining a restraining order or injunction, including temporary restraining orders. Hearings that are held concerning restraining orders and injunctions under this section are allowed to consider inadmissible evidence under the Federal Rules of Evidence.[160]

In *Russello v. United States*,[161] the Supreme Court considered whether "profits and income" were considered an "interest" for purposes of forfeiture. The Court examined insurance money received as a result of a fire loss. The Court noted that although the statute did not specifically define the term "interest," the ordinary meaning of the word encompassed profits or proceeds. The *Russello* Court found that Congress, wanted "to remove the profit from organized crime by separating the racketeer from. . . . dishonest gains." Thus, reading the statute as applying only to interests in an enterprise, would limit its effectiveness and place whole areas of organized criminal activity beyond the reach of the statute. Section 1963(a)(3) codified *Russello* in providing for the forfeiture of the "proceeds" of racketeering activity and the legislative history makes this clear.[162]

Courts have allowed for joint and several liability under RICO's forfeiture provisions. Thus, in *United States v. Caporale*,[163] the Eleventh Circuit held that the government was not required to trace racketeering proceeds to specific assets. All that is necessary is for the government to show the "amount of the proceeds and identify a

---

[160] 18 U.S.C. § 1963 (d)(3).

[161] 464 U.S. 16 (1983).

[162] S Rep. No. 980225, pp. 191–200 (1983).

[163] 806 F.2d 1487 (11th Cir. 1986).

finite group of people receiving the proceeds."[164] With joint and several liability, the government is limited to a set ceiling, but the government can collect up to that amount from each defendant.[165]

In *United States v. Angiulo*,[166] the First Circuit stated that "[b]ecause RICO forfeiture is an *in personam* action, rather than an *in rem* action, it has been held that the government's interest in the forfeitable property vests at the time of the unlawful activity and cannot be defeated by the defendants' subsequent transfer of the property." This is often referred to as the "relation-back" doctrine.

Issues can arise as to the rights of an innocent owner. In *United States v. Parcel of Land, Bldgs., Appurtenances and Improvements, Known as 92 Buena Vista Avenue, Rumson, New Jersey*,[167] the Supreme Court looked at the common-law relation back doctrine in the context of a drug statute, holding that "[t]he government cannot profit from [the] common-law doctrine of relation back until it has obtained a judgment of forfeiture."[168] But it has been noted that this Supreme Court case was premised on a drug statute and this has been distinguished from what is explicitly stated in the RICO statute.[169]

B.   Third Parties

Prosecutors seeking forfeiture are guided by government policy pertaining to issues of third parties, which can be found in the *Asset Forfeiture Policy of the Department of Justice*.[170] The controlling law is found in criminal RICO statute 18 U.S.C. § 1963(i), which provides the procedure for third-parties. It legislates the inability of parties claiming an interest in the property to "intervene in a trial or appeal of a criminal case" or "commence an action at law or equity against the United States concerning the validity of his alleged interest in the property subsequent to the filing of an indictment or information alleging that the property is subject to forfeiture under thus section." But section (l) of this statute does describe the rights of third parties to ultimately protect their property interests.

In *United States v. BCCI Holdings (Luxenbourg, S.A.)*,[171] the District of Columbia District Court looked at a RICO forfeiture under what is called an "L-claim" as it comes under 18 U.S.C. § 1963(l). The court had previously entered a forfeiture order requiring American Express Bank to transfer "over $119 million to the United States Marshals Service." The bank argued for a set off amount of $23,537,303, and after a hearing transferred the money to the United States Marshall. The court was now examining this alleged set off amount in which the bank was arguing that it was a bona fide purchaser for value and that its rights had vested under § 1963(l)(6)(A).

---

[164] Id. at 1508.

[165] See United States v. Masters, 924 F.2d 1362 (7th Cir. 1991).

[166] 897 F.2d 1169 (1st Cir. 1990)

[167] 507 U.S. 111 (1993).

[168] Id. at 129. Congress also passed the Civil Asset Forfeiture Reform Act which provided for an "innocent owner" defense.

[169] See United States v. BCCI Holdings (Luxenbourg), S.A., 961 F.Supp. 287 (D.D.C. 1997).

[170] Available at http://www.justice.gov/criminal/foia/docs/2008policy-manual.pdf.

[171] 961 F.Supp. 287 (D.D.C. 1997).

The court held that the bank had to first establish its standing, and that a state law right of set-off may offer standing. In this case, however, American Express exercised its state law right of set off after regulators shut the bank down and therefore could not prevail under subsection (l)(6)(A).

Equally unsuccessful for the bank was its bona fide purchaser claims under § 1963(l)(6)(B). The court stated that "[i]n this case, American Express Bank reasonably should have known that BCCI's assets were subject to forfeiture based on matters published in the public record. BCCI's troubles were widely reported in, *inter alia,* prominent New York newspapers in 1990 and 1991." The court further stated, "[g]iven the highly publicized nature of BCCI's troubles, the petitioner's claim that a sophisticated banking entity could reasonably be without cause to believe that BCCI's assets were subject to *forfeiture rings hollow.*"[172]

An issue can arise when a prosecutor decides to proceed against an attorney to forfeit his or her legal fee obtained from a client as a result of representation that resulted in a RICO conviction. The First Circuit confronted this issue in *United States v. Saccoccia.*[173] The court allowed post-conviction fees to be forfeited, but remanded the case regarding other fees received by these attorneys. The court stated, "[f]orfeiture is an *in personam* criminal remedy, targeted primarily at the defendant who committed the criminal offense." The court noted that "the implicit limitation in § 1963(m) does not trammel the basic statutory policy by foreclosing all other remedies available to the government, nor does it enable culpable attorneys to dissipate tainted fees with impunity." The court left open that the government could "reach other non-tainted cash of the attorneys by sustaining the somewhat weightier, though not insurmountable, burden of establishing the elements of either contempt or conversion."

C.   Constitutional Challenges

In personam forfeitures are subject to Eighth Amendment challenges under the Excessive Fines Clause. In *Alexander v. United States,*[174] the Supreme Court considered a case involving an owner of sexually explicit materials who was convicted of obscenity and RICO. As part of the penalty, the court ordered forfeiture of nine million dollars and his "wholesale and retail businesses" including all assets of these businesses. The Supreme Court found no First Amendment violation, but did remand the case to the appellate tribunal because they had failed to consider whether the forfeiture was "grossly disproportionate or excessive."

The Supreme Court used a similar analysis in a non-RICO case, *United States v. Bajakajian,*[175] holding that forfeiture "of the entire $357,144 that respondent failed to declare" on a customs currency reporting form to "be grossly disproportional to the gravity of his offense" and therefore violating the Excessive Fines Clauses of the Constitution. Congress, however, came back in the "Uniting and Strengthening America by Providing Appropriate Tools Required to Intercept and Obstruct Terrorism

---

[172] Id. at 300.

[173] 354 F.3d 9 (1st Cir. 2003).

[174] 509 U.S. 544 (1993).

[175] 524 U.S. 321 (1998).

Act of 2001" (USA Patriot Act), creating a bulk cash smuggling offense with new penalties for the undeclared movement of more than $10,000 across U.S. borders.

§ 8.8   CIVIL RICO

18 U.S.C. § 1964 provides for civil RICO which can be brought by both the government and private litigants. The remedy is damages for civil and government litigants, but the government also has the right to obtain equitable relief. Civil RICO allows for threefold damages.

Most civil RICO actions do not require that the defendants be convicted of the predicate acts used to form the basis of the pattern of racketeering.[176] The right to sue for treble damages under RICO, however, does require a showing of injury to the plaintiff. In *Holmes v. Securities Investor Protection Corporation*,[177] the Supreme Court examined when a plaintiff may use RICO's § 1964(c), holding that it is required that "the alleged RICO violation was the proximate cause of the plaintiff's injury." The Court held that a plaintiff needed to show that a predicate offense "not only was a 'but for' cause of injury, but was the proximate cause as well."[178]

In *Anza v. Ideal Steel Supply Corp.*,[179] the Court examined whether this applied when the dispute involved two competing businesses. The Court held that it was required that the alleged violation led to the plaintiff's injuries, thus imposing that it be the proximate cause of the injury. The Court in *Anza* found the fraud alleged and the injury suffered to be "attenuated."

In *Hemi Group LLC v. City of New York, New York*,[180] the Supreme Court examined a civil RICO action brought against a New Mexico company that was selling cigarettes online to City of New York residents without anyone paying cigarette taxes. The Court rejected the City's use of RICO here, holding that the City cannot state a claim under RICO because it "cannot show that it lost the tax revenue 'by reason of' the alleged RICO violation."[181] Chief Justice Roberts, writing for the majority, noted that this case pertained to "RICO liability of a company for lost taxes it had no obligation to collect, remit, or pay, which harmed a party to whom it owed no duty."[182]

In *Beck v. Prupis*,[183] the Supreme Court examined the question of "whether a person injured by an overt act done in furtherance of a RICO conspiracy has a cause of action under § 1964(c), even if the overt act is not an act of racketeering." The Court held that "such a person does not have a cause of action under § 1964(c)."[184] In this case, the plaintiff attempted to use a termination of employment, as an overt act in furtherance of the conspiracy as the basis for the cause of action. This act, however, was not a RICO predicate act.

---

[176] Sedima, S.P.R.L. v. Imrex Co., Inc., 473 U.S. 479 (1985).
[177] 503 U.S. 258 (1992).
[178] Id. at 268.
[179] 547 U.S. 451 (2006).
[180] 559 U.S. 1 (2010).
[181] Id. at 986.
[182] Id. at 994.
[183] 529 U.S. 494 (2000).
[184] Id. 495–96.

Congress amended § 1964(c) so that a civil RICO action could not be premised upon "conduct that would have been actionable as fraud in the purchase or sale of securities" unless the individual was criminally convicted in connection with the fraud. The Supreme Court recently held that a plaintiff in a civil RICO case predicated on mail fraud does not have to "plead and prove" that he or she "relied on the defendant's alleged misrepresentations."[185]

---

[185] Bridge v. Phoenix Bond & Indem. Co., 553 U.S. 639 (2008).

Chapter 9

FALSE STATEMENTS

§ 9.1   INTRODUCTION

A. Overview

False statement statutes are commonly used to prosecute white collar criminality. One finds prosecutors turning to these charges to combat government procurement fraud. The false statement statutes also offer "short-cut" crimes for prosecutors to easily use when the white collar matter is complicated and difficult for a jury to understand. Because false statements do not require a statement under oath, can be premised upon conduct during a criminal investigation, and allow for a mere exculpatory "no" to suffice, prosecutors find these statutes attractive for prosecuting complex white collar matters.

But the false statement statutes have also been criticized as the statements used in the prosecution often occur in an informal noncustodial setting where the individual may be unaware that a false statement could "lead to a felony conviction."[1] These statutes can also be used by prosecutors who might have a weak case or a case with a statute of limitations that has run or is about to preclude proceeding with the prosecution.[2] As noted by Justice Ginsburg in her concurring opinion in *Brogan v. United States*,[3] "[t]he prospect remains that an overzealous prosecutor or investigator-aware that a person has committed some suspicious acts, but unable to make a criminal case-will create a crime by surprising the suspect, asking about those acts, and receiving a false denial."

B. Statutes

There are many false statement statutes that exist within the federal code. The most pervasively used federal false statement statute is located at 18 U.S.C. § 1001. This generic statute has been used in both white collar and non-white collar prosecutions. This statute is extensively discussed in the remaining sections of this chapter, including an overview of its history (see § 9.1(C)) and elements (see § 9.1(D)), followed by examination of each specific element and the cases interpreting this statute (see §§ 9.2–9.7).

But it is important to note that there are also many other specific false statement statutes in the federal criminal code. Some of these statutes are located in Chapter 47 of Title 18, which covers Fraud and False Statements. Others are located in different parts of Title 18, which houses the federal criminal code. Finally there are false

---

[1] Brogan v. United States, 522 U.S. 398, 410–11 (1998) (Justice Ginsburg, concurring).

[2] Id. at 411–12.

[3] Id. at 416.

statement statutes found outside Title 18, as they are associated with false statements in non-criminal areas of the law.

Chapter 47, Title 18 provides statutes that focus on fraudulent acts, and it includes acts related to false statements. For example, 18 U.S.C. § 1011 pertains to false statements relating to the sale of any mortgage to a bank, 18 U.S.C. § 1014 concerns false statements to obtain a federally backed loan, 18 U.S.C. § 1015 criminalizes false statements regarding naturalization, citizenship, or registry of aliens, 18 U.S.C. § 1020 concerns making a false statement with regard to work performed on a highway project, 18 U.S.C. § 1026 criminalizes false statements made in relation to farm indebtedness, and 18 U.S.C. § 1027 relates to false statements on Security Act of 1974 documents that are part of employee welfare and pension benefit plans. One of the more recent false statement statutes in chapter 47 of Title 18 comes from the Emergency and Disaster Assistance Fraud Penalty Enhancement Act of 2007[4] and concerns false statements made in connection with a major disaster or providing emergency benefits. This statute came in the wake of Hurricanes Katrina, Rita and Wilma and sought to criminalize fraud and false statements made by those who improperly obtained government relief or misused the government funds provided to them.

There are also false statement statutes located in other parts of Title 18 of the federal criminal code. For example, 18 U.S.C. § 495 criminalizes false statements in certain contracts, deeds, and powers of attorney that defraud the United States and 18 U.S.C. § 954 concerns false statements made to influence a foreign government. In some instances a fraud statute may provide that giving a false statement is one possible way to commit the criminal conduct. For example, 18 U.S.C. § 1546 includes false statements made as part of a fraud or misuse of visas, permits and other documents under the Immigration and Naturalization Service.

False statement statutes can also be found beyond the federal criminal code. For example, 15 U.S.C. § 645 prohibits false statements made with regard to aid to small businesses, 21 U.S.C. § 331 includes a provision for false statements made with federal food, drug and cosmetic act violations,[5] and the tax code includes a commonly used false statement statute located at 26 U.S.C. § 7206 and relates to false statements on tax returns. (See Chapter 11).

In addition to false statements, prosecutors also use the False Claims Statute, 18 U.S.C. § 287, for prosecuting fraudulent claims made to the federal government. These actions are brought through this criminal statute (see § 9.8), or as a civil action under 31 U.S.C. §§ 3729 et seq.

C. History

The false statement statute emanates from an 1863 Act that made it a criminal offense for a person in the United States armed forces to make a fraudulent claim

---

[4] P.L. 110–179 (2007).

[5] 21 U.S.C. § 331(w).

against the government.[6] It "was drafted in 'the wake of a spate of frauds' on the government."[7] Although it was limited to military personnel, it was an extremely broad statute in that it "cover[ed] the presentation of false claims against any component of the Government to any officer of the Government."[8] In later years the statute was expanded to encompass "every person" and not just those in the military. In *United States v. Gilliland*,[9] the Supreme Court noted that the congressional purpose of the statute was "to protect the authorized functions of governmental departments and agencies from the perversion which might result from" deceptive practices.

There has been some confusion related to the history of the false statement statute. This is reflected in Supreme Court opinions that offer differing interpretations of parts of the statute's history. In one recent Supreme Court case, *Hubbard v. United States*,[10] the Court went so far as to say that the Court's prior decision in *United States v. Bramblett*[11] was based upon "historical misapprehensions." In the end, Congress modified the statute to resolve this difference.

Several amendments to the statute have generated discussion. One amendment that courts have examined is a 1918 amendment to the initial statute. It was considered as keeping the focus of the statute on "financial frauds against the Government." But this amendment also met a growing problem of that time, namely, "false statements made to defraud Government corporations, which flourished during World War I."[12]

A 1934 statutory revision modified the language to include fraudulent claims "in any matter within the jurisdiction of any department or agency of the United States." It "was passed at the behest of 'the Secretary of the Interior to aid the enforcement of laws relating to the functions of the Department of the Interior and, in particular, to the enforcement of relations . . . with respect to the transportation of 'hot oil.'"[13]

In 1948 the legislature divided the statute designating 18 U.S.C. § 287 as the false claims statute (See § 9.8) and 18 U.S.C. § 1001 as the prohibition against the making of false statements. The False Statements Accountability Act of 1996, amended the statute to include "any matter within the jurisdiction of the executive, legislative, or judicial branch" of the United States government.[14]

---

[6] Act of March 2, 1863, ch. 67, 12 Stat. 696; Pub. L. 103–322, Title XXXIII, § 330016(1)(L) (1994); see also Stuart P. Green, Lying, Misleading, and Falsely Denying: How Moral Concepts Inform the Law of Perjury, Fraud, and False Statements, 53 Hastings L.J. 157 (2001).

[7] United States v. Lewis, 587 F.2d 854 (6th Cir. 1978).

[8] United States v. Bramblett, 348 U.S. 503 (1955).

[9] 312 U.S. 86 (1941).

[10] 514 U.S. 695, 707–08 (1995).

[11] 348 U.S. 503 (1955).

[12] Hubbard, 514 U.S. at 706.

[13] United States v. Gilliland, 312 U.S. 86, 93–94 (1941); see also Bramblett, 348 U.S. at 507.

[14] Pub. L. 104–292 § 2 (1996).

D. Elements

1. Specific Provisions

Section 1001 is divisible into three types of conduct. It can apply to one who "[1] falsifies, conceals or covers up by any trick, scheme or device a material fact, [2] makes any materially false, fictitious, or fraudulent statement or representation, or [3] makes or uses any false writing or document knowing the same to contain any materially false, fictitious, or fraudulent statement or entry." "[W]hoever, in any matter within the jurisdiction of the executive, legislative, or judicial branch of the Government of the United States, knowingly and willfully" does one of these acts, commits this crime.

False statements therefore requires proof of the following elements: (1) a statement, (2) falsity, (3) materiality, (4) made knowingly and willfully, (5) within the executive, legislative, or judicial branch of the United States government. The second element can be achieved not only through falsity, but also by concealment or a cover-up. The statute carries a penalty of five years, but allows for an increase to eight years in circumstances such as domestic and international terrorism or for failing to register as a sex offender.

2. Statutory Restrictions

The statute contains two restrictions. It "does not apply to a party to a judicial proceeding, or that party's counsel, for statements, representations, writings or documents submitted by such party or counsel to a judge or magistrate in that proceeding."[15] Also, with respect to legislative branch matters it only applies to:

1) administrative matters, including a claim for payment, a matter related to the procurement of property or services, personnel or employment practices, or support services, or a document required by law, rule, or regulation to be submitted to the Congress or any office or officer within the legislative branch; or (2) any investigation or review, conducted pursuant to the authority of any committee, subcommittee, commission or office of the Congress, consistent with applicable rules of the House or Senate.

There is no statutory right to avoid a conviction by correcting a previously made false statement. Unlike the false declarations statute,[16] the false statements statute fails to include a recantation defense.[17] A court, however, may allow relief when a false statement is "immediately corrected."[18] But this is because the materiality of the false statement may be questionable when the statement is quickly modified.[19] (See § 9.5).

---

[15] 18 U.S.C. § 1001(b).

[16] 18 U.S.C. § 1623; see also § 10.6.

[17] See, e.g., United States v. Sebaggala, 256 F.3d 59, 64 (1st Cir. 2001); United States v. Beaver, 515 F.3d 730 (7th Cir. 2008).

[18] See United States v. Cowden, 677 F.2d 417, 419 (8th Cir. 1982).

[19] See United States v. Kim, 808 F. Supp.2d 44 (D. D.C. 2011).

3. Venue

Prosecutions under a false statement statute are usually brought in the location where the statement was made. Thus, when the statement was made in an interview "began, continued, and ended" in Minnesota, it was held improper to bring the false statement case in Oklahoma.[20] When a statement was made telephonically, and the individual defendant and agent were in two different venues, a court allowed the prosecution to proceed where the agent filed the statement even though the maker of the statement was in a different city.[21] A court also found it proper to bring a false statement charge in the location where there was a material effect of the false statement.[22]

Venue may also be limited by agency regulations. For example, in *Travis v. United States*,[23] the Supreme Court examined a venue question that concerned a § 1001 matter in the context of filings related to Section 9(h) of the National Labor Relations Act (NLRA). The Court found that venue was improper in the place where the affidavits were mailed as it would not be a "matter within the jurisdiction" unless the affidavits were actually on file with the National Labor Relations Board. The explicit language in the NLRA provided jurisdiction only when an item was "on file with the Board."

E. Constitutionality

There have been several constitutional arguments raised with respect to 18 U.S.C. § 1001, the generic false statement statute. Defendants have unsuccessfully claimed violations of the U.S. Constitution's First Amendment, Due Process Clause, Double Jeopardy Clause[24] and the Eighth Amendment's Cruel and Unusual Punishment clause.[25] There have also been unsuccessful challenges arguing that the statute is void for vagueness.[26] Courts have found that using unsworn statements as the basis for the crime does not make the statute overly broad.[27]

The U.S. Constitution's First Amendment protects speech, but it does not protect false speech provided to the government. In *United States v. Alvarez*,[28] the Supreme Court looked at whether the Stolen Valor Act,[29] a statute that prohibited false claims of receiving military decorations or medals, violated the First Amendment. The defendant was accused under this statute of falsely claiming that he won the Congressional Medal of Honor. He pleaded guilty to the charge but reserved the right to challenge his

---

[20] United States v. Smith, 641 F.3d 1200 (10th Cir. 2011).

[21] United States v. Stephenson, 895 F.2d 867 (2d Cir. 1990).

[22] United States v. Oceanpro Indust., Ltd., 674 F.3d 323 (4th Cir. 2012).

[23] 364 U.S. 631 (1961).

[24] See Hudson v. United States, 522 U.S. 93 (1997) (finding no double jeopardy violation for imposition of both civil and criminal punishments with the criminal matter proceeding under false bank entry statute).

[25] See, e.g., Alire v. United States, 313 F.2d 31 (10th Cir. 1962) ("punishment provided is not inhuman, barbarous, nor torturous punishment).

[26] See, e.g., United States v. Matanky, 482 F.2d 1319 (9th Cir. 1973).

[27] See, e.g., United States v. Gilliland, 312 U.S. 86 (1941); United States v. Des Jardins, 772 F.2d 578 (9th Cir. 1985) (statute of making false statements to a customs officer was not overly broad).

[28] 132 S.Ct. 2537 (2012).

[29] 18 U.S.C. § 704.

conviction as invalid under the First Amendment. The Supreme Court supported his position.

In analyzing the Stolen Valor Act as a violation of the First Amendment, the Court distinguished this statute from the false statement statute in 18 U.S.C. § 1001. The false statement statute prohibited statements "made to Government officials, in communications concerning official matters." The Court stated that this "does not lead to the broader proposition that false statements are unprotected when made to any person, at any time, in any context."[30] Although the Court held the Stolen Valor Act unconstitutional, it noted that "[w]here false claims are made to effect a fraud or secure moneys or other valuable considerations, say offers of employment, it is well established that the government may restrict speech without affronting the First Amendment."

The United States Supreme Court in *United States v. Woodward*[31] also found no violation of the Constitution's prohibition against Double Jeopardy when the government charged both a violation of the false statements statute in § 1001 and a currency reporting statute.[32] The Court allowed the defendant to receive consecutive sentences for these two crimes even when the conduct used in the prosecution was the same. The Court found that since congressional intent demonstrated that the statutes were "directed to separate evils" there was no violation of the Constitution's Double Jeopardy Clause. (See § 9.7).

§ 9.2 STATEMENTS

A. Generally

A wide range of statements have been used in false statement prosecutions. The statements can be written or oral, sworn or unsworn. For example, a false name on a Postal Service delivery form has been found to be sufficient for a § 1001 violation.[33] So too, a false incident report by a Federal Protective Service law enforcement officer was considered a false statement sufficient for a violation of § 1001.[34]

False statements that relate to past, present or future activity are also considered covered by the statute. The statement may be either voluntary or made pursuant to a requirement of law. For example, statements made as part of a proffer with the FBI have been found to be false statements under § 1001.[35] In many instances the determination of whether the statement is allowed is premised on whether it is one made within the appropriate jurisdictional confines of the statute. (See § 9.6)

---

[30] 132 S.Ct. at 2546.

[31] 469 U.S. 105 (1985).

[32] 31 U.S.C. § 1101(a).

[33] United States v. Moore, 612 F.3d 698 (D.C. Cir. 2010).

[34] United States v. House, 684 F.3d 1173 (11th Cir. 2012).

[35] United States v. Kozeny, 667 F.3d 122 (2d Cir. 2011).

B. Exculpatory "No"

For many years courts allowed as a defense to a false statement charge instances involving an "exculpatory no," or a mere 'no" response made to a question asked by a federal officer. In *Brogan v. United States*[36] the Supreme Court put a halt to this exception. The Court examined a case involving federal agents from the Department of Labor and Internal Revenue Service who visited the defendant at his home and asked him if he ever received cash or gifts from a certain management corporation. He responded negatively to the question propounded to him by the agents. The agents advised the defendant that "lying to federal agents in the course of an investigation was a crime." Brogan was later indicted for this "no" statement to the agents, a statement that proved to be untruthful. The case eventually made its way to the Supreme Court, where the Court examined whether this exculpatory "no" could serve as the basis for a § 1001 violation.

In *Brogan* the Court, in an opinion authored by Justice Scalia, stated that "we find nothing to support the "exculpatory no" doctrine except the many Court of Appeals decisions that have embraced it." Looking at the plain language of the statute, the Court was unwilling to provide this exception that was nowhere in the text of the statute. Justice Scalia stated "[w]hether or not the predicament of the wrongdoer run to ground tugs at the heartstrings, neither the text nor the spirit of the Fifth Amendment confers a privilege to lie." He noted that a witness has the right to remain silent and not incriminate him or herself, "but there not to swear falsely."[37]

Although the Supreme Court allowed the false statement statute to be used for prosecutions premised on an exculpatory no, the Department of Justice recommends against such prosecutions. In the U.S. Attorneys' Manual it states:

> It is the Department's policy not to charge a Section 1001 violation in situations in which a suspect, during an investigation, merely denies guilt in response to questioning by the government. This policy is to be narrowly construed, however; affirmative, discursive and voluntary statements to Federal criminal investigators would not fall within the policy. Further, certain false responses to questions propounded for administrative purposes (e.g., statements to border or United States Immigration and Naturalization Service agents during routine inquiries) are also prosecutable, as are untruthful "no's" when the defendant initiated contact with the government in order to obtain a benefit.[38]

C. Judicial Function Exception

The false statement statute explicitly states that it "does not apply to a party to a judicial proceeding, or that party's counsel, for statements, representations, writings or documents submitted by such party or counsel to a judge or magistrate in that proceeding."[39] This exception is important since it covers defendants who typically

---

[36] 522 U.S. 398 (1998).

[37] Id. at 404.

[38] USAM § 9–42.160.

[39] 18 U.S.C. § 1001(b).

plead not guilty in open court, when they may eventually enter a plea of guilty. Likewise, attorneys may present arguments in court that test whether the prosecution has proved its case beyond a reasonable doubt. Thus, the exception precludes criminalizing conduct "well within the bounds of responsible advocacy."[40] This exclusion has also been considered warranted as there are many statutes that criminalize false statements made to the judicial branch, such as perjury,[41] false declarations,[42] and obstruction of justice.[43]

This exemption came on the heels of the Supreme Court's ruling in *Hubbard v. United States*,[44] where the Court found that the judicial branch would not be considered a "department" for purposes of § 1001. The Court's opinion in *Hubbard* went beyond its prior decision in *United States v. Bramblett*,[45] where the court held that "department" included all three branches of the government.

In response to the restrictive interpretation provided by the *Hubbard* Court, Congress passed the False Statements Accountability Act of 1996.[46] This Act explicitly allowed for a false statement prosecution for statements made within all three branches of the government.

But concerns were also expressed for conduct that was part of the judicial function. To alleviate these concerns, a judicial function exemption was carved out in the statute. In the legislative history of the False Statement Accountability Act, one finds language that distinguishes between judicial functions and administrative court functions, the latter not being exempted under the statute.[47]

Several courts have considered the breadth of the judicial function exception, and the results have not been consistent. In *United States v. Horvath*,[48] the Ninth Circuit held that a false statement made to a probation officer during a presentence interview was covered by the judicial exemption and could not be the subject of a § 1001 prosecution. In *Horvath*, the defendant stated to the probation officer preparing the presentence report (PSR) that he had served in the United States Marines, when in fact he did not have this military record. The court found that the probation officer had not exercised any discretion in including the false statement in his report. The court stated that a defendant does not lose the protection of the § 1001(b) exemption "simply because he or she hired a courier to take a written statement to the judge." A dissent, however, noted that "if the defendant submits to an interview, and makes a statement,

---

[40] See Julie R. O'Sullivan, The Federal Criminal "Code" Is a Disgrace: Obstruction Statutes as Case Study, 96 J. Crim. L. & Criminology 643, 709 (2006).

[41] 18 U.S.C. § 1621; see also Chap. 10.

[42] 18 U.S.C. § 1623; see also Chap. 10.

[43] 18 U.S.C. § 1501; see also Chap. 6.

[44] 514 U.S. 695 (1995).

[45] 348 U.S. 503 (1955).

[46] Pub. L. No. 104–292.

[47] H. Rep. 104–680, 104th Cong., 2nd Sess. 1996, 1996 U.S.C.C.A.N. 3935, 3937–38.

[48] 492 F.3d 1075 (9th Cir. 2007).

he makes the statement to a probation officer; if he lies, he lies *to* the *probation officer*, not 'to the judge.'"[49]

In the case of *United States v. Manning*,[50] the Tenth Circuit Court of Appeals sided with the dissent from *Horvath*. In *Manning*, the defendant was accused of failing to apprise his probation officer of a 401(k) account that he owned. His omission led to the probation officer leaving this account off of his presentence report (PSR). The question on appeal was whether this false statement to a probation officer met the language of this exception. The court in *Manning* was clear that statements made to the judge, and agents of the judge would be covered by this exception. In this regard, the agents of the judge discussed in the decision were the judge's secretary, law clerk, and "deputy clerk or bailiff." The court noted that "[a]lthough the probation officer acts as the court's agent, it seems the role is certainly more substantive than that of a message bearer; indeed, probation officers can exercise some discretion on their own."[51] In the end, the Tenth Circuit held that prosecutors were not precluded by the statutory exception in § 1001(b) and could prosecute the defendant for the false statement made to the probation officer.

The Sixth Circuit in *United States v. Vreeland*[52] avoided the differing positions taken in *Horvath* and *Manning*, finding that a false statement made to a probation officer "overseeing a defendant's compliance with the terms of supervised release," different from a probation officer preparing a PSR. Lying to a probation officer in this situation is not comparable to making a false statement to a judge. The court held that a false statement to a probation officer during a supervisory meeting does not afford a defendant the protection provided by § 1001(b).

D. Legislative Function Exception

In addition to the exception afforded by a judicial function, § 1001 also provides the legislative functions that can be the subject of a prosecution. The legislative function exception allows prosecutors to reach false statements made on administrative forms such as financial disclosure forms under the Ethics in Government Act. The statute provides that with respect to matters within the jurisdiction of the legislative branch, the statute applies only to:

(1) administrative matters, including a claim for payment, a matter related to the procurement of property or services, personnel or employment practices, or support services, or a document required by law, rule, or regulation to be submitted to the Congress or any office or officer within the legislative branch; or

(2) any investigation or review, conducted pursuant to the authority of any committee, subcommittee, commission or office of the Congress, consistent with applicable rules of the House or Senate.[53]

---

[49] Id. at 1082.

[50] 526 F.3d 611 (10th Cir. 2008).

[51] Id. at 618–19.

[52] 684 F.3d 653 (6th Cir. 2012).

[53] 18 U.S.C. § 1001(c).

In *United States v. Pickett*,[54] the defendant was accused of making a false statement to the United States Capitol Police by allegedly writing a note and leaving it at the security station regarding a white powder that he knew was not anthrax, claiming it to be a training exercise. The District of Columbia Circuit Court reversed the conviction and dismissed the case brought under § 1001 as the government failed to include in the indictment the language of the statute that explicitly controls false statements with the legislature.

On appeal, the government argued that it met the investigation requirement of the statute because there was an investigation of the false statement. The court rejected this claim noting that "[n]ot only was the investigation of the false statement not in existence so that the statement could have been made in it," but also that the government failed to show "evidence supporting the proposition that such investigation was pursuant to the authorities set out in subsection (c)(2)."

§ 9.3 FALSITY

A. False Statement

18 U.S.C. § 1001 requires a false statement. Falsity can be met by either the making of a false statement or concealing or covering up by any trick, scheme or device a material fact. Actual falsity is required and literally true statements cannot serve as the basis for a § 1001 violation. Courts often reference *Bronston v. United States*,[55] a case involving a perjury statute, which held that statements that are literally true cannot be the basis of a perjury prosecution.[56] Ambiguous statements can also prove problematic for the government in achieving a false statement conviction.[57] Here again, courts reference cases discussing this issue in perjury cases.[58] Falsity does require "an intent to deceive or mislead."[59]

Issues of whether the statement is literally true or ambiguous, in the context of the false statement statute, often arise with respect to statements made on government forms. In *United States v. Hixon*,[60] the Sixth Circuit examined what constituted falsity. The defendant was charged with violating § 1001 for stating that he was not self-employed and for allegedly concealing his self-employment in statements made on forms for workers' compensation. The court reversed his conviction finding that as a matter of fact he was not self-employed in that he served as the president of a corporation and that literally true statements could not form the basis of a § 1001 violation. The court found that statements that are subject to more than one interpretation places the burden on the government to prove that the defendant's interpretation was in fact false.

---

[54] 353 F.3d 62 (D.C. Cir. 2004).

[55] 409 U.S. 352 (1973).

[56] Although *Bronston* involved the perjury statute, 18 U.S.C. § 1623, courts have used this line of cases in interpreting falsity for purposes of § 1001. (See § 10.4).

[57] See, e.g., United States v. Rendon–Marquez, 79 F. Supp.2d 1361 (N.D. Ga. 1999).

[58] See, e.g., United States v. Camper, 384 F.3d 1073 (9th Cir. 2004).

[59] See United States v. Boffil–Rivera, 607 F.3d 736 (11th Cir. 2010).

[60] 987 F.2d 1261 (6th Cir. 1993).

In some cases, a defendant will challenge a statement as "fundamentally ambiguous" and therefore an improper basis for a § 1001 violation. In *United States v. Sarwari*,[61] an individual was charged with false statements on three passport applications that he made on behalf of his stepsons. He was accused of listing himself as their father when he was not their birth father and had not adopted any of these children. Charged with a violation of 18 U.S.C. § 1542, the Fourth Circuit held that "[w]hen a question is not 'fundamentally ambiguous' but merely susceptible to multiple interpretations, and a defendant's answer is true under one understanding of the question but false under another, the fact finder determines whether the defendant knew his statement was false." The court found that "in the context of an application for a United States passport" "the word 'father'" was not "fundamentally ambiguous."[62]

B. Concealment

Concealment of a fact can also serve as the basis for a false statement crime. Concealment, however, requires that there be a legal duty to disclose the information. In *United States v. Safavian*,[63] the defendant was charged with the crime of false statements and also a violation of an obstruction of justice statute. The case arose from an investigation into a golfing trip that he took along with lobbyist Jack Abramoff while he was serving as the chief of staff of the General Services Administration (GSA). Safavain had sought ethics advice from the GSA's general counsel "about whether he could accept the air transportation as a gift." Claims were later made that Safavain had concealed certain information regarding Abramoff and his assistance to him in official GSA-related activities. The D.C. Circuit Court of Appeals reversed his convictions finding that concealment cases require a "duty to disclose material facts on the basis of specific requirements for disclosure of specific information." The court noted that "[t]he ethical principles give no indication of the particular facts or information an executive employee must disclose." The convictions premised on concealment, therefore, could not stand when there was no legal duty to disclose this information.

This case can be contrasted with *United States v. Sanford, Ltd.*[64] where the defendant was charged under the false statement statute for allegedly concealing information by failing to record accurate information in an Oil Record Book (ORB), and having a legal duty to do this under specific Coast Guard regulations. As a legal duty existed, concealment could be the basis for a false statement charge. Concealment has also been found to exist when the defendant does an affirmative act such as filing false tax returns.[65]

---

[61] 669 F.3d 401 (4th Cir. 2012).

[62] Id. at 408–09.

[63] 528 F.3d 957 (D.C. Cir. 2008).

[64] 859 F. Supp.2d 102 (D.D.C. 2012).

[65] See United States v. Mubayyid, 658 F.3d 35 (1st Cir. 2011).

§ 9.4   KNOWLEDGE AND INTENT

A. Generally

The crime of false statements under § 1001 requires that the accused acts "knowingly and willfully." This entails proof of the defendant's knowledge of the falsity of the statement, or that the defendant's actions were taken for the purpose of concealing or covering up a material fact. In some cases knowledge is demonstrated by a showing of willful blindness on the part of the accused. There, however, is no need to demonstrate the defendant's knowledge of the federal agency jurisdiction.

The government also needs to prove that the defendant acted with willfulness. The willfulness element of this statute has not been interpreted consistently by the circuits.

B. Knowledge

The government has the burden to prove that the defendant had knowledge that the statement was false or with a conscious purpose of avoiding the truth.[66] "Skimpy" evidence that the defendant knew the information being filed was materially incorrect will not suffice.[67] Making a false statement requires actual knowledge, where concealment requires that "a defendant had a legal duty to disclose the facts at the time he was alleged to have concealed them."[68] When charged with aiding and abetting a principle, the defendant needs to have done an act to aid in the venture. It is insufficient when the appellant lacks the specific intent to violate § 1001.[69]

The level of knowledge required of the defendant can be met by evidence of a reckless disregard of the truth[70] or by a conscious avoidance in learning the truth, often referred to as willful blindness. Actual knowledge of the statement's falsity is not required when willful blindness is asserted. This is to assure that an individual who deliberately avoids reading the form they are signing does not escape criminal liability. In *United States v. Puente,*[71] the defendant claimed that he had never read the HUD form he signed. The court found that this constituted "a reckless disregard of the truth and with the purpose to avoid learning the truth." The court was unwilling to find a lack of knowledge here as "any other holding would write § 1001 completely out of existence." In meeting the knowledge requirement, the government may employ circumstantial evidence.

Recently, the Supreme Court held in *Global–Tech Appliances, Inc. v. SEB S.A.,*[72] a civil patent infringement case, that mere recklessness or negligence would not suffice for willful blindness. To properly show willful blindness it is necessary to show that "[f]irst, the defendant must subjectively believe that there is a high probability that a fact exists. Second, the defendant must take deliberate actions to avoid learning of that

---

[66] United States v. Dick, 744 F.2d 546 (7th Cir. 1984).

[67] United States v. Newell, 658 F.3d 1, 16 (2011).

[68] United States v. Curran, 20 F.3d 560 (3d Cir. 1994).

[69] United States v. Aarons, 718 F.2d 188 (6th Cir. 1983).

[70] See United States v. Salama, 891 F.Supp.2d 1132 (E.D. Cal. 2012).

[71] United States v. Puente, 982 F.2d 156 (5th Cir. 1993).

[72] 131 S.Ct. 2060, 2068–69 (2011).

fact." The Court in the *Global Tech* opinion stated that "a willfully blind defendant is one who takes deliberate actions to avoid confirming a high probability of wrongdoing and who can almost be said to have actually known the critical facts." (See § 1.8(C)(2)).

C. Willfulness

In addition to knowledge, § 1001 also requires willfulness. Willfulness does not mandate proof of an intent to defraud. The false statement statute contains language in the disjunctive: "false, fictitious *or* fraudulent."[73] Thus, willfulness is met with proof that a defendant intended to deceive. But when the government's indictment specifically characterizes the defendant's conduct as fraudulent, as opposed to being false or fictitious, the government could be required to prove this allegation.

When proceeding under the concealment provision of the false statement statute, it is also necessary for the government to present sufficient proof of intent to deceive. Additionally, when the indictment is premised upon concealment, it is necessary for the government to substantiate that the defendant knew of the duty to disclose and intentionally failed to comply with that duty.

Jurisdictions differ on whether the defendant needs to have knowledge of unlawfulness in order to meet the willfulness requirement of the statute. Some courts hold that § 1001 does not require knowledge of the unlawfulness.[74] In contrast, the Third Circuit in *United States v. Starnes*[75] interpreted willfully to require "knowledge of the general unlawfulness of the conduct at issue."[76] The court stated that "when 'willfully' is used in a criminal statute, and particularly where the term is used in conjunction with 'knowingly,' as it is in § 1001(a), it usually requires the government to prove that the defendant acted 'not merely "voluntarily," but with a "bad purpose,"' that is, with knowledge that his conduct was, in some general sense, 'unlawful.'" Although the court set a higher standard in *Starnes* than required by some other jurisdictions, it affirmed the § 1001 conviction for "knowingly and willfully transmitting twelve falsified air-monitoring reports to VIHA [Virgin Islands Housing Authority]," finding that there was sufficient evidence that the defendant "was aware that transmitting falsified air-monitoring reports to VIHA was unlawful."[77]

D. Knowledge of Federal Agency Jurisdiction

Although knowledge and willfulness are required for a violation of § 1001, there is no necessity to show that the defendant had actual knowledge of federal agency jurisdiction. In *United States v. Yermian*,[78] the Supreme Court resolved a then existing jurisdictional dichotomy on whether it was necessary for the government to prove that the defendant actually knew that the matter was before a government agency.

---

[73] See, e.g., United States v. Uphoff, 907 F.Supp. 1475, 1480 (D. Kan. 1995).

[74] See, e.g., United States v. Hsia, 176 F.3d 517, 522 (D.C. Cir. 1999); see also Paul Mogin, The Willfulness Element of a False Statement Charge, The Champion 38 (Sept./Oct. 2012).

[75] United States v. Starnes, 583 F.3d 196 (3d Cir. 2009).

[76] Id. at 211 (citing Bryan v. United States, 524 U.S. 184 (1998)).

[77] Id. at 212–13.

[78] 468 U.S. 63 (1984).

Defendant Yermian was convicted of three counts of making false statements based upon false information supplied to his employer in connection with a Department of Defense security questionnaire. Defendant failed to disclose his mail fraud conviction on the submitted form and additionally listed employment with two companies that had never employed him. The defendant "signed a certification stating that his answers were 'true, complete and correct to the best of [his] knowledge' and that he understood' that any misrepresentation or false statement . . . may subject [him] to prosecution under section 1001 of the United States Criminal Code.'" At trial, defendant admitted to the falsity of the statements, but contended that he did not have actual knowledge that the statements would be given to a federal agency.

The Supreme Court, in a 5–4 decision, found no basis for requiring proof of actual knowledge of federal agency jurisdiction. The Court held that the term "knowingly" following the phrase "in any matter within the jurisdiction of any department or agency of the United States," is merely a jurisdictional requirement. The Court found that "[a]ny natural reading of § 1001, therefore, establishes that the terms 'knowingly and willfully' modify only the making of false, 'fictitious or fraudulent statements,' and not the predicate circumstance that the statements be made in a matter within the jurisdiction of a federal agency."

Unresolved by *Yermian* was whether a lesser degree of *mens rea* would be required with respect to the element of federal agency jurisdiction. In a footnote in the *Yermian* decision, the Supreme Court remarked that the jury had been instructed, without objection from the government, that proof was required that defendant "knew or should have known" that statements were made within the jurisdiction of a federal agency.[79] In this footnote, the Court specifically remarked on the narrowness of the issue being decided. Since the only question before the Court in *Yermian* was whether proof of *actual* knowledge of federal agency jurisdiction was mandated, resolution of the level, if any, of culpable mental state of federal agency jurisdiction remained for future determination. Also left for future interpretation was whether specific inclusion of "executive, legislative, or judicial branch" in the statute alters the required level of knowledge.

In *United States v. Green*,[80] the Ninth Circuit found no abuse of discretion in a trial court's failure to give an instruction on jurisdictional knowledge. The appellate court held that "[n]o culpable mental state must be proved with respect to federal agency jurisdiction in order to establish a violation of section 1001." Other jurisdictions have ruled in accord with this Ninth Circuit decision finding that the government does not need to prove the defendant's knowledge that a federal agency was involved.[81] Courts have referenced *United States v. Feola*,[82] in finding that the federal agency jurisdiction is merely a jurisdictional requirement, and therefore not requiring knowledge on the part of the accused.

---

[79] Id. at 75 n.14.

[80] 745 F.2d 1205 (9th Cir. 1984).

[81] United States v. Hildebrandt, 961 F.2d 116 (8th Cir. 1992); United States v. Suggs, 755 F.2d 1538 (11th Cir. 1985); United States v. Montemayor, 712 F.2d 104 (5th Cir. 1983); United States v. Lewis, 587 F.2d 854 (6th Cir. 1978).

[82] 420 U.S. 671 (1975).

§ 9.5   MATERIALITY

Irrespective of whether the prosecution is premised on subsections (a)(1), (2), or (3) of § 1001, materiality is a necessary element of the crime. Therefore, prosecutors must prove it beyond a reasonable doubt. Originally materiality was only listed in the concealment clause of § 1001. ("Falsifies, conceals or covers up by a trick, scheme or device a *material* fact"). The remaining two misrepresentation clauses of the statute omitted the term. ("(2) makes any false, fictitious or fraudulent statements or representations, or (3) makes or uses any false writing or document knowing the same to contain any false, fictitious or fraudulent statement or entry.") Despite the failure to explicitly require materiality in the second and third clauses of the statute, most courts required proof of materiality to sustain a false statement conviction. Materiality was officially added to subsections (2) and (3) of the statute as part of the False Statements Accountability Act of 1996, so that the statute now reads: "(1) falsifies, conceals, or covers up by any trick, scheme, or device a material fact; (2) makes any materially false, fictitious, or fraudulent statement or representation; or (3) makes or uses any false writing or document knowing the same to contain any materially false, fictitious, or fraudulent statement or entry."

In determining whether a false statement or concealment is material, courts examine whether the statement has "a natural tendency to influence, or [be] capable of influencing, the decision of the decisionmaking body to which it is addressed."[83] It is not necessary to prove that the government agency was actually influenced or that the statement was relied upon by the government.[84] There is also no requirement that the statement be made directly to a federal official. "The false statement must simply have the capacity to impair or pervert the functioning of a government agency."[85]

Some courts have extended this to state that a statement is material if it has a natural tendency to influence, or is capable of influencing, either a discrete decision or any other function of the agency to which it was addressed."[86] For example, giving a false name to the Postal Service and signing a false name on the delivery form, can be considered material as it "may adversely affect the ability of the Postal Service to perform its function."[87]

In *United States v. Gaudin*,[88] the Supreme Court found that the issue of materiality is a mixed question of law and fact that should properly be submitted to the jury. The defendant in *Gaudin* was accused of making false statements on federal loan documents. The district court ruled as a matter of law that the statements were material. The Ninth Circuit, en banc, reversed finding that the issue of materiality should have been submitted to the jury. In affirming the Ninth Circuit, Justice Scalia wrote that "[t]he Constitution gives a criminal defendant the right to have a jury

---

[83] Kungys v. United States, 485 U.S. 759, 770 (1988).

[84] See United States v. Stadd, 636 F.3d 630 (D.C. Cir. 2011).

[85] United States v. Boffil–Rivera, 607 F.3d 736 (11th Cir. 2010); United States v. Lichenstein, 610 F.2d 1272, 1278 (5th Cir. 1980).

[86] United States v. Moore, 612 F.3d 698 (D.C. Cir. 2010).

[87] Id. at 702.

[88] 515 U.S. 506, 509 (1995).

determine, beyond a reasonable doubt, his guilt of every element of the crime with which he is charged."

In *Gaudin*, Justice Scalia stated that "[d]eciding whether a statement is 'material' requires the determination of at least two subsidiary questions of purely historical fact: (a) 'what statement was made?' and (b) 'what decision was the agency trying to make?' The ultimate question: (c) 'whether the statement was material to the decision, requires applying the legal standard of materiality . . . to these historical facts."

An appellate court upheld a statement as material when a defendant improperly stated to a military hospital that he was the lawyer for a restricted prisoner in order to gain access to the prisoner.[89] The statement was "capable of influencing the decision maker to allow the speaker to visit the patient." Likewise, statements "aimed at misdirecting agents and their investigation, even if they miss spectacularly or stand absolutely no chance of succeeding" can satisfy the materiality element.[90] Immediately correcting a false statement, may in some instances provide a defense to the existence of materiality.[91]

In *Gaudin*, the parties had "agreed that materiality was an element of 18 U.S.C. § 1001, but disputed whether materiality was a question for the judge or jury." But not all false statement statutes have a requirement of materiality. In *United States v. Wells*,[92] the Supreme Court found that 18 U.S.C. § 1014, a statute pertaining to false statements to a federally insured financial institution, did not require the government to prove materiality. Likewise, several circuits have found that there is no materiality requirement for 18 U.S.C. § 1542, making a false statement in a passport application.[93]

In determining whether materiality is an element of a particular false statement statute, courts have looked at the text of the statute as indicative of whether Congress intended for a materiality element to be required for this crime. Terms such as "representation" have been found not to be a proxy for requiring materiality in a false statement statute.[94] If the term is omitted, courts also examine whether the statute is a general fraud type of statute that might have materiality as a common law element.[95]

§ 9.6   MATTERS WITHIN THE JURISDICTION OF THE EXECUTIVE, LEGISLATIVE, OR JUDICIAL BRANCH

A prosecution under § 1001 requires that the material false statement be made within the executive, legislative, or judicial branch of the United States government. Several courts have interpreted the scope of this jurisdiction element.

---

[89] United States v. Abrahem, 678 F.3d 370 (5th Cir. 2012).

[90] United States v. Lupton, 620 F.3d 790 (7th Cir. 2010).

[91] United States v. Cowden, 677 F.2d 417, 420 (8th Cir. 1982).

[92] 519 U.S. 482 (1997).

[93] See, e.g., United States v. Najera Jimenez, 593 F.3d 391 (5th Cir. 2010); United States v. Salinas, 373 F.3d 161, 167 (1st Cir. 2004); United States v. Ramos, 725 F.2d 1322, 1323 (11th Cir. 1984).

[94] See United States v. Johnson, 680 F.3d 1140 (9th Cir. 2012).

[95] See Neder v. United States, 527 U.S. 1 (1999) (finding materiality as an element for mail fraud); see also § 4.7.

In *United States v. Rodgers*,[96] the United States Supreme Court provided a broad reading of the term "jurisdiction." The Court noted that § 1001 "expressly embraces false statements made 'in *any* matter within the jurisdiction of *any* department or agency of the United States.'" The defendant who lied to the F.B.I., by telling them his wife had been kidnapped, and lied to the Secret Service, by telling them his wife was involved in a plot to kill the President, was not entitled to have his false statement case dismissed as not within the term "jurisdiction," as used in § 1001. Justice Rehnquist, writing for the Court, held that since the F.B.I. is authorized to investigate crimes, including kidnapping, and the Secret Service is charged with protecting the President, statements to these agencies were within their jurisdiction. The Court noted that reading § 1001 broadly furthered the "valid legislative interest in protecting the integrity of [such] official inquiries."

Determining the scope of "department or agency" has presented controversial questions for the Court. In *United States v. Bramblett*,[97] the Supreme Court found that the Disbursement Office of the House of Representatives was, in fact, a "department or agency of the United States." Defendant Bramblett, a former member of Congress, had been charged with falsely representing to the Disbursement Office that an individual was entitled to compensation for being his official clerk. The Court interpreted the term "department," in this case saying that "as used in this context, [it] was meant to describe the executive, legislative and judicial branches of the government." *Bramblett* opened the door to courts finding that the term "department" included federal government agencies, sub-agencies, and boards.

Forty years later, in *Hubbard v. United States*,[98] the Supreme Court overruled *Bramblett* finding that a court was not an agency or department for purposes of § 1001. The Court noted how the judicial function exception was "almost as deeply rooted as *Bramblett* itself."[99] (See § 9.2(C)). But the Court did not simply endorse a judicial function exception. Instead it decided to speak clearly to "correct *Bramblett's* erroneous construction of § 1001."

Congress immediately reacted to the Court's decision in *Hubbard*, passing the False Statements Accountability Act of 1996. This Act modified the statute to explicitly provide "the jurisdiction of the executive, legislative, or judicial branch" of the United States government. It did, however, specifically codify the judicial exception by excluding "statements, representations, writings or documents submitted by" a party or counsel in a judicial proceeding. (See § 9.2(C)). The new provision also limited the scope of matters of the legislative branch by stating that it applies only to administrative matters or certain Congressional investigations or reviews. (See § 9.2(D)).

The breadth of the existing jurisdiction is seen in the prosecutions of false statements that have been made to an array of different agencies. In *Bryson v. United*

---

[96] 466 U.S. 475 (1984).

[97] 348 U.S. 503 (1955).

[98] 514 U.S. 695 (1995).

[99] Id. at 708.

States,[100] the Supreme Court held that "[b]ecause there is a valid legislative interest in protecting the integrity of official inquiries . . . the term 'jurisdiction' should not be given a narrow or technical meaning for purposes of § 1001."[101]

Statements made to federal agencies like the Federal Bureau of Investigation (FBI), Internal Revenue Service (IRS), or Securities Exchange Commission (SEC) usually present easy findings that the statements were made within the jurisdiction of the statute. Courts have also allowed prosecutions premised on a false statement to an Assistant United States Attorney,[102] an invalid military identification,[103] and a false statement made to a bankruptcy trustee.[104] Prior to the passage of the False Statements Accountability Act of 1996, the statute did not reach as many agencies. For example, a false statement to the Copyright Office was found not to be an executive agency since it was part of the Library of Congress.[105] There have always been questions of whether the false statement statute precludes statements made to a grand jury.[106]

Tougher cases are prosecutions premised upon statements made to a state agent or agency. For example, in *United States v. King*,[107] the Ninth Circuit held that a statement made to a state agricultural officer was within the statute as the defendant knew the Idaho Department of Agriculture was inspecting his wells to determine if he was improperly "injecting water into deep wells without a permit." Since "a willful injection of fluid into a deep well without a permit from the State of Idaho" constituted a federal violation under the Safe Drinking Water Act (SDWA), the defendant's false statement was held to be in a "matter within the jurisdiction" of the United States and therefore within § 1001. In contrast, cases involving fraud upon a state unemployment insurance program have been found not meeting the jurisdiction requirement in § 1001.[108]

The false statement does not need to be made directly to the federal agency. For example, in *United States v. Candella*,[109] the Second Circuit held that false affidavits submitted by movers on city forms were sufficient as the U.S. Department of Housing and Urban Development (HUD) had contracted with the city for this move and the payment of these moving expenses would be by HUD.

---

[100] 396 U.S. 64 (1969).

[101] Id. at 70.

[102] United States v. Tracy, 108 F.3d 473 (2d Cir. 1997).

[103] United States v. Camacho, 506 F.2d 594 (9th Cir. 1974).

[104] United States v. Palmisano, 185 B.R. 476 (D. Vt. 1995).

[105] United States v. Brooks, 945 F.Supp. 830 (E.D. Pa. 1996).

[106] See United States v. Allen, 193 F.Supp. 954, 957–959 (S.D. Cal. 1961) (precluding § 1001 charges for statements made to a grand jury); see also § 9.7.

[107] 660 F.3d 1071 (9th Cir. 2011).

[108] See, e.g., United States v. Holmes, 111 F.3d 463 (6th Cir. 1997) (finding alleged false statements to Michigan Employment Security Commission did not meet jurisdiction requirement); United States v. Facchini, 874 F.2d 638 (9th Cir. 1989) (finding alleged false statements related to state-funded benefits insufficient for § 1001); but see United States v. Herring, 916 F.2d 1543 (11th Cir. 1990) (finding false statement of an application for Georgia unemployment benefits sufficient for § 1001).

[109] 487 F.2d 1223 (2d Cir. 1973).

Neither is it necessary for the accused to know that a federal agency is involved in the matter.[110] One court found that statements made to a private entity trust were within § 1001, when the false statement was made in a letter used to induce the trust to purchase land that would eventually be repurchased by the federal Park Service.[111]

But a disclosure with federal ties was found insufficient when the accused was "not contractually connected to the federal government" and did not have a reporting duty to a federal agency. In *United States v. Ford*,[112] the Sixth Circuit reversed a § 1001 conviction that was premised on a tie to the federal government in that the defendant's financial interests related to TennCare, a Tennessee organization that provided health care to its citizens who were not covered by Medicaid. TennCare was paid predominantly with federal funding and existed "because of a federal waiver from federal Medicaid." The disclosures that the defendant was accused of not making, however, were to state entities, namely the Tennessee Senate and Tennessee Registry of Election Finance. The Sixth Circuit held that "[w]hile the facts that he failed to disclose concerned an entity inseparable from federal ties, the entities to which he failed to disclose those facts were anything but federal." Since the failure to disclose related to state functions, this was not directly related to a federal agency and therefore not within "any matter within the jurisdiction" of the federal government. The court also referenced the rule of lenity as requiring the ambiguity to be resolved in favor of the defendant.

§ 9.7   FALSE STATEMENTS & OTHER CRIMES

In some instances, the government will charge false statements and another federal offense in the same case.[113] For example, the false statement statute is used for prosecuting government procurement fraud. With the passage in 1988 of the Major Fraud Act[114] (18 U.S.C. § 1031), a statute that covers procurement fraud involving one million dollars or more, one sees cases that include both a false statement charge and a major fraud charge.[115] Prosecutors also will charge procurement fraud with both a § 1001 violation and a charge under the false claims statute, 18 U.S.C. § 287.[116] This is particularly noteworthy since the false claims statute[117] was initially a part of the false statement statute. (See § 9.8)

When false statements under section 1001 are charged in conjunction with another criminal offense, courts are left to decide the propriety of the prosecutor's selection of multiple charges. In *United States v. Woodward*,[118] the Supreme Court

---

[110] United States v. Suggs, 755 F.2d 1538 (11th Cir. 1985); see also § 9.4(D).

[111] United States v. Oren, 893 F.2d 1057 (9th Cir. 1990).

[112] 639 F.3d 718 (6th Cir. 2011).

[113] The U.S. Attorneys Manual advises prosecutors in using their prosecutorial discretion to look at whether Congress expressed an intent on the relationship between general and specific statutes. USAM, Title 9, Resource Manual 920, available at http://www.justice.gov/usao/eousa/foia_reading_room/ usam/title9/crm00920.htm

[114] For discussion of the Major Fraud Act see § 4.12.

[115] United States v. Merrill, 685 F.3d 1002 (11th Cir. 2012).

[116] United States v. Adler, 623 F.2d 1287 (8th Cir. 1980).

[117] See § 9.8.

[118] 469 U.S. 105 (1985).

considered the acceptability of indictments under 18 U.S.C. § 1001 and 31 U.S.C. §§ 1058, 1101 for willfully failing to report the carrying of cash in excess of five thousand dollars. The charges arose from the defendant's response of "no" on a customs form followed by a search and finding of monies in excess of five thousand dollars on the defendant and his wife. The Supreme Court found that the government could charge both of these crimes without it being considered multiple punishment for the same offense. The Court found that Congress had the intent to punish under both 18 U.S.C. § 1001 and 31 U.S.C. §§ 1058, 1101 as the statutes were "directed to separate evils."

But when the government charged two different false statement statutes for the same conduct, a Second Circuit court found it to be a violation of the double jeopardy clause to convict and sentence the defendant for both false statements pursuant to § 1001 and making false statements to Customs officials pursuant to 18 U.S.C. § 542. In *United States v. Avelino*[119] the court held that "every element needed to prove a crime under Section 1001 is an element of a Section 542 offense and that there is no clear indication of a congressional intent to provide for cumulative punishments for Sections 1001 and 542."

In contrast, courts have allowed prosecutions using both § 1001 and 1014. In *United States v. York*,[120] the Fifth Circuit found that these two false statement statutes were "directed at different ends." Although the two statutes were close, § 1001 was initially sought "to penalize those who made fraudulent monetary claims against the government." Section 1014, a newer statute, "responded to the expanded role of government."

Court have also dismissed counts when the government used both a § 1001 charge and a perjury charge under 18 U.S.C. § 1623. In *United States v. Butler*,[121] the court held these counts to be multiplicitous stating "there is no basis to conclude that Congress intended § 1001 to penalize false grand jury testimony at all, let alone to permit cumulative punishment or cumulative prosecution for such testimony under both §§ 1001 and 1623."

False statements made during a grand jury, immediately prior to the grand jury appearance, and resulting from a grant of immunity under 18 U.S.C. § 6002 have raised several issues for courts to consider. Some courts have not allowed prosecutions for false statements made before a grand jury, finding that perjury is the appropriate charge for this conduct.[122]

---

[119] 967 F.2d 815 (2d Cir. 1992).

[120] 888 F.2d 1050, 1059 (5th Cir. 1989).

[121] 351 F. Supp.2d 121 (S.D. N.Y. 2004).

[122] In re Grand Jury Witness Sara Baldinger, 356 F.Supp. 153, 160 (C.D. Cal. 1973).

§ 9.8   FALSE CLAIMS

A. Generally

In 1948 Congress split the false statement and false claims statutes, creating 18 U.S.C. § 287, the criminal false claims statute.[123] Congress also provided statutes related to civil false claims, which can be brought by either the government or private individuals.[124] In 2012, the Department of Justice (DOJ) recovered "nearly $5 Billion in [civil] False Claims Act cases."[125] Most of the civil false claims cases arise from the act's whistleblower or *qui tam* provisions. The DOJ saw 647 *qui tam* suits filed in 2012, recovering $3.3 billion in suits that were brought by whistleblowers.[126] Particularly noteworthy here is that many of these cases related to health care fraud, which included the pharmaceutical and medical device industries, mortgage and housing fraud, and procurement fraud.

The criminal false claims statute criminalizes the conduct of "[w]hoever makes or presents to any person or officer in the civil, military, or naval service of the United States, or to any department or agency thereof, any claim upon or against the United States, or any department or agency thereof, knowing such claim to be false, fictitious, or fraudulent." The statute carries a fine and term of imprisonment not to exceed five years. The statute requires the government to prove "(1) that the defendant knowingly made and presented to a department or agency of the United States a false, fraudulent or fictitious claim against the United States, and (2) that the defendant acted with knowledge that the claim was false, fraudulent, or fictitious."[127]

B. Claims

Section 287 requires the presentation of a "claim" to the government. This term has been given a broad reading.[128] It is not necessary for the claim to be honored as the statute criminalizes the mere submission of the claim irrespective of whether the government actually pays on the claim.[129]

Causing the claim to be presented to the government has been found to be sufficient.[130] Thus, if the accused gives the claim to a third party, knowing that this individual will submit the claim to a United States department or agency, it has been found sufficient to meet the element of presenting a claim to the government. Some courts have held that whether the item submitted constitutes a claim against the United States is a legal question for the court to decide. Thus, in *United States v. John*

---

[123] Act of June 25, 1948, §§ 287, 1001, 62 Stat. 698, 749.

[124] 31 U.S.C. §§ 3729 et seq.

[125] Press Release, Department of Justice, Justice Department Recovers Nearly $5 Billion in False Claims Act Cases in Fiscal Year 2012, available at http://ww.justice.gov/opa/pr/2012/December/12–ag–1439.html (Dec. 4, 2012).

[126] Id.

[127] United States v. Kline, 922 F.2d 610 (10th Cir. 1990).

[128] Hubbard v. United States, 514 U.S. 695, 703 n.5 (1995).

[129] United States v. Coachman, 727 F.2d 1293, 1302 (D.C. Cir. 1984).

[130] United States v. Montoya, 716 F.2d 1340 (10th Cir. 1983).

Bernard Industries, Inc,[131] the court found it proper as a matter of law to hold that the sales slips (forms) were properly "claims."

C. Department or Agency

Courts have also found it to be a legal question as to whether the entity receiving the claim was a department or agency for purposes of the statute. Department or agency is defined in 18 U.S.C. § 6 as:

The term "department" means one of the executive departments enumerated in section 1 of Title 5, unless the context shows that such term was intended to describe the executive, legislative, or judicial branches of the government.

The term "agency" includes any department, independent establishment, commission, administration, authority, board or bureau of the United States or any corporation in which the United States has a proprietary interest, unless the context shows that such term was intended to be used in a more limited sense.

Many different entities have been found to be departments or agencies for purposes of this statute. For example, claims to the United States Maritime Commission[132] or Medicaid[133] have been found to be claims made to a department of agency for purposes of this statute. The Internal Revenue Service is a common entity in cases brought under § 287, as making a false claim for refunds on a tax return can meet the statute.[134] There is no requirement that the defendant know that the department receiving the false claim was a federal agency.[135]

D. Materiality

Jurisdictions split on whether there is a requirement of materiality, an element necessary for a prosecution under § 1001.[136] In *United States v. Newell,*[137] the First Circuit examined the issue of whether materiality was required and stated that "§ 287 makes no mention of materiality as an element of the offense." The court in *Newell* then noted that the Eighth and Fourth Circuits had read materiality into the statute, while "the Fifth, Ninth, Tenth, and Second Circuits" found no materiality element in § 287. The Third Circuit had found materiality required in some cases and not in others.[138] Some of the cases taking a position of not requiring materiality were prior to the Supreme Court's decision in *Neder v. United States,*[139] a case that found that

---

[131] 589 F.2d 1353 (8th Cir. 1979).

[132] United States v. Michener, 152 F.2d 880 (3d Cir. 1945).

[133] United States v. Bolden, 325 F.3d 471 (4th Cir. 2003).

[134] United States v. Boyd, 456 Fed. Appx. 752 (10th Cir. 2012); United States v. Davis, 828 F. Supp.2d 405 (D. Mass. 2011); United States v. Nash, 175 F.3d 440, 444 (6th Cir. 1999).

[135] United States v. Gumbs, 283 F.3d 128 (3rd Cir. 2002).

[136] See, e.g., United States v. Taylor, 66 F.3d 254 (9th Cir. 1995) (materiality not required); United States v. Pruitt, 702 F.2d 152 (8th Cir. 1983) (materiality required); see also United States v. White, 27 F.3d 1531 (11th Cir. 1994) (discussing the circuit differences on whether materiality is required for § 287).

[137] 658 F.3d 1 (1st Cir. 2011).

[138] Id. at 16–17.

[139] 527 U.S. 1 (1999); see also § 4.7.

materiality was a necessary component of mail, wire, and bank fraud. Whether this will influence the courts that presently do not require materiality, remains to be seen.

E. Willfulness

The circuit courts are also split on whether willfulness, a necessary element for a § 1001 violation, is also a requirement for cases brought under § 287. In *Johnson v. United States*,[140] the Eighth Circuit held that although one does not need to know the "relevant criminal provisions governing" the conduct, there needs to be sufficient evidence of the accused acting willfully. In this case involving a false claim under § 287, the court found that there was sufficient evidence that "the defendant was well aware of the essential requirements of the contract with the government and that he acted in complete disregard of those requirements both before and after making the claim."

In contrast, in *United States v. Cook*,[141] the Fifth Circuit distinguished § 287 from the willfulness requirement of the false statement statute. The explicit exclusion of this element in § 287, while including it in § 1001, led the court to find that willfulness was not an element for this statute. The *Cook* court referenced the Supreme Court's historical review of the development of §§ 287 and 1001 in *United States v. Bramblett*[142] and its observation "that section 1001 should not be employed to construe section 287's requirements." It noted "that the congressionally approved Form 10 of the Federal Rules of Criminal Procedure designed for section 287 indictments omits willfulness as an element of the offense."[143]

F. Multiple Violations

Courts have allowed each false claim to be separately charged and subject to separate punishment. Thus, in *Swepston v. United States*,[144] the Eighth Circuit allowed each false claim for an income tax refund to be a separate violation of the statute. The court noted that each involved "the name of a different person and was for a separate and different amount."

Using the Supreme Court's decision in *United States v. Halper*,[145] defendants used to argue that it was a violation of double jeopardy to punish with both civil and criminal penalties for the same false claim. In *Hudson v. United States*,[146] the Court disavowed its position in *Halper* finding "that the Double Jeopardy Clause of the Fifth Amendment is not a bar to the later criminal prosecution because the administrative proceedings were civil, not criminal."[147]

---

[140] 410 F.2d 38 (8th Cir. 1969).

[141] 586 F.2d 572 (5th Cir. 1978).

[142] 348 U.S. 503 (1955).

[143] Cook, 586 F.2d at 575.

[144] 289 F.2d 166 (8th Cir. 1961).

[145] 490 U.S. 435 (1989).

[146] 522 U.S. 93 (1997).

[147] Id. at 95–96.

Chapter 10

PERJURY AND FALSE DECLARATIONS

§ 10.1 INTRODUCTION

Perjury is an ancient offense, prohibited by the Code of Hammurabi and under Roman law. In medieval France, false testimony in a capital case was itself punishable by death. Blackstone described the common law offense, a misdemeanor punishable by up to six months imprisonment, as "a crime committed when a lawful oath is administered, in some judicial proceeding, to a person who swears willfully, absolutely and falsely, in a matter material to the issue or point in question."[1] In addition to a prison term, a person convicted of perjury was incompetent to testify in any other judicial proceeding, a prohibition that most states and the federal government have now dropped in favor of allowing cross-examination on the topic. Federal Rule of Evidence 609(a)(2) authorizes the admission of a witness's prior conviction within the past 10 years "if the court can readily determine that establishing the elements of the crime required proving—or the witness's admitting—a dishonest act or false statement." Alabama, on the other hand, continues to recognize an objection to the competency of a witness convicted of "perjury or subornation of perjury."[2]

The Supreme Court expressed its views on the impact of perjury in *United States v. Mandujano*,[3] noting that "[p]erjured testimony is an obvious and flagrant affront to the basic concepts of judicial proceedings. Effective restraints against this type of egregious offense are therefore imperative." It described the purpose of the prohibition in *United States v. Williams*[4] as having been "enacted in an effort to keep the course of justice free from the pollution of perjury." In *ABF Freight System, Inc. v. N.L.R.B*,[5] a case involving false testimony in an administrative proceeding, the Court stated, "False testimony in a formal proceeding is intolerable. We must neither reward nor condone such a 'flagrant affront' to the truth-seeking function of adversary proceedings."

There are two primary federal perjury statutes: 18 U.S.C. §§ 1621 and 1623. Section 1621(a) is traceable to the first federal criminal laws enacted by Congress in 1790, and it embodied the common law offense. The statute now provides:

> Whoever—having taken an oath before a competent tribunal, officer, or person, in any case in which a law of the United States authorizes an oath to be administered, that he will testify, declare, depose, or certify truly, or that any written testimony, declaration, deposition, or certificate by him subscribed, is true,

---

[1] 4 Blackstone's Commentaries on the Law of England *138.

[2] Ala. Code § 12–21–162.

[3] 425 U.S. 564 (1976).

[4] 341 U.S. 58 (1951).

[5] 510 U.S. 317 (1994).

willfully and contrary to such oath states or subscribes any material matter which he does not believe to be true . . . is guilty of perjury. . . .

The penalty in the original statute was one hour in the pillory.[6]

Section 1623 was enacted in 1970 to extend the criminal prohibition to false declarations or testimony in ancillary judicial proceedings, such as depositions, and in appearances before a grand jury. The statute provides, "Whoever under oath in any proceeding . . . before or ancillary to any court or grand jury of the United States knowingly makes any false material declaration or makes or uses any other information, including any book, paper, document, record, recording, or other material, knowing the same to contain any false material declaration, shall be" guilty of perjury. The statute also prohibits false statements in submissions that are unsworn but made "under penalty of perjury," similar to the prohibition in § 1621(b).

A key distinction between the two provisions is that § 1623(d) contains an express retraction defense, that a person who "admits such declaration to be false, such admission shall bar prosecution under this section if, at the time the admission is made, the declaration has not substantially affected the proceeding, or it has not become manifest that such falsity has been or will be exposed." In addition, § 1623(e) expressly dispenses with the "two-witness rule" for proving perjury, an element that applies in § 1621 prosecutions. In 1976, Congress added a second means of committing perjury to § 1621(b) and § 1623(a) for those who submit a declaration "under penalty of perjury" but otherwise not made under oath, when that submission is required or permitted "under any law of the United States or under any rule, regulation, order, or requirement" as authorized by 28 U.S.C. § 1746.[7] The expansion of the perjury prohibition was made to allow perjury prosecutions based on the submission of documents in federal proceedings without requiring the person to have it notarized, so that the prohibition applies to a document that is submitted "under penalty of perjury." In order to enforce this expansion, the perjury statutes needed to be updated to permit prosecution for false statements contained in such documents (see Chapter 9).

The bankruptcy fraud statute[8] makes it a crime for any person who "knowingly and fraudulently makes a false oath or account in or in relation to any case under title 11." Similarly, a false statement on a tax return can be prosecuted as a form of perjury.[9] The statute provides that any person who "[w]illfully makes and subscribes any return, statement, or other document, which contains or is verified by a written declaration that it is made under the penalties of perjury, and which he does not believe to be true and correct as to every material matter. . . . " Perjury is also punishable in military proceedings[10] and immigration matters.[11]

Sections 1621 and 1623 share a number of common elements for establishing the offense. For § 1621, the prosecution must prove (1) the person testified or made the

---

[6] Act of April 30, 1790, ch. 9, § 18, 1 Stat. 116 (1790).

[7] Pub.L. No. 94–550, § 2, 90 Stat. 2534 (1976).

[8] 18 U.S.C. § 152(2).

[9] 26 U.S.C. § 7206(a).

[10] 10 U.S.C. § 931.

[11] 8 U.S.C. § 1357(b).

statement under oath; (2) before a competent tribunal, officer, or person; (3) the person willfully made a false statement; (4) believing the statement was not true; and, (5) the statement was material to the proceeding. A prosecution under § 1623 applies to false declarations in a wider range of proceedings, such as grand jury testimony and civil depositions, and also covers the use of "any book, paper, document, record, recording, or other material, knowing the same to contain any false material declaration." For example, altered records submitted to a grand jury could be the basis for a prosecution under § 1623, even if the person never actually testified. The intent element for § 1623 is limited to just knowledge, with no requirement to prove willfulness as § 1621 requires. That has not proven to be an important difference between the two statutes, however, because showing a defendant acted willfully effectively incorporates proof of the person's knowledge of the statement's falsity. Each provision applies to the use of material containing false statements that was submitted "under penalty of perjury."

Section 1622 prohibits subornation of perjury, an offense that goes beyond mere solicitation of the crime by requiring the witness actually commit perjury in the appropriate proceeding.

§ 10.2 OATH

In *United States v. Debrow*,[12] the Supreme Court explained the oath element as requiring proof that "[t]he oath administered must be authorized by a law of the United States." The Court went on to note that "[t]he name of the person who administered the oath is not an essential element of the crime of perjury; the identity of such person goes only to the proof of whether the defendants were duly sworn." While this sounds like a formalistic requirement, it is crucial to establishing perjury because the oath is the witness's commitment to tell the truth, forming the basis for punishing a person for a false statement.

The oath must be one authorized by "a law of the United States," which includes not only statutes but also "Rules and Regulations which have been lawfully authorized and have a clear legislative base."[13] At one time there was a religious aspect to the oath, but there is no longer any requirement of a religious reference. Federal Rule of Evidence 603 provides: "Before testifying, a witness must give an oath or affirmation to testify truthfully. It must be in a form designed to impress that duty on the witness's conscience." In *Moore v. United States*,[14] the Supreme Court overturned a trial judge's decision not to permit a defendant to testify because he refused to use the word "solemnly" for religious reasons, holding that "there is no requirement that the word 'solemnly' be used in the affirmation."

Identifying that a defendant was under oath at the time of the statement or testimony is required to establish perjury. In *United States v. Jaramillo*,[15] the defendant was convicted for violating § 1623(c) based on contradictory statements made in trial testimony and a subsequent written statement submitted to the government. The Ninth Circuit overturned the conviction because the second

---

[12] 346 U.S. 374 (1953).

[13] United States v. Hvass, 355 U.S. 570 (1958).

[14] 348 U.S. 966 (1955).

[15] 69 F.3d 388 (9th Cir. 1995).

statement was not made "under oath," explaining that "[t]he assistant U.S. attorney's warning that Jaramillo could be prosecuted for perjury is not an administration of an oath. Furthermore, nothing in the witness statement itself indicates that it was made under oath, or that Jaramillo was sworn."

Subscribing to a statement "under penalty of perjury" is the functional equivalent of taking an oath, and therefore is sufficient for a perjury prosecution under § 1621(b) and § 1623. In *Dickinson v. Wainwright*,[16] the Fifth Circuit stated, "One who subscribes to a false statement under penalty of perjury pursuant to section 1746 may be charged with perjury under 18 U.S.C.A. § 1621, just as if the statement were made under oath." The defendant need not be compelled to make the statement under penalty of perjury, so that the person's choice to use this manner of supporting a legal position in a filing, in compliance with 28 U.S.C. § 1746, can trigger a perjury prosecution. In *United States v. Gomez–Vigil*,[17] the Sixth Circuit explained that "[s]ection 1746 authorizes the use of unsworn declarations under penalty of perjury, rather than sworn declarations under oath, whenever the law, rule, regulation, order or requirement *permits* the matter to be supported, evidenced, established or proved by sworn declaration."

§ 10.3 PROCEEDING

Section 1621 punishes false testimony and submissions made to "a competent tribunal, officer, or person, in any case in which a law of the United States authorizes an oath to be administered," while § 1623 covers false information provided "in any proceeding before or ancillary to any court or grand jury of the United States." A competent tribunal is one that has jurisdiction over the case, even if it turns out there were other flaws in the proceeding, such as an improper indictment or lack of venue, which can require reversal of a conviction and dismissal of the case. In *United States v. Williams*,[18] the Supreme Court held that a perjury prosecution under § 1621 was proper for testimony in a conspiracy trial, even though the appellate court later overturned the conviction and dismissed the charge because the agreement did not amount to the violation of a law of the United States. The Court explained that the trial court "had jurisdiction of the subject matter, to wit, an alleged violation of a federal conspiracy statute, and, of course, of the persons charged. This made the trial take place before 'a competent tribunal': a court authorized to render judgment on the indictment."

The testimony of a witness at trial is the paradigm for a perjury prosecution, regardless of whether it is successful. As a matter of policy the Department of Justice requires consultation with the Criminal Division before a United States Attorney's Office pursues an investigation or charges for perjury based on an individual's testimony that resulted in an acquittal in the proceeding.[19] The concern is that the government could appear to be acting vindictively by seeking perjury charges because of the "not guilty" verdict in the case, although that does not preclude pursuing a case if there is sufficient evidence showing that false testimony was given.

---

[16] 626 F.2d 1184 (5th Cir. 1980).

[17] 929 F.2d 254 (6th Cir. 1991).

[18] 341 U.S. 58 (1951).

[19] USAM § 9–69.200.

An oath is authorized in more than just a judicial proceeding, so that a competent tribunal includes a Senate committee,[20] a bankruptcy court proceeding,[21] and investigative testimony in an administrative investigation.[22] In *United States v. Tamura*,[23] the Ninth Circuit noted that the filing of a false tax return does not constitute perjury because it is not provided under oath.

When the case involves a congressional committee, it must be duly constituted according to the rules of the particular chamber. In *Christoffel v. United States*,[24] the Supreme Court overturned a perjury conviction under § 1621 because at the time of the defendant's testimony the government could not prove there was a quorum of committee members present. Under the rules in place at that time, the absence of a quorum meant that the committee could not conduct any legitimate legislative business. The Court stated, "A tribunal that is not competent is no tribunal, and it is unthinkable that such a body can be the instrument of criminal conviction." One possible explanation for the Court's adherence to a strict reading of the congressional rules was that the questioning involved an inquiry into the witness's ties to the Communist Party, and a number of Justices found prosecutions of suspected Communists to be distasteful and so construed statutes and regulations quite narrowly to avoid convictions. For example, in *Yellin v. United States*,[25] the Court overturned the conviction of a witness for refusing to respond to questions posed in a House Un–American Activities Committee hearing due to the failure to follow House rules for the hearing that involved an almost hypertechnical interpretation.

A district court, in a 1959 decision, found that even though the congressional rules were followed there was no legitimate legislative purpose to recall a witness whose prior testimony in a committee's investigation of labor unions was found not to be credible by the committee chairman and its chief counsel. The court entered a judgment of acquittal to a charge under § 1621 because the goal of requiring the second round of testimony was to strengthen a perjury case against the witness, so it was no longer a competent tribunal to administer an oath.[26] In a later case involving the Iran–Contra investigation, the district court refused to dismiss a perjury charge based on testimony before a House committee. The court found that the committee was a competent tribunal because "[e]ven if the members of [the] House committee had access to Mr. Clarridge's testimony before a Senate Committee given just a week earlier, the House of Representatives had the power, the authority, and the duty to investigate this matter separately and independently."[27]

---

[20] See United States v. Norris, 300 U.S. 564 (1937) (Senate subcommittee investigating campaign finance violations); United States v. Weissman, 195 F.3d 96 (2d Cir. 1999) (information provided to Senate Permanent Subcommittee on Investigations); United States v. Dean, 55 F.3d 640 (D.C. Cir. 1995) (nominee's testimony before Senate Banking, Housing, and Urban Affairs Committee); United States v. Haldeman, 559 F.2d 31 (D.C. Cir. 1976) (former Attorney General John Mitchell's testimony before the Senate Watergate Committee).

[21] Bronston v. United States, 409 U.S. 352 (1973); Hammer v. United States, 271 U.S. 620 (1926).

[22] United States v. Polichemi, 219 F.3d 698 (7th Cir. 2000) (SEC investigative testimony).

[23] 694 F.2d 591 (9th Cir. 1982).

[24] 338 U.S. 84 (1949).

[25] 374 U.S. 109 (1963).

[26] United States v. Cross, 170 F.Supp. 303 (D.D.C. 1959).

[27] United States v. Clarridge, 811 F.Supp. 697 (D.D.C. 1992).

Section 1623 reaches proceedings that are ancillary to judicial cases along with those conducted by a federal grand jury. In *Dunn v. United States*,[28] the Supreme Court analyzed what is "ancillary" to a court proceeding when the defendant signed an affidavit "under penalty of perjury" in a private attorney's office which contradicted his prior grand jury testimony. Dunn testified before the grand jury about drug dealing by an inmate in a penitentiary, who was indicted on the basis of that testimony, and later recanted it in a meeting with the inmate's defense lawyer. The government charged Dunn with perjury under 18 U.S.C. § 1623(c), which permits proof of falsity based on two contradictory statements. The government's decision to charge Dunn under § 1623(c) meant that it could not rely on the false declarations basis for a charge under § 1623(a); § 1623(c) is limited to "any proceedings before or ancillary to any court or grand jury of the United States" in which "the defendant under oath" makes two inconsistent declarations. The government's theory was that Dunn's statement to the defense attorney, recorded in the affidavit, was "ancillary" to the prosecution of the inmate then pending in the district court because it could rely on it being sworn "under penalty of perjury."

The government argued for a broad reading of what is ancillary to a judicial proceeding, claiming that the statement in the attorney's office was related to the prosecution for drug dealing, and being given "under penalty of perjury" was sufficient to come within the prohibition of § 1623. Under this expansive approach "the Government contends that any statements made under oath for submission to a court, whether given in an attorney's office or in a local bar and grill, fall within the ambit of § 1623." The Court rejected that position, noting that use of the term "proceeding" by Congress "carries a somewhat more formal connotation." The Court contrasted the affidavit with a deposition, pointing out that "the Government does not and could not seriously maintain that the interview in [the attorney's] office constituted a deposition" because it would require much greater formality, such as notice to the parties and permission of the trial court under Federal Rule of Criminal Procedure 15. The defendant's statement was not made under oath, a requirement for a prosecution under § 1623(c), and "[t]o characterize such an interview as an ancillary proceeding would not only take liberties with the language and legislative history of § 1623, it would also contravene this Court's long-established practice of resolving questions concerning the ambit of a criminal statute in favor of lenity."

It is not clear after *Dunn* whether false statements contained in affidavits or other filings made "under penalty of perjury" can be prosecuted under § 1623(a). That subsection is arguably broader because it specifically provides for charges based on false statements made under oath "(or in any declaration, certificate, verification, or statement under penalty of perjury as permitted under section 1746 of title 28, United States Code) in any proceeding before or ancillary to any court or grand jury of the United States. . . . " The formality necessary for a § 1623(c) prosecution would not appear to be required for one based on a sworn statement submitted as part of a grand jury or judicial proceeding.

Some courts have interpreted *Dunn* to require greater formality for any submission that is the basis for a charge under § 1623(a) in addition to § 1623(c). In

---

[28] 442 U.S. 100 (1979).

United States v. Savoy,[29] a district court rejected the argument that the two subsections should not be treated identically after *Dunn*. According to the court:

> First, nothing in the *Dunn* Court's opinion suggests that *Dunn* does not apply to prosecutions under § 1623(a). The Court's holding explicitly applies to the statute as a whole. Moreover, the operative statutory language relied upon by the Dunn Court to reverse the defendant's conviction—i.e., that the false declarations were not made in a proceeding "before or ancillary to any court"—is found in both § 1623(a) and § 1623(c). Finally, as the Court pointed out in *Dunn*, § 1623(c) is directed at a particular "method of proof"; nothing in the Court's opinion or in the statute itself suggests that § 1623(a) and § 1623(c) are directed at different categories of false statements.

The district court cited to an Eighth Circuit decision, *United States v. Scott*,[30] in which the court stated that" the terms 'deposition' and 'ancillary proceeding' are synonymous under the statute," which implies that only a deposition and not any other statement sworn "under penalty of perjury" that is not the functional equivalent of a deposition would suffice for a prosecution under § 1623. The issue in *Scott* was whether there needed to be a separate jury instruction in a § 1623(c) prosecution to find that a deposition was "ancillary" to a judicial proceeding, and the circuit court rejected that argument by finding the two terms were equivalent so no separate instruction was required. This is a different analysis from whether anything other than a deposition can be the basis for a prosecution under § 1623(a).

In *United States v. Lamplugh*,[31] a district court concluded "the United States Supreme Court has unequivocally stated that an individual may not be prosecuted under § 1623 for submission of a false affidavit to a federal district court." The Sixth Circuit took a different approach in *United States v. Gomez–Vigil*,[32] finding that a defendant could be charged with perjury for a sworn statement because while he "was not required to swear, under oath, to the truthfulness of his statements in his April 3, 1989 'Declaration in Support,' he nevertheless chose to make the statements 'under the penalty of perjury.'"

Courts have consistently found that a deposition in a civil case can be the basis for a perjury prosecution under § 1623. In *United States v. McAfee*,[33] the defendant argued that a civil deposition was less formal than one authorized in a criminal case and did not meet the threshold set in *Dunn* to be "ancillary" to a judicial proceeding in which the defendant was charged with perjury for lying about the quality of cow hides provided to the plaintiffs. The Fifth Circuit rejected that position:

> There is no real substantive difference between federal civil and criminal depositions. Although a court order must be obtained to take a criminal deposition, Federal Rule of Criminal Procedure 15 states that subject to additional conditions provided by the court or the rules, a "deposition shall be taken and filed

---

[29] 38 F. Supp. 2d 406 (D. Md. 1998).

[30] 682 F.2d 695 (8th Cir. 1982).

[31] 17 F. Supp. 2d 354 (M.D. Pa. 1998).

[32] 929 F.2d 254 (6th Cir. 1991).

[33] 8 F.3d 1010 (5th Cir. 1993).

in the manner provided in civil actions." Thus, we hold that § 1623(c) does apply to civil depositions.

In *United States v. Wilkinson*,[34] the Fourth Circuit noted that the "ancillary" element was satisfied "upon sufficient evidence that the defendant made the false statement during a deposition in a federal civil case." Defendants have also been convicted for perjury based on sworn testimony given at a bail hearing,[35] in a bankruptcy examination,[36] the filing of a habeas corpus petition,[37] and a bankruptcy petition containing false statements.[38]

Section 1623 also prohibits the use of "any other information, including any book, paper, document, record, recording, or other material, knowing the same to contain any false material declaration" in a proceeding. While most perjury prosecutions involve testimony or other statements submitted under oath, § 1623 also covers the introduction of false evidence. In *United States v. Walser*,[39] the Eleventh Circuit upheld a defendant's conviction for aiding and abetting perjury when she provided a false document to a witness that she knew he would introduce at trial and testify about. The circuit court held that "[b]y falsifying and back-dating the SCI–013, then introducing it at trial through the innocent testimony of [the witness], Walser knowingly caused a fraudulent document to be entered into evidence during a court proceeding." In *United States v. Norton*,[40] the same court found that the defendants did not merely identify falsified records to a grand jury but also used them. The Eleventh Circuit explained, "The false documents were identified as depicting events and records that were in reality nonexistent. Defendants did more than 'merely identify' the documents as business records . . . The false documents were identified as depicting events and records that were nonexistent."

In *United States v. Gellene*,[41] the defendant, a lawyer, was convicted under § 1623 because he failed to disclose in an application submitted to the bankruptcy court his prior work for a creditor of the bankrupt company, a conflict of interest that must be revealed when seeking appointment to represent a party in the proceeding. The defendant argued that there was no reference to the paragraph involving the omission during a hearing, and therefore he did not "use" the false submission. The Seventh Circuit disagreed, finding that "[h]is reference to—and his reliance upon—the application allowed him to demonstrate not only that he had disclosed the representation of Goldman Sachs but also that he had examined other possible areas of concern and had determined that there were no other similar representations that warranted the court's scrutiny before awarding fees."

---

[34] 137 F.3d 214 (4th Cir. 1998).

[35] United States v. Bova, 350 F.3d 224 (1st Cir. 2003).

[36] Bronston v. United States, 409 U.S. 352 (1973).

[37] United States v. Roberts, 308 F.3d 1147 (11th Cir. 2002).

[38] United States v. Johnson, 325 F.3d 205 (4th Cir. 2003).

[39] 3 F.3d 380 (11th Cir. 1993).

[40] 755 F.2d 1428 (11th Cir. 1985).

[41] 182 F.3d 578 (7th Cir. 1999); see also § 13.2(E) (discussing the bankruptcy fraud aspect of this case).

§ 10.4   INTENT

Section 1621 requires proof that the defendant "willfully . . . states or subscribes any material matter which he does not believe to be true." The statute incorporates two separate intents: (1) willfulness in making the false statement, and (2) knowledge that it was untrue at the time it was made. Section 1623, on the other hand, only requires proof that the defendant "knowingly" made a false declaration, or submitted materials "knowing" they contained false statements.

In *United States v. Dunnigan*,[42] the Supreme Court described the essence of a violation of § 1621 as a witness who "gives false testimony concerning a material matter with the willful intent to provide false testimony, rather than as a result of confusion, mistake, or faulty memory." A willfully false answer is one made with intent to deceive rather than a response that is inadvertently incorrect. In *Beckanstin v. United States*,[43] the Fifth Circuit overturned a defendant's conviction for falsely responding that he had graduated from architectural school when he had only attended it, holding that "although the answer was false, the witness had not grasped the form of the question, and had not knowingly or wilfully made a false answer with intent to deceive."

The requirement that only knowledge need be proven for a violation of § 1623 means the prosecution faces a somewhat lower burden of establishing the requisite intent because it need not also show a defendant's willfulness. In *United States v. Watson*,[44] the Seventh Circuit stated, "[W]hile conviction under the federal perjury statute, 18 U.S.C. § 1621, requires a showing of willfulness, that element is not required to establish a violation of 18 U.S.C. § 1623." In *United States v. Goguen*,[45] the First Circuit explained the difference this way: "Section 1621 requires specific intent to deceive and to violate one's oath. Section 1623 requires only that the false statement be made voluntarily and knowingly as opposed to mistakenly or inadvertently." Note that § 1623 is unlike § 1621 because it contains an express recantation defense that provides a defendant with a measure of protection if the person actually sought to mitigate the impact of a false statement. Thus, requiring only proof of knowledge is a way of accommodating that defense.

§ 10.5   TRUTH AND FALSITY

Pontius Pilate asked rhetorically, "What is truth?" Philosophers have disputed since time immemorial what constitutes "truth," arguing about how it can be established conclusively and ways it can be expressed. The law of perjury does not scale such intellectual heights, focusing on the more prosaic issue of whether there is sufficient evidence for a jury to find that the defendant's statement or submission was actually false.

Section 1621 speaks of testimony a defendant "does not believe to be true," while § 1623 deals with a defendant who makes "any false material declaration." While

---

[42] 507 U.S. 87 (1993).

[43] 232 F.2d 1 (5th Cir. 1956).

[44] 623 F.2d 1198 (7th Cir. 1980).

[45] 723 F.2d 1012 (1st Cir. 1983).

"true" and "false" can have different meanings in other contexts, the courts have interpreted the two provisions identically, along with the subornation statute, so there is no difference regarding the determination of whether a statement comes within the statutory prohibition. As the First Circuit put it, "To constitute perjury, the defendant must have believed when he delivered his testimony that it was apocryphal."[46] Section 1623(c) does not require affirmative proof of falsity, however, when the government proves that a defendant made "two or more declarations, which are inconsistent to the degree that one of them is necessarily false."

The seminal decision on the issue of what constitutes a false statement for perjury is *Bronston v. United States*.[47] The defendant was the sole owner of Bronston Productions, a film company that entered bankruptcy. There were suspicions that Bronston had sequestered money from the company in a private Swiss bank account, and during a bankruptcy examination he had the following exchange with a lawyer for the creditors:

Q.   Do you have any bank accounts in Swiss banks, Mr. Bronston?

A.   No, sir.

Q.   *Have you ever?*

A.   *The company had an account there for about six months, in Zurich.*

Q.   Have you any nominees who have bank accounts in Swiss banks?

A.   No, sir.

Q.   Have you ever?

A.   No, sir.

The answers to questions—except the italicized one—were truthful, and it later came to light that Bronston did have a bank account in Switzerland during the relevant period from which he withdrew more than $180,000. His response that "[t]he company had an account there for six months, in Zurich" was certainly not responsive to the question asked, and may well have been misleading to the average listener. The government's theory at trial was that his misleading answer gave the clear—and false—impression that he did not have a Swiss bank account when he actually did.

The Court began by noting that the defendant had not provided an answer that was untrue, but only one that was "not responsive." It pointed out that while in "casual conversation" the implication that he did not have a Swiss bank account might be a fair inference to draw, "we are not dealing with casual conversation and the statute does not make it a criminal act for a witness to willfully state any material matter that *implies* any material matter he does not believe to be true." Rejecting the government's argument that the perjury statute should be construed broadly, the Court asserted, "we perceive no reason why Congress would intend the drastic sanction of a perjury

---

[46] United States v. Reveron Martinez, 836 F.2d 684 (1st Cir. 1988).

[47] 409 U.S. 352 (1973).

prosecution to cure a testimonial mishap that could readily have been reached with a single additional question by counsel alert—as every examiner ought to be—to the incongruity of petitioner's unresponsive answer." Note that the blame for not pursuing the "testimonial mishap," if that was what occurred, should be put on the attorney interrogating Bronston, who was no average listener. The Court explained that "[i]t is the responsibility of the lawyer to probe; testimonial interrogation, and cross-examination in particular, is a probing, prying, pressing form of inquiry. If a witness evades, it is the lawyer's responsibility to recognize the evasion and to bring the witness back to the mark. . . . "

The Court described what does not constitute perjury: "The cases support [Bronston]'s position that the perjury statute is not to be loosely construed, nor the statute invoked simply because a wily witness succeeds in derailing the questioner—so long as the witness speaks the literal truth." The Court did not explain in any detail what was meant by an answer that was the "literal truth," although in a footnote it did give some indication of how to analyze certain types of answers. In the jury instructions at trial, the district court gave an illustration of a misleading answer that it considered to be false. It involved a question about how many times a person entered a store in a day, and the response was 5 when the person actually entered it 50 times. The Court stated, "it is very doubtful that an answer which, in response to a specific quantitative inquiry, baldly understates a numerical fact can be described as even 'technically true.'" For other types of answers, determining their truth required consideration of the question along with the answer:

> Whether an answer is true must be determined with reference to the question it purports to answer, not in isolation. An unresponsive answer is unique in this respect because its unresponsiveness by definition prevents its truthfulness from being tested in the context of the question—unless there is to be speculation as to what the unresponsive answer "implies."

Bronston's analysis of nonresponsive answers has come to be called the "literal truth" defense, even though it is not what is commonly understood to be an affirmative defense because the burden remains on the government to establish the falsity of the statement in order to prove perjury. Nevertheless, courts treat it as if it were a type of defense, and place the burden of production on the defendant to raise the issue of literal truth in order to support a jury instruction on the issue.[48] In *United States v. Thomas*,[49] the Ninth Circuit stated that "[b]efore an instruction is required on Thomas's theory of literal truth, the theory must have had some foundation in the evidence presented at trial." Similarly, in *United States v. O'Neill*,[50] the Seventh Circuit held that "the district court correctly refused to tender [a *Bronston* instruction] to the jury because none of the false statements O'Neill was charged with making were susceptible of the interpretation that they were literally true but misleading." *Bronston* has been applied to charges under § 1623(a) to the same extent as cases involving § 1621.

---

[48] Unlike other defenses, however, review of a literal truth claim is de novo as a question of law rather than one of fact left to the jury. See United States v. Strohm, 671 F.3d 1173 (10th Cir. 2011); United States v. Ahmed, 472 F.3d 427 (6th Cir. 2006); United States v. Hirsch, 360 F.3d 860 (8th Cir. 2004); United States v. Roberts, 308 F.3d 1147 (11th Cir. 2002).

[49] 612 F.3d 1107 (9th Cir. 2010).

[50] 116 F.3d 245 (7th Cir. 1997).

The District of Columbia Circuit described the effect of *Bronston*'s literal truth analysis this way: "Although it may be, as Mark Twain said, that '[o]ften, the surest way to convey misinformation is to tell the strict truth,' a statement that is literally true cannot support a perjury conviction."[51] Asserting that a response is literally true may well turn on rather fine distinctions regarding the meaning of the terminology used in a question and answer, as President Clinton's famous statement "It depends on what the meaning of the word 'is' is" demonstrates how parsing words can be critical. And even a statement that "I don't recall" can be the basis of a perjury prosecution if the government can show by circumstantial evidence that the person did in fact know the answer to the question at the time.[52]

The Eleventh Circuit's decision in *United States v. Shotts*[53] illustrates the point quite well. During a federal grand jury investigation of corruption in a local court, the defendant, a criminal defense attorney, was called as a witness. He had owned a bail bonds company but closed it down when a new state rule prohibited attorneys from having an interest in that business. He then formed a new corporation with his wife as sole shareholder, although he continued to control its operations. Shotts was believed to have made cash payments to a local judge to sign blank bail bonds issued by the new corporation that could be used to obtain the release of the attorney's clients without incurring any liability if the clients failed to appear as required. In the grand jury, the prosecutor asked Shotts, "Do you own a bail bonds business?", to which he replied, "No, sir." In response to questions about his other possible relationships with a bail bonds business, Shotts asserted the Fifth Amendment privilege and refused to respond.

The Eleventh Circuit overturned the conviction because, under Alabama law, one must be a shareholder of a corporation to be considered its owner, which meant that "[h]is answer to the question whether he 'owned' the company was literally true as a matter of both Alabama and general law." Shotts' response was described by the circuit court as "evasive, nonresponsive, intentionally misleading and arguably false." When the prosecutor used a term like "own," however, which carries a particular legal meaning, then the response was literally true and the perjury charge failed.

The Ninth Circuit reached a similar result in *United States v. Boone*,[54] in which a defendant was asked if he had removed any documents from a company's files. While the defendant had in fact removed documents, the files were not labeled in the company's name at the time of the removal so his denial was literally true even though it was "arguably misleading."

In *United States v. Eddy*,[55] the phrasing of the questions was key when a defendant denied submitting an "official" medical school diploma and a "genuine" college transcript in order to be admitted to the Navy as a physician. The documents were in fact false, and the Sixth Circuit overturned his conviction in light of *Bronston*. The circuit court explained that "Eddy's negative responses to the prosecutor's

---

[51] United States v. Dean, 55 F.3d 640 (D.C. Cir. 1995).

[52] United States v. Chapin, 515 F.2d 1274 (D.C. Cir. 1975).

[53] 145 F.3d 1289 (11th Cir. 1998).

[54] 951 F.2d 1526 (9th Cir. 1991).

[55] 737 F.2d 564 (6th Cir. 1984)

questions were the literal truth" because he could not submit any "official" or "genuine" documents, as the prosecutor asked in the grand jury.

In *United States v. Earp*,[56] the Fourth Circuit applied *Bronston* to overturn a defendant's perjury conviction based on his denial that, as a member of the Ku Klux Klan, he had burned a cross in front of a residence. He had been unable to light the fire, so the circuit court explained that "while he no doubt knew full well that he had on that occasion tried to burn a cross, he was not specifically asked either about any attempted cross burnings or even whether or not he was at or near the . . . home on the night in question or whether he participated in the . . . incident." In *United States v. Tonelli*,[57] a defendant's initial answer was false, but upon the prosecutor's clarification of the terminology used, his revised response was true. The Third Circuit found that the government could not select out the initial answer when the subsequent one was in fact truthful, stating that "by quoting a question and answer in isolation, the indictment did not accurately represent the statements made by the defendant and in ignoring the qualifying definitions used by the prosecutor, it was misleading."

Unless an answer is clearly false based on extrinsic verifiable evidence, e.g. the time the sun rose or the physical location of a building, then the context of the question and answer need to be considered in evaluating a claim that an answer was literally true. As *Bronston* explained, "Precise questioning is imperative as a predicate for the offense of perjury." Determining whether a question had sufficient precision is usually an issue to be decided by the jury unless it is deemed "fundamentally ambiguous," then the court can determine as a matter of law that the defendant could not be convicted of perjury.

A question is ambiguous if it is susceptible to two (or more) plausible interpretations of its operative terms. The *Bronston* analysis applies when the response is literally true with regard to one interpretation, even though it was false for the other. In *United States v. Thomas*,[58] the Ninth Circuit explained the test this way:

> When a defendant claims that her allegedly perjured testimony was literally true based on her own purported understanding of the government's questions, the issue is whether the jury could conclude beyond a reasonable doubt that the defendant understood the question as did the government and that, so understood, the defendant's answer was false.

The defendant in *Thomas* was charged with perjury for testimony before a federal grand jury investigating the use of steroids by professional athletes. In response to the question "Did you take anything that [a trainer] gave you?", she responded "No." In seeking to overturn her conviction, defendant argued that the steroids she received were either bought or bargained for, and that "gave" was ambiguous because it could mean a gift so that her response was literally true under that interpretation. The circuit court noted that "give" is a term with a variety of meanings and therefore potentially ambiguous, so that it was up to the jury to decide what meaning the defendant ascribed to it to determine whether her response was false. The Ninth

---

[56] 812 F.2d 917 (4th Cir. 1987).

[57] 577 F.2d 194 (3d Cir. 1978).

[58] 612 F.3d 1107 (9th Cir. 2010).

Circuit found that "[p]erhaps the government's questions could have been phrased to avoid any ambiguity, but the phrasing actually used was not only plausible, but well within the bounds of ordinary construction." The court rejected a similar argument that her negative response to whether she took "anabolic steroids" was literally true because the items she received had not yet been identified under the law as illegal steroids, holding that the "common understanding" of the term included the items she received.

In *United States v. Lighte*,[59] the Second Circuit explained the jury's proper role in assessing whether a response was false if the question is susceptible to multiple interpretations. The issue is not solely the defendant's subjective understanding "as that would compel the jury to accept as conclusive the meaning a defendant alleges he gave to the stated question, and no perjury prosecutions would ever result in convictions." The test to be applied to the question and answer is an objective one:

> The jury should determine whether the question—as the declarant must have understood it, giving it a reasonable reading—was falsely answered. If the jury has been properly charged that it cannot convict the declarant if he made a false statement by mistake or inadvertence, and that an answer is knowingly false "only if it was untrue when made and known to be untrue by the individual making it," then a reviewing court will not disturb the jury's determination.

The focus on the question being asked is crucial to the analysis because it provides context that can clarify the meaning of the terms used. As in ordinary conversation, questioning by a lawyer, whether in a deposition, grand jury, or trial, will take on a rhythm in which there is often a shared understanding of what is meant in the examination, so that each term need not be defined repeatedly. In *United States v. Serafini*,[60] the importance of context became clear when the defendant was charged with perjury for responding "No" to a question about any potential source of campaign contributions when the prior and subsequent question focused solely on one person who supplied the funds. In upholding dismissal of a perjury count based on the negative answer, the Third Circuit stated:

> The question—awkwardly phrased though it is—might, *standing alone*, be thought as a matter of syntax not to be fatally ambiguous. The problem is that, read in context, the question takes on a particular meaning wholly at odds with the "broad, openended" significance the government now seeks to attribute to it.

Some questions are so flawed that they rise to the level of being "fundamentally ambiguous," which means that a perjury conviction cannot be sustained as a matter of law. In *United States v. Lighte*,[61] the Second Circuit provided the following description of such a question:

> A question is fundamentally ambiguous when it is not a phrase with a meaning about which men of ordinary intellect could agree, nor one which could be used

---

[59] 782 F.2d 367 (2d Cir. 1986).
[60] 167 F.3d 812 (3d Cir. 1999).
[61] 782 F.2d 367 (2d Cir. 1986).

with mutual understanding by a questioner and answerer unless it were defined at the time it were sought and offered as testimony.

In *United States v. Farmer*,[62] the Tenth Circuit noted that "where a prosecutor's question is only 'arguably ambiguous,' a defendant's understanding of the question is for the jury to resolve in the first instance." The subset of "fundamentally" ambiguous questions, which cannot be the basis for a perjury conviction, serves three purposes: "to (1) preclude convictions grounded on surmise or conjecture; (2) prevent witnesses from unfairly bearing the risks of inadequate examination; and (3) encourage witnesses to testify (or at least not discourage them from doing so)."

Unfortunately, as the Second Circuit in *Lighte* recognized, "The phrase 'fundamentally ambiguous' has itself proven to be fundamentally ambiguous." Similarly, the Tenth Circuit in *Farmer* pointed out that "line drawing is inevitable, for to precisely define the point at which a question becomes fundamentally ambiguous, and thus not amenable to jury interpretation, is impossible." The issue is whether the question is so ambiguous that there is no basis on which a jury could decide whether the defendant understood the question in a way that made the answer false, so that a conviction would be based solely on speculation regarding its meaning, which is clearly impermissible under due process. The Tenth Circuit stated in *United States v. Strohm*,[63] however, that "a witness cannot pluck a question from its context and then plead fundamental ambiguity by ascribing a meaning that is contrary to the question as viewed against the backdrop of the entire testimony."

In *Lighte*, the Second Circuit found questions asked of a witness about what "you" did in relation to a bank account to be fundamentally ambiguous because "[t]hroughout the questioning the examiner failed to differentiate between Lighte's actions as trustee and those which he undertook in an individual capacity." In *Farmer*, the question was whether the defendant had "talked" to a person charged in another case about her "testimony here today," and she responded "No" because she had not spoken with the person that day but had a day earlier. The Tenth Circuit found the question fundamentally ambiguous because it was unclear whether the "here today" modified "talked" or "testimony," so that "[o]nly by surmise and conjecture could the jury conclude that Defendant understood the question as the prosecutor did." In *United States v. Lattimore*,[64] the district court dismissed a charge that a defendant committed perjury when he denied being a "follower of the Communist line," explaining:

> To ask twelve jurors to agree and then decide that the definition of the Communist line found in the indictment is the definition that defendant had in mind and denied believing in, is to ask the jury to aspire to levels of insight to which the ordinary person is incapable, and upon which speculation no criminal indictment should hinge.

The interaction of the literal truth analysis and the focus on the context of questions to ascertain the witness's understanding was presented in *United States v.*

---

[62] 137 F.3d 1265 (10th Cir. 1998).

[63] 671 F.3d 1173 (10th Cir. 2011).

[64] 127 F.Supp. 405 (D.D.C 1955).

DeZarn,[65] a challenging decision that raises questions about how far a claim of literal truth can be extended. The defendant was a member of the Kentucky National Guard who conducted potentially illegal fundraising activities for a candidate for governor at a "Preakness Party" in May 1990, before the primary election. An Army investigator took the defendant's sworn testimony, during which he was examined about fundraising activities that focused on the 1990 event. In one set of questions, however, the investigator mistakenly referenced "1991," when there was also a gathering but no fundraising took place then because it was well after the election. In response to the question "was that a political fundraising activity?" the defendant responded "Absolutely not," and when asked if there were any campaign contributions "at that activity" he responded "I don't know."

DeZarn asserted at trial that his answers regarding the 1991 party were literally true, which the jury rejected in convicting him. According to the Sixth Circuit, "[e]vidence was presented at trial, however, to establish that DeZarn was not misled by the 1991 date but had answered the investigators' questions as he had with intent to deceive them," including testimony that there was only one "Preakness Party" and it was held in1990. The circuit court contrasted the case with *Bronston*, pointing out that "[w]hat is presented in this case is not a non-responsive, or only partially responsive, answer. Rather, we have a series of categorical answers to questions with a partially mistaken premise or presupposition." The issue in the case was not whether the answer was literally true, but whether the defendant understood the question in the context of the examination to determine if his response was subjectively untruthful. The circuit court stated:

> The question presented here, then, is whether in a perjury case in which a mistaken premise exists in one of the questions asked of the testifier, the Government is entitled to present, and the jury to consider, evidence of the context of the questioning which would establish that the Defendant—despite the false premise of the question—knew exactly what the questions meant and exactly what they were referring to. We hold that the law of perjury not only permits this, but in cases such as this, requires it.

DeZarn is a correct statement of the law if the question had been ambiguous, which would necessitate consideration of its context. But there did not appear to be any ambiguity in the question asked, only a "mishap" in the investigator's phrasing that changed its temporal focus entirely. The problem with the Sixth Circuit's analysis is that there was no ambiguity in the question, but rather a "mistaken premise" that made the response literally true, which seems to bring the case within *Bronston*. As the Supreme Court noted there, the literal truth analysis is required because "the perjury statute is not to be loosely construed, nor the statute invoked simply because a wily witness succeeds in derailing the questioner."

One could argue that DeZarn was not even a "wily witness" because of the shared understanding of the timeframe of the questions, so that he should not receive a windfall from the inadvertence of the examiner. *Bronston* emphasized the duty imposed on the examiner to frame questions properly, however, and the reference to the wrong year was not attributable to any effort by DeZarn to mislead, so the

---

[65] 157 F.3d 1042 (6th Cir. 1998).

investigator's failure should not necessarily be excused by upholding the conviction. The Sixth Circuit seemed to limit the literal truth analysis to only nonresponsive misleading answers, a position the Supreme Court did not appear to adopt in *Bronston*.

Not every perjury prosecution requires proof that a particular statement was false. Under § 1623(c), the government can prove a violation in the following manner:

> An indictment or information for violation of this section alleging that, in any proceedings before or ancillary to any court or grand jury of the United States, the defendant under oath has knowingly made two or more declarations, which are inconsistent to the degree that one of them is necessarily false, need not specify which declaration is false if—
>
> (1) each declaration was material to the point in question, and
>
> (2) each declaration was made within the period of the statute of limitations for the offense charged under this section.

Not having to prove a statement is verifiably false means that *Bronston*'s literal truth defense does not apply to a prosecution under this theory of perjury, although a defendant can argue that the statements are not sufficiently inconsistent to establish that one of them is necessarily false. Both statements must be under oath to come under § 1623(c), so that declarations, affidavits, and other submission "under penalty of perjury" are not sufficient to constitute one of the contradictory statements. In *United States v. Jaramillo*,[66] the Ninth Circuit held, "Because § 1623(c) specifically uses only the language 'under oath,' we hold that 18 U.S.C. § 1623(c) means what it says, namely that § 1623(c) applies only when both of the contradictory statements were made 'under oath.'"

The Fourth Circuit in *United States v. Flowers*[67] described the standard for finding sufficient contradiction to establish a violation of § 1623(c):

> While § 1623(c) has eliminated the need for extrinsic evidence of falsity, the statutory language "irreconcilably contradictory" and "necessarily false" requires a variance in testimony that extends beyond mere vagueness, uncertainty, or equivocality. Even though two declarations may differ from one another, the § 1623(c) standard is not met unless, taking them in context, they are so different that if one is true there is no way that the other can also be true.

All other circuits that have considered the issue have accepted this formulation of the standard.[68]

The Fourth Circuit applied the standard and overturned the defendant's conviction because the statements were made two years apart, and while there were contradictions between them, they appeared attributable more to faded memory than knowing falsity in the statements. The circuit court explained that "Flowers generally

---

[66] 69 F.3d 388 (9th Cir. 1995).

[67] 813 F.2d 1320 (4th Cir. 1987).

[68] See United States v. Hasan, 609 F.3d 1121 (10th Cir. 2010); United States v. McAfee, 8 F.3d 1010 (5th Cir. 1993); United States v. Porter, 994 F.2d 470 (8th Cir.1993).

manifested uncertainty, forgetfulness, and perhaps even evasiveness about the events in question. These testimonial characteristics, however, do not satisfy the § 1623(c) evidentiary standard." For a prosecution based on contradictory statements, it is important that the subject matter of the questions be the same in order to determine whether the answers did in fact present a sufficient contradiction. In *United States v. Crisconi*,[69] a federal district court dismissed a perjury charge in the following circumstances:

> It is clear from the face of the indictment that the November 3rd discussion was about an impression made by an office stamp, while the January 14th discussion concerned an office stamp of the kind used to make such impressions. The fact that Crisconi on November 3rd had no specific recollection of the impression "as it appears on that letter," if true, does not make "necessarily false" the proposition that Crisconi, on January 14th, thought the stamping device shown to him was similar to one which had been in his office.

An individual who has been granted immunity from prosecution usually cannot have any statement or testimony used against him in a later proceeding. The federal immunity statute, however, specifically exempts perjury and false statement prosecutions from the prohibition on the subsequent use of immunized testimony.[70]

§ 10.6 MATERIALITY

Federal perjury prosecutions require proof that the false statement was material to the proceeding in which it was made. In *Johnson v. United States*, the Supreme Court noted that "there is no doubt that materiality is an element of perjury under § 1623. The statutory text expressly requires that the false declaration be 'material.'"[71] In *United States v. Gaudin*,[72] which involved a false statement charge in the context of bank documents, the Court held that when materiality is an element of an offense, it must be decided by the jury and not by the court as a matter of law.

The standard for what is a material statement is a broad one, as set forth by the District of Columbia Circuit in *United States v. Barrett*: "The test of materiality is whether the statement has a natural tendency to influence, or was capable of influencing, the decision of the tribunal in making a particular determination. Proof of actual reliance on the statement is not required; the Government need only make a reasonable showing of its potential effects."[73] The Ninth Circuit described materiality in *United States v. Thomas*[74] this way: "a false statement need only be relevant to any subsidiary issue under consideration, and the government need not prove that the perjured testimony actually influenced the relevant decision-making body." The Sixth Circuit took an arguably broader approach in *United States v. Wallace*,[75] finding that "a false declaration satisfies the materiality requirement if a truthful statement might have assisted or influenced the . . . jury in its investigation."

---

[69] 520 F.Supp. 915 (D. Del. 1981).

[70] 18 U.S.C. § 6002.

[71] 520 U.S. 461 (1997).

[72] 515 U.S. 506 (1995); see also § 9.5.

[73] 111 F.3d 947 (D.C. Cir. 1997).

[74] 612 F.3d 1107 (9th Cir. 2010).

[75] 597 F.3d 794 (6th Cir. 2010).

Because § 1621 and § 1623 apply in a variety of legal settings, courts focus on the role of the factfinder involved and at what stage of the proceeding the falsehood arose in assessing materiality. In *Gaudin*, the Supreme Court described the materiality analysis this way:

> Deciding whether a statement is "material" requires the determination of at least two subsidiary questions of purely historical fact: (a) "what statement was made?" and (b) "what decision was the agency trying to make?" The ultimate question: (c) "whether the statement was material to the decision," requires applying the legal standard of materiality to these historical facts.

The test is whether the false testimony was capable of influencing the factfinder in deciding the issues before it.[76] In *United States v. Wallace*,[77] the Sixth Circuit explained how a false statement in trial testimony could have impacted the jury's assessment of the witness and support a perjury conviction:

> Had Wallace admitted that she did not use the name "Jean Wallace," the jury would have understood that Wallace was mailing a package with an intentionally false name. Wallace asserted that the package was a gift to a relative of [the defendant]'s, so no reasonable explanation exists to explain why she would use a fake name. The use of a false name and address is certainly relevant to the jury's central inquiry at the first trial concerning whether Wallace was a knowing member of the drug conspiracy. The use of a name she did not normally go by undermines her claim that she thought she was innocently mailing a doll.

The materiality assessment is made at the time the false statement was made, and not by how the proceeding or investigation ultimately turned out. In *United States v. McKenna*,[78] the Ninth Circuit held, "Later proof that a truthful statement would not have helped the [decision-making body] does not render the false testimony immaterial."

A false statement can be material regardless of whether there was actual reliance on it, or even if the tribunal knew it was false when made, so long as it was capable of influencing the outcome. In *United States v. Threats*,[79] in which the defendant testified falsely at a co-conspirator's sentencing hearing about his role in drug distribution, the Sixth Circuit noted "if Threats's testimony merely had the potential to interfere with a line of inquiry, materiality is established regardless of whether the perjured testimony actually served to impede the inquiry." In *United States v. Roberts*,[80] the Eleventh Circuit upheld a perjury conviction based on a defendant's filing of a successive habeas corpus petition in which he disclaimed having filed one previously, which would have subjected it to a different standard of review. Even though the trial judge stated that he would have dismissed the filing regardless of whether it was a second petition, the circuit court upheld the materiality determination because it "fooled the clerk of the

---

[76] United States v. Guariglia, 962 F.2d 160 (2d Cir. 1992)

[77] 597 F.3d 794 (6th Cir. 2010).

[78] 327 F.3d 830 (9th Cir. 2003).

[79] 48 Fed. Appx. 980 (6th Cir. 2002).

[80] 308 F.3d 1147 (11th Cir. 2002)

court into accepting the 'writ' for filing, and led the magistrate judge to consider its merits until she discovered that the 'writ' was a successive § 2255 motion in disguise."

In prosecutions under § 1623 for false testimony in a civil deposition, the Second and Fifth Circuits have adopted a flexible standard for assessing materiality in that context. In *United States v. Kross*,[81] the Second Circuit held, "we see no persuasive reason not to apply the broad standard for materiality of whether a truthful answer might reasonably be calculated to lead to the discovery of evidence admissible at the trial of the underlying suit." In *United States v. Holley*,[82] the Fifth Circuit explained the rationale for linking the materiality standard to the broad discovery available in a civil case:

> Ordinarily, there would appear to be no sufficient reason why a deponent should not be held to his oath with respect to matters properly the subject of and material to the deposition, even if the information elicited might ultimately turn out not to be admissible at a subsequent trial. In assessing the materiality of statements made in a discovery deposition, some account must be taken of the more liberal rules of discovery.

In *United States v. Adams*,[83] the Sixth Circuit took a narrower approach to materiality in a civil case, reversing a defendant's conviction for giving false testimony before a magistrate in a discrimination lawsuit against her employer in which she testified that she determined her income from a tax worksheet rather than from the actual tax form. The circuit court found that "[w]hat that record does not show, at least to our satisfaction, is how more precise answers by Ms. Adams to the questions asked her at the hearing before the magistrate could have had any significant influence on the magistrate's decision." The Sixth Circuit rejected the government's argument that her misstatement could have undermined her credibility in the civil case and therefore was material, holding that "this argument proves too much; the credibility of a witness is always at issue, but not every word of a witness's testimony is invariably material. The materiality of a particular snippet of testimony is not automatically established by the simple expedient of proving that the testimony was given." The testimony in *Adams* took place in front of the court, so the Sixth Circuit's analysis does not necessarily raise the standard for what is material in a civil deposition in which a party can inquire about a much wider range of topics.

In *United States v. Clark*,[84] another case involving testimony in a civil deposition, the Ninth Circuit applied the materiality test adopted for false statements in judicial proceedings that determines whether the false statement had "a natural tendency to influence, or was capable of influencing, the decision of the decisionmaking body to which it was addressed." The circuit court did not adopt the flexible approach endorsed by the Second and Fifth Circuits that focused primarily on the potential impact on discovery by the parties rather than the decision of the fact-finder. But the Ninth Circuit also did not reject that approach because the government did not raise the question of the proper test to apply in such a case. The convictions were upheld under

---

[81] 14 F.3d 751 (2d Cir. 1994).

[82] 942 F.2d 916 (5th Cir. 1991).

[83] 870 F.2d 1140 (6th Cir. 1989).

[84] 918 F.2d 843 (9th Cir. 1990).

the traditional approach, so it is not clear whether the Ninth Circuit intended to apply a uniform standard of materiality in all prosecutions under § 1623, even when the statement was made in a discovery deposition.

For perjury cases involving the grand jury, the potential issues that could be affected by a false statement are much broader because that body can investigate a wide range of activity to determine whether criminal conduct occurred. This is unlike a trial, in which the issues are more clearly defined. The materiality standard in the investigatory phase of a case is whether a false statement had "the potential to impede, influence, or dissuade the grand jury from pursuing its investigation."[85] In *United States v. Regan*,[86] the Second Circuit noted that a "statement in grand jury proceedings is material if a truthful answer could conceivably have aided the grand jury investigation." In *United States v. Gribben*,[87] the same court explained:

> [T]he standard is not whether a perjurious answer with respect to a charge of covering up the facts would likely have resulted in a wrong decision by the grand jury, but rather whether it had the potential or a natural tendency to affect or influence the grand jury in, or impede or dissuade it from, pursuing its investigation.

The Second Circuit overturned the dismissal of perjury charges against two police officers for embellishing the facts about where they found a gun that led to the prosecution of a defendant, even though the defendant could have been charged with possession of the weapon without regard to their false statements. The circuit court explained that "Gribben's alleged false statements to the grand jury and federal officials influenced their decision-making because the truth would have alerted them to the inconsistency between Gribben's testimony and the written reports he filed on the day of Calhoun's arrest."

In *United States v. Gant*,[88] the Seventh Circuit upheld a perjury conviction because the grand jury was not limited to considering just the violation under investigation, and truthful testimony could have corroborated the statements of other witnesses so it met the requirement of materiality.

One type of materiality claim raised in perjury prosecutions based on grand jury testimony is that the government set a "perjury trap" by seeking a sworn statement for the sole purpose of having the person testify falsely while the prosecutor was already aware of the truth of the subject of the investigation. Another aspect of the defendant's argument is that the government's conduct violated due process because it involved an improper use of the grand jury to manufacture a crime. In *United States v. Chen*,[89] the Ninth Circuit described a "perjury trap" claim as follows:

> A perjury trap is created when the government calls a witness before the grand jury for the primary purpose of obtaining testimony from him in order to prosecute him later for perjury. It involves the government's use of its investigatory powers

---

[85] United States v. Gulley, 992 F.2d 108 (7th Cir. 1993).
[86] 103 F.3d 1072 (2d Cir. 1997).
[87] 984 F.2d 47 (2d Cir. 1993).
[88] 119 F.3d 536 (7th Cir. 1997).
[89] 933 F.2d 793 (9th Cir. 1991).

to secure a perjury indictment on matters which are neither material nor germane to a legitimate ongoing investigation of the grand jury.

Courts have generally rejected perjury trap claims if the government can show it called the witness to testify to further a legitimate grand jury investigation into conduct that was arguably criminal which may have occurred in the jurisdiction. For example, in *United States v. Alvarez*,[90] a district court stated, "[I]f information is sought, which is useful to a legitimate investigation, that scenario renders the perjury trap doctrine inapplicable."

Reported cases dismissing charges based on a finding the government set out a "perjury trap" are quite rare, although it may be that the claim is successful in dissuading prosecutors from pursuing a case for which there would be no record of the decision. If the purpose of calling the witness before the grand jury is solely to entice the person into lying and there is no legitimate basis for an investigation, then a perjury charge is subject to dismissal. In *Brown v. United States*,[91] the Eighth Circuit reversed a conviction because the grand jury testimony was for no apparent reason other than to entice the defendant into committing perjury, so that the grand jury was used for an improper purpose. Although the decision does not use the term "perjury trap," the circuit court noted:

> The court is of the opinion that the evidence in this case clearly established that [the prosecutor's] purpose was simply to do what he did, viz., to extract from defendant his testimony about the talk in which he had taken part in St. Louis on May 3, 1950, knowing that his recollection of it differed from that of the others present, and to get him indicted for perjury ... Extracting the testimony from defendant had no tendency to support any possible action of the grand jury within its competency. The purpose to get him indicted for perjury and nothing else is manifest beyond all reasonable doubt.

§ 10.7 RECANTATION DEFENSE

Section 1623(d) provides an express recantation defense for one charged with perjury. The defense is not available in prosecutions under § 1621, although courts may be willing to allow a defendant to argue that recanting prior false testimony establishes a lack of intent to willfully deceive. In *United States v. Norris*,[92] a lower court reversed a perjury conviction because the district court refused to instruct the jury on a recantation defense when the defendant returned to the witness stand a day after he denied receiving any campaign contributions and admitted to receiving them. The Supreme Court reinstated the jury verdict, holding that "[d]eliberate material falsification under oath constitutes the crime of perjury and the crime is complete when a witness' statement has once been made." The Court explained the rationale for denying a recantation defense:

> The argument overlooks the tendency of such a view to encourage false swearing in the belief that if the falsity be not discovered before the end of the hearing it

---

[90] 489 F. Supp. 2d 714 (W.D. Tex. 2007).

[91] 245 F.2d 549 (8th Cir. 1957).

[92] 300 U.S. 564 (1937).

will have its intended effect, but, if discovered, the witness may purge himself of crime by resuming his role as witness and substituting the truth for his previous falsehood. It ignores the fact that the oath administered to the witness calls on him freely to disclose the truth in the first instance and not to put the court and the parties to the disadvantage, hinderance, and delay of ultimately extracting the truth by cross-examination, by extraneous investigation, or other collateral means.

The statutory defense in § 1623(d) can be invoked if the following requirements are met:

> Where, in the same continuous court or grand jury proceeding in which a declaration is made, the person making the declaration admits such declaration to be false, such admission shall bar prosecution under this section if, at the time the admission is made, the declaration has not substantially affected the proceeding, or it has not become manifest that such falsity has been or will be exposed.

Prosecutors are not required to choose one statute over the other, so long as the elements of each can be established, so the recantation defense can be negated if the government chooses to charge the person under § 1621 rather than § 1623. Moreover, § 1623 did not work as a *sub silentio* repeal of § 1621, so a defendant cannot argue that the decision to pursue charges under the older general perjury statute was improper unless a claim for purposeful discrimination can be shown.[93]

The first element of the recantation defense is that it occurred during "the same continuous court or grand jury proceeding" in which the false statement was made. This temporal aspect is designed to ensure that the impact of the false statement is minimized and the recantation is effective in alleviating any harm. In *United States v. McAfee*,[94] the defendant stated in a deposition in 1990 that his statement in a deposition in 1987 was false. The Fifth Circuit found the defense unavailable because the later deposition "was not part of the same proceeding in which the false statement was made."

Second, the witness must fully admit the prior statement was false, and not just call it into question. In *United States v. Sebaggala*,[95] the First Circuit set a high standard for recantation that goes beyond just a bare statement that prior testimony was false. In addition, "In order effectively to recant a prior perjurious statement, the declarant must make an outright retraction and repudiation. He also must explain unambiguously and specifically the respects in which his earlier answer was false." In *United States v. Scivola*,[96] the same court noted that "a mere implicit admission of rendering false testimony does not satisfy the requirements of an effective recantation under section 1623(d)." In *United States v. Goguen*,[97] the First Circuit stated that "for an effective recantation, the accused must come forward and explain unambiguously and specifically which of his answers in prior testimony were false and in what respects they were false."

---

[93] See United States v. Sherman, 150 F.3d 306 (3d Cir. 1998) ("[T]he district court erred when it decided that § 1623 impliedly repealed § 1621.").

[94] 8 F.3d 1010 (5th Cir. 1993).

[95] 256 F.3d 59 (1st Cir. 2001).

[96] 766 F.2d 37 (1st Cir. 1985).

[97] 723 F.2d 1012 (1st Cir. 1983).

The Second Circuit, in *United States v. D'Auria*,[98] explained the rationale for requiring a witness to make "an outright retraction and repudiation" of prior testimony, rather than simply disclaiming its truthfulness, to be eligible for the recantation defense:

> Otherwise a witness, by suggesting that he might be willing to change his perjurious testimony, could still avoid telling the whole truth by engaging in a skillful discussion with the prosecution aimed at finding out what contrary evidence existed in the government's possession and then tailoring his testimony to it rather than give his truthful recollection of the facts. The government is not obligated to engage in any such demeaning process of bargaining, including giving the witness multiple opportunities to testify, for what may turn out to be a revamped version of the perjury.

The circuit court found the defendant's conduct undermined his claimed recantation, finding that "D'Auria's entire conduct throughout the case was that of a person who, far from wanting to recant his false grand jury testimony, unsuccessfully sought through maneuvering and dissimulation to persuade the court and jury that it was essentially the truth."[99]

The third requirement involves an admission of falsity before there was any impact from the false statement on the proceeding in which it was made. Section 1623(d) provides that the admission of prior falsity will be effective if at the time it was made "the declaration has not substantially affected the proceeding, or it has not become manifest that such falsity has been or will be exposed." There is a split in the circuits about whether a defendant must establish both prongs to claim the recantation defense, or whether either will suffice. The issue revolves around whether Congress intended the "or" to be read in the disjunctive, or whether it really meant it to be understood as "and," requiring a defendant to prove each aspect for a successful defense.

In *United States v. Sherman*,[100] the Third Circuit found that the requirements for a recantation defense should be read as equally applicable, despite the use of the term "or" in the statute. The defendant had testified in an earlier medical malpractice trial as an expert witness, listing the states where he was permitted to practice and that none had revoked his license, when in fact on cross-examination he admitted that his licenses to practice medicine had been revoked in all jurisdictions. The district court dismissed perjury charges brought under § 1621 on the ground that the defendant had a valid recantation defense when his false statements had no appreciable impact on the malpractice case because the defense lawyer had brought forth the information about license revocations that the defendant readily admitted. The circuit court rejected the conclusion that charging the defendant under § 1621 rather than § 1623, which deprived him of the recantation defense, violated due process. It held that even if the case had been charged under § 1623, the recantation defense would not be available,

---

[98] 672 F.2d 1085 (2d Cir. 1982).

[99] See also United States v. Anfield, 539 F.2d 674, 679 (9th Cir.1976) ("Testimony which serves to cast doubt as to the truth of that which is perjurious is not a recantation. Being a poor liar does not make one a repentant sinner.").

[100] 150 F.3d 306 (3d Cir. 1998); see United States v. Moore, 613 F.2d 1029 (D.C. Cir. 1979).

stating that if only one prong of the impact element need be satisfied, then "one could commit perjury with impunity." The Third Circuit explained:

> A witness could violate his or her oath in the comfort of knowing that no perjury prosecution was possible so long as he or she recanted as soon as it appeared the perjury would be disclosed. A recantation at that point, under Sherman's interpretation, would shield the conduct even if the judicial proceedings had been substantially affected by the false testimony. Similarly, a witness could escape prosecution even after the false nature of it had been disclosed and hope to successfully argue that the proceedings had not been substantially effected because there had been a recantation.

Although it appeared odd to read "or" to mean "and," the Third Circuit justified its approach by referring to the legislative history of the provision, finding that "[o]nly if both statutory conditions exist at the time of recantation will Congress' dual purpose of deterring perjury through more effective prosecutions and encouraging truthful testimony be furthered." If only one need be shown, then the circuit court said it would give defendants a "get out of jail free card" by allowing witnesses to provide false testimony secure in the knowledge that as long as it was exposed in the proceeding there could be no criminal prosecution.

In *United States v. Moore*,[101] the District of Columbia Circuit looked to the New York statute on which § 1623 was based. The circuit court noted that the state law phrased the two conditions for invoking the recantation defense in the conjunctive rather than the disjunctive, which Congress "inexplicably" changed. In considering whether Congress actually intended that only one condition be met for the defense, the it stated:

> Had so drastic a departure from the New York statute as a switch from combinational to alternative satisfaction of its carefully developed preconditions been really intended, we believe Congress would have said so . . . Had Congress, after making crystal clear its purpose to promote truthtelling to the hilt, intended the almost wide-open door to prevarication that disinjunctive construction of the statutory preconditions would furnish, it hardly would have failed to elucidate its logic.

The District of Columbia Circuit found that "notwithstanding the formulation of Section 1623(d) grammatically, the will of Congress must prevail." By requiring both be shown as the prerequisite to the defense, the circuit court held that "Congress did not countenance in Section 1623(d) the flagrant injustice that would result if a witness is permitted to lie to a judicial tribunal and then, upon only learning that he had been discovered, grudgingly to recant in order to bar prosecution." The First, Second, and Fifth Circuits have taken the same conjunctive approach to the two conditions in § 1623(d).[102]

---

[101] 613 F.2d 1029 (D.C. Cir. 1979).

[102] See United States v. Scivola, 766 F.2d 37 (1st Cir. 1985) ("[I]n order for a recantation to effectively bar a prosecution for perjury pursuant to section 1623(d), it must be made both before the false testimony has substantially affected the proceeding and before it has become manifest."); United States v. Fornaro, 894 F.2d 508 (2d Cir. 1990) ("We therefore hold that recantation is an effective bar to prosecution only if the false

The Eighth Circuit took the opposite approach in *United States v. Smith*,[103] applying a plain meaning analysis in holding that "[t]he ordinary usage of the word 'or' is disjunctive, indicating an alternative. Construing the word 'or' to mean 'and' is conjunctive, and is clearly in contravention of its ordinary usage. Thus, we find the plain language of § 1623(d) controlling and accord the word 'or' its ordinary, disjunctive meaning." In considering the incentives created by its approach to the conditions for recantation, the circuit court explained that "construing the word 'or' to mean 'and' creates a statutory scheme providing a stronger incentive for witnesses to testify truthfully at the outset; however, we defer to Congress's chosen scheme as manifested by its language which balances encouragement of truthful testimony and penalties for perjury." It also relied on the rule of lenity to support its finding that the scope of the perjury prohibition should be read narrowly by recognizing a broader recantation defense.

In assessing whether the false statement had a substantial impact on the proceeding, courts have looked to the timing of the recantation and how the proceeding could be affected, not requiring that the effect lead to a different result. In *United States v. Crandall*,[104] a district court found that a two-month delay in providing the grand jury with truthful testimony was sufficient to preclude the defense "since the original declaration did substantially affect the proceeding." While the statute refers to the recantation "in the same proceeding," courts have been willing to recognize that an admission of prior false testimony, such as by a statement to a law enforcement agent, can be sufficient.

A determination of whether the falsity of the prior statement has been or will be exposed is made from the declarant's point of view, not whether the factfinder involved in the proceeding has learned of it. Section 1623(d) is designed to encourage truthfulness, so the longer a defendant waits to disclose the false statement the greater the risk that facts will emerge exposing the perjury, barring the defense. Courts have read this requirement narrowly, effectively imposing on a declarant the obligation to show that no one else was aware of the perjury when the person admitted to making a false statement. In *United States v. Denison*,[105] the Fifth Circuit held:

> There is little benefit to these investigations in permitting a witness to escape prosecution by recanting after it is clear to him that his perjury will be exposed. Such a rule would encourage a witness to testify falsely knowing he could always recant if evidence of his perjury comes to light. Congress did not intend to create so broad a shield when it passed § 1623(d).

In *United States v. Swainson*,[106] the Sixth Circuit found the defendant's recantation claim insufficient when "[h]is changed testimony came after he had heard

---

statement has not substantially affected the proceeding *and* if it has not become manifest that the falsity has been or will be exposed.") (italics in original); United States v. Scrimgeour, 636 F.2d 1019 (5th Cir. 1981) ("The rule of strict construction also applies to exceptions or provisions of a criminal statute which exempt conduct otherwise within a statute and the exception is to be strictly construed against the defendant seeking to invoke its protection.").

[103] 35 F.3d 344 (8th Cir. 1994).

[104] 363 F.Supp. 648 (W.D. Pa. 1973).

[105] 663 F.2d 611 (5th Cir. 1981).

[106] 548 F.2d 657 (6th Cir. 1977).

transcripts of the testimony of two eyewitnesses to a previous transaction which he had categorically denied in his earlier testimony." Similarly, in *United States v. DeLeon*,[107] the Seventh Circuit found that the defense was unavailable because "[b]y the time DeLeon alerted the district court to the falsity of the caseload statement in his motion to withdraw his guilty plea, its falsity had been exposed by not one but two witnesses." Although the defense may not be available once it is clear the person testified falsely, prosecutors have afforded witnesses the opportunity to recant prior false statements in order to assist in the truth-seeking function of the proceeding.[108]

The circuit courts have determined that recantation is a question of law to be decided by the court rather than the jury because the statute provides that a witness who successfully recants is barred from being prosecuted. In *United States v. Wiggan*,[109] the Ninth Circuit held that "the recantation claim is one that should be raised with the district court before trial," although evidence of the witness's subsequent statements can be introduced to show the defendant did not have the intent to commit perjury.

§ 10.8   THE TWO–WITNESS RULE

The traditional perjury offense imposed a heightened proof standard by requiring that two witnesses testify under oath against the defendant, so that the case did not devolve into a swearing contest as to which person the jury believed. Perjury prosecutions under § 1621 continue to adhere to the two-witness rule, while § 1623(e) dispenses with the requirement entirely by providing that "[i]t shall not be necessary that such proof be made by any particular number of witnesses or by documentary or other type of evidence." The two-witness rule is not a constitutional requirement, unlike that for proving treason,[110] and § 1623(e) has been upheld by all the lower courts that considered constitutional challenges to it.

In *Hammer v. United States*,[111] the Supreme Court explained that "[t]he general rule in prosecutions for perjury is that the uncorroborated oath of one witness is not enough to establish the falsity of the testimony of the accused set forth in the indictment as perjury. The application of that rule in federal and state courts is well nigh universal." In *Weiler v. United States*,[112] the Court rejected the government's invitation to dispense with the two-witness rule, pointing out that this "special rule which bars conviction for perjury solely upon the evidence of a single witness is deeply rooted in past centuries. That it renders successful perjury prosecution more difficult than it otherwise would be is obvious. . . . " In continuing to apply the rule, the Court explained that "[s]ince equally honest witnesses may well have differing recollections of the same event, we cannot reject as wholly unreasonable the notion that a conviction for perjury ought not to rest entirely upon 'an oath against an oath.'"

---

[107] 603 F.3d 397 (7th Cir. 2010).

[108] United States v. Beasley, 550 F.2d 261 (5th Cir. 1977).

[109] 700 F.3d 1204 (9th Cir. 2012). See United States v. Fornaro, 894 F.2d 508, 511 (2d Cir.1990); United States v. Goguen, 723 F.2d 1012, 1017 (1st Cir.1983); United States v. D'Auria, 672 F.2d 1085 (2d Cir. 1982); United States v. Denison, 663 F.2d 611, 618 (5th Cir. Dec.1981).

[110] U.S. Const. Art. III, § 3 ("No person shall be convicted of treason unless on the testimony of two witnesses to the same overt act, or on confession in open court.").

[111] 271 U.S. 620 (1926).

[112] 323 U.S. 606 (1945).

Weiler recognized that the two-witness rule should be softened somewhat, so that it does not strictly require two different individuals testifying to the falsity of the defendant's statement. According to the Court, one witness along with corroborative evidence showing the statement was false can be sufficient to support a perjury conviction so long as the following requirements were met: "(1) that the evidence, if true, substantiates the testimony of a single witness who has sworn to the falsity of the alleged perjurious statement; (2) that the corroborative evidence is trustworthy."

In *United States v. Weiner*,[113] the Second Circuit explained that evidence that "substantiates the testimony of a single witness" should be understood as meaning

> the two-witness rule has not been construed to require the Government, in effect, to prove its case twice over. At the other edge of the spectrum the corroboration of a casual or incidental bit of testimony given by the main witness for the prosecution on a matter which did not tend to show that the accused's statements under oath were false, could not be accepted as complying with the two-witness rule.

To meet the requirements of the rule when the second "witness" is circumstantial evidence, then "the two-witness rule is satisfied by corroborative evidence of sufficient content and quality to persuade the trier that what the principal prosecution witness testified to about the falsity of the accused's statement under oath was correct."

In *United States v. Forrest*,[114] the Fifth Circuit stated the standard for corroboration this way: "To sustain a conviction for perjury the evidence must be strong, clear, convincing and direct. Where the government seeks to establish perjury by the testimony of one witness and corroborating evidence, the latter must be independent of the former and inconsistent with the innocence of the defendant." In *United States v. Stewart*,[115] the Second Circuit upheld a perjury conviction based on the testimony of a witness who spoke with the defendant and a telephone message log that she created, which was admitted by the court as evidence under the business records exception to the hearsay rule. The circuit court found that the message log satisfied the two-witness rule, even though it came from the same source as the testimony used to establish the perjury, because "its reliability and trustworthiness derive from the circumstances under which it was created, rather than the author's recollection." In *Weiner*, the same court overturned a conviction because notes used to refresh the only witness's recollection did not have sufficient corroborative value to establish falsity. Similarly, in *United States v. Freedman*,[116] the Second Circuit overturned a perjury conviction based on a witness's testimony about the purpose of a transaction and the check establishing the payment because "[t]he crucial concern, that of an explanation of the transaction underlying the giving of the check, is not independently explained by proving the check's existence and its negotiation. Absent [the witness]'s definition of the deal, it is devoid in and of itself of any persuasiveness as to why it was given."

---

[113] 479 F.2d 923 (2d Cir. 1973).

[114] 639 F.2d 1224 (5th Cir. 1981).

[115] 433 F.3d 273 (2d Cir. 2006).

[116] 445 F.2d 1220 (2d Cir. 1971).

The two-witness rule gives way when one source of the proof is the defendant's own statements or writings to establish the falsity of the testimony under oath. As early as 1840, in *United States v. Wood*,[117] the Supreme Court stated:

> If it be true, then—and it is so—that the rule of a single witness, being insufficient to prove perjury rests upon the law of a presumptive equality of credit between persons, or upon what Starkie terms, the apprehension that it would be unsafe to convict in a case where there is merely the oath of one man to be weighed against that of another; satisfy the equal claim to belief, or remove the apprehension by concurring written proofs, which existed, and are proved to have been in the knowledge of the person charged with the perjury when it was committed, especially if such written proofs came from himself, and are facts which he must have known, because they were his own acts; and the reason for the rule ceases.

In *Phair v. United States*,[118] the Third Circuit noted that "[a] living witness is no longer necessary to a conviction for perjury where the defendant's own acts, business transactions, documents, or correspondence show that his oath charged to be perjury is false."

Testimony recounting a defendant's admissions that contradict what he stated under oath is insufficient, standing alone, to support a perjury conviction. In *Clayton v. United States*,[119] the Fourth Circuit found that "the only evidence in support of these [charges] is the testimony of two witnesses as to what defendant had told them in private conversation some time before the grand jury met. This was quite insufficient, for the falsity of a sworn statement is not shown by proof of an unsworn contradictory statement." A defendant's statement about the falsity of prior sworn testimony can be sufficient, however, to corroborate a witness's testimony that the defendant committed perjury, thus meeting the two-witness rule.

§ 10.9 SUBORNATION OF PERJURY

Having another person commit perjury is a separate offense, and under § 1622 "[w]hoever procures another to commit any perjury is guilty of subornation of perjury." Unlike the typical case in which one would be guilty as an accomplice for encouraging or enticing another to commit a crime, subornation was viewed as a more serious offense under the common law and received a greater punishment than that prescribed for aiding and abetting another person's crime. Today the maximum punishment for subornation is the same as prescribed in § 1621 and § 1623 for committing perjury, and the Sentencing Guidelines treat the three crimes identically.

Most cases in which one person induces another to commit perjury are prosecuted as an obstruction of justice under 18 U.S.C. 1512(b), which prohibits corruptly persuading another person to impede a proceeding, including any attempt to commit the offense (see § 6.3(C)). If a charge of subornation of perjury is pursued, the elements of the offense are:

---

[117] 39 U.S. (14 Pet.) 430 (1840).

[118] 60 F.2d 953 (3d Cir. 1932).

[119] 284 F. 537 (4th Cir. 1922).

(1) that the testimony of the suborned witness must be false and known to be false by him, and the truth of the matter so falsely testified to must be set forth; (2) the suborner must know or believe that the testimony of the witness about to be given will be false, and he must know or intend that the witness is to give the testimony corruptly or with the knowledge or belief of its falsity.[120]

The first step is establishing that the witness actually committed perjury, which means that any of the defenses that can be offered to negate a violation of § 1621 or § 1623 can be offered by the party accused of suborning perjury, such as a claim that the testimony was literally true. In *Petite v. United States*,[121] the Fourth Circuit explained, "Since proof that perjury was actually committed is a necessary element of subornation, the perjury must be established in the same manner as when the perjurer himself is tried."

In *United States v. Brumley*,[122] the Fifth Circuit overturned a subornation conviction because the evidence of materiality of the witness's statement was completely lacking, and that "[i]t is elemental, of course, that a defendant is not guilty of subornation of perjury unless the perjury is, in fact, committed." Similarly, in *Meyers v. United States*,[123] the District of Columbia Circuit overturned a conviction for suborning perjury when it could not be established that the witness was questioned on the subject matter, holding that "there can be no subornation of perjury if there was no perjury. It is equally true that one cannot be convicted of suborning perjury if the alleged perjurious statement actually was not made by the alleged perjuror."

The two-witness rule, when applicable, can also be a defense to a subornation charge. In *Hammer v. United States*,[124] the Supreme Court applied this evidentiary requirement in overturning a conviction for suborning perjury in a bankruptcy case. The Court explained that "[e]vidence that is not sufficient to warrant a finding of that fact as against the one accused of perjury cannot reasonably be held to be enough as against the other who is accused of suborning the perjury." The two-witness rule does not apply, however, to the procurement element of the offense, only proof of the underlying perjury, so the prosecution can rely on one witness—usually the person suborned—to establish a violation. In *United States v. Cravero*,[125] the Fifth Circuit stated, "In a trial for subornation of perjury, only the falsity of the witness' grand jury testimony must be proved by two witnesses. The inducement of the witness to commit perjury may be established by one witness' uncorroborated testimony."

The person suborning perjury must know, or at least believe, that the testimony given would be false, and that he knowingly induced or procured the witness to give the false testimony. Thus, if the defendant does not know or believe the witness will testify falsely, then there is no subornation even if the witness did in fact commit perjury. Similarly, if the procurer of the testimony believed it would be false, but the

---

[120] Boren v. United States, 144 F. 801 (9th Cir. 1906).

[121] 262 F.2d 788 (4th Cir. 1959).

[122] 560 F.2d 1268 (5th Cir. 1977).

[123] 171 F.2d 800 (D.C. Cir. 1948).

[124] 271 U.S. 620 (1926).

[125] 530 F.2d 666 (5th Cir. 1976).

witness knew it would be truthful, then there would be no subornation because of the witness's belief.

Chapter 11

TAX CRIMES

§ 11.1 INTRODUCTION

A. Constitutional Base

Article 1 § 8 of the Constitution provides "[t]hat Congress shall have power to lay and collect taxes." The ability to tax "income" without apportionment was provided by the Sixteenth Amendment to the Constitution, which allowed for the creation of a body of law that provides intricate statutes and rules concerning topics such as who may tax, what may be taxed, what may be excluded from taxation, how it can be taxed, and the methodology and structure for collecting taxes. At the heart of much of this body of law was what would constitute income for purposes of taxation.

A key aspect of the constitutional power to tax is that it would lack substance if it failed to recognize enforcement. In this regard, both civil and criminal enforcement mechanisms have developed over time. These enforcement measures help to achieve compliance with the tax laws and serve to deter, through punishment, those who fail to abide by the laws that are created.

Within Title 26 of the United States Code, a main product of the Sixteenth Amendment, are the existing criminal tax statutes. There are a relatively small number of criminal tax statutes when compared to the over 4,500 existing criminal statutes in the federal code.[1] But these tax statutes provide a voice to the power offered by the Sixteenth Amendment, and in this regard they are substantively and symbolically crucial aspects of the Internal Revenue Code. They criminalize, for example, attempts "to evade or defeat any tax,"[2] failure to file a tax return,[3] and the filing of a false return,[4] as well as other conduct related to reporting and paying income taxes.[5] Criminal tax statutes also provide criminalization to acts such as structuring transactions to evade reporting requirements.[6]

B. Tax Division

Tax prosecutions are overseen by the Department of Justice Tax Division, in order "[t]o achieve uniform, broad, and balanced criminal tax enforcement . . . "[7] This

---

[1] *See* Mila Sohoni, The Idea of "Too Much Law," 80 Fordham L. Rev. 1585, 1606 (2012) (discussing the problem of overcriminalization); John S. Baker, Jr., Jurisdictional and Separation of Powers Strategies to Limit the Expansion of Federal Crimes, 54 Am. U. L. Rev. 545, 548 (2005) (discussing the expansion of the federal criminal law).

[2] 26 U.S.C. § 7201.

[3] 26 U.S.C. § 7203.

[4] 26 U.S.C. § 7206.

[5] See 26 U.S.C. §§ 7201 et seq.

[6] 26 U.S.C. § 6050I. (See § 12.3).

[7] USAM § 6–4.010.

oversight includes the authorization to prosecute and also to decline investigations.[8] In most instances, a United States Attorney is restricted in proceeding with an investigation or prosecution of a tax matter unless it is authorized by the Tax Division.[9]

At the head of the Tax Division is an Assistant Attorney General. Tax Division cases include ones brought using crimes that are part of Title 26, the tax code, and also crimes that are outside the Tax Code. Thus, Tax Division cases can include charges from Title 18, such as false statements, mail fraud, obstruction of justice or a charge under the Rackeeter Influenced Corrupt Organization Act (RICO). But once a case has been approved by the Tax Division, the "United States Attorney generally has responsibility for handling the case."[10] The Tax Division's Criminal Tax Manual (CTM) serves as a key resource to guide the handling of tax cases.[11]

There are four components to the criminal tax enforcement process: "(1) IRS Criminal Investigation (CI) special agents; (2) attorneys with the IRS's Office of Chief Counsel Criminal Tax Division (CT); (3) TIGTA [Treasury Inspector General for Tax Administration] special agents; and (4) Assistant United States Attorneys."[12] Coordination between these components is essential for an effective process. The CTM states that:

> Within the Tax Division, four sections administer the enforcement of the nation's criminal tax laws: the Criminal Appeals and Tax Enforcement Policy Section (CATEPS) and three Criminal Enforcement Sections—Northern, Southern, and Western—with responsibility over designated geographical regions of the United States. Each section is supervised by a Section Chief, who reports to the Deputy Assistant Attorney General for Criminal Matters and the Assistant Attorney General of the Tax Division.[13]

Cases are typically investigated by IRS special agents, and this administrative investigation is turned over to the "Tax Division and in some cases, the United States Attorney."[14] There is no requirement that the government has to pursue tax cases civilly prior to initiating a criminal prosecution.[15] Because tax cases may be civil, criminal, or both, it is important to consider specific agency investigation law. (See § 17.6 (B)). Issues can also arise regarding parallel proceedings such as the sharing of information in civil and criminal enforcement proceedings. (See Chapter 18). State tax authorities can also be investigating or proceeding against the individual or corporation who may be under federal scrutiny.

---

[8] 28 C.F.R. § 0.70 (Tax Division—General Functions).

[9] USAM § 6–1.110.

[10] Id.

[11] The Criminal Tax Manual (CTM), available at http://www.justice.gov/tax/readingroom/2008ctm/CTM%20TOC.pdf.

[12] CTM § 1.01[4][b] (footnotes omitted).

[13] Id.

[14] USAM § 6–4.110. Direct referrals to the United States Attorney are covered in USAM § 6–4.243. For example, cases premised on 26 U.S.C. § 6050I are considered direct referral matters that can be sent to a United States Attorney. USAM § 6–4.243(E).

[15] See United States v. Ellett, 527 F.3d 38 (2d Cir. 2008).

C. Criminal Tax Prosecutions

Income tax statutes are used against ordinary tax cheats, something that is directly related to enforcing income tax laws. But in other instances, such as prosecutions of drug traffickers, organized crime, and more recently white collar offenders, income tax statutes are used to address conduct beyond the non-payment of taxes. In the past, prosecutors used tax statutes to creatively tackle criminal conduct that might be difficult to prove.

Although the government has used tax offenses creatively over the years, the number of prosecutions with a lead charge being a tax crime has decreased in recent years. For example, charges under 26 U.S.C. § 7201, the basic tax evasion statute, dropped 4.1% from ten years ago and 45.9% from twenty years ago.[16] Likewise, charges under 26 U.S.C. § 7203, willful failure to file a return, are down 37.9% from five years ago and 83.6% from twenty years ago.

The addition of new specialized federal statutes may account for the decreased number of tax prosecutions. Statutes that did not exist fifty years ago, like RICO[17] and Money Laundering,[18] may now cover the criminal conduct that had previously been prosecuted as tax crimes. Statutes focused on particular areas of conduct, such as bank fraud and health care fraud, provide new alternative charges when prosecuting white collar criminality.

Tax crimes, however, are also seen tacked onto criminal indictments, increasing the number of charges against an accused individual. Thus, a defendant may be charged with conduct related to government corruption, but also face tax charges for the improper income that he or she may have failed to report.[19] Recent prosecutions of individuals involved in conduct related to tax shelters may present new issues for the courts.[20]

D. Criminal Tax Statutes

Title 26 of the United States Code provides an array of tax offenses. The key charges used in criminal tax prosecutions are:

26 U.S.C. § 7201–Attempt to Evade or Defeat Tax (tax evasion)

---

[16] TracReports, Tax Convictions for 2012, at http://trac.syr.edu/tracreports/. The Office of the United States Attorneys (USAO) statistical reports provide that for tax fraud there were 741 cases in 2011, 945 cases in 1991, and 1005 cases in 1981. Annual Statistical Reports, available at http://www.justice.gov/usao/reading_room/foiamanuals.html.

[17] 18 U.S.C. §§ 1961 et seq.; see also chapter 8.

[18] 18 U.S.C. §§ 1956; see also chapter 12.

[19] For example, the primary charge under section § 2T1.1 of the U.S. Sentencing Guidelines, for "Tax Evasion, Willful Failure to File Return, Supply Information, or Pay Tax; Fraudulent or False Returns, Statements, or Other Documents," had 580 offenders sentenced in 2011, while 698 were sentenced under this same guideline as a non-primary offense. See U.S. Sentencing Commission, Sourcebook of Federal Sentencing Statistics, available at http://www.ussc.gov/Data_and_Statistics/Annual_Reports_and_Source books/2011/Table17.pdf.

[20] See, e.g., United States v. Coplan, 703 F.3d 46 (2d Cir. 2012); United States v. Daugerdas, 759 F. Supp.2d 461 (S.D. N.Y. 2010).

26 U.S.C. § 7203–Willful Failure to File Return, Supply Information, or Pay Tax (failure to file)

26 U.S.C. § 7206–Fraud and False Statements (filing or aiding and assisting in the filing of a false tax return)

26 U.S.C. § 7207–Fraudulent Returns, Statements, or Other Documents (delivering a fraudulent return)

Additionally, tax offenses can sometimes be prosecuted through general criminal statutes found in Title 18. (See § 11.1(E)).

In addition to these four main criminal tax crimes, there are also tax offenses such as a willful failure to collect or truthfully account for and pay over any tax (26 U.S.C. § 7202), a willful furnishing of a fraudulent statement or failing to furnish a statement to employees as required by section 6051 of the Internal Revenue Code (26 U.S.C. § 7204), and a willful failure to supply withholding information or the supplying of false withholding information to an employer (26 U.S.C. § 7205).

Section 7212 criminalizes two types of behavior. Under § 7212(a), one who corruptly or by force or threats of force endeavors to interfere with the administration of the internal revenue laws is subject to prosecution. Section 7212(b) criminalizes forcible rescue of property seized under the Internal Revenue Code. A tax offense also exists specifically to combat offenses such as extortion and obstruction by officers and employees "of the United States acting in connection with any revenue law of the United States." (26 U.S.C. § 7214).

There are also statutes for specific criminal conduct that arise in the context of tax issues. For example, false statements to purchasers or lessees relating to tax (26 U.S.C. § 7211), failure to obey a summons pursuant to certain sections of the Internal Revenue Code (26 U.S.C. § 7210), and disclosure or use of information by preparers of returns can in certain circumstances result in misdemeanor penalties (26 U.S.C. § 7216). There are also criminal penalties in the tax code for crimes such as structuring transactions to evade reporting requirements (26 U.S.C. § 6050I) (See § 12.3). Additional monetary penalties can be imposed for promoting an abusive tax shelter (26 U.S.C. § 6700).

E.   Generic Statutes

1.   Conspiracy

Tax misconduct may be charged using the conspiracy statute. For example, a conspiracy charge, under 18 U.S.C. § 371, may be brought when the accused conspires with another to commit an offense defined in other federal statutes or conspires to defraud the United States. Conspiracy under the generic conspiracy statute requires an overt act in furtherance of the conspiracy. (See Chapter 3).

Conspiracies to defraud the United States by defrauding the IRS are called "*Klein*" conspiracies, named after the case of *United States v. Klein*.[21] In *Klein* the Second

---

[21] 247 F.2d 908 (2d Cir. 1957).

Circuit found sufficient evidence to support the conspiracy, but cautioned that the "[m]ere failure to disclose income would not be sufficient to the crime charged of defrauding the United States under 18 U.S.C. § 371." Some of the cases following *Klein* have found that the government's use of conspiracy to defraud in a tax case was not warranted. (See § 3.4(B)(3)).

In *United States v. Coplan*,[22] the defendants were convicted of conspiracy to defraud the government, tax evasion, obstruction of the IRS, and false statements to the IRS. The defendants were partners and employees of accounting firm Ernst and Young, LLP, and the case arose from a group that was designing tax shelters. On appeal the defendants challenged the *Klein* conspiracy.[23]

The Court in *Coplan* examined the history of conspiracies to defraud noting the expansive reading given this statutory language in *Haas v. Henkel*.[24] The later decision in *Hammerschmidt v. United States*[25] limited this decision by stating that "[t]o conspire to defraud the United States means primarily to cheat the government out of property or money, but it also means to interfere with or obstruct one of its lawful governmental functions by deceit, craft or trickery, or at least by means that are dishonest."[26] Although the court in *Coplan* accepted the validity of *Klein* conspiracies, it rejected the evidence provided by the government with respect to the defendants.

In some instances the government will charge both a conspiracy to defraud and a conspiracy to commit a specific tax offense. In the case of *United States v. Helmsley*,[27] hotel owner Leona M. Helmsley was charged with conspiracy, tax evasion, mail fraud, and filing false personal tax returns. The conspiracy charge was premised on her and her husband's alleged scheme to charge personal expenses to business entities. The court rejected her arguments, including an argument claiming that since the state tax returns were required to be mailed, this could not be the basis for a mail fraud conviction. Although there is case law holding that required mailings cannot serve as the mailings for a mail fraud charge, the court stated that this case was limited to its particular circumstances.[28] The *Helmsley* court found that the fraudulent misrepresentations were part of the execution of the fraud. The court also allowed a jury instruction that permitted the jury to consider both violations of the defraud clause and specific offense clause in § 371.

2.   *Other White Collar Offenses*

False statements (18 U.S.C. § 1001), false claims (18 U.S.C. § 287), perjury (18 U.S.C. § 1621), and mail fraud (18 U.S.C. § 1341) are some of the offenses that have been used when the conduct involves tax violations. The Department of Justice, however, restrains prosecutorial discretion by internally limiting the application of

---

[22] 703 F.3d 46 (2d Cir. 2012).

[23] The court explored the history of *Klein* conspiracies citing Abraham S. Goldstein, Conspiracy to Defraud the United States, 68 Yale L.J. 405 (1959).

[24] 216 U.S. 462 (1910).

[25] 265 U.S. 182 (1924)

[26] Id. at 188.

[27] 941 F.2d 71 (2d Cir. 1991).

[28] See Parr v. United States, 363 U.S. 370 (1960) (holding that required mailings were not part of the execution of the scheme to defraud).

mail fraud charges to tax offenses, and requires authorization to prosecute tax violations as mail fraud. Further, a Department of Justice guideline states that "absent unusual circumstances [ ] the Tax Division will not approve mail or wire fraud charges if a case involves only one person's tax liability or when all submissions to the IRS were truthful."[29] But the guidance provided to prosecutors also provides that mail and wire fraud "charges may be appropriate if the target filed multiple fraudulent returns seeking tax refunds using fictitious names, or using the names of real taxpayers without their knowledge."[30]

The DOJ restriction on using mail fraud for tax conduct, serves to also limit tax violations that might be prosecuted under RICO. Because mail fraud serves as one of the possible predicate acts for a RICO offense, but tax violations do not, the restriction has the effect of precluding many tax violations from being used in RICO prosecutions. (See Chapter 8). This guideline, as with all DOJ guidelines, are not enforceable as a matter of law in that they are merely internal guidelines of the Department.

Defendants have challenged cases when the prosecution charged both a tax violation and mail fraud charge, arguing that mail fraud should not be used when a more specific crime exists, the more specific legislation being the tax fraud charge.[31] Courts, however, have allowed the crime of mail fraud to be used when the underlying conduct is the mailing of a fraudulent tax return. For example, in *United States v. Mangan*,[32] one defendant, an Internal Revenue Service agent, and his brother, submitted false tax returns in order to obtain the refunds. The government charged the defendants with conspiracy, mail fraud, and the filing of false tax returns under 26 U.S.C. § 7206. The Second Circuit rejected defendants' claim that this was an improper use of the mail fraud statute, stating "[t]he scheme here was to swindle the Government by causing it to pay out money to persons having no entitlement to it, in a fashion similar to those embraced within the historic purpose of the mail fraud statute."[33]

But in *United States v. Henderson*,[34] a district court in the Southern District of New York rejected tax fraud charges brought using the mail fraud statute. Defendant Lyle C. "Skitch" Henderson had donated musical scores to the University of Wisconsin, taking a deduction for this charitable donation. The government contested the documentation and value of this donation and proceeded to charge him with both mail fraud and tax fraud. The court rejected the prosecution's case, finding that mail fraud's "stopgap" device was unnecessary here since "particularized legislation" had been enacted. The court noted the harms of "pyramiding of sentences" that could be

---

[29] USAM § 6–4.210; see also Tax Division Directive No. 128–Charging Mail Fraud, Wire Fraud or Bank Fraud Alone or as Predicate Offenses in Cases Involving Tax Administration, available at http://www.justice.gov/usao/eousa/foia_reading_room/usam/title6/tax00014.htm.

[30] Id. at Tax Division Directive No. 128.

[31] Ellen S. Podgor, Tax Fraud—Mail Fraud: Synonymous, Cumulative or Diverse?, 57 U. Cin. L. Rev. 903 (1989).

[32] 575 F.2d 32 (2d Cir. 1978).

[33] Id. at 49.

[34] 386 F.Supp. 1048 (S.D.N.Y. 1974).

"staggering" and "utterly unrealistic."[35] But many courts have not accepted the position taken by the Southern District of New York court in *Henderson*.[36]

§ 11.2 WILLFULNESS

A. Generally

The term "willfully" is seen in several criminal tax statutes.[37] A long line of Supreme Court opinions have provided the contours for how to interpret this term. Key decisions include *United States v. Murdock*,[38] *Spies v. United States*,[39] *United States v. Bishop*,[40] *United States v. Pomponio*,[41] and *Cheek v. United States*.[42] Other Supreme Court opinions have dealt with related issues such as the role of lesser included offenses.[43] For example, in *Sansone v. United States*,[44] the Court examined differences between tax evasion in § 7201 and misdemeanor offenses in §§ 7203 (willful failure to file) and 7207 (filing a false return) to determine whether the accused was entitled to a lesser offense charge. The discussion here included consideration of the element of willfulness.

To meet the willfulness element, courts require the government to prove that the accused intentionally and voluntarily violated a known legal duty. Whether the accused acted with the requisite intent is a question of fact subject to jury determination. Often the prosecution offers circumstantial evidence as proof of this *mens rea*. A jury may infer willfulness from the facts presented. In practice, juries are often provided with evidence of the accused engaging in fraudulent type conduct, what some might call "badges of fraud." For example, in *United States v. Olbres*,[45] the First Circuit found sufficient evidence by noting the following:

> (1) the defendants signed the 1987 tax return; (2) they knew the contents of the return at the time they signed it, and they knew that it significantly understated their taxable income; (3) they knew their business had made substantially more money than the return reflected; (4) they had received revenues during the tax year which they knew were taxable, such as business receipts and transportation rebates, yet they neither deposited those revenues in the business checking account nor recorded their receipt in the usual manner, but, instead, diverted the revenues to other bank accounts; (5) they deliberately understated the amounts of rental income received when transmitting data to their accountant preliminary to the accountant's preparation of their tax return; and (6) they withheld materials

---

[35] Id. at 1054.

[36] See United States v. Ohle, 678 F. Supp.2d 215, 220–21 n.1 (S.D. N.Y. 2010) (citing cases rejecting *Henderson's* position).

[37] 26 U.S.C. §§ 7201–7207.

[38] 290 U.S. 389 (1933).

[39] 317 U.S. 492 (1943).

[40] 412 U.S. 346 (1973).

[41] 429 U.S. 10 (1976).

[42] 498 U.S. 192 (1991).

[43] Berra v. United States, 351 U.S. 131 (1956); Achilli v. United States, 353 U.S. 373 (1957).

[44] 380 U.S. 343 (1965).

[45] 61 F.3d 967 (1st Cir. 1995).

from the accountant (and, later, from the IRS auditor) that would have pointed to the existence and extent of the undeclared income.[46]

The Supreme Court has also examined how the specific intent required by willfulness can be negated. In *James v. United States*[47] the Court held that willfulness requires proof through independent evidence and that this "cannot be inferred from the mere understatement of income."[48]

Whether willfulness can be negated by uncertainty in the tax law is a subject that courts have considered, although not always with agreement.[49] Oftentimes, expert testimony is requested by the defendant to explain the taxation issues to the jury. For example, in *United States v. Garber*,[50] the Fifth Circuit in an *en banc* hearing, examined the defendant's conviction for tax fraud that stemmed from her alleged failure to report income from the sale of her blood. The court reversed and remanded this § 7201 conviction, finding that the district court had acted improperly in failing to permit experts from testifying on the question of whether the income was taxable. The court also found it improper for the trial court to have refused to instruct the jury that a reasonable misconception of tax law would negate defendant's intent. Because of the novel and unsettled nature of the law, the defendant should have been afforded the opportunity to present this position. The court in reversing Garber's conviction stated:

> The tax treatment of earnings from the sale of blood plasma or other parts of the human body is an uncharted area in tax law. The parties in this case presented divergent opinions as to the ultimate taxability by analogy to two legitimate theories in tax law. The trial court should not have withheld this fact, and its powerful impact on the issue of Garber's willfulness, from the jury.

Some cases, however, limit[51] or reject the position taken in *Garber,* finding uncertainty in the law as an improper defense to a tax charge. For example, the Sixth Circuit in *United States v. Curtis*,[52] rejected *Garber* because it (1) "allows juries to find that uncertainty in the law negates willfulness even when the defendant is unaware of that uncertainty"; (2) "distorts the role of expert witnesses and the purpose of their testimony"; and (3) "requires the jury to assume part of the judge's responsibility to rule on questions of law."[53] The *Curtis* court stated that a jury should not be asked "to read and interpret statutes to determine whether or not the governing law is uncertain or debatable."[54]

---

[46] Id. at 973.

[47] 366 U.S. 213 (1961).

[48] Quoting Holland v. United States, 348 U.S. 121 (1954).

[49] See United States v. Vallone, 698 F.3d 416, 453 n.3 (7th Cir. 2012) (discussing the different positions taken by courts on presenting experts to explain an uncertainty in law).

[50] 607 F.2d 92 (5th Cir.1979).

[51] See United States v. Burton, 737 F.2d 439 (5th Cir. 1984) (limiting Garber to cases where the uncertainty is "approaching legal vagueness").

[52] 782 F.2d 593 (6th Cir. 1986).

[53] Id. at 599–600.

[54] Id. at 600.

B. Court Interpretations

1. *United States v. Murdock*[55]

In *Murdock* the Court interpreted willfulness to mean acts done with "bad purpose or evil intent." Defendant Murdock had been indicted "for [his] refusal to give testimony and supply information as to deductions claimed in his 1927 and 1928 income tax returns for moneys paid to others." The Court stated, "that, where directions as to the method of conducting a business are embodied in a revenue act to prevent loss of taxes, and the act declares a willful failure to observe the directions a penal offense, an evil motive is a constituent element of the crime."[56]

2. *Spies v. United States*[57]

The Court recognized this history from *Murdock* in *Spies*, noting that although the willfulness element remains consistent in all tax fraud prosecutions, it "is a word of many meanings, its construction often being influenced by its context."[58] Defendant Spies had been convicted of attempting to defeat and evade income tax in violation of § 145(b), a predecessor to the current statute. Although he admitted to having sufficient income to pay the tax, he failed to pay or file a return despite the statutory duty. Defendant, however, presented evidence showing specific circumstances to support his lack of willfulness in failing to comply with his legal obligations. He requested an instruction that would advise the jury of there being an affirmative act necessary to meet the element of willfulness. The trial court, however, rejected his requested instruction.

The government in *Spies* argued that a "willful failure to file a return together with a willful failure to pay the tax may, without more, constitute an attempt to defeat or evade a tax within § 145(b).[59] The defendant responded that this only establishes two misdemeanors covered by § 145(a), and that this should not be sufficient for the felony charge under § 145(b).

The *Spies* Court agreed with the petitioner-defendant stating that,

> [t]he difference between willful failure to pay a tax when due, which is made a misdemeanor, and willful attempt to defeat and evade one, which is made a felony, is not easy to detect or define. Both must be willful, and willful, as we have said, is a word of many meanings, its construction often being influenced by its context.

The Court found the difference in the two offenses rested with the "affirmative action implied from the term 'attempt' as used in the felony subsection." The Court held that "[w]illful but passive neglect of the statutory duty may constitute the lesser offense, but to combine with it a willful and positive attempt to evade tax in any manner or to

---

[55] 290 U.S. 389 (1933).

[56] Id. at 395.

[57] 317 U.S. 492 (1943).

[58] Id. at 497.

[59] Id. at 494–95.

defeat it by any means lifts the offense to the degree of felony."[60] The Court concluded its opinion stating:

> The Government argues against this construction, contending that the milder punishment of a misdemeanor and the benefits of a short statute of limitation should not be extended to violators of the income tax laws such as political grafters, gamblers, racketeers, and gangsters. We doubt that this construction will handicap prosecution for felony of such flagrant violators. Few of them, we think, in their efforts to escape tax stop with mere omission of the duties put upon them by the statute, but if such there be, they are entitled to be convicted only of the offense which they have committed.[61]

3. United States v. Bishop[62]

The *Bishop* case dealt with a lawyer who was convicted of three counts of filing a false return in violation of 26 U.S.C. § 7206(1), a felony. His defense at trial was that he was unaware of double deductions and improper deductions taken on his return. The trial court rejected his request for a lesser included instruction on the misdemeanor offense of delivering a fraudulent return under 26 U.S.C. § 7207. He argued that § 7207 was a lesser included offense of the felony and that "willfully" as found in the misdemeanor statute should be construed to require less *scienter* than the term would require in the felony offense.

In rejecting defendant's argument, the Supreme Court in *Bishop* stated that "'willfully' has the same meaning in § 7207 that it has in § 7206(1)."[63] The Court noted the importance of having a consistent definition for willfulness as used in different tax statutes. The Court stated that "consistent interpretation of the word 'willfully' to require an element of *mens rea* implements the pervasive intent of Congress to construct penalties that separate the purposeful tax violator from the well-meaning, but easily confused, mass of taxpayers."[64] While adhering to the historical standard of willfulness, the Court also stated that willfully "connotes a voluntary, intentional violation of a known legal duty."[65]

4. United States v. Pomponio[66]

In *United States v. Pomponio*, the Supreme Court elucidated upon its holding in *Bishop*. Petitioners in *Pomponio* were convicted of willfully filing false income tax returns and like *Bishop*, the case alleged a violation of 26 U.S.C. § 7206(1). The instruction given by the trial court had not required a finding of bad purpose or evil motive. The Court in *Pomponio* stated that *Bishop* did not require "proof of any motive other than an intentional violation of a known legal duty."[67] Thus, the trial court did not err in failing to instruct the jury on bad purpose or evil motive. A later Sixth

---

[60] Id. at 499.

[61] Id. at 500.

[62] 412 U.S. 346 (1973).

[63] Id. at 361.

[64] Id.

[65] Id. at 360.

[66] 429 U.S. 10 (1976).

[67] Id. at 12.

Circuit court using the *Pomponio* decision additionally noted that a *"good-faith motive for willfully committing tax fraud has never constituted a proper defense."*[68]

5. *Cheek v. United States*[69]

Although a "good-faith motive" is not a defense, negating willfulness is possible when the accused has a good faith misunderstanding of the law. In the landmark case of *Cheek v. United States,* the Supreme Court resolved the standard to be used by a jury in deciding whether a defendant had a good-faith misunderstanding of the law that negated willfulness.

Petitioner Cheek, a commercial airline pilot, was convicted by a jury of six counts of failing to file federal income tax returns in violation of 26 U.S.C. § 7203, and three counts of tax evasion in violation of 26 U.S.C. § 7201. He was accused of not filing income tax returns after 1979 and claiming an increased number of withholding allowances on his W–4 forms. His position was that he was exempt from federal income tax. Petitioner, acting pro se at trial, argued that he acted without willfulness in that he believed his actions were lawful and further that he believed that the tax laws were being unconstitutionally enforced.

The district court instructed the jury on three occasions regarding aspects of willfulness. The latter two occasions were as a result of questions submitted to the court by the jury. On appeal Cheek argued that the trial court erred in instructing the jury "that only an objectively reasonable misunderstanding of the law negates the statutory willfulness requirement." The Seventh Circuit rejected Cheek's argument and affirmed his convictions.

The Supreme Court granted certiorari and thereafter vacated the judgment of the Court of Appeals and remanded the case for further proceedings consistent with its opinion. The Supreme Court reaffirmed that the standard for willfulness is the "voluntary, intentional violation of a known legal duty." Justice White, writing the majority opinion, however, also noted that the term "willfully" as used in federal criminal tax offenses served to "carv[e] out an exception to the traditional rule" that ignorance of the law or mistake of law is no defense in a criminal prosecution. The complexity of the tax laws warranted this exception.[70]

In resolving the issues presented in the *Cheek* case, the Court concentrated on the "knowledge" requirement of willfulness. The Court found that the government must prove that the defendant is "aware of the duty at issue, which cannot be true if the jury credits a good-faith misunderstanding and belief submission, whether or not the claimed belief or misunderstanding is objectively reasonable."[71] To characterize a belief as not objectively reasonable transforms the question to a legal issue and precludes the jury from properly resolving this factual question. It was, therefore, improper for the trial court to instruct the jury in such a way that they were precluded from considering petitioner's asserted beliefs that wages were not income and that he was not a taxpayer within the meaning of the Internal Revenue Code. The Court determined that

---

[68] United States v. Aaron, 590 F.3d 405 (6th Cir. 2009).

[69] 498 U.S. 192 (1991).

[70] Id. at 200.

[71] Id. at 203.

these points were rightfully issues to be decided by a jury in considering whether Cheek had acted willfully.

The Court in *Cheek*, however, rejected the defendant's claim that he had a good-faith belief that the income tax laws were unconstitutional as applied to him. Claiming that the law was unconstitutional demonstrated that the accused was not acting from innocent mistakes. Rather, it provided a showing of full knowledge of the law. Since a defendant's view of the law is irrelevant to the issue of willfulness, it was not error for the trial court to instruct the jury to disregard defendant's claims that the tax laws were unconstitutional.

In his concurring opinion, Justice Scalia voiced his dissatisfaction with the Court's test for willfulness. He argued that willfulness should not be interpreted so "that belief in the nonexistence of a textual prohibition excuses liability, but belief in the invalidity (*i.e.*, the legal nonexistence) of a textual prohibition does not."[72]

A dissent authored by Justice Blackmun, and joined by Justice Marshall, criticized the Court for exceeding the limits of common sense. The dissent expressed the view that a person of defendant's intelligence should not be permitted to assert, as a defense to willfulness, that the wages he receives for labor is not income. They stated:

> [I]t is incomprehensible to me how, in this day, more than 70 years after the institution of our present federal income tax system with the passage of the Income Tax Act of 1913, . . . any taxpayer of competent mentality can assert as his defense to charges of statutory willfulness the proposition that the wage he receives for his labor is not income, irrespective of a cult that says otherwise and advises the gullible to resist income tax collections. One might note in passing that this particular taxpayer, after all, was a licensed pilot for one of our major commercial airlines; he presumably was a person of at least minimum intellectual competence.[73]

The Supreme Court remanded the case back to the Seventh Circuit, where the appellate court stated:

> Tax evaders who persist in their frivolous beliefs (such as that wages are not income or that Federal Reserve Notes do not constitute cash or income) should not be encouraged by the Court's decision in *Cheek* or our decision today. While a defendant is now permitted to argue that his failure to file tax returns and to pay his income taxes was the result of his incredible misunderstanding of the tax law's applicability, the government remains free to present evidence demonstrating that he knew what the law required but simply chose to disregard those duties. . . . And, as the Court noted, "the more unreasonable the asserted beliefs or misunderstandings are, the more likely the jury will consider them to be nothing more than simple disagreement with known legal duties imposed by the tax laws and will find that the Government has carried its burden of proving knowledge." . . . [74]

---

[72] Id. at 208.

[73] Id. at 209–10.

[74] United States v. Cheek, 931 F.2d 1206 (7th Cir. 1991).

The Seventh Circuit then remanded the case to the trial court for a retrial of Cheek. At the retrial Cheek attempted to argue a good-faith belief premised upon his reliance on the advice of counsel. The trial court, however, refused his requested instruction on advice of counsel. Cheek was convicted and sentenced to a year and a day and fined $62,000. The Seventh Circuit affirmed this conviction, finding insufficient evidence to warrant the giving of an advice of counsel instruction.[75]

§ 11.3   TAX EVASION

A.   Statutory Base

Tax evasion is considered the "capstone" of the tax offenses. Its purpose is to "induce prompt and forthright fulfillment of every duty under the income tax law and to provide a penalty suitable to every degree of delinquency."[76] "The gravamen of Section 7201 is the specific intent or design to deprive the Government of taxes."[77] The elements of a charge pursuant to 26 U.S.C. § 7201 are: (1) the existence of a tax deficiency, (2) an affirmative act of evasion or attempted evasion of tax, and (3) willfulness.[78] The felony of tax evasion carries a penalty of not more than five years imprisonment and a fine. When the evasion is by a corporation, the statutory fine can be higher than what is provided for by statute to an individual.

The government is required to prove beyond a reasonable doubt the existence of a tax deficiency. In *United States v. Chesson*,[79] the Fifth Circuit stated that "[t]o prove a tax deficiency, 'the government must show that the taxpayer had unreported income, and second, that the income was taxable.'"[80] A civil agency determination of civil collection remedies is not sufficient proof of a deficiency for purposes of a criminal tax evasion case,[81] but "an unchallenged certificate of assessment" has been held to be "prima facie evidence of a deficiency when a taxpayer who filed no return is charged with tax evasion."[82]

Courts differ on whether it is necessary to prove a substantial deficiency to meet the element of an existence of a tax deficiency. Some courts look for a showing of a substantial deficiency,[83] while others note that the "government need not charge a substantial tax deficiency to indict or convict under 26 U.S.C. § 7201."[84] "It simply states that willful attempts to evade 'any tax' under the Tax Code is a felony."[85] Thus, courts may reject a defendant's *de minimis* argument. In reality, the Justice

---

[75] United States v. Cheek, 3 F.3d 1057 (7th Cir. 1993).

[76] Spies v. United States, 317 U.S. 492, 497 (1943).

[77] United States v. DeNiro, 392 F.2d 753, 758 (6th Cir. 1968).

[78] Sansone v. United States, 380 U.S. 343 (1965).

[79] 933 F.2d 298 (5th Cir. 1991).

[80] Id. at 306 (citing United States v. Fogg, 652 F.2d 551, 555 (5th Cir.1981)). Section 7201 does not define the term "deficiency," but 26 U.S.C. § 6211 does offer a definition. See also United States v. Schoppert, 362 F.3d 451 (8th Cir. 2004).

[81] United States v. Silkman, 156 F.3d 833 (8th Cir. 1998), on remand 220 F.3d 935 (8th Cir. 2000).

[82] United States v. Silkman, 220 F.3d 935, 937 (8th Cir. 2000).

[83] United States v. Daniels, 387 F.3d 636, 640 n.2 (7th Cir. 2004) (collecting cases from different circuits which provide guidance on whether a "substantial" tax deficiency is required).

[84] Id. at 641.

[85] United States v. Marashi, 913 F.2d 724, 735 (9th Cir. 1990).

Department seldom prosecutes a tax evasion case absent a showing of a sufficient level of tax due and owing.

A mere tax deficiency will not suffice to sustain an evasion conviction. It is also essential that the government show an affirmative act of evasion and willfulness.[86] The evidence supporting these latter two elements (affirmative act and willfulness) often coalesces. Although a "simple nonpayment of taxes owed cannot sustain a conviction under the statute, acts intended to conceal or mislead [can be] sufficient."[87]

The defendant's signing his or her name to an income tax return with knowledge that it failed to correctly state the defendant's income and tendering that return to the IRS has been held to suffice for an evasion charge.[88] But merely signing a blank return was found to be insufficient evidence absent knowledge of the contents of the return by the individual signing.[89] A court held that it is not, however, necessary for the government to prove that the form filed by the defendant was in fact a "return" in order to establish a tax evasion crime as the "filing of a 'return' is not an element of the crime of tax evasion."[90] Likewise the filing of an accurate return does not preclude an evasion prosecution under § 7201 when the defendant evades paying the taxes due on the reported return.[91]

As to the second element of the crime of tax evasion, the government can meet its burden by proving either an affirmative act of evasion or attempted evasion. As stated in *United States v. McGill*,[92] "[a]n affirmative act is anything done to mislead the government or conceal funds to avoid payment of an admitted and accurate deficiency."[93] Sometimes the alleged conduct will be rejected as insufficient for meeting this element of a § 7201 violation. For example, in *United States v. Romano*,[94] the First Circuit held that taking money out of the country without reporting it, giving evasive answers to customs officials, and failing to file a tax return, did not establish beyond a reasonable doubt an attempt to evade or defeat tax.[95]

In contrast, other cases have found that false statements to an IRS agent constitute an affirmative act. For example, in *United States v. Newman*,[96] the Fifth Circuit held that:

Although defendant did not file any false *returns*, there is ample proof of *statements* made by defendant to Treasury agents denying any income during the years in question. The government's evidence, accepted by the jury, established that these statements were false. It is clear that making false statements to

---

[86] United States v. McGill, 964 F.2d 222 (3d Cir. 1992).

[87] United States v. Voigt, 89 F.3d 1050, 1090 (3d Cir. 1996).

[88] United States v. Hoover, 233 F.2d 870 (3d Cir. 1956).

[89] United States v. Bass, 425 F.2d 161 (7th Cir. 1970).

[90] United States v. Robinson, 974 F.2d 575 (5th Cir. 1992).

[91] United States v. Schoppert, 362 F.3d 451 (8th Cir. 2004).

[92] United States v. McGill, 964 F.2d 222 (3d Cir. 1992).

[93] Id. at 230.

[94] 938 F.2d 1569 (2nd Cir. 1991).

[95] Id. at 1572.

[96] 468 F.2d 791 (5th Cir. 1972).

Treasury agents for the purpose of concealing income constitutes a sufficient affirmative act to satisfy § 7201.[97]

A similar position was taken in a Second Circuit decision which found that a defendant's background as a CPA, making false statements to government agents, and continually underestimating his tax liability served to infer willfulness and met the required affirmative act.[98]

Willfulness is also an element for proving an evasion charge. (See § 11.2). In *Spies v. United States*,[99] the Supreme Court examined the predecessor evasion statute as it relates to the misdemeanor of willful failure to pay a tax. According to the Court, the factor that distinguishes these two offenses is the "affirmative action implied from the term 'attempt,' as used in the felony subsection."[100] While the misdemeanor can be a willful omission, the felony of evasion requires a positive attempt to evade tax.

The willful attempt to defeat or evade tax can be accomplished "in any manner." In *Spies* the Court offered illustrations of conduct (so-called "badges of fraud") from which a willful attempt could be inferred. The examples provided were

> keeping a double set of books, making false entries or alterations, or false invoices or documents, destruction of books or records, concealment of assets or covering up sources of income, handling of one's affairs to avoid making the records usual in transactions of the kind, and any conduct, the likely effect of which would be to mislead or conceal.

The filing of a false tax return has been found to be a sufficient affirmative commission to satisfy this element,[101] as has the filing of a false W–4 tax form.[102] Likewise, concealment of assets may prove sufficient.[103] A consistent pattern of underreporting may also suffice.[104]

B. Methods of Proof[105]

It is necessary for the government to prove a tax deficiency for a prosecution under § 7201. One way this can be accomplished is through the direct or specific item method. Alternatively, the government can use indirect methods of proof. The indirect methods include the net worth method, the expenditures method, and bank deposit method.

The direct or specific item method is considered the simplest method of proving a tax deficiency. It employs specific items to prove the underpayment. For example, a defendant's records could be used to prove that a specific deduction listed on the return was improper.

---

[97] Id. at 794.

[98] United States v. Klausner, 80 F.3d 55 (2d Cir. 1996).

[99] 317 U.S. 492 (1943).

[100] Id. at 498.

[101] Sansone v. United States, 380 U.S. 343 (1965).

[102] United States v. King, 126 F.3d 987 (7th Cir. 1997).

[103] United States v. Hook, 781 F.2d 1166, 1169 (6th Cir. 1986).

[104] United States v. Garavaglia, 566 F.2d 1056 (6th Cir. 1977).

[105] See generally Ellen S. Podgor & Jerold H. Israel, White Collar Crime in a Nutshell 4th Ed. 182 (2009).

Indirect methods of proving a tax deficiency use circumstantial evidence to establish this element. One such method is the net worth method that examines the defendant's net worth at the beginning of a year in contrast to his or her net worth at the end of the year.

In *Holland v. United States*,[106] the Supreme Court examined the use of the net worth method and stated that "requisite to the use of the net worth method is evidence supporting the inference that the defendant's net worth increases are attributable to currently taxable income."[107] This can be accomplished in two ways: (1) by "show[ing] that there is a likely taxable source of the unreported income;" or (2) "it can negate all possible nontaxable sources of that income."[108] The *Holland* Court noted the flaws inherent in using a net worth method, but upheld its legality cautioning that it be subject to the "exercise of great care and restraint."[109] It is essential that the government establish the net worth at the beginning of the year with "reasonable certainty." Because the net worth method rests solely on circumstantial evidence, courts require the government to investigate all reasonable explanations offered by the defendant that are inconsistent with guilt. That said, one court noted that it is not necessary to reduce everything to a certainty. If a defendant's "financial dealings could be precisely determined[,] use of the net worth method would be unnecessary."[110]

In *United States v. Heath*,[111] the Sixth Circuit noted how "a number of courts have held that a substantiality instruction is necessary" when the "net worth" method is used and the amount of tax owed is disputed by the defense.[112] The court reiterated from *Holland* how the net worth method is "fraught with danger for the innocent" in stating that the "phrase 'substantial tax' must be included as part of the first element of § 7201."[113] The court noted that this phrase was not part of the model instructions used by the Sixth Circuit. That said, there was no error found in this case because "there was no dispute at trial over the amount that Heath owed in unpaid taxes."[114] The essence of this case was not about "unreported income" but rather about "his decision to claim that he was exempt from paying taxes on what he reported."[115]

Using the cash expenditures method, a variant of the net worth method, the government shows that the defendant's expenditures exceeded the reported income. Presumably the source of funds for these expenditures must be taxable income.[116]

Finally, the government can use the bank deposit method for proving the tax deficiency. The government examines the bank deposits of the defendant, excluding deposits that are not taxable income. These deposits are then compared to the reported

---

[106] 348 U.S. 121 (1954).

[107] Id. at 137.

[108] United States v. Dwoskin, 644 F.2d 418 (5th Cir. 1981) (citing Holland, 348 U.S. at 138 and United States v. Massei, 355 U.S. 595 (1958).

[109] Holland, 348 U.S. at 129.

[110] Dwoskin, 644 F.2d at 423.

[111] 525 F.3d 451 (6th Cir. 2008).

[112] See United States v. Sorrentino, 726 F.2d 876 (1st Cir. 1984).

[113] Heath, 525 F.3d at 457 (citing Holland, 348 U.S. at 125).

[114] Id.

[115] Id.

[116] See United States v. Citron, 783 F.2d 307 (2d Cir. 1986).

income of the accused. The excess in the amount deposited over the reported income represents the unreported income.

The government also may use a combination of methods. For example, in *United States v. Scott*,[117] the defendant William J. Scott, former Attorney General for the State of Illinois, was convicted of one count of violating § 7206(1). The government used the net worth, cash expenditures, and specific items methods to prove that Scott had falsely reported his adjusted gross income for 1972.

§ 11.4   FAILURE TO FILE A RETURN OR PAY A TAX

Section 7203 criminalizes the willful failure to pay any tax, make any return, keep any records, or supply any information as required by law or regulations. The government must prove beyond a reasonable doubt that the accused, (1) willfully, (2) failed to make a return, to pay a tax, to keep records or supply information, (3) having a legal duty to do so, (4) at the time required by law. This misdemeanor offense carries a penalty of up to one year imprisonment and a fine. Corporate fines can be higher than those permitted against individuals. If the failure to pay involves an estimated tax, the section is inapplicable if there is no addition to the tax under §§ 6654 and 6655. The statute, however, does become a felony offense where the willful violation involves § 6050I of the Code. (See § 12.3). A currency reporting violation under this statute carries a penalty of up to five years imprisonment.

This section is commonly employed to prosecute tax protesters who fail to file a return or who file incomplete returns. It is rare that the government proceeds with a § 7203 case absent a certain threshold of unpaid tax. Failure to file can be proven by testimony of an individual from the IRS stating that a search was made of the government's records and no return was found. As with other tax offenses, the government is required to prove that the accused acted willfully. (See § 11.2).

Section 7203 is considered a lesser included offense of tax evasion under § 7201. As such courts have rejected the defendant being punished for both offenses in the same case.[118]

§ 11.5   FALSE RETURNS

Section 7206 is divided into five separate offenses. Sections one and two are the sections typically used by prosecutors bringing tax charges. Section one is a tax perjury offense in that it prohibits one from willfully making and subscribing a return, statement, or other document under penalties of perjury which the person did not believe to be true and correct as to every material matter. Section two criminalizes the conduct of one who aids or assists in the preparation of a false return. Sections three, four and five focus on specific conduct such as "(3) fraudulent bonds, permits and entries;" "(4) removal or concealment with intent to defraud;" and "(5) compromises and closing agreements."

In order to sustain a conviction under § 7206(1), the government must prove that the accused: (1) willfully (see § 11.2), (2) signed a return, statement, or other document,

---

[117] 660 F.2d 1145 (7th Cir.1981).
[118] United States v. Buckley, 586 F.2d 498 (5th Cir. 1978).

(3) under penalties of perjury, (4) that the return, statement, or document was materially false, and (5) that the accused did not believe it to be true and correct.[119] Section 7206(2) requires the government to prove that the accused: (1) willfully, (2) aided or assisted in, or procured, counseled or advised the preparation or presentation of any document in connection with any matter arising under the internal revenue laws, (3) which document is materially false. Unlike the tax evasion statute found in § 7201, there is no requirement for the government to prove a tax deficiency. It is only necessary to show that the return is materially false. Courts have allowed corporations to be prosecuted under this statute, despite the fact that it is a perjury statute, an offense that typically is limited to individual defendants.[120]

Both of these statute's subsections are felony offenses. They carry penalties of up to three years imprisonment and a fine. Corporate fines can be higher than those permitted to be imposed upon individuals. When the amount of the tax loss to the government exceeds ten thousand dollars, it is considered an aggravated felony for purposes of deportation.[121]

Although cases premised on § 7206(1) are not limited to perjurious tax returns, there is no clear designation of what documents are covered under this statute. Prosecutors have included other documents filed with the IRS, such as a currency transaction form required of trades or businesses receiving cash of ten thousand dollars or more.[122] In *United States v. Levy*,[123] the Fifth Circuit found that this section is limited to "any statement or document required by the Internal Revenue Service or by any regulation lawfully promulgated for the enforcement of the Code."[124] Thus, the court reversed the conviction of a lawyer who filed Form 433–AB when approached by the IRS about taxes owed that he was unable to pay. Other cases, however, take a more expansive view of what documents are covered by § 7206(1) and allow documents beyond those authorized by a statute or regulation.[125]

The falsity of the statement is a question of fact for the jury. A "literally true" statement can raise issues since this is perjury statute, but some cases also may look beyond the statement to see if the tax return was false.[126]

Materiality is also an issue that arises when prosecutors use this statute. Materiality in a false tax return case "is whether a particular item must be reported in order that the taxpayer estimate and compute his tax correctly."[127] In *United States v. DiVarco*,[128] defendants' convictions included violations of § 7206(1). Defendants argued

---

[119] United States v. Perez, 612 F.3d 879 (7th Cir. 2010).

[120] See, e.g., United States v. Ingredient Technology Corp. 698 F.2d 88, 99 (2d Cir. 1983).

[121] Kawashima v. Holder, 132 S.Ct. 1166 (2012).

[122] United States v. Pansier, 576 F.3d 726, 736–37 (7th Cir. 2009).

[123] 533 F.2d 969 (5th Cir. 1976).

[124] Id. at 975.

[125] See, e.g., United States v. Wommer, 2012 WL 1032243, * 3–4 (D.Nev. 2012); United States v. Holroyd, 732 F.2d 1122 (2d Cir. 1984).

[126] See United States v. Reynolds, 919 F.2d 435 (7th Cir. 1990) (finding that Bronston's literally true defense applied to § 7206(1); but see United States v. Gollapudi, 130 F.3d 66 (3d Cir. 1997) (distinguishing Reynolds saying that it involved filing the wrong tax form).

[127] United States v. Klausner, 80 F.3d 55 (2d Cir. 1996).

[128] 484 F.2d 670 (7th Cir.1973).

on appeal that the government's failure to show that they understated their income precluded the use of this statutory provision. The Seventh Circuit noted that although most cases involving misstatement of source of income also involve an understatement of taxable income, "the purpose behind the statute is to prosecute those who intentionally falsify their tax returns regardless of the precise ultimate effect that falsification may have."[129] In *DiVarco*, the court found that misstatement of the source of one's income could be a material matter.

But in *United States v. Greenberg*,[130] the Second Circuit rejected defendant's argument that the misstatements were not material in that "they resulted in, at most, minimal underpayments of taxes."[131] The court found that materiality referred to the impact the statement may have on the ability of the agency to perform its assigned functions. "The question is not what effect the statement actually had, . . . rather whether the statement had the potential for an obstructive or inhibitive effect."[132] The court in *Greenberg* found the false statements of income material, even though they resulted in the minimal underpayment of taxes.

In *Neder v. United States*[133] the Supreme Court reaffirmed its holding from *United States v. Gaudin*[134] that materiality is a jury question. (See § 4.7). The defendant attorney had been charged with mail fraud, wire fraud, and a tax violation under § 7206(1). The Court stated that "a false statement is material if it has 'a natural tendency to influence, or [is] capable of influencing, the decision of the decisionmaking body to which it was addressed.'"[135] Although the trial error in *Neder* was found to be harmless, the Court did hold that "[i]n a prosecution under § 7206(1), several courts have determined that 'any failure to report income is material.'"[136]

A tax preparer can be charged under either subsection of this statute, § 7206(1) or (2). In *United States v. Shortt Accountancy Corp.*,[137] the defendant corporation was convicted of seven counts of violating § 7206(1). The corporation, through its chief operating officer, improperly structured certain investments to appear as if they occurred before a change in the law. This permitted clients to receive an undeserved tax benefit.

On appeal, the corporation argued that a tax preparer could not be charged under subsection one of this statute, but rather § 7206(2) was the applicable offense. The accounting corporation also maintained that the actual subscriber of the return was unaware of the fraud involved and therefore did not have the requisite intent of willfully making and subscribing a false return.

The Ninth Circuit, in *Shortt*, rejected defendant's arguments, finding that § 7206(1) was not limited to taxpayers. Being a perjury statute, the court found that

---

[129] Id. at 673 (quoting United States v. DiVarco, 343 F.Supp. 101, 103 (N.D. Ill. 1972)).

[130] 735 F.2d 29 (2d Cir.1984).

[131] Id. at 31.

[132] Id.

[133] 527 U.S. 1 (1999).

[134] 515 U.S. 506 (1995) (See also § 9.5).

[135] Neder, 527 U.S. at 16.

[136] Id.

[137] 785 F.2d 1448 (9th Cir.1986).

anyone who makes a false return could be prosecuted pursuant to this provision. The court also held that the corporation could be convicted of § 7206(1) even though the particular employee subscribing the return had no knowledge of the fraudulent scheme. To hold otherwise would permit a tax preparer to escape liability "by arranging for an innocent employee to complete the proscribed act of subscribing a false return."[138]

---

[138] Id. at 1454.

Chapter 12

CURRENCY REPORTING CRIMES

§ 12.1 OVERVIEW

Three relatively recent congressional acts set the stage for the currency reporting crimes. Enacted in 1970 was the Currency and Foreign Transactions Reporting Act (CFTRA), commonly referred to as the Foreign Bank Secrecy Act or the Bank Secrecy Act (BSA),[1] which is focused on reporting and recordkeeping by banks. (See § 12.2). Found in title 12 (Banks and Banking) and title 31 (Money and Finance) of the United States Code, the Bank Secrecy Act mandates that financial institutions report certain cash transactions to the government. In *California Bankers Association v. Shultz*[2] the Supreme Court stated that the Act was "designed to obtain financial information having 'a high degree of usefulness in criminal, tax, or regulatory investigations or proceedings.'"[3] The Patriot Act added an additional mission of requiring reports "in the conduct of intelligence or counterintelligence activities, including analysis to protect against international terrorism."[4]

Next came 26 U.S.C. § 6050I in 1984, which focused on reporting certain monetary transactions by those engaged in a "trade or business." Found in the Internal Revenue Code of the United States Code, the section titled *Returns Relating to Cash Received in Trade or Business, etc.*, was intended to focus on individuals who were in a "trade or business" as the Bank Secrecy Act had targeted financial institutions. Like the Bank Secrecy Act, this section of the federal code also criminalized structuring transactions to avoid the reporting requirements.

Moving from financial institutions and those engaged in a "trade or business," Congress in1986 directly criminalized money laundering. 18 U.S.C. § 1956 targets financial transactions undertaken for the purpose of hiding the proceeds of criminal activity, or to promote further criminal activities and 18 U.S.C. § 1957 targets the use of proceeds of criminal activity in excess of $10,000, sometimes referred to as the "money spending statute."

Although some of these statutes were initially focused on drug, terrorism, and organized crime prosecutions, it is now common to see these statutes used in white collar cases. One finds banks prosecuted under the Bank Secrecy Act, lawyers charged with violations of 26 U.S.C. § 6050I and money laundering charges tacked onto white

---

[1] Pub. L. 91–508 (1970).

[2] 416 U.S. 21, 27 (1974).

[3] See also 12 U.S.C. § 1951 (Congressional Findings and Declaration of Purpose)

[4] 31 U.S.C. § 5311.

collar crime cases, such as public corruption, mail fraud, health care fraud, insider trading, and bank fraud.[5]

§ 12.2 BANK SECRECY ACT

A. Generally

The Bank Secrecy Act requires financial institutions to record and report information about customers' transactions, particularly those involving large amounts of currency or other monetary instruments. Congress identified two reasons for requiring banks to maintain and report information about financial transactions, as described by the Supreme Court in *California Bankers Association v. Schultz*: 1) "The absence of such records, whether through failure to make them in the first instance or through failure to retain them, was thought to seriously impair the ability of the Federal Government to enforce the myriad criminal, tax, and regulatory provisions of laws which Congress had enacted;"[6] 2) "Congress was concerned about a serious and widespread use of foreign financial institutions, located in jurisdictions with strict laws of secrecy as to bank activity, for the purpose of violating or evading domestic criminal, tax, and regulatory enactments."[7] It was not employed significantly when initially passed, but in recent years has influenced the banking industry and resulted in prosecutions of financial institutions.

Although many government agencies, such as the FBI and IRS, are involved in the investigation of currency reporting crimes, a key player in investigations under the Bank Secrecy Act is the Financial Crimes Enforcement Agency (FinCEN). Located as a bureau in the U.S. Department of the Treasury, "FinCEN carries out its mission by receiving and maintaining financial transactions data; analyzing and disseminating that data for law enforcement purposes; and building global cooperation with counterpart organizations in other countries and with international bodies."[8]

The Bank Secrecy Act has a Title I and II.[9] Title I of the Act, found in Title 12 of the United States Code, pertains to the requirements of certain financial institutions to keep records, including the maintaining of records of customer identity and the microfilming of checks. Title II of the Bank Secrecy Act, found in Title 31 of the United States Code, requires the reporting to the federal government of certain foreign and domestic transactions.[10] The Act authorizes the Secretary of the Treasury to prescribe via regulation the specified bank recordkeeping and reporting requirements. These regulations can be found on a website maintained by the Department of Treasury's Bureau FinCEN.[11] Effective March 2011, these regulations, previously located at 31 C.F.R. Part 103, were transferred to 31 C.F.R. Chapter X. The regulations are now

---

[5] See Teresa E. Adams, Note, Tacking on Money Laundering Charges to White Collar Crimes: What Did Congress Intend and What are the Courts Doing, 17 Ga. St. L. Rev. 531 (2000).

[6] California Bankers Ass'n, 416 U.S. at 26–27.

[7] Id. at 27–28.

[8] FinCEN, What We Do, available at http://www.fincen.gov/about_fincen/wwd/.

[9] Pub. L. 91–508, Titles I, II (1970).

[10] Initially it was codified at 31 U.S.C. §§ 1051–1122, but in 1982 they were moved to 31 U.S.C. §§ 5311–5322. USAM, Criminal Resource Manual § 2029.

[11] See FinCEN's Mandate From Congress, available at http://www.fincen.gov/statutes_regs/bsa/.

organized by industry. Thus the bank regulations, insurance regulations, and other industries are grouped together.[12]

Title I starts with the Congressional Findings and Declaration of Purpose.[13] It includes recordkeeping and procedures for uninsured banks and uninsured financial institutions.[14] It provides for both civil[15] and criminal penalties[16] for non-compliance. A willful violation of any regulation incurs a criminal fine of "not more than $1,000 or imprisoned not more than one year, or both." This can be increased to "not more than $10,000 or imprisoned not more than five years, or both" when the willful "violation is committed in furtherance of the commission of any violation of Federal law punishable by imprisonment for more than one year."[17]

Title II also starts with a declaration of purpose.[18] It is immediately followed by a statute that provides definitions and application, including the definition of the term "financial institution," a key term in many currency transaction crimes.[19] The recordkeeping and reporting statutes are 31 U.S.C. §§ 5313–5316.[20] (see §§ 12.2(C), (D)). 31 U.S.C. § 5318A focuses on international counter-money laundering activities and also provides for special measures for jurisdictions.[21]

Title II also has provisions for both civil[22] and criminal penalties.[23] The penalties here are greater than those found in Title 12. A willful violation of everything except §§ 5315 and 5324 can receive a fine and imprisonment of up to five years. If it occurs "while violating another law of the United States or as part of a pattern of any illegal activity involving more than $100, 000 in a 12–month period," the allowable penalty is doubled with a fine now of up to $500,000 and a maximum imprisonment that cannot exceed ten years. In computing violations under 31 U.S.C. § 5318A or a regulation under this statute, "a separate violation occurs for each day the violation continues and at each office, branch, or place of business at which a violation occurs or continues."[24] Violations of this statute can also offer an increased fine, of up to $1,000,000, in certain circumstances.[25]

---

[12] See Chapter X, available at http://www.fincen.gov/statutes_regs/ChapterX/.

[13] 12 U.S.C. § 1951.

[14] 12 U.S.C. § 1953.

[15] 12 U.S.C. § 1955.

[16] 12 U.S.C. § 1956.

[17] 12 U.S.C. § 1957.

[18] 31 U.S.C. § 5311.

[19] 31 U.S.C. § 5312.

[20] Reports on Domestic Coins and Currency Transactions (31 U.S.C. § 5313); Records and Exports on Foreign Financial Agency Transactions (31 U.S.C. § 5314); Reports on Foreign Currency Transactions (31 U.S.C. § 5315); Reports on Exporting and Importing Monetary Instruments (31 U.S.C. § 5316). Initially Title II was codified at 31 §§ 1051–1122, but in 1982 they were moved to 31 U.S.C. §§ 5311–5322. USAM, Criminal Resource Manual § 2029.

[21] 31 U.S.C. § 5318A.

[22] 31 U.S.C. § 5321.

[23] 31 U.S.C. § 5322.

[24] 31 U.S.C. § 5322(c).

[25] 31 U.S.C. § 5322(d).

In 1984, a statute was added to reward informants.[26] Whistleblowers can be rewarded for their information if it "leads to a recovery of a criminal fine, civil penalty, or forfeiture, which exceeds $50,000, for a violation of this chapter."[27] In 1986, Congress added 31 U.S.C. § 5324 to criminalize those who structure transactions to evade reporting requirements. (see § 12.2(F)).

B. Constitutionality

Two years after the passage of the Bank Secrecy Act, the constitutionality of the Act was challenged in *California Bankers Association v. Shultz*.[28] At the heart of the suit was a claimed violation of the Fourth Amendment's guarantee against unreasonable searches and seizures. The plaintiffs also claimed violations of the First, Fifth, Ninth, Tenth and Fourteenth Amendments of the Constitution. The Supreme Court rejected these arguments and accepted the breadth of the Bank Secrecy Act's recordkeeping and reporting obligations stating:

> While an Act conferring such broad authority over transactions such as these might well surprise or even shock those who lived in an earlier era, the latter did not live to see the time when bank accounts would join chocolate, cheese, and watches as a symbol of the Swiss economy. Nor did they live to see the heavy utilization of our domestic banking system by the minions of organized crime as well as by millions of legitimate businessmen.[29]

The Court held that the recording-keeping requirements did not impose an unreasonable burden on banks, that a requirement of maintenance of records did not constitute a seizure, and that the application of the reporting requirements to both foreign and domestic transactions was reasonable. The Court also found that the bank depositors lacked standing to challenge the Act under the Fourth and Fifth Amendments.

Other constitutional challenges have been brought against the Bank Secrecy Act and specific provisions therein. In *United States v. Miller*,[30] the Supreme Court held that a bank depositor had no interest protected by the Fourth Amendment in records maintained by a bank that was complying with the mandates of the Bank Secrecy Act. The Court held that the defendants had no legitimate expectation of privacy in these bank business records, stating, "[t]he depositor takes the risk, in revealing his affairs to another, that the information will be conveyed by that person to the Government."[31]

Several circuit courts have examined whether the Bank Secrecy Act violates the individual bank customer's rights under the Fifth Amendment, and these opinions have continually held that it is not unconstitutional.[32] In *United States v. Mickens*,[33]

---

[26] 31 U.S.C. § 5323.

[27] 31 U.S.C. § 5323(a). It also provides the methodology for determining this award.

[28] 416 U.S. 21 (1974).

[29] Id. at 30.

[30] 425 U.S. 435 (1976).

[31] Id. at 443.

[32] See, e.g., United States v. Hurley, 63 F.3d 1 (1st Cir. 1995); United States v. Camarena, 973 F.2d 427 (5th Cir. 1992); United States v. Hoyland, 914 F.2d 1125, 1130 (9th Cir. 1990); United States v. Fitzgibbon, 576 F.2d 279 (10th Cir. 1978); United States v. Dichne, 612 F.2d 632 (2d Cir. 1979).

[33] 926 F.2d 1323, 1331 (2d Cir. 1991).

the defendants argued that the Currency Transaction Reports required by 31 U.S.C. § 5313(a) violated Fifth Amendment privilege against self-incrimination. Finding the statute constitutional, the Second Circuit noted that the defendants were not being compelled to report their transactions.

C. Domestic Financial Institutions

31 U.S.C. § 5313 concerns reports required to be filed by domestic financial institutions. A financial institution is defined in 31 U.S.C. § 5312 and in the regulations of the Secretary of the Treasury. The breadth of this term is apparent in the inclusion of businesses well beyond the typical banking association. For example, financial institutions include "a dealer in precious metals, stones, or jewels," "a pawnbroker," "a travel agency," "a telegraph company," "a business engaged in vehicle sales, including automobile, airplane, and boat sales," and "persons involved in real estate closings and settlements."[34]

Courts have also provided a wide breadth to what will be considered a financial institution. In *United States v. Gollott*[35] the Fifth Circuit upheld a jury finding that the defendants were a financial institution. The court found that the defendants' activities were within the confines of the regulations used to define this term. The court stated that, "[t]his language is broader than and perhaps counterintuitive to everyday understanding of what a financial institution is, but it is not vague as applied to appellants' dealings."[36]

Courts have found individuals to be financial institutions.[37] "Currency dealers or exchangers" can be a financial institution, even if not engaged in the exchange of foreign currency.[38] A financial institution has also been defined to encompass a bank, including each of its branches. Thus, if there are multiple cash transactions at different branches of the same financial institution that meet the reporting requirements, then the bank must file a currency transaction report.[39]

In some instances courts did restrain what would be considered a financial institution. But amended regulations were quick to respond to these limitations. For example, in *United States v. Bucey*,[40] the Seventh Circuit reversed a defendant's convictions premised on 31 U.S.C. §§ 5313 and 5322(b). The court found defendant Bucey, acting in his individual capacity, not to be a financial institution, where the definition of the term included the language "agency, branch, or office." The court in *Bucey* did, however, note that the term financial institution was amended in 1987 after the time of defendant's alleged violations. The amended regulation added the word "agent" prior to "agency, branch, or office."

---

[34] 31 U.S.C. § 5312 (a)(2).

[35] 939 F.2d 255 (5th Cir. 1991).

[36] Id. at 258.

[37] See United States v. Tannenbaum, 934 F.2d 8 (2d Cir. 1991); United States v. Goldberg, 756 F.2d 949 (2d Cir. 1985).

[38] United States v. Levy, 969 F.2d 136 (5th Cir. 1992).

[39] See United States v. Giancola, 783 F.2d 1549 (11th Cir. 1986); See also United States v. Cuevas, 847 F.2d 1417 (9th Cir. 1988).

[40] 876 F.2d 1297 (7th Cir. 1989).

Most circuits find that an individual may be a financial institution. In *United States v. Tannenbaum*[41] the Second Circuit noted that "[t]he regulations define a financial institution in part as 'a person.' There is no indication in the statute or the regulations that a natural person cannot be considered a financial institution, and it seems strained to assume that the term 'person' was intended to exclude natural persons."[42]

The terms "domestic financial agency" and "domestic financial institution" are defined in § 5312 as to "apply to an action in the United States of a financial agency or institution."[43] In *United States v. Mazza–Alaluf*,[44] a district court in the Southern District of New York looked at whether "an unlicensed money-transmitting business" met this definition. The defendant called his business "an auxiliary to the banking system."[45] The court found the activities involved in this case as meeting the definition provided in § 5312(a)(2)(R) which includes as a financial institution, "a licensed sender of money or any other person who engages as a business in the transmission of funds, including any person who engages as a business in an informal money transfer system or any network of people who engage as a business in facilitating the transfer of money domestically or internationally outside of the conventional financial institutions system."

In *United States v. Eisenstein*,[46] the defendant argued that the transactions were not a domestic financial institution because the transactions were "negotiated and completed in Columbia." The Eleventh Circuit held that even though activities occurred in Columbia, the defendants were a domestic financial institution where their currency exchange business deposited money in a United States bank and the bank relayed information concerning each transaction from the United States to Columbia.

D. Recordkeeping and Reporting Requirements

Several statutes within the Bank Secrecy Act require reporting and recordkeeping. For example, section 5313 concerns reports on domestic coins and currency transactions. Section 5314 pertains to the reporting on foreign financial agency transactions and§ 5315 concerns reports on foreign currency transactions.

Section 5313 of title 31 has exemptions with respect to these reporting requirements, such as "a department or agency of the United States, any State, or any political subdivision of any State."[47] The Code of Federal Regulations provides additional guidance in specifying a host of different reports that are required to be made under the Bank Secrecy Act.[48] These include reports for suspicious

---

[41] 934 F.2d 8 (2d Cir. 1991).

[42] Id. at 12.

[43] 31 U.S.C. § 5312(b)(1).

[44] 621 F.3d 205 (2d Cir. 2010).

[45] Id. at 487.

[46] 731 F.2d 1540 (11th Cir. 1984) (using a predecessor statute).

[47] See 31 U.S.C. § 5313(d)(1)(B).

[48] See 31 C.F.R. Chapter X.

transactions,[49] reports of transactions to be made by casinos,[50] reports for foreign financial accounts,[51] and reports relating to currency in excess of $10,000 received in a trade or business.[52]

These reports are called Currency Transaction Reports (CTR) and different Internal Revenue Forms are used depending on the transaction involved. For example, domestic financial institutions under § 5313 in the amount of $10,000 or more are made on IRS Form 4789.[53] Foreign financial agency transactions are reported on treasury form TDF 90–22.1 and on Internal Revenue Form 4683.[54]

Pursuant to § 5316, reports also need to be filed on the exporting and importing of monetary instruments.[55] Those who "with the intent to evade a currency reporting requirement under § 5316, knowingly conceal[ ] more than $10,000 in currency or other monetary instruments on their person" or in what they are carrying, like luggage, "from a place within the United States to a place outside of the United States," or the reverse, can be held criminally accountable under a statute prohibiting bulk cash smuggling into or out of the United States.[56] This statute was written in response to the Supreme Court's ruling in *United States v. Bajakajian*[57] which held that a failure to report funds on a customs currency reporting form would not subject the individual to forfeiture of the entire amount that had not been declared, when the forfeiture was disproportionate to the gravity of the offense. Congress in the Patriot Act,[58] passed 31 U.S.C. § 5332 to criminalize the undeclared movement of $10,000 across U.S. borders and also make the money subject to forfeiture.[59]

There are also recordkeeping requirements.[60] The Code of Federal Regulations again provides details of some of these requirements. For example, financial institutions are required to "retain either the original or a microfilm or other copy or reproduction of" different items such as "[a] record of each extension of credit in an amount in excess of $10,000, except an extension of credit secured by an interest in real property, which record shall contain the name and address of the person to whom the extension of credit is made, the amount thereof, the nature or purpose thereof, and the date thereof."[61]

---

[49] See, e.g., 31 C.F.R. § 1024.320 (reports by mutual funds of suspicious transactions); § 1025.320 (reports by insurance companies of suspicious transactions); § 1020.320 (reports by banks of suspicious transactions); § 1021.320 (reports by casinos of suspicious transactions).

[50] 31C.F.R. § 1021.311.

[51] 31C.F.R. § 1010.350.

[52] 31C.F.R. § 1010.330.

[53] USAM, Criminal Resource Manual § 2030.

[54] USAM, Criminal Resource Manual § 2032.

[55] 31 U.S.C. § 5316.

[56] 31 U.S.C. § 5332.

[57] 524 U.S. 321 (1998).

[58] Pub. L. No. 107–56, § 371, 115 Stat. 272.

[59] 31 U.S.C. § 5332(b)(2). See also United States v. Jose, 499 F.3d 105 (1st Cir. 2007).

[60] See 31 C.F.R. §§ 1010.400 et seq.

[61] 31 C.F.R. § 1010.410.

E. Compliance

The Secretary of the Treasury has authority under the statute to "require any financial institution, and any director, officer, employee, or agent of any financial institution, to report any suspicious transaction relevant to a possible violation of law or regulation."[62] There is also a requirement that each financial institution have an "anti-money laundering program."[63] The program needs to include "(A) the development of internal policies, procedures, and controls; (B) the designation of a compliance officer; (C) an ongoing employee training program; and (D) an independent audit function to test programs."[64] There is also the requirement of "due diligence for United States private banking and correspondent bank accounts involving foreign persons." This requires that "[e]ach financial institution that establishes, maintains, administers, or manages a private banking account or a correspondent account in the United States for a non-United States person, including a foreign individual visiting the United States, or a representative of a non-United States person shall establish appropriate, specific, and, where necessary, enhanced, due diligence policies, procedures, and controls that are reasonably designed to detect and report instances of money laundering through those accounts."[65]

F. Structuring

1. Elements

31 U.S.C. § 5324 makes it a crime "for the purpose of evading the reporting requirements" for financial transactions to cause or attempt to cause the failure to file a required report, or to "structure or assist in structuring, or attempt to structure or assist in structuring, any transaction" with an organization subject to the reporting requirements. This statute was passed to counter individuals who deliberately tried to avoid the reporting requirements with structured transactions below the $10,000 mark. The focus of this statute is on the financial institution that is required to file the report, but an individual who causes or attempts to cause the financial institution from filing, is criminally liable under the statute.

The elements of this offense are: "(1) the defendant must, in fact, have engaged in acts of structuring; (2) he must have done so with knowledge that the financial institutions involved were legally obligated to report currency transactions in excess of $10,000; and (3) he must have acted with the intent to evade this reporting requirement."[66]

2. Mens Rea

Initially the statute required proof that a defendant acted "willfully," the *mens rea* term used for currency reporting violations pursuant to 31 U.S.C. § 5322. In *Ratzlaf v. United States*,[67] the Supreme Court examined the term willfulness in 31 U.S.C. § 5324

---

[62] 31 U.S.C. § 5318(g).

[63] 31 U.S.C. § 5318(h).

[64] 31 U.S.C. § 5318(h)(1).

[65] 31 U.S.C. § 5318(i).

[66] United States v. MacPherson, 424 F.3d 183 (2d Cir. 2005) (citing United States v. Scanio, 900 F.2d 485 (2d Cir. 1990).

[67] 510 U.S. 135, 144 (1994).

and reversed defendant's conviction. The Court held that to willfully violate "the antistructuring law, the Government must prove that the defendant acted with knowledge that his conduct was unlawful." The Court in *Ratzlaf* stated that they were "unpersuaded . . . that structuring is 'so obviously "evil" or inherently "bad" that the "willfulness" requirement is satisfied irrespective of the defendant's knowledge of the illegality of structuring.'"

In response to the *Ratzlaf* decision, Congress modified § 5324 as part of the Riegle Community Development and Regulatory Improvement Act of 1994. The modified statute omits the term willfully. By placing penalty provisions directly in § 5324, the *mens rea* for the structuring statute is now met when the government shows that the defendant intended to evade the reporting requirement.

Courts have allowed proof of structuring through circumstantial evidence. A prosecution for violating § 5324 does not require the government to show that the funds involved in the transaction were related to criminal activity or in any way tainted, which is necessary for a successful prosecution under § 1956 or § 1957. (See § 12.3). In *United States v. MacPherson*,[68] the Second Circuit found sufficient evidence of structuring when a defendant made thirty-two cash deposits at three banks and all of the amounts were for under $10,000, with many of these transactions being in the amount of 9,000 dollars.

3. *Penalties*

Section 5324 contains two levels of criminal penalties for a violation. The general punishment is up to five years in prison and a fine, while an "aggravated" case can result in up to a ten year sentence and a fine twice that authorized for a violation. An "aggravated" case is one that occurs "while violating another law of the United States or as part of a pattern of any illegal activity involving more than $100,000 in a 12–month period."[69] (See chap. 24).

G. Collective Knowledge

Courts allow proof of knowledge through a theory of "collective knowledge." (See § 2.3 (B)). *United States v. Bank of New England*[70] is a case in which a bank was found guilty of thirty-one violations for failing to report structuring even though the jury acquitted the individual who actually made the cash withdrawals. The trial court had given the jury an instruction on the bank's intent that included reference to its "collective knowledge":

[A] corporation cannot plead innocence by asserting that the information obtained by several employees was not acquired by any one individual who then would have comprehended its full import. Rather the corporation is considered to have acquired the collective knowledge of its employees and is held responsible for their failure to act accordingly.

---

[68] 424 F.3d 183 (2d Cir. 2005).

[69] 18 U.S.C. § 5324(d)(2).

[70] 821 F.2d 844 (1st Cir. 1987).

Rejecting the bank's argument that the instruction did not properly reflect the intent requirement for a corporation, the First Circuit stated that "[s]ince the Bank had the compartmentalized structure common to all large corporations, the court's collective knowledge instruction was not only proper but necessary." This approach means that a bank can be held liable for a failure to report transactions even though no one individual employee alone had the requisite knowledge that the report must be filed so long as the aggregate of corporate knowledge showed that the organization was aware of the need to file.

§ 12.3   SECTION 6050I

A. Legislative History

26 U.S.C. § 6050I, an Internal Revenue Code statute, was modeled after the Bank Secrecy Act. Enacted as part of the Deficit Reduction Act of 1984,[71] it was intended to encourage the reporting of cash income in order to reduce the deficit. A shortcoming of the Bank Secrecy Act was that it was limited to financial institutions. It was envisioned that this tax statute would allow the government to extend currency transaction reporting to individuals engaged in a "trade or business." Although intended as a tax measure, this section has become a tool for monitoring criminal activity.[72]

When initially passed, there was no legislative discussion of this statute being used as a criminal enforcement tool in areas of drugs and organized crime. There was also no discussion of it being used against attorneys engaged in the practice of law.[73] After its passage one finds recognition that this statute can offer the government helpful information in enforcing laws.[74] It has become a crime that occasionally falls in the white collar realm and government use of this statute against attorneys has proved controversial.

B. Statutory Mandates

26 U.S.C. § 6050I requires trades or businesses that receive in excess of ten thousand dollars in cash to report these transactions to the Internal Revenue Service. It is not limited to amounts received in one transaction, but instead includes two of more related transactions. Thus, businesses that receive cash for the sale of a boat[75] or an automobile[76] are required to file Form 8300. The Internal Revenue Service's form for complying with § 6050I is found in Form 8300.

A provision of § 6050I prohibits the evading or assisting in the structuring of a transaction to avoid the reporting requirement.[77] Thus, someone who deliberately pays

---

[71] Pub. L. No. 98–369, Title I, § 146(a) (1984).

[72] See generally Ellen S. Podgor, Form 8300: The Demise of Law as a Profession, 5 Geo J. Legal Ethics, 485 (1992).

[73] Id. at 491.

[74] Notice 923, Department of the Treasury, Internal Revenue Service (Aug. 1990).

[75] United States v. Loe, 262 F.3d 427 (5th Cir. 2001).

[76] United States v. McLamb, 985 F.2d 1284 (4th Cir. 1993).

[77] 26 U.S.C. § 6050I(f).

in several transactions to try and avoid the reporting requirements will find him or herself criminally liable under the structuring provision of this statute.

This statute does exclude transactions that would be reported pursuant to the Bank Secrecy Act and also excludes transactions that occur entirely outside the United States.[78] Court opinions have expressed that it is applicable to conduct on an American Indian reservation[79] and acts occurring in Puerto Rico.[80]

C. Application to Attorneys

Section 6050I and Form 8300 have proved controversial in the legal community. Because the statute applies to all trades or businesses, the question has arisen as to the section's applicability to payments received by attorneys. In this regard the Second Circuit in *United States v. Goldberger*,[81] found § 6050I constitutional. Analogizing to cases reported under the Bank Secrecy Act, the court found no Fourth or Fifth Amendment violation. The *Goldberger* court also found that the application of the statute to defense counsel did not result in a deprivation of the right to counsel under the Sixth Amendment. The court stated that section 6050I did not preclude clients from their choice of counsel, "they need only pay counsel in some other manner than with cash."[82]

Courts, including the *Goldberger* court, have found that § 6050I does not conflict with the attorney-client privilege.[83] In *Goldberger*, the court stated that "[a]bsent special circumstances," client identity and fee information were not privileged matters.[84] Since the practice of law is considered a "trade or business" for purposes of the income tax laws and the Sherman Act, *Goldberger* found that absent a specific congressional intent to exclude attorneys, section 6050I applied to lawyers.

In *United States v. Sindel*,[85] the Eighth Circuit examined when the attorney-client privilege might protect client identity and fee information. "Special circumstances" exceptions were found to include "the legal advice exception," "the last link exception," and the "confidential communications exception." "After examining Sindel's *in camera* testimony about [the] client's special circumstances," the court found that the release of information with respect to one client, could not be accomplished without revealing "confidential communication." According to the court, "special circumstances," however, did not exist with respect to a second client.[86]

It is necessary for the government to use the procedural process correctly when seeking to obtain information from an attorney about their client. In *United States v.*

---

[78] 26 U.S.C. § 6050I(c).

[79] United States v. White, 237 F.3d 170 (2d Cir. 2001).

[80] United States v. Casablanca Motors, Inc., 863 F.Supp. 50 (D. Puerto Rico 1994).

[81] 935 F.2d 501 (2d Cir. 1991).

[82] Id. at 504.

[83] See, e.g., United States v. Blackman, 72 F.3d 1418 (9th Cir. 1995). United States v. Leventhal, 961 F.2d 936, 940 (11th Cir. 1992).

[84] Id. at 506.

[85] 53 F.3d 874 (8th Cir. 1995).

[86] Id. at 876.

Gertner,[87] the First Circuit did not address the applicability of § 6050I to attorneys, finding that summons enforcement should be denied in that the government failed to adhere to the proper procedure for the service of a John Doe summonses. But another attorney was denied relief when he paid the penalty for filing Form 8300 with incomplete information, and later sought a refund challenging that special circumstances warranted not providing this information.[88]

§ 12.4 MONEY LAUNDERING

A. Generally

The Money Laundering Control Act of 1986 marked a significant expansion in the use of the criminal law to combat criminal enterprises by making financial transactions the basis for separate prosecutions that carry substantial penalties for facilitating the transfer of the proceeds of illegal conduct. It took currency transaction criminality a step beyond the Bank Secrecy Act's focus on reporting and recording by financial institutions and the tax statute 26 U.S.C. § 6050I's focus on trades or businesses. The two key statutes for criminalizing money laundering are found in the criminal code, title 18, and are §§ 1956 and 1957.

Although some might think of money laundering as crimes exclusive to organized crime or drug offenses, white collar offenders can be charged with these offenses and more commonly have money laundering charges tacked onto their indictments. Financial institutions, ranging from multinational banks to small money transmitting operations, can become involved in money laundering cases because of their central role in processing funds worldwide.[89] Prosecutors have pursued cases when there is evidence an employee or officer has knowingly facilitated transactions that violate the law, such as the prosecution of a former officer of Bank of New York for facilitating billions of dollars of transactions from Russia.[90] In 2005, Riggs Bank pleaded guilty to failing to file suspicious transaction reports related to accounts held by foreign government officials that were used for money laundering, paying a $16 million fine.[91]

B. *18 U.S.C. § 1956*

1. *Elements*

a. *Generally*

Section 1956 is a complex provision with different ways for proceeding with the charging of this offense. Three different types of violations are included in this statute: (1) transactional money laundering; (2) international transportation or transmission money laundering; and, (3) sting operations. Section 1956(a), provides:

---

[87] 873 F.Supp. 729 (D. Mass. 1995).

[88] Lefcourt v. United States, 125 F.3d 79 (2d Cir. 1997).

[89] See United States v. Dinero Exp., Inc., 313 F.3d 803 (2d Cir. 2002).

[90] See, e.g., United States v. $15,270,885.69 on Deposit in Account No. 8900261137, 2000 WL 1234593 (S.D.N.Y. 2000).

[91] U.S. Dept. of Justice, Riggs Bank Enters Guilty Plea and Will Pay $16 Million Fine for Criminal Failure to Report Numerous Suspicious Transactions, Jan. 27, 2005, available at http://www.justice.gov/tax/usaopress/2005/txdv050530.html.

(a)(1) Whoever, knowing that the property involved in a financial transaction represents the proceeds of some form of unlawful activity, conducts or attempts to conduct such a financial transaction which in fact involves the proceeds of specified unlawful activity—

(A)

    (i) with the intent to promote the carrying on of specified unlawful activity; or

    (ii) with intent to engage in conduct constituting a violation of section 7201 or 7206 of the Internal Revenue Code of 1986; or

(B) knowing that the transaction is designed in whole or in part—

    (i) to conceal or disguise the nature, the location, the source, the ownership, or the control of the proceeds of specified unlawful activity; or

    (ii) to avoid a transaction reporting requirement under State or Federal law,

shall be sentenced to a fine of not more than $500,000 or twice the value of the property involved in the transaction, whichever is greater, or imprisonment for not more than twenty years, or both. For purposes of this paragraph, a financial transaction shall be considered to be one involving the proceeds of specified unlawful activity if it is part of a set of parallel or dependent transactions, any one of which involves the proceeds of specified unlawful activity, and all of which are part of a single plan or arrangement.

(2) Whoever transports, transmits, or transfers, or attempts to transport, transmit, or transfer a monetary instrument or funds from a place in the United States to or through a place outside the United States or to a place in the United States from or through a place outside the United States—

(A) with the intent to promote the carrying on of specified unlawful activity; or

(B) knowing that the monetary instrument or funds involved in the transportation, transmission, or transfer represent the proceeds of some form of unlawful activity and knowing that such transportation, transmission, or transfer is designed in whole or in part—

    (i) to conceal or disguise the nature, the location, the source, the ownership, or the control of the proceeds of specified unlawful activity; or

    (ii) to avoid a transaction reporting requirement under State or Federal law,

shall be sentenced to a fine of not more than $500,000 or twice the value of the monetary instrument or funds involved in the transportation, transmission, or transfer whichever is greater, or imprisonment for not more than twenty years, or both. For the purpose of the offense described in subparagraph (B), the defendant's knowledge may be established by proof that a law enforcement officer represented the matter specified in subparagraph (B) as true, and the defendant's subsequent statements or actions indicate that the defendant believed such representations to be true.

(3) Whoever, with the intent—

(A) to promote the carrying on of specified unlawful activity;

(B) to conceal or disguise the nature, location, source, ownership, or control of property believed to be the proceeds of specified unlawful activity; or

(C) to avoid a transaction reporting requirement under State or Federal law,

conducts or attempts to conduct a financial transaction involving property represented to be the proceeds of specified unlawful activity, or property used to conduct or facilitate specified unlawful activity, shall be fined under this title or imprisoned for not more than 20 years, or both. For purposes of this paragraph and paragraph (2), the term "represented" means any representation made by a law enforcement officer or by another person at the direction of, or with the approval of, a Federal official authorized to investigate or prosecute violations of this section.

b.   *Transactional Money Laundering*

The elements of the crime under § 1956(a)(1) have been stated as being: (1) the defendant took part in a financial transaction; (2) the defendant knew that the property involved in the transaction involved funds that were the proceeds of some form of unlawful activity; (3) that the property involved was in fact the proceeds of that illegal activity; and (4) the defendant engaged in the financial transaction knowing that the transaction was designed in whole or in part to conceal or disguise the nature, source, location, ownership, or control of the illegal proceeds.[92]

Not every form of conduct constitutes concealment for purposes of § 1956(a). For example, in *United States v. Naranjo*,[93] the Eleventh Circuit stated that "[t]he spending of illegal proceeds alone is insufficient to prove concealment money laundering."[94] One court provided examples of what might support a finding of the defendant being engaged in transactional money laundering:

[S]tatements by a defendant probative of intent to conceal; unusual secrecy surrounding the transaction; structuring the transaction in a way to avoid attention; depositing illegal profits in the bank account of a legitimate business; highly irregular features of the transaction; using third parties to conceal the real owner; a series of unusual financial moves cumulating in the transaction; or expert testimony on practices of criminals.[95]

---

[92] United States v. Tarkoff, 242 F.3d 991 (11th Cir. 2001).

[93] 634 F.3d 1198 (11th Cir. 2011).

[94] Id. at 1208.

[95] United States v. Garcia–Emanuel, 14 F.3d 1469, 1475–76 (10th Cir. 1994).

Concealment can also be shown by structuring transactions so that multiple small amounts are used, sometimes referred to as "smurfing." Exchanging large bills for smaller ones can also be a ploy to conceal the transaction. In *United States v. Farese*,[96] the Eleventh Circuit held that the defendant had violated § 1956(a) in that "[e]xchanging large-denomination bills for small-denomination bills facilitates concealment of the 'location' of funds because one large-denomination bill is easier to hide than several small-denomination bills of the same total value."[97]

c.   *International Transportation or Transmission Money Laundering*

Section 1956(a)(2) was added as part of the Anti–Drug Abuse Act of 1988 to reach the cross-border movement of funds and monetary instruments, whether by physical transport or electronic transmission, when undertaken for certain illegal purposes.[98] The funds need to travel into or outside of the United States, so funds merely crossing state lines will not suffice. A defendant can be prosecuted as long as one part of a multi-step plan involves movement of monetary instruments into or outside the United States, even if some of the steps in the plan are entirely within the United States.[99]

In *Cuellar v. United States*,[100] the Supreme Court explained that transportation for the purpose of concealing or disguising the nature or source of the proceeds does not require proof that the person sought to make the money appear to be from a legitimate source, only that the defendant intend to achieve the goal of concealment or disguise. Thus, "a defendant who smuggles cash into Mexico with the intent of hiding it from authorities by burying it in the desert may have engaged in transportation designed to conceal the location of those funds, but his conduct would not necessarily have the effect of making the funds appear legitimate."[101]

The Court in *Cuellar* held that transportation "designed" to achieve the illegal purpose meant that "merely hiding funds during transportation is not sufficient to violate the statute, even if substantial efforts have been expended to conceal the money."[102] Therefore, in proving the design to engage in money laundering through transportation, "*how* one moves the money is distinct from *why* one moves the money. Evidence of the former, standing alone, is not sufficient to prove the latter."[103] The manner of transporting the monetary instruments can be circumstantial evidence of the defendant's intent, but simply hiding money while transporting it does not necessarily violate § 1956(a)(2).

d.   *Sting Operations*

18 U.S.C. § 1956(a)(3), added in 1988, authorizes "sting" operations as a means of violating the statute. This section requires proof of the defendant's belief that the money or property is the proceeds of unlawful activity. This allows law enforcement

---

[96] 248 F.3d 1056 (11th Cir. 2001).

[97] Id. at 1060.

[98] 134 Cong. Rec. S17367 (Nov. 10, 1998) (statement of Sen. Biden).

[99] United States v. Dinero Express, Inc., 313 F.3d 803, 806 (2d Cir. 2002).

[100] 553 U.S. 550 (2008).

[101] Id. at 559.

[102] Id. at 563.

[103] Id. at 566.

officers to make representations that the funds are from specific unlawful activities, when that is not the case. Courts have held that the "representation" made by a federal official does not have to be factually specific.[104]

2. *Knowledge of Some Form of Unlawful Activity*

Section 1956(a)(1) makes it a crime to knowingly engage in a broad range of transactions involving the proceeds of criminal activity. The definition of this element in § 1956(c)(1) requires proof that "the person knew the property involved in the transaction represented proceeds from some form, though not necessarily which form, of activity that constitutes a felony under State, Federal, or foreign law, regardless of whether or not such activity is specified" in the definition of "specified unlawful activity." The defendant is not required to know the particular felony that generated the proceeds, only that some felony did so.

Knowledge can be established by proof of the defendant's state of mind, which is usually established by circumstantial evidence.[105] It can also be shown if a defendant was "willfully blind."[106] In *Global–Tech Appliances, Inc. v. SEB, S.A.*, the Supreme Court stated that proof of willful blindness involves "two basic requirements: (1) the defendant must subjectively believe that there is a high probability that a fact exists and (2) the defendant must take deliberate actions to avoid learning of that fact." The Court noted that "a willfully blind defendant is one who takes deliberate actions to avoid confirming a high probability of wrongdoing and who can almost be said to have actually known the critical facts."[107] (See § 1.8(c)(1)).

The depth of a person's understanding of the source of the funds need not be great in order to establish knowledge that they are proceeds of *some* illegal activity.[108] As with any subjective intent element, knowledge can be established by circumstantial evidence, so that a defendant's denial of actual knowledge need not be credited by a jury if other facts establish the high likelihood of the person's understanding of the source of the funds. In *United States v. Turner*,[109] the Seventh Circuit examined a case involving a "prime bank note" operation, and noted how numerous transactions demonstrated the defendant's knowledge. The court stated that "[l]ooking at all of this evidence in combination, it is silly to suggest that Turner did not know that he was dealing with ill-gotten funds. Any reasonable person watching all of these strange dealings would clearly believe something was amiss."[110]

---

[104] United States v. Marbelt, 129 F. Supp.2d 49 (D. Mass. 2000).

[105] See United States v. Cruzado–Laureano, 404 F.3d 470, 483 (1st Cir. 2005) ("A conviction requires evidence of intent to disguise or conceal the transaction, whether from direct evidence, like the defendant's own statements, or from circumstantial evidence, like the use of a third party to disguise the true owner, or unusual secrecy.").

[106] See United States v. Flores, 454 F.3d 149, 156 (3rd Cir. 2006); United States v. Rivera–Rodriguez, 318 F.3d 268, 271 (1st Cir. 2003).

[107] 131 S.Ct. 2060, 2070–2071 (2011).

[108] See United States v. Huezo, 546 F.3d 174, 183 (2d Cir. 2008) ("Based on the complexity and scale of the money laundering scheme, common sense and experience would support an inference that the principals in the conspiracy would not have trusted an outsider (with no knowledge of their criminal purpose) to transport $1 million in laundered funds, to be present when Del Rio removed the first suitcase containing $500,000 from the trunk, and to share a house over several days with witting conspirators.").

[109] 400 F.3d 491 (7th Cir. 2005).

[110] Id. at 498.

In addition to evidence from the transactions, the financial circumstances and educational background of the defendant can be considered in determining the person's knowledge that illegal activity generated the funds. In *United States v. Corchado–Peralta*,[111] the First Circuit found sufficient circumstantial evidence of knowledge because "Corchado knew that the family expenditures were huge, that reported income was a fraction of what was being spent and that legitimate sources were not so obvious as to banish all thoughts of possible illegal origin," along with the fact that "Corchado was herself well educated and involved in the family bookkeeping."[112]

3. *Conduct*

A defendant must "conduct" a monetary transaction in order to engage in money laundering, although that does not require proof of actual personal involvement in every phase of the transaction. Section 1956(c)(2) defines "conduct" to mean "initiating, concluding, or participating in initiating or concluding, a transaction." The Second Circuit explained the scope of the provision in *United States v. Gotti*,[113] in holding that "when a person accepts a transfer or delivery of funds, he has participated in the conclusion of that transfer or delivery, and has therefore conducted a transaction."[114]

Similarly, even if the transaction is not completed, perhaps because the bank did not accept the deposit, the conduct element has been met so long as the transaction was initiated. In *United States v. Li*,[115] a federal district court stated, "There is no requirement that the transaction be both initiated and concluded. Merely initiating a deposit satisfies the conducting a financial transaction element of the offense."[116]

4. *Transaction, Financial Transaction, and Monetary Instruments*

Section 1956(a)(1) refers to "property involved in a financial transaction." The statute contains two interlocking definitions, first providing a broad meaning to "transaction" and then further refining it with regard to what constitutes a "financial transaction." The term "transaction" involves two parts: first, it is a "purchase, sale, loan, pledge, gift, transfer, delivery, or other disposition," and second, when a financial institution is involved, it includes "a deposit, withdrawal, transfer between accounts, exchange of currency, loan, extension of credit, purchase or sale of any stock, bond, certificate of deposit, or other monetary instrument, use of a safe deposit box, or any other payment, transfer, or delivery by, through, or to a financial institution, by whatever means effected."[117]

Courts have read the definition of this term broadly.[118] In one instance where a court read the statute restrictively, Congress followed with an amendment to include

---

[111] 318 F.3d 255 (1st Cir. 2003).

[112] Id. at 258.

[113] 459 F.3d 296 (2d Cir. 2006).

[114] Id. at 335.

[115] United States v. Li, 856 F.Supp. 421 (N.D. Ill. 1994).

[116] Id. at 423.

[117] 18 U.S.C. § 1956 (c)(3)–(4).

[118] See United States v. Hill, 167 F.3d 1055, 1072 (6th Cir. 1999) (finding that the use of a line of credit with a bank constituted a "transaction" under § 1956(c)(3)).

the specified conduct. Thus, following a Seventh Circuit opinion[119] that held that placing money in a safe deposit box at a bank was not a "transaction" within the meaning of the statute, Congress amended § 1956(c)(3) to include "safe deposit box" within the definition.

The statute incorporates the definition of "transaction" into "financial transaction," which has two meanings that focus on providing a basis for federal jurisdiction. It states:

> (A) a transaction which in any way or degree affects interstate or foreign commerce (i) involving the movement of funds by wire or other means or (ii) involving one or more monetary instruments, or (iii) involving the transfer of title to any real property, vehicle, vessel, or aircraft, or (B) a transaction involving the use of a financial institution which is engaged in, or the activities of which affect, interstate or foreign commerce in any way or degree;

Achieving interstate commerce can be relatively easy as one court noted, "at some stage in the life of the check, the utilization of a bank, and banks are all plainly engaged in interstate commerce."[120] Courts have found that the delivery of cash, recording a mortgage on real property, obtaining a car loan, and buying a cashier's check can meet the definition of a "financial transaction" with the requisite effect on interstate commerce.[121]

Section 1956(a)(2) uses the term "monetary instrument," which is defined as "(i) coin or currency of the United States or of any other country, travelers' checks, personal checks, bank checks, and money orders, or (ii) investment securities or negotiable instruments, in bearer form or otherwise in such form that title thereto passes upon delivery." This broad definition brings within § 1956 the use of cash and other untraceable instruments that are frequently used by large-scale organizations to move the profits from illegal activity. For international money laundering prosecutions under § 1956(a)(2), there must be a movement into or out of the United States of monetary instruments generated from specified unlawful activity, and the government need not show a financial transaction.

5. *Financial Institution*

Section 1956(c)(6) defines a "financial institution" to include those organizations "defined in section 5312(a)(2) of title 31, United States Code, or the regulations promulgated thereunder" and also any foreign bank, as provided in the International Banking Act of 1978.[122] The definition in § 5312(a)(2) includes a long list of businesses that can be easily used to launder funds, such as money transfer operations, casinos,

---

[119] United States v. Bell, 936 F.2d 337, 341–342 (7th Cir.1991).

[120] United States v. Canavan, 153 F.Supp.2d 811, 812 (D. Md. 2001).

[121] See United States v. Gotti, 459 F.3d 296, 336 (2nd Cir. 2006) (delivery of cash); United States v. Hall, 434 F.3d 42, 52 (1st Cir. 2006) (recording mortgage); United States v. McGahee, 257 F.3d 520, 527 (6th Cir. 2001) (obtaining car loan); United States v. Reed, 77 F.3d 139, 142 (6th Cir. 1996) (delivery of money to drug currier to obtain additional drugs).

[122] A "foreign bank" includes "foreign commercial banks, foreign merchant banks and other foreign institutions that engage in banking activities usual in connection with the business of banking in the countries where such foreign institutions are organized or operating." 12 U.S.C. § 3101(7).

pawnbrokers, jewelry dealers, insurance companies, law firms, and travel agencies. (See § 12.3).

In *United States v. Ness*,[123] the Second Circuit examined a case where the government had not argued that the defendant's armored car company fit a financial institution under § 5312(a)(2). Rather, they used a regulation promulgated under § 5312, which defined "financial institution" to include a "money services business."[124] The court rejected this theory, noting that the defendant was not as a matter of law a "person engaged as a business in the transfer of funds." A "money transmitter" is "limited to certain 'facts and circumstances.'" The court noted that "[t]he Financial Crimes Enforcement Network ("FinCEN") explained in its Federal Register notice that many commenters sought clarification of the definition of money transmitter and objected to any interpretation that would cause businesses that simply transmit funds as part of their other business activities to be categorized as money transmitters." The court, therefore, reversed this § 1957(a) money laundering conviction, as it was unwilling to extend the term "money transmitter" as the government desired.

6.   *Specified Unlawful Activity*

Money laundering to a large extent is built upon other crimes, or what are called "specified unlawful activity" (SUA). A long list of offenses, that includes both federal and state crimes, serves as the basis for a money laundering charge.[125] White collar crimes are included here, such as frauds involving healthcare, bankruptcy, and securities. Also included are environmental crimes. Section 1956(c)(7)(A) incorporates all the offenses that can form a pattern of racketeering activity in violation of the Racketeer Influenced and Corrupt Organizations Act,[126] better known as RICO, and that list includes state crimes like murder, robbery, kidnapping, and extortion, along with its own laundry list of federal offenses, like mail fraud and bribery.[127] (See § 8.4(A)).

Although § 1956(a)(1) requires proof of a defendant's knowledge that the monetary instruments involved in the financial transaction were the product of some form of unlawful activity, if is not necessary to establish that the defendant knows it was actually a product of a particular offense listed as specified unlawful activity.[128] Thus, the prosecution has to link the funds to a particular identified offense that comes within the broad list of specified unlawful activities, but it is not necessary to show any knowledge on the defendant's part regarding the particular crimes.

7.   *Proceeds*

The money laundering statute is directed at financial transactions that occur once the specified unlawful activity generates "proceeds." Section 1956(c)(9) defines

---

[123] 565 F.3d 73 (2d Cir. 2009).

[124] 31 C.F.R. § 1010.100 (previously 31 C.F.R. § 103.11(n)(3)).

[125] 18 U.S.C. § 1956(c)(7).

[126] 18 U.S.C. §§ 1961 et seq.

[127] See 18 U.S.C. § 1961(1).

[128] A transportation violation under § 1956(a)(2) and the sting operation violation under § 1956(a)(3) also require the proceeds of a specified unlawful activity, but neither require proof of a defendant's knowledge of any connection between the funds and a particular violation.

"proceeds" as "any property derived from or obtained or retained, directly or indirectly, through some form of unlawful activity, including the gross receipts of such activity." This provision was added to the statute following the Supreme Court's decision in *Santos v. United States*.[129]

In *Santos*, the Supreme Court rejected the government's argument that "proceeds" included the funds generated by the "unlawful activity" without regard to whether they were the profits from the conduct. According to the Court, "[f]rom the face of the statute, there is no more reason to think that 'proceeds' means 'receipts' than there is to think that 'proceeds' means 'profits.'"[130] The Court used the rule of lenity in reaching this decision.

Following *Santos*, Congress added language to provide a definition of the term "proceeds." The Senate Report on the new legislation stated:

> The Court's decision [in *Santos*] was contrary to Congressional intent and will lead to criminals escaping culpability simply by claiming their illegal scams did not make any profit. Indeed, proceeds of "Ponzi schemes" like the Bernard Madoff case, which by their very nature do not include any profit, would be out of the reach of the money laundering statutes under this decision. This flawed decision needs to be corrected immediately. . . . [131]

By taking a broad approach to what can constitute "proceeds" for purposes of money laundering, Congress allowed for more white collar activity to be charged as money laundering.

Some courts find that it is not necessary for the government to trace the funds to a specific transaction that constitutes unlawful conduct or specified unlawful activity. The fact that a defendant may have commingled tainted and legitimate funds did not preclude a finding that the transaction involved the proceeds of illegal conduct. In *United States v. Moore*,[132] the Fourth Circuit held that, "[m]oney is fungible, and when funds obtained from unlawful activity have been combined with funds from lawful activity into a single asset, the illicitly-acquired funds and the legitimately-acquired funds (or the respective portions of the property purchased with each) cannot be distinguished from each other; that is, they cannot be traced to any particular source, absent resort to accepted, but arbitrary, accounting techniques.[133]

In *United States v. Loe*,[134] however, the Fifth Circuit referenced a prior decision, *United States v. Davis*,[135] in holding that commingled funds should not automatically be held as tainted. The court stated:

> "[W]hen the aggregate amount withdrawn from an account containing commingled funds exceeds the clean funds, individual withdrawals may be said to be of tainted

---

[129] 553 U.S. 507 (2008).

[130] Id. at 514.

[131] Fraud Enforcement and Recovery Act of 2009 (FERA), S. Rep. No. 111–10, at 4 (2009).

[132] 27 F.3d 969 (4th Cir. 1994).

[133] Id. at 976–77.

[134] 248 F.3d 449 (5th Cir. 2001).

[135] 226 F.3d 346, 357 (5th Cir. 2000).

money, even if a particular withdrawal was less than the amount of clean money in the account." *Davis* also implies the converse—that where an account contains clean funds sufficient to cover a withdrawal, the Government cannot prove beyond a reasonable doubt that the withdrawal contained dirty money.[136]

C. *18 U.S.C. § 1957*

1. *Elements*

Section 1957 targets the use of larger amounts of funds generated from specified unlawful activity, without regard to whether there is an effort to hide the source of the money or the nature of the activity that generated it. Section 1957 is often referred to as the "money spending statute" because the focus is on establishing that a transaction involved $10,000 or more in proceeds of criminal conduct regardless of whether the defendant intended to launder funds. The statute provides that any person who "knowingly engages or attempts to engage in a monetary transaction in criminally derived property of a value greater than $10,000 and is derived from specified unlawful activity, shall be punished" by up to ten years in jail. The essential elements of § 1957 are that "(1) the defendant engage or attempt to engage (2) in a monetary transaction (3) in criminally derived property that is of a value greater than $10,000 (4) knowing that the property is derived from unlawful activity, and (5) the property is, in fact, derived from "specified unlawful activity."[137]

There are two jurisdictional aspects to the offense, covering monetary transactions that "takes place in the United States or in the special maritime and territorial jurisdiction of the United States," or that occur outside the United States "but the defendant is a United States person." Section 1957(d)(2) incorporates the definition of "United States person" used in 18 U.S.C. § 3077, which includes U.S. citizens or permanent resident aliens, any organization "composed principally of nationals or permanent resident aliens of the United States," and corporations—including a foreign subsidiary of a U.S. company—organized under the laws of any state, territory, or possession of the United States.

While § 1956 applies to financial transactions undertaken for one of the specified purposes in the statute, such as concealment or promotion of a specified unlawful activity, § 1957 only requires that there be a "monetary transaction" in an amount greater than $10,000. That term "monetary transaction" means:

> the deposit, withdrawal, transfer, or exchange, in or affecting interstate or foreign commerce, of funds or a monetary instrument (as defined in section 1956(c)(5) of this title) by, through, or to a financial institution (as defined in section 1956 of this title),[138] including any transaction that would be a financial transaction under section 1956(c)(4)(B) of this title, but such term does not include any transaction necessary to preserve a person's right to representation as guaranteed by the sixth amendment to the Constitution;

---

[136] Loe, 248 F.3d at 467.

[137] United States v. Johnson, 971 F.2d 562, 568 n.3 (10th Cir. 1992) (citing United States v. Lovett, 964 F.2d 1029 (10th Cir. 1992).

[138] See §§ 12.2(C) and 12.4(B)(5).

The statute prohibits monetary transactions in "criminally derived property," which according to § 1957(f)(2) "means any property constituting, or derived from, proceeds obtained from a criminal offense." The terms "proceeds" and "specified unlawful activity" have the same meaning as provided in § 1956. (See § 12.4(B)(6) & (7)).

A prosecution for violating § 1957 requires proof of the defendant's knowledge that the funds are proceeds of criminally derived property. A defendant, however, need not believe the monetary transaction itself was illegal, so long as there is proof of knowledge that the proceeds were derived from unlawful activity.

The government is not required to trace the proceeds of criminal activity that constitute the monetary transaction. In *United States v. Mooney*,[139] the defendant was charged with securities violations, mail fraud and money laundering under § 1957. Argued on appeal was that the government had not proved that the money in a certain bank account were proceeds of insider trading and that a sufficient amount of money in the account was "dirty money." The Eighth Circuit rejected this argument stating "that the government need not trace each dollar to a criminal source to prove a violation of 18 U.S.C. § 1957." To hold otherwise, the court stated, "would allow wrongdoers to evade prosecution for money laundering simply by commingling criminal proceeds with legitimate funds."[140]

In *United States v. Johnson*,[141] the Tenth Circuit held that "both the plain language of § 1957 and the legislative history behind it suggest that Congress targeted only those transactions occurring after proceeds have been obtained from the underlying unlawful activity." The court reversed convictions under§ 1957 as "the defendant did not have possession of the funds nor were they at his disposal until the investors transferred them to him." The court said that "[t]he defendant therefore cannot be said to have obtained the proceeds of the wire fraud until the funds were credited to his account."[142]

2.   *Exempt Conduct*

Section 1957(f) specifies that the term "monetary transaction" "does not include any transaction necessary to preserve a person's right to representation as guaranteed by the sixth amendment to the Constitution." In *United States v. Velez*,[143] an attorney was charged with violating § 1957 in a case where he had been hired "to review the source of funds" used to pay another attorney's legal fees, in order to determine if the funds came from criminal proceeds. The attorney reviewing the fee determined that these funds were not criminally derived property. The government differing with the opinion rendered by this attorney, charged him with a violation of § 1957.

The government argued several points on appeal, including that the statute does not "protect the right of a criminal defendant to use criminally derived proceeds for legal fees." The Eleventh Circuit rejected the government position and upheld the

---

[139] 401 F.3d 940 (8th Cir. 2005).

[140] Id. at 947.

[141] 971 F.2d 562 (10th Cir. 1992).

[142] Id. at 569.

[143] 586 F.3d 875 (11th Cir. 2009).

district court's dismissal of this § 1957 charge, finding that this conduct, by the plain language of the statute, was exempt. The court noted that to accept the government's interpretation of the statute would make the exemption "entirely superfluous—to read § 1957(f)(1) as an exemption from criminal penalties for *non-tainted* proceeds spent on legal representation, as those funds can always be used for any legal purpose."[144]

---

[144] Id. at 879.

Chapter 13

BANKRUPTCY CRIMES

§ 13.1 INTRODUCTION

A. History

Bankruptcy crimes in the United States date back to the Bankruptcy Act of 1800. But the predecessor for the present-day bankruptcy crime statutes was the Bankruptcy Act of 1867.[1] These criminal provisions "were enacted to preserve honest administration in bankruptcy proceedings and to ensure the distribution to creditors of as large a portion of the bankrupt's estate as possible."[2] Historically 18 U.S.C. § 152 served as the key bankruptcy crime statute for the prosecution of bankruptcy fraud. This statute concentrates on the concealment of assets, false oaths, and bribery and extortion conduct occurring in connection with a bankruptcy.

Initially when passed, § 152 was not commonly used by prosecutors. Individuals were charged with the substantive offenses that may have led to the bankruptcy as opposed to acts within the bankruptcy matter. Two Department of Justice (DOJ) initiatives increased bankruptcy crime prosecutions. First, in 1992, Attorney General William Barr issued a Department of Justice Memo that placed bankruptcy fraud as one of the DOJ's priorities.[3] Second, Attorney General Reno was a strong advocate for pursuing criminal bankruptcy fraud and had an initiative known as "Operation Total Disclosure" which sparked bankruptcy fraud prosecutions.[4] "'Operation Total Disclosure,' announced by the Attorney General on Feb. 29, 1996, focused on prosecuting bankruptcy filers who illegally concealed assets, filed fraudulent bankruptcy petitions, or otherwise abused the bankruptcy system."[5] Since 2000, the number of bankruptcy fraud convictions has declined.[6]

The DOJ has also reached out to citizens to report bankruptcy fraud and posted a notice requesting individuals to report bankruptcy fraud and explaining how to do this.[7] Most recently President Barak Obama's Financial Fraud Enforcement Task Force included bankruptcy fraud within its initiatives.[8]

---

[1] See Craig Peyton Gaumer, Bankruptcy Fraud: Crime and Punishment, 43 S.D. L. Rev. 527 (1998).

[2] USAM, title 9, Criminal Resource Manual 838, available at http://www.justice.gov/usao/epusa/foia_reading_room/usam/title9/crm00838.htm

[3] Id. at 536.

[4] Ralph C. McCullough II, Bankruptcy Fraud: Crime Without Punishment II, 102 Com. L.J. 1, 5 (1997)

[5] DOJ Press Release, Bankruptcy Fraud, Bank Fraud, Result in 21–month Prison Sentence (April 2, 1998), available at http://www.justice.gov/ust/eo/public_affairs/press/docs/pr040298.pdf

[6] In 2000, the number of bankruptcy fraud convictions was approximately 190. In contrast, in 2012 the government reported 81 new bankruptcy fraud convictions. TracReports, Fraud–Bankruptcy Convictions for 2012, at http://tracfed.syr.edu.

[7] See Report Suspected Bankruptcy Fraud, available at http://www.justice.gov/ust/eo/fraud/

[8] Stopfraud.gov, available at http://www.stopfraud.gov/report.html

B. Bankruptcy Prosecutions

1. Bankruptcy & Generic Statutes

Today bankruptcy crimes are found in §§ 151 through 157 of Title 18. (see §§ 13.2–13.3). These statutes offer crimes for different forms of bankruptcy conduct and include both felonies and misdemeanors to combat improprieties in bankruptcy proceedings.[9]

Bankruptcy crimes are also prosecuted under generic statutes. One finds cases charging false statements (18 U.S.C. § 1001),[10] mail and wire fraud (18 U.S.C. §§ 1341, 1343)[11] and RICO (18 U.S.C. §§ 1961 et.seq.).[12] For RICO it is necessary to have a pattern of racketeering, which includes activities involving fraud connected with a case under Title 11, the Bankruptcy Code. To proceed with a RICO charge it is, of course, necessary for the government to prove all the elements of this offense (see Chap. 8). As a predicate act of RICO, bankruptcy fraud can be pursued in both criminal and civil RICO actions.

When two or more individuals are engaged in the criminal act, prosecutors may decide to proceed with a conspiracy to commit the specific bankruptcy provision under § 371.[13] Thus, one may find a conspiracy to embezzle property from the estate of the debtor charging § 371 for a conspiracy to violate § 153, or a conspiracy with another bankruptcy crime statute.

2. Prosecuting Lawyers

Bankruptcy crimes often include prosecutions against attorneys. From fraudulent conduct to concealing assets, lawyers have faced bankruptcy charges.[14] In some instances their legal knowledge can serve to their detriment as it can be used to show their intent to commit the crime. For example, in *United States v. Goodstein*,[15] the Seventh Circuit upheld convictions, including a violation of section 152, against an attorney with extensive bankruptcy experience. Finding that the accused was a "knowledgeable businessman and lawyer," the court found that this "extensive legal background and integral role in" these bankruptcy affairs indicated that a failure to notify the bankruptcy court and creditors of a transfer was not something done inadvertently.

3. Statute of Limitations

The applicable statute of limitations can arise as an issue in a bankruptcy fraud prosecution. Typically, the statute of limitations for federal crimes is five years,[16] the time allowed for non-capital offenses that are not otherwise specified by statute. Bankruptcy concealment cases, however, have a specific applicable statute. which

---

[9] See § 13.3 for a discussion of crimes beyond § 152.

[10] See Chap. 9.

[11] See Chap. 4.

[12] See Chap. 8.

[13] See Chap. 3.

[14] See, e.g., United States v. McIntosh, 124 F.3d 1330 (10th Cir. 1997); United States v. Dolan, 120 F.3d 856 (8th Cir. 1997); United States v. Bartlett, 633 F.2d 1184 (5th Cir. 1981).

[15] 883 F.2d 1362 (7th Cir. 1989).

[16] 18 U.S.C. § 3282(a).

states, "[t]he concealment of assets of a debtor in a case under title 11 shall be deemed to be a continuing offenses until the debtor shall have been finally discharged or a discharge denied, and the period of limitation shall not begin to run until such final discharge or denial of discharge."[17] This extended statute of limitations is exclusive to concealment cases and does not cover the typical false statement in a bankruptcy proceeding.[18]

As to when the time period actually begins to run in bankruptcy fraud prosecutions presents legal issues. For example, in *United States v. Freeman*,[19] the defendant argued that the time began when he filed a "Notice of Voluntary Dismissal" of his chapter 13 bankruptcy. The government, however, argued that it began the date the court entered the order dismissing the bankruptcy case, which was a later date than what the defendant claimed. Siding with the government in *Freeman*, the court noted that the "five-year limitations period did not begin until the bankruptcy court entered its order dismissing Defendant's bankruptcy case."

More difficult questions can arise in situations when there is no discharge date. In *United States v. Gilbert*,[20] the Eleventh Circuit faced the issue of determining the discharge date of a corporation, which had no final discharge to start the running of the clock. Reversing the conviction of a corporation because it was time-barred, the court followed the lead of other decisions in saying that "where discharge is no longer possible, the date upon which the discharge became impossible is the date upon which the statute of limitations begins to run."[21]

Some cases, however, have held that the failure to receive discharge by the bankruptcy court will toll the statute of limitations. In *Winslow v. United States*,[22] the Ninth Circuit held that the defendant had the "power to apply for, and to secure the entry of, an order denying discharge if it were not possible for him to secure a discharge." In this case, securing the order "would have been sufficient to start the running of the three-year period of limitation."

4. *Venue*

The venue for a bankruptcy fraud prosecution premised on concealment is the location of the bankruptcy proceeding. In *United States v. Gordon*,[23] the defendant argued that the concealment, if any, occurred in New York and that therefore it was improper to prosecute in Connecticut. The Second Circuit, however, held that the situs of the trustee, in Connecticut, was what controlled the venue for the prosecution.

In *United States v. Schireson*,[24] the Third Circuit explored in-depth the question of venue in a bankruptcy concealment case. The defendant made a Sixth Amendment

---

[17] 18 U.S.C. § 3284.

[18] See United States v. Knoll, 16 F.3d 1313 (2d Cir. 1994) (Holding that a non-concealment bankruptcy fraud case is not entitled to the extended statute of limitations offered for concealment cases).

[19] 864 F. Supp.2d 1298 (M.D. Fl. 2012).

[20] 136 F.3d 1451 (11th Cir. 1998).

[21] Id. at 1454–55.

[22] 216 F.2d 912 (9th Cir. 1954).

[23] 379 F.2d 788 (2d Cir. 1967).

[24] 116 F.2d 881 (3d Cir. 1940).

argument claiming that his constitutional rights were violated as the assets initially "came from Illinois, were subsequently moved to New Jersey and were not shown ever to have been within Pennsylvania [the location of the prosecution] at any relevant time." In deciding that the Eastern District of Pennsylvania was the appropriate venue for this prosecution, the court noted that "[t]here can be no concealment from a trustee prior to the appointment of a trustee." The court stated:

> A man who is not a bankrupt may have buried treasure all over the world. He commits no offense under the Bankruptcy Act. Certainly it was no indictable concealment to have valuable objects in a bank vault in New Jersey before bankruptcy. The wrongdoing came only after bankruptcy had supervened.[25]

The court found that since the bankruptcy trustee was in the State of Pennsylvania, this was the proper site for this prosecution, irrespective of where the goods were located.[26] The location for a bankruptcy case premised on a false statement or oath has not been the subject of judicial scrutiny.[27]

§ 13.2   *18 U.S.C. § 152*

A. Overview

1. *The Statute*

Section 152 serves as the main bankruptcy crimes statute and is the most commonly used provision for the prosecution of bankruptcy fraud.[28] The statute includes nine different types of conduct:

(1) knowingly and fraudulently conceals from a custodian, trustee, marshal, or other officer of the court charged with the control or custody of property, or, in connection with a case under title 11, from creditors or the United States Trustee, any property belonging to the estate of a debtor;

(2) knowingly and fraudulently makes a false oath or account in or in relation to any case under title 11;

(3) knowingly and fraudulently makes a false declaration, certificate, verification, or statement under penalty of perjury as permitted under section 1746 of title 28, in or in relation to any case under title 11;

(4) knowingly and fraudulently presents any false claim for proof against the estate of a debtor, or uses any such claim in any case under title 11, in a personal capacity or as or through an agent, proxy, or attorney;

---

[25] Id. at 883–84.

[26] See also United States v. Brimberry, 779 F.2d 1339 (8th Cir. 1985).

[27] Federal District in Which Offense of Concealing Assets from Trustee in Bankruptcy, or Making False Oath with Reference to Assets, Deemed Committed so as to Confer Jurisdiction Upon Court of that District, 132 A.L.R. 1163 (2011).

[28] It is also the number one charge used in prosecuting bankruptcy fraud related crimes. TracReports, Fraud–Bankruptcy Convictions for 2012, at http://tracfed.syr.edu.

(5) knowingly and fraudulently receives any material amount of property from a debtor after the filing of a case under title 11, with intent to defeat the provisions of title 11;

(6) knowingly and fraudulently gives, offers, receives, or attempts to obtain any money or property, remuneration, compensation, reward, advantage, or promise thereof for acting or forbearing to act in any case under title 11;

(7) in a personal capacity or as an agent or officer of any person or corporation, in contemplation of a case under title 11 by or against the person or any other person or corporation, or with intent to defeat the provisions of title 11, knowingly and fraudulently transfers or conceals any of his property or the property of such other person or corporation;

(8) after the filing of a case under title 11 or in contemplation thereof, knowingly and fraudulently conceals, destroys, mutilates, falsifies, or makes a false entry in any recorded information (including books, documents, records, and papers) relating to the property or financial affairs of a debtor; or

(9) after the filing of a case under title 11, knowingly and fraudulently withholds from a custodian, trustee, marshal, or other officer of the court or a United States Trustee entitled to its possession, any recorded information (including books, documents, records, and papers) relating to the property or financial affairs of a debtor,[29]

It has been stated that § 152 was "a congressional attempt to cover all the possible methods by which a debtor or any other person may attempt to defeat the intent and effect of the bankruptcy law through any type of effort to keep assets from being equitable distributed among creditors."[30] A prosecution under this statute provides criminality to acts of concealment (see § 13.2 (B)), false oaths (see § 13.2 (C)), and bribery that occur knowingly and fraudulently (see § 13.2 (E)) and are in relation to a Title 11 case (see § 13.2 (F)).

It is difficult in some cases to distinguish between a false oath and concealment as the making of the false statement may in fact result in a concealment.[31] Materiality has been a component in concealment cases. (See § 13.2 (D)). Section 152 carries a penalty of up to five years and a fine. This criminal bankruptcy statute has been found to be constitutional and when challenged a court held that it was not vague.[32]

2. Multiple Charges

Courts have allowed separate counts for the nine different crimes outlined in the statute, but some have not allowed repetitive counts for the same set of facts. In *United States v. Montilla Ambrosiani*,[33] the court stated that "presumptively Congress favors a

---

[29] 18 U.S.C. § 152; see also USAM, Criminal Resource Manual § 840.

[30] United States v. Johns, 686 F.3d 438 (7th Cir. 2012).

[31] Burchinal v. United States, 342 F.2d 982 (10th Cir. 1965); United States v. Schireson, 116 F.2d 881 (3d Cir. 1940).

[32] See, e.g., United States v. Ballard, 779 F.2d 287, 295 (5th Cir. 1986); United States v. Lawson, 255 F.Supp. 261 (D. Minn. 1996).

[33] 610 F.2d 65 (1st Cir. 1979).

single punishment for a single result, the method of accomplishment being merely incidental." One court reversed a prosecution that used the same conduct for charging multiple parts of the statute, remanding the decision with directions for "the government to elect which § 152 count of the conviction it wish[ed] to leave in effect."[34] But in *United States v. Cluck*,[35] the court allowed different provisions of the statute to be used when the provisions called for different kinds of conduct. The court stated that "[b]ecause each statutory provision 'requires proof of an additional fact which the other does not,' charging the same conduct under both sections does not give rise to a multiplicity problem."

3. *Individuals Charged*

Issues can arise when the individual has provided a power of attorney for the filing of the bankruptcy petition. In *United States v. Spurlin*,[36] one of the defendants argued "that she cannot be convicted of concealment of bankruptcy assets, because the joint bankruptcy petition was filed on her behalf using a general power of attorney and because she did not supply any information for the petition." The court noted the split in caselaw regarding a joint bankruptcy with one party using a general power of attorney, noting that some jurisdictions allowed this practice and others did not.[37] In *Spurlin,* the Fifth Circuit held "that a general power of attorney may be used to file for bankruptcy on another's behalf." The court stated, "[a]lthough certain matters are too personal to be entrusted to another, bankruptcy is primarily for property protection and is not as profoundly personal as divorce or enlistment."

B. Concealment

Concealment is a common basis for a § 152 prosecution. Secreting, falsifying, and mutilating of property or information have been found to be evidence of concealment. To sustain a conviction under the general concealment clause of section 152, the government must prove beyond a reasonable doubt that the accused (1) knowingly and fraudulently, (2) concealed from an officer or the creditors, (3) in a Title 11 case, (4) property belonging to the estate of the debtor.

What constitutes "property belonging to the estate of the debtor" may become an issue for resolution in a case. In *United States v. Cardall*,[38] the Tenth Circuit looked to the Bankruptcy Code, specifically 11 U.S.C. § 541,[39] in stating that this section "is to be broadly construed to include all property interests, whether reachable by state-law creditors or not, and whether vested or contingent." The court held that "clearinghouse funds diverted into interrelated accounts did not lose their status as 'debtor's property' simply because they were held in a PAC [Payable Accounting Company's] account,

---

[34] United States v. Graham, 60 F.3d 463 (8th Cir. 1995).

[35] 143 F.3d 174 (5th Cir. 1998).

[36] 664 F.3d 954 (5th Cir. 2011).

[37] Id. at 959 (citing In re Raymond, 12 B.R. 906 (Bankr. E.D. Va. 1981) (finding bankruptcy to be a "highly personal privilege, similar to divorce or enlistment in the armed forces, that could not be effected by a power or attorney); In re Ballard, 1987 WL 191320 (Bankr. N.D. Cal. 1987) (permitting a wife to sign a joint bankruptcy filing for her husband who was serving in the military).

[38] 885 F.2d 656 (10th Cir. 1989).

[39] Bankruptcy Code § 541 does provide exceptions as to what is "property of the estate" such as "an interest in a trust subject to transfer restrictions enforceable under applicable non-bankruptcy law." United States v. Shadduck, 112 F.3d 523, 528 n.7 (1st Cir. 1997).

rather than on one of the numerous clearinghouse accounts." The jury decides whether the property is part of the bankruptcy estate, as this is a factual issue.[40] "Whether property belongs to the debtor, and therefore the bankruptcy estate is determined by state law."[41]

In *United States v. Persfull*,[42] the Seventh Circuit affirmed a conviction where the accused failed to disclose an inheritance and an account that he used, thus concealing assets from the bankruptcy trustee. Equitable interests have also been found to be property of the debtor.[43] But when the debtor has no legal or equitable ownership interest in property, a failure to report the item will not be sufficient for a bankruptcy concealment conviction.[44] There is no requirement that the assets concealed need to be substantial.[45]

Mere omission of an asset on a bankruptcy schedule does not, however, indicate conclusively the existence of concealment. In *Coghlan v. United States*,[46] the Eighth Circuit discussed the circumstances of when a failure to schedule property would constitute a concealment. The court noted that although omission of assets from a schedule indicates concealment, taken alone this is inconclusive. "The conduct of the bankrupt, the relative extent of the omission, the character of the asset itself, and the reasons given for the difference between financial statements of the business and the bankruptcy schedules are the other circumstances in every case." When these circumstances explain the omission, the element of concealment is lacking. The court in *Coghlan* noted, however, that facts supporting a continued concealment consummate the offense.

Thus, in *United States v. Spurlin*,[47] the Fifth Circuit found sufficient evidence of certain counts regarding concealment despite the defendant not being the one to provide the initial information on the bankruptcy petition. The court stated, "[e]ven if she never supplied false information for the filings, withholding information constitutes concealment, and as a continuing violation, concealment can begin after the bankruptcy proceedings have started." In this case, the defendant had attended the creditors' meeting, a meeting in which she and her husband were asked "whether they had read all the documents in their bankruptcy filing and whether all the schedules and the statement of financial affairs were accurate." Their "no" answer was considered in determining the sufficiency of the evidence.[48]

---

[40] United States v. Dennis, 237 F.3d 1295, 1300 (11th Cir. 2001).

[41] United States v. Lawrence, 189 F.3d 838 (9th Cir. 1999).

[42] 660 F.3d 286 (7th Cir. 2011).

[43] United States v. Weinstein, 834 F.2d 1454, 1461 n.2 (9th Cir. 1987).

[44] United States v. McIntosh, 124 F.3d 1330 (10th Cir. 1997).

[45] United States v. Grant, 971 F.2d 799 (1st Cir. 1992). The court in Grant did note that a "de minimus value may be probative of the absence of intent to defraud." Id. at 809 n.19. If the bankruptcy fraud is premised on § 152(5), then the amount may be an issue since it is necessary that the defendant receive a "material amount of property from a debtor after the filing of a case under title 11, with intent to defeat the provisions of title 11."

[46] 147 F.2d 233 (8th Cir. 1945).

[47] 664 F.3d 954 (5th Cir. 2011).

[48] The court did reverse the husband's conviction for allegedly making false statements on the petition premised on insufficient evidence. Id.

C. False Oaths

The knowing and fraudulent filing of a false account or schedule of assets under oath, also can form the basis of a prosecution under the false oath provision of section 152.[49] To sustain a conviction under the false oath clause of § 152, the government must prove beyond a reasonable doubt that the accused (1) knowingly and fraudulently, (2) made a false oath or account, (3) that was material, (4) in relation to a Title 11 case. When a defendant claims that he was unaware that the bankruptcy petition was inaccurate, the jury gets to resolve this factual issue.[50] But a court will reverse when there is insufficient evidence.[51]

Some courts will specify for an 18 U.S.C. § 152(2) prosecution, that the false statement be a "proceeding under penalty of perjury."[52] There is no requirement that the government has to prove that the fraudulently obtained property is a pre-petition debt.[53]

Although courts have stated that the false oath provision of § 152 does not require proof of all of the elements of a perjury charge,[54] some courts will examine the false oath in the context of perjury law. Where in perjury, literally true but unresponsive answers to questions cannot form the basis for a perjury conviction,[55] false oaths in bankruptcy have used a contextual approach. Thus, a false oath prosecution might be upheld despite the existence of statements that may be literally true in isolation.[56]

Courts have found sufficient evidence when a defendant "fraudulently secured credit cards by listing her friends, without their permission, as the applicants or co-applicants and that she made purchases with those accounts."[57] Sections 152(2) and (3) have been used when the defendants failed to include in their bankruptcy petition "a substantial monetary settlement for a workers' compensation claim" that they had received just prior to filing the bankruptcy petition.[58]

A "subsequent disclosure of the assets before the referee and the trustee's acquisition of knowledge of the existence of said assets" will not negate a false oath charge. In *United States v. Young*,[59] the Seventh Circuit stated that "[t]he offenses of making the false oaths were completed when the knowingly false schedules were sworn to and filed."

---

[49] Goetz v. United States, 59 F.2d 511 (7th Cir.1932).

[50] United States v. Cutter, 313 F.3d 1 (1st Cir. 2002) (claiming that he was unaware that his bankruptcy petition was inaccurate).

[51] United States v. Ward, 197 F.3d 1076 (11th Cir. 1999) (finding insufficient evidence of a false oath on a bankruptcy schedule).

[52] United States v. Marston, 694 F.3d 131 (1st Cir. 2012).

[53] United States v. Knox, 68 F.3d 990 (7th Cir. 1995).

[54] United States v. Lynch, 180 F.2d 696 (7th Cir.1950).

[55] Bronston v. United States, 409 U.S. 352 (1973); see also § 20.5.

[56] United States v. Schafrick, 871 F.2d 300 (2d Cir. 1989).

[57] United States v. Marston, 694 F.3d 131 (1st Cir. 2012).

[58] United States v. Gary, 613 F.3d 706 (7th Cir. 2010).

[59] 339 F.2d 1003 (7th Cir. 1964).

D. Materiality

Courts have required proof of materiality when the case is premised on a false oath. Materiality in this context has been defined as referring "not only to the main fact which is the subject of inquiry, but also to any fact or circumstance which tends to corroborate or strengthen the proof adduced to establish the main fact."[60] Materiality does not require the government to prove that creditors were harmed by the false statement.

Matters "pertinent to the extent and nature of [a] bankrupt's assets, including the history of a bankrupt's financial transactions," have been found material. Statements designed to secure adjudication by a particular bankruptcy court also have been found to be material.[61] Failing to disclose prior bankruptcies has been found to be material in that this information can "impede an investigation into a debtor's financial affairs."[62] Additionally, statements aimed at obtaining a particular status before a court, such as *in forma pauperis*, have been held to be material.[63]

In *United States v. Phillips*,[64] the Ninth Circuit found misstatements in a bankruptcy petition material, and as included in the indictment, these false statements were properly read to the jury. The statements were a false social security number, false prior addresses, and failure to give past names by which the accused had been known. The court stated that the false social security number and fabrication of prior addresses may have misled creditors as to the petitioner's identity and financial background. The failure to provide prior names can obstruct attempts to acquire a full credit history and hinder the determination of assessing one's eligibility for bankruptcy.

E. Knowingly and Fraudulently

Section 152 requires that the defendant act knowingly and fraudulently. This intent requirement mandates proof by the government that the accused acted willfully as opposed to through mistake, excusable neglect, or inadvertence. In some cases willful blindness will be an instruction given to demonstrate that the accused acted knowingly and fraudulently. (See § 1.8(C)(2)).

In *United States v. Zehrbach*,[65] the court stated that "proof of knowledge of illegality is not a burden of the government in a bankruptcy fraud case." The term "knowingly" only required "that the act be voluntary and intentional and not that a person knows that he is breaking the law." The court in *Zehrbach* was unwilling to extend to bankruptcy fraud cases, the holdings in *Cheek v. United States*[66] and *Ratzlaf v. United States*,[67] that required knowledge of the illegality. In the tax and anti-structuring financial reporting requirement cases, mistake of law was a complete

---

[60] Metheany v. United States, 365 F.2d 90 (9th Cir.1966).

[61] United States v. O'Donnell, 539 F.2d 1233 (9th Cir.1976).

[62] United States v. Lindholm, 24 F.3d 1078 (9th Cir.1994).

[63] United States v. Yagow, 953 F.2d 427 (8th Cir.1992).

[64] 606 F.2d 884 (9th Cir. 1979).

[65] 47 F.3d 1252 (3d Cir. 1995).

[66] 498 U.S. 192 (1991); see also § 11.3.

[67] 510 U.S. 135 (1994); see also § 12.2(F)(2).

defense. In contrast, the *Zehrbach* court stated that the "elements making up the offense of bankruptcy fraud, particularly the intent to defraud the creditors or the trustee of the bankruptcy estate," do not include "a defendant's good faith belief in the lawfulness of his conduct." Unlike, the statutes from the *Cheek* and *Ratzlaf* cases, a good faith belief in the lawfulness of one's conduct is not a defense to bankruptcy fraud. (See § 1.8(C)(1)).

Circumstantial evidence is often used to prove the *mens rea* of the crime. The jury is instructed that they may infer intent from the evidence presented. In *United States v. Gellene*,[68] the Seventh Circuit permitted an "intent to deceive" to suffice in meeting the "fraudulent" element of the statute. Gellene, a partner at a New York law firm, had filed "in the bankruptcy court a sworn declaration that was to include all of his firm's connections to the debtor, creditors, and any other parties in interest. The declaration failed to list the senior secured creditor and related parties." Gellene had argued that he "used bad judgment in concluding that the representations did not need to be disclosed," but "that he had no fraudulent intent." The court rejected this argument finding that the "district court treated all elements of the offense fairly and accurately."

Although courts permit intent to be inferred from the circumstances, it is still necessary to have sufficient evidence of the *mens rea*. Where the accused, in a bankruptcy fraud action alleging concealment, lacked knowledge of the bankruptcy order for relief or the appointment of a receiver, a court reversed the defendant's convictions. The defendant in *United States v. Guiliano*[69] was neither the owner or an officer of the debtor. As a salesperson, the court found that he was not required to be familiar with the financial condition of the company. Although it was possible to speculate that when the business closed the accused should have realized that a bankruptcy would follow, mere conjecture was insufficient to meet the knowledge requirement. Likewise, there was insufficient evidence in a case of a wife who was not involved with her husband's business affairs, despite the fact that her signatures were on "different documents attached to the petition—but not on the pages listing the petitioners' assets."[70]

With respect to one count in the *Guiliano* case, the Second Circuit was satisfied that there was evidence to support a jury inference of the defendant's knowledge of the bankruptcy order for relief or the appointment of a trustee. This count accused the defendant of fraudulently concealing certain equipment from the bankruptcy trustee. According to the court, there was evidence that the defendant had been requested to remove this equipment and sell it for as much cash as possible. Upon removal of these items, the defendant knew of the company's financial crisis. The court noted that the defendant also worked closely with another individual after the bankruptcy order for relief and appointment of a trustee. Although the *Guiliano* court found evidence inferring knowledge, this count was reversed and remanded for a retrial in that there was a risk that the jury was influenced in its disposition of this count by improper evidence and by allegations of a reversed RICO count.

---

[68] 182 F.3d 578 (7th Cir. 1999).

[69] 644 F.2d 85 (2d Cir.1981).

[70] United States v. White, 879 F.2d 1509 (7th Cir. 1989).

F. In Contemplation of Bankruptcy

Crucial to a bankruptcy fraud prosecution is a bankruptcy proceeding. Prosecutions under § 152 require the government to prove that the defendant contemplated a bankruptcy. Insufficient proof that the defendant's acts contemplated a bankruptcy proceeding will not support a conviction.[71] A defendant's belief in the invalidity of a bankruptcy proceeding, however, does not negate the bankruptcy fraud.[72]

Courts also use circumstantial evidence to prove that the defendant acted in anticipation of filing a bankruptcy petition. For example, in *United States v. Martin*,[73] the court affirmed the trial court's finding that the defendant's act demonstrated that they "were attempting to secrete and conceal assets [ ] with the intent to defeat the Bankruptcy Laws and that they did this with a knowing and fraudulent intent."

It is necessary that the actions of concealment or false oath relate to the bankruptcy. In an action premised upon the false statement provision within § 152, the Eighth Circuit held that the "in relation to" requirement should be interpreted broadly. The court found that statements made in cases arising from a central bankruptcy proceeding would be "in or in relation to any case under Title 11."[74]

§ 13.3 OTHER BANKRUPTCY STATUTES

A. *18 U.S.C. § 153*

Section 153 pertains to embezzlement by a trustee, officer, or their agent. A penalty of up to five years imprisonment and fine can be imposed. It requires that this individual "knowingly and fraudulently appropriates to the person's own use, embezzles, spends, or transfers any property or secretes or destroys a document belonging to the estate of a debtor." A typical case under this section could include an attorney who may have embezzled funds from individual bankruptcy matters where the attorney was serving as the trustee.[75] Misappropriating a check belonging to the estate of a bankrupt has also served as the basis for this embezzlement charge.[76]

The statute applies to "[a] person . . . who has access to property or documents belonging to the estate by virtue of the person's participation in the administration of the estate as a trustee, custodian, marshal, attorney, or other officer of the court or as an agent, employee, or other person engaged by such an officer to perform a service with respect to the estate."[77] The term "custodian" has been defined to include an attorney who "obtained charge of the property in question."[78]

---

[71] United States v. Tashjian, 660 F.2d 829 (1st Cir. 1981).

[72] United States v. Beery, 678 F.2d 1043 (8th Cir. 1984).

[73] 408 F.2d 949, 954 (7th Cir. 1969).

[74] United States v. Yagow, 953 F.2d 427 (8th Cir.1992).

[75] See, e.g., United States v. Fousek, 912 F.2d 979 (8th Cir. 1990).

[76] United States v. Ivers, 512 F.2d 121 (8th Cir. 1975).

[77] 18 U.S.C. § 153(b).

[78] Jackson v. United States, 72 F.2d 764 (3rd Cir. 1934).

Many of the cases under this section of the federal code occurred prior to revisions of the bankruptcy code. Thus, the applicability of some of these decisions may be questioned. According to *Meagher v. United States*,[79] one of the prior cases, § 153 does not require that the indictment specify the ownership of the property. Nor was it necessary that the bankrupt debtor have had an interest in the property at the beginning of the bankruptcy proceeding. The "estate may acquire an interest in property after the commencement of the case" and this could serve as the basis for "property belonging to the estate of a debtor" for purposes of § 153.[80] In *United States v. Knight*,[81] the Supreme Court held that "[a]ll the consideration which is paid for a bankrupt's assets becomes part of the estate." Justice Douglas writing for the majority stated that "[i]t is the substance of the transaction not its form which controls."[82]

"Knowingly and fraudulently appropriates" has been held not to include unintentional acts. But this is a question for the jury to determine.[83] One court did require that there be a showing of fraud, dismissing the case when it was lacking.[84] The DOJ's Criminal Resource Manual recommends that when evidence of intent to defraud is weak, consideration should be given to proceeding under the general embezzlement statute, as opposed to § 153.[85]

It has been found not to violate the Double Jeopardy clause to charge both § 152 and § 153. In *United States v. Atiyeh*,[86] the Eastern District of Pennsylvania noted that "§ 153 requires proof of embezzlement and § 152 requires proof of concealment and § 153 does not" and thus, the two counts encompass different offenses.

B. *18 U.S.C. § 154*

Section 154 criminalizes three different types of conduct by custodians, trustees, marshals, or other court officers:

> (1) knowingly purchases, directly or indirectly, any property of the estate of which the person is such an officer in a case under title 11; (2) knowingly refuses to permit a reasonable opportunity for the inspection by parties in interest of the documents and accounts relating to the affairs of estates in the person's charge by parties when directed by the court to do so; or (3) knowingly refuses to permit a reasonable opportunity for the inspection by the United States Trustee of the documents and accounts relating to the affairs of an estate in the person's charge,

The penalty here is a fine and forfeiture of the individual's office.

This section of the code emphasizes that a trustee in bankruptcy serves in a fiduciary relationship and owes a duty as an officer of the court to protect the property

---

[79] 36 F.2d 156 (9th Cir. 1929).

[80] United States v. Derryberry, II, 856 F.2d 196 (6th Cir. 1988) (reversed on other grounds).

[81] 336 U.S. 505 (1949).

[82] Id. at 508–09.

[83] United States v. Lynch, 180 F.2d 696 (7th Cir. 1950).

[84] United States v. Sharpe, 996 F.2d 125 (6th Cir. 1993).

[85] USAM, Criminal Resource Manual 870, available at http://www.justice.gov/usao/eousa/foia_ reading_room/usam/title9/crm00870.htm

[86] 330 F. Supp.2d 499 (E.D. Pa. 2004).

of the estate.[87] When an individual is disqualified under this section, it may allow him or her to purchase assets of the estate, since he or she is no longer in a fiduciary role.[88]

C. *18 U.S.C. § 155*

Section 155 prohibits a party in interest from knowingly and fraudulently agreeing with another party in interest to the fixing of a fee or other compensation from the assets of the estate. In *Lutheran Hospitals and Homes Society of America v. Duecy*,[89] the Ninth Circuit stated that the purpose of section 155 was "to keep the fees under the control of the court to prevent trustees, creditors and others, and their counsel, from playing fast and loose with other people's money in courts of bankruptcy." A violation of this provision can result in imprisonment of up to one year and a fine.

This misdemeanor statute "covers all agreements, whether expressed or implied, to pay fees or compensation from the assets of the bankruptcy estate."[90] But it is limited to the assets of a bankruptcy estate and does not include property or debts that are not a part of the bankruptcy estate.

This statute can prove contentious in civil litigation that might be resolving attorney fee payments. The statute has been found not to be an impediment when an attorney is requested to show proof of the reasonableness of his or her fee.[91] It also proved controversial when a court decided to use this statute as a basis for not considering a contingent fee agreement in a civil matter.[92]

D. *18 U.S.C. § 156*

The Bankruptcy Reform Act of 1994 modified §§ 152–155 of the existing statutes and also added new statutes with the passage of sections 156 and 157. Section 156 penalizes a bankruptcy petition preparer "if a bankruptcy case or related proceeding is dismissed because of a knowing attempt" by the preparer to disregard the bankruptcy statutes and rules. The bankruptcy petition preparer, defined as "a person, other than the debtor's attorney or an employee of such attorney, who prepares for compensation a document for filing" faces up to one year imprisonment and a fine for the knowing disregard of a bankruptcy law or rule. The statute also defines the term "document for filing."[93] The Resource Manual for U.S. Attorneys points out that this statute has a lower level of *mens rea* required in that the acts need to be done knowingly, but not done fraudulently.[94] Like the prior section, this statute is a misdemeanor.

---

[87] In re Grodel Manufacturing, Inc., 33 B.R. 693 (Bankr.D. Conn. 1983).

[88] Gross v. Russo, 762 F.2d 239 (2d Cir. 1985).

[89] 422 F.2d 200 (9th Cir. 1970).

[90] USAM, title 9, Criminal Resource Manual § 875.

[91] In re Gianulias, 111 B.R. 867 (E.D. Cal. 1989).

[92] Mullendore v. Mullendore, 527 F.2d 1031 (10th Cir. 1975).

[93] 18 U.S.C. § 156(a)(2).

[94] USAM, title 9, Criminal Resource Manual § 877.

E.   *18 U.S.C. § 157*

Section 157 is modeled after the mail fraud statute.[95] It was added as part of the bankruptcy crimes in the Bankruptcy Reform Act of 1994.[96] It authorizes a penalty of up to five years imprisonment and a fine against individuals who devise or intend to devise a scheme or artifice to defraud.[97] Section 157 is ranked the second most frequently used charge in bankruptcy related prosecutions.[98]

In 2005, Congress inserted "including a fraudulent involuntary petition under section 303 of such title." As a result of this amendment to the statute, it was said to include a "fraudulent involuntary bankruptcy petition. A technical amendment to the statute in 2010 clarified the language in the statute.[99]

This crime, like many fraud related crimes, is focused on the fraudulent activity. It is the use of the bankruptcy process that adds the specificity to this crime. The execution of the scheme can be through filing a bankruptcy petition, bankruptcy document, or the making of a "false or fraudulent representation, claim, or promise concerning or in relation" to a bankruptcy proceeding. The statute requires proof of "1) the existence of a scheme to defraud or intent to later formulate a scheme to defraud, and 2) the filing of a bankruptcy petition 3) for the purpose of executing or attempting to execute the scheme."[100]

The success of the scheme is not required. It is the filing of the petition that is the "forbidden act."[101] In *United States v. DeSantis*,[102] the Sixth Circuit considered whether an unsuccessful scheme to defraud is the equivalent to an attempt for purposes of sentencing under § 157. The courts stated that "[t]he statute makes the crime complete upon the *filing* of the bankruptcy petition when the filing is accompanied by the other two defined circumstances." An unsuccessful scheme is not an attempt. To have an attempted bankruptcy fraud would require "the unusual situation of an unsuccessful attempt to file the bankruptcy petition itself."[103]

Some courts have noted that materiality is required, although there is no *de minimus* exception[104] and no requirement to show an actual reliance.[105] But the broad reach of § 157 led one court to state in a footnote that materiality would be required for

---

[95] See Chap. 4.

[96] P.L. 103–394 (Oct. 22, 1994).

[97] Courts have stated that the "proper loss calculation in bankruptcy fraud cases is the amount of the debt that the defendant sought to discharge in bankruptcy." United States v. Mutuc, 349 F.3d 930 (7th Cir. 2003), see also Chap. 24.

[98] TracReports, Fraud–Bankruptcy Convictions for 2012, at http://tracfed.syr.edu.

[99] The technical amendments in 2010 struck out "bankruptcy" following "involuntary" in subsection 2(b)(1) and struck our "including a fraudulent involuntary petition under section 303 of such title" following "title 11" in paragraphs 2 and 3 of 2(b)(2). Pub. L. 111–327 (2010).

[100] United States v. McBride,362 F.3d 360 (6th Cir. 2004).

[101] Id.

[102] 237 F.3d 607 (6th Cir. 2001).

[103] Id. at 614.

[104] See United States v. Everett, 2008 WL 3843831 (D. Arizona 2008). In *Neder v. United States*, 527 U.S. 1 (1999) the Supreme Court held materiality required for mail fraud. See § 4.7.

[105] United States v. Wagner, 382 F.3d 598 (6th Cir. 2004).

§ 152, but that it did not appear to be required for § 157. But it noted that this issue had not been briefed by the parties to the matter.[106]

In *United States v. Daniels*[107] the Fifth Circuit rejected an argument that the statute was unconstitutionally vague. The defendant had argued that it was unclear in the statute who was to be protected from the fraudulent conduct: the bankruptcy system, creditors, or general public. The court found that as applied to this defendant it was constitutional as "Daniels defrauded not only the homeowners, but also the bankruptcy system and the mortgage companies."[108]

Cases under § 157 have included a scheme based on claims of receiving a Small Business Administration (SBA) loan to pay creditors, when the alleged loan of 10.7 million did not exist.[109] "[P]ark[ing] assets with family members," placing other assets in accounts to avoid creditors, and lying to creditors, the trustee, and bankruptcy court presents a violation of § 157.[110] A non-lawyer paralegal who was giving erroneous advice to clients about the effect of filing a bankruptcy petition was defrauding both his clients and the bankruptcy court.[111]

In *United States v. Holstein*,[112] a case involving a § 157 prosecution for the falsification of documents by an attorney, the Seventh Circuit affirmed the judge's findings following a bench trial. These findings included that the defendant had "solicited clients, accepted fees, and hid from the clients his impending suspension and consequent inability to complete the representation; misrepresented to the bankruptcy court that the debtors were unrepresented by counsel; and made the misrepresentations to conceal that he was practicing without a license."[113]

But courts have also rejected cases under § 157 for failing to meet the statutory requirements or insufficient evidence. In *United States v. Lee*,[114] an Eastern District of Pennsylvania court considered the case of an accused who was alleged to have "failed to disclose that he was receiving indirect payments from [an individual] through his to-be wife." The government alleged that this was a scheme or artifice to defraud. The court referenced the legislative history of this statute stating:

> The Report stresses that specific intent to defraud must be found. On the other hand, according to the Report, the statute would *not* cover either (1) someone who makes a misrepresentation on a financial statement, and then subsequently goes into bankruptcy, so long as the defendant had not, at the time of the misrepresentation, planned the bankruptcy as part of the scheme; and (2) someone who makes a false statement or promise in a bankruptcy proceeding, so long as

---

[106] United States v. Yagman, 2007 WL 4532670 n.3 (C.D. Cal. 2007)
[107] 247 F.3d 598 (5th Cir. 2001).
[108] Id. at 600.
[109] United States v. Wagner, 382 F.3d 598 (6th Cir. 2004).
[110] United States v. Roti, 484 F.3d 934 (7th Cir. 2007).
[111] United States v. Alexander, 135 F.3d 470 (7th Cir. 1998).
[112] 618 F.3d 610 (7th Cir. 2010).
[113] Id. at 611.
[114] 82 F. Supp.2d 389 (E.D. Pa. 2000).

this statement or promise was not made as part of a scheme to defraud involving the bankruptcy proceeding.[115]

Using principles of due process and the rule of lenity, the court rejected the use of § 157 with this conduct. The court held that it could not "find that Lee's post hoc filing was in execution of this antecedent putative fraud." The court held that this statute should not be given the breadth that had been afforded to other fraud statutes, such as the mail and securities fraud statutes.

In *United States v. Milwitt*,[116] the Ninth Circuit rejected the bankruptcy fraud convictions, finding insufficient evidence of the crimes charged under §§ 152 and 157. Like the *Lee* decision, the court stressed the legislative history that required specific intent for a § 157 prosecution. The Ninth Circuit found that "the crime of bankruptcy fraud under 18 U.S.C. § 157 requires specific intent to defraud an identifiable victim or class of victims of the identified fraudulent scheme." Here there was no showing of an intent to defraud creditors. The court stated, "[w]hen the government rested its case, it had presented no proof that there was a scheme to defraud the landlords, much less that the bankruptcy petitions had been filed as a means of executing or concealing the scheme." It is necessary that the fraud is related to the scheme, and merely "filing a voluntary petition under Chapter 13 when the debtor has sufficient means to repay the debts is not viable."

F.   *18 U.S.C. § 158*

Section 158, added in 2005, provides the individuals who will address bankruptcy abuses, including the U.S. Attorney and provides for an agent for each FBI field office. It also provides for bankruptcy courts to "establish procedures for referring" these cases to the designated individuals.

§ 13.4   PONZI SCHEMES AND CLAWBACKS

The Securities Exchange Commission (SEC) defines a Ponzi scheme as:

A Ponzi scheme is an investment fraud that involves the payment of purported returns to existing investors from funds contributed by new investors. Ponzi scheme organizers often solicit new investors by promising to invest funds in opportunities claimed to generate high returns with little or no risk. In many Ponzi schemes, the fraudsters focus on attracting new money to make promised payments to earlier-stage investors and to use for personal expenses, instead of engaging in any legitimate investment activity.[117]

The name used to describe these schemes originates from a scheme of Charles Ponzi who in the 1920s had a scheme that resulted in his receiving a sentence of five years.

More recent Ponzi schemes have received significantly higher sentences, with Bernard Madoff receiving a federal prison sentence of 150 years. The slow response to

---

[115] Id. at 387 (citing House Report 103–835, 1994 U.S.C.C.A.N. 3340, 3366–67).

[116] 475 F.3d 1150 (9th Cir. 2007).

[117] Ponzi Schemes, SEC–Frequently Asked Questions, available at http://www.sec.gov/answers/ponzi.htm.

detect this Ponzi scheme by the SEC resulted in three inspector general reports, one of which is entitled *Investigation of Failure of the SEC to Uncover Bernard Madoff's Ponzi Scheme*.[118]

Both the SEC and DOJ are integral parts in the investigation of Ponzi schemes, many of which result in prosecutors bringing criminal charges. These Ponzi schemes often result in bankruptcy proceedings and this can be followed by bankruptcy receivers distributing any remaining funds.

As a result of fraudulent transfers by Ponzi schemers, clawback actions can result.[119] Clawbacks are aimed at fraudulent transfers and the bankruptcy receiver seeks to claw-them-back into the bankruptcy estate in order to include them within the total funds, and thus diminish the harm caused to innocent investors. Whether it is actual or constructive fraud, the use of state fraudulent transfer laws and fraudulent transfer provisions in the bankruptcy code allow for receivers to proceed on these clawbacks.[120] Clawbacks have proved controversial, as they in some instances involve the taking of funds given to charities or to individuals who may have already lost significant sums of money as a result of the Ponzi scheme.[121]

---

[118] SEC, Office of Investigations, Investigation of Failure of the SEC to Uncover Bernard Madoff's Ponzi Scheme, available at http://www.sec.gov/news/studies/2009/oig–509.pdf.

[119] See, e.g., Wiand v. Morgan, ___ F.Supp.2d ___ (M.D. Fl. 2013), available at 2013 WL 247072; United States v. Petters, 2011 WL 281031 (D. Minn. 2011).

[120] See Miriam A. Cherry & Jarrod Wong, Clawbacks: Prospective Contract Measures in an Era of Excessive Executive Compensation and Ponzi Schemes, 94 Minn. L. Rev. 368 (2009).

[121] See Spencer A. Winters, Note, The Law of Ponzi Payouts, 111 Mich. L. Rev. 119 (2012). Miriam A. Cherry & Jarrod Wong, Clawbacks: Prospective Contract Measures in an Era of Excessive Executive Compensation and Ponzi Schemes, 94 Minn. L. Rev. 368 (2009).

Chapter 14

ENVIRONMENTAL CRIMES

§ 14.1 INTRODUCTION

A. History

Despite the existence of the Rivers and Harbors Act of 1899 (see § 14.3), and a few other statutes that date back to the early 1900s,[1] the development of environmental crimes in the United States is relatively new. The Department of Justice's (DOJ) commentary on the historical development of environmental criminal laws admits that the Rivers and Harbors Act, a strict liability crime, was limited to dealing with the pollutants of an industrial age.[2] Another relatively early Act, the Lacey Act of 1900, served as the "cornerstone of federal criminal enforcement when plants or animals [were] illegally taken."[3] But for the most part, in the early 1900s the expansive array of environmental statutes that exist today, had not been enacted.

Eventually a host of different environmental criminal statutes were passed. These included the Water Pollution Control Act (later called the Clean Water Act) which was first passed in 1948 (see § 14.4), the Resource Conservation and Recovery Act (RCRA) passed in 1976 (see § 14.5) and specialized statutes to deal with specific environmental concerns. Today one finds that most environmental regulatory schemes have an enforcement provision included, and these provisions typically call for criminal penalties as one possible way to deter illegal conduct.

B. Environmental Statutes

There is no single comprehensive set of environmental crimes found in one place within the United States Code.[4] Rather, there are many environmental criminal statutes and they are scattered throughout the federal code.[5] As opposed to being located in title 18, the typical location of criminal statutes, most environmental criminal offenses accompany the environmental statutes that regulate the area of concern. For example, one finds pollution crimes, such as those in the Water Pollution

---

[1] The Migratory Bird Treaty Act (16 U.S.C. §§ 703–12; Ch. 128; July 13, 1918; 40 Stat. 755) was enacted in 1918, although there have been more recent amendments.

[2] DOJ, Historical Development of Environmental Law, Environment & National Resources Division, available at http://www.justice.gov/enrd/5472.htm.

[3] Id.

[4] See also Ellen S. Podgor & Jerold H. Israel, White Collar Crime in a Nutshell 4th Ed. (2009). The basic shell and parts of this chapter emanate from chapter 14 of the Nutshell.

[5] USAM § 5–11.101 provides a listing of a variety of pollution and wildlife crimes that have criminal prohibitions and are considered in the Environmental Crimes section of the USAM. They divide the statutes into the groupings of Pollution Crimes and Wildlife Crimes.

Control Act, located in title 33. The criminal sanction is included with the legislation that has as one of its goals to eliminate pollution.[6]

Because environmental issues span across many different areas, it is difficult to track all of the different crimes and their location. Just looking at pollution related activities, one area designed at the Department of Justice (DOJ), one finds criminal statutes associated with acts pertaining to water, air, and energy. For example, there are pollution statutes with criminal prohibitions included in the Federal Insecticide, Fungicide and Rodenticide Act (FIFRA) Act which is in title 7,[7] the Toxic Substances Control Act (TSCA) found in title 15,[8] the Act to Prevent Pollution from Ships (APPS) in title 33,[9] and the Noise Control Act in title 42.[10]

Wildlife crimes, a second category of environmental crimes designated by the DOJ, are typically located in title 16. For example, there is the Pacific Salmon Fishing Act,[11] the Lacey Act,[12] and the Migratory Bird Treaty Act.[13] But wildlife crimes are not found exclusively in title 16. For example, in title 18 there are criminal penalties for improper activities that take place on wildlife refuges.[14]

In some instances an environmental incident will result in charges under several different environmental crimes statutes. For example, an Alaskan oil spill resulted in charges against Exxon Corporation and the Exxon Shipping Company for alleged violations of the Clean Water Act, the Refuse Act, the Migratory Bird Treaty Act, the Ports and Waterways Act, and the Dangerous Cargo Act.[15]

C. Generic Statutes

Environmental crimes, like so many white collar crimes, are also prosecuted using statutes beyond the specific legislation that criminalizes the conduct. Prosecutors often use generic statutes in white collar cases because they are simplistic and allow the case to proceed without needing to present the complicated white collar crime to a jury.

In some instances a prosecutor will use these general criminal statutes as the sole basis for the case against a defendant. In other instances, these "short-cut" offenses get added as an additional count in the indictment. Thus, one finds prosecutions for conspiracy, pursuant to 18 U.S.C. § 371, when there are two or more offenders who agree to commit a specific offense and an overt act is performed in furtherance of the conspiracy.[16] Environmental crime prosecutions have also added charges of mail or

---

[6] 33 U.S.C. § 1319(c); see also § 14.4.

[7] 7 U.S.C. §§ 136 et seq. There are criminal penalties in 7 U.S.C. § 136*l*(b).

[8] 15 U.S.C. §§ 2601 et seq. There are criminal penalties in 15 U.S.C. § 2615(b).

[9] 33 U.S.C. §§ 1901 et seq. There are criminal penalties in 33 U.S.C. § 1908(a).

[10] 42 U.S.C. §§ 4901 et seq. There are criminal penalties in 42 U.S.C. § 4910(a).

[11] 16 U.S.C. §§ 3631 et seq. There are criminal penalties in 16 U.S.C. § 3631(c).

[12] 16 U.S.C. §§ 3371 et seq. There are criminal penalties in 16 U.S.C. § 3373(d).

[13] 16 U.S.C. §§ 703 et seq. There are criminal penalties in 16 U.S.C. § 707.

[14] 18 U.S.C. § 41(Hunting, Fishing, Trapping; Disturbance or Injury on Wildlife Refuges).

[15] See Jerold H. Israel, Ellen S. Podgor, Paul D. Borman, & Peter J. Henning, White Collar Crime: Law and Practice 3d Ed. 206 (2009) (citing Philip Shabecoff, Federal Statutes Cited in Indictment of Exxon, N.Y. Times, Mar. 1, 1990, A14).

[16] See, e.g., United States v. Fillers, 2012 WL 715256 (E.D. Tenn. 2012) (charging conspiracy to defraud the United States and violate the Clean Air Act); United States v. Templeton, 378 F.3d 845 (8th Cir. 2004)

wire fraud when there is a scheme to defraud and a mailing in furtherance of that scheme. (18 U.S.C. §§ 1341, 1343).[17] There may also be charges for obstruction of justice,[18] false statements,[19] or other criminal offenses. For example, a false reporting of a material fact to a government agency can result in a prosecution under the false statements statute, (18 U.S.C. § 1001), and can avoid needing to present a lengthy trial regarding an oil spill.

Some environmental statutes explicitly provide for conduct such as false statements.[20] For example, the Clean Water Act has a statute criminalizing materially false statements to the Environmental Protection Agency (EPA). The essential elements here mirror much of what is needed for a false statements charge under § 1001. In *United States v. Little Rock Sewer Committee*,[21] a district court for the Eastern District of Arkansas stated that the essential elements of proving a false statement under 33 U.S.C. § 1319(c)(2) are:

> First, that the defendant made a materially false statement in a report required to be filed with the [EPA] and also made a materially false statement in other records required to be maintained under its permit and under the Federal Water Pollution Control Amendments of 1972, for the months designated in the particular counts of the information.

Second, that the defendant knowingly made the materially false statement.[22]

D. Prosecuting Environmental Crimes

1. Generally

In 1982 both the EPA and the DOJ "established units that were dedicated to investigating and prosecuting environmental crimes."[23] In 1987 the Environmental Crimes Section (ECS) "became a fully independent Section within the Environmental and Natural Resource Division" (ENRD). ECS handles both pollution and wildlife cases. It also provides assistance to the individual U.S. Attorneys' Offices in the prosecution of environmental crimes.[24]

The federal government is not the sole enforcers of environmental protection. Many states have also incorporated environmental crimes statutes as part of its laws

---

(charging a conspiracy to violate the Clean Water Act); United States v. Johnson & Towers, Inc, 741 F.2d 662 (3d Cir. 1984) (charging conspiracy under § 371 in addition to RCRA and CWA charges); see also Chapter 3.

[17] United States v. Eidson, 108 F.3d 1336 (11th Cir. 1997); United States v. MacDonald & Watson Waste Oil Co., 933 F.2d 35 (1st Cir. 1991) (defendants faced RCRA, CERCLA, mail fraud, and false statement charges); See also Chapter 4.

[18] 18 U.S.C. §§ 1501 et seq.; See United States v. Atlantic States Cast Iron Pipe Co., 2007 WL 2282514 (D.N.J. 2007) (charging 18 U.S.C. §§ 1505 and 1519); United States v. Royal Caribbean Cruises Ltd., 24 F. Supp.2d 155 (D. Puerto Rico 1997) (charging violations of 18 U.S.C. §§ 371, 1001, and 1512(b) in addition to violations against the Federal Water Pollution Control Act); see also Chapter 6.

[19] See United States v. Atlantic States Cast Iron Pipe Co., 2007 WL 2282514 (D.N.J. 2007); see also Chapter 9.

[20] 33 U.S.C. § 1319(c)(2).

[21] 460 F.Supp. 6 (E.D. Ark. 1978).

[22] Id. at 9.

[23] See supra note 2.

[24] Id.

and U.S. Attorneys are instructed to "familiarize themselves with state environmental enforcement laws and state enforcement officials." In this regard they are advised to consider joint task forces and to recognize that state enforcement agencies may provide "valuable sources of information on suspected violations of federal environmental statutes."[25]

In the federal environmental area there can often be both a civil and criminal investigation as a person violating a federal environmental statute is often subject to civil proceedings, criminal prosecution, or dual civil and criminal actions. Thus, there may be an agency investigation (see Chapter 17) and a parallel proceeding (see Chapter 18), all possibly involving the same conduct. The government recognizes this overlap and advises the U.S. Attorney's Office handling an environmental matter, to contact the ECS to assist in coordinating these parallel matters.[26]

2. Parties Charged

The prosecution of environmental crimes is not limited to individuals. A significant number of prosecutions have concentrated on corporate entities. Principles of corporate criminal liability, as well as personal criminal liability in the corporate setting, play a factor in the environmental arena. (See Chapter 2). Whether one is a responsible corporate officer, and therefore criminally liable, may depend not only on the activities of the individual within the corporation (see § 2.7(B)), but also on whether a designated statute exists allowing for this form of criminal liability. For example, both the Clean Water[27] and Clean Air[28] Acts have incorporated the "responsible corporate officer" doctrine into the statutes. (See § 14.4(D)(1)). Statutes may also specify who can be a "person in charge" and therefore the individual who may be liable for reporting something like a hazardous leak.[29] (See § 14.5(C)).

In 2011 there were 201 guideline offenders in the primary offense category of environmental/wildlife. This is compared to an overall total of 86,201 offenders, of which 8,332 were in the fraud category.[30] Under organization sentencing guidelines, the second highest primary offense category of an organization receiving a fine or restitution was crimes related to environmental-water, which comprised 18.8% of the total number of organizational fines or restitution. If one adds to this number the environmental crimes involving air, hazardous/toxic pollutants, and wildlife, the percentage exceeds the fraud category, which is the highest designated percentage of primary offense categories from organizations receiving fines or restitution.[31] The mean fine or restitution imposed for environmental water crimes was $632, 310.

---

[25] USAM § 5–11.113.

[26] USAM § 5–11.112.

[27] 33 U.S.C. § 1319(c)(6).

[28] 42 U.S.C. § 7413(c)(6).

[29] See United States v. Carr, 880 F.2d 1550 (2d Cir. 1989) (discussing how is a person in charge under the CERCLA statute found in 42 U.S.C. § 9603(a)).

[30] United States Sentencing Commission, Sourcebook Fiscal Year 2011, available at www.ussc.gov, (hereinafter USSC, Statistics), Table 3. See also Chapter 24.

[31] Id. at Table 51.

3. *Pleas and Settlements*

Plea agreements are reached in 94.4% of the cases involving corporations charged with an environmental crime.[32] It is uncertain whether this number includes the deferred and non-prosecution agreements that entities commonly reach with the government. (See § 2.4(C)). The USAM does provide explicit guidance on environmental case settlements stating:

> Without the express approval of the Assistant Attorney General, Environment and Natural Resources Division, in any criminal case arising under the statutes identified in USAM 5–11.101 no plea agreement will be negotiated which compromises the right of the United States to any civil or administrative remedies under those statutes. Efforts by defendants to effect such results may arise in the context of so-called 'global settlement' offers.[33]

The "2010 Deepwater Horizon disaster that killed 11 people and caused the largest environmental disaster in the U.S. history" resulted in BP Exploration and Production Inc. (BP) entering into a record settlement of "$4 billion dollars in criminal fines and penalties." A 14–count information charged "BP with 11 counts of felony manslaughter, one count of felony obstruction of Congress, and violations of the Clean Water and Migratory Bird Treaty Acts." BP entered into a plea agreement and the government stated that "[t]he $4 billion in penalties and fines is the single largest criminal resolution in the history of the United States."[34]

E. International

Like so many of today's crimes, environmental crimes also may extend beyond the borders of the United States. Often the obligations are dependent on the nature of the crime, the countries involved, and the relationship of these countries with the United States. For example, international environmental crimes in the context of warfare[35] can pose different issues than international environmental crimes coming from business endeavors. Issues of state sovereignty, extraterritoriality, and procedural issues can frame the nature of the crime and the ability to proceed with a prosecution. (See § 1.7 (D)).

The Lacey Act, a statute that focuses on the protection of fish and wildlife, is an example of a statute that can present international issues. The statute criminalizes certain activities of importing and exporting fish, wildlife, or plants in "violation of a law or regulation of any State or in violation of any foreign law."[36]

In *United States v. McNab*,[37] several defendants were convicted of "conspiracy, smuggling, money laundering, and Lacey Act violations in connection with the

---

[32] Id. at Table 52.

[33] USAM § 5–11.115.

[34] DOJ Press Release, BP Exploration and Production Inc. Agrees to Plead Guilty to Felony Manslaughter, Environmental Crimes and Obstruction of Congress Surrounding Deepwater Horizon Incident, available at http://www.justice.gov/opa/pr/2012/November/12–ag–1369.html.

[35] See Marcos A. Orellana, Criminal Punishment for Environmental Damage: Individual and State Responsibility at a Crossroad, 17 Geo. Int'l Envtl. L. Rev. 673 (2005).

[36] 16 U.S.C. § 3372(a)(2)(A).

[37] 331 F.3d 1228 (11th Cir. 2003).

importation, sale, and purchase of Caribbean spiny lobsters from Honduras." The convictions were based on the importing of these lobsters being in violation of Honduran law. On appeal, the defendants raised the issue of whether Honduran regulations constituted "any foreign law" for the purposes of the Lacey Act. The Eleventh Circuit, in a 2–1, decision held that the Honduran regulations were covered by the Lacey Act, as the plain language of the statute and the legislative intent was to include these type of foreign regulations within the statute's term "any foreign law."

The *McNab* case had a unique twist, in that on appeal the Honduran government was claiming that the alleged conduct did not violate Honduran law. The majority of the court felt bound by what it believed to be the original position taken by the Honduran government. It was unwilling to overturn the conviction on what it believed to be a "shift" in the Honduran government's position. The dissent, however, wrote that the Honduran government was clearly expressing its position that this resolution was void now and at the time of the alleged conduct. The dissent found it "troubling" to affirm this conviction premised on Honduran law since the "defendants could not be tried and convicted for violation of Resolution 030–95 in Honduras."

§ 14.2 *MENS REA*

A common defense in white collar cases pertains to whether the accused had the designated *mens rea* to commit the crime. Intent can be particularly difficult with environmental statutes as there is no consistent *mens rea* used in the different pieces of environmental legislation. Courts have also struggled with the level of intent needed by the accused, who in some cases may be claiming that he or she was unaware of the illegality and thus did not know that this conduct was criminal, or unaware of the conduct occurring and therefore arguing that he or she should not be held responsible. The latter argument can also trigger a question of whether the accused was willfully blind.

Even when focused on one statute, courts have not always ruled consistently on the issue of intent. This can sometimes be a result of unclear statutory language. For example, the Sixth Circuit in *United States v. Wulff*,[38] found that a felony provision of the Migratory Bird Treaty Act (MBTA), that did not require proof of *scienter*, violated due process. The court found that because the felony was a "crime unknown to the common law" which carried a substantial penalty, the government was required to prove that the defendant acted with some degree of *scienter*. In contrast, the Third Circuit in *United States v. Engler*,[39] found that the absence of a *scienter* requirement in the strict liability provisions of a felony under the MBTA, did "not offend the requirements of due process."

Congress responded to these two cases by clarifying the required *mens rea* in the MBTA, making it a strict liability offense in 16 U.S.C. § 707(a), a misdemeanor provision, and requiring a *mens rea* of knowingly in 16 U.S.C. § 707(b), a felony provision.[40] As such, in *United States v. Gayhart*,[41] a district court in the Eastern

---

[38] 758 F.2d 1121 (6th Cir.1985).

[39] 806 F.2d 425 (3d Cir.1986).

[40] Emergency Wetlands Resources Act of 1986, Pub. L. 99–645, 100 Stat. 3590 (1986).

[41] 2011 WL 4715168 (E.D. Ky. 2011).

District of Kentucky refused to dismiss a case where the defendant claimed that the MBTA was unconstitutional because it lacked a *scienter*. The court stated that the plain language of the statute under which the defendant was charged, now let the defendant know that the charges were a misdemeanor which did not require a *mens rea*.[42]

In *United States v. Pitrone*,[43] one of the defendant's arguments was that the MBTA required the government to prove that the defendant acted with willfulness. This argument was premised on the Supreme Court's decision in *Ratzlaf v. United States*,[44] a structuring case, which held that "knowledge of the unlawfulness of one's conduct"[45] was needed for this structuring crime that required willfulness. The MBTA, however, which originates in response to a treaty between the United States and Canada,[46] does not include the word willfulness. The court in *Pitrone* stated that the defendant's "argument overlooks (or, at least, fails to acknowledge) that the element of willful intent and the element of scienter are birds of a very different feather: the cases which the appellant includes in this string citation stand for the proposition that knowledge of the unlawfulness of one's conduct is required when the statutorily prohibited behavior includes an element of *willful* intent."[47] Finding no element of willfulness in the MBTA, the court rejected Pitrone's argument.

Most environmental crimes, however, do require proof of the defendant acting knowingly. Courts usually permit knowledge to be inferred from the surrounding circumstances. Thus, in *United States v. International Minerals & Chemical Corp.*,[48] the Supreme Court held that "where [...] dangerous or deleterious devices or products or obnoxious waste materials are involved, the probability of regulation is so great that anyone who is aware that he is in possession of them or dealing with them must be presumed to be aware of the regulation."

Knowledge also can be found when there is a deliberate avoidance to learn all the facts. Courts may give a willful blindness instruction in these circumstances. In *United States v. Fillers*,[49] an Eastern District of Tennessee court recognized the willful blindness standard provided by the Supreme Court's decision in *Global–Tech Appliances, Inc. v. SEB*.[50] (See § 1.8(C)(2)). Although the *Fillers* court acknowledged that there was sufficient evidence in this case which included violations of the Clean Air Act, it noted that the government when using willful blindness needed to prove

---

[42] Courts have also not ruled consistently on the activities covered by the MBTA. See United States v. CITGO Petroleum Corp. 893 F.Supp.2d 841 (S.D. Tex. 2012) (finding that the death of migratory birds in open oil tanks could form the basis for a violation of the MBTA); but see United States v. Brigham Oil & Gas L.P., 840 F. Supp.2d 1202 (D.N.D. 2012) (holding that "oil development and production activities are not the sort of physical conduct engaged in by hunters and poachers, and such activities do not fall under the prohibitions of the [MBTA]").

[43] 115 F.3d 1 (1st Cir. 1997).

[44] 510 U.S. 135 (1994).

[45] Pitrone, 115 F.3d at 6.

[46] Convention for the Protection of Migratory Birds in the United States and Canada, Aug. 16, 1916, 39 Stat. 1702.

[47] Pitrone, 115 F.3d at 6.

[48] 402 U.S. 558 (1971).

[49] 2012 WL 715256 (E.D. Tenn. 2012).

[50] 131 S.Ct. 2060 (2011).

that the "defendant subjectively believed there to be a high probability that a fact existed and took deliberate actions to avoid learning of that fact."[51]

Most courts interpreting the term knowledge in the context of environmental statutes have held that there is no requirement that a defendant know the specific law being violated. For example, in examining knowledge in the context of the Comprehensive Environmental Response, Compensation, and Liability Act (CERCLA), a Sixth Circuit Court held that "'knowledge' as used in such regulatory statutes means knowledge that one is doing the statutorily prescribed acts, not knowledge that the statutes or potential health hazards exist."[52]

§ 14.3 REFUSE ACT

A. Generally

The Rivers and Harbors Appropriations Act of 1899 (33 U.S.C. §§ 401 et seq.), commonly referred to as the Refuse Act, has been one tool for prosecutors to use in combatting environmental crimes.[53] The Act, a codification of prior statutes, includes § 13, now codified as 33 U.S.C. § 407,[54] which forbids "the deposit" of all kinds of "refuse matter" into navigable rivers "other than that flowing from streets and sewers and passing therefrom in a liquid state."[55]

Section 407 provides criminal penalties for the improper discharge into navigable or tributary waters of the United States. In *United States v. American Cyanamid Co.*,[56] the court held that it is not necessary for the government to prove that the refuse actually reached the navigable waters if it was likely that it would. The court stated:

> [S]ection 13 prohibits the discharge of refuse into 'any tributary of any navigable water from which the same shall float or be washed into such navigable water. . . . ' The phrase "shall float or be washed" allows for possibility or likelihood. The language "shall float" clearly anticipates a future occurrence. If Congress had intended to require a showing that refuse actually had floated into navigable water before section 13 had been violated, it would have said so explicitly by using the language 'shall have floated or washed.'[57]

The statute allows the Secretary of the Army to grant permits, which serve as exceptions from the statute's prohibitions.[58] A defendant is entitled to present evidence that it was affirmatively misled into not applying for a permit.[59]

---

[51] Fillers, 2012 WL 715256 at * 3.

[52] United States v. Buckley, 934 F.2d 84 (6th Cir. 1991).

[53] Several criminal statutes are found in 33 U.S.C. §§ 403 et seq. such as a misdemeanor statute providing a "Penalty for Wrongful Construction of Bridges, Piers, etc., Removal of Structures." See 33 U.S.C. § 406.

[54] See generally Andrew Franz, Crimes Against Water: The Rivers and Harbors Act of 1899, 23 Tul. Envtl. L.J. 255 (2010).

[55] See United States v. Dexter, 507 F.2d 1038 (7th Cir. 1974) (discussing the exception when it flows "from streets and sewers and passing therefrom in a liquid state").

[56] 480 F.2d 1132 (2d Cir. 1973).

[57] Id. at 1134–35.

[58] "The statute does not purport to provide for permits as of right." United States v. Granite State Packing Co., 470 F.2d 303 (1st Cir. 1972).

The government can charge each separate act of discharging or depositing refuse as a separate count. The number of acts chargeable "cannot be deduced from the mere size or length of time of a discharge without more, unless discontinuity of the flow or change in composition or other evidence indicates that certain actions necessarily were taken to further the discharging or depositing of refuse."[60]

B. Defining Statutory Terms

Refuse has been defined as "all foreign substances and pollutants apart from those 'flowing from streets and sewers and passing therefrom in a liquid state' into the watercourse." In *United States v. Standard Oil Co.*,[61] an oil company was prosecuted for violating the Rivers and Harbor Act. The question for resolution before the Supreme Court was "whether the statutory ban on depositing 'any refuse matter of any kind or description' in a navigable water covers the discharge of commercially valuable aviation gasoline." The Court noted that this case came to it "at a time in the Nation's history when there was greater concern than ever over pollution—one of the main threats to our free-flowing rivers and to our lakes as well." In holding that commercially valuable gasoline, discharged into a navigable river, could be within the definition of "refuse" under the Rivers and Harbors Act, the Court stated that "[o]il is oil and whether useable or not by industrial standards it has the same deleterious effect on waterways."[62] The Court noted that in looking at prior iterations of this Act showed that there was "no distinction between valuable and valueless substances."[63]

A three-justice dissent in *Standard Oil* emphasized that penal statutes should be strictly construed.[64] In the case of *United States v. Millis*,[65] the Ninth Circuit used the rule of lenity to distinguish the *Standard Oil* decision from a case arising from a disposal of waste regulation.[66] In *Mills*, the defendant "plac[ed] full, gallon-sized plastic bottles of water on trails in the Buenos Aires National Wildlife Refuge to help alleviate exposure deaths among undocumented immigrants crossing into the United States." Although the defendant admitted to the conduct, he argued that this conduct did not violate the regulation. The Ninth Circuit held that unlike *Standard Oil*, the regulation at issue here was narrower. The court found that the term "garbage" as used in the regulation was "sufficiently ambiguous" to warrant using the rule of lenity, and therefore reversed the judgment that had been entered against the defendant.[67]

C. Scienter

Most courts find the Rivers and Harbors Act to be a strict liability statute. In *United States v. White Fuel Corp.*,[68] the defendant corporation was convicted for

---

[59] United States v. Pennsylvania Indus. Chemical Corp., 411 U.S. 655 (1973).

[60] United States v. Allied Chemical Corp., 420 F.Supp. 122 (E.D.Va. 1976) (quoting United States v. Tobin Packing Co. Inc., 362 F.Supp. 1127, 1130 (N.D.N.Y. 1973).

[61] United States v. Standard Oil Co., 384 U.S. 224 (S.Ct.1966).

[62] Id. at 226.

[63] Id. at 228.

[64] Id. at 231.

[65] 621 F.3d 914 (9th Cir. 2010).

[66] 50 C.F.R. § 27.94(a).

[67] 621 F.3d at 918.

[68] 498 F.2d 619 (1st Cir. 1974).

violating the Rivers and Harbors Act. White Fuel, upon notification of "possible oil spoilage problems" in the Boston harbor, "immediately undertook to clean up the oil and to trace its source." The source of the problem was determined to be "seeping from an immense accumulation [ ] which had gathered under White Fuel's property." The court denied White Fuel's argument regarding a lack of intent, finding that "intent or *scienter* is irrelevant to guilt." The court stated that "[a]lthough there is no generalized 'due care' defense, a defendant may always, of course, show that someone other than himself was responsible for the discharge."[69] In this regard, the court stated:

> White Fuel might, for example, undertake to prove that oil had percolated through its soil from the supply of an adjacent landowner. If a plane crashed into one of its tanks causing a spill, White Fuel would not be liable. If thieves overpowered its watchmen and somehow caused a pipe to overflow, White Fuel would not be liable. Acts of God would be another legitimate defense. It might be a defense that the spill was caused by an independent contractor who was entirely outside the defendant's control.[70]

In *United States v. United States Steel Corp.*,[71] a district court in the Northern District of Indiana held that depositing refuse in navigable waters is *malum prohibitum*, and as a public welfare offense it was a strict liability statute. "The public is injured just as much by unintentional pollution as it is by deliberate pollution, and it would have been entirely reasonable for Congress to attack both."[72] The court held:

> The Refuse Act has been in existence for more than seventy years now; and as far as the Court can determine, no reported decision has ever imposed a scienter requirement. On the contrary, those courts presented with the question have uniformly held that no such requirement exists.[73]

But in *United States v. Commodore Club, Inc,*[74] a district court in Michigan held that the lack of intent words in the statute did not mean that no *scienter* was required. The court stated:

> Considering the relatively stringent criminal penalties imposed, the serious consequences of a criminal conviction, the vagaries of the scope of the Corps' jurisdiction under the Act and the fact that effective remedies can be achieved through injunctive action against offending parties, this Court believes that general intent to violate the Act must be established as a prerequisite to criminal conviction under § 403 and § 406 of the Rivers and Harbors Act.[75]

In *United States v. Interlake Steel Corp.*,[76] a district court in Illinois took a differing position, holding that the Rivers and Harbors Act did not require a *scienter*. But it did

---

[69] Id. at 624.

[70] Id.

[71] 328 F.Supp. 354 (N.D. Ind. 1970).

[72] Id. at 356.

[73] Id.

[74] 418 F.Supp. 311 (E.D. Mich. 1976).

[75] Id. at 320.

[76] 297 F.Supp. 912 (N.D. Ill. 1969).

state that if the case was premised on aiding and abetting, then a showing of knowledge would be necessary.[77]

§ 14.4 WATER POLLUTION CONTROL ACT (CLEAN WATER ACT)

A. Generally

The objective of the Federal Water Pollution Control Act, commonly referred to as the Clean Water Act, (33 U.S.C. §§ 1251 et seq.), "is to restore and maintain the chemical, physical, and biological integrity of the Nation's waters." It has been stated that "Congress was convinced that uncontrolled pollution of the nation's waterways is a threat to the health and welfare of the country, as well as a threat to its interstate commerce."[78] Passed in 1948, the Act prohibits the discharge of pollutants into navigable waters unless authorized. Significant amendments were made to the Act in 1972 and it was then that it acquired the name Clean Water Act (CWA). It was passed on an override by the legislature after President Nixon vetoed the bill. In 1987, the CWA was again amended, increasing the penalties for violations.[79]

The CWA requires one to have a permit for the discharge of pollutants from a "point source" into "navigable waters."[80] Court decisions have discussed the definition of these terms. (See § 14.4(B)). "The EPA's National Pollutant Discharge Elimination System (NPDES) permit program controls discharges."[81] The CWA also requires certain notifications to an appropriate governmental agency when there is "knowledge of oil or a hazardous substance" that has been improperly discharged.[82]

The CWA provides for the adoption of effluent limitations.[83] Defendants who fail to obtain a permit can be held criminally liable despite the fact that effluent standards were not promulgated against them. The absence of effluent limitations does not nullify the basic prohibition against the discharge of pollutants. It merely places the burden on those discharging pollutants to apply for and to obtain a permit.[84]

Under the CWA both the EPA Administrator and the Secretary of the Army has the administrative responsibility for establishing guidelines for permits. In *United States v. Mango*,[85] the Second Circuit held that the Secretary of the Army could delegate their authority to district engineers or their designees to issue discharge permits.

---

[77] Id. at 914–15.

[78] United States v. Ashland Oil & Trans. Co., 504 F.2d 1317, 1325 (6th Cir. 1974).

[79] P.L. 100–4 (1987).

[80] See generally Environmental Protection Agency (EPA), Summary of the Clean Water Act, available at http://www.epa.gov/lawsregs/laws/cwa.html.

[81] Id.

[82] 33 U.S.C. § 1321(b)(5). See also United States v. Kennecott Copper Corp., 523 F.2d 821 (9th Cir. 1975).

[83] 33 U.S.C. § 1311.

[84] United States v. Frezzo Brothers, Inc., 602 F.2d 1123 (3d Cir. 1979), rev. on other grounds 642 F.2d 59 (3d Cir. 1981).

[85] 199 F.3d 85 (2d Cir. 1999).

In obtaining a permit, companies need to be aware not only of federal standards, but also those applicable in the state where they are operating. In *United States v. Marathon Development Corp.*,[86] the company sought to present evidence that they had a nationwide permit. The court did not allow this defense as the nationwide permit was not applicable in Massachusetts, the site of the alleged violation. The court stated that "[t]he ability of states to enforce their own more stringent water quality standards by denying certification for a nationwide permit is consistent with the legislative purpose and history of the Clean Water Act."[87] The court held that this practice did not violate equal protection rights under the Constitution.

Criminal penalties exist for negligent violations of discharge limits, with increased penalties provided for knowing violations. Repeat offenses also carry increased penalties. When the actions place another individual in "imminent danger of death or serious bodily injury" there is a possible penalty of imprisonment of up to fifteen years and a fine. The fine may be increased when the knowing endangerment is by a corporation.[88]

In *United States v. Borowski*,[89] the First Circuit looked at whether the criminal sanction applied when the imminent danger was "not to people at the publicly-owned treatment works, municipal sewers or other downstream locations affected by the illegal discharge, but rather to employees handling the pollutants on the premises from which the illegal discharge originates." The court held that a knowing endangerment prosecution could not "be premised upon danger that occurs before the pollutant reaches a publicly-owned sewer or treatment works."[90]

The *Borowski* court provided three rationales for its decision. First it noted that "[t]he Clean Water Act is not a statute designed to provide protection to industrial employees who work with hazardous substances."[91] Second, it noted that Congress passed explicit legislation pertaining to "the general handling, treatment and storage of hazardous substances" in the Resource Conservation and Recovery Act (RCRA). (See § 14.5). Finally, the rule of lenity mandated that deference go to the defense when a statute is ambiguous.[92]

B. Defining Statutory Terms

1. Point Source

The term "point source" is defined in 33 U.S.C. § 1362(14) as meaning:

[A]ny discernible, confined and discrete conveyance, including but not limited to any pipe, ditch, channel, tunnel, conduit, well, discrete fissure, container, rolling stock, concentrated animal feeding operation, or vessel or other floating craft, from

---

[86] 867 F.2d 96 (1st Cir. 1989).

[87] Id. at 99.

[88] 33 U.S.C. § 1319(c).

[89] 977 F.2d 27 (1st Cir. 1992).

[90] Id. at 32.

[91] Id. at 30–31.

[92] Id. at 31–32.

which pollutants are or may be discharged. This term does not include agricultural stormwater discharges and return flows from irrigated agriculture.

Although the statute uses non-exclusive words in its description, the terminology and examples provided "evoke images of physical structures and instrumentalities that systematically act as a means of conveying pollutants from an industrial source to navigable waterways."[93] That said, it has been stated that Congress intended a broad definition of "point source."[94] In *United States v. West Indies Transport, Inc.*,[95] the Third Circuit confirmed that "barges" were "floating craft" for purposes of this statute.

In *United States v. Plaza Health Laboratories*,[96] however, the Second Circuit held that a person is not a "point source." The defendant allegedly deposited blood vials in a crevice by the Hudson River, which were later discovered by eighth graders on a field trip. The Second Circuit reversed the defendant's convictions for knowingly discharging pollutants into the Hudson River in violation of §§ 1311 and 1319(c)(2) of the CWA.[97]

The *Plaza Health Laboratories* court stated that "discharge from a point source" is an element of a "knowing" and "knowing endangerment" violation under the statute. Human beings, however, are not a "point source." The court stated:

> We find no suggestion either in the act itself or in the history of its passage that congress intended the CWA to impose criminal liability on an individual for the myriad, random acts of human waste disposal, for example, a passerby who flings a candy wrapper into the Hudson River, or a urinating swimmer. Discussions during the passage of the 1972 amendments indicate that congress had bigger fish to fry.[98]

2. *Pollutant*

The term pollutant is defined by statute as meaning, "dredged spoil, solid waste, incinerator residue, sewage, garbage, sewage sludge, munitions, chemical wastes, biological materials, radioactive materials, heat, wrecked or discarded equipment, rock, sand, cellar dirt and industrial, municipal, and agricultural waste discharged into water."[99] This definition statute explicitly excludes:

> (A) "sewage from vessels or a discharge incidental to the normal operation of a vessel of the Armed Forces" within the meaning of section 1322 of this title; or (B) water, gas, or other material which is injected into a well to facilitate production of oil or gas, or water derived in association with oil or gas production and disposed of in a well, if the well used either to facilitate production or for disposal purposes is approved by authority of the State in which the well is located, and if such State determines that such injection or disposal will not result in the degradation of ground or surface water resources.

---

[93] United States v. Plaza Health Laboratories, Inc., 3 F.3d 643 (2d Cir. 1993).

[94] See United States v. West Indies Transport, Inc. 127 F.3d 299 (3rd Cir. 1997).

[95] Id.

[96] 3 F.3d 643 (2d Cir. 1993).

[97] The government cross-appealed the dismissal of two counts of knowing endangerment. Id. at 643.

[98] Id. at 647.

[99] 33 U.S.C. § 1362(6).

Thus, this definition makes it clear that sewage from a vessel will not be included. It does not matter that the vessel's engines do not work or that it requires towing. Two cases, one from the Third Circuit and the other from the Eighth Circuit, present distinguishing facts for interpreting what constitutes "sewage from vessels" that serves to exclude its coverage under the CWA. In *United States v. Templeton*[100] the Eighth Circuit stated:

> In *West Indies,* [ ][101] the defendants were convicted for discharging sewage into a bay from a barge. The Third Circuit affirmed the convictions, ruling the barge, used to house workers, was not a vessel because it was moored permanently to the shore, could not have been used for transport because it was halfway submerged "with part of [its] hull resting on the bottom" of the bay, had water visible below deck, and "could not be moved from its mooring." [ ] In contrast, the Rand [a vessel owned by the parties in Templeton] was not permanently moored, was floating and had no part of its hull resting on the river bed, and could be moved easily.[102]

Since in *Templeton* it was held that the sewage was from a vessel, the conviction was reversed as it was excluded from criminal liability under the CWA.

3. *Navigable Waters*

The term "navigable waters" is defined in the statute as meaning "the waters of the United States, including the territorial seas."[103] In *United States v. Phillips*,[104] the defendant moved to dismiss the case arguing that the government was required to prove that "the waters are navigable-in-fact." The Ninth Circuit rejected this argument finding that, "[t]he Army Corps of Engineers has long interpreted 'navigable waters' in the CWA 'to include not only actually navigable waters but also tributaries of such waters, interstate waters and their tributaries, and nonnavigable intrastate waters whose use or misuse could affect interstate commerce.'"[105] The court noted that the term "'navigable waters' within the meaning of the CWA has encompassed tributaries for almost thirty years."[106] Whether the term "navigable waters" includes wetlands has been an issue raised in several cases.[107]

In the CWA case of *Rapanos v. United States*,[108] the Supreme Court examined the phrase "navigable waters in the context of a federal enforcement action and in a plurality opinion stated:

> '[T]the waters of the United States' includes only those relatively permanent, standing or continuously flowing bodies of water 'forming geographic features' that

---

[100] 378 F.3d 845 (8th Cir. 2004).

[101] United States v. West Indies Transport, Inc., 127 F.3d 299 (3d Cir. 1997).

[102] Id. at 851.

[103] 33 U.S.C. § 1362(7).

[104] 367 F.3d 846 (9th Cir. 2004).

[105] Phillips, 367 F.3d at 855; see also United States v. Hubenka, 438 F.3d 1026 (10th Cir. 2006).

[106] Phillips, 367 F.3d at 855; see also United States v. Moses, 496 F.3d 984 (9th Cir. 2007) (holding a creek as meeting the statute).

[107] See, e.g., United States v. Johnson, 437 F.3d 157, 159 opinion withdrawn, decision vacated, 467 F.3d 56 (1st Cir. 2006).

[108] 547 U.S. 715 (2006).

are described in ordinary parlance as 'streams[,] . . . oceans, rivers, [and] lakes.' . . . The phrase does not include channels through which water flows intermittently or ephemerally, or channels that periodically provide drainage for rainfall. The Corps' expansive interpretation of the 'the waters of the United States' is thus not 'based on a permissible construction of the statute.'

Because of a four-justice dissent, Justice Kennedy's concurring opinion becomes particularly important. He found that the CWA would extend to wetlands that "possess a 'significant nexus' to waters that are or were navigable in fact or that could reasonably be so made."[109] He said that "[w]hen the Corps seeks to regulate wetlands adjacent to navigable-in-fact waters, it may rely on adjacency to establish its jurisdiction." He opted, however, for a case-by-case basis in those instances when the Corps sought "to regulate wetlands based on adjacency to nonnavigable tributaries."[110] He stated that "[g]iven the potential overbreadth of the Corps' regulations, this showing is necessary to avoid unreasonable applications of the statute."[111]

Proof of the discharge reaching navigable waters can be through circumstantial evidence. Thus, a showing that the waste was pumped into a storm gate, witnesses saying they saw the raw sewage on the dates in question, and tests confirming this raw sewage, have been held to be ample evidence that the discharge reached navigable waters.[112]

C. Mens Rea

In *United States v. Hanousek*,[113] the defendant was charged and convicted under the CWA with negligently "discharging a harmful quantity of oil into a navigable water of the United States." The Ninth Circuit rejected defendant's arguments that "gross negligence" should be required to meet this particular Clean Water Act statute. The court stated that 33 U.S.C. § 1319(c)(1)(A) can be met with a showing of ordinary negligence.

Justices Thomas and O'Connor dissented on the Court's failure to accept certiorari in *Hanousek v. United States*.[114] They pointed out that in this case an "independent contractor retained before petitioner was hired, accidentally struck a petroleum pipeline near the railroad tracks." A pipeline ruptured causing a "spill between 1,000 and 5,000 gallons of oil into the [Skagway River]." These dissenting justices noted that the supervisor, "was off duty and at home when the accident occurred," and that he was the one indicted and convicted. Thomas and O'Connor argued for the Court to accept certiorari as the seriousness of the penalties involved here should be a stumbling block to holding the CWA as a public welfare statute.[115]

---

[109] Id. at 759.

[110] Id.

[111] Id.

[112] United States v. Strandquist, 993 F.2d 395 (4th Cir. 1993).

[113] 176 F.3d 1116 (9th Cir. 1999)

[114] 528 U.S. 1102 (2000).

[115] Id.

In *United States v. Weitzenhoff*,[116] the Ninth Circuit held that "[t]he criminal provisions of the CWA are clearly designed to protect the public at large from the potentially dire consequences of water pollution, . . . and as such fall within the category of public welfare legislation. The court in *Weitzenhoff* found that the government did not need to prove that the defendants "knew that their acts violated the permit or the CWA."[117]

But they do need to have knowingly discharged the sewage into the water. This distinction was highlighted in *United States v. Sinskey*,[118] where the Eight Circuit stated:

> We therefore believe that the underlying conduct of which Sinskey must have had knowledge is the conduct that is prohibited by the permit, for example, that Morrell's discharges of ammonia nitrates were higher than one part per million in the summer of 1992. Given this interpretation of the statute, the government was not required to prove that Sinskey knew that his acts violated either the CWA or the NPDES permit, but merely that he was aware of the conduct that resulted in the permit's violation.

Defendants have argued insufficient evidence that he or she knew of the discharges. Courts respond noting that circumstantial evidence can be used to infer this intent.[119]

It has also been held that a defendant does not have to know that it is "waters of the United States." This is a jurisdictional element that does not necessitate proof of knowledge, merely proof of the jurisdictional element existing. Thus, in *United States v. D.J. Cooper*,[120] the Fourth Circuit held that "the creek's status as a 'water of the United States' is simply a jurisdictional fact, the objective truth of which the government must establish but the defendant's knowledge of which it need not prove."[121]

D. Parties Liable

1. *Responsible Corporate Officer*

Both individuals and corporations have been charged with criminal violations under the CWA. The statute provides an added basis for this liability with respect to individuals in that it provides that responsible corporate officers are statutorily included as "persons" that are subject to criminal penalties under this Act.[122]

In interpreting the responsible corporate officer[123] provisions in the Clean Water Act, the court in *United States v. Iverson*[124] stated that "a person is a 'responsible

---

[116] 35 F.3d 1275 (9th Cir. 1993).

[117] Id. at 1286; see also United States v. Wilson, 133 F.3d 251 (4th Cir. 1997).

[118] 119 F.3d 712 (8th Cir. 1997).

[119] United States v. Agosto–Vega, 617 F.3d 541 (1st Cir. 2010).

[120] 482 F.3d 658 (4th Cir. 2007)

[121] Id. at 668.

[122] 33 U.S.C. § 1319(c)(6).

[123] See also § 2.7(B).

[124] 162 F.3d 1015 (9th Cir. 1998)

corporate officer' if the person has authority to exercise control over the corporation's activity that is causing the discharges." The Ninth Circuit noted that "[t]here is no requirement that the officer in fact exercise such authority or that the corporation expressly vest a duty in the officer to oversee the activity."[125] In *Iverson*:

> The district court instructed the jury that it could find defendant liable under the CWA as a "responsible corporate officer" if it found, beyond a reasonable doubt:
>
> 1.   That the defendant had knowledge of the fact that pollutants were being discharged to the sewer system by employees of CH2O, Inc.;
>
> 2.   That the defendant had the authority and capacity to prevent the discharge of pollutants to the sewer system; and
>
> 3.   That the defendant failed to prevent the on-going discharge of pollutants to the sewer system.[126]

Looking at both this instruction and another given by the trial court, the Ninth Circuit held that the, "'responsible corporate officer' instruction relieved the government *only* of having to prove that defendant *personally* discharged or caused the discharge of a pollutant. The government still had to prove that the discharges violated the law and that defendant knew that the discharges were pollutants."[127]

The inclusion of a provision regarding a responsible corporate officer does not serve to limit the prosecution of individuals who violate the act. In *United States v. Brittain*,[128] the Tenth Circuit referenced the *Dotterweich* and *Park* cases (see § 2.7(B)), two cases that explored the responsible corporate officer doctrine, in holding that "[w]e interpret the addition of 'responsible corporate officers' as an expansion of liability under the Act rather than, as defendant would have it, an implicit limitation." Individuals are clearly subject to liability as responsible corporate officers.

2.   *Person in Charge*

Questions can also arise as who is a "person in charge," for reporting discharges under the statute.[129] The statute provides that it must be reported by "any person in charge." Corporations are explicitly included as a "person" under the Act so courts have allowed them to be considered "any person in charge."[130] In *Apex Oil Co. v. United States*,[131] a Missouri company raised the issue of whether a corporation could be a "person in charge" within the meaning of the statute and whether there was sufficient evidence to support the conviction. The court found the statute provided for corporate

---

[125] Id. at 1025.

[126] Id. at 1022.

[127] Id. at 1026. See also United States v. House of Raeford Farms, Inc., 2012 WL 3283396 (M.D. N.C. 2012).

[128] 931 F.2d 1413 (10th Cir.1991).

[129] 33 U.S.C. § 1321(b)(5).

[130] 33 U.S.C. § 1321(a)(7)

[131] 530 F.2d 1291 (8th Cir. 1976).

liability. Addressing the sufficiency of the evidence, the court found that "the knowledge of the employees is the knowledge of the corporation."[132]

§ 14.5 RESOURCE CONSERVATION AND RECOVERY ACT (RCRA)

A. Generally

The Resource Conservation and Recovery Act (RCRA), enacted in 1976,[133] is considered to be a "'cradle-to-grave' regulatory scheme for toxic materials, providing 'nationwide protection against the dangers of improper hazardous waste disposal.'"[134] Congress enacted RCRA, found in 42 U.S.C. §§ 6901 et seq., to provide a national system for the safe management of hazardous waste and to promote a system that conserved valuable material and energy resources. The law was signed by President Ford, who called hazardous waste disposal "one of the highest priority environmental problems confronting the Nation."[135] The legislation begins with findings in four areas: (a) solid waste; (b) environment and health; (c) materials; and (4) energy.[136] A 1980 addition makes findings concerning used oil recycling and that "it is in the national interest to recycle used oil in a manner which does not constitute a threat to public health and the environment and which conserves energy and materials."[137] This statute authorizes the EPA, through its adoption of regulations, to place controls on solid and hazardous wastes. The Act is divisible into two sections, one pertaining to non-hazardous solid waste management, and another regarding hazardous waste management. Despite the complexity of the regulations that come from the RCRA statutes, they have not been held to be vague.[138]

Federal criminal enforcement is found in 42 U.S.C. § 6928 with criminal penalties in subsections (d) and (e). Although originally the statute authorized misdemeanor penalties for the disposal of waste without a permit, later amendments increased the penalties for noncompliance to felonies. The amendments also expanded coverage to include not only the disposal of waste, but also the improper treatment and storage of waste.

The EPA can allow a state to enact its own hazardous waste management program and once authorized by EPA it supplants the federal system.[139] In *United States v. Elias*,[140] the Ninth Circuit court concluded that "the federal government retains both its criminal and civil enforcement powers," even when there is a state counterpart, if the state regulatory scheme is not authorized by the federal government. When authorized, however, "the Federal Government is barred from

---

[132] Id. at 1295.

[133] P.L. 94–580, see also EPA, New Law to Control Hazardous Wastes, End Open Dumping, Promote Conservation of Resources, available at http://www.epa.gov/aboutepa/history/topics/rcra/05.html.

[134] United States v. Johnson & Towers, Inc., 741 F.2d 662 (3d Cir. 1984).

[135] EPA, New Law to Control Hazardous Wastes, End Open Dumping, Promote Conservation of Resources, available at http://www.epa.gov/aboutepa/history/topics/rcra/05.html.

[136] 42 U.S.C. § 6901.

[137] 42 U.S.C. § 6901A (emanating from Pub. L. 96–463, Oct. 15, 1980).

[138] United States v. White, 766 F.Supp. 873 (E.D. Wash.1991).

[139] 42 U.S.C. § 6926.

[140] 269 F.3d 1003, 1012 (9th Cir. 2001).

enforcing state requirements that have a greater scope of coverage than the federal regulations," but "if a state chooses to makes it regulations 'more stringent' than the federal regulations, the Federal Government's enforcement authority is not restricted."[141]

B. Mens Rea

1. *Knowingly*

Section 6928(d) provides for penalties when one "knowingly," commits certain acts specified by the statute. Although knowledge of the statute is not required, the government does need to prove that the defendant knew the general hazardous character of the waste material being handled.[142] Courts differ on whether knowledge of a permit is necessary for a conviction. But many courts agree that

> 'knowingly' means no more than that the defendant knows factually what he is doing-storing, what is being stored, and that what is being stored factually has the potential for harm to others or the environment, and that he has no permit-and it is not required that he know that there is a regulation which says what he is storing is hazardous under the RCRA.[143]

In *United States v. Hayes Int'l Corp.*,[144] the Eleventh Circuit stated that "it is completely fair and reasonable to charge those who choose to operate in such areas with knowledge of the regulatory provisions." In *Hayes*, the company operated an airplane refurbishing plant that generated waste products, specifically it had to drain fuel tanks from airplanes and eliminate some paint and solvents used in the business. The defendant argued that they did not act "knowingly" because they "misunderstood the regulations," they didn't "'know' that Performance Advantage did not have a permit," and "they believed that Performance Advantage was recycling the waste." The court rejected the three defenses presented. The court stated that to convict "the jurors must find that the defendant knew what the waste was (here, a mixture of paint and solvent), and that the defendant knew the disposal site had no permit." "[I]gnorance of the regulatory status is no excuse," and there was sufficient evidence "for the jury to find the [defendants] knowing transported hazardous waste.[145]

Courts have not ruled consistently on whether knowledge of a permit is required. One court found that although the term "knowingly" is omitted in subsection (2)(A) of the statute, its inclusion in subsection (2)(B) implies that there must be knowledge of the requirement of a permit. In *United States v. Johnson & Towers, Inc.*,[146] the Third Circuit held that, "[i]t is unlikely that Congress could have intended to subject to criminal prosecution those persons who acted when no permit had been obtained irrespective of their knowledge (under subsection (A)), but not those persons who acted

---

[141] United States v. Southern Union Co., 643 F. Supp.2d 201 (D. R.I. 2009).

[142] See United States v. Laughlin, 10 F.3d 961 (2d Cir. 1993) (holding that "the government need prove only that a defendant was aware of his act of disposing of a substance he knew was hazardous.").

[143] United States v. Baytank (Houston), Inc., 934 F.2d 599 (5th Cir. 1991).

[144] 786 F.2d 1499 (11th Cir. 1986).

[145] Id. at 1504.

[146] 741 F.2d 662 (3d Cir. 1984).

in violation of the terms of a permit unless that action was knowing (subsection (B))." The court in *Johnson & Towers, Inc.* concluded that either the word "knowingly" was inadvertently omitted from subsection (A), or that "knowingly" as introducing subsection (2) applies to (B).

Other courts, however, have rejected the view taken in *Johnson & Towers* finding that there is no requirement of knowledge of a lack of a permit for conviction under subsection (A) of this statute. As noted by the Ninth Circuit in *United States v. Hoflin*,[147] "[t]he statute makes a clear distinction between non-permit holders and permit holders, requiring in subsection (B) that the latter knowingly violate a material condition or requirement of the permit. To read the word 'knowingly' at the beginning of section (2) into subsection (A) would be to eviscerate this distinction." Also rejecting the view taken by the court in *Johnson & Towers, Inc.*, the Sixth Circuit in *United States v. Dean*[148] noted that "[t]he 'knowingly' which begins section 6928(d)(2) cannot be read as extending to the subsections without rendering nugatory the word 'knowing' contained in subsections 6928(d)(2)(B) and (C)."

2. *Knowing Endangerment*

Subsection (e) of § 6928 increases the penalty for a RCRA violation when it involves a knowing endangerment. The statute states:

> Any person who knowingly transports, treats, stores, disposes of, or exports any hazardous waste identified or listed under this subchapter or used oil not identified or listed as a hazardous waste under this subchapter in violation of paragraph (1), (2), (3), (4), (5), (6), or (7) of subsection (d) of this section who knows at that time that he thereby places another person in imminent danger of death or serious bodily injury, shall, upon conviction, be subject to a fine of not more than $250,000 or imprisonment for not more than fifteen years, or both. A defendant that is an organization shall, upon conviction of violating this subsection, be subject to a fine of not more than $1,000,000.

The Tenth Circuit, in *United States v. Protex Industries, Inc.*[149] found the "serious bodily injury" provision of this statute not to be unconstitutionally vague when it was applied to a corporate defendant whose employees were alleged to have suffered "psychoorganic syndrome," which may cause impairment to mental facilities. "Serious bodily injury" was also found in *United States v. Hansen*,[150] a case with evidence that employees "suffered serious skin and respiratory conditions from the wastewater on the cellroom floors." Expert testimony in the case provided sufficient evidence including exposure to mercury. Consent to the risks by the person being endangered is an affirmative defense.[151]

---

[147] 880 F.2d 1033 (9th Cir.1989).

[148] 969 F.2d 187 (6th Cir. 1992).

[149] 874 F.2d 740 (10th Cir. 1989).

[150] 262 F.3d 1217 (11th Cir. 2001).

[151] Id. at 1245–46.

C. Parties Liable

The Act's criminal provisions have been found applicable to "any person" that stores, treats, or disposes of hazardous wastes. "Any person" is defined in 42 U.S.C. § 6903(15) as meaning "an individual, trust, firm, joint stock company, corporation (including a government corporation), partnership, association, State, municipality, commission, political subdivision of a State, or an interstate body and shall include each department, agency, and instrumentality of the United States."

Courts have not limited the provisions of the RCRA only to those who are owners or operators of facilities. In *United States v. Johnson & Towers, Inc.*,[152] the Third Circuit stated:

> It would undercut the purposes of the legislation to limit the class of potential defendants to owners and operators when others also bear responsibility for handling regulated materials. The phrase "without having obtained a permit under *section 6925*" (emphasis added) merely references the section under which the permit is required and exempts from prosecution under section 6928(d)(2)(A) anyone who has obtained a permit; we conclude that it has no other limiting effect. Therefore we reject the district court's construction limiting the substantive criminal provision by confining "any person" in section 6928(d)(2)(A) to owners and operators of facilities that store, treat or dispose of hazardous waste, as an unduly narrow view of both the statutory language and the congressional intent.

Federal employees working at a federal facility are considered to be a "person" subject to the mandates of the statute. In *United States v. Dee*,[153] the defendants argued that they should be immune from prosecution "because neither the United States nor an agency of the United States is defined as a person, defendants maintain they cannot be 'persons' in the sense contemplated by § 6928(d)." The Fourth Circuit rejected this argument and found that sovereign immunity did not immunize federal employees from prosecution for criminal acts that violated RCRA.

Some courts have rejected the use of the responsible corporate officer doctrine to establish knowledge under RCRA. The responsible officer doctrine it was feared would allow for a conviction without the necessary intent required by this statute.[154] In *United States v. MacDonald & Watson Waste Oil Co.*,[155] the defendants were charged with RCRA and CERCLA violations. The President and owner of MacDonald & Watson contested the knowledge instruction given to the jury and the court agreed, vacating this conviction. The First Circuit held that proof of a defendant being a responsible corporate officer would be insufficient to show the required knowledge for conviction under RCRA. The court stated:

> [K]nowledge may be inferred from circumstantial evidence, including position and responsibility of defendants such as corporate officers, as well as information provided to those defendants on prior occasions. Further, willful blindness to the

---

[152] 741 F.2d 662 (3d Cir. 1984).

[153] 912 F.2d 741 (4th Cir. 1990).

[154] United States v. White, 766 F.Supp. 873 (E.D. Wash. 1991).

[155] 933 F.2d 35 (1st Cir. 1991).

facts constituting the offense may be sufficient to establish knowledge. However, the district court erred by instructing the jury that proof that a defendant was a responsible corporate officer, as described, would suffice to conclusively establish the element of knowledge expressly required under § 3008(d)(1). Simply because a responsible corporate officer believed that on a prior occasion illegal transportation occurred, he did not necessarily possess knowledge of the violation charged. In a crime having knowledge as an express element, a mere showing of official responsibility under *Dotterweich* and *Park* is not an adequate substitute for direct or circumstantial proof of knowledge.[156]

Courts have also not allowed RCRA to be used "to apply to persons who do no more than receive hazardous waste."[157]

---

[156] Id. at 55.

[157] United States v. Fiorillo, 186 F.3d 1136, 1149 (9th Cir. 1999).

Chapter 15

COMPUTER CRIMES

§ 15.1 INTRODUCTION

A. Overview

With the growth of computers and the Information Age, there has likewise been an increase of computer related crimes. One regularly hears of computer viruses,[1] worms,[2] and hacking[3] that cause problems for computer users throughout the world. Prior to 1984, there was no specific computer criminal statute and prosecutors used then existing statutes, such as wire fraud (18 U.S.C. § 1343), to bring these prosecutions.[4] Computer crimes continue to be brought under a variety of criminal statutes, but there now exists a specific statute focused on this conduct, namely, 18 U.S.C. § 1030. (See § 15.2).

Computer crimes are different from other forms of criminality in that computers can be the "object," the "target," or tangential to the crime.[5] When used as an object, the computer is used to commit the crime. Thus, when the perpetrator uses his or her computer to commit a crime such as committing a fraud or manipulating data on a computer, the computer is the object or tool being used to commit the crime. When the computer is the "target" of the offense, the perpetrator is trying to destroy or damage a computer, network, or the information contained therein. Thus, when a hacker breaks into a military computer, the destination computer is the "target" of the crime. Finally, the computer may be tangential to the crime in that it may be used as storage of illegal information. For example, a drug trafficker or money launderer may keep his or her books or records on the computer, using the computer as part of the criminal activity.

Computer crimes present unique issues in that there are multiple variants of criminal activities and the role of the computer may be different depending on the form of the criminality.[6] For example, computers are often connected with crimes of pornography, piracy, extortion plots, identity fraud, and cyber-stalking. Each of these crimes can present different social harms. Whether or not one should consider the crime to be a white collar offense may depend upon the activity involved.

---

[1] Ellen S. Podgor, Cybercrime: National, Transnational, or International?, 50 The Wayne State L. Rev. 97, 98 (2004) (discussing viruses that have had an effect on computer users throughout the world, such as the "I Love You," "Melissa," "Code Red," and "SoBig" viruses).

[2] United States v. Morris, 928 F.2d 504 (2d Cir. 1991).

[3] See Brian Womack & Michael Riley, Facebook Said to Work With FBI on Malware Attack Probe, Bloomberg News, Feb. 15, 2015, available at http://www.bloomberg.com/news/2013–02–15/facebook-targeted-by-sophisticated-attack-using-malware.html.

[4] See Glenn D. Baker, Trespassers Will Be Prosecuted: Computer Crime in the 1990s, 12 Computer L. J. 61(1993).

[5] Scott Charney & Kent Alexander, Computer Crime, 45 Emory L.J. 931, 934 (1996) (discussing how computers can be "target of the offense," "tool of the offense," or "incidental to the offense").

[6] See Ellen S. Podgor, International Computer Fraud: A Paradigm for Limiting National Jurisdiction, 35 U.C. Davis L. Rev. 267 (2002).

There are also widely differing perpetrators. One finds juveniles hacking into government agencies' computers for amusement. Other computer crime offenders may be terrorists using the computer for terrorist activity. Some may be sophisticated business people who use a computer to commit acts of fraud, such as insider trading. Thus, a computer crime may or may not involve a white collar offender.

Approaches to computer crimes have also differed in that some argue that the computer is merely a method or instrument used to commit the crime, and that the focus should be on the criminal activity. Thus, cyber-stalking, cyber-pornography, cyber-fraud, and other cyber-crimes should focus less on the "cyber" aspect of the crime and more on the underlying activity.[7] In contrast, others argue that computerization makes crimes unique and that cyber activities should not be treated the same as the underlying criminal activity might be treated.[8] For example, the location of the perpetrator and accompanying jurisdiction issues, as well as the type of evidence that will be presented should the case proceed to trial, often differ from cases that do not cyber criminal activity.

The Department of Justice's (DOJ) Computer Crime and Intellectual Property Section (CCIPS), a section of the Criminal Division of the DOJ, "is responsible for implementing the Department's national strategies in combating computer and intellectual property crimes worldwide."[9] The CCIPS has a 213–page manual titled, *Prosecuting Computer Crimes*, that provides prosecutors with explicit guidance for computer related cases.[10] This training guide for federal prosecutors is merely an internal document that explicitly states that "[n]othing in it is intended to create any substantive or procedural rights, privileges, or benefits enforceable in any administrative, civil, or criminal matter by any prospective or actual witnesses or parties."[11] The Manual provides guidance on the computer fraud statute, 18 U.S.C. § 1030, and also "other network crimes" such as identity theft,[12] and access device fraud.[13] There are several appendices to the Manual including ones for "Best Practices for Working With Companies" and "Best Practices for Victim Response and Reporting."

State prosecutors also proceed against individuals who commit computer crimes, with many states now having laws explicitly protecting computer information and prohibiting computer misuse.[14] In some instances, states create crimes to combat theft of information contained on a computer or misuse of a state computer.

---

[7] See Michael Edmund O'Neill, Old Crimes in New Bottles: Sanctioning Cybercrime, 9 Geo. Mason L. Rev. 237 (2000).

[8] See Neal Kumar Katyal, Criminal Law in Cyberspace, 149 U. Pa. L. Rev. 1003 (2001).

[9] Department of Justice, About the Computer Crime & Intellectual Property Section, available at http://www.justice.gov/criminal/cybercrime/.

[10] Prosecuting Computer Crimes, Published by Office of Legal Education Executive Office for United States Attorneys, available at http://www.justice.gov/criminal/cybercrime/docs/ccmanual.pdf.

[11] Citing United States v. Caceres, 440 U.S. 741 (1979); This language is typical for all DOJ guideline manuals. See also § 1.5(A).

[12] 18 U.S.C. § 1028. There is also aggravated identity theft. 18 U.S.C. § 1028(A).

[13] 18 U.S.C. § 1029.

[14] Chris Kim, Barrie Newberger, & Brian Shack, Computer Crimes, 49 Am. Crim. L. Rev. 443, 481n.376 (2012); See also Eli Lederman, Criminal Liability for Breach of Confidential Commercial Information, 38 Emory L.J. 921, 934–36, 940 (1989) (discussing different state approaches to computer crimes).

B. Domestic

1. History of Specific Computer Fraud Legislation

In 1984, Congress passed the Counterfeit Access Device and Computer Fraud and Abuse Act, an Act that exclusively focused on computer offenses. Located in § 1030 of title 18, this statute concentrated on improper computer access as opposed to other improprieties, such as computer use. (See § 15.2). 18 U.S.C. § 1030 was amended in 1986 (the Computer Fraud and Abuse Act of 1986) to cure some of the deficiencies apparent in the initial legislation.[15]

In 1996, as part of the National Information Infrastructure Protection Plan (NIPPA), 18 U.S.C. § 1030 was again amended.[16] With these amendments there are now seven different types of criminal conduct covered, which include both felonies and misdemeanors. Repeat offenders face increased penalties under this statute. (See § 15.2)

The statute is no longer restricted to crimes related to computer access. In the "Uniting and Strengthening America by providing Appropriate Tools Required to Intercept and Obstruct Terrorism Act of 2001(USA PATRIOT Act)," Congress made additional changes to the computer fraud act. For example, computer fraud is now listed as a specified unlawful activity of money laundering (see Chapter 12) and the statute now has extraterritorial application.[17]

In 2012 there were approximately one hundred criminal prosecutions with a lead charge of 18 U.S.C. § 1030. This number has been relatively constant in the past ten years, but it is four times greater than the number of prosecutions under § 1030 in the year 1992 and in the immediately surrounding time frame. Of the prosecutions in 2012, the FBI classified approximately 80% as white collar offenses, with the second highest category classified as computer crimes related to public corruption.[18]

2. Use of Generic Statutes for Computer Fraud Prosecutions

Despite the passage of a specific computer fraud statute in 1984, many computer related prosecutions still are premised on generic statutes such as wire fraud (18 U.S.C. § 1343)(see § 4.9), the National Stolen Property Act (18 U.S.C. § 2314) (NSPA), and the Economic Espionage Act (18 U.S.C. § 1832) (EEA). (See § 15.4).

Prosecutors also have creatively charged computer crimes by using charges of copyright infringement (17 U.S.C. § 506),[19] conspiracy (18 U.S.C. § 371),[20] illegal

---

[15] Other statutory amendments are discussed in Prosecuting Computer Crimes, Published by Office of Legal Education Executive Office for United States Attorneys, see supra note 9.

[16] Pub. L. 104–294 (1996).

[17] See United States v. Ivanov, 175 F. Supp.2d 367 (D. Conn. 2001) (finding the Computer Fraud and Abuse Act's 1996 amendment demonstrated that Congress intended for § 1030 to apply extraterritorially).

[18] TracReports, Prosecutions for 2012—Lead Charge: 18 U.S.C. 1030—Fraud and Related Activity—Computers, available at http://tracfed.syr.edu.

[19] See United States v. Slater, 348 F.3d 666 (7th Cir. 2003).

[20] See Chapter 3.

interception devices and equipment (18 U.S.C. § 2512),[21] and unlawful access to stored communications (18 U.S.C. § 2701).[22] In some instances, statutes may specifically provide for prosecution when the activity involves online or computer conduct. For example, 18 U.S.C. § 1465 criminalizes the production and transportation of obscene matters for sale or distribution, 18 U.S.C. § 1084 criminalizes the transmission of wagering information which often occurs via a computer, and 18 U.S.C. § 1037 pertains to fraud and related activity in connection with electronic mail.[23]

Criminal activity can also come from improper procedural conduct during a criminal investigation. For example, the Wiretap Act, referred to as Title III, provides criminal penalties for both law enforcement officials and others for the prohibited interception, disclosure, or use of wire, oral, or electronic communications. The Wiretap Act, located at 18 U.S.C. § 2511 was amended in 1986 to include "electronic communications."[24]

C. International

Computer crimes are a global problem as the interconnected nature of the global network allows criminal acts in one country to pass easily into another country. As stated by former Attorney General Janet Reno, "a hacker needs no passport and passes no checkpoints."[25]

One basic problem in the international realm is that there is no consistent definition of what is a computer crime. Several international initiatives provide some guidance, such as the U.N. Manual on the Prevention and Control of Computer–Related Crime.[26] There are also international initiatives that foster cooperation in computer-related investigations.[27]

The United States has been at the international forefront in fighting computer crimes, and it participated in the drafting of and is a signatory to the Council of Europe's Convention on Cybercrime, sometimes referred to as the Budapest Convention.[28] The U.S. signed the Convention in 2001, ratified it in 2006, and accepted its entry into force in 2007. The U.S. does have reservations and declarations to this

---

[21] See, e.g., United States v. Biro, 143 F.3d 1421 (11th Cir. 1998); United States v. Splawn, 982 F.2d 414 (10th Cir. 1992).

[22] See United States v. Vevea, 446 F. App'x 63 (9th Cir. 2011).

[23] This latter statute emanates from the Controlling the Assault of Non–Solicited Pornography and Marketing Act of 2003 (CAN–SPAM Act of 2003). P.L. 108–187.

[24] See supra note 9 at 59–87; See also § 21.2.

[25] Keynote Address by U.S. Attorney General Janet Reno on High-tech and Computer Crime, Delivered at the Meeting of the P–8 Senior Experts' Group on Transnational Organized Crime, Jan. 21, 1997, at 5. This same metaphor was also used in a report of one of the Presidents working groups. *See The Electronic Frontier: The Challenge of Unlawful Conduct Involving the Use of the Internet*, A REPORT OF THE PRESIDENT'S WORKING GROUP ON UNLAWFUL CONDUCT ON THE INTERNET 21 (Mar. 2000), available at http://ncsi-net.ncsi. iisc.ernet.in/cyberspace/law/responsibility/cybercrime/www.usdoj.gov/criminal/cybercrime/unlawful.pdf.

[26] See U.N. Manual on the Prevention and Control of Computer–Related Crime, available at http://www.uncjin.org/Documents/EighthCongress.html.

[27] See Action Against Cybercrime, available at http://www.coe.int/t/DGHL/cooperation/economic crime/cybercrime/default_en.asp; see also International Telecommunications Union (ITU) Report, Understanding Cybercrime: Phenomena, Challenges and Legal Response (2012), available at http://www. itu.int/ITU–D/cyb/cybersecurity/docs/Cybercrime%20legislationÉV6.pdf.

[28] Council of Europe Convention on Cybercrime, available at http://conventions.coe.int/Treaty/ Commun/QueVoulezVous.asp?NT=185 & CL=ENG.

Convention. For example, in January 2007, the U.S. declared that with regard to the offense set forth in Article 2 of the Convention (illegal access), U.S. laws had "an additional requirement of intent to obtain computer data."[29] It also reserved certain rights that might be inconsistent with the U.S. Constitution. For example, crimes related to the distribution of material that might or might not be considered obscene under applicable U.S. standards," might raise First Amendment issues.[30] The U.S. did not want to sign an international agreement that would be barred by U.S. constitutional law and thus included reservations in these areas.

The main objective of the Cybercrime Convention "is to pursue a common criminal policy aimed at the protection of society against cybercrime, especially by adopting appropriate legislation and fostering internal co-operation." The Convention covers areas such as definitions of computer terminology, measures that should be taken at a national level, various forms of computer related offenses, and corporate liability. It also covers procedural law regarding computer crimes, including evidence issues related to prosecuting computer crimes. The Convention provides general principles on international cooperation, which includes considerations such as mutual assistance and extradition.

The Cybercrime Convention does not provide an international court for the prosecution of computer crimes. Nor does it provide a definitive and binding answer as to who should have priority jurisdiction in the prosecution of these offenses. In Article 22 of the Cybercrime Convention it states that "[w]hen more than one Party claims jurisdiction over an alleged offence established in accordance with this Convention, the Parties involved shall, where appropriate, consult with a view to determining the most appropriate jurisdiction for prosecution."

§ 15.2   *18 U.S.C. § 1030*

A. Generally

Section 1030(a) contains seven variants of conduct that are subject to prosecution.[31] As opposed to a consistent *mens rea* and jurisdictional predicate, each of the seven subsections specifies its own requisite jurisdiction and *mens rea*. Likewise, the penalties for some of these varying forms of improper computer conduct differ. In addition to imprisonment, the statute also provides for imposition of a fine and forfeiture of property.[32]

Often conduct relating to accessing a computer may qualify under more than one provision of the statute. Additionally, § 1030(b) permits criminal culpability for conspiracies and attempts for the conduct provided for in part (a) of the statute.

---

[29] Declarations and Reservations to the Council of Europe's Cybercrime Convention, available at http://www.ictparliament.org/node/2128.

[30] Id.

[31] See generally Lee Goldman, Interpreting the Computer Fraud and Abuse Act, 13 U. Pitt. J. Tech. L & Pol'y 1 (2012); see also Ellen S. Podgor & Jerold H. Israel, White Collar Crime in a Nutshell 4th Ed. 225 (2009).

[32] 18 U.S.C. § 1030(i) & (j).

The term "protected computer" is used in various parts of § 1030 and is defined in subsection (e)(2) to mean a computer—

(A) exclusively for the use of a financial institution or the United States Government, or, in the case of a computer not exclusively for such use, used by or for a financial institution or the United States Government and the conduct constituting the offense affects that use by or for the financial institution or the Government; or

(B) which is used in or affecting interstate or foreign commerce or communication, including a computer located outside the United States that is used in a manner that affects interstate or foreign commerce or communication of the United States;

Courts have found that using the Internet meets the interstate commerce aspect of the statute.[33]

Despite the statute being located within the criminal code, § 1030(g) provides civil litigants with a cause of action in certain circumstances. It states that, "[a]ny person who suffers damage or loss by reason of a violation of this section may maintain a civil action against the violator to obtain compensatory damages and injunctive relief or other equitable relief." There, however, are limitations with respect to these civil actions, including a rejection of using the statute to bring actions for negligent design of manufacture. The civil statute also has a compressed statute of limitations that differs from what is used in criminal cases.

The United States Secret Service, in addition to other agencies having authority, can investigate crimes under this statute. The Federal Bureau of Investigation (FBI) has the "primary authority to investigate offenses under subsection (a)(1) for any cases involving espionage, foreign counterintelligence, information protected against unauthorized disclosure for reasons of national defense or foreign relations, or Restricted Data", except for certain offenses related to the duties of the United States Secret Service.[34]

B. § 1030(a)(1)

Subsection (a)(1) criminalizes the conduct of one who "having knowingly accessed a computer without authorization or exceeding authorized access," thereby obtained confidential national security information "with reason to believe that such information so obtained could be used to the injury of the United States, or to the advantage of any foreign nation willfully" attempts to or communicates it to someone "not entitled to receive it, or willfully" "fails to deliver it to the officer or employee of the United States entitled to receive it." This electronic espionage provision permits imprisonment of up to ten years. Additionally, a repeat offender is subjected to imprisonment of up to twenty years. (See Chapter 24).

---

[33] See United States v. Drew, 259 F.R.D. 449, 457–58 (C.D. Cal. 2009). The court, however, dismissed this case. See § 15.2(C).

[34] 18 U.S.C. § 1030(d).

C. *§ 1030(a)(2)*

Subsection (a)(2) pertains to one who "intentionally accesses a computer, without authorization or exceeds authorized access, and thereby obtains" financial information of a financial institution or a card issuer, "information from a department or agency of the United States," or "information from a protected computer." This conduct is punishable by imprisonment of up to one year. The statute provides for an increase to five years if the offense is committed for private or commercial gain, "in furtherance of a criminal or tortious act in violation of the Constitution" or federal or state laws, or "the value of the information exceeds five thousand dollars." The statute also provides for an increase to ten years for the repeat offender. (See Chapter 24).

In the case of *United States v. Drew*,[35] a district court in the Central District of California ruled against the government on a defendant's motion to dismiss, finding that a conviction under § 1030(a)(2) could not stand when it was based solely on the defendant's failure to abide by a website's terms of service.

Drew was indicted for her alleged use of an account on the social networking website "myspace.com," where she was alleged to have posed as a teenage boy feigning a romantic interest in a thirteen year old girl.[36] One of the alleged messages she sent to the thirteen year old was discovered after the girl committed suicide. Prosecutors charged Lori Drew, claiming that the messages were contrary to the "myspace.com" agreement. The court found that "if any conscious breach of a website's terms of service is held to be sufficient by itself to constitute intentionally accessing a computer without authorization or in excess of authorization, the results will be that § 1030(a)(2)(C) becomes a law 'that affords too much discretion to the police and too little notice to citizens who wish to use the Internet.'"[37]

D. *§ 1030(a)(3)*

Subsection (a)(3) pertains to browsing in a government computer. It applies to those who access "intentionally, without authorization to access a nonpublic computer" of a federal department or agency, said computer being exclusively for government use or the conduct "affects" the government's use of the computer. The penalty for commission of this offense is one year, but may be increased to ten years for the repeat offender. (See Chapter 24).

E. *§ 1030(a)(4)*

Subsection (a)(4) concentrates on theft from protected computers. It applies to one who "knowingly and with intent to defraud, accesses a protected computer without authorization or exceeds authorized access," furthering the fraud and obtaining anything of value. An exception is provided when the object of the fraud is the computer and the value of such use does not exceed five thousand dollars in any one year period. The statute, in subsection (e), explicitly defines a "protected computer." (See § 15.2(A)) This offense is punishable with up to five years of imprisonment, with an additional five years possible for the repeat offender. (See Chapter 24).

---

[35] 259 F.R.D. 449, 457–58 (C.D. Cal. 2009).

[36] Ellen S. Podgor, Cybercrime: Discretionary Jurisdiction, 47 U. Louisville L. Rev. 727, 731–34 (2009).

[37] Drew, 259 F.R.D. at 467 (citing City of Chicago v. Morales, 527 U.S. 41, 64 (1999).

F. § 1030(a)(5)

Subsection (a)(5) is divided into three parts. A central focus of this subsection is that it pertains to conduct where the defendant is causing damage to a computer. Each of the three subparts contain a different *mens rea* for the "causing of damage," moving from intentionally (a)(5)(A), to recklessly (a)(5)(B), to then no *mens rea* (a)(5)(C).

Subsection (a)(5)(A) pertains to one who "knowingly causes a transmission of a program, information, code or command, and as a result of such conduct *intentionally* causes damage without authorization to a protected computer." Subsection (a)(5)(B) criminalizes the intentional access of "a protected computer without authorization, and as a result of such conduct *recklessly* causes damage." Finally, subsection (a)(5)(C) criminalizes conduct of those who "intentionally" access a "protected computer without authorization, and as a result of such conduct, cause[ ] damage and loss."

Subsection (a)(5)(A) carries a penalty of up to ten years imprisonment in certain specified circumstances with an additional ten years possible for the repeat offender. It can also be increased to a twenty-year sentence when the "offender knowingly and recklessly causes serious bodily injury" resulting from the conduct in (a)(5)(A), and may be increased to a life sentence "if the offender knowingly and recklessly causes or attempts to cause death from conduct in violation of (a)(5)(A)." Subsection (a)(5)(B) carries a penalty of up to five years imprisonment under certain specified circumstances with an additional ten years possible for the repeat offender. Finally subsection (a)(5)(C) provides for an increase to ten years in the case of a repeat offender. All other offenses not explicitly provided for in other provisions under (a)(5) are subject to imprisonment of not more than one year and a fine. (See Chapter 24).

G. § 1030(a)(6)

Subsection (a)(6) of this statute criminalizes interstate trafficking of passwords. The government must show that the defendant "knowingly and with intent to defraud traffics" "in any password or similar information." The trafficking must affect "interstate commerce or foreign commerce," or the computer must be used by or for the federal government. The statute refers to 18 U.S.C. § 1029 for a definition of "traffics," which defines the term as meaning "transfer, or otherwise dispose of, to another, or obtain control of with intent to transfer or dispose of." Section 1030(a)(6) carries imprisonment of not more than one year with the possibility of ten years imposed for the repeat offender. (See Chapter 24).

H. § 1030(a)(7)

Subsection (a)(7) was originally added as part of the National Information Infrastructure Protection Act of 1996 (Economic Espionage Act of 1996, Title II). It criminalizes the conduct of one who:

with intent to extort from any person any money or other thing of value, transmits in interstate or foreign commerce any communication containing any—

(A) threat to cause damage to a protected computer;

(B) threat to obtain information from a protected computer with authorization or in excess of authorization or to impair the confidentiality of information obtained from a protected computer without authorization or by exceeding authorized access; or

(C) demand or request for money or other thing of value in relation to damage to a protected computer, where such damage was caused to facilitate the extortion.

Section 1030(a)(7) carries imprisonment of up to five years, with repeat offenders facing the possibility of ten years. (See Chapter 24).

§ 15.3 PROSECUTING COMPUTER CRIMES

A. "Accessing Without Authorization" and "Exceeding Authorized Access"

1. *Generally*

Several provisions in § 1030 require the accused to have "accessed without authorization" or "exceeded authorized access." Typically outsiders engage in unlawful access and insiders are individuals who exceed their access. Courts, however, have differed on the distinction between "accessing without authorization" and "exceeding authorized access." Courts have also differed in how to interpret the specific terms used here.[38]

In *LVRC Holdings, LLC v. Brekka*,[39] the Ninth Circuit looked at the distinction between accessing without authorization and exceeding authorized access. The court stated:

> an individual who is authorized to use a computer for certain purposes but goes beyond those limitations is considered by the CFAA as someone who has 'exceed[ed] authorized access.' On the other hand, a person who uses a computer 'without authorization' has no rights, limited or otherwise, to access the computer in question. In other words, for purposes of the CFAA, when an employer authorizes an employee to use a company computer subject to certain limitations, the employee remains authorized to use the computer even if the employee violates those limitations. It is the employer's decision to allow or to terminate an employee's authorization to access a computer that determines whether the employee is with or 'without authorization.'[40]

Some courts, however, have focused on whether there was a breach of loyalty by the employee, which might be proven merely by a change in the mental state of the individual from a loyal employee to a disloyal one.[41] This approach, seen in some civil cases, was criticized in the *Brekka* decision.

---

[38] Goldman, supra note 31. (discussing the agency, contract and plain meaning approaches that have been used by different courts).

[39] 581 F.3d 1127 (9th Cir. 2009).

[40] Id. at 1133.

[41] See International Airport Centers, L.L.C. v. Citrin, 440 F.3d 418 (7th Cir. 2006).

2. Accessing Without Authorization

There is no explicit definition in the statute of what constitutes "accessing a computer without authorization." In *United States v. Phillips*,[42] a student with access to his university system, agreed to the "acceptable use" computer policy at his school. He then proceeded to engage in "port scanning" a technique which allowed him to infiltrate hundreds of computers at the school and elsewhere and steal passwords and encrypted data. His indictment included a violation of § 1030 for "intentionally accessing a protected computer without authorization." The Fifth Circuit noted that "typically [courts] analyzed the scope of a user's authorization to access a protected computer on the basis of the expected norms of intended use or the nature of the relationship established between the computer owner and the user."[43] The court, using an "intended-use" approach, found that Phillips's "brute—force attack program was not an intended use of the [school] network within the understanding of any reasonable computer user and constitutes a method of obtaining unauthorized access to computerized data that he was not permitted to view or use." The Fifth Circuit rejected his argument that he had merely exceeded his authorized access saying that he was authorized to use his "email account and other activities defined" by the school's acceptable computer use policy, but he was never authorized to access the TXClass, a secure server for the college's faculty and staff, that he did access.

3. Exceeding Authorized Access

Subsection (e)(6) defines the term "exceeds authorized access" to mean "to access a computer with authorization and to use such access to obtain or alter information in the computer that the accesser is not entitled so to obtain or alter." But even with this definition, courts have struggled with deciding whether specific conduct meets this definition.

In *United States v. Nosal*,[44] an en banc Ninth Circuit considered a clash of position between the defendant and the government on how to interpret § 1030(a)(4) with regard to the definition of "exceeds authorized access." The defendant, a former employee of an executive search firm, was accused of "convinc[ing] some of his former colleagues who were still working" at this firm "to help him start a competing business." He allegedly had "employees use[ ] their log-in credentials to download source lists, names and contact information from a confidential database on the company's computer, and then transfer[ ] that information" to him. The government responded with a twenty count indictment for aiding and abetting the company employees in violating § 1030(a)(4).

The Ninth Circuit noted how the statute's language could be read two ways. The court rejected the government's approach to how this statute should be read. The court stated:

> First, as Nosal suggests and the district court held, it could refer to someone who's authorized to access only certain data or files but accesses unauthorized data or files—what is colloquially known as "hacking." For example, assume an employee

---

[42] 477 F.3d 215 (5th Cir. 2007).

[43] Id. at 219.

[44] 676 F.3d 854 (9th Cir. 2012).

is permitted to access only product information on the company's computer but accesses customer data: He would "exceed [ ] authorized access" if he looks at the customer lists. Second, as the government proposes, the language could refer to someone who has unrestricted physical access to a computer, but is limited in the use to which he can put the information. For example, an employee may be authorized to access customer lists in order to do his job but not to send them to a competitor.[45]

In rejecting this second position advocated by the government, the court stated that taking this approach "would transform the CFAA [Computer Fraud and Abuse Act] from an anti-hacking statute into an expansive misappropriation statute." The court chose to use a definition that would offer a consistent definition throughout the entire statute (§ 1030(a)) and not just a definition limited to § 1030(a)(4), as requested by the government. The court stated "Congress obviously meant 'exceeds authorized access' to have the same meaning throughout section 1030."[46] In ruling against the government in this case, the court stated that "[b]asing criminal liability on violations of private computer use policies can transform whole categories of otherwise innocuous behavior into federal crimes simply because a computer is involved."[47]

Although the government argued that prosecutorial discretion would protect against the prosecution of "minor violations," the court was unwilling to accept these government assurances. The court stated that "we shouldn't have to live at the mercy of our local prosecutor."[48]

The en banc court in *Nosal* recognized that other circuits had taken different positions, including some cases that permit the statute to be used to prosecute "corporate computer use restrictions or violations of a duty of loyalty."[49] A two-judge dissenting opinion focused on cases from the Fifth[50] and Eleventh[51] Circuits that held that "employees who knowingly violate clear company computer restrictions agreement 'exceed authorized access' under the CFAA."

Although the *Nosal* case involved a criminal action, a court recognized this decision in the civil context in a case that was brought under § 1030(a)(2)(C) and (a)(4). The court in *Oracle America, Inc. v. Service Key, LLC*,[52] dismissed a civil action under these provisions on the basis of the decision in *Nosal*.

B. Mens Rea

Several cases have explored whether a *mens rea* is required for the damages or loss resulting from computer activity that forms the basis for the criminal charge. For

---

[45] Id. at 856–57.

[46] Id. at 859.

[47] Id. at 860.

[48] Id. at 862.

[49] Id. at 862–63 (citing United States v. Rodriguez, 628 F.3d 1258 (11th Cir.2010); United States v. John, 597 F.3d 263 (5th Cir.2010); Int'l Airport Ctrs., LLC v. Citrin, 440 F.3d 418 (7th Cir.2006)).

[50] United States v. John, 597 F.3d 263 (5th Cir.2010)

[51] United States v. Rodriguez, 628 F.3d 1258 (11th Cir.2010).

[52] 2012 WL 6019580 (N.D. Cal. 2012).

example, in *United States v. Sablan*[53] the Ninth Circuit held that it was constitutional to omit a *mens rea* for the damages element of the offense in that the defendant "must have had a wrongful intent in accessing the computer in order to be convicted under the statute." Later amendments to the statute provide a *mens rea* for the damages clause in the amended (a)(5)(A) ("intentionally causes damage") and (B) ("recklessly causes damage"). There is no *mens rea*, however, for the damages clause in (a)(5)(C).

Whether a *mens rea* was required for the damages or loss was also an issue in the first appellate case interpreting the computer crime statute, which used a prior version of § 1030. In *United States v. Morris*,[54] defendant Robert Tappan Morris, a graduate student at Cornell University, was alleged to have transmitted a "worm into INTERNET, which is a group of national networks that connect university, governmental, and military computers around the country." He miscalculated the worm's potential capabilities and it had a damaging effect. The Second Circuit was faced with the issue of whether the intent requirement in then subsection (a)(5) applied only to accessing information or also to preventing the authorized use of the computer's information and thereby causing loss.

The court in *Morris* found that "[d]espite some isolated language in the legislative history that arguably suggests a *scienter* component for the 'damages' phrase of section 1030(a)(5)(A), the wording, structure, and purpose of the subsection, examined in comparison with its predecessor provision persuade us that the 'intentionally' standard applies only to the 'accesses' phrase of section 1030(a)(5)(A), and not to its 'damages' phrase."[55] The court also rejected defendant's argument that the statute only covered those who lacked access to any federal interest computer. The court noted that "Congress did not intend an individual's authorized access to one federal interest computer to protect him from prosecution, no matter what other federal interest computers he accesses."[56]

In interpreting § 1030(a)(2)(C), the Tenth Circuit, in *United States v. Willis*,[57] chose not to mirror the *mens rea* that was used in § 1030(a)(4). Unlike § 1030(a)(4), which requires an intent to defraud, under § 1030(a)(2) the government does not need to prove "that the defendant had the intent to defraud the court held that in obtaining the information, or that the information was used to any particular ends."[58]

C. Anything of Value

Subsection 1030(a)(4) contains the language "anything of value." Merely browsing in a government computer has been found not to be sufficient for a charge under § 1030(a)(4). In *United States v. Czubinski*[59] the First Circuit reversed convictions for wire fraud and computer fraud that were premised upon the defendant's alleged browsing in an Internal Revenue Service computer system. Czubinski "was employed as a Contact Representative in the Boston Office of the Taxpayer Services Division of

---

[53] 92 F.3d 865 (9th Cir.1996).

[54] 928 F.2d 504 (2d Cir.1991).

[55] Id. at 509.

[56] Id. at 511.

[57] 476 F.3d 1121 (10th Cir. 2007).

[58] Id. at 1125.

[59] 106 F.3d 1069 (1st Cir. 1997).

the Internal Revenue Service (IRS)." The court found that Czubinski had "exceeded authorized access to a Federal interest computer." He had not, however, received "anything of value," a requirement for the government to prove under the statute. The court stated,

> [t]he value of information is relative to one's needs and objectives; here, the government had to show that the information was valuable to Czubinski in light of a fraudulent scheme. The government failed, however, to prove that Czubinski intended anything more than to satisfy idle curiosity.

The First Circuit court held that viewing information "about friends, acquaintances, and political rivals" in an IRS computer does not merit a computer fraud conviction where there is no evidence showing "that he printed out, recorded, or used the information he browsed."

In a civil case, *In re America Online, Inc.*,[60] a Southern District of Florida District Court judge denied a motion to dismiss that was premised on there being no value to support a claim under § 1030(a)(4). The court contrasted the position taken in *Czubinski* by saying that "customers have been found to be a thing of value" and that the allegations here were for "more than mere satisfaction of [ ] curiosity."

§ 15.4 ECONOMIC ESPIONAGE ACT

A. Generally

Congress passed the Economic Espionage Act (EEA) of 1996 to criminalize economic espionage (18 U.S.C. § 1831) and theft of trade secrets (18 U.S.C. § 1832).[61] In *United States v. Hsu*,[62] the Third Circuit outlined the history of this Act noting that it "became law in October 1996 against a backdrop of increasing threats to corporate security and a rising tide of international and domestic economic espionage." At this time there was no "comprehensive federal remedy targeting the theft of trade secrets, compelling prosecutors to shoehorn economic espionage crimes into statutes directed at other offenses."[63]

Section 1831 criminalizes foreign economic espionage. As stated by the court in *Hsu*, § 1831 "punishes those who knowingly misappropriate, or attempt or conspire to misappropriate, trade secrets with the intent or knowledge that their offense will benefit a foreign government, foreign instrumentality, or foreign agent." The court noted that the legislative history indicates that it "is designed to apply only when there is 'evidence of foreign government sponsored or coordinated intelligence activity.'"[64]

---

[60] 168 F. Supp.2d 1359, 1380 (S.D. Fla. 2001).

[61] Pub. L. 104–294, 110 Stat. 3488 (Oct. 11, 1996); see also Kent B. Alexander & Kristin L. Wood, The Economic Espionage Act: Setting the Stage for a New Commercial Code of Conduct, 15 Georgia St. U. L. Rev. 907 (1999).

[62] 155 F.3d 189 (3d Cir. 1998).

[63] Id. at 194–95.

[64] Id. at 195.

Section 1832 criminalizes the theft of trade secrets, including attempts and conspiracies to do these acts. The *Hsu* court notes three distinctions in this statute that are not included in § 1831:

Section 1832 also contains at least three additional limitations not found in § 1831. First, a defendant charged under § 1832 must intend to convert a trade secret "to the economic benefit of anyone other than the owner thereof," including the defendant himself. This "economic benefit" requirement differs from § 1831, which states merely that the offense "benefit," in any manner, a foreign government, instrumentality, or agent. Therefore, prosecutions under § 1832 uniquely require that the defendant intend to confer an economic benefit on the defendant or another person or entity. Second, § 1832 states that the defendant must intend or know that the offense will injure an owner of the trade secret, a restriction not found in § 1831.... Finally, unlike § 1831, § 1832 also requires that the trade secret be "related to or included in a product that is produced for or placed in interstate or foreign commerce."

Many of the terms used within the two statutes are defined in 18 U.S.C. § 1839. For example, the term "trade secret" is defined to mean:

all forms and types of financial, business, scientific, technical, economic, or engineering information, including patterns, plans, compilations, program devices, formulas, designs, prototypes, methods, techniques, processes, procedures, programs, or codes, whether tangible or intangible, and whether or how stored, compiled, or memorialized physically, electronically, graphically, photographically, or in writing if—

(A) the owner thereof has taken reasonable measures to keep such information secret; and

(B) the information derives independent economic value, actual or potential, from not being generally known to, and not being readily ascertainable through proper means by, the public;[65]

Prosecutions under § 1831 require approval from the Assistant Attorney General for the Criminal Division.[66] Prosecutors are instructed that "[t]he EEA is not intended to criminalize every theft of trade secrets for which civil remedies may exist under state law." Factors for consideration in whether to prosecute under §§ 1831 and 1832 include:

(a) the scope of the criminal activity, including evidence of involvement by a foreign government, foreign agent or foreign instrumentality; (b) the degree of economic injury to the trade secret owner; (c) the type of trade secret misappropriated; (d) the effectiveness of available civil remedies; and (e) the potential deterrent value of the prosecution. The availability of a civil remedy should not be the only factor considered in evaluating the merits of a referral

---

[65] 18 U.S.C. § 1839(3).

[66] USAM § 9–59.100. There is also a federal Manual titled, "Federal Prosecution of Violations of Intellectual Property Rights," that provides additional guidance for prosecutors.

because the victim of a trade secret theft almost always has recourse to a civil action.[67]

Actions under the EEA may involve extraterritorial conduct and this is permitted if "the offender is a natural person who is a citizen or permanent resident alien of the United States, or an organization organized under the laws of the United States or a State or political subdivision, thereof." Extraterritoriality is also permitted for territorial acts committed in the United States that are in furtherance of the offense.[68] In some instances the Attorney General may proceed with a civil action, or obtain injunctive relief, as opposed to proceeding with criminal charges.[69] Prosecutions under the EEA can entail forfeiture of property or proceeds from the activity.[70]

The increased focus on the seriousness of these offenses is noted by Congress' approval of the Foreign and Economic Espionage Penalty Enhancement Act of 2012, which became law on January 14, 2013.[71] This amendment increased the fine for a violation of § 1831 and called upon the United States Sentencing Commission to review the sentencing under the EEA. It states:

> review and, if appropriate, amend the Federal sentencing guidelines and policy statements applicable to persons convicted of offenses relating to the transmission or attempted transmission of a stolen trade secret outside of the United States or economic espionage, in order to reflect the intent of Congress that penalties for such offenses under the Federal sentencing guidelines and policy statements appropriately, reflect the seriousness of these offenses, account for the potential and actual harm caused by these offenses, and provide adequate deterrence against such offenses.[72]

Additionally, in February 2013, President Barak Obama announced the *Administration Strategy on Mitigating the Theft of U.S. Trade Secrets.*[73] Included here is that "DOJ will continue to make the investigation and prosecution of trade secret theft by foreign competitors and foreign governments a top priority."

B. "Used In or Intended for Use In"

In *United States v. Aleynikov,*[74] the government proceeded against the accused with crimes beyond the Computer Fraud and Abuse Act (CFAA). The defendant, a computer programmer for Goldman Sachs & Co. (Goldman), had worked on the development of "computer source code for the company's proprietary high-frequency trading system (HFT)." The confidentiality policies at Goldman required that he keep in "strict confidence all the firm's proprietary information," including the intellectual

---

[67] Id.

[68] 18 U.S.C. § 1837.

[69] 18 U.S.C. § 1836.

[70] 18 U.S.C. § 1834.

[71] P.L. 112–269, 126 Stat 2442 (Jan. 14, 2013).

[72] See also Chapter 24.

[73] White House, Office of Budget Management, Launch of the Administration's Strategy to Mitigate the Theft of U.S. Trade Secrets, available at http://www.whitehouse.gov/blog/2013/02/19/launch-administration-s-strategy-mitigate-theft-us-trade-secrets.

[74] 676 F.3d 71 (2d Cir. 2012).

property that he created. When the defendant left the firm, he was alleged to have uploaded the source code for Goldman's HFT to a foreign server. The three count indictment against Aleynikov included violations of the Economic Espionage Act (19 U.S.C. § 1832(a)), the National Stolen Property Act (18 U.S.C. § 2314), and the Computer Fraud and Abuse Act (18 U.S.C. § 1030). The court granted the defendant's motion to dismiss Count Three, a count premised on § 1030, as the accused was authorized to access the Goldman computer. The trial court held that the misappropriation of information did not present a violation of § 1030. The government did not appeal this dismissal.[75]

Aleynikov was convicted after a jury trial on the remaining two counts, but the Second Circuit reversed these convictions. With respect to the count premised on the NSPA, the court found insufficient evidence of a § 2314 violation, noting that this section does not define the terms "goods," "wares," or "merchandise." The question was "whether the source code that Aleynikov allegedly uploaded to a server in Germany, then downloaded to his computer devices in New Jersey, and later transferred to Illinois, constituted stolen "goods," "wares," or "merchandise." The court found that "[b]ased on the substantial weight of the case law, as well as the ordinary meaning of the words" it did not.[76] The court noted that cases under § 2314 have "always involved physical items" and that caselaw did not extend criminal liability to "purely intangible property."[77]

The Second Circuit in *Aleynikov* also rejected the EEA count. Section 1832(a) requires that "products be "'produced for' or 'placed in' interstate or foreign commerce." The court noted that "Goldman's HFT system was neither 'produced for' nor 'placed in' interstate or foreign commerce." The court held that "[b]ecause the HFT system was not designed to enter or pass in commerce, or to make something that does, Aleynikov's theft of source code relating to that system was not an offense under the EEA."[78] In reversing the convictions, the court stated, "[t]he conduct found by the jury is conduct that Aleynikov should have known was in breach of his confidentiality obligations to Goldman, and was dishonest in ways that would subject him to sanctions; but he could not have known that it would offend this criminal law or this particular sovereign."[79]

Judge Calabresi authored a concurring opinion in the *Aleynikov* case, where he stated that he found it difficult "to conclude that Congress, in this law, actually meant to exempt this kind of behavior." He "expressed the hope that Congress [would] return to the issue and state, in appropriate language, what [he] believe[d] they meant to make criminal in the EEA."[80]

The *Aleynikov* case did in fact end up serving as the impetus for congressional change, as Senator Leahy proposed a bill that would clarify the statute's language. He

---

[75] Id. at 75.

[76] Id. at 77–79 (citing United States v. Brown, 925 F.2d 1301 (10th Cir. 1991); United States v. Stafford, 136 F.3d 1109 (7th Cir. 1998)).

[77] The court referenced the Supreme Court decision in Dowling v. United States, 473 U.S. 207 (1985), noting that in that case "theft and subsequent interstate transmission of purely intangible property [was] beyond the scope of NSPA." Aleynikov, 676 F.3d at 78–79.

[78] The court also used the rule of lenity in resolving any ambiguity in the statute. Id. at 82.

[79] Id. at 82–83.

[80] Id. 82–83.

stated in a congressional hearing that the *Aleynikov* case "casts doubt on the reach of the statute." He offered "clarifying legislation" that he believed would "correct[] the court's narrow ruling to ensure that our federal criminal laws adequately address the theft of trade secrets related to a product or service used in interstate commerce."[81]

On December 19, 2012, President Obama signed the Theft of Trade Secrets Clarification Act of 2012. This amendment to § 1832(a) struck the language "or included in a product that is produced for or placed in" and inserted in its place, "a product or service used in or intended for use in."[82] As such, the crime allows for prosecution of individuals or entities who "attempt to steal, or conspire to steal a trade secret related to a product or service used in or intended for use in interstate or foreign commerce."[83]

C. Confidentiality of Trade Secrets

Prosecutions under § 1832 can present issues of how to prosecute the criminal conduct, yet maintain the confidentiality of the trade secret. Section 1835 provides that:

> In any prosecution or other proceeding under this chapter, the court shall enter such orders and take such other action as may be necessary and appropriate to preserve the confidentiality of trade secrets, consistent with the requirements of the Federal Rules of Criminal and Civil Procedure, the Federal Rules of Evidence, and all other applicable laws. An interlocutory appeal by the United States shall lie from a decision or order of a district court authorizing or directing the disclosure of any trade secret.

In *Hsu*, the defendants were indicted "for their involvement in an alleged conspiracy to steal corporate trade secrets from Bristol–Myers Squibb," particularly "processes, methods, and formulas for manufacturing Taxol, an anti-cancer drug" produced by this company.[84] The defendants argued that they should be entitled to discovery of confidential documents as this prosecution was for alleged attempt and conspiracy conduct. The defendants claimed this information was needed as they were raising a defense of legal impossibility.

The *Hsu* court found that Congress never intended for legal impossibility to be a defense here. To do so would "have the bizarre effect of forcing the government to disclose trade secrets to the very persons suspected of trying to steal them."[85] But the court did remand the case to ascertain whether the documents requested were material to the defense. The district court would be tasked with finding the appropriate balance between the defendant's need for the evidence for its defense, and the need to preserve confidentiality of the trade secret.

---

[81] 158 Cong. Rec. S6978–03, 2012 WL 5932548 (2012).

[82] P.L. 112–236 (Dec. 28, 2012).

[83] White House, Office of the Press Secretary, Dec. 28, 2012, available at 2012 WL 6738523.

[84] Hsu, 155 F.3d at 191–92.

[85] Id. at 202.

Chapter 16

GRAND JURY INVESTIGATIONS

§ 16.1 INTRODUCTION

A. Overview

This chapter addresses the law and practice of the federal grand jury investigation, as used to investigate possible white collar crime. Unlike the term "police investigation", which in literal correctness refers to an investigation conducted by the police, the term "grand jury investigation" does not refer to an investigation conducted by the group of laypersons constituting the grand jury. The grand jury investigation, as various courts realistically have noted, is an investigation conducted in large part by the prosecutor, using investigative tools established under the authority of the grand jury and the unique operational setting of the grand jury. As discussed in § 16.4, the prosecutor's direction of the investigation depends in large part on the acquiescence of the grand jury, although aspects of the investigation may reflect authority vested exclusively in the prosecutor. The grand jury's participation will occasionally extend beyond acquiescence (e.g., where jurors directly question witnesses), but the prosecutor invariably controls the basic content of the investigation, acting within the structure of the grand jury setting.

In the federal system, the grand jury's authority is not limited to investigations. The grand jury also plays a significant role in the decision to charge through its vote on whether or not to issue an indictment. The application and content of the law governing the exercise of this function is not shaped in any significant way by the white collar context of a particular charging decision. In contrast, the application and content of the law governing grand jury investigations is very much influenced by the white collar context. Indeed, grand jury investigations are so significant in the enforcement of white collar offenses that various aspects of the governing law are attributed to the need to facilitate such investigations (although the governing standard typically will be stated as applicable to the investigation of all types of crimes). Accordingly, while the screening and investigative roles of the grand jury will be combined in a single grand jury (see § 16.3(A)), our focus on white collar enforcement by the federal government leads to restricting this chapter's coverage to the investigative role of the federal grand jury.[1]

---

[1] Grand jury investigations also tend to be a staple of state enforcement of white collar offenses. Indeed, in many of the states in which local prosecutors rarely bring charges for white collar offenses, such limited enforcement may be explained, in part, by the grand jury not being a regular part of the state's criminal justice process. So too, in other states with limited white-collar enforcement, grand juries are regularly used in charging by indictment, but the grand jury structure is not conducive to conducting extensive investigations. Where state prosecutors have specialized units that regularly enforce certain classes of white collar crimes, they commonly proceed through grand jury investigations under state law that gives grand juries investigative authority approximating that of federal grand juries. So too where attorneys general have units prosecuting white collar crimes, they often will utilize statewide grand juries with

The operation of federal grand jury investigations is shaped initially by a variety of constitutional, statutory, and court-rule standards applied by the federal courts.[2] The DOJ's internal guidelines, found primarily in the United States Attorneys' Manual,[3] impose additional restrictions upon federal prosecutors in their use of the grand jury's investigative authority. Although these guidelines do not create substantive or procedural rights enforceable by the courts, the DOJ provides an internal enforcement mechanism through the DOJ's office of Professional Responsibility.[4] The DOJ's "Federal Grand Jury Practice" Manual also is influential, as it describes a variety of preferred practices as well as the preferred interpretation of the USAM guidelines.[5]

B. The Grand Jury's Investigative Strengths

The federal grand jury has available to it certain investigative tools and operational features that are particularly advantageous in uncovering evidence of white collar crime. The primary investigative tools are: (1) the subpoena ad testificandum compelling a person to appear and give testimony before the grand jury (see § 16.6); (2) the subpoena duces tecum compelling a person to produce documents or other tangible matter for grand jury consideration (see § 16.7); and (3) the grant of immunity, which replaces the privilege against self-incrimination and therefore eliminates that grounding for refusing to comply with a grand jury subpoena (see § 19.5). These investigative tools are supported by the sanction of contempt (civil or criminal) imposed upon the subpoenaed person (individual or entity) who fails to comply. (See § 16.5(E)).

The primary operational features of the grand jury investigation are (1) the closed grand jury session and (2) grand jury secrecy requirements. The closed session requires the witness to testify under oath, in response to the questions of the prosecutor and grand jurors, with essentially all others excluded (thus the witness may not be accompanied by his lawyer or any member of the public and no judge is present). (See § 16.3(C)). The secrecy requirements preclude disclosure of the content of the grand jury investigation (including witness testimony) by the jurors or government personnel and also severely restrict judicial disclosure of that content when requested in litigation by targets, defendants, and other persons. (See § 16.9).

---

roughly similar authority. Two of the sources cited in note 2 infra, CRIMPROC and GRJUR LAW cover state grand juries.

[2] The description of these standards in this chapter is drawn largely from chapters 8 and 15 of Wayne R. LaFave, Jerold H. Israel, Nancy J. King and Orin S. Kerr, Criminal Procedure Treatise (3d ed. 2007 and updated annually), available on Westlaw under the database CRIMPROC, and hereafter cited as CRIMPROC. Our case citations accordingly have been limited to cases individually discussed, with the reader directed to CRIMPROC for citations supporting more general descriptions of the caselaw. Two other treatises available on Westlaw provide further discussion of the caselaw, legislation, and relevant court rules. See Sara Sun Beale, William C. Bryson, James E. Felman, and Michael J. Elston, Grand Jury Law and Practice (2d ed. 1997 and updated annually), available under the Westlaw database GRJURLAW; Susan W. Brenner and Lori E. Shaw, Federal Grand Jury: A Guide to Law and Practice (2d ed. 2006 and updated annually), available under the Westlaw database FEDGRJURY.

[3] See USAM 9–11.00 (§§ 9–11.010–9–11.330). Various provisions scattered throughout the Criminal Resource Manual, Title 9 of the USAM, also relate to grand jury practice.

[4] See 28 C.F.R. §§ 0.39–0.41. See OPR, Policies and Procedures, available at http://www.justice.gove/opr/reports.htm.

[5] See DOJ, Executive Office for United States Attorneys, Federal Grand Jury Practice (Office of Legal Education Litigation Series, 2008) (hereafter cited as "Federal Grand Jury Practice"). See also the Antitrust Division's "Grand Jury Practice Manual" (1993), available at http://www.justice.gov/atr/public/guidlines.

The grand jury investigation's unique combination of investigative tools and operational setting offer a variety of strengths. These include: (1) forcing statements from persons who will not voluntarily furnish information to the prosecutor or investigators (including, where immunity is granted, persons who would otherwise be able to base their refusal on the privilege against self-incrimination); (2) obtaining statements that will have the added reliability provided by having been made under oath; (3) encouraging more candid and unrehearsed witness responses through various aspects of the grand jury setting—including a confidential forum, the exclusion of the attorney, and the witness speaking directly to the grand jurors, who may themselves ask questions; (4) for witnesses who fear attempts at intimidation or economic or social repercussions (or simply seek to avoid notoriety), providing, through grand jury secrecy requirements, a shield against disclosure to the target or other interested persons; (5) being able to initiate an investigation based on rumor or suspicion with greater assurance that, if nothing is discovered, grand jury secrecy requirements will operate to prevent subsequent public disclosure of the investigation and thereby avoid potential injury to the reputation of the target who was innocent; (6) being able to obtain documents and other physical evidence without the showing of probable cause that would be required for a search warrant, and even where probable cause exists, without having to set forth that probable cause in a document likely to be available to the target (see § 21.3); (7) being able to obtain documents that contain only general background information and therefore do not fit within the category of documents that can be the subject of a search warrant (see § 21.3(A)); (8) obtaining documents by a process that will not result in their subsequent suppression, if Fourth Amendment errors occur, in contrast to obtaining documents through a search warrant (see § 21.7); (9) where the documents sought are voluminous, likely to be intermingled in a mass of irrelevant documents, or scattered in different locations, eliminating logistical difficulties that would be presented in collecting the documents via a search warrant by utilizing a subpoena duces tecum, which shifts to the recipients of the subpoena the task of sorting through masses of documents in multiple locations to identify those covered by the subpoena; and (10) where documents are held by a disinterested third-party, recognizing the third party's legitimate interest in avoiding the disruptive impact of a physical search by police officers (an interest protected in the Privacy Protection Act, (see § 21.2) by instead utilizing a grand jury subpoena to obtain the needed documents (see § 16.7(F)).

It is clear that not all of these advantages work as effectively in practice as they do on paper (see e.g., § 16.9, discussing the limits of grand jury secrecy). Nonetheless, they undoubtedly do operate to provide a substantial advantage over alternatives where investigative success requires some or all of the following tasks: (1) unraveling a complex criminal structure; (2) dealing with potential witnesses who are reluctant to cooperate (or are reluctant to appear to cooperate) notwithstanding their lack of personal liability; (3) obtaining information buried in extensive business records; (4) obtaining the cooperation of third-party service providers who want the protective shield of a legal directive before revealing customer information; and (5) controlling the information revealed about an ongoing investigation—e.g., attempting to keep the target or targets of the investigation "in the dark" to the greatest extent possible, and where media coverage of the investigation would be disruptive, seeking to block media access to relevant sources of information. Criminal activities likely to present such investigative tasks include almost the full range of white collar crimes. As a result, federal prosecutors rely heavily, though not exclusively, on the grand jury investigation in most white collar cases.

C. Investigations by Law Enforcement Agencies

Over 60 federal agencies meet the standard definition of a law enforcement (or "police") agency—their responsibilities include the investigation of possible federal crimes and their personnel include agents who are given the traditional authority of sworn police officers (e.g., arrest authority). Many of these agencies are located in the executive branch (e.g., DOJ or Homeland Security), but some are independent agencies (e.g., the SEC). Federal agencies typically have an enforcement responsibility limited to specific types of crime (e.g., environmental crimes in the case of EPA) or crimes relating to particular institutions (e.g., the financial system in the case of the Secret Service). The major exception is the FBI, which is responsible for enforcing all federal offenses.

Almost all federal prosecutions flow from law enforcement agency investigations. Typically, the prosecution is based entirely on evidence developed in that investigation. In white collar cases, however, investigations by a law enforcement agency are most likely to be only the first step in the investigation. The needs of a white collar investigation are not as readily met by the traditional modes of "police" investigation. The potential for custodial interrogation is illustrative. In white collar cases the investigation commonly will be completed before an arrest is made (indeed, the defendant is usually charged by the grand jury before an arrest is made). Enforcement agencies, with good reason, do not count on gaining incriminating admissions through post-arrest interrogation. The arrestee most often will have been aware of the distinct possibility of being arrested (and charged), and prepared not to make any statement without a lawyer present.

Seeking information through interviews of potential witnesses also tends to be less effective in white collar offenses. These offenses only infrequently present a victim or an uninvolved bystander who reports a crime and is most willing to be interviewed. In white collar cases, a good many potential witnesses have reason not to be cooperative, such as a tie to a potential target (e.g., an employment relationship) or concern that revealing their own involvement in the transaction under investigation will have negative consequences. Disinterested third-parties asked to provide information about their clients or customers may well be prohibited by law from doing so without a legal directive commanding cooperation (and often will insist upon such a directive, in any event, as a matter of internal policy). Where potential witnesses are willing to be interviewed, they sometimes will insist upon the presence of their counsel, leading the agency investigator to request the participation of the prosecutor, who can respond to any witness' demands for assurances regarding possible prosecution.

Not all white collar offenses present such difficulties. For certain types of investigations, the procedures available to federal law enforcement agents are most effective. In the investigation of bribery schemes, for example, "sting" operations, using undercover agents, will often produce cases that need no further investigation. "*The Informant*" (both the book and the play) brought public attention to a related technique employed in uncovering white-collar conspiracies (there a price-fixing conspiracy)—

using a cooperating participant who is "wired."[6] As discussed in §21.2, while grand jury subpoenas duces tecum offer various advantages over searches in obtaining documents, in some settings the search pursuant to a warrant is to be preferred.

Many of the police investigating techniques used in white collar investigations are employed by law enforcement agencies without prior consultation with a prosecutor. Others, almost always involve such consultation. In the case of the search pursuant to a warrant, for example, legal advice is needed in preparing the warrant application, and the search (in contrast to regulatory searches, see § 21.5) may be related to an ongoing grand jury investigation. (See § 16.9(C)). In the case of wiretapping (§ 21.2), prosecutor involvement is legally required as the application must be authorized by a "Main Justice" official.

In the white collar field, the investigation by a law enforcement agency is often coordinated with a grand jury investigation. The law enforcement agency will initiate the investigation, present its initial findings to the prosecution, and the prosecution will then determine that additional investigation through the use of the grand jury is needed. Although there certainly are instances in which police investigative techniques are sufficient in themselves, they often must be supplemented by a grand jury investigation. Often also, some police techniques will be continued, now being used in conjunction with the grand jury investigation. As noted in § 16.3(E), the law-enforcement agency investigators, needing access to information developed by the grand jury in their continuing investigative effort, will become grand jury "personnel," subject to restrictions as to what they can disclose to their agency supervisors. At this point, the supervision of their investigative efforts rests largely with the prosecutor.

D. Investigation by Administrative Agencies

As noted in § 16.1(B), the primary investigative tools of the grand jury investigation are the subpoenas ad testificandum and duces tecum and the immunity grant. As discussed in Chapter 17, numerous federal administrative agencies have a broad subpoena authority, which can be used to investigate possible violations of regulatory provisions that may constitute crimes as well as civil violations. As discussed in § 19.5(C), immunity grants are also possible with the approval of the DOJ. Of course, if the administrative agency uncovers evidence of a criminal violation, it will not be able itself to initiate a criminal prosecution. However, various alternative investigative strategies are presented once the agency recognizes that the conduct being investigated could very well present a criminal offense as well as a civil violation. These include: (1) consulting with the prosecutor and staying the agency investigation if the prosecutor decides to institute a grand jury investigation; (2) consulting with the prosecutor, but continuing with the agency's independent investigation even if the prosecutor decides to institute a grand jury investigation (subject to any special agency limitations, as noted in §§ 17.6, 17.7); and (3) carrying the agency investigation forward until a largely completed case can be presented to the prosecutor (possibly eliminating the need for further investigation by a grand jury).

---

[6] See United States v. Andreas, 39 F. Supp.2d.1048 (N.D.Ill.1998); Kurt Eichenwald, The Informant (2000).

Both the agency and the prosecution have independent authority—the agency as to the continuation of its investigation and the prosecutor as to the initiation of a grand jury investigation. The exercise of that authority may be influenced by different perspectives on the comparative importance of criminal prosecution and the achievement of other regulatory objectives. However, insofar as the focus is on the best means of achieving a successful criminal investigation, the grand jury investigation will provide various advantages over the administrative agency investigation.

The grand jury investigation offers a variety of investigative strengths as compared to the agency investigation. These include: (1) the grand jury requires the witness to testify in a closed proceeding, with the witness' attorney excluded; (2) the grand jury subpoena duces tecum is not subject to some of the restrictions applied to the agency subpoena duces tecum (see §§ 17.4, 17.5, although the Fourth Amendment applies equally to both, and parts of the *Powell* requirement (see § 17.4(A)) merely duplicate Rule 17(c) requirements for grand jury subpoenas (see § 16.12); (3) the procedure for challenging a grand jury subpoena, the motion to quash (see § 16.5(D)) offers the challenger less opportunity for delaying enforcement (e.g., through an appeal), or forcing a government disclosure, than does the separate civil proceeding utilized in enforcing agency subpoenas (see § 17.4(A)); and (4) grand jury secrecy may be useful in various respects (see § 16.9), whereas the full record of administrative proceedings (including immunized testimony) is subject to court-ordered disclosure (in particular, to the target). In many instances, these factors will lead the prosecution to favor initiation of a grand jury investigation as soon as the administrative agency investigation suggests a possible criminal violation.[7] However, where the prosecutor believes that other interests should prevail (e.g., facilitating a sharing of information among various agencies and civil litigators that would be difficult under grand jury secrecy, see §§ 16.9, 18.2(B), 18.3(B)), the prosecutor is free to delay instituting a grand jury investigation and offer advice to the administrative agency as it pursues its administrative investigation. (See § 18.2(A), (B)).[8]

§ 16.2 HISTORICAL TRADITION

A. The Common Law and Colonial Progenitors

In creating the federal judiciary, the First Congress included several statutory provisions governing criminal procedure, but generally relied on the assumption that the federal courts would follow the procedures of the English common law, as those procedures had been followed (with some modifications) in the colonies and had later

---

[7] That conclusion could also lead the prosecutor to prefer that the agency investigation be stayed, so as to avoid undesirable disclosures and overlap; but these concerns might be met by simply limiting the scope of the agency investigation. While, as noted in §§ 17.6, 18.2(B), close coordination is common in many areas, the independent agency remains free to pursue its own path. Similar choices without the potential for clashing decision-makers are presented by several statutes that grant subpoena power directly to prosecutors for the purpose of investigating violations of statues that can be both criminal and civil. See, e.g., 18 U.S.C. § 3486 (production of records relating to "federal healthcare offenses"); 31 U.S.C. § 3733 (fraud in government contracts). Such statutes provide a subpoena authority similar in operation to administrative subpoenas. See CRIMPROC § 8.1(c).

[8] USAM § 9–11.254 similarly advises: "Before issuing a grand jury subpoena, prosecutors should consider ... whether a voluntary request, contractual obligation, inspector general subpoena, civil investigative demand or other compulsory process is available to obtain the information sought. Those methods may be just as effective as a grand jury subpoena in obtaining information but their use may avoid grand jury secrecy issues."

been adopted by the independent states. The grand jury was an important part of that common law procedure. The English grand jury traced its roots back to a body instituted by the Normans in an attempt to strengthen the Crown's authority. A group of twelve "good and lawful men" in each local community were assigned the task of being the eyes and ears of the Crown in the enforcement of the criminal law. They were required, subject to substantial fines, to accuse all who were suspected of having committed crimes, with those persons then subjected to trial by ordeal. When the English later turned to trial by petit jury, this grand jury predecessor became a larger body, sometimes described as *le grand inquest*. This group was initially 24 (twice the size of the petit jury), but then reduced to 23 (to avoid ties, as it proceeded by majority vote). Its function remained that of accusation, based on either its "own knowledge" or information provided by the Crown, with its accusations then followed by a jury trial.

By the end of the seventeenth century, the grand jury had been transformed into an independent body, which met in closed sessions and no longer was beholden to the Crown. Indeed, the grand jury was now viewed as a primary vehicle for achieving lay control of the criminal justice process, roughly equal in importance to the petit jury. It was in later years described as occupying the roles of both "shield and sword" in the criminal justice process. It served as a shield in reviewing charges brought to it for approval by a representative of the Crown (typically a sheriff). It could refuse to approve the charge, and thereby bar prosecution, thus shielding the innocent person from improperly motivated or completely unfounded prosecutions by the Crown (or the guilty person from a prosecution simply thought to be "unjust"). The grand jury served as a sword in its retention of the authority to charge on its "own knowledge." It had the authority to make its own independent inquiry into matters that escaped the attention of the Crown or that the Crown, perhaps for improper reasons, chose not to pursue. This included not only hearing from victims but calling forward possible witnesses to appear before it (in closed sessions) and reveal what they knew about a possible crime.

The dual functions of the English common law grand jury were reflected in the two types of charging instruments that it issued. When the Crown brought before the grand jury evidence supporting a charge it favored, it presented a draft of a proposed charging instrument, titled an "indictment." If the grand jury found that the Crown's evidence was sufficient to justify the proposed charge, it issued the indictment, declaring it to be a "true bill". If the grand majority concluded that the Crown's presentation did not justify prosecution, it returned a finding of ignoramus ("we ignore it"), or in later years, "no bill."

Where the grand jury's charging instrument was based on the grand jury's "own knowledge", it was labeled a "presentment". The presentment could be based on evidence that had been brought to the grand jury's attention by a private complainant or evidence that was the product of the grand jury's own investigation, initiated on the basis of what its members personally knew or had heard (including rumors circulating through the community). The grand jury's public support stemmed in part from the character of its presentments, particularly those based on inquiries into the misconduct of minor officials in matters of local administration. Not all such inquires had resulted in the conclusion that the misconduct by the local officials had been criminal. Grand juries had nonetheless issued findings of official malfeasance, and since these findings were based on the grand jury's authority to conduct an independent inquiry, they often were also characterized as "presentments" (although technically they constituted nothing more than public "reports").

The common law grand jury was transplanted, without modification, to the colonies. The grand jury retained the power to consider indictments and to issue presentments and reports. From the start, its reporting power, as it related to public administration, grew in prominence. During the period leading up to the American Revolution, its independence in considering indictments and presentments also added to its luster. In one of the most famous instances of a grand jury rejecting a proposed indictment, colonial grand juries twice refused to charge Peter Zenger, a newspaper publisher, for criminal libel in his newspaper's criticism of the governor. Similarly, on the other side, the grand jury investigated on its own initiative and issued presentments, over the opposition of Royal officials, against British soldiers who had misused their authority.[9]

B. The Fifth Amendment

When several states, in ratifying the Constitution, insisted upon the addition of a Bill of Rights, it was not surprising, in light of the grand jury's public support, that their recommended criminal process guarantees included grand jury approval of the decision to charge in all serious criminal cases. This proposal was not controversial. Preeminent Federalists, though seeing no need for a Bill of Rights, had praised the grand jury. James Wilson, for example had described it as a "great channel of communication between those who make and administer the laws, and those for whom the laws are made and administered." Madison initially sought to place the proposals on the grand and petit juries in a single amendment, but those provisions eventually were separated. The grand jury clause was added to what became the Fifth Amendment—a cluster of guarantees that could be viewed as aimed at precluding unfairness in the processes that either led to a prosecution (compelled self-incrimination or prior jeopardy) or involved the institution of prosecution (grand jury participation). The grand jury clause guaranteed that prosecution for a capital or otherwise infamous offense (basically, any felony) be based on the grand jury's issuance of a "presentment or indictment," except for certain military cases.

The Fifth Amendment recognizes both forms of charging instruments that were issued by the common law grand jury. It appears to do so, however, only in ensuring that a person will not be accused without the grand jury's approval. Thus the reference to a presentment presumably did not give constitutional status to the grand jury authority that led to the issuance of presentment. It recognized the existence of that authority, and concluded that a charging instrument based on that authority offered sufficient protection for the person to be charged with an offense. However, it did not

---

[9] While the exercise of independence by grand juries in these instances and others became part of the lore of the American Revolution, and advanced a highly favorable image of the grand jury at the time, various modern critics have argued that the significance of the grand jury as either a shield or sword was very much exaggerated as to both the English and colonial experience. They note, for example, that Zenger was eventually charged by information (though acquitted by a petit jury), and that the Crown refused to proceed against the British soldiers. However, federal courts, in discussing the history of the grand jury have almost invariably cited as well deserved the Founders' high regard for grand juries, noting particularly the refusals to indict by colonial grand juries in the Zenger case and by English grand juries in the late 17th century cases involving Stephen Colledge and the Earl of Shaftesbury, two prominent supporters of the Protestant cause.

preclude the federal system from abandoning the presentment as a charging instrument, as it eventually did.[10]

C. The Abandonment of the Presentment

Over the first several decades of the American Republic, grand jury presentments played a prominent role in several of the states and in the western territories. In particular, the grand jury's reputation as a "public watchdog" was enhanced by self-initiated prosecutions and reports relating to corruption in government and widespread evasion of particular laws. In the federal system, however, the presentment authority rarely was utilized. In part, that may have been due to the character of the federal criminal law. Federal offenses often had no victim other than the government, so there was no aggrieved party to bring to the grand jury's attention the need to initiate its own investigation where the federal prosecutor had refused to proceed. Federal judges, in advising the grand jury, did take note of its authority to issue presentments, and a United States Attorney General cited the grand jury presentment as an alternative route in announcing that prosecution was not appropriate in a case involving a tumultuous assemblage before a foreign consulate. At the same time, however, various sources, including an opinion by Chief Justice Marshall (riding circuit), questioned whether a presentment could lead to a prosecution where the federal prosecutor for the particular district was opposed. Those sources suggested that the grand jury presentment could only serve as an accusatory instrument if the prosecutor framed an indictment based on that presentment. Still, the early federal grand juries did issue several notable presentments that led to prosecutions, although the federal grand jury's reputation for independence was more commonly associated with refusals to indict, particularly in politically sensitive cases.

During the nineteenth century, the grand jury was challenged as to both its screening and presentment authority, and many states eliminated the requirement of prosecution by indictment or presentment. As to presentments, a major objection was that the use of law enforcement resources and prosecutorial authority should rest with the professional prosecutor, not a body of laymen. That criticism came to be reflected in the charges that some judges gave to federal grand juries. In perhaps the most prominent of these charges, that by Justice Field,[11] the grand jury was told that a presentment was no more than an "informal charge," upon which an indictment might later be framed. It was also told that "this form of accusation has fallen in disuse since

---

[10] A contrary argument was possible. The grand jury might have been viewed as aimed at preserving the rights of the "people," as expressed in the Ninth Amendment. The Supreme Court has never offered that view of the grand jury clause or of other clauses that might be viewed in that manner. Such a view of the clause arguably would have precluded the elimination of the presentment (as that gave the executive branch, rather than "the people," ultimate control over prosecution) and certain other restrictions of the grand jury's authority over investigations (see § 16.4.B).

[11] 30 Fed.Cas. 992 (C.C.D. Cal. 1872). The Field charge was contradicted by other charges given in the same era, and in several respects, its directions on grand jury practice were later rejected. But it reflected the ultimately prevailing view as to the limited authority of presentments, and the rejection of any right of an alleged crime victim to inform the grand jury of the alleged offense. Indeed, modern rulings making the latter point rely on the Field jury charge. See e.g., the extensive discussion in In re New Haven Grand Jury, 604 F.Supp. 453 (D.Conn. 1985) (noting that a private complaint may request permission from the court or prosecution to send a communication to the grand jury, but direct correspondence without such permission is not allowed and presumptively violates 18 U.S.C. § 1504 (prohibiting an attempt "to influence the action or decision of any grand or petit juror pertaining to his duties by writing, or sending him any written communication")).

the practice has prevailed . . . for the prosecuting officer to attend the grand jury and advise them in their investigations." Justice Field did not state that the grand jury could investigate only matters called to its attention by the prosecutor or the court (although noting that it "may be safely inferred that public justice will not suffer" if the grand jury limited itself to such matters). He did warn, however, that grand jurors were not to allow "private prosecutors to intrude themselves into [their] presence and present accusations."

In 1944, the adoption of the Federal Rules of Criminal Procedure settled the status of the presentment in the federal system. Federal Rule 7 (still in effect) recognized a defendant's right to be prosecuted by indictment for all felonies (apart from the special case of criminal contempts). The Rule did not refer to the alternative of a presentment. The Committee Notes explained that a presentment probably referred only to "a statement of facts by grand jurors upon which an indictment would be framed later by a United States Attorney when available," although it might also have meant "an accusation by grand jurors upon presentation of facts to them by a special prosecutor for a private individual." Presentments had become "obsolete," the Committee noted, because federal prosecutors were readily available to assist the grand jurors in drafting an indictment once they were ready to charge, and prosecutions by private persons were no longer allowed.

Although not mentioned by the Committee, the use of a presentment would be contrary to another aspect of Rule 7 if the presentment were viewed as a true charging instrument, as many common law authorities had suggested. Under Federal Rule 7, even an indictment does not become a charging instrument upon an affirmative vote of the grand jury. That only occurs if the indictment is also signed by "the attorney for the government," and the prosecutor has discretion to withhold that signature if the DOJ concludes that a prosecution should not be brought. Indeed, one federal appellate court has held that, since the prosecutor need not sign, the prosecutor may also refuse to assist the grand jury by drafting an indictment on which it might vote. In other instances, however, the draft has been prepared and the grand jury has been allowed to vote and request that its approved indictment be made public as a "report" or "presentment." The few federal courts considering that issue have divided as to whether they have the authority to grant such a request. In any event, Rule 7 clearly gives the federal prosecutor the authority to veto a grand jury's decision to charge, and that is contrary to the basic character of a presentment that is a true charging instrument.

The end result of Rule 7 is that the presentment is abandoned as a charging instrument, and the grand jury cannot force a prosecution on its own initiative. It does not follow, however, that the federal grand jury therefore has lost the independent investigative powers that so often led to presentments. As discussed in § 16.4(B), the federal grand jury retains the authority to call for evidence beyond that presented by the prosecutor, and to ask witnesses questions beyond those asked by the prosecutor. However, Rule 7, in effect, warns the grand jury that it will not be able to act upon that investigative power to institute a charge that is opposed by the prosecutor.

D. The Relevance of History

Critics of the broad investigative power of today's federal grand jury argue that it cannot be justified by the historical precedent of the common law grand jury. In granting grand juries broad investigative power, it is argued, the common law assumed that the lay grand jurors controlled the investigation and reflected the views of the citizenry. Today, they continue, the grand jury's investigation is basically the prosecutor's investigation. They contend that the federal courts therefore should put aside grand jury history and subject the modern grand jury investigation to constitutional and supervisory limitations similar to those imposed upon other investigative weapons in the government arsenal (in particular, police investigations).

Although occasional lower court decisions have been partially receptive to this approach,[12] the Supreme Court has consistently looked to the authority of the English common law grand jury and its colonial counterpart. Its starting premise has been that, absent a congressional directive to the contrary, the federal grand jury should have the same investigative authority, and be allowed to follow the same procedures, as its historical ancestors. The Court has reasoned that the basic functions of the grand jury remain the same and its powers follow from these functions. This rationale was at the heart of two preeminent Supreme Court rulings in the early 1900s, *Hale v. Henckel*[13] and *Blair v. United States*,[14] and has been cited in almost every subsequent ruling examining challenges to the grand jury's investigative authority.[15]

---

[12] Those cases relied on this perspective in utilizing the federal court's supervisory power to impose restrictions aimed at precluding prosecutorial misuse of the grand jury's investigative authority. Apart from their departure from the perspective noted in the Supreme Court rulings discussed infra, those cases are difficult to reconcile with the Supreme Court's later ruling in the United States v. Williams restricting use of the supervisory authority to regulate grand jury proceedings. (See § 16.4(C)).

[13] 201 U.S. 43 (1906). In *Hale*, the Court rejected the contention that the grand jury's right to subpoena witnesses was limited to situations in which a "specific charge [was] pending before the grand jury against any particular person." That was inconsistent, the Court noted, with the traditional authority of common-law grand juries. The grand jury oath directed the jurors to "diligently inquire" not only as to matters "given to you in charge," but also to matters "as shall come to your own knowledge touching this present service." That "oath of the grand juryman . . . assigns no limits except those marked by diligence itself to the course of [the grand jury's] inquiries." The Court also cited previous recognition of the common law grand jury's authority to "send for witnesses" on its own initiative, and the well-established principle that a presentment could be based on information obtained from grand jury witnesses who had been summoned based on a juror's personal knowledge.

[14] 250 U.S. 273 (1919). As discussed in § 16.12(B). *Blair* held that a witness could not object to grand jury questioning on the ground that the subject of inquiry was beyond the grand jury's investigative authority. The Court stressed the general obligation of a subpoenaed witness to respond to a subpoena valid on its face (the witness thus having no authority to challenge the jurisdiction of the body issuing the subpoena). It emphasized in this connection the history of grand jury subpoenas. "At the foundation of our federal government," it noted, "the inquisitional function of the grand jury and the compulsion of witnesses were recognized as incident of the judicial power of the United States." The grand jury's authority to resort to compulsory process had been recognized in England as early as 1612, and the inquisitional function of the grand jury had been equally well established. Both the Fifth Amendment and the earliest federal statues recognized an investigative authority of the grand jury that included the "same powers that pertained to its British prototype." The Supreme Court would not view that authority with suspicion and subject it to new limitations. The grand jury, the Court concluded, "is a grand inquest, a body with powers of investigation and inquisition, the scope of whose inquiries is not to be limited narrowly by questions of propriety or forecasts of the probable result of investigation."

[15] Thus, the "Anglo–American history" of the grand jury has been cited in most of the Supreme Court rulings discussed in this chapter, including United States v. Williams (§ 16.4(C)), and United States v. Calandra (§ 16.11(F)). That history also has played a prominent role in rulings addressing the screening function of the grand jury. Thus Costello v. United States, 350 U.S. 359 (1956), looked to that history in refusing to prohibit the grand jury from considering hearsay evidence in deciding to indict. The Court noted that the English common law never prescribed the type of evidence that a grand jury could consider, and "there is every reason to believe that our constitutional grand jury was intended to operate substantially like its English progenitor."

§ 16.3 GRAND JURY STRUCTURE

A. Regular and Special Grand Juries

Both Rule 6 of the Federal Rules of Criminal Procedure and 18 U.S.C. § 3331 (adopted as part of the Organized Crime Control Act of 1970) authorize the impanelment of federal grand juries. Rule 6 applies in every federal district, and every district has one or more grand juries established under that Rule. Section 3331, on the other hand, applies only in a limited number of districts. Rule 6 grand juries operate under a legal structure set forth in various provisions of Rule 6, and § 3331 grand juries start with that structure, but then modify it to expand the grand jury's authority. Because § 3331 grand juries would be less common and would expand upon the Rule 6 norm, Congress described these grand juries in § 3331 as "special" grand juries. Rule 6 grand juries, in turn, came to be known as "regular" grand juries.

The Rule 6 grand juries are impaneled in accordance with a directive that a grand jury be summoned "at such time as the public interest requires." In large districts this commonly leads to the impanelment of multiple grand juries at selected intervals so that the terms for the different grand juries do not expire at the same time. Section 3331 applies only to districts of more than four million inhabitants and to smaller districts if the Attorney General or the AG's designee certifies that "a special grand jury is necessary because of criminal activity in the district." Although § 3331 was adopted as part of the Organized Crime Control Act, the Attorney General's determination is not tied to the presence of organized crime, and the grand jury may "inquire into any offenses against the laws of the United States." Where § 3331 applies, the district court is directed to summon a special grand jury "at least once in each period of eighteen months, unless another special grand jury is then serving."

The special grand jury differs from the regular grand jury primarily in the following: (1) a longer term; (2) a statutory responsibility of the prosecutor to convey to the grand jury information received from third persons regarding an alleged offense (in contrast to the prosecutorial discretion as to informing for a Rule 6 grand jury); and (3) a grand jury authority to issue reports on "organized crime conditions" and non-criminal official misconduct involving "organized criminal activity justifying removal or disciplinary action" (in contrast to the unsettled law as to the issuance of reports by Rule 6 grand juries). Although one of the most prominent instances of a special grand jury seeking to issue a report arose in the context of a white collar investigation,[16] the most significant advantage of the special grand jury in conducting white collar investigations is the longer term.

Rule 6 grand juries sit for eighteen months, with an extension possible for another six months; the special grand jury has a term of eighteen months, with three six-month extensions possible (and an even further extension where needed to issue a report). Thus, the longest possible term for a special grand jury as to investigating and issuing

---

As discussed in § 16.10(A), these rulings have not blindly ignored the modern potential for prosecutor dominance of the grand jury's investigative authority. Indeed, prosecution dominance had become a well-known fact of life at the time *Blair* and *Hale* were decided.

[16] See In re Special Grand Jury, 450 F.3d 1159 (10th Cir.2006) (describing the efforts of the "runaway" grand jury that investigated possible environmental crimes by a government contractor at the Rocky Flats Nuclear Weapons Plant in Colorado).

charges is thirty-six months, as compared to a possible twenty-four months for the regular grand jury. Grand jury investigations in white collar cases can easily exceed two years, but limits on the grand jury term are far from an insurmountable hurdle. Under Rule 6, a prosecutor has an automatic right to transfer evidence from one grand jury to another in the form of transcripts and documents. Moreover, the prosecutor may assist the successor grand jury in digesting that material by having it summarized by case agents.[17] While some repetition is involved, and that may be time consuming, the prosecution does not face the much greater burden of having to recall all previous witnesses.

Because the special grand jury is so often associated with long-term investigations, special grand juries are often described as "investigative" grand juries, with the regular grand jury then described as a "charging" grand jury. Both characterizations are misleading if viewed as describing the exclusive function of the particular type of grand jury. A special grand jury engaged in a long-term investigation will eventually have to decide whether charges should be brought, and at that point it has added a "charging" or "screening" function. Regular grand juries often are involved only in the screening function. As discussed in § 16.1(C), for many types of federal offenses, federal enforcement agencies will be able to obtain through police investigative practices all the evidence that can be obtained to support a prosecution. Here, the presentation before the grand jury is likely to consist of a single witness—the investigation supervisor ("case agent"), who describes all the evidence the enforcement agency has obtained through its investigation (e.g., confessions, physical evidence, eyewitness identification). If further witnesses are presented (e.g., the crime victim), the objective is simply to further explain that evidence, but not to develop new evidence. However, as also noted in § 16.1(C), for white collar offenses, the law enforcement investigation often must be supplemented through the grand jury's investigative authority. The grand juries used to conduct these investigations often are Rule 6 "regular" grand juries, even in those districts that also have a special grand jury. Here the regular grand jury is both an investigative and a charging grand jury, and in some instances, the investigative function will rival in scope and length the investigations associated with special grand juries.

B. Grand Jury Composition

The Federal Jury Selection Act of 1968 governs the selection of both petit jurors and grand jurors. The Act requires each district court to adopt a jury selection plan ensuring that both (1) prospective jurors are "selected at random from a fair cross-section of the district" and (2) no citizen is excluded because of "race, color, religion, sex, national origin or economic status." The typical plan uses voter registration and other lists to fill a master wheel from which the group of persons called for possible service (the "array" or "venire") are randomly selected. Excluded from this group are persons who fail to meet basic qualifications for jury service (e.g., residency, age, and literacy) and persons excused on hardship grounds. For grand jury selection, the hardship group is likely to be somewhat larger than for the petit jury because of the much longer term of service.

---

[17] Federal Grand Jury Practice § 4.17 advises that the prosecutor can offer the summary as an alternative to a complete transcript, but "should note for the record that the complete transcripts are available for use by the grand jurors," and "all exculpatory evidence should be re-presented to the new grand jury."

In selecting the petit jury, the next step in moving from the array to the panel of selected jurors presents considerable opportunity for shaping that panel. The prospective jurors are subjected to voir dire (with both sides having input, even if the judge conducts the voir dire) and prospective jurors are eliminated through challenges for cause and peremptory challenges. This step does not apply in grand jury selection, where the non-excused, qualified prospective jurors are directly assigned to panels by random selection.

The Sixth Amendment requires an "impartial" petit juror, but the Supreme Court has never held that the Fifth Amendment requires an indicting grand jury to be impartial (which certainly was not a common law requirement, as a grand jury could charge by presentment "on its own knowledge," with grand jurors acting as complainants). However, the DOJ advises federal prosecutors to conduct a brief inquiry to determine whether any juror has an "interest that may interfere with a fair, impartial, or just decision concerning the indictment." When the grand jury moves to the investigation or screening of a new case, the prosecutor briefly describes the subject matter and asks the jurors if they might have a financial interest in the transactions involved, a social relationship with the participants, or a preconceived viewpoint that precludes an open-minded evaluation of the evidence. If a juror acknowledges such a viewpoint or a significant relationship that raises doubts as to impartiality (more than "the mere fact that a juror knows a witness"), that information will be passed along to the supervising judge. The judge has authority under Rule 6 to excuse a grand juror for "good cause." As to impartiality, the "good cause" standard tends to be interpreted in light of the explanation of disqualifying "bias" in the supervising court's initial charge to the grand jury. That charge typically directs the jurors not to participate if "biased" and offers a detailed explanation of bias that replicates the standards applied under a "for cause" challenge to petit jurors (e.g., "fixed opinion before you hear evidence" or "related by blood or marriage").

Exclusion of grand jurors based on bias appears to be fairly rare, which is not surprising in light of the limited opportunity to explore possible sources of bias (as compared to the petit jury selection process). However, for long-term investigations, the likelihood of a good cause excusal for other reasons (e.g. juror illness or juror moving out of the district) is fairly high. Accordingly, courts commonly impanel alternate jurors, who do not attend sessions, but are ready to replace excused jurors and keep the membership at twenty-three. Although a grand federal jury can continue to operate as long as it has at least 16 jurors (Rule 6 requiring a jury of "16 to 23 members"), it will be more difficult to gain the attendance of a quorum (16 members) as the membership dwindles. An alternate replacing an excused juror may immediately participate in the ongoing investigation and vote on any subsequent indictment. The absence from prior sessions is not a disqualification. The seated alternate is free to examine the recording of those sessions, and, in any event, a grand juror need not be familiar with all the evidence presented; to vote for indictment, the juror simply must be aware of sufficient evidence to support the charge.

C. Grand Jury Sessions

A quorum of sixteen members is needed for a grand jury session. Because grand jury proceedings are secret, those sessions typically are held in a "grand jury room" located in a portion of the courthouse that is not accessible to the general public. The scheduling of grand jury sessions varies, particularly where the grand jury is involved in an investigation. Unlike trial juries, grand juries rarely will meet every day in the week. Indeed, there may be gaps of several weeks between sessions.

Rule 6 states that the only persons who may be present, in addition to the grand jurors, are: "attorneys for the government, the witnesses being questioned, interpreters when needed, and a court reporter or an operator of recording device." This provision operates to exclude a witness' attorney (see § 16.8(A)). It also excludes investigative agents working with the prosecutor, unless they are testifying as a witness.

Rule 6 provides that, "except while the grand jury is deliberating or voting, all proceedings must be recorded by a court reporter or a suitable recording device." This provision is not limited to witness testimony. It includes colloquy between the prosecutor and grand jurors during sessions, and prosecutors are advised to inform the grand jurors that questions relating to the investigation should not be asked until the session starts, so everything will be recorded. Since Rule 6 requires only a recording, the prosecutor may limit the preparation of any transcript to the testimony portion of the recording. A transcript will be useful in making the testimony available to investigative personnel and other attorneys on the prosecutor's staff. Also, a transcript of testimony often would have to be prepared in any event as part of the discovery provided to a defendant at trial.[18]

D. Grand Jury Foreperson

Unlike a petit jury, the grand jury does not select its own foreperson. The court appoints both a foreperson and a deputy foreperson from among the members of the grand jury. The deputy foreperson's primary function is to substitute in the foreperson's absence. In *Hobby v. United States*,[19] in rejecting a defendant's claim that the impaneling court had engaged in gender and racial discrimination in appointing the foreperson of the grand jury that indicted him, the Supreme Court described the foreperson's duties as "essentially clerical in nature—administering oaths, maintaining records, and signing indictments." The Court's reference was to those functions noted in Rule 6 as they related to the decision to indict. Looking to other aspects of the foreperson's duties, the foreperson arguably can play a much more substantive role in the shaping of a grand jury's investigation.

As discussed in § 16.5(A), in some districts the foreperson must "sign off" on the prosecutor's use of grand jury subpoenas. In all districts, it is the foreperson who represents the grand jury in dealing with the testifying witness. Thus, it is the foreperson (not the prosecutor) who instructs witnesses on whether they are excused, whether they may leave the grand jury room to speak with counsel, and whether they must respond to a prosecutor's question or face a request for a contempt citation. While the foreperson ordinarily will follow the prosecutor's lead on these matters, the ultimate decision apparently rests with the foreperson as the spokesperson for the grand jury (see § 16.4(B)). Also, while each grand juror is given the opportunity to

---

[18] As to that discovery, see § 16.6(C). In this connection Federal Grand Jury Practice § 2.17 notes: "Prosecutors should keep in mind, also, that the prosecutor's answers to grand jurors' questions about the law, explanations of foundational facts, organizational structure, or people's names and relationships, etc., should take place without a witness present. When the witness is present, these discussions can become part of the witness's Jencks material [disclosed at trial], when it was not his/her testimony in the first place."

[19] 468 U.S. 339 (1984).

question the witness after the prosecutor has finished, the foreperson goes first and may thereby set the tone for others.[20]

E. Prosecutors and Assisting Personnel

Rule 6 does not use the term "prosecutor." Instead, it refers to the "attorney for the government." That term is used initially in the provision describing the persons who may be present during a grand jury session. It is later used in a Rule 6(e)(3) provision describing disclosures of "grand jury matter" (e.g., grand jury testimony) that may be made without first obtaining judicial approval. That provision recognizes as a general exception to secrecy requirements the "disclosure of a grand jury matter . . . to an attorney for the government in performing that attorney's duty." Rule 1, the provision on definitions, sets forth a definition of "attorney for the government" that encompasses: (1) the legal staff of a United States Attorney, and (2) the legal staff of any of the divisions within Main Justice. As noted in § 18.3(C), the Supreme Court has held that the Rule 6 reference to disclosure to such government attorneys "in performing that attorney's duties" restricts Rule 1's coverage in the context of grand jury proceedings. It adds the requirement that the attorney for the government is performing what the Court has described as "prosecutorial duties"; the attorney for the government who may be present in the grand jury session, and to whom Rule 6(e)(3) disclosures may be made, must be "assisting the grand jury in its [criminal law enforcement] functions."[21] As for the United States Attorneys' office, that function by statute automatically applies to any AUSA assigned to the grand jury team. As for the Main Justice attorneys, an assignment to criminal enforcement responsibilities is not automatically assumed. For divisions such as antitrust, a distinction must be drawn among staff attorneys since their usual function includes civil enforcement. To ensure that the grand jury attorneys have a function only of criminal law enforcement, a special assignment is issued by the Attorney General (or the AG's designee, typically the division chief), pursuant to statue, where the Main Justice attorney will be appearing before the grand jury.[22] A similar statutory assignment is not necessary where the Main Justice Attorney will be only an occasional consultant to an AUSA or Main Justice attorney conducting a grand jury investigation.

The Rule 1 definition of attorney for the government excludes government attorneys working outside the DOJ. Where a case is developed initially by such an attorney (e.g., an SEC attorney), the prosecutor primarily responsible for the grand jury investigation may want to take advantage of that attorney's expertise. That can be achieved by having the non-DOJ attorney appointed a Special Assistant to the Attorney General or Special Assistant to the United States Attorney.[23] While that

---

[20] The foreperson also plays two critical roles should the grand jury run into difficulties in dealing with the prosecutor. Initially, the foreperson is the liaison with the court and may convey the grand jury's concerns to the supervisory judge. Secondly, if the grand jurors find a need to discuss the situation among themselves, the foreperson would be the chairperson for that session.

[21] United States v. Sells Engineering, 463 U.S. 418 (1983), discussed in § 18.3(C).

[22] See 28 U.S.C. § 515(a); USAM § 9–11.241. As to AUSAs assigned to the grand jury, see 28 U.S.C. § 547. As to general consultations with Main Justice attorneys, see USAM, Title 9 (Criminal Resource Manual) § 156.

[23] These appointments are made pursuant to 28 U.S.C. § 515 and 28 U.S.C. § 543. See also USAM § 9–11.242. This authority extends to the appointment of an attorney employed by a state or local government, which is useful where the investigation was initiated by a joint federal-state task force. As part of the appointment process, the requesting grand jury prosecutor must: (1) certify that the appointee "has been

attorney is now an "attorney for the government" for Rule 6 purposes, the same is not true for the attorney's supervisor at his or her home agency. Thus, the special assistant cannot share information relating to the grand jury investigation with the supervisor or other agency attorneys unless court approval is obtained pursuant to one of the secrecy exceptions (see § 16.9). The special assistant is now part of the grand jury team, subject to the supervision of the AUSA or DOJ attorney heading the grand jury investigation.

As discussed in § 16.1(C), very often the transaction that is the subject of a grand jury investigation will have been investigated initially by a federal law enforcement agency. The agents who participated in that investigation often can provide substantial assistance to the prosecutor in shaping the use of the grand jury's investigative tools. Also, as discussed in § 16.1(C), the grand jury investigation often can be facilitated by a continued use of police investigative tools in coordination with the grand jury investigation. Rule 6 recognizes these benefits in allowing the prosecutor's "team" in grand jury investigations to include various personnel from enforcement agencies. The Rule does not go so far as to allow such team members to attend grand jury session with the prosecutor, but its Rule 6(e)(3) provision on disclosures without judicial approval is broad enough to encompass enforcement agency personnel as well as the prosecutor's usual staff (i.e., secretaries, paralegals, etc.).

Rule 6(e)(3) follows its provision on disclosure to "attorneys for the government" with a provision authorizing similar disclosure to: "any government personnel— including those of a state, state subdivision, Indian tribe or foreign government—that an attorney for the government considers necessary to assist in performing that attorney's duty to enforce federal criminal law." This provision covers every possible agency that may have been involved in the investigation that led to instituting the grand jury's investigation. The inclusion of state and local agencies has special relevance for white collar investigations as a result of special units, such as the Interagency Financial Fraud Enforcement Task Force, which are directed to "work with state and local partners." Moreover, the provision does not seek to limit the personnel to those who were involved in the previous investigation. Thus, it covers an agency expert added to the team to analyze a different type of evidence (e.g. financial documents) that will be produced by the grand jury's investigation. It even can include an expert in private practice, converted into "government personnel" by being hired as a temporary employee through the life of the investigation.

Rule 6(e) imposes four conditions for including a particular government agent within the group of personnel to whom disclosures may be made. Initially, the prosecutor must conclude that the assistance of the particular agent is "necessary." This is a prosecutorial determination, not subject to judicial review. Second, the included personnel are limited to using the disclosed grand jury information "only to assist the attorney for the government to enforce federal criminal law." If the particular agency employing the agent is involved in other activities (e.g., regulatory enforcement), the agent cannot use the information for that function. Other agency

---

informed of the grand jury secrecy requirements in Federal Rule 6(e)"; (2) note "whether the agency from which the attorney comes is conducting or may conduct contemporaneous administrative or other civil proceedings" and describe those proceedings; and (3) provide "a full description of the arrangements that have been made to prevent the attorney's agency from obtaining access through the attorney to grand jury maturation the case." See USAM, Title 9 (Criminal Resource Manual) § 155.

investigators may be assigned to achieving other enforcement objectives through a parallel agency investigation, but the agent covered by Rule 6(e)(3) cannot share grand jury information with those agents, unless the court approves pursuant to one of the secrecy provisions discussed in § 16.9(G). To ensure that the court will be able to respond to the claim of unauthorized disclosures by Rule 6(e)(3) personnel, a third condition is imposed—the prosecutor must furnish to the supervising judge "the names of all [personnel] to whom disclosure has been made." A related fourth condition also is aimed at deterring unauthorized disclosures—the grand jury prosecutor must certify that all personnel have been advised of their obligations of secrecy under Rule 6. Such advice is especially important for agents who come from agencies that do not regularly participate in grand jury investigations. The agents must be made aware that grand jury secrecy requirements go far beyond simply not making a public disclosure.

F. The Supervising Judge

Rule 6 assigns a variety of tasks to "the court" (i.e., the federal district court). Each district has its own system for assigning to a single judge the responsibility for executing those tasks and dealing with all other matters relating to the grand jury. That assignment may go to a single judge for all of the district's grand juries (e.g., the Chief Judge) or to a different judge for each grand jury. The assignment is commonly described as "grand jury supervision," with judicial opinions referring to the judge as the "supervising judge." Pursuant to the Magistrates Act,[24] the district may assign some of the functions of the supervising judge to a federal magistrate judge.

Rule 6 assigns to the court such functions as: impaneling the grand jury (including alternate jurors, at the court's discretion); selecting the foreperson and deputy foreperson; assigning such tasks as preserving the record of grand jury votes and retaining control of the recording of the grand jury proceedings; determining whether grand jury matter may be disclosed in the special situations listed in Rule 6(e)(3)(E);[25] discharging the grand jury prior to or at the end of its term; extending the grand jury's term as allowed under the Rule; and excusing a juror for "good cause." As to some of these functions, the Rule simply notes that there is discretion (the court "may" issue a particular order) and as to others, the Rule sets forth standards as to when particular action must be taken (although these standards may be open-ended—e.g., "when the public interest so requires").

Various statutes of general application identify further functions that will fall upon the supervising judge when those statues are applied in a grand jury setting. Thus, the supervising judge will determine whether an interpreter is needed when that request is made for a grand jury witness, and will determine whether statutorily specified procedures have been followed when a grand jury witness is given immunity by the prosecutor. Still other functions of the supervising judge are implicit in the Court's role in impaneling the grand jury. Thus, in the rare instance of disputes

---

[24] 28 U.S.C. § 636.

[25] In the instance of one type of disclosure, the ruling may not rest entirely with the supervisory judge. Under Rule 6(e)(3), when disclosure is sought to aid a party in litigation pending in another district, the petition for disclosure must be made in the district of the grand jury, but the supervising judge will then make a written evaluation of the need for secrecy and transfer the petition to the district of litigation (that court having a better basis for determining the need for disclosure as it relates to the pending litigation). Transfer is not required, however, where the supervising judge has enough information about the pending litigation to "reasonably determine whether disclosure is proper." See FEDGRJURY § 18.10.

between the prosecutor and the grand jury as to appropriate procedure, the supervising judge will often be asked to provide a resolution.[26] Another implicit function is providing juror orientation, which is fairly standard with every impanelment.

Grand jury orientation invariably includes a court charge to the grand jury, typically following either of two prominent model charges.[27] The charge covers such topics as the grand jury's functions, the structure of its operations, its powers (including its independent status), and the obligation of secrecy. In many districts the grand jurors are also given the *Handbook for Federal Grand Jurors*,[28] and asked to view a special orientation film. The *Handbook* is substantially longer than the typical charge, covering in more detail most of the same topics.

Undoubtedly, the most significant function of the supervising judge is to rule on all motions that relate to the grand jury. This includes motions directly addressing the grand jury proceedings (e.g., challenges to subpoenas), and motions for disclosure of grand jury information in connection with other proceedings. It encompasses motions made by witnesses, targets, and the prosecutor on behalf of the grand jury (e.g., directing a witness to answer a particular question or be held in contempt). Under Rule 6(e)(5), "subject to any right to an open hearing in a contempt proceeding, the court must close any hearing to the extent necessary to prevent disclosure of a matter occurring before the grand jury." Since the very subject of the investigation is protected under grand jury secrecy, certain types of objections (e.g., a subpoena challenge) will be entirely closed. When the motion presents an issue in a separate proceeding on which grand jury testimony will be one type of evidence, the motion hearing may be closed only as the discussion of that testimony. Since a description of the challenge to the grand jury proceeding may reveal the nature of the proceeding, the docket itself may be sealed, with the only public record being a generic notation that a grand jury related motion had been filed. The media's First Amendment right of access does not apply to grand jury related matters in light of the long history of grand jury secrecy.

G. Witness Objections to Structural Defects

Federal courts have recognized the right of indicted defendants to challenge indictments based on structural defects in the indicting grand jury (e.g., illegal composition of the grand jury, expiration of its term prior to indictment, violation of the Rule 6 limitation on persons who may be present during grand jury sessions, and participation as a prosecutor by a government attorney who does not qualify as a Rule 1 "attorney for the government"). A witness, however, is in a different situation. As

---

[26] As discussed in § 16.4(A)(B), where the disagreement relates to the use of a particular investigative power, there may well be little or no case law on the division of authority between the grand jury and the prosecutor. Also, the court's authority to impose its own preference under the judiciary's supervisory power is limited. See § 16.4(C). Thus, the judge may prefer to resolve disagreements informally, through mediation, rather than through a legal ruling.

[27] The Model Charge of the Benchbook for United States District Judges, § 7.04 (5th ed. 2007) (also described as the "Judicial Conference charge") is set forth in FEDGRJURY § 5:4. The charge recommended by the Administrative Office of the U.S. Courts is set forth in GRJURLAW § 4:5.

[28] The Handbook was prepared under the supervision of the Judicial Conference of the United States and is distributed by the Administrative Office. See http://www.mdd.uscourts.gov/jury/docs/federalgrand.pdf. It has been cited by federal courts as evidence of the grand jury's standard mode of operation on the premise that jurors follow its directives and suggestions.

discussed in § 16.12(B), the Supreme Court in *Blair v. United States*[29] held that a federal grand jury witness could not object to grand jury questioning on the ground that the subject of the inquiry could not be regulated by the federal government. The reasoning in *Blair* extended beyond subject matter challenges, as the Court emphasized that the witness subpoenaed by the grand jury had had the same "duty to appear and testify" as a witness subpoenaed to testify in court. Thus, "he is not entitled to urge objections of competency or irrelevancy, such as a party might raise, for this is no concern of his. . . . On familiar principles he is not entitled to challenge the authority of the court or the grand jury, provided they have a de facto existence and organization."

Blair has been read by lower courts as precluding witness challenges to various structural defects. Thus, a witness has been held to lack standing to challenge a subpoena based on the unconstitutional composition of the grand jury, and not simply because Rule 6 refers only to composition challenges by "a defendant." Such a challenge also is viewed inconsistent with the lesson of *Blair*—"that a grand jury need only be de facto, as to a witness, while it may be required to be de jure as to a person whom it indicts." Occasional federal court rulings have allowed a grand jury witness held in contempt for refusing to comply with a subpoena to raise the contention that compliance was not required because the participating prosecutor did not meet Rule 6 standards, but these rulings then rejected that contention on the merits, without considering the relevance of *Blair* as to standing.

§ 16.4 DIVISION OF AUTHORITY

A. Prosecution Authority

Federal prosecutors obviously play a dominant role in shaping federal grand jury investigations. They initially determine what part of an investigation will be assigned to law enforcement agencies and what part will depend upon use of the grand jury's investigative tools. They then determine who and what will be subpoenaed, question witnesses who testify before the grand jury, determine whether witnesses who assert the self-incrimination privilege will be granted immunity, and provide legal advice that shapes grand jury decision-making. Indeed, federal lower courts have observed that, "for all practical purposes," the grand jury is "an investigative arm . . . of the executive branch of government." Federal courts also have suggested, however, that this reality has very limited legal significance insofar as it stems from the grand jurors passively accepting the prosecutor's leadership,[30] rather than the prosecutor exercising a legal authority that overrides the grand jury's preferences. Although the caselaw is sparse, other sources suggest that a federal prosecutor acts subject to a potential grand jury

---

[29] 250 U.S. 273 (1919), also discussed in note 14 supra and § 16.12(B).

[30] Commentators offer various explanations as to why federal grand jurors would almost always be passive, both in accepting what the prosecution does in its use of the grand jury's investigative authority and failing to extend investigations beyond that use. One explanation is reliance upon prosecutorial expertise, particularly where the investigation involves a complex criminal scheme. Another is that grand jurors recognize that, without their own counsel or investigative staff, any attempt to move the investigation in another direction would not take it very far. Prosecutors also are seen as commonly developing a rapport with the grand jury which gives the prosecutor significant informal control over the process. It is suggested that prosecutors can readily lead the jurors to identify with the investigative effort by reviewing the investigative goals and strategy and explaining in particular why the grand jury's investigative authority is essential to uncovering the type of crime being investigated.

veto when using most elements of the grand jury's investigative process. Of course, a grand jury is most unlikely to exercise that veto (which might well require its seeking the assistance of the court), and that largely explains why the caselaw is sparse.

There clearly is no grand jury veto as to one significant investigative tool—the grant of immunity. Here the prosecutor clearly is the sole decisionmaker. (See § 19.5(E)). Beyond that, there are varying degrees of uncertainty as to whether typical actions taken by prosecutors must be accepted by the grand jury or could be overridden if the grand jury cared to exercise its full authority.

Rule 6(e)'s wording presents one area of ambiguity, although it arguably is best read as granting the prosecutor an absolute authority to be present during the grand jury session. Rule 6(e) lists "attorneys for the government" among these persons who "may be present," and the "may" could refer to either the prosecutor's discretion or the grand jury's discretion. Support for the former reading is found in both the *Grand Juror Handbook* and the two widely used model grand jury charges.[31] They refer to various roles of the prosecutor that require the prosecutor's presence, and in discussing the grand jury's authority, offer no suggestion that it could exclude the prosecutor (an authority that does exist in a few states).

The scope of the prosecutor's authority as the grand jury's "legal advisor," while not fully explored, is fairly clear in its major attributes. Courts have described the prosecutor's role here as extending beyond simply giving legal advice when the grand jury requests such advice. The prosecutor is free to dispense legal advice as particular issues arise in the course of the investigation (e.g., where a witness asserts a privilege not to testify). The grand jury ordinarily is told in the court's charge that the government's attorney "will provide you with important service in helping you find your way when confronted with complex legal matters," but it is not told that such legal advice must be taken as the final word. Indeed, the *Handbook* in one context notes that "a ruling [also] may be obtained from the court," and the two model charges both cite the grand jury's authority to put a question to the court. Thus, the grand jury apparently cannot prevent the prosecutor from presenting legal advice, but it certainly can seek a second opinion.

The prosecutor's authority to bring before the grand jury such the evidence as it selects is, perhaps, the critical ingredient in shaping the grand jury investigation, even though (as discussed in subsection B) the grand jury has the authority to call for additional evidence. As noted in § 16.5(A), the prosecutor in most federal districts may issue grand jury subpoenas without first gaining the approval of the grand jury. Courts have consistently upheld this practice, but in stating that advance approval is not necessary, they have not suggested that the prosecutor could issue a subpoena over the grand jury's objection. On the contrary, a few rulings suggest that the grand jury has the last word on subpoenas because it is the "party" for whom the subpoena is obtained under Rule 17. (See § 16.5(A)). Thus, the First Circuit held that, in light of the major intrusion upon liberty involved in being directed to appear in a lineup, that "directive has to come from the grand jury itself," rather than on petition of the prosecutor

---

[31] See notes 27 and 28 supra.

claiming to use the grand jury's subpoena authority.[32] So too, local rules in some districts provide that the prosecutor may not issue a grand jury subpoena without first obtaining approval of the grand jury foreperson on behalf of the grand jury. (See § 16.5(A)).

Although these sources indicate that a grand jury could direct the prosecutor not to use a subpoena to compel the attendance of a particular witness or to obtain certain documents, neither the *Handbook* nor the model judicial charges inform the grand jury of any such authority. On the contrary, the jurors are told that government attorney will "subpoena for testimony before you such witnesses as he may consider important and necessary," and that their first task is "hearing testimony and considering documentary evidence" as brought to their attention by the government attorney. The implicit message is that the government has the authority to produce such evidence as it chooses, although the grand jury can request additional evidence. Only in the instance of issuing a subpoena to the target of the investigation is the grand jury advised that its approval is needed. (See § 16.6(G)). If a witness refuses to comply with a subpoena, and a contempt sanction is sought from the court, the grand jury must furnish an affidavit evidencing the witness' non-compliance, but the issuance of that affidavit is not dependent on the grand jury first voting approval of the subpoena directed to that witness.

The *Handbook* and the model jury charges include directions on the questioning of witnesses that arguably suggest an automatic right of the prosecutor to question all witnesses—those produced by the prosecution and any additional witnesses requested by the grand jury. "Ordinarily," it is noted, "the attorney for the government questions the witness first," with any grand juror questions coming after that. The jurors are advised that the questions must be "relevant and proper," and that applies to the prosecutor's questions as well as the jurors' questions. The jurors are not told, however, to seek to stop prosecutorial questioning if they believe the prosecutor is exceeding these boundaries.

In many districts, the jurors are told that the prosecutor may screen their questions in advance to ensure that the questions are legally proper. One common prosecutorial practice is to ask the witness to leave the room, with the prosecutor then reviewing any questions the grand jurors desire to put forth. If a question would be improper (e.g., it would violate secrecy requirements by revealing the testimony of another witness), the prosecutor will then explain to the jurors why it cannot be asked. Grand jurors are informed, however, that if they are not satisfied by the prosecutor's reasoning, they may seek a ruling from the court. Although the grand juror can only be barred from asking a question because it would be legally improper, the prosecutor is free to call to a juror's attention tactical considerations that might advise against asking the particular question.

---

[32] See In re Melvin, 546 F.2d 1 (1st Cir. 1976). Other courts have rejected this special requirement. See CRIMPROC § 8.8(g). However, they have done so where the process would require a grand jury directive if the subpoenaed party so insisted. Here, the prosecution initiates a subpoena directing the individual to appear before the grand jury, where the grand jury will be asked to order the individual to provide an identification exemplar; however, the individual is told that there is no need to appear if he or she voluntarily provides the exemplar (e.g., a handwriting sample). See United States v. Smith, 687 F.2d 147 (6th Cir.1982).

B. Grand Jury Authority

Even if the federal grand jurors should lack authority to restrict the prosecutor in using the grand jury to obtain evidence, the grand jurors clearly have the authority to go beyond the prosecutor's presentation. Initially, as noted above, the grand jurors may ask further questions of witnesses. The grand jurors are informed of that authority in both the *Handbook* and commonly used model charges. Moreover, the DOJ in its Grand Jury Manual notes the investigative value of such questions (they often "aid the attorney") and their importance in keeping the grand jury interested and involved. Of course, prosecutors are urged to screen questioning to ensure that they are legally permissible, and that process, even if it does not discourage questioning by jurors, may limit the free flow of "follow-up" questions.

The grand jurors are also told, both in the *Handbook* and in the model jury charges, that they have the authority to call for additional witnesses. Thus, one model charge notes: "You alone decide how many witnesses you want to hear. You can subpoena witnesses from anywhere in the country, directing the United States Attorney to issue necessary subpoenas." In certain situations, the recommended practice is to ask the grand jury if it wishes to hear from a particular witness. For example, when a case agent summarizes statements obtained from interviewed persons or the grand jury is given a transcription of testimony given before a prior grand jury, the grand jurors are asked whether they would prefer to hear directly from those persons. So too, when an agent summarizes the content of subpoenaed documents, the grand jurors will be asked whether they would prefer to see the documents.

The grand jury's authority to call for additional witnesses most often is associated with developing more fully the evidence relating to the transactions that are the subject of the investigation initiated by the government. However, that authority extends to self-initiated investigations of related or unrelated transactions and jurors are so informed. The *Handbook* notes that the jurors' oath directs jurors "to inquire diligently and objectively into all federal crimes committed within the district of which they may have or may obtain evidence." It adds that the "matters may be brought to [the grand jury's] attention in three ways: (1) by [the attorney for the government]; (2) by the court that impaneled it; and (3) from the personal knowledge of a member of the grand jury or from matters properly brought to member's personal attention." This third source appears to draw on the Supreme Court's discussion of jury-initiated investigations in the *Hale v. Henkel*,[33] which relied on precedent going back to a time when crime victims and other aggrieved persons often directly contacted the grand jury, a practice no longer permitted in the federal system.[34] However "matters properly

---

[33] 201 U.S. 43 (1906), also discussed in note 13 supra and § 16.11(A) at note 139. *Hale* rejected the contention that the grand jury's right to subpoena witnesses was limited to situations in which a "specific charge [was] pending before the grand jury against any particular person." The Court noted that the traditional grand juror oath directs that jurors "diligently inquire" not only as to matters "given you in charge," but also as to matters "as shall come to your knowledge touching this present service." It cited Justice Wilson's comment that the "oath of the grand juryman assigns no limits except those marked by diligence itself to the course of [the jury's] inquiries." As Justice Caton similarly had noted, the grand jury had the authority to "send for witnesses" on its own initiative. The grand jury's authority to go beyond the specific cases brought to it also found support in the well-established principle that a presentment could be based upon a juror's personal knowledge.

[34] See note 11 supra. A limited route of access is guaranteed, however, for special grand juries. See § 16.3(A) and note 42 infra.

brought to a member's personal attention can also come from a variety of other sources (including, in particular, investigative reporting).

The model charge recommended by the Judicial Conference also informs the grand jury of its authority to initiate investigation. It does so, however, with a warning as to some practical limitations. After noting that some cases will be forwarded following an arrest and others will be proposed by the government's attorney, this charge states:

> Those are the two principal manners in which matters will be presented to you for investigation. However, if during the course of your hearings, a different crime other than the one you are investigating surfaces, you have the right to pursue this new crime. Although you can subpoena new witnesses and documents, you have no power to employ investigators or to expend federal funds for investigative purposed. If the United States Attorney refuses to assist you or if you believe he is not acting impartially, you may take it up with me or any Judge of this court. You may use this power even over the active opposition of the government's attorneys, if you believe it is necessary to do so in the interest of justice.

The charge notes the possibility of bringing to the court's attention a prosecutor's refusal to pursue a new line of investigation, but it quite appropriately does not suggest the court will be able to provide the grand jury with the investigative assistance that the prosecutor has refused to provide. A federal supervising judge, unlike judges in several states, may not appoint a special prosecutor (absent specific statutory authorization). At most, the judge may urge the government to reconsider its position.

The charge also does not address another practical limitation: even if a runaway grand jury could by itself uncover evidence sufficient to initiate a prosecution, the final decision on prosecuting belongs to the prosecutor, who may prevent a draft indictment approved by the grand jury from taking effect by refusing to sign that instrument. (See § 16.2(B)). Thus, not surprisingly, over the period since the adoption of the Federal Rules, and the rejection of prosecution by presentment, only a very few instances have come to light in which a federal grand jury took substantial steps to become a "runaway grand jury."

C. Judicial Authority: Supervisory Power

Federal courts clearly can apply constitutional guarantees, federal statues, and federal court rules to the grand jury process. To impose regulations or remedies that go beyond these sources, the federal courts must rely on what has been described as their "supervisory power." In the mid-1940s, the Supreme Court first described a federal court authority to establish decisional rules of criminal procedure in the exercise of the federal judiciary's "supervisory authority over the administration of criminal justice in the federal courts." The federal judiciary, the Court noted, has an obligation of "judicial supervision of the administration of criminal justice in the federal courts" and that allows it to impose remedies, regulations, and sanctions as needed to maintain "civilized standards of procedure and evidence in these courts." After several decades of supervisory authority rulings, the Court characterized its past supervisory rulings as directed at achieving one or the other of three purposes: "(1) to implement a remedy for violation of recognized rights [established apart from supervisory authority]"; (2) "to preserve judicial integrity by ensuring that a conviction rests on appropriate consideration valid before the jury'" and (3) "as a remedy designed to deter illegal conduct."[35]

The Supreme Court's supervisory power rulings focused on judicial proceedings that were part of the criminal justice process, although the rulings were not limited to the trial. Lower court rulings assumed that the grand jury process fit within this line of authority because of the grand jury's reliance on the district court's subpoena power. The Supreme Court, in a different context, had described the grand jury as "an appendage of the court, powerless to perform its investigative function without the court's aid, because powerless itself to compel the testimony of the witness." As an "arm of the court," the lower courts reasoned, the grand jury should be subject to a court's supervisory authority, as was the case for other steps in the criminal justice process that are dependent upon the court but not conducted before a judge (e.g., discovery). Several lower courts cited as an added justification for supervisory authority regulation that the courts "have an obligation to supervise [the prosecutor-grand jury] relationship if the grand jury's own role in the investigatory process is to remain at all meaningful." Both of these rationales were rejected by the Supreme Court in *United States v. Williams*.[36]

Most of the pre-*Williams* lower court rulings applying supervisory authority to grand jury proceedings involved challenges to indictments based on alleged unfairness in the grand jury's screening of the indictment's charges. However, the lower courts also relied on their supervisory authority to regulate grand jury investigations, usually upon a motion of a witness challenging a grand jury subpoena, but sometimes upon motions of other persons (e.g., the target of the investigation) relating to non-subpoena issues. Rulings supporting extensive use of the supervisory authority in these contexts included: a ruling directing the prosecutor to either present to the grand jury a private complaint's allegation of wrongdoing by government agents or allow the complainant's counsel to appear before the grand jury to present these allegations; a ruling requiring a preliminary government showing of legitimacy as a prerequisite for judicial enforcement of a subpoena; a ruling requiring the government to show compelling need for enforcement of a subpoena compelling an attorney to give testimony bearing on an attorney-client relationship; a ruling suppressing grand jury testimony based on the government attorney's failure to adhere to the standard practice of initially warning the witness of various rights (a practice that was required only by DOJ internal regulations); a ruling granting a motion for public disclosure of a portion of the grand jury transcript based on the "public interest" even though Rule 6 did not authorize disclosure.

In *Williams*, the lower court had relied on its supervisory authority over criminal justice to rule that (1) the prosecutor had an obligation to present before the grand jury known exculpatory evidence and (2) the failure to meet that obligation justified dismissal of the ensuing indictment. The Supreme Court held that the lower court could not impose a disclosure obligation under the federal courts' supervisory authority, and therefore the indictment could not be dismissed on that ground.[37] The

---

[35] United States v. Hasting, 461 U.S. 499 (1983), discussed (along with other supervisory power rulings) in CRIMPROC § 1.7(i).

[36] 504 U.S. 36 (1992).

[37] The DOJ's internal standards do require that, "when a prosecutor conducting a grand jury inquiry is personally aware of substantial evidence that directly negates the guilt of a subject of investigation, the

lower court had erred in viewing the grand jury setting as no different than a judicial proceeding in assessing the applicability of supervisory authority.

The *Williams* Court stressed that what was at issue here was the use of the supervisory authority to "fashion rules of grand jury procedure" based on the "judicial integrity" objective of that authority. This was not a case in which the supervisory power was used "as a means of enforcing or vindicating legally compelled standards of prosecutorial conduct before the grand jury," as such standards are established in a Federal Rule of Criminal Procedure or a statute. That use had been sustained in prior rulings, which sustained indictment dismissals implementing "those few clear rules which were carefully drafted and approved by this Court and by Congress to ensure the integrity of the grand jury's functions."[38] A federal court there was not invading the independence of the grand jury by prescribing the process it must follow, but simply utilizing the more limited supervisory authority to implement a remedy for violation of recognized rights.

The *Williams* opinion stressed the grand jury's "functional independence from the judicial branch"; "although the grand jury normally operates . . . under judicial auspices, its institutional relationship with the judicial branch has traditionally been, so to speak, at arm's length." For "the grand jury is a constitutional fixture in its own right"—"belong[ing] to no branch of the institutional government." Although an impaneling court had certain responsibilities, they were far too limited to provide a foundation for a "judicial supervisory power . . . [to] prescribe modes of grand jury procedure." Indeed, the Court noted, "we think it clear that, as a general matter at least, no such supervisory authority exists." A review of past precedents reinforced this conclusion. "These authorities," the Court noted, "suggest that any power federal courts may have to fashion, on their own initiative, rules of grand jury procedure is a very limited one, not remotely comparable to the power they maintain over their own proceedings."

The *Williams* Court dealt with a court's authority to prescribe a procedure viewed as protecting the grand jury's screening function, but the Court's discussion also encompassed the use of supervisory authority to regulate the grand jury's investigative function. The *Williams* opinion stressed the federal courts' traditional recognition of the grand jury's "functional independence" in its "power to investigate criminal wrongdoing." In noting that the Fifth Amendment establishes the grand jury as a "constitutional fixture in its own right, separate from the branches described in the

---

prosecutor must present or otherwise disclose such evidence to the grand jury before seeking an indictment against such a person." USAM § 9–5.001 (also noting that, since internal standards are not enforceable by the judiciary, the violation of this directive "should not result in the dismissal of an indictment"; but warning that "appellate courts may refer violations to the Office of Professional Responsibility for review," see note 4 supra).

[38] Thus the Court had indicated that a violation of Rule 6 requirements by the prosecutor could lead to dismissal of the ensuing indictment when that misconduct had a prejudicial impact upon the grand jury's approval of the indictment. It had also held, however, that the supervisory authority did not allow a federal court to override the provision of a federal statute or court rule in fashioning a means of implementing Rule 6. Accordingly, it could not dismiss an indictment without considering whether the government violation constituted harmless error as to issuance of the indictment, as the application of the harmless error standard was prescribed by statute and court rule. See Bank of Nova Scotia v. United States, 487 U.S. 250 (1988).

The reference to standards "approved by this Court and Congress" excludes local court rules. Therefore, that rule making authority cannot be used to fashion rules of grand jury procedure that would go beyond the supervisory authority recognized in *Williams*.

first three articles," the Court added that "the Fifth Amendment presupposes an investigative body 'acting independently of either prosecuting attorney or judge.'" This "tradition of independence," it noted, had lead the Supreme Court to "insist . . . that the grand jury remain free to pursue its investigations unhindered by external influence in supervision so long as it does not breach upon the legitimate rights of any witness called before it."

Post-*Williams* federal lower courts accordingly have concluded that there is a need to reexamine earlier rulings on the use of supervisory authority to control investigative procedures as well as the screening process. *United States v. Gillespie*[39] illustrates the post-*Williams* approach. The Seventh Circuit there refused to exercise its supervisory authority to suppress the testimony of a grand jury witness who had not been informed that he was a target of the investigation as required by DOJ internal guidelines. Since a target warning is not required by the constitution, a statute, or a court rule, and internal guidelines do not create judicially enforceable rights, the witness argued that the supervisory authority provided grounding for suppression as a means of ensuring uniform treatment of witnesses. The Seventh Circuit acknowledged that pre-*Williams* cases supported such a rationale, but concluded that the rationale could not be sustained after *Williams*. It noted that "*Williams* clearly circumscribes the application of that supervisory power to cases involving the violation of the Constitution, applicable statutes, and Federal Rules of Criminal Procedure." The requested ruling here would require the court to impose a procedural requirement not demanded by those sources. Many other (but not all) pre-*Williams* supervisory rulings have been abandoned under a similar analysis.[40] In some instances courts might hope to obtain similar results by advising grand juries of their authority to control the investigative process, rather than issuing judicial directives.[41]

D. Congressional Authority

Although the Court has described the Fifth Amendment as assuming that the federal grand jury has the investigative powers of the common law grand jury (see § 16.2(D)) and as establishing the grand jury as a "constitutional fixture in its own right" (*Williams*), it has never suggested that Congress cannot reshape the grand jury

---

[39] 974 F.2d 796 (7th Cir. 1992).

[40] In some instances, lower courts have had no occasion to return to these rulings. In others, the courts have turned to a statute or court rule as the source for imposing a restriction "similar to that formerly applied under the judiciary's supervisory authority." (See § 16.12(A)).

[41] *Williams*, while stressing grand jury independence, did not suggest that a federal supervising court would invade that independence by offering no more than an opportunity to the grand jury. Thus, while a court post-*Williams* could not insist that the grand jury be given evidence offered by a private complainant, it could advise the grand jury of its option to hear from that witness if it so chooses. Courts that issued supervisory authority directives pre-*Williams* might readily turn to advising the grand jury of its authority to prohibit the prosecutorial practices that the court formerly proscribed.

At common law, courts sometimes directed the grand jury to investigate a particular matter. Despite its historical foundation, such a directive would appear to be contrary to *Williams*. That would not preclude the court from advancing a suggestion as to a possible investigation. That course was followed in the initiation of one of the most preeminent grand jury investigations—the "Watergate investigation," which eventually led to the resignation of a president. Following the conviction of the Watergate burglars, the trial judge stated publicly that there was need for a "grand jury follow-up" and that he had called to the prosecutor's attention the names of "several persons" (presumably government officials) who should be called to testify before the grand jury. The prosecutor subsequently announced that the grand jury would move on to consider high-level involvement, but a Special Prosecutor, utilizing a new grand jury, subsequently took over the investigation.

process by statute or federal court rule (the adoption of these rules being subject to Congressional veto), provided there is no invasion of the constitutionally guaranteed screening role of the grand jury. Thus, the presentment has been eliminated (see § 16.2(C)), and secrecy requirements have been altered (see § 16.9(B)).

During the 1970s the DOJ's use of the grand jury was sharply criticized, in part because of investigations of the alleged criminal activities of "radicals." A variety of reforms were proposed, both by legislators and professional associations (most notably, the ABA). In general, those reforms were aimed at bolstering the protections offered witnesses, strengthening grand jury independence by demanding more involvement of the jurors in the use of investigative authority, and expanding the authority of the judiciary in supervising grand jury proceedings. Many such reforms were adopted by states; roughly twenty states, for example, enacted statutes allowing at least some grand jury witnesses to be accompanied by their attorneys in the grand jury room. In Congress, however, although reform legislation has been introduced over and over again, those proposals have never come close to passage.[42] Change has come primarily through the Justice Department, which has adopted several measures protective of witnesses as internal policy, and has increased juror participation in limited areas of investigative decisionmaking.

§ 16.5 GRAND JURY SUBPOENAS

A. Federal Rule 17

As noted in § 16.4(C), a grand jury obtains evidence through the process of the court, not its own process. "Grand jury subpoenas" are subpoenas of the district court, issued under Rule 17 of the Federal Rules of Criminal Procedure. Rule 17 authorizes subpoenas for a variety of proceedings relating to the criminal justice process, including trials, motion hearings, and depositions, as well as grand jury proceedings. Paragraph (a) of Rule 17 sets forth the basic requirements for a subpoena ad testificandum, which orders a witness to appear and testify. It directs the clerk of the court to issue such subpoenas "in blank to the party requesting it." That party then must fill in the blanks prior to service—specifying first the name of the person who is "commanded to attend and give testimony"; second the time and place of attendance; and third, the identification of the proceeding (since a grand jury proceeding has no title, unlike a filed case, the direction here simply is to give testimony "before the grand jury"). Paragraph (c) of Rule 17 authorizes the issuance of the subpoena duces tecum, stating that a subpoena "may also command the person to whom it is directed to produce the books, papers, documents, data, or other objects designated therein." The "may also" reference is not read as requiring a subpoena duces tecum to command the person served to both testify and produce the designated items. The subpoena may combine both these directives or simply direct production.

Rule 17 directs issuance of the blank subpoena to "the party requesting it," and the party here is the grand jury, not the prosecutor. However, the practice in most federal districts is for the prosecutor to obtain the blank subpoenas and to fill them out

---

[42] The statute on special grand juries included elements that strengthened the role of the jurors—it ensured that the jurors were made aware of information received from third persons and provided for a grand jury report that is not subject to veto by the prosecutor. However, this legislation was adopted prior to the initiation of the reform movement, and its changes were never extended to the Rule 6 grand juries.

and have them served without first consulting the grand jury. Indeed, in some instances, advance consultation would be impossible because the prosecutor, recognizing that it will take some time to assemble the documents identified in a subpoena duces tecum, will have the subpoena served before the grand jury is impaneled (although the directed return will be when the grand jury is sitting). Thus, prosecutors determine *sua sponte* who will be subpoenaed, what documents will be demanded, and the timing and order of both witness' testimony and the required return of documents.[43]

In some districts, by local rule, the foreperson must initial a copy of each subpoena, signifying that the grand jury has been notified of its issuance. In others, the grand jury must issue an authorization, allowing the prosecutor to obtain and direct subpoenas on its behalf. As noted in § 16.3(A), these practices and a few lower court rulings suggest that a grand jury has the authority to restrict the prosecutor's use of Rule 17 subpoenas (if it so desires).[44] However, the impaneling judge's instructions to the grand jury do not refer to any such authority, and, indeed, suggest that the grand jury has a responsibility to hear whatever evidence the prosecution might desire to produce. Thus, in all districts the grand jury is likely to shape the use of the subpoena power only to the extent that it insists upon hearing additional witnesses—an authority clearly noted in the court's instructions. While grand jury investigations often involve a second (and successive) rounds of subpoenas after the initial group of witnesses have testified, no publicly available record will reveal whether any of these additional witnesses were called at the request of the grand jury.

B. Service of the Subpoena

A Rule 17 subpoena must be personally served on the natural person named in the subpoena or personally served on the agent of an entity named in the subpoena.[45] Rule 17 allows for service "by the marshal, by a deputy, or by any other [adult] person who is not a party." In some districts, the court by local rule will require that service be made by the marshal or deputy marshal. When the prosecutor has a choice, service by the case agent is often preferred as the interaction in serving the subpoena might create an excellent opportunity for interviewing the prospective witness.[46]

Rule 17(e) provides for personal service "at any place within the United States." Location is the key, not residence nor citizenship. A foreign national may be served

---

[43] Under the DOJ's internal guidelines, as set forth in the United States Attorney's manual, some of these decisions, under circumstances, require the prior approval of Main Justice or the United States Attorney. See USAM § 9–2.400 (prior approval chart). So too, if the prosecutor seeks to subpoena the target, the grand jury must agree in advance. (See § 16.6(D)).

[44] As noted in the Grand Jury Practice Manual, § 4.14, grand jurors are usually informed of forthcoming investigative steps, including the subpoenas that have been issued and their expected return date. Thus the opportunity to impose restraints often would be available even after the subpoenas have issued.

[45] The individual or entity can agree to have service made through counsel, and that often occurs in white collar investigations. Not infrequently, after an entity has been served, counsel for the entity will request that service for all entity employees be made through counsel. The government need not accept such a request and will not do so where the directly served employee might not want to inform counsel.

[46] The prosecutor can fill in the blank subpoena as the legal advisor to the grand jury. The same is not true of federal agents, even though they are grand jury "personnel." (See § 16.3(E)). Thus the prosecutor may not give blank subpoenas to federal agents and have them fill in the names as they choose (e.g., using the subpoena only after the individual has refused to be interviewed). (See also § 16.12(F)).

even though his or her presence is fleeting (e.g., an airport stopover in the course of international travel). Since grand jury witnesses receive witness fees, which include reimbursement for travel, the witness cannot challenge the subpoena because it will require attendance in a district quite distant from his or her residence.

For a subpoena duces tecum, the witness must have access to the items to be produced. These items need not be the individual's personal property. It is sufficient that the items are in the custody of the person, even if that is informal (de facto) custody rather than official custody. Where entity records are sought, and the custodian of the records is known, the subpoena is often addressed to that person. However, the subpoena can also be addressed to the entity, in which case service may be made on any officer or managing or general agent of the entity (or where state law so provides, on the Secretary of State of the state in which the entity is doing business).

When the prosecutor seeks the testimony of a person located abroad, or seeks the production of records located abroad, use of the Rule 17 subpoena authority becomes problematic. The special considerations presented when seeking evidence located in a foreign country include the potential for being viewed as offending the sovereignty of that nation and the presence of special agreements with individual countries. Accordingly, DOJ internal guidelines require consultation with the DOJ Office of International Affairs prior to attempting to use a grand jury subpoena to obtain such evidence.

Rule 17(e) states that when the potential witness "is in a foreign country, 28 US.C. § 1783 governs the subpoena's service." That section (known as the Walsh Act) authorizes service in a foreign country "on a national or resident of the United States," but only pursuant to a court order. The term "national" refers to both U.S. citizens and other persons who "owe permanent allegiance to the United States," while "resident" refers to a permanent resident alien. Foreign laws may restrict § 1783 service, particularly when the individual is also a citizen of that country. Where § 1783 is not available, an individual's testimony can be sought through letters rogatory (a request for judicial assistance issued by a U.S. court to the foreign judiciary pursuant to 28 U.S.C. § 1781) or a Mutual Legal Assistance Treaty (where one exists with the particular country). A major obstacle in either case is the need to reveal the basis for the investigation and the relevance of the prospective witness' testimony, which may require the disclosure of grand jury matter, limited by Rule 6. (See § 16.9(E)).

Records located abroad are most readily obtained if the entity possessing the records also has a presence in the United States (e.g., a subsidiary or branch). Federal judicial authority clearly extends to U.S. companies having documents in overseas offices or affiliates, and can also include foreign companies that have a presence in this country. Subpoenas in the latter situation are commonly known as *Bank of Nova Scotia* subpoenas because of their use in an investigation involving that bank. The subpoenas there were enforced even though the Canadian Bank claimed that production of records held in its Grand Cayman Branch would violate the Cayman Islands' bank secrecy law.[47] A foreign nation, however, may not allow the foreign

---

[47] See In re Grand Jury Proceedings (Bank of Nova Scotia), 740 F.2d 817 (11th Cir. 1984), discussed in USAM, Title 9 (Criminal Resource Manual) § 279 (along with other lower court rulings suggesting limitations on the availability of such subpoenas).

holder of the records to respond to the subpoena where disclosure is prohibited by that nation's "blocking statutes." In some instances, a grand jury investigation may be able to avoid application of such a statute through a "consent directive." Here, a subpoenaed person or entity is directed by the grand jury to inform the holder of his records that consent is thereby given, pursuant to the grand jury's order, to disclosure of these records. (See § 19.1(E)). The foreign nation then determines whether that consent will be sufficient under its laws.

C. Advice of Rights

The Rule 17 subpoena simply directs the witness to appear before a grand jury. The federal courts have never held that the witness needs to be given any information as to the subject of the grand jury's inquiry. As discussed in § 19.3(B), the Supreme Court plurality opinion in *United States v. Mandujano*[48] held that a grand jury witness, even if a "putative defendant," is not entitled constitutionally to receive "*Miranda* warnings," and that plurality ruling subsequently has been viewed as binding precedent. The plurality similarly concluded that the witness did not have a Sixth Amendment right to counsel, and that plurality ruling also has been viewed as binding precedent. (See § 16.8(A)). While *Mandujano* had no need to consider whether a grand jury witness must be advised of his right to exercise the privilege against self-incrimination, its reasoning suggested that such advice was not constitutionally required. (See § 19.3(B)). However, the DOJ, in USAM § 9–11.151, sets forth a requirement of notification as to these matters, "notwithstanding the lack of a clear constitutional imperative to do so." USAM § 9–11.151 provides that "an Advice of Rights" form shall be appended to all grand jury subpoenas to be served on any 'target' or 'subject' of an *investigation*."[49] It then sets forth the precise content of that "Advice of Rights" form:

> [A] The grand jury is conducting an investigation of possible violations of Federal criminal laws involving: (state here the general subject matter of inquiry, e.g., conducting an illegal gambling business in violation of 18 U.S.C. § 1955.)[50]

> [B] You may refuse to answer any question if a truthful answer to the question would tend to incriminate you.

> [C] Anything that you do say may be used against you by the grand jury or in a subsequent legal proceeding.

> [D] If you have retained counsel, the grand jury will permit you a reasonable opportunity to step outside the grand jury room to consult with counsel if you so desire.

USAM § 9–11.151 also provides definitions for the two categories of witnesses who must receive this notification, not only in the attachment to the subpoena, but by the

---

[48] 425 U.S. 564 (1976).

[49] USAM § 9–11.151 adds that if a district court "insists that the notice of rights not be appended to a grand jury subpoena the advice of rights may be set forth in a separate letter and mailed to or handed to the witness when the subpoena is served."

[50] Although this illustration refers to a specific statutory provision, other DOJ manuals offer as acceptable a reference to the generic character of the offenses (e.g., "tax offenses") or the general nature of the transaction being investigated (e.g., "zoning in Baltimore").

prosecutor addressing the witness prior to the witness' testimony (with "the witness . . . asked to affirm that the witness understands") A "target" is "a person to whom the prosecutor or the grand jury has substantial evidence linking him or her to the commission of the crime and who, in the judgment of the prosecutor, is a putative defendant." A "subject of an investigation" is "a person whose conduct is within the scope of the investigation." For the purposes of the advice-of-rights requirement, the distinction between a subject and a target has no significance, as the advice is required for both. However, as discussed in § 16.6(G), the distinction is important under other internal standards that require additional warnings for the target and also restrict calling a target as a witness.

Certain witnesses commonly called to testify in grand jury investigations of white collar crimes clearly are not subjects—e.g., government agents and experts. USAM § 9–11.151 notes that "an officer or employee of an organization which is a target is not automatically considered a target even if such officer's or employee's conduct contributed to the commission of the crime." Such persons, however, would clearly be subjects. Only an employee far removed from the transaction (e.g., an employee who will simply testify as to organizational record-keeping) could clearly be classified as a "mere witness" (i.e., a witness who is not a subject or target.)

The advice of rights refers in items [b]–[d] to rights that may be exercised by a testifying witness. Yet USAM § 9–11.151 refers to subpoenas generally, drawing no distinction between a subpoena ad testificandum and a subpoena duces tecum. The explanation of the term "target" notes that organizations (who would receive only subpoenas duces tecum) do not automatically constitute targets simply because they employ or employed persons who are targets. In light of the broad scope of corporate criminal liability, (see § 2.1(A)), corporations in that position often would constitute targets, but if not, they almost certainly would be subjects. Subpoenas duces tecum directed to third-party service providers (see § 26.7(F)), on the other hand, would be viewed as directed to a subject only under unusual circumstances.

Like other DOJ internal policies, the standards on advice of rights do not create rights that are enforceable against the government. Therefore, if prosecutors fail to provide advice of rights in a particular case, that failure does not provide a basis for a court to dismiss an indictment or grant other relief.[51] However, providing the advice is so easily accomplished, and so unlikely to have a bearing on the response of witnesses in white collar cases, that there would appear to be no incentive for prosecutors to read narrowly, or ignore, the notice requirement.

D. Witness Challenges

Rule 17(c), which authorizes the issuance of a subpoena duces tecum, recognizes the subpoenaed person's right to challenge the subpoena by a motion to quash. Rule 17 contains no similar provision recognizing a motion to quash a subpoena ad testificandum, but federal courts have entertained such motions. Rarely, however, will a witness subpoenaed to testify have standing to challenge the obligation to appear, as opposed to challenging individual questions asked of the witness.[52] The most common

---

[51] See the discussion of United States v. Gillespie at note 39 supra.

[52] Perhaps the most prominent exception is the "chilling impact" objection discussed in § 16.12(E), and even there, the availability of the objection may depend on the line of questioning.

witness objection is a claim of evidentiary privilege (see § 16.9(B)) and that claim almost always has to be directed at specific questions. A challenge to the order to appear could be based on a structural defect that deprives the grand jury of its authority to utilize the Rule 17 subpoena, but, as noted in § 16.3(G), witnesses generally lack standing to raise such objections.

Court rulings on challenges by witnesses subpoenaed to testify accordingly will involve two preliminary steps. First the witness will assert the objection to a particular question or line of questioning. Second, that objection will be rejected by the foreperson (on advice of the prosecutor), and when the witness persists, the prosecutor will file a motion in the district court to compel the witness to answer the questions at issue. For the subpoena duces tecum, in contrast, the court ruling will come on the subpoenaed person's motion to quash or modify the subpoena. In either setting, should the court rule against the government, it has a right to appeal, as established by 18 U.S.C. § 3731. On the other hand, should the ruling favor the government, the witness will not be able to appeal, as the court's order will not constitute a "final judgment" under the general statute allowing appeals only from such judgments, 28 U.S.C. § 1291.[53]

Final judgments encompass "collateral orders," but the Supreme Court has rejected the contention that grand jury orders should be viewed as such orders, and thereby treated as independent of the criminal process. In the leading case, *Cobbledick v. United States*,[54] the Supreme Court held that the denial of a witness' motion to quash a grand jury subpoena was not appealable. The Court distinguished the proceeding to enforce an administrative subpoena, which is commonly regarded as an independent action for agency discovery (see § 17.4(A)), thereby rendering orders granting an agency subpoena final and appealable. The ongoing grand jury proceeding, *Cobbledick* noted, was instead part of the ongoing prosecution:

> The proceeding before a grand jury constitutes "a judicial inquiry" . . . of the most ancient lineage. The duration of its life, frequently short, is limited by statute. It is no less important to safeguard against undue interruption the inquiry instituted by a grand jury than to protect from delay the progress of the trial after an indictment has been found. . . . That a grand jury proceeding has no defined litigants and that none may emerge from it, is irrelevant to the issue.

The *Cobbledick* Court did recognize one avenue for appeal by a grand jury witness. In the context of a trial, the Court had held that the rejection of a witness' objection to a subpoena was not a final order. To gain appellate review, the witness had to refuse to comply and be held in contempt, which did produce a final order. The same requirement, *Cobbledick* held, was applicable to the grand jury witness. If the witness "chooses to disobey and is held in contempt," an immediate appeal will be allowed. That appeal "may involve an interruption of . . . the investigation," but allowing it is essential to preserve the witness' rights. "[N]ot to allow this interruption," the Court reasoned, "would forever preclude review of the witness' claim, for his alternatives are to abandon the claim or languish in jail." Accordingly, once held in contempt, the "witness' situation becomes so severed from the main proceeding as to permit an appeal."

---

[53] See CRIMPROC § 27.2, especially § 27.2(e), which discusses the various rulings noted below.
[54] 309 U.S. 323 (1940).

The witness whose objection has been rejected can readily have second thoughts as to standing in contempt in order to pursue an appeal. As discussed in § 16.5(E), the contempt order will be civil rather than criminal. Thus, should the witness lose on appeal, subsequent compliance with the grand jury subpoena will relieve the witness of any further sanctions. However, the now adjudicated contemnor has no assurance that the imposition of contempt sanctions will be stayed pending the appeal. The governing statutory provision, 28 U.S.C. § 1826(a), provides: "Whenever a witness in any proceeding before . . . any grand jury of the United States refuses without just cause to comply with an order of the court . . . , the court . . . may summarily order his confinement." Indeed, § 1826(b) notes that "no person confined pursuant to subsection (a) of this section shall be admitted to bail pending the determination of an appeal taken by him from the order of confinement if it appears that the appeal is frivolous or taken for delay." Where the contemnor is held in confinement pending appeal, § 1826(b) requires that the appeal be expedited, with its disposition coming "no later than thirty days from the filing of such appeal." Hence, the price for pursuing an appeal may be incarceration for thirty days.

The Supreme Court has recognized an exception to the contempt prerequisite which occasionally applies in the white collar context. That exception rests on a court order of disclosure in a grand jury proceeding producing the possible invasion of the protected interest of a third party (typically the target of the investigation) and the subpoenaed party having no substantial interest in challenging the order and therefore not likely to be willing to stand in contempt. This exception was established in *Perlman v. United States*,[55] and is commonly known as the *"Perlman* exception." In *Perlman,* the clerk of a federal court was directed to produce before a grand jury documents that Perlman had deposited with the clerk in connection with a patent infringement suit. Claiming a continuing right to those documents, Perlman challenged the order directed to the clerk and subsequently appealed form the denial of that challenge. As the Supreme Court later explained, Perlman's appeal was allowed without the subpoenaed witness (the clerk) meeting the contempt prerequisite of *Cobbledick* because the witness did not share Perlman's interest in challenging the order. Without immediate review, Perlman would have been "powerless to avert the mischief of the [challenged] order."

In *Perlman,* the intervenor and the witness were total strangers, but the *Perlman* exception is not so limited. Lower courts have applied the exception to a variety of situations in which the relationship between the party subpoenaed and the intervenor produces no similarity of interests. Thus, appeals have been allowed from orders denying an appellant's motion to quash subpoenas directing her treating physician to turn over her medical records, an order denying a bank depositor's motion to quash a grand jury subpoena issued to his bank, and an order denying a record custodian's motion to quash a subpoena issued to a corporation. In addition, employers have been allowed to appeal orders denying their motions to quash grand jury subpoenas issued to employees, and clients have been permitted to appeal orders denying their motions to quash subpoenas issued to their attorneys. The latter two situations, however, have produced conflicting decisions among the lower courts. A minority continue to insist that *Perlman* ordinarily should not apply, because lawyers can be expected to submit to

---

[55] 247 U.S. 7(1918).

contempt in order to preserve the right to appeal for their clients, as can employees for their employers.

E. Enforcement by Contempt

Rule 17(g) provides that a federal district court judge or magistrate can hold "in contempt a witness who, without adequate excuse, disobeys a subpoena" issued, respectively, by the federal district court judge or the magistrate. This provision is viewed as restating the previously recognized inherent authority of a federal court to hold in contempt a person who violates an order of the court without justification. As such, it recognizes the use of both civil and criminal contempt. Civil contempt is used to coerce into compliance the subpoenaed person who refuses to obey with the subpoena directive (either as to producing items or testifying). The witness is sentenced to incarceration or a fine (which may increase daily), but she may purge herself by subsequently complying with the subpoena's directive. It is said that the contemnor "carries the key of the prison in his own pockets," as compliance lifts the sanction. Criminal contempt will also result in incarceration or a fine, but here the court is imposing punishment for the violation of its order in the same manner in which punishment is imposed for violating a criminal statute. The object of the sentence in criminal contempt is "not remedial, and for the benefit of the complainant [the grand jury]," but "punitive, to vindicate the authority of the court."

Rule 17(g) does not suggest how the choice between civil and criminal contempt should be made. In *Shillitani v. United States*,[56] the Court commented that the judge should "first consider the feasibility of coercing testimony through the imposition of civil contempt" and should only resort to criminal contempt "after he determines . . . that the civil remedy would be inappropriate." Where an investigation is ongoing, the DOJ recommends, "as a prudential matter," that the prosecutor initially seek to gain compliance through the use of civil contempt and turn to criminal contempt only where the disobedience continues.

Civil contempt is governed by the "Recalcitrant Witness" statute, 28 U.S.C. § 1826, as well as Rule 17(g). Under that statute, "whenever a witness in any proceeding before . . . any . . . grand jury of the United States refuses without just cause shown to comply with an order of the court to testify or provide other information [covered by a subpoena duces tecum] . . . , the court . . . may summarily order his confinement at a suitable place until such time as the witness is willing to give such testimony or provide such information." The statute adds that "no such period of confinement shall exceed the life of . . . the term of the grand jury, including extensions, before which such refusal to comply with the court order occurred, but in no event shall such confinement exceed eighteen months."

Section 1826 differs from Rule 17(g) in its description of the justification that will excuse the failure to obey—prohibiting refusing without "just cause" rather than disobeying "without adequate excuse." However, both provisions appear to accept only such justifications as had previously been recognized in the application of the court's inherent authority. In white collar cases, these will be claims of privilege, inability to

---

[56] 384 U.S. 364 (1966).

comply (e.g., lack of custody or existence as to subpoenaed documents), or the invalidity of the subpoena.

Section 1826 requires that the contempt finding be based on "a failure to comply with an order of the court." The reference here is to a direct order of the court to do a particular act under the subpoena, not the directive stated in the subpoena or a directive of the grand jury. As noted in § 16.5(D), a witness challenging a subpoena duces tecum will move to quash, and where a witness compelled to testify refuses to provide testimony, the prosecutor will file a motion to compel the testimony. At the hearing on these motions, the witness will be expected to raise any justification that would constitute "just cause" or "adequate excuse" for noncompliance. If the court rules in favor of the government, that directive to the witness will constitute the court order required under § 1826. If the witness refuses to comply, the prosecutor will move to show cause as to why the witness should not be held in contempt. At the hearing on the motion, the prosecutor will have to prove that the witness did not comply, which commonly is achieved thought the affidavit or testimony of the foreperson. The witness must be given the opportunity to respond, but since the validity of the subpoena or directive to answer was litigated on the previous motion, there will be little to add. An exception will be the instance in which the contempt consists of a witness' failure to answer a question by falsely stating, "I don't recall." Here, the government must show purposeful evasion. While such evasion also constitutes perjury, the government might prefer civil contempt in the hope that the ability to purge the civil sanction will convince the witness to acknowledge that she does recall (and to answer the question).

Section 1826 clearly alters the previous use of inherent authority by capping incarceration at eighteen months even though the grand jury remains in session.[57] Eighteen months falls short of the longest term for either a regular or special grand jury (see § 16.3(A)). Section 1826 does not clearly indicate whether the eighteen months is an absolute limit or if the period is renewed each time the government calls the witness before a new grand jury. The few courts to address that issue have construed § 1826 to be setting an absolute limit.

Where a prosecutor anticipates that a subpoenaed witness will stand in contempt and continue to refuse to comply after losing an appeal, care will be taken to avoid requiring an appearance before a grand jury that is late in its term. That becomes a particular concern because of an internal policy. Although *Shillitani* noted the possibility of calling a contumacious witness before successive grand juries, USAM § 9–11.160 announces a "policy . . . generally not to resubpoena a contumacious witness before successive grand juries for the purpose of instituting further contempt proceedings." Prior authorization for resubpoenaing requires approval from Main Justice. The policy notes that "resubpoenaing . . . may be justified . . . when the questions to be asked . . . relate to matters not covered in the previous proceedings," where there is an indication that the witness is now willing to testify, or "the prosecutor believes that the witness possesses information essential to the investigation [and] . . . himself or herself is involved to a significant degree in the

---

[57] Section 1826 does not refer to imposing a fine, but that omission is read as indicating only that Congress did not intend to alter the inherent power to use coercive fines, in contrast to the limit it imposed on incarceration. Where the subpoenaed party is an entity, a fine is the standard coercive sanction, since incarceration is not available. Courts typically utilize a per diem fine, and since the 18–month limitation refers only to incarceration, the fine presumably can continue for the full term of the grand jury.

criminality about which the witness can testify." Where the resubpoenaed witness was incarcerated for a substantial period of time on the first contempt citation, the defense will almost certainly challenge a second civil commitment on the ground that is actually a punitive measure (requiring criminal contempt) because the prior commitment has shown that incarceration will not have a coercive effect. By combining its internal policy with resubpoenaing only where the witness is at least several months away from the eighteen month absolute limit the DOJ has created a significant obstacle for judicial acceptance of that argument.

The imposition of sanctions for civil contempt does not bar a subsequent action for criminal contempt based in the witness' refusal to obey the same subpoena.[58] Double Jeopardy does not apply because the first sanction was not criminal. Criminal contempt proceedings are governed by Rule 42 of the Federal Rules of Criminal Procedure. Since the contempt by the grand jury witness occurs before the grand jury, the authorization of a summary contempt sanction does not apply. There is no statutorily set maximum penalty for this offense and the sentence may be substantially longer than eighteen months. However, if the government seeks a sentence longer than six months, the constitutional right to jury trial applies. The defense will certainly suggest that the previous commitment constituted a sufficient sanction, and while that is not a defense, the required measure of "willfulness" (although it does not demand "malice" or "bad intent") may provide the petit jury a convenient vehicle for nullification.

§ 16.6 OBTAINING WITNESS TESTIMONY

A. Identifying Potential Witnesses

Ordinarily, the investigation by a federal enforcement agency that occurs prior to the institution of a grand jury investigation will have identified various potential grand jury witnesses. The grand jury investigation itself will then add others. Documents subpoenaed as possible evidence (e.g., communications and reports) will often identify other participants previously unknown. Moreover, subpoenas often require the production of documents sought not as evidence of a possible crime, but to identify persons who might be potential witnesses by virtue of their position in the entity under investigation.[59]

Witnesses can also be asked questions aimed only at finding other witnesses, and those questions can go beyond their personal knowledge. Since the rules of evidence do

---

[58] The criminal contempt statute, 18 U.S.C. § 401, applies to "disobedience or resistance" to the court's order. It therefore is broad enough to encompass various acts of obstruction of justice (e.g., the destruction of subpoenaed documents). (See § 6.2(D)). However, in the grand jury setting, prosecutions typically are brought under an obstruction provision, as the Rule 42 summary contempt process, which offers advantages over the standard criminal justice process, does not apply to contempt before the grand jury or actions such as document destruction. See *Harris v. United States* 382 U.S. 162 (1965).

[59] Thus, the Antitrust Division's Manual, note 5 supra, cites the following document demand aimed at identifying persons with potentially relevant information: "Such documents as will show the full name, current home and business addresses and telephone numbers, date of birth, social security number, the account number of each Company credit card, positions, dates of service in each position, duties and responsibilities in each position, annual salary and bonuses, termination date, if applicable, and other reasons for such termination of each officer, employee or other representative of the Company whose duties and responsibilities have related, in whole or in part, to the marketing, pricing, sale or distribution of [___] products."

not apply to grand jury proceedings, witnesses can be asked about general rumors or specific "office gossip." Employees can be asked to speculate based on their experience as to which fellow employees might possibly have knowledge of particular transactions. Since investigators need no particular grounding (not even reasonable suspicion) to request an interview, they can readily follow-up on such information. If the individual declines to be interviewed, he or she can be subpoenaed, as no particular grounding is needed to issue a grand jury subpoena. While courts speak of the grand jury's authority to conduct "fishing expeditions" primarily with respect to subpoenas duces tecum, that authority also applies to subpoenaing witnesses. (See § 16.11(C)).[60] The primary limitation is the potential for wasting grand jury sessions on witnesses who have nothing valuable to add—a hazard that often is reduced through the use of pre-testimony office interviews.

B. Office Interviews

Federal courts frequently have noted that a federal prosecutor cannot use a grand jury subpoena to summon a witness to the prosecutor's office for interrogation. At the same time, federal prosecutors may offer the subpoenaed witness the opportunity to be interviewed in advance of his or her testimony. Prosecutors offer three incentives for accepting such an "invitation." First, the witness may be accompanied by counsel. Second, the witness will receive advance notice of the topics to be covered in the testimony and may be shown documents about which questions will be asked. Third, the interview may reveal all the information the prosecutor needs, or may establish that the witness has no relevant knowledge, leading to a decision not to have the witness testify.

These advantages convince many witnesses to agree to (or even to ask for) a pre-testifying office interview. The interview provides a much better opportunity for counsel to gain an understanding of the investigation (and the witness' role) than utilizing the opportunity for anteroom consultations allowed during the course of the witness testifying. (See § 16.8(C)). Potential mistaken testimony can be avoided as the witness will have more time to review relevant documents (and otherwise refresh her recollection) than is likely to be available while giving testimony, and that review will occur without the added pressure provided by the grand jury's presence. The interviewed witness also often will be more comfortable when later giving testimony. One concern of the witness may be losing the protection of grand jury secrecy that covers testimony, as the lower courts are divided on whether the government's record

---

[60] Where there is concern that the potential witness will leave the country to avoid testifying (e.g., where the person is a foreign national who does not reside in this country), the steps needed to ensure that the testimony is obtained may require more. Under 18 U.S.C. § 3144, the individual may be arrested as a material witness, as the material witness statutes applies to a "criminal proceeding," which includes a grand jury investigation. See CRMPROC § 12.4(g). However this statute requires a showing "that the testimony of [the] person is material," with a probable cause standard applied to that determination.

Another means of ensuring that the witness appears is the "forthwith subpoena." Here, the date of appearance is not set at a convenient time in the future, but instead requires the witness to appear within the hour after being served. Forthwith subpoenas are discussed in § 16.11(D). If the agents serving the subpoena ad testificandum in effect execute a seizure of the person, a Fourth Amendment grounding will be required. The key will be whether the subpoenaed person is given the opportunity to consult with a lawyer and bring a court challenge before the required appearance.

To use either the material witness arrest or the forthwith subpoena, the prosecutor must establish a significant likelihood of flight. One obstacle here is establishing why a person who does not want to testify would choose flight over exercising the self-incrimination privilege.

of the substance of the pre-testimony interview is protected under Rule 6 as "grand jury matter." (See § 16.9(C)).

Prosecutors do not view all prospective witnesses as good candidates for interviews. If a prosecutor believes a witness may be reluctant to testify or may testify falsely, the best strategy may be not giving the witness this opportunity to think in advance about her testimony. Even if interviewed, the prosecutor may prefer not to confront the witness with contrary evidence, so as to avoid giving the witness the time between the interview and testifying to fabricate a new explanation that can be reconciled with that evidence.

C.   Cooperative Witnesses

Where a witness is truly cooperative, having told all he knows to an investigative agent or prosecutor, prosecutors often prefer not to have that witness testify before the grand jury. Since the grand jury can rely upon hearsay, the case agent can testify as to all of the information gathered from the cooperating witnesses, and if the grand jury is satisfied with that testimony, there is no need to call the witnesses. The case agent in this role is described as a "summary witness," in contrast to the investigator who testifies as to first-hand knowledge, (a "fact witness"). The summary witness procedure is supported as expediting the presentation of information and minimizing the burden imposed on victims and other witnesses. It also allows the prosecutor to avoid creating a valuable tool of discovery and impeachment for the defense.[61]

Under the Jencks Act, 18 U.S.C. § 3500, and Rule 26.2 of the Federal Rules of Criminal Procedure, after a government witness has testified, the defense is entitled to any prior "statement" of the witness in the government's possession that relates to the subject matter of the witness' testimony. Under Rule 26.2(g), this disclosure applies to witnesses testifying at various proceedings besides the trial. Also, in various federal districts, to avoid delay in the midst of the trial, disclosure of a trial witness' prior statement is made shortly before trial (rather than after the witness testifies). Thus, federal prosecutors seek to avoid creating statements subject to Jencks/Rule 26.2 not only to keep from the defense a statement that can be used to impeach their witness, but also to avoid pretrial disclosure of the likely testimony of government witnesses (which otherwise is not available).

A "statement" for the purposes of Jencks/Rule 26.2 includes "a substantially verbatim, contemporaneously recorded recital of the witness's oral statement that is contained in any recording or any transcription of a recording." An investigator's report recounting a witness' statement (e.g., an FBI form 302) may or may not meet this definition, depending upon the completeness of the memorialization and the timing of the report. On the other hand, the same witness' grand jury testimony will always be

---

[61] Unlike proceedings in which the sworn testimony of the cooperating witness is given subject to cross examination, this disadvantage is not offset in the grand jury setting by the creation of a statement that may be used as substantive evidence if the cooperating witness should become unavailable at trial. At one time, various federal courts allowed admission of grand jury testimony in that situation on the basis that it presented an "adequate indicia of reliability." That standard was held contrary to the confrontation clause in Crawford v. Washington, 541 U.S. 36 (2004), which conditions admission of prior statements on the opportunity for cross-examination by the defendant. Lower courts are divided as to whether the defense (not subject to the confrontation clause) can use at trial the defense-favorable testimony of a now unavailable grand jury witness. See CRIMPROC § 8.3(b).

subject to Jencks/Rule 26.2 disclosure; the definition of "statement" includes "a witness's statement to a grand jury, however, taken or recorded, or a transcription of such a statement." Since the case agent acting as a "summary witness" will not be called to testify at trial, that agent's grand jury testimony will not be subject to Jencks/Rule 26.2 (and it is not discoverable under the federal rules on pretrial discovery). However, if the cooperating witness himself testifies before the grand jury and later testifies in a covered proceeding, his grand jury testimony will have to be disclosed under Jencks/Rule 26.2. In some instances, the witness' earlier statement to the police or prosecutor will also have to be disclosed, but the added disclosure of the grand jury testimony offers an additional opportunity for variation that can be used to impeach the witness. The conventional wisdom is that the more statements a witness makes the more likely that some inconsistencies will appear.

Special circumstances may lead prosecutors to having fully cooperative witnesses testify before the grand jury.[62] These circumstances might include a grand jury request that it hear directly from the witness, the need to utilize the witness in laying a foundation for certain subpoenaed documents, and special expertise of the witness that cannot be readily be conveyed in a summary witness presentation. In these instances, the prosecutor will often use leading questions in order to both expedite the examination and develop as little impeachment material as possible. Very often detail will be avoided,[63] but to ensure accuracy where detail is required, the witness will be advised to reference documents that provide those details (e.g., a desk calendar). Before testifying, the witness will review carefully prior recorded statements that he gave to investigators. If the grand jury testimony contains substantially less detail, the witness will be asked on the record to confirm that his current testimony is not intended to depart from his former statements.

In some instances, prosecutors may be convinced that supposedly "cooperative witnesses" have not been fully forthcoming in their interviews with investigators. Testifying under oath, having been reminded that false testimony here constitutes perjury, hopefully will convince the witness to provide full disclosure. Persons arguably are likely to be more concerned about the adverse consequences of "shading" their descriptions when testifying under oath than in speaking to investigators. Still another feature of grand jury questioning that might assist in this regard is the prosecutor's ability to be persistent in questioning (in contrast to the interview, the witness cannot simply terminate the conversation). In such cases, the strategy in questioning the witness will come closer to that employed as to reluctant and recalcitrant witnesses (discussed below).

---

[62] In some instances, that witness will be subpoenaed to testify. In others, cooperative witnesses simply appear voluntarily (which is also true of agency investigators). Their testimony remains subject to perjury sanctions as it is given under oath. If the voluntary witness finds the questioning uncomfortable, however, the witness is free to leave.

[63] That is not true where the witness has been entirely cooperative, but there is concern that the witness might be less forthcoming at trial, after being pressured by the target or others. The cooperative witness here is subpoenaed in order to "lock in" his recollection of events. Although the witness has given a prior statement to investigators, repeating that statement under oath is viewed as a strong deterrent to a "changed story." Accordingly, the emphasis will be on gaining as much detail as possible.

D. Reluctant and Recalcitrant Witnesses

Some witnesses although clearly not subjects of the investigation, do not want to be seen as cooperating in the building of a case against a particular target. In the white collar context, that commonly will be due to a business relationship with the target. Such persons may not be willing to speak to investigative agents, or may be less than forthcoming in interviews (including even a pre-testifying interview), particularly when accompanied at the interview by an attorney funded by the target (see § 16.8(E)). Brought before the grand jury in a closed session, with their testimony covered by Rule 6 secrecy requirements, some of these reluctant witnesses will readily provide full disclosure of everything they know. Others, however, will remain reluctant, seeking to be as guarded as they can be while avoiding the potential for contempt (for evasion) or perjury (for lying). Many will be forced to testify, as they are unable to claim the privilege against self-incrimination (for legal or practical reasons) or that privilege has been replaced by immunity. They will seek, however, to provide as few "hard facts" as possible.

The DOJ recommends to prosecutors that they focus on gaining from either type of reluctant witness as much detail as possible. Generalized answers should not be accepted. The constant focus should be on obtaining "the who, what, when, where, and how of matters." At the same time, the prosecutor is directed to "cut off the witness or admonish the witness if the witness is not addressing the question." Because the witness may well desire later to retreat from his answers, the prosecutor is directed to make clear on the record that the witness has not misunderstood the question and has not been misled as to the significance of his answers.

Where the witness disclaims knowledge or claims lack of memory, the prosecutor is directed to continue the line of questioning so that claim is repeated as to each event or element of a specific topic. Thus, if the witness should subsequently testify for the defense, the grand jury testimony will show that the witness has had a "suddenly improved memory" as to each aspect of his testimony. Witnesses are to be reminded that intentionally evasive testimony may constitute perjury and obstruct justice, leading to a criminal prosecution. Where documents refer to the particular events, the witness can be asked to review the documents, so that he has been given every opportunity to refresh his memory.

For reluctant and recalcitrant witnesses, leading questions, though permissible, may be less helpful than for cooperative witnesses. The witness at trial can too readily discount a former "yes" or "no" answer as the product of a question that did not allow the development of the entire truth. Open-ended questions are recommended as they produce more complete answers and such answers provide less room for retreat in later testimony. For witnesses inclined to lie, the more complete answer also has advantages. The conventional wisdom is that "the more a witness talks, the more difficult it is to conceal false testimony. Many witnesses who are lying make slips when answering questions in a narrative form."

As discussed in § 10.6, a "perjury trap" defense to a perjury charge requires more than simply showing that the prosecution subpoenaed a witness although anticipating that he probably would lie. If the witness was a potential source of relevant information, the prosecutor is not required to ignore that potential because the witness has lied in the past. The threat of perjury when testifying under oath may be sufficient to gain a truthful answer even though the past false statement to federal enforcement officers may also have constituted a crime. (See § 9.6). The prosecutor in such cases often will advise the witness as to the consequences of perjury at the outset. If the witness does lie, the prosecutor has no duty to warn the witness and advise her that liability may be avoided by immediate recantation (see § 10.7). Nonetheless, a prosecutor with a primary focus on gaining information will provide that advice. The prosecutor will also call the witness' attention to contradictory evidence. Grand jury secrecy rules, as discussed in § 16.9(D), will restrict the prosecutor's description of that evidence. The prosecutor will not show the witness the transcript of contrary grand jury testimony, but the prosecutor can describe the general character of the contradictory explanation provided by (or expected from) other witnesses. The prosecutor may also call the witness' attention to the contradictory content of documents obtained from the witness or the witness' employer; as to documents obtained from other sources, the prosecutor ordinarily will be limited to either describing the document without reference to its source or showing the witness a copy that has all identifying marks removed.

While Rule 6(e) secrecy restricts the prosecutor somewhat in showing the witness the strength of the grand jury evidence establishing the witness' perjury, the witness has nothing to complain about since the government has no obligation even to advise the witness that such evidence exists. Should the witness recant and testify truthfully, the government has achieved its objective in issuing the subpoena. If the witness stands by the false testimony, notwithstanding the warning, a perjury prosecution will follow. The witness may then express a willingness to recant and testify truthfully. At this point, however, the witness' value as a prosecution witness is likely to be dramatically reduced, so the prosecutor will be far less likely to dismiss the prosecution in return for the witness' testimony.

E. Self–Incrimination Claims

Upon receiving subpoenas, prospective witnesses may inform the prosecutor (typically through counsel) that the witness will assert the privilege against self-incrimination. As discussed in § 19.3(A), the privilege gives no witness, not even the target, the right to refuse to testify. It presents "only an option to refuse and not a prohibition of inquiry." Accordingly, it must be raised in response to individual questions. As discussed below, the DOJ has a general policy as to not issuing a subpoena ad testificandum to a target, and where an exception is made, the target's notification of an intent to assert the privilege ordinarily will result in a withdrawal of the subpoena. As to other witnesses, USAM § 9–11.154 flatly rejects the proposition that advance assertion should excuse the witness from appearance even though the prosecutor does not intend to grant immunity. Such a rule would rest on the "unwarranted assumption" that the witness both knows the precise questions to be asked, and can accurately assume that the privilege will be available as to each of these questions. The prosecution is entitled to call the witness and determine whether the witness, once in the grand jury room with counsel excluded, is "willing to answer some or all of the grand jury's questions without incriminating himself or herself." If the privilege is raised, the prosecutor may conclude that it does not apply under the "potential incrimination" standard (see § 19.2(B)), and challenge its exercise. More commonly, the prosecutor will ask the witness a few more questions, and if the privilege again is asserted, will ask if the witness intends to assert the privilege on all remaining questions concerning the particular topic. If the witness intends to do so, the prosecutor will move to another topic or excuse the witness. This assumes that the prosecutor does not intend to grant immunity. As discussed in § 19.5(F), that determination is usually made in advance of having the witness testify, typically as a result of prior negotiations between the witness' counsel and the prosecutor.

F. Target Testimony

As noted in § 19.3(A), constitutionally a witness who is the target of an investigation is treated no differently than any other witness; there is no self-incrimination barrier to subpoenaing the target to appear as a witness and the subpoenaed person is not entitled constitutionally to be notified of his status as a target. In its internal standards, however, the DOJ includes several provision that take into account the distinct status of a "target" (defined as a "person as to whom the prosecutor or grand jury has substantial evidence linking him or her to the commission of a crime and who, in the judgment of the prosecutor, is a putative defendant"). As discussed in § 16.5(B), where a subpoenaed witness is a target or subject, an advice of rights form must be attached to the subpoena. If the witness is a target, supplemental advice as to target status must be added. This assumes that the target can be subpoenaed, but internal standards impose requirements that limit the subpoenaing of targets. Those standards also encourage accepting target requests to testify and notifying targets of their status, so that they can make such a request.

USAM § 9–11.150 governs the initial question of whether to subpoena the target. Recognizing that target subpoenas "may carry the appearance of unfairness," this standard notes that "before a known 'target' is subpoenaed to testify . . . about his or her involvement in the crime under investigation, an effort should be made to secure the target's voluntary appearance." If the target rejects that opportunity, the target may be subpoenaed only after the grand jury and the United States Attorney (or the appropriate Main Justice official) have approved the subpoena. The participation of the grand jury in this decision is acknowledged in the *Grand Jury Handbook* and the model grand jury charges, which warn the jurors that "the appearance of the accused before you may raise complicated legal problems." The DOJ standards cite three considerations as deserving "careful consideration" in determining whether to subpoena the accused: (1) how important the target's testimony is likely to be in achieving "the successful conduct of the grand jury's investigation"; (2) whether "the substance of the testimony or information sought could be provided by other witnesses" and (3) "whether the questions the prosecutor and the grand jurors intend to ask . . . would be protected by a valid claim of privilege."

If the target is subpoenaed, USAM § 9–11.151 requires that, in addition to the standard "advice of rights," witnesses who are known targets should be advised "that their conduct is being investigated for possible violations of Federal Criminal law." This "supplemental advice of status" is typically included in a "target letter"[64] and will be "repeated on the record" along with the advice of rights." Both advice requirements (as to status and rights) apply to subpoenas duces tecum as well as subpoenas ad

---

[64] See USAM, Title 9 (Criminal Resource Manual) § 160 ("Sample Target Letter") ("you are advised that you are a target of the grand jury's investigation").

testificandum. While targets are rarely subpoenaed to testify, they often are subpoenaed to produce documents, so target notifications are not unusual.

As noted in § 16.6(E), USAM § 9–11.154 in general rejects the treatment of a subpoenaed witness' assertion of an intent to raise the self-incrimination privilege as a basis for excusing appearance. A contrary position is taken as to the target subpoenaed to testify. Here, if a target and his or her attorney "state in writing, signed by both, that the target will refuse to testify on Fifth Amendment grounds, the witness ordinarily should be excused from testifying unless the grand jury and the United States Attorney agree to insist on appearance." In making that assessment, consideration is to be given to the same three factors considered in the initial determination to subpoena the witness. At this point, however, the third factor—the applicability of the privilege—becomes critical because it is known that the target will exercise the privilege. Requiring the target to appear and repeatedly raise the privilege is viewed as highly prejudicial.

USAM § 9–11.152 and § 9–11.153 deal with instances in which the target might initiate his or her appearance before the grand jury. The first provision addresses requests by subjects or targets to testify. As USAM § 9–11.152 notes: "It is not altogether uncommon for subjects or targets of the grand jury's investigation, particularly in white collar cases, to request or demand the opportunity to tell their side of the story." The DOJ warns prosecutors that a rejection of such a request "can create the appearance of unfairness." Accordingly, "under normal circumstances, where no burden upon the grand jury or delay of proceedings is involved, reasonable requests . . . to testify personally before the grand jury ordinarily should be given favorable consideration." This is consistent with the Grand Juror Handbook which notes that "upon request, preferably in writing, an accused may be given the opportunity by the grand jury to appear before it."

Counsel rarely will advise an individual who is a target to seek to testify before the grand jury, where he will be subject to the prosecutor's examination without counsel or judge being present. Only very special circumstances would lead a target in a white collar case to make such a request. Far more common is a target request to allow the testimony of others (e.g., a defense expert). Indeed, where the target is an entity, it can only "testify" through others.

As to such "supplementary requests," USAM § 9–11.152 notes that the ultimate decision "is a matter left to the sound discretion of the grand jury." This suggests that such requests should be conveyed to the grand jury, although that obligation is imposed by law only as to special grand juries.[65] Of course, the prosecutor can call to the grand jury's attention the comment in USAM § 9–11.152 that "the grand jury was never intended to be and is not properly either an adversary proceeding or the arbiter of guilt or innocent." On the other hand, the prosecutor often will see an advantage in gaining this preview of the defense the target would most likely raise if indicted.

USAM § 9–11.153 supplements USAM § 9–11.152, with respect to target requests. USAM § 9–11.153 states that the "prosecutor in appropriate cases is encouraged to notify targets of their status in order to afford them the opportunity to testify before

---

[65] See note 42 supra and § 16.3(A).

the grand jury." It adds that such notification is inappropriate in "routine clear cases" or when "such action might jeopardize the investigation" because of likely "flight, or destruction or fabrication of evidence," but these conditions are unlikely to apply to white collar investigations. On the other hand, in white collar investigations the target is likely to be aware of the ongoing investigation and the opportunity provided by USAM § 9–11.152. Thus notification is most likely to be made when the grand jury needs to invite the target to testify, as required by USAM § 9–11.151, prior to deciding whether to subpoena the target, or the prosecutor wants to preclude the defense from later arguing that it was never given the opportunity to tell its story.

As with other internal standards, the USAM directives on target testimony do not create judicially enforceable rights. In the white collar context, persons who are targets are usually aware of the investigation and have retained counsel, and counsel can readily ensure that her client is not harmed by a prosecutor's failure to follow the USAM directives. Perhaps the most significant prosecutorial omission would be the failure to use the target classification where it should apply.[66] However, the subpoenaed person or entity not given target notification would still be treated as a subject (receiving the "advice of rights" form). Counsel for that person is unlikely to place great weight on the person being a "subject" rather than a "target," for today's subject can readily become tomorrow's target.

A target classification requires that there be both "substantial evidence" against the person and a prosecutor determination that the individual is a "putative defendant". Thus, the prosecutor may characterize one person as a target and another as a subject, notwithstanding the existence of substantial evidence as to both, based on differences related solely to factors influencing the use of prosecutorial charging discretion. Those factors may change as the investigation progresses, or a different prosecutor, having the final say as to prosecution, may weigh the factors quite differently. So too, the prosecutor may be focusing the investigation on the possible liability of several persons, have "substantial evidence" (so far) as to only one or two, and consider the remainder (so far) to be only subjects. Thus, counsel for subpoenaed witness often seek to confirm the witness' current status (target, subject, or uninvolved fact witness), and as to "subjects" seek to identify where in a broad spectrum they belong.[67]

---

[66] Because the target classification places limits and duties on a prosecutor, it appears more likely that prosecutors would underuse than overuse the target classification. Target notification might be viewed in some circumstances, however, as a useful element in a strategy to encourage cooperation by an entity, see § 16.9(E), presenting an incentive for overuse.

[67] Consulting the prosecutor as to status is also common in the representation of persons who have not been subpoenaed. Here, however, the prosecutor has no obligation to classify and may refuse to do so in responding. USAM § 9–11.152 recognizes a right to request the opportunity to testify (or have others testify), but it applies to both subjects and targets, so the prosecutor's recognition of that right suggests only that the individual is one or the other. USAM § 9–11.153 provides for discretionary notice to targets only, but even where the prosecutor decides to notify, it is consistent with the objective of that provision to delay notification until the indictment is about to be sought.

§ 16.7   OBTAINING DOCUMENTS AND DATA

A.   The Scope of the Subpoena Duces Tecum

Rule 17(c) authorizes a subpoena duces tecum that commands the production "of any books, paper, documents, data or other objects designated therein." The term "data" was added by a 2002 amendment in recognition that, "in an increasingly technological culture, the information [to be subpoenaed] may exist in a format not already covered by the more conventional list, such as a book or document." The DOJ had adapted a broad view of the Rule's references to "documents" and "objects" long before the adoption of the 2002 amendment. Thus, in white collar investigations, subpoenas requesting "documents" relating to a particular transaction would define "documents" to include "microfilm, magnetic tapes, punch cards, recording discs, and any other instrument conveying information by mechanical, electronic, photographic, or other means." Subpoenas duces tecum had directed production of hard drives, thumb drives, floppy discs, phones, DVDs, CDs, and under unusual circumstances, laptop and desktop computers.

Subpoenas in white collar investigations today regularly demand production of electronically stored information (ESI). Delivery of ESI may be requested in both hard copy and electronic format. The electronic format will require that the information be unencrypted (or if encrypted, with decryption keys provided). In many instances, the subpoena will demand that the electronic format also include metadata (data about the electronic-file, such as the date the file was last modified), which would not appear in the typical screen or hard copy of a document.[68] If information fits the subpoena's description of the demanded documents, it must be produced if located anywhere on the information network of the subpoenaed party. Thus, files that have been "erased" on an individual's computer are subject to production if (as is typical) they remain elsewhere in the system.

Rule 17 authorizes subpoenas requiring persons to testify, to provide personal physical evidence, or to deliver preexisting documents. Very often, however, the most convenient means of providing the desired information will be through the creation of a new document, and Rule 17 does not refer to such a directive. However a subpoena may direct the subpoenaed party to produce documents from which the government could prepare a list (e.g., of all employees terminated within the last several years), and then note that, in lieu of producing those documents, the subpoenaed party can produce a certified statement that contains that compilation. So too, where the prosecution's objective is to prepare a statistical tabulation, and the subpoenaed party will not have collected those statistics in a current document, the subpoena may direct production of the documents that would be the source of the tabulation, but then allow the subpoenaed party to itself produce the tabulation in lieu of presenting the

---

[68] As explored in various standards developed for E-discovery, the subpoena typically also will address other issues relating to the electronic format in which the ESI is delivered (e.g., original file or an electronic image format, and proprietary software concerns). See DOJ, Joint Electronic Technology Working Group, Recommendations for ESI Discovery in Federal Criminal Cases, (2012), available at ST036 ALI–ABA 17 (on Westlaw). See also Federal Grand Jury Practice Manual § 5.17 (discussing model Subpoena Attachment for Production of Electronically Stored Records), and § 6.11 (noting various sources of DOJ expertise in converting ESI evidence into formats more useful for investigative purposes, including application of special software programs).

documents. Thus, grand jury subpoenas will occasionally operate in much the same fashion as a discovery interrogatory.

B. Subpoena Objectives

A primary objective of the subpoena duces tecum is to obtain documents that establish that a crime was or was not committed (i.e., documents constituting incriminatory or exculpatory evidence). But the subpoena objectives, particularly in white collar cases, can be much broader. As noted in § 16.5(A), the subpoena may also seek documents that will do no more than identify potential witnesses. So too, it may seek documents identifying those outside entities working with the target that may have relevant documents.[69]

The subpoena will also seek documents that assist in interpreting the core documents that describe the transaction under inquiry. A subpoena may, for example, demand both a particular type of record and the document that sets forth the entity's internal standards governing the creation and content of the record. An important aspect of interpreting core documents may be comparing them to similar documents. If a fraudulent practice revealed in possible invoice manipulation was thought to have started in a particular time frame, there may be value in comparing invoices from an earlier time frame. So too, when an investigation was aimed at possible entity misrepresentations on one governmental form, the grand jury subpoena sought information relating to other forms as well, seeking to assess whether the misrepresentation was part of a pattern or an isolated incident.

Another major objective of the subpoena duces tecum is to force the subpoena recipient to preserve records of possible interest in the investigation. Upon receipt of the subpoena, an entity will take steps to ensure that document destruction practices are suspended pending compliance with the subpoena. Thus subpoenas will be issued at the very outset of the investigation, often before the prosecution is in a position to access fully the investigative leads that indicate which documents will be needed. As part of the subpoena demand, the recipient will be required to provide documents that "show the company's practice, procedure, or policy with respect to the destruction of documents." Of course, receipt of the subpoena does not preclude the lawful destruction of documents not called for in the subpoena, but documents do not have to be under subpoena to render destruction an obstruction of justice. (See § 16.2(D)). Criminal liability applies if the destruction was undertaken in anticipation that the grand jury might seek the documents in the future. Caution will lead the subpoena recipient to preserve more documents than subpoenaed, particularly where destruction would not be justified under a previously established destruction policy.

In light of the various objectives of the subpoena duces tecum, it is not surprising that prosecutors are told that, when in doubt, it is "advisable to request more documents than fewer." The thought here is that the subpoenaed party's counsel will call to the prosecutor's attention a description of demanded documents that

---

[69] When a subpoena duces tecum calls for production of a large amount of records that will take considerable time to locate, assemble, and produce, a relatively quick partial production of records may be desirable in order to promptly pursue the leads provided in such documents. Thus, staggered production of documents may be required. This may also be preferred for other types of documents. See Federal Grand Jury Practice § 5.18.

unwittingly covers far more than the prosecutor would have anticipated, but counsel will not call to the prosecutor's attention a "loophole" that omits documents of equal significance to those demanded.

At one time, the conventional wisdom on the other side argued that counsel should not automatically call to the prosecutor's attention (and contest in court, if necessary) the broad sweep of a subpoena. Where the subpoena's demand encompassed an immense quantity of documents (50 tons in one famous antitrust investigation), "information control" might best be practiced by giving the government everything that could possibly fit within the subpoena. The strategic assumption was that the government's lack of the resources needed to carefully screen would work to keep potentially adverse documents "buried in the pile." That strategy is much riskier today, as prosecutors have available the tools needed to convert both paper and ESI into electronic formats that can be readily searched using a variety of software programs.[70]

C. Standard Provisions

1. Generally

The critical content of a subpoena duces tecum will be found in an attachment to the subpoena, which describes both the items demanded and the requirements for compliance. The description of the items demanded will vary with the special characteristics of the investigation. Significant variables include the character of potential offenses, the character of the subpoenaed party (whether an individual or an entity), the type of enterprise involved, and what is known of the record-keeping practices of the subpoenaed party. Nonetheless, the demand typically will include certain "boilerplate" provisions and follow certain guidelines in its description of the demanded documents. The provisions and drafting standards discussed below are illustrative.

2. Originals

Grand jury subpoenas commonly call for "originals" rather than copies. Of course, for ESI, the distinction does not apply, but various documents are likely to have been created originally in paper and kept in that form even though later scanned and stored electronically. The government justifies its demand for originals on several grounds. Although authenticated copies of originals will be admissible in evidence under Fed. R. Evid. 1003, in some instances, issues relating to the document might lead the jury to expect the original. Second, the original will reveal white-outs, erasures, or evidence of alterations not apparent on photocopies. Fingerprints can only be found on originals, and where handwriting analysis may be needed, an original is preferred. Also, originals sometimes contain handwritten notations that are not legibly reproduced on photocopies. If the subpoenaed party has a special business reason for keeping the originals, the government will often accept copies, provided the subpoenaed party

---

[70] The programs go far beyond text searches. They may, for example, take account of patterns, identifying the unusual number of edits for a particular document or a sudden decrease in the communications relating to a particular topic. In major investigations, to facilitate such ESI screening, computer specialists will be part of the government personnel certified under Rule 6(e)(3).(See § 16.3(E)); Federal Grand Jury Practice § 3.55 (also noting use of private contractors).

provides assurances as to the later presentation of the originals and the authenticity of the copies.

3.   Time Frame

The subpoena will demand production of documents dating back from the current date to a specific date. The time period may go back even beyond the statute of limitations to produce relevant background documents, and to identify the initiation of the criminal activities. Where a subpoenaed party seeks modifications based on difficulties in collecting the data, a remote time is often a key element of that party's complaint. In the case of ESI, in particular, older records may be stored on systems not readily accessible, in part because of the limited number of personnel familiar with a now obsolete system.

4.   Describing Documents

Documents are often described by reference to the function of the document. Thus, one demand might ask for all documents that record dates of particular events (e.g., meetings). Added will be an "included, but not limited to" clause that identifies many of those documents (e.g., appointment books, desk calendars, diaries, day books, telephone call books, etc.). Other document demands will be tied to a particular type of transaction, asking for all documents that reflect, refer, or relate to the particular transaction or subject. A broad definition of "documents" will supplement that description (e.g., referring to "all writings of any kind" and listing a variety of items, such as letters, e-mails, reprints, tabulations, etc.). Since returns have to identify documents as responding to particular demands, a major drafting objective is to have demands that do not persistently overlap yet do not leave gaps in coverage.

5.   Location

Subpoenas demands often seek to take into account document location as well as document content. Thus, subpoenas sometimes require production of all documents attached to any document that falls within a particular content description, even though the attached document is not within the description. So too, subpoenas commonly require that the name of the file or folder in which a document was located be noted as part of the return process. This helps in understanding the subpoenaed party's filing system and assessing whether a subsequent subpoena should acquire all other documents located in a particular file or folder.

6.   Privilege Claims

Subpoenas commonly require the return to include an affidavit identifying any documents that are responsive to the subpoena but not returned because of a claim of privilege. Typically, the subpoena asks that the document be described in sufficient detail (apart from content) to enable the government to categorize the missing document. That starts with identifying the subpoena demand to which the document is responsive and adding such features as the author of the document, the persons to whom the document was addressed, the names of persons to whom the document was shown, and the date of the document. Where the claimed privilege is the privilege against self-incrimination some aspect of this information may be covered by privilege (and therefore need not be supplied).

D. Compliance

The grand jury subpoena duces tecum commands the subpoenaed party to appear before the grand jury "and bring with you" the subpoenaed documents. However, the subpoenaed party may be given the option of producing the documents in the office of the staff conducting the investigation. Some prosecutors prefer production before the grand jury, and will not offer this option, particularly if a modest number of documents are involved. In the case of subpoenas for personal records, the person subpoenaed is often a target (who otherwise would not be called) and the appearance is thought to press upon the target "the serious nature of the proceeding." Also, the appearance before the grand jury presents the opportunity to place the document presenter under oath and to ask questions appropriate to ascertaining whether there has been full compliance on the production of the documents (although that questioning typically will be superficial since potential compliance deficiencies usually will come to light only after examining the documents).[71]

Many prosecutors prefer the option of production in the staff office, noting that it "generally saves time, inconvenience and expense—both for the staff and the grand jury."[72] Most subpoenaed parties also will prefer that option as more convenient and avoiding the need to testify before the grand jury as to compliance. Office delivery will be conditioned on submitting an affidavit that substitutes for such testimony. Its contents are prescribed by prosecutor's office and cover the major steps in compliance (full search, delivery of documents demanded, etc.).

Where office production is used, USAM § 9–11.254 requires that the grand jury be "apprised of the location and organization of the documents." While some documents may later be shown to the grand jury or described in the testimony of the investigative staff, courts have held that the grand jury simply being made aware of the existence of the remaining documents (which they can always request) is sufficient to effect a return of the documents "to the grand jury." Accordingly, all documents produced pursuant to the subpoena, whether or not examined or described before the grand jury, may constitute "grand jury matter", making them subject to the secrecy requirements of Rule 6(e).[73]

---

[71] The individual who appears as the custodian of the records has an obligation to explain compliance. That obligation ordinarily precludes refusing to testify on self-incrimination grounds, provided the very production of the documents cannot be precluded on self-incrimination grounds. (See § 20.4(B)).

[72] The Right to Financial Privacy Act, 12 U.S.C. § 3420(a)(1), does not always allow for this option. It provides that financial records about a customer obtained from a financial institution "shall be returned and actually presented to the grand jury unless the volume of such records make such return and actual presentation impractical, in which case the grand jury shall be provided with a description of the contents." The Act also includes a special provision on the return of the documents to the financial institution.

[73] Accordingly, USAM § 9–11.254 makes applicable to documents returned by office delivery, as well as documents presented to the grand jury, the protocols established under the DOJ's 1996 memorandum on "Guidelines for Handling Documents Obtained by the Grand Jury." Those guidelines require that subpoenaed documents be separated from documents the staff obtained by other means, to ensure that Rule 6(e) objections are recognized when the DOJ "receives requests for access to documents from Congress, from individuals or entities filing requests pursuant to the Freedom of Information Act, and from private and government lawyers engaged in civil litigation." As to Rule 6(e) restrictions on disclosures in response to such request, see §§ 16.9, 18.3. As noted in § 18.3(A), where a third party is seeking a document for purposes unrelated to the fact that it was subpoenaed, it may not be covered by grand jury secrecy, but that does not depend upon whether the document was actually presented to the grand jury. (See also § 16.9(B)).

Particularly where the subpoena requires a business entity to produce a large quantity of documents, the subpoenaed party must be prepared to go beyond submitting the standard affidavit, or providing brief testimony, on compliance. If the government has misgivings about compliance after reviewing the records received, or omissions are established, the subpoenaed party will be expected to show that it made a good faith, dedicated effort to comply with the subpoena. The concern here is not simply avoiding an obstruction of justice charge, but also ensuring that the subpoenaed party and its counsel are viewed as trustworthy. Thus, a business entity commonly will create an extensive record of its efforts to ensure compliance, including such steps as: (1) a directive to all employees on document preservation; (2) written instructions sent to appropriate employees as to how to conduct the search (including, for examples, directions on searching computer records that include examining hard drives and back-up files, and consultation with the network administrator as to other possible locations); (3) certifications by employees as to the steps they took in searching for documents; (4) a log showing which employees provided which records; (5) review by outside counsel, and (6) and an established process that will implement the continuing duty to produce documents subject to the subpoena as they are later discovered.[74]

E.   Costs of Compliance

Two statutes require the government to reimburse subpoenaed entities for the cost of searching for, copying, and producing subpoenaed records. The Financial Privacy Act does so for financial institutions directed to produce records of their customers[75] and the Electronic Communications Privacy Act does so for providers of telecommunications or internet services when directed to produce the contents of "communications records and [certain] other information."[76] Apart from these situations, the standard presumption is that the subpoenaed party must bear the costs of compliance. Several lower courts have noted that, in exceptional circumstances, the court can condition enforcement of the subpoena on the government bearing the cost of compliance. Some have based such rulings on the court's inherent authority while others look to the Rule 17(c) provision that authorizes quashing a subpoena if compliance would be "oppressive." The key under both groundings is not the cost of compliance per se, but the bearing of the cost on the entity's financial viability, looking in particular as to how this cost compares to other operating expenses of the entity.

Where a subpoenaed entity needs photocopies of the delivered documents to continue its business operations, the government may respond to a financial-burden claim by agreeing to make an extra photocopy that will be given back to the entity. Government investigators commonly make a copy for their own use, keeping the originals in a separate file to be used at trial. The government can also respond to a claim of excessive burden by offering to have its own agents look through the entity's

---

Separate storage of subpoenaed documents also facilitates fulfilling the government's responsibility to return subpoenaed documents at the later of the close of the grand jury investigation or the close of any ensuing criminal prosecution. See Federal Grand Jury Practice § 6.27.

[74] See Villa, Corporate Counsel Guidelines, § 5.17 (2011), available on Westlaw at CORPCG. The continuing duty may be extended beyond the life of the grand jury by special arrangement, particularly where the investigation is continued before another grand jury, and in some instances, beyond the termination of the investigation.

[75] 12 U.S.C. § 3415. See also § 16.10(D) at note 126.

[76] 18 U.S.C. § 2706. See also § 16.10(D) at note 132.

files, but that amounts to conducting a search; while the entity can certainly accept the offer, such an offer is unlikely to be viewed as a satisfactory response to a claim of excessive burden. In some instances, the entity's basic objection will relate less to the overall cost than to the timing of the return. It will argue, for example, that the return date can be met only by devoting so much staff to the project as to interfere with its business operations. That type of objection usually is met by a modification of the return date.

F.   Third–Party Subpoenas

Subpoenas often seek records relating to activities of the target that may be obtained either from target or a third-party providing services to the target. That is the case, for example, of records relating to monetary transfers, airline travel, telephone calls, e-mails, and electronic information stored "in the cloud". A variety of factors will determine whether the prosecution will seek to subpoena such documents directly from the service provider or from the target.[77] If there is concern that the target might alter the document (notwithstanding knowledge that the service provider has a copy), that will support using a third-party subpoena. If there is a desire to keep the target unaware of the government's interest in the particular document, that might also suggest using a third-party subpoena. As discussed in § 16.9(C), the third-party ordinarily has discretion to inform the target of the subpoena, but some service providers will adhere to a government request not to inform (particularly if the target is no longer a customer), and notification can be prohibited under statutes applicable to certain service providers. If there is concern that the target might have a basis for objecting to the subpoena, that might also lead to a third-party subpoena. The service provider may lack the grounding for making the same objection (as in the case of a self-incrimination objection) and may be less inclined to contest the subpoena even if the ground for objection is available.[78]

As discussed in § 16.10(D), statutory provisions add prerequisites for using subpoenas to obtain customer information from certain types of service providers, and where those prerequisites are burdensome, the prosecution might prefer obtaining that information from the target. In some instances, that may be the only route available. For example, obtaining an e-mail from an electronic communications service may require having the probable cause needed for a search warrant. On the other hand, where the sender or recipient of the e-mail has kept that e-mail in his electronic files, it can be obtained by a traditional grand jury subpoena. Even where the statutory prerequisite could be met, the prosecutor might prefer to use a subpoena to a target first, and if that fails, turn to meeting the special prerequisites for a third-party subpoena.

---

[77] Similar considerations may apply where the target sent or received a document, a copy was undoubtedly kept, and the choice is between subpoenaing the target and the party on the other end of the correspondence.

In some instances, records may be available from a target, a service-provider, and the recipient of the document in question. That is the case for tax returns, as copies typically can be obtained from the taxpayer (the target), the accountant who prepared the return, and the IRS. Because of special limitations that apply to the IRS, see § 16.10(D) at note 130, tax returns will usually be subpoenaed from the accountant or the taxpayer.

[78] As to target interventions to contest subpoenas to third parties, see §§ 16.9(D), 16.10(D), 16.11(C), 16.12(G).

§ 16.8   THE WITNESS' RIGHT TO THE ASSISTANCE OF COUNSEL

A. Constitutional Requirements

Although the Supreme Court has never directly ruled on whether a grand jury witness has a constitutional right to the assistance of counsel, the justices have made major statements on that issue in two cases. Those discussions are widely viewed by federal lower courts as establishing that: (1) a grand jury witness has no Sixth Amendment right to counsel,[79] and (2) no other constitutional grounding grants to a witness the right to be accompanied by an attorney when testifying before the grand jury.

In re Groban[80] presented the Court's first significant comment on a possible witness right to the assistance of counsel. *Groban* was a state case decided prior to the Fourteenth Amendment's incorporation of the Sixth Amendment counsel guarantee and therefore looked to the independent content of due process. The challenge there was not to a grand jury proceeding, but to a special investigative proceeding of a state fire marshall at which the witness was not allowed to be accompanied by counsel. In finding that the exclusion of counsel from that proceeding did not violate due process, the Court majority drew an analogy to the grand jury proceeding. There, it noted, the law was clear that "a witness cannot insist, as a matter of constitutional right, on being represented by counsel." Justice Black, in dissent, agreed that there was no constitutional right to counsel in the grand jury proceeding, but viewed the fire marshall's proceeding as not truly analogous. The witness before the grand jury had the protection of "the presence of jurors," which offered a "substantial safeguard" against abuse.

The second discussion came in *United States v. Mandujano*,[81] where the defendant challenged the state's use of his testimony before the grand jury, raising a right to counsel claim under both the Sixth Amendment and *Miranda v. Arizona* (the Fifth Amendment right to counsel recognized in the setting of custodial police interrogation). Prior to his testimony, Mandujano was told that "he could have a lawyer outside the [grand jury] room with whom he could consult," but he was not offered the assistance of an appointed attorney, although claiming to be indigent. The lower courts held that, as a "putative" or "virtual" defendant, he was in a position akin to an arrestee and should have been given complete *Miranda* warnings, including advice as to appointed counsel. As noted in § 19.3(B), the Court majority upheld Mandujano's subsequent perjury conviction without reaching the lower court's ruling on the insufficiency of the warnings given. Six members of the Court, however, did speak to that ruling.

Four justices, through Chief Justice Burger's plurality opinion, concluded that the advice given Mandujano as to the availability of counsel was fully consistent with any

---

[79] Since a grand jury ordinarily may not call before it an indicted person to testify about the charges currently pending against him, see § 16.12(F), the Court's discussions and the lower court interpretation of these discussions have focused on a witness not under indictment. Once a person becomes an "accused," he has a right to consult with counsel during any governmental interrogation relating to the charged offense. See CRIMPROC § 6.4(e).

[80] 352 U.S. 330 (1957).

[81] 425 U.S. 564 (1976).

constitutional requirements. Since "no criminal proceedings had been instituted," the "Sixth Amendment right to counsel had not come into play." The Court had previously held that a person did not become an "accused" for Sixth Amendment purposes until criminal proceedings were instituted by the "initiation of adversary judicial proceedings" (e.g., filing of an indictment). As for other groundings, *Groban* had noted that "a witness before a grand jury cannot insist, as a matter of constitutional right, on being represented by counsel," and the *Miranda* right to counsel, "fashioned to secure the suspect's Fifth Amendment privilege," also did not apply. *Miranda* was premised upon an "inherently coercive" interrogation setting, clearly distinguishable from grand jury questioning.

Justice Brennan, joined by Justice Marshall, disagreed with the plurality's conclusion, but not all of its reasoning. Although *Miranda* did not apply, the questioning of a putative defendant "inextricably involve[s]" the privilege against self-incrimination, thereby distinguishing the Sixth Amendment starting-point analysis cited by the plurality. The combination of putative defendant status and "the peculiarly critical role of the Fifth Amendment" made the advice in this case deficient as defendant was not told that, "if he cannot afford an attorney one will be appointed for him" and "that he may at any and all times during questioning consult with the attorney ["wait[ing] outside the grand jury room"] prior to answering any question posed."

Federal lower courts have viewed the plurality opinion in *Mandujano* and the two *Groban* opinions as establishing that there is no Sixth Amendment right to counsel, and that there is no other constitutional grounding for insisting upon counsel's presence in the grand jury room. That interpretation finds support in the Court's later opinion in *Conn v. Gabbert*.[82] The *Gabbert* Court rejected an attorney's civil rights claim, which alleged that state prosecutors had conducted a search of his person, pursuant to a warrant, while his client was giving testimony before a state grand jury, and had thereby prevented him from advising his client (who received a short recess to consult with him, but was unable to do so because of the ongoing search). Speaking to the witness' right to the assistance of counsel, the Court noted: "A grand jury witness has no constitutional right to have counsel present during the grand jury proceeding, *United States v. Mandujano*, and no decision of this Court has held that a grand jury witness has a right to have her attorney present outside the jury room. We need not decide today whether such a right exists, because Gabbert clearly had no standing to raise the alleged infringement of the rights of his client."

A scattering of lower court decisions have addressed the issue left open in *Gabbert*, and noted, typically in dictum, that a witness has a constitutional right to seek the advice of counsel located outside the grand jury room. Some of these rulings appear to rely, as did Justice Brennan in *Mandujano*, on the implementation of the privilege against self-incrimination.[83] However, this grounding would also arguably encompass a

---

[82] 526 U.S. 286 (1999).

[83] Some support for this position may be found in Maness v. Meyers, 419 U.S. 449 (1975). In that case, the Supreme Court held that the Fifth Amendment precluded holding a lawyer in contempt "for advising his client, during the trial of a civil case, to refuse to produce material demanded by a subpoena duces tecum when the lawyer believed in good faith the material might tend to incriminate his client." Noting the layman's need for legal advice in determining the "nuances and boundaries" of the Fifth Amendment

right to appointed counsel (as Justice Brennan argued), but the lower court references were only to consulting with retained counsel. In speaking of a due process right to consult, these rulings arguably were suggesting a quite different grounding, recognized in cases that have dealt with claims that the government was interfering with a grand jury witness' right to consult with counsel of choice prior to testifying (e.g., by seeking to disqualify that attorney). The argument there is that an individual has a right to seek the advice of counsel as to any type of legal proceeding, as an aspect of a right to use "every legitimate resource at his command" in presenting his position, and the state cannot interfere with that right absent a reasonable justification.[84] This grounding is tied to the right to retain counsel, and does not require appointment of counsel for the indigent. It also does not provide the type of constitutional right to counsel that allows for challenging counsel's performance as ineffective assistance of counsel.

Since federal grand jury witnesses are allowed to consult with counsel in the anteroom, and disqualifications are possible even if the witness has a constitutional right to counsel of choice, federal courts have not had to rule directly on whether a grand jury witness has a constitutional right to the assistance of counsel, both prior to and during the giving of testimony. Nonetheless, if a constitutional right of some sort does exist, it could certainly have a bearing on the issues discussed in the remainder of this section.

B. Providing Counsel for the Indigent

The Criminal Justice Act, 18 U.S.C. § 3006A, which authorizes the appointment of counsel in criminal cases, does not refer to appointments for grand jury witnesses. Nonetheless, many federal district courts have adopted CJA plans giving the district court the discretion to make such appointments. In some districts, the Federal Defender office will take on that responsibility without an appointment. Prosecutors are advised by the DOJ that "in certain circumstances, . . . it is to the government's advantage to find counsel for a witness, such as where the witness faces possible contempt charges."

At one time, it was thought that the recalcitrant witness could force an appointment by refusing to testify, as that would lead to a civil contempt proceeding, and the potential loss of liberty would create a constitutional right to counsel. However, *Turner v. Rogers*[85] raised doubts about such a constitutional right. *Turner* held that "due process does not automatically require the provision of counsel at civil contempt proceedings to an indigent individual who is subject to a child support order [which he allegedly violated], even if that individual faces incarceration (for up to a year)." The Court's reasoning focused in large part on characteristics of the show cause hearing in non-support cases, but it also pointed to a due process right to counsel that

---

privilege, the Court reasoned that the privilege would be "drained of its meaning if counsel, being lawfully present, . . . could be penalized for advising his client."

[84] This grounding finds support in the suggestion in Powell v. Alabama, 287 U.S. 45 (1932), that due process would be denied, even in a civil case, if the court "were arbitrarily to refuse to hear a party by counsel, employed by and hearing from him." Justice Stewart relied upon this analysis in a concurring opinion in *Manness*, supra note 83, and the Court majority there, noted only that it was unnecessary to consider that grounding in light of the alternative ground on which it relied.

[85] 131 S.Ct. 2507 (2011).

was more flexible in its scope than the Sixth Amendment right (which would be applicable in a criminal contempt proceeding), and to the special character of the loss of liberty in a civil contempt proceeding (the contemnor having the ability to immediately gain his freedom by complying with the underlying court order). The show-cause hearing against a grand jury witness is readily distinguishable from the type of proceeding considered in *Turner*, but prior grand jury civil-contempt cases recognizing a constitutional right to counsel often had relied on reasoning inconsistent with *Turner's* focus on a case-by-case analysis, as *Turner* noted in citing one of those cases as illustrative of the automatic-right analysis it was now rejecting. In the federal system, courts should have no need to determine the bearing of *Turner* on show-cause hearings for grand jury contemnors, as counsel may be appointed under the CJA (because of the connection to the criminal process) without reaching the constitutional issue.

In white collar investigations, few witnesses are likely to qualify as indigent under the CJA. The high cost of defense representation in white collar cases relates primarily to defending against prosecution (where dealing simply with the thousands of documents involved in discovery may require a very rich defendant).[86] Representation of a grand jury witness, even a subject or target, is much more limited. The white collar target of moderate means may eventually become CJA-indigent after spending available resources on counsel and associated costs, but that is likely to occur sometime after indictment—not at the grand jury stage.

C. Anteroom Consultations

The Grand Juror Handbook and both of the model charges advise the grand jurors that witnesses are allowed to confer with their counsel outside the grand jury room and "you can draw no adverse inference if a witness chooses to exercise this right." The Handbook adds that "a witness may confer with counsel after each question, as long as he or she does not make a mockery of the proceedings or does not, by such, make an attempt to impede the orderly progress of the grand jury investigation." The Department of Justice does not view the witness' right to anteroom consultations quite so broadly. The Advice of Rights attachment to subpoenas for subjects and targets states: "the grand jury will permit you a *reasonable* opportunity to step outside the grand jury room to consult with counsel" (emphasis added). The reasonable opportunity limitation is viewed as extending beyond simple excluding interruptions so frequent and lengthy as to disrupt the orderly progress of the proceeding. It requires examining as well to the function of the opportunity to consult—allowing the witness to obtain legal advice. Thus, the DOJ manual suggests that an immunized witness might have less reason for consultation since there is no need for advice on the exercise of the privilege against self-incrimination. Leaving after each question, in particular, suggests an objective other than seeking advice—such as counsel keeping a record of the questions as part of a monitoring project (see subsection (F) infra), or having counsel shape the substance of the witness' answer so as to give away as little

---

[86] See, e.g., United States v. Stein, 435 F.Supp.2d 330, 362 (S.D.N.Y. 2006): "The government thus far has produced in discovery, in electronic or paper form, at least 5 million to 6 million pages of documents plus transcripts of 335 depositions and 195 income tax returns. The briefs on pretrial motions passed the 1,000–page mark some time ago. The government expects its case in chief to last three months, while defendants expect theirs to be lengthy as well. To prepare for and try a case of such length requires substantial resources."

information as possible or to be purposely ambiguous. At trial, it is noted, a testifying defendant cannot break off cross-examination to consult with counsel (and have counsel help him in formulating answers); counsel's role is limited at this point to making legal objections. The grand jury similarly is entitled to the witness' response, not a "parroted response" formulated by counsel.

Where the witness seeks to consult frequently, notwithstanding that the questions being asked are largely follow-ups to previous questions on which consultation was allowed, the prosecutor may ask the grand jury to request that the court rule on whether such requests must be allowed. Only a small group of federal lower court cases address the question of how frequently the witness may consult. Some opinions speak of a right to leave on every question, but others disagree. They suggest that, at best, leaving after every few questions should be satisfactory. One court concluded that, under the facts of the particular investigation, the witness could be questioned for 20 minutes and then given 10 minutes to consult. While the jurors have been advised not to draw an adverse inference, witnesses still may fear that leaving on a regular basis will lead the grand jurors to believe they have "something to hide," and that the focus of the investigation then could shift to their activities. Thus, many witnesses apparently are unwilling to be aggressive in asserting a right to consult.

D. Multiple Representation

Where the same attorney represents more than one witness, a witness and a target, or more than one target, the prosecutor may seek a court order of disqualification. Those motions typically are based exclusively on the court's authority to preclude joint representation of clients with conflicting interests. On occasion, prosecutors have urged, as a supplementary factor, that the joint representation in the particular instance has been used to undermine "the right of the public to an effectively functioning grand jury." This argument has been advanced, for example, where a single lawyer was representing all the critical witnesses and they all refused to testify on self-incrimination grounds. Not surprisingly, since such situations typically also present a conflict of interest (in failing to treat separately the situation of each client-witness) and since the leading Supreme Court rulings on disqualification look only to barring conflicts of interest, courts granting disqualifications in such cases have rested their rulings on the presence of a conflict. Other courts have rejected giving any weight to an "interference factor," noting that "discomfort to the grand jury process, without more, is not sufficient to violate an individual's important right to counsel of his own choosing."

Challenges to multiple representation based on the need to preclude a conflict of interest tend to be resolved in light of the Supreme Court's ruling in *Wheat v. United States*.[87] At issue there was the trial court's authority to preclude joint representation among separately tried codefendants. The grand jury setting presents several distinctions that could impact the use of disqualification authority. Initially, in *Wheat*, the Court recognized that the justification for disqualification had to overcome the defendant's right to counsel of choice. That right rested squarely on the Sixth Amendment, whereas the grand jury witness' underlying constitutional right (if any) rests on a more flexible due process right to seek legal advice from a counsel of choice.

---

[87] 486 U.S. 153 (1988), discussed in CRIMPROC § 11.9(c). See also § 22.4.

Secondly, the advantages to a witness of multiple representation at the grand jury stage may well be greater than the advantages to a defendant of multiple representation at the trial stage. For example, representation by a single lawyer may give a group of witnesses far greater discovery as to the nature of the grand jury proceeding than they would obtain through separate representation; at the trial stage, joint representation is less likely to give co-defendants any substantial advantage in discovering the government's case or in responding to that case. Finally, grand jury secrecy may preclude a full development of all the facts that may have a bearing on the existence of a conflict. Very often, the presence of a conflict depends upon the government's view of the status of the jointly represented individuals (e.g., whether one is a target and another a prime candidate for immunity); however, disclosure of such information to those persons as a group would lose for the government a major advantage it hopes to gain through grand jury secrecy.

While the first and third factors discussed above are occasionally noted, the analysis in grand-jury disqualification cases tends to focus on the key elements of the *Wheat* analysis. First, *Wheat* held that disqualification could be ordered where there is a "serious potential for conflict"; there need not be an "actual conflict". That standard is most readily met when the counsel jointly represents persons who might compete for a grant of immunity. Courts also are likely to find the *Wheat* standard met when represented persons have a difference in status as they relate to the investigation (i.e., the group includes persons in two or more of the separate categories of "uninvolved fact witness," "subject", or "target"). The different status of each person suggests that the best interests of each client might well be served by a different level of cooperation. A fact witness for example, might find it most convenient and less expensive (looking, in particular, to attorney fees) to agree to an interview or to testify without objection, notwithstanding the availability of a possible claim of privilege or a possible legal flaw in the subpoena.

Under the Rules of Professional Conduct, as discussed in § 22.4, joint representation will often be allowed if all of the jointly represented persons consent. *Wheat* concluded, however, that a disqualification could be ordered even if the jointly represented codefendants were willing to waive their rights to conflict-free counsel. It noted in this regard both the difficulty of ensuring that the waiver was made knowingly and freely, and the judicial interest in ensuring that "legal proceedings appear fair to all who observe them." The second factor arguably has less significance for a grand jury proceeding, as opposed to a trial. The first concern, however, is even more pressing at the grand jury stage. Waiver at this stage poses the additional problem that the individuals involved are not fully aware of what is being investigated and, unlike trial defendants, can only guess at what their eventual legal status will be in relation to others represented by counsel.

E. Employer Provided Counsel

As noted in § 2.7(E) and § 22.4, indemnification provisions in employment contracts or charter or by-law provisions (sometimes prescribed by state law) may require an employer to pay the attorneys' fees of employees who will be called to testify before the grand jury. Even if not required to do so, the employer may be willing to offer to pay those fees because doing so will assist it in monitoring the grand jury proceeding. An employee giving testimony cannot ask to leave for an anteroom consultation with his employer's counsel, but can do so to consult with his own counsel (who may, with his client's permission, share what he has learned with the employer's counsel). Where indemnification is mandated, the employer may be prohibited contractually from imposing conditions that limit the selection of counsel or that require cooperation (e.g., joining a joint defense agreement, see § 22.5). But if the employer has no obligation to indemnify, or that obligation specifically allows for the imposition of conditions, the employer may well insist upon such conditions.[88] Doing so, however, may lead to a motion by the government to disqualify the employee's attorney.

At the trial stage, fee payment by a third party that has its own separate interest in the outcome of the proceeding does not require the automatic judicial inquiry that follows from joint representation, but it has been held to require such an inquiry where the prosecution called the situation to the attention of the trial judge.[89] The primary concern, of course, is that the attorney will make trial decisions with a view toward avoiding prejudice to the fee-payer when the interests of the fee-payer and defendant diverge. Two situations, in particular, heighten that potential: (1) where the attorney's representation is subject to being cancelled by the fee-payer, and (2) where the attorney has an interest in gaining future business from the fee-payer. These concerns apply as well to the situation in which the employer is paying the fees for employees' counsel at the investigation stage. Whether or not designated as a target, the employer faces the risk of criminal liability if the investigation uncovers criminal activity by employees in the course of the business activities, and even if criminal liability is not established, civil or regulatory liability may be involved. Thus, the potential for a serious conflict is almost invariably present; the key is whether the arrangement for providing counsel sufficiently ensures that the counsel will act solely out of concern for the best interests of the client.[90] Of course, those best interests may lead to working closely with the employer's counsel, but that cooperation does not justify disqualification if the structure of the retention agreement does not point counsel in that direction.

---

[88] As discussed in § 2.4(A), a different situation is presented where the government pressures the employer into imposing conditions that will favor the government. In United States v. Stein, 541 F.3d 130 (2d Cir.2008), as discussed in § 2.4(A), government pressure was deemed state action, through the employer cutting off indemnification, resulting in a Sixth Amendment violation. The Second Circuit ruling there did not consider the legality of the employer's insistence upon employee cooperation with the government during the investigative stage. However, in United States v. Stein, 440 F.Supp.2d 315 (S.D.N.Y. 2006), the district court held this condition attached to continued reimbursement of attorneys' fees produced unconstitutionally coerced statements when employees gave proffers to government attorneys. See note 6 of § 19.1.

[89] See Wood v. Georgia, 450 U.S. 261 (1981) (employer provided counsel for former employees) discussed in CRIMPROC § 11.9(b).

[90] The limited body of caselaw on disqualification at the grand jury stage includes cases that have cited the presence of "informed consent" statements by employees, certifying that the employee was satisfied with the counsel retained by the employer. However, what is at issue is not simply providing an attorney at the grand jury stage, but providing an attorney to defend criminal charges, the employee most often will be under considerable financial pressure to accept. The factors producing that pressure are extensively explored in one of the lower court rulings in Stein, supra note 88, see United States v. Stein, 495 F.Supp.2d 390 (S.D.N.Y. 2007) (noting that the defense fees that would be provided by the employer were estimated to range from 3.3 million to as high as 24 million; the defendants could not afford to pay similar amounts so as to produce the same quality of representation; the defendants would have to "spend down" their assets to qualify for CJA counsel and those counsel also would not have the same resources available to the defendants as the counsel funded by the employer). Of course, informed consent is a prerequisite under Model Rule 1.8(f), see § 22.4, but its presence does not offset the need for considering the other factors noted in Rule 1.8(f).

To avoid possible disqualifications, retainer agreements will specifically state that: (1) the "sole obligation of the retained law firm will be to the employee," (2) the retained law firm "is not required to disclose any legal strategy, theory, plan of action, or the like" to the employer (and therefore accept billings that did not identify those activities); (3) no condition of cooperation with the employer is imposed; (4) payments will be made pursuant to a schedule (thereby precluding delaying payments to impose pressure on the law firm), and (5) the retention of the law firm cannot be terminated prior to the completion of the representation except with the approval of the court. The concern as to the law firm considering future retention by the employer disappears if the employee selects the law firm, but disqualification does not follow simply because the employer choose the attorney or offered the employee a list of acceptable attorneys. The attorney in those settings might have in mind that the employer similarly will select attorneys for employees in the future, but courts have not viewed that as per se disqualifying. (See also § 22.4, discussing Model Rule 1.8(f)). On the other hand, if the attorney currently is representing the employer in other matters, the incentive to keep that business is more likely to be viewed as presenting a serious conflict potential.

F.   Debriefing Witnesses

In the while collar context, persons or entities who are targets or potential targets of an investigation usually become aware of the investigation in its early stages. From that point on, counsel for that individual or entity will seek to monitor the investigation. That is done, in large part, by seeking information from friendly witnesses. A major aspect of that process is debriefing the witness shortly after the witness has testified, seeking to determine what questions were asked and what documents were discussed. Where that witness was represented by an attorney, this will be done with the permission of the counsel. Indeed, the counsel may be willing to assist in this process by having the witness interrupt his testimony with frequent anteroom consultations in which the witness will review the questions asked (and the witness' answers) since the last consultation.

As discussed above, such frequent anteroom consultations may not be allowed, and even if allowed, the witness' memory may not be reliable. Also, not all friendly witnesses will have counsel. Thus, a desirable element of debriefing is witness note-taking. Whether notes can be taken appears to rest in the discretion of the grand jury. While some prosecutors may have no objection, the DOJ takes the position that note-taking should not be permitted as it threatens grand jury secrecy.[91] While witnesses are not subject to an obligation of secrecy, allowing note taking is viewed as allowing the witness to create what is akin to a partial verbatim transcript. As discussed below, most federal courts hold that transcripts are subject to the Rule 6(e) secrecy requirements.

Debriefing would certainly be easier if a witness had a right to obtain a transcript of his grand jury testimony and to share that transcript with others. The primary argument for that right is based on the exemption of witness from the Rule 6(e) secrecy provision. See 16.9(D). Since the witness is free to disclose to others his complete grand jury experience, including what was asked and how he replied, why not allow the witness to do this through a transcript of his testimony? That argument has been flatly

---

[91] Federal Grand Jury Practice § 7.9.

rejected by most federal courts. They rely on Rule 6(e) having provisions on the allowable disclosure of grand jury matter, including testimony, that do not distinguish between requests by witnesses and requests by other persons; those provisions require court approval for disclosures, granted only on a special showing of need. However, a small group of rulings, as discussed below, have viewed the exemption argument as justifying separate treatment of witness requests, although not establishing an automatic right to a transcript.

The dominant caselaw position is that the witness can obtain a transcription of his testimony only by making a showing that qualifies for disclosure under one of the secrecy exceptions set forth in Rule 6(e)(3). This typically requires a showing of particularized need, roughly similar to that which must be made by a third party (e.g., a civil litigant) in obtaining disclosure of grand jury testimony. (See § 16.9(H), § 18.1(D)). A few courts have suggested that such a need is established when the witness is recalled to again testify before the grand jury, in light of the witness' concern that the prosecutor may be seeking to lay the foundation for a perjury prosecution by leading the witness to inconsistent testimony. Of course, should a grand jury witness subsequently be indicted, he becomes entitled to the transcript of his testimony under traditional discovery rules applicable to defendants. (See § 16.9(I)).

Several federal lower courts have recognized a presumptive right of a witness to receive a transcript of his testimony. They will grant the witness access to the transcript of his testimony unless the government presents a "clear showing . . . that other interests outweigh the witness' right to the transcript." These cases view such access as not subject to the Rule 6(e) restrictions upon disclosure because the witness is only seeking a transcript of what ordinarily may be held secret or not at his personal option. Courts taking the dominant view argue that the general structure of grand jury secrecy rejects this argument. It requires that the right of the witness to reveal his own recollection of his testimony be distinguished from his right to receive a transcription of his testimony, for that carries with it a potential for disclosure to others that bears directly upon the Rule 6(e) limitations upon disclosure of transcripts. They note also that recognizing a witness' presumptive right to a transcript can undercut the protection that grand jury secrecy affords the witness, since a target in a position of authority over the witness can then place pressure on the witness to obtain a transcript so as to permit the target to monitor or even control the witness' testimony. So too, recognizing such a right arguably facilitates circumvention of pretrial discovery standards, which deny the defense the prior recorded statements of witnesses (both defense and prosecution) in the government's possession. A witness who is friendly to the defense (or subject to defense pressure) would be able to provide a transcript of the witness' testimony which would be much more useful than the witness' recollection of that testimony in shaping the witness' trial testimony.[92]

---

[92] The D.C. Circuit, in In re Grand Jury, 490 F.3d 978 (D.C.Cir. 2007), concluded that these arguments against providing a transcript "lac[k] force with respect to a witness merely *reviewing* the transcript in private in the U.S. Attorney's office." It therefore held that "grand jury witnesses are entitled under Rule 6(e)(3)(E)(i) [the particularized need provision] to [such] review," with the district court determining in its "sound discretion whether to allow the witness' attorney to accompany the witness . . . and whether to allow the . . . [taking] of notes." That case involved a witness who had given grand jury testimony earlier in the same investigation, and had argued that he needed to review that testimony in order to "avoid the possibility of inconsistent testimony occasioned by the passage of years since the events in question and many months since the prior grand jury testimony."

§ 16.9   GRAND JURY SECRECY

A.   Underlying Considerations

The common law considered secrecy of grand jury proceedings to be an essential element of the grand jury process. This led to a prohibition against disclosure that was broad, but not absolute. Grand jurors were always allowed, for example, to disclose the testimony of a witness for the purpose of charging that witness with perjury before the grand jury. The courts recognized at a very early point that grand jury secrecy was not an end in itself. It was to be imposed only insofar as it might contribute to the grand jury's effectiveness in performing its investigative and screening functions.

Courts today see grand jury secrecy as contributing in several ways to the grand jury's dual roles. The most frequently quoted list of secrecy objectives is that set forth by the Supreme Court in *United States v. Procter & Gamble Company*.[93] The Court there listed five different objectives of secrecy requirements:

> (1) to prevent the escape of those whose indictment may be contemplated; (2) to insure the utmost freedom to the grand jury in its deliberations,[94] and to prevent persons subject to indictment or their friends from importuning the grand jurors; (3) to prevent subornation of perjury or tampering with the witnesses who may testify before grand jury and later appear at the trial of those indicted by it; (4) to encourage free and untrammeled disclosures by persons who have information with respect to the commission of crimes; (5) to protect the innocent accused who is exonerated from disclosure of the fact that he has been under investigation, and from the expense of standing trial where there was no probability of guilt.

If the federal law on grand jury secrecy looked only to these factors, secrecy requirements would have a much broader reach than under the current law. Over the last half of the twentieth century, Congress and the Supreme Court moved in the direction of relaxing rigid rules of secrecy. They frequently sought to strike a new balance in weighing the justifications for grand jury secrecy against the various interests served by disclosure (particularly the criminal defendant's interest in being able to uncover all favorable evidence). In some instances, they created new basic exceptions to secrecy and in others they introduced a flexibility in secrecy standards that could produce case-by-case exceptions.

In In re Grand Jury, 566 F.3d 12 (1st Cir.2009), the First Circuit, although refusing to adopt the D.C. Circuit's standard, found persuasive the distinction between "reviewing access" and receiving a copy of the transcript and concluded that a "less demanding requirement of particularized need would suffice for reviewing access." Note taking, however, would be viewed as similar to receiving a transcript and require the traditional "strong showing" of particularized need.

[93] 356 U.S. 677 (1958), discussed in § 16.12(F).

[94] As Justice Scalia noted in Butterworth v. Smith, 494 U.S. 624 (1990): "[Secrecy] helps to assure that the grand jurors will not be intimidated in the execution of their duties by the fear of unjustified public criticism to which they cannot respond." Indeed, secrecy was originally adopted at common law to protect the grand jury against not only criticism but judicial sanctions should it refuse to indict when the court viewed the evidence as sufficient. The resulting secrecy protection was not limited to instances in which the grand jury did not indict. Secrecy was thought to be needed as well when the grand jury decided to indict, as that decision too could be the subject of public "second guessing" and criticism. The evidence introduced at trial might lead to questioning why the grand jury chose one charge rather than another, or why it chose any charge (where the trial evidence was so insufficient as to produce a directed acquittal). However, as long as the grand jury evidence could not be disclosed, the critics could not be certain that the trial evidence matched the evidence before the grand jury.

Over the same period, a series of precedents, starting with *Procter & Gamble*, introduced what has been described as a sixth justification for grand jury secrecy. As discussed in § 16.12(F), *Procter & Gamble* noted that an otherwise permissible disclosure, to government attorneys would be prohibited where the prosecutor misused the grand jury process by seeking to develop evidence for purposes other than criminal prosecution (there, for use in a civil case). Restricting the disclosure of grand jury evidence outside its use in a criminal case removes any incentive for the prosecutor to engage in such misuse of the process to assist civil and administrative enforcement objectives.

B.   Rule 6(e)

Grand Jury secrecy is largely governed by Federal Rule 6(e), one of the most frequently amended provisions in the Rules of Criminal Procedure. Rule 6(e) currently contains: (1) a general prohibition of disclosure of "a matter occurring before the grand jury," applied initially to all persons present in the closed grand jury proceeding except the witness (i.e., to the grand jurors, prosecutor, court reporter, and any interpreter) and then extended to other "attorneys for the government" and "government personnel" assisting the prosecutor (see 16.3(E)); (2) a list of numerous specified exceptions authorizing disclosure of grand jury matter, with some requiring court authorization and others allowing disclosure without prior judicial approval; (3) procedural provisions governing applications for court approved disclosures (see note 25 supra); (4) a provision authorizing the sealing of indictments until the defendant has been taken into custody or released pending trial; (5) a provision requiring the closing of judicial hearings where needed to avoid disclosure of grand jury matter, "subject to any right to an open hearing in a contempt proceeding" (see § 16.2(F)); (6) a provision requiring grand jury records to be kept under seal as needed to prevent secrecy violations; and (7) a provision making a "knowing violation of Rule 6 * * * punish[able] as a contempt of court".

Notwithstanding its length, Rule 6(e) does not provide the totality of the regulation of federal grand jury secrecy. Initially, other provisions of the Federal Rules may bear upon that subject. Thus Federal Rule 16 (pretrial discovery) and Federal Rule 26.2 (on disclosure of prior recorded statements of witness) both extend to grand jury testimony and establish further exceptions to grand jury secrecy.

Second, federal statutes must be examined. The Rule 6(e)(3) provision on secrecy exceptions refers to two statutory provisions that create exceptions—the Financial Institutions Reform, Recovery, and Enforcement Act (FIRREA) and the national security disclosure provisions of the Patriot Act. Those statutes refer specifically to grand jury proceedings in their provisions on disclosure of particular types of evidence. Ordinarily, statutes addressing governmental disclosures are presumed not to create exceptions to grand jury secrecy by implication. In the case of the Freedom of Information Act, granting public access to judicial documents (which would include a grand jury transcript), Congress did not rely on that presumption, as it included a provision specifically exempting from the Act's provisions materials governed by statutory disclosure prohibitions, including Rule 6(e).

Where statutory provisions *add* to Rule 6(e) secrecy requirements, either by specific reference to grand jury matter or by reference to the general character of material, whether obtained by grand jury subpoena or by other means, those statutory provisions are not cross-referenced in Rule 6(e). Such provisions are found the Right to Financial Privacy Act, the Electronics Communications Privacy Act (Stored Communications Act), The Family Education Privacy Act, and the Tax Reform Act section on the disclosure of tax information obtained from the IRS.[95]

Finally, there remains the possibility that federal courts can order disclosure, in the exercise of their "inherent authority" over the grand jury process, where the court concludes that disclosure would not undercut the groundings of grand jury secrecy and would be in the "interest of justice," even though no statutory provision or court rule specifically authorizes disclosure. In one of the two leading cases relying upon such authority, the court authorized disclosure of the grand jury testimony of a political candidate, given in an investigation that had been closed, where that testimony had become a matter of public controversy and both the candidate and the government favored disclosure In the other, disclosure was authorized to the Investigating Committee of the Judicial Council for the federal circuit, which was investigating alleged misconduct by a federal judge. Other courts have questioned whether such authority exists, however, and that position finds further support in the Supreme Court's narrow reading of supervisory authority in *United States v. Williams.* (See § 16.4(C)).

C. "Grand Jury Matter"

The basic non-disclosure directive of Rule 6(e) prohibits disclosure of "a matter occurring before the grand jury." As explained in § 18.3(A), this is a "term of art" and encompasses far more than what actually takes place in the grand jury room. Indeed, Rule 6(e)(3), setting forth exceptions to the general secrecy directive, so indicates in its short hand reference to disclosure of "a grand-jury matter." Still, "grand jury matter" has not been viewed so broadly as to bar all disclosures that might reveal critical information about the nature of the grand jury investigation. That is especially the case as to those disclosures, described in § 18.3(A), that a prosecutor may make in describing the DOJ's own investigation, as opposed to the grand jury's investigation. In the white collar field in particular, where a prosecutor's office announces that it is investigating a particular transaction (often naming the participants), it is almost inevitable that the grand jury has been or will be involved. The secrecy objective of protecting the reputation of the target who might later be exonerated thus is easily evaded. The DOJ recognizes this concern and has adopted standards for its media releases discussing pending investigations.[96] Two of the primary justifications for authorized public disclosures—"matters that have already received substantial publicity," and "[matters] about which the community needs to be reassured that the appropriate law enforcement agency is investigating the incident"—can readily apply to white collar investigations. While some courts have pointed to the first factor as relevant even as to disclosures that refer specifically to the grand jury's activities ("there comes a times when information is sufficiently widely known that it has lost its

---

[95] As to the RFPA, the ECPA and the Family Education Privacy Act, see note 72 supra, and the text at notes 99, 102, and 103 infra. As to tax information governed by the Tax Reform Act, 26 U.S.C. § 6103 imposes special requirements for obtaining the information for both tax and nontax criminal investigations, and adds special restrictions on further disclosure. These requirements do not apply if the tax information is obtained from a source other than the IRS. See note § 16.10(D) at note 130.

[96] USAM, Ch. 1–700 sets forth a variety of guidelines, with special reference to ongoing investigations in §§ 1–7.111, 1–7.401, 1–7.530. See also CFR. § 50.2.

character as Rule 6(e) material"), the DOJ's media standards clearly allow for public disclosures regarding DOJ investigations that would not be permitted as to grand jury investigations.

Grand jury matter also does not encompass information gathered by investigators prior to the initiation of the grand jury's investigation. Courts are split, however, as to subsequent police procedures that are instituted in conjunction with the grand jury process. Thus, while Rule 6(e) generally does not apply to documents obtained by a search warrant, that may not be true where the search is conducted to further an ongoing grand jury investigation and the search warrant affidavit is based on grand jury testimony.

Especially critical for grand jury secrecy is the status of a prosecutor or investigator memorandum recording the interview statement of a witness under subpoena to testify. As noted in § 16.6(B), such interviews are an important part of the grand jury's investigative process, and for some subpoenaed witnesses, coverage under Rule 6(e) may be critical in deciding whether to accept the invitation to participate. Some courts have reasoned that, since the statement was given in anticipation of the witness testifying before the grand jury, it should be treated as grand jury matter if the witness did testify or a summary of his statement was presented to the grand jury in the case agent's testimony. Although the subsequent grand jury testimony might differ from the interview record, disclosure of the interview may nonetheless reveal the substance of that testimony. Other courts suggest that as long as the interview statement was not itself presented to the grand jury, the fact that it might suggest the content of witness' subsequent testimony is irrelevant, as it was not part of "what transpired in the grand jury room." A similar division may arise as to a post-testimony interview. Where the interview statement is not considered grand jury matter, investigators may show that statement to prospective witnesses, which would not be done with the same person's grand jury testimony. (See § 16.9(E)).

Section 18.3(A) notes the division among federal courts in determining whether grand jury matter includes subpoenaed documents. These rulings come in a special context which limits their impact on grand jury secrecy even where the particular circuit has concluded that such documents are not "grand jury matter." The documents in question are sought from the government only because the subpoenaed party could not produce the documents in response to a legitimate request by a civil litigant seeking the documents. Thus, it is the subpoenaed witness (often a target) who directs that litigant to the grand jury and reveals that the documents had been subpoenaed (a disclosure that might have been avoided through the government's return of the requested originals to the witness). What is revealed as to the grand jury investigation is information that the witness was always free to reveal. These cases do not suggest that the subpoenaed documents are outside of Rule 6(e) for other purposes (e.g., the prosecution making a public disclosure on its own initiative, or showing the documents to prospective witnesses).

D. The Witness Exception

1. General Principles

Federal Rule 6(e) doesn't just fail to include the grand jury witness in its list of persons ordinarily barred from disclosing grand jury matters; it adds that "no obligation of secrecy may be imposed on any person" except in accordance with Rule 6(e). Thus, while the listed participants may not disclose the testimony of a witness, the witness herself, if she so choses, can reveal publicly or privately her account of what went on in the grand jury room (in particular, the questions asked and her responses), the content of any subpoena duces tecum she received, and the content of the documents she returned in response to that subpoena.

Although the "witness exception" has been criticized as creating a gigantic loophole in grand jury secrecy, it has been justified on grounds of practical necessity and the need to prevent grand jury abuses. Imposition of a witness secrecy requirement has been characterized as "impractical and unreal—a partner, an employee, a relative, a friend called on to testify will come back and tell the person concerning whom he testified, and it should be so." The key to encouraging "free and untrammeled disclosures" by witnesses, it is argued, is to afford secrecy to the witness who wants that protection, not to require secrecy from those who feel duty bound to disclose. The witness has the right to refuse to reveal the content of his grand jury testimony, even if deposed in a separate proceeding.[97] That protection is hardly sufficient, however, if the witness can readily be placed in a position where she will face adverse consequences if she exercises her right to refuse to disclose her testimony. This concern requires, in turn, that the witness be assured that both her appearance before the grand jury and the substance of her testimony there will never become known to persons in a position to impose such adverse consequences.

Even if grand jury secrecy ensured that the witness' appearance before the grand jury would not be revealed to anyone other than the prosecution personnel sworn to secrecy, that would not prevent the target or other interested persons from learning that there is an ongoing investigation either from other witnesses or from a subpoena that person received (in the case of a target, most likely a subpoena duces tecum). If the witness is an individual who might well be subpoenaed, considering the nature of the investigation, that interested party may then ask the witness whether he has (or will) testify, and if so, to reveal what occurred in the grand jury room. In many situations, the relationship between the witness and the party making the inquiry will prevent a curt "none-of-your-business" response. The witness here wants grand jury secrecy to allow him to misrepresent, without that misrepresentation ever coming to light. He wants to be able to deny that he was subpoenaed to testify, and if that is not believable, to misrepresent his testimony to the extent necessary to remain on good terms with the person making the inquiry (or others to whom that person will disseminate the witness' response). In the most extreme situation, the witness wants to be able to accept counsel provided by the target, have anteroom consultations with that counsel, and not need to worry about subsequent revelations in leading that counsel to believe the witness testified as favorably to the target as he possibly could (including adhering to counsel's specific directions in framing responses to questions).

Federal judicial districts were divided on the issue of binding witnesses to secrecy prior to the 1946 adoption of the Federal Rules. In refusing to do so, the original

---

[97] In compelling the witnesses to testify before the grand jury, the judicial system offers the witness the protection of its secrecy provision, allowing the witness to refuse to reveal her testimony in a subsequent judicial or administrative proceeding unless the party seeking that disclosure is able to gain access pursuant to one of the Rule 6(e)(3) exceptions to the secrecy provision. Where that party qualifies under exception, it obtains a transcript of the witness' testimony, and the witness then can be questioned about that testimony.

version of Rule 6(e) did not add secrecy provisions so broad as to give the witness who desired not to disclose the full protection described above. The Rule recognized from the outset several of the secrecy exceptions, described below, that are most likely to produce disclosures that identify persons who testified and reveal the substance of their testimony. Subsequently adopted exceptions have further diluted the Rule's protection. Nonetheless, where the government is willing to take all steps within its power to prevent disclosure that a person testified, and if that becomes known, prevent disclosure of the substance of the testimony, it can provide assurance that will be fairly convincing for many witnesses who are reluctant to testify for fear that their cooperation will become known.[98]

2. Gag Orders

Notwithstanding the Rule 6(e)(2) prohibition against imposing a secrecy obligation except in accord with that provision, several federal lower courts have suggested that the judiciary's inherent authority over grand jury proceedings permits a court to issue a protective order prohibiting witness disclosures during an ongoing investigation upon a government showing of "compelling necessity" (i.e., that the investigation will be undermined without continuing secrecy). Other courts, however, view such orders as beyond the court's authority in light of Rule 6(e)(2)'s specific prohibition against imposing additional secrecy requirements. Federal courts uniformly hold that it is not contrary to Rule 6(e)(2) for the prosecutor to request that the witness not make disclosures to the target—provided it is made clear that it is only requesting, not requiring, non-disclosure.

Congress has specifically authorized imposing a ban on witness disclosures in several settings involving third-party subpoenas. The Right to Financial Privacy Act (RFPA) included the first statutory "gag order" provisions. The RFPA governs subpoenas directed to financial institutions to obtain customer records.[99] The Act ordinarily requires the financial institution to notify the customer of the subpoena, but Congress provided from the outset that this notification requirement did not apply to grand jury subpoenas. When many financial institutions nonetheless decided to provide notice as a courtesy to their customers, Congress added two gag order provisions. The stronger provision applies only where the grand jury subpoena is issued in the investigation of possible crimes committed against a financial institution. The RFPA here automatically prohibits the financial institution and its employees from "notifying any person named in the grand jury subpoena * * * about the existence or contents of such subpoena, or information that has been furnished to the grand jury in response to such subpoena."[100] This prohibition appears to be permanent, as the statue does not refer to a later point in time when disclosure would be allowed. In *Butterworth v. Smith*,[101] the Supreme Court sustained a First Amendment challenge to

---

[98] This assumes that government will not make all of the disclosures it would be allowed to make under Rule 6(e)(3), will not call the witness to testify at any subsequent trial of the target, and will argue against disclosures requested by others that require court approval. It also assumes that a witness will have to obtain judicial permission to receive a transcript of his testimony, and that the government can oppose such disclosure. (See § 16.8(F)).

[99] As to the scope of the RFPA, see § 16.10(D) at note 126.

[100] See 12 U.S.C. § 342(1) (setting forth the prohibition and providing for a sanction of loss of licensed depository status); 18 U.S.C. § 1510 (criminal sanctions). See also § 6.3(B).

[101] 494 U.S. 624 (1990).

a state statute that imposed a secrecy ban on a grand jury witness insofar as that ban extended beyond the discharge of the grand jury. However, that state ban was broader than the ban imposed under the RFPA, which refers only to disclosing the subpoena and response by the financial institution. In *Butterworth*, the state sought to prevent the witness from discussing the "content, gist, or import" of his testimony, which was read as barring the witness from "mak[ing] a truthful statement of information he acquired on his own" simply because the subject matter was also covered in his testimony.

When the subject under investigation is an offense other than fraud against a financial institution, the RFPA provides for a gag only if approved by the court. Moreover, the gag order is limited to ninety days, although extensions are possible. To obtain the gag order the court initially must find that the "investigation being conducted is within the lawful jurisdiction of the [grand jury]" and "there is reason to believe that records being sought are relevant to a legitimate law enforcement investigation." It then must conclude that there is "reason to believe" that giving notice to the customer "will result" in either: (1) endangerment to any person; (2) flight from prosecution; (3) "destruction or tampering with evidence"; (4) "intimidation of potential witnesses"; or (5) "otherwise seriously jeopardizing" the investigation. When the gag order expires, this customer must be sent a prescribed notification which states with "reasonable specificity" the "nature of the law enforcement inquiry" and notes that records were supplied and notification delayed pursuant to court order.

As discussed in § 16.10(D), the Electronic Communication Privacy Act governs the issuance of grand jury subpoenas to providers of electronic communication service (both wire and internet) and certain providers of remote computing services (including cloud storage and other services). Where the ECPA (also known as the Stored Communication Act) requires prior notification to the customer of a subpoena (including a grand jury subpoena) demanding customer data, it also provides for a 90–day-court-ordered delay in notification.[102] The finding required for delaying notification is a "reason to believe" as to the same dangers as noted in the RFPA delayed-notification provision. The Family Educational Privacy Act provides for a gag order on somewhat easier terms (a showing of "good cause") where an educational institution is subpoenaed to produce educational records and other information protected by that Act.[103]

In the white collar context, a scenario likely to lead the government to seek a court-ordered notification delay is that in which the government anticipates that the target would respond to a subpoena duces tecum by destroying its documents, but the government currently lacks the probable cause needed to obtain those documents through a search warrant. The government may be able to obtain the information needed to establish probable cause from a subpoena directed to a third party, but if

---

[102] 18 U.S.C. §§ 2703(b), 2705. The ECPA does not require prior notification when a subpoena is used to obtain basic subscriber information and the delayed notification provision is tied to the mandatory notification requirement in obtaining the contents of wire or electronic communications. Although the policy underlying that provision would support a judicial gag order precluding notification as to a subpoena demanding basic customer information, judicial authority to issue such an order without specific statutory authorization remains an open issue. A similar issue arises when stored content is subpoenaed from a remote service provider not subject to the Act because its services are not available to the public. (See § 16.10(D)).

[103] 20 U.S.C. § 1232q.

that party immediately notifies the target, the documents could be destroyed before the search warrant can be obtained and executed. A similar situation is presented where the records of the third party service provider might identify witnesses currently unknown to the government, but there is concern that the target would intimidate these persons through threat of economic reprisals once it learned that the government might be interested in their testimony. The hope here is to identify the potential witnesses and compel their testimony before the target learns of the subpoena that led to their identification.

One consequence of restricting notification is that the target loses the opportunity to challenge the subpoena in advance of the subpoenaed party's response. As discussed in § 16.11(C), the target ordinarily would not be able to raise a Fourth Amendment objection, even if the records subpoenaed from the third party were originally created by the target. However, the target will have standing to present challenges based on the misuse of subpoena authority insofar as that misuse affects the target's interests (see § 16.12(G)). Similarly, where a statute creates certain prerequisites for use of a grand jury subpoena to obtain customer information, the customer can object to the failure to comply with these prerequisites (see § 16.10(D)). Of course, the subpoenaed third-party often can raise those same objections, but that party often will have little interest in presenting such a challenge—viewing the customer as the more appropriate challenger. Whether the preclusion of notification allows the target/customer to object at a later point may depend upon the character of the objection. Where the target/customer could have objected to disclosure based on an evidentiary privilege, that objection is preserved by the standard doctrine that a claim of privilege is not defeated by a disclosure that was compelled "without opportunity to claim the privilege."

E. Disclosures to Further Federal Criminal Law Enforcement

As discussed in 16.3(E), grand jury matter will be disclosed to government attorneys and other personnel who are part of the prosecutorial "team." Rule 6(e)(3) allows for disclosure without a court order to: (1) "an attorney for the government in performing that attorney's duty" (which has been read as limited to "prosecutorial duties"), and (2) designated assisting personnel (including investigators) to "assist the attorney for the government to enforce federal criminal law." The disclosure to these team members in itself does not threaten the secrecy of the grand jury process. However, in granting that disclosure to further the enforcement of the "federal criminal law," Rule 6(e)(3) obviously anticipates further disclosures by these persons as needed for enforcement purposes—e.g., the prosecution's use of grand jury testimony to impeach a witness at trial. The critical issue from the perspective of a person who would benefit from grand jury secrecy (e.g., a witness who would prefer his testimony not be known or a target who would not want the investigation publicly revealed) is what additional disclosures are allowed as being in furtherance of federal criminal law enforcement. Of course, the prosecutor has discretion not to make such disclosures even if legally permissible, but persons interested in the protection of secrecy may want the assurance of a legal prohibition against disclosure.

Initially, the question arises as to what prosecutors and investigators may disclose in the course of developing further evidence. Prosecutors and investigators often will desire to refer to information obtained from the grand jury investigation in the course of discussions with witnesses, potential witnesses, and even targets. That may occur in investigators questioning persons to determine whether they are possible witnesses and should be subpoenaed, in prosecutors discussing proffers with persons seeking immunity, in prosecutors questioning witnesses before the grand jury, and in prosecutors convincing targets to accept liability and cooperate with the investigation. Although such disclosures are quite common, the caselaw addressing their legality is sparse.

One factor contributing to the absence of more caselaw is the DOJ's advice to prosecutors and investigators that they avoid references to the grand jury, if at all possible, in discussing with all third parties the investigation and the evidence it has produced. Indeed, if feasible, the identity of the person providing the information being discussed will not be revealed.[104] That practice finds support in the small group of cases commenting on such disclosures. They have reasoned that secrecy provisions are not violated when prosecutors or investigators refer to grand jury matter in interviewing prospective witness without identifying the matter as coming from the grand jury. Indeed, these and other cases suggest that reference to the material as having come from the grand jury would not render the disclosure a secrecy violation where that reference was necessary to achieving the purpose of the interview. On the other hand, federal lower courts have held that prosecutors lack authority to reveal grand jury matter (identified as such) to private investigators who might assist the government in developing investigative leads, although those rulings rely in part on the fact that such investigators do not fall within the federal provision on disclosures to assisting personnel.

Another set of disclosures presenting the question of what is allowed in the enforcement of the criminal law are disclosures of grand jury matter to a court. Some prosecutors prefer to avoid this issue and seek a judicial order under Rule 6(e)(3) authorizing such a disclosure. Others, however, argue that a court order is not needed as disclosures made in judicial proceedings are per se made in furtherance of federal criminal law enforcement. Courts have allowed many such uses, but questioned others. Thus, they have sustained disclosing grand jury matter in a search warrant affidavit, disclosure at trial to refresh the recollection of a witness or to impeach the witness, disclosure at trial in offering a defendant's grand jury testimony as substantive evidence (e.g., to establish perjury), and disclosure to establish a factual basis for a guilty plea. Such disclosures may be limited by the court, however, to avoid gratuitously exposing aspects of the investigation (e.g., unindicted participants) that are not essential to the particular proceeding. Some courts have reasoned that, once the guilty plea is entered, the prosecution is ended, so use of grand jury matter at later proceedings (e.g., sentencing and parole revocation) requires a court order under Rule

---

[104] See Federal Grand Jury Practice § 3.13 (in describing nature of the investigation, reference should be made to the prosecution's investigation, rather than to the grand jury, and "the identities of the targets of the investigation should not be disclosed"); § 3.45 (in contrast to the authority to show a grand jury witness his own prior testimony, "because it is unsettled whether a prosecutor may disclose grand jury testimony of one witness to another grand jury witness, the prosecutor may wish to seek a court order under 6(e)(3) to permit disclosure"); § 3.51 (when showing a grand jury witness a document subpoenaed from another company, safeguards commonly are employed so as not to reveal the source of the document); § 6.16 (recognizing criticism of the view that the Rule 6(e)(3) references to disclosure for use "in performing the attorney's duty" allow further disclosures by that attorney to third persons, since disclosures to third parties otherwise are expressly authorized in Rule 6(e)(3), and concluding: "Given the uncertainty of the law, AUSAs should exercise caution in disclosing grand jury materials to third parties before indictment without a court order").

6(e)(3). Other courts, however, accept disclosures for sentencing without a Rule 6(e)(3) court order, provided the material is filed under seal. As discussed below in subsection (G), if disclosure in a judicial proceeding requires a Rule 6(e)(3) court order, the disclosure must be justified under a "particularized need" standard. However, that should not prove difficult for the prosecutor if the grand jury matter is relevant to the issue presented in the proceeding.

F. Target Notification

As discussed in § 16.6(F), DOJ internal standards require that a subpoenaed target be informed of that target status. Those standards also encourage notifying targets of their status in order to afford them the opportunity to testify. USAM § 9–11.155 adds that the prosecutor "has discretion to notify an individual who has been the target of a grand jury investigation that the individual is no longer considered to be a target."[105]

The DOJ warns prosecutors and investigators not to reveal the identities of targets, to others, "since one of Rule 6(e)(3)'s specific aims is to protect individuals who ultimately are not indicted from unfavorable publicity."[106] Target notification is considered a justified exception, as the disclosure is limited to the target and is aimed at protecting the interests of the target. Thus, it may be seen as another type of disclosure by the prosecutor furthering the enforcement of the criminal law.[107] In some instances, however, that disclosure may work against the Rule 6(e) objective of protecting against unfair publicity. Where the target is an entity subject to regulation under securities laws or other regulatory structures, the entity may have a duty to report that notification, which will lead to its public disclosure.[108]

G. Disclosures to Further Other Governmental Enforcement

1. Generally

Rule 6(e)(3) has several provisions under which the federal prosecutor can disclose grand jury matter to other governmental officials, federal and state, having responsibility for enforcement of laws other than federal criminal law enforcement. These provisions deal with: (1) disclosures allowed without a court order; (2) disclosures requiring a court order, but limited to specified purposes; and (3)

---

[105] USAM § 9–11.155 notes that notification may be appropriate where the individual previously has been notified of target status and the investigation has been concluded with no indictment being returned or evidence before the grand jury "conclusively establishes" that target status has ended. It adds that other circumstances may also justify notification, "as when government action resulted in public knowledge of the investigation." However, the prosecutor retains "discretion to decline to issue notification" if the notification would "adversely affect the integrity" of the investigation or there are "other appropriate reasons."

[106] Federal Grand Jury Practice § 3.13.

[107] In United States v. Smith, 787 F.2d 111 (3d Cir.1986), the release of a transcript revealing that the trial witness had received a target letter was characterized as not revealing grand jury matter. The court noted that the target letter did not emanate from the grand jury but the prosecutor and it constituted only the prosecution's expression of opinion as to the status of the investigation based on information known to it, which might or might not include grand jury testimony. While the USAM § 9–11.151 definition of target does fit this description, the target letter is accompanied by a subpoena or invitation to testify, and together they convey that the grand jury is investigating the activities of this person, which does constitute grand jury matter. The *Smith* opinion also recognized justifications for disclosure under the circumstances of that case which would apply to disclosing target letter viewed as grand jury matter.

[108] Villa, Corporate Counsel Guidelines § 5.22 (available on at Westlaw CORPCG);

disclosures requiring a court order under the general provision on third-party disclosures.

2. Disclosures Without a Court Order

Unlike disclosures to further federal criminal law enforcement, disclosures to implement the enforcement of other laws generally must be approved by the court supervising the grand jury. Two exceptions have been created by statute and are now incorporated in Rule 6(e)(3).

One exception was created by the Civil Asset Forfeiture Reform Act.[109] It allows disclosure to "an attorney for the government * * * for use in connection with any civil forfeiture provision of federal law." This provision presumably allows the civil DOJ to "use" the grand jury matter in a variety of ways, including disclosure to the target in negotiating a forfeiture or use in a forfeiture proceeding. Of course, it is dependent upon the prosecutor's initiative, and the prosecutor may assign a higher priority to preserving secrecy as to certain aspects of the grand jury evidence.

The second exception was adopted as part of the USA PATRIOT ACT.[110] This exception gives the prosecutor the authority to disclose without court order "grand jury matter involving foreign intelligence, * * * counterintelligence, or foreign intelligence information" with each of these categories defined in detail as to content (e.g., "information relating to the capabilities, intentions, or activities" of "foreign governments"). The disclosure may be made to federal, state, local, and foreign officials with those officials then limited to using the information "only as necessary in the conduct of that person's official duties." State and local officials are further limited by federal guidelines. While here too disclosure rests in the discretion of the prosecutor, it seems unlikely that the interests of grand jury secrecy will trump the national security interests served by the disclosure. Thus for the witness in a white collar investigation who desires the protection of Rule 6(e) secrecy, this provision does not present a significant threat only because it is most unlikely that a white collar investigation will present information in any of the covered categories.

3. Court Orders for Specified Enforcement Purposes

Three provisions in Federal Rule 6(e)(3) authorize court ordered disclosures, on prosecutor initiated requests, to allow for use in the enforcement of specific types of laws. They deal with: (1) disclosure of grand jury matter "sought by a foreign court or prosecutor for use in an official investigation"; (2) disclosure of grand jury matter that "may disclose a violation of State, Indian tribal, or foreign criminal law" to an appropriate official of these government bodies "for the purpose of enforcing that law"; and (3) disclosure of grand jury matter that "may disclose a violation of military law to the appropriate military official for the purpose of enforcing that law." These disclosure authorizations were separated from the general provision on third-party disclosures (discussed below) in order to avoid the particularized need standard applied to those disclosures. The standard here appears to focus simply on relevancy. In contrast to particularized need, there appears to be no room for weighing such factors as

---

[109] See 18 U.S.C. § 3322(a) (included in FIRREA disclosures provision); Rule 6(e)(3)(A)(iii).

[110] See § 203 of Pub. L. 107–56, 115 stat. § 162 (20d); Fed. R. Crim. P. 6(e)(3)(D).

alternative means of obtaining the information by the other government body. Thus, for the person interested in the protection of grand jury secrecy, the key is how the prosecutor will approach requesting disclosure under these provisions, rather than the judicial review involved in gaining court approval.[111]

Very often, when a witness provides testimony or documents relating to a federal white collar crime, that evidence also will relate to a violation of state criminal law. Thus the grounding for disclosure to state officials is often present, with the critical issue being whether the federal prosecutor will use that opportunity. Where the prosecutor intends to proceed on a federal prosecution while seeking not to reveal the identity of certain cooperating witnesses, that concern is likely to carry over to any decision on providing information to state or foreign federal prosecutors. The primary issue for such witnesses is what will the prosecutor do where the only offense revealed is a state or foreign offense, and proceeding there will result in disclosing the identity of the witness (and even if the witness' identity is already known, adding to that disclosure the full content of the witness' testimony).

4. Court Orders Under the General Provision on Disclosures to a Third Party

The most common prosecutor initiated disclosure to implement regulatory enforcement other than the federal criminal law occurs under the general provision on disclosure to third persons, Rule 6(e)(3)(E)(i). This provisions, also discussed in § 18.3(D)(E), allows for court ordered disclosure "preliminary to or in connection with a judicial proceeding." Apart from two statutory exceptions, that is the provision that governs disclosure to other DOJ attorneys charged with the enforcement of federal laws through civil actions.[112] It also is the provision that governs where the prosecutor seeks to disclose grand jury matter to administrative agencies (federal and state) charged with regulatory enforcement. To gain court approval, the disclosure must meet two basic requirements: it must have a sufficient relationship to anticipated or pending litigation to be characterized as made "preliminary to or in connection with a judicial

---

[111] Of course, a court may examine the grand jury matter and conclude that some or all of it could not possibly be relevant to a foreign criminal law investigation, and couldn't possibly disclose a violation of state, trial, foreign, or military criminal law. It must do so, however, without the benefit of an adversary presentation. The provisions involved do not require that notice of the government's motion be given to interested parties (e.g., the grand jury witness whose testimony will be disclosed). The motion will be filed under seal and considered ex parte.

[112] One exception is the disclosure for use in civil forfeiture enforcement, allowed without a court order, as discussed at note 109 supra. The other exception was established in the Financial Institutions Reform, Recover, and Enforcement Act, 18 U.S.C. § 3322, which is cross-reference in Federal Rule 6(e)(3)(A)(iii). Section 3322(b) authorizes a court, on motion of the grand jury prosecutor, to order disclosures of grand jury matter to financial institution regulatory personnel. The only prerequisite for judicial issuance of the order is a "finding of substantial need." This provision eliminated two barriers to ordering such disclosure under the general third-party provision. It allows disclosure to the state regulatory personnel even if that disclosure is not "preliminary to a judicial proceeding." It also substitutes the less demanding "substantial need" standard for the general provision's "particularized need" provision. As to the § 3322(b) standard, Federal Grand Jury Practice § 6.21notes: "Congress [in the legislative history] suggested that courts consider a number of factors in connection with such orders, including (1) the public interest served by disclosure, particularly the protection of the public health or safety or the safety or soundness of a federally insured financial institution; (2) the burden or cost of duplicating the grand jury investigation; (3) the potential unavailability of witnesses; (4) the fact that the department or agency already has a legitimate independent right to those materials; (6) the need to prevent ongoing violations of law; and (7) the expiration of an applicable statute of limitations."

proceeding"; it must be justified by a "particularized need," a standard that looks to whether the need for the disclosure outweighs the public interest in secrecy.

The leading case on the "preliminary to" requirement, *United States v. Baggot*,[113] is discussed in § 18.3(D). While that requirement forecloses disclosures to regulators who take administrative actions without judicial involvement, disclosures to regulators that need a judicial determination for enforcement of their rulings would be "preliminary to" a judicial proceeding. Also distinguishable are administrative proceedings described as quasi-judicial in character.

As discussed § 18.3(E), disclosures for government enforcement purposes automatically present certain factors favorable to disclosure under the particularized need standard (including the public interest in regulatory enforcement and the initiation of the disclosure request by the prosecutor, who has a vested concern in grand jury secrecy). Also, such disclosures tend to be requested after the grand jury investigation has ended, which reduces (but does not eliminate) secrecy concerns. Still, there often will be countervailing considerations, including the possibility that the government regulator could obtain the underlying information without invading grand jury secrecy, and the concern that allowing such disclosures will encourage grand jury prosecutors to "manipulate the grand jury's powerful investigative tools to root out additional evidence useful in the [regulator's] civil suit." The latter concern is particularly strong when the grand jury investigation ended without indicting the individual who is the subject of the grand jury evidence that would be disclosed to regulators.

In light of the competing concerns, meeting the particularized need standard is far from automatic. When given the opportunity to challenge the government's motion,[114] a witness or target may be successful in precluding or narrowing the requested disclosure. Nonetheless, the best protection for a party seeking to ensure that grand jury secrecy will be maintained, as to government initiated disclosure motions under Rule 6(e)(3)(E)(i), is to gain a commitment from the prosecutor not to seek such disclosures.[115]

---

[113] 463 U.S. 476 (1983), discussed in § 18.3 at note 28.

[114] Federal Rule 6(e)(3)(F) provides that petition for court ordered disclosure under the "preliminary-to" provision may be filed and heard ex parte when the government is the petitioner for disclosure. No standard is stated as to when the court should permit an ex parte presentation, but lower courts suggest that the government must establish need, such as the potential concerns that apply to the imposition of a witness "gag." See the text at note—supra. Where an ex parte hearing is not justified, Rule 6(e)(3)(F) requires that notice be given to "(i) an attorney for the government, (ii) the parties to the judicial proceeding, and (iii) any other person when the court may designate." This provision covers both motions by civil litigants and government initiated motions. The parties to the judicial proceeding on a government initiated motion would be the government unit that would bring the civil suit or regulatory proceeding and persons identified in the grand jury matter against whom regulatory action would be taken. The "other persons" could include the persons who provided to the grand jury evidence to be disclosed. The hearing on disclosure will be closed since it will discuss grand jury matter. (See § 16.2(F)).

[115] For the target, such a commitment may be a part of a plea agreement or a deferred prosecution agreement, both of which may be judicially enforced. Typically the target would also have to agree to the types of restrictions of financial obligations that might otherwise be imposed through the regulatory action. See §§ 2.4(C), 24.2(D), 24.7.

H. Court Ordered Disclosures to Civil Litigants

As discussed in § 18.3(D), the general "preliminary to" provision is also commonly used by a civil litigant who seeks disclosure of grand jury testimony. In many instances, the litigant requesting disclosure is a plaintiff suing a former target,[116] but disclosure can also be sought by a former target in presenting a defense or bringing a civil action against others. The key here will be the application of the "particularized need" standard as formulated in *Douglas Oil Co. v. Petrol Stops Northwest*.[117] That standard, discussed in the § 18.3(E), takes into account the protection of grand jury witnesses, particular where revealing their testimony could result in retaliation. Under the applicable procedure, the government will be in a position to oppose the disclosure if that concern or other functions of grand jury secrecy would be adversely impacted by the disclosure. On the other hand, a witness will not be allowed to take advantage of grand jury secrecy to mislead a factfinder. Thus, disclosure will be allowed where the moving party seeks that portion of the grand jury testimony of a trial witness that relates directly to the witness' trial testimony and the court, on in camera review, concludes that the grand jury testimony might be viewed as inconsistent with the trial testimony. In the end, where the prosecutor has not otherwise disclosed the identity of a witness who testified before the grand jury and that witness has not stepped forward to testify in the civil suit, a civil litigant's motion for disclosure is not very likely to pierce the shield of secrecy as to that witness.

I. Disclosures to Defendants

1. *Generally*

Federal Rule 16 sets forth the basic standards governing pretrial discovery by the defendant. At one time, grand jury matter received special protection. Thus it was more difficult for a defendant to obtain disclosure of grand jury testimony than recorded statements given to investigators. That special protection has largely been overturned through the combined force of two rationales: (1) the "traditional reasons for grand jury secrecy" are "largely inapplicable" to post-indictment disclosure of the type of information made available under federal criminal discovery law, and (2) the central focus of federal discovery law—eliminating trial by surprise and thereby making trials more effective in revealing the truth—has a substantially higher priority than preserving grand jury secrecy. Notwithstanding this movement, Rule 16 still contains a special provision on disclosing grand jury transcripts. Rule 16(a)(3) provides: "This rule does not apply to the discovery or inspection of a grand jury's recorded proceedings, except as provided in Rules 6, 12(h), 16(a)(i), and 26.2." Rule 12(h) simply notes that Rule 26.2 will apply to suppression hearings, allowing the disclosure there of a grand jury transcripts where the prerequisites of Rule 26.2 are met. Each of the other cited provisions provides the grounding for one or more exceptions to grand jury secrecy as applied to defendants.

---

[116] Typically, grand jury material will be sought where the investigation did not result in a criminal trial, as there much of the government's case would have been disclosed in that trial.

[117] 441 U.S. 211 (1979), discussed in § 18.3(E) at note 35.

2. *Rule 26.2 Disclosures*

Federal Rule 26.2 addresses the disclosure of prior recorded statement of both defense and prosecution witnesses. As applied to prosecution witnesses, it duplicates the Jenks Act, discussed in § 16.6(C). Like the Jenks Act, it includes in its definition of "statement" a witness' testimony before a grand jury. Like the Jencks Act, it authorizes disclosure of the witness' prior statement after the witness testifies in the current proceeding. Unlike the Jencks Act, Rule 26.2 does not address the possibility of earlier disclosure, but that is not necessary because Rule 16.2, governing pretrial discovery, incorporates the Jencks rule on prior disclosure. Rule 16.2 states that, aside from the special provision for entity defendants under Rule 16(a)(l) (discussed infra), Rule 16 does not authorize "the discovery or inspection of statements made by prospective government witnesses except as provided in 18 USC.2500 [the Jencks Act]." The Jencks Act, in turn, provides that no statement made by a "prospective Government witness" shall be subject to "discovery or inspection until said witness has testified on direct examination." In practice, some district courts encourage prosecution disclosure shortly in advance of the witness testifying so as to avoid delays in the start of cross-examination.

The timing restriction of Rule 26.2 and the Jencks Act have an important bearing on the risk faced by a cooperating grand jury witness as to the eventual disclosure of his or her grand jury testimony. Initially, if the government is willing to proceed to trial without using the witness, there is no provision in Rule 16 authorizing disclosure of the witness' grand jury testimony. If the government needs the witness at trial, then Jencks and Rule 26.2 will require disclosure, but only if the witness does in fact testify. If the prosecution is resolved without a trial, the witness' testimony will not be disclosed, as it is not included in the pretrial discovery granted to the defense.

Indeed, aside from capital cases, the government is not required in pretrial discovery to list its prospective witnesses. Federal courts do have discretion to order production of a witness list pretrial, but the burden placed on the defendant is especially heavy, with the court's assessment starting with a presumption that witness-list disclosure generally is not available (Congress having rejected a proposal to add witness-lists to Rule 16's mandated disclosures). Of course a defendant who eventually enters a guilty plea may be told in the course of plea bargaining that a particular person will be a government witness, and that witness' likely testimony may be described, but such disclosure lies in the discretion of the prosecutor. A prosecutor can commit to not revealing a witness' cooperation before the grand jury unless the case goes to trial and the witness' testimony is then needed. For many potential witnesses, that may be sufficient to gain complete cooperation.

3. *Rule 16(a)(1) Disclosures*

Rule 16(a)(l) has three pretrial discovery provisions that impact grand jury secrecy. The least significant is paragraph B, which requires pretrial disclosure of the "defendants recorded testimony before a grand jury relating to the charged offense." Since the defendant is aware of his own testimony, although he may not recall all of the details, this disclosure does not adversely affect the objectives of grand jury secrecy.

On the other hand, paragraph C does significantly impact grand jury secrecy objectives in its extension of the defendant's right to his own statement (including grand jury testimony) to the defendant who is "an organization." Paragraph C provides for the disclosure of the statements of the organization's "director, officer, employee, or agent" if "the government contends that the person making the statement: (i) was legally able to bind the defendant regarding the subject of the statement because of that person's position * * *, or (ii) was personally involved in the alleged conduct constituting the offense and was legally able to bind the defendant regarding that conduct because of that person's position." Both situations give the organizational defendant pretrial discovery of grand jury testimony that otherwise would be disclosed only when (and if) these witnesses testified at trial. In the first setting, the organizational defendant is more likely to have previously been aware of that testimony. Since the witness when testifying must currently have occupied a position which allows the government to contend that the organization is bound by the witness' statements, the organization is likely to have been aware of the witness' testimony. (See § 16.8(F)). The second setting, on the other hand, applies to the grand jury testimony of witnesses who had participated in the criminal activity but were ex-employees or ex-officers when they testified. These persons are much less likely to have cooperated with the organization at the time they gave testimony, and quite often will be key government witnesses (sometimes immunized and sometimes testifying pursuant to a plea agreement).

Paragraph E of Rule 16(a)(l) does not refer to the grand jury process, but it bears upon grand jury secrecy because it governs pretrial disclosure of documents in the government's possession, including those obtained by grand jury subpoena. Since the government in making disclosures need not identify how the documents were obtained, no reference to Rule 6(e) secrecy is made in paragraph E. However, the character of grand jury investigation, including the government's sources, will be evident in the documents disclosed under paragraph E.

Paragraph E requires disclosure of three classes of documents; (1) documents that were obtained from or belong to the defendant; (2) documents the government intends to use at trial in its case in chief; and (3) documents "material to preparing the defense." It is the third category that reveals information about the grand jury investigation that otherwise would not be known to the defense, even after a trial. However, the burden is on the defense to demonstrate that a particular document likely to be in the government's possession would be material to preparing the defense. Thus, a defendant cannot successfully demand inspection of all records of his former employer subpoenaed by the grand jury; the demand must specify particular types of documents (e.g., reports on a specific subject) and explain why the contents might be helpful in rebutting the prosecution's case or supporting a particular line of defense. The court, if it so chooses, may examine the specific document *in camera* to determine whether it might have such significance.

4. *Rule 6 Discovery*

Although Rule 6(e)(3) contains two provisions under which a defendant may obtain access to grand jury testimony, only one of those provisions authorizes disclosure as a matter of pretrial discovery—the previously discussed Rule 6(e)(3)(E)(i) provision on court ordered disclosure" preliminary to or in connection with a judicial proceeding." Prior to the adoption of the Jencks Act, the Supreme Court held that a defendant who could establish "particularized need" would be entitled under the Rule 6(e)(3)(E)(i) to disclosure of the grand jury testimony of government witnesses for impeachment use at trial. Subsequent lower court rulings concluded that defendants could utilize that provision, on a showing of particularized need, to obtain grand jury testimony for general pretrial discovery purposes. Most of these rulings, however, also held that disclosure under Rule 6(e)(3)(E)(i) must be read in conjunction with the restrictions on pretrial discovery contained in Rule 16 and the Jencks Act. In addressing pretrial discovery of prior recorded statements other than grand jury testimony, some federal courts have recognized a discretionary authority to order disclosure as to persons who are not prospective government witnesses and therefore not within the Jencks prohibition.[118] Rule 6(e)(3)(E)(i) provides a grounding for similar disclosure of the grand jury testimony of persons who are not prospective government witnesses. That authority encompasses a variety of grand jury witnesses, but court ordered disclosure is rare except for the disclosure of the prior statements of codefendants and even there, disclosure requires special circumstances.

5. *Rule 6 Disclosure for an Indictment Challenge*

Rule 6(e)(3)(E)(ii) authorizes court ordered disclosure "at the request of a defendant who shows that a ground may exist to dismiss the indictment because of a matter that occurred before the grand jury." This provision potentially presents the greatest threat to grand jury secrecy through disclosure to the defendant, for it can extend to the disclosure of the entire grand jury transcript. In part because of that potential, the requirements for disclosure under Rule 6(e)(3)(E)(ii) are very rigorous.

In developing the standards applied under 6(e)(3)(E)(ii), courts have recognized the distinct possibility that a defense motion may be characterized as aimed at supporting a motion to dismiss when its actual purpose is to gain valuable pretrial discovery that goes beyond what Rule 16 permits. They also recognize that, since a successful motion to dismiss requires a showing that the legal error in the grand jury process had a prejudicial impact upon the decision to indict, the case for dismissal often can be made only by examining all of the evidence brought before the grand jury. Thus, the needed disclosure will often include witnesses and information that will not be presented at trial, and much more than other disclosures, Rule 6(e)(3)(E)(ii) disclosures commonly undermine the promise of secrecy that encourages "free and untrammeled" testimony by witnesses. Accordingly, while the announced standards for disclosure vary somewhat in wording, they all require a high level of justification. A typical standard states that disclosure will be ordered only if the defense can establish preliminarily "a substantial likelihood of gross or prejudicial irregularities in the conduct of the grand jury."

Applying this type of standard, federal courts find insufficient a showing that does no more than point to surrounding circumstances that evidence a "potential" for irregularities in the government's presentation before the grand jury. To be successful, the defendant must be able to produce such "hard evidence" as the affidavit of a

---

[118] Lower courts have divided as to whether they have authority, notwithstanding the Jencks Act, to order pretrial disclosure of prior recorded statements of prospective government witnesses when those statements constituted "*Brady*" material" (i.e., material exculpatory evidence, which the government has a due process obligation to disclose). See CRIMPROC § 20.3(m). The same division arises under Rule 6(e)(3)(E)(i) as to exculpatory grand jury testimony.

witness who was present when misconduct occurred or the clear suggestion of impropriety in a portion of the transcript released to defendant in the course of pretrial discovery. Of course, such sources of "direct proof" are rarely available, leading courts to acknowledge that the preliminary showing requirement places the defendant in "something of a 'catch 22' [situation]." As a result, a potential grand jury witness concerned that his testimony will eventually be disclosed to the target is not likely to be concerned about the possibility of disclosure under Rule 6(e)(3)(E)(ii).

J.   Remedies for Secrecy Violations

What relief is available when there has been an unauthorized disclosure of grand jury matter? Relying on the structure of Federal Rule 6(e), the Fourth Circuit concluded that there is no private cause of action arising from a secrecy breach. Under this view, an interested party (e.g., a witness whose testimony was disclosed or a person discussed in the disclosed testimony, typically the target of the investigation) may call the unauthorized disclosure to the attention of the supervisory court, but it then rests in the court's discretion as to what further action is taken. While the court has a duty to protect the integrity of the grand jury proceedings, it may conclude that the most appropriate procedure is initially to submit the matter to the Department of Justice for its internal investigation and application of internal sanctions.

Other circuits have held that a private person may maintain a civil action to remedy an unauthorized disclosure prejudicial to that person. The potential remedies include injunctive relief to preclude further disclosure, civil contempt sanctions where the information was purposefully leaked, a prohibition against use by a civil litigant to whom it was improperly disclosed, and providing disclosure to civil litigation opponents to offset the benefit obtained by the party who was the recipient of an unauthorized disclosure. Since the grand jury's decision to indict is not likely to have been influenced by the unauthorized disclosure of information brought before it, disclosure violations ordinarily will not provide an adequate grounding for a defense challenge to the indictment. To some extent, the nature of the disclosure will determine the range of remedies to be considered. Thus, where the disclosure was made openly by a government official in the belief (now found to be incorrect) that the disclosure was not prohibited by Rule 6, contempt would be inappropriate and there ordinarily would be no need for injunctive relief.

In cases in which the disclosure was not made openly, but was leaked by government personnel to the press, contempt sanctions would be appropriate, but courts rarely reach that issue because of the almost insurmountable hurdle that the complaining party (usually the target of the investigation) faces in establishing that there was such a leak. Initially, to establish the grounding even for an evidentiary hearing, the complaining party must make a prima facie showing both that the information disclosed constituted grand jury matter as defined by Rule 6(e) and that the sources of the leaked information were government personnel. Although this burden has been described as "relatively light," meeting it depends largely on the willingness of reporters to implicate their sources in their reports. Media reports that refer only to the general character of the investigation (rather than to grand jury testimony or grand jury actions) fail to establish that grand jury matter was disclosed. If the reports do reveal grand jury matter, but fail to identify the source as government personnel and the information reported is not of type known almost exclusively by government personnel, the showing will fail because the information could very well have been furnished by a witness or someone with whom a witness shared information.

Should a prima facie case be established, the government will be required to respond at an evidentiary hearing. While the supervisory court has discretion in determining the scope of that hearing, appellate courts have prohibited giving the complaining party significant access to the information produced by the government or the opportunity to "conduct direct or cross-examination of government personnel." The "norm" they note, should be an ex parte presentation by the government, reviewed in camera. Since journalists will not reveal their sources, the court's determination often will rest on accepting or rejecting affidavits by relevant government personnel denying disclosure on their part. As a result, it will be a rare case where the complaining party is able to make the showing needed to impose sanctions (as opposed to the imposition of safeguards to preclude further leaks), but the challenge process itself maybe benefit the target in a high-profile case.

§ 16.10 THE RIGHT TO EVERY MAN'S EVIDENCE

A. The Public's Right and the Grand Jury

The grand jury's investigative authority is commonly said to rest largely on "the long standing principle that 'the public has a right to every man's evidence.'" Indeed, no aspect of grand jury power is more frequently extolled by federal courts, particularly in cases rejecting challenges to subpoenas, than its right to compel the testimony of any person, subject only to "constitutional, common law or statutory privilege." The Supreme Court has stated this authority is recognized not only because it is "historically grounded" (see § 16.2(D)), but also because it ranks "[a]mong the necessary and most important of the powers * * * [that] assure the effective functioning of government in an ordered society." While the Court has never stated precisely why it views this authority as so essential to the "welfare of society," it presumably accepts the view of grand jury supporters that effective law enforcement requires the cooperation of the public, and that there are many instances in which such cooperation would not be forthcoming if it could not be compelled. The Court has noted that the "obligation of every person to appear and give testimony" is "indispensable to the administration of justice." Without it, criminal activity could be hidden behind a "wall of silence" that finds no justification in legal privilege, but is grounded simply in the individual's desire not to get "involved," fear of retaliation, dislike for the substantive law, or private code against "snitching."

Assuming that the authority to compel cooperation must of necessity be lodged somewhere, the federal courts find wisdom in the traditional delegation of that authority to the grand jury—an independent body, composed of laymen and having a membership that shifts from one term to the next. The structure of the grand jury, it is noted, provides assurance that investigations will be carried out free from political pressures. The capacity of a grand jury to take an investigation wherever it may lead serves to counteract suspicions of corruption and partisanship in criminal law enforcement. The grand jury therefore has the capacity not only to ferret out hidden crimes, but to relieve public concern generated by false rumors. The courts stress, however, that to achieve these objectives, the grand jury must be free to carry forward wide ranging investigations.

Two points in particular have been stressed with respect to the necessary breadth of grand jury investigations.[119] First, the grand jury must be "free from any restraint comparable to * * * [a] specific charge and showing of probable cause." It must be able to investigate "merely on suspicion that the law is being violated, or even just because it wants assurance that it is not." The jurors must be able to "act on tips, rumors, evidence offered by the prosecutor, or their own personal knowledge." They must have the capacity to "run down every available clue" and to examine "all witnesses * * *in every proper way." It is recognized, in this connection, that "if the investigation is to be meaningful, some exploration or fishing necessarily is inherent and entitled to exist."

Second, courts frequently note that the grand jury must be free of technical rules that would cause grand jury proceedings to be punctuated by litigation and delay. Judicial rulings must not provide the recalcitrant witness with a long list of challenges that can be used "to tie the grand jury into knots—to drag out the proceedings with technicalities instead of matters of substance." In determining whether a particular objection should be recognized, a court must consider whether its holding "would saddle a grand jury with minitrials and preliminary showings [that] would assuredly impede its investigation and frustrate the public's interest in the fair and expeditious administration of the criminal laws." The grand jury must be left "free to pursue its investigations unhindered by external influence or supervision so long as it does not trench upon the legitimate rights of a witness called before it."

The Supreme Court has acknowledged that the obligation of the citizen to appear and testify before the grand jury is not without its burdens. Appearance may be "onerous at times" and required answers "may prove embarrassing or result in an unwelcome disclosure of * * * personal affairs"; but such personal sacrifices, the Supreme Court has noted are "part of the necessary contribution of the individual to the welfare of the public." In this regard, the duty to testify before the grand jury, is sometimes compared to the duty to testify at trial, which is imposed simply upon a determination of one of the parties that a particular person should be subpoenaed. There are, of course, certain distinctions in the two situations. The witness summoned to testify at trial knows the subject to be considered, and is not himself the target of inquiry. In the grand jury setting, the subject under inquiry may not be revealed, and the person summoned may well be a prospective defendant. The witness at trial testifies in public while the witness before the grand jury testifies in a closed proceeding.

Courts have recognized that such distinctions may require somewhat different treatment of the grand jury witness in a few situations, but they also have concluded that the protection afforded the grand jury witness is sufficient to impose a general duty to appear similar to that imposed upon the trial witness. That protection is said to stem from four sources. First, the grand jury witness retains the same constitutional, statutory and common law privileges as the trial witness. Second, the secrecy of the grand jury proceeding affords the witness protection against damage to his reputation and mitigates any elements of embarrassment in his testimony. Third, the witness has the protection afforded by the presence of the grand jurors. Justice Black, in particular, gave considerable weight to this factor:

---

[119] See, e.g., the discussions in United States v. R. Enterprises, 498 U.S. 292 (1991); United States v. Dionisio, 410 U.S. 1 (1973); Branzburg v. Hayes, 408 U.S. 665 (1972).

They [the grand jurors] have no axes to grind and are not charged personally with the administration of the law. No one of them is a prosecuting attorney or law-enforcement officer ferreting out crime. It would be very difficult for officers of the state seriously to abuse or deceive a witness in the presence of the grand jury.[120]

Finally, grand juries remain subject to judicial supervision. Thus, the Supreme Court noted in one of its earliest opinions recognizing broad grand jury investigative authority: "Doubtless abuses of this power may be imagined * * * but were such abuses called to the attention of the court, it would doubtless be alert to repress them."

B. Privileges

Federal grand jury witnesses have always had available the same evidentiary and constitutional privileges as a trial witness. Rule 1101(d)(2) of the Federal Rules of Evidence follows this path in providing that "these rules—*except for those on privileges*—do not apply to * * * grand jury proceedings." Rule 501 of the Evidence Rules, in turn, provides that in criminal cases (including grand jury proceedings) "the common law—as interpreted by United States Courts in light of reason and experience—governs a claim of privilege unless [the Constitution, a federal statute, or "rules prescribed by the Supreme Court"] provide otherwise." Thus, the privileges of a federal grand jury witness are determined by federal law, and apart from a constitutional privilege (e.g., the self-incrimination privilege) and a rare statutory privilege, the focus is on the common law. Since that law is capable of growth based on its interpretation "in light of reason and experience," it can add privileges in situation that did not exist in the past, as occurred in the recognition of a federal psychotherapist-patient privilege.

Looking to the common law, the federal courts have refused to recognize various privileges often recognized in state law, including an accountant-client privilege, a physician-patient privilege, and a parent-child privilege.[121] The recognized federal common law privileges include the attorney-client privilege, the psychotherapist-patient privilege, the clergyman-penitent privilege, the marital confidential communications privilege, the marital adverse testimony privilege, and various governmental privileges (e.g., informer's privilege). The federal courts are divided as whether the common law establishes a reporter's privilege.[122]

The Supreme Court has noted that "privilege claims that shield information from a grand jury proceeding or a criminal trial" are not to be "expansively construed, for they are in derogation of the search for the truth."[123] This theme has been reflected in various contexts. Federal courts have held, for example, that a government attorney's lawyer-client privilege has a narrower scope when information is sought by a grand jury investigating possible wrongdoing (see § 22.9). So too, where the privilege at issue

---

[120] In re Groban, 352 U.S. 330 (1957) (Black, J., dissenting).

[121] However, USAM § 9–23.211 does recognize a "close-family exception" in forcing a person to testify by granting self-incrimination immunity. A close family relative is a "spouse, parent, child, grandparent, grandchild or sibling" of the person against whom testimony is sought. "The Department will ordinarily avoid seeking to compel the testimony" of such a person "absent specific justification." One of the listed justifications is: "the witness and the relative participated in a common business enterprise and the testimony to be elicited relates to that enterprise or its activities."

[122] See note 173 of § 16.12(E).

[123] Cheney v. United States District Court, 542 U.S. 367 (2004).

provides only a qualified immunity to withhold disclosure, the grand jury's investigative function has been held to outweigh the privilege's protective function.[124]

C. Other Protected Interests

Federal courts have recognized certain other interests which, though not privileges, deserve similar protection against compelled disclosure even in the context of a grand jury investigation. Typically, these interests do not absolutely preclude grand jury inquiry, but place upon the prosecution a burden of showing a special investigative need that will override the protected interest. Work product protection, discussed in § 23.4, imposes what arguably is the most stringent showing of need. Even as to fact work product, the need standard is difficult to meet because the grand jury often will have the capacity to obtain a "substantial equivalent" to the information contained in the work product.[125]

As discussed in § 18.2(C), the federal circuits are divided as to whether a civil protective order constitutes a protective shield, requiring a special showing to sustain a grand jury subpoena of records covered by such an order. Similar divisions are found elsewhere. Thus, § 16.12(E) discusses a division as to whether a special showing is needed to sustain a subpoena where compliance might have a chilling impact on the exercise of First Amendment rights.

Federal lower courts have been fairly uniform in rejecting claims that interests protected under state privilege law, but not federal privilege law, should be given a protected status. Granting such protection, it is argued, would undermine the principle that only federal privileges apply to federal grand jury proceedings. A few courts, however, have been willing to apply case-by-case balancing that would preclude disclosure where the evidence sought appears to have only a limited value in the grand jury's investigation. Where the Rule 17 subpoena authority reaches documents belonging to a foreign national because those documents are located in this country, federal courts have sustained the subpoena notwithstanding that foreign law prohibits disclosure. In refusing to provide special protection out of concern for foreign relations, courts note that it is the executive branch which "is charged exclusively with this nation's diplomacy."

D. Statutory Limitations

1. Generally

Previous sections have taken note of statutes that alter Rule 6 procedures where grand jury subpoenas compel production of third-party records that the holder of the records otherwise may not disclose. Thus, the previously discussed Right to Financial

---

[124] See, e.g., In re Grand Jury Investigation (Detroit Police Department Cash Fund), 922 F.2d 1266 (6th Cir.1991) (city police official could not rely on informer's privilege to withhold from federal grand jury names of informants and thereby thwart inquiry into possible corruption).

[125] But consider In re Grand Jury Subpoena Dated July 6, 2005, 510 F.3d 180 (2d Cir.2007) (where the subject of a grand jury investigation secretly recorded his conversation with another participant in the same real estate transaction, and did so in anticipation of litigation, that recording was "fact work product," but it was subject to a grand jury subpoena because the government showed a "substantial need" for the recording, as the recording could establish the respective roles of the two participants, and the government had "exhausted other means of obtaining [that information]," as questioning the participants about the conversation was not equal to obtaining a "unique memorialization of the conversation").

Privacy Act, governing the disclosure of the records of "customers" by "financial institutions,"[126] includes provisions (1) requiring reimbursement for costs incurred in collecting the records, (2) imposes special requirements as to the production of the records before the grand jury and the subsequent return of the records, and (3) alters secrecy requirements by imposing an automatic gag order and authorizing a court-issued gag order.[127] The RFPA, however, does not limit the grand jury's authority to obtain customer records by grand jury subpoena. It specifically provides that, except for the special procedural requirements, "nothing in this title shall apply to any subpoena or court order issued in connection with grand jury proceedings." Various other statutes that restrict third-party disclosure of records similarly contain provisions stating that the statute's restrictions to not apply to grand jury subpoenas.[128] Other statutes, however, permit the disclosure of information by third-party record holders only under conditions that do not include a grand jury subpoena.

Statutes imposing more restrictive conditions for disclosure typically insist upon a court order. An exception is the Privacy Act,[129] governing the disclosure by federal agencies of various records pertaining to individuals. That Act allows for disclosures pursuant to a court order, but also authorizes disclosure to another federal agency for criminal law enforcement upon a written request from the head of the agency. The Act does not, however, include disclosure pursuant to a grand jury subpoena in its list of authorized disclosures.

Several of the statutes requiring court orders cover information unlikely to be sought in a white collar investigation (e.g., drug treatment records, and "records revealing cable subscriber selection of video programing"). However, two statutes imposing special requirements (discussed below) involve records that are likely to be sought in white collar investigations (but which also might be sought from other sources, see § 16.7(F), not governed by the statute).

2.   *Tax Returns and Return Information*

The Internal Revenue Code section on "confidentiality and disclosure,"[130] § 6103, sets forth the requirements for obtaining "tax returns" and "tax return information" from the IRS. "Tax return information" is broadly defined to include such matters as the tax payers' identity, nature and source of income, net worth and related financial information. It includes information obtained from both the taxpayer and other sources.

---

[126] The RFPA, 12 U.S.C. §§ 3401–3422 defines financial institution to include a "card issuer" as defined in 15 U.S.C. § 1602, as well as a variety of banking institutions. "Card issuers" include both traditional credit card companies and retailers issuing company-specific credit cards to consumers. However, the term "customers" includes only individuals or partnerships of five or fewer individuals. See 12 U.S.C. § 3401(4). Thus the RFPA does not apply to the bank accounts of corporations or larger partnerships.

[127] See § 16.6(E) (payments of costs); 16.6(D) at note 72 (delivery and return); § 16.9(D) (gag orders).

[128] See, e.g., 20 U.S.C. § 1232g (Family Educational and Privacy Rights Act), (funding sanction if educational institution releases educational records and "personally identifiable information"); 15 U.S.C. § 1681(b) (consumer reporting agency disclosing credit information); 18 U.S.C. § 2710(b) (Video Privacy Protection Act) (service provider disclosing "personally identifiable information concerning any consumer"). Other statutes use broader exemptions to disclosure prohibitions, "e.g., allowing disclosure for "law enforcement purposes," that encompass grand jury subpoenas. See e.g. 18 U.S.C. § 2721(b) (personal information obtained in connection with a motor vehicle record).

[129] See 5 U.S.C. § 552a.

[130] See 26 U.S.C. § 6103.

Section 6103(h) governs DOJ access to IRS information for "tax administration" purposes, which includes the enforcement of the "internal revenue laws or related statutes." Here, returns and return information, upon DOJ request or IRS referral, are available without a court order, but "solely for their use in any proceeding before a Federal grand jury or preparation for any proceeding (or investigation which may result in such a proceeding) before a Federal grand jury." The disclosure is further conditioned on a relationship of the material sought to the subject of the investigation, which is not limited to determining the taxpayer's liability, but also includes a "transactional relationship between the person who is or may be a party to the eventual proceeding and the third-party whose return or return information is requested." Section 6103(h) does not refer to further disclosures by the DOJ beyond use in the grand jury, but the reference to DOJ use in an investigation indicates that further disclosures are permissible where needed to obtain additional evidence or to effectively prosecute the tax offense.

Section 6103(i) governs disclosure for use in criminal investigations other than revenue law violations. Here two avenues of access are provided. First, under paragraph (1), tax returns and all types of return information may be obtained pursuant to an ex parte order issued by a federal district court judge or magistrate. The disclosure is allowed only to personnel directly engaged in enforcement activities, including "any Federal grand jury proceeding" pertaining to "a designated federal criminal statute (not involving tax administration)." To issue the order, the court must conclude that there is reasonable cause to believe (1) a specific crime has been committed, (2) the information sought "is or may be relevant," and (3) the information is sought "exclusively for use in a criminal investigation or proceeding" and "cannot be obtained, under the circumstances, from another source."

Under paragraph (2), a second, easier route is available, where the government seeks "return information other than the taxpayer return information" (i.e., not information that was "filed with, or furnished to, the [IRS] by or on behalf of the taxpayer"). Here the disclosure can be made by the Secretary of the Treasury upon a request from a designated DOJ official (including a U.S. Attorney). The request must be for use by DOJ personnel engaged in criminal law enforcement, including a grand jury investigation. It must identify the information sought, cite the statutory authority under which "the proceeding or investigation" is being conducted," and set forth "the specific reason or reasons why such disclosure is, or may be, relevant to such proceeding or investigation." Since a primary objective of the confidentiality section is to give taxpayers assurance as to the confidentiality of the information they provide, this easier route is allowed only as to information developed by the IRS from other sources.[131] The Secretary has the last word, but the DOJ request can gain access with only a slightly stronger grounding than would justify issuing a grand jury subpoena.

---

[131] B. Bittker & L. Lokken, Federal Taxation of Income, Estates and Gifts § 111.2 (2012) note that two concerns underlie the provisions governing disclosure of returns and return information to government. "First, taxpayers must disclose to the IRS their financial affairs, as well as [certain] . . . personal matters . . . and this suggests restraint in allowing government agencies that have not been granted similar legal powers to ride piggyback on the IRS statutory powers." This concern does not apply to the grand jury, with its broad subpoena power. Second, "the unrestrained use of tax information for nontax purposes could undermine the self-assessment system on which the flow of federal revenue depends by inducing tax payers to withhold information that they fear would be put to other uses." This rationale largely explains the different requirements of paragraph (1) and (2).

3. Stored Communications

The Stored Communications chapter in the Electronic Communications Privacy Act (a chapter often described as the Stored Communications Act) governs access to both more and less than the two titles might suggest.[132] Initially, "electronic communications" is defined as also including "wire transfers." Thus, the Stored Communications Act (STA) applies to stored information relating to telephone calls, include cellular, text messages, and voice mails, as well as the traditional electronic communications, such as e-mails. The key is that the SCA refers to "stored communications." It does not provide for accessing communications in transit, as in the case of the Wiretap Act, but governs access as to the record of a previously transmitted stored communication.[133] The SCA's reach here goes beyond the stored content of the communication; it also includes information relating to the subscriber's account with the service that transmitted the communication and other non-content information about transmitted communications. The term "communication" might suggest a message sent to be heard or read by the recipient, but the SCA also encompasses information "communicated" electronically only for the purpose of electronic storage on a computer recipient. The SCA does not, however, govern access to all these records of different kinds of communications from the universe of sources possessing such records. It is applies only to access from two types of service providers: (1) providers of electronic communications service (ECS), and (2) providers of remote computing service (RCS).

An ECS provider is "any service which provides to users thereof the ability to send or receive wire or electronic communications." The most common ECS providers are telephone companies and electronic mail companies, but any company or government entity that provides others with the means to communicate electronically can be an ECS provider, even if that is not its primary business. Thus an insurance company that provided e-mail service to its employees and a city providing pager service to its police officers were both held to be ECS providers. An ECS provider, unlike an RCS provider, need not be offering the service to the public. However, companies that offer traditional products and services over the internet are treated as simply using ECS, not providing it; their electronic service is limited to allow customers to communicate with the company through the web page (as distinguished from providing customers with the capacity to communicate with third parties).

An RCS is defined as the "provision to the public of computer storage or processing services by means of an electronic communications system." A key factor in this definition is that the service be offered "to the public." Many providers of storage on

---

[132] The Stored Communication provisions are found in 18 U.S.C. §§ 2701–12. The SCA was title II of the EPCA of 1986. That Act also amended the Wiretap Act and created the Pen Register Act. The definitions section of the Wiretap Act, 18 U.S.C. § 2510, includes definitions that also apply to the SCA. The SCA is discussed at length in Chapter 3 of, DOJ, Office of Legal Education, Searching and Seizing Computers and Obtaining Electronic Evidence in Criminal Investigations (2009), available at http://www.justice.gov.

[133] As noted in the DOJ publication on Obtaining Electronic Evidence, supra note 132: "Some providers retain very complete records for a long period of time; others retain few records, or even none." The SCA includes a provision, 18 U.S.C. § 2703(f), directing providers, "upon the request of a government entity," to "take all necessary steps to preserve records . . . pending the issuance of a court order or other process." The time frame for preservation is 90 days, with a 90 day extension. The DOJ publication notes that § 2703(f) may not be "used prospectively to order providers to preserve records not yet produced." That is viewed as akin to interception in transit, requiring use of provision in the Wiretap Act authorizing such interception. See also *United States v. Warshak*, 631 F.3d 266, 333 (6th Cir. 2010) (Keith, J., concurring).

remote computers do so only for their employees or persons in a special business relationship. Congress apparently concluded that the presence of that relationship gives the provider its own, separate interest in the content of the stored record, which both reduces the privacy interest of the person who stored the record, and makes access from the provider more like access directly from a record owner. Commercial providers of "cloud computing" probably are the most common RCS providers.

The ECS and RCS categories are not exclusive. Many commercial internet service providers (ISPs) provide both services. Indeed, as discussed below, courts have held that an ISP can be first an ECS provider and later an RCS provider as to the same communication. The distinction as to type of provider becomes important only where the information the government seeks is classified as "content."

The SCA distinguishes between access to three different types of information: (1) basic subscriber information; (2) other information pertaining to subscriber use, exclusive of content; and (3) the content of the communication. The prerequisites for access are greater for "other information" than for the subscriber information. As to content, the prerequisites are greater still for some content possessed by an ECS provider, but not other content possessed by an ECS provider or by a RCS provider.

The SCA defines basic subscriber information as limited to the following information concerning a "subscriber or customer": "(A) name; (B) address; (C) local and long distance telephone connection records, or records of session times and durations; (D) length of service (including start date) and types of service utilized; (E) telephone or instrument number or other subscriber number or identity, including any temporarily assigned network address; and (F) means and source of payment for such service (including any credit card or bank account number)[.]" This information can be obtained by a grand jury subpoena (or an administrative subpoena). It is placed at the lowest level of confidentiality because it largely does no more than identify the subscriber's relationship with the ECS or RCS provider. It does include limited transactional information in item (C), but that provision does not encompass logging information that would reveal the addresses contacted. The item (E) reference to a "temporarily assigned national address" merely refers to the internet address used by the subscriber in accessing her e-mail address.

The SCA's "other information" category encompasses "a record or other information pertaining to a subscriber or to a customer of such service (not including the contents of communications)." This is a catch-all provision that encompasses all other non-content information contained in the records of the ECS or RCS provider. Common examples of information in this category include the list of e-mail addresses contacted, the list of internet protocol addresses that the individual sought to contact while surfing the web, phone numbers called, and cell-site data for cellular calls. Here, a subpoena is not sufficient to gain access. The government must obtain a court order under § 2703(d) or a search warrant. To obtain the order, the government must provide "specific and articulable facts showing that there are reasonable grounds to believe" that the information to be compelled is "relevant and material to an ongoing criminal investigation." This is less than the probable cause required for a search warrant, but considerably more justification than is needed for use of grand jury subpoena.

The SCA provides the greatest protection for the contents of certain communications possessed by an ECS provider. Here, a search warrant is required if two prerequisites are met: (1) the contents are in "electronic storage," and (2) the contents have been in electronic storage 180 days or less. Electronic storage is defined as "(A) any temporary, intermediate storage of a wire or electronic communication incidental to the electronic transmission thereof; and (B) any storage of such communication by an electronic communication service for purposes of backup protection of such communication." Part (A) of the definition reflects the specific function of ECS providers: servers make temporary copies of e-mails in the course of transmission, and Part (A) protects these temporary copies pending completion of the transmission of the communication. This record is "temporary" in the sense only that it lasts until the communication is received and opened, for it may not be opened for months. After 180 days, this record loses its special status even though it remains in "temporary" storage waiting to be opened.

Part (B), the backup provision, has produced a division in court interpretation.[134] System administrators commonly make a backup copy for their own files as a safeguard against systems malfunctions. Unlike the originals, these are not designated as temporary, but they arguably are as essential to the communication process as the original and therefore deserve the same protection. Another form of "back-up" arises when an e-mail is opened by the user and stored on the ISP's server. At this point, the interpretation of the backup provision becomes critical because the open e-mail is no longer stored under Part (A) of the definition, which is limited to "storage incidental to the electronic transmission." Courts have divided as to whether the backup provision covers this type of user backup. If the backup provision does not apply, then the e-mail stored by the user on the ISP server is simply in "remote storage," and the search warrant requirement, as discussed below, does not apply.

The SCA allows use of a subpoena to obtain the content of communications held in "electronic storage" by an ECS provider for more than 180 days. The apparent assumption of Congress was that a person who failed to open an e-mail for 180 days effectively abandoned any privacy interest deserving special protection. The SCA also allows use of a subpoena to obtain the contents of a communication held in storage by an RCS provider.[135] Here the subscriber or customer has voluntarily placed the communication (which can be a document as well as an opened e-mail) on a remote computer controlled by another party. Congress apparently viewed that act as also reducing the individual's privacy interest, and thereby not requiring the protection of a court order. The Sixth Circuit, relying on the Fourth Amendment, has rejected such a "reduced-privacy" analysis for remotely stored e-mails, adopting instead an analysis that arguably would also reject the SCA's 180–day dividing line.

In *United States v. Warshak*,[136] the Sixth Circuit held unconstitutional as applied the SCA provision authorizing government access to communications in remote storage through a subpoena (or a court order). The communications at issue were e-mails that had been opened and placed in remote storage, and the court held that the Fourth

---

[134] See CRIMPROC § 4.8(d).

[135] Since the subpoena also would be used to obtain records from a remote service provider that is a non-public provider, the SCA does not adopt a higher standard for the commercial RCS provider. However, it does impose other regulations that would not apply to the non-public provider. These include the requirement of notification, the potential for a gag order, and the order to preserve records. See note 133 supra, and § 16.9(D).

[136] 631 F.3d 266 (6th Cir.2010), also discussed in § 16.11 at note 152.

Amendment required a warrant to obtain them. The e-mails (approximately 27,000) had been obtained by both subpoena and court order from the ISP which served the defendant Warshak's various companies. The court reasoned that "the e-mail is the technological scion of tangible mail," with the "ISP * * * the functional equivalent of a post office." Longstanding Fourth Amendment precedent required a warrant to justify opening a sealed letter seized in transit, and "it would defy common sense to afford e-mails lesser Fourth Amendment protection." The Fourth Amendment analysis was not altered by the fact that the ISP "contractually reserved the right to access Warshak's emails for certain purposes." A subscriber agreement "might, in some cases, be sweeping enough to defeat a reasonable expectation of privacy in the content of an email account," but the agreement here merely indicated that the ISP "may access and use individual subscriber information in the [ISP's] operation of the service as necessary to protect the service."[137]

Warshak had no reason to address the provision on ECS providers disclosing the content of e-mails held in electronic storage more than 180 days, as the ISP there was viewed as operating as an RCS provider when the subscriber left copies of sent and received e-mails on the IPS system. However, the *Warshak* analogy to the opening of letters appears to be equally applicable to e-mails that remain "electronically stored" for more than 180 days because not yet opened by the recipient. On the other hand, the *Warshak* analogy is itself problematic. It is inconsistent with the result in a significant line of lower court rulings that have accepted the provision in the SCA allowing the use of subpoenas to obtain content from RCS providers. That result has been supported, in some instances, on the ground that the subscriber's expectation of privacy was lost by voluntarily exposing the e-mail content to the ISP when placing it in remote storage. The *Warshak* opinion focused on rebutting this argument, but did not consider another possibility.

Assuming that the third party exposure does not eliminate the subscriber's expectation of privacy, other precedents hold that a grand jury subpoena is sufficient under the Fourth Amendment to obtain directly from the owner even very private papers. These cases readily sustain the subpoena if it is viewed not as intercepting a communication, but as seeking either the sender's copy of the communication or the original in the possession of the recipient after being opened. A grand jury subpoena could obtain these documents, along with other private papers, from the sender, the recipient, or a third party holding them in storage (here the ISP). *Warshak* failed to consider this alternative analogy for sustaining the use of a subpoena under the Fourth Amendment.

4.   *Remedies*

Where statutes modify Rule 6 practice by imposing special requirements or restricting subpoena access as to subpoenas directed to third party service providers, the intended beneficiary of these restrictions is the subscriber or customer (often also the target of the grand jury's investigation). Accordingly, that person may object to the subpoena or procedure that violates the statutory requirement. The SCA facilitates

---

[137] The Court compared this authority to that of telephone companies to monitor calls in special situation, which had not diluted Fourth Amendment protection against the interception of those calls. *United States v. Miller* was distinguished, as discussed in § 16.11 at note 152.

that standing by ordinarily requiring the service provider to provide notice of the government demand to the customer. However, as discussed in § 16.9(D), the SCA also provides for delaying that notice, and other statutes leave providing notice in the discretion of the third party service provider. Thus, the subscriber or customer will often become aware of the subpoena only after being indicted. If the subscriber or customer can establish a violation of the statute at this point, its preferred remedy will be suppression of the evidence obtained in violation of the statute. However, federal courts regularly reject suppression as inappropriate for a nonconstitutional violation unless the statute involved specifically calls for suppression. A long line of cases, for example, have held that suppression does not apply to SCA violations. That Act does provide for civil damages (including, in some cases, punitive damages), and after the fact, that is often the most likely remedy. In cases of willful violations, internal discipline through DOJ office of Professional Responsibility is also possible.

§ 16.11 FOURTH AMENDMENT CHALLENGES TO SUBPOENAS

A. Applicability of the Fourth Amendment to Subpoenas for Documents

The application of the Fourth Amendment to court orders requiring production of documentary evidence began with *Boyd v. United States*,[138] a case widely celebrated for that holding, but largely rejected today as to its reasoning. *Boyd* involved a customs forfeiture proceeding in which the government sought to utilize an 1847 statutory provision allowing it to gain documentary evidence from the importer of the property to be forfeited. The provision authorized the trial judge, on motion of the government describing a particular document and indicating what it might prove, to issue a notice directing the importer to produce that document. The petitioners in *Boyd* challenged a notice that directed them to produce the invoice for thirty-five cases of plate glass allegedly imported without payment of customs duties. The Supreme Court sustained their challenge, holding that the notice and the statute authorizing it violated both the Fourth Amendment and the self-incrimination clause of the Fifth Amendment.

Speaking to the Fourth Amendment, the *Boyd* Court acknowledged that the notice procedure "lacked certain aggravating incidents of actual search and seizure, such as forcible entry into a man's house and searching among his papers," but stressed that it nonetheless "accomplish[ed] the substantial object of those acts in forcing from a party evidence against himself." Accordingly, a "compulsory production of a man's private papers" would be treated as "within the scope of the Fourth Amendment to the constitution, in all cases in which a search and seizure would be." Having found the Fourth Amendment applicable, the *Boyd* opinion turned to the question of whether this particular "search and seizure, or what is equivalent thereto," was unreasonable within the meaning of that Amendment. It concluded that the compelled production of a document was per se unreasonable.

Boyd cited several factors in concluding that the Fourth Amendment simply did not allow a search, or its equivalent, as to private papers. The Court initially noted that the searches for contraband or instrumentalities of crime allowed in past cases involved "totally different things from a search for and seizure of a man's private books

---

[138] 116 U.S. 616 (1886), also discussed in § 17.3 at note 7 and § 20.1 at note 2.

and papers for the purpose of obtaining information therein contained or of using them as evidence against him." The former involved situations in which "the government is entitled to the possession of the property," but that was not true of the latter. The Court then turned to the landmark English ruling in *Entick v. Carrington & Three Other King's Messengers,* which had found a trespass in government officials entering the plaintiff's home and breaking open his boxes and examining his papers. This decision, which undoubtedly influenced "those who framed the Fourth Amendment," had spoken of the individual's papers as his "dearest property," and it was the invasion of the individual's indefeasible right in that property, rather than the "breaking of his doors and the rummaging of his drawers" that was the "essence" of the violation of individual liberty in that case. Finally, the "compulsory extortion" of private papers to be used as evidence to convict the individual was parallel to compelling testimony for the same purpose, and here, "the Fourth and Fifth Amendments run into each other." What "is condemned in the Fifth Amendment throws light on * * * what is an 'unreasonable search and seizure'" and renders per se unreasonable a search which is not "substantially different from compelling [a person] * * * to be a witness against himself."

The *Boyd* ruling was soon extended to grand jury subpoenas commanding the production of documents, but its position on per se unreasonableness was rejected as part of that extension. In *Hale v. Henkel,*[139] decided twenty years later, the Supreme Court rejected per se unreasonableness, but reaffirmed the applicability of the Fourth Amendment to a "compulsory production of a man's private papers." *Hale* presented a grand jury subpoena directing production of a variety of corporate records in connection with an investigation into possible criminal antitrust violations. The *Hale* majority initially noted that *Boyd* had erred in reading together the Fourth and Fifth Amendment protections. Any absolute prohibition against compelled production of documentary items lay in the self-incrimination clause alone, and that clause had no application in the case before it; the challenged subpoena was directed to corporate documents and corporations did not have the benefit of the privilege.[140] However, the Court continued, the corporation was entitled to the protection of the Fourth Amendment, and "an order for the production of books and papers" could still constitute "an unreasonable search and seizure." While it was true that "a search ordinarily implies a quest of an officer of the law, and a seizure contemplates a forcible dispossession of property, still, as was held in *Boyd*, the substance of the offense is * * * [unreasonable] compulsory production, whether under a search warrant or a subpoena duces tecum."

Turning to the application of the Fourth Amendment in the case before it, *Hale* found that the subpoena duces tecum constituted an unreasonable search because it was "far too sweeping in its terms to be regarded as reasonable." The subpoena had required production of corporate papers relating to transactions with various different companies, and such a broad request was capable of preventing the corporation from

---

[139] 201 U.S. 43 (1906).

[140] Notwithstanding *Hale's* rejection of per se unreasonableness in a search for documents, its reliance on the Fourth Amendment in a context where the Fifth Amendment did not apply led the lower courts to question whether a traditional search could be directed at documents where the owner did have a self-incrimination privilege. It was not until the 1970s that the Court squarely held that a search for documents was permissible. The Fifth Amendment had no bearing on such a search since the owner was not compelled to himself to produce the documents. See § 21.2 at note 1.

carrying on its business. Reasonableness for a subpoena, like reasonableness for a search warrant, required "particularity" in the description of the documents to be produced. While the government might have need for many of these documents, it would have to make some showing of "materiality" before it could "justify an order for the production of such a mass of papers."

Justice McKenna, concurring separately in *Hale*, argued that the Fourth Amendment should not apply in any respect to a subpoena to compel the production of documents. The majority had acknowledged that the subpoena did not involve a "quest" by the officer or a "forcible dispossession of the owner." Did not that distinction in itself establish the inapplicability of the Fourth Amendment? The service of the subpoena involved "no element of trespass or force," nor was it "secret and intrusive." The subpoena could not be "finally enforced except after challenge, and a judgment of the court upon the challenge." These safeguards and limitations, from Justice McKenna's perspective, clearly distinguished the subpoena from the search. Justice McKenna also considered the possibility that the majority was saying that a subpoena did not involve a search except where it was "too sweeping," but he could not understand how that quality alone, improper though it may be, could transform the subpoena into a search.

The *Hale* Court's only response to Justice McKenna was to briefly restate a portion of *Boyd's* analysis: "While a search ordinarily implies a quest by an officer, and a seizure contemplates a forcible dispossession of the owner, as was held in the *Boyd* case, the substance of the offense is the compulsory production of private papers, whether under a search warrant or a subpoena duces tecum." The Court offered no explanation of another point implicit in its analysis: reasonableness for a subpoena duces tecum "search" does not require probable cause (at the time the only permissible grounding for a traditional search), but it does prohibit overbreadth. *Hale* described that overbreadth prohibition as an application of the "general principle of law with regard to the particularity required in the description of documents necessary to a search warrant or subpoena." The Court did not explain, however, why particularity here goes beyond requiring specificity in description, its usual function in search warrants, and also prohibits excessiveness (a prohibition that applies as well to search warrants, but there through the application of the probable cause requirements to limit the items that may be seized). Lower courts have advanced various answers to these questions, looking to hints in *Hale* and *Boyd*, as well as later Fourth Amendment developments.

One explanation builds upon Justice McKenna's suggestion that the *Hale* majority found the Fourth Amendment applicable only when the subpoena was overly broad. The theory here is that the subpoena which is too sweeping, which calls for a mass of documents without regard to what is relevant, necessarily requires a sifting through the documents to obtain those that are needed. Whether that sifting takes place on the premises of the owner or in the offices of the prosecutor assisting the grand jury, it constitutes a search. Thus, *Hale* and other courts compared the overbroad subpoena to a "general warrant." The issue of particularity here is not particularity of description. In *Hale*, for example, a subpoena for all of the documents located in the corporation's office would not have presented difficulties in identifying the documents. The problem of particularity lies in failing to identify the specific documents that would be relevant to the investigation, but instead compelling production of a mass known to include both relevant and irrelevant, and then identifying the relevant through what would amount to a physical search. While this explanation arguably fits the fact situation in *Hale*, it fails to explain the various lower court rulings that have applied *Hale*'s condemnation of subpoena overbreadth to subpoenas that did not require a large volume of documents.

A second explanation relies in part on Fourth Amendment concepts that had not been articulated at the time of the *Hale* ruling, but arguably were hinted at in *Boyd's* famous passage on the "duty of courts to be * * * watchful * * * against any stealthy encroachments" upon constitutional values, being guided by the "motto * * * of *obstra principus*." That passage urged rejection of "close and literal" interpretations in favor of "liberal constructions" that reach all practices contrary to constitutional substance even though the invasion may be in its "mildest and least repulsive form." Consistent with this approach, decisions more than a half-century later concluded that Fourth Amendment analysis should focus on governmental invasion of a reasonable expectation of privacy rather than the physical invasion associated with traditional police searches. At the same time, the decisions brought within the regulation of the Fourth Amendment a variety of non-police investigative practices, such as regulatory inspections. These developments also produced standards for reasonableness that varied with the character of the search. One illustration of this approach is found in allowing certain administrative searches without any showing of probable cause or reasonable suspicion, as described in § 21.5.

The *Hale* standard, under this explanation, reflects the "balancing approach" applied to many non-traditional forms of privacy invasion that constitute a search. One crucial element in striking that balance is the more limited invasion of privacy in obtaining documents by subpoena. The subpoena does force the disclosure of documents (including personal papers) that are not voluntarily exposed, but the government looks only at that those papers (not the premises, and in particular, not the files in which those documents were located).

Another important factor under this "balancing explanation" is the historically grounded right of the grand jury to "every man's evidence." The *Hale* opinion extensively discussed the grand jury's investigative authority in rejecting petitioner Hale's contention that he did not have to appear before the grand jury because it was not investigating a specific charge.[141] The Court noted that the grand jury's "inquisitorial" investigative authority was not limited to investigating specific charges; the grand jury could pursue an inquiry based on information from any source that might lead to a yet unknown offense. Later cases used even broader descriptions of that authority—stating that the grand jury "may act on tips [and] rumors" and pursue investigations "merely on suspicion that the law is being violated, or even because it wants assurance that it is not."[142]

Under this second explanation of the *Hale* standard, a grand jury subpoena requiring the production of documents constitutes a search, but a less invasive search than the traditional police search. That factor, along with the grand jury's special

---

[141] See § 16.2 at note 13.

[142]   *United States v. Dionisio*, 410 U.S. 1 (1973), discussed at note 154 infra; *United States v. R. Enterprises*, 498 U.S. 292 (1991), discussed in § 16.12 at note 165.

investigative role, produces a reasonableness standard limited to *Hale's* overbreadth prohibition. This explanation justifies application of that prohibition even where large quantities of documents are not sought, as the search is not dependent on the sifting process. It also explains court decisions that apply the overbreadth prohibition more rigorously where the documents sought might include irrelevant information of a highly personal nature.[143] However, the emphasis on privacy protection in this explanation raises the question as to why *Hale* gave great weight, in a Fourth Amendment analysis, to the economic burden imposed upon the entity in relinquishing the documents.

Forty years after *Hale*, in *Oklahoma Press Publishing Co. v. Walling*,[144] the Supreme Court suggested still a third explanation—that the Fourth Amendment had no direct application but was looked to only by analogy to protect against a different form of "officious intermeddling by government officials." In that case, which involved an administrative agency subpoena duces tecum, the Court acknowledged that certain misconceptions had arisen due to the failure of lower courts to distinguish between "so-called 'figurative' or 'constructive'" searches by subpoena and "cases of actual search and seizure." The Court noted that "only in * * * [an] analogical sense can any question related to search and seizure be thought to arise" in subpoena cases. It stressed that the Fourth Amendment, "if applicable," did no more than "guard against abuse only by way of too much indefiniteness or breadth" in the subpoena. The interests to be protected were "not identical with those protected against invasion by actual search and seizure" but arose out of the right of persons to be free from "officious examination [that] can be expensive, so much so that it eats up men's substance," and thereby "become[s] persecution when carried beyond reason." Thus, the *Oklahoma Press* explanation focuses not on privacy interests, but on property rights and the burden that comes with unnecessarily being required to gather and then relinquish large quantities of documents that bear no potential relevancy to the subject of the inquiry.

In its post-*Oklahoma Press* rulings the Supreme Court has returned to referring to the prohibition against "overbreadth" in the subpoena of documents as a Fourth Amendment requirement. It has not, however, retreated from *Oklahoma Press's* explanation of the function of the overbreadth limitation. Thus, lower courts applying the overbreadth limitation to grand jury subpoenas continue to look, in part, to the avoidance of undue burdens upon the subpoenaed party. A survey of those lower court rulings is set forth below. Because a very similar limitation is found in Federal Rule 17(c), which provides protection against subpoenas duces tecum that are "unreasonable or oppressive," the decisions applying that limitation, discussed in § 16.12, must also

---

[143] See note146 infra. Critics argue, however, that a focus on privacy concerns should require more than a stronger showing of relevancy where the documents reveal highly personal information, but demand also some grounding (if not probable cause) as to the possible offense and the individual's relationship to that offense. As discussed in § 20.1(D), subpoenas seeking personal documents not exposed to others are problematic, but the concern here is the application of the self-incrimination clause, not the application of the Fourth Amendment (provided the document is clearly relevant). In white collar cases, subpoenas commonly require production of such potentially private items as "reminder pads, notepads, diaries, calendars, day books, telephone directories, [and] telephone call logs." See DOJ Antitrust Division, Grand Jury Practice Manual 125 (1991). See also § 20.1(D).

[144] 327 U.S. 186 (1946), discussed also in § 17.3 at note 11.

be considered in assessing the potential for successful objections based upon the "too sweeping" reach of a subpoena.[145]

B. Applying the Overbreadth Prohibition

Courts applying the constitutional prohibition against overly broad subpoenas duces tecum frequently start out by noting that the stated standard, proscribing breadth "far too sweeping * * * to be regarded as reasonable," necessarily requires a fact-specific judgment, with each ruling tied to the circumstances of the individual case. At the same time, the courts have sought, with limited success, to develop some general criteria to guide that judgment. Initially, the question arises as to whether the party challenging the subpoena must establish sufficient breadth to suggest that compliance will be burdensome. While there is language in Supreme Court opinions suggesting that is a prerequisite, and most successful challenges have involved such subpoenas, a small group of rulings have struck down subpoenas that would have presented no significant burdens in collecting and relinquishing the records. Those cases involved subpoenas that suggested on their face that no effort had been made to limit the subpoena to what was needed and often dealt with sensitive information.[146]

Assuming some potential for overbreadth, the court then will turn to the three "components" of reasonableness initially developed by the lower federal courts:

> (1) the subpoena may command only the production of things relevant to the investigation being pursued; (2) specification of things to be produced must be made with reasonable particularity; and (3) production of records covering only a reasonable period of time may be required.

The second element of the above formulation is commonly described as having "two prongs": first, "particularity of description" so that the subpoenaed party "know[s] what he is being asked to produce"; and second, "particularity of breadth" so that the subpoenaed party "is not harassed or oppressed to the point that he experiences an unreasonable business detriment." The requirement of adequate notice rarely poses significant difficulty, although ambiguities may arise where documents are described by their relationship to a particular event. Accordingly, courts looking to the second component tend to focus on the second factor, the degree of burden imposed by production.

---

[145] As to strategic considerations advising against raising such an objection, see the last paragraph of § 16.7(B).

[146] See e.g., In re Horowitz, 482 F.2d 72 (2d Cir.1973) (where grand jury was investigating possible fraud of petitioner's now defunct company, and learned from petitioner's accountant that concealed company records were stored in three locked cabinets that also contained petitioner's personal papers, subpoena demanding production of the total contents of the three cabinets was overbroad, as it failed to draw any distinction as to content or time frame, and thereby included personal documents such as wills and trust agreements and documents that antedated the possible inception of the fraudulent scheme by more than a decade); In re Certain Chinese Families Benevolent and District Associations, 19 F.R.D. 97 (N.D. Cal.1956) (where grand jury was investigating possible fraud by various persons in claiming derivative citizenship as offspring of U.S. citizen-fathers, subpoena was overbroad in requiring various Chinese family associations to produce available membership lists, income records, and membership photographs dating back to the association's origin; although associations acknowledge that compliance would not be burdensome as the quantity of records "is not very great in any single case," the subpoena failed by seeking records, "without relation to time, place, or person" where the records were personal, in contrast to business records, and the "result . . . had the effect of being a mass inquisition of the family records of the substantial portion of the Chinese population of San Francisco").

While many courts have treated the elements of relevancy, sufficient particularity to avoid an undue burden of production, and reasonableness of time period as separate requirements of reasonableness, so that deficiency as to any one element can invalidate the subpoena, it is clear that the three elements are interrelated. Greater particularity, by narrowing the range of documents to be produced, will extend the time period into which the subpoena may reach. On the other hand, as a subpoena reaches farther into the past, a court is more likely to require a stronger showing of relevancy. So too, the significance of the burden of production will be weighed against the strength of the showing as to relevancy and the reasonableness of the time period. Thus, courts have noted that a subpoena that clearly meets the relevancy and time-period requirements will be rejected on the basis of a substantial burden of production only in the most extreme cases.

While the subpoenaed party bears the ultimate burden of establishing that a challenged subpoena is unreasonable, many courts insist that the government make an initial showing of relevancy since it alone knows the precise nature of the grand jury inquiry. Ordinarily, this showing requires no more than a general description of the relationship of the material sought to the subject matter of the investigation. A critical factor here will be the character of that subject matter. Some activities (e.g., crimes involving the illicit use of funds) will render relevant all financial records, as total income and receipts must be traced. The possibility of unknown conspirators similarly opens up the range of documents relating to other parties. Similarly, antitrust investigations demand a broad range of documents since the violation may be reflected in many different aspects of a company's business.

Courts generally give grand juries considerable leeway in judging relevancy. They recognize that "some exploration or fishing necessarily is inherent" since the grand jury will not ordinarily have a "catalog of what books and papers exist" nor "any basis for knowing what their character or contents immediately are." Similarly, the grand jury cannot be expected to anticipate the full range of criminal activity that might be connected with a possible criminal enterprise. With computer programs now exploring comparative patterns in records, relevancy may readily be expanded to include records created prior to the earliest date of the potential crime, and records of transactions that are related to those under inquiry only in that they involve the same persons, as such records provide potentially useful comparisons.[147] Thus, courts have spoken of relevancy requiring only "some possible relationship, however indirect."

The government's showing on relevancy also provides a foundation for determining the reasonableness of the time span covered by the subpoena. That period must bear "some relation to the subject of the investigation," which readily can go beyond the statute of limitations. Even in antitrust investigations, where the greatest leeway exists, a period beyond ten years is ordinarily suspect. However, where courts have held such a substantial time period to be unreasonable, they generally also have left open the possibility of reconsideration in light of a request for a narrower range of documents or a stronger showing of relevancy based on subsequently received information.

---

[147] See § 16.7(A) at note 70.

Objections to a subpoena duces tecum based solely upon the burden and expense of assembling a large quantity of records today are almost always doomed to failure. With the advent of photocopying and electronic storage, the possibility that the subpoenaed party will be unable to carry on its business without the relinquished records—a major concern in *Hale*—is largely mooted. As discussed in § 16.7(E), the cost of compliance, including the cost of making copies, will occasionally be beyond the financial capacity of the recipient, but that concern is met by having the government bear that cost.

C.   Third–Party Subpoenas

As discussed in § 16.7(F), subpoenas often seek records relating to the activity of the target that may be obtained from either the target or a third-party providing services to the target. *United States v. Miller*[148] held that where the government directed the subpoena to the third-party service provider, the target could not raise a Fourth Amendment because it had no reasonable expectation of privacy in the records obtained from the service provider. *Miller* involved a grand jury subpoena directed to a bank, prior to the adoption of the Right to Financial Privacy Act, which provides special protection for customer financial records.[149] The *Miller* subpoena demanded both records that the bank had created based on information supplied by Miller and records created by Miller, such as deposit slips and checks. After the bank had complied with the subpoena (without informing Miller), Miller moved to suppress the records as obtained in violation of the Fourth Amendment. That claim was not based on alleged overbreadth, but on the combination of the Bank Secrecy Act requiring the bank to make copies of depositors' personal checks (thereby facilitating obtaining these records from the bank) and the use of an allegedly defective subpoena to obtain those copies. The Court found no need to address that Fourth Amendment contention because "there was no intrusion into an area in which [Miller] had a protected Fourth Amendment interest." The Court noted in this regard that (1) the records involved had become the business records of the bank, leaving the depositor with no claim of "ownership," (2) the documents "contain[ed] only information voluntarily conveyed to the banks and exposed to their employees in the ordinary course of business," and (3) a "depositor takes the risk, in revealing his affairs to another, that the information will be conveyed by that person to the government."

Miller also noted that the checks "were negotiable instruments to be used in commercial transactions," but the *Miller* principle clearly is not limited to records that were exposed to the public before reaching the third-party service provider. Thus *Couch v. United States*[150] held that the taxpayer had no expectation of privacy in records subpoenaed from his accountant, as he furnished those records knowing that the accountant then had the discretion to disclose most or all of the information contained therein to the IRS in filing an accurate tax return. So too, *Smith v. Maryland*[151] held that the telephone caller voluntarily informs the telephone company of the number to be called, and therefore has no expectation of privacy as to the telephone company's subsequent disclosure of those numbers.

---

[148]   425 U.S. 435 (1976), also discussed in § 17.5.

[149] See § 16.10(D) at note 126.

[150]   409 U.S. 322 (1973).

[151]   442 U.S. 735 (1979).

Although lower courts have extended the *Smith* analysis to various types of transactional information provided to an ISP in sending and receiving e-mails, the Sixth Circuit, as discussed in § 16.9(D),[152] has held the *Miller* principle does not further extend to the contents of an e-mail obtained from an ISP, even after the subscriber opens the e-mail and decides to store it with the ISP. *Miller* is distinguishable, the Sixth Circuit reasoned, because (1) *Miller* involved "simple business records" as opposed to "the potentially unlimited variety of confidential communications at issue here," and (2) *Miller* involved information conveyed to the bank for its use in the "ordinary course of business," while the ISP was simply an "intermediary, not the intended recipient of the e-mails." Although the ISP did retain a right to examine the content in special circumstances, the reasonable expectation was that the e-mail would remain in storage without examination by any individual (as opposed to a computer). The Sixth Circuit noted, however, that a different result might be reached under a subscriber agreement giving the ISP a general right to "inspect and monitor" e-mails. Assuming no such provision, the *Warshak* analysis would recognize the standing of the customer in a variety of storage situations, including both electronic and physical storage.

From the government's perspective, the primary danger in recognizing customer standing to raise Fourth Amendment objections to third-party subpoenas arises where the customer is not given notice prior to compliance with the subpoena. Here, lacking an opportunity to object beforehand, the customer may object when the government subsequently seeks to utilize the information obtained through the subpoena. Where the subscriber receives prior notice and objects prior to compliance, the subscriber's Fourth Amendment overbreadth objection fundamentally is the same objection that the third-party service provider could raise (although the subscriber is more likely to raise the objection than the service provider). If the subscriber succeeds in that objection, the subpoena can be modified so as to be acceptable under the overbreadth limitation. In contrast, if the Fourth Amendment challenge can be raise after compliance and the court finds that the overbreadth prohibition was violated, the government then faces the potential of an exclusionary remedy. As discussed in § 21.7, that result can be avoided where a warrant was used, as the magistrate's issuance of the warrant provides the basis for a good faith exception. However, a subpoena, although a court order, lacks the judicial involvement that would justify applying the good faith exception.[153]

D. Application of the Fourth Amendment to Other Subpoenas: *Dionisio* and *Mara*

In *United States v. Dionisio*[154] and *United States v. Mara*,[155] the Court left no doubt that the Fourth Amendment ordinarily does not apply to subpoenas apart from the overbreadth limitation upon subpoenas for documents. *Dionisio* and *Mara* were companion cases arising from separate grand jury investigations. In *Dionisio*, the

---

[152] See § 16.9(D) at note 136, discussing *United States v. Warshak*, 631 F.3d 266 (6th Cir. 2010). *Warshak* held that a warrant was required to obtain the stored e-mail, but that aspect of the ruling may be questioned.

[153] In *Warshak*, supra note 152, the good faith exception was held to apply because the government had relied on the SCA provision allowing use of a subpoena.

[154] 410 U.S. 1 (1973).

[155] 410 U.S. 19 (1973).

grand jury had subpoenaed approximately 20 persons, including *Dionisio*, to give voice exemplars for comparison with recorded conversations that had been received in evidence. In *Mara*, the witness was directed to produce handwriting exemplars for the purpose of determining whether he was the author of certain writings. Both witnesses claimed that the subpoenas constituted unreasonable searches and seizures because they had not been supported by any showing of reasonableness. The Court of Appeals agreed. It held that the government needed to establish that the grand jury investigation was properly authorized, that the information sought was relevant to that inquiry, and that the request for exemplars was adequate but not excessive for the purposes of the relevant inquiry. These requirements, the Court of Appeals reasoned, were a logical extension of the prohibition of the *Hale* doctrine.

The Supreme Court rejected the lower court rulings in both *Dionisio* and *Mara*. The majority opinion noted that the Fourth Amendment did prohibit the "sweeping subpoena duces tecum," as noted in *Hale*, but there was no such extreme breadth of production required in either subpoena here. The Court of Appeals had erred in analogizing the subpoena in *Dionisio* to the action of police in detaining or arresting a person for the purpose of obtaining identification exemplars. "It is clear," the Court noted, "that a subpoena to appear before a grand jury is not a 'seizure' in the Fourth Amendment sense." As a different Court of Appeals had recently explained, there was a dramatic difference in the "compulsion exerted" by a subpoena as opposed to an "arrest or even an investigative stop":

> The latter is abrupt, is effected with force or the threat of it and often in demeaning circumstances, and, in the case of arrest, results in a record involving social stigma. A subpoena is served in the same manner as other legal process; it involves no stigma whatever; if the time for appearance is inconvenient, this can generally be altered; and it remains at all times under the control and supervision of a court.

The Court majority acknowledged that a grand jury subpoena, though differing from the arrest or investigative stop, could be both "inconvenient" and "burdensome." Any "personal sacrifices" required, however, were merely incidental to the "historically grounded obligation of every person to appear and give his evidence before the grand jury." The addition here of directives to give identification evidence did not alter the nature of the burden imposed. Neither the voice exemplar nor the handwriting sample invaded a privacy interest protected under the Fourth Amendment. Both related to physical characteristics "constantly exposed to the public" and were to be distinguished, for example, from the taking of a blood sample.

Having found that the Fourth Amendment had no application to either the summons to appear nor the directive to provide identification exemplars, the Court concluded that there was "no justification for requiring the grand jury to satisfy even the minimal requirement of 'reasonableness' imposed by the Court of Appeals." The grand jury "could exercise its 'broad investigative powers' on the basis of 'tips, rumors, evidence offered by the prosecutor, or [the jurors] own personal knowledge,'" and it should not be required to explain the basis for each of its subpoenas. To "saddle a grand jury with minitrials and preliminary showings would assuredly impede its investigation and frustrate the public's interest in the fair and expeditious administration of the criminal laws."

E. "Forthwith" Subpoenas

A "forthwith" subpoena is a subpoena that compels the witness to appear before the grand jury "forthwith" (or within hours after being served), often directing the witness to produce specified records at that time. A forthwith subpoena duces tecum is used when there is reason to believe that, given an ordinary return date, the witness will destroy, hide, or alter the demanded records. Ordinarily a search warrant is the preferred response to that possibility, but a search warrant requires probable cause and a subpoena does not. A forthwith subpoena ad testificandum is used where there is reason to believe that, over the time provided under a normal return date, the witness might flee. Here, an alternative is a material witness arrest, but that requires a probable cause showing as to materiality.[156] The DOJ requires prior approval of the U.S. Attorney to use a forthwith subpoena. It also suggests that the prosecutor "explain the nature of the exigent circumstances to the grand jury" and get its approval and "carefully instruct the agents serving the subpoena that it is not a search warrant."

The forthwith subpoena does not allow the agent serving the subpoena to enter the premises and search for the documents the witness is required to produce.[157] The argument has been advanced, however, that the forthwith subpoena produces a "seizure" (of the witness or the documents produced by the witness) and therefore is subject to Fourth Amendment requirements. Looking in part to *Dionisio's* explanation of the distinction between an arrest and a witness appearance pursuant to subpoena, lower courts have rejected that contention. They note that the forthwith subpoena does not deprive the witness of the opportunity to contest the subpoena before complying. The witness may appear before the grand jury, as directed by the subpoena, and there note his willingness to comply only if ordered by the court to do so. An implicit condition of this reasoning is that the witness have the opportunity to consult with counsel if he so chooses.

As a practical matter, almost all cases presenting challenges to forthwith subpoenas involve situations in which the subpoenaed party relinquished documents to agents upon receiving the subpoena and then subsequently sought to suppress on Fourth Amendment grounds. The federal courts have rejected the contention that such compliance is so suspect as to assume an involuntary relinquishment of rights. They look to the circumstances of the case, asking whether the agents coerced the consent. In assessing whether coercion was present, courts have looked to such factors as the number of agents serving the subpoena, the length of their presence, the granting of an opportunity to consult with counsel, the use of verbal or physical threats, and the

---

[156] See note 60 supra.

[157] The primary protection against the witness destroying the documents is the absence of time to do so. The agent cannot insist upon watching the witness while he looks for the records. See In re Nwamu, 421 F.Supp. 1361 (S.D.N.Y.1976) (agent's actions in demanding immediate compliance resulted in Fourth Amendment violation). A special difficulty is presented, in this regard, in seeking records stored on a computer. Forthwith compliance concerns might suggest requiring production of the computer itself or the entire hard drive. However, a subpoena demanding production of the hard drive is likely to fail under the overbreadth doctrine. See e.g., In re Grand Jury Subpoena Duces Tecum Dated November 15, 1993, 846 F.Supp. 11 (S.D.N.Y.1994) (not all of the contents would be relevant, and relevant documents could readily be identified through key word searching, but government made no effort to limit its demand). Where probable cause is available, the search warrant can authorize removing the hard drive and subsequently conducting a search for the types of documents specified in the warrant through a designated protocol. While a similar protocol may be utilized in a subpoena to identify the relevant documents, the subpoena process gives the witness, not the government, the right to apply that protocol in identifying documents.

experience and knowledge of the subpoenaed party. The totality of the circumstances prevails, but assuming a legitimate grounding for use of the forthwith subpoena, coercion is not likely to be found absent action that prevented the party from preserving his right to initially contest the subpoena.

F.   Prior Fourth Amendment Violations

In *United States v. Calandra*,[158] a divided Supreme Court held that the exclusionary rule could not be invoked by a grand jury witness to bar questions based on unconstitutionally seized evidence. Viewing the Fourth Amendment's exclusionary rule as basically a prophylactic remedy, the *Calandra* majority concluded that its applicability in the grand jury setting should be determined by weighing "the potential injury [in the rule's application] to the historic role and functions of the grand jury" against the potential for increased deterrence of illegal searches.

On the one side, "it [was] evident that this extension of the exclusionary rule would seriously impede the grand jury": "permitting witnesses to invoke the exclusionary rule before a grand jury would precipitate adjudication of issues hitherto reserved for the trial [as to the legality of the search] ... and would delay and disrupt grand jury proceedings." On the other side, the incremental deterrent effect that might be achieved by applying the rule in grand jury proceedings was "uncertain at best." Any "incentive to disregard the requirements of the Fourth Amendment" as to grand juries, the Court noted, "is substantially negated by the inadmissibility of the illegally-seized evidence in a subsequent criminal prosecution of the search victim." On balance, the Court would not "embrace a view that would achieve a speculative and undoubtedly minimal advance in the deterrence of police misconduct at the expense of substantially impeding the role of the grand jury."

In *Gelbard v. United States*,[159] the Court recognized an exception to *Callandra* created by statute. The federal "Wiretap Act,"[160] (which also covers "bugging") refers to grand jury proceedings as among those hearings at which "no evidence derived from [an illegal interception] may be received." *Gelbard* held that this prohibition allows a grand jury witness to refuse to respond to questions based on illegal interceptions. However, Justice White, the crucial fifth vote in *Gelbard*, made clear that this right is limited as to the challenge presented where the interception was based on a court order, and the claimed illegality is in the issuance of the order. Here, the witness can refuse only if the order is legally flawed due to basic defects apparent on the face of the key documents (e.g., the probable cause affidavit) that led to the issuance of the order. Also as to interceptions made without a court order (and therefore more likely to be illegal), most lower courts require the witness to point to factors suggesting the presence of wiretaps or bugging before the government is required to determine whether investigators did use electronic surveillance in the particular case.

Another *Calandra* exception flows from the Court's ruling in *Silverthorne Lumber Co. v. United States*,[161] a pre-*Calandra* ruling which was distinguished in *Calandra*.

---

[158]   414 U.S. 338 (1974).

[159]   408 U.S. 41 (1972).

[160] See § 21.2 at note 6.

[161]   251 U.S. 385 (1920).

Silverthorne upheld the right of indicted defendants to refuse to respond to a grand jury subpoena duces tecum which would have required them to produce the same documents that had been returned to them following their successful Fourth Amendment challenge to the police seizure of those documents. *Silverthorne* reasoned that the subpoena was the fruit of the poisonous tree, as knowledge of the documents came from the illegal search, and that knowledge was thereby rendered permanently inaccessible to the government. A *Calandra* footnote cited three distinguishing characteristics of *Silverthorne*: (1) "there, plaintiffs in error had previously been indicted * * * and thus could invoke exclusionary rule on the basis of their status as criminal defendants"; (2) the "government's interest in recapturing the original documents was founded on a belief they might be useful in the criminal prosecution already authorized by the grand jury," rather than a "need to perform its investigatory or accusatorial functions"; and (3) "prior to the issuance of the grand jury subpoenas, there had been a judicial determination that the search and seizure were illegal" (in contrast to petitioner Calandra's claim of an illegal search "raised for the first time on a pre-indictment motion to suppress requiring interruption of grand jury proceedings").

Lower court opinions examining the "*Silverthorne* exception" suggest that all three distinguishing factors must be present to challenge a grand jury subpoena as derived from an illegal search. In the few cases where witnesses have raised such an objection based upon a previously successful suppression motion, courts have held that the objection fails because the movant was not an indicted defendant, as were the movants in *Silverthorne,* and because the objection did not pose a clear relationship between the subpoena and search previously held illegal and therefore would require an interruptive hearing on the "fruits" issue. In a case in which an indicted defendant challenged the grand jury's use of the actual evidence obtained from a previously adjudicated illegal search, the Seventh Circuit rejected that challenge because, unlike *Silverthorne*, the evidence here was used to assist the grand jury in its investigation of an additional crime, as it was considering (and eventually issued) a superseding indictment. Thus, the *Silverthorne* exception appears to be reduced to situations in which the subpoena would be subject to challenge in any event as aimed at post-indictment discovery. See § 16.12(F)(3).

§ 16.12 RULE 17(C) AND RELATED CHALLENGES

A. Rule 17(c)(2)

Federal Rule 17(c)(1) states that subpoenas may order the production of "books, papers, documents, or other objects." Rule 17(c)(2) adds that, "on motion made promptly, the court may quash or modify the subpoena if compliance would be unreasonable or oppressive." The subsections that follow largely address objections that make subpoena compliance "unreasonable" or "oppressive" under Rule 17(c)(2). In some instances, those objections have a more frequently cited alternative grounding other than Rule 17(c)(2), although they can also be presented under Rule 17(c)(2).

Rule 17(c)(2) on its face appears to refer only to the Rule 17(c)(1) subpoena duces tecum. Rule 17(a) refers to the subpoena ad testificandum, and it does not include a similar provision on quashing subpoenas. Some of the objections discussed below are commonly raised by witnesses as a grounding for refusing to testify entirely or refusing to answer certain types of questions. Where those objections have been recognized under Rule 17, the courts typically have not addressed the relationship between Rule

17(c)(2) and Rule 17(a), apparently assuming that unreasonableness and oppressiveness in compliance are not issues that can logically be limited to the subpoena duces tecum. Where the objection clearly has an alternative grounding, as in claims based on a "chilling impact" upon the exercise of a constitutional right (see subsection (E) infra), there is no need to consider the relationship between Rule 17(c)(2) and Rule 17(a). However, one alternative grounding offered in many of the "misuse cases" (see subsection (F) infra) has been the exercise of the district court's supervisory power, and after *United States v. Williams* (see § 16.4(C)), that grounding may be questioned insofar as the "misuse" is not prohibited by statute or court rule.

B. Improper Subject of Investigation

It generally is conceded that "a subpoenaed [grand jury] witness has no right to know the subject matter of the inquiry or the person[s] against whom the investigation is directed." Ordinarily, however, the witness will become aware of at least the general area of inquiry through a designation of the subject matter in the "advice-of-rights" form (see § 16.5(C)), the questions asked, or the documents requested. In rare instances, this information may suggest that the federal grand jury is investigating an activity for which it cannot indict. In general, however, federal caselaw states that this is not an objection that can be raised under Rule 17(c) or any other source of judicial authority. *Blair v. United States*,[162] though it involved a rather convoluted subject matter objection, is viewed as barring all witness challenges to the grand jury's "jurisdiction" to investigate.

In *Blair*, the witness claimed that the transaction under investigation was beyond the grand jury's investigative authority because the applicable federal criminal statute was unconstitutional. The Supreme Court initially noted that consideration of the constitutionality of the statute at this point, prior to any indictment, would be contrary to the long-established practice of "refrain[ing] from passing upon the constitutionality of an act of Congress unless obliged to do so." It then proceeded, however, to speak in quite general terms of a witness' lack of capacity to challenge the "authority * * * of the grand jury," provided the grand jury had "de facto existence and organization." The Court treated the position of the grand jury witness as analogous to that of the trial witness. Neither could raise objections of "incompetency or irrelevancy," for those matters were of "no concern" to a witness, as opposed to a party. For the same reasons, witnesses also should not be allowed "to take exception to the jurisdiction of the grand jury or the court over the particular subject matter that is under investigation." The grand jury operates as a "grand inquest," which requires broad investigative powers. It must have the authority, in particular, "to investigate the facts in order to determine the question of whether the facts show a case within [its] jurisdiction." The witness could not be allowed "to set limits to the investigation that the grand jury may conduct."

Relying upon *Blair*, federal courts have refused to recognize witness challenges alleging that the grand jury inquiry concerned offenses as to which prosecution would be barred by the statute of limitations, offenses that occurred outside the grand jury's judicial district, or offenses by persons immunized from prosecution. A few federal decisions have suggested openness to subpoena challenges alleging that the grand jury

---

[162] 250 U.S. 273 (1919), also discussed in § 16.2 at note 14.

is investigating offenses that occurred outside the jurisdiction, but they also note that leeway must be given to the grand jury in evaluating such challenges. Given the broad expanse of federal venue provisions, the court must recognize the possibility that a grand jury investigation of an offense seemingly committed elsewhere may disclose some event that places venue in the grand jury's district, and also the possibility that information relating to crimes committed elsewhere may be relevant to the investigation of related or similar crimes, involving the same or different actors, that occurred in the grand jury's district.

C. Relevancy Objections

In commenting upon the objections of a witness, either at trial or before the grand jury, *Blair* noted that "[h]e is not entitled to urge objections of incompetency or irrelevancy, such as a party might raise, for this is no concern of his." This statement was commonly viewed by federal courts as barring all witness objections to the relevancy of information sought by grand jury questioning. Of course relevancy remained a factor considered in determining whether a subpoena duces tecum violates the Fourth Amendment because it was "too sweeping to be reasonable," but that requirement had a separate grounding. Also, where a subpoena duces tecum was sufficiently limited in its overall scope, the Fourth Amendment did not provide a grounding for challenging production of an individual document because it contained information not relevant to the inquiry. *Blair* similarly established that a witness could not object to individual questions put to him on the ground that they had no bearing upon the grand jury's inquiry.

The absence of a general relevancy objection in federal courts appeared to be reaffirmed in *United States v. Mara*.[163] As discussed in § 16.11(D), the *Mara* Court, having found the Fourth Amendment inapplicable to a subpoena demanding handwriting exemplars, concluded that there was "no justification" for the lower court's ruling that the government had to establish that the information sought was "relevant" to the grand jury's inquiry and that demanding those exemplars was "not excessive." The *Mara* opinion relied heavily on the *Blair* analysis of the breadth of the grand jury's investigative powers, and added that there was a need not to "saddle the grand jury with * * * preliminary showings [that] would assuredly impede its investigation." Neither the Constitution nor the Court's prior cases required "a preliminary showing of reasonableness" to compel testimony from a recalcitrant witness and there was no reason to distinguish compelling compliance with an order to produce identification exemplars.[164]

---

[163] 410 U.S. 19 (1973), discussed in § 16.11(D).

[164] Shortly after *Mara* was decided, the Third Circuit adopted a preliminary showing requirement similar to that rejected in *Mara*. The Third Circuit viewed *Mara*, and the companion ruling in *Dionisio*, as limited to the interpretation of the Fourth Amendment, and imposed its requirement as an exercise of the court's supervisory authority and its control over the contempt sanction. To obtain a contempt sanction against a recalcitrant witness, the "government [would] be required to make some preliminary showing by affidavit that each item [sought] is at least relevant to an investigation being conducted by the grand jury and properly in its jurisdiction, and is not sought primarily for another purpose." This ruling was originally applied to a witness who refused to provide identification exemplars, but later extended to witness refusals to testify based upon the general subject matter covered in a grouping of questions (as opposed to information sought in a specific question). Various other circuits refused to adopt such a requirement, viewing it as inconsistent with the reasoning of *Mara* and *Dionisio*. Further support for rejection is found in the *R. Enterprises* discussion of the assessment of relevancy as to a subpoena compelling the production of

In *United States v. R. Enterprises, Inc.*,[165] the Supreme Court considered the possibility of a relevancy objection in a context not presented in *Blair* or *Mara*—challenging a subpoena duces tecum requiring production of a wide variety of records (there, business records). The witness there sought to quash the subpoena under Rule 17(c), arguing that the subpoena failed under the standard that the Supreme Court had applied to Rule 17(c) trial subpoenas. That standard required the party seeking the subpoena (defendant or prosecution) to show that the documents sought were adequately specified, admissible in evidence, and relevant. The lower court had sustained an objection on the ground that the government had failed to show admissibility and relevance.

The Supreme Court was unanimous in rejecting application of the Rule 17(c) standard for trial subpoenas to grand jury subpoenas. That approach was inconsistent with numerous rulings holding that grand juries could consider evidence that would be inadmissible at trial. It also was contrary to the warning in *Dionisio* and *Mara* that the grand jury should be free of the delays that accompany preliminary-showing requirements. The Court added that requiring the government "to explain in too much detail the particular reasons underlying the subpoena" would "compromise the indispensable secrecy of the grand jury proceeding."

Having rejected application of the trial standard, Justice O'Connor's opinion for the Court turned to the more complex task of "fashioning an appropriate standard of reasonableness" in the application of Rule 17. Here, relevancy should have a role. It was well established that "the investigatory powers of the grand jury are * * * not unlimited." The grand jury could not, for example, "engage in arbitrary fishing expeditions" or "select targets of investigation out of malice or an intent to harass." Applying such limits, however, required consideration of conflicting elements in the grand jury process. On the one hand, the decision as to the appropriate charge "is routinely not made until after the grand jury has concluded its investigation," and "one simply cannot know in advance whether information sought during the investigation will be relevant and admissible in the prosecution for a particular offense." On the other hand, the party to whom the subpoena is directed "faces a difficult situation" in challenging the improper use of a subpoena. Grand juries ordinarily "do not announce publicly the subjects of their investigations," and the subpoenaed party therefore "may have no conception of the Government's purpose in seeking production of the requested information." Thus, what was needed was a standard of reasonableness that "gives due weight to the difficult position of subpoena recipients but does not impair the strong governmental interests in affording grand juries wide latitude, avoiding minitrials on peripheral matters, and preserving a necessary level of secrecy."

Turning to the specific guidelines that give substance to such a standard, Justice O'Connor noted initially that "the law presumes, absent a strong showing to the contrary, that a grand jury acts within the legitimate scope of its authority."

documents, particularly its discussion of the limited burden that might be placed upon the government when relevancy is challenged. The Third Circuit, however, continued to insist upon a preliminary showing of relevancy in a post-*R.Enterprises* ruling. See In re Grand Jury Subpoena, 223 F.3d 213 (3d Cir. 2000).

[165] 498 U.S. 292 (1991). *R. Enterprises* involved a challenge to subpoenas directed to three companies owned by the same proprietor, one of which clearly had shipped sexually explicit material. The challenged ruling had rejected the inclusion of the records of the other two companies. The lower court had not considered an additional First Amendment challenge, which was resolved on remand. See note 174 infra.

Consequently, "a grand jury subpoena issued through normal channels is presumed to be reasonable, and the burden of showing unreasonableness must be on the recipient who seeks to avoid compliance." In this case, the recipient "did not challenge the subpoena as being too indefinite, nor did [it] claim that compliance would be overly burdensome."[166] The challenge was strictly on relevancy grounds and for such a challenge, the presumption of regularity produced the following standard: "[T]he motion to quash must be denied unless the district court determines that there is no reasonable possibility that the category of materials the Government seeks will produce information relevant to the general subject of the grand jury's investigation."

Recognizing that the above standard imposed an "unenviable task" upon the party raising a relevancy challenge, Justice O'Connor suggested that the district court had authority to ease that task through appropriate procedures. Her opinion noted in this regard:

> It seems unlikely, of course, that a challenging party who does not know the general subject matter of the grand jury's investigation, no matter how valid that party's claim, will be able to make the necessary showing that compliance would be unreasonable. After all, a subpoena recipient "cannot put his whole life before the court in order to show that there is no crime to be investigated." Consequently, a court may be justified in a case where unreasonableness is alleged in requiring the Government to reveal the general subject of the grand jury's investigation before requiring the challenging party to carry its burden of persuasion. We need not resolve this question in the present case, however, as there is no doubt that respondents knew the subject of the grand jury investigation pursuant to which the business records subpoenas were issued. In cases where the recipient of the subpoena does not know the nature of the investigation, we are confident that district courts will be able to craft appropriate procedures that balance the interests of the subpoena recipient against the strong governmental interests in maintaining secrecy, preserving investigatory flexibility, and avoiding procedural delays. For example, to ensure that subpoenas are not routinely challenged as a form of discovery, a district court may require that the Government reveal the subject of the investigation to the trial court in camera, so that the court may determine whether the motion to quash has a reasonable prospect for success before it discloses the subject matter to the challenging party.

Although the Court in *R. Enterprises* was unanimous in rejecting application of the trial-subpoena standard, there was division as to the specific guidelines advanced in Justice O'Connor's opinion. Justice Scalia did not join the paragraph discussing the district court's possible authority to require the prosecution to set forth the general subject of the investigation. Three justices, in a separate opinion by Justice Stevens, rejected in its entirety what they described as "the Court['s] * * * attempt[t] to define the term reasonableness in the abstract, looking only at the relevance side of the balance."

---

[166] Both of these restrictions are considered in Fourth Amendment overbreadth analysis, see § 16.10(B), and interpreted similarly under Rule 17(c)(2). A subpoena recipient who raises a particularly objection may find that the uncertainty in the description of the documents is corrected by using criteria that reach a broader group of documents [though not so broad as to violate Rule 17(c)(2)]. See subsection (D) infra.

Justice Stevens argued that the burden imposed upon the challenging party will vary with the nature of the subpoena. A more rigorous relevancy standard would be needed where other significant interests are involved. This would be true, for example, where the "subpoena would intrude significantly on * * * privacy interests, or call for the disclosure of trade secrets or other confidential material," or where "the movant might demonstrate that compliance would have First Amendment implications." Admittedly, Justice O'Connor's opinion did not propose a standard for such special circumstances, but Justice Stevens expressed concern that the Court's opinion "not be read to suggest that the deferential relevance standard the Court has formulated will govern decision in every case, no matter how intrusive or burdensome the request." As lower courts had noted, the application of Rule 17(c) called for a balancing process, similar to that applied under the Fourth Amendment. Thus, there should be, in effect, a varying standard of relevancy, with Justice O'Connor's "no-reasonable-possibility" standard limited to subpoenas that are in no significant way either burdensome or intrusive.

As discussed in subsections that follow, the balancing approach described by Justice Stevens has been applied by lower courts, typically in asking whether compliance with the subpoena would be "oppressive." However, that claim initially requires a showing by the movant of a significant burden in complying or a chilling impact upon the exercise of some specially protected interest. Only then will the government be asked to make some showing beyond what is required under the *R. Enterprises* standard of relevancy.

In the leading lower court discussion of the *R. Enterprises* standard, the Tenth Circuit emphasized the restrictions that the standard imposes upon the district court in assessing relevancy.[167] Initially, the district court must assess relevancy by reference to the categories of documents described in the subpoena. If the documents that fit within a particular category, assessed as a general subject-matter grouping, meet the relevancy standard, that ends the district court's inquiry. The district court below therefore had erred when it created its own sub-categories to identify documents within the group that had a greater likelihood of not being relevant.[168] It had erred further in engaging in a "document-by-document and line-by-line analysis of relevancy after finding categories of material relevant" (a task undertaken, in part, to identify and redact "family information" contained in "otherwise relevant producible documents").[169] The end result had been the imposition of a "much more exacting assessment of relevancy than the relaxed categorical approach articulated by *R. Enterprises*," and that was harmful because it could restrict "the grand jury's broad investigative powers, undermine its secrecy [as the government had to justify

---

[167] In re Grand Jury Proceedings, 616 F.3d 1186 (10th Cir. 2010).

[168] The grand jury subpoenas at issue related to the investigation of possible fraud in the submission of government forms. The Tenth Circuit identified some of the categories, such as all "questionnaires/forms including drafts completed for a [redacted] process." One illustration of a district court created subcategory was the effort to separate materials related to answering each of the different questions on the government form, apparently because the investigation was concentrating on misrepresentations on particular questions. The Tenth Circuit noted that materials relating to the answers on all questions met the "reasonable possibility" standard, since the misrepresentations need not have been limited to particular questions, and what was done elsewhere, could "reflect on motive and intent." While the government was engaged in a "type of fishing," that was not contrary to *R. Enterprises*, which spoke only of prohibiting "arbitrary fishing."

[169] The court acknowledged that "there may be a limited need [for a district court] to examine some documents to determine other issues, such as privilege," but that concern was not before the court.

relevancy of individual documents], and cause unnecessary delay." The court added: "We can sympathize with the district court's desire to prevent the grand jury from subpoenaing wholly irrelevant information * * * [but] incidental production of irrelevant documents * * * is simply a necessary consequence of the grand jury's broad investigative power and the categorical approach to relevancy adopted in *R. Enterprises.*"

D. Oppressiveness Objections

Federal Rule 17(c)(2) also authorizes quashing subpoenas duces tecum where compliance would be "oppressive." In setting forth oppressiveness as an alternative ground, Rule 17(c) implicitly recognizes that a demand may be reasonable as measured by the *R. Enterprises* standard of relevancy, yet nonetheless be oppressive. The paradigm of this objection is the claim that oppressiveness lies in the alleged chilling impact of compliance on the exercise of some constitutional right. That claim is discussed in subsection (E) infra.

Still other oppressiveness claims are tied to the unique circumstances of the particular case, as illustrated by *In re Grand Jury Proceedings (Danbom).*[170] That case involved a challenge to a subpoena requiring Western Union to produce documents identifying all wire transfers of $1,000 or more from its major Kansas City office over a two year period. The Eighth Circuit initially rejected a Fourth Amendment overbreadth claim, concluding that such information was material to the grand jury's investigation of drug trafficking and would not significantly impair the office's daily operations. The court went on, however, to consider Western Union's concern that its response to the subpoena would make available to the grand jury the records of many innocent people, and that the publicity resulting from that production could lead such persons to stop transmitting funds through Western Union. The Eighth Circuit stated in this regard that the "expectations of innocent customers that their financial records will be kept confidential" was recognized in the "common law protection" of the privacy of such records. Moreover, while "that common law right does not in any way restrict the grand jury's access to records for which the government can make a minimal showing of general relevance," the district court "may consider the policy concerns evidenced by the common law" in determining whether the subpoena was challengeable under Rule 17(c). The court suggested that the district judge under Rule 17(c) might therefore "appropriately limit the subpoenas to matters having a greater degree of general relevance to the subject matter of the inquiry" (e.g., by asking the government to identify those patterns or characteristics of transfers that would "raise suspicions").

A subsequent Fourth Circuit ruling similarly took account of the confidentiality concerns of the creator of a record in determining that a district court did not abuse its discretion in quashing a grand jury subpoena for obviously relevant material under Rule 17(c)(2).[171] There, a grand jury conducting a civil rights investigation sought to require a local police department to produce the records of an internal investigation of an excessive-force complaint filed against a particular officer. Weighing the limited value of the report in furthering the grand jury's investigation (as acknowledged by the

---

[170] 827 F.2d 301 (8th Cir.1987).

[171] In re Grand Jury, John Doe No. G.J. 2005–2, 478 F.3d 581 (4th Cir.2007).

prosecutor) against the police department's interest in adhering to the promise of confidentiality provided to police officers willing to cooperate in the investigation (thereby overcoming "the so-called 'blue wall of silence'"), the district court acted within its authority in denying access to the internal report.

E. "Chilling Effect" Objections

1. *Generally*

Grand jury witnesses in several contexts have argued that even where the testimony or documents demanded of them clearly would be relevant, the grand jury should be required to show a "compelling need" for that information because the impact of its inquiry would be to chill the exercise of a constitutionally protected right. Those challenges commonly are grounded on the court's authority to protect the constitutional right said to be chilled. They also may be framed, however, as Rule 17(c) challenges to the oppressiveness of the subpoena. The two claims of this character receiving the most attention involve the alleged chilling impact of grand jury subpoenas upon the exercise of First Amendment rights and upon the lawyer-client relationship.

2. *First Amendment Claims*

"Chilling impact" claims based upon the First Amendment stand apart from any testimonial privileges that may bear upon the exercise of rights of free speech, freedom of association, and the free exercise of religion. These claims look to the First Amendment itself to restrict grand jury access to information on the theory that forcing disclosure of information relating to the exercise of a First Amendment right will chill the exercise of that right. Such claims have been raised by a variety of persons with respect to a variety of activities, including: reporters contending that being forced to reveal their sources, to produce their notes, or simply to be required to appear before the grand jury would chill their capacity to gather and report news; sellers of sexually explicit materials contending that their First Amendment right to convey non-pornographic materials would be chilled by subpoenas that require them to disclose copies of the materials distributed or business records that reveal the identity of their customers; religious organizations objecting to grand jury demands for various records as chilling their organizational decisionmaking and adversely impacting their capacity to attract new members; organizations engaged largely or partly in political advocacy contending that being required to furnish documents that identify their members would chill the participation of those members and restrict their capacity to attract new members; a private association of a controversial character (Hells Angels Motorcycle Club) contending that a grand jury demand for information relating to its membership, funding, and organizational structure would chill the members' freedom of association; a public official contending that his right of association was chilled by a grand jury demand that he produce his calendar and schedule for past years; and the author of a book who contended that a subpoena requiring him to produce records of alleged interviews cited in the book would chill future publications. With few exceptions, such challenges have not succeeded in obtaining the quashing of the grand jury directive. However, the courts have been far less consistent in their analysis of the legal standards applicable to these "chilling-impact" claims than in their disposition of the claims.

The one Supreme Court decision directly addressing such a challenge is *Branzburg v. Hayes*,[172] involving the First Amendment claims of reporters who had been subpoenaed to testify before state and federal grand juries. In each instance, newspaper articles written by the reporters indicated that they had knowledge of specific criminal activities, based upon either personal observations or interviews of the alleged participants. The reporters contended that they should not be compelled to testify, in breach of their promises of confidentiality to their sources, absent a special showing of a "compelling need" for the information the reporters might provide. Justice White's opinion for a closely divided Court majority rejected that contention. Justice White acknowledged that requiring the reporters to testify might deter future confidential sources, but noted that the extent of that deterrence was "unclear." Moreover, even if there would be some negative impact upon news gathering, that impact did not outweigh the interest of the public in the grand jury's investigation of crime.

Justice White's opinion noted that the Court was not leaving "news gathering" without any "First Amendment protections." Judicial control of the grand jury process always was available to provide an appropriate remedy if the grand jury process was misused to harass the press. Justice Powell (who provided the majority's fifth vote and joined Justice White's opinion) offered some illustrations of what might be deemed harassment in his separate concurring opinion: "If a newsman believes that the grand jury investigation is not being conducted in good faith he is not without remedy. Indeed, if the newsman is called upon to give information bearing only a remote and tenuous relationship to the subject of the investigation, or if he has some other reason to believe that his testimony implicates confidential source relationships without a legitimate need of law enforcement, he will have access to the court on a motion to quash and an appropriate protective order may be entered."[173]

Lower courts have varied on their reading of *Branzburg*. Some courts stress that *Branzburg* did not consider a situation in which there was an obvious chilling impact on a well-established First Amendment right, such as political association. They view as the more relevant Supreme Court precedent cases that presented such an impact as an inevitable consequence of government compelled disclosures (e.g., cases in which state legislative investigative committees sought to require disclosure of membership information from groups such as the NAACP). Those cases held that the state can

---

[172] 408 U.S. 665 (1972).

[173] Various federal lower courts have concluded that *Branzburg* does not preclude recognition of a qualified, common law reporter's privilege in a context other than a criminal prosecution or criminal investigation. Those cases generally have held, however, that *Branzburg* prevails as to grand jury investigations, and the only available challenge there is for harassment. However, a few opinions have suggested that *Branzburg* forecloses only a First Amendment privilege, and a qualified common law privilege can be extended to grand jury investigations. That position has been advanced in separate opinions at the Court of Appeals level, where the qualified privilege was described as overriden only by a showing that (1) the information sought from the reporter is essential to the investigation, and (2) alternative sources for obtaining that information have been exhausted. See CRIMPROC § 8.8(d).

Under the guidelines of the Department of Justice, USAM § 9–13.400, and 28 C.F.R. § 50.10, federal prosecutors may not issue subpoenas to members of the news media in criminal investigations before (1) reasonable attempts are made to secure the information sought from alternative sources, (2) negotiations with the media outlet (seeking voluntary cooperation) have failed, and (3) the approval of the attorney general is obtained. Attorney general approval will look to whether (1) reasonable grounds exist to believe that a crime has occurred and (2) alternative sources for obtaining the information have been exhausted. These limitations also apply to subpoenas for telephone toll records of members of the media.

prevail only upon showing a "substantial relationship" between the information sought and a "compelling state interest." Lower courts reading *Branzburg* narrowly hold that a similar test applies once the party challenging the subpoena makes a prima facie showing that compliance will chill the further exercise of a First Amendment protected activity, notwithstanding the secrecy attached to grand jury disclosures. These courts vary, however, in their application of such a standard. A few appear to insist upon a showing that the information sought is critical and that other sources of information will be inadequate in exploring criminal liability. Others give more weight to the governmental interest in criminal investigation, treating it as a per se "compelling state interest," and recognize as well "a presumption of regularity" that attaches to the grand jury subpoena (absent a strong showing that the investigation was undertaken in bad faith). To establish that information sought has a "substantial relationship" to that compelling interest, the government must advance a linkage more substantial than the *R. Enterprises* standard of a "reasonable possibility" of relevance, but it need not establish that the need for the information is critical or that alternative sources are clearly inadequate. This showing, moreover, may be made *in camera*.

Other courts have rejected entirely the contention that the government must ordinarily make a special showing to sustain a subpoena that has the potential for chilling the exercise of First Amendment rights. The Fourth Circuit adopted that position upon remand in the *R. Enterprises* case,[174] considering a First Amendment challenge that had not been presented to the Supreme Court. The Fourth Circuit concluded that adoption of a substantial relationship test was contrary to the reasoning of *Branzburg*. In particular, Justice Powell, in explaining the Court's decision, had stated that the district court's capacity to respond to a "bad faith exercise of grand jury powers" would allow for "striking * * * a proper balance between freedom of the press and the obligation of all citizens to give relevant testimony with respect to criminal conduct," but that balance would be struck on a case-by-case analysis of the facts, not through a threshold imposition of "constitutional preconditions." This indicated that the Supreme Court did not believe it necessary to impose any special burden on the government, as would be imposed under a "substantial relationship test," in order to protect adequately First Amendment interests. The Supreme Court cases that developed the substantial relationship standard in other contexts had been relied upon unsuccessfully by the reporters in *Branzburg*, as the Court there obviously viewed the grand jury setting as distinguishable. Thus, it is sufficient that the district court apply, "with special sensitivity where values of expression are potentially implicated," the standards of *R. Enterprises*, keeping in mind the "traditional rule," as set forth in *R. Enterprises*, that "'grand juries are not licensed to engage in arbitrary fishing expeditions, nor may they select targets out of malice or an intent to harass.'"

3. *Attorney–Client Relationships*

Chilling impact objections have also been raised in connection with grand jury subpoenas requiring attorneys to testify in connection with the investigation of past or current clients. Of course, insofar as questions posed to the attorney/witness seek information protected by the attorney-client privilege, that privilege can be relied upon to refuse to furnish that information. However, certain essential facts that are likely to be sought by the grand jury (e.g., client identity and fee information) commonly are not

---

[174] In re Grand Jury 87–3 Subpoena Duces Tecum, 955 F.2d 229 (4th Cir.1992).

protected by the privilege. Here, attorneys have argued that, because of the chilling impact that such disclosure would have upon the attorney-client relationship, the grand jury should not be allowed to force disclosure from the attorney in the absence of an initial showing of special need and relevance. This position has been consistently rejected by the lower federal courts.

In refusing to require that the government make a showing of need in order to compel an attorney to provide non-privileged information relating to the representation of a client, the federal courts have noted that: (1) the attorney-client privilege and work product doctrine provide adequate protection of the attorney-client relationship; (2) even where the subpoenaed attorney currently is representing the client, that representation typically is at a point where the client is simply a target of the investigation and therefore has no Sixth Amendment right to representation; (3) neither is the subpoena likely to interfere with target/client's future Sixth Amendment right to counsel (assuming a subsequent indictment) because the possibility that the attorney's grand jury testimony will lead to the attorney's disqualification at trial tends to be no more than an "abstract possibility," hinging upon the happenstance of a variety of speculative occurrences; and (4) the attorney/witness is asking for exactly the kind of preliminary showing that the Supreme Court warned against in *Dionisio* and *Branzburg* as causing indeterminate delays in grand jury investigations. The Second Circuit has suggested that the first and fourth factors are sufficient in themselves to reject a "compelling need standard," as it has refused to require such a showing even where the information sought relates to a currently represented criminal defendant and could conceivably lead to counsel's disqualification in the criminal case. Appellate opinions do note, however, that the supervisory court has sufficient discretionary authority under Rule 17(c) to quash or delay enforcement of a subpoena to an attorney where it will interfere with counsel's representation of the defendant in a currently pending trial. In such situations, the supervisory judge may insist that the government make some showing of a need to obtain the information sought prior to that trial, at least where counsel shows that compliance with the subpoena will disrupt preparation for the trial.

In 1991, the ABA added to Rule 3.8 of the Model Rules of Professional Conduct a provision limiting prosecutors in seeking to subpoena lawyers in grand jury or other criminal proceedings for the purpose of obtaining information "about a past or present client." Prosecutorial use of such a subpoena would constitute unprofessional conduct unless the following conditions were met: (1) the information sought is not protected by an applicable privilege; (2) the "evidence sought is essential to the successful completion of an ongoing investigation or prosecution"; (3) "there is no other feasible alternative to obtain the information"; and (4) "the prosecutor obtains prior judicial approval after an opportunity for an adversarial proceeding." The requirement of prior judicial approval for issuance of an attorney subpoena was deleted from Rule 3.8 in 1995, but several states stayed with the 1991 version. When federal district courts incorporated the different versions of Rule 3.8 in local rules establishing federal-court ethical standards, two courts of appeals split on whether the district court had exceeded its authority. The courts were divided on the permissible scope of local rules in light of the Supreme Court's statements on the federal courts' limited supervisory power with respect to grand jury practice (see § 16.4(C)). Since the Supreme Court had noted that the supervisory power could be used to hold federal prosecutors to standards approved by Congress, Congress' subsequent adoption of the Citizen's Protection Act presented the possibility of having mooted that issue.

Adopted in 1998, the Citizen's Protection Act (28 U.S.C. § 530B) subjects an "attorney for the [federal] government" (including United States Attorneys) to the "state laws and local federal court rules governing attorneys in such State where such attorney engages in that attorney's duties, to the same extent and in the same manner as other attorneys in that State." Legislative history makes clear that the objective of the Citizen's Protection Act (CPA) was to make applicable to federal prosecutors standards of professional responsibility contained in state rules and local district court rules, thereby overturning a Justice Department claim of exemption from those rules. However, the CPA did not clearly identify what it meant by a "rule governing attorneys" and what remedies would be available for violations of such rules by federal prosecutors.

In *Stern v. United States District Court*,[175] the First Circuit held that the CPA did not encompass a district court rule that incorporated the 1991 version of ABA Model Rule 3.8. The First Circuit concluded, as had other courts, that the CPA extended only to "ethical standards." Rule 3.8, however, "though doubtless motivated by ethical concerns," is "more than an ethical standard"; "it adds a novel procedural step—the opportunity for a pre-service adversarial hearing—and to compound the matter, ordains that the hearing be conducted with new substantive standards in mind." Accordingly, the local rule did not fall within the shelter of the CPA, and it would not be rescued by that Act if it went beyond the district court's rulemaking authority. The local rule did so here as it conflicted with the subpoena requirements of Rule 17(c) in "impos[ing] new substantive requirements for judicial preapproval of grand jury subpoenas."

In *United States v. Colorado Supreme Court*,[176] the Tenth Circuit held within the CPA a state professional responsibility rule adopting the later version of Model Rule 3.8 (i.e., not including a requirement of judicial pre-approval) as that rule applied to a trial subpoena. The district court had specifically exempted grand jury proceedings from the application of the Rule 3.8 standard, to avoid possible conflict with Rule 17, and the Tenth Circuit therefore did not consider that application. Although concluding that the professional responsibility standard before it could be made applicable to federal prosecutors under the CPA, the Tenth Circuit viewed the standard only in the context of its possible application in a disciplinary proceeding. Various federal courts have concluded that the CPA deals only with the disciplinary process and does not provide an enforcement mechanism within the criminal justice process. Thus a subpoena cannot be challenged on the ground that it does not meet the prerequisites of Model Rule 3.8. As an ethical standard, however, Rule 3.8 does impose a prerequisite for an attorney subpoena that exceeds the DOJ internal standard imposed under

---

[175] 214 F.3d 4 (1st Cir. 2000). The First Circuit had upheld a district court local rule applying a version of Rule 3.8, but that ruling had not assumed the application of the substantive restrictions Rule 3.8 places upon attorney subpoenas.

[176] 189 F.3d 1281 (1999).

USAM § 9–13.140[177] as to the need for the information to be obtained from the attorney.

F. Misuse Objections

1. *Generally*

Relying on various Supreme Court discussions of the possible misuse of the grand jury subpoena to further ends other than the grand jury's investigative function, federal lower courts have concluded that such misuses would constitute grounds for challenging a subpoena under Rule 17. The primary forms of misuse, as they relate to white collar investigations, are discussed below.

2. *Obtaining Evidence to Assist Civil or Administrative Enforcement*

In *United States v. Procter & Gamble Co.*,[178] the lower court granted broad disclosure of grand jury testimony to the defendants in a civil antitrust suit brought by the government. The lower court's ruling appeared to be influenced by its conclusion that the grand jury investigation, which had not produced an indictment, was used "to elicit evidence" that could later be used by the Antitrust Division in a civil action. The Supreme Court rejected the disclosure order as not supported by a showing of particularized need, but it also acknowledged that the alleged government subversion of the criminal process could constitute "good cause" warranting extensive disclosure to the opposing party in the civil suit. There had been no finding, however, that the grand jury proceeding had in fact "been used as a short cut to [civil discovery] goals otherwise barred or more difficult to reach." If the grand jury had been employed in that fashion, the Court noted, the government clearly would have been guilty of "flouting the policy of the law," both as to the grand jury's proper function and the prescribed procedures for civil discovery. On the other hand, if the grand jury investigation were legitimate, there was no need to deny the government the incidental benefit of civil use of properly acquired evidence.

Lower courts applying the civil misuse standard of *Procter & Gamble* agree that the concern here relates to aiding administrative agency actions as well as traditional DOJ civil actions. They agree also that whether or not an abuse exists depends upon the prosecutor's purpose in using the grand jury process, rather than the relevancy of the requested information to possible civil or administrative enforcement. They recognize that a proper criminal investigation may readily encompass elements that also relate to such enforcement, and that in some areas of the law (e.g., antitrust), the overlap between the criminal and civil investigation will be substantial. Here, however, lower court descriptions of prohibited misuses suggest differing views as to how "pure" the government's purpose must be.

---

[177] USAM § 13.140 requires that such subpoenas ordinarily be cleared with the Assistant Attorney General for the Criminal Division. In determining whether to grant approval, the AAG will apply the following principles: [1] the information sought shall not be protected by a valid claim of privilege; [2] all reasonable attempts to obtain the information from alternative sources shall have proved to be unsuccessful; and [3] in a criminal investigation or prosecution, there must be reasonable grounds to believe that a crime has been or is being committed, and that the information sought is reasonably needed for the successful completion of the investigation or prosecution (i.e., the subpoena must not be used to obtain "peripheral or speculative information"). Rule 3.8 requires that the information sought be "essential" to successful completion, as opposed to the DOJ standard of "reasonably needed."

[178] 356 U.S. 677 (1958).

Several courts have suggested that the *Procter & Gamble* standard is violated only when the investigation was aimed "primarily" at civil enforcement. The issue, as they see it, is whether the grand jury proceedings were a "cover" or "subterfuge" for a civil investigation. Under this view, an investigation directed at concurrent criminal and civil uses would be acceptable, at least where the criminal use was at least equal in significance. Other courts suggest that the grand jury can be used only to conduct investigations that are in their inception "exclusively criminal." This standard arguably would bar an investigation that is initiated with "a completely open mind as to what the appropriate remedy should be, criminal, civil, or both." If so, it probably goes beyond what the Supreme Court had in mind in *Procter & Gamble*. Read in light of the lower court rulings in that case, the language of *Procter & Gamble* suggests that the Court there was considering only that situation in which the prosecutor clearly anticipated the government bringing a civil suit and viewed an indictment "as merely an unexpected bare possibility."

Claims of misuse of grand jury proceedings to implement civil or administrative enforcement are most commonly raised: (1) after a completed investigation, in connection with a Rule 6(e) motion for disclosure of the grand jury testimony (where a former targets claims misuse either to bar disclosure to a government unit intending to bring a civil or administrative action, or to gain disclosure for itself after ex parte disclosure to that unit); or (2) during an ongoing investigation, by motion of the witness, or the target, to quash a subpoena. On occasion, targets have sought remedies beyond quashing the subpoena, such as terminating the grand jury investigation or disqualifying the offending prosecutor. The lower courts have not granted those remedies, and have not suggested that they would be appropriate. Quashing the subpoena provides a sufficient remedy at the moment, as it is always possible that a change in events subsequently will produce a legitimate grand jury interest in the possibility of prosecution.

Whatever the procedural context, the party claiming misuse must overcome the traditional "presumption of regularity," and the burden of overcoming that presumption clearly is greater as to the motion to quash. Courts hesitate to project the purpose of an investigation while it is still ongoing. Even where the surrounding circumstances strongly suggest misuse (e.g., where the grand jury investigation was instituted shortly after the target's legal challenges stymied a civil investigation), courts have been willing on a motion to quash to accept a prosecution affidavit of good faith as a sufficient response. A more appropriate assessment, it is argued, can be made after the investigation is ended, with adequate relief still available to the target. If the grand jury should return an indictment, that act will constitute strong evidence "that there has been no perversion of grand jury processes." If an indictment has not been returned, the target retains the opportunity to challenge the proceeding when and if a Rule 6(e) motion seeks disclosure for use in connection with a civil or administrative action. At that point, a more detailed government affidavit may be required, or the court may hold an evidentiary hearing. Exactly how much explanation will be demanded from the government will vary with the strength of the suggestion of possible misuse in the surrounding circumstances. As one court noted, in the end, the judge's ruling on a misuse objection must seek to strike an equitable balance between "(1) the need of the [prospective civil] defendants to ascertain whether there has been an abuse of the grand jury process, and (2) the policies of grand jury secrecy and freedom in government decisionmaking."

3. Obtaining Post–Indictment Criminal Discovery

The grand jury is given its broad investigative powers to determine whether a crime has been committed and an indictment should issue, not to gather evidence for use in cases in which indictments have already issued. Accordingly, lower courts agree that a subpoena should be quashed if the grand jury process is being used "for the sole or dominating purpose of preparing an already pending indictment for trial." This prohibits both exploring additional sources of incriminating evidence that were not known (or not available) prior to the indictment and gaining a preview of what appears post-indictment to be the defendant's' trial defense through subpoenaing possible defense witness. The latter objective achieves discovery unavailable under federal discovery law, which does not require the defense to list its witnesses or identify its defense, outside of alibi, a public-authority defense, an insanity defense, and expert witness testimony.[179]

On the other side, lower courts also agree that where the primary purpose of the investigation is to determine whether others not indicted were involved in the same criminal activity, or whether the indicted party committed still other crimes, the government may go forward with the inquiry even though one result may be the production of evidence that could then be used at the trial of the pending indictment. Also, prior to indictment, nothing prevents the prosecution from bringing before the grand jury evidence that will fully explore the case, beyond what is needed for probable cause, although one consequence is to better prepare the prosecution to meet the defense that will be posed if the indictment is issued. That is consistent with the grand jury's authority to track down every clue, whether incriminatory or exculpatory.

A claim of a dominant purpose of post-indictment discovery may be raised in various procedural settings, including a witness' motion to quash a subpoena, an indicted target's motion for a protective order restricting the scope of an investigation, and a defense objection at trial to the admission of evidence arguably derived from such grand jury misuse. In evaluating such claims, the general approach of the courts has paralleled that applied to claims of the misuse of a grand jury to obtain civil discovery. Here too, courts start with the principle that a "presumption of regularity" attaches to the grand jury proceeding and that the objecting party bears the burden of overcoming that presumption. Courts also have noted their reluctance to interfere with an ongoing investigation, suggesting that the true purpose of the investigation can best be assessed after it is completed. Where the objecting party can point to surrounding circumstances highly suggestive of improper use, the court may require a government affidavit explaining the purpose of the post-indictment investigation or it may examine the grand jury transcript in camera to determine that purpose.

Courts note that establishing a misuse claim is extremely difficult. "Absent some indicative sequence of events demonstrating an irregularity, a court has to take at face value the Government's word that the dominant purpose of the Grand Jury proceedings is proper." Not surprisingly, reported cases finding an improper purpose are rare. Though a few cases suggest that the potential for abuse is heightened where the grand jury post-indictment seeks evidence bearing upon the pending charge from

---

[179] See Fed.R.Crim P. 12.1 (alibi), 12.2 (insanity), 12.3 (public-authority defenses), 16(6)(1)(B) (expert reports and testimony, required only where the defense sought similar discovery from the prosecution).

the indicted person himself, the government can often point to the potential for a superseding indictment involving further activity as a reason for seeking evidence from the indicted person.

4. *Harassment*

In the course of upholding the broad investigatory powers of the grand jury, courts frequently note that, of course, use of those powers for the purpose of "harassment" is always subject to judicial remedy. Precisely what a court has in mind by this reference to "harassment" is often left open, but it apparently refers to something more than simply using the grand jury process for some unauthorized purpose, such as civil discovery. Courts that have offered illustrations of harassment tend to stress a vindictive element in the use of the grand jury, usually a use designed to intimidate the witness. Thus, illustrations are offered of "bad faith harassment of a political dissident" by imposing the burdens (political and otherwise) of a grand jury appearance with "no expectation that any testimony concerning a crime would be forthcoming." Similarly, repeated subpoenas to appear before one grand jury after another may reflect harassment. So too, subpoenas utilized to provide leaks to the press would constitute harassment. It has also been argued that calling a witness before the grand jury solely to trap him into committing perjury constitutes a form of harassment.[180]

As with other misuse claims, harassment claims pose difficulties for the movant both as to timing and proof. A court may hesitate to quash a subpoena where the alleged harassment, if it materializes, can be remedied at a later stage, as in the case of dismissing an indictment that is the product of a perjury trap. To overcome the presumption of regularity, the moving party must establish that there was no legitimate ground for the subpoena. The fact that the witness was called before a third grand jury, after having twice previously refused to testify, may suggest no more than a continuing need for the information and a hope that he may have changed his mind. Similarly, successive appearances required of a testifying witness may evidence no more than an investigation that has moved from one subject to another, all of which relate to the witness. The publication in the press of matters previously disclosed to the grand jury does not necessarily indicate that there have been leaks by government personnel, and that the government has a strategy of creating adverse pretrial publicity. That a witness was called by the prosecutor with the anticipation that he might commit perjury does not necessarily suggest an "ambush"; the prosecutor's intent may have been to "flush out the truth," by confronting the witness with his own lies.

G. Target Standing

In contrast to Fourth Amendment objections (see § 16.11(C)), the target of an investigation often will have standing to intervene and object to a subpoena on the basis of Rule 17(c) and related misuse challenges. As illustrated by the majority's analysis in *In re Grand Jury*,[181] a variety of considerations bear upon determining whether target-standing will be allowed. A divided Third Circuit there recognized the standing of the victims of a privately executed wiretap to seek to quash a grand jury

---

[180] See §§ 10.6, 16.6(D).
[181] 111 F.3d 1066 (3d Cir. 1997).

subpoena directing the perpetrator of the wiretap to produce the intercepted communications. Although the claim there was based on the statutory prohibition against use of illegally intercepted wire communications before the grand jury (see § 16.11(F)), rather than a Rule 17(c) objection, the court relied on the reasoning of a previous Third Circuit Rule 17(c) misuse case in examining the "jurisprudential concerns" of standing doctrine as applied to the grand jury setting.

As the earlier case had noted: "Third party standing to assert claims of grand jury abuse cannot be determined by categorizing the claimed interest as one of property or privilege, but only by examining the nature of the abuse, and asking whether, and in what manner, it impinges upon the legitimate interests of the party allegedly abused." Once the legitimate interest of the party is identified, traditional third-party standing issues will be addressed. Was that interest separate from the interest of the subpoenaed witness; did the claim present "a precise question arising from a specific grievance," rather than an abstract question; was the intervener best suited to challenge the subpoena; and would these considerations be outweighed by the disruptive impact upon the grand jury investigative process. With respect to the latter element, the Third Circuit majority noted that, while the Supreme Court had warned against allowing objections that delay and disrupt grand jury proceedings,[182] a motion to quash "ha[s] not traditionally been regarded as an unreasonable burden on grand jury proceedings where filed by the subpoena recipient, and should not be so viewed where filed by "a third party with an important interest at stake."

Under a similar analysis, third party standing has been allowed on a variety of Rule 17(c) type claims. Thus reporters have been allowed to challenge subpoenas directing telephone service providers to reveal the telephone numbers of sent and received calls; an employer could challenge subpoenas directed to its employees on the ground that the prosecutor's objective was to harass the employer by disrupting its operations; and an indicted defendant could challenge a subpoena directing his travel agency to produce records of his airline travel on the ground that the objective was to obtain discovery as to the criminal case pending against him.

---

[182] See, e.g., the analysis in *Dionisio* discussed in § 16.11(D). The dissent in the Third Circuit relied on that Supreme Court warning.

Chapter 17

ADMINISTRATIVE AGENCY INVESTIGATIONS

§ 17.1 INTRODUCTION

Administrative agencies have proliferated at the federal level as the national government has taken on a broader role in regulating many facets of the economy. Agencies are usually created in the first instance in response to a particular need or crisis. In the late nineteenth century, the issue of railroad rates led to the creation of the Interstate Commerce Commission, the first federal administrative agency. The Federal Trade Commission and the Food and Drug Administration trace their roots to the early twentieth century as Congress sought to address anticompetitive behavior and the need to protect the public from unsafe products in the market. The New Deal era witnessed an explosion of federal agencies to regulate important areas of the economy, such as the Securities and Exchange Commission and the Federal Deposit Insurance Corporation. With the expansion of social programs in the 1960s came the growth of public welfare efforts that led to the creation of the Departments of Health and Human Services (formerly the Department of Health, Education and Welfare) and Housing and Urban Affairs, while in 1970 concerns about the environment led to the formation of the Environmental Protection Agency. The Department of Homeland Security brought together a number of different agencies under one roof in response to the September 11 attacks.

An important statute that provides a framework for how agencies operate is the Administrative Procedure Act,[1] adopted by Congress in 1946. The law sets standards for the consideration and promulgation of regulations, which can have an enormous impact on the day-to-day lives and operations of individuals and businesses. If an agency tries to enforce compliance with its regulations, or seeks a penalty for a violation, then the APA provides the broad structure for that process, including judicial review of its decision. Congress grants most agencies the power to compel the production of information, an authority that is similar to the power of a grand jury to require that documents be produced and witnesses testify. There are, however, important limits on the authority of an agency to obtain information. Under the APA, compulsory process to obtain information "may not be issued, made, or enforced except as authorized by law."[2] The courts play a crucial role in the enforcement of agency demands for information because only the judiciary is authorized to issue an order compelling compliance with an administrative demand for testimony and documents.

The starting point for an analysis of an administrative investigation is the legislative grant of authority. For federal agencies, Congress has typically provided broad power to the agency to gather information and conduct investigations consistent with the laws it administers. For example, the SEC "may, in its discretion, make such

---

[1] 5 U.S.C. §§ 701 et seq.
[2] 5 U.S.C. § 555(c).

investigations as it deems necessary to determine whether any person has violated, is violating, or is about to violate any provision of this chapter, [and] the rules or regulations thereunder. . . . "[3] Similarly, the EPA can compel a business to create and maintain records related to air pollution, and inspectors have the authority to enter the premises to review the records and a facility's compliance with the law.[4] If the demand for information comes within the agency's authority, then the court will not inquire further into the subject matter of the investigation. As the Third Circuit held in *University of Medicine and Dentistry of New Jersey v. Corrigan*,[5] an administrative demand for information was "of a kind that is squarely within the broad authority of the inspector general to audit providers for the purpose of preventing fraud and abuse within the Medicare program."

§ 17.2 CONSTITUTIONAL LIMITATIONS ON AGENCY INVESTIGATIONS

Federal administrative agencies were unknown at the time of the framing of the Constitution, so there are no specific provisions devoted to this important facet of the federal government. Congress has the authority under the Necessary and Proper Clause to pass laws to execute its constitutional authority by placing powers "in any Department or Officer thereof," so the starting point in any analysis of an administrative action is ascertaining whether it is a proper exercise of the agency's power granted by Congress. Many agencies are authorized to issue a subpoena, summons or civil investigative demand as part of an investigation, and an important preliminary issue is whether the investigation is sufficiently related to the statutory authorization to be a proper exercise of the agency's authority.

The Fourth Amendment's prohibition on unreasonable searches and seizures has provided a small measure of protection in regulatory investigations. However, only a few agencies, such as the Occupational Health and Safety Administration, execute search warrants or conduct on-site inspections, so this constitutional requirement is often inapplicable when an agency uses its investigative authority to compel the production of documents and testimony. Most agencies have a broad grant of regulatory authority, and courts focus on whether the demand comports with more general due process requirements in determining whether to enforce a demand for records or a witness appearance. In addition, the Fifth Amendment privilege against self-incrimination is applicable in any proceeding in which a witness is compelled to testify by the government, and may provide a means to resist producing evidence sought by an agency. (See § 20.1). The federal immunity statute[6] authorizes an administrative agency to obtain an order of immunity with the approval of the Attorney General compelling a witness to testify in the agency's investigation. This immunity operates the same way as that provided to a witness to testify before the grand jury. (See § 19.5).

---

[3] 15 U.S.C. § 78u(a).

[4] 42 U.S.C. 7414(a).

[5] 347 F.3d 57 (3d Cir. 2003).

[6] 18 U.S.C. § 6004.

§ 17.3 THE FOURTH AMENDMENT AND ADMINISTRATIVE SUBPOENAS

The first Supreme Court case to consider the government's authority to compel the production of records in a civil investigation was *Boyd v. United States*,[7] which involved an inquiry into whether customs duties had been paid on imported plate glass. The Court found that the order compelling production of the invoice violated both the Fourth Amendment's prohibition on unreasonable searches and the Fifth Amendment privilege against self-incrimination. While noting that the order compelling production of the records was different from a forcible entry into a home to remove evidence, the Court concluded:

> [A] compulsory production of a man's private papers to establish a criminal charge against him, or to forfeit his property, is within the scope of the fourth amendment to the constitution, in all cases in which a search and seizure would be, because it is a material ingredient, and effects the sole object and purpose of search and seizure.

This led the Court to hold that the compelled production of the records violated both the Fourth and Fifth Amendments because "any forcible and compulsory extortion of a man's own testimony, or of his private papers to be used as evidence to convict him of crime, or to forfeit his goods, is within the condemnation of that judgment. In this regard the fourth and fifth amendments run almost into each other." Justice Brandeis once described *Boyd* as "a case that will be remembered as long as civil liberty lives in the United States." As discussed in § 16.11(A), the Court's analysis has been largely undermined in criminal investigations by subsequent decisions rejecting the amalgamation of the Fourth and Fifth Amendments to protect private papers from being disclosed, or prohibiting their seizure pursuant to a warrant.

In administrative investigations, the Supreme Court in *FTC v. American Tobacco Co.*[8] continued to consider the Fourth Amendment as a potential constraint on the authority of agencies to compel the production of records. The Federal Trade Commission sought a broad range of corporate records related to tobacco industry practices, demanding all letters and telegrams received from or sent to certain customers during 1921. In rejecting the agency's demand to compel the production of the records, the Court noted:

> Anyone who respects the spirit as well as the letter of the Fourth Amendment would be loath to believe that Congress intended to authorize one of its subordinate agencies to sweep all our traditions into the fire and to direct fishing expeditions into private papers on the possibility that they may disclose evidence of crime.

The Court refused the F.T.C.'s request for a writ of mandamus directing the district court to enforce its order for production, signaling that it would consider the breadth of the demand as a basis for assessing the reasonableness of the agency's actions.

---

[7] 116 U.S. 616 (1886). (See § 16.11(A)).

[8] 264 U.S. 298 (1924).

With the growth of the federal regulatory state in the New Deal and World War II, the Supreme Court became much more amenable to the authority of the administrative agencies to implement the law and conduct investigations to determine compliance, moving away from its earlier application of the Fourth Amendment. In *Endicott Johnson Corp. v. Perkins*,[9] the Court upheld a broad subpoena for records, rejecting out of hand a claim that the scope of the subpoena violated the Fourth Amendment. The opinion explained that "[t]he subpoena power delegated by the statute as here exercised is so clearly within the limits of Congressional authority that it is not necessary to discuss the constitutional questions urged by the petitioner." The Court found that the "evidence sought by the subpoena was not plainly incompetent or irrelevant to any lawful purpose of the Secretary in the discharge of her duties under the Act, and it was the duty of the District Court to order its production for the Secretary's consideration." The case proved to be an important turning point because it "established that an agency could conduct an investigation even though it had no probable cause to believe that any particular statute was being violated."[10]

In *Oklahoma Press Publishing Co. v. Walling*,[11] the Court moved further away from application of the Fourth Amendment to administrative subpoenas when it upheld a demand for records by the Department of Labor as part of an investigation of possible violations of the Fair Labor Standards Act. Rejecting the approach taken in *Boyd*, the Court stated:

> [T]he Fifth Amendment affords no protection by virtue of the self-incrimination provision, whether for the corporation or for its officers; and the Fourth, if applicable, at the most guards against abuse only by way of too much indefiniteness or breadth in the things required to be "particularly described," if also the inquiry is one the demanding agency is authorized by law to make and the materials specified are relevant. The gist of the protection is in the requirement, expressed in terms, that the disclosure sought shall not be unreasonable.

The Court noted that the Fourth Amendment only applied in an "analogical sense" by requiring that the demand be reasonable and not arbitrary or overbroad, but that establishing probable cause was unnecessary. In that regard, "It is enough that the investigation be for a lawfully authorized purpose, within the power of Congress to command." Thus, whether an administrative subpoena was reasonable, and therefore enforceable, depends on whether the "specification of the documents to be produced [was] adequate, but not excessive, for the purposes of the relevant inquiry."

Oklahoma Press Publishing did not sanction unbounded administrative authority to conduct investigations, although the usual limits of the Fourth Amendment did not apply to a demand for documents. The Court noted that requiring a subpoena to meet a flexible test of reasonableness would provide sufficient protection to "the interests of men to be free from officious intermeddling, whether because irrelevant to any lawful purpose or because unauthorized by law, concerning matters which on proper occasion

---

[9] 317 U.S. 501 (1943).

[10] United States v. Construction Products Research, Inc., 73 F.3d 464 (2d Cir. 1996).

[11] 327 U.S. 186 (1946).

and within lawfully conferred authority of broad limits are subject to public examination in the public interest."

This approach is similar to the Fourth Amendment overbreadth analysis applied to grand jury subpoenas (see § 16.11). Agencies must have independent power to determine when to exercise their authority to conduct an investigation without having to establish in advance probable cause that a violation has occurred, otherwise the congressional purpose supporting the laws and regulations in a field might be thwarted at the outset. The role of the courts is limited to assessing whether the demand is reasonable and relevant to the laws it oversees, not whether the inquiry is necessary or relevant.

In *United States v. Morton Salt Co.*,[12] the Court reiterated this accommodating approach to enforcement of administrative demands for information by upholding a broad FTC order for documents to determine whether a company was in compliance with an administrative cease-and-desist order. The Court noted that an agency's investigative authority is more closely analogous to a grand jury rather than a court, which is necessarily limited to compelling the production of relevant information in a particular proceeding. In determining whether an investigation came within the congressional grant of authority, "it is sufficient if the inquiry is within the authority of the agency, the demand is not too indefinite, and the information sought is reasonably relevant." On the issue of what is required before an agency can exercise its authority to compel the production of information, the Court gave a fairly wide berth to the regulators, explaining that "[e]ven if one were to regard the request for information in this case as caused by nothing more than official curiosity, nevertheless law enforcing agencies have a legitimate right to satisfy themselves that corporate behavior is consistent with the law and the public interest." Nevertheless, there are limits to an agency's power to compel the production of records, as discussed below.

§ 17.4 SUBPOENA ENFORCEMENT

A. Generally

Administrative subpoenas and related demands for records and testimony can only be enforced if the agency goes to federal district court to invoke the judicial authority to compel the action sought. The courts require the government to justify the demand by establishing that it is authorized to pursue the investigation and the information or witness testimony sought comes within the purview of its congressional grant of power. Either the agency or the subpoena recipient can pursue a direct appeal of the decision on enforcement; the recipient need not refuse to comply and be held in contempt to pursue an appeal, as is required to challenge the district court's decision to enforce a grand jury subpoena (see § 16.5(D)).

The leading case establishing the framework for judicial review of an agency subpoena is *United States v. Powell*, which established a four-part test for determining whether to enforce the demand:

---

[12] 338 U.S. 632 (1950).

1.   Is the investigation being conducted pursuant to a legitimate purpose;

2.   Is the information or documents sought relevant to that purpose;

3.   Does the agency already possess the information sought; and

4.   Have the requisite administrative steps been followed.

Powell involved an Internal Revenue Service summons for records of a taxpayer related to the operation of a laundry business. The Court rejected the taxpayer's argument to impose a probable cause requirement before compelling the production of records, noting that the courts should not be called upon to oversee tax investigations. Although the *Powell* test arose in the context of an IRS summons, courts have since found that it provides the applicable framework for determining the enforcement of any administrative subpoena.

B. Procedure

The process of enforcing an administrative subpoena begins with the agency filing an action in district court seeking an order to compel compliance with its subpoena. In *United States v. Gertner*,[13] the First Circuit outlined a three-step analysis to determine whether to enforce an administrative demand: first, the agency must make out a prima facie case that "it is acting in good faith and for a lawful purpose," which can be provided in an affidavit from the agency outlining the basis for enforcing the demand. The circuit court noted that this requirement is "minimal." Second, the burden shifts to the subpoena recipient to rebut the government's claim of good faith that requires articulation of "specific allegations of bad faith and, if necessary, produce reasonably particularized evidence in support of those allegations." Third, if such information is available, then "the district court weighs the facts, draws inferences, and decides the issue" of whether to enforce the agency demand. The First Circuit noted that it is not clear who bears the burden of establishing the enforceability of the subpoena at the third stage, and while it said that the agency should be responsible for establishing the propriety of its summons, it did not conclusively decide the issue. In *United States v. Monumental Life Insurance Co.*,[14] the Sixth Circuit put the burden on the IRS to establish it did not have the records from the taxpayer already in its possession, holding that "[b]ecause Monumental has successfully rebutted the government's prima facie showing as required by *Powell,* the IRS must prove that, on balance, the . . . documents cannot be practicably accessed."

Subpoena enforcement actions are summary proceedings, so that the usual discovery rights provided by the Federal Rules of Civil Procedure are not available absent extraordinary circumstances. In *SEC v. McGoff*,[15] the recipient of an SEC subpoena argued that he had been targeted for investigation because he was a vocal critic of the President, and sought discovery to support his claim of bad faith in the investigation. The District of Columbia Circuit held that discovery was only available

---

[13] 65 F.3d 963 (1st Cir. 1995).

[14] 440 F.3d 729 (6th Cir. 2006).

[15] 647 F.2d 185 (D.C.Cir. 1981).

in extraordinary circumstances, and this case did not qualify as one allowing the subpoena recipient to obtain information from the agency issuing the subpoena. In *United States v. Aero Mayflower Transit Co., Inc.*,[16] the same court stated that discovery may be permitted "where the circumstances indicate that further information is necessary for the courts to discharge their duty." The Sixth Circuit noted that "[t]he Circuits appear to agree that the summary nature of enforcement proceedings must be preserved by limiting discovery."[17]

C. Legitimate Purpose

In *Powell*, the Supreme Court pointed out that "a court may not permit its process to be abused," so an inquiry into the reason for the agency's investigation was proper. A demand may not be enforced "if the summons had been issued for an improper purpose, such as to harass the taxpayer or to put pressure on him to settle a collateral dispute, or for any other purpose reflecting on the good faith of the particular investigation." Although a claim of bad faith is sometimes described as a separate ground for challenging an administrative subpoena, it is better understood as part of the determination that the agency seeks the information for a legitimate purpose.

In challenging the legitimacy of the investigation, subpoena recipients may argue that the agency is acting vindictively in pursing them for an illegitimate purpose, so that the subpoena constitutes a form of harassment denounced in *Powell*. The fact that an agency may have improperly disclosed information during its investigation does not necessarily establish bad faith to demonstrate the subpoena is not for a legitimate purpose. In *United States v. Texas Heart Institute*,[18] the Fifth Circuit held that "even accepting as true that improper disclosures occurred, any alleged improper disclosures do not rise to the level necessary to demonstrate bad faith in the issuance of the summonses or lack of a legitimate purpose for the investigation." Similarly, the Second Circuit in *United States v. White*[19] rejected a requirement that the IRS show a taxpayer's deduction was improper before a summons would be enforced, stating that "[t]he function of the district court and of this Court in an enforcement proceeding is not to test the final merits of the claimed tax deduction, but to assess within the limits of *Powell* whether the IRS issued its summons for a legitimate tax determination purpose."

Challenges to the agency's jurisdiction, or the relationship of the information or testimony sought to its regulatory authority, have been rejected for the most part in the context of arguing that the subpoena is not for a legitimate purpose. In *United States v. Construction Products Research, Inc.*,[20] the Second Circuit dismissed a challenge to a Nuclear Regulatory Commission subpoena related to employment practices involving whistleblowers. The circuit court found that the agency investigation was proper if it would "assist . . . in exercising any authority provided" by statute, and so an inquiry into employment practices might lead to rulemaking or

---

[16] 831 F.2d 1142 (D.C.Cir. 1987) (quoting SEC v. Dresser Industries, 628 F.2d 1368 (D.C.Cir. 1980)).

[17] United States v. Markwood, 48 F.3d 969 (6th Cir. 1995).

[18] 755 F.2d 469 (5th Cir. 1985).

[19] 853 F.2d 107 (2d Cir. 1988).

[20] 73 F.3d 464 (2d Cir. 1996).

other administrative actions related to that authority. The agency's primary focus was nuclear safety, but the subpoena was for a legitimate purpose because unless it was "permitted to investigate whether an employer regularly stifles disclosure of possible nuclear hazards, this practice could go unchecked—a situation rife with safety ramifications." A claim that the agency could not successfully pursue an enforcement action as a result of the information obtained is similarly unavailing in determining whether it was for a legitimate purpose. In *Mollison v. United States*,[21] the Second Circuit stated, "In applying the 'legitimate purpose test,' we are not concerned with whether any subsequent enforcement action is likely to be meritorious, jurisdictionally or otherwise."

D. Relevance

The broad authority granted to agencies to conduct investigations is not limited to evidence that would be admissible in court. In *E.E.O.C. v. Shell Oil Co.*,[22] the Supreme Court noted that the limitation on an agency's power to subpoena only "relevant" information "is not especially constraining" because "courts have generously construed the term 'relevant'" and have afforded the Commission access to virtually any material that might cast light on the allegations against the employer. In *United States v. Arthur Young & Co.*,[23] the Court explained that "an IRS summons is not to be judged by the relevance standards used in deciding whether to admit evidence in federal court."

The Sixth Circuit stated in *Doe v. United States*[24] that "the question of an administrative subpoena's relevance is not a question of evidentiary relevance, but rather is simply a question of whether the documents requested pursuant to the subpoena are relevant to the health care fraud investigation being undertaken." In *United States v. Harrington*,[25] the Second Circuit set forth a pithy measure for when the agency's demand to produce information meets the test of relevance: whether the subpoena gives "an indication of a realistic expectation rather than an idle hope that something may be discovered."

An agency does not have a license to obtain every document imaginable, similar to the Supreme Court's recognition in *United States v. R. Enterprises* that a grand jury subpoena cannot be used for an "arbitrary fishing expedition." (See § 16.12). In *E.E.O.C. v. Ford Motor Credit Co.*,[26] the Sixth Circuit stated that the "task is to weigh the likely relevance of the requested material to the investigation against the burden to Ford of producing the material." The circuit court found that the subpoena failed to meet the relevance requirement when it sought "the name, sex, date of hire, job title, starting grade level and salary, assignments or promotions with the company including job title, salary, and salary grade, address, telephone number, termination date, and discharge reason" for every employee of a single plant over a twelve-year period.

---

[21] 481 F.3d 119 (2d Cir. 2007).

[22] 466 U.S. 54 (1984).

[23] 465 U.S. 805 (1984).

[24] 253 F.3d 256 (6th Cir. 2001).

[25] 388 F.2d 520 (2d Cir. 1968).

[26] 26 F.3d 44 (6th Cir. 1994).

Courts have also applied greater scrutiny to administrative subpoenas for personal financial information when the connection to the investigation appears to be tenuous. This is more of a privacy concern than a restriction on the agency's authority to investigate, reflecting the balance the judiciary tries to strike when an administrative demand appears to be especially intrusive for an individual rather than a business. In *Resolution Trust Corporation v. Walde*,[27] the District of Columbia Circuit refused to enforce a subpoena issued to officers and directors of a failed bank to determine their financial situation so that the agency could decide whether they had sufficient net worth to sue them for the bank's demise. The circuit court pointed out that leading cases like *Morton Salt* and *Oklahoma Press Association* involved investigations of corporations, and more importantly "they dealt with the power to investigate suspicions of wrongdoing whereas in the cases now before us, the agency is attempting to subpoena information relevant to wealth rather than liability." It held that the statute authorizing the investigation did not address an investigation into an individual's net worth, and so "we think that the RTC must have at least an articulable suspicion that a former officer or director is liable to the failed institution before a subpoena for his personal financial information may issue." Personal financial information relevant to a director's potential liability for a violation, such as suspicious transactions with the bank's funds, would fall within the agency's grant of authority and could be obtained.

The Second Circuit took a similar approach in *In re McVane*[28] to a subpoena for personal financial records, noting that "[w]hile applying the relevance test, however, we have not lost sight of the fact that agency subpoenas directed at individuals do implicate privacy rights." The circuit court upheld the subpoena for records of former bank officers to determine their potential liability, but refused to enforce it for records of family members whose only connection to the case was that relationship. The circuit court stated, "A person does not involve him or herself in matters foreseeably the object of agency inquiry simply by being a member of another's family. Conjugal or familial association with a corporate participant does not, by itself, strip an individual of his or her expectation of privacy." The Second Circuit applied an "intermediate" level of scrutiny to subpoenas directed at private information of someone not directly involved in the potential violations, holding that "before it may subpoena the personal financial information of a potential target for the purpose of determining that individual's net worth, the FDIC must articulate specific grounds for its suspicion of liability."

The Ninth Circuit adopted the *McVane* standard in reviewing a subpoena for personal financial records of family members when the agency's affidavit identified documents that implicated individuals in the potential misconduct. That evidence "[w]hen combined with the highly specific allegations of malfeasance by the targeted Directors . . . [meant] the subpoenas satisfy the 'intermediate standard' of scrutiny set forth by *McVane*."[29] The Sixth Circuit took the same approach in *Doe v. United States*, noting that it was "more troubled by the government's request for personal financial documents of the children of the target of a health care fraud investigation."[30] The

---

[27] 18 F.3d 943 (D.C. Cir. 1994).

[28] 44 F.3d 1127 (2d Cir. 1995).

[29] F.D.I.C. v. Garner, 126 F.3d 1138 (9th Cir. 1997).

[30] 253 F.3d 256 (6th Cir. 2001).

circuit court enforced a subpoena that was "sufficiently narrowly-tailored to pass the reasonable relevance standard" when the financial records were those of minor children because "[j]ust as Doe could easily commingle assets between his personal and business financial accounts, so also could he transfer ill-gotten gains into the personal accounts of his unsuspecting minor children."

E. Agency Possession of Information

The requirement that an agency not already possess the information it is trying to obtain reflects a desire by courts to avoid burdensome demands by the government when they have ready access to the information sought. There is not, however, an absolute prohibition on an agency requiring production of information some of which may already be in its possession. In *United States v. Davis*,[31] the Fifth Circuit explained:

> When a summons as a whole is not harassing, when the bulk of the materials summoned is not demonstrably in the possession of the IRS, and where the marginal burden of supplying information which might already be in the possession of the IRS is small, as was the case here, enforcement of the summons in its entirety is not an "unnecessary examination or inspection."

The balancing approach looks at the scope and availability of the information already in the agency's possession and the breadth of the demand the court is being asked to enforce. As with other elements of the *Powell* test, the burden is on the subpoena recipient to establish that the information is already available. In *United States v. Texas Heart Institute*,[32] the Fifth Circuit noted that "a mere showing by the taxpayer that the IRS has previously examined the taxpayer's own records is not sufficient to show either that the IRS *possesses* that information or that it *possesses* information in the custody of parties other than the taxpayer."

Even if the government has copies of the records, there may be instances in which it can seek the originals to determine their authenticity, date of creation, and other issues that may be relevant to an investigation. In *Xelan, Inc. v. United States*,[33] the district court found that the "IRS is entitled, and it is a legitimate purpose to summon, original documents so as to check their consistency and completeness with those obtained elsewhere." But if the government has in its possession the records it needs to conduct its investigation, then that may be a basis to limit or preclude enforcement of a demand. In *United States v. Monumental Life Insurance Co.*,[34] the Sixth Circuit found that once the subpoena recipient rebuts the agency's case regarding the unavailability of the records, then it was up to the agency to show that even if it did possess them they remained inaccessible. Although the IRS claimed the documents "have been locked in a file somewhere," the circuit court held:

---

[31] 636 F.2d 1028 (5th Cir. 1981).

[32] 755 F.2d 469 (5th Cir. 1985).

[33] 397 F. Supp. 2d 1111 (S.D. Iowa 2005).

[34] 440 F.3d 729 (6th Cir. 2006).

The government should bear this burden because Monumental has successfully shown that the IRS does, in fact, possess some of the requested materials in a form it can use in this investigation. Because Monumental has successfully rebutted the government's prima facie showing as required by *Powell,* the IRS must prove that, on balance, the Neonatology documents cannot be practicably accessed.

F.   Administrative Steps Followed

Before the IRS can issue a summons, there are important steps the agency must follow, especially if the summons is issued to a third party for information about a taxpayer. This element of the *Powell* test focuses on whether those fairly detailed procedures have been properly adhered to in issuing the summons. For other agencies, the requirements for issuance of a subpoena or other demand for information are much less formal, often requiring only that the agency approve the use of compulsory process that authorizes the staff to issue a subpoena. It is the rare subpoena that does not comply with the minimal requirements for issuance imposed on an agency, so the question is often whether the court is willing to have its authority invoked in support of the demand for information.

Outside the context of IRS investigations, in looking at whether the agency has complied with the relevant statutory requirements and any internal procedures for issuance of a demand for information, courts will sometimes use this factor to examine whether there is an abuse of process that should prevent a court from ordering enforcement, even if the other elements of the analysis support requiring compliance. In *Doe v. United States,*[35] the Sixth Circuit noted that it was uncomfortable with a third subpoena being issued in a two-year period for records as part of a healthcare fraud investigation. Nevertheless, the circuit court concluded:

> While we are troubled by the fact that the government, after two years of investigation and two subpoenas, has now imposed yet another document request on Doe, Doe has proffered no evidence, nor is there any in the record, that would support a conclusion that the DOJ was motivated by an improper purpose when issuing this subpoena.

§ 17.5 THIRD–PARTY SUBPOENAS

Like a grand jury, an administrative agency will often seek information from third parties who are not the subject of an investigation but have information relevant to it. For example, an investigation involving potential financial wrongdoing may require an agency to review bank and brokerage records, while an antitrust review will often entail looking at transactions and market share of other members of an industry. As discussed in § 16.10(D), Congress has enacted statutes that limit the power of the government to obtain bank records and electronic communications without first notifying the person whose information is being sought and giving an opportunity to challenge the subpoena.

---

[35] 253 F.3d 256 (6th Cir. 2001).

There are procedures prescribed in civil tax investigations by the IRS when it seeks information or records from third parties. If a summons seeks records related to an unidentified taxpayer from a third party, such as an accountant or lawyer, then the taxpayer must receive notice and a copy of the summons, and can file a motion to quash it.[36] The IRS can also seek a court order *ex parte* to issue a "John Doe" summons under which it obtains information from a third party relating to unnamed taxpayers. The IRS must establish:

(1) the summons relates to the investigation of a particular person or ascertainable group or class of persons,

(2) there is a reasonable basis for believing that such person or group or class of persons may fail or may have failed to comply with any provision of any internal revenue law, and

(3) the information sought to be obtained from the examination of the records or testimony (and the identity of the person or persons with respect to whose liability the summons is issued) is not readily available from other sources.[37]

For non-tax investigations, the courts have not imposed notice requirements on agencies similar to what the IRS must comply with to subpoena a third party. In *SEC v. Jerry T. O'Brien, Inc.*,[38] the Supreme Court rejected the argument of the subject of a SEC investigation that it was entitled to prior notice of who the agency intended to subpoena so that it could challenge them. The Court found no basis for any constitutional right to notice, stating that "neither the Due Process Clause of the Fifth Amendment nor the Confrontation Clause of the Sixth Amendment is offended when a federal administrative agency, without notifying a person under investigation, uses its subpoena power to gather evidence adverse to him." There was no basis in the broad grant of investigatory authority from Congress to find any ground to infer a prior notice requirement, especially in light of the fact that in only one instance had Congress required prior notice—the Right to Financial Privacy Act (15 U.S.C. § 78u(h)). The Court concluded that "administration of the notice requirement advocated by respondents would be highly burdensome for both the Commission and the courts" and "would substantially increase the ability of persons who have something to hide to impede legitimate investigations by the Commission."

The Supreme Court has also concluded that when a person communicates information to a third party, even if there is an understanding that the communication is confidential, he cannot object under the Fourth Amendment if the third party conveys that information or records to the government in connection with an investigation. In *United States v. Miller*,[39] the Court held that a bank customer did not have a reasonable expectation of privacy in bank records to raise a Fourth Amendment challenge to their admission when they had been obtained by the Government from his bank pursuant to allegedly defective subpoenas about which he had not received prior

---

[36] 26 U.S.C. § 7609(a)–(b).

[37] 26 U.S.C. § 7609(f).

[38] 467 U.S. 735 (1984).

[39] 425 U.S. 435 (1976).

notice. The Court stated, "The depositor takes the risk, in revealing his affairs to another, that the information will be conveyed by that person to the Government."

Outside of a Fourth Amendment claim, the Court assumed in *Jerry T. O'Brien* that the subject of a subpoena could challenge the lack of notice, but the likelihood of success is quite low if there is no independent statutory notification procedure. This approach has important implications for newer methods of storing information digitally, such as "cloud" computing, which may mean that documents a person might have once been able to shield from an investigation by storing them at home or in a secure location could now be subject to a subpoena because they are accessible by third parties. The Supreme Court has indicated it will take a very cautious approach to the privacy implications of newer technologies for storing information, pointing out that "[t]he judiciary risks error by elaborating too fully on the Fourth Amendment implications of emerging technology before its role in society has become clear."[40]

§ 17.6 PARALLEL CRIMINAL AND CIVIL INVESTIGATIONS

A. Generally

In some cases the Department of Justice will pursue a grand jury investigation while an agency conducts its own independent inquiry. Because of the strict grand jury secrecy rules (see § 16.9), the prosecutors cannot share information subject to Federal Rule of Criminal Procedure 6(e) with their civil counterparts, except in very limited circumstances. There are no such restrictions on information-sharing from the civil to the criminal, however, and in some instances the investigations are coordinated. The administrative agency often has much greater expertise in a particular field, such as securities, banking, and environmental law, and so the prosecutors will defer to that investigation before assessing whether there is a potential criminal case.

B. Tax Investigations

An important exception to the general proposition that civil and criminal investigations can proceed together is when the IRS conducts a civil tax examination and determines there are "firm indications of fraud" pointing to the need for a criminal inquiry. In *United States v. LaSalle National Bank*, the Supreme Court held that in applying the *Powell* factors for a tax summons enforcement, a prerequisite is that "the summons must be issued before the Service recommends to the Department of Justice that a criminal prosecution, which reasonably would relate to the subject matter of the summons, be undertaken." After the Court's decision, Congress amended the law by adopting a bright line test under which "[n]o summons may be issued under this title . . . with respect to any person if a Justice Department referral is in effect with respect to such person."[41] A "referral" occurs when there is a recommendation by the IRS for "a grand jury investigation of, or the criminal prosecution of, such person for any offense connected with the administration or enforcement of the internal revenue laws," or a request for disclosure of tax return information in connection with a pending criminal investigation.

---

[40] City of Ontario, Cal. v. Quon, 130 S.Ct. 2619 (2010).
[41] 26 U.S.C. § 7602(d).

IRS regulations prohibit a revenue agent, who is responsible for civil enforcement of the tax laws, from undertaking an investigation to aid in a criminal prosecution. Pursuant to internal IRS procedures, an examination must be suspended "[o]nce there is a firm indication of criminal fraud." The reason for the strict separation between civil and criminal tax investigations is that the tax system relies on the voluntary cooperation of individuals, and so taxpayers are encouraged to provide information that they otherwise might be reluctant to disclose. If a civil examination were used as a façade for a criminal inquiry, then individuals would conclude they were being misled and might cease all cooperation in the collection of taxes.

The courts have found that the division of cases into civil and criminal categories means that if a taxpayer is misled as to the nature of the inquiry, there may be grounds to suppress any statements made or information disclosed even though there would not be a violation of the Fifth Amendment privilege against self-incrimination. Instead, courts view the protection afforded to taxpayers as an extension of their due process rights. In *United States v. McKee*,[42] the Sixth Circuit rejected a challenge to the use of a civil tax audit to gather information later used in a criminal prosecution, finding that it was "satisfied that the Manual's rule, requiring suspension of a civil investigation once the revenue agent has a 'firm indication of fraud,' is the type of rule that is designed to protect the taxpayer's constitutional rights."

Even though a case should have been referred for criminal investigation does not necessarily mean that a defendant's due process rights were violated, requiring suppression of statements made during a civil tax audit. In *United States v. Rutherford*,[43] the Sixth Circuit held that "[a]lthough the civil examiners may have been negligent in failing to refer the case to the IRS's Criminal Division, the district court found no evidence that they deliberately disregarded the manual in order to mislead the defendants." In *United States v. Peters*,[44] the Seventh Circuit explained that "courts must remember that the 'firm indications of fraud' rule is but a tool for courts to utilize in determining whether the revenue agents made an *affirmative misrepresentation* to a defendant or her representatives concerning the nature of their investigation." Similarly, in *United States v. Kontny*,[45] the same circuit court stated, "A failure to terminate a civil investigation when the revenue agent has obtained firm indications of fraud does not without more establish the inadmissibility of evidence obtained by him in continuing to pursue the investigation."

C. Other Administrative Investigations

The lower courts have not read *LaSalle National Bank* as applicable to other agencies, in part because tax investigations involve sensitive personal information that is often not at issue in other cases. In *SEC v. Dresser Industries*,[46] the District of Columbia Circuit rejected a company's argument that a civil securities fraud investigation should be stayed once the grand jury had begun gathering evidence

---

[42] 192 F.3d 535 (6th Cir. 1999).

[43] 555 F.3d 190 (6th Cir. 2009).

[44] 153 F.3d 445 (7th Cir.1998).

[45] 238 F.3d 815 (7th Cir. 2001).

[46] 628 F.2d 1368 (D.C. Cir. 1980).

regarding the same transactions. The circuit court distinguished tax investigations, for which there is more limited authority to issue a summons, from the broad grant of investigative authority afforded the SEC to pursue investigations of corporate fraud. The circuit court held, "The language of the securities laws and the nature of the SEC's civil enforcement responsibilities require that the SEC retain full powers of investigation and civil enforcement action, even after Justice has begun a criminal investigation into the same alleged violations." Although the investigations involved the same underlying conduct related to overseas bribery, the SEC retained a substantial interest in protecting investors that is beyond the concern of the criminal prosecutors. Thus, the District of Columbia Circuit found that "the securities laws offer no suggestion that the scope of the SEC's investigative authority shrinks when a grand jury begins to investigate the same matters."

§ 17.7 AGENCY BAD FAITH

One limitation on an administrative investigation is if it is undertaken in bad faith for the sole purpose of aiding the criminal inquiry but with no effort to advance the agency's mission. The bad faith standard is a difficult one to establish, as *Dresser Industries* explained: "Where the agency has a legitimate noncriminal purpose for the investigation, it acts in good faith under the *LaSalle* conception even if it might use the information gained in the investigation for criminal enforcement purposes as well." The power of a grand jury to investigate is quite broad, often exceeding what the agency can gather because of its more limited subject-matter jurisdiction, so it will be the rare case that the administrative investigation will be a stalking horse for prosecutors because they cannot obtain the same information. As one district court noted in rejecting a defendant's request to stop the SEC from seeking materials on behalf of prosecutors, "The investigative powers of the grand jury far exceed the scope of civil discovery, so that the United States Attorney's Office and the grand jury have no need to 'exploit' the SEC's discovery."[47]

Close cooperation between an agency and the Department of Justice does not mean there has been bad faith in the conduct of either investigation. In *United States v. Educational Development Corp.*,[48] the Third Circuit rejected the corporate defendant's argument that evidence obtained through the use of an Inspector General's administrative subpoena and search should be suppressed because it was done to aid a grand jury investigation. The circuit court stated:

> We do not minimize the concerns appellants express about the USAO's criminal division's conceded express avoidance of the grand jury by choosing instead to use the Inspector General's civil investigative powers in the investigation of crime, but they fail to direct us to any statutory, regulatory, or case law that prevents the USAO from doing so.

The Ninth Circuit in *United States v. Stringer*[49] overturned a lower court decision dismissing an indictment on the ground that the SEC misled corporate executives

---

[47] S.E.C. v. First Jersey Securities, Inc., 1987 WL 8655 (S.D.N.Y. 1987).

[48] 884 F.2d 737 (3d Cir. 1989).

[49] 535 F.3d 929 (9th Cir. 2008).

about the status of the Department of Justice's interest in the case. An SEC attorney had met with prosecutors before taking the testimony of the executives, and at the urging of the United States Attorney's Office for the District of Oregon the meeting took place in Portland so that office would have jurisdiction in case the witness committed perjury. The prosecutor requested that the SEC attorney not disclose the potential criminal interest in the case. Prior to the start of the testimony, defense counsel for an executive inquired whether there was a pending criminal investigation. The SEC attorney replied that the lawyer should contact the Department of Justice directly, and noted that a standard SEC document, Form 1662, furnished to all witnesses stated that the agency could share information with a number of other offices, including federal prosecutors.

The Ninth Circuit rejected the district court's conclusion that the SEC should have informed the executive's lawyer about the interest of prosecutors in the case, and that by not responding affirmatively to defense counsel's inquiry, the SEC attorney gave a misleading response. The circuit court stated, "The SEC Form 1662 used in this case alerts SEC investigative witnesses that the information can be used in a criminal proceeding. Defendants were on sufficient notice, and so were their attorneys." On the issue of whether the SEC acted in bad faith, the court found that "[i]t is significant to our analysis that the SEC began its civil investigation first and brought in the U.S. Attorney later. This tends to negate any likelihood that the government began the civil investigation in bad faith, as, for example, in order to obtain evidence for a criminal prosecution." While the SEC attorney was not fully forthcoming in response to defense counsel's question, that alone was insufficient to warrant dismissal of the charges because the "SEC engaged in no tricks to deceive defendants into believing that the investigation was exclusively civil in nature."[50]

The Fifth Circuit reached a similar conclusion in *United States v. Posada Carriles*[51] when it overturned a district court's finding that questioning during a naturalization interview was designed solely to gather evidence for a criminal prosecution. The defendant was warned that he could assert the Fifth Amendment privilege in response to questions, and "the 'mere failure' of a government official to warn that an investigation may result in criminal charges does not constitute fraud, deceit, or trickery." Like *Stringer*, the circuit court noted that "while the government may not make affirmative material misrepresentations about the nature of its inquiry, it is under no general obligation of disclosure."

In *SEC v. ESM Government Securities, Inc.*,[52] the Fifth Circuit refused to enforce a subpoena until a determination of whether an SEC investigator engaged in fraud,

---

[50] A district court dismissed a perjury charged based on the defendant's testimony in an SEC investigation because of improper coordination with the Department of Justice. It stated, "[T]he S.E.C. civil investigation became inescapably intertwined with the criminal investigation conducted by the Department of Justice and Mr. Seiden of the S.E.C. This commingling . . . negated the existence of parallel investigations. Because the Government manipulated the simultaneous investigations for its own purposes, including the transfer of Mr. Scrushy's deposition into this district for venue purposes, the court finds that the utilization of Mr. Scrushy's deposition in this case departs from the proper administration of justice." United States v. Scrushy, 366 F. Supp. 2d 1134, 1140 (N.D. Ala. 2005).

[51] 541 F.3d 344 (5th Cir. 2008).

[52] 645 F.2d 310 (5th Cir. 1981).

trickery, and deceit. The investigator pretended to seek the assistance of a brokerage firm's employees to explain how certain securities transactions worked in an effort to gather information that could be used to later compel the production of records from the firm. The circuit court stated:

> [It was] clearly improper for a government agent to gain access to records which would otherwise be unavailable to him by invoking the private individual's trust in his government, only to betray that trust. When that government agency then invokes the power of a court to gather the fruits of its deception, we hold that there is an abuse of process.

Unlike *Educational Development Corp., Stringer,* and *Posada Carilles*, all of which were criminal prosecutions, *ESM Government Securities* involved a subpoena enforcement action by the administrative agency responsible for the alleged misconduct. The *Powell* test puts the burden of establishing the propriety of the demand on the agency, and gives courts greater authority to police administrative agencies to ensure their conduct conforms to accepted norms of fairness and equity. Dismissing criminal charges often requires meeting a much higher standard of demonstrating actual prejudice to the defendant. Courts appear to be more reluctant to grant a remedy that would hamper a criminal prosecution, such as suppression of evidence or dismissal of charges, absent substantial evidence of misconduct, even while expressing concerns about the investigative tactics used.

Chapter 18

PARALLEL PROCEEDINGS AND ADMINISTRATIVE REMEDIES

§ 18.1 INTRODUCTION

Conduct can be the subject of concurrent or consecutive criminal and civil investigations and enforcement proceedings. Corporate conduct in particular often involves common law torts, issues of state law fiduciary duties and corporate governance, and violations of statutes or administrative codes that may lead to civil sanctions, damage actions, and shareholder derivative suits. This leads to the issue of "parallel proceedings" when multiple agencies are involved in a case and can pursue remedies. As discussed in § 17.4, administrative agencies have broad investigative authority to gather information about possible violations of the laws within their jurisdiction, similar to a grand jury's power to compel the production of evidence. Information developed in private litigation, especially *qui tam* claims filed under the False Claims Act and other whistleblower actions, can be used in subsequent enforcement actions.

There is a strong potential for an individual or company to face simultaneous or seriatim criminal, civil, and administrative proceedings because a number of regulatory statutes contain provisions allowing for criminal prosecution for a violation if a particular intent can be shown. This is especially true in securities cases, such as insider trading and violations of the Foreign Corrupt Practices Act, in which the Department of Justice and the Securities and Exchange Commission have a particularly close working relationship. A number of other civil regulators work with the Department of Justice to coordinate their investigations. Once they determine a violation has occurred, parallel criminal and civil cases can be pursued, often filed on the same day that target the same underlying conduct. As the Fifth Circuit noted in *SEC v. First Financial Group of Texas, Inc.*,[1] "The simultaneous prosecution of civil and criminal actions is generally unobjectionable because the federal government is entitled to vindicate the different interests promoted by different regulatory provisions even though it attempts to vindicate several interests simultaneously in different forums."

In addition to parallel proceedings at the federal level, there is a potential for state regulatory and licensure proceedings, particularly in areas such as insurance, banking, securities, and health care. Lawyers may be subject to state bar disciplinary actions for their conduct in representing a client in a transaction. Private claims can be brought by victims of alleged misconduct, most commonly in the securities field in which class actions by shareholders and purchasers (or sellers) can seek redress. Thus, a defendant, particularly a corporation, can face multiple proceedings in different

---

[1] 659 F.2d 660 (5th Cir. 1981).

jurisdictions, each seeking information and perhaps testimony that would be useful in a parallel criminal proceeding.

§ 18.2   OBTAINING INFORMATION

A.   Generally

An important initial issue is whether information can be shared by different agencies, and whether prosecutors can obtain information gathered in a civil case to use in a criminal investigation. As a general matter, information gathered as part of a grand jury investigation cannot be disclosed to civil regulators, but can be shared if it was obtained separately by an investigative agency, such as the FBI, or the prosecutor's office. Federal Rule of Criminal Procedure 6(e)(3) contains a broad prohibition on disclosure of any "matter occurring before a grand jury" except to the extent it will assist in the enforcement of federal criminal law. Moreover, because of the broad civil discovery rules, prosecutors are often reluctant to share information gathered by criminal investigators, even if it is not covered by the grand jury secrecy requirement, because it may be subject to disclosure in civil litigation. Although there are exceptions, it is frequently the case that information usually flows freely from the civil side to the criminal, but less often in the other direction, at least until the criminal proceeding has been concluded.

B.   Sharing Information Between Agencies

Federal agencies are empowered to share information with the Department of Justice regarding possible criminal violations of the statutes they are responsible for administering. For example, the SEC is authorized to "transmit such evidence as may be available concerning such acts or practices to the Attorney General who may, in his discretion, institute the necessary criminal proceedings. . . . "[2] The SEC also has a less formal mechanism for disclosing information to criminal investigators by providing access to its investigative files. In a form provided to all witnesses, the agency states that one of the routine uses of information it receives is to provide it to other agencies, including those involved in criminal enforcement, and also foreign regulators and prosecutors when appropriate. In *United States v. Fields*,[3] the Second Circuit described the reasons for allowing close cooperation between the SEC and federal prosecutors:

> [T]he procedure permitting preliminary communications with the United States Attorney has significant advantages. Allowing early participation in the case by the United States Attorney minimizes statute of limitations problems. The more time a United States Attorney has, the easier it is for him to become familiar with the complex facts of a securities fraud case, to prepare the case, and to present it to a grand jury before expiration of the applicable statute of limitations. Earlier initiation of criminal proceedings moreover is consistent with a defendant's right to a speedy trial. We decline, as the district court likewise declined, to interfere with this commendable example of inter-agency cooperation.

Thus, when a witness is called to testify as part of a civil investigation or required to furnish records, there is a good chance that some or all the information provided will be

---

[2] 15 U.S.C. § 77t(b); 15 U.S.C. § 78u(d).

[3] 592 F.2d 638 (2d Cir. 1978).

shared with the Department of Justice if there are indications that a criminal violation occurred.

In *United States v. Educational Development Network Corp.*,[4] the Third Circuit rejected a defense argument that prosecutors acted in bad faith by obtaining information through a civil subpoena issued by the Department of Defense Inspector General's office as part of a joint criminal/civil investigation of a contract. The government admitted that it chose to use a civil subpoena so that the information could be shared between the criminal and civil investigations rather than using a grand jury subpoena, which would limit use of the evidence obtained. The circuit court found no violation of Rule 6(e) because the information was not provided to the grand jury until after it was obtained through the civil subpoena. Regarding alleged misuse of a civil investigation to obtain information for a criminal prosecution, the court explained:

> We do not minimize the concerns appellants express about the USAO's criminal division's conceded express avoidance of the grand jury by choosing instead to use the Inspector General's civil investigative powers in the investigation of crime, but they fail to direct us to any statutory, regulatory, or case law that prevents the USAO from doing so.

C. Civil Protective Orders

Information obtained as part of civil litigation can be obtained by federal prosecutors in most instances by means of a grand jury subpoena, even if it is subject to a civil protective order. There is a split in the circuits on the appropriate standard to be applied when such an order is in place prohibiting a party from releasing evidence. The Second Circuit took the most protective approach in *Martindell v. International Telephone and Telegraph Corp.*,[5] holding that "absent a showing of improvidence in the grant of a Rule 26(c) protective order or some extraordinary or compelling need . . . a witness should be entitled to rely upon the enforceability of a protective order against any third parties."

The Fourth, Ninth, and Eleventh Circuits take the opposite approach, applying a per se rule that a grand jury subpoena overcomes a civil protective order and the records must be produced.[6] The Fourth and Ninth Circuit applied this rule to require the production of materials sent into the United States by a foreign company as part of civil litigation against its American subsidiary, documents that would not have been subject to a grand jury subpoena if they had remained outside the country.[7] The Ninth Circuit stated, "By a chance of litigation, the documents have been moved from outside the grasp of the grand jury to within its grasp. No authority forbids the government from closing its grip on what lies within the jurisdiction of the grand jury."

---

[4] 884 F.2d 737, 741 (3d Cir. 1989).

[5] 594 F.2d 291, 293 (2d Cir. 1979).

[6] See In re Grand Jury Subpoena, 836 F.2d 1468 (4th Cir. 1988); In re Grand Jury Subpoena Served on Meserve, Mumper & Hughes, 62 F.3d 1222 (9th Cir. 1995); In re Grand Jury Proceedings, 995 F.2d 1013 (11th Cir. 1993).

[7] See In re Grand Jury Subpoena, 646 F.3d 159 (4th Cir. 2011); In re Grand Jury Subpoenas, 627 F.3d 1143 (9th Cir. 2010).

The First and Third Circuits adopted a modified per se rule, providing that the grand jury subpoena is enforceable unless the recipient can demonstrate "exceptional circumstances."[8] No courts have found exceptional circumstances that would allow a court to refuse to enforce a grand jury subpoena, and this is a very difficult standard to meet to keep records subject to a civil protective order from being turned over to prosecutors.

One means by which a party in civil litigation can protect documents is to include the Department of Justice in a protective order, so that its terms apply to criminal prosecutors. In *SEC v. Merrill Scott & Associates, Ltd.*,[9] the Tenth Circuit enforced a protective order issued in a civil securities fraud enforcement action. The circuit court stated:

> The U.S. Attorney/DOJ was specifically named in the protective orders and it is clear that its receipt of documents from the SEC, which was unquestionably a party to the protective order and bound by its terms, was permitted only because the U.S. Attorney/DOJ was permitted to act "in concert with" the SEC in sharing information.

This approach is available in litigation involving a federal agency willing to include such a limitation in a protective order. Otherwise, a civil protective order would not bind a non-party who does not agree to its terms.

D. Department of Justice Policy

The Department of Justice issued a policy memorandum in January 2012 addressing parallel proceedings.[10] It notes that parallel proceedings are likely to arise "in many of the Department's white collar enforcement priorities, and it is essential that an effective and successful response involve an evaluation of criminal, civil, regulatory, and administrative remedies." Therefore, the Department of Justice takes the position that "it is important that criminal, civil, and agency attorneys coordinate in a timely fashion, discuss common issues that may impact each matter, and proceed in a manner that allows information to be shared to the fullest extent appropriate to the case and permissible by law."

The local United States Attorney's offices and sections in the criminal division are encouraged to adopt written policies on parallel proceedings to address the following issues:

> • *Intake*: "From the moment of case intake, attorneys should consider and communicate regarding potential civil, administrative, regulatory, and criminal remedies, and explore those remedies with the investigative agents and other government personnel."

---

[8] See In re Grand Jury Subpoena, 138 F.3d 442 (1st Cir. 1998); In re Grand Jury, 286 F.3d 153 (3d Cir. 2002).

[9] 600 F.3d 1262 (10th Cir. 2010).

[10] U.S.A.M. Title 1, Organization and Functions Manual No. 27 (Jan. 30, 2012), available at http://www.justice.gov/usao/eousa/foia_reading_room/usam/title1/doj00027.htm.

• *Investigation*: "In cases where civil, regulatory, or administrative remedies may be available, prosecutors should, at least as an initial matter, consider using investigative means other than grand jury subpoenas for documents or witness testimony."

• *Resolution*: "Effective and timely communication with representatives of the agency authorized to act on the agency's behalf, including suspension and debarment authorities, should occur so that agencies can pursue available remedies at an appropriate time."

§ 18.3　LIMITATIONS ON DISCLOSING GRAND JURY INFORMATION

A.　Generally

As noted at the outset of this Chapter, while an administrative agency can provide information to criminal investigators, there is usually not reciprocal sharing of information from the criminal investigation before a resolution of the matter. Once a criminal case is concluded, then prosecutors are more willing to disclose information obtained during the investigation. A significant limitation on sharing any information is the requirement of grand jury secrecy in Federal Rule of Criminal Procedure 6(e)(2)(b) (see also § 16.9). That provision provides that the government attorney, a grand juror, and anyone else authorized to be present in the grand jury room to assist in the testimony "must not disclose a matter occurring before the grand jury." Under Rule 6(e)(7), a knowing violation of the grand jury secrecy requirement "may be punished as a contempt of court." The prohibition on disclosing grand jury information applies even after the completion of a case. The Department of Justice's policy on parallel proceedings encourages prosecutors to segregate grand jury material to avoid any problems with sharing information with civil regulatory agencies for use in their investigations.

B.　Grand Jury Material

The secrecy requirement applies to any "matter occurring before the grand jury." This is a term of art that encompasses more than just what actually takes place in the grand jury room, although as the Sixth Circuit noted in *United States v. Rutherford*,[11] "Mere contact with a grand jury, however, does not change every document into a matter 'occurring before a grand jury' within the meaning of Rule 6." The disclosure that a grand jury investigation has been initiated is not necessarily a violation of the secrecy requirement "unless revelation of its existence would disclose the identities of the targets or subjects of the grand jury's investigation and by doing so either incite them to flee or, should they never be indicted, subject them to undeserved bad publicity."[12]

As discussed in § 16.7, a grand jury investigation involves gathering documents and physical evidence along with having witnesses testify under oath. Prosecutors play a central role in the process of determining what evidence to present to the grand

---

[11] 509 F.3d 791 (6th Cir. 2007).
[12] In re Cudahy, 294 F.3d 947 (7th Cir. 2002).

jurors, and when to seek a determination that there is probable cause to support an indictment. Courts have recognized that information related to the grand jury process also falls within the parameters of a grand jury matter subject to the secrecy requirement.

In *In re Motions of Dow Jones & Co.*,[13] the District of Columbia Circuit stated that the phrase "grand jury matter" includes not only "what has occurred and what is occurring, but also what is likely to occur" before a grand jury, including "the identities of witnesses or jurors, the substance of testimony as well as actual transcripts, the strategy or direction of the investigation, the deliberations or questions of jurors, and the like." In *In re Sealed Case No. 99–3091*,[14] the same court considered whether a prosecutor's revelation that the office was considering seeking an indictment in the near future constituted disclosure of a "matter occurring before the grand jury." The District of Columbia Circuit noted that it was "necessary to differentiate between statements by a prosecutor's office with respect to its own investigation, and statements by a prosecutor's office with respect to a *grand jury's* investigation, a distinction of the utmost significance. . . . " It held that "internal deliberations of prosecutors that do not directly reveal grand jury proceedings are not Rule 6(e) material." The Fifth Circuit reached a similar conclusion in *In re Grand Jury Investigation (Lance)*,[15] when it stated:

> A discussion of actions taken by government attorneys or officials, e. g., a recommendation by the Justice Department attorneys to department officials that an indictment be sought against an individual does not reveal any information about matters occurring before the grand jury. Nor does a statement of opinion as to an individual's potential criminal liability violate the dictates of Rule 6(e). This is so even though the opinion might be based on knowledge of the grand jury proceedings, provided, of course, the statement does not reveal the grand jury information on which it is based.

Once grand jury information becomes public, disclosure of material that would otherwise be subject to the secrecy requirement can be allowed. Rule 6(e)(6) provides that information related to a grand jury proceeding "must be kept under seal to the extent and as long as necessary to prevent the unauthorized disclosure of a matter occurring before the grand jury." In *In re Grand Jury Subpoena*,[16] the District of Columbia Circuit authorized the release of a portion of the transcript of grand jury testimony on the ground that the indictment returned in the case "reveals some grand jury matters, and we see little purpose in protecting the secrecy of grand jury proceedings that are no longer secret." The circuit court required that other grand jury information remain secret, however, because "[i]ts publication at this juncture could identify witnesses, reveal the substance of their testimony, and—worse still—damage the reputations of individuals who may never be charged with crimes."

Information gathered by investigators does not normally come within the scope of a "matter occurring before the grand jury," at least not until presented to that body.

---

[13] 142 F.3d 496 (D.C.Cir. 1998).

[14] 192 F.3d 995 (D.C. Cir. 1999).

[15] 610 F.2d 202 (5th Cir. 1980).

[16] 438 F.3d 1138 (D.C. Cir. 2006).

Thus, evidence obtained by means of a search warrant or voluntarily turned over may be shared with other agencies so long as the information was obtained independently of the grand jury's investigation. In *In re Grand Jury Subpoena*,[17] the Fourth Circuit rejected the argument that prosecutors improperly used a search warrant to avoid Rule 6(e)(3) in order to share information with a civil tax investigation. The circuit court found that "the initial IRS investigation and the grand jury investigation were not indiscriminately merged but that the initial IRS investigation was conceived and initiated without any connection to a grand jury proceeding," and therefore sharing documents obtained in the search did not violate the secrecy requirement. The Tenth Circuit reached a similar conclusion in *Anaya v. United States*[18] in finding that "[t]he IRS was in pursuit of a legitimate investigation, and revelation of information learned by other governmental agencies in a parallel investigation without disclosure of what had been submitted to the grand jury was not improper."

Documents provided pursuant to a grand jury subpoena will not necessarily be protected from disclosure in investigations conducted by civil agencies. In *In re Grand Jury Investigation*,[19] the Third Circuit stated that "[d]ocuments such as the business records sought by the Commission here are created for purposes independent of grand jury investigations, and such records have many legitimate uses unrelated to the substance of the grand jury proceedings." Similarly, the District of Columbia Circuit found in *Lopez v. Department of Justice*[20] that an interview of a potential grand jury witness was not necessarily subject to the secrecy requirement "[b]ecause a preliminary interview may serve the distinct interests of the prosecutor *qua* prosecutor or of the prosecutor *qua* 'grand jury facilitator,' the date of a preliminary interview does not on its face convey any information about 'some secret aspect of the grand jury's investigation.'"

Some lower courts look to the purpose for obtaining records in civil litigation that were previously provided to the grand jury investigation in deciding whether they constitute a "matter occurring before the grand jury." The foundational decision in this area is *United States v. Interstate Dress Carriers, Inc.*,[21] a 1960 Second Circuit decision, which stated:

> [W]hen testimony or data is sought for its own sake—for its intrinsic value in the furtherance of a lawful investigation—rather than to learn what took place before the grand jury, it is not a valid defense to disclosure that the same information was revealed to a grand jury or that the same documents had been, or were presently being, examined by a grand jury.

In *United States v. Dynavac, Inc.*,[22] the Ninth Circuit held that "if a document is sought for its own sake rather than to learn what took place before the grand jury, and if its disclosure will not compromise the integrity of the grand jury process, Rule 6(e) does not prohibit its release."

---

[17] 920 F.2d 235 (4th Cir. 1990).

[18] 815 F.2d 1373 (10th Cir. 1987).

[19] 630 F.2d 996 (3d Cir. 1980).

[20] 393 F.3d 1345 (D.C. Cir. 2005).

[21] 280 F.2d 52 (2d Cir. 1960).

[22] 6 F.3d 1407 (9th Cir. 1993).

The Sixth Circuit took a different approach in *In re Grand Jury Proceedings*,[23] holding that the party seeking disclosure of materials previously subpoenaed by the grand jury can rebut the presumption of secrecy "by showing that the information is public or was not obtained through coercive means or that disclosure would be otherwise available by civil discovery and would not reveal the nature, scope, or direction of the grand jury inquiry, but it must bear the burden of making that showing. . . . "

C. Disclosure to Other Government Attorneys

There are exceptions to the secrecy rule that permit prosecutors to disclose grand jury information. Most relate to disclosure to assist law enforcement at the federal level. Rule 6(e)(3)(A) permits disclosure, other than the grand jury's deliberations or vote, to "an attorney for the government for use in performing that attorney's duty," to government personnel (including state law enforcement officers) who will assist in prosecuting violations of the federal criminal law, to another grand jury, and for pursuing civil asset forfeiture. Disclosure in this context does not require prior judicial approval. The government attorney making the disclosure must provide the court that impaneled the grand jury with the names of those to whom disclosure of grand jury material was made and a certification that they have been advised of the secrecy obligation.

In *United States v. Sells Engineering, Inc.*,[24] the Supreme Court held that this provision "is limited to use by those attorneys who conduct the criminal matters to which the materials pertain." If the same attorney is involved in a grand jury investigation and then a subsequent civil proceeding, "[t]he Rule does not contain a prohibition against the continued use of information by attorneys who legitimately obtained access to the information through the grand jury investigation."[25] The Third Circuit explained the rationale for permitting disclosure to other government attorneys involved in federal criminal law enforcement: "Congress apparently determined that inter-district disclosures between AUSAs in support of their criminal law enforcement responsibilities, but without court supervision, could materially increase the efficiency of criminal law enforcement efforts without jeopardizing the interests that grand jury secrecy seeks to protect."[26]

Grand jury information involving foreign intelligence or counterintelligence can be disclosed under Rule 6(e)(3)(D) to "any federal law enforcement, intelligence, protective, immigration, national defense, or national security official. . . . "

D. Discretionary Disclosure

Rule 6(e)(3)(E) gives the court discretion, subject to limitations it deems appropriate, to disclose grand jury material in the following circumstances:

(1) when it is sought by a defendant to show a basis to dismiss an indictment;

---

[23] 851 F.2d 860 (6th Cir. 1988).

[24] 463 U.S. 418 (1983).

[25] United States v. John Doe, Inc. I, 481 U.S. 102 (1987).

[26] Impounded, 277 F.3d 407 (3d Cir. 2002).

(2) when the government requests its release to assist in an official foreign criminal investigation; and

(3) when the government requests the release of information showing a violation of state, Indian tribal, military or foreign law that is made to an appropriate official.

Rule 6(e)(3)(E) is not the only means by which a defendant can receive grand jury material. Under Federal Rule of Criminal Procedure 16(a)(1)(B)(iii), a defendant has the right to receive the "recorded testimony before a grand jury relating to the charged offense." Similarly, under the Jencks Act and Rule 26.2, a defendant has the right to receive a "witness's statement to a grand jury, however taken or recorded, or a transcription of such a statement" after the person testifies at trial, or at such earlier time as the trial court may require.[27]

The broadest ground for disclosing grand jury material is in Rule 6(e)(3)(E)(i), which allows a court to authorize disclosure of grand jury material "preliminary to or in connection with a judicial proceeding." This provision has been the basis for disclosing information to other government agencies at the federal and state level and in private litigation involving facts similar to those at issue in a criminal investigation or prosecution. This provision is the most heavily litigated basis for disclosing grand jury material.

If the civil proceeding has been filed, or is nearly ready to commence, then the courts have found that it comes within Rule 6(e)(3)(E)(i) and disclosure can be authorized. If the civil matter is an administrative proceeding and not one filed in court, then it may fall outside the scope of permissible disclosure of grand jury material.

In *United States v. Baggot*,[28] the Supreme Court held that disclosure to the I.R.S. for a civil audit was not permissible under Rule 6(e)(3)(E)(i) because it was not associated with any judicial proceeding. The Court explained that "the Rule contemplates only uses related fairly directly to some identifiable litigation, pending or anticipated. Thus, it is not enough to show that some litigation may emerge from the matter in which the material is to be used, or even that litigation is factually likely to emerge." The chance that the audit could result in litigation was not enough because the government takes any number of actions that might end up in court, but "[w]here an agency's action does not require resort to litigation to accomplish the agency's present goal, the action is not preliminary to a judicial proceeding." The Court explained that it was not deciding that the government or a private party must show that litigation was required or imminent to allow for disclosure of grand jury material. It stated:

> We also do not hold that the Government (or, for that matter, a private party who anticipates a suit or prosecution against him) may never obtain [Rule 6(e)(3)(E)(i)] disclosure of grand jury materials any time the initiative for litigating lies

---

[27] For a detailed discussion of discovery rights in federal criminal prosecutions, see CRIMPROC § 20.3.
[28] 463 U.S. 476 (1983).

elsewhere. Nor do we hold that such a party must always await the actual commencement of litigation before obtaining disclosure.

If there is a significant judicial role in the operation of the regulatory or administrative program, that can be sufficient to establish that the matter is "preliminary to or in connection with" litigation to permit a court to authorize disclosure. In *Doe v. Rosenberry*,[29] Judge Learned Hand described a "judicial proceeding" as "any proceeding determinable by a court, having for its object the compliance of any person, subject to judicial control, with standards imposed upon his conduct in the public interest." The judicial proceeding must be distinct from the request seeking disclosure of grand jury material.

The issue of whether an administrative proceeding comes within Rule 6(e)(3)(E)(i) has come up with some frequency in state bar disciplinary proceedings against lawyers, and a number of lower court decisions have found that disclosure is permissible.[30] But in *In re Grand Jury 89-4-72*,[31] the Sixth Circuit held that Michigan's attorney disciplinary process did not meet the requirement to allow disclosure of grand jury material "because the disciplinary proceedings are neither carried out before a judicial body, nor subject to sufficient judicial control." An administrative review under the Ethics in Government Act was found to qualify as a "judicial proceeding,"[32] along with impeachment hearings in Congress.[33]

E. Particularized Need

If a matter meets the "preliminary to or in connection with a judicial proceeding" requirement, the party seeking disclosure of the information must establish a particularized need to overcome the presumption in favor of maintaining the secrecy of grand jury material. In *United States v. Procter & Gamble Co.*,[34] the government filed a civil antitrust complaint after a grand jury investigation that concluded without charges being filed. When government attorneys used a transcript from a witness's grand jury testimony to prepare its case, the defendants sought access to it to assist in preparing their case. In deciding whether to allow disclosure of grand jury material, the Supreme Court stated that lifting the veil of secrecy that attaches to grand jury proceedings "must not be broken except where there is a compelling necessity. There are instances when that need will outweigh the countervailing policy. But they must be shown with particularity." According to the Court, the typical situation in which a party will show the requisite need for grand jury material is "to impeach a witness, to refresh his recollection, to test his credibility and the like." While the defendants in *Procter & Gamble* established the usefulness of the grand jury material, that alone was insufficient if they could not also show "that without the transcript a defense would be greatly prejudiced or that without reference to it an injustice would be done."

---

[29] 255 F.2d 118 (2d Cir. 1958).

[30] See In the Matter of Federal Grand Jury Proceedings (United States v. Doe), 760 F.2d 436 (2d Cir.1985); In re Barker, Wolf v. Oregon State Bar, 741 F.2d 250 (9th Cir.1984); In the Matter of Disclosure of Testimony Before the Grand Jury, 580 F.2d 281 (8th Cir.1978).

[31] 932 F.2d 481 (6th Cir. 1991).

[32] In re Sealed Motion, 880 F.2d 1367 (D.C. Cir. 1989).

[33] In re Request for Access to Grand Jury Materials Grand Jury No. 81–1, Miami, 833 F.2d 1438 (11th Cir. 1987).

[34] 356 U.S. 677 (1958).

In *Douglas Oil Co. v. Petrol Stops Northwest*,[35] the Supreme Court returned to the issue of particularized need in a private antitrust case in which the plaintiff sought an order directing the Department of Justice to release copies of grand jury transcripts of employees of the defendant corporations taken during a completed criminal investigation. In analyzing the standard for disclosure of grand jury material, the Court established the following principles for invoking Rule 6(e)(3)(E)(i):

> Parties seeking grand jury transcripts under Rule 6(e) must show that the material they seek is needed to avoid a possible injustice in another judicial proceeding, that the need for disclosure is greater than the need for continued secrecy, and that their request is structured to cover only material so needed.

The Court emphasized that even when a grand jury has concluded its investigation, there remain important institutional reasons to maintain the secrecy of its proceedings, so "the courts must consider not only the immediate effects upon a particular grand jury, but also the possible effect upon the functioning of future grand juries."

A significant concern in deciding whether to permit disclosure would be the impact on witnesses if there was a good chance testimony would be disclosed because "[f]ear of future retribution or social stigma may act as powerful deterrents to those who would come forward and aid the grand jury in the performance of its duties." In deciding whether to authorize release of the grand jury material, the Court stated, "[D]isclosure is appropriate only in those cases where the need for it outweighs the public interest in secrecy, and that the burden of demonstrating this balance rests upon the private party seeking disclosure." In balancing the competing interests, *Douglas Oil* explained that as the need for secrecy diminished, then so too did the burden of showing the requisite justification for disclosure. The Court also emphasized that "a court called upon to determine whether grand jury transcripts should be released necessarily is infused with substantial discretion," which makes it difficult to successfully challenge a district court's ruling on a disclosure motion under Rule 6(e)(3)(E)(i).

An important consideration in the balance is the scope of the request, and the knowledge of the judges involved in the civil and criminal cases. *Douglas Oil* pointed out that assessing the needs of a party for access to information and the concern for preserving grand jury secrecy may require "a coordinating of the informed views of both the civil trial court and the grand jury court concerning the propriety of disclosing portions of the grand jury minutes." The broader the information sought, the more likely a district court will reject it because the need must be particularized. The Supreme Court noted that "disclosure can be limited strictly to those portions of a particular witness' testimony that bear upon some aspect of his direct testimony at trial."

When the government seeks authorization to disclose grand jury material to a regulatory agency or civil attorneys in the Department of Justice, the public interest can be taken into consideration in balancing the need for the information. The Supreme Court applied a lower threshold to establish the "particularized need" in

---

[35] 441 U.S. 211 (1979).

United States v. John Doe, Inc. I.[36] The Court stated, "[T]he concerns that underlie the policy of grand jury secrecy are implicated to a much lesser extent when the disclosure merely involves Government attorneys." The Court also recognized an efficiency rationale for permitting disclosure of grand jury material:

> [B]ecause the contemplated use of the material was to make a decision on whether to proceed with a civil action, the disclosure here could have had the effect of saving the Government, the potential defendants, and witnesses the pains of costly and time-consuming depositions and interrogatories which might have later turned out to be wasted if the Government decided not to file a civil action after all.

Similarly, in *Illinois v. Abbott & Associates, Inc.*,[37] the Supreme Court noted "the district court may weigh the public interest, if any, served by disclosure to a governmental body—along with the requisite particularized need—in determining whether" the interest in secrecy was overcome. And in *Sells Engineering*, the Court gave an example that "a district court might reasonably consider that disclosure to Justice Department attorneys poses less risk of further leakage or improper use than would disclosure to private parties or the general public." But disclosure to civil attorneys in the Department of Justice is not automatic, and a district court "in weighing the need for disclosure . . . could take into account any alternative discovery tools available by statute or regulation to the agency seeking disclosure" in deciding whether to authorize disclosure of grand jury material.

§ 18.4   FIFTH AMENDMENT PRIVILEGE ISSUES

A significant concern when there are parallel criminal and civil investigations or proceedings is that an individual may be called upon to testify in the civil case before the conclusion of the criminal matter. If the person testifies, then the statements can be used by prosecutors in a subsequent criminal case. On the other hand, if the person asserts the Fifth Amendment privilege against self-incrimination in the civil case, then a court in a civil case, an administrative agency, a licensing body, or a self-regulatory organization may draw a negative inference based on the refusal to provide information.

Once a witness chooses to testify, the person waives the Fifth Amendment regarding the responses so the statements can be provided by the agency to the Department of Justice even though the person might not have testified had the likelihood of a criminal investigation or prosecution been clear. In *Brown v. Walker*,[38] the Supreme Court explained the impact of the decision to testify: "[I]f the witness himself elects to waive his privilege, as he may doubtless do, since the privilege is for his protection and not for that of other parties, and discloses his criminal connections, he is not permitted to stop, but must go on and make a full disclosure."

In *Baxter v. Palmigiano*,[39] the Supreme Court took a position "consistent with the prevailing rule at that time," and held that in prison disciplinary proceedings an

---

[36] 481 U.S. 102 (1987).

[37] 460 U.S. 557 (1983).

[38] 161 U.S. 591 (1896).

[39] 425 U.S. 308 (1976).

adverse inference may be drawn from the invocation of the Fifth Amendment. The Court explained, "the Fifth Amendment does not forbid adverse inferences against parties to civil actions when they refuse to testify in response to probative evidence offered against them."

Courts recognize that invoking the Fifth Amendment by itself is insufficient to establish grounds for a civil or administrative sanction, and there must be independent evidence to support drawing the adverse inference. The government cannot make it a condition of continued employment or receiving a government contract that a person respond to questioning or risk losing a job by invoking the Fifth Amendment.

In *Lefkowitz v. Cunningham*[40] the Court explained that "silence in *Baxter* was only one of a number of factors to be considered by the finder of fact in assessing a penalty, and was given no more probative value than the facts of the case warranted. . . . " In *Spevack v. Klein*,[41] the Court found that the Fifth Amendment applied to a lawyer's records, so he could assert the privilege against self-incrimination and his disbarment for not turning over the records could not stand on the ground that he had no privilege. An assertion of the Fifth Amendment privilege in a civil or administrative proceeding can be considered by an agency in reaching its decision, although there is no requirement that an adverse inference be drawn. In *Pyles v. Johnson*,[42] the Fifth Circuit noted "the fact that the Fifth Amendment does not *prohibit* such inferences does not imply that the fact-finder is *required* to make them."

In *SEC v. Jasper*,[43] a civil fraud enforcement action, the Ninth Circuit upheld a district court's decision to admit a defendant's videotaped deposition in which he asserted the Fifth Amendment over 150 times, holding that the repeated invocations of the privilege was not unfairly prejudicial. The circuit court also rejected the argument that the court had to give a separate instruction for each invocation of the Fifth Amendment regarding the propriety of drawing an adverse inference, holding that the trial court properly treated them in a general fashion that permitted the jury to consider the entire deposition in deciding how to treat the defendant's responses.

If an individual refuses to cooperate in an investigation by a state licensing board or a federal regulatory agency, the person's livelihood may be threatened because the refusal may be an indication that the person does not meet the requirements to continue to participate in the profession. For example, a professional who practices before the SEC may be barred from future appearances before the Commission for asserting the Fifth Amendment because that can be used with other facts developed in the investigation to institute an administrative proceeding against the person to show he or she is unfit to practice.[44] Similarly, those who are subject to regulation by the Financial Industry Regulatory Authority (Finra) must provide information or testimony in an investigation, and failure to do so can result in a bar from being associated with a brokerage or investment advisory firm.[45] So the decision to assert the

---

[40] 431 U.S. 801 (1977).

[41] 385 U.S. 511 (1967).

[42] 136 F.3d 986 (5th Cir. 1998).

[43] 678 F.3d 1116 (9th Cir. 2012).

[44] 17 C.F.R. § 201.102(e).

[45] D.L. Cromwell Investments, Inc. v. NASD Regulation, 279 F.3d 155 (2d Cir. 2002).

privilege against self-incrimination in a civil or administrative proceeding is fraught with danger, and carries serious consequences for the witness either way.

An adverse inference may not be permissible if the person subsequently responds to questions or requests for information after initially asserting the Fifth Amendment. In *In re Enron Corp. Securities, Derivative & Erisa Litigation,*[46] the district court stated that it may exclude evidence of invocation of the Fifth Amendment privilege, even though it generally allows adverse inferences against parties in civil actions when they refuse to testify in response to probative evidence, e.g., when that party subsequently testifies or cooperates with an investigation.

A person's decision to respond to an inquiry in a civil or administrative investigation for fear that any failure could be used as evidence does not constitute a Fifth Amendment violation that requires prohibiting subsequent use of the statements. In *State v. Horton,*[47] the Maine Supreme Court reversed an order suppressing a lawyer's statements made in a bar disciplinary proceeding investigating the same conduct for which he was charged. The court held:

> [T]he fact that a lawyer's decision to invoke the privilege and remain silent can be used as evidence in the disciplinary proceeding does not render the lawyer's decision to speak involuntary. Disciplinary proceedings are civil in nature, and a lawyer has no constitutional right to prevent the factfinder in that proceeding from considering the implications of his silence, along with other evidence against him, in making a determination.

Similarly, in *United States v. McKinney,*[48] the district court found that a physician appearing at a hearing about whether to revoke his license was not compelled to testify because "potential silence was only one of a number of factors to be considered by the ALJ when making her determination, and his potential silence would have been given no more probative value than the facts of his case warranted."

In civil litigation, other potential remedies available if a party asserts the Fifth Amendment and refuses to provide information during discovery include limiting the type of evidence that party can introduce, entering factual findings on the issues in which discovery was not provided, dismissing claims or defenses, or entering a judgment in favor of the opposing party. As a general matter, a court will not allow a party to assert the privilege and seek to keep that information from the factfinder if it is relevant to the issues. A party asserting the privilege against self-incrimination can seek to limit or exclude reference to that act by arguing that disclosure would be so prejudicial that it outweighs the probative value of the evidence. One factor to be considered in the decision to exclude evidence of an invocation of the privilege is whether the party later responded to questions by waiving the Fifth Amendment privilege, and the timing of that disclosure.[49] New Hampshire goes a step further by prohibiting any adverse inference being drawn from the exercise of any privilege.[50]

---

[46] 762 F. Supp. 2d 942 (S.D. Tex. 2010).

[47] 561 A.2d 488 (Me. 1989).

[48] 695 F. Supp. 2d 182 (E.D. Pa. 2010).

[49] Harris v. City of Chicago, 266 F.3d 750 (7th Cir. 2001).

[50] N.H. R. Evid. 512(a)(1). This rule was based on proposed Federal Rule of Evidence 513(a).

When a non-party reveals that he or she will assert the Fifth Amendment privilege and refuse to testify, courts may preclude a party from calling the witness to do so in front of the jury and bar reference to the witness's conduct unless that person is an agent of the party, or so closely allied with one that the assertion can reasonably be attributed to that party. In *LiButti v. United States*,[51] the Second Circuit identified the following factors for determining whether to permit a jury to draw an adverse inference against a party from a third-party witness's assertion of the privilege against self-incrimination: (1) the nature of the relevant relationships; (2) the degree of control of the party over the non-party witness; (3) the compatibility of the interests of the party and non-party witness in the outcome of the case; and, (4) the role of the non-party witness in the litigation. The witness in *LiButti* disclaimed ownership of property placed in his daughter's name to avoid having a levy placed on it for his failure to pay taxes. In finding that an adverse inference could be drawn when the father refused to testify about who controlled the property, the circuit court explained that "the overarching concern is fundamentally whether the adverse inference is trustworthy under all of the circumstances and will advance the search for the truth."

In *In re High Fructose Corn Syrup Antitrust Litigation*,[52] the Seventh Circuit explained that the assertion of the Fifth Amendment by former corporate officers convicted of price fixing could be used against the company in civil litigation for the same conduct. The circuit court pointed out that the refusal to testify concerned a conspiracy with the company, which "would justify and explain their taking the Fifth and it would also entitle a jury to treat their refusal to answer as evidence that there indeed was such a conspiracy." Similarly, the Eighth Circuit held in *Cerro Gordo Charity v. Fireman's Fund*[53] that "it was permissible to allow the invocation of the privilege to be made known to the jury when it is invoked by a non-party who was a former employee of a company a party to the litigation." In *FDIC v. Fidelity & Deposit Co. of Maryland*,[54] the Fifth Circuit found that a district court properly allowed an adverse inference to be drawn from the invocation of the Fifth Amendment by borrowers who received improper loans from a bank. The circuit court stated, "[T]he fact that the witness no longer serves the party in an 'official capacity' does not present a bar to requiring the witness to assert the privilege in front of the jury."

§ 18.5   STAYING PARALLEL PROCEEDINGS

A.   Generally

A person involved in concurrent criminal, civil, and regulatory cases can seek to limit the potential for having to choose between providing testimony and documents or asserting the Fifth Amendment privilege by having the non-criminal proceedings stayed until the criminal case is complete. That allows the person to address the proceeding with the greatest potential consequence—the loss of liberty—while not suffering the impact of an adverse decision in other cases, such as a civil monetary penalty or loss of a professional license.

---

[51] 107 F.3d 110 (2d Cir. 1997).
[52] 295 F.3d 651 (7th Cir. 2002).
[53] 819 F.2d 1471 (8th Cir. 1987).
[54] 45 F.3d 969 (5th Cir. 1995).

It is not just individual defendants who might have an interest in staying civil cases until the criminal prosecution is concluded. There may be a benefit to the government from postponing parallel civil proceedings when a criminal case is pending. The District of Columbia Circuit noted in *Afro–Lecon, Inc. v. United States*[55] that "[t]he broad scope of civil discovery may present to both the prosecution, and at times the criminal defendant, an irresistible temptation to use that discovery to one's advantage in the criminal case." Under Federal Rule of Criminal Procedure 16, discovery in criminal prosecutions is limited so that the parties cannot depose prospective witnesses, except in very limited circumstances. If an agency has filed a parallel case, such as an SEC injunctive action based on the same underlying transactions, the defendant and the prosecutor could use the more liberal civil discovery rules to obtain information and statements that might not be available in the criminal prosecution. Thus, the prosecutor may seek to intervene in a civil case and request a stay, often in conjunction with the regulatory agency, to prevent discovery of information that might not be available under the criminal rules.

B. No Right to a Stay

The Supreme Court held in *United States v. Kordel*[56] that it did not violate an individual defendant's due process rights to allow parallel civil and criminal cases even though permitting both to proceed can put an individual defendant in a difficult position regarding whether to respond to information requests. In *Kordel*, the Department of Justice filed a civil suit against a company to seize and condemn two food products after the Food and Drug Administration conducted an investigation. In connection with that suit, the United States Attorney's Office served on the corporation extensive interrogatories prepared by the FDA. Shortly thereafter, the FDA notified the corporation and its president and vice president (Kordel and Feldten) that it was considering recommending a criminal prosecution and that they had the opportunity to present their views in opposition. The corporation sought to stay further proceedings in the civil action, or in the alternative to extend the time it had to answer the interrogatories until after the disposition of any potential criminal charges. The motion was denied, however, and the corporation was ordered to answer the interrogatories, which was done through Feldten. The civil case was subsequently settled, and Feldten and Kordel were then prosecuted and convicted at a trial in which the government used Feldten's answers to the interrogatories to "provid[e] evidence or leads useful to the Government."

Finding no constitutional violation from the government's use of the civil discovery as evidence in the criminal prosecution, the Court stated:

> Feldten need not have answered the interrogatories. Without question he could have invoked his Fifth Amendment privilege against compulsory self-incrimination. Surely Feldten was not barred from asserting his privilege simply because the corporation had no privilege of its own, or because the proceeding in which the Government sought information was civil rather than criminal in character. To be sure, service of the interrogatories obliged the corporation to "appoint an agent who could, without fear of self-incrimination, furnish such

---

[55] 820 F.2d 1198 (Fed. Cir. 1987).

[56] 397 U.S. 1 (1970).

requested information as was available to the corporation." The corporation could not satisfy its obligation under Rule 33 simply by pointing to an agent about to invoke his constitutional privilege.

The Court noted that requiring the government to choose between civil or criminal actions would be harmful to the need to protect the public: "It would stultify enforcement of federal law to require a governmental agency such as the FDA invariably to choose either to forgo recommendation of a criminal prosecution once it seeks civil relief, or to defer civil proceedings pending the ultimate outcome of a criminal trial."

C. Discretion to Grant a Stay

Trial courts have discretion whether to grant a stay of a civil case or to permit the criminal case to move forward first. The burden is on the party seeking the stay to demonstrate the need to delay the civil case. A court must balance the competing concerns of the private or governmental plaintiff in the civil case with the potential harm to the defendant, particularly the Fifth Amendment privilege, from allowing both cases to move forward at once. The First Circuit pointed out in *Microfinancial, Inc. v. Premier Holidays International, Inc.*[57] that "[t]he touchstone, of course, is that a district court's discretionary power to stay civil proceedings in deference to parallel criminal proceedings should be invoked when the interests of justice counsel in favor of such a course."

Delaying the civil case until the criminal proceeding is complete may allow the defendant to participate fully in the civil discovery if the threat of a criminal case is dissipated. In addition, a court will consider any prejudice that would be caused to both parties and non-parties if the civil suit were delayed.

Along with potential Fifth Amendment issues if the civil case is allowed to proceed, courts consider the following factors outlined by the Ninth Circuit in *Keating v. Office of Thrift Supervision*:[58]

> (1) the interest of the plaintiffs in proceeding expeditiously with this litigation or any particular aspect of it, and the potential prejudice to plaintiffs of a delay; (2) the burden which any particular aspect of the proceedings may impose on defendants; (3) the convenience of the court in the management of its cases, and the efficient use of judicial resources; (4) the interests of persons not parties to the civil litigation; and (5) the interest of the public in the pending civil and criminal litigation.

In *Louis Vuitton Malletier S.A. v. LY USA, Inc.*,[59] the Second Circuit held that a district court's decision granting or denying a stay will not be overturned on appeal "absent demonstrated prejudice so great that, as a matter of law, it vitiates a defendant's constitutional rights or otherwise gravely and unnecessarily prejudices the defendant's ability to defend his or her rights." The circuit court noted that the

---

[57] 385 F.3d 72 (1st Cir. 2004).

[58] 45 F.3d 322 (9th Cir. 1995); see Judge Milton Pollack, Parallel Civil–Criminal Proceedings, 129 F.R.D. 201 (1989).

[59] 676 F.3d 83 (2d Cir. 2012).

different factors "can do no more than act as a rough guide for the district court as it exercises its discretion. They are not mechanical devices for churning out correct results in overlapping civil and federal proceedings . . . ."

The procedural posture of the criminal case is often an important consideration in balancing whether to grant a stay of the civil case. If criminal charges have been filed, then there may be a greater need to postpone the civil case. As the District of Columbia Circuit pointed out in *SEC v. Dresser Industries, Inc.*:[60]

> Other than where there is specific evidence of agency bad faith or malicious governmental tactics, the strongest case for deferring civil proceedings until after completion of criminal proceedings is where a party under indictment for a serious offense is required to defend a civil or administrative action involving the same matter. The noncriminal proceeding, if not deferred, might undermine the party's Fifth Amendment privilege against self-incrimination, expand rights of criminal discovery beyond the limits of Federal Rule of Criminal Procedure 16(b), expose the basis of the defense to the prosecution in advance of criminal trial, or otherwise prejudice the case.20 If delay of the noncriminal proceeding would not seriously injure the public interest, a court may be justified in deferring it.

The fact that the plaintiff in a civil case asks for the stay so that it need not produce evidence does not preclude a court from granting one. In *Afro–Lecon Inc. v. United States*,[61] a company was involved in a contract dispute with the government when it learned of a grand jury investigation. Its officers and former employees asserted their Fifth Amendment privilege by refusing to provide information for an accounting ordered in the civil case. The District of Columbia Circuit rejected the government's argument that a plaintiff cannot seek a stay because it initiated the case, stating that it "decline[d] to accept the wooden plaintiff-defendant distinction." The circuit court held that granting a stay at the company's request would not "raise the problem of placing the defendant in the position of maintaining a defense without necessary discovery."

If there is an ongoing criminal investigation but charges have not been filed, then courts may be less willing to postpone the civil case based only on the prospect that criminal charges could arise. In *C.F.T.C. v. A.S. Templeton Group, Inc.*,[62] a district court refused to stay a civil enforcement action because the "[d]efendants' countervailing interest in avoiding the use of their Fifth Amendment privilege is minimal at this time because any parallel criminal proceeding is purely speculative." On the other hand, in *Ashworth v. Albers Medical, Inc.*,[63] the district court granted a stay when the Department of Justice disclosed that charges were likely to be filed in the near future.

Another consideration that can play a role in the analysis is whether the prosecutor sought to stay in the civil case. Judges are generally unwilling to allow a civil case to interfere with a criminal case, and a statement by the prosecutor that a

---

[60] 628 F.2d 1368, 1375 (D.C. Cir. 1980).

[61] 820 F.2d 1198 (Fed. Cir. 1987).

[62] 297 F. Supp. 2d 531 (E.D.N.Y. 2003).

[63] 229 F.R.D. 527 (S.D.W. Va. 2005).

stay in the civil case will allow the criminal case to move forward unimpeded can carry great weight. In *SEC v. Nicholas*,[64] a district court granted a stay requested by the prosecutors even though the Department of Justice and the SEC coordinated the filing of their cases and chose to proceed with each. The court found that "[t]he criminal case is also of greater relative importance to the named Defendants . . . Staying the civil case, which carries only civil sanctions and monetary penalties, is not of an equally pressing nature." But courts will not automatically accede to a prosecutor's request for a stay. In *SEC v. Saad*,[65] the district court denied a stay at the government's request, pointing out the oddity that discovery was broader in a civil case than a criminal prosecution, and "it is stranger still that the U.S. Attorney's Office, having closely coordinated with the SEC in bringing simultaneous civil and criminal actions against some hapless defendant, should then wish to be relieved of the consequences that will flow if the two actions proceed simultaneously."

If a party to the civil case is not named in the parallel criminal prosecution, then the court will consider whether that party will be prejudiced by the grant of a stay. In *SEC v. Doody*,[66] in which a father and son were sued for civil securities fraud violations but only the son was charged in the criminal case, the district court noted that it "would have to be unimaginably naïve to suppose that Doody Sr. is not a stalking horse for Doody himself" in determining whether to grant the government's request for a stay. Rather than completely stopping the civil suit, the court limited the stay to precluding discovery of information and witnesses related to the son's criminal case. This approach highlights the district court's power to fashion the terms of a stay according to the needs of each party.

§ 18.6   CRIMINAL–CIVIL COORDINATION

When faced with a demand for testimony in a civil investigation or adjudicatory proceeding, a key issue is determining whether the Department of Justice is also reviewing the conduct for a possible criminal prosecution. Statements made in the civil case can be used against the declarant in the criminal investigation, so a witness must decide whether to provide information or assert the Fifth Amendment privilege against self-incrimination. Apart from the Internal Revenue Service (see § 17.6), regulators can freely share information with prosecutors conducting a grand jury investigation. There is a possibility that a criminal investigation will await completion of a civil inquiry because the agencies have greater expertise to determine whether there was a violation and its seriousness. Once that determination is made, then prosecutors can review the evidence to decide whether to move forward with a criminal investigation that may lead to charges.

It can be difficult to determine whether there is interest in a civil case on the part of criminal investigators. The staff at a civil agency is unlikely to confirm the existence of a criminal investigation, and usually respond to inquiries from a witness or counsel by directing them to contact the Department of Justice directly, which as a matter of policy refuses to confirm the existence of an investigation. The issue of whether the

---

[64] 569 F. Supp. 2d 1065 (C.D. Cal. 2008).

[65] 229 F.R.D. 90 (S.D.N.Y. 2005).

[66] 186 F. Supp. 2d 379 (S.D.N.Y. 2002).

agency has actively deceived a witness is important in determining whether information provided in a civil investigation can be used in a subsequent criminal case.

In *United States v. Stringer*,[67] the Ninth Circuit concluded that the district court should not have dismissed criminal securities fraud charges because the SEC did not act improperly in responding to an inquiry by a witness's lawyer about whether there was an impending criminal investigation. The SEC staff and prosecutors from the United States Attorney's Office in Portland, Oregon, met about a pending civil investigation of accounting violations, and decided that the SEC would complete its investigation first without disclosing the potential for a criminal inquiry. The prosecutors asked that the witness testimony be taken in Oregon so that perjury charges could be brought there if anyone lied. They also discussed different lines of inquiry the SEC should pursue in the testimony. During the civil investigation, the SEC staff provided a form to all witnesses stating that any information gathered in the case could be provided to the Department of Justice. When asked by a witness's lawyer whether there was a criminal investigation, the SEC attorney said it was the agency's policy not to respond to such questions and directed the attorney to contact the Department of Justice.

The district court found that response to be deceptive, but the Ninth Circuit concluded that "[t]he record does not show the SEC did anything to impede an inquiry, nor does it disclose that any inquiry was made. The record reflects that the government never furnished defendants with any false information concerning the existence of a criminal investigation." Dismissal of charges or suppression of evidence would be appropriate "to the extent that the individual defendants may have been led through trickery or deceit to turn over documentary or physical evidence in their possession or to use their official authority to turn over evidence in the possession of the corporation, the defendants could state a claim under the Fourth Amendment." But the SEC's conduct did not rise to that level, and the circuit court noted that the form provided to the witnesses alerted them "that the information can be used in a criminal proceeding. Defendants were on sufficient notice, and so were their attorneys."

In *United States v. Scrushy*,[68] the district court precluded prosecutors from pursuing a perjury charge based on statements the defendant made while testifying in a SEC investigation. The district judge found that the government violated the requirements of the proper administration of justice when it manipulated the simultaneous civil and criminal investigations, including the transfer of the defendant's deposition in order to create venue for the perjury prosecution that would be added to other charges the prosecutors were already planning to file. At that point, the "civil investigation became inescapably intertwined with the criminal investigation" so that failure to inform the defendant was done in bad faith. Although there was no evidence that the government engaged in an "outright lie to" the defendant, the district court stated that it "cannot take such a limited view of bad faith" in determining whether the government acted properly. Unlike *Stringer*, in *Scrushy* there was clear evidence that the defendant was misled, or at least manipulated, into testifying in aid of the criminal investigation when the Department of Justice was already planning to file charges.

---

[67] 535 F.3d 929 (9th Cir. 2008).

[68] 366 F. Supp. 2d 1134 (N.D. Ala. 2005).

In *United States v. Setser*,[69] the Fifth Circuit rejected a defendant's claim that he was misled about parallel investigations, finding that he "was not lured into any cooperation by the false premise that the investigation was purely civil." The circuit court acknowledged that "[d]eception as to the purposes of the investigation, or using otherwise meaningless civil proceedings as a pretext for acquiring evidence for a criminal prosecution, taking advantage of a person who does not have counsel, or other special circumstances may invalidate the prosecution." The Fifth Circuit stated in *United States v. Posada Carriles*[70] that "while the government may not make affirmative material misrepresentations about the nature of its inquiry, it is under no general obligation of disclosure."

§ 18.7 COLLATERAL CONSEQUENCES

A. Generally

A criminal conviction can result in civil and administrative penalties beyond the punishment given at sentencing. The penalties are usually imposed after an administrative hearing or ordered by a federal court at the conclusion of a civil case. The imposition of civil penalties is triggered by a finding of a violation, and evidence from the criminal case can often be used to establish a civil infraction. In many cases, a defendant in a criminal prosecution will settle an administrative action by agreeing to a civil penalty, which may be imposed in conjunction with a plea agreement to resolve the criminal case, sometimes described as a "global settlement." The range of sanctions that can be imposed by an administrative agency are established by its governing statute. These usually include monetary penalties, suspension or revocation of a license or participation in government programs, forfeiture of goods or compensation, and a prohibition on future involvement in government contracts.

Administrative agencies have also begun using deferred and non-prosecution agreements similar to those employed by the Department of Justice to resolve cases (see § 2.4). In its Enforcement Manual,[71] the SEC authorizes the use of a deferred prosecution agreement that foregoes pursuing civil charges if an individual or company agrees to the following conditions:

> 1) cooperate truthfully and fully in the Commission's investigation and related enforcement actions; 2) enter into a long-term tolling agreement; 3) comply with express prohibitions and/or undertakings during a period of deferred prosecution; and 4) under certain circumstances, agree either to admit or not to contest underlying facts that the Commission could assert to establish a violation of the federal securities laws.

B. Constitutional Issues

Civil penalties can trigger constitutional challenges under the Double Jeopardy Clause of the Fifth Amendment and the Excessive Fines Clause of the Eighth

---

[69] 568 F.3d 482 (5th Cir. 2009).

[70] 541 F.3d 344 (5th Cir. 2008).

[71] Securities & Exchange Commission, Enforcement Manual § 6.2 (2012), available at http://www.sec.gov/divisions/enforce/enforcementmanual.pdf.

Amendment. In *United States v. Halper*,[72] the Supreme Court held that a fixed civil penalty imposed after a criminal conviction based on the same underlying conduct violated the prohibition on double jeopardy as an impermissible second punishment because the civil penalty was considered punitive, not remedial. The Court overruled that broader application of the Fifth Amendment to civil penalties in *Hudson v. United States*.[73] It held, "*Halper's* deviation from longstanding double jeopardy principles was ill-considered." After *Hudson*, the test for "[w]hether a particular punishment is criminal or civil is, at least initially, a matter of statutory construction. A court must first ask whether the legislature, in establishing the penalizing mechanism, indicated either expressly or impliedly a preference for one label or the other." Under this approach, most penalties imposed by regulatory agencies will be considered civil and therefore not limited by the Double Jeopardy Clause.

The proscription on excessive fines applies when a monetary penalty constitutes a punishment. In *Austin v. United States*,[74] the Supreme Court explained, "The Excessive Fines Clause limits the government's power to extract payments, whether in cash or in kind, as *punishment* for some offense." The Court found that an in rem civil forfeiture proceeding was designed to be punishment and not just remedial, and therefore subject to the Eighth Amendment. The issue is not whether the "civil" or "criminal" label applies to the proceeding, but whether the punitive nature of the penalty warrants application of the Excessive Fines Clause.

In *United States v. Bajakajian*,[75] the Court held the forfeiture of over $350,000 in cash because the owner had not declared it when attempting to leave the country was a fine in violation of the Eighth Amendment. The Court then found the amount was "grossly disproportionate" to the violation, and therefore excessive. While the Eighth Amendment imposes an outer limit on the size of a monetary penalty, the Court noted that "[t]he text and history of the Excessive Fines Clause demonstrate the centrality of proportionality to the excessiveness inquiry; nonetheless, they provide little guidance as to how disproportional a punitive forfeiture must be to the gravity of an offense in order to be "excessive." The test is whether the fine is grossly disproportionate to the gravity of the violation, which the Court noted was "inherently imprecise" for distinguishing permissible from excessive penalties. Thus, to establish an Eighth Amendment violation for a civil penalty, a defendant would have to show it constituted a criminal punishment due to its severity, and then that it was "grossly disproportionate" to the impact of the violation.

C. Suspension and Debarment

Suspension and debarment are administrative actions that limit or prohibit an individual or organization from doing business with federal agencies and programs. A suspension is a temporary exclusion imposed upon a suspected wrongdoer pending the outcome of an investigation and any ensuing judicial or administrative proceedings. Debarment is a sanction that prohibits an individual or organization from doing

---

[72] 490 U.S. 435 (1989).

[73] 522 U.S. 93 (1997).

[74] 509 U.S. 602 (1993).

[75] 524 U.S. 321 (1998).

business with the government for a specified period, usually up to three years.[76] These sanctions are imposed to protect the government by ensuring that it only contracts with "presently responsible" parties. Suspension and debarment can be imposed for engaging in wrongful conduct, which includes a criminal conviction, or for violating the rules imposed by a contract or for participation in a program. A person or business subject to suspension or debarment cannot be awarded a contract, nor can they conduct business with the government as an agent or representative of another contractor.[77]

A suspension can only be imposed "on the basis of adequate evidence, pending the completion of investigation or legal proceedings."[78] An interim suspension is usually imposed pending a final determination of whether the respondent should be debarred, and cannot last longer than eighteen months without consent.[79] A criminal indictment can be sufficient grounds to issue a suspension pending the outcome of the case.

The primary grounds for debarment are a conviction or civil judgment for fraud in connection with a government contract, antitrust violations, or "[c]ommission of any other offense indicating a lack of business integrity or business honesty that seriously and directly affects the present responsibility of a Government contractor or subcontractor."[80] Other types of violations that can lead to suspension and debarment include willful failure to perform a contract, drug violations by the contractor, a failure to comply with the Immigration and Nationality Act's employment provisions, and unfair trade practices under the Defense Production Act. There is also a catch-all provision authorizing suspension and debarment "based on any other cause of so serious or compelling a nature that it affects the present responsibility of the contractor or subcontractor."[81]

Debarment is not designed as a punishment, instead being imposed to safeguard the integrity of government contracting and programs. The central issue in determining whether to debar a contractor or program participant is the "present responsibility" of the individual or organization. If there are sufficient grounds for debarment, then the burden is on the person or organization to establish present responsibility to avoid the sanction. Debarment or suspension of an organization usually covers all of its divisions or "other organizational elements" of the company unless an order is explicitly limited to a particular facet of the organization.[82] The issue of a possible suspension or debarment is usually subject to negotiation before a criminal case or civil charges are resolved as part of a global settlement.

In assessing present responsibility, the agency considers past conduct, although a prior violation does not necessarily establish grounds for debarment. As explained by the district court in *Burke v. Environmental Protection Agency*:[83]

---

[76] 48 C.F.R. § 9.406.
[77] 48 C.F.R. § 9.405(a).
[78] 48 C.F.R. § 9.407–1(a).
[79] 48 C.F.R. § 9.407–4(b).
[80] 48 C.F.R. § 9.404–2(a).
[81] 48 C.F.R. § 9.406–2(b)–(c).
[82] 48 C.F.R. § 9.406–1(b).
[83] 127 F. Supp. 2d 235 (D.D.C. 2001).

Debarment is a discretionary measure taken to protect the public interest and to promote an agency's policy of conducting business only with responsible persons. Debarment cannot be used to punish an individual; rather, it serves a remedial purpose of protecting the federal government from the business risk of dealing with an individual who lacks "business integrity or business honesty." The initiation of a debarment proceeding requires the existence of past misconduct; however, the final decision to debar an individual must focus on that individual's present business responsibility. In addition, the debarring official must determine whether any mitigating factors show that the business risk to the government has been eliminated to the extent that debarment would be unnecessary.

Federal regulations provide that the "existence of a cause for debarment, however, does not necessarily require that the contractor be debarred; the seriousness of the contractor's acts or omissions and any remedial measures or mitigating factors should be considered in making any debarment decision."[84] They list ten factors the agency should consider in deciding whether to issue an order of debarment, including whether a contractor disclosed the violation in a timely manner, cooperated with the government, paid all fines and penalties, disciplined employees responsible for the violation, and "recognizes and understands the seriousness of the misconduct giving rise to the cause for debarment and has implemented programs to prevent recurrence."

D. SEC Administrative Remedies

The SEC is authorized to seek permanent or temporary injunctions in federal court "whenever it shall appear to the Commission that any person is engaged or about to be engaged in acts or practices constituting a violation of any provision" of the securities laws or the rules of one of the self-regulatory agencies.[85] A defendant found in violation of an injunction can be prosecuted for civil or criminal contempt, which may result in the imposition of monetary penalty or imprisonment.[86]

In addition to monetary penalties, the SEC usually seeks an order of disgorgement for any gain from the violation. This form of relief had been based on the court's traditional equity power to deprive a defendant of ill-gotten gains.[87] To strengthen the SEC's power in insider trading cases, the Insider Trading Sanctions Act granted the SEC the power to seek up to a triple monetary penalty for a violation in addition to disgorgement of profits.[88] Congress added to the the Commission's remedial power in the Securities Enforcement Remedies and Penny Stock Reform Act of 1990, which authorized the Commission to seek civil monetary penalties or disgorgement, bar or suspend a person from serving as an officer or director of a publicly-traded company, issue cease-and-desist orders, or require audits, accounting for frauds, or special supervisory arrangements. The law also allowed the SEC to require disgorgement in

---

[84] 48 C.F.R. § 9.406–1(a).

[85] 15 U.S.C. § 78u(d) (Securities Exchange Act of 1934). Similar provisions granting authority can be found in 15 U.S.C. § 77t(b) (Securities Act of 1933);15 U.S.C. § 80a–41(d) (Investment Company Act); 15 U.S.C. § 80b–9(d) (Investment Advisers Act).

[86] 18 U.S.C. § 401.

[87] 15 U.S.C. § 78u(d)(5).

[88] 15 U.S.C. § 78u(d)(3)(B).

administrative proceedings in cases against securities firms in which it had the authority to impose monetary penalties.[89]

The Dodd–Frank Act,[90] adopted in 2010, further expanded the SEC's remedial authority by allowing the agency to seek the same penalties in an administrative proceeding as it could in an injunctive action filed in federal district court. Prior to the statute's enactment, the SEC's authority to impose a monetary penalty in any administrative proceeding was limited to only "regulated persons," such as a broker-dealer or investment adviser, along with individuals associated with the firm.

Administrative proceedings are viewed as providing the SEC with certain advantages in comparison with federal court enforcement actions. One is the absence of formal discovery provided by the Federal Rules of Civil Procedure, such as the right to depose witnesses and obtain documentary evidence, with the evidence limited to what was gathered during the SEC's administrative investigation. In addition, the administrative proceeding does not allow for the right to trial by jury, with the case being heard by an administrative law judge on an expedited schedule. Review of a decision by the administrative judge is heard by the full Commission first, and only after that can a respondent seek judicial review in the court of appeals. At that stage, the appeals court defers to the factual findings of the administrative law judge under the abuse of discretion standard.

The SEC also has the authority to pursue administrative sanctions against professionals, such as attorneys and accountants, who appear and practice before it. The remedy available for a violation is denial of the privilege of appearing or practicing before the agency. It can bar future appearances for a specified period of time or permanently if it determines after a hearing that the professional (1) did not possess the requisite qualifications to represent others; (2) was lacking in character or integrity, or had engaged in unethical or improper professional conduct; or (3) had willfully violated, or willfully aided and abetted a violation of, a provision of the federal securities laws.[91] In *Altman v. SEC*,[92] the District of Columbia Circuit upheld the permanent bar of an attorney who represented a client in an investigation and offered to have her refuse to cooperate or remember transactions. The circuit court stated, "By its plain terms [the rule] authorizes the Commission to deny the privilege of appearance upon finding improper professional conduct." This conclusion can be based on the SEC's determination that the conduct violated a state professional responsibility rule even if there is not a separate bar disciplinary proceeding.

E. Other Agency Sanctions

Other federal agencies are empowered to impose substantial sanctions on individuals and companies. For example, the Federal Energy Regulatory Commission can impose a civil penalty of up to $1,000,000 per day for violations of the Energy Policy Act of 1992.[93] The Federal Deposit Insurance Corporation has the authority to

---

[89] Pub.L. No. 101–429, 104 Stat. 951 (1990).

[90] Pub.L. No. 111–203, 124 Stat. 1376 (2010).

[91] 17 C.F.R. § 200.102(e).

[92] 666 F.3d 1322 (D.C. Cir. 2011).

[93] 15 U.S.C. § 717t–1(a).

suspend or remove a director or officer of a bank if that person "engaged or participated in any unsafe or unsound practice" or breached a fiduciary duty that meant the bank "has suffered or will probably suffer financial loss or other damage" and the executive or director's conduct involves dishonesty or shows a "willful or continuing disregard" of the bank's safety and soundness.[94]

In the healthcare area, mandatory exclusion from the federal Medicare and Medicaid programs is triggered by a conviction for a "program-related crime," patient abuse, felony conviction relating to healthcare fraud, or a felony conviction related to controlled substances.[95] The mandatory exclusion can last from five years for a single violation to ten years for convictions of two offenses, and permanent exclusion for convictions of three offenses. Permissive exclusion from the federal healthcare programs may be imposed for excessive charges or unnecessary services, failure to disclose required information, kickbacks, and fraud.[96]

F.   Recovery in *Qui Tam* and Whistleblower Cases

In addition to enforcement and remedial proceedings filed by governmental agencies, individuals can take action when they are aware of violations. A civil lawsuit can be brought in federal court under the False Claims Act against companies and other organizations when they have filed false claims with the federal government.[97] Congress enacted the first False Claims Act in 1863, when it was called "Lincoln's Law" to combat fraud in the sale of goods during the Civil War.[98]

A claim filed by a private party on behalf of the federal government is called a *qui tam* action, short for the Latin phrase *qui tam pro domino rege quam pro se ipso in hac parte sequitur*, which means "who pursues this action on our Lord the King's behalf as well as his own."[99] To establish a violation, the plaintiff must show that the defendant (1) presented a false fictitious or fraudulent claim to a federal agency or department, and (2) the defendant knew the claim was false at the time of submission.

To initiate a private *qui tam* action, an individual, known as a "relator," acts as a private attorney general and brings the suit "in the name of the government" with the hope of sharing in any recovery. The plaintiff files the case under seal, and informs the government about the action. The government then has 60 days to decide whether to intervene and litigate the case on its own, although it frequently seeks an extension. The relator's recovery depends on whether the government intervenes and the level of contribution provided by the relator to the prosecution of the claim. When the government intervenes, a relator is awarded 15% to 25% of the recovery from the case.[100] When the government does not intervene, the relator receives 25% to 30% of any settlement or fine.[101] Along with a potentially substantial award, some of which have been in the tens of millions of dollars, the False Claims Act also provides

---

[94] 12 USC § 1818(e)(1).

[95] 42 U.S.C. § 1320a–7(a).

[96] 42 U.S.C. § 1320a–7(b).

[97] 31 U.S.C. § 3730(b)(1).

[98] Act of March 2, 1863, 12 Stat 696 (1863).

[99] Vermont Agency of Natural Resources v. United States ex rel Stevens, 529 U.S. 765 (2000).

[100] 31 U.S.C. § 3730(d)(1).

[101] 31 U.S.C. § 3730(d)(2).

protection to an employee who was "discharged, demoted, suspended, threatened, harassed, or in any other manner discriminated against" as a result of reporting a false claim.[102]

In the Dodd–Frank Act, Congress extended the concept of whistleblowing to violations of the federal securities laws by requiring the SEC to adopt rules awarding between 10 percent and 30 percent of any disgorgement or penalty over $1 million.[103] Under Rule 21F–3(a), a whistleblower will receive an award if the person "(1) Voluntarily provide[s] the Commission (2) With original information (3) That leads to the successful enforcement by the Commission of a federal court or administrative action (4) In which the Commission obtains monetary sanctions totaling more than $1,000,000." A number of companies complained that the whistleblower program encourages employees to bypass internal compliance systems for reporting misconduct. The final rule, however, did not require internal reporting to receive a whistleblower award, although the SEC in its discretion can consider any such reporting in determining the amount of an award above the 10 percent floor.

G. Collateral Estoppel

If an agency successfully proves a person or company violated federal law in a district court action or an administrative proceeding, that determination may have collateral estoppel consequences in private actions arising from the same facts or transactions. This is often seen in shareholder lawsuits and securities class actions in which there was a determination of a violation in an SEC case could be used against a company and its officers or directors in parallel private litigation. A defendant found to be in violation of the law cannot re-litigate that issue if there was a full trial on the claim. Similarly, a defendant convicted in a criminal trial is precluded from disputing, in a subsequent civil action, the violation established in the criminal proceeding, including a conviction by guilty plea.

In *Parklane Hosiery Co., Inc. v. Shore*,[104] minority shareholders filed a lawsuit against a company and its officers and directors. Before trial, the SEC instituted an injunctive action alleging violations of the proxy rules, which was the same claim filed by the minority shareholders. The district court found a violation of section 14(a) of the Securities Exchange Act based on the issuance of a misleading proxy statement. The shareholders in the private action argued that under principles of collateral estoppel they were entitled to summary judgment on their claims based on the findings in the SEC action. The Supreme Court considered whether the offensive use of collateral estoppel was proper when the party seeking to use it had not been involved in the prior litigation. The Court held that a trial judge should not permit offensive collateral estoppel if a plaintiff could have joined the prior suit without difficulty, or if the offensive use of collateral estoppel would be unfair to the defendant. In this case, however, the Court found:

> The application of offensive collateral estoppel will not here reward a private plaintiff who could have joined in the previous action, since the respondent

---

[102] 31 U.S.C. § 3730(h).

[103] 15 U.S.C. § 78u–6.

[104] 439 U.S. 322 (1979).

probably could not have joined in the injunctive action brought by the SEC even had he so desired. Similarly, there is no unfairness to the petitioners in applying offensive collateral estoppel in this case. First, in light of the serious allegations made in the SEC's complaint against the petitioners, as well as the foreseeability of subsequent private suits that typically follow a successful Government judgment, the petitioners had every incentive to litigate the SEC lawsuit fully and vigorously. Second, the judgment in the SEC action was not inconsistent with any previous decision. Finally, there will in the respondent's action be no procedural opportunities available to the petitioners that were unavailable in the first action of a kind that might be likely to cause a different result.

Parklane Hosiery was particularly important for private plaintiffs because the Court eliminated the mutuality requirement that limited the use of offensive collateral estoppel to cases in which the parties were the same as in the prior proceeding. At least in the limited circumstances outlined by the Court, nonmutual offensive collateral estoppel was permissible. But the doctrine cannot be used against the government, as the Court held in *United States v. Mendoza*[105] when it stated, "*Parklane Hosiery's* approval of nonmutual offensive collateral estoppel is not to be extended to the United States." An acquittal in a criminal case does not affect a parallel civil case because of the different burdens of proof in the two actions.

The settlement of a civil suit or administrative proceeding generally does not have the same effect as a conviction or a finding of a violation after an adjudicatory proceeding because in most instances the agreement is reached under which the private party settles "without admitting or denying the alleged misconduct." Thus, there is no finding of a violation, even if a company or individual pays a civil penalty and agrees to other remedial measures, so private parties cannot use the settlement for collateral estoppel purposes.

The SEC has a policy that while a settling party need not admit to a violation, neither can it deny the findings contained in an administrative order or federal court judgment. The policy statement provides:

> [I]n any civil lawsuit brought by it or in any administrative proceeding of an accusatory nature pending before it, it is important to avoid creating, or permitting to be created, an impression that a decree is being entered or a sanction imposed, when the conduct alleged did not, in fact, occur. Accordingly, it hereby announces its policy not to permit a defendant or respondent to consent to a judgment or order that imposes a sanction while denying the allegations in the complaint or order for proceedings. In this regard, the Commission believes that a refusal to admit the allegations is equivalent to a denial, unless the defendant or respondent states that he neither admits nor denies the allegations.[106]

While a defendant in civil litigation will sometimes assert that it did not violate the law but only settled a case to save the costs of litigation, which is not permissible when settling with the SEC.

---

[105] 464 U.S. 154 (1984)

[106] 17 C.F.R. § 202.5(e).

Chapter 19

THE SELF–INCRIMINATION PRIVILEGE AND TESTIMONY

§ 19.1 BASIC PRIVILEGE DEFINITIONS

A. Generally

The law governing the self-incrimination privilege consists in large part of judicial responses to a series of basic questions about the meaning of the terms used in the Fifth Amendment. The doctrinal standards developed in the course of those responses are discussed at length in this chapter and chapter 20, as they relate to persons testifying and producing documents pursuant to a subpoena.[1] What follows is a brief overview of the basic terms and related aspects of the privilege.

B. Being a Witness in a Criminal Case

The self-incrimination privilege protects only a person compelled to be a "witness against himself in a criminal case." One possible reading of this phrase would restrict the privilege to the "accused" in a criminal prosecution since the accused is the person against whom a witness testifies in a criminal case.[2] Under this view, the self-incrimination clause would simply prohibit the government from compelling the accused to give incriminating testimony as a witness in a judicial proceeding that is a part of his own prosecution. It was not until 1892, in *Counselman v. Hitchcock,*[3] that the Court flatly rejected this restricted reading of the privilege. *Counselman* held that the privilege protected a person called to testify before a grand jury, even though that person was not an accused. Unlike the Sixth Amendment, which refers to "the accused" in a "criminal prosecution," the Fifth Amendment refers to the rights of "a person" with respect to a "criminal case" (a broader term than "criminal prosecution"). The grand jury, the Court noted, was part of a criminal case, so compelling the witness to incriminate himself there clearly was contrary to the Amendment. The *Counselman*

---

[1] The description of these standards is drawn largely from §§ 2.10, 8.10–8.13 of Wayne R. LaFave, Jerold H. Israel, Nancy J. King, and Orin S. Kerr, Criminal Procedure Treatise (3d ed.2007 and updated annually), available on Westlaw under the database CRIMPROC. Citations supporting this chapter's general descriptions of lower court and Supreme Court rulings can be found there. See also ABA Section of Antitrust Law, the Right Against Self–Incrimination in Civil Litigation (2001).

[2] The self-incrimination privilege was established in English common law at a time when defendants were not allowed to testify at trial, so it obviously was not aimed at protecting the defendant from being forced to testify at trial. However, the English common law also utilized a pretrial committal procedure (the "Marian pretrial examination") at which the magistrate examined the accused. The self-incrimination privilege was viewed as prohibiting a magistrate from forcing the accused to testify under oath. The initial development of the privilege extended to an even earlier stage. The privilege originated in opposition to the inquisitorial procedures of the Fourteenth century ecclesiastical courts and the Privy Council's Court of Star Chamber. Both brought persons before the tribunal without any prior accusation or charges and forced them to take an oath—the oath *ex officio*—to answer questions which essentially forced self-accusation. This subsequently abolished procedure resulted in the initial formulation of the privilege as a prohibition against self-accusation (the *nemo tenetur* maxim).

[3] 142 U.S. 547 (1892).

opinion also offered a separate rationale, however, that extended beyond grand jury proceedings.

Counselman reasoned that a person compelled to give testimony in any judicial proceeding was protected by the privilege, even if that proceeding was not itself part of a "criminal case." The compulsion of testimony and the use of that testimony in a criminal case need not occur simultaneously. The privilege, *Counselman* noted, protects against compelling the testimony of a person in any proceeding where that testimony is later used by the government in a criminal case brought against that person (thereby making him a "witness against himself"). Based on *Counselman*, the Court later held that the privilege protects witnesses in a variety of settings not part of the criminal case (e.g., civil cases and administrative hearings), provided that the testimony that would be compelled from the witness might realistically be used against the witness in a subsequent criminal prosecution.[4]

C. The Protected "Person"

As discussed in § 20.4, the Supreme Court has held that, in the context of the self-incrimination clause, the Fifth Amendment's reference to the rights of a "person" encompasses only natural persons. The privilege is not available to artificial "persons," though they can claim various other constitutional rights. Thus, it does not protect all types of corporations (including a sole-shareholder corporation) and various unincorporated organizations that exist as collective entities (e.g., unions, political associations, and almost all partnerships). This limitation is commonly described as the "entity exception" to the application of the privilege.

Of course, an entity, unlike an individual, cannot give testimony from the witness stand, but the self-incrimination clause also applies to compelling other forms of testimonial evidence. Entities as well as individuals are subjected to compulsion to produce such evidence in various settings. The most significant is the subpoena requiring the production of documents, and it is in eliminating the self-incrimination objection to the production of documents belonging to entities that the entity exception has its greatest practical impact. Grand jury and administrative investigations both commonly use such subpoenas.

The entity exception also bears upon the dynamics of parallel civil proceedings. As discussed in §§ 18.4–18.5, individuals facing such civil suits have to weigh the pros and cons of relying upon the privilege to refuse to respond to civil discovery procedures, and consider the possibility of avoiding that dilemma by obtaining a stay of the civil action. Disclosures commanded in civil litigation often are based on procedures that apply to entity litigants as well as individual litigants. In particular, responses may be required from the entity itself (as opposed to its individual officers) by interrogatories and

---

[4] *Counselman* quoted with approval several state court rulings that held the privilege applicable in civil proceedings. Consequently, subsequent Supreme Court opinions treated the application of privilege in noncriminal proceedings (including both civil cases and administrative proceedings) as settled, and sometimes did and sometimes did not explain why the privilege applied even though the proceeding was not itself part of a "criminal case." Also, cases summarizing the general features of the privilege almost invariably noted its availability to a witness in "any proceeding." See, e.g., United States v. Balsys, 524 U.S. 666 (1998) (privilege "can be asserted in any proceeding, civil or criminal, administrative or judicial, investigatory or adjudicatory" in which "the witness reasonably believes that the information sought, or discoverable as a result of his testimony could be used in a subsequent state or federal criminal proceeding").

requests for admissions. Since the entity cannot rely on the privilege, it has no choice (absent a stay) but to make the disclosure even if it is incriminating (and might subsequently be used in a criminal case). While a stay remains a possibility, the entity, unlike the individual, cannot advance in favor of a stay the need to preclude adverse consequences attaching to the exercise of the privilege in the civil suit.

D. Compulsion

The privilege applies only to a person "compelled" to produce testimonial evidence. When the government seeks to obtain information from an individual, that person can properly assert the privilege only if there is an element of compulsion in the government's efforts. So too, a defendant who asserts the privilege to prevent the prosecution from using against him a prior statement must be able to show that the statement was a product of governmental compulsion. A statement not compelled is deemed "voluntary" for Fifth Amendment purposes, and the self-incrimination clause does not prohibit the government's subsequent use of a person's voluntary statement to make him, in effect, a witness against himself in a criminal case.

The paradigm for compulsion is the subpoena ad testificandum. That subpoena produces what the Court has described as the "core" unfairness which led to the adoption of the privilege—"subject[ing] those suspected of crime to the cruel trilemma of self-accusation, perjury or contempt." The person under subpoena who is asked a question that would require an incriminating response, if lacking the privilege, would face precisely that trilemma: (1) testifying truthfully, and in effect, acknowledging facts that could give rise to criminal liability (i.e., "self-accusation"); (2) lying under oath and therefore committing the crime of perjury; or (3) refusing to answer and being held in contempt for disobeying a court order. This is true whether the subpoena is issued on behalf of the government or on behalf of a civil litigant. The compulsion must be a product of state action, but the subpoena is issued under judicial authority, and that is sufficient to constitute "state action."

Compulsion can also exist by force of law without creating this "cruel trilemma." It can be present, for example, where the law imposes regulatory sanctions on a person who fails to provide to the government information that may be incriminating. Illustrative is a law requiring a government employee to choose between disclosing incriminatory information in response to a government inquiry and being discharged for failing to respond to that inquiry. In the leading ruling on such compulsion, *Garrity v. New Jersey*,[5] where police officers had been warned that they would be removed from office if they did not waive their privilege and testify in an official inquiry, the Court drew an analogy to police coercion of a confession. Although the compelled statement may not be given under oath (thereby eliminating the potential for a perjury prosecution), the individual is still forced to choose between self-accusation and the government's imposition of a substantial sanction. The self-incrimination clause thereby applies, and the statement cannot be used against the individual in a criminal prosecution.[6] Similar compulsion exists where the government requires submission of a

---

[5] 385 U.S. 493 (1967).

[6] Since the privilege requires "state action" in the compulsion as well as the use of the statement, a private employer's threat to discharge an employee unless he discloses incriminatory information, even as to disclosure to the government, would not violate the *Garrity* principle. However, if the government is heavily involved in the employer's decision to threaten that employee, the employer can be viewed as the agent of the

form containing incriminating information, with the consequence of failure to file being criminal liability.[7]

Government compulsion may also exist when governmental actors threaten actions that are not authorized by law. The coerced confession cases typically involve such threats.[8] Under *Miranda v. Arizona*[9] custodial interrogations raises a presumption of such compulsion if the interrogation is not accompanied by *"Miranda* warnings." Fifth Amendment doctrines addressing custodial interrogation only rarely need be considered in white collar investigations, as those investigations commonly are complete before a target is arrested and taken into custody. Thus, any interrogation by investigators is likely to have occurred in a non-custodial setting. At one time an offer of leniency was viewed as sufficient to produce an involuntary (i.e., coerced) confession, but in white collar cases such offers are made with the approval of the prosecutor and in a setting where the individual has the opportunity to consult with counsel (if desired) before accepting. Hence, where such offers result in a confession (and typically, an agreement to cooperate), they are viewed in much the same fashion as a plea bargain (where the Supreme Court has noted that, in light of the "give-and-take" negotiation process, a charging or sentencing concession does not produce a plea compelled in violation of the Fifth Amendment).[10]

E.   Protection of "Testimonial" Evidence

The self-incrimination clause speaks of compelling a person to be a "witness" against himself, and the Court has held, most notably in *Schmerber v. California*,[11] that the term "witness," read in light of the common law, restricts the protection of the privilege, The Fifth Amendment does not prohibit the state from compelling production (and subsequently using against a person) all types of evidence, but only evidence of a type that would be provided by a "witness"—evidence which is "testimonial" in character. *Schmerber* held that the privilege therefore did not prohibit the compelled extraction of a blood sample and the subsequent admission of the lab analysis of that sample as incriminatory evidence at trial. The Court acknowledged that the self-incrimination clause went beyond compelling verbal testimony. It reaches "an accused's communications, whatever form they may take," including the compulsion of non-

---

government. See United States v. Stein, 440 F.Supp.2d 315 (S.D.N.Y.2006) (finding such a relationship where the government's conditions for non-prosecution forced the employer to modify its policy on paying legal fees for employees and condition further payments on the employees' cooperation with the government).

[7] See Marchetti v. United States, 390 U.S. 39 (1968) (recognizing self-incrimination objection to statute requiring registration as a gambler, in conjunction with an occupation tax, with the failure to register constituting a crime). As discussed in subsection (I) infra, where the government imposes a sanction for a non-disclosure that was justified under the privilege, and that sanction is not contempt or criminal liability, the Court sometimes has framed the issue presented as whether the sanction unduly burdens the exercise of the privilege, rather than as whether the sanction is so significant as to constitute the "compulsion" prohibited under the Fifth Amendment.

[8] The prohibition against government use of confessions obtained through unlawful police coercion was initially described as based on due process, but today is recognized as grounded also in the self-incrimination privilege. See Dickerson v. United States, 530 U.S. 428 (2000).

[9] 384 U.S. 436 (1966).

[10] See CRIMPROC §§ 6.2, 21.2; Brady v. United States, 397 U.S.742 (1970) (plea bargain offer of lesser sentence distinguished from an earlier coerced confession case, as there the defendant was "in custody, alone and unrepresented by counsel"; promise of leniency was "deemed sufficient to bar the confession not because the promise was illegal as such, but because defendants at such times are too sensitive to inducements and the possible impact on them too great to ignore and too difficult to assess").

[11] 384 U.S. 757 (1966).

verbal responses "which are also communication." However, the compelled act here constituted no more than the production of physical evidence. The "petitioner's testimonial capacities were in no way implicated," as the blood analysis, though the product of that compulsion, was "neither petitioner testimony nor evidence relating to some communicative act."

The *Schmerber* analysis of the testimonial limitation was subsequently applied in two Supreme Court rulings involving aspects of white collar investigations. As discussed in § 20.1(C), the Court later held that the act of producing documents pursuant to a subpoena could have communicative aspects, making the self-incrimination privilege applicable. The key was whether the act-of-production would be used to establish the existence of the documents demanded, that the documents fit the description set forth in the subpoena, or that the subpoenaed party had possession or control of the documents. As discussed in § 20.2, whether these testimonial characteristics are implicated in the production of the documents depend upon the particular subpoena and the government's u *Schmerber v. California* se of the act of production.

In *Doe v. United States*,[12] the Court again emphasized that function rather than form determines whether what is compelled is testimonial. The Court there held that a court order requiring a grand jury witness to sign a form directing any foreign bank to release the records of any account he might have at the bank did not compel testimony. While the individual was being compelled to issue a written statement, the contents of the statement was dictated by the government and did not reveal the "contents of [the individual's] mind." Also, it was not to be used as the individual's "factual assertion." The form was drafted so that the signing party noted that he was acting under a court order and did not acknowledge the existence of any account in any particular bank. The government was not relying on any "truth telling" in the content of the document, and if the bank produced records, the statement could not be used to authenticate those records.

Dissenting in *Doe*, Justice Stevens noted that "in some cases" (presumably where possession is known), a person may be compelled "to surrender the key to a strongbox containing incriminating documents" because that act would not be testimonial; but the same could not be said for compelling the person to "reveal the combination to his wall safe—by word or deed," as that would be testimonial. Justice Stevens viewed the directive at issue in *Doe* as similar to providing a combination, but the majority responded that since the directive did not force the individual "to express the contents of his mind," it was more like forcing surrender of the key. The Supreme Court again pointed to the same distinction in *United States v. Hubbell*,[13] in characterizing a response to a subpoena which required the subpoenaed party to use his knowledge of the background of documents in determining whether they fit within the particular categories of documents identified in the subpoena. The assembly of these documents, the Court noted, "was like telling an inquisitor the combination to a wall safe, not like being forced to surrender the key to a strongbox." Lower courts have also looked to that

---

[12] 487 U.S. 201 (1988).

[13] 530 U.S. 27 (2000), also discussed in § 20.2(B).

distinction in various contexts (e.g., in finding that the process of decryption is like revealing a combination and therefore is testimonial).[14]

F. Prohibited Uses of Compelled Testimonial Evidence

The Fifth Amendment prohibits compelling a person to be a witness "against himself" in a "criminal case." This prohibition clearly is met when a person's compelled statement is used as part of the state's proof of guilt in a subsequent criminal prosecution of the person. The Court has held, however, that the prohibition also encompasses other prosecution uses that operate to the detriment of the individual in his subsequent prosecution. Thus, the privilege bars use of an individual's compelled statement to impeach him when he later testifies as a defendant in his criminal trial. So too, it bars use of the compelled statement as a source leading to other evidence "derived" from the compelled statement.

G. "Criminal Case"

The privilege prohibits the use of the compelled statement only as to a "criminal case." It does not prohibit use in non-criminal proceedings, and a witness cannot claim the privilege when the potential use of the statement does not include use in a criminal case. A criminal case necessarily involves the determination of criminal liability and the imposition of criminal sanctions. Thus *Allen v. Illinois*[15] held that the privilege was not available to preclude use of a coerced confession in a civil commitment proceeding for sexually dangerous persons.

As discussed in § 19.2(D), under the "separate sovereign" doctrine, the privilege against self-incrimination is not violated when the government compels testimonial evidence and that evidence is used against the person in a criminal prosecution in a foreign nation. Thus, a witness cannot claim the privilege when the potential incriminating use of his response is limited to a foreign prosecution. The federal government and the individual state governments are not, for this purpose, treated as separate sovereigns. Thus, a witness in a federal proceeding can claim the privilege, even though protected from incriminating use by the federal government, if the compelled testimony could be used against him in any of the states.

H. Invoking the Privilege

The language of the Fifth Amendment prohibits use of compelled testimonial evidence against a defendant in a criminal case, but that does not necessarily set the point at which the privilege must be invoked. The Supreme Court, influenced by concerns of judicial administration (as well as the Fifth Amendment's core prohibition), has formulated varying standards for invoking the privilege. Those standards differ according to the timing and type of compulsion.

Where the compulsion is directed at gaining the testimony of the defendant in his own criminal prosecution, the privilege is invoked by refusing to give testimony. The

---

[14] See. In re Grand Jury Subpoena Duces Tecum Dated March 25, 2011, 670 F.3d 1335 (11th Cir.2012) (but also noting that the production of unencrypted contents could be compelled if the government can establish the existence of the documents in question as a "foregone conclusion," see § 20.2(B) at note 14).

[15] 478 U.S. 364 (1986).

defendant's self-incrimination privilege entitles him not only to avoid being compelled to give incriminating responses to particular inquires, but to resist being placed in a position where the inquires can be put to him while he is under oath. Neither the prosecution nor the court can force the defendant to testify at trial or be subjected to a pretrial deposition. As a practical matter, no such effort will be made, since the privilege stands as an absolute bar. Instead, the defendant invokes the privilege by simply "remaining silent," by not taking the stand in his own behalf. If he does testify, he then waives the privilege, allowing for cross-examination "reasonably related to the subject matter of his direct examination," which includes a general challenge to his credibility.

The right to refuse to testify is limited to testifying as the accused in a judicial proceeding that is part of the criminal prosecution. Where a person is subpoenaed simply to testify as a witness in a judicial or administrative proceeding, the privilege cannot be invoked by refusing to be sworn. The witness intending to exercise the privilege must take the stand and assert the privilege separately as each question calling for an incriminating response. Indeed, if the witness is to assert the privilege, he must do so at this point. He cannot simply respond, and then raise the privilege to bar government use of his testimony at a subsequent criminal trial. As the Court explained in *Chavez v. Martinez*,[16] the witness is required to assert the privilege at this point to make clear that the statement is not "voluntary" (for simply being under subpoena to testify does not preclude voluntarily offering testimony without regard to possible incrimination). Allowing the assertion at this point serves to "memorialize the fact that the testimony has indeed been compelled" (if the witness, after the assertion, is nonetheless ordered to testify), and thereby enables a court in a subsequent criminal proceeding to distinguish between statements that were compelled and statements that were voluntary.[17]

Once the witness asserts the privilege as to an individual question, the court, to determine whether the privilege is properly available, must consider whether the witness' possible response could indeed be put to incriminating use in some future criminal prosecution of the witness. As discussed in § 19.2(B), the prevailing standard here gives the witness every benefit of the doubt as to that possible use. If the witness' claim of the privilege is sustained, and the government is a party to the proceeding, it can remove the potential for incrimination (and render the privilege unavailable) by providing the witness with immunity—i.e., a government commitment, enforced by court order, that will restrict use of the witnesses testimony in a manner "coextensive with the scope of the privilege." As discussed in § 19.5, such a commitment will preclude use and derivative use of the witnesses testimony as to any subsequent prosecution of the witness.

---

[16] 538 U.S. 760 (2003).

[17] The penalty exception noted in Minnesota v. Murphy, note 19 infra, would indicate that the witness, in response to an erroneous denial of his asserted privilege and a court order to testify, need not challenge that order by standing in contempt, but may instead answer the question to which he objected and later challenge any attempt by the government to use that answer against him in a criminal prosecution. Maness v. Meyers, 419 U.S. 449 (1975), explains, however, why the witness may prefer to refuse to respond, stand in contempt, and pursue an appeal. See § 16.5(D). That procedural route allows the witness to prevail without ever revealing the incriminating evidence, and the language in other cases suggests that it could be the required vehicle for preserving the self-incrimination objection.

Where an individual is not an accused and the compulsion comes in a form other than a subpoena to testify, the individual ordinarily must invoke the privilege at the point of compulsion, just as a subpoenaed witness must do. Thus, if the defendant in a civil suit, in filing an answer to a complaint, would reveal incriminatory information, he must invoke the privilege at that point. So too, if an individual taxpayer concludes that information which must be furnished on a tax return would be incriminating, he must state on the return that the information is not being provided based upon his privilege against self-incrimination.[18] However, as discussed in *Minnesota v. Murphy*,[19] for reasons peculiar to each situation, the Court's rulings recognize three exceptions to the requirement of an affirmative assertion at the point of compulsion: (1) "confessions obtained from suspects in police custody"; (2) situations in which "the assertion of the privilege is penalized so as 'to foreclose a free-choice to remain silent, and compel incriminating testimony,'"—as illustrated by *Garrity v. New Jersey*,[20] where the individual "succumbed to the pressure placed upon him, failed to assert the privilege, and disclosed incriminating information"; and (3) the special "context of federal occupational and excise taxes on gamblers," where "the Court has held that the privilege may be 'exercised by silence,'" as illustrated by *Marchetti v. United States*.[21] In the first two settings, the consequence is that the individual can exclude incriminating statements even though the privilege was not previously asserted. In the third situation, the individual is not held liable for failing to respond even though he remained silent (rather than stating that he would not respond based on the privilege).

I. Unconstitutional Burdens

In an extensive line of cases, the Court has considered what adverse consequences may or may not be attached to the exercise of the privilege against self-incrimination. To be barred, an adverse consequence need not be so significant as to constitute compulsion to testify or produce an involuntary waiver of the privilege. Rather, the key is that the interest supporting the adverse consequence does not justify the burden imposed on the exercise of the privilege.

Brooks v. Tennessee[22] relied on this "undue burden" rationale in holding unconstitutional a state law requiring the defendant to choose at the outset of the presentation of his defense whether he would testify or exercise the privilege by not taking the stand. Requiring the defendant to choose before he heard the testimony of his defense witnesses (and the prosecution's cross-examination of those witnesses) placed "a heavy burden on a defendant's otherwise unconditional right not to take the stand," and that burden could not be justified by the state's interest. As illustrated by *Brooks*, while the Court often speaks of a prohibition against "penalizing" the exercise of the privilege, an adverse consequence may be prohibited constitutionally even

---

[18] See Garner v. United States, 424 U.S. 648 (1976).

[19] 465 U.S. 420 (1984).

[20] See the text at note 5 supra.

[21] See note 7 supra. As noted in Garner v. United States, supra note 18, this third exception rested on the tax and the required reporting requirement being directed at persons "inherently suspect of criminal activities." In the typical regulatory situation, where the individual is required to fill out a particular form, and that would require an incriminatory disclosure, the form must be submitted and privilege invoked as to that disclosure. See also § 20.6 (required record exception, precluding application of the privilege even if content is incriminatory).

[22] 406 U.S. 605 (1972).

though the state has an objective other than imposing a penalty (in *Brooks*, the objective was placing the defendant in a position similar to sequestered witnesses, who testify without having first heard the testimony of others). On the other hand, if the state can advance a legitimate regulatory interest in attaching an adverse consequence to the individual's failure to disclose certain information, that consequence does not invariably fail (as does a penalty).

The Court has concluded that drawing an adverse inference from the exercise of the privilege constitutes an unconstitutional burden in some settings, but not in others. *Griffin v. California*[23] held unconstitutional a state practice allowing the prosecutor and trial court to comment adversely on the defendant's failure to take the stand. The state there argued that it was only logical to draw an adverse inference from a defendant's failure to come forward and testify on critical facts "peculiarly within the accused's knowledge," and that the jury would draw that inference whether or not the court or prosecutor suggested it do so. The Court responded that various factors could explain a failure to testify (e.g., concern as to impeachment by reference to prior convictions), and in any event, allowing adverse comment impermissibly operated as a "penalty imposed by courts for exercising a constitutional privilege." The Court subsequently held that the concerns underlying the *Griffin* rule extended to the sentencing process, and therefore invalidated a sentence imposed by a sentencing judge who stated that he was "holding against [the defendant] that he didn't come forward and explain [his] side of issue [as to the quantity of drugs involved]."[24] *Baxter v. Palmigiano*,[25] however, allowed an adverse inference to be drawn in a prison disciplinary proceeding, and, as discussed in § 18.4, adverse inferences are also permissible in civil suits and administrative proceedings. On the other hand, as further noted in § 18.4, the exercise of the privilege may not be penalized by the automatic imposition of regulatory sanctions on a person who refuses on self-incrimination grounds to provide requested information to a regulatory agency.

§ 19.2   THE INCRIMINATION ELEMENT

A.   Personal Criminal Incrimination

A witness invoking the privilege must claim that his responsive testimony has the potential to be used against him in a criminal case (i.e., a potential for self-incrimination). While the potential for self incrimination encompasses a broad range of content, extending substantially beyond an admission of guilt, it also has very clear limits. It does not encompass responses that subject the witness to "degradation and infamy," economic loss, or even civil penalties, if those responses will not also contribute to criminal liability.

The privilege also does not encompass a response that will potentially incriminate a third party, but not the witness. If the witness claims the privilege, alleging potential personal incrimination, but the witness is concerned solely about providing evidence against another, the privilege is being misused. While the privilege undoubtedly is claimed in many instances by witnesses who only are concerned about protecting

---

[23] 380 U.S. 609 (1965).

[24] Mitchell v. United States, 526 U.S. 314 (1999), discussed in § 24.5 at note 145.

[25] 431 U.S. 801 (1977), discussed in § 18.4 at note 39.

another, establishing that motivation is extremely difficult. The threshold for claiming personal incrimination is so low that a response which provides evidence against another commonly will meet that threshold as to the witness as well. With the claim of the privilege assessed before the precise response is known, it is almost impossible to say with certainty that the witness is concerned solely about providing evidence against another and the privilege is being misused. Thus, as a practical matter, most often, the only way to defeat such a claim is to grant the witness immunity, thereby eliminating the potential for self-incrimination, and placing the witness in a position where he or she must testify (and incriminate the person the witness sought to protect) or be held in contempt. That solution, however, is available only to the government, as immunity in the federal system can be granted only on application of the government. See § 19.5(C).

B. The *Hoffman* Standard

The Supreme Court has repeatedly noted that the self-incrimination privilege is available only when the risk of self-incrimination is "substantial and real and not merely trifling or imaginary." Moreover, a witness' assertion of the privilege is not conclusive: "It is for the court to say whether [the witness'] silence is justified." However, the standard of review, as set forth in *Hoffman v. United States*,[26] gives the witness every benefit of the doubt. Thus, *Hoffman* noted that the witness' claim would be rejected only if it is "perfectly clear, from a careful consideration of all the circumstances in the case, that the witness is mistaken and that the answers cannot possibly have such a tendency to incriminate." Such a lenient review standard, the Court explained, was a product of procedural limitations, the breadth of the causal connection encompassed by possible incrimination, and the constitutional status of the privilege. The Court noted:

> This provision of the [Fifth] Amendment must be accorded liberal construction in favor of the right it was intended to secure. The privilege afforded not only extends to answers that would in themselves support a conviction . . . but likewise embraces those which would furnish a link in the chain of evidence needed to prosecute the claimant for a federal crime. . . . [T]his protection must be confined to instances where the witness has reasonable cause to apprehend danger from a direct answer. . . . However, if the witness, upon interposing his claim, were required to prove the hazard in the sense in which a claim is usually required to be established in court, he would be compelled to surrender the very protection which the privilege is designed to guarantee. To sustain the privilege, it need only be evident from the implications of the question, in the setting in which it is asked, that a responsive answer to the question or an explanation of why it cannot be answered might be dangerous because injurious disclosure could result.

The Supreme Court has applied the *Hoffman* standard in a handful of cases, discussed in the next subsection. Lower court rulings, far more numerous, look to the lessons of those cases, and not infrequently seek to compare the setting before the court to those presented in the Supreme Court rulings. Most often, however, a witness' self-

---

[26] 341 U.S. 479 (1951).

incrimination claim so obviously fits within the *Hoffman* standard that no challenge is made.

C. Applying the *Hoffman* Standard

1. *Considering Context*

Hoffman notes the need to consider the setting in which the question is asked, and the *Hoffman* Court itself placed considerable emphasis on the setting presented there in sustaining the witness' reliance on the privilege. Hoffman, a grand jury witness, looked to the privilege (1) to refuse to identify his current occupation and (2) to refuse to state when he had last seen a person that he acknowledged knowing for over 20 years. The lower court had rejected the claim because *Hoffman* had offered no explanation as how his answers could be incriminatory, but the Supreme Court held that such an explanation was not needed in light of the circumstances known to the lower court. The grand jury was investigating racketeering and the witness Hoffman was called as a "known underworld figure," with an extensive police record. Accordingly, a response as to occupation readily could have been incriminatory, considering that "the chief occupation of some persons [with links] to racketeering involves evasion of federal criminal laws." As for questions about contacts with an acquaintance, that acquaintance was currently a fugitive, and answers relating to recent contacts might furnish a link in a chain of evidence as to assisting the fugitive. The lower court had erred in failing to recognize that these implications of the context were sufficient to justify Hoffman's claims.

Hoffman generally is viewed as indicating that, in the grand jury context, it will be a rare case in which the privilege cannot be successfully claimed as to questioning that might associate the witness with the transactions or persons being investigated. Even where the witness appears to be an uninvolved fact witness (e.g., a third-party service provider), a court cannot discount the possibility that there was a deeper connection. The context also is viewed as establishing likely incrimination in those civil cases in which the civil claim dovetails with a criminal offense. Here, however, a court may insist upon some explanation where the information being sought is basic background information (e.g., the witness' education and professional background) rather than information directly related to the transactions that are the subject of the civil action.

Where the civil suit centers on activities that appear to have no relationship to criminality, the court examining a privilege claim is more likely to shift the burden to the witness to explain why he believes a response could be incriminating. The court may allow the witness to make such a showing *in camera*, but that process does not eliminate concern that requiring the disclosure of too much information would negate the very protection that the privilege is intended to provide. The court can, however, expect the witness' counsel to at least identify general information that points to the possible application of a specific criminal statute under a possible scenario consistent with that information.[27]

---

[27] In re Morganroth, 718 F.2d 161 (6th Cir. 1983), concluded that more was needed where a witness refused on self-incrimination grounds to answer deposition questions that related to the same transactions covered in previous testimony in other proceedings. The witness claimed that his responses might be

2. *Absolute Bars to Conviction*

The possibility that a response will provide a link in the chain of evidence needed to prosecute ordinarily is enough to support a self-incrimination claim. While the risk of prosecution must be "substantial and real," that standard does not invite speculation as to whether a prosecutor would proceed, provided the prosecutor *could* proceed. The requirement that the risk not be "trifling and imaginary" is read as referring to settings in which a prosecution would be prohibited, except, perhaps, for some "barely possible" legal exception. Thus, the focus is on the likely application of legal barriers to prosecution, such as the statute of limitations, double jeopardy, and immunity. Here, the party objecting to the exercise of the privilege must establish that the witness' response would be incriminating only as to an offense for which an absolute bar to prosecution almost certainly exists.

As for double jeopardy, the witness' prior acquittal or prior conviction (if final[28]) for the offense at issue could preclude relying upon the privilege if the incriminating response would be limited to that offense. However, as the Supreme Court noted in *Malloy v. Hogan*,[29] that limitation is difficult to achieve. The lower courts there had held that the self-incrimination privilege was not available to a witness who had pled guilty to a gambling charge and was now being asked about the circumstances surrounding his arrest and plea. The questions were obviously directed to determining the identity of his employer, and the lower court had erred in failing to recognize the possibility of a continuing relationship: "If this person were still engaged in unlawful activity, disclosure of his identity might furnish a link in a chain of evidence sufficient to connect the [witness] with a more recent crime for which he still might be prosecuted."

Malloy v. Hogan was decided before the Supreme Court held that the self-incrimination clause extended to liability in other United States jurisdictions (see subsection (D) infra). After that ruling, a federal court considering whether a witness' prior federal conviction precludes application of the privilege must take account of potential liability under state law. Even if the response to the question would be limited to the transaction that produced the conviction, and no further federal criminal liability would attach, the privilege will be available if that transaction could give rise to state criminal liability. The federal double jeopardy clause does not preclude separate federal and state prosecutions for the same basic offense, although various

---

inconsistent with that prior testimony and thereby lead to his being charged with perjury in his prior testimony. The court majority distinguished *Hoffman*, as the setting here did not inherently suggest the possible presence of perjury in the prior testimony. The witness would have to establish a "foundation" for reasonably fearing a perjury prosecution, pointing to something more than possible inconsistencies with current testimony, which might reflect no more than a different "current memory" of the transactions. Moreover, that foundation had to be provided by the witness "under oath, in person or affidavit, . . . because the present penalty of perjury may be the sole assurance against a spurious assertion of the privilege." The court expressed concern that unless such a showing is required, "no witness would ever have to testify twice because the possibility of perjury would always exist in theory."

[28] The double jeopardy bar is tied to the finality of the conviction. Thus, if a witness has pleaded guilty to an offense, but has not yet been sentenced, the self-incrimination privilege will be available even if the question and response bear only on that offense. See Mitchell v. United States 526 U.S. 314 (1999). Various lower courts have stated that a conviction does not become "final" for this purpose until the opportunity for direct appeal is completely exhausted.

[29] 378 U.S. 1 (1964).

states have statues prohibiting state prosecutions following a federal prosecution for the same offense (or even the same transaction).[30]

A grant of immunity in the state or federal systems will prohibit the use of the immunized testimony and derivative evidence in the other system. Prior to the Supreme Court's ruling in *Pillsbury Co. v. Conboy*,[31] lower courts had relied on the broad scope of that prohibition to hold that a witness could not utilize the privilege in response to questions basically identical to the questions that produced immunized responses in an earlier proceeding. They reasoned that answers to the questions asked in the second proceeding, typically a civil suit, would be derived from the immunized testimony in the earlier action and therefore could not be used against the witness in a future criminal proceeding, federal or state. The *Pillsbury* Court overturned these rulings, concluding that the privilege is available in the second proceeding. It was not necessary to decide whether the answers to the civil deposition questions were derived from the immunized responses in the first proceeding or from the witness' "current, independent memory." The immunity granted by the government in the first proceeding could not be extended, consistent with the immunity statute, by the private litigant in the second proceeding. Control over the scope of the immunity is given exclusively to the government through its framing of the questioning in the proceeding in which the immunity is granted. Accordingly, the immunity only precludes the witness from advancing the privilege in answering those questions in that proceeding. Of course, the government can force testimony in a second proceeding through a new grant of immunity where it is a litigant, but the court cannot do so at the behest of an non-governmental litigant.

3. *Innocence*

As the Supreme Court noted in *Ohio v. Reiner*,[32] a person who claims under oath to be innocent does not thereby preclude exercising the privilege as to the same event. *Reiner* found that the state had erred in concluding that the privilege would have been unavailable to a babysitter who had testified under immunity as to injuries inflicted upon two infants. While the babysitter had testified that she was "unaware of and had nothing to do with the . . . injuries," she also had acknowledged in her testimony that she had "spent extended periods of time alone with the children in the weeks immediately preceding discovery of their injuries" and "was with [the deceased infant] within the potential timeframe of [his] fatal trauma." In light of such acknowledgements, it could hardly be said that she lacked "reasonable cause to apprehend danger from a direct answer" when she initially announced her intention to exercise the privilege (then supplanted by the immunity grant) simply because she also denied involvement in the injuries. It was well established, the Court noted, that the privilege "serves to protect the innocent . . . who otherwise might be snared by ambiguous circumstances" and "that truthful responses of an innocent witness, as well as those of a wrongdoer, may provide the government with incriminating evidence from the speaker's own mouth."

---

[30] See CRIMPROC § 25.5.

[31] 459 U.S. 248 (1983).

[32] 532 U.S. 17 (2001).

4.   *Question–By–Question Application*

Courts commonly note that the *Hoffman* standard does not allow a "blanket" claim of the privilege, as the court must look to the implications of a response to a particular question. A witness presenting oral testimony must assert the privilege on a question-by-question basis; a witness compelled to produce documents must assert the privilege as to the production of a specific document; a civil defendant raising the privilege in responding to a complaint must invoke it as to particular allegations in that complaint.

Very often the privilege will clearly be available as to all requests for information relating to a particular transaction or a particular relationship. The witness bears the burden of identifying the requests that he or she views as seeking that information. In giving testimony, the witness often will exercise the privilege as to a particular question and indicate that the privilege will thereafter be raised as to all further questions touching upon the same subject matter. This will commonly lead to discontinuing questions on that subject (see § 16.6(E)). Where the questioning occurs before a jury or grand jury, to continue to raise question after question in obvious anticipation that the witness will respond by exercising the privilege suggests an improper effort to use that exercise against the witness and against persons associated with the witness.

D.   Incrimination Under the Laws of Another Sovereign

For many years, American courts took the position that the privilege protected only against incrimination under the laws of the sovereign which was attempting to compel the incriminating testimony. In applying this rule, which was said to be derived from the English common law, the individual states and federal system were treated as separate sovereigns. Thus if a witness appearing before a federal grand jury was granted immunity against federal prosecution, he could not refuse to testify on the ground that his answers might be incriminating under the laws of a state. In *Murphy v. Waterfront Commission*,[33] the Supreme Court rejected this "separate sovereign" doctrine as applied to state and federal prosecutions. Noting that a contrary position would allow a witness to be "whipsawed into incriminating himself under both state and federal law," the Court concluded that the "policies and purposes" of the Fifth Amendment required that the privilege protect a "state witness against incrimination under federal as well as state law and a federal witness against incrimination under state as well as federal law." This meant that the immunity granted to replace the privilege had to extend to both state and federal prosecutions. As discussed in § 19.5(A), *Murphy* established that thereafter federal and state immunity grants would meet that standard; they would bar use and derivative use of the immunized testimony in federal and state courts.

The *Murphy* opinion contained language suggesting that the separate sovereign limitation was flawed even in excluding consideration of incrimination under the laws of other nations. That would have made the privilege available where the witness realistically feared that his responses could lead to prosecution in a foreign country. However, the Court noted shortly afterwards that *Murphy's* rejection of the separate sovereign limitation related only to American jurisdictions and that the issue remained

---

[33] 378 U.S. 52 (1964).

open as to incrimination under the laws of foreign countries. In *United States v. Balsys*,[34] that issue was squarely presented by a case in which a resident alien, subpoenaed to testify at a deposition concerning his possible participation in Nazi persecutions during World War II, sought to claim the privilege because of a "real and substantial" danger that his answers could lead to criminal prosecution in either Lithuania or Israel. A divided Court concluded that the incrimination under the laws of foreign country was beyond the protection afforded by the self-incrimination privilege.

The *Balsys* majority rejected the contention that the phrase "any criminal case" in the self-incrimination clause literally encompasses all prosecutions, no matter where they might occur. That phrase, the Court noted, must be read in the context of a Fifth Amendment which encompasses various other guarantees (grand jury indictment, double jeopardy, due process, and just compensation), all of which are only implicated "by action of the government that it binds." In the absence of "legislative history" or "common law practice at the time of the Framing" which suggested otherwise, the Court would "read the Clause contextually as apparently providing a witness with the right against compelled self-incrimination when reasonably fearing prosecution by the government whose power the Clause limits, but not otherwise."

The *Murphy* reading of the privilege as applicable to incrimination under both federal and state law was characterized in *Balsys* as a product of the application of the self-incrimination privilege to the states via the Fourteenth Amendment. Once the states become bound by the Fifth Amendment guarantee, the self-incrimination clause "could no longer be seen as framed for one jurisdiction [i.e., state or federal government] alone, each jurisdiction having instead become subject to the same claim of privilege flowing from the one limitation." The self-incrimination privilege carried with it "a feature unique to the guarantee," an "option to exchange the privilege for an immunity to prosecutorial use of any compelled testimony," which could only be upheld, consistent with the dual applicability of the privilege, by viewing the state and federal jurisdiction "as one." That reasoning, the majority noted, had no bearing on the treatment of potential incrimination in a foreign nation.

§ 19.3   THE GRAND JURY TARGET

A. Exercise of the Privilege

As discussed in § 19.1(H), the defendant in a criminal case can exercise the privilege by refusing to to take the stand at trial, but that is not true of mere witnesses. They are said to have "an option of refusal [to answer] and not a prohibition of inquiry." They must take the stand and exercise the privilege as to individual questions. As discussed in § 16.6(F), the DOJ's internal regulations treat differently the target of a grand jury investigation. Those regulations initially allow for subpoenaing a target only if special circumstances justify doing so and special procedures have been followed. Then, if the target informs the prosecutor that he or she intends to exercise the privilege, the target ordinarily will be relieved of the obligation to appear. As to other witnesses, the internal standards reject the practice of excusing the witness from appearance where the witness has informed the prosecutor that the witness intends to exercise the privilege.

---

[34] 524 U.S. 666 (1998).

Federal courts have uniformly rejected the contention that targets have a constitutional right to refuse to testify, analogous to defendants at trial. The courts note that witnesses cannot make a blanket assertion of the privilege in advance because: (1) witnesses cannot presume to know the precise questions that will be put to them, and (2) the *Hoffman* standard cannot be applied without examining at least the initial inquiry directed to the witness. These reasons, the courts conclude, apply equally to the target.

The courts add that grand jury is in an investigative stage, which is quite different from the trial stage at which a defendant can refuse to testify. The defendant's right of silence grew out of the early common law rule on the incompetency of parties to testify, which had bearing only on the trial. It also rested in part on the fear that a defendant "forced in open court to refuse to answer questions" might be viewed by the jury as having something to hide. This concern has less significance in the grand jury setting; since the grand jury looks only to the issue of probable cause, its proceedings need not be conducted "with the assiduous regard for the preservation of procedural safeguards which normally attends the ultimate trial of the issues." Also, when the target/witness appears before the grand jury and exercises the privilege, that silence may not be used against him if he should later become a defendant. In particular, if the defendant should testify at trial, the exercise of the privilege before the grand jury does not present an inconsistency that would allow its use for impeachment.

Some courts have further argued that the right to subpoena targets is inherent in the grand jury's combined investigative and shielding roles. Having an obligation to "run down every available clue," the grand jury cannot ignore the possibility that any one participant in a criminal enterprise may be willing to identify others. Having an obligation to "shield against arbitrary accusation," the grand jury has a right to be certain that the target's own testimony might not explain away the evidence against him. Another concern is that the establishment of a right not to appear based upon whether the prosecutor knew or should have known someone was a "target" would create a new source of tangential disputation.

Once the target is indicted, quite distinct legal difficulties arise in calling the now indicted target before the grand jury for questioning relating to the subject of the indictment. While some opinions suggest that the indicted target receives Fifth Amendment protection equivalent to that afforded the defendant at trial (and therefore cannot be called to testify), the leading cases rely on other grounds. Initially, there is the prohibition against using the grand jury subpoena for post-indictment discovery. See § 16.12(F). Some courts have suggested that under some circumstances (e.g., where the grand jury witness does not realize he has been indicted), the prosecution's misconduct in this regard rises to the level of a due process violation.

B. Privilege "Warnings"

Witnesses in general need not be advised that they can refuse to respond to questions or document production where they fear self-incrimination. *Miranda v. Arizona*[35] recognized an exception to this principle in the instance of custodial

---

[35] 384 U.S. 436 (1966). See also CRIMPROC § 6.8 as to *Miranda's* requirement of Fifth Amendment "warnings."

interrogation. The Court reasoned, in part, that advice as to rights was needed to offset the special compulsive force of custodial interrogation, as the advice not only informed the arrestee but also conveyed police willingness to respect the privilege. In *United States v. Mandujano*,[36] the lower court held that the "*Miranda* warnings" also applied to a grand jury witness who was a "putative defendant." The Supreme Court, however, unanimously rejected the extension of *Miranda* to the grand jury setting.

Mandujano did leave open the question of whether the Fifth Amendment required some type of advice on the availability of the self-incrimination privilege for a target witness. The Court held that, even if such advice was required, the lack of that advice could not constitute a defense to a perjury charge based on the witness' false grand jury testimony. Six justices, however, went on to speak to the need for Fifth Amendment warnings for the target witness. Four, in what has proven to be a highly influential opinion, advanced a rationale indicating that such warnings are not required constitutionally.

Although the witness in *Mandujano* had been informed of both his privilege against self-incrimination and his right to consult with counsel, the district court had held that warning was insufficient. Since the witness was a "putative defendant," the district court reasoned, he should have been given full *Miranda* warnings, including notification of a right to appointed counsel. Chief Justice Burger's plurality opinion, speaking for four members of the Court, rejected the district court's reasoning. *Miranda*, he noted, applied only to "custodial interrogation," which clearly did not include questioning before the grand jury. The position of the subpoenaed witness could hardly be compared to that of the arrestee subjected to interrogation in the "hostile" and "isolated" setting of the police station. The appropriate analogy was to the questioning of a witness in an administrative or judicial hearing. As noted by Justice Frankfurter in *United States v. Monia*,[37] a witness in that setting "if . . . he desires the protection of the privilege, . . . must claim it or he will not be considered to have been 'compelled' within the meaning of the Amendment."

Chief Justice Burger added that, since Mandujano had been given self-incrimination warnings, there was no need to rule on whether such warnings were constitutionally required. Nevertheless the Chief Justice's reliance on *Monia* would suggest that the plurality viewed grand jury witnesses, whether targets or non-targets, as not entitled to any special notification of rights. Rather, they would seem to bear the obligation, like witnesses generally, to assert the privilege on their own initiative. Justice Brennan, joined by Justice Marshall, viewed the Chief Justice's reference to *Monia* in this way, and responded that the plurality had read the privilege too narrowly. The *Monia* principle, he argued, rests on the assumption that the government ordinarily had no grounds for assuming that its compulsory processes are eliciting incriminating information. However, where the prosecutor is questioning a target witness, he is "acutely aware of the potentially incriminating nature of the disclosures sought." This knowledge, Justice Brennan reasoned, carries with it an obligation to advise the witness of his rights so as to ensure that any waiver of the privilege is "intelligent and intentional." Thus, though *Miranda* did not extend to the

---

[36] 425 U.S. 564 (1976), also discussed in § 16.8 at note 81.

[37] 317 U.S. 424 (1943) (Frankfurter, J., dissenting). See also § 19.1 at note 11.

grand jury setting, the self-incrimination clause on different grounds required *Miranda*-like warnings.

In two subsequent rulings, the Supreme Court again treated the constitutional necessity for warnings as an open issue. In *United States v. Washington*,[38] the primary issue was whether a witness who was a target had to be informed of his target status. Since the witness had been warned of his privilege against self-incrimination, the Court found no need to rule on what was needed in that regard.[39] As for the additional notification that the witness was the target of the inquiry, that was not needed to put the witness in a position to exercise the privilege if he chose to do so. The failure to so inform him did not put him at a "constitutional disadvantage," as the target status "neither enlarge[ed] nor diminish[ed]" the scope of his constitutional protection. Thus, the witness here "knew better than anyone else" whether his answers would be incriminating, and he also knew, having been given the warnings, that anything he did say, after failing to exercise the privilege, could be used against him.

In *Minnesota v. Murphy*,[40] the issue before the Supreme Court was the constitutional necessity of giving *Miranda*-type warnings to a probationer being questioned by a probation officer at his office. In holding that the warnings were not required, the Court drew an analogy to the grand jury setting. The interview setting in *Murphy*, the Court noted, subjected the probationer to "less intimidating pressure than is imposed upon a grand jury witness," and the Court had "never held that [warnings] must be given to the grand jury witness." This "expansive dictum," along with the reasoning of Chief Justice Burger's plurality opinion in *Mandujano*, has led the Seventh Circuit to conclude that "the Supreme Court would be reluctant to extend a warning requirement to grand jury proceedings."[41]

As discussed in § 16.5 (C), internal DOJ policy requires that an advice of rights statement be attached to any subpoena issued to a "target" or "subject," and that advice is then repeated when such a witness testifies.[42] Adherence to this policy largely moots the constitutional issue left open in *Mandujano*. Of course, internal standards do not create rights that are enforceable against the government; if a witness seeks to exclude from evidence a statement made before the grand jury because he was a target and the government failed to advise him of his right to exercise the self-incrimination privilege, that will require consideration of the constitutional issue. However, with the internal standard applicable to subjects as well as targets, and the advice of rights form attached to subpoenas as standard practice, such a situation is unlikely to arise.

---

[38] 431 U.S. 181 (1977).

[39] The Court rejected the contention that self-incrimination warnings, if required, could not be given satisfactorily at the time the witness takes the stand. That the warnings were given in the presence of the grand jury, or without any advance notice, was not crucial, provided the witness fully understood the warnings.

[40] 431 U.S. 181 (1977).

[41] United States v. Gillespie, 974 F.2d 796 (7th Cir. 1992). Other Circuits have reached a similar conclusion.

[42] As discussed in § 16.6(G), witnesses who are targets are also notified of their target status.

§ 19.4   WAIVER

A. Basic Requirements

A waiver of the privilege against self-incrimination must be voluntary. Thus, threats of various types of sanctions if the witness exercises the privilege can result in an invalid waiver. *Garrity v. New Jersey*,[43] where the state threatened to automatically discharge its employees if they exercised the privilege, presented such an involuntary waiver.[44] Other adverse consequences that flow from exercise of the privilege, such as the consequences that attach in civil litigation (see § 18.4), are permissible and therefore do not produce an involuntary waiver.

While federal courts, in various contexts, refer to the self-incrimination privilege being waived "knowingly" as well as "voluntarily," the structure of the law governing the invocation of the privilege in various settings indicates that the individual need not be aware that he has waived the privilege in providing the requested information. As discussed in § 19.3(B), the individual need not be advised of the availability of the privilege in most settings. Where warnings are required, the Court has not insisted upon more than a general awareness of the privilege's availability, provided by the warning, to sustain a waiver.[45] In the settings in which warnings are not required, the privilege is often described as a "fighting clause"—a party or witness must affirmatively invoke the privilege to receive its benefit. Apart from the few exceptions noted in § 19.1(H), the privilege is "waived" (or forfeited) when the question is answered, or information provided. Accordingly, when a witness provides an obviously incriminating response, there is no need to ask whether his intent is to relinquish the privilege.[46]

B. The *Rogers* Doctrine

In *Rogers v. United States*[47] the witness testified before a grand jury that, as treasurer of the Communist Party of Denver, she had been in possession of party records, but had subsequently delivered those records to another person. She refused, however, to identify the recipient of the records, asserting that would be incriminating. A divided Supreme Court affirmed her contempt conviction, holding the privilege inapplicable. The Court noted that Rogers had already incriminated herself by admitting her party membership and past possession of the records; disclosure of her "acquaintanceship with her successor present[ed] no more than a 'mere imaginary possibility' of increasing the danger of prosecution." A witness would not be allowed to

---

[43] 385 U.S. 493 (1967), discussed in § 19.1 at note 4.

[44] As discussed at note 20 supra, *Garrity* presented one of the exceptional instances in which the individual was not required to raise the privilege at the point of compulsion. Accordingly, the Court was required to determine whether the employee's decision to testify in the Attorney General's inquiry constituted a voluntary waiver. In other contexts, the failure to object when required to testify is viewed as a "waiver."

[45] See CRIMPROC § 6.9(b), discussing individual competence and waivers in custodial interrogation.

[46] So too, federal courts have uniformly held that a defendant who chooses to testify at trial need not be asked whether he realizes that he has a right to remain silent. This position may reflect, in part, a concern that the court not be seen as interfering with the lawyer client relationship. Even where the defendant proceeds pro se, however, federal courts have not insisted upon an on-the-record colloquy, although a judicial response is needed where the defendant obviously is confused. See United States v. Ly, 646 F.3d 1307 (11th Cir.2011).

[47] 340 U.S. 367 (1951).

disclose a basic incriminating fact and then claim the privilege as to "details." To uphold such a claim of the privilege would "open the way to distortion of facts by permitting a witness to select any stopping point in her testimony."

Rogers directs the district court to ask "whether the answer to the [additional] question would subject the witness to a 'real danger' of further incrimination." Justice Black, in dissent, argued that further incrimination was present here because the witness' answer would identify persons who might provide additional evidence against her.[48] However, such a broad reading of further incrimination is inconsistent with the *Rogers* directive that the witness cannot withhold details and thereby risk a distortion of the facts. Additional detail will often provide even stronger incriminating evidence than the original disclosure. Hence, lower courts have read the "further incrimination" standard more narrowly, looking to incrimination as to an additional offense, although some cases have held that incrimination as to an additional element of the same offense is sufficient to preclude waiver.

Although *Rogers* often is described as posing a great danger for the witness who answers even seemingly "innocuous questions," the decision as applied by lower courts tends to be fairly limited. The fact that the second question asked for further detail as to the same event is not deemed to conclusively establish a prior waiver as to that question. Courts look as well to the character of that further detail. Indeed some courts ask whether the initial statement "creates a significant likelihood that, absent further testimony [responding to the additional questions], the finder of fact will be left with, and prone to rely upon, a distorted version of the truth stemming from the earlier testimony."[49] Here, waiver is tied to the distortion component of the *Rogers* rationale.

C. Separate Proceedings

Rogers presented a witness who sought to invoke the privilege after waiving it in the same proceeding. The defendant Rogers could have returned to claim the privilege in a separate proceeding. Moreover, the dominant position in the federal courts is that the grand jury investigation and the criminal prosecution are separate proceedings.

§ 19.5 IMMUNITY AND COMPELLED TESTIMONY

A. Constitutionality

The use of immunity grants to preclude reliance upon the self-incrimination privilege predates the adoption of the constitution. The English adopted an immunity procedure, known as providing "indemnity" against prosecution, soon after the privilege against compulsory self-incrimination became firmly established, and a similar practice was followed first in the colonies and then in the states. The first federal immunity act was not adopted until 1857, however, and the first Supreme Court ruling upholding immunity grants did not come until 1896, when *Brown v. Walker*[50] was decided. In that case, a sharply divided Court concluded that the

---

[48] Justice Black's main contention was that nothing in the record suggested that the witness intended to relinquish the privilege. Justice Black acknowledged, however, that the "Court's holding" rested on the premise that waiver occurred automatically, as to "all related questions," "regardless of her intention."

[49] See E.F. Hutton & Co. v. Jupiter Development Corp. Ltd., 91 F.R.D. 110 (S.D.N.Y. 1981).

[50] 161 U.S. 591 (1896).

immunity procedure was consistent with the history and function of the Fifth Amendment privilege. The history of the Amendment clearly indicated that its object was only to "secure the witness against criminal prosecution." Thus, the self-incrimination privilege had been held inapplicable where the witness' compelled testimony would relate only to an offense as to which he had been pardoned or as to which the statute of limitations had run. So too, the privilege had been held not to apply where the witness' response might tend to "disgrace him or bring him into disrepute" but would furnish no information relating to a criminal offense. Such rulings implicitly sustained the constitutionality of the immunity procedure. Since the immunity grant removed the only danger against which the privilege protected the witness, the witness could no longer claim that he was being compelled to incriminate himself.

In *Counselman v. Hitchcock*,[51] decided prior to *Brown*, the Court struck down a federal immunity statute that granted the witness protection only against admitting his immunized testimony into evidence in a subsequent prosecution. The Court stressed that there was no statutory protection against derivative use of the witness' testimony. Thus, the statute "could not, and would not, prevent the use of his testimony to search out other testimony to be used in evidence against him." At the conclusion of its opinion, the Court spoke in terms of even broader protection than prohibiting derivative use. "To be valid," it noted, an immunity grant "must afford absolute immunity against future prosecution for the offense to which the question relates." This statement was taken as indicating that a valid immunity grant must absolutely bar prosecution for any transaction discussed in the witness' testimony. Accordingly, Congress adopted a new immunity statute providing for such "transactional immunity." That statute provided that a witness directed to testify or produce documentary evidence pursuant to an immunity order could not be prosecuted "for or on account of any transaction, matter, or thing concerning which he may testify or produce evidence." The constitutionality of this provision was upheld in *Brown*, and subsequent federal immunity statutes were largely patterned upon the *Brown* statute.

Later decisions—and the language of the later statutes—recognized two limitations in transactional immunity. The witness may still be prosecuted for perjury committed in his immunized testimony. Similarly, the immunity does not extend to a transaction noted in an answer totally unresponsive to the question asked. Thus, the witness could not gain immunity from prosecution for all previous criminal acts by simply including a reference to those acts in his testimony without regard to the subject on which he asked to testify.

In *Murphy v. Waterfront Commission*,[52] the Court first upheld immunity that was not as broad in scope as the traditional transaction immunity. *Murphy*, as discussed in § 19.2(D), held that the self-incrimination privilege extended to possible incrimination under both federal and state law. Accordingly, to be constitutionally acceptable, the immunity granted to a witness had to provide adequate protection against both federal and state prosecutions. If that protection had to encompass transactional immunity, the state immunity provisions would necessarily fail. Congress had the power, in authorizing federal immunity grants, to preempt state prosecutions, but the states

---

[51] 142 U.S. 547 (1892).

[52] 378 U.S. 52 (1964), also discussed at note 33 supra.

lacked authority to prohibit federal prosecutions. The *Murphy* Court held, however, that the immunity grant need not absolutely bar prosecution in the other jurisdiction. It was sufficient that the witness was guaranteed that neither his testimony nor any fruits derived from that testimony would be used against him in any criminal prosecution. The Court, to accommodate "the interests of State and Federal Governments in investigating and prosecuting crime," would exercise its supervisory power to prohibit the federal government from using in federal courts state immunized testimony or the fruits thereof. The federal immunity statute was to be read as implicitly extending its immunity to state prosecutions.

Following *Murphy*, Congress adopted a new immunity provision for federal witnesses, replacing transactional immunity with a prohibition against use and derivative use as to both federal and state prosecutions. The statute provided that "no testimony or other information compelled under the [immunity] order (or any information directly or indirectly derived from such testimony or other information) may be used against the witness in an criminal case, except a prosecution for perjury, giving a false statement, or otherwise failing to comply with the order."[53] In *Kastigar v. United States*,[54] a divided Court upheld the new federal provision. The "broad language in *Counselman*," which suggested the need for transactional immunity, was discounted as inconsistent with the "conceptual basis" of the *Counselman* ruling. The crucial question, as *Counselman* noted, was whether the immunity granted was "coextensive with the scope of the privilege against self-incrimination." Both the immunity upheld in *Murphy* and the traditional Fifth Amendment remedy of excluding compelled statements and their fruits (as, for example, in the coerced confession cases) indicated that the privilege did not require an absolute bar against prosecution. A prohibition against use and derivative use satisfied the privilege by placing the witness "in substantially the same position as if . . . [he] had claimed his privilege."

The *Kastigar* majority rejected the argument, relied upon by the dissenters, that the bar against derivative use could not be enforced so effectively as to ensure that the witness really was placed in the same position as if he had not testified. The statute's "total prohibition on use," it noted, "provides a comprehensive safeguard, barring the use of compelled testimony as an 'investigatory lead,' and also barring the use of any evidence obtained by focusing investigation on a witness as a result of his compelled disclosures." Appropriate procedures for "taint hearings" could ensure that this prohibition was made effective. Those procedures, the Court noted, would be identical to the procedures prescribed in *Murphy*:

> As stated in *Murphy*: "Once a defendant demonstrates that he has testified, under a state grant of immunity to matters related to the federal prosecution, the federal authorities have the burden of showing that their evidence is not tainted by establishing that they had an independent, legitimate source for the disputed evidence." This burden of proof, which we reaffirm as appropriate, is not limited to a negation of taint; rather, it imposes on the prosecution the affirmative duty to prove that the evidence it proposes to use is derived from a legitimate source wholly independent of the compelled

[53] 18 U.S.C. § 6002.

[54] 406 U.S. 441 (1972).

testimony. This is very substantial protection, commensurate with that resulting from invoking the privilege itself.

B. Applying the Use/Derivative-Use Prohibition

Federal case law developments since *Kastigar* have cast considerable light on the protections afforded by *Kastigar* in a subsequent prosecution of an immunized witness. Initially, the lower courts have held that the prosecution's burden of establishing that its evidence was derived from an independent source and not from the defendant's immunized testimony is subject to a preponderance of the evidence standard (rather than a higher burden of persuasion). Typically this burden must be carried at an evidentiary hearing (commonly described as a "taint hearing" or a "*Kastigar* hearing"), although in exceptional cases (e.g., where the government relies upon evidence produced in a prior trial), affidavits alone may be sufficient. Many courts insist that the hearing be held prior to trial, which incidentally gives the defense far broader pretrial discovery than it would ordinarily obtain, but others will allow the government to make its showing after the trial is completed and all of its evidence has been seen. As *Kastigar* noted, the government burden at the hearing is not limited to "negation of taint," but must include a showing that it has "an independent legitimate source for the disputed evidence." Mere denials of prosecutor access to the testimony is insufficient, as it does not establish that the government's sources also were free of taint. Typically, "to establish a 'wholly independent source,' the government must demonstrate that each step of the investigative chain through which the evidence was obtained is untainted."

Federal caselaw applying *Kastigar* suggests that the prosecution is most likely to meet its burden of showing an independent source when the investigation of the defendant was completed or substantially completed before the defendant was compelled to give immunized testimony. The preferred practice in such cases is for the prosecutor to make a record of all of the evidence collected prior to the grant of immunity, to file that record with the court, and then at the taint hearing, note its intent to utilize only the previously acquired evidence and further evidence directly derived from that evidence. That procedure, however, is hardly foolproof.

One potential difficulty is illustrated by *United States v. North*.[55] In that case, the Independent Counsel, conducting a grand jury investigation of the Iran–Contra affair, followed the above described procedure for "canning" all previously uncovered evidence prior to Congress' initial public hearings at which it granted immunity to the defendant (at that point, a key target of the grand jury investigation). Although the government's subsequent criminal prosecution rested on the testimony of witnesses who had previously testified before the grand jury, and Independent Counsel had established a "Chinese Wall" to ensure that its staff was not exposed to the immunized testimony at the Congressional hearings,[56] that was held insufficient to meet the

---

[55] 910 F.2d 843, modified in part, 920 F.2d 940 (D.C. Cir.1990).

[56] The Chinese Wall serves two functions. First, it lends support to the claim that investigators and prosecutors developed evidence independently of the immunized testimony. Second, it precludes the possibility that the prosecution, although relying on independently obtained evidence, made tactical use of the immunized testimony in framing its trial strategy. Lower courts have divided over whether *Kastigar* bars "nonevidentiary uses of immunized testimony" (e.g., the decision not to pursue a certain line of questioning in cross-examination).

Kastigar burden. The district court had found that the "witnesses had their memories refreshed with [defendant's] immunized testimony by 'hearing the testimony, reading about it, being questioned about aspects of it before the Select Committees and, to some extent, by exposure to it in the course of responding to inquiries within their respective agencies.'" Insofar as the testimony of the witnesses was shaped by their memories having been refreshed, the government was making "use" of the immunized testimony, contrary to *Kastigar*. Accordingly the case was remanded for further proceedings to see if "it is possible . . . to separate the wheat of the witness' unspoiled memory from the chaff of North's immunized testimony."[57]

C.   The Immunity Statute

The primary federal immunity statute has separate sections for immunity grants in administrative agency proceedings and "proceedings before or ancillary to a court . . . or a grand jury."[58] For agency proceedings, the agency may issue the order, but it must first obtain approval of the Attorney General. For judicial proceedings, the order is issued by the court but only on application of a U.S. Attorney with the approval of a designated Main Justice official.[59]Although it is common for the witness to take the stand and claim the privilege before the immunity order is issued, that is not required as to either administrative or judicial proceedings. Both statutory provisions authorize granting immunity to a person "who may be called to testify or provide other information," and both include as a condition that the person has refused "or is likely to refuse" to testify or provide information on the basis of the privilege.

Both sections require a determination that "the testimony or other information from such individual may be necessary to the public interest." That determination for administrative proceedings rests in the "judgment" of the agency. For judicial and grand jury proceedings that determination rests in the "judgment" of the U.S. Attorney seeking the immunity order. Thus, the court reviewing the application plays a limited role. Its sole function is to determine whether the U.S. Attorney has complied with the statute (e.g., received the proper approval). It may not inquire into whether the immunity order serves the public interest, as the statute gives conclusive effect to the determination of the United States Attorney.

Both statutes are read as authorizing proceeding specific immunity orders. Thus, if an order is issued for grand jury testimony, and the government desires to have the witness testify at trial as well, it must obtain a new order. In *Pillsbury Co. v. Conboy*,[60] the Supreme Court accordingly refused to allow civil litigants to extend the impact of

---

[57] In *North*, the government was unable to meet this burden and the charges against the defendant were dismissed. In United States v. Slough, 641 F.3d 544 (D.C. Cir. 2011), another case in which witnesses had been exposed to immunized statements, the D.C. Circuit found that the district court had erred in striking the testimony of those witnesses without more careful examination as to whether (1) parts of their testimony did not overlap with the immunized testimony and (2) their testimony could be attributed to an independent source insofar as it did overlap.

[58] 18 U.S.C. §§ 6001–6005 are the primary immunity provisions. Section 6001 sets forth the general scope of the immunity, see note 53 supra, while § 6002 covers agency proceedings, § 6003 covers court and grand jury proceedings, and § 6005 covers Congressional proceedings.

[59] The statute allows designation at the level of Assistant Attorney General or Deputy Attorney General, and the officials holding those positions in various DOJ divisions have been given approval authority. However, all requests must be cleared by the Criminal Division. USAM § 9–23.130.

[60] 459 U.S. 248 (1983), discussed at note 31 supra.

the immunity order through the contention that the witness could not exercise the privilege when asked the same questions that had put to him in earlier proceedings under a grant of immunity.

Once the immunity order is granted, the witness must either testify or face contempt sanctions, unless the witness has some legal justification (e.g., the attorney-client privilege) for refusing to respond. The witness may not refuse to testify because his answers will subject him to substantial civil liability. Neither may he refuse to testify because he is fearful of physical or economic retaliation by associates or others. Some courts have suggested a duress defense could be available where the witness reasonable feared a sufficiently immediate threat of death or serious bodily harm, but the government can then respond by making available its witness protection program.

D. DOJ Guidelines

The DOJ sets forth in USAM § 9–23.210 a list of factors to be considered in deciding whether an immunity order is in the public interest. Those factors are: (1) the seriousness of the offense and the importance of the case in achieving effective enforcement of the criminal law; (2) the value of the witness' testimony to the investigation or prosecution; (3) the likelihood that the witness will comply promptly with the immunity order and provide useful testimony; (4) the witness' culpability relative to other possible defendants; (5) the possibility of successfully prosecuting the witness without immunity; and (6) the possibility of adverse collateral consequences for the witness if the witness is compelled to testify.[61] This list is not "all-inclusive." Other relevant considerations include a previous grant of immunity by a state (which would make it difficult under *Kastigar* to prosecute the witness and therefore reduce the "cost" of forgoing federal prosecution), and how a jury might view the immunity grant (in particular, whether the grant seems "unfair" when compared to proceeding against the target).

The "cost" of immunity (noted in the fifth factor) is basically eliminated in one very common scenario for immunity grants: the individual initially is convicted (at trial or through a guilty plea) and then is given immunity when he refuses to testify against other participants in the general criminal activity. As discussed in § 19.2(C), a conviction often will not preclude raising the privilege, either because the conviction is not final or a potential exists for further liability (e.g., under state law). On the other hand, with the defendant already convicted, the immunity grant will not allow a culpable person to escape without criminal sanction.

As discussed below, prosecutors often prefer using informal immunity rather than statutory immunity. However, where the witness is not willing to testify in exchange for promised immunity, statutory immunity becomes the prosecution's only option. In many instances the witness' recalcitrance is due to the witness' loyalty to a target who

---

[61] In the white collar setting, a primary concern is economic repercussions, including possible retaliation by the target. If the witness will be compelled to testify before the grand jury, a relevant consideration in this connection is whether grand jury secrecy can operate to protect the witness' identity. See § 16.9

Adverse consequences (as well the likelihood that the witness will not comply) also are a critical consideration where the witness is a "close family relative" of the target or subject. USAM § 9–23.211 sets forth a general policy against compelling testimony from such persons subject to several exceptions. See note 121 of § 16.10.

is a friend or employer. Such loyalty often may lead to the exercise of the privilege by persons who are not concerned about their own liability, concluding that their participation (if any) was not criminal or that their role was too insignificant to attract a federal prosecutor's interest. Rather than dispute such a witness' reliance on the privilege, the prosecutor may choose to force the witness to testify through statutory immunity. The primary hope of the person who seeks to avoid testifying is that the prosecutor will conclude that the person's testimony is not worth the effort involved in obtaining statutory immunity, particularly if others in the same position are willing to provide the same basic information without claiming the privilege (or in exchange for informal immunity).

E.   Informal Grants of Immunity

Where the witness is willing to testify under a grant of immunity, the prosecutor may prefer to provide immunity through an agreement whereby the witness agrees to testify in exchange for a promise of non-prosecution or non-use. For the prosecutor, non-statutory immunity offers primarily two advantages. First, it bypasses the statutory procedure for obtaining an immunity order, a procedure which often is cumbersome and time-consuming. Second, it permits the prosecutor to tailor the scope of the immunity to the needs of the case. Thus, a prosecutor may believe that federal transactional immunity will be more effective in gaining witness cooperation, and that can be provided only through informal immunity. In other situations, the use/derivative-use immunity provided by statute may be more than the witness requires or the prosecutor is willing to give; an informal grant may be limited to barring prosecution only as to certain aspects of a transaction, or it may provide only use and not derivative-use immunity. Finally, the prosecution can condition the immunity on full cooperation, allowing for use of that information already provided should the defendant fail to provide that cooperation.

For the witness, informal immunity has an advantage primarily where it will permit him to obtain broader protection than would otherwise be available. Sometimes informal immunity may be broader in certain respects and narrower in others. It may provide transactional immunity, rather than use/derivative-use immunity, but that transactional immunity may be limited to only a certain offense or to prosecution by the particular U.S. Attorney office that offers the informal immunity.[62] Unlike statutory immunity, informal immunity cannot restrict state prosecution, as the federal prosecutor has no preemptive authority (in contrast to Congress). However, the possibility of state prosecution is slight (or non-existent) for many types of federal offenses.

For informal immunity, unlike statutory use/derivative-use immunity, issues relating to the scope of the immunity cannot be answered by reference to the commensurate protection provided under the self-incrimination privilege. Here, the scope may be broader or narrower than what would be required to supplant the privilege, and the crucial question is what scope was agreed to by the parties. The primary source of assistance in answering that question is the terms of the written

---

[62] The Antitrust Division's Amnesty Program includes a promise of non-prosecution as to current employees of the entity that qualifies for amnesty, but this transactional immunity is limited to the particular antitrust violation being disclosed under the program. See DOJ, Antitrust Division, Corporate Leniency Policy and Leniency Policy, available at http://www.justice.gov.

immunity agreement,[63] but not infrequently courts find ambiguity in those terms. That ambiguity may relate to whether the immunity promised was as to use alone or use and derivative-use, what types of uses were to be prohibited by an agreement barring derivative-use, what crimes and jurisdictions were included in an agreement not to prosecute, and whether certain action or inaction by the prospective defendant constitutes a material breach of the conditions set forth in the agreement. The lower courts tend to resolve these issues by reference to general principles of contract law, keeping in mind the special context in which such agreements are made. Because the government is the author of the agreement and has the capacity and experience needed to anticipate difficulties and limit the agreement so as to protect its interests, courts often take the position that ambiguities generally should be construed against the government and in favor of the defendant.

F. Proffers

A witness seeking to secure either statutory or informal immunity must be prepared to make a "proffer" describing the substance of the testimony that he or she can provide. While a prosecutor may be willing to grant immunity based on what available evidence suggests as to the witness' knowledge and participation, that often presents certain dangers, reflected in its common characterization as "blind immunity." Prosecutors prefer to know precisely what information the witness can provide and to be able to question the witness as to his or her participation in the transactions being investigated. That can be achieved through a proffer.

The witness' counsel will often prefer to provide the requested information in what is described as a "hypothetical proffer." This is a statement by counsel phrased in "conjectural terms," conveying detail about the testimony that the witness can offer without attributing the information it conveys directly to the witness on whose behalf it is submitted. Prosecutors very often want more from a proffer—in particular, the opportunity to interview the witness. This leads to the need for a proffer agreement as to what subsequent use can be made of the proffer if the witness does or does not receive immunity.[64] The government will invariably insist that the statement may be used for impeachment should the individual later offer inconsistent testimony. It also often will reserve the right to charge the witness with making a false statement if the witness lies.

Other provisions on government use vary with the U.S. Attorney's office and the bargaining position of the witness. Under the fairly common "Queen for a Day," agreement, the government agrees not to make "direct use" of the individual's statement if an immunity agreement is not reached, but reserves the right to make

---

[63] These agreements are commonly set forth in "immunity letters," leading to informal immunity often being described as "letter immunity." The treatment of the individual's forthcoming testimony also may be addressed in a deferred prosecution or non prosecution agreement, see § 2.4(C), relating to the individual. Plea agreements also can address the defendant's agreement to testify and the government's subsequent use of that testimony against the defendant.

[64] This agreement serves to avoid the issue of whether the particular proffer is governed by Federal Rule 11(f). That Rule provides that the admissibility or inadmissibility of a "plea discussion and any related statement is governed by Federal Rule of Evidence 410." Rule 410, in turn states that any statements made in the course of plea discussions which do not result in a plea of guilty may not be admitted in evidence against the person making the statement, except for a prosecution for perjury. United States v. Mezzanatto, 513 U.S. 196 (1995), holds that the benefit of Rule 410 can be waived by agreement. Thus, even if Rule 410 would otherwise be applicable, the proffer agreement prevails.

derivative use. Under a significant modification of that direct-use prohibition, the witness' statement can be used in evidence against him if the witness later is charged and presents a position at trial "inconsistent with the proffer." The Seventh Circuit held that this language does not eliminate the use prohibition whenever the witness (now defendant) contests his guilt (i.e., contesting guilt is not itself "inconsistent" even if the proffer statement acknowledged guilt). However, it does allow use of the proffer statement where the trial defense offers a factual position (even if offered only through witness cross examination) that is inconsistent with factual statements in the proffer statement.[65]

---

[65] See United States v. Krilich, 159 F.3d 1020 (7th Cir.1998).

Chapter 20

SELF–INCRIMINATION AND THE COMPULSORY PRODUCTION OF DOCUMENTS[1]

§ 20.1 FROM *BOYD* TO *FISHER*

A. The *Boyd* "Principle"

Although a subpoena duces tecum may be used to compel production of various types of physical evidence, its most frequent use in white collar investigations is to require the production of documents. *Boyd v. United States*,[2] decided in 1886, was the first Supreme Court case to consider the applicability of the self-incrimination privilege to court ordered production of documents. Although *Boyd* involved a different form of court order, the reasoning of the Court clearly encompassed the subpoena duces tecum. Under the analysis adopted in *Boyd*, a subpoena requiring the production of a document was subject to challenge under both the Fourth Amendment and self-incrimination clause of the Fifth Amendment. As noted in § 16.11(A), *Boyd*'s Fourth Amendment analysis was soon thereafter modified so as to limit the Fourth Amendment challenge to subpoenas that were overly broad in the documents requested. *Boyd*'s Fifth Amendment analysis survived for a considerably longer period and provided a far more significant barrier to the compelled production of documents.

Under current precedent, very little, if anything, remains of *Boyd*'s Fifth Amendment analysis. Yet the *Boyd* analysis remains a universally accepted starting point for understanding the many strands of current Fifth Amendment doctrine applicable to the subpoena duces tecum. For much of the current doctrine was developed in the process of first limiting and then replacing the *Boyd* analysis. Moreover, some uncertainty remains as to whether the privacy aspect of the *Boyd* analysis might continue to apply in limited situations.

Boyd upheld a self-incrimination challenge to a court order requiring an importing firm organized as a partnership to produce the invoice it had received for items allegedly imported illegally. Quoting from the famous English case of *Entick v. Carrington*, the *Boyd* opinion noted that papers are an owner's "dearest property," respected by a well established common law prohibition against forcing such evidence "out of the owner's custody by process." Allowing the state to compel production of private books and papers, even where necessary to convict for the most serious crime, would be "abhorrent to the instincts" of an American or Englishman and "contrary to the principles of a free government." Just as the Fifth Amendment prohibited "compulsory discovery by extorting the party's oath," it also prohibited discovery by

---

[1] This chapter, along with Chapter 19, is based on the more extensive discussion in CRIMPROC §§ 8.12, 8.13, which provide additional citations. See note 1 of § 19.1.

[2] 116 U.S. 616 (1886), also discussed in § 16.11 at note 138.

"compelling the production of his private books and papers." The challenged documentary production order was simply another form of "forcible and compulsory extortion of a man's own testimony."

Boyd relied on what has been described as a "property oriented" view of the Fourth and Fifth Amendments, built upon the owner's right of privacy in the control of his lawfully held possessions. It recognized a special Fifth Amendment interest in the privacy of documents, viewing the forced production of their content as equivalent to requiring a subpoenaed party to reveal that content through his testimony. Although the Court spoke of "private books and papers," it obviously was not referring only to confidential documents relating to personal matters. The document at issue in *Boyd* was a business record that had not been prepared by the partners themselves but by the shipper of the item alleged to have been illegally imported.

Insofar as it relied upon the self-incrimination privilege, the *Boyd* ruling could be read as limited to documents. As documents contain words, the compelled disclosure of their content could be seen as more closely analogous to the compelling of testimonial utterances than compelling the disclosure of other forms of property possessed by the subpoenaed party. Yet, the key to the Court's analysis appeared to be the invasion of the individual's privacy interest in his possession of property to which the public had no entitlement (such entitlement existing, the Court noted, only where a third-party had a superior right, as with stolen property, or the state had a superior interest, as with records required to be kept by law). Although the invasion might be more serious as to the individual's "dearest property" (i.e., his papers), the same principle would appear to forbid the forced production of any form of personally held property where there was no such public entitlement and the property could be used as incriminating evidence. Thus, the Supreme Court later spoke of the self-incrimination privilege as protecting the individual "from any disclosure, in the form of oral testimony, documents, *or chattels*, sought by legal process against him as a witness."

B. Post–*Boyd* Developments

Starting with *Hale v. Henkel*,[3] decided only two decades after *Boyd*, the Court gradually developed a series of doctrines that chipped away at the broad implications of *Boyd*'s property-rights/privacy analysis of Fifth Amendment protection. Finally, in *Fisher v. United States*,[4] decided close to a century after *Boyd*, the Court majority was forced to conclude that all that remained of *Boyd* was a "prohibition against forcing the production of private papers" that had "long been a rule searching for a rationale."

Hale recognized what has come to be known as the "entity exception" to the self-incrimination clause. An artificial entity (a corporation in *Hale*) was not entitled to the benefit of the privilege. The entity-exception cases did not directly question the *Boyd* analysis, although they did render that analysis inapplicable to the production of documents belonging to entities, including partnerships. As the Court later noted, "[i]t would appear that under [the entity exception], the precise claim sustained in *Boyd* would now be rejected for reasons not there considered."

---

[3] 201 U.S. 43 (1906), discussed at note 17 infra.

[4] 425 U.S. 391 (1976), discussed at note 6 infra.

Certain aspects of the Court's reasoning in establishing the entity exception did implicitly raise questions as to the soundness of *Boyd's* analysis, even though that analysis continued to be applied to the individual. *Hale* and other entity-exception cases stressed features of business records that appeared to undermine *Boyd's* inclusion of those records when speaking of an individual's "dearest property." Initially, the entity opinions stressed the government's regulatory interest in inspecting such documents. The rulings also questioned the relationship of business documents to the primary function of the self-incrimination clause. Thus, a major ruling on the entity exception noted that the Fifth Amendment serves to protect "'a private inner sanctum of individual feeling and thought'—an inner sanctum which necessarily includes an individual's papers and effects to the extent that the privilege bars their compulsory production and authentication." However, it also noted, a "substantial claim of privacy or confidentiality . . . cannot often be maintained with respect to financial records of an organized collective entity." Control of such records is typically regulated by the entity, with "access to the records . . . generally guaranteed to others in the organization." Much the same could be said of business records possessed by an individual proprietor.

Though it did not restrict the *Boyd* ruling as such, the limitation of the Fifth Amendment to "testimonial" compulsion, as held in *Schmerber v. California,*[5] did raise further questions as to the scope of the *Boyd* analysis. As discussed in § 19.1(E), *Schmerber* held that the privilege did not prohibit the compelled extraction of a blood sample from an accused. The history of the privilege limited its application to compelled production of an accused's "communications" or "testimony." While this protection extended beyond words compelled from "a person's own lips" and extended to "communications . . . in whatever form they may take," it did not encompass "compulsion which makes a suspect or accused the source of 'real or physical' evidence." Citing *Boyd*, the *Schmerber* opinion distinguished the "compulsion of responses which are also communications, for example, compliance with a subpoena to produce one's papers." It did not explain, however, how such compliance could constitute a communication of the individual through his forced disclosure of contents of the subpoenaed document. Arguably, a document authored by the individual might be seen as "speaking" for him, as it contains his words. In *Boyd*, however, the required production was of a document written by another, an invoice sent to the *Boyd* partnership by a supplier.

C. *Fisher*: A New Rationale

In *Fisher v. United States,*[6] sole owners of separate businesses had delivered to their attorneys various workpapers that had been prepared by their accountants in the course of filing tax returns. The IRS issued a summons (the equivalent of a subpoena) to the attorneys, requiring production of the workpapers. The taxpayers, relying on *Boyd*, raised a self-incrimination objection. That objection failed under the third-party production principle announced in *Couch v. United States.*[7] As discussed in § 20.5, the owners of documents ordinarily cannot raise the privilege when the compulsion is

---

[5] 384 U.S. 757 (1966), discussed in § 19.1(E) at note 11.

[6] 425 U.S. 391 (1976).

[7] 409 U.S. 322 (1973), also discussed at note 28 infra.

directed at a third-party, who will produce the documents. In the *Fisher* situation, the third-party attorneys did not fear incrimination, and therefore could not raise their personal privilege. So too, they could not raise the self-incrimination privilege to protect their clients. However, under the attorney-client privilege, the attorneys could refuse to produce the documents if those documents "would have been privileged in the hands of the client by reason of the Fifth Amendment." Thus, the Court found itself in the position where it had to decide the self-incrimination issue that the taxpayers had advanced—whether *Boyd* rendered the privilege applicable to the compelled production from the taxpayers of the type of record subpoenaed in this case.

In separate concurring opinions, Justices Marshall and Brennan argued that the *Boyd* rule was inapplicable under the facts of this case. Ever since *Boyd*, they noted, the Fifth Amendment had protected a privacy interest that "extends not just to the individual's immediate declarations, oral or written, but also to his testimonial materials in the form of books and papers." That protection, however, read in light of the entity cases, was limited to the compelled production of papers that fell within the "zone of privacy recognized by the Amendment." Some business records of a sole proprietor could fall within the protected category of "personal" or private papers, but that was not true of the records subpoenaed here. "Given the prior access by the accountants" and the "wholly business rather than personal nature of the papers," the compelled production of the documents in question was not barred by the privilege.

Justice White's opinion for the Court in *Fisher* also ejected the taxpayer's reliance upon *Boyd*, but on much broader grounds. Justice White noted that *Boyd* had relied on a combined Fourth and Fifth Amendment theory that had "not stood the test of time." Much of *Boyd's* Fourth Amendment analysis had been flatly rejected and the rulings in cases like *Schmerber* and the entity cases had adopted a different view of the Fifth Amendment. What was left was a "prohibition against forcing the production of private papers [that] has long been a rule searching for a rationale consistent with the proscriptions of the Fifth Amendment against compelling a person to give 'testimony' that incriminates him." In light of *Schmerber*, that prohibition could not rest on the incriminating content of the subpoenaed records. The court order of production of preexisting records does not require the subpoenaed party to author those records. Where the preparation of subpoenaed records was voluntary, those records "cannot be said to contain compelled testimonial evidence." The records may contain incriminating writing, but whether the writing of the subpoenaed party or another, that writing was not a communication compelled by the subpoena. Accordingly, the prosecution's acquisition of that writing by subpoena is no more compelling testimony than its acquisition by subpoena of physical evidence with a similar incriminating content.

Having found that the application of the privilege could not rest on the declarations contained in the writings, the Court then turned to what it viewed as a more appropriate explanation of the *Boyd* rule. The act of producing subpoenaed documents, the Court noted, "has communicative aspects of its own, wholly aside from the contents of the papers produced." Compliance with a subpoena "tacitly concedes the existence of the papers demanded and their possession or control by the [subpoenaed party]." It also would indicate that party's "belief that the papers are those described in the subpoena," and in some instances this could constitute authentication of the papers. Indeed, post-*Boyd* decisions suggested that such "implicit authentication" was the "prevailing justification for the Fifth Amendment's application to documentary subpoenas." These three elements of production—acknowledgment of existence, acknowledgment of possession or control, and potential authentication by identification—are clearly compelled, but whether they also are "testimonial" and "incriminating" would depend upon the "facts and circumstances of particular cases or classes thereof." The resolution of that question, the Court reasoned, should determine whether a particular compelled documentary production is subject to a Fifth Amendment challenge.

Upon examining the implications of the act of production in the case before it, the *Fisher* Court, for reasons explored in § 20.2, concluded that the taxpayer did not have a valid self-incrimination claim. "In light of the records now before us," the Court noted, "however incriminating the contents of the accountant's workpapers might be, the act of producing them—the only thing which the taxpayer is compelled to do—would not itself involve testimonial self-incrimination." The Court also added, however, a comment that might significantly limit its ruling. It noted: "Whether the Fifth Amendment would shield the taxpayer from producing his own tax records in his possession is a question not involved here; for the papers demanded here are not 'private papers,' see *Boyd v. United States.*"

Following *Fisher*, some lower courts saw the act-of-production doctrine and *Boyd*'s content-based analysis as alternative grounds for sustaining a self-incrimination challenge to the compelled production of the business records of a sole proprietor. In *United States v. Doe (Doe I)*,[8] the Court went out of its way to point out that this approach was mistaken. The rationale of *Fisher*, the Court concluded, implicitly rejected application of a content-based analysis of the privilege in such a situation.

Doe I involved a subpoena directing a sole proprietor to produce for grand jury use a broad range of records, including billings, ledgers, canceled checks, telephone records, contracts and paid bills. The district court sustained the proprietor's claim of privilege. It concluded that compliance with the subpoena would require the proprietor to "admit that the records exist, that they are in his possession, and that they are authentic" and that each of these testimonial elements of production was potentially incriminatory. The Third Circuit agreed with this reasoning, but also added that the privilege applied because compelled disclosure of the contents of the documents violated the Fifth Amendment. Relying upon a privacy analysis it found in *Boyd*, the Third Circuit reasoned that the contents of personal records were privileged under the Fifth Amendment and that "business records of a sole proprietorship are no different from the individual's personal records."

Justice Powell's opinion for the Court in *Doe I* affirmed the rulings below insofar as they relied on the act-of-production doctrine. *Fisher* had recognized that the act of production could be testimonial and incriminatory under the facts of a particular case, and here two lower courts had so found. That finding would be accepted in accordance with the Court's traditional "reluctan[ce] to disturb findings of fact in which two courts below concurred." Three concurring Justices argued that, in light of the acceptance of

---

[8] 465 U.S. 605 (1984), often described as *Doe I* to distinguish the later decision *Doe v. United States*, discussed in § 19.1 at note 12.

this finding, there was no reason to speak to the alternative grounding of the Third Circuit's opinion, but the Court majority concluded that it was desirable to resolve the "apparent conflict" between that grounding and "the reasoning underlying this Court's holding in *Fisher*." That resolution resulted in the majority's flat rejection of the Third Circuit's conclusion that the contents of the subpoenaed documents were protected by the privilege.

Justice Powell initially acknowledged that the Court in *Fisher* had "declined to reach the question whether the Fifth Amendment privilege protects the contents of an individual's tax records in his possession." The "rationale" underlying *Fisher*'s holding, however, was equally persuasive here. *Fisher* had emphasized that "the Fifth Amendment protects the person asserting the privilege only from compelled self-incrimination." That a record was prepared by a subpoenaed party and is in his possession is "irrelevant to the determination of whether its creation ... was compelled." The business records here, like the accountant's workpapers in *Fisher*, had been prepared voluntarily, and therefore only their production, and not their creation, was compelled. The contention that the Fifth Amendment created a "zone of privacy" that protected the content of such papers had been rejected in *Fisher*. The respondent could not avoid compliance with a subpoena "merely by asserting that the item of evidence which he is required to produce contains incriminating writing, whether his own or that of someone else."

D. The Remnants of *Boyd*

Although *Doe I* flatly rejected the Third Circuit's "zone of privacy" analysis, the Court had before it only a subpoena to compel the production of business records. Arguably, the most private records of an individual could be treated differently. Justice White had noted at one point in *Fisher* that that case did not raise "the special problems of privacy which might be presented by subpoena of a personal diary." In his *Fisher* concurring opinion Justice Brennan had argued that both "history and principle" made the privilege applicable to the individual's "immediate declaration, oral or written." No rational principle, he maintained, would support the view that the constitution "does not permit compelling one to disclose the contents of one's mind but does permit compelling the disclosure of the contents of that scrap of paper [on which] ... persons would, at their peril, record their thoughts and the events of their lives."

The *Doe I* majority opinion did not offer any opening for separate treatment of personal recollections in confidential documents. It emphasized that the key to the application of the self-incrimination clause was the testimonial and incriminating aspects of the act of production, not the content of the voluntarily prepared document. Based upon that analysis, if intimate personal papers were to receive greater production, it was only because the confidential nature of those papers made it more likely that their production would have those attributes that made the production of the document "testimonial." This reading of *Doe I* was made explicit in Justice O'Connor's concurring opinion in that case, which led to a responding concurring opinion by Justice Marshall, who argued for a much narrower reading of the majority's position.

Justice O'Connor, in her concurring opinion, suggested that the *Doe–Fisher* rationale rejected a content based analysis as to all types of documents. She noted:

I write separately . . . to make explicit what is implicit in the analysis of [Justice Powell's] opinion: that the Fifth Amendment provides absolutely no protection for the contents of private papers of any kind. The notion that the Fifth Amendment protects the privacy of papers originated in *Boyd v. United States*, but our decision in *Fisher v. United States*, sounded the death-knell for *Boyd*. "Several of *Boyd's* express or implicit declarations [had] not stood the test of time . . . and its privacy of papers concept ha[d] long been a rule searching for a rationale." *Fisher*. Today's decision puts a long overdue end to that fruitless search.

Justice O'Connor's opinion brought forth a response from Justice Marshall, joined by Justice Brennan. "This case," Justice Marshall noted, "presented nothing remotely close to the question that Justice O'Connor eagerly poses and answers." The documents in question here were business records, "which implicate a lesser degree of concern for privacy interests than, for example, personal diaries." It accordingly could not be said that the Court had "reconsidered the question of whether the Fifth Amendment provides protection for the content of 'private papers of any kind.'"

In the years since *Doe I*, lower courts usually have found it unnecessary to decide whether anything remains of Boyd. "If the contents of papers are protected at all," they note, "it is only in rare situations, where compelled disclosure would break the heart of our sense of privacy." That might be the case as to subpoena compelling production of "intimate papers such as private diaries and drafts of letters or essays," but it certainly would not cover the business and other financial records that typically are in issue.

A growing number of courts, however, have come to the conclusion that the rationale of *Doe* and *Fisher* precludes self-incrimination protection of the contents of a voluntarily prepared document, no matter how personal the document. Thus, courts have held that the act-of-production doctrine provides the only protection for such personal records as diaries and pocket calendars. In all of those cases, however, once the concept of a *Boyd*-based content protection was rejected, the government was able to overcome an act-of-production objection because the documents had been shared with others and their existence, possession, and authentication were established as foregone conclusions. Ordinarily such documents are kept more privately and the individual required to produce them would implicitly be giving testimony as to those elements and therefore be entitled to the protection of the privilege.[9]

---

[9] In *United States v. Hubbell*, 530 U.S. 27 (2000), discussed at note 13 infra, Justice Thomas, joined by Justice Scalia, suggested that the Court should reexamine *Fisher* in light of historical evidence indicating that the self-incrimination privilege was intended to protect against "the compelled production not just of incriminating testimony, but of any incriminating evidence." Justice Thomas argued that the understanding of the word "witness" at the time of the adoption of the Constitution, the "history and the framing of the Fifth Amendment privilege," and the use of the term "witness" in the Sixth Amendment, all pointed in the direction of protecting a person against being compelled to furnish incriminating physical evidence, such as "books and papers," without regard to whether the production has a testimonial component. Justice Thomas noted that such a reading would restore *Boyd* in full force, and would render irrelevant the "difficult parsing of the act of responding to a subpoena duces tecum" required by *Fisher*. Although the Court majority did not respond directly to Justice Thomas' criticism of "*Fisher's* fail[ure] to examine the historical backdrop of the Fifth Amendment," it did cite in a footnote to other rulings which had described as historically sound the limitation of the privilege to "compell[ing] incriminating communications . . . that are 'testimonial' in character." The *Hubble* majority applied *Fisher* and did not even mention *Boyd*.

§ 20.2 APPLICATION OF THE ACT-OF-PRODUCTION DOCTRINE

A. Testimonial Character and the Foregone Conclusion Standard

As discussed in § 20.1(C), *Fisher v. United States*[10] concluded that the act of producing subpoenaed documents could have "communicative aspects of its own, wholly aside from the contents of the papers produced." Compliance with a subpoena "tacitly concedes the existence of the papers demanded and their possession or control by the [subpoenaed party]." It also indicates that party's "belief that the papers are those described in the subpoena," and in some instances this could constitute authentication of the papers. These three elements of production—acknowledgment of existence, acknowledgment of possession or control, and potential authentication by identification—are clearly compelled, but whether they are "testimonial" and "incriminating," *Fisher* noted, would depend upon the "facts and circumstances of particular cases or classes thereof."

The *Fisher* opinion itself provided the basic analytical structure for determining whether the elements of the act of production are testimonial in character in the particular case. The Court there concluded that there was no basis for holding "testimonial" the implicit admissions as to existence and possession that would be made in that case with the taxpayer's production of his accountant's workpapers. Relying upon what came to be known as the "foregone conclusion" standard, the *Fisher* Court reasoned:

> It is doubtful that implicitly admitting the existence and possession of the papers rises to the level of testimony within the protection of the Fifth Amendment. The papers belong to the accountant, were prepared by him, and are the kind usually prepared by an accountant working on the tax returns of his client. Surely the Government is in no way relying on the "truthtelling" of the taxpayer to prove the existence of or his access to the documents. The existence and location of the papers are a foregone conclusion and the taxpayer adds little or nothing to the sum total of the Government's information by conceding that he in fact has the papers. Under these circumstances by enforcement of the summons "no constitutional rights are touched. The question is not of testimony but of surrender."

Justice Brennan, in his concurring opinion, sharply criticized the Court's reliance on this "foregone conclusion" rationale. He argued that the Court was holding, in effect, that an admission as to existence and possession is not testimonial "merely because the Government could otherwise have proved [those facts]." Such a position rested on the untenable proposition that "one's protection against incriminating himself . . . turn[s] on the strength of the Government's case against him." Undoubtedly, as Justice Brennan noted, in assessing whether compelled testimony falls within the privilege, courts have never deemed it significant that the government could otherwise establish the incriminating information that might be disclosed in the witness' testimony; the

---

[10] 425 U.S. 391 (1976), discussed at note 6 supra.

critical question is simply whether the witness's testimony would be usable against him.

However, the *Fisher* Court was not dealing with a traditional form of testimony, but with what it viewed as a quite different issue—whether the incidental communicative aspects of a physical act (production) were "testimonial." The Court cited by analogy its rulings holding the Fifth Amendment inapplicable to a court order requiring an accused to submit a handwriting sample. Incidental to the performance of that act, the Court noted, the accused necessarily "admits his ability to write and impliedly asserts that the exemplar is his writing." But the government obviously is not seeking this information—the "first would be a near truism and the latter self-evident"—and therefore "nothing he has said or done is deemed to be sufficiently testimonial for purposes of the privilege." Where the existence and possession of the documents to be produced are a "foregone conclusion," the act of production similarly "adds little or nothing to the sum total of the government's information" and therefore is no more testimonial than other compelled physical acts. The government in such a case obviously is not seeking the assertions of the subpoenaed party as to the facts of existence and possession, and his incidental communication as to those facts, inherent in the physical act that the government had the authority to compel, therefore does not rise to the level of compelled "testimony." To allow the privilege to be claimed simply because the required act incidentally provided information, even though the government did not seek that information, would be to make every compelled act a testimonial communication, contrary to the *Schmerber* rule.

Fisher spoke of the foregone conclusion doctrine as a means of establishing that the act of production was not testimonial as to the elements of existence and possession. *Doe I* indicated that the doctrine applied as well where the act of production would provide evidence of authentication by communicating that the documents produced were those designated in the subpoena. The lower courts in *United States v. Doe* (*Doe I*)[11] had found that the act of production there had a testimonial element as to authentication, as well as a testimonial element as to existence and possession. The Supreme Court noted that the government could have "rebut[ed] this finding by showing that possession, existence and authentication were foregone conclusions," but it had not done so.

Doe I's inclusion of authentication in the foregone conclusion analysis follows logically from *Fisher's* explanation of the foregone conclusion concept. As with possession and existence, the government can readily have independent sources which establish authenticity, rendering any acknowledgment of authenticity through production an unrequested, incidental product of the act of production. Indeed, in some instances the character of the record sought makes it clear that the government will have no need to resort to the act of production to establish authenticity. The records on their face will establish their authenticity (i.e., they are self-authenticating) or their

---

[11] 465 U.S. 605 (1984), discussed at note 8 supra.

authenticity will be established by other sources obviously available to the government (e.g., a handwriting analysis where the records are handwritten).[12]

As illustrated by *Fisher*, the government will not always need to look to the foregone conclusion doctrine on the authentication element, as the act of production will not invariably have the potential for assisting the government in establishing authenticity. In *Fisher*, the Court noted that the production there would not provide the government with evidence that would be useful in authenticating the subpoenaed workpapers since production by the taxpayer would "express nothing more than the taxpayer's belief that the papers are those described in the subpoena," and that was not the belief of an individual with personal knowledge. The taxpayer "did not prepare the papers and could not vouch for their accuracy."

Lower courts have added that even where the party producing the documents has critical knowledge as to the origination of the document, that knowledge may not be reflected in the act of production. A subpoena may describe the document to be produced so particularly and objectively that the only acknowledgment made by the person producing the documents is that he has the capacity to identify that which would be obvious to any uninformed third-party observer. For the subpoenaed party's act of production to be testimonial, it must reflect a cognition that incorporates historical fact (typically something about the background, use, or content of the document) in identifying the document produced as that demanded by the subpoena. The typical subpoena description of documents (see § 16.7(C)) will require the subpoenaed party to draw upon such knowledge in identifying and categorizing those documents.

B. Establishing a Foregone Conclusion

The *Fisher* Court concluded that the existence and location of the accountant's workpapers were a foregone conclusion, but the Court never explained why that was so—apart from noting that the papers were of the kind usually prepared by an accountant. In *Doe I*, in contrast to *Fisher*, the Court sustained the lower courts' conclusion that the testimonial aspects of the act of production prevailed, as the government had not shown "that possession, existence, and authentication were a foregone conclusion." However, the *Doe I* Court did not provide an extensive analysis of what was needed to meet the foregone conclusion standard. Rather, it relied basically on the presence of the "explicit finding of the District Court that the act of producing the [subpoenaed] documents would involve testimonial self-incrimination." That finding rested essentially "on the determination of factual issues" and it had been affirmed by the Third Circuit. The Supreme Court had "traditionally been reluctant to disturb findings of fact in which two courts below have concurred" and there was no reason to do so here.

---

[12] Federal Rule of Evidence 901 governs "the requirement of authenticity or identifying an item of evidence." It sets forth various examples of evidence that will meet this requirement, including "testimony of a person with knowledge," expert opinions (e.g., handwriting analysis), and "distinctive characteristics of the item, taken together with all the circumstances." Rule 902 adds a list of documents that are "self-authenticating," including "commercial paper and related documents." The function of the authenticity requirement is to ensure that the documents are what they are represented to be.

In light of the *Doe I* Court's emphasis on its limited role in reviewing the lower courts' findings, the significance of the lower courts' reasoning in reaching those findings is unclear. The Supreme Court did note that such a finding would be overturned if it had "no support" in the record, and it did set forth at length the reasoning of the lower courts. The district court had concluded that compliance with the subpoena would require respondent to "admit that the [subpoenaed] records exist, that they are in his possession, and that they are authentic," and that each of these elements was potentially incriminatory. The district court had added that while the government had argued that "existence, possession and authenticity . . . can be proved without [Doe's] testimonial communication," it was not satisfied "as to how that representation can be implemented." The Third Circuit had found "nothing in the record that would indicate that the United States knows, as a certainty, that each of the myriad documents demanded . . . in fact is in the appellee's possession or subject to his control." The "most plausible inference," it had noted, was that the government was "attempting to compensate for its lack of knowledge by requiring the appellee to become, in effect, the primary informant against himself."

Fisher had been read by some lower courts as suggesting that possession and existence should be presumed to be a foregone conclusion whenever the material subpoenaed consisted of the type of records commonly used in business transactions (in *Fisher*, workpapers were so characterized as to the preparation of tax returns). *Doe I* seemingly rejected this reading, as the records there were typical business records and the government nonetheless had failed to "produce [the] evidence" necessary to meet the foregone conclusion standard. However, *Doe I* might also be viewed as an unusual case in which some additional showing was needed because it was not obvious that the subpoenaed party had any relationship to the businesses involved. More likely, however, its reasoning followed from a line of lower court cases holding that, even when the subpoenaed records are of a type commonly kept by businesses, the government does not establish existence and possession as a foregone conclusion unless it can establish the existence of these particular records, not just the general class of records. *Fisher* also was consistent with this approach, since the government there had additional evidence of the existence and possession of the workpapers. The subpoenaed attorneys, in supporting their clients' Fifth Amendment privilege via the attorney-client privilege, had to establish that they had received the particular records in question from their clients.

Subsequent to *Doe I*, lower court rulings generally insisted that the foregone conclusion standard be met by the government "demonstrat[ing] with reasonable particularity that it knows of the existence and location of subpoenaed documents." Those rulings recognized, however, that there are a variety of ways in which such a demonstration may be made. These include: some prior action by the subpoenaed party acknowledging that the particular documents existed and were in his possession; identification of some person (as in the case of the accountants in *Fisher*) who can testify that the particular documents were previously in the possession of the subpoenaed party; documents or similar evidence in the government's possession which would indicate that the subpoenaed documents exist and are in the subpoenaed person's possession; and the fact that the documents are of a type regularly sent to the subpoenaed person by a particular entity in the course of business, combined with the absence of any dispute as to whether the documents were received. Similarly, as to authentication, courts held that the foregone conclusion standard is met where the government can point to another person (e.g., the preparer of the document) who can authenticate, or where authentication can be achieved by other means (e.g., comparison with other documents independently authenticated or matching the handwriting with that of the subpoenaed party).

In its latest consideration of the act-of-production doctrine, *United States v. Hubbell*,[13] the Supreme spoke briefly to the foregone conclusion doctrine, suggesting an analysis similar to that applied in the post-*Doe I* lower court rulings. At issue in *Hubbell* was a government claim that its evidence was not barred by a grant of act-of-production immunity. As discussed in § 20.3(B), the Court found that the immunized act of production in *Hubbell* contained various testimonial disclosures which assisted the government in locating its evidence. In reaching this conclusion, the Court also rejected the government's contention that the "communicative aspect of respondent's act of producing ordinary business records is insufficiently 'testimonial' . . . because the existence and possession of such records by any businessman is a 'foregone conclusion.'" It reasoned:

> Whatever the scope of this "foregone conclusion" rationale, the facts of this case plainly fall outside of it. While in *Fisher* the Government already knew that the documents were in the attorneys' possession and could independently confirm their existence and authenticity through the accountants who created them, here the Government has not shown that it had any prior knowledge of either the existence or the whereabouts of the 13,120 pages of documents ultimately produced by respondent. The Government cannot cure this deficiency through the overboard argument that a businessman such as respondent will always possess general business and tax records that fall within the broad categories described in this subpoena. The *Doe* [I] subpoenas also sought several broad categories of general business records, yet we upheld the District Court's finding that the act of producing those records would involve testimonial self-incrimination.

The *Hubbell* ruling supports the broad reading of *Doe I* adopted by the lower courts. The *Hubbell* Court turned to *Doe I* in rejecting the contention that a foregone conclusion exists simply because the records involved were of a type commonly used in business. It did not describe *Doe I* as involving a special situation because the government had failed to tie respondent Doe to the particular business involved. Neither did the Court draw such a distinction in discussing the failure to meet the foregone conclusion standard in the case before it. Several of the categories of subpoenaed documents concerned activities with which the defendant's connection was yet to be established, but others involved his known activities, such as his travel and telephone calls. Yet, that knowledge did not establish the presence of the records as a foregone conclusion without a government showing that went beyond the common practice of businessmen to keep such records.

Hubbell did not announce a standard as to what additional showing would be needed to establish the existence and possession of such records as a foregone conclusion. The lower court in *Hubbell* had applied the "reasonable particularity"

---

[13] 530 U.S. 27 (2000), also discussed at note 16 infra.

standard developed in the aftermath of *Doe I*. Post-*Hubbell* lower court rulings have continued to apply this standard. The government must point to its prior knowledge that a group of documents described with "reasonable particularity" exist and were in the possession of the subpoenaed party.

The reasonable particularity standard does not require that the foregone conclusion proof go to each document the government seeks. It is sufficient that the independent source establish the existence and possession of a set of documents readily distinguishable by one or more key features (e.g., location, function, or authorship).[14] Support for prior knowledge as to a general grouping of documents is found in *Hubbell's* description of the foregone conclusion showing held acceptable in *Fisher*. There, the *Hubbell* opinion noted, the IRS summonses had sought "production of working papers prepared by the taxpayers' accountants that the IRS knew were in the possession of the taxpayers' attorneys," and the IRS "could independently confirm their existence and authenticity through the accountants who created them." The *Hubbell* opinion thus described the government's prior knowledge in *Fisher* as relating to the working papers as a group, not as relating to specific documents within that grouping. The "working papers" grouping apparently was sufficiently identified by reference to function, timing (identified by tax year), source (the accountants) and current location (being held by the attorneys).

The *Hubbell* opinion discussed *Fisher* only in the course of pointing to factors that clearly distinguished the situation in *Fisher* from that in *Hubbell*. In *Hubbell*, the "Government had not shown that it had any prior knowledge of either the existence or the whereabouts of 13,120 pages of documents ultimately produced by the respondent." Also, in contrast to *Fisher*, where the documents were readily identified and, indeed, had already been assembled in the course of their transfer to the attorneys, the *Hubbell* subpoena used descriptions requiring "respondent to make extensive use of 'the contents of his own mind' in identifying the hundreds of documents responsive to the subpoena."

The pre-*Hubbell* and post-*Hubbell* lower court rulings relying on the foregone conclusion doctrine avoid the flaws cited in *Hubbell*. Those rulings, like *Fisher*, rely on case-specific sources referring to the existence of a particular group of documents and their possession by the party subpoenaed. So too, they tend to identify the documents in a manner that does not require the subpoenaed party in the course of assembling the documents to refer to his or her special knowledge of historical fact (i.e., the "contents of his own mind"), as opposed to identifying documents by reference to such

---

[14] In re Grand Jury Subpoena Duces Tecum Dated March 25, 2011, 670 F.3d 1335 (11th Cir. 2012), indicated that the "set" could be as broad as to encompass a computer file of undetermined size. The grand jury subpoena there required the target to produce "the unencrypted contents of the hard drives on his computer." The Eleventh Circuit initially concluded that the decryption and production would be testimonial since it would "require the use of the contents of the [target's] mind." See § 19.1 at note 13. Accordingly, the target's self-incrimination claim prevailed absent a showing under the foregone conclusion doctrine that would negate the testimonial aspects of production. That would not require that the government establish its knowledge of the contents of the encrypted files, but it would have to show with some "reasonable particularity that it seeks a certain file and is aware, based on other information, that the file exists on the target's computer." That had been done in other cases where the individual had confirmed that the file was in his computer or an agent had seen (but not fully examined) the file. Here, however, the government could not establish that the encrypted portion of the hard drives contained any files.

features as letterhead, signature, or location. On the other hand, few of those lower court rulings involved as strong a showing as to current existence and possession as did *Fisher* (where the lawyers had acknowledged both); but there is nothing in *Hubbell's* discussion of the foregone conclusion doctrine that mandates such a conclusive showing on the temporal components of existence and possession.

C. Potential Incrimination

To raise a successful self-incrimination claim based on the act of production doctrine, the subpoenaed party must establish not only that the communicative aspects of production rise to the level of testimony, but also that such testimony would meet the traditional standard of potential incrimination. Thus, in *Fisher*, after indicating that act of production there would not be testimonial, the Court went on to conclude that the Fifth Amendment claim failed in any event because there had been no showing that the communicative aspects of production posed a "realistic threat of incrimination to the taxpayer."

The *Fisher* Court examined separately the potential incrimination stemming from implicit authentication and implicit acknowledgment of existence and possession. As to authentication, it noted that production would not provide the government with evidence that could be used to authenticate the subpoenaed workpapers since production by the taxpayer would "express nothing more than the taxpayer's belief that the papers are those described in the subpoena" and the taxpayer could not thereby authenticate as he "did not prepare the papers and could not vouch for their accuracy." As to existence and possession, "surely it was not illegal to seek accounting help in connection with one's tax returns or for the accountant to prepare workpapers and deliver them to the taxpayer." Accordingly, "at this juncture," the Court noted, it was "quite unprepared to hold that either the fact of the existence of the papers or their possession by the taxpayer" posed a sufficient threat to raise a legitimate self-incrimination claim. In focusing upon the general character of the documents subpoenaed, rather than the possible incriminating content, the Court may have been suggesting that the content is irrelevant, or it may have been suggesting no more than that the taxpayer had the burden of suggesting a potential for incriminating content (which would, in turn, make possession potentially incriminatory).

In *Doe I,* the Court returned to the issue of incrimination in a footnote that appeared to reject a broad reading of the *Fisher* discussion. In that footnote, the *Doe I* Court responded to the government's contention that even if the act of production there were viewed as having sufficient "testimonial aspects," any incrimination would be "so trivial" that the Fifth Amendment would not be implicated. The Court agreed that the Fifth Amendment would only be implicated if the risk of incrimination were "substantial and real," not merely "trifling or imaginary." It rejected, however, the government's claim that the risk of incrimination here clearly did not meet that standard. Respondent Doe had never conceded that the records subpoenaed actually existed or were within his possession. As respondent also noted, "even if the government could obtain the documents from another source, by producing the documents, respondent would relieve the government of the need for authentication." The potential prosecution uses of respondent's production, the Court noted, "were sufficient to establish a valid claim of the privilege."

Doe I's comment on the incriminatory potential of production as authentication evidence put to rest any suggestion that *Fisher* be read as holding that the act of production can be used to assist the government (and thereby incriminate) only where the person identifying the document is its author. Although the Court did not comment on the fact, many of the records subpoenaed (which included billings, ledgers, telephone records, and paid bills) obviously had not been authored by respondent Doe. Read in light of *Doe I*, the distinguishing feature in *Fisher* may have been the obvious availability there of the accountants as the most likely source of authentication testimony (although the availability of that independent source of authentication would more appropriately seem to relate to establishing authentication as a foregone conclusion, rather than to establishing the absence of sufficient incriminatory potential in the possible use of the act of production in authentication).

Doe I's discussion of the incrimination element also made clear that the acknowledgment of the existence and possession of records legally possessed could have a sufficient incriminatory potential to give rise to a "valid claim of the privilege." The records described in the *Doe I* subpoena were as innocuous on their face as the accountant's workpapers subpoenaed in *Fisher*. The potential for incrimination existed in tying the subpoenaed party to the contents of those records through his acknowledgment that he was aware of their existence and possessed them—factors that were significant to the government's case as the respondent had never conceded that the records existed or were in his control. What distinguished this case from *Fisher*, the *Doe I* Court noted, was the finding of the District Court, affirmed by the Court of Appeals, that the potential for incrimination through the testimonial aspects of production was "substantial and real." The Court stated that this conclusion was based on a "determination of factual issues" which it would not revisit, but its description of the lower court proceeding suggested at least a few of the factors that contributed to the lower court's determination. The subpoena was issued by a grand jury investigating corruption in the awarding of government contracts; the government had "conceded [before the District Court] that the materials sought in the subpoena were or might be incriminating"; and the government was seeking through the act of production to establish a connection between Doe and several businesses under investigation (a link it apparently otherwise could not establish).

Doe I's analysis seemed to indicate that *Fisher* should not be viewed as excluding from consideration the possible incriminatory content of the records in question. Rather, it should be read as a case in which that potential was not before the Court, since the taxpayer had raised no more than a blanket claim of the privilege as it related to the records as a whole. In stating that it was unprepared "at this juncture" to find a realistic threat of incrimination, the Court was leaving the door open for the taxpayer to make a more particularized showing of possible incrimination (as was done in *Doe I*). Thus, a valid self-incrimination claim arguably could have been presented in *Fisher* if the taxpayer had pointed to particular records that posed a real and appreciable threat of containing incriminatory information and had indicated that the government was seeking to link the taxpayer to those potentially incriminatory records through his act of production.

The Supreme Court's latest discussion of the act-of-production doctrine, in *United States v. Hubbell*, appears to confirm the implications of *Doe I*. Although *Hubbell* was concerned primarily with consequences of immunity, it did consider whether the subpoena there had been subject to a valid self-incrimination objection. That question, however, was viewed as raising the single question of whether the foregone conclusion doctrine was applicable. Having found that it did not apply, and the act of production therefore was testimonial in acknowledging existence and possession and identifying the documents sought, the Court characterized that testimonial act as clearly incriminatory. It noted in this regard that "testimony inherent in the act of producing these documents" had led the government to the documents and the documents in turn had produced the evidence that the government was now using in a criminal case. Through the act of production, the government had elicited "information about the existence of sources of potentially incriminating evidence" and that clearly was incriminatory. The Court did not explain why the documents identified in the subpoena were viewed as "sources of potentially incriminating evidence" (in contrast to the working papers in *Fisher*), perhaps because they had in fact proven to be just that. Undoubtedly this characterization depended upon the content of the documents, as it was that content which led to the derivative evidence the government intended to use at trial. *Hubbell* noted that whether the privilege protects the information as to "existence, custody, and authenticity" which is provided by the act of production "is a question distinct from the question whether the unprotected contents of the documents are incriminating." However, once it determined that the information provided was "testimonial" for Fifth Amendment purposes, the Court apparently did turn to the "unprotected contents of the document" in determining whether that information posed a sufficient likelihood of incrimination. If there was any doubt after *Doe I* that potential content could be considered for this purpose, it was put to rest by *Hubbell*.

Lower court cases, analyzing the self-incrimination issue in light of the Supreme Court's rulings, have rejected "blanket claims" of self-incrimination based on the testimonial aspects of the act of production. Where the documents to be produced are innocuous on their face, the witness has been asked to make a "contextual" showing indicating how the linkage to the documents established by the act of production (or further evidence derived from that linkage) "would, in any sense, create a hazard of prosecution against him or a link in a chain of evidence establishing guilt." The lower courts have allowed that showing to be made *in camera*, have permitted the showing to be made by reference to different categories of documents (rather than as to production of each individual document), and have noted that the "showing will be sufficient if the court can 'by the use of reasonable inference or judicial imagination, conceive a sound basis for a reasonable fear of prosecution.'" Nonetheless, the witness seeking to claim the privilege against a subpoena to produce documents would appear, as a practical matter, to carry a greater burden in establishing potential incrimination than the witness claiming the privilege in the course of testifying. Compare § 19.2(C).

§ 20.3 ACT–OF–PRODUCTION IMMUNITY

A. Limiting Immunity to Document Production

United States v. Doe (Doe I)[15] also considered the possibility that the government could obtain and make use of documents, even where the self-incrimination privilege

---

[15] 465 U.S. 605 (1984), also discussed at notes 8 and 11 supra.

applied to the act of production, by granting act-of-production immunity. The government there maintained that, accepting arguendo the lower court's finding of testimonial self-incrimination, the subpoena nevertheless should have been enforced by the district court, with that court granting respondent immunity as to the act of production. The government contended that it had, in effect, requested such an order, since it "stated several times before the district court that it would not use the respondent's act of production against him in any way." Responding to this position, the Supreme Court conceded that the government "could have compelled respondent to produce the documents" by utilizing the federal immunity statute providing for use/derivative-use immunity. Moreover, that immunity need not have covered the contents of the documents, but could have been limited to the act of production since "immunity need be only as broad as the privilege against self-incrimination." However, the government here had not used the immunity statute. Instead, it was asking the Court to adopt a doctrine of "constructive use immunity," whereby the federal courts could bypass the immunity statute and simply direct the government not to make use of the incriminatory aspects of production. This the federal courts could not do, since the decision to grant immunity involved a delicate balancing of interests that Congress had expressly delegated to appropriate Justice Department officials rather than the judiciary.

B. Derivative Use

The critical aspect of the *Doe I* ruling was the Court's acknowledgment that the necessary immunity need go only to the act of production itself, and not to the contents of the subpoenaed records. That such limited immunity was acceptable clearly followed from the mainspring of *Fisher*'s reassessment of the "*Boyd* rule." A significant question remained, however, as to what uses of the records and their content would be treated as derived from the information conveyed by the act of production.

Concurring in *Fisher*, Justice Marshall suggested that production immunity commonly would "effectively shield" the contents of the documents, as the contents would be a "direct fruit" of the "immunized testimony" contained in the act of production. Justice Marshall's assumption was that the testimonial component of the act of production would usually include an implicit admission of existence and possession, and the document itself would be the fruit of those admissions. The situation would be different, however, where the act of production was testimonial only because of its implicit authentication of the document (i.e., where existence and possession were foregone conclusions, but authentication was not a foregone conclusion). Here, the immunity would not bar use of the document, as its existence would be independently established. The government would be precluded from using the act of production to authenticate, but if it found through the document's contents another means of authenticating (e.g., a reference to a third person who could authenticate or a handwritten entry that could be matched against the producer's handwriting sample), then it could use the document.

In contrast to Justice Marshall, the Department of Justice viewed act-of-production immunity as having no bearing on the use of the contents, irrespective of the range of the testimonial components in the particular act-of-production. Its position, quite simply, was that the contents of the record are not privileged, and that immunity therefore is fully satisfied if the government is prohibited from in any way (investigative or evidentiary) looking to the act of production itself. The subpoenaed documents must be treated as if they "magically appear[ed] before the grand jury" from an unknown source. At this point, it was argued, the documents speak for themselves in establishing their existence. The government can use them and their contents, provided that use is not guided by the knowledge that they were produced by a particular person. If the contents of the documents (or the contents combined with information possessed prior to production) lead to a means of authentication, the documents can be used in evidence against the producer even if their existence had been uncertain prior to the immunized production. So too, the government could use the contents to establish that the documents were possessed by that person even if that too was not a foregone conclusion prior to immunized production. Thus, depending upon what is revealed by the contents (combined with the information previously known), the government would be able to use the documents as evidence against the producer in much the same fashion as where the documents were produced by a third party.

Such a narrow view of act-of-production immunity was rejected by the Supreme Court in *United States v. Hubbell*.[16] The government there had granted the respondent act-of-production immunity for compliance with a subpoena calling for eleven categories of documents (totaling 13,120 pages), but it contended that this immunity grant did not impact its subsequent prosecution of the respondent. It was not using the documents produced by the respondent, but other evidence discovered through an examination of the contents of the produced documents, and there would be no need to "advert to respondent's act of production in order to prove the existence, authenticity, or custody of any documents that it might offer in evidence." The Court found this showing insufficient because the government could not also show that it had not made "derivative use" of the "testimonial aspect[s]" of the respondent's act of production "in obtaining the indictment against respondent and in preparing its case for trial."

It was "apparent from the text of the subpoena itself," the Court noted, "that the prosecutor needed respondent's assistance both to identify potential sources of information and to produce those sources." That assistance had come from elements of the act of production that were clearly testimonial, as it was "unquestionably necessary for respondent to make extensive use of 'the contents of his own mind' in identifying the hundreds of documents responsive to the subpoena." "Given the breadth of description of the 11 categories of documents called for by the subpoena, the collection and production of the materials demanded was tantamount to answering a series of interrogatories asking a witness to disclose the existence and location of particular documents." If such interrogatory answers were compelled under a grant of immunity, the government could not utilize evidence derived therefrom and the consequence was no different when the information as to "existence and location" was provided by the testimonial aspects of production. It had been argued, the Court noted, that the government should be able to utilize the produced documents as if they "magically appear[ed] in the prosecutor's office, like 'manna from heaven'." However, in fact, those documents "arrived there only after respondent asserted his constitutional privilege,

---

[16] 530 U.S. 27 (2000), also discussed at note 13 supra.

received a grant of immunity, and . . . took the mental and physical steps necessary to provide the prosecutor with an accurate inventory of the many sources of potentially incriminating evidence sought by the subpoena."

The *Hubbell* case presented certain special circumstances that conceivably could be utilized in limiting its scope. The subpoena, as the Court emphasized, was broadly stated, calling for the respondent to make critical distinctions among documents and to convey through the act of production information as to the use of the documents produced and their relationship to particular transactions. The Court also noted that the record made obvious the role of that particular information in providing the "first step in the chain of evidence that led to the prosecution"; after the act of production conveyed that information, the grand jury investigation moved in a new direction that led to an indictment in a different judicial district for an offense unrelated to that originally investigated.

On the other hand, the *Hubbell* opinion also contains language indicating that neither of the above factors is essential to clothing with immunity documents produced under act-of-production immunity. Thus, the Court described the critical link between the act-of-production and the government's evidence as follows: "It was only through respondent's truthful reply to the subpoena that the Government received the incriminating documents of which it made 'substantial use . . . in the investigation'." A critical component of that truthful reply in producing the documents was the testimonial acknowledgment that the documents did exist. That acknowledgment, under the Court's rationale, leads to the government receiving the document, which in turns leads to the evidence derived from the contents of the documents. Thus, except for the situation in which existence is a foregone conclusion, and therefore not protected by the privilege, the act-of-production immunity should encompass the testimonial component of acknowledging existence and thereby make the document itself derivative evidence. As lower courts have noted, this may be true even where, in contrast to *Hubbell*, the subpoena is "narrow and specific."

Arguably the same result follows even where the existence of the document may be established as a foregone conclusion, if the government's prior knowledge does not similarly establish as a foregone conclusion possession by the subpoenaed party. The Court in *Hubbell* stated at several points that the act of production had provided testimony as to both "existence" and "whereabouts" (or existence and "location"), and certainly truthtelling as to location in respondent's files was as critical to respondent producing the documents as truthtelling as to existence. Thus, *Hubbell* would appear to have attached to act-of-production immunity the consequence that Justice Marshall predicted—prohibiting the government from making use of the contents of the produced document except in the limited situation where immunity was granted only because the prior knowledge that otherwise established a foregone conclusion could not be extended to the element of authentication.

§ 20.4   THE ENTITY EXCEPTION

A.   Grounding

Hale v. Henkel[17] not only reconstructed *Boyd*'s Fourth Amendment analysis, but also added a major exception to its Fifth Amendment rationale. *Hale* held that the self-incrimination privilege was not available to a corporation and therefore *Boyd* did not bar a grand jury subpoena duces tecum requiring production of corporate records. The Court's refusal to allow a corporation to utilize the privilege rested basically on two grounds. First, the self-incrimination privilege is designed in large part to protect interests unique to the individual. Thus, in a later case, the privilege was described as designed to prevent "inhumane" methods of compulsion, to ensure "respect for the inviolability of the human personality," and to maintain the "right of each individual to a private enclave where he may lead a private life." A corporation, as a fictional entity, needs no such protection.

Second, *Hale* spoke of the state's greater regulatory power over corporations, which were merely "creature[s] of the state." The individual, it noted, "owes no duty to the State . . . to divulge his business, or to open his doors to an investigation, so far as it may tend to incriminate him." The corporation, in contrast, "is a creature of the State," and exercises it franchise subject to the "reserved right" of the State to compel its assistance in ensuring that it has not "exceeded its powers." Although here a federal grand jury was investigating activities of a corporation created under state law, the federal government has the same right to ascertain that a corporation complied with its laws as the State would have with respect to the corporation's abuse of the privileges granted to it under state law.

The Court in *Hale* took special note of the enforcement needs of the government in compelling the production of corporate records; if such production were precluded by a self-incrimination claim, "it would result in a failure of a large number of cases where the illegal combination was determinable only upon such papers." In light of this concern, it was not surprising that, in *Wilson v. United States*,[18] the Court rejected the claim of a corporate officer possessing subpoenaed corporate records that he could refuse to produce those records because they would personally incriminate him. The State's "reserved power of visitation," the Court noted, "would seriously be embarrassed, if not wholly defeated in its effective exercise, if guilty officers could refuse inspection of the records and papers of the corporation." As the records were those of the corporation, not personal records, and were held "subject to the corporate duty," the official could "assert no personal right . . . against any demand of the government which the corporation was bound to recognize." The subpoena in *Wilson* was directed to the corporation, but the Court later held that the result was the same where the subpoena was directed to a specific individual in his capacity as corporate custodian.

---

[17] 201 U.S. 43 (1906), also discussed in § 16.11 at note 139.

[18] 221 U.S. 394 (1911).

In *United States v. White*,[19] the Court concluded that the grounding advanced in *Hale* logically extended beyond corporations. *White* held that the president of an unincorporated labor union could not invoke his personal privilege to a subpoena demanding union records. Characterizing *Hale's* reliance on the State's visitorial power as "merely a convenient vehicle for justification of governmental investigation of corporate books and records," the *White* Court concluded that the exception recognized in *Hale* was derived primarily from the inappropriateness of affording the privilege to an impersonal collective entity, whether or not that entity took the corporate form. The privilege against self-incrimination, the Court noted, "was essentially a personal [privilege], applying only to natural individuals," as evidenced by its history. The privilege was "designed to prevent the use of legal process to force from the lips of the accused the evidence necessary to convict him or force him to produce and authenticate any personal documents that might incriminate him," and "thereby avoided . . . physical torture and other less violent but equally reprehensible modes of compelling the production of incriminating evidence." These concerns did not apply to the entity, which lacked the qualities of human personality and therefore could not suffer the "immediate and potential evils of compulsory self-disclosure."[20]

B. Range of Entities

The *White* opinion characterized the labor union as an organization with "a character so impersonal in the scope of its membership and activities that it cannot be said to embody or represent the purely private or personal interests of its constituents, but rather to embody their common or group interests only." In *Bellis v. United States*,[21] however, the Court concluded that the entity exception remained applicable even though the entity embodied personal as well as group interests. The functional key was that the organization "be recognized as an independent entity apart from its individual members." Thus, a small law firm, organized as a partnership, was an entity for this purpose even though it "embodie[d] little more than the personal legal practice of the individual partners." The partnership was not an "informal association or a temporary arrangement for the undertaking of a few projects of short-lived duration," but a "formal institutional arrangement organized for the continuing conduct of the firm's legal practice." State law, through the Uniform Partnership Act, imposed a "certain organizational structure"; the firm maintained a bank account in the partnership name; it had employees who worked for the firm as such; and, the firm "held itself out to third parties as an entity with an independent institutional identity."

---

[19] 322 U.S. 694 (1944).

[20] Although discounting the significance of the state's visitorial power as to corporations, *White* stressed, as had *Hale* and *Wilson*, the state's need to "regulate effectively" the economic activities of both "unincorporated and incorporated organizations." In a statement that played a significant role in later discussions of the entity exception (see e.g., note 23 infra), the Court noted: "The greater portion of evidence of wrongdoing by an organization or its representatives is usually to be found in the official records documents of that organization. Were the cloak of the privilege to be thrown around these impersonal records and documents, effective enforcement of many federal and state laws would be impossible. The framers of the constitutional guarantee against compulsory self-disclosure, who were interested primarily in protecting individual civil liberties, cannot be said to have intended the privilege to be available to protect economic or other interests of such organizations so as to nullify appropriate governmental regulations."

[21] 417 U.S. 85 (1974).

Bellis left open the possibility that a "small family partnership" might be treated differently, as might a temporary arrangement for undertaking a short-lived project, or an association based on some "pre-existing relationship of confidentiality among the partners." Lower courts view any such exceptions as quite narrow. Indeed, even when there is no formal partnership, a structured organization operating as a joint entity will be held to fall within the entity exception. Also, a corporation, even a one-person corporation or a closely held family corporation, will be viewed as an entity no matter how closely it would otherwise resemble the possible "small-family-partnership" exception noted in *Bellis*. The same is true of a statutory structure that provides limited liability (e.g., an LLP) even if it reflects a single person operation. On the other hand, a person operating a business as a sole proprietor can rely on the privilege, as in the case of *Doe I* and *Hubbell*. The state's regulatory interests, stressed in part in the Court's explanation of the grounding for the entity exception, may be no less significant here than as to an entity operating the same business, but the sole proprietor remains a natural person rather than an artificial person.

C. Claims by Entity Agents

In many instances, the person subpoenaed to produce entity records may himself be incriminated by what is to be found in those records. Prior to the adoption of the act-of-production doctrine, the Court, in *Wilson* and its progeny, had firmly established that an entity agent may not rely upon his personal privilege to refuse to produce the entity's records. The individual who holds the entity records (whether or not a formally designated custodian) does so in a representative rather than individual capacity. By voluntarily accepting the custodianship of the records, he assumed the entity's responsibility for making the records available to a government agency (including a grand jury) entitled to see them. If the rule were otherwise, the Court noted, the entity exception would be meaningless.

In *Braswell v. United States*,[22] the petitioner, a corporate president and sole shareholder who had been subpoenaed to produce various corporate records, argued that the act-of-production doctrine provided a new grounding for recognizing a corporate custodian's exercise of the privilege, distinguishing the Court's earlier rulings. A closely divided Supreme Court rejected that contention and reaffirmed the unavailability of the privilege to a custodian of entity records. The *Braswell* majority concluded that the earlier rulings had not ignored the testimonial aspects of the act of production, but rather had considered any testimonial elements of that act to be properly attributed to the entity rather than to the agent acting on its behalf. *Fisher* itself had accepted this distinction in the course of analyzing the act-of-production rationale. Thus, the *Braswell* majority noted, "whether one concludes—as did the Court [in *Fisher*]—that a custodian's production of corporate records is deemed not to constitute [personal] testimonial self-incrimination, or instead that a custodian waives the right to exercise the privilege, the lesson of *Fisher* is clear: A custodian may not resist a subpoena for corporate records on Fifth Amendment grounds." To rule otherwise, as the Court had noted in its earlier rulings, would "substantially undermine the unchallenged rule that the organization itself is not entitled to claim

---

[22] 487 U.S. 99 (1988).

any Fifth Amendment privilege, and largely frustrate legitimate government regulation of such organizations."[23]

Braswell, however, added an evidentiary limitation not mentioned in the earlier cases that had rejected self-incrimination claims by entity agents. Since the agent's act of production is an act of the entity and not the individual, the government "may make no evidentiary use of the 'individual act' against the individual." Illustrating this point, the Court noted that "in a criminal prosecution against the custodian, the Government may not introduce into evidence before the jury the fact that the subpoena was served upon and the corporation's documents were delivered by one particular individual, the custodian." The government would be limited to showing that the entity had produced the document and to using that act of the entity in establishing that the records were authentic entity records that the entity had possessed and had produced. Admittedly, if the defendant's position in the entity were such that it could be assumed that he had possession or knowledge of the documents, the jury might make that assumption; it would not be doing so, however, because of defendant's act of production but would be relying on reasonable inferences applicable without regard to who produced the documents.

In its discussion of the limited use the government might make of the act of production in a subsequent prosecution of the custodian, the Court, in a footnote, added what could be a very important caveat: it was "leav[ing] open the question [of] whether the agency rationale supports compelling a custodian to produce corporate records when the custodian is able to establish, by showing for example that he is the sole employee and officer of the corporation, that the jury would inevitably conclude that he produced the records." The petitioner in *Braswell* might himself have fit that description, but no showing directed at the inevitability of such a jury conclusion was made there.

Lower courts addressing the issue left open in *Braswell* have offered two responses, neither favorable to the custodian. One response is that an inevitable adverse jury conclusion is readily avoided. Initially, the government need not explain how it obtained the documents as long as it can independently authenticate, without reference to the act of production. Second, even if it is necessary to inform the jury that the documents were obtained by subpoena directed to the entity, that will lead only to a "strong inference," not an "automatic conclusion," that the sole corporate participant was the person who responded. The jurors "might infer that the corporation engaged a third party to search its records and make the production on its behalf." Thus, the sole-participant/custodian is not entitled to any special protection.

---

[23] The majority further noted in this regard that "recognizing a Fifth Amendment privilege on behalf of record custodians of collective entities would have a detrimental impact on the Government's effort to prosecute 'white collar crime' . . . as the greater portion of evidence of wrongdoing by an organization or its representatives is usually found in the official records and documents of that organization." The majority rejected the dissent's suggestion that the government could always grant the custodian use/derivative-use immunity. It characterized such immunity as substantially different from the prohibition against use it was imposing, and likely to constitute a serious impediment to subsequently proceeding against the custodian. It rejected as a "chimera" petitioner's solution that the subpoena be directed only to the corporation, which could then appoint an alternative custodian, as the petitioner also insisted that he could "not be required to aid the appointed custodian in his search for the demanded records."

Other courts acknowledge that a particular setting may lead a jury to "inevitably conclude" that the production was based on at least the knowledge of the sole-participant/custodian (e.g., in assisting the third party custodian in locating and categorizing the documents). These courts conclude, however, that the sole participant simply is stuck with that consequence, as it is a product of his free choice in deciding to operate in "the corporate form." *Braswell*, in leaving the issue "open," did not foreclose the conclusion that, in the end, the jury's inevitable conclusion should not matter. The government should not be subjected to restrictions beyond the use prohibition as to the act of production simply because the entity in the particular case has only a single participant.

Lower courts also have differed on an issue not mentioned in *Braswell*—whether the analysis there extends to the production of entity documents by a former entity employee who retained those documents. On the one side, courts reason that the documents remain the entity's documents and therefore the former employee cannot raise his personal privilege, even though he does not possess the documents as the entity's custodian. To conclude otherwise, it is noted, "create[s] a perverse incentive" for an employee to leave the entity with the documents that "he knows may contain evidence of his wrongdoing and then resist production . . . by asserting a claim of privilege" that could not be raised if the documents had been left with the entity. On the other side, *Braswell* is held not to apply because it is limited to persons who hold documents in their representative capacity, and the "former employee is no longer an agent" of the entity. The privilege is not lost simply because the former employee's removal and continued possession of the documents may be wrongful. The entity has a right to recover the documents if that is the case, and the government may then subpoena the documents from the entity (with the privilege unavailable). Also, "there is nothing that prevents the government from proceeding to recover the documents itself . . . by means of a search warrant."

D. Custodian's Duty to Testify

The custodian's responsibility to produce the subpoenaed records ordinarily will encompass a duty to testify for the limited purpose of identifying the material produced. In *Curcio v. United States*,[24] the Supreme Court distinguished such testimony from what was required there. In that case, defendant Curcio, a secretary-treasurer of a union, had informed the grand jury that he could not produce the subpoenaed records because they were not in his possession. Without challenging the truth of his statement, the prosecution sought to compel him to testify as to the whereabouts of the documents. Although Curcio exercised his privilege against self-incrimination at this point, the government argued that the custodial duty that required the production of the documents also carried with it a relinquishment of the privilege as to "auxiliary testimony" that would permit the government to locate the documents. The Supreme Court rejected that argument, noting that an entity agent did not "waive his constitutional privilege as to oral testimony by assuming the duties of his office."

---

[24] 354 U.S. 118 (1957).

The *Curcio* Court distinguished the Second Circuit's decision in *United States v. Austin–Bagley*[25] that had developed the auxiliary testimony concept, noting that it "need not pass on [*Austin–Bagley's*] validity." It then went on to strongly suggest the correctness of an auxiliary testimony obligation as to the authenticating testimony involved in *Austin–Bagley*. The Court noted:

> The custodian's act of producing books or records in response to a subpoena duces tecum is itself a representation that the documents produced are those demanded by the subpoena. Requiring the custodian to identify or authenticate the documents for admission in evidence merely makes explicit what is implicit in the production itself. The custodian is subjected to little, if any, further danger of incrimination.

This language has been read by lower courts to impose upon the custodian an obligation to provide basic authentication testimony—i.e., to testify as to "the location of the documents produced and that the produced records are those called for in the subpoena." The Sixth Circuit has extended that obligation to testimony as to how records were kept, thereby qualifying the records for admission under the business records exception to the hearsay rule, although such testimony seemingly goes substantially beyond what *Curcio* characterized as testimony "implicit in the act of production."[26]

Braswell v. United States[27] arguably adopts a narrow reading of what is permitted under *Curcio*. The Court there stated that, in *Curcio*, "the line drawn was between oral testimony and other forms of incrimination" [i.e., the act of "producing the books of which he is custodian."] The *Curcio* Court had not viewed the custodian's obligation as going beyond "produc[ing] corporate records and merely identify[ing] them in oral testimony." *Braswell's* description suggests that very detailed authentication testimony, as well as testimony beyond authentication, may not be compelled unless the government can successfully argue that the testimony does not add to the incrimination provided by the act of production. Very often, detailed additional testimony on matters such as the precise location of the documents readily may provide additional leads incriminating to the custodian. *Braswell* also indicates that whatever authentication testimony may be compelled, that testimony may not be admitted against the custodian should he later be prosecuted.

E. Distinguishing "Personal Records"

An employee subpoenaed to produce what are supposedly entity records can assert the privilege if those records are actually his personal documents. Thus, a substantial body of lower court opinions consider the question of whether, under the circumstances of the case, such documents as employee desk and pocket calendars are personal rather than corporate records. The burden is on the subpoenaed employee to show that the

---

[25] 31 F.2d 229 (2d Cir.1959).

[26] In re Custodian of Records of Variety Distributing, 927 F.2d 244 (6th Cir.1991). Compare In re Grand Jury Investigation of Possible Violation of 18 U.S.C. § 1461, 706 F.Supp.2d 11 (D.D.C. 2009) (self-incrimination privilege precludes compelling custodian to provide Rule 803(b) testimony, as that is not truly "auxiliary" to production).

[27] 487 U.S. 99 (1988), discussed at note 22 supra.

records are personal rather than entity records. In making that determination, courts commonly examine the documents *in camera* to determine their content. A multi-factored analysis is employed, with the court seeking to determine the "essential nature" of the document by looking at such criteria as: "who prepared the document; the nature of its contents; its purpose or use; who possessed it; who had access to it; whether the corporation required its preparation; and whether its existence was necessary to or in furtherance of corporate business." The clearest case of a personal document is a diary containing an individual's end-of-the-day reflections on social and business experiences, not used in conducting office affairs and not shared with others, though kept in the office.

§ 20.5   THIRD–PARTY PRODUCTION

Couch v. United States[28] and *Fisher v. United States*[29] both involved situations in which an individual had transferred records to an independent professional who was then served with an IRS summons requiring production of those records. In *Couch*, the sole proprietress of a restaurant had delivered various financial records to her accountant for the purpose of preparing her income tax returns. In *Fisher*, sole owners of separate businesses had delivered to their attorneys various workpapers that had been prepared by their accountants in the course of filing income tax returns. In both cases, the taxpayers relied upon *Boyd*, arguing that the government was seeking to obtain disclosure of papers of an even more confidential nature than the invoice subpoenaed in *Boyd*. The taxpayers acknowledged that the IRS summonses required their agents rather than the taxpayers themselves to produce the documents, but contended that factor was irrelevant since they had maintained a reasonable expectation of privacy in the documents even after delivered to the agents.

The Supreme Court rejected the taxpayers' position in both cases.[30] The Fifth Amendment applied only to personal compulsion and there was none here. Unlike the importers in *Boyd*, the taxpayers here were not themselves required "to do anything." The Court was not persuaded by the contention that its focus on personal compulsion was too formalistic to serve adequately the goals of the privilege. Responding in *Fisher*, it noted: "We cannot cut the Fifth Amendment completely loose from the moorings of its language and make it serve as a general protector of privacy—a word not mentioned in its text and a concept directly addressed in the Fourth Amendment." The Fifth Amendment, it continued, "protects against 'compelling testimony, not the disclosure of private information.'"

Both *Fisher* and *Couch* acknowledged that "situations might exist where constructive possession is so clear or the relinquishment of possession is so temporary and insignificant as to leave the personal compulsions upon the accused substantially intact." Lower courts have suggested, however, that where documents have been delivered to an independent third party, this "constructive-possession exception" will

---

[28] 409 U.S. 322 (1973).

[29] 425 U.S. 391 (1976), also discussed at note 6 supra.

[30] As discussed following note 7 supra, the attorney client privilege allowed the attorneys to resist the subpoena if it could be established that the clients could have resisted their own production under the self-incrimination clause.

be available only if the third party received the records strictly for custodial safekeeping and the owner retained ready access to the records. Constructive possession is more likely to be found where a sole proprietor seeks to raise the privilege in response to a subpoena directing an employee to produce company records kept by that employee. Even here, however, a constructive possession argument may be denied, and the employer barred from raising the privilege, where, for example, the employer was an absentee proprietor who had delegated exclusive responsibility for the records to the subpoenaed employee. Indeed, the argument has been rejected even where the employer shared the offices in which the records were kept, and directly supervised the employee who kept the records, but delegated to the employee considerable control over the preparation and distribution of the records.

§ 20.6   THE REQUIRED RECORDS EXCEPTION

Building upon dictum in certain entity cases, to the effect that the privilege did not extend to corporate records because they were required by law to be kept for the public benefit, *Shapiro v. United States*[31] held that the same principle could apply to the records of individuals engaged in regulated businesses. *Shapiro* upheld against a self-incrimination objection a subpoena directing production of records of commodity sales that the petitioner, a wholesale fresh produce dealer, was required to keep, and to make available for inspection by federal regulators, under the wartime Emergency Price Control Act. The Court acknowledged that "there are limits which the Government cannot constitutionally exceed in requiring the keeping of records which may be inspected by an administrative agency and may be used in prosecuting statutory violations committed by the record-keeper himself," but it concluded that there was no need in that case to define precisely where those limits might lie. For, the Court noted, "no serious misgivings that those bounds were overstepped would appear to be evoked where there is a sufficient relation between the activity sought to be regulated and the public concern so that the Government can constitutionally regulate or forbid the basic activity concerned." This broad description of the acceptable nexus between the records and regulating authority offered the possibility of a far reaching required records doctrine. Justice Frankfurter, dissenting in *Shapiro*, argued that the Court was stating that "all records which Congress may require individuals to keep in the conduct of their affairs, because they fall within some regulatory power of Government, become 'public records' and thereby, ipso facto, fall outside the protection of the Fifth Amendment." However, in the 1968 companion cases of *Marchetti v. United States*[32] and *Grosso v. United States*,[33] the Court made clear that the required records doctrine could not be carried to that extreme.

Unlike *Shapiro*, *Marchetti* and *Grosso* did not present a government attempt to force production of existing records, but prosecutions for failure to comply with statutory schemes that included a reporting requirement. In both cases, self-incrimination challenges were presented to federal wagering tax statutes that required gamblers to identify themselves by registering with the government and by paying an occupational tax. Initially, the Court concluded that, in light of the comprehensive

---

[31] 335 U.S. 1 (1948).
[32] 390 U.S. 39 (1968).
[33] 390 U.S. 62 (1968).

system of federal and state prohibitions against wagering activities, the required disclosure presented a "real and appreciable" hazard of self-incrimination. It then rejected the contention, suggested in earlier cases, that since the defendant had no constitutional right to gamble, the individual intending to engage in the wagering business could not complain because the government insists that he first inform it of his intended activities. Utilizing such a forced waiver or "antecedent choice" analysis, the Court noted, could abrogate the privilege's protection in numerous situations where it had historically been recognized. The privilege was designed to shelter "the guilty and imprudent as well as the innocent," and a state could not avoid its application by simply requiring that the potential criminal identify himself in advance. This left the government with the contention that the disclosure requirements were nonetheless constitutional because they fit within the rationale of the required records doctrine. The Court found that contention totally unpersuasive.

In rejecting the government's required records contention, the Court noted that it was unnecessary here to "pursue in detail the question left open in *Shapiro* of what limits the Government cannot constitutionally exceed in requiring the keeping of records." It was "enough that there [were] significant points of difference between the situations here and in *Shapiro*." There were "three principle elements" of the required records doctrine, as it was "described in *Shapiro*," and all three elements were missing in *Marchetti*, while at least two were missing in *Grosso*. As described in *Grosso*, those three elements, which furnished the "premises of the [required records] doctrine," were: "[F]irst, the purpose of the United States' inquiry must be essentially regulatory; second, information is to be obtained by requiring the preservation of records of a kind which the regulated party has customarily kept; and third, the records themselves must have assumed 'public aspects' which render them at least analogous to public documents."

With respect to the first of these elements, both the "characteristics of the activities about which information is sought" and the "composition of the groups to which inquiries are made" readily distinguished the wagering tax system at issue in *Marchetti* and *Grosso* from the price control regulations at issue in *Shapiro*. The wagering tax provisions were not dealing with "an essentially non-criminal and regulatory area," and their disclosure requirements were directed to a "selective group inherently suspect of criminal activities." As for the second requirement, at least in the *Marchetti* case, the contested disclosure requirements were not based on information contained in records that the person otherwise would have kept in the course of his occupation.

The Court also thought it obvious that the third element of the required records doctrine—that the records have assumed "public aspects" analogous to public records had no bearing in the cases before it. Indeed, a contrary conclusion could be reached only by gutting the distinguishing character of such documents. In concluding that the record in question in *Shapiro* had "public aspects," the Court majority had noted that "the transaction which it recorded was one in which petitioner could lawfully engage solely by virtue of the license granted to him under the statute." An analogy had been drawn to state statutes requiring druggists to keep records of sales of intoxicating liquor. The *Shapiro* dissent had argued that even such qualities failed to make the records sufficiently analogous to public records. *Marchetti* concluded that "whatever public aspects there were to the records at issue in *Shapiro*, there are none to the information demanded [here]." The only basis for claiming that the information sought was public was the presence of a governmental demand "formalized . . . in the attire of a statute." If that were sufficient, "no room would remain for the application of the constitutional privilege."

Although decided in 1968, *Marchetti* and *Grosso* remain the Supreme Court's leading discussions of the required records doctrine. A later case, *California v. Byers*,[34] although not relying directly on the required records doctrine, did help to put that doctrine in perspective. In *Byers*, the Court upheld a "hit and run" statute which required a driver involved in an accident to stop at the scene and leave his name and address. The plurality noted that, in judging the constitutionality of regulatory schemes requiring disclosures that might conceivably lead to criminal prosecutions, the Court had to "balanc[e] the public need on the one hand, and the individual claim to constitutional protections on the other." That balancing approach presumably was at the core of the required records doctrine as well. Under such an approach, the critical factors in defining the limits of the required records doctrine, assuming a truly regulatory scheme, would be the significance of the government's regulatory interest, and the importance of the disclosure to making that interest effective. Such factors may readily be considered in determining whether the records can be characterized as having "public aspects." However, the importance of the second *Shapiro* element—that the records be of a type customarily kept—is problematic under such a balancing analysis. Arguably, the presence of that element may support the government's claim that its interest is truly regulatory, but there certainly may be instances, as suggested by *Byers*, in which a regulatory interest requires the keeping of records of activities that would not otherwise be recorded in the normal course of business. Of course, the starting assumption, as indicated in the first of the three elements, is *Shapiro's* requirement that government's interest truly be "regulatory," reflecting some interest other than facilitating the prosecution of crime.

Lower court rulings assessing the scope of the required records doctrine largely have been consistent with above analysis. A regulation that required automobile dealers to report altered serial numbers was held to extend beyond the limits of the doctrine; the regulation had no statutory purpose independent of a desire to "ferret out criminal activities." So too, check and deposit slips required by regulation to be kept as substantiation for a tax return were held not to have sufficient public aspects to constitute required records because the keeping of such records was not an ongoing condition of operating the taxpayer's business under a comprehensive regulatory scheme. On the other hand, found to be required records were records of a custom-house brokerage service kept pursuant to customs regulations, records relating to cattle purchases that licensed cattlemen were required to keep as part of a government program for controlling communicable diseases in domestic animals, and medical records as to patient treatment required for the purpose of reviewing professional competency. The thrust of these decisions is that a person who fears incrimination has no special exemption from record keeping duties imposed generally upon a regulated class that is not by its nature suspected of criminal activity. In some instances, the

---

[34] 402 U.S. 424 (1971).

regulations can go beyond a limited regulated class, as in the acceptance of the Bank Secrecy Act requirement that taxpayers keep and share with the IRS various basic account-holder information as to foreign bank accounts (similar to the information U.S. banks would provide to the IRS).

Chapter 21

SEARCHES

§ 21.1 INTRODUCTION

The use of search warrants in white collar crime investigations was almost completely unknown at one time. Grand jury subpoenas were the primary vehicle through which documents were obtained by compulsory process. As discussed in Chapter 20, the Fifth Amendment's act-of-production and collective entity doctrines were developed in the context of grand jury investigations and civil enforcement actions to deal with the right of subpoena recipients to resist a demand for records. Over the past two decades, however, prosecutors have used search warrants with increasing frequency to obtain business records from individuals and organizations under investigation, sometimes because of the danger that items may not be produced in response to a subpoena.

The Fourth Amendment provides for "[t]he right of the people to be secure in their persons, houses, papers, and effects, against unreasonable searches and seizures. . . . " In white collar cases, the inclusion of "papers" is of greatest importance because the items most often sought in a search will be the records maintained by a business or individual, which now includes both physical documents and electronic files. The Fourth Amendment also requires that "no warrants shall issue, but upon probable cause, supported by oath or affirmation, and particularly describing the place to be searched, and the persons or things to be seized."

While there are a number of well-developed exceptions to the Fourth Amendment's warrant requirement, such as those for automobiles and exigent circumstances, they are largely inapplicable to searches in white collar crime cases. Almost all searches in this area involve warrants, so the primary focus is on meeting the requirements for a valid warrant, and whether materials seized pursuant to it came within its scope or were in plain view during the search. Issues also arise related to administrative searches of businesses.

§ 21.2 ADVANTAGES AND DISADVANTAGES

During the investigative phase of a case, gathering documents to determine whether a crime was committed is paramount. Using a search warrant rather than a grand jury subpoena presents certain advantages and disadvantages for the government. These are not mutually exclusive options in an investigation, and in some cases both methods for obtaining records will be used. For example, the government may commence an investigation by issuing subpoenas and then obtain a search warrant if there is an indication that documents have been withheld. Similarly, after executing a warrant, the prosecutor can issue a grand jury subpoena requiring the production of records that might not have been at the location searched or that were created subsequently.

A threshold issue in deciding how to obtain records is whether a search warrant can be obtained, or whether only a grand jury subpoena can be issued. In order to issue a warrant, the government must establish probable cause that a crime has been committed and that evidence of the offense can be found at the place to be searched. If an investigator has only a suspicion that a violation occurred, or that documents might be found in a particular location, that would usually not be sufficient to obtain a search warrant without developing more information. A grand jury subpoena does not require probable cause for its issuance, so it is often a better vehicle for obtaining records when information about whether a crime occurred or the location or relevance of records is incomplete. Assuming there is sufficient information available to obtain a search warrant, then the issue is whether to pursue that option rather than issuing a grand jury subpoena (see § 16.5).

There are a number of benefits to using a search warrant to obtain records. Execution of a warrant carries the element of surprise because the party whose premises will be searched need not be given prior notice of its issuance. This can be particularly important when prosecutors fear evidence will be destroyed or sequestered in an inaccessible location if a grand jury subpoena is issued. The government agents executing a warrant determine which records to seize, unlike a subpoena that puts the burden on the recipient to identify responsive records. Agents may also be able to obtain a wider array of records with a warrant because they will see first hand what is available, including items that might indicate other potential violations that can be seized pursuant to the "plain view" doctrine, discussed below.

During the execution of the search warrant at a business, investigators often ask employees present if they would be willing to be interviewed. Valuable information about the operation of the business and location of important records can be obtained from them that might not otherwise be available. Upon completion, the government has immediate access to the records, unless there is a claim of privilege to prevent review of the records, and does not have to await compliance with the subpoena.

There is no Fifth Amendment privilege to resist the execution of a search warrant, while a subpoena recipient may be able to claim that the act of production will be personally incriminating as a means to avoid compliance. In *Andresen v. Maryland*,[1] the Supreme Court rejected a motion to suppress records seized pursuant to a warrant as a violation of the defendant's Fifth Amendment privilege because he "was not asked to say or to do anything. The records seized contained statements that petitioner had voluntarily committed to writing."

While not directly tied to the warrant, searching for records can send a message about the seriousness of the investigation and the government's willingness to commit greater resources than would be involved in simply issuing a grand jury subpoena. Because it is a more public act, which can draw significant media attention when a large company or high-profile individual is involved, the search can be a signal about the direction of a case and the potential for criminal charges to be filed. A grand jury subpoena, on the other hand, is a private document, subject to the secrecy requirement of Federal Rule of Criminal Procedure 6(e), and so there may be no publicity related to

---

[1] 427 U.S. 463 (1976).

it unless the recipient chooses to disclose it or there is an improper leak from a government official.

There are burdens to using a search warrant that prosecutors consider before undertaking this method of gathering evidence. While there is immediate access to records, it is likely that a large volume could be seized because the description in the warrant is likely to be broad. Moreover, the agents executing the search often will be as inclusive as possible in taking records, leaving it to the prosecutor to sort out what is relevant. Along the same lines, records could be overlooked or not be found at the location searched, something that may not be immediately apparent in the volume of material seized. If the records sought are not in the place where agents believed them to be, then a new warrant must be obtained if information can be gathered indicating their location. A search is limited to evidence of a crime, while a grand jury subpoena can be for a wider range of records, and can be used for other purposes, such as obtaining voice and handwriting exemplars.

Perhaps the greatest barrier to obtaining a search warrant is establishing probable cause that a violation has occurred and the records sought are related to it. The government must provide to a neutral and detached magistrate a detailed recitation of the information gathered in the investigation and the likely offenses involved in the case. This information is generally considered to be open to the public, although the court can order it sealed if necessary upon a showing of need. But even if the documents related to the search are sealed, the person or organization searched can challenge the seizure of records through a motion for the return of seized items under Federal Rule of Criminal Procedure 41(g) if no charges have been filed yet, a proceeding that will eventually reveal details about the investigation and its progress. Thus, a search warrant is much more likely to expose the scope of an investigation and the likely targets.

If a search warrant was improperly issued, or the agents executing it exceeded the authorization to seize records, a court can suppress the records from use at trial under the exclusionary rule if charges are filed. A challenge to a subpoena, on the other hand, is usually raised prior to the production of records through a motion to quash, so no evidence will be lost if a court finds the subpoena was unreasonable or oppressive, and prosecutors can reissue it to cure any problems.

Even if the Constitution does not prohibit the use of a search warrant, Congress can impose restrictions on their use. The Supreme Court recognized in *Zurcher v. Stanford Daily*[2] that a search warrant can be used to obtain documentary materials in the possession of a disinterested third party, a case involving a search of a college student newspaper's offices for materials that could identify protesters who clashed with the police. Congress enacted the Privacy Protection Act[3] in response to *Zurcher*. The Act provides protection for materials used for journalistic purposes unless there is probable cause the person is involved in illegal activity, and requires the Attorney General to issue guidelines for using search warrants to obtain materials from a third party not suspected of any involvement in criminal conduct. Subject to specified exceptions, rules adopted by the Department of Justice provide:

---

[2] 436 U.S. 547 (1978).

[3] 42 U.S.C. § 2000aa.

A search warrant should not be used to obtain documentary materials believed to be in the private possession of a disinterested third party unless it appears that the use of a subpoena, summons, request, or other less intrusive alternative means of obtaining the materials would substantially jeopardize the availability or usefulness of the materials sought. . . . [4]

Similarly, the Wiretap Act imposes heightened requirements beyond the Fourth Amendment's probable cause standard when the government wants to listen to and record conversations, which constitutes a search under the Supreme Court's decision in *Katz v. United States*.[5] The statute limits the types of offenses that can be investigated by intercepting wire, oral, or electronic communications, and further requires that the government establish that that normal investigative techniques have been tried and have failed, or that they reasonably appear to be unlikely to succeed if tried or would be too dangerous if undertaken.[6] The statute also provides for suppression of evidence from an unlawful interception of wire and oral communications but not electronic communications.

§ 21.3 THE WARRANT REQUIREMENT AND BUSINESS RECORDS

A. Generally

In federal investigations, Federal Rule of Criminal Procedure 41 provides that a magistrate judge, or if one is not available then a state court judge in the district, has the authority[7] to issue a warrant for any of the following:

(1) evidence of a crime;

(2) contraband, fruits of crime, or other items illegally possessed;

(3) property designed for use, intended for use, or used in committing a crime; or

(4) a person to be arrested or a person who is unlawfully restrained.

The government submits an affidavit or sworn testimony detailing the information it has gathered to establish probable cause to conclude that a criminal violation occurred and that the items to be seized are in the place described. The description for a search warrant must be made with sufficient particularity to avoid the issuance of a "general" warrant.

B. Probable Cause

The Supreme Court explained the meaning of the term "probable cause" in *Illinois v. Gates*[8] as "a fluid concept—turning on the assessment of probabilities in particular factual contexts—not readily, or even usefully, reduced to a neat set of legal rules." The

---

[4] 28 C.F.R. § 59.4(a)(1).

[5] 389 U.S. 347 (1967). See CRIMPROC § 4.3 for a detailed discussion of the procedures for a wiretap.

[6] 18 U.S.C. §§ 2510 et seq. See CRIMPROC § 4.6.

[7] Fed. R. Crim. P. 41(c).

[8] 462 U.S. 213 (1983).

decision whether to issue a search warrant is based on a "practical, common-sense" consideration of the information presented by the government to determine whether "there is a fair probability that contraband or evidence of a crime will be found in a particular place." The Court described this as a "flexible, easily applied standard" that is based on the totality of the circumstances. Thus, review of a warrant will depend on the particulars of the situation, and it is hard to draw broad conclusions from a particular case.

In establishing probable cause to believe a crime was committed, the time frame in which the violation occurred must be established, not just that at some point in the past there was criminal conduct. This is a more frequent issue in white collar investigations like fraud or tax evasion because it may not be clear when the violation occurred, unlike a crime of violence or illegal narcotics sales that often occur at a specific point in time. For example, in *United States v. Diaz*,[9] the First Circuit criticized prosecutors for not providing information to the magistrate about when a fraudulent scheme may have started in seeking authority to seize records before the first date on which an allegedly fraudulent transaction occurred. The circuit court stated:

> We find that the government should have advised the magistrate of its belief regarding the duration of the suspected scheme, and the basis for that belief. This would have allowed the magistrate to reach a reasoned decision as to the first date on which there is probable cause to believe that evidence of criminal acts was recorded in [the company]'s business records.

Nevertheless, the probable cause regarding a potential violation does not mean the search warrant should be limited to only those records related to illegal transactions alone. A district court noted that "courts have often found probable cause for the seizure of the records of 'innocent' transactions when those records made the fraudulence of other transactions clear."[10] For example, a warrant can seek all records created in a specified time frame to show what transactions were proper and which constituted a part of an illegal scheme, or to show the absence of records for particular transactions under investigation.

C. Particularity

The Fourth Amendment requirement that a warrant not be issued except for those "particularly describing the place to be searched, and the . . . things to be seized" requires the government to provide enough information to protect against "general, exploratory rummaging in a person's belongings."[11] This requirement addresses concerns about the vagueness of the description that limits what can be seized. Requiring sufficient particularity in the description ensures the authority to search is congruent with the probable cause, preventing the issuance of an overbroad warrant that would permit the seizure of items for which the government did not have adequate grounds to believe they were related to criminal conduct. In *Andresen v. Maryland*,[12]

---

[9] 841 F.2d 1 (1988).

[10] United States v. Cohan, 628 F.Supp.2d 355 (E.D.N.Y. 2009).

[11] Coolidge v. New Hampshire, 403 U.S. 443 (1971).

[12] 427 U.S. 463 (1976).

the Supreme Court said that the warrant must describe the place to be searched and items to be seized with enough detail to leave "nothing . . . to the discretion of the officer executing the warrant." But that statement cannot be read literally because the warrant need not go into so much detail that it precludes the exercise of an officer's reasonable judgment. Instead, the warrant must give the officer executing it sufficient guidance to identify the items that come within its scope. In addition, the affidavit can provide additional descriptive detail of the items to be seized by being incorporated into the warrant, giving the framework for a lawful search. In *Groh v. Ramirez*,[13] the Court stated:

> We do not say that the Fourth Amendment prohibits a warrant from cross-referencing other documents. Indeed, most Courts of Appeals have held that a court may construe a warrant with reference to a supporting application or affidavit if the warrant uses appropriate words of incorporation, and if the supporting document accompanies the warrant.

A warrant for business records will often contain very broad descriptions of the items to be seized, including both physical and electronic files along with a definition of what can constitute a record to include almost any means of recording and communicating information, such as notes, calendars, drafts, electronic messages, and the like. The government is generally not required to identify the particular information that is contained in the record that makes it subject to a search because many white collar crimes involve ordinary business transactions that are part of a course of conduct that may constitute a violation. Therefore, courts require identification in the warrant of the particular types of documents to be seized or the transactions at issue, such as sales of a specified item or wire transfers from certain locations or companies, along with the time period in which the violations allegedly took place.

The use of broad catchphrases in a warrant will not necessarily invalidate it. In *Andresen*, the Court held that including in a warrant for business records the phrase "together with other fruits, instrumentalities and evidence of crime at this (time) unknown" did not undermine its validity because the language must be read in context with the more particular description related to a specific offense described in it. The case involved a "complex real estate scheme whose existence could be proved only by piecing together many bits of evidence," and the Court explained that the complexity of the potential violation could "not be used as a shield to avoid detection when the State has demonstrated probable cause to believe that evidence of crimes is in the suspect's possession."

Courts have generally been less exacting in their review of warrants in white collar investigations because of the difficulty the government faces in giving more than broad outlines of the types of records to be seized when the case involves complex financial transactions over an extended period of time. As a district court once noted, "Few people keep documents of their criminal transactions in a folder marked 'crime records'."[14] In *United States v. Yusuf*,[15] the Third Circuit upheld a warrant that

---

[13] 540 U.S. 551 (2004).

[14] United States v. Triumph Capital Group, Inc., 211 F.R.D. 31 (D. Conn. 2002).

[15] 461 F.3d 374 (3d Cir. 2006).

included authorizing the seizure of evidence of money laundering and other violations over more than 10 years from a number of different corporations and "any affiliated companies as well as their principals, officers, managers, and employees." The circuit court pointed out that "[g]iven the nature of the crime and the limitation on the items to be searched, the warrant here was drafted with sufficient particularity." Despite the apparent breadth of the description of the items subject to seizure, the Third Circuit noted that "[w]e have repeatedly stated that the government is to be given more flexibility regarding the items to be searched when the criminal activity deals with complex financial transactions."

Of great importance is the description of the alleged offense for which there is probable cause, the persons and entities involved, and the time frame within which the violation occurred, which will provide the focus for the types of records that are subject to seizure. In *United States v. Mathison*,[16] the Eighth Circuit upheld a warrant for all records related to 17 corporations controlled by the defendant and 11 customers in an investigation of sham loans. The circuit court held, "[F]raud, by its nature, entails concealment ... Because the first search warrant limited the search to all records pertaining to the specified corporations and to certain individuals' financial records, we find that it was sufficiently particular." In *United States v. Davis*,[17] the Fifth Circuit noted that "warrants using generic categories of evidence are adequately particular where the crime being investigated is likely to require examination of all of a business's records."

But in *United States v. Abboud*,[18] the Sixth Circuit found a warrant overbroad when it authorized searching for records from 1996 through 2002 but the affidavit only described a check-kiting scheme over a much shorter period. The circuit court stated, "Here, law enforcement knew that the evidence in support of probable cause in the affidavit revolved only around a three-month period in 1999; the authorization to search for evidence irrelevant to that time frame could well be described as 'rummaging.'" In *United States v. Kow*,[19] the Ninth Circuit invalidated an entire warrant when "[t]he government did not limit the scope of the seizure to a time frame within which the suspected criminal activity took place." The circuit court found "[t]o the extent that it provided any guidance to the officers executing the warrant, the warrant apparently sought to describe every document on the premises and direct that everything be seized," and concluded that "[b]y failing to describe with any particularity the items to be seized, the warrant is indistinguishable from the general warrants repeatedly held by this court to be unconstitutional."

Even if a limited time frame is incorporated into the warrant, the description of the categories of documents subject to seizure must also be sufficiently particular. In *United States v. SDI Future Health, Inc.*,[20] the same circuit court suppressed evidence covered by certain portions of a search warrant while allowing the rest, finding that by failing to "describe the crimes and individuals under investigation, the warrant provided the search team with discretion to seize records wholly unrelated to the

---

[16] 157 F.3d 541 (8th Cir. 1998).
[17] 226 F.3d 346 (5th Cir. 2000).
[18] 438 F.3d 554 (6th Cir. 2006).
[19] 58 F.3d 423 (9th Cir. 1995).
[20] 568 F.3d 684 (9th Cir. 2009).

finances of SDI or Kaplan." Another category that authorized the seizure of all "rolodexes, address books, and calendars" was improper because it amounted "to the laziest of gestures in the direction of specificity. Again, this category practically begs the search team to find and to seize the contact information of every person who ever dealt with SDI."

Courts have had to deal with the challenge of applying the particularity requirement to computers and electronic storage systems, which can hold vast amounts of data. Some courts have simply analogized a computer to a file cabinet or other closed container, so that if the warrant authorizes a search of the computer then its entire contents can be viewed.[21] But in *United States v. Walser*,[22] the Tenth Circuit noted how technology is challenging the traditional application of Fourth Amendment principles: "Analogies to other physical objects, such as dressers or file cabinets, do not often inform the situations we now face as judges when applying search and seizure law."

In *United States v. Adjani*,[23] the Ninth Circuit rejected a challenge to a warrant that permitted an extensive search of computer files in a case involving threats to a business to reveal its confidential information. The circuit court pointed out that "[t]o require such a pinpointed computer search, restricting the search to an email program or to specific search terms, would likely have failed to cast a sufficiently wide net to capture the evidence sought."

Whether the protocol for searching electronic files should be set out in the warrant to meet the particularity requirement has not yet been decided. In a concurring opinion in *United States v. Comprehensive Drug Testing, Inc.*,[24] Circuit Judge Kozinski asserted that "the warrant application should normally include, or the issuing judicial officer should insert, a protocol for preventing agents involved in the investigation from examining or retaining any data other than that for which probable cause is shown." Professor Orin Kerr argued that "*ex ante* limits on the execution of computer warrants are constitutionally unauthorized and unwise."[25] In *United States v. Richards*,[26] the Sixth Circuit explained that "given the unique problem encountered in computer searches, and the practical difficulties inherent in implementing universal search methodologies, the majority of federal courts have eschewed the use of a specific search protocol and, instead, have employed the Fourth Amendment's bedrock principle of reasonableness on a case-by-case basis. . . . "

D. "Permeated by Fraud"

The lower courts have approved warrants containing a very broad description of the records that effectively permits the seizure of every document at a business if it is found that the operation was "permeated by fraud." Although sometimes described as an "exception" to the specificity requirement of the Fourth Amendment, it operates more as a recognition that everything connected to a completely fraudulent business will be tainted by the violation, so that its records are like contraband and subject to

---

[21] See United States v. Runyan, 275 F.3d 449 (5th Cir. 2001).

[22] 275 F.3d 981 (10th Cir. 2001).

[23] 452 F.3d 1140 (9th Cir. 2006).

[24] 621 F.3d 1162 (9th Cir. 2010).

[25] Orin S. Kerr, Ex Ante Regulation of Computer Search and Seizure, 96 Va. L. Rev. 1241 (2010).

[26] 659 F.3d 527 (6th Cir. 2011).

wholesale seizure. The government is not relieved of its obligation to identify the items subject to seizure, but its description of the violations must demonstrate that the operation had virtually no legitimate purpose so that everything connected to it may be considered evidence of the criminal violation. Typical situations in which the "permeated by fraud" analysis applies are boiler rooms selling worthless investments, telemarketing schemes peddling counterfeit or worthless goods, and health care clinics in which no medically necessary services are provided to patients.

In *United States v. Brien*,[27] the First Circuit held "that where there is probable cause to find that there exists a pervasive scheme to defraud, all the business records of an enterprise may be seized, if they are, as here, accurately described so that the executing officers have no need to exercise their own judgment as to what should be seized." Similarly, in *United States v. Offices Known As 50 State Distributing Co.*,[28] the Ninth Circuit upheld a warrant described as "extraordinarily broad" that permitted the seizure of every record of a business because "[i]t was not possible through more particular description to segregate those business records that would be evidence of fraud from those that would not, for the reason that there was probable cause to believe that fraud permeated the entire business operation of 50 State." In *United States v. Bentley*,[29] the Seventh Circuit found that "[t]his is the rare case in which even a warrant stating 'Take every piece of paper related to the business' would have been sufficient. Universal was fraudulent through and through." Other lower courts have also upheld broad warrants that effectively authorize the seizure of all of a business's records.[30] The Eleventh Circuit stated in United States v. Bradley[31] that the issue is not whether every aspect of the business was illegal, but "the extent to which fraud has permeated the scope of the defendant's business. That is, the doctrine is concerned with the breadth of the alleged fraud—whether evidence of fraud is likely to be found in records related to a wide range of company business."

Whether or not a business is "permeated by fraud" is a factual issue that must be established in the affidavit supporting the warrant application. If the business has both legitimate and illegitimate aspects, then the warrant cannot simply authorize the seizure of all records because then it is overbroad. In *In re Grand Jury Investigation of Solid State Devices, Inc.*,[32] the Ninth Circuit rejected the government's argument that the warrant was sufficient because of the breadth of the false statements. The circuit court noted that "[w]here a business appears, as SSDI does here, to be engaged in some legitimate activity, this Court has required a more substantial showing of pervasive fraud than that provided by the Government in the instant case."

---

[27] 617 F.2d 299 (1st Cir. 1980).

[28] 708 F.2d 1371 (9th Cir. 1983).

[29] 825 F.2d 1104 (7th Cir. 1987)

[30] See United States v. Martinelli, 454 F.3d 1300 (11th Cir. 2006) ("there were allegations of a 'pervasive scheme' to defraud sufficient to justify the seizure of all company documents."); United States v. Hurwitz, 459 F.3d 463 (4th Cir. 2006) (seizure of all records from doctor whose "practice was permeated with the illegal distribution of drugs.").

[31] United States v. Bradley, 644 F.3d 1213 (11th Cir. 2011).

[32] 130 F.3d 853 (9th Cir. 1997).

The Tenth Circuit refused to follow the "permeated by fraud" analysis, although it did not preclude the possibility that a warrant could properly authorize the seizure of all the records of a business. In *Voss v. Bergsgaard*,[33] the circuit court explained:

> Where a warrant authorizes the seizure of particularly described records relevant to a specific crime and all of an organization's records, in fact, fall into that category, they may all lawfully be seized. However, a warrant that simply authorizes the seizure of all files, whether or not relevant to a specified crime, is insufficiently particular.

§ 21.4   EXECUTION OF THE WARRANT

A.   Requirements

Once a warrant is secured, it must be executed in accordance with its terms, or a court may order suppression of the evidence seized. Federal Rule of Criminal Procedure 41(e)(2)(A) requires that the warrant be executed "within a specified time no longer than 14 days," and the search be conducted during the daytime unless expressly authorized at another time. It is uncommon for a warrant to search a business to be executed in the evening because the officers often seek to interview employees who are present during normal business hours. If the warrant is for electronically stored information, then Rule 41(e)(2)(B) authorizes "a later review of the media or information consistent with the warrant" and does not require that the storage media be reviewed within the 14–day period to conduct the search.

Once the warrant is executed, Rule 41(f)(1) directs that an officer must prepare an inventory of any property seized and give a copy of the warrant, the inventory, and a receipt for any items removed with the person from whom the items were seized or whose premises were searched. Once the search is completed, an officer must also return the warrant and inventory to the designated magistrate judge.

Violation of the requirements of Rule 41 for execution of a warrant will not always result in suppression of any evidence unless the agents deliberately disregarded the rule or the defendant was prejudiced by the violation. In *United States v. Gantt*,[34] the Ninth Circuit held that evidence would be suppressed "because the violation was deliberate . . . The agents failed to show Gantt the complete warrant even after she asked to see it."

B.   Privileged Material

Even if materials come within the description of the warrant, they may be subject to a claim of privilege, such as the attorney-client privilege. In that situation, the party whose materials were seized should notify the government agency responsible for the investigation and the district court that issued the warrant that specified items are subject to a claim of privilege. This issue arises most often when an attorney's offices are searched or a computer is seized that contains correspondence and legal documents of an attorney or client.

---

[33] 774 F.2d 402 (10th Cir. 1985).

[34] 194 F.3d 987 (9th Cir. 1999).

Law offices are not immune from being searched, but there are special dangers to a defendant's Sixth Amendment rights when the search involves ongoing representation. Department of Justice policy[35] requires prior approval of a search warrant for a law office, and that "in all cases a prosecutor must employ adequate precautions to ensure that the materials are reviewed for privilege claims and that any privileged documents are returned to the attorney from whom they were seized." When government agents are aware that privileged materials are likely to be subject to seizure, then protocols should be put in place before issuance of the warrant to protect those items from exposure when the search is conducted.

One means to deal with claims of privilege for seized material is for the government to appoint a "taint team" that will review any materials seized during the search to ascertain whether there is a basis for withholding the document. Defense lawyers object to having a government agent involved in the process of judging whether items seized should be withheld because they are privileged because of the potential conflict of interest. As the Sixth Circuit pointed out in *In re Grand Jury Subpoenas*[36]:

> [T]aint teams present inevitable, and reasonably foreseeable, risks to privilege, for they have been implicated in the past in leaks of confidential information to prosecutors. That is to say, the government taint team may have an interest in preserving privilege, but it also possesses a conflicting interest in pursuing the investigation, and, human nature being what it is, occasionally some taint-team attorneys will make mistakes or violate their ethical obligations.

This is a particular concern when a law office has been searched because privileged materials of innocent clients might be exposed. In that circumstance, courts often appoint a special master who is not affiliated with either side to recommend to the court the proper resolution of any privilege issues.

C. Responding to Searches

As search warrants have become a more common feature in white collar crime investigations, companies have adopted procedures for the organization's response if agents appear with a warrant and begin to conduct a search. Because there is no prior warning that a search will be executed, companies often adopt guidelines to help employees to respond properly while protecting the company's interests until it has additional information and can begin to formulate a response.

There is no single set of procedures for when agents appear with a warrant, but some of the most common suggestions for dealing with the situation are:

• Notify corporate counsel immediately, and if possible have a lawyer on the scene to deal with the agents conducting the search.

• Have counsel or a corporate officer review the warrant and meet with the agents conducting the search to minimize any disruption while allowing for the proper execution of the warrant.

---

[35] USAM § 9–13.420.

[36] 454 F.3d 511 (6th Cir. 2006).

• Try to establish a working relationship with the agent overseeing the search and the prosecutor assigned to the matter so that information can be communicated quickly and accurately.

• If an agent seeks to interview employees during the search, ask to be present to observe. Some companies provide that all employees except those essential to responding to the search are sent away from the premises.

• If employees seek guidance about how to respond to questions posed by agents, provide careful guidance that they can voluntarily choose to answer, but that corporate counsel cannot represent them in an interview.

• If privileged materials may be seized, immediately notify the agents and the prosecutor responsible for the investigation that a claim of confidentiality will be made and that the materials should be segregated and not reviewed.

• Prepare a separate inventory of the materials seized that can be compared to the inventory required by Rule 41.

• If the premises searched are those of a publicly traded corporation with reporting obligations, or there is media attention on the search, prepare a statement that can be issued quickly.

§ 21.5 ADMINISTRATIVE SEARCHES

A. Generally

Although the Fourth Amendment's warrant and probable cause requirements appear to apply to all searches, the Supreme Court recognizes limitations on the scope of the constitutional protection in certain circumstances. Among the situations in which a lesser probable cause showing is permitted are searches performed by authorities for non-penal purposes, such as regulatory inspections, those conducted at the border or its equivalent, and when there are "special needs." The Court has not required that searches in these contexts be based on a particularized suspicion of wrongdoing, and warrants, when they are required, need not be based on the typical probable cause determination. While the searches can be quite invasive, such as the taking of a urine sample, the Court permits them even though the targets are not viewed as being involved in criminal activity. Indeed, one element for these searches to be found permissible is the *lack* of any indication of the person's involvement in a crime, which otherwise should trigger the Fourth Amendment's protections. The standard applied by the Court assumes that the searches are not for the usual law enforcement purpose, although in many cases the Fourth Amendment issue arises in a criminal prosecution based on the fruits of such an administrative search.

B. Regulatory Searches

Administrative agencies can be granted authority to conduct inspections as part of a regulatory regime. While these are similar to searches conducted as part of a criminal investigation, there are important differences in the application of the Fourth Amendment when the object is civil enforcement rather than for penal purposes. The

Supreme Court's decisions in *Camara v. Municipal Court*[37] and *See v. City of Seattle*[38] are the foundational decisions setting forth the application of the warrant requirement for inspections and searches by agencies related to enforcement of civil and regulatory provisions.

Camara involved an inspection of an apartment in which the leaseholder refused entry to a health inspector looking for housing code violations without a warrant. The Court held that administrative searches "are significant intrusions" on the privacy interests of those searched and required a warrant before one can be undertaken. The probable cause requirement for a regulatory inspection, however, is different from that applicable in a criminal investigation. The Court explained that there was sufficient probable cause for issuing this type of warrant "if reasonable legislative or administrative standards for conducting an area inspection are satisfied with respect to a particular dwelling."

See involved the warrantless inspection of a warehouse by the fire department for potential fire code violations. The Court explained that the privacy interests in a private dwelling at issue in *Camara* were the same for a business because "[t]he businessman, like the occupant of a residence, has a constitutional right to go about his business free from unreasonable official entries upon his private commercial property." The probable cause standard was reduced, so that an "agency's particular demand for access will of course be measured, in terms of probable cause to issue a warrant, against a flexible standard of reasonableness that takes into account the public need for effective enforcement of the particular regulation involved."

In light of *Camara* and *See*, the probable cause requirement for an administrative warrant does not require the agency to have a particularized suspicion that the location involved some measure of wrongdoing, and the warrant can cover a wider area than the usual authority granted to criminal investigators to search a particular location. Although the probable cause standard is reduced, it has not been eliminated entirely for regulatory inspections. In *Marshall v. Barlow's, Inc.*,[39] the Court rejected the proposition that inspections by the Occupational Safety and Health Administration conducted under the authority of administrative guidelines furnished the same protection as an administrative warrant. The Court concluded that the regulatory authority to conduct warrantless entries of a business gave the agency too much discretion, while "[a] warrant, by contrast, would provide assurances from a neutral officer that the inspection is reasonable under the Constitution, is authorized by statute, and is pursuant to an administrative plan containing specific neutral criteria." It rejected the government's argument that requiring a warrant put an undue burden on the agency.

C. Pervasively Regulated Businesses

A warrant is not required in every non-emergency situation, as the Court explained in *Colonnade Catering Corp. v. United States*.[40] The Court recognized an

---

[37] 387 U.S. 523 (1967).

[38] 387 U.S. 541 (1967).

[39] 436 U.S. 307 (1978).

[40] 397 U.S. 72 (1970).

exception to the requirement for an administrative warrant when the business to be searched is subject to pervasive government regulation. In *Barlows, Inc.*, the Court explained that "when an entrepreneur embarks upon such a business, he has voluntarily chosen to subject himself to a full arsenal of governmental regulation." The company in *Colonnade Catering* had a liquor license, and a statute prohibited a license holder from refusing to allow a warrantless entry to inspect the premises. The Court found "the liquor industry long subject to close supervision and inspection," so the statute was not unconstitutional because "Congress has broad authority to fashion standards of reasonableness for searches and seizures" involving businesses related to alcoholic beverages.

In *United States v. Biswell*,[41] the Court applied *Colonnade Catering* in rejecting a challenge to a warrantless search of a gun dealer's locked storeroom under the authority provided by statute. The Court stated:

> Federal regulation of the interstate traffic in firearms is not as deeply rooted in history as is governmental control of the liquor industry, but close scrutiny of this traffic is undeniably of central importance to federal efforts to prevent violent crime and to assist the States in regulating the firearms traffic within their borders.

The finding that the Fourth Amendment did not proscribe the search of the gun dealer was permissible because "the possibilities of abuse and the threat to privacy are not of impressive dimensions."

What constituted a closely-regulated business was clarified further in *New York v. Burger*.[42] The Court described three criteria for determining whether a warrantless inspection was reasonable under the Fourth Amendment:

> (1) There must be a substantial government interest informing the regulatory scheme that is the basis for the inspection;

> (2) a warrantless inspection is necessary to further the regulatory scheme; and

> (3) the statute authorizing the warrantless inspection fulfills the two core requirements of a warrant by advising the owner of the premises that a search is made pursuant to that law with a properly defined scope, and it limits the discretion of those who will conduct the inspection.

In explaining these criteria, the Court held that warrantless inspections are permissible if requiring the agency to obtain a warrant in advance would alert the business owner to the impending inspection and allow it to be impeded. A valid regulatory scheme that allows entry to the premises without a warrant must provide fair warning that the business is subject to extensive regulation that includes periodic inspections, and any entry to conduct the inspection must be limited in time, place, and scope.

---

[41] 406 U.S. 311 (1972).

[42] 482 U.S. 691 (1987).

The business involved in *Burger* was an automobile junkyard, and the Court found that the state had a substantial interest in regulating it because of the problems caused by auto theft. Although the statute dealt with potential criminal activity, and police officers conducted the inspection, the Court held that the warrantless entry was reasonable under the Fourth Amendment. The Court focused on the statutory scheme and not the particular inspection, which ultimately resulted in a criminal prosecution, concluding that it was not "designed to gather evidence to enable convictions under the penal laws." Similarly, the defendants in both *Colonnade Catering* and *Biswell* were convicted of crimes based on evidence gathered in the administrative search. There was no Fourth Amendment violation because the original purpose of the government inspection was regulatory, not penal. These cases demonstrate that an administrative investigation can furnish evidence to be used in a criminal prosecution, at least when the agency's primary purpose was not to gather evidence of a criminal violation.

After *Burger*, the Supreme Court upheld the warrantless inspection of mines in *Donovan v. Dewey*[43] because "the Mine Safety and Health Act applies to industrial activity with a notorious history of serious accidents and unhealthful working conditions." The lower courts have concluded that other businesses and industries meet the requirements to be viewed as pervasively regulated, and therefore subject to warrantless administrative inspections. These include commercial trucking, nursing, fishing docks, animal research facilities, and airline passengers.

If evidence is obtained in violation of the Fourth Amendment in a regulatory inspection or search, it will be excluded from being used in a subsequent criminal prosecution of the person whose rights were violated. However, the exclusionary rule does not apply to an administrative proceeding before the agency. In *Pennsylvania Board of Probation and Parole v. Scott*,[44] the Court stated that "we are asked to extend the operation of the exclusionary rule beyond the criminal trial context. We again decline to do so." The Court explained that applying the exclusionary rule outside of prosecutions "would provide only minimal deterrence benefits in this context, because application of the rule in the criminal trial context already provides significant deterrence of unconstitutional searches."

§ 21.6 CHALLENGING A SEARCH OF A BUSINESS

Although the Fifth Amendment privilege against self-incrimination cannot be asserted by an organization under the collective entity doctrine (see § 20.4), a business is protected by the Fourth Amendment. In *Go–Bart Importing Co. v. United States*,[45] the Supreme Court held that the prohibition on unreasonable searches "protects all, those suspected or known to be offenders as well as the innocent, and unquestionably extends to the premises where the search was made and the papers taken." In *See v. City of Seattle*,[46] the Court explained that a "businessman, like the occupant of a residence, has a constitutional right to go about his business free from unreasonable official entries upon his private commercial property."[47]

---

[43] 452 U.S. 594 (1981).

[44] 524 U.S. 357 (1998).

[45] 282 U.S. 344 (1931).

[46] 387 U.S. 541 (1967).

[47] For a complete discussion of standing issues under the Fourth Amendment, see CRIMPROC § 9.1.

The more difficult issue in cases involving a search of a business is whether an employee has a reasonable expectation of privacy to challenge a search of the person's workspace. *Mancusi v. DeForte*[48] considered whether a union official could challenge the search of an office when the person worked in a large room occupied by others. It was not clear that the official had exclusive control of the area searched, although he had possession of the records when they were seized. The Court pointed out that "if DeForte had occupied a 'private' office in the union headquarters, and union records had been seized from a desk or a filing cabinet in that office, he would have had standing." But that was not a prerequisite to being able to raise the Fourth Amendment claim because

> [i]t seems to us that the situation was not fundamentally changed because DeForte shared an office with other union officers. DeForte still could reasonably have expected that only those persons and their personal or business guests would enter the office, and that records would not be touched except with their permission or that of union higher-ups. This expectation was inevitably defeated by the entrance of state officials, their conduct of a general search, and their removal of records which were in DeForte's custody.

In *United States v. Ziegler*,[49] the Ninth Circuit found that an employee had a reasonable expectation of privacy to challenge a search when he worked in an office that was not shared with co-workers and kept his door locked, noting that "while there was a master key, the existence of such will not necessarily defeat a reasonable expectation of privacy in an office given over for personal use."

The fact that a person is a controlling shareholder of a business or one of its managers does not necessarily confer standing to challenge a search of its premises. In *United States v. Anderson*,[50] the Tenth Circuit set forth the following circumstances as relevant to analyzing whether an individual can challenge a search of a business: "(1) the employee's relationship to the item seized; (2) whether the item was in the immediate control of the employee when it was seized; and (3) whether the employee took actions to maintain his privacy in the item." In *United States v. SDI Future Health, Inc.*,[51] the Ninth Circuit pointed out that "security measures that SDI took to ensure the privacy of its business records are relevant only to the standing of the corporation itself, not of its officers. As for [individuals], their ownership and management do not necessarily show a legitimate expectation of privacy."

In *O'Connor v. Ortega*,[52] the Supreme Court applied the same analysis to offices of public employees, holding that "[i]ndividuals do not lose Fourth Amendment rights merely because they work for the government instead of a private employer." But they may have a reduced expectation of privacy, and the Court concluded that neither a warrant nor probable cause is required when the search is for a work-related purpose and not a criminal investigation, even one involving misconduct. The Court stated, "public employer intrusions on the constitutionally protected privacy interests of

---

[48] 392 U.S. 364 (1968).

[49] 474 F.3d 1184 (9th Cir. 2007).

[50] 154 F.3d 1225 (10th Cir. 1998).

[51] 553 F.3d 1248 (9th Cir. 2009).

[52] 480 U.S. 709 (1987).

government employees for noninvestigatory, work-related purposes, as well as for investigations of work-related misconduct, should be judged by the standard of reasonableness under all the circumstances."

§ 21.7 THE GOOD FAITH EXCEPTION

When a warrant is executed to seize business records, its validity can be challenged on the grounds outlined above. Even if a warrant is found to be invalid, that does not mean the exclusionary rule will be automatically applied to preclude use of the records at trial. In *United States v. Leon*,[53] the Supreme Court held that "the Fourth Amendment exclusionary rule should be modified so as not to bar the use in the prosecution's case-in-chief of evidence obtained by officers acting in reasonable reliance on a search warrant issued by a detached and neutral magistrate but ultimately found to be unsupported by probable cause." The Court took this approach because the purpose of the exclusionary rule is to deter police misconduct, so that if the officer acted in reasonable reliance on the judgment of a judicial officer issuing the warrant, then precluding use of the evidence seized would not serve any significant societal interest. In *Massachusetts v. Sheppard*,[54] the companion case to *Leon*, the Court applied the good faith analysis to permit the use of evidence when a warrant was found invalid because it was overly broad.

The Court recognized four situations in which a search pursuant to an invalid warrant would still result in the exclusion of evidence from the government's case-in-chief despite the good faith exception: (1) a knowing or reckless falsehood in the affidavit or information provided by the officer seeking the warrant; (2) the magistrate must perform the role of providing a neutral and detached review and not act "merely as a rubber stamp for the police"; (3) the warrant "was so facially deficient—i.e., in failing to particularize the place to be searched or the things to be seized—that the executing officers cannot reasonably presume it to be valid"; and, (4) when no officer would rely on an affidavit "so lacking in indicia of probable cause as to render official belief in its existence entirely unreasonable." The third and fourth elements of the *Leon* analysis are the ones most commonly raised in challenges to search warrants for business records. But note that *Leon* does not apply to improper execution of a search, only to flaws in the warrant itself or the basis for its issuance.

Courts have relied on *Leon* to permit a broad description of the records subject to seizure in fraud cases because the statutes involve a range of technical issues and the category of records subject to seizure will be comprehensive. In *United States v. Diaz*,[55] the First Circuit overturned a district court's conclusion that the warrant was facially deficient in meeting the particularity requirement for a valid warrant. The circuit court explained:

> The complexity of the fraudulent scheme, its description as an ongoing enterprise bolstered by evidence that illegal activity had continued for at least seven months, and the agent's reasonable belief that the fraud had begun already at IRSI's

---

[53] 468 U.S. 897 (1984).

[54] 468 U.S. 981 (1984).

[55] 841 F.2d 1 (1st Cir. 1988).

inception, all demonstrate that a reasonably well trained officer would not necessarily have known that the search was illegal.

The First Circuit recognized the challenge faced in drafting a proper warrant in a fraud case involving complex transactions over a significant period of time. It noted that courts must "recognize that the inherent difficulty in segregating 'good' from 'bad' records, and consequently in drawing up an adequately limited warrant," and that even a well-trained investigator "is not expected to be a legal technician and is entitled to rely on the greater sophistication of the magistrate—to know precisely where to draw the line." Similarly, in *United States v. Ninety–Two Thousand Four Hundred Twenty–Two Dollars*,[56] the Third Circuit applied *Leon* to an overbroad warrant authorizing the seizure of over ten years of records:

> The Magistrate Judge in this case believed that the warrant was proper and thus issued it. When a Magistrate Judge has made such a determination, law enforcement officers, who are rarely attorneys, are entitled to rely on the Magistrate Judge's judgment, except in rare circumstances, such as where the warrant is so plainly defective in form that even a lay officer could not believe in good faith that the warrant was proper.

Leon is a means for the government to avoid application of the exclusionary rule to a criminal trial, but business searches often occur well in advance to the filing of any charges in a case. A person "aggrieved by an unlawful search and seizure of property or by the deprivation of property may move for the property's return" by filing a motion under Federal Rule of Criminal Procedure 41(g). If the motion is granted, then the court "must return the property to the movant, but may impose reasonable conditions to protect access to the property and its use in later proceedings." Thus, *Leon*'s good faith analysis does not apply to the determination of whether the seizure was unlawful because the records can be maintained for later use if charges are filed and the court finds them admissible in the government's case-in-chief.[57]

In *In re Search of Office of Tylman*,[58] the district court ordered the government to provide copies of the records that had been seized because of a finding that the search was illegal. Rejecting the claim that all the documents must be returned, the Seventh Circuit stated, "The procedures involved in Rule 41[(g)] are not intended to deny the government the use of evidence it needs during its investigations and prosecutions, and here the government is continuing to conduct an investigation into, if true, serious violations of federal law." Similarly, in *United States v. Comprehensive Drug Testing, Inc.*, the Ninth Circuit explained:

> The return of seized property under Rule 41(g) and the exclusionary rule serve fundamentally different purposes. Suppression helps ensure that law enforcement personnel adhere to constitutional norms by denying them, and the government they serve, the benefit of property that is unlawfully seized. Rule 41(g) is concerned with those whose property or privacy interests are impaired by the

---

[56] 307 F.3d 137 (3d Cir. 2002).

[57] Matter of Search of Kitty's East, 905 F.2d 1367 (10th Cir. 1990).

[58] 245 F.3d 978 (7th Cir. 2001).

seizure. Suppression applies only to criminal defendants whereas the class of those aggrieved can be . . . much broader.

§ 21.8 PLAIN VIEW

Under the plain view doctrine, when an officer observes an item from a legitimate vantage point, then it can be seized without a warrant so long as it was immediately apparent there was probable cause to believe it was evidence of a crime. The doctrine developed in cases involving the execution of a search warrant or when officers were otherwise legitimately present.[59] In white collar crime investigations, the doctrine arises most often when an item is seized during the execution of a search warrant. If it does not come within the warrant's description of what can properly be seized, the taking of the item can still be justified if it was found in "plain view" during the execution of the warrant. Thus, the first issue is determining whether the challenged seizure was authorized by the warrant, and if not, then whether it was in plain view and therefore subject to being taken under that doctrine.

In *Horton v. California*,[60] the Supreme Court upheld the seizure of weapons used in a robbery that were in plain view in the defendant's home during the execution of a search warrant for stolen jewelry. Although the police knew about the weapons, the warrant only identified the jewelry in the search warrant as subject to seizure. In permitting the seizure of the weapons, the Court explained that "[i]f an article is already in plain view, neither its observation nor its seizure would involve any invasion of privacy." It also rejected any requirement that would limit the plain view doctrine to those instances in which an officer inadvertently discovered the item. The Court, "The fact that an officer is interested in an item of evidence and fully expects to find it in the course of a search should not invalidate its seizure if the search is confined in area and duration by the terms of a warrant or a valid exception to the warrant requirement." Thus, application of the plain view doctrine focuses on whether the officer was authorized to view the item, and whether its incriminating character was "immediately apparent."

The plain view doctrine has been particularly important when business records are the object of a search and evidence of other crimes is discovered among them. This is especially true when electronic files on computers and other storage devices are involved. In *Andresen v. Maryland*,[61] the Supreme Court noted that "[i]n searches for papers, it is certain that some innocuous documents will be examined, at least cursorily, in order to determine whether they are, in fact, among those papers authorized to be seized."

When the search involves a computer, there is a danger that the plain view doctrine can essentially trump the terms of the search warrant because every file could conceivably contain evidence of a crime, and so all records could be searched. In *United States v. Williams*,[62] the Fourth Circuit took a broad approach to the plain view doctrine in a computer search, finding that the warrant effectively permitted agents to

---

[59] Coolidge v. New Hampshire, 403 U.S. 443 (1971).

[60] 496 U.S. 128 (1990).

[61] 427 U.S. 463 (1976).

[62] 592 F.3d 511 (4th Cir. 2010).

view every file for evidence of the crimes identified in the search warrant. The circuit court stated:

> [The] search could not be limited to reviewing only the files' designation or labeling, because the designation or labeling of files on a computer can easily be manipulated to hide their substance. Surely, the owner of a computer, who is engaged in criminal conduct on that computer, will not label his files to indicate their criminality.

Thus, the Fourth Circuit held, "Once it is accepted that a computer search must, by implication, authorize at least a cursory review of each file on the computer, then the criteria for applying the plain-view exception are readily satisfied."

In *United States v. Stabile*,[63] the Third Circuit noted the two competing principles at issue when the government relies on the plain view doctrine to justify searching electronic files beyond those directly related to the search warrant authorization. The circuit court stated, "On one hand, it is clear that because criminals can—and often do—hide, mislabel, or manipulate files to conceal criminal activity, a broad, expansive search of the hard drive may be required." But, "granting the Government a carte blanche to search every file on the hard drive impermissibly transforms a limited search into a general one." The search involved viewing images of child pornography during a financial fraud investigation. The Third Circuit pointed out, rather unhelpfully, that "the exact confines of the doctrine will vary from case to case in a common-sense, fact-intensive manner. What is permissible in one situation may not always be permissible in another." At least with regard to examining the file names in which the pornography was found, the circuit court held that the plain view doctrine allowed the detective to view them "because a thorough computer search requires a broad examination of files on the computer to ensure that file names have not been manipulated to conceal their contents." It avoided deciding whether the actual viewing of the files was permissible as a plain view examination of evidence because the inevitable discovery and independent source doctrines would have resulted in seizure of the files.

The Ninth Circuit, sitting en banc, expressed misgivings about the use of the plain view doctrine for computer searches in *United States v. Comprehensive Drug Testing, Inc.*[64] The majority opinion stated:

> We recognize the reality that over-seizing is an inherent part of the electronic search process and proceed on the assumption that, when it comes to the seizure of electronic records, this will be far more common than in the days of paper records. This calls for greater vigilance on the part of judicial officers in striking the right balance between the government's interest in law enforcement and the right of individuals to be free from unreasonable searches and seizures. The process of segregating electronic data that is seizable from that which is not must not become a vehicle for the government to gain access to data which it has no probable cause to collect.

---

[63] 633 F.3d 219 (3d Cir. 2011).

[64] 621 F.3d 1162 (9th Cir. 2010).

In a concurring opinion, Circuit Judge Kozinski argued that as a prerequisite to issuing a search warrant, "Magistrate judges should insist that the government waive reliance upon the plain view doctrine in digital evidence cases."

In *United States v. Carey*,[65] the Tenth Circuit took a restrictive approach to application of the plain view doctrine once the search turns up evidence in electronic files of crimes that fall outside the search warrant. During the course of a search for evidence of narcotics sales, an officer opened files on the defendant's computer containing images of child pornography, conducting a 5–hour search for other files containing pornography after opening the initial file containing the image. The circuit court stated, "Where officers come across relevant documents so intermingled with irrelevant documents that they cannot feasibly be sorted at the site, the officers may seal or hold the documents pending approval by a magistrate of the conditions and limitations on a further search through the documents."

The Tenth Circuit appeared to adopt an inadvertence requirement, finding that the officer's broad search of the computer after discovering the illegal file meant that "we cannot say the contents of each of those files were inadvertently discovered." *Carey*'s analysis seems to conflict with the Supreme Court's rejection in *Horton* of any to show inadvertence, but the circuit court's approach reflects the concern that a warrant authorizing a search of electronic files not be a license to look at everything stored on a computer regardless of any indication that it is connected to the possible violation. The plain view doctrine works well in the context of physical searches because the location available to be seen is limited, while electronic storage media can contain huge amounts of information and there is no physical proximity to limit application of the doctrine. A legitimate search of a computer will open up a great deal of information to scrutiny, but to the extent a review is more akin to wholesale "rummaging" through electronic files then a court should recognize at least some limitations to the government's authority to use a warrant as a license to view every electronic file.

---

[65] 172 F.3d 1268 (10th Cir. 1999).

Chapter 22

ATTORNEY–CLIENT PRIVILEGE

§ 22.1 INTRODUCTION

The attorney-client privilege is among the most important privileges recognized under the common law, and one of the most heavily litigated. As the Second Circuit once noted, "Narrowly defined, riddled with exceptions, and subject to continuing criticism, the rule affording confidentiality to communications between attorney and client endures as the oldest rule of privilege known to the common law."[1] It has a special importance in white collar crime investigations because of the pervasive presence of lawyers in business transactions, where they play a variety of roles in advising companies and individuals.

The Supreme Court summarized the rationale of the privilege in the leading case of *Upjohn Co. v. United States*[2] as encouraging "full and frank communication between attorneys and their clients and thereby promote broader public interests in the observance of law and administration of justice." The Court explained that "sound legal advice or advocacy serves public ends and that such advice or advocacy depends upon the lawyer's being fully informed by the client." That rationale supported the Court's conclusion in *Swidler & Berlin v. United States*[3] that the privilege survives the death of the client, in which it stated "knowing that communications will remain confidential even after death encourages the client to communicate fully and frankly with counsel."

The roots of the privilege can be traced to Roman law, and under the English common law it developed into a client-oriented protection designed to keep the client's secrets from being revealed through the lawyer. The Supreme Court embraced the privilege as a facet of federal law in *Connecticut Mutual Life Insurance Co. v. Schaefer*,[4] an 1876 decision upholding a trial court's order precluding a lawyer from testifying about his client's statements in an earlier divorce action. It stated, "If a person cannot consult his legal adviser without being liable to have the interview made public the next day by an examination enforced by the courts, the law would be little short of despotic. It would be a prohibition upon professional advice and assistance." A few years later, in *Hunt v. Blackburn*,[5] the Court stated:

> The rule which places the seal of secrecy upon communications between client and attorney is founded upon the necessity, in the interest and administration of justice, of the aid of persons having knowledge of the law and skilled in its practice, which assistance can only be safely and readily availed of when free from the consequences or the apprehension of disclosure.

---

[1] United States v. Schwimmer, 892 F.2d 237 (2d Cir.1989).

[2] 449 U.S. 383 (1981).

[3] 524 U.S. 399 (1998).

[4] 94 U.S. 457 (1876).

[5] 128 U.S. 464 (1888).

Like any privilege that protects against the disclosure of information, it also frustrates a party's search for evidence and so makes it more difficult to ascertain the truth. Thus, the Court noted in *Fisher v. United States*[6] that "since the privilege has the effect of withholding relevant information from the fact-finder, it applies only where necessary to achieve its purpose." While courts state that the attorney-client privilege should be narrowly construed, in reality judges are generally solicitous of privilege claims and will review a request for disclosure of attorney-client communications quite carefully.

There are four basic requirements to assert the attorney-client privilege, as outlined in District Judge Charles Wyzanski's famous decision in *United States v. United Shoe Machinery Corp.*:[7]

> The privilege applies only if (1) the asserted holder of the privilege is or sought to become a client; (2) the person to whom the communication was made (a) is a member of the bar of a court, or his subordinate and (b) in connection with this communication is acting as a lawyer; (3) the communication relates to a fact of which the attorney was informed (a) by his client (b) without the presence of strangers (c) for the purpose of securing primarily either (i) an opinion on law or (ii) legal services or (iii) assistance in some legal proceeding, and not (d) for the purpose of committing a crime or tort; and (4) the privilege has been (a) claimed and (b) not waived by the client.

The focus on protecting communications means that the privilege does not apply to the underlying facts discussed with counsel or any documents prepared by or on behalf of the client unrelated to the attorney-client relationship.

§ 22.2 COMMUNICATIONS

A. Generally

The attorney-client privilege protects confidential communications from a client to the lawyer, and those from the lawyer to the client if disclosure would reveal the substance of a client communication. While it is easy to understand why the client's communications are protected, the privilege extends to the attorney's communications because of the likelihood that revelation of the legal advice given to a client will result in disclosure of what was communicated by the client, even if the exact statements are not revealed. The District of Columbia Circuit explained in *In re Sealed Case*[8] that an "attorney's communications (his advice) to the client must also be protected, because otherwise it is rather easy to deduce the client's communications to counsel." The privilege also protects communications with prospective clients who meet with a lawyer for the purpose of determining whether to retain the person to provide legal advice.[9]

---

[6] 425 U.S. 391 (1976).

[7] 89 F.Supp. 357 (D.Mass. 1950).

[8] 877 F.2d 976 (D.C. Cir. 1989).

[9] Westinghouse Electric Corp. v. Kerr–McGee Corp., 580 F.2d 1311 (7th Cir. 1978). See ABA Model Rule of Professional Conduct, Rule 1.18.

B. Legal Advice

Information an attorney gathers from a third party and conveys to a client is not necessarily protected if disclosure would not reveal any client communications.[10] But "advice does not spring from lawyers' heads as Athena did from the brow of Zeus," so that "[i]n a given case, advice prompted by the client's disclosures may be further and inseparably informed by other knowledge and encounters."[11]

Whether an attorney's discussion of legal issues is privileged can be important in the corporate context when counsel may make presentations about the state of the law for the benefit of employees. In *Upjohn*, the Supreme Court explained the scope of the attorney-client privilege for corporations: "the privilege exists to protect not only the giving of professional advice to those who can act on it but also the giving of information to the lawyer to enable him to give sound and informed advice." The Third Circuit took a broad approach in *United States v. Amerada Hess Corp.*,[12] stating that "[l]egal advice or opinion from an attorney to his client, individual or corporate, has consistently been held by the federal courts to be within the protection of the attorney-client privilege." But the circuit court found that a list of employees interviewed as part of an internal investigation and attached to counsel's report to a corporate committee was not protected by the privilege because it did not contain any legal advice or disclose client communications. And in *Hartford Life Insurance Co. v. Bank of America Corp.*,[13] a district court found that a document prepared by corporate counsel for a bank dealing with its due diligence policies in securities transactions was not protected by the privilege because it did not "apply any of these generalized legal principles to specific factual situations nor does it indirectly disclose any inquiry by or concern of [the bank] that would not be self evident from the nature of [its] business." So while in most circumstances the lawyer's communications with a client are protected by the privilege, there may be situations in which the protection afforded can be challenged if the legal advice can clearly be separated from any client communications.

While the communications between the lawyer and client are privileged, the underlying facts communicated do not become privileged merely because the client conveyed them to counsel. In *Upjohn*, the Supreme Court stated that the privilege "does not protect disclosure of the underlying facts by those who communicated with the attorney." In *City of Philadelphia v. Westinghouse Electric Corp.*,[14] quoted with approval in *Upjohn*, a district court explained the distinction between facts and communication this way: "The client cannot be compelled to answer the question, 'What did you say or write to the attorney?' but may not refuse to disclose any relevant fact within his knowledge merely because he incorporated a statement of such fact into his communication to his attorney."

In *In re Six Grand Jury Witnesses*,[15] outside counsel used corporate employees to conduct an analysis of the company's performance of a government contract in

---

[10] Brinton v. Department of State, 636 F.2d 600 (D.C.Cir. 1980).

[11] In re Sealed Case, 737 F.2d 94 (D.C. Cir. 1984).

[12] 619 F.2d 980 (3d Cir. 1980).

[13] 2007 WL 2398824 (S.D.N.Y. 2007).

[14] 205 F.Supp. 830 (E.D. Pa. 1962).

[15] 979 F.2d 939 (2d Cir. 1992).

response to a grand jury subpoena for records. Those employees had also worked on the contract, and so had information about how the company had performed. In rejecting an attorney-client privilege claim related to questions about the company's performance that did not reference communications with corporate counsel, the Second Circuit stated:

> To begin with it seems plain that merely by asking witnesses to conduct an analysis defense counsel may not thereby silence all the key witnesses on the cost aspects of the Fox contracts under either claim of privilege. Were counsel to succeed in such a tactic, the government would never be able to conduct a full and complete investigation of an alleged crime because the critical witnesses would have been effectively silenced, nor for the same reason would the government be able to present all the evidence at trial regarding a defendant's guilt or innocence.

In addition to witnesses, pre-existing corporate records are not protected by the attorney-client privilege when a client transfers them to counsel, even when it is provided to obtain legal advice. If the client could have asserted a claim of privilege for the documents under the Fifth Amendment to prevent turning them over to the government (see § 20.1), then providing them to the attorney will not waive that privilege and the lawyer can assert the privilege on the client's behalf for the records. In *Fisher v. United States*,[16] the Supreme Court considered a taxpayer's claim that the Fifth Amendment protected records provided to an attorney to secure legal advice. While the attorney could not assert the privilege against self-incrimination because the records were not personally incriminating, the Court explained that "[s]ince each taxpayer transferred possession of the documents in question from himself to his attorney in order to obtain legal assistance in the tax investigations in question, the papers, if unobtainable by summons from the client, are unobtainable by summons directed to the attorney by reason of the attorney-client privilege."

C. Client Identity and Fee Information

Not all information related to the attorney-client relationship is privilege. As a general rule, the identity of a client and information about fees arrangements are not privileged. Courts have determined that, in most instances, a client's identity and fee information does not involve any communication with the lawyer, and so falls outside the protection of the privilege. Information about a client's identity and arrangements for compensating the lawyer may be of particular interest when an undisclosed third party is paying the fees for defendants or targets of an investigation. The source of an attorney's fee and the amounts being paid can be important in a white collar crime investigation if an issue is whether the target may be trying to hide assets or launder the proceeds of illegal activity.

Subpoenas to lawyers for client identity and fee information have increased, and courts have struggled to establish limits on the government's right to learn this information to prevent undue interference with the attorney-client relationship while preserving the power of a grand jury to obtain evidence. An early case focusing on this issue was the Ninth Circuit's decision in *United States v. Hodge & Zweig*,[17] written by

---

[16] 425 U.S. 391 (1976).

[17] 548 F.2d 1347 (9th Cir. 1977).

then-Circuit Judge Anthony Kennedy. The circuit court acknowledged the general rule that client identity and fee information was not privileged, but asserted that a "client's identity and the nature of that client's fee arrangements may be privileged where the person invoking the privilege can show that a strong probability exists that disclosure of such information would implicate that client in the very criminal activity for which legal advice was sought." The trigger for invocation of the privilege was whether disclosure would incriminate the client. The problem with this analysis was that whether information was inculpatory does not determine whether the attorney-client privilege should apply. The Ninth Circuit backed away from a broad reading of *Hodge & Zweig* in *Tornay v. United States*,[18] describing the incrimination approach to client identity and fee information as "dictum."

The Fifth Circuit refined the incrimination analysis in *In re Grand Jury (Pavlick)*[19] by offering the "last link" exception that would protect client identity and fee information "when the disclosure of [his] client's identity . . . would have supplied the last link in an existing chain of incriminating evidence likely to lead to the client's indictment." This approach narrowed the incrimination analysis by requiring that the information lead directly to an indictment of the client. One weakness is that if only a "final" link would cloak client identity and fee information with the privilege, then prosecutors would have an incentive to seek the information at an earlier stage of the investigation so that it would be more likely to be subject to disclosure. The Fifth Circuit stated in a subsequent case, *In re Grand Jury Subpoena for Attorney Representing Criminal Defendant Reyes–Requena*,[20] that the "last link" language was not meant to create a new test based on whether the information was incriminating as the basis for recognizing that it was privileged, but was instead tied to a determination whether the information reflected a confidential communication.

The predominant view is that the determination whether client identity and fee information is protected from disclosure depends on whether compelling the attorney to reveal it would also disclose a client communication that is otherwise subject to the attorney-client privilege. In *In re Grand Jury Subpoena*,[21] the Fifth Circuit stated, "We protect the client's identity and fee arrangements in such circumstances not because they might be incriminating but because they are connected inextricably with a privileged communication—the confidential purpose for which he sought legal advice." Similarly, in *Matter of Grand Jury Proceeding, Cherney*,[22] the Seventh Circuit held, "The proper question is whether the revelation of the identity of the fee payer along with information regarding the fee arrangement would reveal a confidential communication between Cherney and the fee payer." In *In re Grand Jury Proceedings 88–9 MIA*,[23] the Eleventh Circuit found that compelling disclosure of who provided a $30,200 cashier's check for an unnamed client would not reveal any confidential communications when the client had retained the attorney in a separate matter, and the third-party payment did not reveal any other communication, motive or strategy of the client.

---

[18] 840 F.2d 1424 (9th Cir. 1988).

[19] 680 F.2d 1026 (5th Cir. 1982).

[20] 913 F.2d 1118 (5th Cir. 1990).

[21] 926 F.2d 1423 (5th Cir.1991).

[22] 898 F.2d 565 (7th Cir. 1990).

[23] 899 F.2d 1039 (11th Cir.1990).

D. Communications by Agents

The classic view of the attorney-client relationship is an individual client meeting in the lawyer's office discussing legal issues related to the representation. While this certainly happens every day, the business world is much more complex for both attorneys and clients involved in interactions that do not fit within this simple view. For lawyers, they may need the assistance of accountants, investigators, consultants, and support staff to adequately represent a client. The client may be an organization that ranges from a single-shareholder company with a few employees to a multinational business with subsidiaries spread throughout the globe, using outside contractors as a regular part of its operations. The attorney-client privilege can be raised in connection with a number of communications that do not fit the paradigm of the individual lawyer meeting with a single client.

The attorney-client privilege does not apply to communications between a lawyer and a third party who is not a client, except if the third party is an agent of the attorney or client. The foundational case on this issue is the Second Circuit's decision in *United States v. Kovel*,[24] which involved a contempt prosecution of an accountant employed by a law firm for refusing to answer questions before a grand jury about what he was told by a client by asserting the attorney-client privilege. The circuit court noted that employing a non-lawyer to assist on a legal issue would not bring all communications with that person within the attorney-client privilege, but "the complexities of modern existence prevent attorneys from effectively handling clients' affairs without the help of others; few lawyers could now practice without the assistance of secretaries, file clerks, telephone operators, messengers, clerks not yet admitted to the bar, and aides of other sorts." The Second Circuit held:

> [I]f the lawyer has directed the client, either in the specific case or generally, to tell his story in the first instance to an accountant engaged by the lawyer, who is then to interpret it so that the lawyer may better give legal advice, communications by the client reasonably related to that purpose ought fall within the privilege; there can be no more virtue in requiring the lawyer to sit by while the client pursues these possibly tedious preliminary conversations with the accountant than in insisting on the lawyer's physical presence while the client dictates a statement to the lawyer's secretary or is interviewed by a clerk not yet admitted to practice.

Since *Kovel*, lower courts have found the privilege applicable to communications by clients with paralegals,[25] psychiatrists,[26] investigators,[27] public relations consultants,[28] and patent agents,[29] so long as there was a close nexus to aiding the attorney in rendering legal advice.

Communication with the third party must be related to rendering legal advice, but that alone is not sufficient to bring it within the privilege. In addition, it must be made

---

[24] 296 F.2d 918 (2d Cir. 1961).

[25] In re Grand Jury Proceedings, 786 F.2d 3 (1st Cir. 1986).

[26] United States v. Alvarez, 519 F.2d 1036 (3d Cir. 1975).

[27] NLRB v. Harvey, 349 F.2d 900 (4th Cir. 1965).

[28] In re Grand Jury Subpoenas, 265 F. Supp. 2d 321 (S.D.N.Y. 2003).

[29] Golden Trade v. Lee Apparel Co., 143 F.R.D. 514 (S.D.N.Y. 1992).

on the lawyer's or client's behalf and not simply communicate information that the attorney will find helpful to assist in the representation. In *United States v. Ackert*,[30] the Second Circuit rejected a privilege claim regarding a discussion the lawyer had with an investment banker about the potential tax consequences of a transaction. The circuit court explained that "a communication between an attorney and a third party does not become shielded by the attorney-client privilege solely because the communication proves important to the attorney's ability to represent the client." A privilege claim can be made under *Kovel* "if the purpose of the third party's participation is to improve the comprehension of the communications between attorney and client." The discussions at issue in *Ackert* were not designed to help the lawyer interpret the client's communications, but were more like the type of investigation counsel would conduct to evaluate the case, which usually falls outside the privilege.

In dealing with agents and advisers to a corporate client, communications with the lawyer may come within the protection of the attorney-client privilege if the third parties are viewed as the functional equivalent of the client. In *In re Bieter*,[31] the Eighth Circuit found that communications by a partnership's lawyer with a consultant who acted as the sole representative of the partnership at various meetings which were the focus of the litigation were covered by the attorney-client privilege. The circuit court held that "when applying the attorney-client privilege to a corporation or partnership, it is inappropriate to distinguish between those on the client's payroll and those who are instead, and for whatever reason, employed as independent contractors." Dean John Sexton offered a principle for interpreting the scope of the privilege for a corporate client that "[t]he information-giver must be an employee, agent, or independent contractor with a significant relationship to the corporation and the corporation's involvement in the transaction that is the subject of legal services."[32]

It is also important to note that even if the attorney-client privilege does not apply because a third party was involved in the communication who is not considered an agent of either the attorney or the client, there may still be a basis to withhold the information under the protection afforded to attorney work product (see Chapter 23).

E. Business Advice

The attorney-client privilege protects against the disclosure of communications designed to assist the attorney in formulating and presenting legal advice. Attorneys now play a key role in a wide range of transactions, and virtually every organization of any size has an in-house counsel who is consulted on a regular basis. The fact that an attorney is involved in a discussion does not necessarily mean that it is protected by the privilege, but determining where to draw the line between legal and business advice is fraught with imprecision. As the district court noted in *United States v. Chevron Texaco Corp.*,[33] "Because the purported privileged communications involve attorneys who apparently performed the dual role of legal and business advisor,

---

[30] 169 F.3d 136 (2d Cir. 1999).

[31] 16 F.3d 929 (8th Cir. 1994).

[32] John E. Sexton, A Post–*Upjohn* Consideration of the Corporate Attorney–Client Privilege, 57 N.Y.U. L. Rev. 443 (1982).

[33] 241 F. Supp. 2d 1065 (N.D. Cal. 2002).

assessing whether a particular communication was made for the purpose of securing legal advice (as opposed to business advice) becomes a difficult task."

In *Zenith Radio Corp. v. Radio Corp. of America*,[34] the district court stated, "When he acts as an advisor, the attorney must give predominantly legal advice to retain his client's privilege of non-disclosure, not solely, or even largely, business advice." In *United Shoe Machinery Corp.*, Judge Wyzanski noted that "the privilege of nondisclosure is not lost merely because relevant nonlegal considerations are expressly stated in a communication which also includes legal advice." One danger from a broad application of the privilege in this context is that a company may be able to cloak information ordinarily subject to discovery from disclosure merely by having an attorney involved in the transaction or discussion. In *First Chicago International v. United Exchange Co.*,[35] the district court pointed out that "[a]ny standard developed, therefore, must strike a balance between encouraging corporations to seek legal advice and preventing corporate attorneys from being used as shields to thwart discovery." The focus is on the role of the lawyer, and whether obtaining legal advice was a facet of the communication, a highly fact-specific approach in which the party asserting the privilege bears the burden of establishing its applicability.

§ 22.3 CORPORATE ATTORNEY–CLIENT PRIVILEGE

The scope of corporate criminal liability is broad (see § 2.1), and the need to investigate misconduct within the organization is of great importance to a company hoping to avoid being charged with a crime or mitigate any punishment. The attorney-client privilege allows corporate counsel to speak with employees who have knowledge of transactions that may have violated the law but are reticent about speaking to government investigators, shielding those discussions at least until the corporation decides whether or not to waive the privilege.

A corporation can only operate through its agents, even though it is a separate legal entity. An important question concerned the scope of the attorney-client privilege for a corporate client, whether it covered communications with any employee of an organization or only those with decision-making authority. The lower federal courts had developed the "control group test" to limit the privilege to communications between counsel and those in a position to establish corporate policy, such as the directors or senior managers of the business. *City of Philadelphia v. Westinghouse Electric Corp.*,[36] a 1962 district court decision, was the first opinion to set forth the basic parameters for when a corporation could invoke the attorney-client privilege under the control group approach:

> [I]f the employee making the communication, of whatever rank he may be, is in a position to control or even to take a substantial part in a decision about any action which the corporation may take upon the advice of the attorney, or if he is an authorized member of a body or group which has that authority, then, in effect, he is (or personifies) the corporation when he makes his disclosure to the lawyer and the privilege would apply.

---

[34] 121 F.Supp. 792 (D. Del. 1954).

[35] 125 F.R.D. 55 (S.D.N.Y. 1989).

[36] 210 F.Supp. 483 (E.D. Pa. 1962).

The Supreme Court rejected the control group test in *Upjohn Co. v. United States*[37] because it "overlooks the fact that the privilege exists to protect not only the giving of professional advice to those who can act on it but also the giving of information to the lawyer to enable him to give sound and informed advice." The case arose when the IRS sought to obtain documents from an internal investigation of overseas bribery conducted by corporate counsel, including notes of interviews with employees involved in the payments. The Court focused on the rationale of the attorney-client privilege as fostering free and open discussion between the attorney and the client, finding that the narrower control group test "frustrates the very purpose of the privilege by discouraging the communication of relevant information by employees of the client to attorneys seeking to render legal advice to the client corporation." The Court also questioned the uncertainty of the test, noting that it was hard to determine exactly where to draw the line, which could discourage companies from seeking legal advice to comply with the law.

In concluding that the communications came within the attorney-client privilege, the Court said that it would "not undertake to draft a set of rules" for ascertaining when the protection applied. Instead, it highlighted factors indicating when the communications were of the type usually subject to the privilege, noting for example that the "communications at issue were made by Upjohn employees to counsel for Upjohn acting as such, at the direction of corporate superiors in order to secure legal advice from counsel." The Court highlighted that the "communications concerned matters within the scope of the employees' corporate duties, and the employees themselves were sufficiently aware that they were being questioned in order that the corporation could obtain legal advice." The company also emphasized that its investigation was "highly confidential," which was consistent with maintaining the confidentiality required for the attorney-client privilege.

Upjohn ensured a much wider application of the attorney-client privilege by allowing companies to assert it whenever corporate counsel communicates with an employee or agent of the organization for the purpose of rendering legal advice. Importantly, the privilege applies to gathering information in an internal investigation and not just the actual furnishing of legal advice to the organization. Much like an individual provides the lawyer with the information necessary for the representation, the corporate attorney needs to speak with employees and agents to gather the information that management may not have access to in order to determine what legal avenues are available to it. By allowing the company to assert the privilege for all communications with corporate counsel related to an internal investigation, the Court noted that it "puts the adversary in no worse position than if the communications had never taken place." The government was free to speak with the employees on its own, and they could not assert the attorney-client privilege because that only proscribes disclosure of communications with counsel, not the underlying facts.

Upjohn left open the question whether the attorney-client privilege applied to communications with former employees. In a concurring opinion, Chief Justice Burger took the position that "as a general rule, a communication is privileged at least when, as here, an employee or former employee speaks at the direction of the management with an attorney regarding conduct or proposed conduct within the scope of

---

[37] 449 U.S. 383 (1981).

employment." After *Upjohn*, the Fourth Circuit noted in *In re Allen* that "[m]ost lower courts have followed the Chief Justice's reasoning and granted the privilege to communications between a client's counsel and the client's former employees."[38] In order to come within the organization's privilege, the former employee must have been with the company during the time period at issue and possessed information relevant to the attorney's investigation.

The rule on communications with a former employee as being considered privileged is not unanimous. A district court stated in *Infosystems, Inc. v. Ceridian Corp.*[39] that as a general proposition "counsel's communications with a former employee of the client corporation generally should be treated no differently from communications with any other third-party fact witness." The district court noted, however, that the privilege would apply when the communication concerned a "confidential matter that was uniquely within the knowledge of the former employee when he worked for the client corporation, such that counsel's communications with this former employee must be cloaked with the privilege in order for meaningful fact-gathering to occur." Thus, this approach looks to the particular circumstances to permit a company to assert the privilege, rather than applying the broader approach advocated by Chief Justice Burger in *Upjohn*.

The Supreme Court's analysis in *Upjohn* on the availability of the attorney-client privilege for organizations was an application of the federal common law under Federal Rule of Evidence 501 and thus applies to all federal cases. Investigations involving multinational companies may raise issues regarding the availability of the privilege because it may not apply to certain communications made outside the United States. The European Court of Justice held in *AM & S Europe Ltd. v. Commission*[40] that the privilege does not apply to in-house counsel because the communication must "emanate from independent lawyers . . . not bound to the client by a relationship of employment."

§ 22.4   CONFLICTS OF INTEREST AND MULTIPLE REPRESENTATION

Privileged communications can trigger conflict of interest issues when a lawyer or single law firm represents multiple parties in an investigation or legal proceeding. It is common for the officers and directors of a corporation to be represented by one firm during the early stages of an investigation, when it is not clear who are the likely targets or whether it will develop into a criminal prosecution. Once the investigation reaches a stage at which the government can identify who is likely to be involved in a potential case, either as a defendant or as a witness, then under the professional responsibility rules of the legal profession each individual who is likely to be prosecuted will need separate counsel. In some investigations, there may be individuals viewed by prosecutors as only fact witnesses unlikely to be considered targets or subjects of an investigation based on current information. One lawyer or law firm may be able to represent a number of witnesses because it is unlikely they will be

---

[38] In re Allen, 106 F.3d 582 (4th Cir. 1997).

[39] 197 F.R.D. 303 (E.D. Mich. 2000).

[40] Case No. 155/79, 1982 E.C.R. 1575, 2 C.M.L.R. 264 (1982).

in adverse positions that would limit the ability of the lawyers to continue to represent them.

Model Rule of Professional Conduct 1.7(a) provides that a current conflict of interest exists when "there is a significant risk that the representation of one or more clients will be materially limited by the lawyer's responsibilities to another client, a former client or a third person. . . . " In *Cuyler v. Sullivan*,[41] the Supreme Court stated, "Defense counsel have an ethical obligation to avoid conflicting representations and to advise the court promptly when a conflict of interest arises during the course of trial." A common scenario is when there are privileged communications between a lawyer and client, so the attorney's obligation to one person is likely to limit the ability to represent another person involved in the case because of the prohibition on revealing or using confidential information. Even if there are no issues regarding confidential information, the duty of loyalty owed to a former client may constrain the lawyer's ability to adequately represent another client when there is a conflict of interest between their positions, requiring the lawyer to withdraw from the case completely. For example, in *United States v. Self*,[42] two lawyers from the same firm represented brothers in a prosecution, until one partner withdrew because of a conflict between their trial strategies. The Third Circuit upheld the disqualification of the other partner from the case, finding that "[t]here can be little doubt that this 'blame the co-defendant' strategy created a potentially serious conflict of interest" that could not be overcome because the two lawyers worked together closely.

In corporate crime investigations, it is often the case that directors or officers have different levels of involvement and their positions may become adverse if one were to provide information that incriminated others. Therefore, a single lawyer or law firm could not represent multiple clients who may be in a conflicting position, and each individual would have to retain separate counsel.

An attorney's representation of different individuals involved in a case, including the investigatory phase, can result in a motion to disqualify from any further involvement in the matter. Even if there is no actual conflict of interest at that time, a potential conflict can be sufficient to allow a court to disqualify the lawyer from further representation, even if the client is willing to waive any conflict of interest. In *Wheat v. United States*,[43] the Court considered whether the Sixth Amendment protected a defendant's choice to be represented by an attorney with a potential conflict of interest arising from his representation of other parties to a drug conspiracy. The Court held that trial judges have broad discretion to disqualify attorneys because of the "institutional interest in the rendition of just verdicts in criminal cases that may be jeopardized by unregulated multiple representation." That discretion is not limited to just actual conflicts of interest, and a defendant's waiver of the conflict is not controlling, so that the trial courts are "allowed substantial latitude in refusing waivers of conflicts of interest not only in those rare cases where an actual conflict may be demonstrated before trial, but in the more common cases where a potential for conflict exists which may or may not burgeon into an actual conflict as the trial progresses."

---

[41] 446 U.S. 335 (1980).

[42] 681 F.3d 190 (3d Cir. 2012).

[43] 486 U.S. 153 (1988).

In corporate investigations, the company is often required to pay the attorney's fees of employees under an indemnification provision in an employment contract or provided in the corporate charter or by-laws. (See § 2.7(C)). The company's payment to an individual's lawyer does not necessarily violate the conflict of interest rules. Under Model Rule 1.8(f), a lawyer can be paid by someone other than the client if (1) the client gives informed consent, (2) "there is no interference with the lawyer's independence of professional judgment or with the client-lawyer relationship," and (3) the lawyer maintains the confidentiality of information received from the client. The organization cannot control the conduct of counsel in the case, nor may it demand access to information that would be protected by the attorney-client privilege as a condition of paying for the lawyer.

A lawyer for a corporation, whether in-house or from an outside firm, represents the entity, not its individual employees unless there is a separate agreement to do so. Model Rule of Professional Conduct 1.13(a) provides that "[a] lawyer employed or retained by an organization represents the organization acting through its duly authorized constituents." It is important that the lawyers conducting an internal investigation for a company make clear in dealings with employees that they are not representing that person individually, unless there is an agreement to do so. Model Rule 1.13(g) provides that "[a] lawyer representing an organization may also represent any of its directors, officers, employees, members, shareholders or other constituents, subject to" the requirement to avoid a conflict of interest, and with the express consent of the organization. Although it may be permissible to represent both the company and an individual officer or director in an investigation, that is often unadvisable if there is any indication that the lawyer may have to identify an individual as being responsible for any wrongdoing in order to establish the company's cooperation to avoid or limit criminal charges (see § 2.4).

When corporate counsel conducts an internal investigation, it is a common practice to advise employees that all communications are confidential in order to preserve the attorney-client privilege. Employees being interviewed are often given what is known as an "*Upjohn* warning" to inform them that counsel represents the corporation and not the individual, and any discussions with counsel may not be disclosed without the company's permission. In addition, the warning should inform the employee that the organization controls the attorney-client privilege, which can be waived resulting in disclosure of any statements the person made.

There is sometimes a dispute about whether corporate counsel also represented an individual employee during an investigation, which would allow that person to object to the company's disclosure of communications coming within the attorney-client privilege. The usual rule about whether there is an attorney-client relationship is to consider whether the individual has an honest and reasonable belief that the lawyer was acting as his or her counsel. A different approach applies in the corporate counsel context, however, as the First Circuit noted in *In re Grand Jury Subpoena*[44] that "[t]he default assumption is that the attorney only represents the corporate entity, not the individuals within the corporate sphere, and it is the individuals' burden to dispel that presumption."

---

[44] 274 F.3d 563 (1st Cir. 2001).

The leading case on determining the scope of the privilege when it is claimed for communications with corporate counsel is *In re Bevill, Bresler & Schulman Asset Management Corp.*,[45] a bankruptcy case in which the trustee for the company waived the privilege to allow disclosure to the SEC of communications between officers and corporate counsel. The officers challenged the disclosure on the ground that they were part of a joint-defense agreement that resulted in personal representation by the company's lawyers, and therefore they would also have to waive the privilege. The Third Circuit took a limited view of whom corporate counsel represents, so that "[a] corporate official thus may not prevent a corporation from waiving its privilege arising from discussions with corporate counsel about corporate matters." The circuit court upheld the application of the following test by the district court to determine whether the company's lawyer also represents individual employees as well:

> First, they must show they approached [counsel] for the purpose of seeking legal advice. Second, they must demonstrate that when they approached [counsel] they made it clear that they were seeking legal advice in their individual rather than in their representative capacities. Third, they must demonstrate that the [counsel] saw fit to communicate with them in their individual capacities, knowing that a possible conflict could arise. Fourth, they must prove that their conversations with [counsel] were confidential. And, fifth, they must show that the substance of their conversations with [counsel] did not concern matters within the company or the general affairs of the company.

Other circuits have adopted the *Bevill, Bresler* analysis for determining individual attorney-client privilege claims for communications with corporate counsel.[46]

The key limitation in the *Bevill, Bresler* analysis is the fifth one, regarding statements made by the individual about "the general affairs of the company" as falling outside the privilege. In *Grand Jury Proceedings v. United States*,[47] the Tenth Circuit considered a privilege claim of an individual employee related to communications about a corporate document. Rather than completely preclude assertion of the privilege, the circuit court stated, "[i]f the communication between a corporate officer and corporate counsel specifically focuses upon the *individual officer's* personal rights and liabilities, then the fifth prong of *In Matter of Bevill* can be satisfied even though the general subject matter of the conversation pertains to matters within the general affairs of the company." In *In re Grand Jury Subpoena*, the First Circuit noted that even if corporate counsel represented an employee along with the organization, that person "may only assert an individual privilege to the extent that communications regarding individual acts and liabilities are segregable from discussions about the corporation."

Even if there is joint representation of the corporation and an executive during an internal investigation, that does not necessarily mean statements made to corporate counsel will be privileged. In *United States v. Ruehle*,[48] the Ninth Circuit found that

---

[45] 805 F.2d 120 (3d Cir. 1986).

[46] United States v. Graf, 610 F.3d 1148 (9th Cir. 2010); In re Grand Jury Subpoenas, 144 F.3d 653 (10th Cir. 1998); United States v. International Brotherhood of Teamsters, 119 F.3d 210 (2d Cir. 1997); In re Sealed Case, 29 F.3d 715 (D.C. Cir. 1994). The Fourth Circuit reserved decision on whether to adopt the five-part test in In re Grand Jury Subpoena: Under Seal, 415 F.3d 333 (4th Cir. 2005).

[47] 156 F.3d 1038 (10th Cir. 1998).

[48] United States v. Ruehle, 583 F.3d 600 (9th Cir. 2009).

statements made by a company's chief financial officer at the start of an investigation into its accounting practices were not intended to be kept confidential because the statements were made "for the purpose of disclosure to the outside auditors." The circuit court found the attorney-client privilege inapplicable because

> Ruehle readily admits his understanding that all factual information would be communicated to third parties, which undermines his claim of confidentiality to support invoking the privilege. Ruehle's subjective shock and surprise about the subsequent usage of the information he knew would be disclosed to third-party auditors—e.g., information subsequently shared with securities regulators and the Justice Department now used to support a criminal investigation and his prosecution—is frankly of no consequence here.

§ 22.5 JOINT DEFENSE AGREEMENTS

The benefits provided by the attorney-client privilege have been extended in the multi-party context through joint defense agreements that permit counsel for one party to gather information from other parties without fear that the government can force disclosure of those communications. Called by various names, including the "common interest," "community of interest," and "joint defense" privilege, it is actually an extension of the attorney-client privilege to a particular situation in which parties with closely allied interests who can work together without foregoing the benefits of the privilege by communicating with non-clients. To qualify for protection, the Third Circuit stated in *Bevill, Bresler* that the communications must meet the basic requirements of the attorney-client privilege and demonstrate that "(1) the communications were made in the course of a joint defense effort, (2) the statements were designed to further the effort, and (3) the privilege has not been waived." The Restatement (Third) of the Law Governing Lawyers states the requirements for application of the privilege in "common-interest arrangements" this way:

> If two or more clients with a common interest in a litigated or nonlitigated matter are represented by separate lawyers and they agree to exchange information concerning the matter, a communication of any such client that otherwise qualifies as privileged. . . . that relates to the matter is privileged as against third persons. Any such client may invoke the privilege, unless it has been waived by the client who made the communication.[49]

The parties need not be in the exact same position, nor are they precluded from having certain conflicting interests among themselves. But there must be a significant degree of congruity between them to permit a court to find that they have agreed to act jointly in pursuing their legal position. In *F.D.I.C. v. Ogden Corp.*,[50] the First Circuit stated that the parties must have an "identical (or nearly identical) legal interest as opposed to a merely similar interest." A comment in the Restatement (Third) of the Law Governing Lawyers states that "[t]he interests of the separately represented clients need not be entirely congruent." Determining how closely allied the position of the participants in the joint defense must be remains vague, but co-defendants charged in the same case seem to clearly come within the scope of the privilege.

---

[49] Restatement (Third) of the Law Governing Lawyers § 76(1) (2000).

[50] 202 F.3d 454 (1st Cir. 2000).

The privilege can attach to communications before litigation commences, and applies in both criminal and civil cases. In *In re Grand Jury Subpoenas*,[51] the Fourth Circuit stated, "Whether an action is ongoing or contemplated, whether the jointly interested persons are defendants or plaintiffs, and whether the litigation or potential litigation is civil or criminal, the rationale for the joint defense rule remains unchanged. . . . " The privilege has been extended to cooperative efforts in SEC investigations,[52] private class actions,[53] and parent-subsidiary transactions.[54]

A key step in determining whether communications come within the attorney-client privilege is this relation to a legal issue about which the parties intend to act jointly. In *In re: Santa Fe International Corporation*,[55] the Fifth Circuit held that "there must be a palpable threat of litigation at the time of the communication, rather than a mere awareness that one's questionable conduct might some day result in litigation" in order for a communication to be considered part of a joint defense. In *United States v. BDO Seidman*,[56] however, the Seventh Circuit stated that "communications need not be made in anticipation of litigation to fall within the common interest doctrine." The distinction between the cases centers on whether there is a common legal interest at stake, and not just similar commercial or economic interests that tie the parties together and would result in their being in the same position if litigation developed later on. Thus, while a lawsuit need not imminent, there must be some legal issue that joins the different parties together, which will often involve a potential investigation or government enforcement proceeding, including criminal charges.

To protect communications on the basis of a joint defense or common interest, there must be an agreement for the parties to act together, although it need not be in writing or have other formalities attached. In *United States v. Bay State Ambulance and Hospital Rental Service*,[57] the First Circuit found that a written outline of conduct provided by the defendant to counsel for the corporation was not privileged because there was no evidence of an agreement between them. In *United States v. Melvin*,[58] counsel for one defendant asked another defendant, who was secretly cooperating with the government and stated that he did not have counsel, to attend meetings to discuss the case. The Fifth Circuit held that the communications were not intended to be confidential because the informant had not become a member of the defense team. Therefore, "Only those communications made in the course of an ongoing common enterprise and intended to further the enterprise are protected."[59]

The government may seek to learn the content of discussions among joint defendants or investigative targets and attorneys by arguing that there was no agreement permitting application of the attorney-client privilege, or that there was no

---

[51] 902 F.2d 244 (4th Cir. 1990).

[52] In re LTV Securities Litig., 89 F.R.D. 595 (N.D. Tex. 1981).

[53] Schachar v. American Academy of Opthamology, 106 F.R.D. 187 (N.D. Ill. 1985).

[54] Medcom Holding Co. v. Baxter Travenol Laboratories, 689 F.Supp. 841 (N.D. Ill. 1988).

[55] 272 F.3d 705 (5th Cir. 2001).

[56] 492 F.3d 806 (7th Cir. 2007).

[57] 874 F.2d 20 (1st Cir. 1989).

[58] 650 F.2d 641 (5th Cir. 1981).

[59] United States v. Schwimmer, 892 F.2d 237 (2d Cir. 1989).

intention to keep the communications confidential. To show the existence of a joint defense agreement, parties involved in governmental investigations often enter into written agreements that reflect their common interests in the investigation and set forth the basic framework of the relationship, including provisions for sharing work product among counsel and apportioning among different participants. But there is no requirement that it even be an express agreement. In *United States v. Gonzalez*,[60] the Ninth Circuit stated "it is clear that no written agreement is required, and that a JDA may be implied from conduct and situation, such as attorneys exchanging confidential communications from clients who are or potentially may be codefendants or have common interests in litigation." The parties must enter into an agreement to work together for a common purpose before communications will be protected, and the timing of the agreement can be crucial to determining whether a communication is protected by the privilege. In *United States v. Weissman*[61] and *In re Grand Jury Subpoena: Under Seal*,[62] the Second and Fourth Circuits refused to extend the privilege when the parties had not yet entered into a joint defense agreement at the time of the communications with corporate counsel.

The privilege covers all communications made within the scope of the joint defense to any counsel, not just those with one's own lawyer. When communications are protected by a joint defense agreement or common interest, then the attorney-client privilege can only be waived by the members of the common group because each shares in the protection. In *In re Grand Jury Subpoena*,[63] the First Circuit stated that the agreement "prevents disclosure of a communication made in the course of preparing a joint defense by the third party to whom it was made." Thus, one participant cannot reveal the communications made in the course of the common action by other participants in the joint defense. However, because each participant controls the attorney-client privilege regarding his or her own communications, the person can waive the privilege as to those statements. In *United States v. Almeida*,[64] the Eleventh Circuit explained the scope of the protection:

> [E]ach party to a joint defense agreement is represented by his own attorney, and when communications by one co-defendant are made to the attorneys of other co-defendants, such communications do not get the benefit of the attorney-client privilege in the event that the co-defendant decides to testify on behalf of the government in exchange for a reduced sentence.

A joint defense agreement is like any contact, so its terms are subject to the interpretation of the courts and can be modified with the agreement of the parties. In *United States v. LeCroy*,[65] the district court found that a written joint defense agreement had been orally modified by one of the parties, the corporate employer, who informed the two employees that it intended to turn over to prosecutors the notes of an interview with them. By agreeing to the interview, the court found that the agreement

---

[60] 669 F.3d 974 (9th Cir. 2012).

[61] 195 F.3d 96 (2d Cir. 1999).

[62] 415 F.3d 333 (4th Cir. 2005).

[63] 274 F.3d 563 (1st Cir. 2001).

[64] 341 F.3d 1318 (11th Cir. 2003).

[65] 348 F. Supp. 2d 375 (E.D. Pa. 2004).

had been altered to permit the disclosure without violating the attorney-client privilege.

The privilege does not extend to communications among the defendants or investigative targets outside the presence of counsel, at least where those communications would not otherwise be covered by the attorney-client privilege. Statements outside the presence of counsel are generally considered to not be made in connection with seeking legal advice, a condition for invoking the attorney-client privilege. In *In re Teleglobe Communications Corp.*,[66] the Third Circuit held that "to be eligible for continued protection, the communication must be shared with the *attorney* of the member of the community of interest. Sharing the communication directly with a member of the community may destroy the privilege." Similarly, in *United States v. Gotti*,[67] the district court refused a defense claim that recordings of conversations between defendants when no lawyers were present should be suppressed because it violated the joint defense privilege, holding that "[s]uch an extension is supported neither in law nor in logic and is rejected."

A joint defense agreement can cause problems for the lawyers if one party withdraws and agrees to cooperate with government by testifying against the remaining member(s). Because counsel for the other participant(s) is likely to have received privileged communications from the cooperating witness, those must remain confidential, absent a waiver. Information gained through the agreement cannot be used against the withdrawing person, for example by cross-examining about inconsistencies between the testimony and prior statements made during the course of the joint defense. Thus, the remaining lawyers can have a conflict of interest that prevents them from representing other defendants adequately because of the obligation to the withdrawing party.

In *United States v. Henke*,[68] the Ninth Circuit stated that "[a] joint defense agreement establishes an implied attorney-client relationship with the co-defendant." In that case, the district judge refused to allow the lawyers for the remaining defendants to withdraw because of the conflict with the cooperating witness who had been a party to the joint defense agreement. The district court reasoned that the defendants would be in no worse position than if new counsel who did not receive confidential communications were appointed—in either situation, the communications would not be available for use by the defense. This approach was rejected because it did not address the impact of the conflict, which resulted in ineffective assistance of counsel who could not effectively cross-examine the cooperating witness. The circuit court pointed out that it was not adopting a blanket rule requiring disqualification of all defense counsel when one member of a joint defense agreement testifies for the government. It noted that "[t]here may be cases in which defense counsel's possession of information about a former co-defendant/government witness learned through joint

---

[66] 493 F.3d 345 (3d Cir. 2007).

[67] 771 F.Supp. 535 (E.D.N.Y. 1991).

[68] 222 F.3d 633 (9th Cir. 2000).

defense meetings will not impair defense counsel's ability to represent the defendant or breach the duty of confidentiality to the former co-defendant."[69]

In *Roosevelt Irrigation District v. Salt River Project Agricultral Improvement and Power District*,[70] the district court pointed out that "an attorney may be disqualified from a proceeding if the attorney is both in actual possession of confidential information, and by virtue of having this information, is either incapable of adequately representing the new client or will breach the duty of confidentiality owed to the former co-defendant." Thus, defense lawyers have to determine whether their ability to adequately defend a client has been impaired because of an obligation to maintain the confidentiality of communications when a member of the joint defense agreement defects to the government.

A joint defense agreement can contain a provision providing that there is no implied attorney-client relationship between the lawyers and non-clients participating in the common undertaking, and that the withdrawal of a member will waive any privilege claim regarding communications with counsel for the remaining defendants. Those provisions can obviate any potential conflict of interest that would require counsel for the remaining defendants to withdraw. In *United States v. Stepney*,[71] a large-scale drug and weapons prosecution, the district court required that "[e]ach joint defense agreement must contain provisions conditionally waiving confidentiality by providing that a signatory attorney cross-examining any defendant who testifies at any proceeding, whether under a grant of immunity or otherwise, may use any material or other information contributed by such client during the joint defense." If the parties do not have a written agreement, however, then it can be difficult to establish any waiver of confidentiality, so there is a greater risk the defense lawyers may have a potential conflict that can result in disqualification from further representation in the case.

An issue can arise when a cooperating witness who participated in a joint defense agreement becomes privy to the defense strategy. The prosecutor may not intentionally "invade the defense camp" for information, although the Supreme Court recognized in *Weatherford v. Bursey*[72] that the government can authorize a cooperating witness to attend a meeting with counsel for other defendants to maintain the witness's cover. *Weatherford* required a defendant to show prejudice arising from the informant's presence at a meeting with the defense attorney to constitute a violation of the Sixth Amendment right to counsel. In *United States v. Mastroianni*,[73] an unindicted informant attended a meeting with counsel for a defendant out of fear that revealing his cooperation would endanger his safety. The First Circuit held that the government bears the burden of proving the necessity of the informant's attendance at the meeting to avoid a Sixth Amendment violation. It held that any "advantage that the government gains in the first instance by insinuating itself into the midst of the defense meeting must not be abused."

---

[69] See United States v. Executive Recycling, Inc., 908 F.Supp.2d 1156 (D. Colo. 2012) (attorney not permitted to withdraw because potential conflict with co-defendant who left joint defense agreement but was not cooperating with the government was minimal).

[70] 810 F. Supp. 2d 929 (D. Ariz. 2011).

[71] 246 F. Supp. 2d 1069 (N.D. Cal. 2003).

[72] 429 U.S. 545 (1977).

[73] 749 F.2d 900 (1st Cir. 1984).

§ 22.6   WAIVER

A.   Express Waiver

The attorney-client privilege, like all privileges, can be waived by its holder, which is the client, through a knowing and voluntary relinquishment of the protection. Thus, a client can choose to reveal protected communications with counsel, thereby removing any claim to confidentiality afforded by the law. As the agent for the client, an attorney also can waive the privilege even without the client's prior authorization. Once waived, formerly privileged communications can be used in any civil or criminal proceeding.

The same waiver rule applies to organizations, although the analysis is complicated by the fact that no one individual usually speaks on behalf of the organization. In *CFTC v. Weintraub*,[74] the Supreme Court considered the authority to waive a corporation's attorney-client privilege. It noted that for a solvent corporation "the power to waive the corporate attorney-client privilege rests with the corporation's management and is normally exercised by its officers and directors." Similarly, if a company is acquired, its new management decides whether to waive the privilege, even if former managers object because it is the organization that controls the privilege and determines whether to permit disclosure of confidential communications.

Although a corporation's board usually decides whether to waive the privilege, the conduct of a senior corporate officer may result in a waiver of the privilege. In *Velsicol Chemical Corp. v. Parsons*,[75] the Seventh Circuit held that in-house counsel's testimony before a grand jury about confidential communications by employees to corporate lawyers waived the company's privilege because he "was nonetheless possessed of the office of house counsel of the corporation and as such was an agent of the client corporation with authority to waive the attorney-client privilege." But in *In re Grand Jury Proceedings*,[76] the Second Circuit found that the grand jury testimony of a corporate officer did not waive the organization's privilege when the person did not have the authority to waive, testified in a personal capacity rather than on the company's behalf, and corporate counsel had expressly informed prosecutors that it did not intend to waive the attorney-client privilege.

When a company is placed into bankruptcy, a trustee may be appointed under federal law to administer the reorganization or dissolution process, effectively taking control of the organization. In that context, the Supreme Court in *CFTC v. Weintraub* held that "vesting in the trustee control of the corporation's attorney-client privilege most closely comports with the allocation of the waiver power to management outside of bankruptcy without in any way obstructing the careful design of the Bankruptcy Code." This authority can be important in corporate criminal investigations because a company may suffer significant financial difficulties due to the misconduct of its management, resulting in a bankruptcy. The trustee will usually be willing to waive the attorney-client privilege to allow investigators to obtain access to corporate counsel to determine who might be responsible for any violations.

---

[74] 471 U.S. 343 (1985).

[75] 561 F.2d 671 (7th Cir. 1977).

[76] 219 F.3d 175 (2d Cir. 2000).

An issue arose about whether the Department of Justice was improperly pressuring corporations to waive the attorney-client privilege to demonstrate their cooperation in order to avoid being charged with a crime or obtain a favorable settlement. In that situation, it was questionable whether the waiver was truly voluntary. As discussed in § 2.4(A), prosecutors are now prohibited by Department of Justice policy from seeking a waiver of the privilege, although companies continue to feel pressure to disclose confidential communications to generate goodwill with prosecutors.

Apart from express waiver, there are a number of issues that arise when the circumstances may indicate an implied waiver of the privilege. In this context, the term "waiver" was described by the First Circuit in *United States v. Massachusetts Institute of Technology*[77] as a "loose and misleading label for what is in fact a collection of different rules addressed to different problems." The circuit court noted that the waiver issue covers cases "as divergent as an express and voluntary surrender of the privilege, partial disclosure of a privileged document, selective disclosure to some outsiders but not all, and inadvertent overhearings or disclosures."

B. Partial and Selective Waiver

The protection afforded by the attorney-client privilege requires a party to maintain the confidentiality of the communications, and the usual rule is that once a party discloses them their confidentiality is irretrievably lost and cannot be restored. In *In re Martin Marietta Corp*,[78] the Fourth Circuit stated that "any disclosure of a confidential communication outside a privileged relationship will waive the privilege as to all information related to the same subject matter." Although unintended, a client can engage in conduct that operates as an implied waiver of the privilege.

There may be an issue about the scope of any implied waiver concerning whether it was a partial waiver, requiring disclosure of additional information, and whether disclosure to one party necessarily entails a complete loss of the privilege in relation to others. A partial waiver "permits a client who has disclosed a portion of privileged communications to continue asserting the privilege as to the remaining portions of the same communications,"[79] such as part of a memorandum or a portion of a discussion with counsel. Selective waiver is the intentional disclosure to a third person of privileged communications after which the party seeks to assert the privilege to prevent disclosure to others. The issue usually arises in white collar crime cases when a corporation discloses the results of its internal investigation to a government agency that includes privileged communications with its employees, and a third party seeks to obtain from the company the information it revealed to the government.

The partial disclosure of confidential communications waives the privilege not only with respect to what was actually revealed, but may also encompass related information that the party continues to withhold. Courts can require disclosure of additional privileged communications if the disclosed information would be favorable to the privileged party such that it would be unfair to an opponent not to give it the

---

[77] 129 F.3d 681 (1997).

[78] 856 F.2d 619 (4th Cir. 1988).

[79] Westinghouse Electric Corp. v. Republic of Philippines, 951 F.2d 1414 (3d Cir. 1991).

opportunity to explore fully the context of the disclosure. In *In re Martin Marietta Corp.*, the Fourth Circuit required disclosure of the communications and data underlying a report prepared by a company's counsel and then submitted to the government. This is similar to the "rule of completeness" under Federal Rule of Evidence 106, which provides: "If a party introduces all or part of a writing or recorded statement, an adverse party may require the introduction, at that time, of any other part—or any other writing or recorded statement—that in fairness ought to be considered at the same time."

Federal Rule of Evidence 502(a), adopted in 2008, puts this approach into practice when considerations of fairness related to a waiver of a privileged communication can extend to an undisclosed communication. When the waiver was made in a federal proceeding, which includes both judicial and administrative matters, or is made "to a federal office or agency," then the waiver can extend to other communications only if three conditions are met:

(1) the waiver is intentional;

(2) the disclosed and undisclosed communications or information concern the same subject matter; and

(3) they ought in fairness to be considered together.

Rule 502(f) makes this provision specifically applicable to both federal and state proceedings, one of the rare instances when a federal rule governs evidence in a state case, regardless of whether it involves any issues of federal law. The rationale for extending it to state court proceedings, as explained in the Advisory Committee Note, was "[t]o assure protection and predicatability." The Advisory Committee scaled the rule back from the original proposal that would have applied a uniform rule in all federal or state proceedings, opting instead to limit the waiver to instances in which the initial disclosure was at the federal level.

Rule 502(d) authorizes a court to issue an order providing "that the privilege or protection is not waived by disclosure connected with the litigation pending before the court—in which event the disclosure is also not a waiver in any other Federal or State proceeding." This effectively allows the court to institute a rule of selective waiver in the particular case before it that will govern other proceedings in federal or state court. The rule does not enable parties to agree in advance to a selective waiver of the attorney-client privilege and then seek judicial approval in a separate proceeding, so Rule 502's protections can only be implemented in the context of ongoing litigation.[80]

While parties have argued that disclosure to one party should not operate as complete waiver of the privilege, all the circuit courts except one endorse the rule that disclosure of privileged materials to any third party outside the protections afforded by Rule 502, including to a government agency or a company's outside auditor, waives the attorney-client privilege.[81] In *Permian Corp. v. United States*,[82] the District of

---

[80] Cong. Rec. H7818 to H7819 (Sept. 8, 2008) (House Judiciary Committee clarifications to scope of Rule 502(a)).

[81] In re Pacific Pictures Corp., 679 F.3d 1121 (9th Cir. 2012); In re Qwest Communications Int'l, 450 F.3d 1179 (10th Cir. 2006); Burden–Meeks v. Welch, 319 F.3d 897 (7th Cir. 2003); In re Columbia/HCA

Columbia Circuit rejected the concept of selective waiver, explaining that it was inconsistent with the rationale of the attorney-client privilege that sought to encourage full disclosure to lawyers by requiring strict confidentiality of communications:

> The client cannot be permitted to pick and choose among his opponents, waiving the privilege for some and resurrecting the claim of confidentiality to obstruct others, or to invoke the privilege as to communications whose confidentiality he has already compromised for his own benefit. . . . The attorney-client privilege is not designed for such tactical employment.

The Eighth Circuit is the only court to have recognized that a client may reveal privileged communications to a government agency without thereby waiving the privilege with respect to third parties. In *Diversified Industries v. Meredith*,[83] the circuit court stated the reason for allowing disclosure to a government agency that would not completely vitiate the attorney-client privilege: "To hold otherwise may have the effect of thwarting the developing procedure of corporations to employ independent outside counsel to investigate and advise them in order to protect stockholders, potential stockholders and customers." The Ninth Circuit questioned this rationale in *In re Pacific Pictures Corp.*[84] in rejecting the selective waiver approach, stating that "[t]his apprehension has proven unjustified. Officers of public corporations, it seems, do not require a rule of selective waiver to employ outside consultants or voluntarily to cooperate with the government."

Congress has adopted a selective waiver provision for banks and credit unions that disclose privileged communications to regulators. A provision of the Financial Services Regulator Relief Act, enacted in 2006, provides:

> The submission by any person of any information to any Federal banking agency, State bank supervisor, or foreign banking authority for any purpose in the course of any supervisory or regulatory process of such agency, supervisor, or authority shall not be construed as waiving, destroying, or otherwise affecting any privilege such person may claim with respect to such information under Federal or State law as to any person or entity other than such agency, supervisor, or authority.[85]

The Judicial Conference of the United States considered adding Rule 502 to the Federal Rules of Evidence that would have recognized selective waiver when privileged communications were provided to a federal agency.[86] Due to strong opposition to the proposal, however, it never advanced to the Supreme Court for consideration.

Healthcare Corp. Billing Practices Litigation, 293 F.3d 289 (6th Cir. 2002); United States v. Massachusetts Institute of Technology, 129 F.3d 681 (1st Cir. 1997); In re Steinhardt Partners, LP, 9 F.3d 230 (2d Cir. 1993); Westinghouse Electric Corp. v. Republic of the Philippines, 951 F.2d 1414 (3d Cir. 1991); Permian Corp. v. United States, 665 F.2d 1214 (D.C. Cir. 1981).

[82] 665 F.2d 1214 (D.C. Cir. 1981).

[83] 572 F.2d 596 (8th Cir. 1977).

[84] 679 F.3d 1121 (9th Cir. 2012).

[85] 12 U.S.C. § 1828(x)(1). The provision for credit unions can be found at 12 U.S.C. § 1785(j)(1).

[86] Advisory Committee on Evidence Rules, Minutes of the Meeting of November 16, 2006, available at http:// www.uscourts.gov/uscourts/RulesAndPolicies/rules/Minutes/EV11–2006–min.pdf.

C. Inadvertent Disclosure

The prevalence of electronic files for documents, and the use of e-mail, text messaging, and other electronic forms of communication, has substantially increased the possibility that otherwise privileged communications will be inadvertently disclosed to an opponent during litigation. Although the usual rule is that any disclosure of a privileged communication waives confidentiality, there has been a general reluctance to adopt a broad rule of "accidental" waiver through inadvertent disclosure that does not permit a party to protect communications. Federal Rule of Evidence 502(b) now provides for dealing with this issue in federal cases:

> When made in a Federal proceeding or to a Federal office or agency, the disclosure does not operate as a waiver in a Federal or State proceeding if:
>
> 1.   the disclosure is inadvertent;
>
> 2.   the holder of the privilege or protection took reasonable steps to prevent disclosure; and
>
> 3.   the holder promptly took reasonable steps to rectify the error, including (if applicable) following Federal Rule of Civil Procedure 26(b)(5)(B).

Federal Rule of Civil Procedure 26(b)(5)(B) provides a set of procedures in civil litigation if a party is notified that otherwise privileged information has been unintentionally disclosed. Under the rule, the receiving party

> must promptly return, sequester, or destroy the specified information and any copies it has; must not use or disclose the information until the claim is resolved; must take reasonable steps to retrieve the information if the party disclosed it before being notified; and may promptly present the information to the court under seal for a determination of the claim.

ABA Model Rule of Professional Conduct 4.4(b) requires that a "lawyer who receives a document relating to the representation of the lawyer's client and knows or reasonably should know that the document was inadvertently sent shall promptly notify the sender." Note that the obligation under the Model Rule is not as broad as Rule 26(b)(5)(B), which requires much greater action by an attorney to ensure the privileged information is not available. Moreover, some state bar authorities may permit limited use of information inadvertently provided by an opponent in representing the client.[87]

Most courts reviewing claims that inadvertent disclosure waives the attorney-client privilege have tended to adopt a middle-of-the-road approach reflective of Rule 502(b) that eschews a categorical approach to finding waiver in all circumstances or no waiver once inadvertence is shown. In *Ciba–Geigy Corp. v. Sandoz Ltd.*,[88] the district court described the analysis: "While an inadvertent disclosure is, by definition, an unintentional act, if such a disclosure results from gross negligence, courts . . . will

---

[87] See Colorado Bar Op. 108 (2000); D.C. Bar Op. 256 (1995); Maryland Op. 2007–09 (2007); Philadelphia Bar Ass'n Op. 94–3 (1994).

[88] 916 F.Supp. 404 (D. N.J. 1995).

deem the disclosure to be intentional, thus constituting a waiver of the privilege." In *United States v. Keystone Sanitation Co., Inc.*,[89] a pre-Rule 502 case, the district court described the factors taken into consideration to determine whether a party was grossly negligent in disclosing privileged information:

> (1) the reasonableness of the precautions taken to prevent inadvertent disclosure in view of the extent of the document production; (2) the number of inadvertent disclosures; (3) the extent of the disclosure; (4) any delay and measure taken to rectify the disclosure; and (5) whether the overriding interests of justice would or would not be served by relieving a party of its error.

In *Edelen v. Campbell Soup Co.*,[90] applying Rule 502, the district court held, "Given that only four pages out of a more than 2000 page production were privileged, the documents were checked by three different attorneys prior to production, and counsel immediately sought the return of the documents once they discovered their mistake, return of the documents is required." In *Callan v. Christian Audigier, Inc.*,[91] on the other hand, the district court rejected a claim of inadvertence, finding that the party failed to show that it "reviewed the allegedly privileged documents before producing them to plaintiff or what precautions they took to prevent the disclosure of allegedly privileged documents to plaintiff; thus, defendants have not shown their production of any document was 'inadvertent.'" The cases are very fact-intensive, and almost all of the decisions in this area have come in civil litigation, in which document production is much broader than in a criminal prosecution.

D. Advice of Counsel Defense

A defendant can offer what is sometimes termed an "advice of counsel" defense to certain types of charges that require proof of a specific intent in which good faith is a defense. Relying on legal advice is not an affirmative defense asserting that the defendant acted properly, but a basis to argue the defendant acted in good faith, and therefore should not be found guilty because of reliance on the advice of an attorney. In *United States v. Joshua*,[92] the Seventh Circuit explained that offering such evidence "is not a stand-alone defense; rather, information about advice of counsel sheds light on the question whether the defendants had the required intent to defraud." In order to use legal advice as a basis for establishing good faith, the Eighth Circuit explained in *United States v. Rice*[93] that a defendant must show that he "(i) fully disclosed all material facts to his attorney before seeking advice; and (ii) actually relied on his counsel's advice in the good faith belief that his conduct was legal." Merely consulting an attorney is not enough to establish good faith, as the circuit court noted when stating that "a defendant is not immunized from criminal prosecution merely because he consulted an attorney in connection with a particular transaction."

By asserting reliance on the lawyer, courts have determined that this operates as an implied waiver of the attorney-client privilege, so that the defendant cannot seek to

---

[89] 885 F.Supp. 672 (M.D. Pa. 1994).
[90] 265 F.R.D. 676 (N.D. Ga. 2010).
[91] 263 F.R.D. 564 (C.D. Cal. 2009).
[92] 648 F.3d 547 (7th Cir. 2011).
[93] 449 F.3d 887 (8th Cir. 2006).

keep the attorney from testifying about the advice given. In *United States v. Bilzerian*,[94] the Second Circuit rejected a defendant's argument that the trial court erred when it would not permit him to testify that he consulted with an attorney before engaging in conduct without waiving the attorney-client privilege regarding what was actually said. The circuit court noted "the attorney-client privilege cannot at once be used as a shield and a sword," so that the defendant's "conversations with counsel regarding the legality of his schemes would have been directly relevant in determining the extent of his knowledge and, as a result, his intent."

§ 22.7 CRIME–FRAUD EXCEPTION

Communications between the targets of criminal investigations and their attorneys can be fertile ground for gathering incriminating statements because clients can be expected to be honest with their lawyers and reveal their true intentions. The attorney-client privilege protects such communications except when the client seeks legal advice in furtherance of a pending or future crime or fraud. In *Clark v. United States*,[95] which concerned whether the privilege for jury deliberations could be vitiated because a juror failed to disclose important information, the Supreme Court said that "[a] client who consults an attorney for advice that will serve him in the commission of a fraud will have no help from the law. He must let the truth be told."

Because lawyers often have a continuing role in advising business organizations, there is a real possibility that an attorney may be an unwitting—or perhaps even a witting—participant in criminal activity. The crime-fraud exception to the attorney-client privilege has grown in importance in white collar crime investigations as attorneys are consulted more frequently about business activities and sought out when there is even just the potential for a criminal or regulatory investigation. As a well-known white collar defense practitioner once noted, "The government invokes [the crime-fraud exception] because lawyers have a prominent role in complex transactions in areas which are the subject of increasing criminal investigations, such as tax, banking, and securities."[96]

The first step in the analysis is to determine that the communication meets the requirements for being privileged, and the burden is on the party asserting it to establish that it is protected. If that is done, then the burden shifts to the party seeking disclosure of the communications to show (1) that they were related to an ongoing or contemplated crime or fraud and (2) the attorney was consulted "in furtherance" of that crime or fraud. The client's intent at the time of the consultation must be to obtain legal advice to assist in the pending or future crime, not that the person later determined to act improperly after consulting counsel. Because the focus is on the client's intentions, that is usually established through circumstantial evidence and, as discussed below, the content of the communications.

The crime-fraud exception cannot be applied to communications about completed acts for which a client sought legal advice, because that is the core of the protection

---

[94] 926 F.2d 1285 (2d Cir. 1991).

[95] 289 U.S. 1 (1933).

[96] Earl J. Silbert, The Crime–Fraud Exception to the Attorney–Client Privilege and Work–Product Doctrine, the Lawyer's Obligations of Disclosure, and the Lawyer's Response to Accusation of Wrongful Conduct, 23 Am Crim. L. Rev. 351 (1986)

afforded by the privilege. In *In re Federal Grand Jury Proceedings*,[97] the Eleventh Circuit held that "although communications otherwise covered by the attorney-client privilege lose their privileged status when used to further a crime or fraud, post-crime repetition or discussion of such earlier communications . . . may still be privileged even though those earlier communications were not privileged because of the crime-fraud exception." But if a client were to seek legal advice regarding pending or future illegal or fraudulent conduct and in the course of the discussion recounted prior criminal activity, then that could lose the protection of the attorney-client privilege.

The communication must be related to the illegal or fraudulent acts of the client, although the attorney need not be aware that the legal advice sought was in furtherance of improper conduct. The Ninth Circuit stated in *In re Grand Jury Proceedings* that "the attorney need know nothing about the client's ongoing or planned illicit activity for the exception to apply." The communication must relate to the client's misconduct and not that of a third party. The District of Columbia Circuit pointed out in *In re Sealed Case*,[98] "The privilege is the client's, and it is the client's fraudulent or criminal intent that matters. A third party's bad intent cannot remove the protection of the privilege."

The types of conduct that can constitute a crime or fraud are quite broad, and do not require the party seeking the communications to show an actual prosecution, or even that the party to the communications viewed the pending or proposed conduct as illegal. In *Rambus, Inc. v. Infineon Technologies AG*,[99] a civil case, the district court found spoliation of evidence sufficient misconduct to invoke the crime-fraud exception because "destruction of documents of evidentiary value under those circumstances is wrongful and is fundamentally at odds with the administration of justice." The illegal or fraudulent act only has to be one objective of seeking the legal advice, and the client need not succeed for the crime-fraud exception to be invoked. As the Second Circuit noted in *In re Grand Jury Subpoena Duces Tecum Dated Sept. 15, 1983*,[100] "If a fraudulent plan were ineffective, the client's communications would not thereby be protected from disclosure." The question whether an alleged course of conduct qualifies as a crime or fraud is rarely an issue because the criminal law potentially encompasses most acts of questionable legality, and a fraud can be perpetrated in almost any context.

The "in furtherance" requirement is established when the documents or oral communications "containing the privileged materials bear a close relationship to the client's existing or future scheme to commit a crime or fraud."[101] The party seeking disclosure of the communications usually will not know its content, and therefore courts do not require proof showing conclusively the connection between the privileged communication and the intended illegal or fraudulent act. Nevertheless, the mere proximity in time between the consultation with an attorney and the crime or fraud does not necessarily establish the requisite nexus to overcome the privilege. As the

---

[97] 938 F.2d 1578 (11th Cir. 1991).

[98] 107 F.3d 46 (D.C. Cir. 1997).

[99] 222 F.R.D. 280 (E.D. Va. 2004).

[100] 731 F.2d 1032 (2d Cir. 1984).

[101] In re Grand Jury Proceedings #5 Empanelled January 28, 2004, 401 F.3d 247 (4th Cir. 2005).

Second Circuit stated in *In re Grand Jury Subpoenas Duces Tecum*,[102] it is insufficient to invoke the crime-fraud exception "merely upon a showing that the client communicated with counsel while the client was engaged in criminal activity."

The relationship between the privileged communications and the crime or fraud is often based on an inference about what the client may have learned from the attorney and how it could be related to the misconduct at issue. In *In re Grand Jury Investigation*,[103] the Third Circuit reviewed a district court's finding that the crime-fraud exception applied to legal advice given to an executive of a non-profit organization about the need to retain e-mails that were called for by a grand jury subpoena investigating the organization. When it came to light that e-mails continued to be deleted after consulting with the attorney, the government sought to learn the conversations between the attorney and the executive. The circuit court found that the communications from the lawyer could have been used in furtherance of a crime:

> If, with knowledge of the Government's interest in retrieving any remaining emails, Jane Doe continued to receive emails that were arguably responsive to the subpoena and failed to use her position as an executive of the Organization to direct that all email deletions stop immediately, she may be viewed as furthering the obstruction of the grand jury's investigation or the obstruction of justice.

The key issue in applying the crime-fraud exception is the quantum of proof the party asserting it must proffer to establish that the communications are not protected by the attorney-client. The rule is that the party seeking the privileged communications must make a prima facie showing that the communication was in furtherance of a crime or fraud. In *In re Grand Jury Proceedings*,[104] the First Circuit made the wry observation that "'[p]rima facie' is among the most rubbery of all legal phrases; it usually means little more than a showing of whatever is required to permit some inferential leap sufficient to reach a particular outcome."

The lower courts have used a number of different formulations to describe the level of proof required to meet this standard: "reasonable cause to believe" a crime or fraud was intended,[105] "a reasonable basis to suspect the perpetration of a crime or fraud,"[106] "evidence which, if believed by the fact-finder, would be sufficient to support a finding that the elements of the crime-fraud exception were met,"[107] evidence "such as will suffice until contradicted and overcome by other evidence,"[108] and "evidence that, if believed by a trier of fact, would establish the elements of some violation that was ongoing or about to be committed."[109] The Second Circuit referred to a probable cause standard rather than a prima facie test, but noted that regardless of the terminology used, "[b]oth require that a prudent person have a reasonable basis to suspect the perpetration or attempted perpetration of a crime or fraud, and that the

---

[102] 798 F.2d 32 (2d Cir. 1986).

[103] 445 F.3d 266 (3d Cir. 2006).

[104] 417 F.3d 18 (1st Cir. 2005).

[105] In re Grand Jury Proceedings (Corporation), 87 F.3d 377 (9th Cir. 1996).

[106] In re Antitrust Grand Jury, 805 F.2d 155 (6th Cir. 1986).

[107] Haines v. Liggett Group, Inc., 975 F.3d 81 (3d Cir. 1992).

[108] In re Grand Jury Subpoena, 419 F.3d 329 (5th Cir.2005).

[109] In re Grand Jury Proceedings #5 Empanelled January 28, 2004, 401 F.3d 247 (4th Cir. 2005).

communications were in furtherance thereof."[110] The First Circuit explained the standard in *In re Grand Jury Proceedings* this way: "The circuits—although divided on articulation and on some important practical details—all effectively allow piercing of the privilege on something less than a mathematical (more likely than not) probability that the client intended to use the attorney in furtherance of a crime or fraud." What is clear about the standard of proof to establish the crime-fraud exception is that the party seeking to obtain the privileged communications need not meet the "beyond a reasonable doubt" or even the "preponderance of the evidence" thresholds applied to factual and evidentiary determinations.

The prima facie (or probable cause) standard begs the question of what evidence a court can consider in determining whether the exception should apply. It is often the case that the privileged communication itself is the best proof of whether the legal advice was in furtherance of a crime or fraud, yet the privilege ensures the confidentiality of the communications or its value is severely diminished. In *United States v. Zolin*,[111] the Supreme Court held that a trial court can conduct an *in camera* review of an attorney-client communication to determine whether the crime-fraud exception applied. The Court rejected the Ninth Circuit's rule that the party seeking disclosure of privileged communications must adduce "independent evidence" of the crime or fraud without relying on the communications at issue.

Zolin refused to adopt a blanket rule permitting *in camera* review upon the request of the party opposing the privilege, explaining that such an approach would permit parties "to engage in groundless fishing expeditions, with the district courts as their unwitting (and perhaps unwilling) agents." Instead, the Court required the party seeking disclosure to provide the trial court with a factual basis "'adequate to support a good faith belief by a reasonable person'" that *in camera* review "may reveal evidence to establish the claim that the crime-fraud exception applies." The Court noted that this preliminary standard is lower than the prima facie case necessary to a determination of whether the crime-fraud exception should be invoked. The impact of *Zolin*'s approach is to make the threshold issue of whether the court can consider the privileged communication critical to the outcome. Once the party seeking disclosure provides enough evidence showing a factual basis to meet the good faith belief threshold, then the *in camera* review will often provide the evidence necessary to meet the prima facie standard for vitiating the attorney-client privilege.

The procedure for pursuing a crime-fraud claim in a criminal case often involves the government making an *ex parte, in camera* submission of grand jury materials to establish the potential misconduct to which the privileged communication relates. A district court can consider this evidence, along with any other submissions by the government, in making either the preliminary *Zolin* determination to review the communications at issue, or to decide that there is a prima facie case of a crime or fraud sufficient to vitiate the privilege.

Courts have rejected claims of a due process violation for not allowing the defendant to review the government's *ex parte* submission, including grand jury material otherwise subject to the strict secrecy requirement, in order to challenge the

---

[110] In re Grand Jury Subpoena Duces Tecum Dated Sept. 15, 1983, 731 F.2d 1032 (2d Cir. 1984).
[111] 491 U.S. 554 (1989).

good faith belief or prima facie standard for application of the crime-fraud exception. In *In re Grand Jury Proceedings, Thursday Special Grand Jury Sept. Term, 1991*,[112] the Fourth Circuit noted that it has "expressly held that a court's *in camera* examination of evidence supporting the applicability of the crime-fraud exception is not violative of due process." In *In re John Doe Inc.*,[113] the Second Circuit held that "[i]n light of the district court's legitimate concern that the secrecy of the grand jury be preserved, its *in camera* examination of the attorney was the most effective method of determining that the crime-fraud exception had been established." The circuit court also noted, however, that "where concerns for secrecy are weak, an *in camera* proceeding may not be justified." All other circuit courts that have considered the issue have upheld a district court's decision not to disclose the government's *ex parte, in camera* submission made to establish the prima facie case, at least where it contains grand jury material for which secrecy must be maintained.[114] In civil cases, on the other hand, the party opposing the crime-fraud claim will be afforded the opportunity to rebut the prima facie case because there is no danger that secret grand jury information will be revealed.[115]

Once it is determined that the crime-fraud exception applies, the trial court must determine which communications lose the protection. The fact that a client consulted an attorney for the purpose of engaging in misconduct does not mean every communication falls outside the privilege. In *In re Grand Jury Subpoena*,[116] the Fifth Circuit held that "the proper reach of the crime-fraud exception when applicable does not extend to all communications made in the course of the attorney-client relationship, but rather is limited to those communications and documents in furtherance of the contemplated or ongoing criminal or fraudulent conduct."

Once a district court determines that the crime-fraud exception applies, it will have to assess which documents or statements can be disclosed. In *In re Richard Roe, Inc.*,[117] the Second Circuit outlined what the district court was required to do:

> [It] shall determine which, if any, of the documents or communications were in furtherance of a crime or fraud. . . . If production is ordered, the court shall specify the factual basis for the crime or fraud that the documents or communications are deemed to have furthered, which of the parties asserting claims of privilege possessed a criminal or fraudulent purpose with respect to those documents or communications, and, if appropriate, whether the crime-fraud exception applies to an innocent joint privilege-holder.

If the lawyer will be called before the grand jury to testify, then the trial judge has the discretion to conduct a preliminary review to determine the scope of the privilege, even though that inserts the court into the grand jury's investigation. In *In re Grand*

---

[112] 33 F.3d 342 (4th Cir. 1994).

[113] 13 F.3d 633 (2d Cir. 1994).

[114] See In re Grand Jury Subpoena as to C97–216, 187 F.3d 996 (8th Cir. 1999); In re Grand Jury Proceedings, 867 F.2d 539 (9th Cir. 1989); In re Special September 1978 Grand Jury (II), 640 F.2d 49 (7th Cir. 1980).

[115] See In re Napster, Inc. Copyright Litigation, 479 F.3d 1078 (9th Cir. 2007); Haines v. Liggett Group, Inc., 975 F.2d 81 (3d Cir. 1992).

[116] 419 F.3d 329 (5th Cir. 2005).

[117] 68 F.3d 38 (2d Cir. 1995).

Jury Subpoenas,[118] the Tenth Circuit stated that "if, before ordering testimony in front of the grand jury, the district court, within its discretion, believes an in camera examination of the witness or the questions to be asked of the witness is needed to ensure the scope of the inquiry will not be too broad, it may do so." In *Mohawk Industries, Inc. v. Carpenter*,[119] the Supreme Court held that a district court's disclosure order that is adverse to the attorney-client privilege is not immediately appealable under the collateral order doctrine, so the lawyer whose testimony is sought would have to refuse to respond and suffer a criminal contempt in order to obtain appellate review of the issue.

§ 22.8 FIDUCIARY EXCEPTION

A civil proceeding that often accompanies a white collar crime prosecution involving corporate misconduct is a shareholder derivative suit seeking damages from the directors and officers of the company for a breach of fiduciary duty. If a senior officer or director was directly involved in the misconduct, then there can be a claim for a breach of the duty of due care and loyalty owed to the corporation. In addition, under the law of Delaware, the state in which many larger publicly traded companies are incorporated, the directors are required to create and implement a compliance program to prevent and detect wrongdoing by employees, and a failure to create such a program or adequately monitor it can result in a breach of their fiduciary duty. This is known as a *Caremark* claim, after the decision of the Delaware Chancery Court in *In re Caremark Int'l Inc. Derivative Litigation*,[120] which stated:

> [I]t is important that the board exercise a good faith judgment that the corporation's information and reporting system is in concept and design adequate to assure the board that appropriate information will come to its attention in a timely manner as a matter of ordinary operations, so that it may satisfy its responsibility.

Thus, any criminal case against a corporation, even one settled by a deferred or non-prosecution agreement, is likely to trigger a shareholder derivative suit.

The company is the nominal plaintiff in a shareholder derivative suit because it was harmed by the alleged misconduct. A corporation's management and board of directors are responsible for deciding how the corporation should act, including whether to pursue a lawsuit. But a derivative suit is authorized in recognition of the potential conflict of interest if the harm were caused by corporate officials. It is a procedural device that gives shareholders a means to police the conduct of corporate directors and management by allowing them to file a lawsuit on the company's behalf against officers and directors who would probably be unwilling to sue themselves. Any recovery from the derivative suit goes to the corporation rather than the individual shareholders because the violation only harmed the organization.

Communications with corporate counsel are privileged under *Upjohn*, but in a derivative suit the courts have recognized a "fiduciary exception" that permits

---

[118] 144 F.3d 653 (10th Cir. 1998).

[119] 558 U.S. 100 (2009).

[120] 698 A.2d 959 (Del. Ch. 1996).

disclosure of otherwise privileged communications to the shareholder plaintiffs because the true beneficiary of the legal advice are the owners of the corporation. The roots of the fiduciary exception are in the common law in cases in which the party seeking disclosure was the "real client" while the trustee who received the confidential communications was a "mere representative" of the beneficiaries of a trust. In *United States v. Jicarilla Apache Nation*,[121] the Supreme Court explained the factors to be considered in determining whether the beneficiary is the "real client" who can have access to privileged communications:

> (1) when the advice was sought, no adversarial proceedings between the trustees and beneficiaries had been pending, and therefore there was no reason for the trustees to seek legal advice in a personal rather than a fiduciary capacity; (2) the court saw no indication that the memorandum was intended for any purpose other than to benefit the trust; and (3) the law firm had been paid out of trust assets.

Similar to the beneficiary of a trust, shareholders of a corporation have a claim to obtain communications by management with corporate counsel to establish the breach of fiduciary duty owed to the corporation because they are the owners of the business and therefore receive the benefit of the privileged communications. But unlike a trust beneficiary, who has a direct stake in the assets, a shareholder does not have control of the corporate assets or even a say in the management of the organization. Thus, shareholder derivative suits are not always in the best interest of the company, and so courts have not recognized an automatic right to obtain privileged communications involving the corporate client. Instead, the shareholders pursing the derivative action must establish "good cause" before the company would be compelled to disclose privileged communications.

The seminal decision on the fiduciary exception is *Garner v. Wolfinbarger*,[122] a Fifth Circuit decision in 1970. The case involved claims of securities fraud in the issuance of stock by an insurance company, and the corporation refused to disclose the legal advice it had received from corporate counsel related to the issuance in connection with a shareholder derivative suit claiming the directors breached their fiduciary duty. The circuit court recognized the competing concerns in a shareholder derivative suit, noting that "management does not manage for itself" but that "a corporation must be free to seek legal advice without fear of indiscriminate disclosure to disgruntled shareholders."[123] It adopted the good cause requirement to balance the "competing interests of confidentiality and full disclosure."

The Fifth Circuit set forth a non-exclusive list of factors a court can consider in deciding whether to compel disclosure of privileged communications with corporate counsel:

> [1] the number of shareholders and the percentage of stock they represent; [2] the bona fides of the shareholders; [3] the nature of the shareholders' claim and whether it is obviously colorable; [4] the apparent necessity or desirability of the

---

[121] 131 S.Ct. 2313 (2011).

[122] 430 F.2d 1093 (5th Cir. 1970).

[123] See Edna Selan Epstein, The Attorney–Client Privilege and the Work–Product Doctrine (5th ed. 2007).

shareholders having the information and the availability of it from other sources; [5] whether, if the shareholders' claim is of wrongful action by the corporation, it is of action criminal, or illegal but not criminal, or of doubtful legality; [6] whether the communication related to past or to prospective actions; [7] whether the communication is of advice concerning the litigation itself; [8] the extent to which the communication is identified versus the extent to which the shareholders are blindly fishing; [9] the risk of revelation of trade secrets or other information in whose confidentiality the corporation has an interest for independent reasons.

In *Fausek v. White*,[124] the Sixth Circuit extended *Garner* to a lawsuit by shareholders in an individual capacity rather than through a derivative suit, explaining "[t]he fact that shareholder-plaintiffs seek recovery for themselves only may render their motives more suspect than if they bring a derivative action. Nevertheless, this is just one factor to be considered in determining whether good cause exists to deny the application of the privilege in a particular case." The Ninth Circuit took the opposite approach in *Weil v. Investment/Indicators, Research and Management, Inc.*,[125] a lawsuit against a mutual fund by a former investor claiming violations of the federal securities laws. The circuit court stated, "Weil is not currently a shareholder of the Fund, and her action is not a derivative suit . . . [Unlike *Garner*], Weil seeks to recover damages from the corporation for herself and the members of her proposed class. *Garner*'s holding and policy rationale simply do not apply here."

In *Cox v. Administrator U.S. Steel & Carnegie*,[126] the Eleventh Circuit assumed that *Garner* applied to a lawsuit by union members against their union, but declined to compel disclosure of privilege communications because of "the fact that only a tiny percentage of the defendant Union's members are members of the plaintiff class; and the fact that the interest of the plaintiff class is adverse to those who are not in the class." The fiduciary exception analysis has also been applied in a corporate bankruptcy case,[127] to an ERISA fiduciary,[128] and for beneficiaries of an ESOP.[129] In *Jicarilla Apache Nation*, however, the Supreme Court rejected the application of the fiduciary exception to permit disclosure of privileged communications by government attorneys acting on behalf of an Indian tribe. The Court held, "Congress may style its relations with the Indians a 'trust' without assuming all the fiduciary duties of a private trustee, creating a trust relationship that is 'limited' or 'bare' compared to a trust relationship between private parties at common law."

§ 22.9   GOVERNMENT ATTORNEYS

Like any organization, a governmental unit can assert the attorney-client privilege for communications between its officials and attorneys made for the purpose of obtaining legal advice, at least in the civil context. Section 74 of the Restatement (Third) of the Law Governing Lawyers states that the "attorney-client privilege extends to a communication of a governmental organization" to the same extent it

---

[124] 965 F.2d 126 (6th Cir. 1992).

[125] 647 F.2d 18 (9th Cir. 1981).

[126] 17 F.3d 1386, opinion modified on reh'g, 30 F.3d 1347 (11th Cir. 1994).

[127] In re Teleglobe Communications Corp., 493 F.3d 345 (3d Cir. 2007).

[128] Wachtel v. Health Net, Inc., 482 F.3d 225 (3d Cir. 2007).

[129] In re Occidental Petroleum Corp., 217 F.3d 293 (5th Cir. 2000).

could be asserted by a private entity under *Upjohn*. The Freedom of Information Act, which requires disclosure of most government records, specifically exempts "inter-agency or intra-agency memorandums or letters which would not be available by law to a party other than an agency in litigation with the agency."[130] This effectively shields communications between a government attorney and officials to the extent they would be privileged in dealing with a private client. Similarly, Federal Rule of Criminal Procedure 16(a), which provides for discovery in criminal cases, "does not authorize the discovery or inspection of reports, memoranda, or other internal government documents made by an attorney for the government or other government agent in connection with investigating or prosecuting the case."

The federal courts are split on whether the attorney-client privilege shields communications from a grand jury investigation into wrongdoing by a government official who consulted with government counsel. The Seventh, Eighth, and District of Columbia Circuits have held that a government lawyer cannot assert the attorney-client privilege regarding communications with another government official in the course of performing their duty. This approach is broader than the crime-fraud exception because there is no requirement to show the government official intended to commit a crime when seeking legal advice. The Second Circuit, however, has recognized that a state government lawyer could assert the privilege to resist responding to a grand jury subpoena, rejecting the approach of the other circuits on the issue.

In *In re Grand Jury Subpoena Duces Tecum*,[131] the Eighth Circuit rejected extending *Upjohn*'s analysis to a subpoena for notes of conversations between a White House lawyer and First Lady Hillary Rodham Clinton related to the Whitewater investigation. The circuit court found "important differences between the government and nongovernmental organizations such as business corporations weigh against the application of the principles of *Upjohn* in this case" that precluded invocation of the privilege. The White House could not be subjected to a criminal prosecution, unlike a corporation, and "executive branch employees, including attorneys, are under a statutory duty to report criminal wrongdoing by other employees to the Attorney General." The Eighth Circuit cited to 28 U.S.C. § 535(b), which provides that any information received by an executive branch employee "relating to violations of Federal criminal law involving Government officers and employees shall be expeditiously reported to the Attorney General by the head of the department or agency, or the witness, discoverer, or recipient, as appropriate." Another important distinction from *Upjohn* was "the general duty of public service calls upon government employees and agencies to favor disclosure over concealment." Thus, the circuit court refused to permit the government lawyer to invoke the attorney-client privilege to resist the subpoena because "the strong public interest in honest government and in exposing wrongdoing by public officials would be ill-served by recognition of a governmental attorney-client privilege applicable in criminal proceedings inquiring into the actions of public officials."

---

[130] 5 U.S.C. § 552(b)(5).

[131] 112 F.3d 910 (8th Cir. 1997).

The District of Columbia Circuit considered a similar claim in connection with an investigation of the White House in *In re Lindsey*[132] and reached the same conclusion as the Eighth Circuit. While recognizing the attorney-client privilege applied to government lawyers, the circuit court held that "government attorneys stand in a far different position from members of the private bar. Their duty is not to defend clients against criminal charges and is not to protect wrongdoers from public disclosure." Because of the government attorney's role to represent the public interest, when there is an investigation of misconduct by an official, then "if there is wrongdoing in government, it must be exposed" without regard to the attorney-client privilege. The Seventh Circuit took the same approach in *In re a Witness Before the Special Grand Jury 2000–2*[133] involving a grand jury subpoena to the legal counsel to a state official related to an investigation of corrupt payments. In rejecting the attorney-client privilege claim, the circuit court found that "[i]t would be both unseemly and a misuse of public assets to permit a public official to use a taxpayer-provided attorney to conceal from the taxpayers themselves otherwise admissible evidence of financial wrongdoing, official misconduct, or abuse of power."

The opposite approach was taken by the Second Circuit in *In re Grand Jury Investigation*,[134] involving a grand jury subpoena to a governor's chief legal counsel for testimony in an investigation of whether the governor accepted gifts for awarding public contracts. Unlike the view of the role of the government attorney as different from the private lawyer, the circuit court stated:

> We cannot accept the Government's unequivocal assumption as to where the public interest lies. To be sure, it is in the public interest for the grand jury to collect all the relevant evidence it can. However, it is also in the public interest for high state officials to receive and act upon the best possible legal advice.

The circuit court pointed to a state statute providing that confidential communications with a government attorney are privileged and the lawyer cannot disclose them "unless an authorized representative of the public agency consents to waive the privilege and allow such disclosure." Although the issue of the attorney-client privilege arose under federal law because a federal grand jury subpoena was at issue, the Second Circuit concluded that the government's interest in disclosure did not necessarily outweigh that state's determination to protect confidential communications; indeed, "[o]ne could as easily conclude, with the Connecticut legislature, that the protections afforded by the privilege ultimately promote the public interest, even when they might impede the search for truth in a particular criminal investigation." On the question of whether recognizing the privilege would undermine the criminal investigative process, the Second Circuit took a stance almost diametrically opposed to the approach in the Seventh, Eighth, and District of Columbia Circuits when it stated, "Upholding the privilege furthers a culture in which consultation with government lawyers is accepted as a normal, desirable, and even indispensable part of conducting public business. Abrogating the privilege undermines that culture and thereby impairs the public interest."

---

[132] 158 F.3d 1263 (D.C. Cir. 1998).

[133] 288 F.3d 289 (7th Cir. 2002).

[134] 399 F.3d 527 (2d Cir. 2005).

Chapter 23

WORK PRODUCT PROTECTION

§ 23.1 INTRODUCTION

A close relation to the attorney-client privilege is the protection afforded to attorney work product that keeps confidential, with certain important exceptions, materials created by or on behalf of a lawyer in anticipation of litigation. Each is based on the attorney-client relationship, and is designed to afford a measure of confidentiality to the representation of a client. Because work product often incorporates client communications, privilege claims are frequently asserted along with the work product doctrine to resist disclosure of material. While there can be a significant overlap between them, it is important to separate a privilege claim from the protection afforded to work product because they have different rationales, and a finding that one does not apply does not preclude finding that the other is available. While many cases may involve claims of both the attorney-client privilege and the protection of attorney work product, they are distinct and must be analyzed separately.

In *United States v. American Telephone & Telegraph Co.*,[1] the District of Columbia Circuit explained that unlike the attorney-client privilege, "[t]he purpose of the work product doctrine is to protect information against opposing parties, rather than against all others outside a particular confidential relationship, in order to encourage effective trial preparation." The protection afforded work product is not based on the need to permit full and candid communication between a lawyer and a client, and it does not provide the same measure of confidentiality from compelled disclosure as the evidentiary privilege because an opposing party can obtain some work product upon a showing of sufficient need. On the other hand, the scope of what can constitute work product is broader than what comes within the attorney-client privilege, covering documents and information gathered by an attorney that may not contain any direct reference to a client communication.

An important distinction between the attorney-client privilege and the work product doctrine are the differing rationales for each. The attorney-client privilege encourages full and frank communication between the lawyer and the client, and once the privilege applies there is no basis for compelling disclosure absent waiver or an exception to its application, such as a communication made for the purpose of a client engaging in a crime or fraud. The work product doctrine is designed to permit the attorney a measure of privacy related to the representation of the client so that the lawyer need not fear there will be a disclosure of materials to an opponent that were created as part of the litigation process. The Supreme Court described the scope of the work product protection in the foundational case of *Hickman v. Taylor*[2] this way: "Proper preparation of a client's case demands that he assemble information, sift what he considers to be the relevant from the irrelevant facts, prepare his legal theories and

---

[1] 642 F.2d 1285 (D.C. Cir. 1980).
[2] 329 U.S. 495 (1947).

plan his strategy without undue and needless interference . . . to promote justice and to protect [the] clients' interests." Unlike the privilege, which focuses on the needs of the client, the work product doctrine benefits both the client and the lawyer, and each can assert a claim to preclude disclosure of materials that qualify for the protection.

The work product doctrine is closely related to the litigation process, but it is not limited solely to protection of material from pretrial discovery. A lawyer or client can invoke the doctrine to resist producing materials in response to a grand jury or regulatory agency subpoena, or to require its return if it is seized pursuant to a search warrant. The protection is particularly important in white collar crime cases because the government's access to work product during an investigation could provide crucial evidence of a client's potential misconduct that would not otherwise be available and that is not protected by the attorney-client privilege.

§ 23.2 DEVELOPMENT OF THE WORK PRODUCT DOCTRINE

The adoption of the Federal Rules of Civil Procedure in 1937 created broad discovery rights for parties in civil litigation. The rules did not limit what type of information could be obtained from an opponent, and so lawyers sought internal memoranda and reports created by opposing counsel in order to learn how the other side planned to approach the case. The Supreme Court dealt with this issue in *Hickman v. Taylor*, where it recognized a protection for attorney work product to prevent it from being subject to discovery even though that topic was not addressed explicitly in the rules at that time. The case arose from the death of five crewmen on a tugboat that had sunk, and its owner retained a law firm that interviewed four survivors shortly after the accident. The estate of one of the drowned crewmen filed a lawsuit nine months later and sought copies of all the statements and memoranda prepared by attorneys from the interviews.

The Court began its analysis by noting that "the protective cloak of [the attorney-client] privilege does not extend to information which an attorney secures from a witness while acting for his client in anticipation of litigation." Nevertheless, the requested material "falls outside the arena of discovery and contravenes the public policy underlying the orderly prosecution and defense of legal claims. Not even the most liberal of discovery theories can justify unwarranted inquiries into the files and the mental impressions of an attorney." The Court explained that permitting discovery of an attorney's work product would mean that "[i]nefficiency, unfairness and sharp practices would inevitably develop in the giving of legal advice and in the preparation of cases for trial."

Hickman v. Taylor did not recognize a new privilege for attorney work product, however, because the Court held that in certain situations a party could be compelled to disclose otherwise protected materials upon a showing of good cause. It stated, "Where relevant and non-privileged facts remain hidden in an attorney's file and where production of those facts is essential to the preparation of one's case, discovery may properly be had." But there is a presumption in favor of protecting work product, so that the "burden rests on the one who would invade that privacy to establish adequate reasons to justify production through a subpoena or court order." The Court had no problem in recognizing the protection for work product even though the rules made no mention of it, explaining that "this Court and the members of the bar in general certainly did not believe or contemplate that all the files and mental processes of lawyers were thereby opened to the free scrutiny of their adversaries."

Congress codified the protection for attorney work product in Rule 26(b)(3), which provides that "[o]rdinarily, a party may not discover documents and tangible things that are prepared in anticipation of litigation or for trial by or for another party or its representative (including the other party's attorney, consultant, surety, indemnitor, insurer, or agent)." Attorney work product can be obtained if the materials are relevant to a claim or defense in the litigation, and "the party shows that it has substantial need for the materials to prepare its case and cannot, without undue hardship, obtain their substantial equivalent by other means."

Rule 26(b)(3)(B) incorporates a critical distinction that developed after *Hickman v. Taylor* between two types of attorney work product: "fact" (or "ordinary") and "opinion" work product. Under the rule, even if the court orders disclosure of attorney work product, "it must protect against disclosure of the mental impressions, conclusions, opinions, or legal theories of a party's attorney or other representative concerning the litigation." This has come to be known as opinion work product, and it receives nearly complete protection from disclosure.

In *Upjohn Co. v. United States*,[3] the Supreme Court considered an effort by the IRS to obtain memoranda prepared by corporate counsel from interviews with company employees as part of an internal investigation into overseas bribery, documents that contained the legal analysis and impressions of the attorneys. Rejecting the trial court's finding of substantial need, the Court pointed out that Rule 26 and *Hickman v. Taylor* both supported finding that opinion work product is subject to a higher level of protection than fact work product, although it was unwilling to recognize an absolute protection because that would make the protection for opinion work product the equivalent of a privilege. The Court came very close to doing so, however, when it asserted "we think a far stronger showing of necessity and unavailability by other means than was made by the Government or applied by the Magistrate in this case would be necessary to compel disclosure." How much of a showing will meet this vague "stronger" standard is not clear, but the implication of the Court's position is that the "substantial need" requirement in Rule 26(b)(3) is not sufficient on its own to authorize disclosure of opinion work product, and that is already a significant barrier to disclosure.

The term "work product" covers a wide range of documents and electronic records, such as drafts of memoranda, notes of meetings, and internal communications. Documents and files obtained in discovery or voluntarily provided by a third party to the lawyer are usually not viewed as protected work product unless there is some type of special organization or selection of the records that reveals counsel's thought-process or legal strategy. In *In re Grand Jury Subpoenas Dated March 19, 2002 and August 2, 2002 (The Mercator Corporation)*,[4] prosecutors subpoenaed a law firm for records from a client's Swiss bank account, and the firm tried to resist producing them on the ground that they constituted fact work product for which the government had not established a sufficient need. The Second Circuit held that "[n]ot every selection and

---

[3] 449 U.S. 383 (1981).

[4] 318 F.3d 379 (2d Cir. 2003).

compilation of third-party documents by counsel transforms that material into attorney work product." The circuit court stated that third-party documents are generally not covered by the work product protection if they were not created at the instigation of counsel, so "the party asserting the privilege must show a real, rather than speculative, concern that counsel's thought processes in relation to pending or anticipated litigation will be exposed through disclosure of the compiled documents." Even if the records contain notations of the attorney that would qualify as opinion work product, a court may order disclosure to the extent the protected materials can be redacted from the records.

Rule 26(b)(3) does not cover all types of work product because it only speaks directly to discovery of "documents and tangible things" prepared by the attorney, and not the personal recollection of a lawyer that may not have been memorialized. The rule does not supplant *Hickman v. Taylor*'s statement that recognized a protection for "written statements, private memoranda and personal recollections prepared or formed" by an attorney, so this type of work product cannot be compelled. The rule is also broader than the Supreme Court's analysis because it covers work by more than just the attorney, reaching materials created in connection to litigation by the lawyer's or client's "consultant, surety, indemnitor, insurer, or agent."

The Rule only applies in civil litigation, and does not govern the operations of a grand jury, which is entitled to "every man's evidence" in its investigation of potential violations of federal law. In *United States v. Nobles*,[5] the Supreme Court stated that "[a]lthough the work-product doctrine most frequently is asserted as a bar to discovery in civil litigation, its role in assuring the proper functioning of the criminal justice system is even more vital." The principles in *Hickman v. Taylor* are equally applicable to a criminal case, from the investigation of a potential violation through the conclusion of the prosecution.

§ 23.3   IN ANTICIPATION OF LITIGATION

A.   Generally

Both *Hickman v. Taylor* and Rule 26(b)(3) condition the availability of the protection afforded to work product on it having been created "in anticipation of litigation." The scope of the doctrine is much narrower than the attorney-client privilege in this regard because of the requirement of a link to an adjudicatory proceeding, while the privilege applies to any communication related to obtaining legal advice, including business development. Because of the potential threat of litigation in almost any context, a key issue has been to identify the situations in which the document has a sufficient link to a judicial or administrative proceeding to afford the protection for work product without allowing it to shroud from discovery virtually any document related to an attorney's work.

The Advisory Committee Note to Rule 26(b)(3) provides that "[m]aterial assembled in the ordinary course of business, or pursuant to public requirements unrelated to litigation, or for other non-litigation purposes are not under the qualified immunity provided" for attorney work product. Documents created for current litigation are easy

---

[5] 422 U.S. 225 (1975).

to identify, and often the prospect of a lawsuit or adjudicatory proceeding, such as the tort claim in *Hickman v. Taylor*, is sufficiently clear that there is no question that documents are protected from discovery. The involvement of lawyers in a wide range of business activities on behalf of a client raises thornier issues regarding the availability of the work product doctrine, which can make it difficult for an opposing party to obtain information about transactions or policies in which a lawyer had some measure of participation. The circuit courts have applied three tests for determining whether a document was created "in anticipation of litigation" or involves ordinary business conduct that falls outside the protection. The majority of courts apply the "because of" test, while the Fifth Circuit considers whether the "primary motivating purpose behind the creation of the document was to aid in possible future litigation," and the First Circuit looks to whether the material was "prepared for use in litigation." The differences between the tests are subtle, and it can be difficult to predict under any test whether documents will be protected from discovery when the connection to potential litigation is not clear.

B. "Because Of"

The broadest protection for work product is afforded under the "because of" test, which looks to whether the document would have been created in the ordinary course of business without regard to potential litigation, or whether its creation or structuring was designed, at least in part, to address the possibility of future litigation. In *United States v. Adlman*,[6] the Second Circuit considered whether a memorandum prepared for corporate counsel that analyzed tax issues from a proposed restructuring that included an assessment of likely outcomes from potential litigation over the transaction was attorney work product that need not be produced in response to an IRS summons. The circuit court noted that determining whether a document was created "in anticipation of litigation" was unclear "as to documents which, although prepared because of expected litigation, are intended to inform a business decision influenced by the prospects of the litigation."

The circuit court took a broad approach to the issue because "it would oddly undermine its purposes if such documents were excluded from protection merely because they were prepared to assist in the making of a business decision expected to result in the litigation." It adopted the test from the Wright & Miller treatise *Federal Practice and Procedure*, which recognized the application of the work product protection if "in light of the nature of the document and the factual situation in the particular case, the document can fairly be said to have been prepared or obtained *because of* the prospect of litigation." The Second Circuit pointed out the limits of the "because of" test, that it "withholds protection from documents that are prepared in the ordinary course of business or that would have been created in essentially similar form irrespective of the litigation."

This formulation of the test for determining whether a document was created "in anticipation of litigation" has been adopted in the Third, Fourth, Sixth, Seventh, Eighth, Ninth, and District of Columbia Circuits.[7] For example, in *In re Grand Jury*

---

[6] 134 F.3d 1194 (2d Cir. 1998).

[7] See In re Grand Jury Proceedings, 604 F.2d 798 (3d Cir. 1979); National Union Fire Insurance Co. v. Murray Sheet Metal Co., Inc., 967 F.2d 980 (4th Cir. 1992); United States v. Roxworthy, 457 F.3d 590 (6th Cir. 2006); Binks Manufacturing Co. v. National Presto Industries, Inc., 709 F.2d 1109 (7th Cir. 1983); Simon

Subpoena (Mark Torf/Torf Environmental Management),[8] the Ninth Circuit applied the test in assessing whether documents created to aid a company in determining its compliance with a previous settlement with a federal agency was protected work product. The circuit court held that they were "entitled to work product protection because, taking into account the facts surrounding their creation, their litigation purpose so permeates any non-litigation purpose that the two purposes cannot be discretely separated from the factual nexus as a whole."

C. "Primary Purpose"

The Fifth Circuit adopted a much narrower test that looks to whether the "primary purpose" for creating a document was for potential litigation, so that records that are related more to the conduct of a business and its transactions are less likely to receive the protection of the work product doctrine. In *United States v. Davis*,[9] the circuit court held that documents related to an attorney's work in preparing a tax return for a client were not work product because their primary purpose was not to assist in future litigation. The test was phrased as "litigation need not be imminent . . . as long as the primary motivating purpose behind the creation of the document was to aid in possible future litigation."

In *United States v. El Paso Co.*,[10] the circuit court rejected a claim for work product protection for a company's tax analysis because "the primary motivation is to anticipate, for financial reporting purposes, what the impact of litigation might be on the company's tax liability. El Paso thus creates the tax pool analysis with an eye on its business needs, not on its legal ones." It noted that the documents involved "weighing legal arguments, predicting the stance of the IRS, and forecasting the ultimate likelihood of sustaining El Paso's position in court," but that "[t]he legal analysis is not an end in itself: the memoranda underlying the tax pool analysis do not map out El Paso's actual litigating strategy." In contrast to the Second Circuit's "because of" test applied to similar documents in *Adlman*, the "primary purpose" test requires a much closer connection to impending litigation, so that documents created for a business that are only tangentially related to possible—but not imminent—litigation will not be protected from discovery.

D. "Prepared for Use in Possible Litigation"

In *United States v. Textron*,[11] the First Circuit, sitting *en banc*, rejected a claim that tax accrual workpapers related to reserves that would not have been created by a company but for litigation were protected by the work product doctrine when the documents were "not in any way prepared 'for' litigation but relate[d] to a subject that might or might not occasion litigation." The circuit court noted that "the immediate motive of Textron in preparing the tax accrual work papers was to fix the amount of the tax reserve on Textron's books and to obtain a clean financial opinion from its

---

v. G.D. Searle & Co., 816 F.2d 397 (8th Cir. 1987); In re Grand Jury Subpoena (Mark Torf/Torf Environmental Management), 357 F.3d 900 (9th Cir. 2004); Senate of Puerto Rico v. United States Dep't of Justice, 823 F.2d 574 (D.C. Cir. 1987).

[8] 357 F.3d 900 (9th Cir. 2004).

[9] 636 F.2d 1028 (5th Cir. 1981).

[10] 682 F.2d 530 (5th Cir. 1982).

[11] 577 F.3d 21 (1st Cir. 2009) (en banc).

auditor," thus distancing them too much from the "in anticipation of litigation" requirement. To invoke the protection, "[i]t is not enough to trigger work product protection that the *subject matter* of a document relates to a subject that might conceivably be litigated."

The First Circuit took a more visceral approach to the work product analysis, pointing out that "[e]very lawyer who tries cases knows the touch and feel of materials prepared for a current or possible (*i.e.,* 'in anticipation of') law suit." When it came to tax reserve calculations, those records have "in ordinary parlance only that purpose: to support a financial statement and the independent audit of it." To come within the "in anticipation of litigation" requirement, that phrase "did not, in the reference to anticipation, mean prepared for some purpose other than litigation: it meant only that the work might be done *for* litigation but *in advance of* its institution." The link to litigation must be clear from the creation and purpose of the documents, and in *Textron* the First Circuit refused to find that the tax accrual workpapers were protected.

E.   Determining "In Anticipation of Litigation"

The source of the different circuit rules were cases involving tax documents that relate to the ordinary business of a company that later became the subject of an IRS inquiry. Outside the tax context, the courts have been more willing to apply the work product doctrine to prevent discovery of documents, particularly those created by an attorney, when a clear link to potential litigation can be established. The Sixth Circuit in *United States v. Roxworthy*[12] noted that the work product analysis has both a subjective and objective component: "1) whether a document was created because of a party's subjective anticipation of litigation, as contrasted with an ordinary business purpose, and (2) whether that subjective anticipation of litigation was objectively reasonable." In considering whether a memorandum prepared by an accountant after the completion of a transaction that identified possible tax issues could qualify as work product, the circuit court found that "[t]he company's decision to obtain a legal opinion only after it had completed a series of transactions could easily lead to the conclusion that the opinion was *more* likely to be in anticipation of litigation as opposed to being used for ordinary business purposes."

Documents created in advance of litigation can be protected if there is evidence of at least a potential threat of a lawsuit. In *Equal Rights Center v. Post Properties, Inc.,*[13] the district court found that an accessibility analysis prepared by an attorney for a multi-family property developer later sued for not complying with federal law was protected work product because "[w]hile Post could not have been certain that ERC would file suit against it, the fact that ERC had filed suit against four other housing developers and sought media attention for this 'series' of lawsuits supports a finding that Post had a subjective and objectively reasonable belief that litigation was a real possibility."

---

[12] 457 F.3d 590 (6th Cir. 2006).
[13] 247 F.R.D. 208 (D.D.C. 2008).

§ 23.4   SUBSTANTIAL NEED

Even if a particular document or file constitutes work product, that does not mean it is absolutely protected from disclosure. A court can order the production of work product if the party seeking disclosure makes a sufficient showing of necessity. *Hickman v. Taylor* spoke of "good cause" for requiring that it be released, while Rule 26(b)(3) states that a party can obtain discovery if it "shows that it has substantial need for the materials to prepare its case and cannot, without undue hardship, obtain their substantial equivalent by other means." Determining whether "good cause" or "substantial need" were shown led one district judge to note that "the determination must rest upon the balance struck in the particulars of a concrete case between the competing interests of full disclosure and protection for the fruits of the lawyer's labor."[14]

The type of work product at issue is the first step in the analysis. Rule 26(b)(3)(B) requires that if a court orders production of work product, "it must protect against disclosure of the mental impressions, conclusions, opinions, or legal theories of a party's attorney or other representative concerning the litigation." Thus, opinion work product receives near absolute protection from disclosure, while fact work product can be ordered disclosed to a party if the other requirements of the rule are established.

A court will condition a finding of "substantial need" on proof that the information contained in the work product is important, perhaps even crucial, to the case, and not merely something a party believes is relevant to trial preparation. In *Hickman v. Taylor*, the Supreme Court noted that the plaintiff's request for reports of witness interviews was to aid the attorney in preparing depositions "and to make sure that he has overlooked nothing," a reason that was found wanting. In *Director, Office of Thrift Supervision v. Vinson & Elkins, LLP*,[15] the District of Columbia Circuit rejected an effort to obtain attorney notes of a client interview with law enforcement officials to confirm deposition testimony. The circuit court held, "Appellant's need, as we understand its position, reduces to nothing more than its desire to find corroborating evidence. It is the rare case where corroborative evidence can be thought 'necessary.'"

In *In re HealthSouth Corp. Securities Litigation*,[16] on the other hand, the district court ordered the disclosure of a lawyer's notes of a former client's interviews with the FBI because of a claim that memoranda prepared by the FBI from the interviews were inaccurate, so there was no other evidence to determine what was said during the sessions. In order to make the requisite determination of substantial need, district courts can order a party to submit the work product *in camera* for review to assess whether disclosure should be ordered.

To determine whether denial of discovery would constitute an "undue hardship," courts often consider whether the witness is available and willing to provide information. This often comes up in the context of a lawyer or investigator for one party obtaining a statement from a witness who late becomes unwilling to speak with an opposing party so a copy of a report on the interview is sought. Most of the caselaw

---

[14] United States v. Swift & Co., 24 F.R.D. 280 (N.D. Ill. 1959).

[15] 124 F.3d 1304 (D.C. Cir. 1997).

[16] 250 F.R.D. 8 (D.D.C. 2008).

in this area involves civil litigation because a prosecutor can give a witness immunity in order to compel the testimony before a grand jury or at trial. If the witness has an impaired memory, has died, cannot be located, or a substantial amount of time has passed, then there is a stronger basis to show an "undue hardship" if the person's statement has been recorded at a time closer to the events in question.

A "substantial equivalent" to the information contained in the work product must not be available from another source before a court can order disclosure. In a grand jury investigation, the government can use any available evidence, including hearsay and items subject to the exclusionary rule, to establish probable cause that a person committed an offense. Therefore, it is often more difficult to show a need for work product when prosecutors can use a wider range of evidence than at trial. In *In re Grand Jury Subpoena Dated Oct. 22, 2001*,[17] prosecutors sought the testimony of corporate counsel present at an interview of an officer to help establish that the officer made false statements. An IRS agent was also present at the interview, but the government wanted the attorney's testimony to help establish the falsity of the statements and avoid a "swearing contest" between the officer and the agent, which might well preclude a jury finding guilt beyond a reasonable doubt. The Second Circuit quashed the subpoena because the attorney's recollections constituted work product, and "the Government's arguments as to its substantial need for Attorney's testimony to resolve a swearing contest at trial are not directly pertinent to its need to compel Attorney's testimony before the grand jury" at which "the Government does not need to prevail in a swearing match."

§ 23.5 WAIVER

Similar to the attorney-client privilege, the protection afforded to work product can be waived expressly or through disclosure. The standard for finding an implied waiver based on revealing work product is different from that applied to the attorney-client privilege, which requires strict adherence to maintaining confidentiality of the attorney-client communications. The District of Columbia Circuit explained the approach to waiver through disclosure in *United States v. American Telephone & Telegraph Co.*:[18]

> A disclosure made in the pursuit of such trial preparation, and not inconsistent with maintaining secrecy against opponents, should be allowed without waiver of the privilege. We conclude, then, that while the mere showing of a voluntary disclosure to a third person will generally suffice to show waiver of the attorney-client privilege, it should not suffice in itself for waiver of the work product privilege.

Because fact work product is not afforded the same degree of protection as privileged communications, courts have been less willing to find a waiver when information is disclosed because an avenue for discovery still exists if a party can make a showing of substantial need. The work product protection is designed to protect the attorney's labors within the adversary system, so the waiver analysis undertaken by courts involves different considerations than for application of the attorney-client

---

[17] 282 F.3d 156 (2d Cir. 2002).

[18] 642 F.2d 1285 (D.C. Cir. 1980).

privilege. The First Circuit in *United States v. Massachusetts Institute of Technology*[19] described the contrasting approach to work product and privileged communications this way: "The privilege, it is said, is designed to protect confidentiality, so that any disclosure outside the magic circle is inconsistent with the privilege; by contrast, work product protection is provided against 'adversaries,' so only disclosing material in a way inconsistent with keeping it from an adversary waives work product protection." Similarly, the District of Columbia Circuit in *United States v. Deloitte LLP*[20] explained that the privilege "protects the attorney-client relationship by safeguarding confidential communications, whereas [work product] promotes the adversary process by insulating an attorney's litigation preparation from discovery." Another important difference in the analysis is that both the client and the lawyer can resist an effort to discover work product, so a waiver by one will not necessarily eliminate the protection.

Disclosure of work product to an adversary means that the protection cannot be asserted to prevent discovery by others. Determining who is an "adversary" requires looking at the relationship of the parties and the likelihood that they will be on opposing sides in future litigation. In *United States v. Deloitte LLP*, the District of Columbia Circuit considered whether a report prepared by a company's outside auditor and its in-house counsel on potential tax litigation involving a partnership investment was protected work product because it was made available to the accounting firm. The circuit court rejected the government's argument that independent auditors are potential adversaries of a corporate client because they have the power to issue adverse opinions and that disputes can arise between them regarding the proper accounting treatment of items on the financial statements. It found that there was no realistic likelihood of litigation between the company and its auditor, which would necessitate the accountant resigning from the engagement, and that "Deloitte's power to issue an adverse opinion, while significant, does not make it the sort of litigation adversary contemplated by the waiver standard." The District of Columbia Circuit's focus on the current relationship between the party claiming the protection and the recipient regarding the work product that was transmitted means that the mere possibility of a future dispute on another issue that could ripen into litigation is not enough to turn the recipient into an adversary. The circuit court held that the work product protection had not been waived because "the question is not whether Deloitte could be Dow's adversary in any conceivable future litigation, but whether Deloitte could be Dow's adversary in the sort of litigation the [work product] address."

Most district courts have taken the same approach to disclosure of work product to a company's outside auditor, finding that it does not waive the protection because, while independent, the accountant is not an adversary.[21] A district court reached the opposite conclusion in *Medinol, Ltd. v. Boston Scientific Corporation*,[22] denying protection to materials drafted by the special litigation committee of a company's board of directors that had been disclosed to its outside auditor in connection with its audit of the company's litigation exposure. It found that disclosure waived the work product

---

[19] 129 F.3d 681 (1st Cir. 1997).

[20] 610 F.3d 129 (D.C. Cir. 2010).

[21] Lawrence E. Jaffe Pension Plan v. Household Int'l, Inc., 237 F.R.D. 176 (N.D. Ill. 2006); Frank Betz Associates, Inc. v. Jim Walter Homes, Inc., 226 F.R.D. 533 (D.S.C. 2005); Merrill Lynch & Co., Inc. v. Allegheny Energy, Inc., 229 F.R.D. 441 (S.D.N.Y. 2004); In re Honeywell Int'l, Inc. Securities Litigation, 230 F.R.D. 293 (S.D.N.Y. 2003).

[22] 214 F.R.D. 113 (S.D.N.Y. 2002).

protection because "in order for auditors to properly do their job, they *must* not share common interests with the company they audit." The focus on "common interests" is different from a determination of whether one is a current or likely adversary, which the District of Columbia Circuit found crucial in *Deloitte LLP.*

In *United States v. Massachusetts Institute of Technology*, the First Circuit held that a university's disclosure of financial information to a federal audit agency required for compliance with the terms of government contracts waived the work product protection when the IRS later sought the information as part of an investigation of whether the school was in compliance with the requirements for a tax-exempt organization. The circuit court held that "MIT doubtless hoped that there would be no actual controversy between it and the Department of Defense, but the potential for dispute and even litigation was certainly there." Unlike *Deloitte LLP*, in which there was a closer relationship between the outside auditor and the company, a government contract does not put the parties on the same side when the agency will review the performance and can pursue a range of remedies in court for a potential breach.

Rule 26(b)(3) by its terms only applies to discovery, but the Supreme Court held in *United States v. Nobles*[23] that "[a]lthough the work-product doctrine most frequently is asserted as a bar to discovery in civil litigation, its role in assuring the proper functioning of the criminal justice system is even more vital." In *Nobles*, the defense called an investigator to testify about contradictory statements made by key prosecution witnesses, and the government sought to obtain a copy of the investigator's report on the interviews to use in cross-examining him. Similar to an implied waiver through disclosure to an adversary, calling the investigator to testify resulted in the Court finding that the defendant had "waived the privilege with respect to matters covered in his testimony." It analogized this to a defendant's decision to testify at trial, which waives the Fifth Amendment privilege against self-incrimination and requires the person to respond to cross-examination. But use of information at trial does not necessarily open up all work product to discovery. The Court pointed out that "[c]ounsel necessarily makes use throughout trial of the notes, documents, and other internal materials prepared to present adequately his client's case, and often relies on them in examining witnesses. When so used, there normally is no waiver."

If the adversary to whom disclosure is made is a federal government office or agency, or it is made in a federal proceeding, then Federal Rule of Evidence 502(a) provides that the disclosure only extends to other undisclosed information if the waiver was intentional, it concerns the same matter, and "they ought in fairness to be considered together." This is the same analysis for disclosure of communications that come within the attorney-client privilege. Similarly, the approach to inadvertent waiver in the attorney-client privilege context applies for work product under Rule 502(b). Courts also apply the same rule of selective waiver of the work product protection as that for the attorney-client privilege when it has been disclosed to an adversary. But work product shared with a bank or credit union regulator will not result in a waiver of the privilege even though the agency would be viewed as an adversary.[24]

---

[23] 422 U.S. 225 (1975).
[24] 12 U.S.C. § 1828(x)(1) (banks); 12 U.S.C. § 1785(j)(1) (credit unions).

§ 23.6   CRIME–FRAUD EXCEPTION

When a client consults with a lawyer for the purpose of obtaining legal advice that can be used to commit a pending or future crime or fraud, the law recognizes that the protections afforded to the lawyer-client consultation should not be permitted to shield information. Much like the application of the crime-fraud exception to communications covered by the attorney-client privilege (see § 22.7), so too is attorney work product subject to disclosure if it was created as a result of work on behalf of a client who was engaged in illegal or fraudulent conduct.[25] If the information sought constitutes work product, then the party seeking disclosure of the materials can overcome the protection by showing (1) that they were related to an ongoing or contemplated crime or fraud by the client and (2) the attorney was consulted "in furtherance" of that crime or fraud that resulted in the production of the work product. If the crime-fraud exception is established, then there should be no need to establish a "substantial need" for the materials under Rule 26(b)(3) because the protection afforded to work product is no longer available to preclude discovery.

The standard for establishing that the work product relates to a client's crime or fraud are the same as that for the attorney-client privilege: the party seeking disclosure must make a prima facie showing that the communication was in furtherance of a crime or fraud. The quantum of proof necessary is less than a preponderance of the evidence, and the government can rely on grand jury information to show the crime or fraud that is submitted to a court *ex parte* and *in camera* to comply with the secrecy requirements. In addition, the Supreme Court's rule in *United States v. Zolin*[26] also applies so that a trial court can conduct an *in camera* review of the work product to decide whether it relates to a pending or future crime or fraud that will result in loss of the protection.

There is an important difference in the application of the crime-fraud exception when opinion work product is involved. Because both the client and the lawyer can assert the protection, the attorney can keep confidential any work product that reflects his or her thought process and legal analysis even if the client sought legal advice to engage in a crime or fraud.[27] In *In re Grand Jury Proceedings, G.S., F.S.*,[28] the Eighth Circuit stated that "even when an attorney's clients have used the attorney's services to commit a crime or fraud, the government cannot compel production of an attorney's opinion work product if the attorney was unaware of his client's wrongful activities."

If the attorney was involved, however, then all work product can be discovered, including opinion work product. In *In re Grand Jury Proceedings, G.S., F.S.*, the circuit court found that there was sufficient evidence to show an attorney aided the criminal conduct of his clients when he advised against a transfer of property to relatives to avoid reporting it to the bankruptcy court, and then assisted in the transfer, to require disclosure of all documents related to the representation, including the lawyer's legal

---

[25] See United States v. Under Seal (In re Grand Jury Proceedings #5), 401 F.3d 247 (4th Cir. 2005); In re Special September 1978 Grand Jury (II), 640 F.2d 49 (7th Cir. 1980).

[26] 491 U.S. 554 (1989).

[27] See In re Grand Jury Proceedings, 867 F.2d 539 (9th Cir. 1989); In re Antitrust Grand Jury, 805 F.2d 155 (6th Cir. 1986).

[28] 609 F.3d 909 (8th Cir. 2010).

analysis. On the other hand, in *In re Green Grand Jury Proceedings*,[29] the Eighth Circuit upheld a lower court's determination that an attorney's notes and memoranda need not be turned over to a grand jury because they were opinion work product when "the client knowingly lied to the attorney by providing the attorney with a false back-story for the monies the client had allegedly improperly received." On that basis the court held that "an attorney who is not complicit in his client's wrongdoing may assert the work product privilege with respect to his opinion work product."

---

[29] 492 F.3d 976 (8th Cir. 2007).

Chapter 24

SENTENCING

§ 24.1 OVERVIEW

The sentence is one of the key features differentiating criminal liability from civil liability. For the class of behavior loosely characterized as "white collar crime," the financial burden of a criminal sentence is not necessarily more severe than a civil or administrative award or penalty, as both may include payments well beyond what is required for remediation and restitution.[1] But only criminal liability carries the risk of incarceration. Criminal convictions also carry greater reputational harm than civil liability, as well as more severe collateral consequences that can affect an offender's citizenship, livelihood, and civil rights.

State white collar prosecutions, including cases of fraud, identity theft, embezzlement, bad checks, and bribery, far outnumber federal white collar cases. For example, more than 90% of the convictions for fraud each year are in state court, not federal.[2] Nevertheless, there are several reasons to profile federal sentencing in some detail in this chapter. Federal sentencing is relatively uniform; the variation in state sentencing law and practice limits the utility and accuracy of generalizations. Federal sentencing has long been a focus of practitioners who specialize in white collar cases. Law school classes on white collar crime tend to cover federal, not state sentencing, and media attention tends to gravitate to sentencing in federal cases as well. That said, in addition to its analysis of federal sentencing, this chapter provides both an overview the constitutional rules that apply to sentencing in every jurisdiction, and some information on key features of state sentencing in white collar cases.[3]

The sentencing of offenders convicted of white collar crimes in federal court is governed by the same law that controls the sentencing of other federal offenders: the United States Constitution, the Sentencing Reform Act of 1984,[4] the individual statutes that define each offense, the Federal Rules of Criminal Procedure, and the judicial Sentencing Guidelines promulgated by the United States Sentencing Commission. Like punishments for other types of crime, the authorized penalties for white collar offenses are often adjusted following notorious incidents of criminality. For

---

[1] See Chapters 1 and 18.

[2] See Motivans, Federal Justice Statistics, 2009, December 2011, NCJ 234184, Fig. 10, p. 18.

[3] The material on constitutional rules is drawn in part from Chapter 26 of Wayne LaFave, Jerold Israel, Nancy King, & Orin Kerr, Criminal Procedure Treatise (3d ed., 2007 & annual updates), available on Westlaw under the database CRIMPROC and hereafter cited as CRIMPROC. Citations have been limited to cases discussed individually in the text, with the reader directed to CRIMPROC for additional authority and discussion.

[4] 18 U.S.C. §§ 3551 et seq., 28 U.S.C. §§ 991–998.

example, the collapse of Enron and other accounting catastrophes prompted Congress to boost the sentences for fraud in the Sarbanes–Oxley Act of 2002.[5]

Nevertheless, there are differences between white collar sentencing and sentencing for other types of crime. Because white collar crime frequently involves pecuniary loss, white collar sentencing often involves greater attention to restitution. Congress has authorized civil or criminal forfeiture of certain assets for several white collar offenses, forfeiture that is not always available for other property crimes. White collar prosecutions also involve the challenge of crafting sentences for organizational defendants, entities that cannot be incarcerated and are less likely to be prosecuted for other types of offenses. Finally, although conviction and sentence by negotiation is the norm throughout the criminal justice system, the context within which negotiations take place is often different in white collar cases, involving simultaneous litigation of multiple criminal, civil, and agency actions for the same wrongdoing.

The chapter begins with a review of the many different types of punishments that make up white collar sentencing today (§ 24.2), and a summary of federal constitutional limits on the use of such penalties (§ 24.3). The next sections cover the sentencing of individuals convicted of white collar offenses in federal court, first introducing the federal Sentencing Guidelines (§ 24.4), and then the procedural rules for sentencing, including constitutional regulation (§ 24.5) as well as procedures established by statute and court rule (§ 24.6). The final three sections turn to the sentencing of organizations (§ 24.7), sentencing appeals (§ 24.8), and the modification of sentences (§ 24.9).

One caveat: This chapter addresses sentencing in felony cases only. The sentencing of petty offenses is governed by separate statutes and rules in both the federal and state systems. There are no sentencing guidelines for such cases in federal court, for example.[6] In most jurisdictions, moreover, petty offense and misdemeanor sentences are even more likely than felony sentences to be the product of negotiation.

§ 24.2 TYPES OF SANCTIONS

A. Incarceration

Legislation in each jurisdiction will provide, for each offense, the minimum and maximum term of any incarceration authorized as a sentence for that offense. Statutes in every jurisdiction also specify whether sentences will be indeterminate or determinate. The difference between indeterminate and determinate sentencing turns on the timing and method of release. Indeterminate sentencing includes a paroling authority with the discretion to release an offender prior to the maximum sentence. By contrast, the determinate sentence sets a definite term of incarceration that the offender must serve with a release date that is not subject to the discretion of a paroling authority. Many states employ a combination of the two types of sentences, allowing discretionary release for less serious offenders, but prohibiting it for recidivists and more serious offenders. When determinate sentences are used, as in the federal system, a period of conditional release under supervision often follows

---

[5] See, e.g., §§ 6.1, 6.3.

[6] The United States Sentencing Guidelines do not apply to any count of conviction that is a Class B or C misdemeanor or an infraction. U.S.S.G. § 1B1.9.

incarceration, but the term of release is served in addition to, and not as a partial substitute for, the sentence of incarceration.

In several states using both determinate and indeterminate systems, lawmakers have adopted judicial sentencing guidelines or other mechanisms for structuring the judge's discretion to select an initial sentence from within the authorized statutory range. Judicial sentencing guidelines provide judges with recommended or mandatory sentences and apply to most felony offenses, including white collar crimes. The advisory sentencing guidelines applied in the federal courts are examined in detail later in this chapter.

Incarceration is a common punishment for white collar offenders and has been for some time. For example, nearly 80% of the more than 8000 offenders sentenced under the federal sentencing guidelines for fraud during fiscal year 2011 received a sentence of imprisonment.[7] Inmates serving sentences for white collar offenses make up less than 10 percent of the federal prison population. The median incarceration term imposed for economic offenses (fraud, embezzlement, forgery/counterfeiting, bribery, tax offenses, and money laundering) during the years 2007 through 2011 in federal courts was about a year and a half.[8] Both state and federal judges have imposed lengthy terms of imprisonment for white collar offenders that far exceed this median, however, such as a sentence of 54 years for a defendant convicted of a Ponzi scheme, and the sentences of over one hundred years imposed in recent prosecutions for fraud.[9]

B. Probation and Supervised Release

Probation, discretionary parole, and supervised release following a set term of incarceration are intended to prevent and detect additional criminal behavior by the offender, provide restitution to victims, and enable the offender to abide by the law. These goals are addressed by allowing the offender to reside in the community, conditioned upon compliance with conditions, some that are mandated by statute and others that are tailored to an individual offender and offense.[10]

Federal law authorizes probation as a sentence for most white collar offenses, at least those that do not carry mandatory minimum terms of incarceration or maximum terms greater than 25 years.[11] About one-fifth of the more than 8000 offenders sentenced for fraud in the federal courts during 2011 received a sentence of probation.

Conditions of probation and supervised release typically include drug testing,[12] payment of restitution[13] and fees, and residence and travel restrictions. A defendant

---

[7] United States Sentencing Commission, Sourcebook Fiscal Year 2011, available at www.ussc.gov, (hereinafter USSC, Statistics), Table 12.

[8] USSC Statistics, Figure E.

[9] See, e.g., http://sentencing.typepad.com/sentencing_law_and_policy/2012/04/unusual-but-justified-three-strikes-25–to-life-sentence-for-repeat-california-fraudster.html. See also Daniel C. Richman, Federal White Collar Sentencing in the United States—A Work in Progress (May 20, 2012), http://ssrn.com/abstract=1999102, at 2 n. 8, noting state sentence of 54 years for Ponzi scheme upheld in Reeves v. Indiana, 953 N.E.2d 665 (Ind.App. 2011).

[10] E.g., 18 U.S.C. § 3563.

[11] 18 U.S.C. § 3561(a). The federal guidelines recommend probation as an option when the recommended guideline range includes no incarceration. See U.S.S.G. § 5B1.1(a), § 5C1.1(b).

[12] 18 U.S.C. §§ 3563(a)(5), (a)(9), 3583(d).

may be required to reside in "a community corrections facility" or halfway house, called Residential Reentry Centers (RRCs) in the federal system,[14] or in "home detention."[15] A defendant may be barred from liquidating assets, or engaging in other specified financial transactions.[16] Intermittent confinement such as weekend terms may also be imposed as a condition of probation for federal offenders.[17] Convicted organizations, as well as individuals, may be placed on probation.[18]

Discretionary parole has been abolished for federal offenders, but the Guidelines recommend that a federal judge impose a term of supervised release (up to five years) following any term of imprisonment more than a year.[19] More than 91 percent of fraud sentences imposed between 2005 and 2009 included a term of supervised release, averaging 37 months.[20] A judge may terminate a period of supervised release early but this is not common.[21] If an offender violates a condition, a court may revoke release and sentence the defendant to incarceration for the term of supervised release. Section 24.9 examines the modification and revocation of supervised release.

C. Fines

The authorized punishment for most state and federal crimes includes a fine, and the fine is one of the primary sanctions for organizations convicted of criminal offenses. In felony cases against individuals, fines are sometimes imposed in addition to terms of conditional release or incarceration.

For crimes punishable by fine, the legislature typically defines an upper limit, either a set dollar figure, a multiplier of the financial gain achieved by the offender or the financial loss to the victim, or a per diem penalty. Unless otherwise provided by the statute defining the offense, federal fines for individuals are capped at $250,000 for a felony, $100,000 for a Class A misdemeanor, and $5,000 for less serious crimes.[22] Alternative fines based on gains or losses are also available.[23] Fine ceilings in the states tend to be lower than those under federal law, although several states also provide alternative fine ceilings based upon gain or loss. For example, New York

---

[13] See § 24.3(d), discussing restitution. Federal courts have discretion to impose restitution as a condition of supervised release at least in some cases where one or more victims have been harmed. 18 U.S.C. § 3583(d).

[14] See 18 U.S.C. § 353(b)(11).

[15] The Guidelines allow home detention as a substitute for imprisonment in certain instances. U.S.S.G. § 5C1.1(c)–(e).

[16] USSC, Federal Offenders Sentenced to Supervised Release (2010) (hereinafter USSC, Supervised Release, available at http://www.ussc.gov.

[17] 18 U.S.C. § 3563(b)(10); U.S.S.G. § 5C1.1(c)(3).

[18] See § 24.7(a) on the sentencing of corporations and other organizations.

[19] U.S.S.G. § 5D1.1(a); 18 U.S.C. § 3583(b) (noting maximum supervised-release terms). Supervised release begins on the day the defendant is released from imprisonment and runs concurrently with any other term of release, probation, or parole. 18 U.S.C. § 3624(e); United States v. Johnson, 529 U.S. 53 (2000).

[20] USSC, Supervised Release.

[21] Id.; 18 U.S.C. § 3583(e)(1).

[22] 18 U.S.C. § 3571(b).

[23] E.g., 18 U.S.C. § 3571(d), known as the Alternative Fines Act. See also United States v. Sanford Ltd., 878 F. Supp.2d 137 (D.D.C.2012) (interpreting "gross gain" "derived from" to mean "monetary proceeds which are additional before-tax profit to the defendants that was proximately caused by the relevant conduct of the offense").

permits a fine up to double the amount of the defendant's gain.[24] In Florida, where the fine limit is ordinarily $5000 to $15,000, depending upon the degree of felony, a court may impose any higher amount equal to double the pecuniary gain derived from the offense or loss suffered by the victim.[25]

The statutory fine limit for organizations convicted in federal court is twice that for individuals, and fines for organizations are calculated differently under the Guidelines than those for individuals. States that have separate provisions for the sentencing of organizations also tend to authorize higher fine amounts. Arizona, for example, which caps fines for individuals at $250,000, provides a special set of fines applicable to offenses committed by an enterprise,[26] up to one million dollars.

The Guidelines for individuals sentenced in federal court provide that a sentence must include a fine unless the defendant lacks the financial resources to make payments.[27] A court cannot require that a fine be paid as a precondition for release from imprisonment,[28] and before imposing any financial penalty, the court must consider the defendant's ability to pay.[29] If a defendant willfully fails to pay a fine, he may be sentenced to any term of imprisonment that might have been imposed originally.

Although most individuals sentenced for white collar offenses in federal court actually do not receive a fine as part of their sentence,[30] most organizations do. During 2011, 113 of the 160 organizations sentenced in federal court were ordered to pay a fine; the median fine for all offenses was $100,000.[31]

D.　Restitution

1.　*Generally*

Restitution is a routine element of white collar sentencing in both state and federal courts, in part because of the ubiquity of victims' rights provisions in state constitutions and criminal codes. Restitution may be imposed when authorized by statute, and is often included as a condition of probation, parole, or supervised release.

Before restitution may be imposed, the court must identify the "victim" entitled to restitution. This is a simple matter if the crime inflicted immediate harm upon a particular individual, but it becomes more complicated if the offense implicates the interests of the public in general, as do many regulatory offenses. Restitution statutes generally define the "victim" as someone who has suffered actual property or pecuniary loss as a direct result of the defendant's criminal conduct, excluding those who took

---

[24] N.Y. Penal Law § 80.00(2).

[25] Fla.Stat.Ann. § 775.083(1).

[26] Ariz.Rev.Stat. § 13–803.

[27] See U.S.S.G. § 5E1.2. See also the discussion of *Bearden* in § 24.5, at note 142.

[28] See Pub. L. 110–177, § 505, amending 18 U.S.C. § 3624(e) by deleting prohibition on release unless inmate agreed to adhere to an installment schedule to pay for any court-ordered fine imposed for the current offense.

[29] 18 U.S.C. § 3572; United States v. Gonzales, 620 F.3d 475 (5th Cir. 2010).

[30] USSC Statistics, Table 15.

[31] Id., Table 52.

part in the crime.[32] When the victim is unidentifiable, a defendant may be required to pay restitution to a victim's compensation fund.[33]

Once the victim is identified, the court must determine which losses can be considered in measuring the amount of restitution. Restitution typically is not permitted for mental anguish—it is limited to measurable economic loss. In some jurisdictions, a special statute governs restitution from corporate defendants.

2. *Restitution in Federal Cases*

The provisions governing restitution in federal criminal cases are collected in 18 U.S.C. §§ 3663 and 3663A. First established by the Victim and Witness Protection Act of 1982,[34] the provisions in Section 3663 provide *discretionary* authority to order restitution to order restitution to victims of most federal crimes. The statute authorizes restitution for four categories of costs: (1) the value of lost property; (2) the expenses of recovering from bodily injury, such as medical expenses; and (3) funeral costs, and, added in 1994, (4) "lost income and necessary child care, transportation, and other expenses related to participation in the investigation or prosecution of the offense or attendance at proceedings related to the offense."[35] Authority to order restitution to victims of identity theft in "an amount equal to the value of the time reasonably spent by the victim in an attempt to remediate the intended or actual harm incurred by the victim from the offense" was added in 2008.[36]

Section 3663A, added by the Mandatory Victims Restitution Act of 1996,[37] *requires* that restitution for the same four categories of costs be included in sentences for certain offenses, including property crimes. Litigation over whether specific expenditures fall within these categories is voluminous.

Both the VWPA and the MVRA define a victim as "a person directly and proximately harmed as a result of the commission of an offense for which restitution may be ordered including, in the case of an offense that involves as an element a scheme, conspiracy, or pattern of criminal activity, any person directly harmed by the defendant's criminal conduct in the course of the scheme, conspiracy, or pattern." The scope of compensable losses is limited to the loss caused by the specific conduct that is the basis of the offense of conviction.[38] However, if a "scheme, conspiracy, or pattern of criminal activity" is an element of the offense, or if a plea agreement allows for a greater amount, restitution can be ordered for losses that are considered "relevant conduct" even if the victim is not named in the indictment.[39]

---

[32] See 18 U.S.C. § 3663(a)(1)(A) (authorizing restitution to a third party if agreed upon in the plea agreement); United States v. Reifler, 446 F.3d 65 (2d Cir.2006) (vacating restitution award because it included restitution to persons who were clearly beyond the MVRA's definition of victims).

[33] 18 U.S.C. § 3663(c)(1).

[34] Pub.L. No. 97–291 § 3579, 96 Stat. 1248, 1253.

[35] 18 U.S.C. § 3663(b)(4).

[36] 18 U.S.C. § 3663(b)(6).

[37] Pub.L. No. 104–132 § 204, 110 Stat. 1214, 1227.

[38] See Hughey v. United States, 495 U.S. 411 (1990).

[39] E.g., United States v. Brown, 665 F.3d 1239 (11th Cir.2011) (amounts lost were caused by conduct that was part of the scheme, conspiracy, or pattern or criminal behavior underlying the offense of conviction, that restitution can cover losses for "relevant conduct" including both indicted and unindicted schemes, here

If the offense involved is one for which restitution is required, restitution must be imposed as a condition of supervised release. If a statute authorizes restitution but does not require it, the Guidelines provide that a sentencing court nonetheless "shall . . . enter a restitution order for the full amount of the victim's loss."[40]

3. *Procedures for Determining Restitution*

It is up to the prosecutor to prove both the amount of loss and that the loss was caused by the defendant's conduct. In general, courts have held that due process is satisfied when these factual issues are adjudicated with the procedures ordinarily applied to other historical facts that judges consider when selecting a sentence of incarceration from within the range authorized by statute. Facts such as causation and loss amounts are routinely decided by judges, who require such facts to be established by a preponderance of the evidence. Lower courts have thus far rejected arguments that the Supreme Court's *Apprendi* line of cases (discussed in § 24.5(e)) provides to the defendant a right to insist that those facts be established beyond a reasonable doubt to a jury. The Court has yet to address this issue directly, however. Some states use trial-type hearings to resolve factual issues concerning restitution.

E. Criminal Forfeiture

1. *Generally*

Criminal forfeiture is a form of punishment allowing the government to seize specified assets of the defendant. Forfeiture may be part of sentencing for white collar offenses in both state and federal court. The scope of assets subject to forfeiture is limited by statute to property that has a prescribed relationship with the criminal activity. In many white collar cases prosecuted in federal court, forfeiture extends to property "involved in" the offense,[41] a term that includes "proceeds" of the underlying criminal activity and property used to "facilitate" that activity. The forfeiture of "substitute assets" of the defendant may be authorized if the designated property is no longer available.[42] Increasingly, government attorneys use both civil and criminal forfeiture to provide restitution to crime victims in white collar cases in federal court.

2. *Procedure in Federal Cases*

Forfeiture statutes provide special procedures for determining which assets are subject to forfeiture. These procedures, including notice and jury trial, tend to be more protective of the defendant's interests than those followed in typical sentencing. For example, Federal Rule 32.2 governs criminal forfeiture in federal cases and requires that the government provide notice of its intent to employ forfeiture as part of a sentence in the indictment or information. Because that notice need not identify the specific property or the amount of any forfeiture money judgment that the government seeks, the court may direct the government to file before trial a bill of particulars that

---

others were "victims" under MVRA even though they were not named in the indictment); United States v. Thomas, 862 F.Supp.2d 19 (D.D.C.2012).

[40] U.S.S.G. § 5E1.1(a)(1).

[41] 18 U.S.C. § 982.

[42] 18 U.S.C. § 982(b)(1).

provides that information, the statutory basis for the forfeiture claim, and the nexus the government will seek to establish between the property and the offense.

As for proving the amount of proceeds or the relationship between the assets and the defendant's criminal activity, unless a higher threshold is specified by statute, the government need only prove these factual issues to a judge by a preponderance of the evidence, like other sentencing facts, held the Court in *Libretti v. United States*.[43] Numerous commentators have argued that *Apprendi* has since undermined *Libretti's* rationale, but the Court has yet to address the question.[44]

Jurisdictions that do provide for the trial of forfeiture issues by jury employ a bifurcated procedure, with the determination of forfeiture issues postponed until after the trier of fact first finds the defendant guilty of the underlying crime. Federal Rule 32.2 presently provides for a bifurcated proceeding in cases that go to jury trial, using a special verdict form and requiring a party to request retention of the jury for the forfeiture phase prior to the beginning of deliberations. A defendant may waive the jury's determination of forfeiture facts, but the Court in *Libretti* declined to hold that such a waiver must pass the standards enforced for guilty pleas. Whether the hearing is before a judge or a jury, evidence admitted to prove the requisite nexus between property and offense need not be admissible under the rules applicable at trial, and need only be determined by the court to be "relevant and reliable."[45]

Under Rule 32.2, ordering forfeiture in a federal case is a multi-step process. If the requisite nexus between property and offense is established by hearing as described above, the court enters a preliminary order that permits seizure of the property as well as time to make corrections to the order in advance of sentencing. At sentencing, the preliminary order becomes part of the final order against the defendant and must be included in the judgment, permitting appeal. The preliminary order also provides notice to third parties who may claim an interest in the property involved and resolve contested claims in an "ancillary" proceeding, after which the forfeiture order is amended as needed. Finally, the court may amend a forfeiture order "at any time" to include substitute property when substitute property is permitted by statute,[46] or additional property that was located and identified following the preliminary order. This provision is helpful to the government in cases in which it has not completed its investigation to locate the forfeitable property by the time of sentencing. The court in such a case may issue a forfeiture order describing the property in "general" terms, and amend it later when additional specific property is identified, although that authority that should be used only in unusual circumstances.[47] The statutory jury right does not apply to the forfeiture of substitute assets or to the addition of newly-discovered property to an existing order of forfeiture.

---

[43] 516 U.S. 29 (1995).

[44] See § 24.5(e).

[45] Rule 32.2(b)(1)(B).

[46] 18 U.S.C. § 982(b)(1).

[47] Rule 32.2, Committee Note, citing United States v. BCCI Holdings (Luxembourg), 69 F.Supp.2d 36 (D.D.C.1999) (ordering forfeiture of all of a large, complex corporation's assets in the United States, permitting the government to continue discovery necessary to identify and trace those assets).

F.   "Collateral Sanctions"

Although not technically part of the criminal sentence itself, many severe collateral consequences can follow from conviction for a white collar offense.[48] Some federal judges have imposed reduced sentences where the collateral consequences of a conviction are extraordinary. But even when there is no chance that collateral consequences of conviction will affect the judge's selection of sentence, they should always be considered by counsel in prosecuting and defending white collar cases.

As the Court stated in *Padilla v. Kentucky,*[49] deportation is "sometimes the most important part . . . of the penalty that may be imposed on noncitizen defendants who plead guilty to specified crimes." White-collar crimes that may carry immigration consequences such as removal and denial of reentry for noncitizens fall into two categories. The first comprises offenses defined as "aggravated felonies,"[50] and includes money laundering or fraud over $10,000, RICO violations, commercial bribery, forgery, obstruction of justice, perjury, bribery of a witness, and conspiracy.[51] The second category includes crimes of "moral turpitude," usually involving fraud or evil intent, that carry a sentence of at least one year.[52]

A white collar conviction may lead to the loss of many other rights and benefits, including the right to vote, participate in a jury, hold political office, or own or possess a firearm. A person convicted of a felony white collar offense may not reside in an Armed Forces Retirement Home or serve as a representative payee for a beneficiary entitled to social security benefits. A government employee convicted of fraud in the application for benefits for a work related injury may lose benefits for earlier injuries.

Any criminal record may affect job opportunities generally, and being convicted of a white collar crime can severely impact employment prospects for an offender. A wide variety of work may be specifically prohibited for a person convicted of a white collar offense. This includes work in ports or airports, labor organizations, employee benefit programs, investment companies, banks, insurance companies, private transport companies that transport prisoners, state departments of motor vehicles, or customs brokerages. Conviction may also mean revocation or denial of a license or registration by federal agencies such as the Commodity Futures Trading Commission, the FCC, or the SEC.

White collar convictions can also lead to debarment from federal programs. For example, a health care provider must be excluded from federally funded health care programs for at least five years if convicted of a program-related crime or health care fraud, and may be excluded for up to three years if convicted of fraud, theft, embezzlement, breach of fiduciary duty, or other financial misconduct related to health care. An individual who is convicted of fraud, certain antitrust violations, embezzlement, theft, forgery, bribery, falsification or destruction of records, making

---

[48] See § 18.7.

[49] 559 U.S. 356 (2010).

[50] 8 U.S.C. § 1101(a)(43).

[51] 8 U.S.C. 1101(a)(43)(M). See Kawashima v. Holder, 132 S.Ct. 1166 (2012) (stating that to determine whether an offense "involv[e] fraud or deceit" court employs a categorical approach by looking to the statute defining the crime of conviction).

[52] 8 U.S.C. § 1227(a)(2).

false statements, tax evasion, receiving stolen property, making false claims, or obstruction of justice may face debarment from federal procurement programs. Convictions may also lead to prohibitions on contracting with the Department of Defense, or participation in certain aspects of the drug industry. The statutory provisions governing these rules and more can now be found on an interactive website providing a comprehensive listing of collateral consequences.[53]

§ 24.3 CONSTITUTIONAL LIMITATIONS ON TYPE, AMOUNT, OR SEVERITY OF PUNISHMENT

A. Cruel and Unusual Punishment Clause

The United States Constitution places few substantive limits on the use of these various sanctions as punishment for crime. The Eighth Amendment's Cruel and Unusual Punishment Clause is unlikely to restrain non-capital sentences of incarceration for adult offenders in white collar cases. According to the Court, no Eighth Amendment proportionality analysis is warranted unless a threshold comparison of the gravity of the offense with the severity of the sentence "leads to an inference of gross disproportionality."[54] Not surprisingly, ever since the Court struck down a sentence of life without parole for defendant's conviction of a seventh non-violent felony in *Solem v. Helm,*[55] subsequent applications of the Clause suggest that relief will be available, if at all, only in the most "extreme cases."[56] Long sentences for adults,[57] even those dooming offenders to life in prison, have so far withstood attack.[58]

B. Excessive Fines Clause

Criminal forfeitures and fines are subject to being challenged as "grossly disproportionate to the gravity of the offense" under the Excessive Fines Clause of the Eighth Amendment.[59] The Court in *United States v. Bajakajian,*[60] found that forfeiture of over $350,000 in cash because the owner had not declared it when attempting to leave the country was unconstitutionally excessive, but it is unusual for a challenge on this ground to succeed. Several circuits have treated the proceeds of an illegal activity differently than other forfeitures and have held that the proceeds of an illegal activity will never exceed Eighth Amendment limits.[61] The federal courts have generally looked

---

[53] The website was created by the ABA with funding from the Department of Justice. See http://www.abacollateralconsequences.org/CollateralConsequences/index.html.

[54] Graham v. Florida, 560 U.S. 48, 130 S.Ct. 2011, 2022 (2010) (citing Harmelin v. Michigan, 501 U.S. 957, 1005 (1991) (opinion of Kennedy, J.)).

[55] Solem v. Helm, 463 U.S. 277 (1983).

[56] Harmelin v. Michigan, 501 U.S. 957 (1991) (upholding life sentence for defendant convicted of possession of cocaine with no prior felony convictions); Ewing v. California, 538 U.S. 11, 22 (2003) (upholding life sentence for defendant convicted of stealing three golf clubs, his fifth conviction).

[57] For the separate treatment of juveniles, see Miller v. Alabama, 132 S.Ct. 2455 (2012).

[58] See, e.g., United States v. Hoyt, 47 Fed.Appx. 834, 836–37 (9th Cir.2002) (upholding 235 month sentence for conspiracy to commit fraud, mail fraud, and bankruptcy fraud despite the defendant's age and condition).

[59] Stefan D. Cassella, Asset Forfeiture Law in the United States 839 (2007).

[60] 524 U.S. 321 (1998).

[61] See e.g., United States v. Betancourt, 422 F.3d 240, 250 (5th Cir.2005). Compare United States v. Jalaram, 599 F.3d 347, 354–55 (4th Cir. 2010) (clause applies, but it would be very difficult, and perhaps impossible, for a defendant to show that the forfeiture of proceeds was grossly disproportional to the gravity of his offense).

to four factors in determining whether a forfeiture is "grossly disproportional" to the offense of conviction: (1) the essence of the crime of the defendant and its relation to other criminal activity, (2) whether the defendant fit[s] into the class of persons for whom the statute was principally designed, (3) the maximum sentence and fine that could have been imposed, and (4) the nature of the harm caused by the defendant's conduct.[62] Additionally, at least one circuit has also considered whether forfeiture would deprive the defendant of his livelihood.[63] Courts have presumed constitutionality when the amount to be forfeited falls within the congressionally mandated range of fines,[64] but do not presume unconstitutionality when the forfeiture exceeds that range.[65]

C. Double Jeopardy Clause

The Double Jeopardy Clause of the Fifth Amendment also places few restraints on punishment. As noted in Chapter 18, it does not prevent the imposition of punitive civil penalties and a criminal fine for the very same conduct, even when payments are made to the very same government. It does not bar multiple punishments or prosecutions for the same crime by different "sovereigns," that is, by both the federal government and a state, or by more than one state.[66]

A judge does not violate a defendant's rights under the Double Jeopardy Clause by imposing a higher sentence on one charge because of a prior conviction for another,[67] or because of conduct with which the defendant was never charged, or was previously acquitted.[68] Likewise, a defendant may be separately prosecuted and sentenced for an offense that had previously been the basis for an enhanced sentence for a different offense.[69] Finally, double jeopardy does not forbid the government from seeking a higher sentence on appeal, or seeking a higher sentence at resentencing if the defendant is reconvicted after successfully appealing his conviction.[70]

D. Ex Post Facto Clause

Retroactive application of changes in sentencing law may violate the Ex Post Facto Clause, if the change is substantive and disadvantages a defendant. If a change in the law increases the punishment for an offense beyond that provided on the date

---

[62] United States v. Castello, 611 F.3d 116 (2d Cir.2010) (upholding forefeiture); United States v. Malewicka, 664 F.3d 1099 (7th Cir.2011) (upholding forfeiture).

[63] United States v. Levesque, 546 F.3d 78 (1st Cir.2008). Compare United States v. Aguasvivas–Castillo, 668 F.3d 7 (1st Cir.2012) (upholding 20 million dollar forfeiture when defendant failed to present facts on future deprivation of livelihood and forfeiture was not disproportional to the gravity of the defendant's offense).

[64] E.g., United States v. Fifty Nine Thousand Dollars, 282 Fed.Appx. 785, 789 (11th Cir.2008).

[65] United States v. Seher, 686 F.Supp.2d 1323, 1331–32 (N.D.Ga.2010).

[66] CRIMPROC § 25.5. On when crimes are the "same," see note 140.

[67] Almendarez–Torres v. United States, 523 U.S. 224 (1998).

[68] United States v. Watts, 519 U.S. 148 (1997); Williams v. New York, 337 U.S. 241 (1949).

[69] Monge v. California, 524 U.S. 721 (1998).

[70] A higher sentence after appeal may be limited by due process, however, see notes 147-148. See also CRIMPROC § 26.8.

when the defendant committed the offense, even an increase in an advisory sentencing guideline range, it may not be applied when sentencing the defendant.[71]

§ 24.4 FEDERAL GUIDELINES SENTENCING FOR INDIVIDUALS

A. The Advisory Sentencing Guidelines—Overview

1. History

Dissatisfied with what it perceived as unwarranted disparity in sentencing in the federal courts, Congress passed the Sentencing Reform Act of 1984.[72] The Act was designed to increase transparency, uniformity, and predictability in federal sentencing by restricting judicial sentencing discretion, limiting good time, and abolishing discretionary parole release. As Justice Breyer later phrased it, "Instead of a parole commission and a judge trying to second-guess each other about the time an offender will actually serve in prison, the SRA tries to create a sentencing system that will require the offender actually to serve most of the sentence the judge imposes."[73] The Act created the United States Sentencing Commission to write guidelines that judges were required to use to determine sentences.[74] The resulting Guidelines, discussed in more detail below, identify and categorize offense and offender characteristics, and assign a specified weight to each in determining a narrow sentence range for each case. The hope was that the Guidelines would increase the probability that offenders who engage in roughly the same criminal conduct would receive roughly the same sentence. White collar offenses were given particular attention under the Guidelines, as the Commission sought to remedy what many considered to be undue leniency extended to white collar offenders.[75]

2. Relevant Conduct

The Guidelines were intended to restrict the discretion of judges when selecting as sentence from within the statutory range authorized for each offense, by requiring judges to follow consistent rules for weighing information about the offender, the offense of conviction, and "relevant conduct." Relevant conduct includes criminal activity other than that established by the elements of the offense of conviction. To qualify as "relevant" under the Guidelines, conduct must have been (1) the part of the same court of conduct or common scheme or plan; or (2) in preparation for, during the commission, or in the course of attempting to avoid detection or responsibility for offense of conviction; or (3) in cases of "jointly undertaken criminal activity," conduct that the defendant aided and abetted, and "reasonably foreseeable acts and omissions *of others* in furtherance of the jointly undertaken criminal activity."[76] In other words, the recommended sentence under the Guidelines is based not upon conduct proven

---

[71] See Johnson v. United States, 529 U.S. 694, 699–701 (2000); Peugh v. United States, 133 S.Ct.2072 (2013) ("District courts must begin their sentencing analysis with the Guidelines in effect at the time of the offense and use them to calculate the sentencing range correctly.").

[72] 98 Stat. 1987.

[73] Setser v. United States, 132 S.Ct. 1463, 1475 (2012) (Breyer, J., dissenting).

[74] 28 U.S.C. §§ 991, 994.

[75] 12 S. Rep. No. 98–225, at 91–92 (1983), reprinted in 1984 U.S.C.C.A.N. 3182, 3274–75.

[76] U.S.S.G. 1B1.3(a)(I).

beyond a reasonable doubt by trial or admitted by guilty plea, but instead upon the actual conduct of the defendant and any co-conspirators.[77] Crimes that qualify as relevant conduct can be taken into account when setting a defendant's sentence regardless of whether the defendant was charged, convicted or even acquitted of those crimes.[78] This modified "real offense" system, drafters hoped, would help to reduce disparity in punishment that results from charging and bargaining decisions of the prosecution.

3.   *Advisory Status*

As designed, sentencing in accordance with the Guidelines was mandatory. Sentences that did not comply with the Guidelines could be, and frequently were, reversed on appeal. That changed in January of 2005 when the Supreme Court in *United States v. Booker*,[79] decided that judicial fact finding under the mandatory Guidelines was unconstitutional. *Booker* held that because the Sentencing Reform Act dictated specific sentencing ranges, and prohibited more severe sentences above those ranges unless certain facts were found, those facts must be found by juries beyond a reasonable doubt. The Act authorized fact finding by judges, not juries, and thus violated the Sixth Amendment right to jury trial. By dictating narrow sentencing ranges conditioned upon a specific set of factual findings, Congress had essentially replaced the criminal code with a much more detailed set of nested lesser and greater offenses, each separated by specific Guidelines factors. As a remedy, the Court "excised" those parts of the Act that made the Guidelines binding. With the Guidelines advisory only, a judge was free to sentence within the entire statutory range authorized by offense of conviction.

Under the now advisory Guidelines, judges must continue to calculate properly and consider the recommended Guidelines sentence, comply with sentencing statutes and Federal Rule 32, and give reasons for each sentence. The failure to do so can result in reversal on appeal and resentencing. But federal judges need not impose sentences that fall within the recommended Guidelines range or that are authorized by the Guideline's departure provisions. Instead, as the Court has explained, the Guidelines are "the starting point and the initial benchmark" only, and "district courts may impose sentences within statutory limits based on appropriate consideration of all of the factors listed in § 3553(a), subject to appellate review for "reasonableness."[80]

Section 3553(a) requires judges to impose a sentence sufficient, but not greater than is necessary to reflect the seriousness of the offense, promote respect for the law, provide just punishment, afford adequate deterrence, protect the public from further crimes of the defendant, and provide the defendant with needed educational or vocational training, medical care, or other correctional treatment in the most effective manner. The information that a judge can consider in applying these many factors is much broader than the range of information permitted under the Guidelines. Post-sentence rehabilitation, for example, can be considered when relevant to the selection

---

[77] § 1B1.3(a)(1)(B); § 1B1.3, comment. (n.2); United States v. McClatchey, 316 F.3d 1122, 1128 (10th Cir. 2003).

[78] United States v. Watts, 519 U.S. 148 (1997).

[79] 543 U.S. 220 (2005).

[80] Pepper v. United States, 131 S.Ct. 1229, 1241 (2011) (quoting Gall v. United States, 552 U.S. 38, 49–51 (2007)).

of an appropriate punishment should an offender be resentenced, even though the Guidelines provide that it should not be considered.[81] A separate provision bars a judge from imposing or lengthening a prison term in order to promote a criminal defendant's rehabilitation, however.[82]

Even after *Booker* lifted the mandate to abide by the Guidelines, the vast majority of sentences continue to fall within a range authorized by the Guidelines. This is not surprising considering federal judges had been using the Guidelines to select sentences for more than a quarter century prior to the *Booker* decision. Most federal judges surveyed in 2010 thought that the Guidelines ranges for fraud were appropriate.[83] But the proportion of guideline-compliant sentences has steadily dropped,[84] and for the past several years judges in white collar cases have imposed on average 5–7 months less incarceration than the minimum sentence called for by Guidelines.[85] The Department of Justice has expressed concerns about inconsistent sentencing in high-loss fraud cases, and high-profile white collar crimes promise to keep white collar sentencing in the spotlight.

B. The Guidelines and Mandatory Minimum Sentences

Beginning in the 1970s, legislatures began to regulate sentencing by enacting statutes that require a minimum sentence of imprisonment for any offender who commits a particular offense. In operation, these "mandatory minimum" statutes limit the discretion of sentencing judges and provide leverage to prosecutors in plea bargaining. Some mandatory minimum statutes require a certain minimum term for offenders who commit offenses under specified conditions. The federal "three strikes" law, for example, like similar laws in several states, mandates a sentence of life imprisonment for a defendant's third offense.[86] Prosecutors often use mandatory minimum sentencing in charge bargaining, promising to dismiss or declining to bring a charge with a mandatory sentence in exchange for the defendant's agreement to plead guilty to a different charge.

Mandatory minimums have had an enormous impact. Because the statutory range designated by Congress for the offense of conviction trumps any recommended sentence under the Guidelines, a mandatory minimum sentence statute will prohibit a judge from sentencing the defendant to a lesser sentence, even if the judge's evaluation of factors under § 3553(a), or an accurate calculation of the recommended sentence under the Guidelines, suggest that a lower sentence would be appropriate. Section 3553 authorizes a sentence below a statutory minimum only when the government makes a

---

[81] Id. at 1242. On the potential scope of mitigating information, see Todd Haugh, "Can the CEO Learn from the Condemned? The Application of Capital Mitigation Strategies to White Collar Cases," 62 Am.U.L.Rev. 1 (2012).

[82] Tapia v. United States, 131 S.Ct. 2382 (2011) (lengthening a defendant's sentence to provide for particular drug treatment program violated 18 U.S.C. § 3582(a), which instructs sentencing courts to "recogniz[e] that imprisonment is not an appropriate means of promoting correction and rehabilitation").

[83] USSC, Results of Survey of United States District Judges January 2010 through March 2010 (June 2010), available at www.ussc.gov, hereinafter USSC, 2010 Survey.

[84] Prepared Testimony, Subcommittee on Crime, Terrorism, and Homeland Security Committee on the Judiciary Cong. (2011) (testimony of Judge Patti B. Saris).

[85] For example, nationwide, sentences for fraud are within the Guidelines 54.6% of the time. USSC Statistics, Table 27.

[86] 18 U.S.C. § 3559(c).

motion based on the defendant's cooperation.[87] As one judge put it, "the government's unreviewable decision to invoke the mandatory sentencing provision ma[kes] the actual facts irrelevant."[88] Criticism that the continued proliferation and use of mandatory minimum sentencing statutes undermines the rationality of judicial sentencing Guidelines, including complaints by Supreme Court justices and the Sentencing Commission itself, has yet to gain traction in Congress.[89]

C. Calculating the Offense Level–Base Offense Level and Specific Offense Adjustments

The recommended sentence range under the Guidelines depends upon two scores: the offense level, reflecting the seriousness of the defendant's conduct, and the criminal history score, reflecting the defendant's criminal record. To determine the offense level, a judge must begin by calculating the "base offense level," using the appropriate guideline for the particular offense of conviction.[90] Chapter 2 of the Sentencing Guidelines Manual contains different Guidelines for different types of offenses. Many white collar offenses fall within the guideline for fraud, § 2B1.1, a provision that covers simple thefts and embezzlements to complex securities frauds, and which designates, for most of these crimes, a base offense level of 6 or 7. Tax offenses, contempt, obstruction of justice, perjury, and environmental crimes each have separate guidelines.

The base offense level is then modified up or down by "specific offense adjustments,"—points added or subtracted from the base offense level for aggravating and mitigating features tailored to the particular crimes covered by that particular Chapter 2 guideline. For example, commonly used specific offense adjustments under the fraud guideline include the number of victims,[91] and the use of sophisticated means to accomplish the offense.[92] But the most important factor under this guideline is the amount of loss resulting from the crime.[93] In nearly half of the cases sentenced in 2011 in which loss was calculated under § 2B1.1, losses were $70,000 or less, adding up to 6 levels to the base offense level. In nine cases, however, the offense level was increased by 30 levels for losses over 400 million dollars.[94]

Because of its potential influence upon the adjusted offense level that is used to determine the advisory sentence range, loss amount drives the sentence in many white

---

[87] See also Fed. R. Crim. P. 35 and U.S.S.G. § 5K1.1.

[88] United States v. Dossie, 851 F.Supp.2d 478, 485 (E.D.N.Y.2012).

[89] E.g., Barbara S. Vincent & Paul J. Hofer, Federal Judicial Center, The Consequences of Mandatory Minimum Prison Terms: A Summary of Recent Findings (1994); Stephen Breyer, Federal Sentencing Guidelines Revisited, 11 Fed.Sent.Rep. 180, 184 (1999); USSC, Report to Congress: Mandatory Minimum Penalties in the Federal Criminal Justice System (2011), available at www.ussc.gov (recommending several changes to statutes that the Commission concluded may be excessively severe).

[90] U.S.S.G. § 1B1.2(a).

[91] U.S.S.G. § 2B1.1(b)(2). For example, more than 50 victims is a four-level increase. Victims include those who have been compensated or reimbursed for their losses. See Comment, "Once Victim, Always Victim," Compensated Individuals Under the Amended Sentencing Guidelines on Fraud, 108 Mich.L.Rev. 445 (2009).

[92] U.S.S.G. § 2B1.1(b)(9).

[93] U.S.S.G. § 2B1.1(b)(1). Under the Guidelines, a court may use the gain that resulted from the offense as an alternative measure only if the loss cannot be determined. U.S.S.G. § 2B1.1, comment. (n. 3(B)).

[94] USSC, Use of Guidelines and Specific Offense Characteristics, FY 2011, available at www.ussc.gov.

collar cases. This focus on loss has been criticized as arbitrarily skewing sentences, allowing a "quantifiable task" like loss determination to "distort the larger qualitative project" of selecting an appropriate sentence.[95] Disapproval of this aspect of the Guidelines has not been limited to academic commentary; judges, too, have argued that the fraud guidelines' "fetish with abstract arithmetic" can cause unjust punishment.[96] What counts as "loss" under the Guidelines has unsurprisingly become a topic of continual litigation.

"Loss" is defined as "the greater of actual loss or intended loss."[97] "Actual loss" is "the reasonably foreseeable pecuniary harm that resulted from the offense."[98] "Intended loss" is defined as "pecuniary harm[99] that was intended to result from the offense"[100] even if that harm "would have been impossible or unlikely to occur (e.g., as in a government sting operation, or an insurance fraud in which the claim exceeded the insured value)."[101] Courts measure the amount of loss under the Guidelines using not only losses resulting from the offense of conviction, but also losses from "relevant conduct" of the defendant and any coconspirators.[102]

The Guidelines specify no particular method of calculating loss in securities or commodities cases, leading to conflicting loss-calculation methods among the circuits. For example, circuits do not agree on if or how the principles used for determining loss in civil fraud cases should apply to guidelines loss calculations.[103] Difficulties faced by courts include how to measure loss to investors who hold investments over time during ongoing fraud, how to measure and exclude losses from causes other than the fraud,[104]

---

[95] See Richman, supra note 9. See also Alan Ellis, John R. Steer and Mark H. Allenbaugh, At a "Loss' for Justice, Federal Sentencing for Economic Offenses, Criminal Justice (Winter 2011), at pp 35–40 (criticizing the application of the loss guidelines); Ellen S. Podgor, The Challenge of White Collar Sentencing, 97 J.Crim.L. & Criminology 731 (2007).

[96] See United States v. Adelson, 441 F.Supp.2d 506, 512 (S.D.N.Y.2006) (noting "the utter travesty of justice that sometimes results from the guidelines' fetish with abstract arithmetic, as well as the harm that guideline calculations can visit on human beings if not cabined by common sense").

[97] U.S.S.G. § 2B1.1, cmt. n.3(A).

[98] U.S.S.G. § 2B1.1, cmt. (n.3(A)(i)). For a helpful resource in understanding loss under the Guidelines, see USSC, Loss Primer (§ 2B1.1(b)(1)) (2012), available at http://www.ussc.gov, hereinafter USSC, Loss Primer.

[99] U.S.S.G. § 2B1.1, cmt. (n.3(A)(iii)).

[100] U.S.S.G. § 2B1.1 cmt. (n.3(A)(ii)).

[101] Id.

[102] See U.S.S.G. § 1B1.3(a)(1)(A). See also USSC, Loss Primer (collecting authority). Reasonably foreseeable is defined by U.S.S.G. § 2B1.1 cmt. (n.3(A)(iv)) as those losses that the defendant "knew or, under the circumstances, reasonably should have known, was a potential result of the offense." See U.S.S.G. § 1B1.3(a)(2). Loss is based on "all acts and omissions . . . that were part of the same course of conduct or common scheme or plan as the offense of conviction."

[103] Compare United States v. Olis, 429 F.3d 540, 545–6 (5th Cir.2005) (citing Dura Pharmaceuticals, Inc. v. Broudo, 544 U.S. 336, 341–43 (2005)); United States v. Nacchio, 573 F.3d 1062, 1078–79 (10th Cir.2009) (suggesting that the Olis approach would be appropriate); and United States v. Rutkoske, 506 F.3d 170, 179 (2d Cir.2007); with United States v. Berger, 587 F.3d 1038, 1042–45 (9th Cir.2009). See also John D. Esterhay, Apples and Oranges: Securities Market Losses Should Be Treated Differently for Major White– Collar Criminal Sentencing Under the Federal Guidelines, 76 Mo. L. Rev. 1113–1142 (2011).

[104] United States v. Ebbers, 458 F.3d 110 (2d Cir.2006) (explaining problems with using simplistic "market capitalization test" for ongoing frauds).

and when to use gain as a substitute for loss when calculation of loss proves too difficult.[105]

Litigation over loss calculations in non-securities cases is also ongoing, including such issues as determining the "fair market value" of a loss, and whether unforeseen decreases in the value of collateral should offset fraudulent loan loss amounts.[106] Conflicting authorities are collected in the Sentencing Commission's helpful primer on loss calculation, which is periodically updated.[107]

D. Calculating the Offense Level—Adjustments Not Specific to the Offense

1. *Generally*

In addition to the offense-specific adjustments listed in each Chapter 2 guideline, there are several other adjustments to the offense level that are considered in all cases, contained in Chapter 3 of the Guidelines Manual. Of these, the following are frequently applied in white collar sentencing.

2. *Acceptance of Responsibility*

The most frequently applied adjustment in Chapter 3 is a reduction for the acceptance of responsibility. A defendant who "clearly demonstrates acceptance of responsibility for his offense" receives a two-level reduction.[108] The Guidelines provide that a guilty plea is "significant evidence" of acceptance of responsibility. The Guidelines state that a defendant who goes to trial is not "automatically preclude[d]" from receiving this credit, but in practice the credit is reserved for those who plead guilty. A defendant who "falsely denies, or frivolously contests, relevant conduct that the court determines to be true has acted in a manner inconsistent with acceptance of responsibility."[109] For those defendants with an offense level of 16 or more, an additional third level may be subtracted if the government files a motion stating that the defendant has timely notified authorities of his intention to plead guilty.[110] The courts do not agree whether the additional level reduction is mandatory once the government makes the motion.[111] Not surprisingly given the overwhelming proportion of offenders who plead guilty, all but 8% of offenders sentenced under the guideline for fraud in 2011 received some credit under this provision.

---

[105] United States v. Parris, 573 F.Supp.2d 744 (E.D.N.Y.2008) (difficulties inherent in calculating loss to the market made use of gain appropriate).

[106] Compare United States v. Turk, 626 F.3d 743 (2d Cir.2010) (in case of fraudulent loans, court rejected defendant's argument that loss should exclude unforeseen decrease in value of collateral, concluding, "a defendant may not reasonably count on the expected sale value of collateral to save himself from the foreseeable consequences of his fraudulent conduct").

[107] USSC, Loss Primer.

[108] U.S.S.G. § 3E1.1(a); § 3E1.1, cmt. (n.3).

[109] U.S.S.G. § 3E1.1, cmt. (n.1(a)).

[110] U.S.S.G. § 3E1.1(b).

[111] Compare United States v. Mount, 675 F.3d 1052 (7th Cir.2012), with United States v. Williamson, 598 F.3d 227 (5th Cir.2010).

3.   Role in Offense

White collar offenses often involve multiple participants. In such cases, even when the other participants are never charged, a defendant's sentence can be increased or decreased by up to four levels depending upon his "role in the offense" and the number of participants.[112] Of economic crime offenders in 2011, about one in ten received a sentence increase, and about one in twenty a sentence decrease, under this guideline.

4.   Obstruction

In a small number of cases (approximately 4% of those sentenced under the fraud guideline in 2011), a defendant's recommended guideline range will be increased using the adjustment for obstruction of justice. The government must show the defendant "willfully obstructed, or impeded or attempted to obstruct or impede, the administration of justice with respect to the investigation, prosecution, or sentencing of the instant offense of conviction." Perjury, destroying evidence, encouraging another to avoid complying with a grand jury subpoena,[113] and providing false information to a probation officer are all examples of conduct that will support this sentence enhancement.[114] If the basis for the enhancement is the defendant's alleged perjury, however, the court must first find that the defendant (1) gave false testimony, (2) concerning a material fact, (3) with the intent to deceive, rather than as a result of confusion, mistake or faulty memory.[115]

5.   Abuse of Trust

Section 3B1.3 of the Guidelines authorizes an increase if the defendant occupied a position of trust that he used to facilitate the commission or concealment of the offense. This increase was applied in 16% of of the sentences for fraud-related offenses in 2011. A position of trust is characterized by (1) professional or managerial discretion and (2) minimal supervision, and is not applicable to ordinary bank tellers, secretaries, or janitors who have access to credit cards.[116]

6.   Multiple Counts

In cases with multiple counts, there may be further additions to the offense level. When multiple counts involve "substantially the same harm" the counts will be grouped together for sentencing so that a defendant has only one offense level for the

---

[112] U.S.S.G. Ch.3, Pt.B, intro. comment.

[113] United States v. Snipes, 611 F.3d 855 (11th Cir.2010) (upholding enhancement when defendant Wesley Snipes told a former employee not to respond to a grand jury subpoena or else "pay the consequences").

[114] U.S.S.G. § 3C1.1, cmt. (n.4). See also U.S.S.G. § 3C1.2 (adjustment for endangering another while fleeing); United States v. Byors, 586 F.3d 222 (2d Cir.2009) (money laundering sentence can be increased to reflect obstruction regarding underlying crimes).

[115] See United States v. Dunnigan, 507 U.S. 87, 94 (1993).

[116] United States v. Ollison, 555 F.3d 152 (5th Cir.2009).

entire group,[117] namely, the level for the most serious offense in the group.[118] The offense level will be based on the combined losses for all grouped counts.[119]

E. Criminal History/Prior Convictions

A defendant's criminal history is a common consideration in all sentencing systems, as it is considered an important measure of culpability and the need for specific deterrence, as well as relevant to likely rehabilitation and future offending. Not surprisingly, criminal history plays a substantial role in federal sentencing of all offenders, including those convicted of white collar crimes. The two main determinants of a recommended sentence for an individual convicted in federal court are the adjusted offense level, described above, and the defendant's criminal history. Each forms an axis on the grid of recommended ranges known as the sentencing table.

There are six categories of criminal history on the sentencing table, ranging from the lowest for first offenders to the highest for career offenders. The appropriate category in each case depends upon the calculation of criminal history points under Chapter 4 of the Guidelines manual.[120] Points for a defendant's prior convictions and juvenile adjudications may vary based on the sentence received, how long ago the defendant was convicted, and whether the offense was committed shortly after release or under supervision. Sentences for organizations, although not determined using a sentencing table like sentences for individuals, are also influenced by the criminal history of the organization, as described in § 24.7, below.

White collar defendants, compared to defendants convicted of many other types of federal crime, tend to have both lower criminal history scores and lower recidivism rates following release.[121]

F. The Recommended Sentencing Range, Departures, and Variances

The recommended sentence range is the number of months found at the intersection of the defendant's criminal history and adjusted offense level on the sentencing table.[122] The table contains four "zones," each designating certain sentencing options. For cases falling within zone A—less serious criminal histories and offense levels—a sentence of straight probation is available and the recommended sentence range is six months or less. The Guidelines recommend that defendants falling within the highest zone—Zone D—be sentenced to prison. Those in the middle, in Zones B or C, may receive a split sentence—combining some confinement with release on conditions.

---

[117] U.S.S.G. § 3D1.2. See also U.S.S.G. § 5G1.2 (providing rules for sentencing on multiple counts, and for imposing statutorily required consecutive sentences).

[118] U.S.S.G. § 3D1.3(a).

[119] U.S.S.G. § 3D1.3(b).

[120] U.S.S.G. § 4A1.1.

[121] USSC, Measuring Recidivism: The Criminal History Computation of the Federal Sentencing Guidelines (2004); USSC, Recidivism and the "First Offender" (2003), both available at www.ussc.gov.

[122] U.S.S.G. ch. 5, pt. A, Sentencing Table, §§ 5E1.2, 7B1.4. See also U.S.S.G. § 1A1.4(h), at 11.

As explained in more detail in the next sections, after the Court's decision in *Booker*, neither the Guidelines, ranges nor the zone options are binding upon sentencing judges. A judge may impose any sentence within the statutory range consistent with the factors in Section 3553(a).[123] Yet even before *Booker*, when the Guidelines sentence was mandatory, the sentencing table was not the last word on what the sentence would be. The Guidelines have always included permissible upward and downward departures from the recommended range for factors not adequately taken into consideration by the Commission in determining that range. Departures were intended to provide needed flexibility to accommodate circumstances or a kind or degree not already included in the Guidelines' calculus. The general departure provision, as well as various specified reasons for departure were, and still are, part of the Guidelines manual. Most are located in Chapter 5,[124] but another popular basis for departure appears in Section 4A1.3, which permits a court to downgrade or upgrade the criminal history category if the category recommended by the Guidelines substantially under- or over-represents the defendant's criminal history or the likelihood that the defendant will commit other crimes.

Before *Booker*, a decision to depart from the Guidelines range was scrutinized closely on appeal. After *Booker* rendered the Guidelines no longer binding, many federal judges have continued to consider in each case whether a departure is warranted, and at times invoke a departure guideline, but the use of a departure receives the same "reasonableness" review as any sentence. For example, in one recent case from the District of Nevada the defendant was convicted of bank fraud, a crime carrying a statutory maximum sentence of 30 years. The judge rejected the recommended sentence range—41 to 51 months. Instead, finding that the defendant murdered his wife in order to defraud the bank and obtain her assets, the judge imposed a sentence of nearly twenty-two years citing Section 5K2.1 of the Guidelines, a policy statement authorizing an upward departure "if death resulted."[125]

Not all judges use the departure provisions to explain a sentence that falls outside of the recommended Guidelines range. In some circuits, the court of appeals has instructed district judges that *Booker* made the concept of departures obsolete, and that they should apply a "two-step" process that skips departures: consider the guidelines range, then § 3553. Even where district judges are expected to use a "three-step" process—considering guidelines range, then potential departures, then § 3553—many judges prefer to explain sentences outside the recommended guideline range by referring solely to the factors in § 3553(a) rather than the specific departures authorized by the Guidelines. According to a recent survey, district judges explained that they opt for "variances" under § 3553 rather than departures under the Guidelines because the departure provisions do not always include the reason the judge wishes to sentence outside the range, and because departures are subject to stricter procedural

---

[123] 18 U.S.C. § 3553(b); U.S.S.G. §§ 1A1.2, at 1–2; U.S.S.G. § 1A1.4(b), at 6–7.

[124] U.S.S.G. §§ 5K1.1–5K3.1.

[125] See United States v. Fitch, 659 F.3d 788 (9th Cir.2011). For more on why the Constitution does not bar a judge from adding nearly 18 years to a defendant's sentence for a crime that was never charged or proven beyond a reasonable doubt, see § 24.5(e).

requirements, including notice to the defendant prior to sentencing, as well as closer appellate review.[126]

The one exception to this post-*Booker* trend away from reliance on departures is the continuing application of § 5K1.1. This guideline authorizes a downward departure if the defendant "has provided substantial assistance in the investigation or prosecution of another person who has committed an offense." It also allows a judge to impose a sentence that is less than what would otherwise be a mandatory minimum,[127] but a motion by the government is required.[128] One high-profile example of this departure is the lenient two-year sentence for Stuart Levine, who had faced a potential life sentence for a career of scams, but was rewarded for his cooperation in the prosecution of several other defendants, including former Illinois Governor Rod Blagojevich.[129] In 2011, about 15% of federal defendants sentenced under the guideline for fraud received sentence reductions for substantial assistance, with a median decrease of 18 months from the minimum guideline sentence.[130]

G.   Concurrent and Consecutive Sentences

When a defendant is subject to more than one sentence, federal judges and those in most states retain the discretion to determine whether those sentences must be served consecutively (one after the other) or concurrently (simultaneously). This choice can arise when a defendant is convicted of multiple offenses at the same trial, or when a defendant is convicted while subject to a sentence for a different offense in the same or another jurisdiction.[131]

This discretion to "stack" punishment creates the risk of grossly disparate terms of incarceration for similarly situated offenders. To guard against disparity, statutes typically limit judicial discretion by establishing a presumption of either consecutive or concurrent sentences, mandating consecutive sentences for specified offense combinations, or laying out conditions under which concurrent or consecutive sentences may be imposed. Under the Sentencing Reform Act, a federal judge may run multiple terms of imprisonment either concurrently or consecutively, with the exception of attempt and another offense that was the object of the offense. There is a presumption that simultaneously imposed terms are concurrent, and terms imposed at different times are consecutive, unless the court indicates otherwise, as well as a Sentencing Guideline that provides for concurrent sentencing of multiple counts in

---

[126] 2010 Survey, supra note 84. On notice for departures, see § 24.6(b). On the departure variance debate, see Paul J. Hofer, Beyond the "Heartland": Sentencing Under the Advisory Federal Guidelines, 49 Duquesne L.Rev. 675, 697–700 (2011).

[127] U.S.S.G. § 5K1.1, p.s.; *cf.* 18 U.S.C. § 3553(b)(2)(A)(iii). See also 28 U.S.C. § 994(n) (instructing Commission to assure that Guidelines "reflect the general appropriateness of imposing a lower sentence than would otherwise be imposed, including a sentence that is lower than that established by statute as a minimum sentence, to take into account a defendant's substantial assistance in the investigation or prosecution of another person").

[128] See Wade v. United States, 504 U.S. 181, 185 (1992) (dictum).

[129] Peter Nickeas, "Prosecutors: Levine among 'most valuable' witnesses in 3 decades," Chicago Tribune, June 16, 2012.

[130] USSC, Statistics, Tables 28, 30.

[131] 18 U.S.C. § 3584.

most cases.[132] A federal court may also order a federal sentence to run consecutively or concurrently to a state sentence that has yet to be imposed.[133]

§ 24.5 CONSTITUTIONAL CONSTRAINTS ON THE SENTENCING PROCESS

A. Constitutionally Required Procedure—Right to Counsel

Compared to the detailed constitutional regulation of investigation and trial, relatively few constitutional rules constrain the sentencing process. Instead, sentencing law is primarily statutory. This subsection summarizes most constitutionally based procedural protections afforded both state and federal defendants for sentencing. Other constitutional limitations on the punishment itself (as opposed to the process by which it is determined and imposed) are discussed in earlier in the chapter.

The Sixth Amendment right to the effective assistance of counsel extends through the sentencing phase of a criminal prosecution, at least in cases where the defendant's sentence includes imprisonment.[134] The Court has noted that its general approach of extending the right to counsel for "critical stages" of the prosecution is consistent with enforcing the right to counsel at sentencing.[135] Lower courts have rejected a constitutional right to counsel during a typical presentence interview by a probation officer, however, reasoning that this non-adversarial interview by a neutral party is not a "critical stage" requiring counsel's assistance. Statute or court rule may authorize counsel's attendance at the interview although the Constitution does not require it, as does Rule 32 of the Federal Rules of Criminal Procedure.

B. Limits on Sentencing Information and Reasons for Sentence

The Constitution has little to say about what a judge may consider when setting a sentence. In 1949, in *Williams v. New York*,[136] the Court made this clear, reasoning that when sentencing, a judge should be able to draw on information concerning "every aspect of a defendant's life." For example, constitutionally derived exclusionary rules do not apply at sentencing.[137] Nor does a court violate due process when, in setting a sentence within the statutory maximum for one offense, it considers other criminal conduct of the defendant, regardless of whether that conduct resulted in a criminal conviction.[138] *Williams* itself rejected a challenge to a death sentence based in part

---

[132] Id. See also U.S.S.G. § 5G1.2(c) ("If the sentence imposed on the count carrying the highest statutory maximum is adequate to achieve the total punishment, then the sentences on all counts shall run concurrently, except to the extent otherwise required by law.").

[133] Setser v. United States, 132 S.Ct. 1463 (2012) (noting § 3584 does not speak to this situation, so a court retains its discretion).

[134] Glover v. United States, 531 U.S. 198 (2001). See CRIMPROC § 26.4(e).

[135] Lafler v. Cooper, 132 S.Ct. 1376, 1381 (2012).

[136] 337 U.S. 241, 246–247 (1949).

[137] CRIMPROC § 25.6(a).

[138] See United States v. Watts, 519 U.S. 148 (1997); Nichols v. United States, 511 U.S. 738 (1994) (noting that because the defendant could have "been sentenced more severely based simply on evidence of the underlying conduct" which the state need prove only by a preponderance of the evidence, it must be "constitutionally permissible to consider a prior uncounseled misdemeanor conviction based on the same conduct, where that conduct had to be proven beyond a reasonable doubt").

upon allegations that the defendant had engaged in multiple crimes other than the crime for which the defendant was being sentenced.

The Fifth Amendment prohibits the imposition of multiple sentences by the same sovereign for the "same offence." But the "same elements" test that the Court has adopted for determining when two crimes are the "same offence" does not ensure that a defendant will face only one sentence for any given set of conduct. Instead, that test permits separate punishment and prosecution for multiple offenses so long as each offense contains an element not found in the other.[139] Because the offense definitions available for white collar prosecutions are often complex and overlapping, defendants may face multiple charges for what is essentially the same conduct. Double jeopardy has been held to include the concept of collateral estoppel, but that will bar prosecution only in the highly unusual case where a defendant was previously acquitted, it was clear from the record that the basis for the verdict of not guilty was its rejection of a particular factual element, and the government seeks conviction on a charge with that very same element.[140]

Some reasons for sentencing are off-limits, however. The Equal Protection Clause forbids a judge from imprisoning an indigent probationer who fails to pay a monetary sanction unless alternatives to incarceration are first considered,[141] and prohibits a judge from conditioning a more lenient sentence on the payment of restitution.[142] Lower courts have upheld sentences of incarceration, contempt, or community service following an indigent's failure to pay a monetary sanction, but only if the judge determines first that the defendant was unable to make payments despite bona fide efforts.[143] The Equal Protection Clause also prohibits judges from basing a sentence upon the race or gender of defendant or victim, or upon the defendant's exercise of a fundamental right.[144] Also forbidden by the process clause is vindictive sentencing, that is, imposing a higher sentence as punishment for a defendant's exercise of a procedural right. Finally, under the Self–Incrimination Clause, a judge may not draw an adverse inference about a factual issue from the defendant's assertion of the privilege against self-incrimination at sentencing.[145]

The challenge for courts and litigants in all of these contexts has been determining when the unconstitutional reason and not some alternative explanation was the basis

---

[139] United States v. Dixon, 509 U.S. 688 (1993); CRIMPROC § 17.4(b).

[140] Ashe v. Swenson, 397 U.S. 436 (1970); CRIMPROC § 17.4(a).

[141] Held the Court, "If the probationer could not pay despite sufficient bona fide efforts to acquire the resources to do so, the court must consider alternative measures of punishment other than imprisonment. Only if alternate measures are not adequate to meet the State's interest in punishment and deterrence may the court imprison a probationer who has made sufficient bona fide efforts to pay." Bearden v. Georgia, 461 U.S. 660 (1983).

[142] Tate v. Short, 401 U.S. 395 (1971). See e.g., DeLuise v. State, 72 So.3d 248 (Fla.App.2011) (in offering to reduce the defendant's sentence if he and his family came up with $100,000 of the restitution owed to the victims within 60 days, the court violated the equal protection rights of the defendant, citing *Tate*).

[143] See 18 U.S.C. § 3614, a defendant may be "resentenced to any sentence which might originally have been imposed" if the defendant "willfully refused to pay or failed to make sufficient bona fide efforts legally to acquire the resources to pay." See United States v. Johnston, 595 F.3d 292 (6th Cir.2010) (upholding increase of mail fraud defendant's sentence from 25 months to 51 months).

[144] CRIMPROC § 26.4(b).

[145] Mitchell v. United States, 526 U.S. 314 (1999); CRIMPROC § 26.4(c).

for the sentence. For example, though the Court has forbidden factual inferences from a defendant's silence at sentencing, it has not foreclosed the use of silence for other purposes, such as assessing the defendant's character or willingness to cooperate.

Alternative explanations for sentences have made the prohibition on vindictiveness less protective than it might appear as well. Take a case in which a judge imposes a higher sentence after a successful appeal and reconviction. A reviewing court will presume that the higher sentence is vindictive if the same judge imposed both the first sentence and the higher sentence.[146] But vindictiveness will not be presumed in circumstances that suggest that other reasons for the differing sentences are likely, such as when a different judge resentenced the defendant after appeal, when the defendant pleaded guilty and did not insist on trial, or when only the sentence and not the underlying conviction was overturned.[147]

Nor is vindictiveness for asserting the right to trial presumed when judges sentence those who are convicted after trial more severely than those who plead guilty. Reducing sentences for defendants who admit guilt is not considered to be a tax on trial. Rather than a trial penalty, the difference in sentence is considered a "plea discount," typically justified by the objectives of individualizing punishment, promoting rehabilitation, and rewarding cooperation. Similarly, enhancements for defendants who commit perjury during trial are permitted as a response to the additional culpability demonstrated by deliberate perjury, despite the chilling effect this may have upon the right to testify.[148]

C. Notice of and Access to Sentencing Information

Generally, there are few constitutionally mandated procedural safeguards to ensure that sentencing information is accurate. The Court has held that notice of sentencing information *before* a sentencing hearing is not required as "there is no general constitutional right to discovery in a criminal case."[149] In capital sentencing, surprise information is permitted, but secret information is not; the Court has barred a judge from considering information without any notice at all to the defendant.[150] The application of this rule to non-capital sentencing is unsettled.[151]

Although there may be no general right to discovery of sentencing information, if information favorable to the defendant and material to the sentence is possessed by the government, it must be disclosed to the defendant under the Court's *Brady* doctrine.

---

[146] North Carolina v. Pearce, 395 U.S. 711 (1969).

[147] CRIMPROC § 26.8(a).

[148] United States v. Dunnigan, 507 U.S. 87 (1993) (consideration permissible so long as the court makes an independent finding that the defendant gave false testimony concerning a material matter with the willful intent to provide false testimony, action that suggests a heightened "need for incapacitation and retribution" as "compared with the defendant charged with the same crime who allows judicial proceedings to progress without resorting to perjury"); CRIMPROC § 26.4(c).

[149] Gray v. Netherland, 518 U.S. 152 (1996).

[150] Gardner v. Florida, 430 U.S. 349 (1977).

[151] See Lankford v. Idaho, 500 U.S. 110 (1991) (stating that "the need for notice is even more pronounced" in capital cases than in non-capital cases); O'Dell v. Netherland, 521 U.S. 151 (1997) (stating that Justice White's concurring opinion in *Gardner* states its holding, and rested upon the Eighth Amendment, not due process). In the past, some justices have suggested that due process may govern the disclosure of sentencing information in non-capital cases, but the justices who have reached this issue have not agreed on the appropriate analysis. CRIMPROC § 16.4(d); Burns v. United States, 501 U.S. 129 (1991).

Lower courts have assumed this rule also applies to non-capital cases although there is little case law on the application of *Brady* to non-capital cases because statute or rule routinely mandates the disclosure to defendants of sentencing information in presentence reports.

D. Opportunity to Contest and Submit Sentencing Information

1. *Contesting Information, Confrontation*

Given the uncertainty about whether the Constitution requires sentencing information to be disclosed to a defendant in non-capital cases, it is perhaps not surprising that there is no constitutional rule mandating that defendants be given the opportunity to test that information. Ever since the Court in *Williams* rejected the defendant's assertion that he was entitled to cross examine allegations relied upon by the judge in sentencing, it has not revisited this issue.[152] Even after state and federal Guidelines systems, unlike the discretionary sentencing examined in *Williams,* tied the severity of a sentence to particular findings of fact, and even after the Court reinvigorated the confrontation right for trial in 2004,[153] lower courts have refused to extend confrontation rights to the sentencing phase. As a result, hearsay assertions in presentence reports and victim letters are routinely considered, and only a "minimum level of reliability" is required.[154]

2. *Presenting Evidence and Argument in Mitigation*

Every jurisdiction provides some opportunity for the defendant to make a statement before sentence is pronounced, commonly known as allocution. As the Court has observed, "The most persuasive counsel may not be able to speak for a defendant as the defendant might, with halting eloquence, speak for himself."[155] But the Court has yet to decide whether denying a defendant this chance to speak at sentencing is constitutional error. In *Hill v. United States*,[156] the Court held that in a case where the defendant is represented by counsel, absent "aggravating circumstances," the failure of a judge to comply with Rule 32 of the Federal Rules of Criminal Procedure and ask the defendant whether he wished to say anything before imposition of sentence "is not a fundamental defect which inherently results in a complete miscarriage of justice" necessitating that the sentence be vacated.

As for whether a defendant must be given the opportunity to present other evidence on his own behalf at sentencing for a non-capital crime, the Court has issued conflicting statements.[157] The constitutional issue may remain unresolved for some

---

[152] CRIMPROC § 26.4(f).

[153] Crawford v. Washington, 541 U.S. 36 (2004).

[154] See, e.g., United States v. Powell, 650 F.3d 388 (4th Cir.2011).

[155] Green v. United States, 365 U.S. 301 (1961).

[156] 368 U.S. 424 (1962).

[157] Compare Mempa v. Rhay, 389 U.S. 128 (1967) ("counsel was necessary to assist defendant in marshaling the facts, introducing evidence of mitigating circumstances and . . . present[ing] his case as to sentence . . . "); Miller v. Alabama, 132 S.Ct. 2455 (2012) (requiring consideration of mitigating evidence before imposing life without parole sentence on juvenile offender); with McGautha v. California, 402 U.S. 183 (1971) (any constitutional right to present evidence was not violated when counsel could argue for mercy and no defense evidence was excluded as relevant only to sentence).

time, because defendants commonly are provided some opportunity to submit sentencing information to the court by statute or court rule. A hearing at which defense evidence and argument may be presented is also routinely provided by statute and rule, although the Constitution requires no such entitlement. Federal Rule 32(i) provides for a sentencing hearing at which the court "may" permit the parties to introduce evidence on objections to the presentence report.[158] If a sentencing hearing is held, the defendant has both a constitutional and a statutory right to be present.[159]

E. Fact Finding at Sentencing—Jury or Judge; Burden of Proof

1. Generally

The Supreme Court's interpretations of the scope of two constitutional procedural protections at sentencing deserve special attention: the burden of proof and the right to jury. The Court's rulings on these points during the first decade of this century have had a profound impact on federal sentencing.

2. Facts Used to Set Sentence Within Statutory Maximum

Unlike elements at trial, the Court has held that facts used in setting the sentence within the statutory range authorized for the offense of conviction need only be proven by a preponderance of the evidence and need not be submitted to a jury. In *Alleyne v. United States*,[160] the Court reiterated that judges retain "broad discretion" "to select a sentence within the range authorized by law." Nor is it unconstitutional to increase a sentence based upon conduct for which the defendant had been previously tried and acquitted, held the Court in *United States v. Watts*.[161] The Court reasoned that "application of the preponderance standard at sentencing generally satisfies due process" and that "a jury's verdict of acquittal does not prevent the sentencing court from considering conduct underlying the acquitted charge, so long as that conduct has been proved by a preponderance of the evidence."

3. Facts That Authorize a Sentence Beyond the Statutory Range

A legislature cannot avoid the jury right and beyond a reasonable doubt standard by disguising an element of a separate, aggravated offense as a sentencing factor, however. Even if a legislature labels a fact as a sentencing factor, if the presence of that fact authorizes the imposition of a penalty that is more severe than the penalty authorized by law for the offense of conviction alone, the Court held in *Apprendi v. New Jersey*,[162] the Constitution guarantees the defendant the right to require the government to prove that fact beyond a reasonable doubt to a jury. Any fact, other than prior conviction, that increases the penalty for a crime beyond its prescribed "statutory maximum," the Court held, must be treated like an element and either be admitted by the defendant or submitted to a jury and proved beyond a reasonable doubt.

---

[158] Fed.R.Crim.P. 32. U.S.S.G. § 6A1.3 states that the "parties shall be given an adequate opportunity to present information" as to any factor "reasonably in dispute." The commentary to this guideline adds that an "evidentiary hearing may sometimes be the only reliable way to resolve disputed issues."

[159] For federal authority, see United States v. Williams, 641 F.3d 758 (6th Cir.2011). See also CRIMPROC § 24.2(f).

[160] 133 S.Ct. 2151 (2013).

[161] 519 U.S. 148 (1997).

[162] 530 U.S. 466 (2000).

In *Apprendi,* the defendant's offense of possession of a weapon for an unlawful purpose was punishable by up to ten years' incarceration. Under a state statute that allowed an even higher sentence if the judge found at sentencing that the defendant had been motivated by racial bias, Apprendi was sentenced to 12 years. The United States Supreme Court found that Apprendi had been denied his right to a jury determination beyond a reasonable doubt of each offense element. Essentially, the majority reasoned, the state had convicted Apprendi of one offense but had sentenced him for a more serious crime without proving the more serious crime to a jury beyond a reasonable doubt.

The Court soon extended the logic of *Apprendi* to mandatory sentencing guidelines systems, holding in *Blakely v. Washington*[163] that Washington state's mandatory guidelines ranges set the statutory sentence ceilings for each offense, so that aggravating factors that raised the ranges had to be proven to a jury beyond a reasonable doubt. The Court explained: "[T]he 'statutory maximum' for *Apprendi* purposes is the maximum sentence a judge may impose solely on the basis of the facts reflected in the jury verdict or admitted by the defendant." In 2005, in *United States v. Booker,*[164] the Court held that the federal sentencing guidelines violated *Apprendi* as well. As a remedy, the Court "excised" the provisions in the Sentencing Reform Act that *required* judges to impose a sentence within the applicable Guidelines, rendering the Guidelines "effectively advisory." Without mandatory guidelines capping the permissible sentence, judges could select a sentence within the entire statutory range, based on facts not found by a jury or admitted by the defendant.

The Court has consistently exempted the fact of a prior conviction from the *Apprendi* rule. Statutes permitting judges to boost a defendant's maximum sentence based on a prior conviction, without a jury finding that the defendant had been convicted before, have a long historical basis. And, unlike any other type of fact, the Court reasoned in *Almendarez–Torres v. United States*, a prior conviction "must itself have been established through procedures satisfying the fair notice, reasonable doubt, and jury trial guarantees."[165] Lower courts have divided over the necessity of jury trial and proof beyond a reasonable doubt for various ancillary facts about a prior conviction that may be specified by a recidivist enhancement provision. For example, proof that a prior conviction be committed while under supervision would appear to fall outside the bare exception for the fact of the prior conviction itself.[166]

Relying primarily upon its analysis of historical practice as a guide for the scope of the Sixth Amendment right to jury, the Court in *Southern Union v. United States*[167] extended the rule in *Apprendi* to facts upon which fine amounts are conditioned.[168] A

---

[163] 542 U.S. 296 (2004).

[164] 543 U.S. 220 (2005).

[165] Almendarez–Torres v. United States, 523 U.S. 224 (1998); *Booker.*

[166] See CRIMPROC § 26.4(i).

[167] Southern Union Co. v. United States, 132 S.Ct. 2344 (2012) (vacating $18 million fine imposed for storing hazardous material without a permit in violation of the Resource Conservation and Recovery Act, which provides for "a fine of not more than $50,000 for each day of violation.").

[168] See United States v. Sanford Ltd., 878 F. Supp.2d 137 (D.D.C. 2012) (applying *Southern Union* and concluding that the "Constitution requires that the jury find beyond a reasonable doubt that this amount constituted a "gross gain" to Sanford and that this amount was "derive[d] . . . from" the charged offenses").

different majority of the Court in *Alleyne v. United States* overruled earlier precedent to hold that a fact triggering a mandatory minimum sentence must also be proven to a jury beyond a reasonable doubt, because such a fact "produces a higher range, which, in turn, conclusively indicates that the fact is an element of a distinct and aggravated crime."[169] The Court has declined to extend the *Apprendi* rule to facts required before a sentence can be run consecutively rather than concurrently with another sentence.[170] As lower courts work through sentencing challenges by defendants whose sentences may have been imposed contrary to either *Southern Union* or *Alleyne*, it is important to keep in mind that neither applies to a defendant whose appeal was final before the decision was announced,[171] and that violations of the *Apprendi* rule are subject to harmless error review.[172]

As for what is an admission for purposes of *Apprendi* and its progeny, a fact is not admitted merely because the defendant fails to object to its allegation in a presentence report. A fact is admitted by a defendant who pleads guilty if it is included in the terms of a plea agreement, or is part of the charging document. A stipulation in connection with a guilty plea will also bind the defendant, as will an oral admission at a plea hearing.[173]

4. Mitigating Facts

A statute or guideline may designate certain facts as mitigating factors, operating to reduce the sentence. The burden of proving mitigating facts may be placed on the defendant.[174] The Court has not addressed whether it would be unconstitutional to require the defendant to prove mitigating facts by more than a preponderance of the evidence, but lower courts have upheld more demanding burdens for mitigating facts.

§ 24.6 THE FEDERAL SENTENCING PROCESS UNDER RULE 32 AND SENTENCING REFORM ACT

A. Sentence Agreements

Most white collar defendants, both individuals and organizations, are convicted by guilty plea, and most enter into plea agreements.[175] In both federal and state courts, plea agreements often include agreements about the sentence as well as the charges. The defendant may agree to plead guilty in exchange for a prosecutor's promise to recommend a sentence to the court. The court is free to reject the parties' sentencing

---

[169] Alleyne v. United States, ___ S. Ct. ___ (2013).

[170] Oregon v. Ice, 555 U.S. 160 (2009).

[171] See Schriro v. Summerlin, 542 U.S. 348 (2004) (holding that decision applying *Apprendi* to death sentencing was not retroactive).

[172] Washington v. Recuenco, 548 U.S. 212 (2006) (*Blakely* error can be harmless).

[173] Cf. Shepard v. United States, 544 U.S. 13 (2005) (interpreting statute to avoid constitutional question).

[174] Kansas v. Marsh, 548 U.S. 163 (2006); *Apprendi*, 530 U.S. at 490 n.19 ("If the defendant can escape the statutory maximum by showing, for example, that he is a war veteran, then a judge that finds the fact of veteran status is neither exposing the defendant to a deprivation of liberty greater than that authorized by the verdict according to statute, nor is the judge imposing upon the defendant a greater stigma than that accompanying the jury verdict alone. Core concerns animating the jury and burden-of-proof requirements are thus absent from such a scheme.").

[175] See USSC Statistics, Table 11 (only about 8.9% of tax convictions and about 5.5% of fraud and bribery convictions went to trial). See also Chapter 1 and 3.

recommendation, but if that happens the defendant may not withdraw the plea for that reason. Alternatively, the agreement may make the plea *contingent* on the court's acceptance of a certain sentence, sentence ceiling, or sentence factor. If the court does not accept the stipulated sentencing term, the deal is off and the defendant may withdraw his plea—the court does not have the power to retain the plea and discard the agreed-upon sentence. Rule 11 of the Federal Rules of Criminal Procedure authorizes both of these types of agreements—those that don't bind the judge's sentencing discretion, under Rule 11(c)(1)(B), and those that do, also known as "c" pleas under Rule 11(c)(1)(C).

As the Court noted in *Freeman v. United States*,[176] before accepting any plea agreement, the Guidelines require a federal judge to carefully consider the recommended guidelines sentencing range. The court may reject a charge bargain if it concludes that the agreement is not in the interests of justice or does not adequately reflect the seriousness of the actual offense behavior.[177] Victims may intervene and object to an agreement as too lenient or providing insufficient restitution. Despite these considerations, judges ordinarily accept plea agreements.

If the parties submit a "c" plea for approval, the court must either accept or reject the agreement, or defer consideration until after it can review the presentence report. The court may not alter the terms of the sentence in the agreement.[178] For this reason, some federal judges will not accept any "c" pleas, preferring to retain the discretion to set the sentence. Others accept them routinely. Once they do, at sentencing "the court simply implements the terms of the agreement it has already accepted."[179] Sometimes a judge will reject a "c" plea agreement because of disagreement with the sentence. In *United States v. Guidant LLC*,[180] for example, the judge rejected a "c" plea because it contained no term of probation and the court wanted to add as conditions of probation that the defendant pay restitution and strengthen its compliance and ethics program. The parties later drafted an amended agreement including a three-year term of probation, which the judge accepted.

As Chief Justice Roberts explained in *Freeman*, when parties enter into a "c" plea, they "could well have had quite different reasons for concluding that [the selected sentence] was a good deal. Perhaps the prosecutor wanted to devote the limited resources of his office to a different area of criminal activity, rather than try this case. Perhaps the defendant had reason to question the credibility of one of his key witnesses, and feared a longer sentence if the case went to trial. Indeed, the fact that there may be uncertainty about how to calculate the appropriate Guidelines range

---

[176] 131 S.Ct. 2685 (2011).

[177] U.S.S.G. § 6B1.2. See also Missouri v. Frye, 132 S.Ct. 1399, 1411 (2012) ("A State may perhaps [choose] to preclude a trial court from rejecting a plea bargain.").

[178] Fed. R. Crim. P. 11(c)(3)(A).

[179] *Freeman*, 131 S.Ct. at 2696 (Sotomayor, J., concurring in the judgment) (providing fifth vote for conclusion that "the term of imprisonment imposed pursuant to a (C) agreement is, for purposes of § 3582(c)(2), "based on" the agreement itself).

[180] 708 F.Supp.2d 903 (D. Minn.2010).

could be the basis for agreement on a fixed term in a plea under Rule 11(c)(1)(C). . . . "[181]

B. The Presentence Investigation Report

Federal judges, like state judges, obtain most of the information they use in sentencing from presentence investigation reports, prepared by probation officers.[182] The officer recommends findings of fact, calculates the recommended sentencing range under the advisory Guidelines, and may recommend departures or discuss reasons under § 3553(a) to sentence outside the recommended guideline range. The report is also used by the judge to set conditions of probation or supervised release. The Bureau of Prisons, too, uses the report when managing a defendant's confinement, including determining custody level, placement, and education and work assignments.

The presentence report is usually prepared after conviction before sentence. It may be prepared prior to the defendant's guilty plea and disclosed to the judge prior to the judge's consideration of a plea agreement, if the defendant consents.[183] Preparation of a report may be waived only if the judge finds that the information in the record enables it to meaningfully exercise its sentencing authority under 18 U.S.C. § 3553, and the court explains its finding on the record.

Probation officers must complete each report within two months of conviction.[184] Most will interview the defendant early in their preparation of the report. Defense counsel has the right to attend this interview,[185] and normally should do so. The officer will obtain additional information about the offense and offender from the prosecutor. Employment, criminal history, and other facts will be verified.

Once the report is completed, it is disclosed to the parties, at least 35 days prior to sentencing. Rule 32 requires that certain information must not be included in what is disclosed to the defendant, namely (1) "any diagnoses that, if disclosed, might seriously disrupt a rehabilitation program," (2) "sources of information obtained upon a promise of confidentiality," or (3) "any other information that, if disclosed, might result in physical or other harm to the defendant or others." The underlying sources of information in the report need not be disclosed to the defendant, and sentencing information need only have "sufficient indicia of reliability to support its probable accuracy."[186]

The parties have two weeks to serve any objections to the report upon each other and also upon the probation officer, who may investigate further or attempt to address the objections in an amended report. Any unresolved objections will be addressed by the judge at a sentencing hearing. If after reviewing the report the court anticipates applying a departure, it must provide reasonable notice to the parties of this

---

[181] *Freeman*, at 2703 (Roberts, C.J., dissenting).

[182] 18 U.S.C. § 3552(a); Fed. R. Crim. P. 32(c).

[183] Rule 32; cf. Gregg v. United States, 394 U.S. 489 (1969) (finding no evidence that judge saw the report before the jury verdict was returned).

[184] 18 U.S.C. § 3552(b).

[185] Fed. R. Crim. P. 32(c)(2) (requiring that probation officer give counsel notice and reasonable opportunity to attend interview).

[186] U.S.S.G. § 6A1.3(a), p.s.

possibility.[187] If the judge intends not to use a departure, but plans to impose a sentence outside the Guidelines for a reason under 3553(a), no notice is required.[188]

Access to presentence reports by third parties, including victims, is strictly limited by courts.[189] The party seeking disclosure usually must demonstrate a particularized compelling need, similar to the showing required for access to grand jury proceedings, in order to protect the privacy and safety of defendants, victims, and other sources of sentencing information.

C. Hearings and Findings

A defendant is entitled to a hearing before he is sentenced. There, the court must ensure that both sides have had an opportunity to review the report, provide a summary of any information excluded from the report on which the court will rely in sentencing, and give the parties a reasonable opportunity to comment on that information, the report, and the appropriate sentence. The court may permit the parties to introduce evidence and testimony, but need not do so. Both defendants and victims are entitled to speak to the judge at the sentencing hearing.

At the hearing, the court must rule on each disputed factual matter or indicate that resolution is not needed because it wouldn't make any difference in the sentence imposed. Rule 32 requires that a record of the court's rulings on disputed matters must be appended to the report, which allows the Bureau of Prisons to learn of any allegations in the report the court concluded were unreliable or false.

The judge must state in open court the sentence and the reasons for selecting that sentence, and if full restitution is not ordered, the reasons for that decision as well.[190] The facility in which the defendant will be confined is up to the Bureau of Prisons, not the judge.[191]

§ 24.7 SENTENCING OF ORGANIZATIONS

A. Organizational Guidelines—Generally

The Sentencing Commission promulgated a separate set of sentencing guidelines for organizations. The Commission concluded that existing sanctions for corporations and other organizations were not providing enough incentive to avoid law breaking. In crafting sentencing guidelines for entities, the Commission adopted a carrot and stick approach to enforcement that it hoped would incentivize organizations to adopt internal reforms to prevent criminal conduct. The organizational Guidelines seek to promote compliance with the criminal law by combining stiff sentences for organizations that tolerate criminal activity with substantial sentencing breaks for entities that demonstrate that they had previously put in place effective compliance programs, promptly reported the offense conduct, and had no high-level officers

---

[187] Burns v. United States, 501 U.S. 129 (1991); U.S.S.G. § 6A1.4, p.s. See also Fed. R.Crim. P. 32(h).

[188] Irizarry v. United States, 553 U.S. 708 (2008).

[189] CRIMPROC § 26.5(c). Neither the Crime Victims Rights Act nor the constitutional right to access court proceedings entitles victims to access presentence reports. See, e.g., In re Siler, 571 F.3d 604 (6th Cir.2009).

[190] 18 U.S.C. § 3553(c).

[191] 18 U.S.C. § 3621.

involved in criminal activity. Like the Guidelines for individuals, the organizational Guidelines are advisory only following *Booker*. (See § 24.4 (a)).

As Chapter 2 mentioned, the number of organizations sentenced in federal court is relatively small—only 160 between October 2010 and October 2011. According to the Commission, most organizations sentenced in federal court are modest in size; few have more than 200 employees. Many of these organizations are not actually even sentenced under the Guidelines. The organizational Guidelines cover sentencing for some of the more common white collar offenses such as fraud, but do not govern sentencing for crimes involving environmental pollution, consumer products, contempt, obstruction of justice, and perjury. Sentences for organizations convicted of these other crimes are determined based Sections 3553 and 3572.[192]

The Guidelines, particularly the compliance program outlined as the basis for leniency and examined in more detail below, have had influence far beyond these modest numbers. Some have hailed the Guidelines as inspiring a "major culture change"[193] toward compliance planning and programming by businesses. It is difficult to isolate the impact of the Guidelines, however, because the charging policy of the Department of Justice and developments in corporate law have also independently pushed businesses to adopt and enforce similar compliance policies.

There are several key differences between the organizational Guidelines and those governing the sentencing of individuals. The Guidelines make remediation the first priority in sentencing an organization, through restitution or other means.[194] A judge may reduce or not impose a fine if its imposition would impair the organization's ability to make restitution.[195] Nearly half of the 36 organizations sentenced for fraud in 2011 were ordered to pay restitution only and no fine.[196]

Fine calculations are different for organizations than for individuals,[197] with differing aggravating and mitigating factors. The presence of a compliance program, discussed in more detail below, and role that senior personnel play in the offense may have a significant influence on the recommended sentence, for example.[198]

Like an individual, a convicted organization may be placed on probation, so that compliance with conditions can be enforced. Probation terms must be between one and five years in length, and may include steps the court decides are necessary to ensure payment of a fine or restitution, such as opening its books for examinations, and adopting or changing its program for compliance and ethics. More than two thirds of convicted organizations receive probation as part of the sentence.[199]

---

[192] U.S.S.G. § 8C2.10.

[193] Ethics Resource Center, The Federal Sentencing Guidelines for Organizations At Twenty Years (2012), avail: http://www.ethics.org/files/u5/fsgo-report2012.pdf (hereinafter F.S.G.O. 2012 Report), at ii.

[194] See U.S.S.G., Ch.8, Pt.B, intro. comment.

[195] See U.S.S.G. § 8C3.3(a).

[196] USSC, Statistics, Table 51.

[197] See U.S.S.G. § 8A1.2(b).

[198] U.S.S.G. § 8C2.5(f)(3)(A).

[199] USSC Statistics, Table 53.

There is also a rarely applied provision, known as the "corporate death penalty," or "death sentence," that calls for divesting any organization operated primarily for a criminal purpose or primarily by criminal means of all its net assets.[200] Examples of such an organization include "a front for a scheme that was designed to commit fraud or a hazardous waste disposal business that had no legitimate means of disposing of hazardous waste. "Net assets" means the assets remaining after payment of all legitimate claims against assets by known innocent bona fide creditors.[201]

B.　Calculating the Fine

The Guidelines for organizations provide a recommended fine range[202] in cases that involve an offense for which pecuniary loss can be readily quantified, such as fraud.[203] Fines for other offenses, such as those involving environmental pollution, consumer products, contempt, obstruction of justice, and perjury, are not governed by specific Guidelines, but are determined based on the provisions in §§ 3553 and 3572.[204]

The recommended range under the Guidelines is determined by multiplying the "base fine" by a minimum and maximum multiplier. These multipliers, in turn, are derived from the organization's "culpability score." Unless otherwise provided in the Chapter 2 guideline for the specific offense, the "base fine" is the greater of (1) the fine amount keyed to the appropriate base offense level in the fine table in Chapter 8[205]; (2) the pecuniary gain to the organization from the offense; or (3) the pecuniary loss caused by the organization, to the extent that such loss was caused intentionally, knowingly, or recklessly.[206] If calculating gain or loss "would unduly complicate or prolong the sentencing process," a court may skip that step.[207]

An organization's culpability score may be increased for the involvement of officers or other personnel with substantial authority[208]; a prior history of misconduct by the organization[209]; the violation of a judicial order or condition of probation[210]; or obstruction of justice.[211] It may be reduced if the organization had an effective compliance and ethics program in place at the time of the offense[212]; and if it promptly reported the offense the offense to the appropriate governmental authorities, fully cooperated in the investigation, and clearly demonstrated recognition and affirmative

---

[200] See U.S.S.G. §§ 8A1.2(b)(1), 8C1.1.

[201] See U.S.S.G. § 8C1.1, comment (n.1). If the extent of the assets of the organization is unknown, the guidelines instruct the court to impose the maximum fine authorized by statute, absent innocent bona fide creditors. See U.S.S.G. § 8C1.1, comment (backg'd.).

[202] The Sentencing Commission has published a helpful "primer" for calculating the recommended fine for organizations, entitled "Chapter Eight Fine Primer: Determining the Appropriate Fine under the Organizational Guidelines," available at http://www.ussc.gov and hereinafter USSC, Fines Primer.

[203] U.S.S.G. §§ 8C2.2—8C2.9.

[204] U.S.S.G. § 8C2.10.

[205] U.S.S.G. § 8C2.3; § 8C2.4(d).

[206] U.S.S.G. § 8C2.4(a)(1)–(3), comment.

[207] U.S.S.G. § 8C2.4(c).

[208] U.S.S.G. § 8C2.5(b)(1)–(5).

[209] U.S.S.G. § 8C2.5(c).

[210] U.S.S.G. § 8C2.5(d)(1)–(2).

[211] U.S.S.G. § 8C2.5(g).

[212] U.S.S.G. § 8C2.5(f)(1).

acceptance of responsibility for its conduct.[213] A table identifies the minimum and maximum multipliers that correspond to the resulting culpability score.[214] The minimum recommended fine is the product of the base fine and the minimum multiplier, the maximum recommended fine is the product of the base fine and the maximum multiplier.[215]

Finally, like the Guidelines for individuals, the organizational Guidelines include a number of grounds for departing from the recommended range. Among these is a departure downward for substantial assistance to the government in its prosecution of another defendant not part of the organization, and various upward departures.

C. The Importance of Compliance and Ethics Programs

Under the organizational Guidelines, an effective compliance and ethics program can substantially influence the culpability score given to a corporation, as well as conditions of probation. An effective compliance program is important not only for judges when calculating the advisory sentence under the Guidelines for a convicted offender, but also for prosecutors in deciding whether or not to charge, and for civil liability and agency enforcement actions as well.

To receive credit under the Guidelines for such a program, a firm must "exercise due diligence to prevent and detect criminal conduct," as well as "promote an organizational culture that encourages ethical conduct and a commitment to compliance with the law."[216] Due diligence under the sentencing Guidelines requires a program with high-level corporate oversight that has specific individuals "delegated day-to-day operational responsibility for the compliance and ethics program." Those who have engaged in misconduct within the entity should not be involved in the program. The Guidelines call for training programs, periodic evaluation of the program's effectiveness, and a system for whistleblowers to report misconduct anonymously. Due diligence also requires promotion of the program within the entity and reasonable responses whenever improper conduct is detected. The fact the program does not correct all offenses does not render it ineffective.[217]

Seven key criteria for establishing an "effective compliance program" are set forth in the Guidelines.[218] These standards have been quite influential. In 2004, following the high profile scandals involving top executives at corporations including Enron and WorldCom, the Commission adopted several amendments to Chapter 8, recommended by a special advisory committee. The amendments include for the first time a role for a company's board of directors in ensuring compliance. Section 8B2.1(a) requires that an effective compliance and ethics program requires a program that "reasonably designed, implemented, and enforced so that the program is generally effective in preventing and detecting criminal conduct," and that a company "exercise due diligence to prevent and

---

[213] U.S.S.G. § 8C2.5(g)(1).

[214] U.S.S.G. § 8C2.6. For instance, a culpability score of 10 or more results in a minimum multiplier of 2.00 and a maximum multiplier of 4.00, while a lower culpability score of 3 results in a minimum multiplier of 0.60 and a maximum multiplier of 1.20.

[215] See U.S.S.G. § 8C2.7(a), (b).

[216] U.S.S.G. § 8B2.1.

[217] U.S.S.G. § 8C2.1, comment (bkgnd).

[218] U.S.S.G. § 8B2.1.

detect criminal conduct," "otherwise promote an organizational culture that encourages ethical conduct and a commitment to compliance with the law." Specifically, Section 8B2.1 provides:

(1) The organization shall establish standards and procedures to prevent and detect criminal conduct;

(2) (A) The organization's governing authority shall be knowledgeable about the content and operation of the compliance and ethics program and shall exercise reasonable oversight with respect to the implementation and effectiveness of the compliance and ethics program.

(B) High-level personnel of the organization shall ensure that the organization has an effective compliance and ethics program, as described in this guideline. Specific individual(s) within high-level personnel shall be assigned overall responsibility for the compliance and ethics program.

(C) Specific individual(s) within the organization shall be delegated day-to-day operational responsibility for the compliance and ethics program. Individual(s) with operational responsibility shall report periodically to high-level personnel and, as appropriate, to the governing authority, or an appropriate subgroup of the governing authority, on the effectiveness of the compliance and ethics program. To carry out such operational responsibility, such individual(s) shall be given adequate resources, appropriate authority, and direct access to the governing authority or an appropriate subgroup of the governing authority.

(3) The organization shall use reasonable efforts not to include within the substantial authority personnel of the organization any individual whom the organization knew, or should have known through the exercise of due diligence, has engaged in illegal activities or other conduct inconsistent with an effective compliance and ethics program.

(4) (A) The organization shall take reasonable steps to communicate periodically and in a practical manner its standards and procedures, and other aspects of the compliance and ethics program, to the individuals referred to in subparagraph (B) by conducting effective training programs and otherwise disseminating information appropriate to such individuals' respective roles and responsibilities. (B) The individuals referred to in subparagraph (A) are the members of the governing authority, high-level personnel, substantial authority personnel, the organization's employees, and, as appropriate, the organization's agents.

(5) The organization shall take reasonable steps—(A) to ensure that the organization's compliance and ethics program is followed, including monitoring and auditing to detect criminal conduct; (B) to evaluate periodically the effectiveness of the organization's compliance and ethics program; and (C) to have and publicize a system, which may include mechanisms that allow for anonymity or confidentiality, whereby the organization's employees and agents may report or seek guidance regarding potential or actual criminal conduct without fear of retaliation.

(6) The organization's compliance and ethics program shall be promoted and enforced consistently throughout the organization through (A) appropriate incentives to perform in accordance with the compliance and ethics program; and (B) appropriate disciplinary measures for engaging in criminal conduct and for failing to take reasonable steps to prevent or detect criminal conduct.

(7) After criminal conduct has been detected, the organization shall take reasonable steps to respond appropriately to the criminal conduct and to prevent further similar criminal conduct, including making any necessary modifications to the organization's compliance and ethics program.

D. Avoiding Sentence: Deferred Prosecution Agreements; Non Prosecution Agreements

Most larger corporations suspected of criminal activity are not convicted or sentenced for their wrongdoing. Instead, if investigation reveals likely criminal liability, in recent decades prosecutors have preferred to negotiate a settlement that avoids conviction—either in the form of a deferred prosecution agreement or non-prosecution agreement.[219] Department of Justice policy instructs prosecutors to take the existence of an effective ethics and compliance program into account when deciding whether to bring criminal charges or negotiate one of these agreements, but some have criticized the lack of publicly available evidence that this key feature has actually affected charging decisions.[220]

These agreements tend to have common elements. First, if charges have not already been filed, these agreements do not require any sort of judicial approval. The lack of transparency and potential for inconsistency has been an ongoing source of concern for critics.[221] Second, the organization avoids criminal liability only by agreeing to help the government prosecute its officers and employees, by waiving its rights (including privileges), and by agreeing to other sanctions, including fines and restitution. Companies often agree to structural reforms involving changes in corporate governance and compliance programs.[222] Firms may be required to hire "independent monitors with sweeping powers to implement compliance programs and access documents."[223] The threat of prosecution awaits any firm that breaches its agreement.

§ 24.8 APPELLATE REVIEW OF SENTENCES

A. Review of Compliance With Procedural Rules

Both parties may appeal a sentence,[224] although the number of defense appeals far exceeds the number of government appeals.[225] The Supreme Court held in *United*

---

[219] F.S.G.O. 2012 Report, at 37–38. See also § 2.4(C).

[220] Id. at 39–44.

[221] For an analysis of the advantages and disadvantages of greater judicial oversight of DPAs and NPAs, see U.S. Government Accountability Office. (Dec. 18, 2009), Corporate Crime: DOJ Has Taken Steps to Better Track Its Use of Deferred and Non–Prosecution Agreements, But Should Evaluate Effectiveness. (Publication No. GAO–10–110), available at: http://www.gao.gov.

[222] Brandon L. Garrett, Structural Reform Prosecution, 93 Va. L. Rev. 853 (2007).

[223] Brandon L. Garrett, Globalized Corporate Prosecutions, 97 Va.L.Rev. 1775, 1797 (2011).

[224] See 18 U.S.C. § 3742.

[225] USSC Statistics, Tables 55 & 56A.

States v. DiFrancesco[226] that it does not violate the Constitution for the government to seek a higher non-capital sentence on appeal,[227] as resentencing does not raise the same sort of harms as those raised by retrial. If the defendant appeals and the government does not, however, the court of appeals may not on its own increase a sentence for a reason the defendant did not raise. Both the initial sentence and any new sentence after revocation of release may be appealed.

Parties may seek appellate review of the sentence itself, contesting its duration, severity, or type, or seek review of the procedure followed in imposing the sentence. Procedural errors include violations of constitutional protections, statutes, and court rules. The more elaborate the sentencing procedure mandated by statute and court rule, the more potential violations there are to review on appeal. In the federal system, errors of law, such as a court's failure to consider the Guidelines at all, incorrect Guidelines calculations, or failure to consider the defendant's non-frivolous reasons for imposing a different sentence, are reviewed de novo. Factual findings made during the process of sentencing, such as the amount of money lost by a victim of fraud or the number of people employed by a defendant, are also subject to appeal for clear error.

A procedural error in setting a sentence, like a procedural error in determining guilt, will not require resentencing if the error was harmless. Harmless error review in the federal courts is governed by Rule 52(a). Constitutional errors, such as a violation of the defendant's privilege against self-incrimination or right to equal protection, will require relief unless the government can demonstrate beyond a reasonable doubt that the error did not affect the sentence.[228] Statutory and rule errors require relief unless the government can show that the error had no substantial influence on the sentence.[229] Similar standards govern state appellate review of timely raised allegations of procedural error in state courts.[230]

When a party fails to raise a procedural objection on time in the trial court, the more deferential "plain error" standards of Rule 52(b) apply. Relief will be denied for claims forfeited in the trial court, unless the defendant can show that the error was not expressly waived, was clear, more likely than not influenced the outcome, and, if left unremedied, would create a miscarriage of justice.[231]

B. Reasonableness Review of Sentence Imposed

In addition to enforcing compliance with sentencing procedure, appellate courts in the federal system and in many states are authorized to review the sentence itself. Federal sentences, including terms of probation, imprisonment, and supervised release, as well as monetary penalties, are reviewed for "reasonableness." A federal appellate court conducting "reasonableness review" of a federal sentence "asks whether the trial

---

[226] Greenlaw v. United States, 554 U.S. 237 (2008).

[227] 449 U.S. 117 (1980); CRIMPROC § 26.7(a).

[228] E.g., Washington v. Recuenco, 548 U.S. 212 (2006).

[229] E.g.,United States v. Lane, 474 U.S. 438 (1986); United States v. Vonn, 535 U.S. 55 (2002).

[230] CRIMPROC §§ 26.3(g) (appeal of sentence), 27.6(b) (harmless error review).

[231] Id. at § 27.5(d) (plain error review).

court abused its discretion."[232] This review is quite deferential, as the Court has made clear in a series of cases. Assuming a trial court's Guidelines analysis is correct, the reviewing court may presume that a sentence within the recommended Guidelines range is "reasonable."[233] But a sentence outside the Guidelines cannot be presumed unreasonable. Trial judges may disagree with a guideline or guideline policy and disregard it.[234]

Not surprisingly, most sentences survive appellate review.[235] Even under this deferential "abuse of discretion" review, occasionally sentences for white collar offenders have been overturned as substantively unreasonable. Examples include a case in which the judge made it clear that the only reason he did not incarcerate the defendant was to preserve the defendant's ability while on probation to earn enough to pay restitution,[236] and another case in which a judge imposed a sentence of five years' probation for a defendant who played a leading role in the massive accounting fraud at Health South.[237]

C. Appeal Waivers

The explosion of sentencing appeals in the federal courts following the adoption of Guidelines contributed to the popularity of sentencing appeal waivers. An appeal waiver is an agreement as part of a plea deal to waive the right to challenge the yet-to-be-imposed sentence and any errors that might occur later at sentencing, or perhaps the right to challenge both his conviction and sentence. Waivers are usually signed before conviction, well before the presentence report is prepared and any errors in sentence can be identified. Although several courts and commentators have criticized such waivers as permitting prosecutors to insulate themselves from scrutiny and impeding the appellate development of sentencing law and norms (a problem particularly acute for white collar cases, already infrequent compared to other crimes[238]) appeal waivers have been upheld by every circuit. Federal Rule 11 requires the court to include in the plea colloquy notice to the defendant if his agreement includes an appeal waiver.

In upholding as "knowing" the waiver of future errors, courts often rely on the Supreme Court's holding in *Brady v. United States*.[239] Brady had entered a guilty plea in order to avoid the death penalty, a punishment that the kidnapping statute at the time authorized only for those who were convicted following a trial. After the Supreme Court announced in a different case that imposition of the death penalty under this statute was an unconstitutional penalty on the exercise of the right to trial, *Brady* challenged his prior guilty plea as unknowing and involuntary, because it had been

---

[232] Gall v. United States, 552 U.S. 38 (2007) (in determining whether trial court abused its discretion in imposing a sentence outside the range recommended by the Guidelines, an appellate court may not require extraordinary circumstances to justify the variance from the Guidelines).

[233] Rita v. United States, 551 U.S. 338 (2007).

[234] Spears v. United States, 555 U.S. 261 (2009); Kimbrough v. United States, 552 U.S. 85 (2007).

[235] E.g., United States v. Tomko, 562 F.3d 558 (3rd Cir.2009) (en banc) (upholding probation sentence for tax evasion).

[236] United States v. Engle, 592 F.3d 495 (4th Cir.2010).

[237] United States v. Livesay, 587 F.3d 1274 (11th Cir.2009).

[238] See Richman, supra note 9, at 18 ("The relative infrequency with which non-fungible white collar cases are brought will always limit our ability to develop stable, transparent, and fair sentencing doctrine").

[239] Brady v. United States, 397 U.S. 742 (1970).

based on the faulty assumption that he would be subject to the death penalty if he had been convicted after trial. The Court rejected Brady's claim. Three decades later in *United States v. Ruiz*,[240] the Court reiterated its rationale from *Brady* when it upheld a plea agreement's waiver of the right to disclosure of information that could be used to impeach government witnesses, stating that a court may "accept a guilty plea, with its accompanying waiver of various constitutional rights, despite various forms of misapprehensions under which a defendant might labor."

An appeal waiver will not foreclose appellate review of allegations that the waiver itself was not knowing or voluntary, or that a sentence was imposed in violation of the plea bargain. In some states waivers of the right to raise claims of ineffective assistance or prosecutorial misconduct are considered unethical. In many federal districts the standard appeal waiver term is limited so that is that a defendant does not waive his right to appeal any sentence that exceeds the "statutory maximum." This phrase, some circuits have held, will not bar the appeal of certain restitution orders.[241]

§ 24.9 POST–COMMITMENT SENTENCING

A. Post–Commitment Judicial Reductions in Sentence

Unlike some states where legislatures have provided to trial judges broad discretion to grant a reduction in sentence upon the defendant's motion,[242] in the federal system, this authority is extremely limited. First, § 3553(e) and Rule 35 authorize a judge to grant a government motion to reduce an offender's sentence as a reward for assisting in the investigation or prosecution of another defendant. The sentence may be reduced even below a mandatory minimum if the government requests.[243] Only a small percentage of defendants sentenced under the Federal Guidelines (about 2.4 percent in 2010) will receive a judicial reduction in sentence under these provisions.

A judge may also reduce a sentence for "extraordinary and compelling reasons" on motion of the Director of the Bureau of Prisons.[244] In practice, however, these motions have been filed only for inmates with terminal or severe and debilitating illnesses.[245] Finally, a judge may resentence a defendant to a lesser term if an amendment to the Guidelines that lowered the defendant's sentencing range is made retroactive.[246]

---

[240] United States v. Ruiz, 536 U.S. 622 (2002).

[241] United States v. Tsosie, 639 F.3d 1213 (9th Cir.2011).

[242] See CRIMPROC § 26.3(g).

[243] See Fed. R. Crim. P. 35(b)(4).

[244] 18 U.S.C. § 3582(c). The Court recently suggested that this provision could be used in other circumstances as well. See Setser v. United States, 132 S.Ct. 1463, 1472 (2012) (stating that "when the district court's failure to 'anticipat[e] developments that take place after the first sentencing,' . . . produces unfairness to the defendant," Section 3582 "provides a mechanism for relief").

[245] See Human Rights Watch, Families Against Mandatory Minimums, The Answer is No (2012), at (reporting 444 motions over an eleven year period, of which 60% were granted), available at http://www.hrw.org/sites/default/files/reports/us1112ForUploadSm.pdf.

[246] For an example of retroactive application of new sentencing law, see Dorsey v. United States, 132 S.Ct. 2321 (2012).

B.   Post–Commitment Executive Reductions in Sentence

1.   *Discretionary Early Release on Parole*

In the majority of states indeterminate sentences of incarceration for at least some offenses allow for early release on parole at the discretion of the paroling authority, and that authority plays an important role in determining the actual term of imprisonment.[247] Discretionary release on parole is no longer an option for federal prisoners sentenced under the Sentencing Reform Act.

2.   *Good Time Credit*

Good time or earned time credit can also reduce a term of incarceration. The Sentencing Reform Act[248] allows a federal prisoner who is serving a term of imprisonment of more than a year but less than life to receive credit of up to 54 days per year toward their sentence at the end of each year. Credit is calculated by the Bureau of Prisons, based upon actual time served and the prisoner's "compliance with institutional disciplinary regulations." [249] Credits in both state and federal systems may be revoked for a violation of prison rules.[250] When a prisoner's release date depends, as in the federal system, upon the calculation of good time, a prisoner is entitled to some due process protections before credits are revoked, although not the full range of procedural requirements demanded for the revocation of supervised release.[251]

3.   *Clemency*

An offender may also receive relief from a sentence through reprieve, remission, commutation, or pardon, procedures collectively known as "clemency." A reprieve delays the execution of a sentence, remission relieves the offender of the responsibility of paying a fine or forfeiting property, and commutation reduces a term of imprisonment. Pardon absolves the defendant of guilt and thereby eliminates the basis for imposing any punishment. Clemency power in most states is shared between the governor and an administrative board or advisory group. The President has clemency power for federal defendants; applications are reviewed by the United States Pardon Attorney.[252] There appears to be no constitutional entitlement to procedural safeguards before clemency is denied. Instead, clemency is a "matter of grace committed to the executive authority."[253]

---

[247] Nancy King, "Procedure at Sentencing," in Joan Petersilia and Kevin Reitz, The Oxford Handbook of Sentencing and Corrections, 315, 328 (2012) (collecting authority).

[248] See 18 U.S.C. § 3624(b). See also 28 C.F.R. § 523.20.

[249] Barber v. Thomas, 130 S.Ct. 2499, 2506–07 (2010). See sentence computation manuals available at http://www.bop.gov/inmate_programs/sentence_computations.jsp; United States v. Wilson, 503 U.S. 329 (1992).

[250] E.g., Pepper v. United States, 131 S.Ct. 1229, 1248 n.14 (2011).

[251] Superintendent, Mass. Correctional Institution at Walpole v. Hill, 472 U.S. 445 (1985); Wolff v. McDonnell, 418 U.S. 539 (1974). For procedures followed in federal prisons, see 28 CFR §§ 541.1–8.

[252] U.S. Const., Art. II, sec. 2 ("The President . . . shall have Power to grant Reprieves and Pardons for Offenses against the United States, except in Cases of Impeachment); 28 CFR §§ 1.1–1.11. For details on all past presidential grants of clemency, see http://www.justice.gov/pardon/statistics.htm.

[253] Ohio Adult Parole Authority v. Woodard, 523 U.S. 272, 285 (1998); District Attorney's Office for Third Judicial Dist. v. Osborne, 557 U.S. 52, 68 (2009).

C.   Revocation of Release; Failure to Pay Restitution

A defendant who has been released subject to conditions of supervision, either on probation or following a term of incarceration, may face a more severe sentence if he violates those conditions. Upon finding a violation of the conditions of release, a federal judge may either revoke release and resentence the defendant, or continue release with the same or modified conditions. Revocation of release and incarceration is mandatory, however, for possessing weapons or drugs, or refusing to comply with drug testing.[254]

The Constitution entitles a defendant to an adversarial hearing with several trial-like protections before release can be revoked. As the Court has explained, the revocation determination requires two decisions—"a wholly retrospective factual question" about whether the defendant in fact violated one or more conditions, and a sentencing decision concerning whether he should be recommitted.[255] At the revocation hearing the exclusionary rule and the rules of evidence do not apply, although there are some limits on the use of hearsay. The prosecution need only prove the violation by a preponderance of the evidence.[256] Revocation of release for failure to pay a fine or restitution requires a finding that the defendant willfully did not pay or failed to pay in bad faith.

In the federal courts, revocation is governed by Rule 32.1, which provides for a first appearance and a preliminary hearing before the revocation hearing. The defendant has a statutory right to counsel for these proceedings.[257] If revoked, a court may sentence the defendant after considering the factors in § 3553(a), to a period of imprisonment for up to the maximum term of supervised release that was authorized by statute for the offense of conviction, without credit for the supervised release already served,[258] and may imposed a new term of supervised release to follow that incarceration.[259]

---

[254] 18 U.S.C. §§ 3565(b), 3583(g). See 18 U.S.C. § 3553(a)(4)(B) (requiring court to consider Guidelines and policy statements applicable to revocation). The Sentencing Commission's policy statements regarding revocation are in U.S.S.G. Ch.7. For violations leading to revocation, policy statement § 7B1.4 sets out a sentencing table formatted like the initial sentencing table.

[255] Greenholtz v. Inmates of Nebraska Penal and Correctional Complex, 442 U.S. 1, 9 (1979).

[256] See CRIMPROC § 26.10.

[257] 18 U.S.C. § 3006(a)(1)(E).

[258] USSC, Supervised Release (collecting authority, also noting some courts limit incarceration to the length of the original term of supervised release actually imposed).

[259] 18 U.S.C. § 3583(h).

Table of Cases

Table of Statutes

Index

References are to Sections